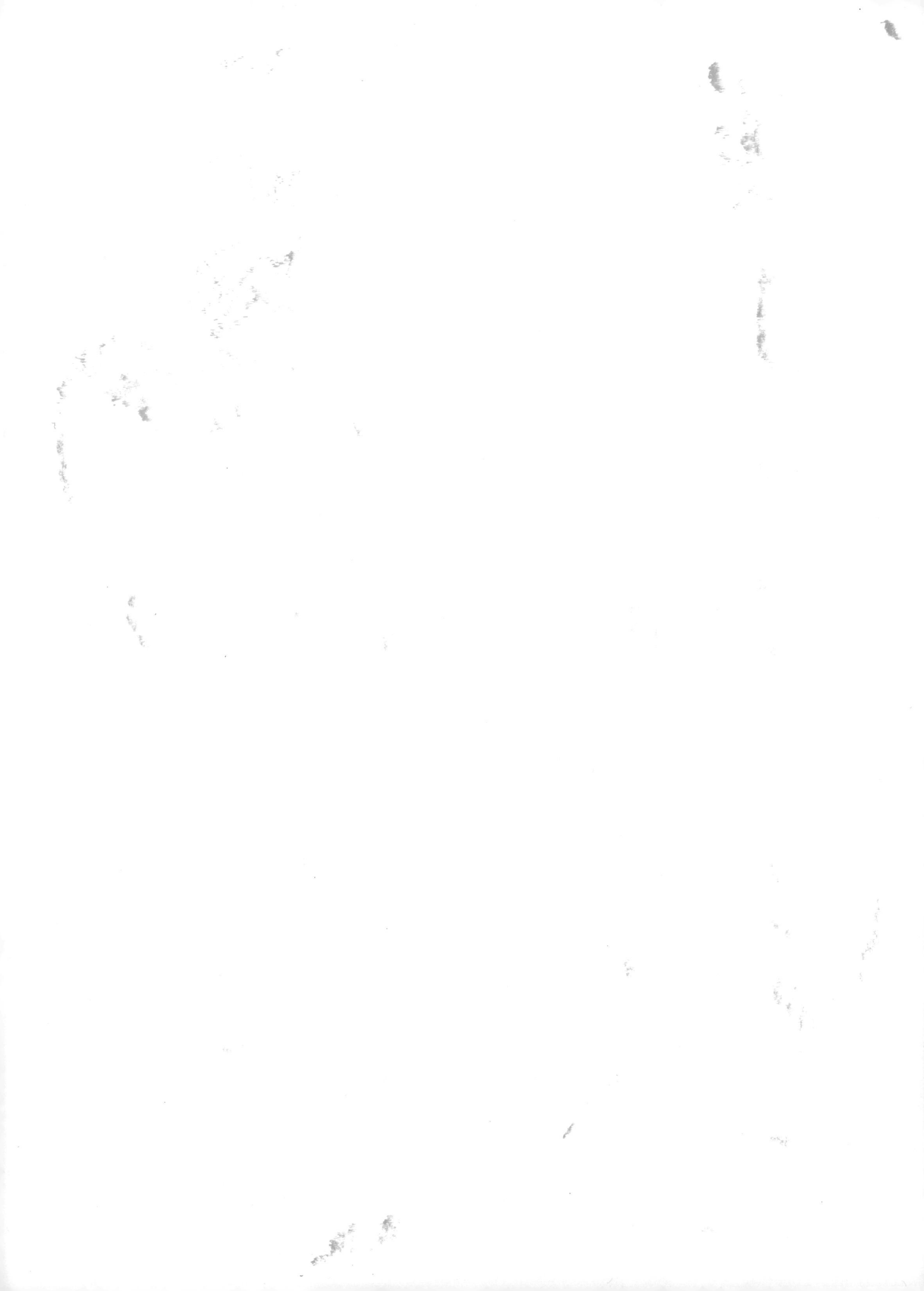

Darkness and Desolation

In Memory of the Communities of Braslaw, Dubene, Jaisi, Jod, Kislowszczizna, Okmienic, Opsa, Plusy, Rimszan, Slobodka, Zamosz and Zaracz (Belarus)

Translation of
Emesh Shoah: Yad Le-Kehilot/Gevidmet di Kehiles Braslav . . .

Original Memorial Book Edited by Ariel Machnes and Rina Klinov

Published in 1986 by the Association of Braslaw and Surroundings in Israel and America;
Ghetto Fighters House and Hakibbutz Hameuchad Publishing House

JewishGen
מרכז עולמי לגנאלוגיה יהודית
The Global Home for Jewish Genealogy

A Publication of JewishGen
Edmond J. Safra Plaza, 36 Battery Place, New York, NY 10280
646.494.2972 | info@JewishGen.org | www.jewishgen.org

JewishGen is the Genealogical Research Division
of the Museum of Jewish Heritage—A Living Memorial to the Holocaust

MUSEUM OF JEWISH HERITAGE
A LIVING MEMORIAL TO THE HOLOCAUST

Memorial Book for 12 Communities in the Braslav Region
Translation of *Emesh Shoah: Yad Le-Kehilot/Gevidmet di Kehiles Braslav . . .*, published in Israel in 1986

Copyright © 2024 by Jeff Deitch, All Rights Reserved
First Printing October 2024, Tishrei 5785
Editors of Original Memorial Book: Ariel Machnes and Rina Klinov
Editor of the English Translation/Translation Project Manager: Jeff Deitch
Cover Design: Rachel Kolokoff Hopper

JewishGen Press is not responsible for inaccuracies or omissions in the original work and makes no representations regarding the accuracy of this translation. Digital images of the original book's contents can be seen online at the Yiddish Book Center website or the New York Public Library Digital Collections website.

The mission of the JewishGen organization is to produce a translation of the original work, and we cannot verify the accuracy of statements or alter facts cited.

Library of Congress Control Number (LCCN): 2021947074

ISBN: 978-1-954176-20-1 (hardcover: 618 pages, alk. paper)

About JewishGen.org

JewishGen is a Genealogical Research Division of the Museum of Jewish Heritage—A Living Memorial to the Holocaust, and it serves as the global home for Jewish genealogy.

Featuring unparalleled access to 30+ million records, it offers unique search tools, along with opportunities for researchers to connect with others who share similar interests. Award-winning resources such as the Family Finder, Discussion Groups, and ViewMate are relied upon by thousands each day.

In addition, JewishGen's extensive informational, educational and historical offerings, such as the Jewish Communities Database, Yizkor Book translations, InfoFiles, Family Tree of the Jewish People, and KehilaLinks, provide critical insights, first-hand accounts, and context about Jewish communal and familial life throughout the world.

Offered as a free resource, JewishGen.org has facilitated thousands of family connections and success stories, and is currently engaged in an intensive expansion effort that will bring many more records, tools, and resources to its collections.

Please visit https://www.jewishgen.org/ to learn more.

Vice President for JewishGen: Avraham Groll

About the JewishGen Yizkor Book Project

Yizkor Books (Memorial Books) were traditionally written to memorialize the names of departed family and martyrs during holiday services in the synagogue (a practice that still exists in many synagogues today).

Over the centuries, as a result of countless persecutions and horrific atrocities committed against the Jews, Yizkor Books (*Sefer Zikaron* in Hebrew) were expanded to include more historical information, such as biographical sketches of famous personalities and descriptions of daily town life.

Following the Holocaust, the idea of remembrance and learning took on an urgent and crucial importance. Survivors of the Holocaust sought out other surviving residents of their former towns to memorialize and document the names and way of life of those who were ruthlessly murdered by the Nazis. These remembrances were documented in Yizkor Books, hundreds of which were published in the first decades after the Holocaust.

Most of these books were published privately, or through *Landsmanshaftn* (social organizations comprised of members originating from the same European town or region) that still existed, and were often distributed free of charge. The languages used to document these crucial histories and links to our past were mostly Yiddish and Hebrew. JewishGen has undertaken the sacred responsibility of translating these books into English so that the culture and way of life of these communities will be preserved and transmitted to future generations.

In 1986, a group of farsighted JewishGenners started a project to pool their efforts together in groups based upon their ancestors' towns and donate funds to translate the Yizkor Books of their ancestral towns into English. As the translated material became available, it was made accessible for free at https://www.JewishGen.org/Yizkor. Hardcover copies can be purchased by visiting https://www.jewishgen.org/Yizkor/ybip.html (see below).

It is our hope that the translation of these books into English (and other languages) will assist the countless Jewish family researchers who are so desperately seeking to forge a connection with their heritage.

Director of JewishGen Yizkor Book Project: Lance Ackerfeld

About JewishGen Press

JewishGen Press (formerly the Yizkor Books-in-Print Project) is the publishing division of JewishGen.org and provides a venue for the publication of nonfiction books pertaining to Jewish genealogy, history, culture, and heritage.

In addition to the Yizkor Book category, publications in the Other Non-Fiction category include Shoah memoirs and research, genealogical research, collections of genealogical and historical materials, biographies, diaries and letters, studies of Jewish experience and cultural life in the past, academic theses, and other books of interest to the Jewish community.

Please visit https://www.jewishgen.org/Yizkor/ybip.html to learn more.

Director of JewishGen Press: Joel Alpert
Managing Editor: Jessica Feinstein
Publications Manager: Susan Rosin

Notes to the Reader

The images in the original book were reproduced from photographs from the time of the first edition. These reproductions were already of poor quality, being prewar and at least 30 or more years old. As a result, the images in the book are the best achievable.

A reader can view the original scans of the book on the websites listed below. The original book can be seen online at the Yiddish Book Center website:

https://www.yiddishbookcenter.org/collections/yizkor-books/yzk-nybc313711/machnes-ariel-klinov-rinah-emesh-sho-ah-yad-li-kehilot-gevidmnt-di-kehiles-braslav

OR

at the New York Public Library Digital Collections website:

https://digitalcollections.nypl.org/items/15e88750-58a9-0133-cf62-00505686a51c

To obtain a list of Shoah victims from **Braslav (Belarus) and the 11 other Jewish communities** in the memorial book, the reader should access the Yad Vashem website listed below; one can also search for specific family names using the family name option. These lists are continually updated by Yad Vashem, so it is worthwhile to periodically search them.

There is more valuable information (including the Pages of Testimony, etc.) available on this website: https://yvng.yadvashem.org/

A list of all books available from JewishGen Press along with prices is available at: https://www.jewishgen.org/Yizkor/ybip.html

Cover Photo Captions

Row 1 (from left):
- Braslav's main thoroughfare: Pilsudsky Street; undated/presumably 1930s

- Young Jews in Braslav, 1935

- Jewish inhabitants of Dubina, 1930s

- Street in Opsa, 1937

Row 2 (from left):
- Site of the massacre of 18-25 people (all but one of whom were Jewish) near Dubina in July 1941

- Memorial at the massacre site in Yod in December 1941. The inscription reads: "Here lie victims of fascism / 500 children, women and men. Peaceful Soviet citizens from Yod of Jewish nationality. Brutally shot to death by Nazi executioners. December 17, 1941 / [Erected by the] Rescued and friends."

- Memorial at the site of the massacres in Braslav in June 1942 and March 1943. The inscription reads: "Here are buried more than 4,500 people of the Jewish population from the town of Braslav and environs, brutally tortured to death by the German monsters in 1942-1943."

- One of the pits at Ponar outside Vilnius, Lithuania, where an estimated 100,000 Jews and Gentiles were killed and buried between 1941 and 1944 (and later dug up and burned). The dead included many Jews from Slobodka, Plusy and Dubina, who were shot at Ponar on April 5, 1943.

Row 3 (from left):
- Partisans (including Mottel Vishkin of Dubina at far right) in a forest in Belorussia or Lithuania, October 1943; said to be the Rudnicki/Rudninkai forest south of Vilna. Mottel Vishkin (Max Wischkin) survived the war. He didn't give an account for this memorial book, but the account of his wife, Yetta/Yentka, appears on pages 117-119 of this memorial book.

- Partisan Benyamin Movshenzon of Rimshan (first on the right) with his wife, Sara, from Braslav and Sara's son, Luba. Sara Movshenzon's account appears on pages 164-216 of this memorial book.

Row 4 (from left):
- Postwar reburial in Holon Cemetery near Tel Aviv, Israel of earth from the massacre site in Braslav

- Reunion of survivors and their descendants at the Ghetto Fighters' House in Israel, 1992

Row 5 (from left):
- Jewish cemetery from the prewar era, Braslav region, as it looks today

- Typical landscape outside Braslav, as it looks today

Photos courtesy of the Ghetto Fighters' House, Mira Lotz, the family of Max Wischkin, Yuri Dorn, and Jeff Deitch.

Back cover: Wojskowy Instytut Geograficzny

[Cover and title page of the Hebrew-language memorial book published in Israel in 1986]

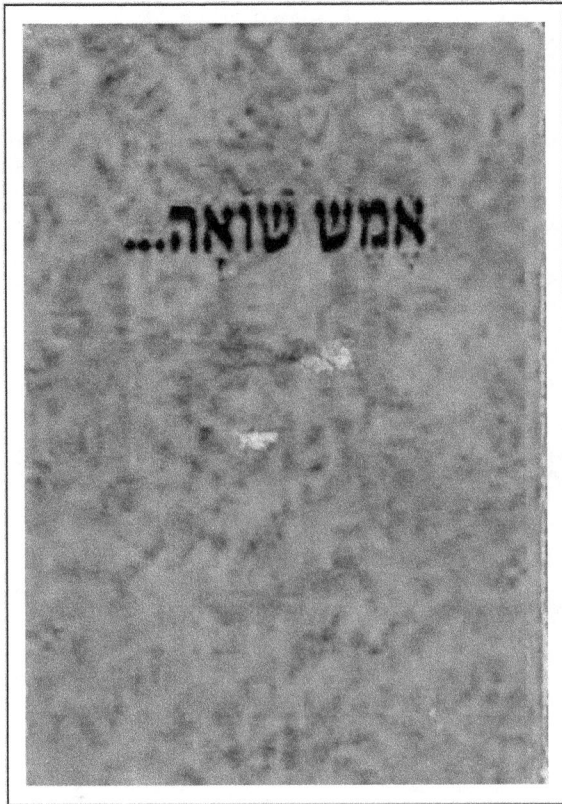

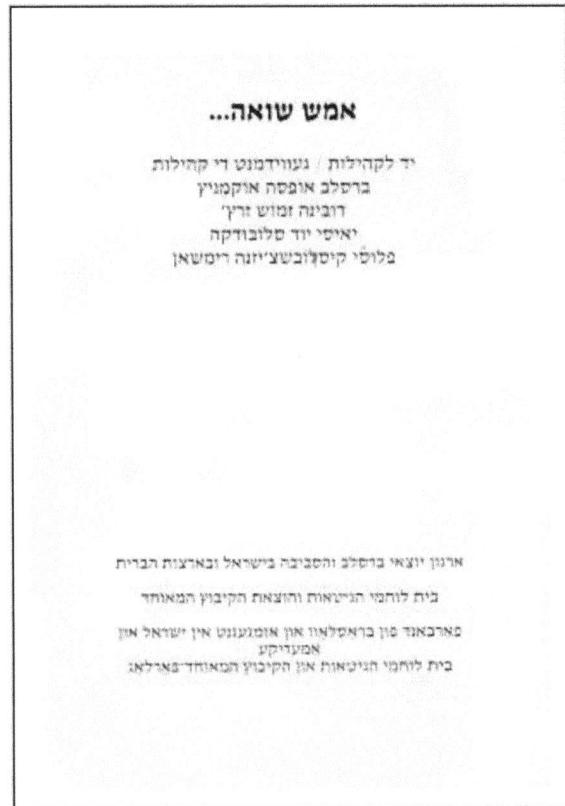

<table>
<tr><td>

אמש שואה...

</td><td>

אמש שואה...

יד לקהילות / געווידמענט די קהילות
ברסלב אופסה אוקמנין
רוביגה זמוש זרץ'
יאוסי יוד סלובודקה
פלולי קיסלובשצ'יזנה רימשאן

ארגון יוצאי ברסלב והסביבה בישראל ובארצות הברית

בית לוחמי הגיטאות והוצאות הקיבוץ המאוחד

פארבאנד פון בראסלאוו און אומגעגנט אין ישראל און אמעריקע
בית לוחמי הגיטאות און הקיבוץ המאוחד בארלאג

</td></tr>
</table>

[Map of the region: detail of the inside front cover of the Hebrew-language memorial book published in Israel in 1986, indicating the 12 Jewish communities covered in the book]

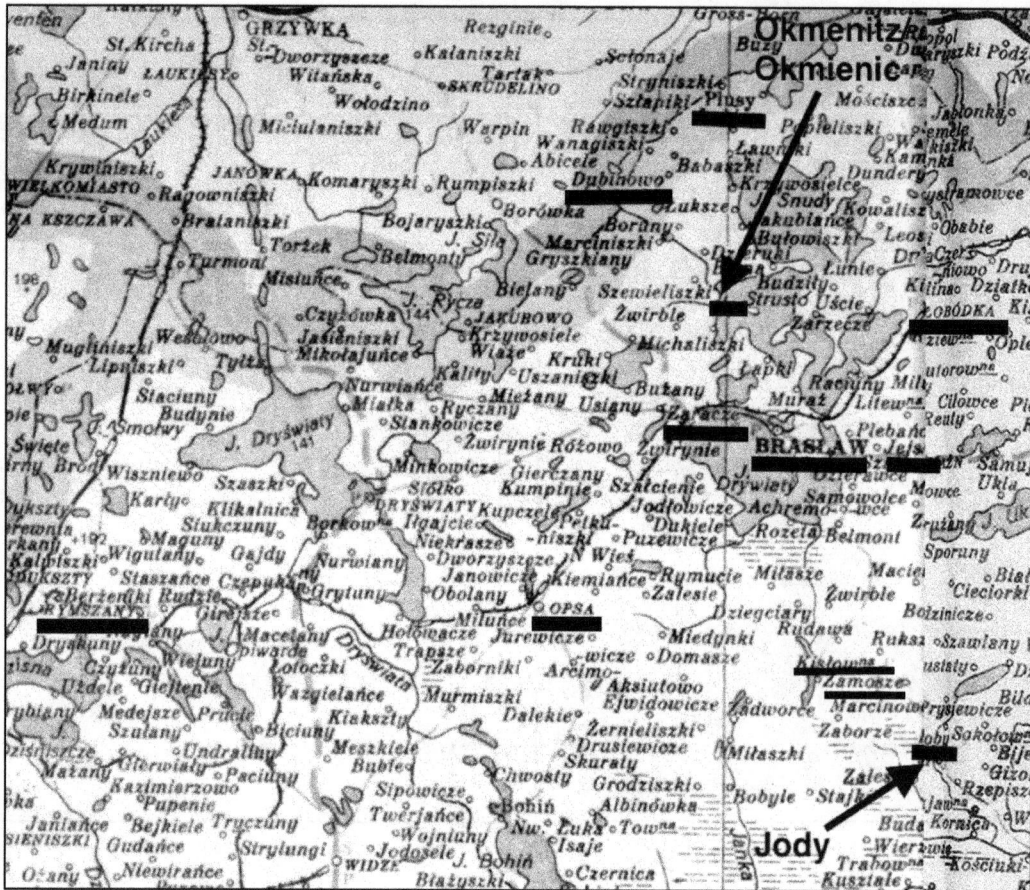

[Page 1 of the Hebrew-language memorial book published in Israel in 1986]
Emesh Shoah . . .

[Page 2]
[Dedication in the original memorial book in 1986]

Translated from the Hebrew by Laia Ben-Dov

My contribution to the book is a memorial candle for my family that was killed in the Holocaust with all the Jews of Braslav.
My father, Zerach Bogomolski.
My mother, Chasia-Rachel.
My sister, Sara-Leah.
And in memory of my good and devoted wife, Clara, of blessed memory, who passed away on 26 Shevat 5743 [February 9, 1983].

--- Moshe Bogomolski

[Dedication for the English translation of the memorial book in 2024

The translations were donated to commemorate with love a people and a region, and to make the record of tragic sacrifice and heroic resistance more fully available in English.

Many thanks to the translators of the 85 sections that I commissioned from 2019: Laia Ben-Dov (who translated about three-fourths of the book), Jerrold Landau, Ida Schwarcz, Yaacov David Shulman and Aaron Krishtalka. And to those at JewishGen who handled the uploading of the web version in 2020-21, including Lance Ackerfeld. The present book, published in 2024, is a revision of the web version.

Thank you to the donors/translators of seven sections completed independently before I began: Jon Seligman, Eilat Gordin Levitan, Guy Elitzur, and the translator Joshua Leifer (whose section was donated by Joshua Levkowicz). And to Eilat Gordin Levitan, who served as project coordinator for the web version until 2019.

Most of all, thank you to Yaacov Aviel, Moshe Bogomolski, Ariel Machnes, Rina Klinov and all of the others who produced the original book that this English translation was made from.

In memory of all the families in this book, my relatives among them. And in memory of the survivors; a meeting years ago with two of them --- Mira Lotz and her husband, Mendel Lotz --- set in motion the process that led to these translations.

--- Jeff Deitch]

[Page 3: Title page]

Darkness and Desolation

Memorial Book for 12 Communities in the Braslav Region: Braslav, Dubina, Kislovshchitzna, Opsa, Okmenitz, Plusy, Rimshan, Slobodka, Yaisi, Yod, Zamosh and Zarach

[Original book title was *Emesh Shoah: Yad Le-Kehilot/Gevidmet di Kehiles Braslav, Opsa, Okmenitz, Dubina, Zamosh, Zarach, Yaisi, Yod, Slobodka, Plusy, Kislovshchitzna and Rimshan*]

Association of Braslav and Surroundings in Israel and America, Ghetto Fighters' House, and Hakibbutz Hameuchad Publishing House

[Page 4]

Editors: Ariel Machnes, Rina Klinov

Book Editorial Board: Yaacov Aviel, Moshe Bogomolski, Yaacov Levin, Aharon Shmutser

Book Committee: Yaacov Aviel, Moshe Bogomolski, Chaim Band, Boris Berkman, Moshe Goldin, Moshe Vishkin, Zalman Charmatz, Yaacov Levin, Arieh Munitz, Yehuda Chepelevitz, Isser Rabinovitz, Aharon Shmutser

Members of the Committee in the United States: Leib-Shmuel Bernamov, Tsala [Charles] Witkin, Leib Chanin, Mendel Maron, Tuvia Fisher, Michael Kopach, Yehoshua Shuran

Translations into Hebrew (from Yiddish, Polish and Russian) and Initial Editing: Yaacov Aviel, Moshe Bogomolski, Chaim Band, Yaacov Levin, Aharon Korner, Aharon Shmutser

Yiddish Abridged Version: Yaacov Levin

Editing of the Yiddish Version: Zvi (Tzvi) Eisenman

Translation of the Abridged Version into English: Rachel Mann [Rachman]

Map of Braslav (Drawn from Memory): Chaim Band

Map of Opsa (Drawn from Memory): Yaacov Aviel

Photographs: Private collections

Gathering of Material: Moshe Bogomolski

Graphic Editing: Arieh Velleman

[Total of 640 pages, comprising 496 pages in Hebrew, a Yiddish-language section of 72 pages, and an English-language section of 72 pages]

Copyright by the Ghetto Fighters' House
Printed in Israel 1986 (5746)
Chidekel Printers Ltd., Tel Aviv

[Pages 5-8]

TABLE OF CONTENTS

Translated from the Hebrew by Laia Ben-Dov
Donated by Jeff Deitch

[Page 9]

Introduction

Translated from the Hebrew by Jerrold Landau
Footnote Added / Donated by Jeff Deitch

"Then they spoke . . . each to his friend . . . and a book of remembrance was written . . ."

--- Malachi 3:16

The terrible tragedy that afflicted our nation with the destruction of European Jewry in general and Polish Jewry in particular --- the destruction, the annihilation of hundreds of large and small communities in Eastern Europe, the physical and spiritual liquidation the like of which had never occurred in either Jewish history or general human history, carried out by the Nazis and their collaborators --- will not be forgotten, will never be erased from the annals of humanity.

The storm of destruction that passed over the Jewish nation must be chronicled by the Holocaust survivors who were living witnesses to the terrible atrocities perpetrated by the Nazis.

In the preface to his book *Kiddush Hashem*, Sholem Asch, the renowned Yiddish writer, conveyed a sentence from an old book on the Chmielnicki uprising.[1] These were his words: "We are embarrassed to describe everything that the enemies, may their names be blotted out, did to us, so as not to degrade man, who was created in the image of G-d."

Is it possible for us not to tell, write or publicize the deeds of the Nazis? Not to describe the torture, humiliation, murder, gas chambers, valleys of murder?

The story of the historian Simon Dubnow spread through the ghettos. As he was being taken to his death [in 1941], he turned to Jews near him and said, "Write and record!"

With holy trembling, we fulfill the command --- to write, to leave something in writing about what happened to us, to our parents, our children, youths, elders --- for those coming after us, our children and grandchildren, for generation after generation.

--- Yaacov Levin [member of the Editorial Board]

Footnote:

1.   *Kiddush Hashem*, published in Yiddish in 1919, was a historical novel on the Chmielnicki uprising of Cossacks against the Polish-Lithuanian Commonwealth that began in 1648 and continued intermittently into the 1650s. In the course of the rebellion, mass atrocities were committed against the civilian populations --- Jewish and Polish-Lithuanian --- mainly in what's now Ukraine, which was part of the commonwealth at that time. Several hundred Jewish communities were destroyed, with current estimates of deaths and refugees each running into the tens of thousands at a minimum. The uprising saw the first mass murder of Jews in Eastern Europe.

Gathering of Braslav natives on the Memorial Day

[The banner at the top says in Hebrew: "A meeting of Braslaver survivors on the fifth
anniversary of the deaths / 18 Sivan 5707 / June 6, 1947 / in the camp Herzog [in] Hesse-
Litau" (The Herzog camp was near Kassel in central Germany.)
The placard at bottom says in Hebrew: "May G-d avenge the blood of the martyred souls of
Braslav and environs who were murdered at the hands of Hitler, may his name be blotted out
/ 18 Sivan 5702 to 2 Tammuz 5702 [June 3, 1942 to June 17, 1942] in the town
of Braslav" (The last two words in the placard are indecipherable in the photo.)]

[Page 10]

From the Editorial Board

Translated from the Hebrew by Jerrold Landau
Footnotes Added / Donated by Jeff Deitch

The book before you for Braslav and the surrounding area --- *Emesh Shoah*[1] [*Darkness and Desolation*] --- includes testimony, memoirs and accounts from many natives of Braslav, Opsa, Okmenitz, Dubina, Zamosh, Zarach, Yaisi, Yod, Slobodka and Kislovshchitzna [as well as Plusy and Rimshan], written by people who experienced indelibly the events of the Holocaust perpetrated upon us by the Nazi enemy. Some were put into ghettos and survived by hiding in various places, some were deported to forced labor and death camps, and some joined the partisans and fought against the cruel enemy and its local collaborators, while others fought in the allied Red, Polish and British armies.

This book is being published almost a generation later, 40 years [1986]. Time hasn't blunted the pain, nor has it eased the horror of destruction, annihilation and the death of individuals as well as entire communities. In it you'll find descriptions of strength and bravery, heroism, self-sacrifice and the will to survive. It deals with the relentless struggle of individuals and groups who fought --- the few against the many, the unarmed against a well-oiled war machine. The courage of all contributed in no small way to victory against the forces of darkness --- the Nazi enemy.

The book includes descriptions of events in the towns, stories and images of Jews as they're etched in the writers' memories. It portrays everyday Jews and Jews of festivals and holy days, poor Jews struggling for a livelihood, Jews in relation to Gentiles, and Jews in relation to other Jews in a range of community activities, a full spectrum, as well as childhood pastimes.

And after the Holocaust:

Decades haven't washed away the blood nor quieted people's cries. Let the pages of this memorial book serve as a monument, a testimony and a sign of the honor that we, the survivors and our descendants, owe to them.

The idea of publishing a memorial book to the Holocaust victims of Braslav and the surrounding region was formed many years ago. Impressions of events and the gathering of testimony commenced as early as in the displaced people's camps on conquered German soil, which the first survivors reached soon after the war's end. There, in the U.S. and British occupation zones, the first memorial ceremony for the martyrs of Braslav and the region was conducted in 1947. The memorial was organized by Zusman Lubovitz [Lubowicz] in the Eschwege camp. The next memorial took place on 17 Sivan [June 24] 1948 in the Herzog camp.[2] It was organized by Zalman Charmatz, Tuvia Fisher, Eliahu Shmidt, Bentzion Charmatz, of blessed memory, and David Sztrimling, of blessed memory.

In 1949, after the survivors made *aliyah* to Israel, a memorial ceremony was organized in the home of David Sztrimling in Haifa. A year later, a committee of natives of Braslav and the region was set up through the efforts of David Sztrimling, Zusman Lubovitz and Zalman Charmatz. From this time, annual memorial ceremonies were organized at various locations in Israel.

The idea of publishing a memorial book was discussed on many occasions during the meetings and memorial ceremonies, but actualization of the plan was long deferred due to the size of the undertaking.

The members of the committee deserve praise. They include the head Yehuda Chepelevitz [Cepelewicz], Moshe Goldin, Moshe Vishkin [Wishkin] and Arieh Munitz. They gave of their time and abilities to convene the memorial ceremonies and meetings. The crowning achievements of their vital activities in the latter years were two endeavors of great worth: (1) With the assistance of Yitzchak Reichel [Rajchel], they obtained an urn of soil saturated with the blood of our martyrs. It was brought to Israel from the killing pits in Braslav by Shlomo Reichel and buried in Holon Cemetery, and a monument was erected to the martyrs' memory [in June 1981]. (2) Through their tireless, blessed efforts, the decision to publish the book *Emesh Shoah* was realized --- another monument to our martyrs. Our friends Mendel Maron, Charles Witkin and Tuvia Fisher, from the committee of Braslav natives in the United States, were also brought into this important endeavor. They took upon themselves a full partnership in funding the pages of the book. Mendel Maron began the good deed and

[Page 11]

the treasurer of the committee, Tuvia Fisher, gave a great deal of his time and abilities to the fundraising effort --- he deserves our appreciation and gratitude.

To edit the literary material and forge the form, scope and content of the book, an editorial board was selected, composed of Yaacov Levin, Yaacov Aviel, Moshe Bogomolski and Aharon Shmutser. The latter, a member of Kibbutz Ein Carmel, was brought in to help us on account of his wife, Monka, a native of Braslav. He united his efforts with ours, working extensively to translate and collect testimony. The material that reached us was written mainly in Yiddish, with some in Hebrew. There were also testimonies in Polish and Russian. The members were involved in rewriting, translating into Hebrew, formulating the text, and performing the first editorial pass on the material. An extended committee was set up especially for the purposes of the book, to deliberate fundamental issues.

Blessings shall come to the following:

Thanks and appreciation to the natives of Braslav and the region who wrote about the story of their lives during the period of the Holocaust.

We appreciate and recognize the activities of the director of Beit Lochamei HaGetaot [the Ghetto Fighters' House in Israel], Zvi Shner, of blessed memory, who encouraged, guided and helped to actualize the idea of publishing the book.

We extend our thanks to Sarah Shner, Zvika Dror and Yitzchak Sternberg, members of Kibbutz Lochamei HaGetaot, for whom the topic of the Holocaust is close to their hearts, for reading the manuscripts, sharing their impressions and encouraging publication.

To Benjamin Anolik, a member of the Ghetto Fighters' House board of directors who worked to obtain photocopied sections from the Polish National Library and who photocopied sections from the book *Historja Powiatu Brasławskiego* [*History of Braslav County*, published in Polish in 1930] by Otton Hedemann and copies of microfilms from the Yashinski trial,[3] we owe much gratitude.

To Yaacov Levin, who wrote the abridged Yiddish section; to Zvi Eisenman of Beit Lochamei HaGetaot, who edited it; and to Rachel Mann, a native of Braslav living in Johannesburg who translated the abridged version from Yiddish to English --- we thank them.

We were assisted by

The Library of the Ghetto Fighters' House
The National Library of Jerusalem University
The Archives of Yad Vashem
The Archives of the Ministry of Defense
The YIVO Archive in New York
The Library of Congress in Washington, D.C.

We received financial assistance from

The Amos Foundation, Office of the President of the State of Israel
The Fund for the Perpetuation of the Memory of Polish Jewry
The U.S. association of the Jews of Braslav and the surrounding region

To all of them, our thanks and blessing.

--- The Editorial Board

[Page 12]

For them, for them . . .

A shiny precious stone amid green forests, surrounded on all sides by blue ponds, with the skies peering down upon them as if into a mirror, with stars twinkling and flickering on moonlit nights. The depths of silence and calm enveloped all creation, imparting feelings of melancholy and mystery.

And in the winter, during the months of Tevet and Shevat, everything was covered with a white blanket, as strong ice overcame the waters of the surrounding ponds. Roads and houses slept under the cover of snow. From time to time, a few sounds could be heard --- the cracking of ice and the sound of wind singing in the oak trees ---

. . . In this way, memories of a small town in northeastern Poland rise up and take wing --- one town out of many, whose sons and daughters remained after the final destruction, bearing its memory in their hearts . . .

Our town [Braslav] wasn't large: approximately 400 families, scattered in the land around the mountain --- Castle Hill, rising from the center of the town, nestled between ponds, rivers and forests.

It wasn't large but was full of life, bustling and struggling for centuries, with all its institutions: a yeshiva, schools, clubs, factions, clergy, toilers, merchants, shopkeepers, and inquisitive youth who were thirsty for knowledge and wisdom . . .

Decades have passed since it was destroyed and its Jews were annihilated . . . Decades, years of eclipse for European Jewry . . .

Decades . . .

Is it possible to forget, to remove from memory, to not remember and memorialize?! With trembling and awe, we have come to gather, collect and preserve a small part of the events of our town so that coming generations will know, for the sake of those that follow us, for the sake of those who didn't see the events and the history.

For those who come after us, and for those who are no longer, for all those whose souls are with us, for them, for their memory, let this book serve as an eternal memorial and monument.

In memory of our martyrs ---

Let us remember . . .

Footnotes:

1. The title of this memorial book was taken from the Book of Job 30:3: *"B'chesed ub'kaffan galmud haorkim tziya,* **emesh shoah** *um'shoah"* ("In poverty and hunger, alone they flee to the desert, a place of darkness, a desert wasteland").

2. The Eschwege camp was a displaced persons (DP) camp near Frankfurt, Germany, in the American-occupied zone, that operated from 1946 to 1949. The Herzog camp was a DP camp near Kassel, Germany, also in the American-occupied zone, that operated during the same period.

3. The 1963 trial of Stanislav Yashinski (Stanislaw Jasinski), a Gentile who served the Nazis in Braslav as head of the town's local police in 1941-44, is described on pages 134-142 of this memorial book.

[Page 13]

Braslav [Braslaw]: Chapters from Its History

Emblem of the town of Braslav

[Page 14 = Blank in the original]

[Page 15]

Braslav: Historical Notes[1]
By Yaacov Levin

Translated from the Hebrew by Jerrold Landau
Footnotes Added / Donated by Jeff Deitch

The history of Braslav [Braslaw] lies hidden in the mists of the distant past. According to information in our possession, Braslav was first noted in 1065, almost 300 years before the founding of Vilna.

In the 11th century Braslav belonged to the principality of Polotsk,[2] in the borderland between what's now Poland, Russia and Lithuania. It appears that its name derives from Duke Bryachislav [Bryachislaw], who ruled the area at that time. We can assume that Braslav originated as a border town, with all that this entails. Its geographical location was well suited to protecting the border, due to the hills and bodies of water around it, with marshland to the east, lakes and a ridge of consecutive peaks. Its proximity to the Dvina (Daugava) River [some 28 kilometers to the north and flowing east-west], an artery for transportation and commerce and a link to the Baltic Sea, also contributed greatly to its development.

During the 13th century, Braslav belonged to the Grand Duchy of Lithuania and was under the rule of the renowned Grand Duke Gediminas.[3]

During the time of union between Poland and Lithuania, in the era of the Jagiellonian rulers in 1410,[4] Braslav was annexed to the Vilna district, and it was one of the five administrative areas (*powiaty*) in the district. Incidentally, the name of Braslav appears as "Braslaw Litewski" [the Braslav of Lithuania] in all official documents, to distinguish it from the Ukrainian (Moscovite) Breslov near Uman.[5] Braslav suffered greatly from battles and fires due to the continual feuds and disputes between the rulers of Poland and Russia (known at that time as Moscovia). The Tatar invasion also left its mark on the town: residents had to pay heavy taxes to the conquerors, whose flag was raised atop the mountain [Castle Hill],[6] the fortress mountain upon which the Tatar army was stationed.

In the 16th century, the town was under the guardianship of the Polish prince Sapieha. Braslav passed from hand to hand, from one prince to the next through the years, as a result of the sale of the land and its residents.

The fortress mountain that stood in the heart of Braslav served as the town center in those days. The military barracks for the local troops was built on it, and it was also the center of the Christian faith, site of a church and monastery.

During the 17th century, the town suffered from a flood that damaged and destroyed the majority of the buildings. The damage was so great that the central authorities in Warsaw freed the town from all taxes and duties for the next 40 years, through a special decree.

A proclamation from the year 1792 testifies to Braslav's strategic importance --- a special edict of the Polish King Stanislav August [Stanislaw August Poniatowski, who ruled from 1764 to 1795] noted the town's uniqueness and its contribution to the crown. In his proclamation, the king designated the town's emblem as a radiant triangle with an eye in its center --- the "Eye of Providence" (*oko opatrznósci*) [pictured on page 13]. We have no additional information on the town's development for several centuries. As one historian noted, the lack of information is due to the many wars, and particularly to the invasion of Vilna [in 1812] by Napoleon's army, which burned most of the historical documents of the region.[7]

[Page 16]

> **Excerpt from the Newspaper *HaMelitz*,[8] 20th Year, 12 Shevat 5644 [February 8, 1884, in Hebrew]:**
>
> From Braslav: (Kovno District). Mr. Shlomo-David Sherman states that an edict was issued by the authorities to close three Hebrew houses of worship, as they were built without government permission. They were given a period of grace of one month only. The writer urges his townsfolk to rise up against this travesty through intercession before the time passes --- after which they will be like those who cry out and are not answered.

> **Excerpt from the Newspaper *HaMelitz* No. 39, 20th Year, 9 Sivan 5644 [June 2, 1884, in Hebrew]:**
>
> From Braslav (Kovno District) --- Previously I published in *HaMelitz* something on the great dispute in our town between the Hasidim and the Mitnagdim [opponents of the Hasidim], in which people are causing ruin to each other and bringing petitions to government officials.[9] It is because of this that all the synagogues in the town have been closed. And is it not serious that nine people involved in the strife have been sentenced to six months in prison for signing a request to the district minister? For all the houses of worship in the town had been built through permits from imperial officials, and they [presumably the Hasidim] still requested to open their own special house of worship (for the Hasidim), whose opponents have said that they're building without government permission in the year 5639 (1879). When it became known to the district minister that this was a lie and that people had sworn falsely, they were sentenced to six months in prison.[10]
>
> I hereby inform the public that all the houses of prayer that had been closed have now been "opened," not through the edict of the imperial officials but rather through the great fire that afflicted the town for many days. Approximately 100 structures, including houses of worship, some 150 years old, were burnt.
>
> --- David-Shlomo Sherman

Jews of the Town and Its Environs

The few documents we have show that Jews were mentioned in Braslav in the 16th century. For example, a document dealing with the census of 1559 [sic] listed several Jewish families, including those named Bik, Nemirovitz [Nemirowicz] and Kravitz [Krawiec].[11]

In general, the primary occupation of the Jews was commerce. Some of them were also tradesmen, such as tailors, saddlers and shoemakers.

According to the document, the Jews of Braslav and its environs were organized into [main] communities and secondary communities. The independent communities were Braslav, Druya and Vidz [Widze], while the smaller, secondary communities were Opsa, Slobodka, Drisviati [Dryswyaty] and Druysk.[12]

It appears that at the time the Jews enjoyed the same rights extended to the rest of the population. We can assume this from a report published by a researcher from the royal office of King Stanislav August, who wrote that the Jews of the community enjoyed conditions similar to those in England and Holland.

[Page 17]

Excerpt from the Newspaper *HaMelitz* No. 13, 25th Year, 12 Adar 5645 [February 27, 1885, in Hebrew]:

Braslav (Kovno district) --- The extent to which the level of Torah and its upholders has declined in these years can be understood by anyone who sees the notices posted on the walls of the synagogue in our town by the local rabbi. From his soul he pleads, like a pauper at the door, for people to think of him and have mercy on him, so that he and his family members do not die of starvation. Whose heart would not be moved when it hears of the condition of such a person, who is visited by many people and asked for words of Torah from his mouth! The people of our town, who would find it easy to collect 20 silver rubles weekly for their far-off *tzaddikim* [righteous ones] and *rebbes* [Hasidic spiritual leaders], find it difficult and do not gather five silver rubles weekly for their rabbi who lives among them, to keep him from being afflicted by hunger . . . Where is the money from their tax that they imposed on the poor of the town: from meat, salt and yeast? Great men of the town, if you are dissatisfied with the rabbi and complaints against him, it will still be considered a great sin if you turn your eyes away from him, he who has occupied the rabbinical seat here for some 20 years and is now old and weak, and can no longer travel around. You have the duty and obligation to guide him with bread, even if you appoint another rabbi in his place.

I will now use this place to alert the Hasidim of our town to not stand in castigation against the Mitnagdim in building their own Beit Midrash in place of the Beit Midrash that was burnt last summer [in 1884]. If that which is heard in the town is true, that hundreds of Hasidim petitioned the district minister to not grant the Ashkenazim (as the Mitnagdim are known) a permit to build the Beit Midrash, it will be considered a great travesty on your part, especially at such a bad time in our country for the House of Israel. We must band together as one and not incite one against the other. Only through peace, the vessel that holds blessing, can we stand up and exist without allowing our enemies to harm us.

--- David-Shlomo Sherman

However, the report [from the royal office for King Stanislav August mentioned on page 16] may not have been objective. Other documents show that the lives of the Jews under the Polish and Russian governments in those times were not at all comfortable. There are documents that include complaints and libels accusing the Jews of being spies and haters of Christians, especially during the times of change in government. One historian wrote that he simply couldn't put on paper a description of the lowly conditions the Jews endured in those places. It's possible to understand the Jews and their feelings in those times and explain some of the accusations against them as follows: On account of the continual wars that afflicted the district, given that Braslav was a border town and there were frequent changes in government (Poland, Russia, Lithuania, the Tatars), the Jews always found themselves between a hammer and an anvil. Each of the new rulers could accuse them of disloyalty, spying and the like.

Innkeeping (*karczma*) was one of the sources of the Jews' livelihood. Innkeepers were scattered along the roads, in the villages, and even in the town, with some of them leasing businesses from the estate owners.[13]

We have no verified information about the exact number and status of the Jewish population, but there are

[Page 18]

several written testimonies stating that there was an attempt to settle Jews on the soil, in independent villages, some of which carried on until they were destroyed during the Holocaust that overtook Polish Jewry in general.

For example, in the years 1847-48 the government of Russia allotted lands to the Jews and set up village settlements such as Druysk, Plissa [Plusy], Dubinovo [Dubinowo, a.k.a. Dubina], Yaisi [Jaisi], Ikazn and others.[14] We can surmise that this succeeded, for these settlements later developed into small towns focused on agriculture and existed up until World War II.

The rapid development of Braslav and its surroundings began during the first years of the present century. The number of families increased, after declining following pogroms and the Russo-Japanese War [in 1904-05], which had caused a portion of the town's population to move to Danzig, and even to far-off America and other places.

After World War I, many families that had moved to places in central Russia began to return. The returnees both increased the Jewish population and were a factor in the town's development.

Between the Two World Wars: The Image of the Town

The houses of the town were scattered among the sand dunes, nestled between the large Lake Driviata [Drywiaty, a.k.a. Dryviaty] (40 square kilometers) and the small Lake Noviata [Nowiata] (three square kilometers) --- like mushrooms, nestling against the mountain --- the fortress mountain [Castle Hill], like a hoop. The main street used to be called Large [Bolshaya] Street. After World War I [when Poland regained its independence] its name was changed to honor Marshal Pilsudski, the leader of the new Poland.

The street was long and straight. On its eastern side, from the hill on which the windmill stood silent like a statue, the street descended below over a wooden bridge over the banks of a nameless rivulet joining the two lakes. The street continued, paved with uncut stones. There were sidewalks of wooden boards on both sides that shook with every step. All the houses were wooden, except for two or three white brick houses. There were houses that looked as if they'd been swallowed in mud from age: low and grayish brown, with their squashed roofs covered by greenery. There were houses that stood out with pride, as if boasting of their thick pine walls and tall windows. Between the houses there were stores for haberdashery, linens and oils, as well as butcher shops and small workshops. There were also a few general stores that carried all sorts of merchandise, including food as well as merchandise for the farmers of the area such as harnesses, saddles, plows, sickles, ropes, wagon grease and so on.

The Catholic church jutted out on one side, at the entrance to Third of May Street (named for the day in 1791 that the Polish constitution had been issued), on a low hill. It was built of red bricks and pierced the skies with its thin crosses. Opposite it, on the other side of the street, on the banks of the large lake, was the Pravoslavic [Eastern] Orthodox church. It was situated between green lawns, appearing short and modest with its five onion domes.

All day, it would sound as if the church bells were competing with each other, calling out to their listeners for prayers morning and evening.

[Page 19]

Not far from them, on the slope of the street, was the synagogue courtyard. There were four synagogues in the town, and for some reason they were referred to as *minyanim* [prayer quorums]: the New Minyan, the Old Minyan, the Sandy Minyan, and the Beit Midrash [all but the Sandy Minyan were between Castle Hill and Lake Driviata]. The Sandy Minyan was located further away from the other synagogues --- on a sandy sidestreet [around one side of Castle Hill], which gave it its name. The three minyans were for the Hasidim; only the Beit Midrash was for the Mitnagdim.

The street continued on until Bik's flourmill. There was located the local power mill, which provided electricity and light to the town.

The main street was paved as a narrow strip along the large lake, whose waters irrigated the vegetable gardens of the householders. Sometimes during winter storms, when the strong winds blew, blue hailstones fell noisily upon the town, striking the houses at the edge of the lake like a thirsty beast without restraint. Then tumult arose as the residents of the town gathered ---

firefighters and ordinary people --- armed with rods, bayonets and other such vessels, fighting the forces of nature for two or three days before the eyes of the curious onlookers.

The two lakes that surrounded the town, as if grasping it from both sides, were among the most beloved places for the residents, especially the youth, as places for enjoyment and meeting each other. On clear summer nights, they'd go out in boats. Loud singing could be heard, now approaching, now moving away, until the early hours of the morning.

The lakes served mainly as places for bathing and swimming. Each year, there were drownings. When this happened residents would gather at the banks, and swimmers armed with fishing nets and other implements worked day and night searching for the bodies, as heavy mourning enveloped the town. "The lake drowns our relatives," people whispered through tears.

At the western edge, the street merged with the road, paved with limestone and gravel, that led to Vilna through Jewish towns, villages, estates of landowners, sand dunes, and oak and fir forests.

Several streets and alleyways branched off from the north side of the main street. Third of May Street ran from the Catholic church, passed opposite the small lake, and connected with the Gentile suburb of Gumnes until the small railway station, for travel from the nearby town of Druya to the intersection of the Warsaw-Zemgale international train.[15] There, opposite the narrow railway tracks, a sandy road meandered to the small Jewish settlement of Dubinovo, whose residents were occupied in agriculture, trade and commerce with Braslav.

Several secondary streets crossed the town's length and breadth, passing by the central market, the post office, the Magat Brothers Printing House, toward the old cemetery, and further on in the direction of the neighborhood of the government officials --- a green, cultivated neighborhood, with new houses and paved roads. The neighborhood was surrounded by the Karpovitz [Karpowicz] pine forest --- one of the places where the town residents went for excursions and enjoyment. However, because of its proximity to the neighborhood of the officials, Jews didn't particularly like that forest. They preferred the Dubkes forest, which was situated on the shore of the large lake, with golden sands on the shore. Young people and children would spend time there on Sabbaths and festivals. Later, during the time of the Nazi occupation [1941-44], the forest, spread over a large area, was one of the important places for partisans to gather.

[Pages 20-21: Map of Braslav]

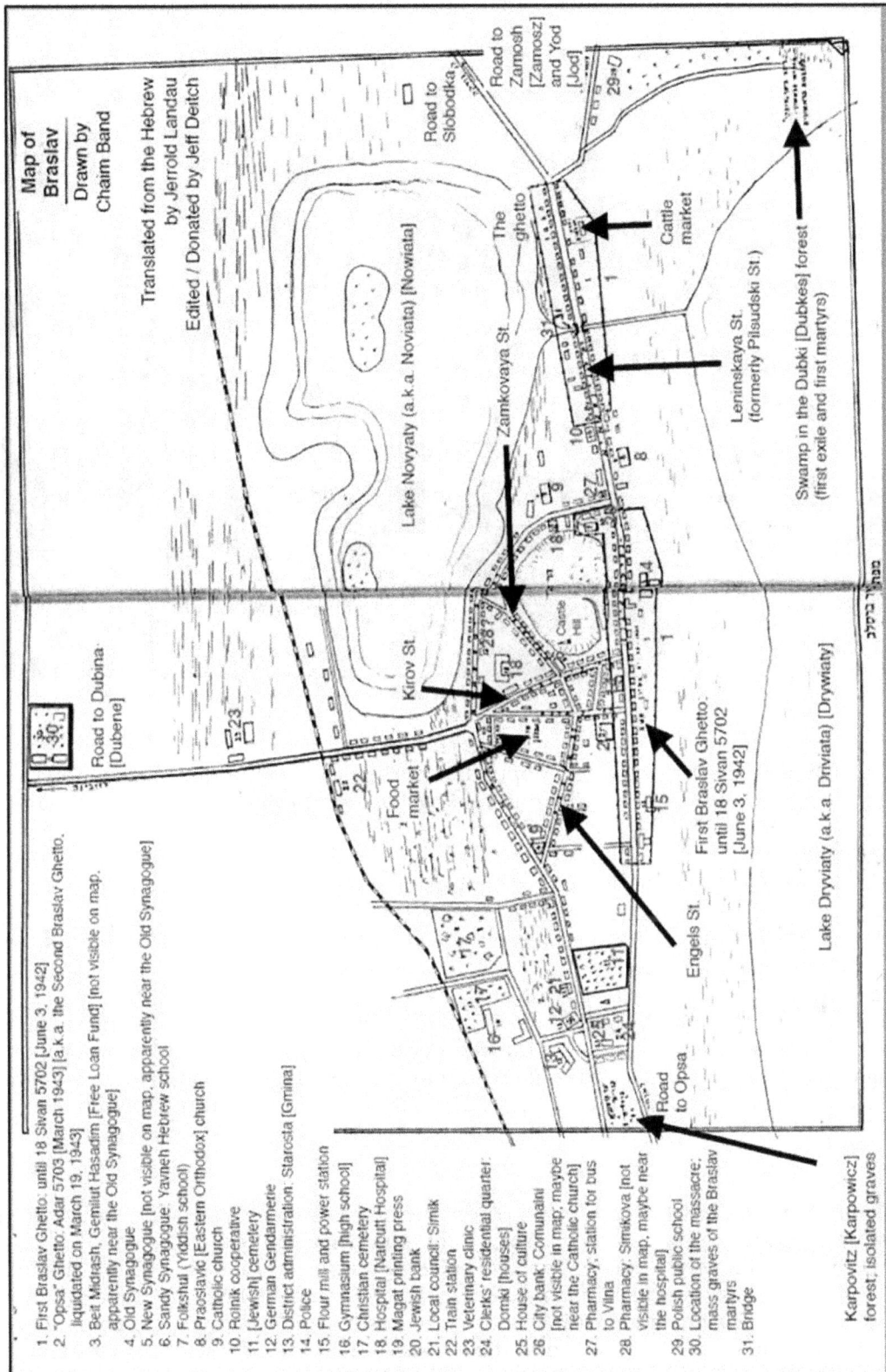

Map of
Braslav
Drawn by
Chaim Band

Translated from the Hebrew
by Jerrold Landau

Edited / Donated by Jeff Deitch

Road to Zamosh [Zamosz] and Yod [Jod]

Road to Slobodka

Road to Dubina [Dubene]

Lake Novyaty (a.k.a. Noviata) [Nowiata]

The Zamkovaya St.

ghetto

Cattle market

Leninskaya St. (formerly Pilsudski St.)

Swamp in the Dubki [Dubkes] forest (first exile and first martyrs)

Kirov St.

Castle Hill

Food market

Engels St.

First Braslav Ghetto, until 18 Sivan 5702 [June 3, 1942]

Lake Dryviaty (a.k.a. Drviata) [Drywiaty]

Road to Opsa

1. First Braslav Ghetto: until 18 Sivan 5702 [June 3, 1942]
2. "Opsa" Ghetto: Adar 5703 [March 1943] [a.k.a. the Second Braslav Ghetto, liquidated on March 19, 1943]
3. Bet Midrash, Gemilut Hasadim [Free Loan Fund] [not visible on map, apparently near the Old Synagogue]
4. Old Synagogue
5. New Synagogue [not visible on map, apparently near the Old Synagogue]
6. Sandy Synagogue: Yavneh Hebrew school
7. Folkshul [Yiddish school]
8. Praoslavic [Eastern Orthodox] church
9. Catholic church
10. Rolnik cooperative
11. [Jewish] cemetery
12. German Gendarmerie
13. District administration: Starosta [Gmina]
14. Police
15. Flour mill and power station
16. Gymnasium [high school]
17. Christian cemetery
18. Hospital [Narcutt Hospital]
19. Magat painting press
20. Jewish bank
21. Local council: Simik
22. Train station
23. Veterinary clinic
24. Clerks' residential quarter: Domki [houses]
25. House of culture
26. City bank: Comunalni [not visible in map; maybe near the Catholic church]
27. Pharmacy, station for bus to Vilna
28. Pharmacy: Smakova [not visible in map, maybe near the hospital]
29. Polish public school
30. Location of the massacre: mass graves of the Braslav martyrs
31. Bridge

Karpovitz [Karpowicz] forest: Isolated graves

[Page 22]

View of Braslav

Paths covered with limestone led from the town to the surrounding villages. One of them was the Jewish village of Yaisi, which was populated by several tens of families who earned their livelihood from agriculture --- primarily from raising goats and selling their products to the town.

The Market

Unlike other towns, most of the shops in Braslav weren't concentrated in and around the marketplace. Instead, nearly all were on the main street. The market was situated in a large area, not paved or fenced off. Houses bordered it on all sides. The only place empty of houses was the entrance, opposite the post office.

On Wednesdays and Fridays, the days designated as market days, the area's farmers streamed into the town. Amid bustle, noise and the neighing of horses, the town merchants wandered about, negotiating, conducting business and shaking hands. All types of products were on the wagons: fowls, pig bristles, hides, flax, animal fodder, hay, firewood, fruits and vegetables.

Business was especially vibrant and loud during the autumn, when the town residents went out to buy

[Page 23]

provisions to store during the winter. Then the market was filled with housewives, and children wandered among the wagons to search for what they wanted.

In the bustle and din, the "*chinomi*" always called attention to himself. He got this nickname because he was always shouting, "*Chinom, chinom, hakol chinom!*" ["Free, free, everything's free!"] . . . as he stood on his wagon laden with brushes, creams, cheap perfumes and colored kerchiefs. He'd demonstrate the strength, benefit and usefulness of his products with his teeth and hands, as he called out his motto in a hoarse, cracked voice, "Free! Free! Everything's free!" The village women, old and young, gathered around him, enjoying and imitating his clownish movements. Sometimes, when he was unsuccessful at publicizing his merchandise, or when a comb broke or a kerchief tore, they'd burst out laughing. With an embarrassed look on his face, he'd laugh with those around him, wiping the sweat from his brow.

At times, two or three "*chinomis*" would come to the market. Then a dizzying competition, accompanied by mutual mocking and insults, would break out. This was one of the most beloved spectacles for the market-goers.

The farmers of the region, especially those whose lands were divided between Poland and Latvia after World War I and whose relatives lived on the other side of the border, also occupied themselves with smuggling. One of the most lucrative products for this was sugar, which was "protected" due to government taxes and duties. Sugar was brought to town [by the smugglers] and sold to the shopkeepers at a price that was much cheaper than the government price. On market days, farmers would arrive in wagons laden with fodder or hay, with sacks of sugar buried beneath. The shopkeepers knew the smugglers by sight and would purchase the contents of the entire wagon, including what was hidden inside them. Sometimes a farmer would be caught by the police with his load and forced to drive from the market to the police station. The distance was sufficiently far that the farmer, knowing the hidden goods would be confiscated in any case, would secretly cut open the bags. The sugar would spill on the route without the police realizing it, since they were traveling in front of the wagon holding the reins of the horse --- all to the general amusement of the shopkeepers and onlookers.

Employment and Economy

Not a small number of heads of households earned their livelihoods by driving wagons. The closest large city was Vilna, 180 kilometers away.[16] Shipping merchandise to and from Vilna by train was complicated, due to the transfer stations between the "small" train and the regular one. It was easier and more comfortable to transport merchandise and loads directly from seller to purchaser through a caravan of wagons. Loading and unloading was also more comfortable and cheaper. In the winter, the autumn mud was frozen and snow covered the routes. Giant sleds hitched to horses of burden would transport fish, flax, wool and hides to the big city and would return with cloth, salt, haberdashery and groceries.

The most important branch of business, in which tens of families earned their livelihood, was fruit. A significant number of town residents were employed during the summer and autumn in guarding, harvesting and transporting apples and pears

[Page 24]

from the orchards and estates to the town [Braslav], for export to the large cities as well as for sale in the local market.

Fishing played an important role in the livelihoods of the town residents. The residents themselves were involved directly in it. In other words, since they were close to many surrounding lakes, they were able to earn their livelihoods from the purchase and sale of fish, and the transport and marketing.

Several individuals directed this business. Shneiur Aron, the primary lessee of fishing permits [in Braslav], was at their head. He maintained fishing staff in nearly all the villages of the area, equipped with nets and boats. The main fishing activities took place in the winter months, when the lakes froze and were covered by a thick layer of ice. Then the workers would go out, bore holes through the ice, and cast their fishing nets into the water. They'd remove the nets after two or three days with a bounty of silver fish.

Among the [Gentile] farmers, those adhering to the old group[17] of the Eastern Orthodox religion stood out; they were tall, thin men with long, thick beards. They'd gather and come to the town from all corners of the country, as well as from outside, to celebrate their traditional festival, which was unique to them, the Gromnitsa [Candlemas] holiday celebrated annually on February 23 [sic].[18] They'd arrive in decorated sleds, hitched to fine horses decorated with bells and colored ribbons tied to their manes. They'd travel through the town streets throughout the entire day. Maidens dressed in expensive furs and shiny, leather boots would stroll through the road in pairs. Sturdy lads in hats and sheepskin coats paced behind them.

Suddenly a lad would appear, sitting on a sled, snatch one of the girls, and disappear with his beloved as quick as an arrow. Of course, all this was organized from the beginning, according to the accepted custom as a form of courtship leading to marriage. This was a performance that everyone waited for; it was an enjoyable attraction.

During the early afternoon hours, a horse race took place on the ice of the frozen lakes. Many residents of the town were present at this competition.

The relations between the Jews of the town and the farmers of the area were generally proper and polite. In many cases, they were also friendly. On more than one occasion, they stood up to the wild incitement from anti-Semitic factions, especially after the Endeks --- the Polish national fascist party, a racist party --- increased their own activity.[19] This organization was set up with the help of the Nazi government that had then started its rule in Germany [sic]. Later, during the time of the Nazi occupation, it became clear that several leaders of the party, residents of the town, were Nazi infiltrators who assisted the deeds of murder and annihilation. However, there were also demonstrations of strong bonds between the Jews and the villagers. For example, in the village of Zahoria on the shore of Lake Ukla [about 18 kilometers southeast of Braslav], the Kagan family was attacked by Polish agitators, who wished to pillage their property and murder them. The head of the family was the lessee of fishing on the lake. All the people of the town, armed with pitchforks, sickles and axes, repelled the attackers and saved the Jewish family.

[Page 25]
Religious, Social and Cultural Life
A yeshiva with several tens of students functioned in two of the four synagogues of the town: the New Minyan and the Old Minyan. Approximately 60 students, some from the nearby settlements, studied in the yeshiva until the Russians came in 1939. A kitchen was set up for the students alongside the yeshiva. Some of the yeshiva lads ate their meals on a daily rotation basis: an old, accepted custom at most yeshivas. Of course, the portion of the lad depended on the economic situation of the host family. No small number of verses and humorous sayings have been written on this topic.

The head of the yeshiva was Rabbi Chaim Tarshish of the village of Yaisi near Braslav. From an economic perspective, the situation of the yeshiva was very difficult. This is confirmed by the extensive correspondence between the principal of the yeshiva, Henech Veinshtein, and the yeshiva committee. The correspondence is full of requests and complaints about the situation of the yeshiva. The yeshiva's circumstances declined further with the opening of the Yavneh school,[20] which led to a drop in donations to the yeshiva by local residents. The complaints of the yeshiva activists increased, growing bitter and more urgent.

Despite this, this Torah institution added to the character of the town. Many of its students went on to acquire Torah in the large yeshivas of other cities.

The Etz Chaim Yeshiva of Braslav
[The sign in the photo says the year is 5690, that is, October 1929 to September 1930.]

[Page 26]

Questionnaire on the Yeshiva's Condition and Quality
The Yeshiva Committee Center of Vilna
Place: Braslav
Questionnaire on the situation and quality of the yeshiva

a. Distance of the place from the railway line: Station[?] Braslav [original is hard to read]
b. Name of the institution: Etz Chaim Yeshiva
c. Number of grades and classes: Five grades
d. Order and quality of the students of each grade: [reply illegible]
e. Total number of students, and detailed list of all students by year: 61
f. Number of students in each grade: *aleph* = 16; *beit* = 18; *gimel* = 10 *daled* = 8; *he* = 9
g. Number of local students: 22
h. Number of students from the area: 35
i. Number of students from distant places: ---
j. Number of students who came from outside the country: ---
k. Number of students who take their meals at householders: 35
l. Number of students who are supported by the kitchen: 23
m. Who directs the kitchen, the yeshiva principal or a householder:
n. Number of students who receive support, and the amount of support for each: ---
o. Number of teachers: 5
p. Number of principals and spiritual supervisors: 1
___ day of the month of Sivan 5690 [May or June 1930], place: Braslav

Signature of the yeshiva head and principal: Henech Veinshtein, Braslav

[Page 27]

The Hebrew Yavneh school in Braslav
[Sitting in the group are two leaders of the town's Jewish community: Rafael-Yaacov Munitz at far left and Shneiur Aron at center-right; they also appear on page 30.]

Sixth grade, 1935

[Page 28]

There were two rabbis in Braslav, who led the community for many years. The rabbi of the Mitnagdim was Rabbi Hershel Valin, a tall, strong man, with a thin, black beard, streaked with gray hair. He was a fine orator. He busied himself with matters of religion and Torah, and served as the prayer leader on festivals and the High Holy Days. In the 1930s he left the town to move to the neighboring country of Latvia, where he was appointed rabbi of one of the communities there [Goldingen; see pages 66-67 of this memorial book]. The second rabbi, Rabbi Abba Zahorie, a very old man, served as the rabbi of the congregants of the Hasidic *minyanim*. He was quiet and introverted. His blue eyes always appeared as though they were scanning the surrounding world and caressing those to whom he was speaking. He was as innocent as a child. During the great disaster that overtook the town [on June 3-5, 1942; see pages 68-69 of this memorial book], he went to slaughter together with all of the people, as if accepting the judgment of the Creator with faith and love.

The synagogues served not only as a place for prayer and Torah study. The Yiddish school was also housed there. Classes took place in the women's gallery of the *minyanim*. Of course, this caused friction between the students of the yeshiva and the school on account of the different modes of dress, the wearing of head coverings, and other such things.

At the beginning of the 1930s, it was decided to set up a school [the Folkshul, with education in Yiddish] with the help of the TSYSHO, the Central Yiddish School Organization, and with the participation of the parents and supporters of the school.[21]

The school was set up in a large yard on the slope of the fortress mountain [Castle Hill] next to the Jewish bank, whose director Levi-Yitzchak Veinshtein was a supporter of the school. He not only assisted in its establishment but also did a great deal on behalf of the graduates when they continued their studies in the high school in Vilna.[22] In essence, the Folkshul in Braslav was the workbench upon which the intelligentsia of the town was forged. Graduates of the school went on to study in secondary and post-secondary schools in other towns. Some graduated from gymnasiums, real schools and technical schools, and returned to become teachers. They became the primary channels for disseminating knowledge and progressive ideas among the youth.

Aside from the activities in the classroom and the gym, the school organized various clubs. One was the drama club, which on occasion put on enjoyable performances, naturally in Yiddish. The chief bookkeeper of the bank, [Gershon] Viderevitz [Wydrowicz], as well as Shayke Deitch, were the living spirits of the drama club. Both were highly skilled actors; many of the youth gathered around them. Shayke Deitch would be murdered in Ponar[23] during one of the German Aktions in Vilna.

Wide-ranging party activity began to sprout in the town during the early 1920s. Through the influence and direction of the Hebrew teacher Reb Rafael Munitz, a veteran lover of Zion, the first HeChalutz [Pioneer] group was established.[24] It began practical work, such as the preparation of land for agriculture, fishing, study of Hebrew and the Tanach [the Hebrew Bible], and especially disseminating the idea of a return to Zion among the young people. Several young people received certificates and made *aliyah* to the Land of Israel, including Moshe Valin, a son of the town rabbi. He was an actor in the theater and performed in Ansky's *The Dybbuk*, *Uriel Acosta*, *Yehudit* and other plays.[25] Later, in Israel, he became active in the Li La Lo Theater [in Tel Aviv] and a well-known impresario.

The Revisionist movement arose later, headed by deputy defense attorney Shimon Gelishkovski [Geliszkowski].[26]

Supporters and friends of the Yiddish school were known as Folksists (populists). Their ideology tended toward the Bund Party [the Jewish socialist party in Poland, which was anti-Zionist], which had a great influence in metropolitan centers in those days. Its influence weakened, however, with time. The only thing that testified to its existence in Braslav

[Page 29]

was the daily newspaper *Folks-Tsaytung*. The more accepted and widely read newspapers were generally *Der Moment* and *Haynt* from Warsaw and *Vilner Tog* from Vilna.[27]

Despite the shortage of manufacturing enterprises and a civic proletariat, activities of the Communist Party in the town and area were not lacking. Following World War I, a large part of the lands of Belorussia was annexed to Poland, along with a rural population numbering approximately one million. The lack of agricultural land for village farmers, the enslavement of entire villages in semi-permanent work for landowners and the Russian and Polish nobility, and the lack of work for rural youth who abandoned their villages due to poverty and government neglect --- all of these factors were fruitful ground for the growth and development of revolutionary ideas, as well as the desire for connection to the "large land" --- Soviet Russia. In the 1920s, an underground revolutionary group called Gromada was organized in the villages of the region. Jewish youth of the town also played an active role in it until the organization was crushed by the Polish police, and its heads and activists were arrested and given long prison sentences. From among those arrested, I'll mention Mantzik Balonov [Balonow] and Efraim Amdur, who was later appointed mayor when the Soviets entered Braslav. He fell as a fighter in the battle for Leningrad during the time of the Nazi occupation.

[In the years before World War II] the Communist Party continued to operate. Its primary activities included the dissemination of revolutionary announcements, issuing proclamations and providing flags for revolutionary holidays, collecting money for prisoners, and so on.

Despite the political divisions, there was no strangeness or actual split among the youth groups. Only on occasion, during factional assemblies, did debates or disturbances take place. In general the atmosphere was proper and warm, marked by joint entertainment and parties.

In September 1939 the community of Braslav, like others, fell within the boundaries of Soviet occupation. This led to a decline in cultural, religious and communal activities and marked the beginning of the end.

Slowly, one by one, echoes about the fate of the Jews who were trapped in the German-occupied areas began to reach the eastern areas of the country. The few refugees who succeeded in crossing the border told of the difficult situation and uncertainty that afflicted the Jews of central Poland [under German occupation in 1939-1941]. In contrast, the situation of the Jews to the east of the Bug River [under Soviet occupation in 1939-41 and including Braslav] wasn't bad from an economic perspective, even though the way of life had changed radically --- as if the vitality of their lives had been taken away. Slowly the cultural institutions, schools, *chederim* [Hebrew primary schools] and yeshivas were closed. No small number of people were deported to distant areas and separated from their families. Even members of the local Communist Party, who'd had great hopes that with the Red Army's entry they'd be able to help establish a local Soviet regime, were thrown into confusion and not greatly trusted by the Soviet Communist Party.

This existence in limbo continued for nearly two years for the Jews of Poland [in 1939-41], Braslav included, as they lived through this whirlwind of events that ended in destruction and obliteration.

[Page 30]

Leaders of Braslav's Jewish Community

Liber Chepelevitz

Baruch Fisher

Rafael-Yaacov Munitz

Shimon Gelishkovski

Zerach Bogomolski

Levi-Yitzchak Veinshtein

Shneiur Aron

Gershon Klioner

[Page 31]
Images:
Reb Shlomo-Itza [Shlomo-Yitzchak] Eidelson

He was a stocky man, as if hewn from the root of a tree. His white beard flowed over his chest and highlighted his short stature even more. He walked very cautiously between the houses and shops of the town, with a red handkerchief in his hand.

He neither begged or urged, but everyone knew: If Shlomo-Itza had come, it was a sign that someone needed immediate help. He was a type of charitable and benevolent institution --- whether to help bring a poor bride to the wedding canopy, assist a family whose head had fallen ill, buy a horse for a wagon driver whose animal had died, or simply aid someone in need.

Nobody asked the reason he was collecting the money, or for whom. With an expressionless face, he didn't even glance at the sum of money placed in his handkerchief, as if he understood the power of silence. Only on rare occasions, if someone asked whether he'd collected the needed amount, would he answer with a quiet voice and shy smile, "The needs of our nation are great, but I don't pass over anyone. I'll grant everyone the merit of giving charity, I don't want to embarrass anybody." Then he'd continue on his way.

At times, he was summoned for help in the dark of night. Then he'd go only to the wealthy people of the town and explain the reason for his visit, without mentioning the name of the person in need.

The residents of the town were accustomed to his figure. When they saw him walking on the side of the street, day or night, they knew that someone was in trouble, and they'd whisper and wonder, "Who, where, what happened?"

The Girl

Nobody knew where she came from or who she was. They didn't even know her name. She appeared one snowy, winter day, covered in rags, wearing torn overshoes, tied with rope. Her hair was cropped short, covered with a netted shawl wrapped over her shoulders and arms. Under them, she carried a small package attached to her shoulders.

Her prominent eyes testified to her insanity. She'd walk in the middle of the street, trampling through the deep snow, quietly muttering words that nobody understood. Toward evening, approaching a shopkeeper who stood wondering at her appearance, she'd utter in a hoarse voice, "The girl is hungry, the girl wants to eat."

She remained in the town for many years. Everyone got used to her, and no one bothered her. Many people, especially women, tried to meet her modest requests. She accepted everything in silence, occasionally uttering, "The girl, the girl."

At times, benevolent women took her to the bathhouse. They removed the rags that were covered with lice and insects, burned them, and dressed her in clean clothes. But she'd toss them away, find new rags, and cover herself in them once more.

At night, when quiet fell over the town, she'd wander through the streets with her small sack in her hand, singing a long, bright tune, wailing some sort of cradle song in her hoarse, cracked voice. At times she'd stop and raise her head toward the star-filled sky. With tears flowing

[Page 32]
down her wrinkled face, she'd ask, "Where are you, where?"

Someone said that she was from a faraway town, had once been married, and had lost her mind when her children died. And that she had wandered from place to place, filled with illusions and longing for her lost children. Finally she disappeared as she'd come; nobody knew where she'd gone. Only her voice remained as an obscure echo to her existence as "the girl" . . .

Dr. Narbutt[28]

The mountain [Castle Hill] that rose up in the center of town was much loved by all the residents as a place for excursions, games and enjoyment, especially for the children and young people. From the mountain it was possible to look far away, over the entire area, with its dense forests and blue lakes scattered around, to the gray horizon.

There were no buildings on the mountain, only dense, aromatic greenery. At the western side, literally at the end of the slope, a tall monument jutted out, thin as a needle, fenced in by thick chains. This was the grave of Dr. Narbutt, who'd been buried there at his own request.

Already in his lifetime, Dr. Narbutt was a legend. It was rumored that he was a Jew and this was why he'd asked to be buried on the mountain instead of in the Christian cemetery. He didn't want to be buried in the Jewish cemetery, it was said, to avoid causing problems for his son and daughter, who were considered to be Poles.

He limped slowly, holding a knotted cane in his hand, as he walked along the streets, mingled with the people of the town, and often took part in their conversations. At times, as a joke, he'd approach a group of students and join in their games. He'd jump on one foot and laugh, chatting in Yiddish with the children and giving them candies. Sometimes on summer evenings, he'd dive discreetly into the blue waters of the lake, emerging suddenly and unexpectedly among the bathing women, before disappearing again into the water as they screamed in surprise.

He took payments in a roundabout way for tending to the sick. He not only avoided taking money from poor people but also would sometimes give them a note for the pharmacy to provide the medication on his account.

He served as physician of the town for many years, and took part in all that happened there. He often visited the homes of Jews and spoke Yiddish like a Jew.

His death in 1928 [sic] was a heavy loss for the Jews of the town, who regarded him as a friend and intermediary.

Shmuel-Yosef Milutin

In general, good relations obtained between the Jewish population and the surrounding villages, with the exception of isolated incidents that demonstrated hidden anti-Semitic feelings among certain segments of the population.

During the times between regimes, when the town was left with no ruling authority --- such as happened during World War I, when the czarist Russian army retreated but the army of the German Kaiser hadn't yet entered the town --- the villagers and run-of-the-mill hooligans attacked with the aim of pillaging and killing Jews. In response, the town established a defense force of young Jews who got even with the perpetrators. There were injuries on both sides. In one case, a lad from the local self-defense force was even killed ---

[Page 33]

Yerachmiel-Mendel Meirson. The pervading atmosphere was difficult and oppressive. Then a brave, strong man arose, Shmuel-Yosef Milutin. Riding on a horse, with a gun in one hand and a sword in the other, he burst into the group of hooligans, striking with his sword right and left, and firing his gun. He chased off the attackers, scattering them in all directions. After this, the town quieted down until the arrival of a permanent government.

He was of the stock of the *nephilim*.[29] His son Chaim was among the first to be murdered by the Germans before the eyes of all the Jews of the town [in late June 1941], and many of his family members were active in the anti-Nazi underground and the partisans.

Members of the Bikur Cholim Society of Braslav for visiting and helping the sick [sitting in the center is a leader of Braslav's Jewish community, Shimon Gelishkovski, who also appears on page 30]

[Page 34]

Betar's Hachshara
[Hachshara, from the Hebrew word for "preparation," referred to organizations/programs
that prepared young Zionists for settlement in Palestine; the one pictured here was
affiliated with Betar, the youth movement of the Revisionist Zionists.]

Betar and Brit Hachayal
[Revisionist Zionist Association of Jewish veterans of the Polish army]

Footnotes:

1. A footnote in the original Hebrew says that the history in this section was drawn from the book *Historja Powiatu Brasławskiego (The History of Braslav County)*, written by the historian Otton Hedemann (1887-1937) and published in Vilna in 1930. Anyone interested in the history of Braslav should refer also to pages 576-627 of this memorial book, as they contain an English-language summary that includes some details not mentioned on pages 15-34.

2. The principality of Polotsk, also called the Kingdom of Polotsk and the Duchy of Polotsk, was a medieval state established by the early Eastern Slavs, with a capital in what's now Polotsk, Belarus. The date of the principality's origin is uncertain; the first recorded mention was in 862. The Kingdom of Polotsk experienced a golden age in the late 1000s as a trade center between Kievan Rus to the south and Scandinavia to the north. At its peak, it controlled northern and central Belarus and parts of southeastern Latvia. Thereafter it fell into decline, becoming part of the Grand Duchy of Lithuania in 1240, after the rise of the Lithuanian state.

    The town of Braslav, said to have been founded by Duke Bryachislav, who ruled the Kingdom of Polotsk from ca. 1001 to 1044, was originally called Bryachislav.

3. Gediminas ruled the Grand Duchy of Lithuania from 1316 until his death in 1341. A pagan, he battled the Christian Teutonic Knights and incorporated many Slavic lands into his domain; at his death, the territory of Lithuania stretched from the Baltic Sea to the Black Sea. According to legend he was the founder of Vilna, whose first recorded mention was in the 1300s.

4. The Polish-Lithuanian Commonwealth was established in 1385, when the Polish Queen Jadwiga, a Christian, contracted to marry the pagan Lithuanian Grand Duke Jogaila, grandson of Gediminas, and Jogaila agreed to become a Christian. Thereafter, Jogaila (Jagiello in Polish) was baptized and took the Polish Christian name of Wladyslaw. The union created the largest state in Europe, bordering Bohemia and Hungary to the west, the Teutonic Knights to the north, the Black Sea to the south, and the Duchy of Moscovy to the east.

    The Jagiellonian dynasty would rule the Polish-Lithuanian Commonwealth from 1386 to 1572. (Rulers after 1572 were from other dynasties, during which Poland became the dominant power over Lithuania.) From the Jagiellonian period the commonwealth was a great power in Europe, with ethnic diversity and a high degree of religious tolerance compared to Western Europe. This made the commonwealth an attractive place for Jews from other lands.

    As the U.S. scholar Harold Segel noted in his book *The Stranger in Our Midst* (1996):

    > "In the history of the Polish-Lithuanian Commonwealth . . . the political structure of the state, with its decentralization and powerful noble class, acted as a virtual guarantee of Jewish security. Jews were allowed into the country in ever greater numbers in the wake of the Inquisition in Spain, the plague . . . and the frenzy of religious conflict in the German world. Not only were Jews [in the commonwealth] given legal protection . . . but they were permitted the free exercise of their faith and free conduct of their own affairs. What this meant, in effect, was that the Jews were allowed to live as Jews in a Jewish environment." (p. 3)

5. The **Breslov** (a.k.a. Bratslav) near Uman, located in what's now central Ukraine, was the home of the venerated Rabbi Nachman (1772-1810), who established the Breslov Hasidic movement and left behind many teachings and enigmatic tales. The **Braslav** in Belarus, described in this memorial book, is sometimes confused with Rabbi Nachman's Breslov in Ukraine as well as with the city of **Breslau** (now Wrocław in southwestern Poland).

6. Schloss Berg, also known as Castle Hill and the Zamek. It was called a mountain by locals, even though it stood only 15 meters or so above the town.

7. A corps of Napoleon's army, commanded by Marshal Michel Ney, passed through the Braslav region in July 1812, on the way to Moscow. A letter written by an officer in the army, Prince Friedrich-Wilhelm of Wurttemberg, said that the countryside had been stripped bare (as described in *With Napoleon in Russia*, published in English in 2001). A journal kept by Jakob Walter, an infantryman, mentioned marching through Drisviati and Braslav on the way east to Disna and Polotsk, and said that the army typically stripped the towns and left them half burned (*The Diary of a Napoleonic Foot Soldier*, published in English in 1991). But if Braslav's historical documents were burned during the invasion, somehow the destruction spared documents such as the 1550s census mentioned later in this account; the Grand Duchy of Lithuania's 1784 poll tax for Braslav, which listed 242 Jews in the Braslav *kahal* (community); and the 1811 Russian revision list (census) for the town of Braslav.

It's true, however, that during the 1812 invasion the area of what's now Belarus suffered a heavy loss in population and severe economic damage. Modern-day estimates of civilian deaths during the invasion, in and around the area of what's now Belarus, run as high as one million, about one-quarter of the regional population, and it's said that several decades passed before the population recovered to its pre-invasion level. The disastrous invasion is reflected in the steep decline in the Jewish population of Braslav, which fell from 329 in the 1811 revision list to 205 in the 1816 revision list.

8. *HaMelitz* (*The Advocate*) was the first Hebrew-language newspaper published in the Russian Empire. It was published intermittently from 1860 to 1904, first from Odessa and later from St. Petersburg. It represented the Haskalah movement (the Jewish Enlightenment), which sought to modernize the condition of Jews in Russia.

    In the Hebrew original, in the three excerpts from *HaMelitz* that appeared in this memorial book, Mr. Sherman's name was identified in the first excerpt as Shlomo-David and in the second and third excerpts as David-Shlomo; it isn't clear which version of his name is correct.

9. The Hasidim and Mitnagdim were two important branches within Ashkenazi Judaism. Hasidism (Pietism) emerged in the 1700s in what's now western Ukraine as a movement for spiritual revival, spreading through Eastern Europe. Besides knowledge and observance of the Torah and Talmud, it emphasized immediate religious experience. By the late 1700s, the Mitnagdim (Opponents) came to refer to traditionalist Ashkenazi Jews who opposed Hasidic Judaism, emphasizing intensive study of the Talmud. Opposition to Hasidism was centered in Lithuania, particularly in Vilna.

10. The language in the newspaper in the original Hebrew is hard to follow and doesn't make completely clear which side (Hasidim or Mitnagdim) was swearing falsely against the other, or the sequence of events. The excerpts appear to suggest that the Mitnagdim in Braslav accused the Hasidim before the fire in 1884, and after the fire the Hasidim in Braslav asked the government to refuse the Mitnagdim's petition to rebuild their own synagogue.

11. The census in Braslav took place in 1554, not 1559. The assertion above that this early census in Braslav mentioned several Jewish families --- which comes from the Polish-language book by Otton Hedemann described in Footnote 1 --- has several problems, as pointed out recently by Dr. Alexander Beider, a contemporary authority on Jewish names.

    In the original Polish, Hedemann's book said that the three Jews were "Bik, Joszko Niemirowicz and Joszko *krawiec* [Joszko the tailor]." But (1) here Bik could be a first name or a nickname and wasn't necessarily Jewish; (2) Niemirowicz was typically a Christian name, not a Jewish one; and (3) here *krawiec* described an occupation (tailor), not a name. Also, (4) if the three people mentioned by Hedemann were indeed Jews in the 1554 Braslav census, it's strange that they weren't mentioned in exhaustive collections of old documents on Jews in the Russian territories that were published in Russia between 1899 and 1913. For these reasons, the assertion by Hedemann that several Jews were mentioned in the 1554 Braslav census should be regarded as mistaken, and the three people Hedemann mentioned shouldn't be considered to have had Jewish hereditary surnames. Many thanks to Dr. Beider for this analysis.

    What surviving documents for the Braslav area suggest instead is that Jews in the Braslav area didn't have hereditary surnames until the early 1800s. In 1784, the government poll tax for Braslav listed 242 Jews in the Braslav *kahal* (community) --- men, women and children --- none of them with surnames. (From lists for other areas besides Braslav, it appears that informal surnames were in use at this time, such as Shlama Shmerkovitz, meaning "Shlama son of Shmerka"; but such surnames weren't hereditary and changed with each generation, since they were formed from the first name of a person's father.) In 1784, at the time the poll tax list was compiled, Braslav was in the Grand Duchy of Lithuania, which was part of the Polish-Lithuanian Commonwealth; in 1795, the territory was taken by Russia in the third partition of Poland and Lithuania.

    In 1804, the Russian government required all Jews in its territory to adopt a hereditary family name for use without change in all registers and transactions. However, it appears that some years passed before the requirement was widely obeyed. For example, in 1811 the Russian revision list (census) for the town of Braslav showed 329 Jews, of whom 144 --- fewer than half --- had surnames.

    In 1816, the Russian revision list (census) for the town of Braslav showed 205 Jews, of whom 201 had surnames. This suggests that the adoption of hereditary surnames by Jews in the Braslav area had become near-universal by 1816, after becoming compulsory in 1804.

12. In relation to Braslav: Druya was 34 kilometers northeast, Vidz was 40 kilometers southwest, Opsa was 18 kilometers southwest, Slobodka was 11 kilometers northeast, Drisviati was 24 kilometers west, and Druysk was 19 kilometers northeast.

13. According to the *YIVO Encyclopedia of Jews in Eastern Europe*, Jews in Poland began leasing taverns and breweries in the 1500s. By the late 1600s/early 1700s, there was a significantly greater

proportion of Jews involved in activities related to the production and sale of beer and vodka in Poland than elsewhere in Europe. According to a Polish census of Jews taken in 1764-65, about 80% of the Jews living in villages and about 14% of those living in towns were involved in such activities. Further background on the subject can be found in the book *Yankel's Tavern*, published in 2014 by the scholar Glenn Dynner.

Typically, a Polish nobleman would establish one or more taverns at a crossroads on his estate --- comprising villages or towns that he owned --- and put Jews in charge of the tavern as well as the provisioning of spirits. The Jews, who were preferred for their sobriety and reliability, had to pay the nobleman for the privilege. The nobles held a monopoly on the production and sale of alcohol, which meant that the surrounding Gentile peasants had to buy beer and vodka exclusively at landowners' taverns and were banned from importing these items from the estates of other lords. Because the taverns, frequented by the local Gentile peasants, tended to draw criticism for encouraging drunkenness and wasteful spending, over the decades local governments imposed fees, restrictions and bans in attempts to counter the taverns. But nobles frequently helped their Jewish operators to circumvent such regulations, sometimes by installing a Gentile as the face of the operation.

In Russia (which took over the Braslav region in the third partition of Poland-Lithuania, in 1795), a law was passed in 1804 prohibiting Jews from holding leases on taverns and selling liquor. It's uncertain how strictly this ban was enforced by government authorities in subsequent decades, given the opposition of nobles as well as concern that zealous enforcement would send a flood of rural Jews into cities and towns. In 1840 and 1843, laws were passed in Kovno calling for Jews to be removed from all village taverns, which suggests that the ban of 1804 was being circumvented. Coincidentally or otherwise, agricultural settlements for Jews were set up by the government soon afterward in the Braslav region, in 1847-48. (For more information on the settlements, see page 18 of this memorial book.)

14. In relation to Braslav: Plusy was 21 kilometers north, Dubina was 16 kilometers northwest, Yaisi was seven kilometers east, and Ikazn (a.k.a. Ikazna) was 14 kilometers east.

According to a memoir by the Vilna educator Hirsz Abramowicz, *Profiles of a Lost World* (published in Yiddish in 1958 and translated into English in 1999), beginning in 1835 the Russian government of Czar Nicholas I encouraged the establishment of Jewish agricultural colonies in the northwestern territories of the Russian Empire, a large area that included the Braslav region. Unfortunately, the soil in these colonies was often poor and sandy:

> Buckwheat was the only crop that could be sown in these sandy fields. Summer rye and other grains yielded very small harvests. Potatoes could only grow if the fields were well fertilized. It was some of these spartan fields that the government of Tsar Nicholas I found possible to spare for the Jews . . . .
>
> The sandy fields did not provide enough for a living. The Jewish colonists had to supplement their incomes by working as drivers, peddlers, or working in some cottage industry, such as spinning, dyeing cloth, making harnesses, and the like. Still, they lived in poverty. It was impossible to develop their cottage industries to any considerable extent. They lacked money, raw materials and, most of all, community support. (p. 109)

15. Zemgale (located, in terms of the borders formed after World War I, in Latvia near the border with Lithuania) was a station about two kilometers north of Turmont (now Turmantas, in Lithuania). From the 1920s trains ran between Zemgale station, passing through Vilna, to Warsaw, 530 kilometers to the southwest. From Zemgale, going in the opposite direction, it was possible to get a train connection to Dvinsk (now Daugavpils, in Latvia), which was about 17 kilometers north of Zemgale. Druya was 58 kilometers east of Dvinsk, and Braslav was about 34 kilometers southwest of Druya.

16. Presumably this refers to the distance by road; as the crow flies, Vilna was about 165 kilometers southwest of Braslav.

17. This was an offshoot of the Eastern Orthodox Church in Russia that had split from the main church in the 1600s over differences in liturgy and ritual. In Polish, its adherents were called *Starowiery* (Old Believers).

18. This appears to be a mistake in the Hebrew original; the festival takes place on February 2, not 23.

19. The Endeks were members of the Narodowa Demokracja (National Democracy) or N.D. Party, a chauvinistic political party. Contrary to what the Hebrew original said above, this party was established in Poland in 1897, long before the Nazi Party was formed.

20. The Yavneh school was part of a network of more than 200 schools established throughout Poland by Mizrahi, the Religious Zionist movement that had been founded in 1902 in Vilna to promote Zionism among Orthodox Jews. Yavneh schools emphasized Hebrew (in place of Yiddish), Torah and Talmud study, and reconstruction of Jewish life in Palestine. In the interwar years, the flagship of the Yavneh school network was the Tachkemoni Rabbinical Seminary in Warsaw.

21. Di Tsentrale Yidishe Shul-Organizatsye (Central Yiddish School Organization), abbreviated as TSYSHO or CYSHO, had been established in Warsaw in 1921 and continued to operate until 1939. It sought to create a network of secular Yiddish schools under socialist auspices. It was led mainly by members of the Bund (the Jewish socialist party in Poland) and Left Poale Zion (the left wing of the Labor Zionists). (The Bund and Left Poale Zion differed politically --- the former was Marxist and anti-Zionist, the latter was Marxist and Zionist --- but each supported the use of Yiddish.)

    TSYSHO was administered by a central office in Warsaw and a central education committee in Vilna (which between ca. 1920 and 1939 was part of Poland, as was Braslav). According to the *YIVO Encyclopedia of Jews in Eastern Europe*, the curriculum consisted of Yiddish language and literature, Jewish history and culture, the sciences, math, music, physical education, arts and crafts and, in some cases, Hebrew. In addition, Polish language, literature and history were taught in Polish.

    At its peak in the late 1920s, TSYSHO maintained 219 institutions with 24,000 students spread across 100 locations. These included 46 kindergartens, 114 elementary schools, 6 high schools, 52 evening schools, and a pedagogical institute in Vilna. The Vilna Realgymnazye, the crown jewel of Yiddish secular education in Poland, was the first modern high school in which Yiddish was the language of instruction. The pedagogical institute (the Vilna Teachers' Seminary) played a major role in the secular Yiddish school system, as both a training institute and a center for communicating new ideas in Jewish teaching.

22. Presumably this refers to the Realgymnazye operated in Vilna by a branch of the TSYSHO.

23. Ponar (Ponary in Polish, Paneriai in Lithuanian), located outside the city of Vilna in Lithuania, was the major execution site in the Vilna region during World War II and the largest execution site in Lithuania. Between July 1941 and August 1944 an estimated 50,000-70,000 Jews, 2,000-20,000 ethnic Poles and 5,000-8,000 Soviet prisoners were killed there.

24. Reb is an honorific term, something like an exalted "Mr." HeChalutz was a youth movement of the Labor Zionists.

25. These refer to S. Ansky's play *The Dybbuk*, written in the 1910s in Russian and first performed in Yiddish in 1920. *Uriel Acosta*, another classic of the Yiddish theater, was based on the 1846 play by the Gentile author Karl Gutzkow, written in German, that advocated emancipation of the Jews. The reference to *Yehudit* is uncertain but might refer to a play about Judith and Holofernes written in 1892 by Abraham Goldfaden, the father of modern Yiddish theater.

26. The Revisionist Zionists were established by Vladimir (Zeev) Jabotinsky in 1925. In the late 1920s and 1930s, they were the chief opponent of the World Zionist Organization, which was dominated by the socialist-oriented Labor Zionists. Secular, liberal and nationalist, the Revisionists opposed socialism and sought to establish a Jewish state in Palestine on both sides of the Jordan River. The youth movement of the Revisionist Zionists was Betar, that of the Labor Zionists was HeChalutz.

27. The *Folks-Tsaytung* (*People's Newspaper*) was published in 1921-39 and 1946-49 in Warsaw in Yiddish; it was the central paper of the Bund, the Jewish socialist and anti-Zionist party. *Haynt* (*Today*), published in 1908-39, and *Der Moment* (*The Moment*), published in 1910-39, were the two major Warsaw newspapers published in Yiddish. *Vilner Tog* (*Vilna Day*) was published in Vilna in Yiddish between 1912 and 1939.

28. Dr. Stanislav Ostyk-Narbutt (1853-1926) was a prominent resident of Braslav. In 1906, he opened a hospital in the town that he managed until his death. There he treated the poor for free. In addition to his hospital work he led a volunteer fire brigade, supported an insurance fund, published a newspaper, and directed and acted in an amateur theater. For all of his efforts he was loved and respected by town residents, and a street was named for him (later renamed Kirov Street under the Soviets). After Narbutt's burial on the western side of Castle Hill, town residents paid for an obelisk to be erected on the hill at his grave. His hospital remained in use in Braslav until 1994.

29. Beings mentioned in the Torah that can be interpreted as giants or warriors.

[Page 35]
In Memory of Yerachmiel-Mendel Meirson
By Miriam (Mariashka) Rotenberg, Daughter of Velvel and Gitel Reichel

Translated from the Hebrew by Dr. Ida Schwarcz
Footnote Added / Donated by Jeff Deitch

This happened in 1917 or 1918 --- toward the end of World War I. Our town, Braslav [Braslaw], passed from hand to hand: The Russians captured it from the Poles, the Germans and Lithuanians also ruled there for short periods, but there were times when there was no ruling authority at all in the town. Then the gangs of bandits, composed of Gentiles from the area, raised their heads and sought to steal the property of the Jews and murder them. This is what my mother told me when I was 10 years old. Meanwhile, groups of Jews organized themselves to defend the town. One of these was my uncle, Yerachmiel-Mendel Meirson --- the only son of my grandparents Yitzchak-Yaacov and Chaya-Sara (there were also five girls).

On a summer day in 1918, when there was no ruling authority in Braslav, hooligans and bandits burst in, beat up Jews and stole their property. There was tumult and a great outcry in the town. Everyone was afraid. Many hid in their homes, attics, stables and the like.

Then the group of defenders went to attack the gang and drive it away.

On that day, Shmuel-Yosef Milutin excelled in heroism and beat the leaders of the bandits. Avraham Lubovitz [Lubowicz], a member of the group, was injured in the leg and remained crippled for the rest of his life. More Jews joined the defenders, struck the bandits with fierce blows and chased them out of the town. But during the clash between my uncle and the angry bandits who came to rob the store of Zalman Ulman, my uncle [Yerachmiel-Mendel Meirson] was shot and killed. My uncle was a good man, well liked by all, and especially active in working on behalf of the Yiddish school.

Years went by but Yerachmiel-Mendel wasn't forgotten, and on the 10th anniversary of his death a tombstone was put up for him. The schoolchildren and their teachers attended its unveiling. Merchants, tradesmen and storekeepers closed their businesses and joined in;

housewives and others joined in. We marched in rows to the rhythm of the mourners' march played by the band, followed by the schoolchildren. They carried wreaths, and many held flowers to put on his grave.

There were speeches, Yerachmiel's mother unveiled the tombstone (his father was no longer among the living). At the top of a canopy made from red bricks, there was a plaque of black marble on which was engraved

[Page 36]
in golden letters: "Here rests Yerachmiel-Mendel Meirson, who fell while defending the Jewish community at the age of 18" [in Yiddish, followed by the same sentence in Hebrew]. There was a religious ceremony, and Kaddish was said.

May the name of this Jewish fighter be exalted and sanctified.

As is known, the old Jewish cemetery in Braslav was later vandalized, and the tombstones were removed for various purposes.[1]

May these words serve as a tombstone and candle to his memory.

Footnote:
1. This refers to the old Jewish cemetery in Braslaw that was in the western part of the town, number 11 in the map on page 21 of this memorial book. This cemetery was destroyed during World War II, and after the war the area was turned into a park. The newer Jewish cemetery of Braslav lies north of the town, where the Jews of the town were killed on and after June 3-5, 1942 and on March 19, 1943.

The [old] Jewish cemetery in Braslav, before it was vandalized and destroyed

**[This photograph shows the tombstone not of Yerachmiel-
Mendel Meirson but of Esther Kremer, who died on October 26,
1929. Standing next to the tombstone in Braslav in 1930 are
Feiga/Fania (née Kremer), who was the daughter of Esther. With
Feiga are her husband, Rafael Fisher of Braslav, and (it is thought) their son
Yaacov/Yankel. The account of Yetta, a daughter of Rafael and Feiga
who survived the war, is on pages 117-119 of this memorial book.]**

[Page 37]

Perke (Perel-Mina) Fisher
Daughter of Chaya-Golda and Bentzion Charmatz

Translated from the Hebrew by Laia Ben-Dov
Footnotes Added / Donated by Jeff Deitch

The image of the town of my birth comes up in my memory with affection and longing, and with a terrible rending of the heart. The place of my childhood no longer exists. Its friendly, pleasant people have passed and are no more, as are the young, who once were lively and hungry for knowledge. Only memories remain, memories of the lovely days of the long-ago past.

Until World War I Braslav [Braslaw] belonged to Russia as part of Belorussia, but after the Polish-Russian War in 1921[1] the town and entire region were annexed to Poland. The residents of the surrounding villages were all Belorussian and spoke it [the Belarusian language] as their mother tongue, but the official language was Polish.[2]

Braslav was one of the most beautiful towns in Poland. Because of its unique climate and geographic location [in what was then the nation's northeast corner], people called it the "Polish Siberia." In winter, severe cold and snowstorms were very common.

Two lakes surrounded the town --- the large Lake Driviata [to the south] and the small Lake Noviata [to the north]. In the center of town the lakes were connected by a river, over which there was a wooden bridge. The lakes were full of many kinds of fish. Many residents earned a living from fishing, marketing and selling the fish. For young people these lakes were an excellent place for recreation, in both summer and winter. They were a wonderful place for sailing, skiing and skating. On summer days, students from the center of Poland came to Braslav from the universities of Warsaw, Krakow and other cities. They'd organize parties of bonfires (*ogniska*) in the evenings, and many of the townspeople would gather and enjoy plays and entertainment under the starry skies until the wee hours of the night. The authorities sought to instill the spirit of Polish nationalism among both the Belorussian population and the Jews, residents of the country's northeast region.

On both sides the town was surrounded by thick forests, most of them trees of pine and fir. To the southeast --- the Dubki [Dubkes] forest, and to the west --- the Karpovitz [Karpowicz] forest. The forests served the residents of the town as a place for hikes and meetings, mainly on the Sabbath, when large numbers of young people and children would go out to relax and play.

In the town center stood Castle Mountain.[3] Around it

[Page 38]

the wooden houses of the inhabitants lay scattered like mushrooms. At the western edge of the mountain was a monument at the grave of the physician, the supporter of the Jews, Dr. Narbutt.[4] The Jews of the town loved and respected him, because of the warm feelings he showed toward the Jews and especially to the locals. A street was even named for him --- Narbutt Street.

On each side of Braslav stood a flour mill. On one side of town was the windmill, which stood silently for many years; only its arms projected into the blue sky. In a strong wind the arms would turn slowly, as if they lacked will to do so. On the other side of town was an active flour mill, which belonged to a Jew and operated day and night.

There were four synagogues in the town. Three of them stood in the heart of Braslav, on the main street, and one synagogue (the Sandy Synagogue) stood on the other side of the mountain.

Next to the [three] synagogues was a fire station. In the station was a large hall used for shows, plays, meetings and ceremonies for celebration. Nearby, on the shore of the large lake, stood the ruins of a house. This was the community bathhouse, which served the Jews of the town on Thursdays and Fridays.

There were also a Jewish bank and a Gemilut Hesed [Free Loan Fund] in Braslav. Locals in need could receive loans from it without interest.

In our town were three schools: one for the Yiddish language [the Folkshul, with education in Yiddish]; the second one, Yavneh,[5] based on the purity of Hebrew; and the third, a Polish school.

Important offices were concentrated in a new, exclusive neighborhood, green and well looked after, that was built near the Karpovitz forest [in the western part of the town], especially for the Polish officials.

Braslav was a regional town (*powiat*[6]), and the nearby settlements and forests belonged to it: Druysk [Drujsk], Yod [Jod], Miory, Dubina [Dubene], Slobodka, Yaisi [Jaisi], Opsa and smaller places.[7] Braslav belonged to the Vilna district; the major city of Vilna had a large concentration of Jews and served as not only a cultural and Jewish spiritual center (the Jerusalem of Lithuania) but also a trade center.

There were no factories in Braslav. The main business of the residents was trade: small stores, small workshops of shoemakers, tailors, blacksmiths and the like. In the town were several guest houses, hostels that were called "hotels," bakeries and processing houses for leather. There were two markets. For some reason the first was called the "bread market," even though everything that came to hand was traded there. The second was called the "horse market."[8] The means of transportation indeed was mainly horse and wagon, in which merchandise would be taken to and from Braslav from other towns.

In the years before World War II --- due to unfair competition by the Poles, mainly the government --- the economic situation of the Jews worsened. During these years, with the help of the authorities the Poles opened a giant department store with a varied inventory and engaged in extensive anti-Semitic propaganda about not buying from the Jews. Despite this they couldn't defeat the Jewish shop owners, mainly because of the credit that these shop owners gave to farmers. Because of the good relations between the Jews and the Gentiles from the surrounding villages, the authorities failed in their attempt to oppress the Jews.

And so life went on in the town, amid work, problems and worries. Each day of the week, people were busy and troubled. On Fridays, all of the tumult stopped and it grew quiet. From every window the Sabbath candles winked and capered, candles of rest and tranquility.

[Page 39]

I can remember my town many, many years ago: without electricity, without roads or sidewalks, in deep mud on dark nights . . . Most of the Jews lived in poverty. Even the small children tried to assist their families, through handwork or by helping in the house. Because of this, many children were unable to finish primary school.

Especially difficult were the lives of the women. They were always busy next to the stove, cleaning the house, caring for the children, and helping the head of the family earn their daily bread.

In those [very early] days, the school had lacked a building; lessons took place in the women's section of the synagogue. The overlapping boundaries that resulted caused arguments between the praying congregation and the teachers and students of the school. These problems ended when a nice, large building was constructed, one with comfortable classrooms and an exercise hall. A real school.

The years of study are engraved in my consciousness forever. I'll never forget the dedication and sacrifice of the teachers, who always treated us as if we were members of their own families. Despite the tiny salary, which they [often] didn't receive on time, despite the freezing cold in the classrooms and the lack of teaching aids and books --- they always carried out their work as if it were a sacred mission.

I remember how on cold winter days we --- all the children of the class --- decided to "drag" wood for heating from our parents' homes to warm the classrooms. The Polish government didn't support the Jewish educational institutions or set aside funds for them, and these schools existed on tuition payments and donations. Next to the school was a large library, with whose help we enriched our knowledge and formed our outlook on the world. Sometimes, when a teacher was sick and couldn't come to class, we --- the children of the higher grades --- took the initiative and taught the children of the lower ones. After completing school (seven grades), some of the young people would leave for other places, mainly to the district city, Vilna, to continue their studies. Of course this depended on financial support that only a few families could manage, but several young people did succeed in gaining knowledge and a profession at the ORT[9] school, an abridged technion [technological institute], teachers' seminary, and the like.

A few of the young people studied at the Jewish [teachers'] seminary in Vilna, the only one in Poland.[10] But to their great dismay, its gates were closed some time before the end of the last semester, and the students attending supplementary courses didn't receive their completion certificates and were unable to work as teachers.

Next to our school there was a drama club, whose purpose was to help the teachers financially by means of plays, parties for entertainment and so on. At the head of the club was a very talented young man who guided and taught us. We presented mainly classic plays. We also organized Purim and Hanukkah parties for other institutions, and with this we filled gaps in the school's budget. I'm writing about this in detail because the school was the center of our life and experience.

Sometimes there came to our town [Jewish] preachers and speakers of all kinds and from differing political parties. A large crowd would gather, and each orator spoke on the importance and superiority of his party. Usually these gatherings were accompanied by interruptions, shouting and even an exchange of blows between the righteous of one party and its opponents . . .

I loved our holidays, especially Hanukkah. There were parties, our father, of blessed memory, would light

[Page 40]
the holiday candles and we, the children, would enjoy the tasty special foods for each holiday.

At the end of the 1920s [or the early 1930s], a power station was built in the town. The houses and streets were lit with electric lights. The roads were [finally] paved, and this brought an end to the ever-present mud. At this time, several Jews established a printing press that gave employment to a number of young men of the town. Sometime later, a bulletin appeared --- a local newspaper.

At this time, anti-Semitism and hatred of the Jews grew stronger in the town. The Poles, mainly from the racist-nationalist party, the N.D.,[11] established hooligans as guards [in the town], and these prevented buyers from entering Jewish stores, broke windows and so on.

Such events caused agitation among the Jewish young people. A not-insignificant part of them saw a solution to the problem in *aliyah* to the Land of Israel. Another part searched for redemption in the socialist idea of Soviet Russia. In this way, the social situation worsened. Many young people stood at a crossroads. The Communist youths weren't able to do much; occasionally the police would arrest many of them.

A few of the Zionist youth received certificates and made *aliyah* to the Land of Israel.[12] For a time, there was also in our town a preparatory kibbutz of the General Zionists.[13] The period was filled with events, and we felt that something important was about to happen. Newspapers printed editorials, men in the street talked and argued, but the situation wasn't completely clear.

The drama society of Braslav

[Handwritten in Yiddish at the top of the photo are the words "At the departure of member Shayke, Braslav, May 11, 1935." This refers to Shayke (Shaya) Deitch, who was from Braslav but is said to have worked as a theater actor in Vilna. Shayke, marked by the arrow in the photo, is also pictured on pages 41 and 229 of this memorial book. Yiddish caption translated by Aaron Krishtalka and Jerrold Landau.]

[Page 41]

With the rise of Hitler to authority in Germany [from 1933], persecution of the Jews had begun. Several refugees reached us, telling of the troubles and suffering of the Jews under the Nazi regime. At the time, we didn't fully understand the seriousness of what was being said. Warnings were heard from Jewish leaders, but people didn't take them seriously.

In late 1939 [on September 1], Germany attacked Poland. A few days later [sic], the country surrendered.[14] Many of our young men had been drafted into the Polish army, and we didn't know what was happening to them.

I remember the day the Red Army entered our town [in late September 1939]. The soldiers marched in all their strength; they stood up straight on the backs of cars and tanks, waved to us, and announced they'd come to free us from the yoke of the Polish *shliachta* [*szlachta*].[15] The Jewish population received them with satisfaction, thinking it was better to live under Russian rule than to be persecuted and oppressed by the Germans.

Members of the drama club after a performance in 1937
Standing (from right): Hirshke Chepelevitz, Mariashka Reichel, Tzipka Levin, Perke Charmatz
[the author of this account] and Daniel Karasin
Sitting (from right): An unidentified man with glasses, Shayke Deitch and Shimon Viderevitz

[Handwritten in Yiddish on one side of the photo is a hard-to-read caption with the words
"Producers of the revue evening of [19?]37, direction Shayke, missing is V. Gershon" (referring
perhaps to Gershon Viderevitz). Yiddish translated by Aaron Krishtalka and Jerrold Landau.]

[Page 42]

There were no bounds to the excitement of the local Communists. Many people who'd spurned Communism until then now changed their faces overnight and joined the sycophants. Immediately after entering, the Russians began their system of propaganda with the help of films, presentations, songs and other forms of communication.

I belonged to no party. In addition, after the [Soviet] occupation I wasn't tempted to register with the youth organization, the Komsomol.[16] I remembered all the trials and confessions of senior [Soviet] officers and leaders [in the 1930s] who'd admitted to being capitalist agents and traitors with the evil intention of attacking the Soviet "Garden of Eden" and establishing a fascist state in Russia.[17] I couldn't understand how it was possible for these people, who'd dedicated their lives to the Revolution and suffered so much for the socialist idea, to suddenly reverse course and turn traitor.

Immediately with the coming of the Russians, we began to feel a shortage of food. The shops emptied out. We began to stand in line to buy bread and other food products. Once, in a line for bread, a woman made scornful, derogatory statements about what was happening. For this, she was immediately arrested. She was only freed thanks to the efforts of several respected men of the town, who managed to convince the authorities of her apparent insanity.

This was how we lived under Soviet rule, until the coming of the terrible loss and destruction of the Jews of my town of Braslav.[18]

Footnotes:

1. This war between Poland and the Soviet Union began in 1919, when Poland invaded Belorussia and parts of the Ukraine in an attempt to expand its eastern border. A peace treaty signed in 1921 gave Poland territory about 200 kilometers east of its prewar border. This new Polish territory included the Braslav region, which was part of Poland between 1921 and 1939. After World War II, most of the territory won by Poland in 1921 became part of the Soviet Union again, included in the Belorussian Soviet Socialist Republic. In 1991, following the breakup of the Soviet Union, it became part of independent Belarus.

2. Like Russian, Belarusian is an East Slavic language that uses the Cyrillic alphabet, while Polish is a West Slavic language that uses the Latin alphabet. It's estimated that Belarusian has 75% mutual intelligibility with Russian and 55% mutual intelligibility with Polish.

3. Schloss Berg, also known as Castle Hill and the Zamek. It was called a mountain by locals, even though it stood only 15 meters or so above the town.

4. Dr. Stanislav Ostyk-Narbutt (1853-1926) was a prominent resident of Braslav. In 1906, he opened a hospital in the town that he managed until his death. There he treated the poor for free. In addition to his hospital work he led a volunteer fire brigade, supported an insurance fund, published a newspaper, and directed and acted in an amateur theater. For all his efforts he was loved and respected by town residents, and a street was named for him (later renamed Kirov Street under the Soviets). After Narbutt's burial at the edge of Castle Hill, town residents paid for an obelisk to be erected on the hill at his grave. His hospital remained in use until 1994.

5. The Hebrew-language Yavneh school was part of a network of more than 200 schools established throughout Poland by Mizrahi, the Religious Zionist movement that had been founded in 1902 in Vilna to promote Zionism among observant Jews. Yavneh schools emphasized modern Hebrew (in place of Yiddish), religious education and reconstruction of Jewish life in Palestine. The flagship of the Yavneh school network was the Tachkemoni Rabbinical Seminary in Warsaw.

6. *Powiat*: County or district. In Poland, it was a larger unit of administration than a *gmina* (commune or municipality) but smaller than a *województwo* (voivodeship or province).

7. In relation to Braslav: Druysk was about 19 kilometers northeast, Yod was 25 kilometers southeast, Miory was 40 kilometers east, Dubina was 16 kilometers northwest, Slobodka was 11 kilometers northeast, Yaisi was 7 kilometers east, and Opsa was 18 kilometers southwest. Vilna was about 165 kilometers southwest of Braslav.

8. Mrs. Fisher here wrote "bread market" and "horse market," while the map of Braslav on pages 20-21 of this memorial book, made by Chaim Band, referred to these two places as "food market" and "cattle market."

9. ORT: Obshchestvo Remeslennogo i zemledelcheskogo Truda (Society for Trades and Agricultural Labor), an organization founded in St. Petersburg, Russia in 1880 to provide employable skills for Russia's impoverished Jews.

10. Presumably this refers to the Yiddish Teachers' Seminary, which had been established in Vilna in 1921 to produce teachers for the TSYSHO network of secular Yiddish schools. TSYSHO was led mainly by the left wing of Poale Zion (the more radically socialist wing of the Labor Zionists) and the Bund (the Jewish socialist party in Poland), which was anti-Zionist but supported the use of Yiddish. Although official state recognition was granted to the Yiddish Teachers' Seminary in the 1920s, later governments in Poland proved less supportive and in 1931 the seminary was forced to close.

11. Narodowa Demokracja (National Democracy), also called Endek: A Polish political movement founded in the late 1800s initially to champion Polish sovereignty against the Russian, Prussian and Austro-Hungarian regimes that had partitioned Poland. Following Polish independence in 1918, the party's right-wing nationalism and anti-Semitism become increasingly pronounced.

12. In Palestine under the British Mandate, immigration was strictly controlled; the British allowed in only those with official permission, in the form of the certificate. Such permission was difficult to obtain.

13. General Zionism: A center-right Zionist movement, established in 1922 within the Zionist Organization, which had been started in 1897 on the initiative of Theodor Herzl. The General Zionists' establishment in 1922 took place around the time that Zionism was becoming polarized between the Labor Zionists on the left and the Revisionist Zionists (led by Vladimir Jabotinsky) on the right. General Zionists were identified essentially with liberal, middle-class supporters of capitalism.

14. The fighting lasted from September 1 to October 6 and the Polish government went into exile instead of formally surrendering. After Germany invaded Poland from the west on September 1, the Soviet Union invaded Poland from the east on September 17. The two aggressors then divided Poland between them, in line with the secret Molotov-Ribbentrop Pact that had been signed before the

outbreak of war. Polish attempts at armed resistance led eventually to the creation of the Armia Krajowa (Polish Home Army).

15. *Szlachta*: Literally "nobles," the Polish land-owning class of hereditary nobles that enjoyed many legal privileges and political/economic power until 1795, when its position was significantly eroded by the third and final partition of Poland. For centuries, it was primarily the nobles who protected the Jews in Poland against other groups such as the clergy, peasants and burghers. Presumably the Soviets used *szlachta* as shorthand for "feudal oppressor."

16. The All-Union Leninist Young Communist League, the youth division of the Communist Party of the Soviet Union.

17. This refers to the wave of purges by Joseph Stalin of rival power centers in the Soviet government in 1936-38. The purges included a series of trials --- which received great publicity abroad --- at which the Communist defendants confessed to treason against Stalin and the Soviet state.

18. In connection with prewar Braslav, it should be mentioned that Chaim Bermant (1929-98), a native of Braslav who immigrated to Great Britain in 1938 and went on to become an English-language author of note, left a memoir of his 1930s childhood in Braslav and in Borovka, a Latvian village some 23 kilometers to the north. The memoir, *Genesis: A Latvian Childhood*, was published in 1998.

   Although his memoir mainly discussed Borovka, Bermant also lived in Braslav in 1929-32 (with his parents) and in 1937-38 (with his grandmother). His memoir included descriptions of Jewish life in the region and recollections about family members who were in Braslav in the 1930s. There were brief descriptions of Braslav and some of the residents that he remembered, such as the attorney Shimon Gelishkovski and the businessman Shneiur Aron, as well as recollections of his own experiences at the Yavneh school. Bermant mentioned reading *Emesh Shoah* soon after it was published in Israel in 1986, and in 1990 he visited Braslav from Great Britain, finding the house where his grandmother had lived.

   Bermant was the son of Rabbi Azriel-Baruch Bermant of Kraslava and Feiga-Tziril Deitch of Braslav. Surviving records from Braslav show that at least two earlier generations of Feiga-Tziril's Deitch family had lived in the town: her father (Chlavna, born ca. 1860s) and her grandfather (Aharon-Matityahu, born ca. 1830s). Feiga-Tziril's mother, Tayba, was also a Deitch.

[Page 43]

Yehuda Chepelevitz
Son of Tzvia and Liber

Translated from the Hebrew by Laia Ben-Dov
Footnotes Added / Donated by Jeff Deitch

Our house stood in the center of the town, at 121 Pilsudski Street, a small distance from the three synagogues, the fire department and the Polish police.[1] Opposite, at a distance of about 100 meters, rose the eastern side of Castle Mountain (the Zamek).[2]

Our house was large and wide; the bakery was on the bottom floor, a sort of half-basement, and above it was a spacious dwelling and a shop for bakery products and confections, delicacies, soft drinks and light meals.

Our house wasn't only large, it was also an open house. All of the family members had comrades and friends who would visit frequently and were honored with a glass of tea in our shop. Almost all of them had a clear connection, being graduates and friends of the Folkshul [Yiddish school] in Braslav [Braslaw]. On this point father, who was a supporter and active member of the management of the school, brooked no compromise. Whoever didn't support the Folkshul, at least passively, wasn't considered a close friend. And so, as I remember, our house was a meeting place for young people and adults from the circles close to the Folkshul. In our house it was possible to meet the outstanding youth of the town: Shayke [Shaya] Deitch, a talented dramatic actor, a tailor by profession; his cousin Yerachmiel Deitch, who had a clever sense of humor; Tsipka Levin, who was also a member of the drama club; Daniel Karasin, who worked as a printer and was a talented sportsman; Netzka Lin; Luska Segal; Munka Munitz, with her braids, who was active in HeChalutz HaTzair [The Young Pioneer, a movement for socialist-oriented Labor Zionist youth and an offshoot of the earlier HeChalutz] until she immigrated to the Land of Israel; Reinka Bank; Avromitske Ulman, a tailor and member of the drama club; Meir Kort; Machla Eidelson; Sara-Mirka [Sara-Miriam] Veif; Mashka Katz; the quiet and smart Beilka Goldin; her sister Dvairka [Dvora] Goldin, a talented dancer; and many more.

The living spirit among them was Shayke Deitch, who knew how to tell jokes and was always filled with the joy of life. This was a lively group. Father loved them and enjoyed seeing them in our house; he didn't miss even one show that was put on by the drama club. Father personally had a group of close friends who would visit our home: Zelig Ulman, who took part in all of the pranks of the town; Leibke Michals, who seemed born to partner Zelig Ulman in their pranks;

[Page 44]

Meishke Biliak, one of the young people in the group, who today is in Canada; the brothers Nachke [Nachman] and Leizer Fisher, cattle dealers whose fists were well known among drunken Gentiles; Chona Munitz, a fish trader; Falka [Rafael] Fisher, a trader of crops and leather; Chona Biliak, a cattle dealer; Yoske Ulman, owner of the community bathhouse; Chaim-Aizik Maron, a wise and joyful Jew, a flax trader, whose two sons, Mendel and Yosef, are now in New York; and many others. I remember them on their visits to our house or in the shop, gossiping and mocking each other and, of course, arguing about public and political matters. Father, who was a regular and devoted reader of the daily newspaper *Der Tog* and well informed as to what went on in the world, was the life of these arguments.[3] Almost always these meetings would end with a gentlemanly card game and not a little tension, and pranks were also played during the games.

In his soul and his actions, father was a proletarian; he loved his people and treated the Gentiles who worked for us in the bakery as members of the family, working with them hand in hand. They'd eat with us at one table, and they had a spacious room to rest in; they deposited their savings with father until there was enough to buy a cow, a horse or tools for their families in one of the local villages. Two of them continued to work for us until the war broke out. At the time of the "education talks" that father gave me, sometimes with the addition of a slap on the cheek, he emphasized every man's obligation to work for his livelihood. And so all of us worked in the bakery during vacations from our studies. But he spared no effort or money to give us more than an ordinary, basic education. He sent my sister Sheyndel to study in the *gymnasium* [secondary school] in Vilna. For many years my brother Hirshke studied the violin, performing well; I preferred the fire department's orchestra of wind instruments. More than once, I greatly enjoyed looking at father as he listened with happiness to my brother's playing, especially when my brother played a rhapsody by Liszt. Father was an emphatic anti-Zionist. When I returned from the club of HeChalutz HaTzair, he'd ask me jokingly when we were setting out for Palestine. But while viewing the socialist wing of Zionism with some tolerance, he actively opposed [the anti-socialist] Betar and its leaders in the town, missing no opportunity to argue against them.[4] He'd go with friends to the meetings of Betar that took place in the synagogues and interrupt them, arguing with the local heads of Betar of the time --- Shimon Gelishkovski, Shneiur Aron and Zusman Lubovitz, who's now in Israel --- and sometimes the exchanges grew very heated. But fate had a surprise in store for father. My brother Hirshke began to pursue Chana, the daughter of Shimon Gelishkovski, and the relationship between the young couple grew more serious. Father remarked with disdain, "Just my luck if [Gelishkovski] has to be my in-law."

Father wasn't religious, but he observed Sabbath night and the Sabbath as days of rest. In the New Synagogue (Der Neier Minyan) [of the Hasidim] we had an honored place next to the Holy Ark, and father visited the synagogue on the Sabbath and holidays. Rafael Munitz was a good leader of the prayers. Father appreciated him very much and would join him frequently with his own pleasant voice in special prayers.

To the chapter on father's public activities should be added his membership in the fire department and in the leadership of the artists' association guild. In general, there was almost no public event in the lives of Braslav's Jews in which father, of blessed memory, wasn't involved. For him, public activity seemed to fill a deep spiritual need.

And then --- war broke out between Poland and Germany [in September 1939]. My brother Hirshke, who served in the Polish army, was sent to the front. For

[Page 45]

many months, we received no news from him. Suddenly old age caught up with father, and worriedly he paced in silence. When the Red Army entered Braslav, we received word that my brother Hirshke had been taken prisoner by the Germans. Father recovered a bit and devoted himself entirely to the family and his granddaughter, but soon the decrees of the Soviet government arrived. Our bakery was confiscated, and we became the hired help in it. The officer in charge of supplying bread to the Russian army was appointed owner of our house, and each day he demanded that father bring him some vodka. He took orders for the bakery without understanding a thing about the profession, and in a rare moment father revealed to us with great bitterness his heart-felt feelings about the Soviet government, in language that went something like this: "A wild beast has arisen in Russia, and its name is Communism. This new situation has quickly revealed itself in all of its sharpness and cruelty." Father's thick moustache began to turn white. He talked a great deal. He worked day and night, living in hope that my brother would be released from the German imprisonment.

In the Russian-German war [that began in June 1941], father was cruelly taken from us, never to return. After the war, I met Jews who told me how father and his sister Sara from Zamosh had been killed. His dear image is preserved in my heart. May these pages be a monument to his blessed memory.

My Braslav

Forty-one years have passed since we left you in fear and haste [in 1941], but also with the hope and belief that we'd quickly return home after the Red Army pushed back the Germans. But history decided otherwise. We didn't return, and I see you with unusual clarity in the eyes of my soul: undestroyed, untrampled, beautiful as you were before the bloodthirsty monster trod over you with his nailed boots.

If I succeed in putting on paper your story and all that I remember, then maybe I can contribute something to the erection of a spiritual monument to the memory of the extended Chepelevitz family in Braslav and the surrounding area; for father and my dear brother, whose burial place is unknown; and to the entire holy community of the Jews of Braslav and the region, innocents who were killed for no reason. May their memory be blessed forever!

Four thousand Jews lived in Braslav, earning a living in trade as well as from small businesses that were hardly sufficient to merit the description but somehow supported their owners: craftsmen, shoemakers, carpenters, harness-makers, tanners, hatters and bakers. The intelligent ones among them were without a doubt the tailors. They were divided into two types: the lower-level tailors who sewed clothing for ordinary Jews and the farmers in the area; and tailors like Yekutiel Kanfer, Benyamin Beilin, Falka Katz, Charat and Stavski, who sewed suits and coats for the wealthy people of the town, and mainly for the officials of the Polish government in the regional offices (*starosta*). A Jewish lad who wanted to learn the profession from these tailors spent the first year of his apprenticeship helping the tailor's wife with household duties in the kitchen and caring for the children. Only in the second year was he allowed to touch the buttons and buttonholes. But after a number of years the apprentices debuted as excellent professionals, whose name preceded them.

David and Efroike [Efraim], members of the Zarzhevski family, were unique professionals. They were painters and artists, and their special business was to draw portraits of the Christian saints on the ceilings and walls of the churches in Braslav and the surrounding area.

[Page 46]

The Gentile woman Fima lived on Pilsudski Street across from the storerooms of the Kovarski family, and her business was curing *shoshana* [erysipelas, a bacterial infection of the skin]. A person who was sick with *shoshana* (which mostly affected the feet) would order a treatment from Fima, and the ceremony would be carried out at sunrise or sunset. Fima would cover the afflicted area with blue paper from the packages of Sabbath candles, whispering words whose meaning only she herself understood. But it worked, and many patients were cured by her treatment.

In Braslav there was a Polish policeman whose name was Bednarski. He was short of stature, fat, and nice to the Jews of the town. He liked gefilte fish, vodka and sweet Sabbath *challah*,[5] and when he wanted these he'd come to the shop owners to check the cleanliness of the sidewalk and the shop, and all of them knew what he intended. He'd inform the traders and shop owners of bad intentions toward them on the part of anti-Semitic government officials.

The shops were spread out over the entire length of Pilsudski Street [the main street of Braslav], but the commercial center was in the square at the corner of Pilsudski and Third of May streets. In this square, which was near the two Christian churches, the Catholic and the [Eastern] Orthodox, were the shops and storerooms of Levi-Itza Veinshtein, Betzalel-Yankel Dagovitz, Luba Sheiner, Hertzka Shtol [Hirsh Stol], Velvel Mindlin, Hillel Fisher, Berta Rabinovitz, the Fridman family, Zalman Ulman, Leiba Zeif, two hotels of the Band family and the Ulman family, the alcoholic beverage store of the Lubovitz family, the large store of books and writing equipment under Polish ownership, the Polish community center --- Dom Ludzi [House of the People] --- the beer house and billiard table of the Charmatz family, the bakeries of the Chepelevitz family, Blacher and Shmushkovitz, Fisher's shoe store, and below them the factory for soft drinks, soda pop and beer of the Gans family who came from Vilna and --- opposite them --- the store of Yisrael Levin. Five hundred meters from the commercial center, the large store (known as Rolnik) was established by the Polish farmers' union in a large, splendid two-story house; there were storehouses for seeds, agricultural tools, and a modern bakery. One of the unofficial purposes of its establishment was to compete with the Jewish trade in the town. And indeed, the Fridman family's store, which was opposite the Rolnik, nearly went bankrupt.

On Wednesdays and Fridays, there was a fair [market day] in our town. Two large lots were allocated for this purpose, one for a fair of cattle and horses, next to the municipal slaughterhouse, and a second lot on the market street opposite the post office, for a fair of agricultural products. Early in the morning, the farmers from the area's villages were already there with bundles and sacks of flax, produce, chickens, fruit, milk products, eggs and the like. Peddlers stationed themselves along the fences and presented their merchandise on stands and tables; they called out loudly to the villagers to buy "everything good for half free." Their voices mixed with the sounds of the bargaining conducted by the town's traders over prices of agricultural produce that they wished to buy from the farmers.

Toward noon, the Gentiles and their wives would go on a shopping expedition to the peddlers and shopkeepers of the town, finishing a successful market day with a cup of vodka and dessert of the cheapest kind of salted fish (*taranes*), which was large, tough as wood and very salty. The town's traders stayed busy for another long hour packing up their purchases and preparing them to be sent to Vilna by the train, which came to our town twice a day.[6]

At the fair for agricultural products, the tone was set mainly by traders from the families Fisher, Deitch, Maron, Lotz, Veinshtein, Sherman and Ulman, who bought the majority of the crops and flax, which

[Page 47]

after suitable processing were sent to Lodz [some 660 kilometers southwest of Braslav and in Poland]. On the other hand, the fair of cattle and horses was dominated by the family of Baruch Fisher and his strong sons Tevka [Tuvia], Motka [Mottel-Hirsh], Velfka [Zalman-Volf] and Avramka [Avraham-Yosef] --- the main suppliers of meat to the units of the Polish army in the area --- together with the extended Biliak family, traders of cattle, sheep and leather that were sent to the big cities. In addition to working together closely and living near each other, the members of the Biliak family were known for their warm temperament and great physical strength; Gentiles felt their fists many times when they tried to plot against the Jews. A well-known and unique figure in the horse-trading market was Maishke *der barishnik* [peddler or horse dealer]. In Maishke's hands a weak, thin horse would turn into one that was almost purebred. For some reason, Maishke wore his hat with the brim always behind. The gypsies, who were expert horse traders, also respected Maishke *barishnik* because of his expertise with horses.

A respected name among the horse traders and wagoners, and even among the Polish *szlachta* (nobility) who owned purebred horses, was the blacksmith Nachman-Chaim Gurevitz, because of his great expertise in shoeing wild horses. He carried out the shoeing with the help of his two strong sons, Mendel and Meir, who could subdue the wildest horses. Mendel and Meir would first honor the horse with several strong blows on the back with a flat hand, and sometimes also with a huge "pat" on the nose. After that, they'd grab the horse's foot and not let go until the shoeing was finished. The horses seemed to feel that not even they could play tricks on the Gurevitz boys.

Yoske Ulman was a unique character with a sense of humor; he managed the community bathhouse in Braslav. On Thursdays, the men's day in the bathhouse, he'd join actively in the conversations and gossip among the naked men sitting in the front room, after they'd absorbed a reasonable amount of steam and lashes with a broom of twigs. He'd hurry to inform the group that Shlomo-Itza the teacher and Berel-Shachna were coming to the *mikvah* [ritual bath]; both of them were well known in the town because each had an enormous *kila* [hernia]. All of the men, normally serious heads of families, turned quickly into joyful boys who wanted to see the two Jews immersing themselves in the *mikvah*. There, in the airing room of the bathhouse, I heard many funny stories from the unique lore of Braslaver humor.

I remember several funny stories from this lore: One concerned Feivush Fisher [a brother of Baruch], an honest man who worked hard all week cleaning and selling cattle intestines. He liked to eat a lot, and he especially enjoyed *cholent* and *kishke* [respectively a traditional Jewish stew, simmered overnight and eaten for lunch on the Sabbath, and sausage/stuffed intestine with fillings]. He was accustomed to finishing his Sabbath-night meal immediately after returning from prayers in the synagogue, a very abundant meal. After eating, he'd get up on the hot stove to sleep, and it was known that he'd wake up early on the Sabbath morning.[7] The smell of the *cholent* rising from the stove all night would dance in his nostrils. So he'd get up quietly, take out the *cholent*, eat until he was satisfied, and put the rest back in the oven. His family knew that he did this, and so they prepared a very large amount of *cholent* beforehand. The residents of the town also knew this; only Feivush, of blessed memory, thought that no one knew. This was a secret that came out in the airing room of Yoske Ulman's bathhouse, and here there was no reason to be jealous.

Here's another story about a famous eater in the town: Yoske Yarom, the owner of a softdrink factory, arrived with other traders from Braslav at a hostel in the town of Turmont [Turmantas, about 40 kilometers west of Braslav and in Lithuania], to attend a fair. The owner prepared for them an omelet of 20 eggs in a single frying pan. When he put the pan on

[Page 48]

the table, Yoske Yarom got up and said to him approximately this: "What an omelet you made, *tfoo* [ugh] on an omelet like this" --- and he spit on it. This upset the others at the table, and they demanded that he eat the omelet. To which he replied, "So, good, I'll eat it." And indeed, he ate the whole thing himself.

And a story about Zalman Ulman, owner of a large store, who was scolding his sons Davidke, Abrashke and Itzke, three grown lads, because they didn't want to learn Torah; the teacher Rafael Munitz, one of the best teachers in the town, had said of them that they wouldn't even know how to say Kaddish for their father after he passed away. This they denied absolutely. So what did Zalman Ulman, of blessed memory, do? He lay down on the floor in the living room of his apartment, covered himself with a sheet, and said to his three sons, "Here, I'm dead. Let's see if you know how to say Kaddish." Naturally this story and others became material for jokes and laughs by the wags of the town.

The next story involves Leibke Michals, who convinced the dental technician Yakobson to buy from him the lot next to his house, because he, Leibke Michals, had found salt in a pit that he dug on that lot [presumably a good omen]. Leibke showed Yakobson the pit, into which he'd earlier poured a large amount of salt. By the way, the technician Dr. Yakobson would frequently go out to fish on Lake Noviata [Nowiata], which wasn't far from his house, and he always brought home a respectable catch. A group of jokers began to take an interest in the matter and found that Mr. Yakobson, of blessed memory, (I should be forgiven for revealing this) was buying fish from the Gentile fishermen to take home.

The behavior of the gang of pranksters reached a peak in the commotion they caused involving the dentist [Shimon] Bergazin and family, when it came to driving a *dybbuk* from the dentist's house.[8] This is what happened: Leibke Michals, Zelig Ulman, Liber Chepelevitz, Nachke Fisher, Chona Munitz and other members of the gang were playing cards one evening at the home of the Bergazin family, a few days after a neighbor of the Bergazins had died. Leibke Michals asked Bergazin and his wife if they'd poured out the water from all of the vessels in their house, as was the Jewish custom, and the couple replied that they hadn't known it was necessary. In that case, Zelig Ulman said with a completely straight face, he was worried that they were likely to find a *dybbuk* in the house. In view of the fright that took hold of the dentist and his wife on hearing this, the men promised to help them drive out the *dybbuk*. The couple were asked to keep the matter secret until the men could consult with the only person capable of carrying out the expulsion. The Bergazin couple believed every word. The next day, the two were told to get ready and prepare refreshments for everyone, as the expert had consented to carry out the ceremony. And indeed, Moishe-Baruch Bank, a grown man with a black beard, had been drafted to expel the *dybbuk*. He and the group arrived at the Bergazins' house, carrying a large collection of brooms from the bathhouse. The group stood the couple in the middle of the living room, covered them with a sheet and gathered around them, with each one waving a broom at the couple while Moishe-Baruch recited verses in a thick voice. After several rounds of this, the couple were told that the *dybbuk* had been expelled and now they could set out the meal. The talk that went on in the town after the expert's mission to drive out the *dybbuk* can easily be imagined.

[Page 49]
The Folkshul

In Braslav there were three elementary schools: the Polish (*powszechny*) ["comprehensive" or seven-grade school, with instruction in Polish]; the Yavneh school [with instruction in Hebrew]; and the Folkshul, in which the language of instruction was Yiddish, and which was connected to the network of TSYSHO schools in Poland.[9] The great majority of the Jewish children in our town received their basic education at this school. The school was located in two buildings, one of which had two stories, in a spacious, well-fenced-in yard on Third of May Street, opposite the Catholic church. The diplomas of the graduates of the school were recognized at institutions of higher learning. The staff of teachers, among them residents of Braslav, consisted of graduates of the Yiddish Teachers' Seminary in Vilna. Their salaries were low in comparison to other institutions of learning, but they spared no effort to provide the students with proper Torah and communal customs: They inspected the cleanliness of hands, nails and clothing; there were nature hikes outside the town, to the forests in the area, sports and group games. It's impossible to talk about Braslav without mentioning the teachers: Goldberg, short of stature, serious and very strict, who didn't hesitate to slap the ears of the students; the smiling, full-figured teacher Tutengerber; the teacher Koritzki from Sventzion, who's today at Kibbutz Gvat [in northern Israel]; the bespectacled teacher Bergman, who pursued Tsipka Levin in all seriousness; the teacher Chaim Munitz,[10] a resident of the town who taught us to draw; the teacher Itka Fisher, a resident of Braslav and graduate of the seminary in Vilna, who had a thunderous voice and a hearty laugh; the red-headed teacher Eliahu Yonas, who was also a talented dramatic actor and took part in the drama club that was next to the school; the fat teacher Rabinovitz, who was amazingly light on his feet; the teacher Genia Fishfeder (Rabinovitz), who is today in Israel, married to a native of Braslav, Isser Rabinovitz; and the young and lovely teacher, whose name I don't remember, who married Shneiur Kovarski, one of the wealthy men of the town, owner of wholesale storerooms for food products and a supporter of the Folkshul.

School wasn't just an institution for education, it was also a center of cultural activity. It drew around it the youth and graduates of the school in a large drama club that operated intensively all year round and staged productions at a high, artistic level, of the best Yiddish repertoire, such as *Chasia the Orphan*, *Urke Nachalnik* and *The Dybbuk*, as well as plays for the students of the school.[11] Besides the actors, all the members of the club took part in the preparations and rehearsals, busying themselves preparing the lighting and costumes for the actors. A number of excellent actors came from this dramatic club, such as Shayke Deitch in "Young Vilna,"[112] Dveirka Goldin, a talented ballet dancer, and the two sons of Rabbi Hirshel Valin, Meishke [Moishe] and Yisraelke [Yisrael], who immigrated to Israel and for many years were well-known faces in the world of the Tel Aviv theater and were among the founders of the Li La Lo theater in Tel Aviv. Outstanding members of the drama club were Gershon Viderevitz [Wydrowicz], Tsipka Levin, Ishike Levin, the Gilenson sisters, Leibke Band, Hirshke Chepelevitz, Danielke Karasin, Itzka Fisher, Chaike Bank, Avromitske Ulman, Baska Arklis and others.

The preparations for the traditional Purim party began two months before the holiday. All of the clubs and those close to the Folkshul took part in the preparations for the large party, which was a major event in Braslav. The party was held in one of the large halls (the card hall) next to the government offices. The

[Page 50]

distribution and sale of tickets among the residents of the town and smaller places in the area (Slobodka, Zamosh [Zamosz], Dubina [Dubene]) were done by friends of the school and members of the clubs.[113] The party was always a great success. The dancing continued until after midnight, with the accompaniment of two bands: the fire department's band of wind instruments and, alternatively, playing by Niuta Kantor on the piano, Hirshke Chepelevitz on the violin and Yaacov Feldman on drums. Significant profits were brought in by the buffet, which was prepared by women activists and wives of activists for the school. All of the profits were dedicated to operation of the Folkshul.

A regular, respected guest at the party was a representative of the regional government, Mr. Etrushko, who was short of stature, almost a dwarf. He was the son of a cattle and sheep shepherd from Slobodka, and had been adopted by the landowner who was his father's boss. He was sent to be educated and rose to the high position of manager of the tax division in the regional offices. At the party he'd invite the tall girls to dance, and after the dance he would gallantly kiss their hand.

The Yiddish Folkshul in Braslav:

First graduation class, 1921

[Page 51]

Seventh grade, 1929

[Handwritten in Hebrew on the photo are the words "Class VII of the school in Braslav, November 1929." At the left-center of the photo, the adult male with the wide-brimmed hat is Levi-Yitzchak Veinshtein, a prominent supporter of the Folkshul who is also described on page 28 of this memorial book and whose photo appears on page 30.]

Second grade, 1931

[Page 52]

Another exalted project was customary during the last years of the school: During the long recess, the students received a glass of warm milk and a large roll. All of the students, without regard to economic standing, ate together. This contributed to unity among the students. The project required a lot of money, and the management of the school and its supporters made every effort to keep it going without interruption. A library operated next to the school. For a token fee, the residents of Braslav, mainly the young people, received books and the freedom to read in the hall of the library. The young took advantage of the library and its services in the best way, reading many books in Yiddish and translations of Russian and Polish literature. Chatzkele [Yechezkel] Vinokur is well remembered for his dedicated work in the library, which contributed a great deal to enriching the spirits and broadening the minds of the towns' citizens.

Beilka Deitch, the sister of Shayke Deitch, managed a kindergarten and earned great appreciation. After she completed her pedagogic studies in this field in Vilna, she returned to Braslav and established a kindergarten. Within a short time, she was beloved by both the children and their parents. The song "Unter di Grininke Beymelech" ["Under the Little Green Trees"], sung by the children in her kindergarten, became virtually an anthem of the children of Braslav.[14]

Youth

When their primary education ended, young people in Braslav didn't have many options. Only a small proportion of them continued with secondary school; these were the most talented and strong willed, those whose parents had the means to finance their education in the big city of Vilna. Most of the young people, on the other hand, joined their parents in their local businesses or began to learn a trade with the craftsmen of the town. The hope for a better future, and for a way of life different from the one they saw their parents leading, was an important reason why many joined the Zionist youth groups. And indeed, dozens of young people joined the branch of

HeChalutz HaTzair, whose clubhouse was open every day in the hours of the afternoon and evening, and where notable and varied events were held: talks between members, gatherings and lectures by emissaries from the movement's center in Vilna, evenings of song and dancing the hora, and trips to the local forests. There were summer camps in the village at the edges of the Dubkes [Dubki] forest that included camp life and guard duty at night. A number of members were accepted into kibbutzim in Vilna and other towns, to prepare for *aliyah* to the Land of Israel: Munka Shmutzer (Munitz), who made *aliyah* to Israel before the war; Shimon Modlin, who was active in the Braslav branch and also made *aliyah* before the war broke out; Arke Deitch, who made *aliyah* before the war and was among the first who landed in Haifa; the brothers Moshe and Yisrael Valin, who made *aliyah* long before the war broke out. All are in our community in Israel. There also was a branch of Betar in the town; one of its active officers, Zusman Lubovitz, is also in Israel. Occasionally, very heated arguments would break out between the two Zionist parties as to the rightness of their opinions and approach, but the Communist ideology enchanted many of the youth no less than the Zionist idea.[115] Despite the fact that it was forbidden and dangerous, many young people in Braslav were drawn to it, and not only those who were poor; these were the best of the youth, who believed with perfect faith in the Communist redemption, and many of them found themselves under preventive arrest on the eve of May 1 [International Workers' Day, when political demonstrations were frequent]. Nevertheless, somehow young people succeeded in hanging red flags on telephone lines in the town and its approaches. In several incidents, residents of Braslav were put on trial for Communist activity. They

[Page 53]
were defended by Dr. [Joseph] Chernikov from Vilna, who was renowned for his ability to quash accusations by the police and the Polish criminal investigators; for most of the accused, he obtained a complete acquittal. Who can understand the ways of fate? The lawyer Chernikov, who successfully defended dozens of Jewish youths, sometimes without payment, rescuing them from the clutches of the Polish criminal investigation department, was arrested by the Soviets in 1940. He was sent to Siberia and never returned.

Braslav was blessed with forests and lakes, and it was chosen by the Central Institute of Physical Education in Poland (Centralny Instytut Wychowania Fizycznego, or CIWF), as a suitable place for summer camps for vacation and sports training for the best sportsmen in Poland. Accordingly, for a few years before the war, both the Dubkes and Karpovitz [Karpowicz] forests were turned into camps of tents, sports fields and cultural installations; the shores of Lake Driviata, plentiful with clean white sand, became an anchorage with a huge number of kayaks, trampolines and racing boats. Groups of muscular, suntanned "*shkotzim* and *shiksas*" [dismissive Yiddish terms for Gentile men and women] were seen in the town wearing short sports pants, which was shocking to the people of Braslav. After a while, it became known that these young people were the "cream of the crop" of the academic youth and the best sportsmen in Poland, most of them from the big cities: Warsaw, Lodz, Poznan, Lublin, Krakow. After completing their studies, these sons and daughters of the Polish nobility were destined for the highest positions in central government.

Every Sunday evening, there was an artistic show for the residents of the town and the surrounding area, which was called the bonfire (*ognisko*). In the bonfire's light, singers, dancers and acrobats appeared before thousands of onlookers. Among these were a total of two Jewish performers --- one of them, Dr. Rapaport, would visit the synagogue on the Sabbath [the day before the show], drawing most of the residents to pray on that Sabbath. We, the young people, would spend a long hour each day next to the anchorage of the athletes, watching with fascinated curiosity as they jumped into the water and rowed in the kayaks.

In the winter, both lakes were covered by ice half a meter thick. The youth of the town spent many hours in good weather gliding over the ice on ice skates and snow sleds. A unique pastime was to go out to the middle of the frozen lake, about three kilometers from shore, to observe the groups of fishermen (*Starowiery*[116]), grown Gentiles with beards and light-colored hair, who worked for the big landowner of Braslav, Shneiur Aron. Aron hired dozens of fishermen from the villages of Matseshe [Maciesze, 13 kilometers southeast of Braslav] and Ozravtzi [Ozierawce, six kilometers southeast of Braslav].

Shneiur Aron was a big exporter of fish to all the cities in Poland. To the Gentiles who worked for him, he behaved like a landowner. He was accustomed to visit the fishermen in an elaborate sleigh, harnessed to a thoroughbred horse with a special wagoner. When he appeared in the distance, the fishermen would take off their hats to him. The wagoner would take out a crate of vodka from the sleigh and give it to the head of the group, and the head of the fishermen would kiss Shneiur Aron's hand.

We'd end the winter day sometimes also by pulling the big sled that belonged to Yankel Levin's grandfather, with all of the friends in the sled in a big pile, sliding down the hill of Vilcha Street to the corner of Pilsudski Street, next to Ber-Leib Milutin's house, across from the house of Shimon Gans.

[Page 54]

Young people of HeChalutz and HeChalutz HaTzair

Yitzchak Zuckerman (known as Antek) visits the HeChalutz HaTzair branch in Braslav (1936).

[In 1936, the year the photo was taken, Zuckerman (1915-81) --- seated in the center ---
was working for the HeChalutz HaTzair Zionist youth movement, headquartered in Warsaw, Poland.
Two years later, he would become secretary general. In April 1943, he would help to prepare the
Warsaw Ghetto Uprising, and in August 1944 he took part in the Warsaw Polish Uprising.
Zuckerman survived the war and immigrated to Palestine in 1947. There he established near Acre
the Ghetto Fighters' Kibbutz and the Ghetto Fighters' House museum. The Ghetto Fighters' House
is the organization that produced this memorial book in 1986.

Several Braslav residents in the photo were identified as follows in the Ghetto Fighters'
House archive in Israel. Front row: Heschel Zeif (seated first from left), Eliahu Munitz (leaning
down between an unidentified woman and Zuckerman), Feiga/Fania Band (seated second from
right, wearing a beret) and Moshe-Chone Lin (seated first from right). Second row: Shimon Modlin
(standing first from left), Bracha Smushkovitz (standing second from left), Yechiel Sherman
(standing in the center, in a light-colored shirt), David Ulman (standing second from right) and
Shachna Band (standing first from right). Feiga/Fania Band is known to have died in Israel in
1969. Heschel Zeif is described further on pages 316-317 of this memorial book.]

[Page 55]
Fire Department

The fire department in our town was a volunteer organization; 99% of its members were Jews,
only the chief was a Pole, a retired officer whose name was Motel. His deputy was Beinish Milutin,
a strong and bold Jew. When a fire broke out, the firemen were called by ringing a bell and
blowing trumpets. In later years, an electric siren was installed. When they heard the alarm, the
firemen would start to run to the fire department building, holding uniforms, a special axe and
a shiny copper helmet. Here the great show began of grabbing horses to pull the firemen's tools
and equipment to the location of the fire. Beinish Milutin, riding a horse, and next to him Shimon
Per with a trumpet in his hand, first grabbed the horses of the Gentiles, on the strength of a
town ordinance granting firemen the authority to take a horse from its owner when a fire broke
out. In most cases, by the time everything was ready and the firemen arrived at the scene, there
was nothing left to extinguish. If a fire broke out at the house of a Gentile with an orchard of
fruit trees beside his house, the firemen arrived to find baked apples.

There also was an orchestra of wind instruments next to the fire department. Among the 26 players there was just one Gentile, a flute player whose name was Leon. He spoke Yiddish like we did. On official holidays of the country, such as Constitution Day [May 3] and Independence Day [November 11], the orchestra led the parade and played Polish marches. The orchestra was also invited to play at dance parties held by the clerical staff and high officers in the officers' casino [café, club or mess hall] or in the card hall. For us, the players, it was an experience to watch drunken Poles jumping around at length while dancing the *mazurka* and *oberka* and then, at the end, gallantly kissing the hands of their partners.

Electricity

An electricity station was erected in Braslav in the early 1930s [or the late 1920s]. Within two or three years, kerosene lamps disappeared from the houses of Braslav. Electric lights appeared on the streets, in truth dimly, but this was still great progress. After electricity arrived, the first cinema opened in Braslav. The owner of the cinema, a Pole by the name of Bokovski [Bokowski], showed films twice a week, on Saturdays and Sundays --- silent movies accompanied on the violin by the teacher Shimon Efron from Kozian [Koziany, about 40 kilometers southwest of Braslav] and on the piano by Niuta Kantor. The hall would be full from one side to the other. The first movies shown in Braslav were "The Black Pirate" with Douglas Fairbanks and "The Son of the Sheik" with Rudolph Valentino [both released in 1926]. Parallel with the electricity and the cinema, the motor car appeared in Braslav; the first passenger car, a model Ford, belonged to the Polish ruler of the region, Vendof, and the driver, a Pole named Borkovski [Borkowski], drove proudly through the streets, followed by all the children of the town.

The train station was located at the end of Koliova Street at the edge of the town, and the way to it passed through streets populated by Gentiles. Twice a day, a passenger train came to our town, once in the direction of Duksht [Dukstas, about 45 kilometers southwest of Braslav and in Lithuania] and stopping on the way in the towns of Opsa and Turmont, and the second time in the [opposite] direction of the town of Druya [Druja, about 34 kilometers northeast of Braslav] and stopping in the towns of Slobodka and Druysk [Drujsk, about 19 kilometers northeast of Braslav]. Since the train had narrow tracks, passengers who wanted to go to Vilna had to transfer in Duksht to a train with wide tracks. The station also served as a destination for a Sabbath walk for the citizens of Braslav, for them to see who was coming to town.

[Page 56]

The Braslav fire brigade

The fire department commanders:
Standing (from left): Efraim Zarzhevski, Reuven Deitch, Zusman Lubovitz, Yankel Band
Sitting (from left): Uriel Karasin, Beinish Milutin, Moshe-Chone Lin

[Page 57]

In the winter, heavy snow covered the train tracks, and the train frequently got stuck. When this happened, convoys of sleighs were organized to maintain the connection to Vilna. In these convoys, hundreds of tons of merchandise and agricultural produce were transported to that city. When they returned, they brought merchandise for our town's traders. This was a difficult and exhausting trip that took almost a week altogether, there and back; it was 180 kilometers in each direction [this was presumably the road distance; as the crow flies, Vilna was about 165 kilometers southwest of Braslav]. Often the owners of the horses walked alongside their sleighs for many kilometers, pushing the sleigh up the hills with a strong shoulder. But such a trip provided a nice profit. Many stories circulated in our town about the troubles of the journey and their heroes; the brothers Leiba and Feivush Levin; Leiba-Meir Barmapov with his sons Maishke [Moshe] and Itzka; the extended Milutin family, who were known for their audacity and strength; the Shkolnik family, who were quick to anger and sought out any insolent Gentile who needed to be taught manners; Yudka [Yudel] Fisher, the strong man, who once rolled a drunken Gentile, together with his sled and his horse, into a ditch by the side of the road when the drunkard didn't want to open the lane so that a convoy could pass; the Biliak boys, who took part in the convoy to Vilna until they bought a car, which was the second motorized vehicle in the town (the first one belonged to Shmuel-Yosef Milutin, who opened the age of a motorized link to the city of Vilna); Hirshke Maron, a trader of flax and hay; tall Falka [Rafael] Fisher, a trader of cattle and leather; Yankel Amdur, owner of a shop and a leather trader, the son of the *shochet* [ritual slaughterer] Shalom-Zavel Amdur; members of the family of Arke Veinshtein, owner of a shop and a trader of chickens and eggs; Zalman Eliahu, and more whose names I don't remember, who were faithful representatives of the folk in our town and who didn't hesitate to protect their honor, even when danger was involved.

The Draft (*Priziv*[17])

Young men close to the age of 21 were obligated to report to the medical committee of the Polish army. In the runup to this date, tension would grow among the youths, who preferred not to serve in the army because of the anti-Semitism, as well as the rigid attitude that officers took toward new draftees in general and Jews in particular. The candidates for the draft would go at night through the streets of the town, carrying out all kinds of practical jokes. They'd collect all of the outhouses, which in our town were located in the yards of the houses, and stand them in the commercial center, hanging on them the signs that belonged to the craftsmen and shop owners. They'd mix up the horses in the stables and other pranks of this type. But everyone took this in good spirit because it had been the custom for many years, and despite all their efforts to earn the rejection of the doctors of the medical committee and forgo army service, many of the young men of Braslav did serve in the army. Their stories of exhausting training, together with journeys made on foot over great distances in full equipment, were fascinating but frightened the parents whose sons stood to be drafted.

Spring and Passover

In Braslav, no one needed a calendar to know that spring was approaching --- and with it the Passover holiday. It was possible to see and feel the coming of spring; the heavens opened more frequently to the warmth of the sun, even though sometimes there was still light snow that changed immediately into water and mud. The windows of the houses began to be opened for a short time during the day, after having been closed all winter long

[Page 58]

in a double frame, with a filling of cotton wool and sawdust stuffed between the frames. Housewives brought out the warm mattresses and quilts to air on the windowsills. In the streets appeared the first wagons of the farmers from the villages. In the morning, the wagoners of the town found it hard to decide what to harness the horse to: the wagon or the sleigh.

The time arrived for the *matzoh* bakers in our town to prepare and make the bakeries kosher for baking *matzot* [unleavened bread]. In Braslav there were three permanent *matzoh* bakeries: Moishe *der baker*, whose house was at the end of Pilsudski Street next to the leather trader

Hertzke Skopitz, and where *matzoh* was baked by hand; another baker, Aba Katz, whose house was on Third of May Street next to the officials' casino and who also baked by hand; and the bakery of Zerach Bogomolski, who dealt all year with the sale and repair of clocks and who installed a machine to make *matzoh*. Zerach Bogomolski's bakery enjoyed unusual success. First, everyone wanted to see how the machine worked. Second, the *matzoh* there was tastier. The place from which professional *matzoh* bakers came was the village of Dubina. Most of Dubina's Jews worked in Braslav in this profession, each year when the holiday approached.

Before the War --- And the War

In the first years after Hitler rose to power in Germany [in 1933], the Jews of Braslav didn't feel especially worried. But on the eve of the war between Poland and Germany [in September 1939], they were shocked when Jewish refugees from Czechoslovakia and Austria began to appear in Braslav on their way to the Baltic seaport of Klaipeda [the major port city of Lithuania and formerly known as Memel, it was about 370 kilometers west of Braslav]. When they saw that these Jewish refugees, who appeared well off and intelligent, were fleeing the Nazis with nothing, the people of our town felt --- maybe for the first time --- that anti-Semitism meant more than just being called *"Zhid"* ["Jew"] or the throwing of a stone, that it posed a threat to the very lives of the Jews. The community committee organized assistance for the refugees and helped them on their way to Lithuania. Statements began to be heard about the war to come. When the war broke out [in September 1939], the young men were drafted and sent to the front. On Polish radio, all day long just two sentences were heard: "Listen, listen, he's coming" and "Listen, listen, he has passed" (referring to German airplanes).

On the first day of the fourth week of the war, the Polish government began to evacuate the town, because the Russian army had crossed the border in the town of Disna [Dzisna], 80 kilometers from Braslav [actually about 72 kilometers east of Braslav]. The government officials informed the Jews of Braslav that they were leaving, and they left a number of weapons for protection against the villagers of the area who wanted to use the absence of government authority to carry out robberies and maybe even a pogrom. The Jews organized immediately in self-defense. The strong men, with Beinish Milutin at their head, blocked all the entrances to Braslav and stood patrol on all the roads leading to the town. In fact, groups of villagers made several attempts to enter the town, but they turned back when they saw Jews armed with axes, metal rods and a few rifles. The lack of government authority continued for a week, while the armed Jewish guards kept order. Then the Soviet government arrived, in the form of a military vehicle carrying a commissar accompanied by several armed soldiers, who took over the police building. Army units entered the town after them, and the Communist era in Braslav began.

Footnotes:

1. The three synagogues were the Beit Midrash of the Mitnagdim and the Old Synagogue and New Synagogue of the Hasidim, which were near one another on the side of Castle Hill facing Lake Driviata (Drywiaty). Some distance from them, around one side of Castle Hill, was a fourth synagogue: the Sandy Synagogue of the Hasidim.

   The Hasidim and Mitnagdim were two important branches within Ashkenazi Judaism. Hasidism (Pietism) emerged in the 1700s in what's now western Ukraine as a movement for spiritual revival, spreading through Eastern Europe. Besides knowledge and observance of the Torah and Talmud, it emphasized immediate religious experience. By the late 1700s, the Mitnagdim (Opponents) came to refer to traditionalist Ashkenazi Jews who opposed Hasidic Judaism, emphasizing intensive study of the Talmud. Opposition to Hasidism was centered in Lithuania, particularly in Vilna.

2. Schloss Berg, also known as Castle Hill and the Zamek. It was called a mountain by locals, even though it stood only 15 meters or so above the town.

3. *Der Tog (The Day)*, also called *Der Vilner Tog*, was a Yiddish newspaper published in Vilna between 1912 and 1939, edited during the interwar years by the scholar Zalman Reisen (1887-1941).

4. Betar was the youth movement of the Revisionist Zionists, who were led by Vladimir (Zeev) Jabotinsky. The Revisionist Zionists were classically liberal in economic orientation and thus opposed to the socialists. Their other major aims, as set forth in 1929, included immigration to Palestine, compulsory military training, a commitment to learning Hebrew, and the establishment of a Jewish state on both sides of the Jordan River.

5. Specially made bread, typically eaten on ceremonial occasions such as the Sabbath and major Jewish holidays except for Passover.

6. Vilna was about 165 kilometers southwest of Braslav and --- in the 1920s and 30s --- like Braslav, was part of Poland.

7. In Russia, Belorussia and the Ukraine, ovens were traditionally made of brick masonry that retained heat for long periods of time, and their outer surface was safe to touch. In winter, people would sleep on top of the oven to keep warm.

8. A *dybbuk* was believed to be the wandering soul of a dead person that sought to enter and take over the body of a living person, as a refuge from the demons pursuing it. In S. Ansky's 1920 play *The Dybbuk*, for example, a bride became possessed by the soul of a man who had died and began speaking with his voice.

9. The **Yavneh** school was part of a network of more than 200 schools established throughout Poland by Mizrahi, the Religious Zionist movement that had been founded in 1902 in Vilna to promote Zionism among Orthodox Jews. Mizrahi's religious focus set it apart from many of the other Zionist movements, which were secular. The youth movement of Mizrahi was Tse'ire Mizrahi. The Yavneh school program emphasized Hebrew (in place of Yiddish), Torah and Talmud study, and reconstruction of Jewish life in Palestine. In the interwar years, the flagship of the Yavneh school network was the Tachkemoni Rabbinical Seminary in Warsaw. Secular Zionists on the political left/center, on the other hand, operated the **Tarbut** school network, with instruction in Hebrew.

    Di Tsentrale Yidishe Shul-Organizatsye (Central Yiddish School Organization), abbreviated as TSYSHO or CYSHO, had been established in Warsaw in 1921 and continued to operate until 1939. Led mainly by members of the Bund (the Jewish socialist party in Poland) and Left Poale Zion (the left wing of the Labor Zionists), it sought to create a network of secular Yiddish schools under socialist auspices. (The Bund and Left Poale Zion differed politically --- the former was Marxist and anti-Zionist, the latter was Marxist and Zionist --- but each supported the use of Yiddish.) TSYSHO was run by a central office in Warsaw and a central education committee in Vilna (which between ca. 1920 and 1939 was part of Poland, as was Braslav). According to *The YIVO Encyclopedia of Jews in Eastern Europe*, the curriculum consisted of Yiddish language and literature, Jewish history and culture, the sciences, math, music, physical education, arts and crafts and, in some cases, Hebrew. In addition, Polish language, literature and history were taught in Polish.

    At its peak in the late 1920s, TSYSHO maintained 219 institutions with 24,000 students spread across 100 locations. These included 46 kindergartens, 114 elementary schools, 6 high schools, 52 evening schools, and a pedagogical institute in Vilna. The Vilna Realgymnazye, the crown jewel of Yiddish secular education in Poland, was the first modern high school in which Yiddish was the language of instruction. The pedagogical institute (the Vilna Teachers' Seminary) played a major role in the secular Yiddish school system, as both a training institute and a center for communicating new ideas in Jewish teaching.

10. An account of Chaim Munitz appears on pages 70-71 of this memorial book.

11. *Chasia the Orphan*, published in 1903, was a famous play by the Russian-born American playwright Jacob Gordin (1853-1909). *Urke Nachalnik* was the dramatization of memoirs by the Jewish ex-con Yitzchak Farbarowicz (1897-1939) that were popular in Poland in the 1930s. *The Dybbuk*, by the Russian-born author S. Ansky (1863-1920), was written in the 1910s and first performed in 1920, in Yiddish by the Vilna Troupe.

12. "Young Vilna" might refer to either (1) a prominent group of writers and artists associated with Vilna from 1929, such as Chaim Grade, Avrom Sutzkever and Shmerke Kaczerginski, or (2) the magazine *Yung-Vilne*, published in Vilna in Yiddish between 1934 and 1936, which included many of these writers and artists.

13. In relation to Braslav, Slobodka was about 11 kilometers northeast, Zamosh was 16 kilometers south, and Dubina was 16 kilometers northwest.

14. This was a poem written in Yiddish by Chaim Nachman Bialik and published in 1901. It was later set to music by Platon Brounoff in two distinct melodies, composed in 1905 and 1914. The song became popular throughout the Yiddish-speaking world. Beila/Beilka Deitch, mentioned elsewhere in this memorial book (pages 126, 168, 228, 235, 254 and 263), appears in a photo on page 229.

15. The two Zionist parties were the World Zionist Organization (dominated by the socialist-oriented Labor Zionists, whose youth movement was HeChalutz) and their chief opponent in the late 1920s and 1930s: the Revisionist Zionists, led by Vladimir Jabotinsky (whose youth movement was Betar). Secular, liberal and nationalist, the Revisionist Zionists were opposed to socialism.

16. This referred to an offshoot of the Eastern Orthodox Church in Russia that had split from the main church in the 1600s over differences in liturgy and ritual. In Polish, its adherents were called *Starowiery* (Old Believers).

17. *Priziv*, a Yiddish word derived from the Russian, meant military conscription.

[Page 59]

Ziska (Reuven) Shmushkovitz
Son of Gitel and Leib

Translated from the Hebrew by Dr. Ida Schwarcz
Footnotes Added / Donated by Jeff Deitch

Today is Rosh Hashanah [the Jewish New Year], and standing wrapped in my *tallit* [prayer shawl] I pour out my heart before the Master of the Universe. Forgotten images rise out of the mist of years, faces and experiences. I hear within me the melodies of Shlomo [Zilber] the *shochet* [ritual slaughterer], the choir of Chaim-Aizik Maron and his sons on Kol Nidre night, and memories from my childhood and adolescence stand before my eyes like beloved guests . . .

Our lives in those days weren't easy. My family wasn't among the rich. Poverty and hardship were frequent companions.

My father was a wagoner, on the roads for an entire week. The work was difficult and exhausting, requiring much effort, and also fraught with danger. In the wintertime, amid the cold and snowstorms, my father and the other wagoners would take merchandise from our town to the big city of Vilna [165 kilometers to the southwest] and then return. They'd load the wagons with their merchandise after the Sabbath, set out on the long journey and come back on Friday, exhausted, rushing to the bathhouse to wash from their bodies the sweat and dust that had accumulated during the week.

Many years later, I met the old bathhouse attendant --- Anton --- and he spoke nostalgically of those days when the wagoners would come to the bathhouse. "They were heroes," he said, "everything shook when they stood in the steam room and whipped each other with the birch branches in their hands --- they were great men." They and some other families, like the Biliaks, always came out to defend the Jews of the town during the pogroms, opposing the anti-Semitic hooligans.

We lived in a small house, very narrow and almost fallen down. In the wintertime the snow came up to the windows and we had to work hard to clear a path to leave the house. In those days, I remember, I used to run to school in good spirits, because during the break we got a fresh roll and a glass of warm milk. We didn't always get this at home. We didn't always have wood for a fire to warm the house, and we children would go to the flax warehouses of Avraham-Leib Fisher and take from there, for a small price, the leftover waste of the flax and bring it home. We used to go there after the Sabbath, when the workers weren't around, and we --- children of all ages --- would stuff the dusty waste matter into large sacks that had been sewn for that purpose.

[Page 60]

We tried to stuff the sacks quickly, to beat the other children. The dusty waste turned us into "ghosts"; our ears, noses and mouths became clogged and covered with a thick layer of dirt. Heating with this waste wasn't easy. We had to stir the burning material with a stick, otherwise thick smoke would burst from the oven. After a while, a tinsmith named Moshe-Aharon [Etzin] invented a special device that made it easier to use the waste.

I remember Moshe-Aharon [Etzin], a short thin man, who worked in his shop from morning until evening. He had a strange, funny nickname: "Moshe-Aharon Puff-Up." The origin of the nickname, as I heard it, was in a story about his wife Chana: On the Sabbath, after the afternoon rest, he and his wife used to take a walk on the main street dressed in their Sabbath clothes. As they approached the richest man in town, Chana would tell her husband to puff up his cheeks and stick out his chest so that he'd make his thin body look more important. Thus, the nickname "Moshe-Aharon Puff-Up" became permanent. Both he and his wife were murdered together with all the Jews of Braslav [Braslaw].

In our house we had a large wide oven --- especially for cooking *cholent* [traditional Jewish stew]. Many housewives would bring their pots with the *cholent* on Friday before Sabbath and on the next day, after the morning prayers, they'd come to take them. Once it happened that a maidservant took a pot by mistake that didn't belong to her mistress, and the poor family was delighted to find the delicious meal that had been prepared . . .

I remember the fire in our town. Many houses burned down and we, the children dragged whatever we could to the shore of the lake. The men were busy trying to put out the fire, and we were happy to serve as important helpers in a time of trouble.

The problem of clothing was very difficult. Every holiday eve, we had rosy dreams of new shoes or new outfits.

Mother used to buy used clothing and give them to Reb Tsale-Nahum to alter. He was an old and very religious man. His house was always full of all kinds of rags that he repaired for poor children. He was so pious that he took care to avoid, G-d forbid, sewing a cross when he sewed a button, and his stitches were always straight and not crossed. He had a mentally handicapped daughter; she was an innocent soul who would never harm anyone and who said to everyone she met, "Milky golem boo boo boo."[1] Her name was Gita, and her nickname was "Gitka Boo."

The [Jewish] community council was located in the building of the study house of the Mitnagdim,[2] where people came to receive assistance. The heads of the council, may their memory be honored --- to my sorrow I don't recall their names --- tried to help the needy graciously, whether it meant buying a horse for a wagoner whose horse had died, or with *ma'ot hitim* [money to buy food for Passover], or any other type of assistance.

I will commemorate the good Jews of the town: Shneiur Aron, who leased the lakes and gave fish to the poor every Sabbath eve; and the baker Aba Shmushkovitz (not a relative), who always gave me *challot* [loaves of bread] for Sabbath when I came to buy them, telling me my mother had already paid for them. His image appears before my eyes, as he stood in the synagogue on Sabbath and holidays, handing out prayer books to the children.

We were children, and we yearned for bicycles such as other children had. Bicycles, of course were just a dream for us. We did everything we could to earn a few moments of happiness when we borrowed bicycles for an

[Page 61]

hour or two from Mendel the mechanic. He used to build bicycles from junk and would rent them for a short time to children like me. We earned the money, a few pennies, on market days from the farmers who paid us to water their horses at the lake.

I'll mention Moshe-Baruch, who took any job, even the lowliest, to earn his bread honestly, as the saying goes: "Flay a carcass outside, and you won't need other people." [In other words, it's better to take on even work that's degrading to avoid handouts]. He used to give poor children haircuts for free, on condition that they keep their *payot* [sidelocks]. I used to sneak into the barn afterward and cut them off with my mother's scissors.

And also Chaim-Aizik Maron, a cheerful and friendly man who once met a farmer who asked where he could buy an English saw. Maron said, "Come with me" and took the farmer to his own house. There he showed him his wife (who was English) and said, "Here's an English saw, she cuts me up every day."

The days of my childhood and the years of my youth have passed and gone, never to return, but the memories remain, memories full of sadness and also feelings of sweet pain.

I survived the terrible war, from Stalingrad until the victory. I was wounded twice. I always dreamed and hoped to return to my town and to find it as I remembered it and as it was engraved in my heart, with the candlelight dancing in the windows on Sabbath eve . . .

I returned to Braslav, the place where I'd lived and dreamed, but found neither my beloved town nor its people.

Footnotes:

1. In Jewish folklore, a golem was a superhuman but slow-witted creature created from mud or clay. In Yiddish, it's used to describe someone considered to be simple minded or sluggish.
2. Mitnagdim (Opponents) referred to traditionalist Ashkenazi Jews who resisted Hasidic Judaism, emphasizing intensive study of the Talmud. Opposition to the Hasidim was centered in Lithuania.

[Page 62 = Blank in the original]

[Page 63]

The Community of Braslav
during the Holocaust

Translated from the Hebrew by Laia Ben-Dov
Donated by Jeff Deitch

". . . For behold,
Your enemies stir,
and those who hate You
raise their heads.
Against Your people
they plot cunningly,
and they take counsel
against Your protected ones.
They said, 'Come let us
destroy them as a nation,
and the name of Israel
will no longer be remembered.'"

--- Psalm 83:3-5

[Page 64 = Blank in the original]

[Page 65]

Deep, Deep Pits and Red, Red Loam
By Shmuel Halkin[1]

Deep, deep pits, and red, red loam ---
Once I too had a home ---
Where the orchards bloomed in spring
And in autumn birds took wing
And in winter soft snow fell.
Now --- the wind his moan howls there.

A disaster struck my home!
Open wide flung doors and gates
The vile murderers, the butchers,
They who slaughter little children,
They who hang the old, the weak,
They who leave no one to speak . . .

Deep, deep pits, and red, red loam ---
Once I too had a home.

The years come, the years go,
Brimful are the pits
And redder still the loam.
That loam is now my home.
There my brothers, sisters lie ---
Torn limb from limb
Cut down on the spot
Shot down beside the pit.

Deep, deep pits, and red, red loam ---
Once I too had a home.

Brighter days will dawn again
Fortune will yet smile again
And the pain will slowly wane.
Once again will children sprout
Once again will play and shout
Near the graves of the holy dead
Graves so deep, so full, so red ---
And with the wind will sigh your moan.

Deep, deep pits, and red, red loam ---
Once I too had a home.

Deep, deep pits, and red, red loam ---
Once I too had a home . . .

Yes, once I too had a home . . .

Footnote:

1. Shmuel Halkin (1897-1960) was a Soviet Yiddish poet from Rogachev, Belorussia. His poem (in Yiddish, "Tife Griber, Royte Laym") is an iconic work on the Holocaust, begun in 1943 after he visited what was left of his native town. The English version of this poem also appears on pages 628-629 of this memorial book.

[Page 66]

In Memory of My Father,
Rabbi Zvi-Hirsh [Valin],
of Blessed Memory
By Yisrael Valin

Translated from the Hebrew by Laia Ben-Dov
Footnotes Added / Donated by Jeff Deitch

Today, when we say the Yizkor prayer, full of horror for our loved ones who were destroyed, murdered, slaughtered and burned, we must remember that the voices of our brothers' blood are shouting to us from within the earth. They're demanding that we continue to keep their memory . . .

As one of those who was blessed to live for 20 years --- from the dawn of my childhood --- in our town of Braslav [Braslaw], I recall as a sacred obligation the image of my father, my teacher, the brilliant Rabbi Zvi-Hirsh (the son of Avraham-Yitzchak Valin), may G-d avenge his blood, the former rabbi of Braslav (who last served as the rabbi of the town of Goldingen, in Courland, Latvia [now called Kuldiga, about 370 kilometers northwest of Braslav]).

My father, my teacher, the rabbi, the Gaon, Rabbi Zvi-Hirsh Valin, was born in our town of Braslav to his father, Rav Avraham-Yitzchak Valin, one of the distinguished men of the town. In his childhood, superior talents were recognized in him. He studied at the Volozhin Yeshiva[1] and at the Knesset Beit Yitzchak Yeshiva in Slabodka,[2] and he received Torah from the head of the yeshiva, the Gaon Rabbi Yitzchak-Elchanan [Spektor] [1817-96], of blessed memory. His wonderful skills and great diligence shaped him and made him one of the great Torah scholars. After his marriage to my mother, the *rebbetzin* [wife of the rabbi] Sara-Hinda, may G-d avenge her blood, the daughter of the honored wealthy man Reb Yehuda-Leib from Sventzion [Swieciany, about 85 kilometers southwest of Braslav; now in eastern Lithuania], he continued to study Torah in his home and became a great man of stature, with a majestic appearance and a mouth that produced jewels. While he was still studying at the yeshivas, he won goodwill through his talent for speaking and practical initiative, and as a community worker and faithful Zionist. At all of the assemblies of the yeshivas and the rabbis, he was always among the main speakers, and everywhere he appeared he made a great impression. He had the strength to speak for three continuous hours without fatigue. With the magic of his oratory, with fiery words, he enthralled his audience.

When he was still young, he was accepted as a rabbi in Krasnopolia (Suvalk sector) [Krasnopol in the Russian province of Suwalki Gubernia, now in northeast Poland], and after several years he was invited to take a position in the rabbinate in Nei-Sventzion (Vilna sector) [Nowo-Swieciany in Polish/Svencioneliai in Lithuanian, in the Russian province of Vilna Gubernia, now in eastern Lithuania; Nei-Sventzion was about 86 kilometers southwest of Braslav]. After a time, the distinguished men of the town of my birth, Braslav, turned to him and asked him to take office as the rabbi of Braslav and the surrounding area. He did much, promoting and looking after the daily life of the residents of the town. He also established a grand yeshiva, to which streamed young men of talent from Braslav and the surrounding area, as well as young men who came to learn from the yeshivas in the cities of Poland, who were fleeing from being drafted into the Polish army. To enable the yeshiva students to cross the border into Latvia and continue their Torah studies there, my father formed a connection with a trader from Braslav, Reb Velvel the flax dealer, may G-d avenge his blood, who smuggled flax over the border. My mother, the *rebbetzin* Sara-Hinda, may G-d avenge her blood, should be remembered for her goodness; she did a lot to help the yeshiva students as well as the brides in the town who were in straitened circumstances. Among these yeshiva students were two lads who were wonderful in Torah and in their character. One of them was Rabbi Eliezer-Yehuda Nidzviadovitz[?] from the Chofetz Chaim Yeshiva in Radun [about 240 kilometers southwest of Braslav; now in Belarus]. My father chose him as a bridegroom for my elder sister Brayna, may G-d avenge her blood. She and her husband and their children were killed in the Holocaust in Luzhki [Luzki, about 65 kilometers southeast of Braslav] (near Gluboki [Glubokoye]), where he served as the rabbi. The second lad was Rabbi Moshe Shtern (called the "young genius of Rassishk") and he was among the yeshiva students who fled from the army draft. I, the writer of these lines, crossed the border together with him [into Latvia], with the help of Reb Velvel the flax dealer, and from there I went on *aliyah* to Israel.

My father also took an interest in the local youth, and he was original in his influence . . . I remember that one day

[Page 67]

the non-religious youths gathered to paint the [building of the] HeChalutz[3] organization; there also was a drama club in Braslav and at their head was my brother Moshe, of blessed memory (the prominent Israeli impresario, who passed away in 1979).[4] The matter became known to my father, and suddenly he appeared among the youths painting the building and said to them, "Is there some reason you didn't invite me into your group? . . . As the town rabbi, I'd be glad to serve at your head." When they heard this, the youths were embarrassed and they dispersed . . . the next day my father brought out a *kol-korei* [rabbinic statement]: "To build up the precious faith and warm hearts of the youngsters, gather to us every pioneer, every generous soul who finds in himself the desire for the Land of Israel, who's prepared to choose Zion and Jerusalem. Come, together we can consult and unite the scattered strengths into one camp, with the assistance of the Helper of Israel in Zion . . ." and so on.

In the pamphlet *Otzar HaAretz* [*Treasures of the Land*], published by Knesset Jerusalem in the year 5686 [1926], we find the signature of my father, my teacher, the genius, on the proclamation of the rabbis of Poland on behalf of Keren Hayesod.[5] At that time, my father volunteered to go abroad for a collection campaign for the Vaad HaYeshivot [Council of Yeshivot],[6] which was then facing a difficult economic situation. For this purpose he traveled to Latvia, where the heads of the community in the town of Goldingen recognized and appreciated him, and they chose him to be the rabbi of their town. The young man Reb Moshe Shtern came to us, and my father chose him to marry my young sister Beila, may G-d avenge her blood. He [Shtern] was chosen to hold office in the rabbinate of the town of Schonberg in Latvia [now Skaistkalne in central-southern Latvia, some 180 kilometers northwest of Braslav], where he served until the day of the Holocaust.

The day of parting from Braslav was hard for us and for the residents of the town. The entire large community felt in its soul that it was parting from something precious and holy. When my father gave his farewell sermon in the synagogue, from which the residents of the town accompanied him to the train, they all felt a holy feeling enveloping their hearts . . . and a holy splendor poured over all of those who gathered there, who were ready to break down in weeping . . . the impression was so strong and so dramatic . . . that at that hour all of them felt a hidden spiritual value in this true rabbinate . . .

In Goldingen, my father served as rabbi until the bitter day when the Holocaust came. Then all of them gathered together. My brother-in-law, Rabbi Gaon Moshe Shtern, his wife the *rebbetzin* (my sister Beila) and their children, my brother Mordechai, his wife and their children, my brother Betzalel, all of them went to my parents, who'd already managed to flee from Goldingen to Riga. There all of them were murdered by the Nazi oppressor and burned while they were still alive, together with other rabbis of Latvia, in the great synagogue in Riga.[7] May G-d avenge their blood.

. . . We will remember the comrades, the relatives and the friends who were killed in Braslav during the Holocaust and gave their lives as martyrs for the Sanctification of the Holy Name. To all of them, I read the words of Jonathan to David: "You will be remembered, because your place will remain empty" [I Samuel 20:18] . . . we won't forget you, your places remain empty . . .

Rabbi Rav Zvi-Hirsh Valin

Footnotes:

1. The Volozhin Yeshiva, also called the Etz Chaim Yeshiva, was a Lithuanian yeshiva located in what's now Valozhyn, Belarus. Established in 1806 by Rabbi Chaim Volozhin, a student of the famed Vilna Gaon, it operated from 1806 to 1892 and from 1899 to 1939. It served as a model for yeshivas established thereafter in Lithuania and was called the Oxford/Cambridge of Judaism. The building housing the yeshiva survived World War II and in 1989 was returned to the Jewish community of Belarus.

2. This prominent yeshiva was located in Slabodka in what's now Vilijampole, a suburb of Kovno [Kaunas], Lithuania. It operated from the late 1800s until World War II.

3. HeChalutz (The Pioneer) was a Jewish youth movement that trained young people for agricultural settlement in Palestine. It was part of the Labor Zionist youth movement.

4. This refers to Moshe Valin, a founder and director of the Li La Lo theater group in Tel Aviv.

5. Keren Hayesod was the Foundation Fund, founded in London in 1920 as a funding arm of the World Zionist Organization to help the Jews return to Palestine, following the Balfour Declaration in 1917.

6. This organization, based in Vilna and active from 1924-39, was authorized by the Polish government to provide spiritual and financial support to the Orthodox yeshivas in Poland's five eastern provinces: Bialystok, Nowogrodek, Polesie, Vilna and Volhynia. It comprised a network of about 70 yeshivas with a total of about 6,000 students, with a supporting membership of more than 350 Jewish communities in the region.

7. The Great Choral Synagogue, completed in 1871, the largest synagogue in Riga, was burned on July 4, 1941, three days after the Nazis occupied Riga; it's estimated that as many as 300 Jews were killed in the conflagration. Also burned on July 4 were other synagogues in Riga, including the Old-New Synagogue, the city's oldest. Only the Peitav Synagogue escaped destruction.

[Page 68]

In Memory of the
Rabbi Rav Avraham-Abba-Yaacov Zahorie,
of Blessed Memory
By Tuvia Fisher

Translated from the Hebrew by Laia Ben-Dov
Footnotes Added / Donated by Jeff Deitch

This rabbi, who reached his high position not because of the authorities but on the strength of his moral standing in the Jewish community, wasn't a man who studied Torah for a limited time, but one who dedicated his entire life to sacred studies and immersed himself in serving the Creator heart and soul, day and night. The rabbi's house was a study hall for learning Jewish law and was separated from the external, materialistic world. The rabbi's wish was to lead his community and influence it with words of honesty and holiness, to be a leader and set a personal example in his morality, in daily life in ordinary times and in times of calamity, G-d forbid. The rabbi sat among the people, although his conduct set him apart. He taught the members of his congregation "on his right, the fire of religion . . ."[1] Thus are scholars of the law recognized, "by their speech and their clothing in the marketplace" (Sefer Bracha). Everything said thus far, and much more than this, was embodied in the character of our rabbi, Rav Avraham-Abba-Yaacov, of blessed memory. With heart and soul, he was deeply tied to the Jews of the place. He shared all of their celebrations and felt all of their sorrows. With difficulty, he supported his family by selling yeast to housewives on the eves of the Sabbath and holidays. The economics of the household were the concern of the *rebbetzin* [his wife]. Rabbi Avraham-Abba-Yaacov was immersed entirely in his spiritual world, the world of Torah, and he didn't know the shape of a coin or its worth. When I was a yeshiva student living outside Braslav, I'd always make my first visit, when I came home for the holidays, to the house of Rabbi Avraham-Abba, to say to him "*Shalom aleichem*" ["Peace be upon you"] and wish him well. Always I found him sunk in his learning. Rav Avraham-Abba-Yaacov was satisfied even with very little. His main food was bread dipped in salt and boiled water.

There were four minyans in Braslav --- four locations of prayer in which the Jews of the town prayed on weekdays and holidays: the Old Minyan, the New Minyan, the Sandy Minyan called Der Zamdiker [The Zodiac], and the Beit Midrash [study hall]. In three of these minyans, they prayed according to the Sephardic custom --- Nusach HaAri Hakadosh --- and only in the Beit Midrash did they pray according to the Ashkenazi custom.[2] Rabbi Avraham-Abba-Yaacov prayed in the Old Minyan, but he was accepted and very much honored by all of the prayer houses and congregations. The *gabbai* [caretaker] of the Old Minyan synagogue was my father, Reb Baruch Fisher, of blessed memory. Many of the men of the town would come to listen to Rav Avraham-Abba-Yaacov's sermons, which he gave in the Old Minyan. The place was always full from end to end with members of all the minyans. All the men of Braslav paid great respect to their Rabbi Rav Avraham-Abba-Yaacov Zahorie, of blessed memory, or, as he was called with affection by the people, Rav Abba der Rav. In his sermons, he didn't pain his listeners and he didn't moralize. He always saw before him holy, pure Jews, not sinners, G-d forbid. He explained Torah in new ways connected to a Jew's daily life led in terms of charity and honesty.

In the summer of 1939 I was drafted into the Polish army, which was about to go to war against Nazi Germany. Before I left home, my father sent me to ask Rav Avraham-Abba-Yaacov for his blessing, and of course I did this willingly. When I entered the Rav's house I found him, as always, immersed in the Gemarah.[3] Out of respect, I stood and waited until he sensed that I was there. I blessed him with the greeting, "*Shalom aleichem*," and stated my request. The Rav listened with great attention and then told me to say three times the verses

[Page 69]

"Do not fear sudden terror or destruction"[4] that are recited after the prayer "It is our duty to praise the Master of all . . ." [from the Aleinu L'Shabeach prayer]. In the difficult moments I had over the years that followed, I always repeated to myself these words of the Rav's blessing. The shining face of Rav Abba and his spiritual image were with me on every path. With G-d's help and the Rav's merit I arrived at old age, when the years of the war and the Holocaust that the Nazis brought upon our people were behind me.

Rabbi Rav Avraham-Abba-Yaacov, his wife the *rebbetzin* and his two sons, Reb Eliezer-Yitzchak and Reb Mendel, met their death in the massive slaughter that the Nazis and their collaborators carried out in the Braslav Ghetto on Wednesday, 18 Sivan 5702 --- June 3, 1942.

May G-d avenge their blood.

Rabbi Rav Avraham-Abba-Yaacov Zahorie

Footnotes:

1. Deuteronomy 33:2, associating fire with the Torah.
2. This reflected the spread of Hasidic Judaism, which from the 1700s had led to the application of Kabbalistic concepts to Jewish daily ritual. Before Hasidism emerged, most East European Jews had followed the generally non-Kabbalistic prayer liturgy inherited from West European Jewry: the Nusach Ashkenaz. The Hasidim, on the other hand, believed that the more Kabbalistically oriented Sephardic prayer liturgy (Nusach Sepharad) was superior, and they changed the prayer liturgy from the Ashkenazic tradition to the Sephardic one. Acceptance or rejection of this change was one of the major differences between the Hasidim and the Mitnagdim.

    HaAri Hakadosh refers to Rabbi Isaac Luria of Safed (1534-72), the scholar of Kabbala whose Sephardic teachings were adopted by Hasidic Judaism in the 1700s.
3. Talmudic literature comprising rabbinical analysis of and commentary on the Mishnah.
4. Proverbs 3:25-26: "Do not fear sudden terror or destruction caused by the wicked, when it comes; for you can rely on G-d; he will keep your foot from being caught in a trap."

[Page 70]

About Chaim Munitz, of Blessed Memory
(Son of Sheitel and Rafael-Yaacov)
By Leyzer Ran

Translated from the Hebrew by Laia Ben-Dov
Footnotes Added / Donated by Jeff Deitch

Chaim Munitz was born in 1911 in Braslav in the Vilna district. After World War I broke out, he moved with his parents to the city of Kerch on the Crimean peninsula. In 1921, his family returned to Minsk in Belorussia. His father managed a *cheder* [Hebrew primary school], and Chaim studied there in the oldest class. In 1922, he returned to Braslav and studied at the Jewish public school.

In 1922 he was accepted into the Vilna Jewish teachers' seminary, and he also attended an art school where he learned cartography and photography inking [touching up]. In 1932, he finished his studies at the teachers' seminary and worked as a teacher in the Jewish school in Braslav. That same year, he took part in an autobiography contest sponsored by YIVO[1] (the Yiddish Scientific Institute), winning second prize.

In 1933 he worked in Vilna (together with a teacher named Biber) on the preparation of a Yiddish geographical atlas of Poland, supporting himself by inking photographic portraits. In 1937 he was accepted into the second graduation class as a research student (aspirant) at YIVO, and in the years 1937-1940 he prepared a research project on the subject "Jewish Attire in Eastern Europe in the First Half of the 19th Century," which included an album of his drawings on the subject. Of this project, only one chapter was published: "Di Vaybershe Koptsirung" ("Women's Head Jewelry"), in the anthology *Dos Tsveyte Yor Aspirantur* (*The Second Year of Research-Students*) (Vilna: YIVO, 1938), pages 81-92.

In 1936, Munitz prepared the tables and illustrated sections of the writings of Mendele Mocher Sforim[2] for the Mendele exhibit at YIVO that year. He prepared for print volume five of *Filologishe*

Shriftn fun YIVO: Yidishe Folklor (*Philological Studies from YIVO: Jewish Folklore*) (Vilna, 1938). He also drew the map of the area from which the folklore was gathered. In addition, he drew the geographic maps of the collected materials for a questionnaire that YIVO distributed on the subject "Min Fun Substantiv" ("Gender of Substantives"). Munitz was also involved in the illustration of Yiddish books. Among others, he drew the frontispiece and illustrated the book by Dr. M[ax]. Weinreich, *Di Geshikhte fun Beyzn Beyz* (*The Story of Big Bad Beyz*) (Warsaw, 1937). He also wrote poetry. His first poem, "Frost," was printed in *Der Vilner Tog* [the newspaper *Vilna Day*] on January 31, 1936.

[Page 71]

In the anthology *In Zich*, No. 19 (New York, 1935), a poem of his was published in the series "Dos Lid fun Khodesh" ("Poem of the Month"). In 1938, Munitz published a translation from Polish of a poem by Antoni Slonimski, "Two Homelands."[3]

Munitz was especially active in the Vilna group of ethical socialists that was called "Fraye Shriftn" ("Free Writings").

When the Nazis conquered Vilna, Munitz returned to Braslav, his birthplace. There he was appointed secretary of the Judenrat [Jewish Council] and kept a diary of events.

He was killed together with his wife and family [his wife Asya and their young son Rafael] in the massacre of the Jews of Braslav in June 1942.[4]

The above was written originally in Yiddish as an article for the *Leksikon fun der Nayer Yidisher Literatur* [*Biographical Dictionary of Modern Yiddish Literature*], published by Der Alveltlekher Yidisher Kultur-Kongres [World Congress for Jewish Culture] (New York, 1963).

Footnotes:

1. Yidisher Visnshaftlekher Institut (Yiddish Scientific Institute), founded in 1925 and based in Vilna before the war, where it preserved, studied and taught the history of European Jews and Yiddish. During World War II the headquarters was moved to New York City, where it continues to operate. It's now known in English as the Institute for Jewish Research.
2. Mendele the Book Peddler, the pen name of Sholem Abramovich (1835-1917), a founder of modern Yiddish and Hebrew literature.
3. Slonimski (1895-1976) was a Polish author of Jewish descent who expressed his love for both Palestine and Poland and was frequently critical of Polish nationalists and Jews alike. His poem was published in 1933.
4. The account by a sister of Chaim Munitz (Chana Lubovitz) appears on pages 217-226 of this memorial book. In addition, Lucy Dawidowicz, the U.S. scholar of modern Jewish history who befriended Chaim Munitz while she was studying in Vilna at YIVO in the 1930s, left a brief description of him in her memoir of Vilna, *From That Place and Time* (1989):

> Chaim Munitz wasn't a historian at all, but an artist. Originally from Braslaw, a small town not far from Vilna, he'd studied at the Yiddish Teachers' Seminary and for a while at an art school. He was tiny --- about my height, thin to the point of emaciation, with a beautifully expressive face, dark eyes, and a rich head of dark wavy hair off his high forehead. He was a person of fine sensibility and was known to write poetry. He lived at the edge of penury. Sometimes he had work drawing maps or retouching and at the YIVO he did whatever artwork or design was wanted. His Aspirantur project, in the field of social history, suited his visual and graphic talents. He was preparing a lexicon of Jewish clothing in the first half of the nineteenth century.
>
> In February 1939, at twenty-eight, Munitz decided to get married. The *aspirantn* [research students] were invited to the wedding. We were his family. His mother was dead, and his father, seriously ill in Braslaw, was being cared for there by Munitz's only sister [sic; Chaim had several sisters, but Dawidowicz knew only one of them]. The bride, a seamstress, was as small, thin, and dark as he, and just as poor. She had only her parents, who lived in an old-age home, which was where the wedding ceremony, canopy and all, was held. (p. 95)

[Page 72]

Masha Maron
Daughter of Brayna-Malka and Chaim [Maron]

Mendel Maron
Son of Sofia and Chaim-Aizik

Translated from the Hebrew by Laia Ben-Dov
Footnotes Added / Donated by Jeff Deitch

In June 1981, survivors of the ghettos and extermination camps met in Israel. In this month, on the 17th of Sivan [June 19], our memorial day, a ceremony was held in Holon Cemetery to unveil a monument to the memory of more than 4,500 Jews of Braslav [Braslaw] and the surrounding area, who were cruelly annihilated by the Germans and their collaborators.

Under the monument an urn was buried, containing a container of earth taken from the graves of the martyrs and smuggled from Russia to Israel by an immigrant from Braslav --- Shlomo Reichel.

The chairman of the U.S. association of the Jews of Braslav and the surrounding region, Mendel Maron, came to the meeting and ceremony with his wife, Masha. We took advantage of their presence here and wrote down a small part of their description of what happened to them during the years of the German occupation.

Mendel speaks: The war broke out [in 1941]. The speech of Soviet Foreign Minister [Vyacheslav] Molotov on the radio shocked everyone. What now? . . . What should we do? . . . Russian officers swore that their army was unconquerable and would repel the attackers within a few days, but the situation was otherwise; the German army advanced without meeting any real opposition. Already on the fourth day of the war, we saw Russian army units retreating eastward and then Communist Party members, Soviet clerks and police began to leave Braslav in disorder. We watched them with worry and fear about our own fate. We knew of the cruel, degrading attitude of the Nazis toward the Jews of Germany and the areas they occupied. Part of the Jewish population, mainly some of the young people, decided to leave the town and flee into the depths of Russia. The fortunate ones, who owned horses, hitched them to their wagons and set out. Some people managed to leave on the train before it stopped running. A few took advantage of the transportation afforded by the withdrawing Russian army, but the majority went on foot.

My family had an additional concern: Two months before the war broke out, my older brother Hirshke had been drafted, along with many other Jews of Braslav. They were busy building an airport next to the town of Skidel near the German border.[1] None of them had returned, and we had no information or news. Though our parents decided to remain, I harnessed our horse, we loaded

[Page 73]

the wagon with a few clothes and some food, and left Braslav: I, my little brother Mulka [Shmuel] and my brother Hirshke's wife Batia and their little daughter [Sara].

The roads were full of people, with everyone rushing eastward. We wanted to cross the old (pre-1939) border between Disna [Dzisna] and Polotsk as soon as possible.[2] We thought that at the Dvina River maybe the Russians would succeed in halting the invaders and we'd quickly return home. When we approached Miory, 40 kilometers [east] from Braslav, our horse grew tired and we were forced to stop and rest. In Miory we heard that the bridge over the Dvina had been destroyed by German bombing and their army was already there. Having no choice, we returned home, and there . . . were the Germans.

Masha speaks: We didn't know much about the Germans and their behavior toward the Jews. Geographically we were far from them, and we'd only read in the newspapers about their treatment of Jews; we didn't always believe what was written. We'd begun to hear of fearful events when the Germans occupied most of Poland [in September 1939]. Fortunately, the Russians also occupied parts of Poland where most of the population was Belorussian or Ukrainian --- and so we were saved from the clutches of the Nazis [until June 1941]. Then, everything changed. The Germans invaded Russia and advanced quickly. Many Jews fled eastward.

In our house, we were seven children. I was the oldest girl. My mother suggested that she stay to watch over the house and our possessions, while father would travel with the children (with the hope that it wouldn't be for long). But in the end, we all remained at home.

A few days after the Germans entered Braslav, a young German soldier visited our house. He boasted that no army in the world could conquer the German army. Their goal was to take

Russia, and after that, England. Nor would America withstand their army's pressure. They wished to bring a new order to the world, in which the Germans would rule. He thought the fate of the Jews was sealed: "They'll be slaves." On his visit, he brought us some bread and fish. Apparently the silver hair of my mother and my sister Sonia's blond hair misled him and he took us for Gentiles, but when he saw me and my black hair, he realized his mistake. I ran out of the house immediately, and he didn't visit us again.

The first to enter the town were patrols on motorcycles. After them came battle units. One unit remained in Braslav and took over the government. Many of the local Gentiles volunteered to help the Germans; some of them even put on police uniforms.[3] The first order was that the Jews must mark their houses with the word "*Jude*" (I think the German soldier visited us because we hadn't yet written this "special name" on the wall of the house). The next order was that every Jew had to wear yellow patches on his chest and back. Once, when I went to work, the policeman [Stefan] Zhuk caught me. I was terrified of him. With his bayonet he moved aside my hair, which covered my back, to make sure I was indeed wearing a yellow patch.

Mendel: The decrees followed one after another. One Friday, about two weeks after the Germans entered Braslav, they ordered the Jews to gather in the square of the Pravoslavic [Eastern Orthodox] Church.[4] They separated the men from the women and children, and arranged all of them in rows of five. The line was so long that it reached the Skuriat windmill at the edge of town. For their amusement, the Germans pulled from the line the elderly *shochet* [ritual slaughterer] Reb[5]

[Page 74]

Aharon-Zelig Singalovski, cut off his beard, sat him on a motorcycle and drove him at dizzying speed the length of the line and the streets, back and forth a number of times. The next day, the man had a heart attack and died.

[That day] they took all of us to a deep swamp in the Dubki [Dubkes] forest [just outside the town]. On the way, despite the prohibition against talking, we told each other we were about to be killed. We were surrounded by SS men and policemen armed with rifles and machine guns. Two men among us tried to escape, my friend Chaim Milutin and Reb Shlomo [Zilber] the *shochet*. Both were caught and killed before our eyes.

Masha: Within the line of women, a German policeman saw a beautiful, blond girl [Masha's sister Sonia]. He was convinced she was Aryan. "*Was machst hier?*" ("What are you doing here?") he shouted at her. "*Gehen schnell heraus!*" ("Get out of here quick!"), "*Gehen zurück*" ("Go back"), he ordered her. He ordered the other patrols to help her leave the place. My aunt Chana, who was watching what was happening and didn't understand, grew frightened and shouted to her, "Sonialeh! Where are they taking you?" Sonia explained to the German that the woman was a little "crazy." Sonia was my younger sister. The patrol accompanied her to the pharmacy [in the town center] and then returned to work. Sonia ran home, frightened by the events; the street was empty of people, and no one was in the house. Our house stood near Lake Noviata [Nowiata], and on the shore was a boat that had been turned over. Sonia's first thought was to sail to the other side of the lake, and from there to continue on foot to the village of Dubina [Dubene a.k.a. Dubinovo, 16 kilometers northwest of Braslav], to our grandfather and grandmother, but she changed her mind lest the enemy suspect she was fleeing from the Aktions and shoot her. She spent the rest of the day and that night under the overturned boat. We found her the next day, when they freed us from the swamp and we returned home. This time, the matter ended merely with threats and intimidation. Those who knew how the Germans operated said that we'd been saved from certain death.

That black Friday became a holiday for the Gentiles. While we were away, they treated our houses like they were their own. They stole everything they could, and what was impossible to take away they broke. We found our houses empty of possessions and were left without resources. We had to set things up anew, get a bit of food and clothing, something for the bedrooms and something for the kitchen and the house.

Anything was permitted when it came to oppressing the Jews. In the evenings, we shut ourselves up in our houses, afraid to go outside. Children didn't study. The stores had been closed. Occasionally people were grabbed and put to work at various kinds of labor. The Germans and their collaborators abused us at every turn, as they liked. It's true that among them were also men who were "human"; I knew one German like this. He was a veterinarian by profession and responsible for the horses. In the winter, out of concern for the horses, he'd "merely" take coats off of the Jews and put the coats over the horses. Later in the war, at a suitable opportunity, a girl from the partisans killed him.

Mendel: They ordered us to organize a Judenrat [Jewish Council]. Through the Judenrat, the [German] authorities channeled all their decrees, claims and demands regarding the Jewish population. At the head of the Judenrat stood Yitzchak Mindel, and with him other men who were known to the Jewish community: the teacher [Eliezer] Mazeh, Sasha Tempelman, the translator Ribash, Leib Valin, Yaacov Feldman and others. A few of them served as policemen and helped the Judenrat to carry out the orders of the Germans.

Masha: But all of them were good people.

[Page 75]
Every day or two, a "list of requests" was presented to the Judenrat indicating how many Jews to send to assorted jobs: to clear the snow or load wood on the train cars, send girls to clean the Germans' quarters; women to knit hats and gloves for the army, and so on. Each request was accompanied by threats that if the matter wasn't carried out at the specified time and speed, a certain number of Jews would be killed. Once they really did murder 13 or 18 Jews [at the train station], who they said were careless at work. By the same method, they also squeezed out bribes in the form of money, gold and other valuables as well as clothing. In situations like these, no one envied the members of the committee [the Judenrat], who did everything they could to meet the requests so as not to give the Germans a reason to carry out their threats.

Mendel and Masha: The worst thing for the general community was the [formation of the] ghetto. On Passover Eve 1942 [April 1, 1942], we were commanded to leave our homes [outside it]. We went out to find a corner in one of the crowded houses on Pilsudski Street; this was the area appropriated to become the ghetto, and all the Jews of Braslav were concentrated in it. Our houses and property [outside the ghetto] were confiscated by the authorities.

Masha: During our last two years in Braslav, we were fated to move three times. All the years up to then [1942], my family had lived in our own private house on the lake shore. In the yard was another building --- a bakery, the source of our livelihood. There our family grew over the years: seven children and the parents. When the place had become too small to contain everyone, my father built a new house, large and spacious. How happy we were in this new place. But we lived there less than two years. Our last dwelling place was the house of Chaim-Aizik and Sofia [Maron] in the ghetto; in other words, the house of my husband Mendel's parents.

Mendel: The real troubles began in the ghetto. The crowding was terrible; two or three families to an apartment. It was forbidden for farmers to trade with the Jews or sell us food. Only those who were sent to work outside the ghetto succeeded sometimes in exchanging valuables and clothing with the farmers for a bit of food. The locals excelled at oppressing us. Yesterday they'd been our neighbors, but now they took a major part in eliminating Jews from the neighboring villages.

We weren't so naive as to believe they wouldn't murder us. Our concentration in the ghetto was the first step toward physical annihilation. It was only a matter of time and the proper order to carry it out. The Jews in the ghetto began to prepare. In every possible place --- under the houses, in chicken coops, cowsheds, stables, under garbage dumps and toilets --- they dug pits, camouflaged cellars, built hiding places. Many people did this, and everyone took care that others didn't see their preparation. Under our house was a cellar, and we began to convert it into a hiding place. During the days of destruction to come, three families would find shelter in this cellar: my family, Masha's family, and Tuvia Vishkin's family. The days of the ghetto were numbered, a total of three months.

On Wednesday, the 18th of Sivan 1942 [Wednesday, June 3], toward morning, [German] gendarmes and [local] policemen surrounded the ghetto. With them were Lithuanians, Latvians and local residents. With threats and bestial shouts, curses and other degrading words, beatings with rods and shooting, they drove the Jews from their houses. Everyone ran about in fear: men and women, the elderly, children, youths, women with babes in their arms. All were made to run toward the train station, into a small wood [north of the town]. There, giant pits had been prepared for destruction. [In this commotion] our three families rushed into the cellar. We covered the entrance with a wooden panel and put a chair on top of it,

[Page 76]

to hide it. The killing of the ghetto's Jews continued for three days, and after that came the hunt for solitary Jews who'd succeeded in escaping.

A street in the Braslav Ghetto: The building on the right is the police station.

Masha: Two days before the massacre, the Judenrat had received an order to send 100 young girls out to work. On the third day [the day of the massacre], in the morning, the girls were taken to Slobodka (10 kilometers from Braslav).[6] There they cleaned, washed and polished the army barracks. Among these girls was my sister Sonia. My little brother Lusik, one of the twins in our family, volunteered to accompany his sister. On the fourth day [the second day of the massacre] they were returned to Braslav and taken straight to the pits. They took their last journey by way of the outskirts of the town, outside the ghetto, an area where only a day earlier it had been forbidden for Jews to go.

On our third day in the hiding place, we heard someone enter the house. There was talking in German, while they searched and turned over everything. In a corner stood a sack of potatoes, which they tumbled to the floor. A few of the potatoes rolled away and touched the board covering the entrance to our cellar, and they noticed the board was wobbling. They approached and lifted the board, and shouted that we had to come out immediately or they'd throw a hand grenade inside. We trembled in fear. The parents began to say their goodbyes to us and to each other. Someone quickly pulled out the pipe for ventilation, and a few stones in the wall came with it.

We burst outside through the opening and ran in every direction. They surrounded us. Father ran in the direction of the lake, maybe he decided it was better

[Page 77]

to drown than to fall into the hands of the murderers. But there wasn't time, a bullet caught him before he reached the lake. My brother Mosheleh ran far; they caught him next to the bathhouse and killed him. He was only seven years old. My sister Etzinka, who was eight years old, managed to run to the Milutins' house, and there she fell from a murderer's bullet. Mendel's mother [Sofia] was murdered when she came out of the hiding place. I managed to hide in a nearby storage shed without them seeing me. In the cellar remained my grandmother, my mother [Brayna-Malka] and my brother, the second twin, Abrashka [Avraham, the twin of Lusik]. This was the year of their bar mitzvah. Also there were Mendel's father [Chaim-Aizik], my sister Rachla, who was 12, and Moshe Vishkin's mother [Sara-Leah]. Meanwhile, they found me and a policeman shot at me. His bullet hit a tree, and a splinter from it must have hit my ear. I fainted from the strength of the blow. Thinking I was dead, the policeman rushed off. When I awoke later, it was quiet. I went outside. What I saw is indescribable. Before me was a field of destruction. The first one I found was my father; his head had been smashed by bullets. A little further on lay my sister Etzinka, like an animal. A bullet had penetrated her skull. I took her in my arms, but then I saw a policeman approaching. I laid her down and fled.

On the third day after the start of the massacre, the murderers had announced that they wouldn't kill any more and whoever remained alive should come forward to register with the police. Later I learned that my mother [Brayna-Malka] and grandmother, my sister Rachla, my brother Abrashke and Mendel's father [Chaim-Aizik] had been arrested by the police. I ran to see them. Mother didn't yet know that father and four of her children [Sonia, Lusik, Etzinka, Mosheleh] were no longer alive. She was angry that I'd come to see the family [at the police station] and told me to get away from there. To the police [station], she said, there was only an entrance, not an exit. [At the police station, after seeing my mother] I asked for permission to go to the washroom. An unarmed policeman accompanied me, but it was dark outside, so I was able to flee. In the streets outside, I saw the bodies of people who'd been murdered. I succeeded in reaching the Milutins' house. I went up into the attic, and from there they took me to a hiding place. Mendel was there too. The hiding place was big and wide, and many people were hiding there, children also.

The people who the police had gathered from their hiding places, and others who'd believed the Germans and come out (after the Germans said they wouldn't kill any more), were all concentrated in the Folkshul. On Monday morning [June 8], the fifth day since the beginning of the massacre, we heard policemen searching the house. All of us remained in our hiding places, not moving. The children did the same. The police turned the house upside down, searching for a hidden entrance to a bunker. But without intending to, they managed to hide the entrance even better, by moving a truck seat that was in the house to the area in front of our hiding place. Finding nothing, they left the house. We were very lucky; we were several dozen people. That day, we were saved from certain death.

Toward evening, I got a strong feeling that my mother was near our hiding place. To this day, I'm convinced that it was my mother and she was looking for me, having risked her life by escaping from the Folkshul. I whispered to the others, "My mother's here," but they didn't let me communicate with her. I'm convinced that I heard her footsteps, though the others thought it was the police. We lay as quiet as the dead, and my mother went away like [I felt] she'd come. I never saw her. The next day, Tuesday [June 9], they took all the people who'd been in the Folkshul to the pits and shot them. And so, of all my large family, only I was left. Until my last day I'll remember the words of my mother, who'd said --- two days before the Germans entered the town --- "I'll stay to watch over the house and the farm; you, father, take the children and flee . . ." [Neither of the other siblings of Masha (Abrasha and Rachla) survived the war.]

. . . After the war, when I returned to Braslav, a Christian neighbor told me this: They took the Jews from the Folkshul down the street where our house stood, on the way to the pits. Suddenly, my mother broke from the line and ran toward the house. The oppressors grabbed her and put her back in the line that was being led to slaughter. I don't

[Page 78]

know what she was thinking when she ran toward the house. Did she want to flee? To be saved? Or did she just want to enter the house and tell the walls that Chaim Maron, the 17-year-old blond beauty Sonialeh, the twins Lusik and Abrasha, Rachla, who'd reached the age of *mitzvot* [age 13], 8-year-old Etzinka, and Mosheleh, the smallest at 7 years old, were no more and she was on her way to them?

Mendel: The massacre lasted a week. Only a few dozens were saved, the living witnesses to the destroyed Jews of Braslav. Masha is the only one left of her family. Of our family, I and my brother Mulka remained. Somewhere, in a hiding place, in the attic or in a pit under the house, others were hiding. Now we had to flee. We made plans. A few had a Gentile acquaintance in one of the villages who agreed to help. The others, who lacked an address [to flee to], escaped somehow, fleeing at night on back roads without knowing where they were going. The main thing was to avoid getting caught by the haters of Israel. If you fell into the hands of one of those --- you were lost. For each Jew he'd receive a reward --- a sack of salt (16 kilograms).

I, my brother Shmuel [Mulka] and Moshe Milutin resolved to stay together. We also persuaded Masha to come with us. Not far from the town hospital was a garage belonging to the gendarmes. The one responsible for it was a Pole, a very honest Gentile. Moshe Milutin, a blacksmith by profession, had sometimes been sent by the Judenrat to work at this garage. Above it was an attic, and this was our destination. The danger was great. Moshe and I went first; at night, through the alleys. The next day, the same way, Masha and my brother Mulka came to us. It didn't occur to the gendarmes that Jewish survivors were hiding in their attic. The next day, when the Polish manager came to work, we spoke with him and promised him that within a certain number of days we'd leave. He agreed and even brought us some bread and water. Five days passed; we had to go. In our hands was an address in the village of Krasnosletzi [Krasnosielce, four kilometers west of Braslav]. This time, I and Masha went first. At night we sneaked through the quarter where the Polish clerks had lived. It was a beautiful area: solitary houses, with red tile roofs, in a sea of flowers. We passed through the Karpovitz [Karpowicz] forest and arrived at Krasnosletzi, to the farmer to whom Moshe Milutin's father sent us before we left the small dam. But this time we failed; the farmer wouldn't receive us and drove us away with curses and mockery. Disappointed and depressed, we left not knowing where to go. Moshe and Mulka received a similar welcome and went off in another direction. Our paths separated. Later, I found out that my brother Mulka had been murdered in Ponar.[7]

We crossed a forest and entered a village. We spent the day in the small village bathhouse, continuing on at night. Toward morning, we approached another village. When the sun came up, we found a pit in a field and climbed down into it. In the afternoon hours children played outside, and one of them jumped into our pit and grew very frightened [on seeing us]. We begged him not to reveal our presence to anyone. At night we again continued onward. We approached a house at the edge of the village, and Masha knocked on the door: "We're hungry," we said. The man took us inside, gave us some food and agreed that we could sleep in his house. We were impressed by his decency and asked him to hide us. He didn't reply, but neither did he send us away; he went out by himself. Later we learned his name --- Ignacy Matul --- and we found out that he was hiding a few Jews from Dvinsk [in Latvia, 42 kilometers northwest of Braslav]. Toward evening he returned, accompanied by his nephew, who took us to his house. Our path that night was through the swamps. Before we left Matul's house, he calmed us by saying that everything was arranged and we were going to a safe place.

[Page 79]

Masha: We arrived at the village of Kochanishek [Kochaniszki, about eight kilometers northwest of Braslav] and the Chesnoviski [Czesnowicki] family. A young lad took us into a small house with one room and a stable. There were three people in the house: two sisters, Emilia and Jadzia [Jadwiga], and the young lad, whose name was Alfons. They weren't married, they were religious and orphans. They received us nicely. A heavy stone was lifted from our hearts. It's hard to comprehend that during those days there were people who put their own lives at risk to rescue Jews. For 22 months, they hid us in their attic and shared their scanty food with us, without payment. Occasionally they'd host me in the house, on the stove.[8] The only thing that

I gave them was a watch I'd received from my grandmother. To this day, I don't know how to explain why they did all this for us. Maybe they wished to convert us to Christianity? Maybe they acted in good faith? One thing I know: The two sisters and their brother saved our lives.

Mendel: They didn't save only us. When they began to destroy the second ghetto in Braslav,[9] Chana and Tuvia Fisher, Baruch's Motka [Motka the son of Baruch Fisher] and Zalman-Yankel's Motka [Motka the son of Zalman-Yankel Fisher] succeeded somehow in fleeing from it. The Chesnoviski family wanted with all their hearts to help the escapees, but their house was small and it was dangerous to take all of them. But the Chesnoviskis didn't send away escapees from death. These friends of the Jews suggested that we build a hiding place under the cowshed. We dug a pit, camouflaged it well and there we hid, six souls, until the liberation.

Conclusion

Mendel: Spring 1944; the Soviet army was advancing. The Germans were withdrawing and destroying everything in their path. In July, Braslav was liberated. Fierce battles took place; villages went up in flames. A stray bullet hit the straw roof of the Chesnoviski family, setting the house on fire. But we'd gone through too much to be burned alive now or suffocated by smoke. We burst outside and, crawling through fields of grain, moved toward the lake we saw in the distance. Next to a cemetery, we met a Russian soldier who told us that Braslav had just been liberated.

We knew the way home. After hours of walking, after three years of hardship, we arrived back in Braslav. It was a strange feeling, to see Braslav with no Jews. Each step was soaked in the blood of our dear ones. From the other side of Lake Noviata, the Germans were continuing to rain fire on the town. We had to leave again temporarily for the forest and live with the partisans. After the Germans were driven out of the area for good, we returned.

Masha: We knew we couldn't remain in Braslav. It was impossible to build a life in a cemetery, when memories tormented you day and night, when every step you took was on earth soaked in blood. With tears and thankful gratitude, we parted from our saviors, Jadzia, Emilia and Alfons. Before we left Braslav, I gave them my parents' house as a gift. To this day, we write to each other and we provide them with as much material help as we can.

In 1973, I went to Vilna [about 165 kilometers southwest of Braslav] and Braslav. My purpose was to visit the graves of our dear ones and meet with our saviors. I left Braslav with a small bag of earth that I took with me from the graves of the martyrs. May their memory be blessed!

Footnotes:

1. Skidel (Skidziel), then in Poland, was about 310 kilometers southwest of Braslav.
2. This refers to the pre-1939 border between Belorussia and Poland, which lay to the east of Braslav. Disna was about 72 kilometers east of Braslav, and Polotsk was about 35 kilometers southeast of Disna.
3. According to the *Encyclopedia of Camps and Ghettos, 1933-1945*, Volume II-B (2012), on June 30, 1941 the German commandant in Braslav began recruiting a local police unit from among local ruffians sympathetic to the Germans. Stanislaw Jasinski, a Pole, was the commander. Other policemen included Kriwko, Stefan Zhuk, Malinowski, Masara, Czeslaw Kolkowski, Zarniewicz, and Stanislaw Nowicki. A man named Sucharewicz was described as one of the most brutal participants.

    In autumn 1941 responsibility for the local police was transferred from the Germany army to the German Gendarmerie, after a civil administration had been established. Among the men based at the Gendarmerie outpost in Braslav were Johannes Czapp, Willy Dittmann, Otto Haymann, Paul Kontny, Leo Leidenroth, Ludwig Müller, Ernst Schreiber and Waldemar Schultz.
4. Other survivors recall this event as happening on June 27 (Saturday), the day after the Germans arrived in Braslav.
5. Reb is an honorific term, something like an exalted "Mr."
6. Slobodka was about 11 kilometers northeast of Braslav.
7. Ponar (Ponary in Polish, Paneriai in Lithuanian), located outside Vilna in Lithuania, was the major execution site in the Vilna region during World War II and the largest execution site in Lithuania. Between July 1941 and August 1944 an estimated 50,000-70,000 Jews, 2,000-20,000 ethnic Poles and 5,000-8,000 Soviet prisoners were killed there.

8. In Russia, Belorussia and the Ukraine, ovens were traditionally made of brick masonry that retained heat for long periods of time, and their outer surface was safe to touch. In winter, people would sleep on top of the oven to keep warm.
9. After the first Braslav Ghetto was liquidated on June 3-5, 1942, the Germans repopulated it in August or early September 1942 by bringing in some 50 Jews from Opsa, many of them craftsmen. Because these people were from Opsa, this second Braslav Ghetto was also called the "Opsa" Ghetto. It would be liquidated by the Germans on March 19, 1943.

[Page 80]

Chaim Band
Son of Chaya-Chana and Avraham-Leib

Translated from the Hebrew by Laia Ben-Dov
(Yiddish Translated by Aaron Krishtalka)
Footnotes Added / Donated by Jeff Deitch

My childhood and the years of my youth passed without any problems. My life, like the lives of many children and of my town and its young people, was full of hope for the future until . . . until the fateful days that turned my world and the world of many, many others into disappointment and isolation, suffering and torture.

September 17, 1939: In the morning, it was announced on the radio that the Red Army had crossed the Polish border. The purpose --- to free the western provinces of Belorussia and Ukraine from Polish rule and join them to the Soviet Union. During the day, squadrons of Polish border-guard soldiers passed through the town going west, accompanied by the police and high-level Polish officials. Our town was left without a government.

In the evening we learned that in the neighboring village, Zbornie-Gomnie [Zaborne-Gumna, three kilometers southeast of Braslav], farmers of the place were gathering in the house of the fisherman Semyon Voyevoda, to attack the Jews of Braslav [Braslaw] and steal their possessions. Many Jews armed themselves with iron rods and other improvised weapons, and went to the edge of town to protect it and keep the hoodlums from putting their plans into effect. We gathered next to the old windmill. Someone, I think it was Shmuel Biliak, brought with him an old rifle from World War I, in which there was just one bullet. Due to carelessness, the bullet was fired. We remained on guard until morning and waited for the rioters, but they didn't come. The next day, we learned that they'd heard the shot and this was what had deterred them.

September 18, 1939: We were still without a government. The Poles had fled, and the Russians had yet to arrive.

The men of the fire department took it upon themselves to keep order in the town. Most of them were Jews. The outstanding ones among them were Beinish Milutin, Uriel Karasin, Zusman Lubovitz, Yerachmiel Milutin and Liber Chepelevitz. A few of them traveled to the Polish army camp in Ritzki-Bor, five kilometers from town, found rifles and ammunition, and brought them to Braslav for protection. Jewish youths organized themselves into groups and went out to guard the approaches to the town.

Wednesday was the market day, to which the Gentiles of the surrounding area would come. The provisional leaders of the town decided to cancel the market day out of concern that there would be riots, and ordered the guards of the approaches to the town to notify

[Page 81]

the Gentiles that market day was canceled. The entry from the direction of Belmont [about seven kilometers southeast of Braslav] was guarded by a group that included Shmuel Lubovitz, Yitzchak Tos, Yitzchak Ulman, Chaim Lif, and the one responsible for them was Chalvina [or Chlavna] Tzinman. At dawn, the Gentiles began to arrive. A few listened to the explanation and then returned the way they'd come. But there also were those who refused to listen, arguing, cursing and uttering disgraceful, anti-Semitic slogans. When the atmosphere heated up and people were about to come to blows, Chalvina Tzinman ordered the guards to fire into the air. When they saw that the matter was serious, the Gentiles returned on foot to their villages. Somebody decided, rightly, to destroy the stock of vodka in the storerooms and shops [in Braslav]. This task was carried out by the fire department. I remember Liber Chepelevitz, sword in hand, driving away the rabble. Crates of bottles of vodka and wine were taken out, broken, and their contents were poured onto the road. Several drunkards laid themselves on the ground and licked up the liquid together with the mud.

On September 19, a Red Army unit appeared in Braslav. Opposite our house was Aharon Zeif's fabric store. The owner of the store brought rolls of red fabric outside, tore them into ribbons and distributed them with cheer for every necessity.

Already on the first day of their arrival, the Soviets began to manage information and organize political propaganda. In the streets and markets, films were shown every evening, and political agents explained their content. After some time, we began to notice the absence of many essential products. The stores emptied out.

Then, after a relative calm that continued for nearly two years, once again we faced a storm of fateful events. On the morning of Sunday, June 22, 1941, we learned that the Nazis had invaded and a war between Germany and the Soviet Union had begun. Toward evening, there was a public gathering on the shore of Lake Driviata [Drywiaty], opposite the Jewish cemetery. The speakers, the heads of the Communist Party in the town, promised solemnly that the Nazi enemy would be conquered and we could sleep in peace without fear.

June 23, 1941: Soviet tanks and trucks passed through the town, going west. The announcer Levitan[1] admitted that there'd been heavy fighting and large losses. But in the evening, artillery and tanks begin to flow in the opposite direction, from west to east. Men of the NKVD,[2] armed and drunk, circulated in the town and calmed the residents.

June 24, 1941: Trucks loaded with the household goods and families of Soviet officers left the town and withdrew to the east.

All of us were tense and frightened.

June 25, 1941: The government representatives who remained in town no longer hid the seriousness of the situation. They were burning documents.

At noon, men of the NKVD came to the fire department garage where I worked, ordered us to take the equipment out of the only truck we had, and confiscated the truck. Several hours later we saw it leave town, loaded with household goods and the families of Soviet officers.

In the town: fear. Nobody knew what to do, and there was no one to consult. Several friends --- the brothers Moshe and Yisrael Bogomolski and I --- decided to leave. Each of us went to his home to say goodbye. I found all the members of my family --- my father, mother, sister Chiena [or Chiuna] and brothers Shachna and Yehoshua --- loading household goods onto a wagon and planning to go to a nearby village (where we had a farm) until the troubles passed.

[Page 82]

My father argued that he'd known the Germans during World War I, and it was impossible for such a cultured nation to commit the atrocities that people were attributing to them. My sister Chiena wanted to come with me, but I was sure I'd be drafted immediately into the [Red] army and this would leave her on her own. She was only 17 years old.

And so, they all remained. Only I parted from them and left. As I said, the decision to leave Braslav was made by the three of us: I and the two Bogomolski brothers. My father opposed my leaving, arguing that there was no need to flee, but in the Bogomolski family it was completely different. Their father pleaded with them to go. He believed everything that was said of the Nazis, but he also believed that in the end the Russians would win and we'd return. He encouraged us. His words stayed with us continually and gave us strength and hope.

On the night of June 25-26, the three of us left and headed toward the town of Disna (many people headed for Druya, but they returned).[3] On the way, we caught up with Peretz Levin, Batia Deitch (Arklis), Liuba Maler with her toddler son Reuven, and Galia Kanfer, Shmuel Lubovitz, Ziska Shmushkovitz and others.

After walking for two hours, Peretz Levin remembered that a stamp from the office where he worked as an accountant remained in his pocket. He headed back to Braslav to return the stamp to his supervisors.

During the first few kilometers, we encountered signs of "sympathy" from the village populations. My father had many acquaintances among villagers in the area, mainly near the village of Ikazna [Ikazn, about 14 kilometers east of Braslav]. I knocked on a few doors and asked them to drive the women and their little children, who'd grown tired, a few kilometers in exchange for payment, but not one of the villagers agreed. And so we continued to walk. From the direction of the Dvina River [a.k.a. the Daugava River, to the east and north], we heard the echoes of shelling and we hurried to cross to the eastern side of the river, which was the old [pre-1939] border of Poland-Russia. We were sure that on the old border the Red Army would stop the Nazi invaders and after that we'd be able to return home. We wanted to reach the town of Polotsk [115 kilometers east of Braslav]. In Disna we met Esther Munitz who, to her misfortune, forgot her identification card and returned to Braslav.

We continued to advance. We passed Polotsk, Vitebsk [some 200 kilometers east of Braslav], Smolensk and Tambov until, after a long journey, we reached Uzbekistan [some 2,500 kilometers southeast of Braslav]. There we were visited by hunger and illness, torture and hard labor. In April 1944 I was drafted into the army, and I was at the front until May 1945. I learned of the liberation of Braslav from the Nazis on the day of liberation, July 9, 1944. I wrote home immediately, despite lacking a specific address. Weeks later I received a postcard, soaked in tears, from my sister Chiena.

When I was a soldier, around Baranovich [Baranowicze, 300 kilometers south of Braslav], one night I received 10 days of leave and traveled to Braslav. This was in mid-August 1944. In Braslav I found my sister and some families who'd been saved. It's difficult to describe the destruction. During the few days I stayed in the town, I heard from my sister about the atrocities that had befallen them. I'll try to describe briefly what I remember from the events of those terrible days:

That night [in June 1941] after I parted from my family and left the town with my friends, the family packed a few movables on a harnessed wagon and traveled to our farm in the village of Dubki [perhaps Dabki, about 4.5 kilometers southeast of Braslav]. After the Germans entered, my family returned to Braslav.

My parents continued to take care of the farm, but the Germans confiscated the crops. At that time, the first

[Page 83]

martyrs fell: Shlomo Zilber, the *shochet* [ritual slaughterer], and the young man Chaim Milutin [on June 27, 1941, when the Jews of Braslav were taken to a swamp outside Braslav but released the next day]. Later, 13 Jews were murdered at the train station. Among them was a relative of my family, Yitzchak Blacher. Before the destruction of the first ghetto [on June 3-5, 1942], a group of youths was taken to the town of Slobodka [about 11 kilometers northeast of Braslav] to work as cleaners. All of them were murdered.

I heard the story about the blacksmith Nachman-Chaim Gurevitz, who was *"ein nützlicher Jude"* (a useful Jew[4]) --- and who continued to work in his smithy. Once he shoed the horse of a German officer. After the work was finished, the German said he wanted to pay for the work. He took out his pistol and killed the blacksmith.

In the village of Dubki, two families of farmers lived --- Labuti was their name. The family of Yisrael Zeif hid at Nikolai Labuti's house. Nikolai's neighbor, Michael Labuti, saw them and notified the police, who grabbed them and murdered them. The denouncer Michael was later tried and imprisoned by the Soviets. This was told to me by Nikolai's son --- Bronislav.

Before the ghetto was destroyed, when rumors were spreading about the destruction to come, the head of the [Braslav] Judenrat [Jewish Council], Yitzchak Mindel, asked a German officer who was friendly with him if the rumors were true. When the officer acknowledged that they were, Mindel asked the officer to kill him and his family in his house. The "merciful" officer fulfilled the request, shooting the entire family the day before the destruction of the ghetto.

In the Yavneh school there was a teacher of Hebrew, Eliezer Mazeh. He too was a member of the Judenrat. When he learned of the ghetto's approaching destruction, he managed to warn many, who concealed themselves in their hiding places. That night, he was in my parents' house. They [the Germans] grabbed him, and in the yard of the Gmina [district administration] they split his head with an axe.

On the day of the Aktions [June 3-5, 1942], when they took everyone out to be killed, Anton Burak, a Gentile resident of Braslav, came to the house of Shimon Per, drove his wife Fridel outside, grabbed their young son by the leg and split his head open on a tree.

After the Aktions, which continued for a few days, that same Anton Burak, who'd grown up among the Jews and spoke Yiddish, went around between the houses and called, *"Yidn, geyt aroys, mer harget men nisht"* ("Jews, come out, they aren't killing any more"). Some people believed this lie, came out of their hiding places and immediately were murdered.

In one of the hiding places was the elderly rabbi of Braslav, Rabbi Abba Zahorie. When the Germans led them all to slaughter, he recited the prayer "Out of the depths I have called you, O G-d" [Psalm 130:1]. He left his hiding place, joined them all --- and was murdered.

After my parents had been warned by Eliezer Mazeh, all of them --- my father, Avraham-Leib; my mother, Chaya; my sister Chiena; and my two brothers, Shachna and Yehoshua --- managed to hide and after that to leave the town and hide themselves. I don't know the circumstances, but after some time they were scattered.

My father hid in the villages until the second ghetto was established (the "Opsa" Ghetto).[5] He returned to the ghetto and passed away two days before the general destruction [liquidation of the second ghetto on March 19, 1943]. He was buried next to the Bogomolski family's house (their house was inside the area of the "Opsa" Ghetto). In August 1944, I found in that place four graves of Jews whose fate had led them to die in that house.

My mother hid somewhere in a village, together with Shachna and Yehoshua, until March 1943. When her feet froze, Shachna and Yehoshua took her on a sled to the town [Braslav]. On the way to the ghetto they [the Germans] grabbed her and killed her in the Karpovitz forest [Karpowicz forest, near the western entrance to Braslav]. I never found her grave, but I did find signs of graves in the forest, pieces of clothing

[Page 84]
and shoes.

My brothers Shachna and Yehoshua succeeded in leaving the town after the Aktions and wandered around the villages. I learned that in the summer of 1943 they entered the house of a farmer, Parmon was his name, near Ikazna in the village of Druvnishki [probably Dyrwaniszki, about two kilometers northwest of Ikazna]. He gave them a loaf of bread. That same night they also visited Samyonov Agai's house in the village of Ikazanskiya Chutra, and from there they went to the village of Kashinza-Polia [perhaps Ksiezopol, about 2.5 kilometers northwest of Ikazna, on the road between Ikazna and Slobodka] and hid in a shed. The people of the village

noticed them, notified the *starosta* [village elder], whose name was Katzinovski, and he ---
together with his brothers and a few others --- grabbed them, tied their hands with barbed wire,
put them in a wagon and traveled toward Slobodka [about 11 kilometers northeast of Braslav] to
hand them over to the police. (There they'd get a reward for grabbing a Jew --- eight kilograms
of cooking salt.) On the way, near the village of Admovo [Adamowo, about 13 kilometers northeast
of Braslav], they met several policemen, who forced Shachna and Yehoshua to dig a grave and
then shot them. In 1946, by chance, I met one of the Katzinovski brothers who'd taken part in
the murders of Shachna and Yehoshua (the second Katzinovski brother had been killed by
Jewish partisans from Yod [about 25 kilometers southeast of Braslav]). I wrote about the brother
to the police (the NKVD). I also had a witness who'd seen the murder --- David Gans, who'd been
hiding in his house at that time. Several months later, I heard from the NKVD that there was no
reason to take up the matter. I never found the place of my brothers' burial. The field [where they
were killed and buried] was plowed and planted.

When I was pursuing the murderer of my brothers Shachna and Yehoshua, I visited the secret
police [the NKVD]. There they showed me a picture of five bodies they'd taken out of a pit on the
Lishishki farm. They told me that these were members of the family of Yaacov Kastrel, who lived
opposite the Sandy Synagogue [in Braslav]. I learned that this family had requested shelter with
the local forester Artiom, and he was the one who'd killed them.

My sister Chiena hid for a few days in Yitzchak Kort's baking oven (he was outside the ghetto),
and with the help of a Russian prisoner of war named Borin, who served both the Germans and
the partisans, she left Braslav. A farmer named Voronov, from the village of Zapolosia [perhaps
Zapolosie, about 30 kilometers northeast of Braslav], got her out of the town; he hid her under
a pile of hay in a wagon and took her to his house in the village. After a few months, however,
she had to leave the village because of growing suspicions from the neighbors. She fled to the
forest near the village of Perebrodia [Pirabrod/Perebrodye, a.k.a. Przebrodzie, about 25
kilometers east of Braslav] in search of the partisans. There my sister met a Christian by the
name of Irina Ivanova [Iwanowa]. The woman understood what was happening and suggested
that Chiena wait for her until she returned with food and clothing; if the members of her
household agreed, she'd take her to her house. Worried that the woman would notify the police,
Chiena ran from the place. The woman indeed returned as she'd promised, but Chiena found
her again only after much searching. The woman took Chiena to her house, which was two
kilometers from the village of Zatzirevia [Zaczerewie], which was near Perebrodi[a].[6]

Only Irina and her father, Vasil Ivanov [Iwanow], knew about the guest. For a long time, the
rest of the members of her family didn't know Chiena was in their house. It's worth mentioning
that one of Vasil's sons, Timofei, was a policeman. All summer they hid Chiena in the storehouse
for hay, and when winter came they dug a deep pit under the bed and hid her there. Only then
did the family learn about her, except for Timofei. After the war I was a witness in the trial of this
Timofei, the policeman. He was accused of treason and sentenced to death, but the verdict was
lightened because his parents had saved a Jewish girl and it was thought that he'd known about
it. He was sentenced to 15 years in prison and returned home after seven years.

It's impossible to describe then what happened to my sister: hunger, cold, tortures of the body
and soul to the point of despair.

At the beginning of July 1944, she left the pit and returned to Braslav.

[Page 85]

As I've said, in August 1944 I was given leave and arrived in Braslav for a few days. My sister
Chiena and I found many photos of residents of the town. The identity cards of the Jews had
been thrown in the garbage by the German police, apparently after the Jews were murdered.
After liberation, some of the identity cards were found in the yard of the police station. My sister
took the photos out of these cards. At the time, she was getting letters from natives of Braslav
from all over Russia. Among the first ones who wrote to Braslav, and whose letter reached her,
was Moshe Bogomolski. In her answer, I don't know if she told him the horrible truth about his
family, but she sent him the pictures of his family members who were murdered, the photos that
she'd succeeded in removing from the identity cards.

My sister remained in Braslav until the end of 1946. In 1946, she left the town. Today she lives with her family in Leningrad.

Footnotes:

1. Yuri Levitan, the foremost announcer on Radio Moscow during World War II and for several decades thereafter. His name and voice were known throughout the Soviet Union.
2. Narodnyi Komissariat Vnutrennikh Del (People's Commissariat for Internal Affairs): The Soviet law enforcement and intelligence agency that existed from 1934 to 1946, after which it evolved into the KGB.
3. Disna (Dzisna) was about 72 kilometers east of Braslav. Druya (Druja) was 34 kilometers northeast of Braslav.
4. Jews working in jobs considered by the Nazis to be economically useful: chemists, blacksmiths, tailors, butchers, painters and so on.
5. After the first Braslav Ghetto was massacred on June 3-5, 1942, the Germans repopulated it in August or early September 1942 by bringing in some 50 Jews from Opsa, many of them craftsmen. Because these people were from Opsa, this second Braslav Ghetto was also called the "Opsa" Ghetto. It would be liquidated on March 19, 1943.
6. Zatzirevia was two kilometers west of Perebrodia.

[Page 86]

Yaacov Levin
Son of Chaya-Shayna and Leib-Meir

Translated from the Hebrew by Laia Ben-Dov
Footnotes Added / Donated by Jeff Deitch

A Simple Story: Prison Camp, Exile and Struggle

In the short, cruel war between Poland and Germany [that began in September 1939], I was drafted into the Polish army, but the days of my service were brief. After a few days of battle, we learned that the Red Army had crossed the eastern border. As if caught in giant pincers, trapped with no way out, mired in disappointment and despair, we were taken prisoner by the Russians. We then traveled a long, exhausting road until arriving near Smolensk [370 kilometers east of Braslav/Braslaw], where we were put in a huge camp housing tens of thousands of war prisoners. As fate would have it, we didn't stay long in the camp. Most of the men were freed after a few months and returned home, but the time was enough for all of us to get the taste of a prison camp and the rough conditions that prevailed there. However, we had little time to live quietly; the Germans attacked Russia.

That day, the day the horrible disaster began [June 22, 1941], I was in Bialystok [some 400 kilometers southwest of Braslav]. Somehow I managed to return to Braslav and was immediately drafted into the Red Army. All was in chaos, everything was mixed up. After a few days, we fled in every direction like sheep without a shepherd, and each of us had to take his fate into his own hands. From the place where the Red Army draftees had been gathered, I returned to Braslav with the aim of locating and helping my mother or other relatives, but I found no one. The town was without a government; army officers and those from the local authority fled in panic, leaving the inhabitants in uncertainty and fear.

I left the town and headed [east] toward the old border between Poland and the Soviet Union, to somehow find a way into the Soviet Union. On the road I met Beinish Milutin, traveling in a wagon hitched to a horse, coming from the other direction. He and his family had been staying for days in the village of Ukla, near Ikazna [Ikazn, about 14 kilometers east of Braslav], and now he was returning to Braslav to get some possessions. I described the situation to him and added that Braslav was deserted; hoodlums might riot, it wasn't worth putting himself in danger. He listened to my advice, and together we returned to the village [Ukla, about four kilometers southeast of Ikazn].

We were confused and didn't know what to do: stay in the village until

[Page 87]

the hostilities passed (we thought the war would end in a month or two) or flee with the entire family (Beinish's family was in the village, as well as Iska, my brother Yehoshua's wife). In the end, we decided to take the road toward the old border: the men only, because a rumor had spread that the Germans were killing only men.

We parted from our dear ones and left them. The three of us --- Beinish, his son Katriel and I --- traveled in a wagon from village to village, town to town. When we passed the villages, we felt strongly the depth of the hatred toward the Soviets and the Jews that beat in the hearts of the Christian population.

We traveled day and night, awake and listening to every sound, until we reached the old border. But here we were disappointed --- we weren't allowed to cross. Under ceaseless bombing from the German planes, we were forced to lie for hours in boggy swamps. At the time, the Red Army was withdrawing toward the Soviet Union to reorganize. We were helped by Jewish-Lithuanian soldiers, who joined us to a convoy of artillery, and with them we passed into Russia. Again we wandered from town to town, from place to place. The roads were crowded, and we advanced slowly amid thick, choking dust, deep into the Soviet Union. At every place we arrived, the officer of the town sent us onward, onward.

In Vitebsk [some 200 kilometers east of Braslav] we sold the horse and wagon for a sack of rye bread, and after many hardships we arrived by freight train at the city of Ufa [1,830 kilometers east of Braslav and near Kazakhstan], the capital of Bashkiria. There, our paths parted: Beinish and his son remained there and were put to work by a relative. Together with other young men from my town who we'd met on the road, I was sent to a village, to a *kolkhoz* [Soviet collective farm].

During the winter months of 1942, I found my brother Peretz. Like me he'd reached the Ural Mountains, and he was working as an accountant at an agricultural machine station (M.T.S.).[1] I traveled to him, and after staying there a number of months both of us were drafted into the army. After a short time, though, we were released as unreliable, since we were "westerners" [from Poland] and the Soviet authorities didn't trust us.

Peretz was then sent east, into the heart of the Ural Mountains, to the region of coal mines, and I was drafted into a labor battalion. In just a few months, I and many others turned into living skeletons. The scarce food, poor living conditions, illness and isolation took their toll.

It was forbidden to leave the workplace; this was regarded as desertion. It was also forbidden to travel in a train without an official permit. Despite this, one day I decided to burn all my bridges; with a small piece of whole-wheat bread, a can of *makhorka* [cheap-cut tobacco] and a towel, I left. I took my fate into my hands; I'd nothing to lose, and I fled. After many troubles, hungry and crawling with fleas, I reached my brother Peretz. A thorough disinfection and a hot meal gave me renewed strength and hope. I began a new chapter of my life, together with my brother Peretz, until we were drafted into the army [again] and sent to the front in 1944.

[This happened in the following way.] As essential workers in the coal mines, Peretz and I had "armor": We weren't drafted into the army. But then an incident occurred in which Peretz showed his Jewish pride: The coal miners' union failed to meet its production quota. At the time, Peretz was working in the union as the chief accountant. The manager was afraid of being reprimanded and removed from his high post for failing to meet the quota, so he ordered Peretz to fake the production results and add thousands of tons of coal to the lists to cover the deficit.

[Page 88]

Yaacov Levin: Citation of valor from the Red Army for his action in the capture of Gdansk

[Page 89]

Peretz refused, saying that forgery wasn't part of his job. The manager reacted with clenched fists and slanders about his Jewishness, threatening to draft him and send him to the front. Peretz replied that for him the front wasn't a punishment; he'd be happy to avenge the blood of his son, wife and relatives, rifle in hand. With that, he left the manager's office.

I waited for Peretz in the hallway. When the incident became known, we went together to the officer of the town (who by the way was a Jew named Levit), and I asked that the "armor" be removed from me as well. And so it happened. We were drafted at about the same time and sent to nearby battalions, and from there to the front.

Peretz didn't return. He fell on February 8, 1945, a few months before the end of the war, in eastern Prussia. Later I heard that he'd been wounded in the arm [or hand] during an attack; an officer then ordered him to go to the field clinic, but he refused. A few minutes later, he was hit and killed by a shell fragment. [Additional information about Peretz Levin appears on pages 300-301 of this memorial book.]

I fought until the end of the war.

The news of the victory reached me at the Elbe River.

Footnote:

1. *Mashinno-traktornaya stantsiya*: Machine and tractor station, a state enterprise that oversaw agricultural machinery used in collective farms.

[Page 90]

Mottel-Hirsh Fisher
Son of Beila-Zelda [née Katz] and Baruch

Translated from the Hebrew by Laia Ben-Dov
Footnotes Added / Donated by Jeff Deitch

The chapter of our family's life covers many years. Our home was a traditional one, in which the principles of the religion were strictly observed.

My father was a strong, tall, healthy man, with something of a squint.[1] Since the time I was a boy, I remember him being occupied with trade. His business was the trade of meat and live animals, and the rental of orchards from farmers of the area. He provided meat to units of the Polish army that were camped in the region, and he also sent meat and live animals to large towns in Poland. Despite his many occupations, he always found time to devote himself to the needs of the community. For years he served as the head of the Jewish community, took care of the Gemilut Hasadim [Free Loan Fund] and was the *gabbai* [caretaker] in the Old Synagogue. He helped the yeshiva in our town materially and offered help to people in need: in buying a new horse for a wagoner to replace a horse that had died; in supplying wood for heating to widows in the winter; *maot hitim* [donation of money to buy food] for Passover, and clothing and school supplies for the needy.

My mother was also very busy taking care of our large family; she enjoyed inviting a guest to her home and feeding daily a few yeshiva students. I remember the day of the bar mitzvah of my brother Velvel [Zalman-Volf] of blessed memory, the oldest in our family, the hospitality that mother prepared, and the oration that my brother made before more than 100 guests. Mother melted with pleasure when my brother went up to the synagogue platform to read the Torah. When I and my brother Tuvia traveled to yeshivas far from home to study Torah, her happiness and care went with us.

When I arrived home for vacations, my father would put in my hand a number of gold coins, for giving as a donation to beggars, to the synagogue and to the *shamash* [sexton] Reb[2] Uri, of blessed memory.

I remember the happiness in the house when, after six sons (two of whom died when they were small), three daughters were born. Thus we lived in our house until the Polish-German War broke out in September 1939: Baruch [Fisher] our father, Beila-Zelda our mother, the brothers Velvel [Zalman-Volf] and Avramke [Avraham] and the sisters Gutka [Guta], Rivka and Zlata, all of whom were killed most cruelly by the Nazi oppressor and his collaborators. May G-d avenge their blood. Of them all, there remained only my brother Tuvia and me to remember and speak. When the Russians took over western Belorussia [from mid-September 1939], we continued to lead our lives as usual for a number of months.

[Page 91]

As mentioned, my father was the supplier of meat and other provisions to the Red Army in the area. Our brother Velvel was manager of the office for procuring animals, but within a number of months everything changed. The [Soviet] regime established itself, and the problems began. Our brother Velvel was arrested following a denunciation and put in jail (but later freed because of a lack of proof). They began to send to Siberia people [who were considered] disloyal to the regime; these included merchants and of course those with hostile political opinions. Among large segments of the population, Siberia became a frightening word. Many nights our family lay down to sleep without getting undressed; we were prepared for any eventuality. It's possible that our good name among the population kept the authorities from harming us. Now, after all that happened, I can say: If only they'd exiled us to Siberia, it would have averted our family's tragic destruction. But fate decreed otherwise.

Immediately after the Germans entered Braslav [in late June 1941], they took Jews out of their houses for various types of work --- mainly to clean storerooms and stables. After they'd been in the town for some time, they ordered all the Jews to gather on one Friday at the end of Pilsudski Street.[3] Most of the Jews showed up, and the Germans took them, organized in rows of four, to the [Dubkes] swamp outside the town. There they were ordered to enter the swamp and sit in the water. From time to time, the Germans threatened to kill the frightened Jews. [Earlier] when the Jews had gathered on Pilsudski Street, I'd hidden in one of the houses, despite the great danger. Through a small opening in my hiding place, I saw how the Gentiles of the town and the surrounding area went wild and did whatever they wished, as if the town belonged to them. They robbed our houses, taking from them every valuable that they could, without interference. "The Jews won't return," they cried. The next day, on the morning of the Sabbath [June 28], the Jews were freed from the swamp, knowing neither why they'd been taken there nor why they'd been released. They returned to their homes, which had been emptied of everything. That same day fell the first two martyrs of the Braslav Jews --- Reb Shlomo [Zilber] the *shochet* [ritual slaughterer] and Chaim Milutin.

All of the irresponsible and criminal Gentiles of the town and the surrounding area armed themselves and became the new authority in Braslav [under the Germans].[4] The lives of the Jews became forfeit; danger threatened us at every turn. How sad it is to recall today those few among the Jews who for some reason fostered the deception that with the coming of the Germans, following the Russian retreat, people's lives would be easier.

Every day brought new decrees. A Judenrat [Jewish Council] was established, and at its head stood [Yitzchak] Mindel. They tried to help the Jews, but they were powerless. Jews arrived in Braslav from other places where the Germans had [already] conducted Aktions to destroy the ghettos. The Jews who succeeded in escaping these massacres were received in Braslav with brotherly love. They were lodged among families in the town and lived there like members of the family. With these refugees, Rav [Rabbi Yisrael-Alter] Fuchs and the daughter of the Rogatchover Gaon, who was a *rebbetzin* in Jerusalem, also arrived from Latvia.[5] They put their trust in the saying, "He who changes his location changes his luck." The Germans issued new decrees: Every Jew had to wear a yellow patch; it was forbidden for a Jew to walk on the sidewalk together with non-Jews; it was forbidden for a Jew to buy products in the marketplace, and it was forbidden to exchange various items for food. Each time, they demanded a "contribution" from the Jews

--- a ransom --- in gold and silver and expensive items. In this way, matters continued until Passover Eve 1942.

On Passover Eve 1942 [April 1], the Germans decided to establish a ghetto in Braslav.[6] The Jews from Dubina [Dubene], Slobodka and isolated families from the surrounding villages were brought to Braslav.[7] The killing began [in the following way]. Following a denunciation by a Gentile, Zelig Ulman was arrested, together with his wife and family. Their son wasn't in the house at the time, and so he was saved. The Judenrat

[Page 92]

tried to free them, but failed. Several days after their arrest, they were shot to death. Another day, a group of Jews was taken from among the Jewish laborers that worked loading wood [at the train station] and shot for no reason.

In the yard of Leizer [Eliezer] Fisher,[8] the Germans established a field bakery for bread. The workers were Jews. They divided among the workers the bread that was baked poorly. My father also worked in the bakery. It happened that one day he didn't feel well, and to revive himself he took a piece of bread. A German from among the supervisors saw this and immediately drew his pistol, wanting to kill my father. After much pleading, my father succeeded in stopping him. He returned home pale as whitewash, saying, "Today I was saved by a miracle from certain death."

The crowding in the [Braslav] ghetto grew from day to day. Despite this, people believed that the evil would pass. Many Jews prepared secret places for themselves and their families, bunkers in which to hide during a crisis. One Tuesday [June 2] Germans came to the ghetto, accompanied by local police, and demanded from the Judenrat a large group of girls to work as cleaners. The girls who reported were taken, as became known afterward, to Slobodka, where they were held for a day and night. When they returned to Braslav they saw the destruction and ruin, the empty houses without Jews. A few of them lost their minds, running into the nearby lake and committing suicide. Witnesses related that my sister Guta was among them.[9]

The day after the girls were taken, on Wednesday, the 18th of Sivan [June 3, 1942], the Germans surrounded the ghetto on all sides. With shouts like those of wild animals, they called to the Jews to come outside. The panic was terrible. The majority came out, and only a few managed to enter their hiding places. Then a few [Jews] said: "Come, let us set our houses on fire." Others replied that this might harm those who'd hidden inside the bunkers. Our Avramke as well as Naftali, the son of Zalman-Yaacov [Fisher],[10] tried to flee from the ghetto and were shot near the cattle market [a.k.a. the horse market].[10] I and my father hid [in a pit] under the floor in the Skuriat granary. We didn't know what happened to the rest of the family. Three days passed.

On Wednesday, Thursday and Friday [June 3-5, 1942], the Nazis massacred the Jews of Braslav. They took the Jews to pits they'd prepared ahead of time near the train station and shot them. Many of the Jews were thrown into the pit while still alive. From our hiding place, we heard voices of Jews who were being taken out of hiding places nearby. For three days, my father and I lay in hiding, and after that we went out to look for food and water. We walked during the night and arrived at [the house of] a Gentile woman, Helena was her name, who'd once been a servant in our house. We received a bit of bread and water from her. From there, we went on to another farmer and hid in his stable without his knowledge. My father, who all his life had been a proud Jew, was completely broken and became indifferent to life.

Fearful that the farmer's family would find us, we left the stable and entered a small deserted house nearby. I went up to the attic and asked my father to come up also. I rigged a small scaffold to make it easier for him. But a little girl appeared and saw father, putting us in danger. She let out a great scream and ran to call the police, who were searching in the area for Jews. They came immediately and took away my father. I was sitting above, hidden. I heard my father's last words to the police, "Don't take me anywhere. Kill me here." They removed him from the building, and after a few more steps they shot him. A witness told me afterward that a local policeman named Milavski [Milawski] was the one who shot my father. In the moments when the police were removing my father, I succeeded in getting away and reaching the nearby forest. When the police returned to look for me, I was gone.

At night, despite the danger, I again entered the granary of one of the farmers. In the morning, he entered and found me. To my surprise

[Page 93]

he didn't drive me out, but said he'd bring me some food and water. After I stayed in the granary for several hours, the farmer's sons came and told me that the Germans had announced they were no longer shooting Jews. They said they'd been told this by a policeman.

That night I left the farmer's yard and returned to Braslav. When I got there, I grew afraid; it was a place of ghosts. One of the survivors told me that my mother and my two sisters, Zlata and Rivkeleh, were alive and hiding in a pit in the yard of Leizer [Eliezer], the son of Feivush [Fisher]. My brother Tuvia and his wife Chana were hiding in the yard of Falka [Rafael] Fisher.[11] They also told me that the son of Zalman-Yaacov Fisher --- Motka [Mottel Fisher, the brother of Chana Fisher] --- Mottel's wife Liuba and their two children were alive. All of us gathered together and went up in the attic in the house of Berel the teacher, to discuss what to do and where to go. Was there a place to go? We all knew that the statements of the Germans were only lies and tricks. We agreed that none of us would leave the house, to avoid revealing ourselves. The people in the attic, who'd been in the ghetto during the fateful hours, said the Germans had wanted to leave the head of the Judenrat, [Yitzchak] Mindel, alive, but he'd asked to die; he didn't want to remain alive without the [other] Jews. So they shot him first. The Germans had also wanted to leave alive Rabbi [Yisrael-Alter] Fuchs, the rabbi of Dvinsk, because of his vast knowledge of German. The rabbi asked them to also spare the life of the *rebbetzin* from Jerusalem [Rachel Citron], but the Germans wouldn't agree to this. So the rabbi asked to die, and they shot him immediately. The cruelest policeman was a man by the name of [Stefan] Zhuk. This murderer said to Moshke, the son of Leiba-Meir, who was lying seriously wounded in his stomach and asked to be killed, "For a Jew, it's not worth wasting even one bullet."

And an incident that I saw with my own eyes from the attic where we sat: Policemen brought Moshe-Baruch, the chimney-sweeper of Braslav, tied up with ropes, with some other men, women and children, to kill them. This was what the "amnesty" looked like.[12]

At night I went down below, and without anyone seeing I entered the apartment where we'd lived. I found a piece of dry bread there and gave it to my mother. We told her we'd go out to search for a hiding place with one of the farmers in the area, and return immediately to take them all there. We walked only at night. We came to the village of Achremovtzi [Achremowcy a.k.a. Achremowce, seven kilometers southeast of Braslav]; there one of our acquaintances told us he was prepared for us to come to him, the entire family: mother and my sisters, and Motka's wife and two daughters. With that same farmer, we found Falka Fisher. We were overjoyed that the farmer was so good-hearted and immediately set out for Braslav to summon our dear ones. On the way, from time to time we had to hide from farmers who were traveling in their wagons to and from Braslav. In one place, we found the young daughter of Natke [Natan] Biliak, who'd escaped from Braslav. She told us that a farm woman had revealed to the enemy the hiding place of our family; the Germans had come and murdered them all. Hearing this news shocked us to the depths of our souls. We didn't want to believe a tragedy such as this. We continued toward Braslav. A Gentile we met confirmed what Natke Biliak's daughter had told us. If we'd gotten there a day earlier --- just one day --- we could've saved them all. What a cruel fate it was!

We remained with the farmer in Achremovtzi for several months. Since he was a poor farmer, we had to get our food from somewhere else. At night, we spread out to vegetable gardens in the area and took all kinds of vegetables. We cooked cabbages and pickles. Somehow we survived. But what would we do in the winter, which was already approaching? Our Gentile occasionally traveled to Braslav for fairs, and when he came back he'd give us the news. Once he told us they'd brought Shachna Band and his brother Yehoshua to the city tied with rope. Another day he told us they'd brought Rachka Lans [sic],[13] her husband and their son to the town in handcuffs. He made sure to tell us about the Gentiles' hunt for Jews who'd escaped from death, tying them up and handing them over to the Germans.

[Page 94]

One day, he came with news: "In Braslav Jews are running around, completely free." He'd seen them in the streets of the town and in the markets. I asked the Gentile, on his next visit to Braslav, to find out who these Jews were and if any members of our family were among them. We waited anxiously for a week, until his next visit to Braslav. When he returned, he told us that the Germans had established another ghetto, a new one, on the sands of Braslav, which extended from the house of Benjamin the tailor along the entire right side of Pilsudski Street and on the hills, and they'd fenced it in with a fence two meters high.[114] They made an entrance gate next to Benjamin the tailor's house, with a permanent police guard. Those in the ghetto were mostly Jews from Vidz [Widze] and Opsa who the Germans had driven out of their homes [Vidz and Opsa were respectively 40 kilometers and 18 kilometers southwest of Braslav]. After we heard the farmer's words, we didn't know what to do. True, all of us felt that during the coming winter months we wouldn't be able to continue at the farmer's. But what brought us to the crucial decision to enter the ghetto was the knowledge that Falka Fisher, his wife Fania, their two daughters and son Neftel were there.

One night, we walked to Braslav and entered the ghetto. During the first days there, we didn't go outside. I stayed in Benjamin the tailor's house with Falka Fisher and his family. My brother Tuvia, his wife Chana and her brother lived together with a family from Opsa. After we stayed several days in the ghetto, they registered us as residents and we went out with everyone to work. In the ghetto there were about 1,000 [sic][115] Jews, entire families and single individuals. There were a few Jews from Braslav. I, Tuvia and his wife Chana, Mottel [i.e., Mottel Fisher, the brother of Chana], Falka [Fisher], his wife Fania, their son Neftel and two daughters [Esther and Rivka]. We worked at different jobs, near the train [station], where the farmers brought different seeds --- tax for the lands that they worked. The registrar of the tax was a Jewish lad from Opsa, and thanks to him we occasionally received food from the farmers. The danger was great, but the will to stay alive made us risk our lives to get food. Life in the ghetto got worse from day to day. There was nothing to eat, and sickness increased. Only from time to time did the Germans distribute a bit of flour, potatoes and a small amount of wood for heating.

One day --- it seems to me it was a Tuesday in the month of February [1943] --- a great panic arose in the ghetto. Everyone saw this as the beginning of the second ghetto's destruction. That day, Falka and Fania Fisher spoke to their son Neftel, [to convince him] to leave the ghetto and return to the farmer in Achremovtzi, where all of us had been staying when the first [Braslav] ghetto was destroyed [on June 3-5, 1942]. They said to him, "If you go, then maybe at least one of our family will remain alive." They dressed Neftel in the clothing of the village farmers, so that he'd look like a villager returning home from the market. Mottel, Chana's brother, accompanied him to the house of Hertzke Skopitz. From there, he went out on the road alone. As I've said, this was in February. Everything was covered with a great deal of snow; he had to walk in the tracks made by the farmers' sleds. After he'd been walking for some time, policemen and Germans, who were returning from one of the villages, approached him from the opposite direction. Even though to us Neftel looked like a real villager, one of the policemen recognized him as a member of the Fisher family and, without asking anything, shot and killed him.[116] That day in the ghetto, despite the great fear that took hold of everyone, nothing unusual happened. "Life" continued as before. (When we returned to Braslav after it was liberated by the Russians, the farmers showed us the temporary burial place of Neftel, of blessed memory. We transferred his bones for burial next to the pits where the martyrs of Braslav had been killed.)

Jews of the ghetto who could do so prepared hiding places. But in the house where we lived, there was no chance of doing this. As mentioned the house stood next to the ghetto gate, and police were

[Page 95]

always near the gate. Everyone continued to go out to work each day. Matters went on in this way until two days before Purim 1943 [March 19, 1943]. It was a Friday. Toward morning, a great noise of vehicles was heard. A glance outside showed Germans and police surrounding the ghetto. We understood what was about to happen. I quickly left the house and got over the fence, running [northeast] in the direction of the Sandy Synagogue and Lake Noviata [Nowiata]. The police and Germans fired many rounds at me, but luckily I wasn't hit. It was a miracle: I don't understand how I was left unharmed. At the lakeshore, I reached the house of Zalman-Yaacov [Fisher]. In the house lived a Gentile woman who'd worked for the family before the war. I went inside and told her what had happened. I asked her to explain what was being done to the Jews in the ghetto. They [presumably the Gentile woman was with her own family, now living in the house] said that in the ghetto the police and Germans were preparing a great massacre of the Jews, and that Leizer, the son of Meir-Yossel Biliak, had shot the policeman Milavski, who'd died of his wounds. (As mentioned previously, this same Milavski had killed my father. May this be the fate of all our enemies.)

During that entire Friday and Sabbath, I lived in great fear. I didn't know what had happened to my relatives, who I'd left in the ghetto. When the Sabbath ended, the Gentile went out, as was always his habit in the evening, to lock the cowshed [presumably this refers to the Gentile woman's husband]. He immediately came back inside, looking happy, and said, "Mottel, we have guests." Behind him my brother Tuvia came in with Chana his wife and her brother Motka. They'd stayed in their hiding place for two days. In the evening, they came out and reached us safely.

The Jews who survived after the massacre in the second ghetto [on March 19, 1943] were few. With deceit and lies, the Germans had gathered the Jews who remained alive after the first ghetto. Now they'd killed them also. There were no more Jews in Braslav, none. We were their mourners.

We remained hidden with the Gentiles in Zalman-Yaacov's house for some time. After that, we left the house and began to wander from place to place and from farmer to farmer. I don't have the strength to describe what happened to us during that time, until the region was liberated by the Russians [in July 1944]. Someday I'll do this, if G-d grants me long years and strength. Many have researched and written about the Holocaust, and the survivors, who by a miracle remained alive, have told much in their accounts. But does anyone have the strength to tell everything that the Germans and their collaborators did to the Jews? They're the remnants of hell on earth, branches broken from rootless trees. Their descendants lack complete families; they've no grandfather or grandmother, no uncles spread out in different places in the city and neighboring towns. They've no knowledge of the existence of the Jewish family in general, and of the holidays in particular. The destruction harmed the soul and spirit of the nation and will never be forgotten.

People ask, and have asked me, why didn't we protest? I don't have a clear, unequivocal answer. Not for others, and not for myself. Only some thoughts about it:

1. The Germans weakened us with threats and tortures. They took everything from us. Each day, they threatened death. They degraded us to dust.
2. The will to live in man, the miracle that each one of us believed --- or wanted to believe --- would happen, the miracle of survival, the connection to the entire family [kept people from acting]. Concern for the children, the thought that maybe they'd succeed in rescuing the children from death, more than once stopped those in whom the fire burned to fight and take revenge.
3. When we believe in Divine Providence, we see the destruction as a decree from Heaven. Who are we to question what and why?

Footnotes:
1. The father, Baruch Fisher, was a son of Zelik Fisher and Guta and a grandson of Morduch Fisher. This Fisher family had lived in Braslav [Braslaw] since at least the time of Morduch, born ca. 1800. Mottel-Hirsh Fisher was a brother of the Tuvia Fisher whose accounts appear on pages 68-69 and pages 108-110 of this memorial book.
2. Reb is an honorific term, something like an exalted "Mr."
3. Other survivors recall this event as happening on June 27 (Saturday), the day after the Germans arrived in Braslav.
4. According to the *Encyclopedia of Camps and Ghettos, 1933-1945*, Volume II-B (2012), on June 30, 1941 --- a few days after entering Braslav --- the local German commandant began to recruit a local police unit from among local ruffians who were sympathetic to the Germans. A Pole named Yashinski [Stanislaw Jasinski] was made the unit's commander. Other policemen in the unit

included Kriwko, Stefan Zhuk, Malinowski, Masara, Czeslaw Kolkowski, Zarniewicz and Stanislaw Nowicki. A man named Sucharewicz was one of the most brutal participants in the persecution of the local Jews.

    In autumn 1941 responsibility for the local police was transferred from the German army to the German gendarmes, after a civil administration had been established to replace the military administration. (That is, the German gendarmes supervised the local police unit.) Among the men based at the German gendarmes' outpost in Braslav were Johannes Czapp, Willy Dittmann, Otto Hayman, Paul Kontny, Leo Leidenroth, Ludwig Müller, Ernst Schreiber and Waldemar Schultz.

5.   *Rebbetzin* is the title used for the wife of a rabbi. Rachel Citron, a widow, was the daughter of the late Hasidic rabbi of Rogatchov, the Gaon Rabbi Yosef Rosen (1858-1936). Around 1936, Mrs. Citron traveled from Palestine to Dvinsk in Latvia to help compile and safeguard her late father's writings. Working in Dvinsk with Rabbi Fuchs (also known as Safern-Fuchs), a devoted student of her father and his successor, she was able to publish several volumes of her father's writings and send copies of his notes and correspondence to New York City, before fleeing with Rabbi Fuchs to Braslav following the German invasion on June 22, 1941. In accounts in this memorial book she's described as being from Jerusalem, but other sources say that she was from Petah Tikva.

6.   April 1, 1942 was the approximate date the Braslav Ghetto was fenced in or formally established. But Jews had begun to be concentrated in the area of the ghetto since approximately August 1941; see, for example, the account of Alexander Dagovitz on page 357 of this memorial book and the account of Chalvina Pinchov on page 393.

7.   Dubina was 16 kilometers northwest of Braslav, Slobodka was about 11 kilometers northeast of Braslav. A number of Jews from Dubina stayed in Braslav only a short time and were then taken to the Vidz [Widze] Ghetto, as is clear from the accounts of survivors from Dubina in this memorial book. These Dubina Jews remained in the Vidz Ghetto until around the autumn of 1942, when it was closed and the inmates were transferred to the Sventzion Ghetto. (The exceptions were mainly those who escaped from the Vidz Ghetto, died in Vidz from privation, or were removed and sent to labor camps.)

    In March 1943, it was announced that the Sventzion Ghetto would be shut down. On April 4, 1943, the Jews in the Sventzion Ghetto, on the pretext of being taken to the Kovno and Vilna ghettos, were instead taken in freight cars to the execution site at Ponar outside Vilna, where they were shot on April 5. Only a very small number survived this massacre. For a number of Jews from Dubina, this was the path to destruction.

8.   Eliezer Fisher was a son of Feivush Fisher and a grandson of Zelik Fisher, as well as a great-grandson of Morduch Fisher. Eliezer Fisher's account is on pages 155-158 of this memorial book.

9.   Other accounts say that the girls were marched to the pits outside Braslav and shot, although they differ on whether this happened on the day the massacre began (June 3) or the day after.

10.   Naftali Fisher was a son of Zalman-Yankel Fisher and a grandson of Neftel Fisher and Lana, as well as a great-grandson of Morduch Fisher.

11.   Rafael Fisher was a son of Neftel Fisher and Lana and a grandson of Morduch Fisher. Chana Fisher was a daughter of Zalman-Yankel Fisher, a granddaughter of Neftel Fisher and Lana, and a great-granddaughter of Morduch Fisher. Chana was thus a cousin of her husband, Tuvia Fisher, the brother of Mottel-Hirsh (the person giving this account), since Tuvia and Mottel-Hirsh were also great-grandchildren of Morduch.

    Chana Fisher also had a brother named Mottel Fisher, described later in this account, and he too survived the war.

12.   After the first few days of killing the Jews of Braslav (June 3-5, 1942), the Germans and their collaborators announced that the killing would stop and those Jews who emerged from their hiding places would be registered. However, they soon killed most of those who'd emerged.

13.   The surname Lans doesn't appear in the list of victims in this memorial book, nor in the Yad Vashem database of victims. It's possible that it's a misprint in the memorial book and the surname was actually Gans/Gens, which does appear in the memorial book and the database.

14.   In August or early September 1942, some 50 Jews in Opsa were transferred to the former ghetto in Braslav, to repopulate it after the original inmates had been slaughtered on June 3-5, 1942. Because the members of this second, new ghetto in Braslav were from Opsa, the ghetto was also called the "Opsa" Ghetto. It would be liquidated on March 19, 1943.

15.   The number 1,000 appears to be an overestimate for the second ghetto. Other accounts say that only 50 or so survivors from Opsa were brought to Braslav to make the second ghetto. The size of the second ("Opsa") Ghetto as shown on the map on pages 20-21 of this memorial book also was very small.

16.   This killing was also described on page 119 of this memorial book by Neftel Fisher's sister Yetta.

[Page 96]

Yerachmiel Biliak
Son of Sara-Gitel and Chaim-Leib

Translated from the Hebrew by Laia Ben-Dov
Footnotes Added / Donated by Jeff Deitch

I was born in Braslav [Braslaw] in 1904. Here I lived with my family until the end of June 1942.

It was on Friday, June 27, 1941 that the Germans arrived in my town. Fear embraced us all; we ran about in confusion. We received the first portion of dread immediately: We were ordered to come out into the street. They took us to a large swamp beyond the town [in the Dubkes forest]. On the way, they warned us that if even one man tried to flee, they'd kill 10 of us in his stead. They threatened to pour boiling oil on us and burn us alive. Two among us who tried to run were caught and shot before our eyes: Shlomo Zilber (the *shochet* [ritual slaughterer]) and the lad Chaim Milutin. On the way to the swamp, the Germans forced the men to take off their boots and hand them over. They fenced in the marshy swamp with barbed wire and mounted machine guns around us, then put us into the swamp. We sank in up to our knees, and we sat like this, wet and frightened, from Friday until the Sabbath. On the Sabbath, they said that they were waiting for the judgment of the mayor. If he testified that we were good and useful Jews, they'd free us. And indeed, at 11:00 in the morning [on Saturday] we were told that we were free to go home.

While we were in the swamp, our Christian neighbors went wild; they robbed our homes and took everything of value that they needed. We were happy to have returned alive.

The first two who'd been killed [Zilber and Milutin] were buried on Sunday. On Monday, toward evening, the mayor gathered us at a certain location. He told us that now everything had changed. The government was different, as were the rulers, and the treatment of the Jews would be different as well. We'd have to obey each instruction, order and request without argument or appeal. "Know," he said, "that your good years have ended. Now you're under German authority. From tomorrow, Tuesday, all of you will go out to work. You must choose a Judenrat [Jewish Council], and through it you'll receive all future instructions." He finished speaking and left. For the Judenrat we chose Yitzchak Mindel, Eliezer Mazeh, Rafael Fisher, Gershon Klioner and others.

On Tuesday morning, we went out to work. They took everyone. They even forced the elderly rabbi [Rabbi Avraham-Abba-Yaacov Zahorie], who was 80 years old, to go to work. We

[Page 97]

were divided into groups. Some worked at repairing and improving the roads. I was joined to a group that worked at the train station, loading ammunition. People worked continuously at these jobs, also at night. On Friday, toward evening, again they ordered us to gather in the field behind the Pravoslavic [Eastern Orthodox] church near the lake. A German, the officer Steinhaltz, arrived with his staff in his hand, and ordered us to divide ourselves: separately into women [without infants], women with infants, children, and men. Again we were seized with terror, and once more we thought that our end had come. In a frightening voice, he screamed at us: "We know who you Jews are . . . soon I'll command you to run to the lake and go into the water . . . I'll check your attitude toward work . . ." and before finishing his threats he added, "Now I'll blow a whistle and you must disappear immediately from this place." And so it happened. Once more, we returned home alive. On the Sabbath, we went out to work. One day, they had us move stones from place to place. After two days of dragging the stones, we were ordered to return them to their previous location. This was how we worked and how they oppressed us. Our supervisors were two Belorussians. At the end of a day of hard labor, a German Unteroffizier [sergeant or squad leader] arrived on a bicycle. He pulled one of the young men from the group, and ordered him to run after him while he sped on his bike down the streets of the town.

One day we noticed that one of the supervisors was recording people's names. The next day, when we got to work, 13 of the men received no tools. Within a short time, a gendarme arrived; he took these men, put them into a freight car and closed it. We, the remaining men, continued to work. We were on edge. At the noon break, one of the supervisors noticed me saying something that to him seemed suspicious; actually I was expressing concern to my friends about the ones who'd been arrested, saying that we should do something to free them. Suddenly the supervisor approached, grabbed me and began to drag me away. I told him that I could walk by myself, and for this remark he hit me on the head with his staff. He took me over to the boxcar of prisoners. Fortunately, a Gentile acquaintance and a member of the Judenrat showed up, and with effort they were able to get me away from the murderer.

The member of the Judenrat went to try to free the prisoners, but they were already dead. Here are their names, as engraved in my memory: Boris Karas, Yitzchak Blacher, Nachman Zubovich, Shalom Budzin, Hirsh Goldman, Velvel Deitch, Chatzkel [Yechezkel] Vinokur, Zalman Lif, Chaim Todres, Chona and Gedalia Shapira, one man from Opsa, and one man from Dubina.[1]

After the incident with the supervisor, I went to the Judenrat and asked for my work location to be changed, so that I wouldn't encounter murderers who intended to do evil to me. In this way passed 10 months of oppression, killing, suffering and fear.

By profession, I was a driver. One day I was called to the Judenrat and ordered to drive Belorussian policemen to the town of Gleboki [Glubokoye], about 100 kilometers from Braslav [actually about 70 kilometers southeast of Braslav]. They gave me an exit permit, and we started out. During the trip, snatches of the policemen's conversation reached my ears, and suddenly I realized that I was transporting murderers to destroy the Jews of Dokshits [Dokshitsy, about 20 kilometers south of Gleboki]. When I arrived in Gleboki, I hurried to tell the members of the Judenrat, and they tried to inform Dokshits of what was going to happen. Some of the Jews succeeded in fleeing. After reaching Dokshits, the murderers killed 496 Jews.[2] When I returned home, I was happy to be with my family again.

[On June 2, 1942, Tuesday] the day before the destruction of the [Braslav] ghetto, they gathered 80 young people, children of the town (among them my daughter Gitka [Gita]), and took them, supposedly, to work in the nearby village of Slobodka [about 11 kilometers northeast of Braslav]. On Wednesday toward morning,

[Page 98]

they brought them back, confined them in the fenced area of the cattle market [a.k.a. the horse market], and murdered them all. I know that Neftel, the son of Feivush and Chaya Fisher, and also Tevka [Tuvia], the son of Chava and Chonka [Chona] Biliak, succeeded in escaping, but Gentiles grabbed them and killed them.[3] That same morning, Wednesday, 18 Sivan 5702 [June 3, 1942], saw the start of the utter destruction of the Jews of the Braslav Ghetto. I and three of my children [Chaim-Leib, Leizer-Itza and Sara-Esther] succeeded in fleeing. My brother Chontza [Chona] and his children, who hid at the Gebelman family's house during the days of the massacre, left their hiding place on Sunday and succeeded in slipping out of the town.[4]

We were helped a lot by the Gentile Vintza Kolkovski [Vincenty Kolkowski] from Belmont [a locality a few kilometers southeast of Braslav, near Lake Driviata]. ---

From a distance, we saw a bridge. We approached the house of a Gentile acquaintance and asked him to check if anyone was on the bridge. Yes, he told us, there were police. Having no choice, we moved about a kilometer away and crossed the river by swimming it. As we were dressing ourselves after crossing the river, we saw a man standing not far from us. I said to my friend loudly, in Russian: "*Vozmi v ruki vintovku*" ("Grab the rifle!"), even though we had only a shovel for digging . . . The man heard this and ran away, as did we.

We approached Braslav [presumably from Belmont, to which they had fled]. We took off our shoes and quietly entered the town. It was night-time: silence. We walked slowly. We heard footsteps and hid behind a house. A patrol passed by, and we continued on to my house. When we entered, we saw that it had been plundered and destroyed. I didn't find a thing that I'd wanted to take, and my soul despaired. We went back [presumably toward Belmont]. On the way, we entered [the house of] a Gentile where I'd hidden some items. I took away something and brought it to the Gentiles where I was hiding.

We went back to the children [apparently the children had been left somewhere around Belmont]. There was nothing to eat. From a piece of wood I made a scale, which helped me divide correctly what little food we had. We, the four adults,[5] received 50 grams each. The children, who were smaller --- 40 grams, and the littlest ones --- 30 grams. This was three times a day.

One day, after we'd stayed 73 days in a pit, the local Gentile came and showed me an order, according to which he had to put in his hayshed --- which contained the pit where we were hiding --- 21 horses belonging to the German cavalry. He explained to us that we had to leave, because he was in great danger. ---

My son Chaim-Leib died of a heart attack. I asked my daughter Sara-Esther what had happened, and she told me: "After you left us in the stable and went away, that evening there was a party in the village. The Gentiles became drunk and quarreled, and then the police arrived. Shooting began not far from the stable; he took fright and died." We took him for burial in the forest nearby. The next day my brother Chontza went with Fisher [sic], and I remained with my 10-year-old son Leizer-Itza and my eight-year-old daughter Sara-Esther. I stayed in that place for 82 days [with the Gentile Francis Kolkovski], until the winter. The local Gentile woman hinted to me once that it was preferable for us to find another place for the winter. Aronchik and Fridman came to me and repeated the words of the woman who'd told them as well that she didn't have a place to keep us in the winter. "Maybe we should go to the ghetto? In Braslav there's a second ghetto,"[6] they said. I said that I'd think about it.

I waited until evening. I took my son [Leizer-Itza] with me, and we went down to the river. There we found a rowboat. We sailed in it to a Gentile, who'd suggested earlier that we come to him. I asked the Gentile if the offer was still good, and he replied, "Yes, but only on condition that no one else knows about it." We determined that I'd return to him with the children on Sunday. We waited until evening and then rowed back. I said to "my" Gentile that on Sunday we'd leave him, but I didn't tell him where we'd go. On Thursday, the Gentile prepared a boat for us. On Thursday and Friday the frost increased, and it continued to do so on the Sabbath as well. On Sunday, besides the frost, there was a strong wind. The Gentile warned me that on the bridge there was sometimes a police guard --- after some time, he came to me looking very worried and told me the following. Twenty Germans had been traveling on the Kozian [Koziany]-Peltrova road [Kozian was about 40 kilometers southwest of Braslav]. Partisans had attacked them from the nearby forest, shot at them

[Page 99]

and killed them all, to the last one. The partisans then stripped the clothing from the Germans, leaving them naked, and wrote on a nearby post, "Don't touch the bodies." Someone had notified the gendarmes of the German dead. The gendarmes immediately drafted 80 wagons and set out on the road with a German escort; "my" Gentile had been among those drafted. When they reached the place and found the dead Germans, the German officer ordered that all the villages near the forest be set on fire; the local young people were to be taken away, and an order was given to burn the elderly along with the houses. The cows and horses were also taken.

And that's what happened: The gendarmes went from village to village, taking out the young people and the animals. They gathered the old people in one house, raining fire on it with machine guns until it went up in flames. This was the fate of dozens of villages in the area. My Gentile acquaintance told me all this, and because of it he was afraid to shelter me any longer. The Germans had notified all the villages that if they discovered a partisan or a Jew in any of the villages, they'd burn the entire village. The Gentile asked that I leave and look for another place. I promised to do so, but asked for permission to stay with him for just one more day.

I sat and considered where to go. The time --- the days of Hanukkah [December 1942]. It was getting colder. The children were naked and barefoot. I had to go --- but where? I heard someone knocking on a door [nearby]. When it opened, I heard the local Gentile woman saying [to someone], "Go to that house, he's there." Darkness. Then I heard the voice of my brother [Chontza Biliak] calling me: "Yerachmiel, where are you?" He approached us, and I asked him what was happening. He told me he had no hiding place, and for a few weeks he'd been wandering from place to place each day with the children, and he hadn't a crumb of food. He'd heard that Jews from Opsa had been brought to Braslav [around August-September 1942] and a ghetto had again been established. But they didn't let Jews enter from outside, unless they succeeded in sneaking in, and woe to the Jew who got caught entering without permission by a policeman or a German. The punishment for this was shooting. Because I had a hiding place, my brother asked me to take his little girl [Sara-Gitka], so that maybe at least she'd remain alive. To my question of where were the [other] children, he answered, "In the bathhouse of Francis Kolkovski," the Gentile where I'd stayed earlier for 82 days. I told him that the Gentile didn't want to keep me either. It was a bad and bitter time for us. I waited until morning and then went inside to speak with the Gentile. I said to him, "What should I do? My brother has a good hiding place [sic], and I know that you also wanted to save us, but you cannot, and now you're telling us to leave. I can't go, because they'll certainly catch us. I won't tell others where I've been hiding, but I can't guarantee what the children will say. I suggest that you hitch up the horse to take us to Braslav." I knew he wouldn't agree to this --- and indeed he didn't. Then I said to him [with sarcasm], "Maybe I'll warm up the bathhouse; shall I take the children inside and we can be suffocated there by the gas?" He replied that he didn't agree. I said, "I see that you want me to live, so I have a suggestion. With your agreement, I'll dig a pit in the *punia*[7] (hayshed). Today my brother's here and he'll assist me, and maybe with your help my children and I can stay alive." The Gentile spoke as if talking to himself --- "The ground is frozen" --- and he told me to wait a bit. After a short time, he called me into the house and suggested that I move the hay to another place with my brother's help, and dig a pit there. Until the evening, we worked at moving the hay aside. Now we were sitting and thinking: We must dig the pit; we must go to my brother's children --- they were alone in the bathhouse [of Francis Kolkovski], and the Gentile didn't even know about it. I decided to go again to my homeowner. This time I told him, "We're hiding some things in a certain place. We agreed with the owner of the place not to allow one brother

[Page 100]

to take any of the things unless the other brother is also present. With your consent, we'd like to go now and take some of them." He agreed. I explained to the children that I and my brother were going and would return the next night, bringing with us Sara-Gitka [Chontza's daughter].

"When we knock on the window, open the door for us, and we'll bring her inside without the Gentile knowing there's another girl with us."

My brother and I set out. We walked through the fields and came to the bathhouse. The children [of Chontza] were there. We waited for dawn and sent two of the oldest children to the ghetto: the 10-year-old daughter Feiga-Tzipka and the eight-year-old boy Tevka [brother of Feiga-Tzipka]. Nechama Gebelman, who was 23 years old, went with them. We remained, waiting in the bathhouse. Toward evening, the boy [Tevka] came back and told us that the ghetto had received them nicely. They'd gotten food, and the Judenrat had divided them among several families. It grew late: It was night. We kept the boy with us until morning, and then he returned to the ghetto while we went back to our place. One of us brought a package with him, and the other put the girl [Sara-Gitka] into a sack, and we proceeded. Outside there was snow and a stormy wind. The distance wasn't great, only five kilometers, but it was hard to walk in such weather. We progressed slowly. Finally we knocked, and my child came out and opened the door for us. We went inside, and the Gentile didn't realize we were there. We waited until morning. I heard them [the Gentiles] walking around in the house. I went inside and gave them the package with the items that we'd brought. The woman took the package willingly, and the Gentile brought us to the hayshed to dig the pit. Somehow he realized that we'd brought the additional girl [Sara-Gitka]. He grew very angry. "I've no room for you," he said, "and you do to me a thing like this?" I explained to him, "My brother fled the massacre with an older daughter [Feiga-Tzipka], and she was tormenting this little girl. I already told you that he has a place and food. But the older daughter was hitting the younger one. When she saw me, this girl began to cry and beg me to take her with me. Her words touched my heart, and I couldn't refuse her. I've taken her only for a limited time and I won't ask for food for her." We began to dig. Toward evening, the Gentile came back to us and said, "I have bad news: They caught Berel Miaisi with my neighbor Blaika. They tied him up and took him to Braslav. They also announced that everyone must lock up the granaries, bathhouses and stables properly, so that undesirables can't hide in them." He was already regretting that he'd given us permission earlier to dig the pit. Dejected by events, he insisted that we finish digging that same evening. It was hard to dig; the ground was frozen. It was forbidden to make any noise; we dug with our teeth [sic] and nails. We padded the pit with a bit of straw and put the children inside. Later the Gentile came, forced my brother to leave, and closed the hayshed. After two hours, I broke a board off the fence and my brother entered through the opening. Now there were five of us in the pit, without the Gentile knowing it. They brought us food once a day, sometimes twice. After the Sabbath, my brother went to a Gentile acquaintance, Vincent Kolkovski [Vincenty Kolkowski], who went to church in Braslav on Sundays. Through him, my brother passed a note to his children in the ghetto, asking them to come to him, because he was waiting for them. The Gentile returned with a note from the children that it was better for them in the ghetto than in the pits, and they didn't want to come out to us.

At the end of a week, my brother went to the Gentile and sent another note, asking his son and daughter [Feiga-Tzipka and Tevka] to just come and talk to him; he wouldn't take them out of the ghetto. Again the son refused, but the daughter agreed to come and see her father. After talking with him, she wanted to hurry and return to the ghetto, but the father delayed her from going, begging her to remain with him. Meanwhile, it grew dark. The father said to her: "I'll return at midnight to the pit and you'll return in the morning to the ghetto." At midnight, the father suggested that she get dressed and come to see me and the children. At first the girl refused, but eventually she gave in to his pleas and came with her father to the pit.

[Page 101]
There was no shortage of fleas in the pit, and they attached themselves to her in droves. She began to cry out loud. I tried to calm her: "Don't cry, when day breaks you'll be able to return to the ghetto." In the morning, she asked to go. I answered that she could go when it got dark, because in the daylight someone was likely to see her. In this way, a number of days passed. We cut her hair, and finally she remained with us.

My cousin Leizer Biliak was in the ghetto. At night, I'd go out with my brother Chontza. We'd go to Francis Kolkovski, take two loaves of bread from Francis and send a note with him to our cousin [Leizer], to the ghetto, and he [Francis] would bring notes to us. In the notes we described the place where we were located and suggested that if anything happened, he [Leizer] should take the boy [Tevka, the son of Chontza] and come to us. "When you enter the granary," I wrote, "knock three times on the post and I'll come out to you." One day while we were lying there, we heard someone crawl through the opening that we used, and then there were three knocks on the post. I wanted to go out and see, but my brother wanted to stop me. Finally I went out and asked, "Who is it?" And Leizer answered, "It's me." We went down into the pit --- he was barefoot and hatless, with only a shirt on his body. I saw that a finger on his right hand had been injured by a bullet. It was Sabbath night. He told me that everyone had been shot [on March 19, 1943, when the "Opsa" Ghetto in Braslav was liquidated] and Chontza's son [Tevka] had been burned [alive]. He said that when they were in Bogomolski's house [in Braslav], toward morning a German approached a window from outside, knocked on it and signaled to him to come out. Leizer had a pistol and shot the German through the window, killing him. Two more policemen attacked the house. Leizer killed one of them and seriously wounded the other. As he jumped over a fence to flee, a bullet injured his right hand, and he dropped the pistol. This had been on Thursday, the night of the Fast of Esther, 5703 [the 11th of Adar II, or March 18, 1943]. The next day, on Friday [March 19, 1943], the massacre took place.

That same Friday, the Gentile came and asked me to look for another hiding place. Again he argued that he was worried about keeping me. On Sunday, he returned. He told me that the ghetto had been destroyed and "your Leizer killed a German and two policemen. In public places, they posted notices about a big reward that would be given to anyone who turned Leizer Biliak over to the authorities. Many people know I had friendly relations with you, and I'm afraid that they'll come and search near me. You must go and look for another place." In the evening, the Gentile came back. He told me that Leizer had been caught and handed over to the gendarmes (at this time, Leizer was in fact lying near me in the pit). A number of days passed, and the Gentile calmed down. We talked among ourselves about looking for another place. In the hayshed, flax was stored. I twisted some rope from it and made Leizer some slippers. We went out into the field and found a deep pit that remained after potatoes had been stored in it. We dug and deepened the pit further, added posts to support it, and inside it we dug a second pit. We laid boards, brought in straw, and covered the second pit with sand, so that no one would find it. In a word, we did an excellent job. Everyone agreed that it was possible to stay in this hiding place for a number of days; meanwhile, Leizer and my brother set out to look for another place, and to find out if there were partisans in the area. They set out on Wednesday evening, planning to return after the Sabbath. On Friday morning, the Gentile came, frightened, and told me that the village was being searched. He quickly covered the exit [of our shelter]. Inside the pit, we lacked enough air. Somehow I poked a small hole in the wall and we were able to breathe through it. Toward evening, the Gentile returned. "Are you alive?" he asked, and he told us that they'd searched the entire area of the village and left only when it became dark. He was worried that they might return and "then they'll also search near me. I've kept you for as long as it possible, I can't do any more." I asked him to give us a few more hours; it was too early. "In another two hours, we'll go," I argued. He left. Meanwhile, I took my brother's two children [Feiga-Tzipka and Sara-Gitka] and pushed them

[Page 102]

through an opening that was made by moving the board. I brought them to the pit and sat them inside it. I returned. I sat and waited for the Gentile to come back. He returned, bringing with him two loaves of bread and six onions, and in a bag a little salt.

All day on the Sabbath, I waited for Chontza and Leizer to come, but they didn't show up. Nor did they return on Sunday. I didn't know what to think. More than a week went by with no sign of them. So I took the boy with me [Yerachmiel's son Leizer-Itza], left the three girls in the pit [Yerachmiel's daughter Sara-Esther and his brother Chontza's daughters Feiga-Tzipka and Sara-Gitka], and we went out. I knocked on the door of the house of a Gentile acquaintance. There was no answer. I asked them to come to the window, but nobody appeared. I raised my voice: "If Petra [Petro] doesn't come to the window, I won't move from here." I waited next to the window for another hour, maybe more, and finally he came out of the house and said, "Yerachmiel, what do you want? Why are you crying?" I asked him, "Did you hear anything about my brother and Leizer?" He replied, "On Thursday they shot both of them in the village of Rudva."[8]

You can imagine what I felt. The farmer brought out about four kilos of beans and gave them to me. I didn't know what to do or where to go. I no longer had a brother, a place to stay, or a slice of bread in my hands. I remained in the pit with the four "chicks." For me, the heavens had collapsed. I entered [the house of] a farmer and cried about my bitter fate. I received a loaf of bread from him, and we [Yerachmiel and his son Leizer-Itza] returned to the children [Yerachmiel's daughter Sara-Esther and his brother Chontza's daughters Feiga-Tzipka and Sara-Gitka]. On the way, we discussed whether to reveal the truth to them. I decided that I had an obligation to tell them, I couldn't keep all of it dammed up inside me. When we entered [the pit], I told them, "Children, I beg you not to cry; you no longer have a father, and Leizer also is no more. They shot them. As long as I live I'll protect you, and we'll live together. But if you cry now, I won't be able to stand firm." And so they didn't cry out loud. I saw only how tears fell silently from their eyes.

A number of days passed. The food was gone. I was lying in the pit and thinking: what to do? To go to the farmers' houses and ask for something was too dangerous. I was afraid that if they caught me, all of us would be killed. Late at night, I went out with my son to look for some food. We found another pit. In addition to a belt, I had a piece of rope. I tied them together, tied the rope under my son's arms and lowered him into the pit. Inside it were potatoes and beets. I passed him a sack, and he gathered these items into it. I pulled out the sack and the boy, and we returned to the children. We ate potatoes until we felt sick; they contained a lot of starch. Then we tried the beets and found that they were edible. Our meal became one beet in the morning, one at noon and one at night, a total of three beets per day for five people. From the beans [received earlier from the Gentile], I passed out 45 seeds to each child, taking for myself 55 seeds a day. When the beets were gone, I went out with the boy [Leizer-Itza, his son] to look for food in other pits. We didn't gather any more potatoes, only beets, radishes and carrots. One time the rope broke, and the boy fell into a deep pit. I got him out with difficulty. We found another place where there were vegetables, and we returned to the children.

Several days later, we went out again at night. It was dark and rainy. Hearing footsteps, we sought cover in the grass. Not far from us a policeman passed by, armed with a rifle. Later, we took a few more beets and returned to the children. I lived this way with the children for 102 days, on raw beets. The pit wasn't deep. The children could sit up in it, but I could only lie down or sit while bent over.

One Friday, I heard someone wandering around outside and saying, "What's this? Where did these footsteps come from?"

[Page 103]

and then moving away. I considered what to do, and decided to go and speak with the Gentile. I waited until Sunday. Early in the morning, I parted from the children and went out into the fields. I lay down in the standing wheat, not far from the farmer's house, and waited. I saw the Gentile woman take the cows out to pasture; after her, the Gentile went out with sheep. When he approached, I called out to him, "Jozef, Jozef!" He saw me: "Rachmiel, is that you? Maybe you want something to eat?" I answered that I didn't want to eat but wanted to talk to him about something else. "In a little while I'll come back," he said. He returned and asked what I wanted. I said to him, "I ask that you give me a place to hide." He answered, "It's summer now, why do you need a place with me? Here, all around you are many pits, go into one of them and live." And he pointed to one pit and another pit, and another one. I asked him who the pits belonged to, and he answered, "They're mine, but it's impossible for you to keep living in them. If I didn't know you were here, I wouldn't have to deal with it. But as it is --- tomorrow, Monday, I'll come to take apart your hiding place." I began to explain to him that I and the children were located there and asked him to give us permission to stay there, but he insisted that we leave immediately, that night. Finally, he agreed that we could remain for one more night. I found another pit; I and the boy brought boards and twigs. It became clear that this pit was very deep. I looked around the fields and found two chains for hitching horses. I attached them and went down inside the pit. Within two nights, I and my son prepared the place for ourselves. We returned to the children, and I told them that at night we'd move to the new shelter.

When it got dark, the Gentile came to me and said, "If you forsake your religion, I'll bless you." He took a prayer book out of his pocket, told me to kiss the book and continued, "Not far from here, near a tree, there's half a loaf of bread. Go and take it." We went there, took the bread, and continued to the other pit that we'd prepared. I put the children inside; I went down myself, and we all sat in the pit. I didn't notice that the Gentile was following us. Early in the morning, I heard someone walking around near the pit and then going away. After an hour someone came and called, "Yerachmiel, Yerachmiel!" I recognized the voice and replied, "Jozefa, what do you want?" "The place isn't for you," she said, "Leave here." I answered, "Today I won't go. Outside it's raining hard; I'll go tomorrow. Bring the police if you want, they can throw a grenade down on us. But today I won't go." To the children, I said, "Not far from here there's a cemetery. Maybe we'll go and dig a hiding place there: a pit?" The children agreed. I took the boy. We passed through the entire area of the cemetery to find a suitable place, but we had nowhere to put the sand that we dug while making a pit. So I gave up the idea.

The next day, Jozefa returned. I asked her to get her brother [Jozef]. She went to call him, but immediately came back and said that her brother was sick, but he'd ordered us to leave the village immediately. "They know you're located here and they'll catch you," she said. Her brother suggested that we go to the Zamosh [Zamosz] forest, where there were partisans.[9] She brought us a lighter as well as bread, butter and cheese. When it got dark, I took the children and set out on the road. After a short stay outside, the clear air began to affect the children and they fainted. I cared for them, and little by little they recovered and continued walking slowly. Daylight began to appear. I gave each child a little slice of bread. On our way, I found a field sown with peas. I laid the children between the furrows, covering them all with greenery, and we stayed there until evening. When it got dark, we continued to walk through fields and swamps, until we arrived at the bathhouse of Mikola Markovitz [Markowicz] on Saturday night. Without his knowing it, we crowded inside it until Monday morning. On Monday morning, I found the shepherd who was taking the cows out to pasture. I asked him to send

[Page 104]

his father to me. He came immediately. I began to plead that he rescue me and the children and permit me to build a hiding place near him. "I don't have a space for a hiding place," he answered, and continued, "I think you don't need one. Partisans come to me from time to time. I'll talk to them." I was very glad to hear this, but didn't show it. "When did they come?" I asked. "and when are they supposed to return?" "Maybe tonight," he replied. "Meanwhile, stay here in the bathhouse." The next day, he came and told me that they hadn't showed up. I asked for permission to stay an additional night in the bathhouse, but again no one came. Then I asked for permission to leave the children so that I could go out and look for the partisans myself, and to this he agreed. I put the three girls in the attic of the bathhouse; in the evening, I and the boy set out. We passed through 20 kilometers of fields and swamps, and arrived in the village of Okolitsa [Okolica, about 13 kilometers southeast of Braslav, near Rudawa]. I knocked at the house of a farmer. In reply to my question, he told me that there were partisans three kilometers away, in Zamosh [to the southwest of Okolitsa]. He suggested that I not go there at night, because they were likely to kill me [in the dark]. I waited for the daylight, and we set out. In Zamosh, they told us that there were no partisans. I asked a farmer again, quietly: "Are there partisans in the area?" and he answered that there were some eight kilometers away, in the village of Babiles [perhaps Bobyle, about eight kilometers southwest of Zamosh, in the middle of the forest]. We went there. I met a lad and asked, "Where are the partisans?" and he showed me a house nearby. I entered it. A man wearing a hat was sitting and sewing a saddle. He asked what I wanted, and I asked for the commander. He suggested that I sit down. He raised his face toward me and continued, "Are you interested in seeing some of yours (that is, Jews)? They're here, sitting in the stable." I hurried to the stable and indeed found many of my acquaintances; among them Shalom Gans from Slobodka, Yitzka Samovar, Yankel Shneider and his brother, and two more from Ikazna [Ikazn, about 14 kilometers east of Braslav]. To my question about when they'd arrived, they answered, "Just two days ago." From them I learned that the partisans weren't prepared to accept them into the *otriad,*[10] but they were giving them food and drink. I was also told that a commander and a commissar were there. I waited for evening, until they returned from somewhere and all of the men of the village gathered to hear the news. The commissar got up on a chair. In his speech, he promised to drive out Hitler even from Germany. The commander followed him and continued in the same vein, promising that someday the red flag would fly over Berlin. Afterward, I approached him and asked to be accepted into the *otriad*. He asked if I had a rifle; I said I didn't. "And whose boy is that?" he asked. "Mine," I answered, "and I've three more children with me." "I can't take you into the *otriad*, but there's a Jewish family camp here, join them," he said, and he went away.

I calculated my next step. I decided to move the children to the camp and hope for the best. I passed through fields and swamps and returned to the bathhouse. "Children, are you here?" I asked. "Yes," they replied. They told me that during the daylight hours a German unit had passed by, stopped a while to rest, and then moved on. I waited for the night; I took with me the four children [Yerachmiel's son Leizer-Itza and daughter Sara-Esther, and his brother Chontza's daughters Feiga-Tzipka and Sara-Gitka], and we set out on the road. I turned toward the villages that were under partisan control.

We walked slowly. Within two nights we arrived at Zamosh, and from there we continued to the village in daylight --- we had no place to stop and rest. I was accepted to work at a farmer's place [under partisan control]. I plowed fields and gathered crops; finally the children had something to eat. I didn't allow them to run around outside, because the partisans didn't want strangers to be seen in the village. After three weeks of work at the farmer's place, a sergeant of the partisans approached me and asked if I wanted to join them to work at the mill, and I agreed. There we did the grinding

[Page 105]

using the village method. The grindstones were operated using horses. I kept busy with the grinding, and the children sped up the horses when they were changed every hour. I continued to do this for a number of weeks. Once I saw three riders approaching the headquarters. After some time, the sergeant came and told me to bring oats for the three horses, 15 kilograms per horse. I asked, "Why such a large amount? The allocation is three kilograms per horse." "These are high-ranking officers," he explained. When I went to bring the oats, I went past the house where the officers were sitting and looked in --- and who did I see among them? The chairman of the regional committee who I'd worked for in Braslav as a driver. I put down the sacks, entered the room and stood next to the door. He recognized me and shouted, "Rachmiel, you're alive?!" "I'm alive," I replied, "and I'm glad to see that you're alive." He invited me to sit next to him with all the officers and commissars. After that, we went outside to talk. He introduced himself to me --- he was the top-ranking officer of the partisan movement in the region. He wanted to know about my situation. We talked a lot. I told him I had four children with me and couldn't get into the *otriad*. We reentered the room. "Who in the *otriad* do you wish to serve?" he asked me. I pointed to the officer Antonov.[11] He introduced me to Antonov as one who'd been his driver in the past, adding that I was very responsible and could do any job. The officer called the commander to him and ordered the sergeant to hand over to me responsibility for all quartermastering of the partisans [storage and distribution of provisions]. I was appointed to oversee the farm sector [farms that supplied the partisans], and carried out my work successfully. Things continued like this for three months. Then, one fine morning, our patrol returned and told us that the German army had been sighted in the villages nearby. The next day, the enemy approached the forest where we were located. We organized a defense and fought them for nine days, until our ammunition began to run out. We began to withdraw, keeping intact the framework of the brigades and the *otriads*. The Germans didn't pursue us; they preferred not to enter the forest. The officer [Antonov] suggested that I remain with him in the base. "What about the children?" I asked. "Take a wagon and send them into the forest --- to the partisans!" And so I did. I put them in a wagon, and told them what to do and gave them the password. But the guards wouldn't allow them to enter the area and sent them back.

News arrived that a large German army was preparing to lay siege to the forest. The officer suggested that I take the children to the family camp and then return. Patrols reported that the

Germans were close by and numbered in the thousands; the commissar ordered us to evacuate. I asked one of the partisans to take the children and avoid the field of fire. We'd only just left when the entire village went up in flames. I got the children and traveled with them to the Kozian forest, where the family camp was located. When I arrived, it became clear to me that it was in great confusion. I spoke with many people, asking them to take care of my children temporarily because I had to return to the *otriad*, but no one would help. I saw people gathering in groups and asked where they were going. Confused, they replied that they themselves didn't know. Night fell; we found a hut and went inside. During the night, I adopted another three children. They told me that everyone had left the camp.

At dawn, we went outside and heard the crying of a child, who'd certainly been forgotten. We returned to the camp. There we found nine partisans and two compassionate nurses. One was a Jewish woman from Kozian, Peshka Hoffman, and the second one was named Galina; with them was a wounded officer. They were angry that I'd brought the children to such a dangerous place. I promised to take the children far into the forest, to the area of the swamps, to a piece of higher ground between

[Page 106]

the swamps. I found a good place where I left the children and then returned to the base. I'd visit them at night, and this pattern continued for a number of days. Then German airplanes arrived and bombed the area. Fires broke out, and German soldiers hit us in a series of attacks. The children said, "Father, if they get close to us, start running and we'll run after you." Suddenly, enemy soldiers appeared! I began to run, and the children ran after me. While running, I heard my son shouting, "Father, wait for me; you watched over us all this time and now you're leaving us?" I stopped; I knew it was hard for them to run barefoot. When they reached me, we entered a dense wood, where we hid. We heard the shouts of the Germans. The sound of shooting reached us. And here . . . a German bullet passed through my daughter's head scarf [without harming her]. What luck!

After a rest, we kept going. Finally we escaped the encirclement! Then we encountered a farmer and his family, the two compassionate nurses from the *otriad*, and a partisan. Once more we entered the bushy vegetation so that we wouldn't be seen. From a distance, we saw how German soldiers trapped the partisan and the nurses. To the question "Who are you?" the nurses answered, "We're villagers from the area." The soldiers replied, "No, you're partisans!" and took them prisoner.[112] I think these soldiers were Ukrainians who were serving the Nazis. We stayed in the bushes for three days, and for three days we licked a bit of flour from a bag that I had with me. The shooting stopped, and we started to return to the base. I and the Gentile farmer were first, and the others followed us. The *zemlyanka*s [cabins partly buried in the ground] had been burned, and the supply storerooms for people and animals were still burning. We began to put out the fires. When the Germans returned and attacked the base, we fled once more to the swamps and hid in the tall grass. The children's feet froze. This time, the Germans wounded and killed Froika Boretz --- a lad from Gleboki who'd joined us. Again we returned to the base. We had food and everything good: potatoes, flour, salt, lard and beef in wooden barrels. Everything was protected, [buried] in the ground. I knew that a wounded officer had remained in the area, and I went to look for him. I reached the approximate place and called his name, "Kolya, Kolya!" but got no answer. I didn't know what had happened to him. As I turned to go back, I heard him calling my name: "Bilka, Bilka!" and indeed, it was he. I carried him to the children's hiding place. The partisans came to us occasionally to equip themselves with necessities for their units. In the forest I found our horses tied to trees, and I took them to the base. I received a letter from the officer of the *otriad*, in which he wrote, "I was glad to hear that you and the children weren't hurt in the attacks. In the last battles 22 partisans were killed, and there are many wounded." He asked that I continue to care for the wounded officer, and said that in a number of days he and his men would return to the base.

Two days later, I was asked to report to a certain place. I went there with Kanoil [sic, it's unclear who this refers to; perhaps Kolya, the wounded officer]. An officer and three soldiers who'd arrived from the east suggested that a few of us go eastward, toward the Soviet Union. But

I told them that when the liberation came, I wanted to return home. I asked that they take with them the wounded officer; I parted from him and went back to the partisans.

The reserves of supplies were almost used up. Sixteen fighters were sent to Belmont to bring cattle. They returned with 36 cows. Our *otriad* was allocated 10 of them. I and Leizer [Eliezer] Fisher[13] killed them, cut the meat, salted it, put it in barrels and buried them in the ground. Except for a few partisans who were killed in operations, the surroundings were generally quiet. A few weeks later, the scouts came again and told us that a German unit was preparing to attack the base. The commissar himself, at the head

[Page 107]

of a partisan unit, went out to meet the enemy, who was stationed in the nearby village. At dawn, the signal was given and the partisans went out to battle. They pushed the Germans back eight kilometers and caused them many losses. We killed 170 Germans. We took booty: artillery, machine guns, automatic rifles, ordinary rifles and pistols. We lost two partisans, and two others were wounded.

In a formation after the battle, the commissar praised a few of the fighters, among them Yankel Shneider. The commissar was also promoted. The next day, we went out to bury the German soldiers and their horses that had been killed in the battle and were spread out over the area, then we returned to the base and the daily routine.

Footnotes:

1. All of the men identified by name appear in the memorial book's list of victims in Braslav, except for Gedalia Shapira. Opsa was about 18 kilometers southwest of Braslav, and Dubina (Dubene) was 16 kilometers northwest of Braslav.
2. According to the *Encyclopedia of Camps and Ghettos 1933-1945*, Volume II-B (2012), the Dokshits Ghetto was established in November 1941 and suffered three Aktions in the course of its existence. In the first Aktion, in mid-March 1942, some 60 Jews were killed. In the second Aktion, in early May 1942, some 400-600 Jews were killed; presumably this is the event to which Mr. Biliak referred. In the third Aktion, on May 29, 1942, the Dokshits Ghetto was liquidated, with the loss of some 2,600 lives. The liquidation of the Braslav Ghetto began a few days later, on June 3.
3. Chona Biliak, also called Chonka and Chontza later in this account, was Yerachmiel's brother.
4. The account on pages 159-163 of this memorial book of Tzipora (Feiga-Tzipka) Toker (née Biliak), daughter of Chontza Biliak and niece of Yerachmiel Biliak, adds more detail to some of the events mentioned here.
5. The adults aren't identified here; the account is hard to follow.
6. In August or early September 1942, some 50 Jews in Opsa were transferred to the former ghetto in Braslav, to repopulate it after the original inmates had been slaughtered on June 3-5, 1942. Because the members of this second, new ghetto in Braslav were from Opsa, the ghetto was also called the "Opsa" Ghetto. It would be liquidated on March 19, 1943.
7. Belarussian word for shed.
8. This was presumably Rudawa, about 13 kilometers southeast of Braslav, near Belmont.
9. Zamosh was about 16 kilometers south of Braslav and about 10 kilometers south of Belmont. From Zamosh, large forests extended to the south and west, and southwest as far as Kozian, which was about 40 kilometers southwest of Braslav.
10. Russian word for a partisan military unit.
11. Presumably this was the leader of the Antonov detachment of the Shirokov brigade, which operated in the region to the south of Braslav.
12. The nurse called Peshka Hoffman in this account was perhaps Pesia Hochman from Kozian, a combat medic for the Spartak brigade. According to the *Lexicon Hagevura* (Biographical Dictionary of Jewish Resistance), published in Israel in 1965, she was captured at a partisan base while caring for the sick and wounded, and then tortured and shot. According to the Organization of Partisans, Underground Fighters, and Ghetto Rebels in Israel, she was killed in the Koziany forest on November 13, 1943.
13. The account of Eliezer Fisher, another native of Braslav who survived the massacre of the Braslav Ghetto in June 1942 and later joined the partisans, is on pages 155-158 of this memorial book.

[Page 108]

Tuvia Fisher
Son of Beila-Zelda [née Katz] and Baruch

Translated from the Hebrew by Laia Ben-Dov
Footnotes Added / Donated by Jeff Deitch

A.

Our survival after the destruction, which I, my wife [Chana, née Fisher], my brother Mottel [Mottel-Hirsh Fisher] and my brother-in-law Mottel [Fisher] experienced first-hand, is a miracle. Otherwise, it can't be understood: our flight from death at the time the ghettos in Braslav [Braslaw] were liquidated; the wandering from one Christian to another, begging for a place to sleep and a slice of bread; the running from place to place in the forest for weeks and months --- a place where we stayed during the day and moved at night. Entering, at great risk to our lives, the farmers' storehouses at night to warm up a bit and maybe get a piece of bread, because the hunger was great; and eating, more than once, food that was meant for cattle. We were pursued by the murderers day and night. Death lay in wait for us at each moment, and every careless movement endangered our lives.[1]

Yet despite everything, we survived. How? It shouldn't be assumed that our remaining alive was the result of bravery or wisdom granted to us or to others. In our family, we were four brothers and three sisters. Until the war broke out, I was a yeshiva student. I lived modestly in the atmosphere of the yeshiva, cut off from all else around me. I didn't strive for the good life. My existence was for my parents and for helping the community, "days" in the Ivia [Ivye] Yeshiva, the kitchen in the Slonim Yeshiva, and *chaluka*[2] money in the Mir Yeshiva. My brothers Zalman-Volf and Avraham differed from me completely. They were courageous activists fighting for a better life. Likewise, my sisters: Guta, Zlata and Rivka, young and full of life, striving for comfortable lives. All of them were lost in the storm of the Nazi destruction and I, the weak one, remained. How did it happen? I've thought about it for many years and have no answer except this: A higher power warned me at crucial moments and helped me through all my troubles. Religious feeling and faith assisted me during the fateful moments.

B.

When the Germans came to Braslav [in late June 1941], they took many Jews for labor on the railroad. We were about 200 Jews, who worked at stripping the bark from large logs. We did this in groups. Sometimes the Germans took out from among us groups of 10-12 men for so-called other work, and shot them. They also

[Page 109]

took Jews from my group, but passed over me. Once, after the railroad work, I was visiting the home of my father-in-law, Zalman-Yaacov Fisher. Because of the great heat, I left the house for a few minutes without my coat, on which was sewn the yellow Magen David [Shield of David]. As fate would have it, at that moment a Nazi supervisor passed by and asked me for my *Jude-schein* [labor permit]. As he did this, I saw his hand move to his pistol; it was clear to me that my life was in danger. The blood froze in my veins. Suddenly, I felt as if a hand pushed me backward and a voice called to me: "Flee!" I began running with all my strength, and the German ran after me. I ran a long way, until I came to an outhouse and rushed into it. For some reason, the German didn't see this and he lost me. My life was saved.

After four months of wandering from place to place [outside Braslav], in the cold and wet, thirsty and hungry, we who had survived the liquidation of the [Braslav] ghetto [on June 3-5, 1942] learned from a farmer that a second ghetto was being established in Braslav.[3] The Jews from Opsa were already in this ghetto. We decided to enter the ghetto despite the German prohibition. We were four people: me, my wife Chana [née Fisher], my brother Mottel [Mottel-Hirsh Fisher] and my brother-in-law Mottel [Fisher]. Torn and worn out, tired and hungry, the men among us with beards, we set out on the road to Braslav. The danger of being caught was great. Nevertheless, we entered the ghetto without being noticed by the murderers. For a time, we were invisible.

In the ghetto [the second ghetto in Braslav, also called the "Opsa" Ghetto], I got the idea of digging under the floor of the house. I disposed of the dug-out material by taking it up into the attic. A certain power pushed me to start the job immediately, even though by nature I wasn't a man of action. I devoted every minute to the work. Before the bunker was finished my brother-in-law Mottel came, frightened, and said the Germans were intending to liquidate the second ghetto. They surrounded the ghetto [around March 19, 1943]. The unfinished bunker saved our lives in these moments. When it became dark, we escaped from the place. We went into the house of Hertz Skopitz, which stood on the hill [of Braslav] next to the great cross. A Christian woman with her two daughters had already moved into the house, and my wife Chana knew them. We hid in this house, but after we'd been there two days the Germans turned it into a police station for locals who cooperated with them. Our situation grew very dangerous. At any moment, we could be discovered. To leave the house, we had to cross a high fence, hidden from the policemen who guarded it. They'd certainly start firing if they saw us, and it was unlikely that any of us would survive that. But here too, we escaped without injury. Many times, I felt guilty to have survived; I should have gone together with all my dear ones and loved ones. I was calmed only by the faith that my life depended not on me, but on a higher power that watched over me.

C.

[This paragraph jumps back in time, discussing the first Braslav Ghetto before it was massacred on June 3-5, 1942.] It's terrible to see the suffering of your daughter without being able to help her. I consider the binding of Yitzchak to be the cruelest test in the history of mankind, when Our Father, Abraham, took his only son to be bound at the command of the Creator. Many of us were tested by a similar fate, not through a command of G-d but by the German oppressor. With our own eyes we saw the suffering of our daughter [Chasia], who was just an infant in the ghetto [before June 3-5, 1942]. My father-in-law, Zalman-Yaacov [Fisher], would sometimes put his life in danger by going out in search of a drop of milk to keep her alive, but sometimes he couldn't find any. It was hard to see her suffering; we looked for different ways to help her. We knew the day would come when the Germans liquidated the ghetto, but we didn't know when it would happen. We wanted to take the child out of the ghetto. In discussion with Rabbi Avraham-Abba Zahorie,

[Page 110]
we said we'd put her in a Christian orphanage that was managed by a woman who was an acquaintance of Dr. Baretzki [Barecki]. We thought that --- when the war finally ended --- we'd be able to remove her from there with the help of an identifying mark on her body. We made all the arrangements to transfer her to the orphanage. We also transferred there the few possessions she had, but parting from her was very hard and was put off from day to day. She was the only ray of light for us in those dark days. Things were put off one day and then another day . . . until it was too late. Zalman-Yaacov carried her in his arms when the Jews of Braslav were marched to the pits [on June 3-5, 1942], led by the German beasts in human disguise.[4] Our daughter was among the million innocent Jewish children who were killed by the Nazis.

D.

At the time the Dvinsk Ghetto in Latvia was liquidated [sic] in 1941, some Jews who'd succeeded in escaping arrived in Braslav.[5] With these Jews came Rabbi Yisrael-Alter Fuchs, a learned man, great in Torah and knowledge of the world. Rabbi Fuchs, who was from Vienna in Austria, had become the rabbi of Dvinsk after the passing of the [Hasidic] rabbi of Rogatchov, the Gaon Rabbi Yosef Rosen [1858-1936]. Together with Rabbi Fuchs, the daughter of the Gaon, Mrs. [Rachel] Citron, now arrived in Braslav. She'd come to Dvinsk from the Land of Israel, from Jerusalem, to her father's grave.[6] The war had trapped her in Dvinsk. Both of them stayed in our house, which was a religious home. Our father was connected to all matters of religion and the congregation in Braslav. He was active in the yeshiva, a *gabbai* [caretaker] in the Old Synagogue and active in all the charitable matters in the town. When they [Rabbi Fuchs and Mrs. Citron] were in our house, we shared our meager food and made sure they had everything. Food was scarce and barely enough to sustain the soul. My mother, in poor health, took care of everyone. She'd get up early to prepare food for Rav [Rabbi] Fuchs, which was mostly potatoes. The Rav ate only one meal toward morning and would fast all day. He was sunk in Torah until late at night. Both of them, Rav Fuchs and Mrs. Citron, were with us until the ghetto in Braslav was liquidated on June 3, 1942 (18 Sivan 5702). They met their death on that day, together with [most of] the Jews of Braslav.

Footnotes:

1. Tuvia Fisher and his wife, Chana Fisher (whose photo appears above his on this page), were second cousins. Tuvia was the son of Baruch Fisher and Beila-Zelda Katz, grandson of Zelik Fisher and Guta, and great-grandson of Morduch Fisher. Chana was the daughter of Zalman-Yaacov Fisher and Chasia, granddaughter of Neftel Fisher and Lana, and great-granddaughter of Morduch Fisher. Their Fisher families had lived in Braslav since at least the time of Morduch, born ca. 1800.

   Both of the men named Mottel Fisher who are mentioned in Tuvia Fisher's account survived the war: Tuvia's brother Mottel-Hirsh (whose account is on pages 90-95 of this memorial book) and Mottel the brother of Tuvia's wife, Chana Fisher.

2. Before World War II, charity funds collected from Jews throughout the world for Jewish residents in Palestine. Ivia and Slonim were about 205 kilometers and 305 kilometers southwest of Braslav, respectively, and Mir was about 230 kilometers south of Braslav.

3. In August or early September 1942, some 50 Jews in Opsa were transferred to the ghetto in Braslav, to repopulate this ghetto after its inmates had been slaughtered on June 3-5, 1942. Because the members of this second, new ghetto in Braslav were from Opsa, the ghetto was also called the "Opsa" Ghetto. It would be liquidated on March 19, 1943. At the beginning of this account, when Mr. Fisher refers to "the time the ghettos in Braslav were liquidated," it's these two liquidations to which he's referring.

4. Rabbi Zahorie was also killed in the massacre on June 3-5, 1942, thus it's clear that in this paragraph Mr. Fisher is discussing events before June 1942.

5. Dvinsk, in Latvia, was 42 kilometers northwest of Braslav. Today it's called Daugavpils.

6. Rachel Citron, a widow, had come to Dvinsk from Palestine around 1936 to help compile and safeguard her late father's writings. Working in Dvinsk with Rabbi Fuchs, a devoted student of her father and his successor, she was able to publish several volumes of her father's writings and send copies of his notes and correspondence to New York City before fleeing to Braslav with Rabbi Fuchs after the German invasion on June 22, 1941. In accounts in this memorial book she's described as being from Jerusalem, but other sources say that she was from Petah Tikva.

   According to the *Encyclopedia of Camps and Ghettos 1933-1945*, Volume II-A (2012), the Dvinsk Ghetto was formed in July 1941 and the Jews of Dvinsk suffered large-scale massacres in July-August 1941 (with 5,400 to 7,600 killed) and November 1941 (with 3,000 to 6,000 killed). The ghetto wasn't liquidated in 1941 but continued to function, suffering a further massacre in May 1942. In October 1943 the ghetto was cleared, and the remaining ghetto inmates were transferred to concentration camps in Kaiserwald and Stutthof.

[Page 111]

Henka (Chana) Fisher
Daughter of Rachel and Leib Gurevitz

Translated from the Hebrew by Laia Ben-Dov
Footnotes Added / Donated by Jeff Deitch

A short time before the war broke out, our father, Leib, passed away after a continuous illness. We remained: my mother, Rachel; three daughters, Henka, Rivka and Chaya; and one brother, Idel-Meir. I was the oldest child in the family and also its only supporter, working as a seamstress. I was 20 years old when the war broke out [in June 1941]. We supported ourselves with great difficulty.

Our troubles began with the outbreak of war. The Germans, with the help of the local residents who were drafted to help them, drove us out of our house, took us behind the town and made us enter the large and boggy swamp. On the way, two of the Jews of the city were shot and killed.[1] They kept us in the swamp all night. The next day we were freed, and when we returned home we found that the Gentiles had stolen all of our possessions. We had no place to lay our heads.

After a short while, the Germans established the ghetto [formally on April 1, 1942]. It was located on [the former] Pilsudski Street. There they gathered the Jews from all the other streets and closed its entrances with barbed wire. With its establishment, the decrees began: Jews were forbidden to walk on the sidewalks and were ordered to attach yellow patches with the word "*Jude*" on their clothing. At night Germans or local police would come and arrest Jews to frighten them, releasing them the next day.

Two days before the destruction of the ghetto [on June 3-5, 1942], representatives of the Judenrat [Jewish Council], the teacher Mr. [Eliezer] Mazeh and Levi-Yitzchak Veinshtein, came to our house and told us that according to an order from the Germans they had to transfer a large group of young girls to Slobodka [about 11 kilometers northeast of Braslav] to clean an army barracks. We couldn't object to this; we also had no idea of what would happen. Our sister Chaya parted from us and set out; we never saw her again. [Later] we tried to investigate and find out, but we never learned anything. And so we never knew where she was buried. She was killed together with the entire group of girls.

Our brother Idel-Meir, who was 16 years old, and his friend Falka [Rafael] Kharat understood that it was dangerous to remain hidden [in Braslav]. They decided to leave the place and go to the town of Glubok [Glubokoye, about 70 kilometers southeast of Braslav], where two of our aunts lived. They thought, for some reason, that the situation would be better there, but in fact it wasn't so. The end was tragic; our brother was killed in the Glubok Ghetto.[2]

Hiding with us [in Braslav] were refugees from Kovno [about 230 kilometers southwest of Braslav]; a woman named Etel Vorin

[Page 112]
and Hirsheleh, her three-year-old son. The boy was hungry and thirsty and cried without stopping. The mother understood that her child's crying could reveal all the residents of the shelter to the Germans, and she asked that one of us strangle him. No one was prepared to do this. With her own hands, the mother strangled her son.

When the Jews of Yod [Jod, 25 kilometers southeast of Braslav] were massacred [on December 17, 1941], the Tzipin family, Chaim-Leizer and Chava, relatives and good acquaintances of ours, fled and came to us [in Braslav]. But pain and suffering were their lot. When the Jews of Yod were massacred, their three lovely daughters [Mina, Dvera and Tziva] had been caught and killed; they went to their deaths holding each other's hands.

When they began to discuss the coming destruction of the Braslav Ghetto, Chaim-Leizer suggested installing a hiding place in the cellar. They said it and did it: A number of neighbors got together, dug and built the hiding place. The dirt was spread between the garden beds of the vegetable garden behind the house. When the destruction began [June 3-5, 1942], 15 of us hid in the shelter. Because time was short, we were unable to prepare food beforehand. At night mother would go out, with her head wrapped so no one would recognize her, and bring drinking water from the well in the yard. This is how we lived.

Chaim-Leizer and Chava found no rest from their suffering and blamed themselves constantly for not doing enough to rescue their girls. They said that without them their lives weren't worth living, and they decided to leave the shelter and meet their deaths. One night, in complete darkness, they left the shelter carefully so that no one would see where they'd come from, and they disappeared.

My uncle Nachman-Chaim [Gurevitz] had a different end. First he had to pay for the poison, so to speak, before receiving it. Nachman-Chaim was a blacksmith, and this profession made him one of those who were necessary to the Germans. On the day when the destruction of the [Braslav] ghetto began [June 3-5, 1942], a gendarme came to his house early in the morning, woke him from his sleep and called him to shoe his horse. Nachman-Chaim got up, went to his smithy and faithfully did his work. When he finished shoeing the horse, the German said, "Now I'll pay you," pulled out his pistol and shot him to death.

From our hiding place, we'd hear people going around the house, breaking things and looking for Jews who were in hiding. We concluded that they'd find us before too much longer, so we decided to leave the shelter and flee, each going his own way to his own fate. We had nowhere to go, because we had no Christian acquaintances in the villages.

One very rainy night, we left the shelter and spread out, with each heading in a different direction. Very frightened, my mother, my sister and I snuck out of the town, and continued to walk along the shore of the lake. In this way, we arrived at the village of Krasnosletzi [Krasnosielce, about four kilometers west of Braslav]. In the darkness we saw a bathhouse; we went inside and took off our wet clothes. We were very tired and hungry, and we fell asleep. The next morning, we sat there and took care so that nobody saw us, but there was no reason to stay there; we knew that in the end people would find us. After midnight, when we were very hungry, we left the bathhouse and walked along the road leading to Dvinsk [42 kilometers northwest of Braslav and now called Daugavpils]. Once in a while, when a car appeared, we went down off the road so that no one would see us. And so we walked until we reached the village of Urban [Urbany, 11 kilometers northwest of Braslav]. Next to the road stood a house with small windows, from which a weak light was shining. Trembling from cold and fear, we knocked on the door and waited. The door opened and an elderly woman, a Christian, asked, "What do you want?" We told her that we'd come from Braslav and were very hungry, and we asked for a bit of bread. She took us into her house and gave each of us a slice of bread. When we stood up to leave, she said to us, "Where will you go on such a rainy night?" She took pity on us and gave us a place to sleep on the warm stove.[3] We felt like we were in the Garden of Eden. When we woke in the morning, we saw that the woman wasn't

[Page 113]

there and we were alone in the closed house. We grew very frightened with worry that she had gone to the police to tell them Jewish women were hiding in her house. We waited for what would happen. Suddenly, we heard her opening the door and coming in. She looked at us and said, "I understand your situation; if you leave the house, they'll catch you and kill you. So please stay in the house, and with G-d's assistance I'll help you as much as I can." She told us she was very poor, life was hard but her food was just enough for her. She was religious, a nun, and was always crossing herself and praying.

The same morning that she shut us in her house, it became clear to us that she'd gone to the village priest and told him she'd taken us into her house out of pity, but she didn't know what to do next. The priest, a good-hearted man, listened to her and said, "You've done nothing bad. On the contrary, hide them if you're able, and I'll help you as much as I can. When you come to confession, if they're still with you just say in Polish 'They're here,' and I'll know they're with you." The woman returned home, satisfied that the priest didn't object to what she'd done and had even promised to help her. In the house, she raised a number of boards in the ceiling and told us to go up into the attic and sit there quietly. She warned us not to talk among ourselves and not to cough, Heaven forbid, so that no one would know we were up there. She brought a few rags and gave them to us to cover ourselves. Once a day, she brought up a slice of bread and some water. We knew that she was sharing with us the little she had, and that without the priest's help she too would face starvation. We couldn't pay her a thing, since we had nothing; we'd escaped with only our souls.

The name of this good woman was Josefa Savitzkia [Sewickaja]. Since she was religious, she'd bring us Christian holy books and ask that we read them and learn the prayers by heart. She hoped that if we remained alive we'd convert to her faith, and perhaps I and my sister would marry Christian boys. She said she had two nephews who we could marry; G-d would certainly forgive us and we'd be as if born again.

She listened to news from the villagers and told us how Jews from Braslav and other places were seized and killed, and also how the Germans executed Christian families for hiding Jews in their houses. She knew that her life too was in great danger.

In the attic there was a small opening, through which we could see everyone who passed by or traveled on the road. We saw a large German army: tanks, artillery and machine guns going to the front. We saw the local police, who sometimes were more terrible than the Germans. We dreamed of a day when the war would end, though sometimes we lost sight of that hope.

Then winter arrived. Strong winds, with falling snow piling up on the roof and in the village. It turned cold. It was difficult to stay strong in these conditions. When she saw us frozen with cold, Josefa darkened her two small windows and took us down into the house at night, but this continued for only a short time. One night, her nephew knocked on the door. We were very frightened. She gave him what he wanted and he left without seeing us, thanks to the dark. But from then on, she was afraid to let us stay in the house. Under the floor there was a pit dug for storing potatoes in the winter, and so we went down there. It was warmer there than in the attic under the roof; this was a small consolation.

Our problem was my little sister, Rivka. She was 12 years old. The hunger bothered her very much and made her cry. Usually we were very hungry and wanted to leave the pit and eat bread

[Page 114]

until we were full. We'd look at each other and see how very thin we were getting, growing weak from our troubles and hunger. It was a long time since we'd washed in a bathhouse, and the lack of personal hygiene was a great burden.

More than once we asked ourselves, why is fate so cruel to us? What was our sin? We hadn't stolen, we hadn't killed. Our lives had only just begun, why did we have to struggle with death? Why didn't we lose hope that G-d would hear the cries from our hearts and the day would come when we too would be free like all the nations of the world? Sometimes we'd hear the playing of a harmonica, the singing and dancing of the villagers; our eyes would tear up and we'd lose heart.

I remember we were in great danger when the Germans conducted a hunt for the partisans. A large army took part in the sweep, and German soldiers were billeted in the villagers' houses. Our Christian woman came running and ordered us down into the pit, covering the opening with a rug. Six Germans slept on the floor of the house for three nights, while we sat below in the pit, hungry and frightened. Then they left the house and moved away from the village.

Fierce battles took place in our region when the Germans withdrew, after unceasing pressure from the Red Army. Shells whistled above us, and houses in the village were burned. We were afraid that our house too would be burned. We went out with the Christian woman and lay in a ditch. Suddenly three German soldiers appeared and asked us, in German, if we'd seen any Russian soldiers in the area. We told them in Polish that we didn't understand. When they saw that we were only women, they left us and went away.

After fierce battles, the Germans withdrew and the Russian army arrived [around July 1944]. Out of fear, we continued to sit in our hiding place. The Christian woman came and said to us, "Now you don't need to be afraid, you're free. The Russians are here. The Germans left and they won't return." We hugged her, and all of us burst into tears of joy. I never kept a diary, but I remember very well all the trials and tribulations we experienced from the beginning of the war. How could I not remember this wonderful woman, Josefa Savitzkia, who shared her poor bread and humble house with us and put her own life in danger for our sake? We said goodbye to Josefa; we resolved to stay in touch with her and invited her to visit us in Braslav. Then we set out on the road.

The problem was how to get to Braslav. We went out to freedom after two years and two months, during which we'd been hidden by the Christian woman. Because we'd been sitting in one place for such a long time, it was difficult to walk. We moved step by step, arm in arm so as not to fall. Whoever saw us would stop and rub his eyes, because we looked like living skeletons, only skin and bones and stumbling feet; our feet could hardly carry us. We sat on the side of the road for a short rest. We saw a car approaching; it stopped nearby and inside it were Russian soldiers. They looked at us and couldn't believe their eyes, they'd never seen people as thin as we were. They asked where we came from and where we wanted to go. Then they helped us get into the car and made a place for us to sit. At the entrance to Braslav, they dropped us off. We walked looking in all directions, hoping we might see someone we knew. Near the flour mill, we met the first Jew we'd seen since leaving the house. This was Elchik [Eliahu] Shmidt. We were happy to see him and cried from excitement. He took us to the house of Falka Katz, where we found Chaim Kagan, Yankel-Velvel Shapira and his brother Shlomo, Chalvina Pinchov[4] and others, who like us had come out from their hiding places and reached the town. Elchik gave us food, but we were afraid to eat lest it harm us, since we'd eaten so little for so long.

[Page 115]

After a week had passed, a man came from the town government and asked that everyone who owned a house to go to live in it, to prevent others from taking possession of it. We went to our house, and there we found destruction. The windows and doors were broken; the walls were destroyed; the roof leaked, and rain was coming inside. The rooms were empty and deserted --- no beds, tables, chairs, bedding or clothing --- and hadn't we left an orderly home filled with good things? A few men came to help us, and somehow we organized the house. At night we were afraid to stay in it, because rumors were being spread about gangs of murderers, mainly men who'd served in the German police. Therefore, we asked Shlomo Shapira and his wife to sleep at our house. Elchik visited us frequently and tried to help as much as he could.

Not far from us, large-scale fighting was still taking place. Institutions hadn't yet organized themselves to provide food to the population. Bread was passed out only according to ration slips and sometimes there weren't even any potatoes, but we were glad that we were free.

I began to work as a seamstress. Rivka started working as a telephone operator at the post office. While working for the villagers I also received food from them: milk, eggs, butter and cheese. Sometimes we'd join together and go to "the pits" --- the place where the Germans and their collaborators had killed our dear ones: thousands of Jews from the town and the surrounding area. They were taken like sheep to be slaughtered: We'd had no weapons to protect ourselves and weren't prepared spiritually to do so. One's heart broke at seeing the large pits where those pure, innocent souls were buried. These visits would end with the prayer "El Malei Rachamim"[5] ["G-d, Full of Mercy"] and the Kaddish. My request, my wish and my prayer are that our children and all the children of Israel --- wherever they are --- will never know and never experience the things that happened to us.

We continued to stay in touch with Josefa; she was like a dear mother to us. Despite the scarcity, we shared our few possessions with her. She'd visit us frequently and never went home with empty hands. We also visited her and brought her things that she needed. When guests came to us, we'd travel with them to her village to show them the little attic and the potato pit under the floor where we'd hidden.

The miracle that we experienced was one of the rarest things in the world. Equally rare was to find a woman, a nun, religious and faithful like Josefa. She saved our lives.

One day toward morning, when it was still dark outside, we heard knocks on the door. This frightened us. In fear, we approached the door and asked, "Who's there?" "It's me, Josefa," came the answer. We were very happy she'd come. She entered, frozen and wet from the rain, looking tense. "What happened?" we asked, and she told us in a choked voice that the priest had been arrested. During the night men of the NKVD[6] had come, taken him from his house and imprisoned him in Braslav. We calmed her down and promised to do everything that we could to free him. We gave her clothes to change into and ate breakfast together. Afterward, I went to the house of the police [NKVD] officer and was received nicely. I knew his Jewish wife; I'd sewn all her clothes. I told them the purpose of my visit and asked for their help in freeing the priest. I pointed out that thanks to him we'd been saved from the clutches of the Germans, and he'd helped the partisans a great deal. The officer promised to help and invited me to return in the evening. Before going off to work, he told me he'd received an order to arrest all the priests, because it was known that they'd cooperated with the Germans and now they were acting against the Soviet government. I remained sitting with his wife, and again I asked for her help. It seemed to me that they were convinced this priest was a decent man

[Page 116]

and we had enough reasons to testify to his goodness.

Toward evening, I returned to the police officer's house. He told me the priest was well and suggested that the three of us --- me, my mother and my sister --- write and sign a statement that the priest had rescued us and that thanks to him we remained alive, and also that he'd helped the partisans.

We went to the NKVD and signed such a document, with two of the partisans. The next day, the priest was freed from prison. Josefa hadn't returned to her house, because she didn't believe he'd be released. Suddenly the door opened, and the priest walked in. The joy in the house was tremendous. He knew we'd worked on his behalf, and he said that he'd never forget our help. We replied that we'd never forget his help in saving us. We made a nice reception for the priest and the Christian woman; we accompanied them to the bus and parted from them there. Sometime later, in 1958, the priest received permission to emigrate to Poland. Before his journey, he came to say goodbye. He gave us his address in the city of Gdansk [about 580 kilometers southwest of Braslav] and asked that we visit him if we came to Poland.

Until we left Braslav, we helped Josefa Savitzkia with everything. After we made *aliyah* to Israel in 1960, we managed to send her two packages. In 1961, we received a letter that Josefa had passed away. We will always remember her and what she did for us.

One day, representatives from the town institutions [in Braslav] visited us and asked if we could host a few soldiers in our house for a number of days. These soldiers came to gather potatoes for their units. Of course, we agreed. Among those who came was a Jewish officer who was a lieutenant, in his civilian life an engineer. While he was with us, he fell in love with my sister Rivka, and a short time later they were married and settled in the city of Sverdlovsk [now Yekaterinburg, some 2,200 kilometers east of Braslav].

I too was lucky. Zalka Fisher from Yod, who I knew from the years of my childhood, was released from his service in the Red Army after the war and returned to Yod, but he didn't find anyone from his family. He moved to Braslav, and within a short time we were married.

In 1960, we made *aliyah* to Israel: I and my husband, my sister and her husband, and our dear mother. We have a son, a daughter and four grandchildren.

Footnotes:

1. The two were the ritual slaughterer, Shlomo Zilber, and Chaim Milutin. Their killings are said to have taken place on June 27, 1941, shortly after the Germans entered Braslav (Braslaw).

2. According to the *Encyclopedia of Camps and Ghettos, 1933-1945*, Volume II-B (2012), a ghetto had been established in Glubokoye in October-November 1941; Jews from nearby towns were also brought there, raising the ghetto population to 6,000. On June 19, 1942, a massacre of some 2,200-2,500 of them was carried out, but unlike the Braslav Ghetto a large population was also kept alive to work.

   Later the Germans decided to raise the population of the Glubokoye Ghetto, as a way to attract the Jews who were scattered among the region's forests. Eventually the ghetto population rose again, to 7,000. By 1943, Glubokoye was serving as a temporary refuge for Jews in western Belorussia who weren't in the forests. As partisan activity in the region increased, the Germans finally decided to liquidate the ghetto, announcing a deportation on August 20, 1943. When the ghetto responded with armed resistance, the Germans set fire to it, killing some 5,000 inmates. Some Jews managed to break out and join the partisans; it's estimated that about 60-100 ghetto inmates survived the war.

3. In Russia, Belorussia and the Ukraine, ovens were traditionally made of brick masonry that retained heat for long periods of time, and their outer surface was safe to touch. People could sleep on top of the oven to keep warm.

4. The account of Chalvina Pinchov is on pages 393-396 of this memorial book. The Hebrew in this memorial book gives his first name as Chalvina; a more common variant of the name is Chlavna.

5. A Jewish prayer for the soul of the deceased, usually recited at the graveside.

6. Narodnyi Komissariat Vnutrennikh Del (People's Commissariat for Internal Affairs): The Soviet law enforcement and intelligence agency that existed from 1934 to 1946, after which it evolved into the KGB.

[Page 117]

Yetta (Yentka) Vishkin[1]
Daughter of Fania and Rafael Fisher

Translated from the Hebrew by Laia Ben-Dov
Footnotes Added / Donated by Jeff Deitch

Our family in Braslav [Braslaw] was eight souls: my parents, Rafael and Fania; my two brothers, Yankel and Naftali [Neftel]; and my three sisters: Esther, Rivka and a baby girl named Chasia, who was born in [January] 1943 in the second ghetto;[2] I never saw her. I was the oldest girl and the only survivor of all my family.

My father dealt in the meat trade, and our economic situation was quite good. My parents planned to immigrate to the United States; the documents were already prepared, but the war that broke out disrupted our plans. Conditions changed for the worse, life became difficult. Many people were exiled to Siberia. Private commerce was forbidden, and it became hard to obtain food. But nobody thought that even worse times lay ahead.

In the summer of 1941 [June], the Germans entered our town. A few days later, they gathered all the Jews of the town and took us to the swamps. On the way, they killed Shlomo [Zilber] the *shochet* [ritual slaughterer] and the young man Chaim Milutin. They kept us in the swamps all night while allowing the Christian residents to rob our houses. The next morning, they allowed us to go home.

The Germans demanded that the Jews work for them. The women were drafted to clean their lodgings, and the men were kept busy loading logs at the train station for shipping to Germany and doing other jobs.

Life became very difficult. It was hard to obtain food and wood for heating. Opposite us were Fisher's storerooms for flax, and we'd take the refuse from there for heating.

Rumors reached us of the destruction of Jewish communities in the nearby towns, and the shipment of Jews to the death camps. Many fled from the massacres and arrived in Braslav. We accepted them and shared with them the little we had. My mother's cousins Leib, Gitta and Ida Gravitz fled from the city of Dvinsk[3] in Latvia, and crowded in with us. Ida's husband and her two children were killed in Dvinsk. The Gravitzes knew a Christian family named Shcherbinski [Szczerbinski] who bought in the market in Braslav. This family had a farm near the village of Ikaznia [Ikazn, 14 kilometers east of Braslav], and they agreed to hide the Gravitz family.

My father decided to build a hiding place in the basement of our house. With my cousin Mottel Fisher, the two of them installed double walls in the basement.[4] The entrance

[Page 118]

was through a clothes closet in our house. My father, who was a member of the Judenrat [Jewish Council], tried to request that the Germans ease up a bit on the living conditions in the ghetto --- but without success.

On June 3, 1942, the Germans surrounded the [Braslav] ghetto and took the Jews out to be slaughtered. Collaborators from the local Christian population helped them. All of us entered our hiding place, and together with us came some of our relatives: Chana and [her husband] Tuvia Fisher, Chona and [his wife] Sonia Fisher and their sons Avrameleh and Berka, my cousin Mottel Fisher and his wife Liuba and their daughters Sonia and Racheleh; my cousin Chaya-Merka [Fisher] and a couple from the town of Yod [Jod, 25 kilometers southeast of Braslav].[5]

From the hiding place, we heard the Germans entering and taking our grandmother Lana [Fisher] and her two sons, Zalman-Yaacov and Yehoshua. My grandmother was a lovely woman, a nice, elderly lady. She was killed by the Nazis. I remember more, that when we were sitting in the hiding place we suddenly heard footsteps and a man's voice: "Fisher, if someone's hiding here, come out --- the Germans promise they won't kill anyone else. This is Ribash speaking to you." I don't know who this Ribash was, but I'll never forget his voice. The Germans took him to all the houses to look for Jews who were hiding. They forced him to do this.

My father signaled to us with his hand to be quiet. At that moment, Sonia Fisher's boy began to cry [which one, Avrameleh or Berka, isn't stated]. Avraham, from Yod, closed the boy's mouth with his hand and quieted him. When the Germans and Ribash left, it became clear that the boy had suffocated from lack of air. He was buried behind our house.

We stayed in the hiding place for two nights. On the third night, we went outside and left Braslav. I don't know where the rest of the people went. My father sent me and my brother Naftali to the Shcherbinski family, where the Gravitz family was hiding. My father divided us among different places, with the idea that family members shouldn't all be in one place during the searches. My mother, and with her the rest of the children, hid at a farmer's house in the village of Matseshe [Maciesze, 13 kilometers southeast of Braslav]. My father went to look for a hiding place for himself, and stayed for a length of time with the Christian Matulka. When my brother and I arrived at the place, they took us into the storehouse, where there was a hidden pit covered with straw.

The Shcherbinskis were wonderful people. The head of the family, Danat, and his wife, Josefa, had two small daughters and a nephew, whose name was Vladek [Wladek]. They brought us food every day. Partisans or Jews who'd succeeded in fleeing came to their house more than once, and they helped and fed each one. Once, during the night, partisans came to Shcherbinski's farm and demanded weapons from him. He told them he didn't have any. They didn't believe him and threatened to kill him. Having no choice, he told them that Jews from Dvinsk and Braslav were hiding in his house. One of the partisans said he was from Braslav and wanted to see the hidden people, to make sure. After Shcherbinski revealed the hiding place to them, the partisans left him alone. The partisan from Braslav was Chaim Burat.

I don't have the words to describe the big hearts of these people. Unfortunately there weren't many like them. They lived always in fear and put their lives in danger. Even their small children didn't know we were there. But their maid began to suspect that her masters were hiding Jews; she told the village head that she'd seen Josefa entering the storehouse with a pail of food. The head of the village was a friend of the Shcherbinskis, and he told them of the defamation. After that, he invited the family and the maid to come see him. When Josefa heard the accusation, she demanded that a search of their house be made, and if the maid's accusation proved false and there were no Jews, she asked the village head to put the maid in prison and even have her shot. The maid was terrified and apologized for everything. She said that she'd invented the story and begged for forgiveness.

[Page 119]

At the beginning of 1943, we learned that a second ghetto had been established in Braslav for the Jews who had nowhere to go and had returned to the town. We also found out that our parents were there. We wanted to see them, and we decided that Naftali would go to them. Vladek Shcherbinski drove him to the approaches to the town, and my brother arrived in the ghetto on his own. After a few days, my parents sent him from there to return to me. He left the ghetto, went out of the town and was supposed to meet Vladek on the way and return with him to us. Unfortunately, Germans and local police who knew him encountered him on the way. They shot him and buried him right there. At the war's end, I transferred his body to the pits, to the place of the [Braslav] massacre, and buried him there.

I wrote to my parents and asked them to flee. Vladek, who traveled to Braslav, took the letters and smuggled them into the ghetto. My father also wrote several letters to me. Then, in March 1943, we heard that the Germans had liquidated the second ghetto.

In the summer of 1944 we already knew the Germans were losing the war, and they were burning the villages as they withdrew. We learned that a German unit was located nearby, in Ikaznia, and was sweeping through the neighboring villages. Because of the risk of fire, we were forced to leave the storehouse. In the yard of our house was a giant tree, with a thick, hollow trunk and an entrance that allowed hiding inside it. The four of us went inside the tree. The owners piled furniture and other items in front of the opening, as if to rescue their property from a fire. The Germans arrived and stayed in the yard for two days. We stood, squeezed together, inside the tree without moving. When we finally came out, we were swollen, exhausted and broken.

The Germans fled, and the Russians entered and freed the region. A few days later, my cousin Mottel Fisher, who'd been hiding with some villagers with his sister Chana and her husband Tuvia [Fisher] and Masha and Mendel Maron, came to the Shcherbinskis' house. Mottel told me about the destruction of the second ghetto in Braslav, and brought me the sad news of the death of my parents and my little sister Chasia, who hadn't yet reached a year of her life, as well as the rest of the members of the family. It became horribly clear that I was the only survivor of all my family. I went to live with my cousins in the city of Dvinsk. The Shcherbinski family left the village of Kamionka [13 kilometers northeast of Braslav]; the head of the family, Danat, passed away. His wife Josefa, her daughters and Vladek left Russia, moved to Poland and they live in the city of Konin [this might refer to a city of that name in central Poland].

At the end of the war, I immigrated to the United States. From there, I traveled to visit them [the Shcherbinski family]. I'll never forget them. They put their lives and the lives of their children in danger to save Jews.

Footnotes:

1. A prewar photo of Yetta's father, Rafael Fisher, and her mother, Fania/Feiga (née Kremer), appears on page 36 of this memorial book. They're standing in the old Jewish cemetery in Braslav next to the gravestone of Fania's mother, Esther.
2. "Second ghetto" refers to the second Braslav Ghetto, which contained some 50 Jews from Opsa who'd been transferred to Braslav in August or early September 1942 to repopulate it, after the inmates of the first Braslav Ghetto had been slaughtered on June 3-5, 1942. The second ghetto was also known as the "Opsa" Ghetto, since it contained residents of Opsa. This second Braslav Ghetto would be liquidated on March 19, 1943.
3. Dvinsk, now called Daugavpils, was 42 kilometers northwest of Braslav.
4. Yetta Fisher was the daughter of Rafael Fisher and Fania Kremer, granddaughter of Neftel Fisher and Lana, and great-granddaughter of Morduch Fisher. Neftel and Lana Fisher were also the grandparents (through their son Zalman-Yaacov) of Mottel Fisher and his sister Chana, making Mottel and Chana first cousins of Yetta.

Chana Fisher was married to her second cousin, Tuvia Fisher, and Yetta was also a second cousin of Tuvia's. Tuvia Fisher's account appears on pages 108-110 of this memorial book. The account of Mottel-Hirsh Fisher, a brother of Tuvia's, appears on pages 90-95. The account of Eliezer Fisher, their first cousin, appears on pages 155-158. (The Chana Fisher married to Tuvia differs from the Henka/Chana Fisher who was the daughter of Leib Gurevitz and whose account appears on pages 111-116.)

5. Chana Fisher and Tuvia Fisher, as mentioned in the earlier footnote, were Yetta's married cousins. Chona/Chonon Fisher, a brother of Chana Fisher and Mottel Fisher, was married to Sonia. Mottel Fisher, the brother of Chana and Chona, was married to Liuba. Chaya-Merka was a sister of Chana, Chona and Mottel.

Of this group, the survivors were Chana and Tuvia Fisher, and Mottel Fisher. The identity of the couple from the town of Yod isn't known for certain.

[Page 120]

Like Arrows in the Hands of a Warrior Are the Children of One's Youth . . .[1]

Translated from the Hebrew by Jerrold Landau
Footnotes Added / Donated by Jeff Deitch

The young people ́ . . .

Like a pink crystal palace; dreams and hopes, hopes for the future, enchantment and magic. All of these were wiped out, trampled under the cruel, barbaric hooves of the Nazi beast.

In terrible conditions, in hunger, oppression, and degradation, in the shadow of torture and death, the Jewish young people in the ghetto found the force of will and a ray of bright light in meetings and incidental discussions. They didn't lose hope, the faintest hope, for a better tomorrow. We see testimony to this in the "memento" albums they wrote to each other, to their male or female friends, in the darkness of oppression.

Here are some of these mementos written in Hebrew, Polish, Russian and Lithuanian by young people from Braslav [Braslaw] and other places, in the album of Yenta [Yetta] Fisher.[2]

It's important to note that these mementos are from the end of 1941 until June 1944, just before liberation, through all the tribulations of hell --- slaughter, torture, hunger and utter want.

A free translation of the mementos has been made, although the content has been strictly preserved.

A Memento!!!

Oh! Do not tell of the depth of your suffering
Do not say that you are desperate and lost
That the cruel world has frozen your heart.
Oh! Think only: I will find calm.

As the pain in your heart grows
Even if your spirit often falls
The ground will support you even more strongly
And your soul will absorb more calmness and quiet.

So on with the journey!
In the battle for truth you will suffer for your relatives,
Raise up your desire for happiness for your fellow Jews
And pay no heed if you are met with revulsion.

--- Written to you by your friend: G. S. (Skopitz)

A Memento!!!

Hey, to you with a Jewish heart and the soul of an angel
Love your fate with suffering and storms
Do not lower your head in the face of disaster
Hey, comfort to broken hearts . . .

--- Written by your friend: H. S. in Braslav, October 20, 1941

[Page 121]

To the honorable Vladislav [Wladyslaw] on his birthday!
We, your friends, bring you flowers from our land
And wish you perpetual happiness
We will never forget you
For your good feelings and ties
We will thank you without bounds
We will love you and wish you happiness
Until the wedding and after
Enjoy good life with love, friendship and peace.
Be blessed by G-d
As you deserve,
In wealth, good luck, and praise
With diamonds in a golden frame.

--- Your friend, June 27, 1944

This refers to the nephew of Danat and Josefa Shcherbinski [Szczerbinski], who hid and saved several families. [The nephew was Wladyslaw, nicknamed Wladek; Danat and Josefa also hid and saved people.]

A Memento!

There are many more drops in the cup of your fate
That you must suffer, and drink slowly to the end . . .

--- Written by H. S., October 20, 1941
The writer was Hirsh Skopitz.

A Memento!

We do not find our friends through conversation
It is possible to identify them only in hard times
When hardship overtakes them and they shed tears
This is your friend, the one who weeps with you.

--- Writer: Ida, October 15, 1943
Written by Ida Gurevitz while she was hidden by the farmer Shcherbinski.

[Page 122]

A Memento!

Do not be sad, my friend, that is not for you,
All your life is still ahead of you
You shed many tears
And you do not know
When you will return home.
Everything is so sad and cruel,
Everything happened suddenly
However, the time will come
When we take revenge against the enemy
Therefore, gird yourself, my friend, with patience
The day of liberation will arrive
And we will go up on the shining path
And you will be able to rest from all the tribulations.
Then we will remember and exalt the friendly people
Who saved us.
We will spread throughout the world the names of the saviors
And to vex our enemies, the saviors will receive their due
As we wish them ---
Much happiness, health, praise
And diamonds in gold frames.

--- Written by Ida: September 25, 1943

The sun is shining, spring has arrived
The flowers are blooming, nature has risen to life
Why am I so sad and heavy of heart?
Why am I waiting, for whom do I have pity?

No! I am not waiting for anything from G-d,
But I am sorry over the past,
I am searching for freedom and peace
I want to forget and fall asleep
So that I can wake up and take revenge on the enemy executioners
For the innocent blood that they spilled
May the murderous executioners not remain alive,
May the truth be perpetuated
In a place where hatred reigned,
May the blood of the murderers be spilled as rain from the sky
And their leader be destroyed along with them.

Written by Ida: May 10, 1943

[Page 123]

I am prepared to kill the enemy
And to destroy the executioner
May they receive their due
He murdered many people
And he must be wiped from the face of the earth
Guess, who killed him?

--- Written by A. N., October 10, 1943
Apparently the words refer to a collaborator who was taken out to be killed.

When these difficult times pass,
When the deep tragedies and tribulations pass
And you find yourself in a different world,
Before you a new era opens.
You will live and enjoy
Love and rejoice,
And then ---

Do not forget all that happened
Try to help
All the unfortunate and oppressed
All those alone, childless, and degraded
All who are lost and depressed . . .

--- The signature of the writer can't be deciphered. November 10, 1943

A Memento!!!

It was good that we knew each other
It was good to live together
But it is difficult for us to part
When we must
Say the word "Shalom."

--- From your friend R. Tzirlin, October 19-21, 1941

Footnotes:
1. Psalm 127:4.
2. Her account of her experiences during the war is on pages 117-119 of this memorial book.

[Page 124]

Anna (Niuta) Zelikman
Daughter of Rachel and Yaacov Kantor

**Translated from the Hebrew / Donated by Jon Seligman
(Dedicated to relatives from Slobodka who perished
and to Yasha and Ewa Zelikman, the children of Anna)**

**Revised Based on Laia Ben-Dov's Translation /
Footnotes Added by Jeff Deitch**

I remember that sunny Sunday morning, a day of rest and rosy thoughts. [June 22, 1941, the day the USSR was invaded.] As was usual in those days, the radio was on. The speech by the Soviet foreign minister, [Vyacheslav] Molotov, struck us like thunder on a clear day and changed our lives in an instant. There was no panic at first; most people trusted in the strength of the Red Army. Everyone hoped that the battles would be short, ending in a Soviet victory.

A few days passed, and the news that reached us was incomplete and discouraging. Some people tried to flee to the east, gathering up what they could in whatever was available: wagons and bicycles. The young people left on foot, and in some cases adults accompanied their children.

The members of my family, who worked with Soviet citizens, succeeded in organizing a truck. My mother, my brother, my sister, I and all the rest of the family members loaded onto it some of our possessions. We set out full of hope, but our happiness was short-lived indeed. The police stopped us and ordered us and our possessions out of the truck; they needed the vehicle for themselves --- to catch saboteurs. Broken and disappointed, we returned home. I want to emphasize that this didn't happen only to us; some other families (Kort, Eidelson and others) reached the [pre-1939] border only to be turned back by the Red Army. During these days, some kind of authority remained in Braslav [Braslaw] to keep order, and there was no looting.

A few shells fell on the town, there were deaths and injuries, but all of it seemed unreal. We lived in continuous shock and fear about what was to come. Everything was happening so fast that it seemed unbelievable, as if we were in the midst of a kaleidoscope.

If my memory isn't mistaken, German patrols entered the town a few days after the war broke out, but they only passed through, ignoring the residents. A number of days later, we awoke to the sound of heavy artillery moving through the town and the clattering hooves of huge horses. The German army was entering Braslav in full force: well-built, healthy soldiers with rough features, against a background of massive red flags with the swastika at their center. Fear and discouragement took hold of us.

I'm unable to remember the events that

[Page 125]

followed. It seems to me that the first thing the Germans did was to take all the Jews to the swamps [around June 27]. Someone else has doubtlessly written about this event and all that happened that night. None of us thought we'd return alive. It was said that [the Gentiles] Kovalski [Kowalski] and Dr. Baretzki [Barecki] saved all of us except for two men [Chaim Milutin and Shlomo Zilber]. We learned of the horrible murder of the Jews of Yaisi (a Jewish village near Braslav).[1] Zelig Ulman learned that in the shtetl of Borovka in Latvia the Germans had driven 200 Jews --- children, women, the elderly and young people --- into the lake and shot them.[2] After a few days, all the Jews of Braslav were gathered at the shore of Lake Driviata [Drywiaty] and the women, children, men and people from other places were separated from each other. We were collected in this way a number of times, by Germans with huge guard dogs. To this day, I don't know why they gathered us. Especially engraved in my memory is the time when groups of Poles gathered --- clerks, teachers, many of the "good" Polish youth --- dressed as if for a holiday, all of them happy and joyful. Already at this time, they seemed to hope for our destruction. It's easy to understand what we were in their eyes: Our death --- the death of men, women and children --- was a form of entertainment for them. In our home lived two families of refugees from Lithuania. They wanted to flee eastward but didn't have enough fuel. They were "stuck" in Braslav and murdered there, except for a few people who survived by hiding with farmers in the area.

After entering Braslav, the Germans found more than enough people who were prepared to carry out all of the criminal dirty-work on their behalf. These were Poles and Belorussians, many villagers and residents of the town, who dreamed of looting and murdering the Jews. They collaborated with the Germans up until the time the German Reich began to fall apart. Only a few of them turned down the chance to become hangmen.

The Judenrat [Jewish Council] was organized, headquartered in the Yiddish school [the Folkshul] that was opposite our home. The members of the Judenrat would often come to our house, because we were better informed than others about what was happening in the town. On the Polish side, an administration was organized to cooperate with the Germans. Thus, we were caught between a hammer and an anvil. On one side was the Judenrat, and on the other were the local collaborators.

At the head of the local administration was the chief of police, a Belorussian who'd arrived from somewhere and was essentially a puppet. Other persons who grabbed high positions in the administration were the teacher Pavlik [Pawlik] and his wife, who were *Volksdeutsche* [ethnic Germans].

The most enthusiastic collaborators were the deputy police chief, Yashinski [Stanislaw Jasinski] (he'll be discussed below), the mayor Kovalski [Kowalski], and the jail director Shliachchik, a *Volksdeutscher* and a sadist. Under the Soviet administration, he'd worked at repairing typewriters and lived modestly. With the entry of the Germans, however, he began to show his murderous nature and enjoyed unlimited authority.

I'd like to point out that at the beginning the Germans were received enthusiastically by the Christian residents. Even Dr. Baretzki was swept away by the general euphoria and welcomed the Germans with a splendid banquet that he gave at the municipal hospital. This was his great sin. Dr. Baretzki, who hid the family of [Shlomo] Ustyev the tinsmith for a long period, acknowledged this to me when he came to Vilna with his wife in the 1950s. After the war, when the Soviet authorities arrested Dr. Baretzki, all of the survivors signed a petition, after which he was released. Dr. Baretzki tried to help the Jews. He worked to raise their bread allowance. He also risked his own life by operating on a growth that my mother was suffering from. The operation was carried out in the hospital after the ghetto had been established.

The Germans exploited the Jews for labor: repairs in the workshops, cleaning wood at the train

[Page 126]

station, and so on. The women knitted socks and gloves and worked at cleaning. Sometimes the work assignments were used to humiliate and torture. The terror was indescribable.

After the regular German army soldiers left the town, some of the SS soldiers remained near the train station with their commander, Officer Bucholtz. Everyone was afraid of him, because of his sadism and his officer's baton, which he used to hit people indiscriminately. After some more time had passed, this officer and his platoon left the town. The administration remained in the hands of the local collaborators and several SS officers. At this point, the most degenerate characters raised their heads. In their eyes, we weren't human beings but something to be trampled on.

During the months I stayed in Braslav, a number of murders took place before the ghetto was destroyed [on June 3-5, 1942]. At this time the family of Zelig Ulman, a member of the Judenrat, was killed. Shlomo [Zilber] the *shochet* [ritual slaughterer] and Chaim Milutin were killed on the way to the swamps [around late June 1941]. At about the same time, Frida Ulman, Beilka Deitch and Yaacov Musin were murdered. Other victims were 5-6 people who were peeling bark from logs [at the train station]. This murder was the basis for my lawsuit against Yashinski [in 1963].[3]

The family of Zelig Ulman had deposited jewelry and other valuables with a villager outside Braslav, in the hope that they'd be able to hide at his house in the village. The farmer, who wanted to take all of the property for himself, reported that Zelig Ulman was listening to radio news from the Soviet Union and circulating the information. Zelig, his wife and daughter were thrown in jail, at the mercy of the sadist Shliachchik. There they were held for some time. They were cruelly tortured and finally murdered. Boris, their only son, succeeded in escaping death.

It should be emphasized: Friendly relations between Jews and Poles were utterly forbidden. Special notices were posted in this regard.

The winters of 1941-43 were especially cold in all the areas of the occupation. Temperatures dropped to 42 degrees below zero. The initial German victories turned to stalemate, and the German armies suffered greatly from the cold: Their clothing was unsuited to the Russian climate. For this reason, the Germans ordered the Judenrat to collect warm clothes and demanded a very high ransom for allowing the Jews to remain alive. The Judenrat appointed me and N. Fridman to record on special lists the clothing that was gathered. As usual, the Germans promised that the greater the amount of gold, silver and clothing, the greater the chance the Jews would live. And they said that hardworking people, such as those in Braslav, had nothing to fear.

I'll never forget the occasion when the clothes were collected. Everyone came to show their presence, bringing piles of warm clothing, expensive furs for men and women, sheepskin coats, hats, and gold and silver valuables. Poor families brought Passover goblets, trays, candlesticks, gold coins, earrings and so on. These were items that they'd kept all their lives to serve as a dowry for their daughters. The wealthier people handed over only a part of their possessions. The wife of Betzalel-Yaacov [Dagovitz] cried bitterly when they took her caracul fur coat. In this way a very large amount of property was collected, and the Judenrat said the Germans were very pleased.

Life went on, with pressure, extortion and torture at every step. But people weren't discouraged and would try to encourage one another. From the front, we received encouraging rumors.

[Page 127]

Sasha Tempelman, who we'd known for a long time, would often come to us and tell us that Yashinski was passing him news heard on the radio. And that Yashinski had promised to help him and warn of any impending trouble. For such information Yashinski received a lot of gold, but over time people began to lose their faith in miracles and understood that they were the "walking dead."

It was known that the Jews of Lithuania and Latvia had been exterminated by the Germans immediately after their invasion. It's impossible to describe the brutal methods of murder that the Lithuanians and Latvians carried out. To save bullets, these killers would cut the throats of small children or bash their heads against the wall. Adults met a similar fate. In Vilna, Kovno and Riga, only a handful of Jews were left in each of the ghettos after the massacres. The residents of southern Latvia were taken to Dvinsk [42 kilometers northwest of Braslav] and immediately killed there. This was also the fate of the Jews of Kraslava, a fairly large town [30 kilometers north of Braslav and in Latvia, across the Dvina River].

After all the Jews of Kraslava had been taken to Dvinsk,[4] there remained only one very wealthy and respectable family --- the Barkan family --- who were hidden by the Catholic priest of Kraslava in the church. The condition for their rescue was that the family renounce Judaism and convert to Christianity. This difficult condition was accepted by the family. I'm sure that those who condemn them would've done the same thing if placed in a similar situation. Who could stand seeing their child torn to pieces? And I'm sure that G-d, in His great mercy, would forgive them. The Barkan family included the couple, Zusia and Liuba; the son Yasha (Yaacov), age 9; the daughter Rafaela, age 6; and Liuba's mother --- Mrs. Dinerman, a very respectable matron. They were saved.

After some time had passed, the priest concluded that even their conversion wouldn't guarantee their survival and the area around Braslav had become very dangerous. He decided to move the family to a safer place. For this, he contacted the priest in Plusy [12 kilometers southwest of Kraslava, south of the Dvina River]. There the situation was a bit calmer. The priest in Plusy turned to one of the poorest, most religious families --- the M[ichael] Kizlo family from the village of Shemelki [Szemielki] --- pointing out that the Barkans had converted and must be saved.[5] And also that the Barkans were wealthy and owned a lot of property, and they would certainly compensate the family generously if they survived. But these weren't the only things that influenced the farmer. The main reason for his agreement was his deep religiosity, together with that of his entire family: the grandfather, the grandmother, his wife and his two children. Each of them was filled with compassion for all living things, and they were moral people to the depths of their hearts.

With the agreement of the Kizlo family, the Barkan family crossed the Dvina River on a dark night and was given accommodations in the village [Shemelki]. The mother, Mrs. Dinerman, refused to eat non-kosher food. As we were related to them, her son-in-law decided to bring her to us in Braslav. The peasant Michael [Kizlo] brought her to us at the end of 1941. She was happy to be among Jews. She knitted socks with all of the women and was relatively content. Things continued in this way until December 1941, until the destruction of the Jews of Yod [Jod, 25 kilometers southeast of Braslav].

I remember that the Braslav *Schutzpolizei* [police force] under Yashinski took part in that destruction. People saw the trucks returning to Braslav, loaded with the possessions of those who'd been murdered.[6] The killers, Yashinski among them, sat on the loot, drunk and singing merrily. This was a reminder of the frightening reality, after months of anticipation.

Michael, our farmer, who was always well informed, learned of the massacre [in Yod]. He was brave and didn't hesitate. He came to Braslav and took back Mrs. Dinerman. Panic and fear gripped

[Page 128]

us all. My family asked Michael to also take me with him to the village, as I was the youngest daughter and without a family of my own. Only later did I understand the noble sacrifice they made. The farmer, an open and warm-hearted man, didn't refuse, and I agreed to leave my loved ones. To this day, I can neither forget nor forgive myself for my decision.

It was December 24, 1941. When it got dark we crept, covered in large shawls, to the sleigh. My brother-in-law Yaacov Feldman accompanied us to the other side of Lake Noviata [Nowiata].

After a dramatic goodbye, he disappeared into the fog with all my dearest ones, who I never saw again.

I arrived in Shemelki on Christmas Eve. The entire Kizlo family, together with the Barkan family, waited for us beside the festive table. My arrival was no surprise, as all had believed that Michael would want to save another person.

The village of Shemelki was divided into separate farms, each of them far from the next. In the village lived several Kizlo families, all related to each other. One of them, Yosef, was told of our presence. He was an honest, good-hearted man. We had three hiding places, which Michael prepared ahead of time. One was a pit under the cowshed, covered with boards, into which air entered through a hidden opening. Food was brought to us when the cows were fed. Most of the time, we lived there. The second hiding place was a concealed room in one part of the house, with its own toilet. The third place was located in an attic, with a hidden entrance. We hid there only in the most dangerous situations, because it was cramped and very narrow.

Our hosts shared with us their last crust of bread. The winter was hard, the summer harvest had been very poor, and it was difficult for them to support us. But there was a more challenging problem: Michael's neighbors would often visit him for friendly conversation, and they could see the large quantity of food that was cooking and the smoke that rose from the chimney at unusual hours. Even the two small children in the family might let a word slip out by mistake. The smallest thing might arouse suspicion, and in addition two families of policemen lived in the village.

We lived in constant fear, hoping only to survive. This feeling was shared by our host. He'd received no prize or payment in advance from us. The end of the war wasn't yet in sight, and worse --- each day he endangered the lives of his family, all of whom could be killed because of our presence.

But through a miracle, all went well. The children never gave us away, even though they knew about us and in calmer times even played with us, when they took us from the hiding place into the house so that we could warm ourselves in the kitchen on the coldest days.

In June 1942, as we lay in our hiding place, we heard someone ask our host, "Michael, do you need any plunder? "Why?" Michael asked, and the other replied, "They're killing the Jews of Braslav today, there will be a lot of loot." These words were spoken by a man called Josef Buzo, the manager of the "steshelets" [*strzelec*] (sharpshooter) association in Braslav. He was originally from Plusy. He sometimes visited Michael and was known as a respectable man.

I didn't have the right or the will to shout, wail or even bang my head against the wall. I could only

[Page 129]

sit quietly in despair. After some time had passed, a woman of the village came to visit the grandmother and spoke about the same event: "Jews, cats, rubbish --- they're all the same." This view was shared by 95% of the Christian population. Nearly all of them thought this way.

The wife of the watchmaker Kshidzianek [Krzyzanek] --- a Christian family that lived near the house of the Christian parish house (*dom parafialny*) near the Catholic church --- told me, when I returned to Braslav after the liberation, that from the window of her house she'd seen the destruction of the ghetto. She said that the Jews had been brought there and filled the parish house. They'd been placed under guard and held for three days without a drop of water as they awaited their fate: to be taken to the pits. She saw the elderly rabbi, Rav Abba Zahorie, marching calmly at their head during their last journey. She also saw my mother Rachel and my sister Fania walking together. Fania's husband, Yaacov Feldman, died later.

We lived suspended between life and death. I suffered greatly from asthma. Sometimes I received medicine with the help of the priest Bilsher. I'd lie down with a pillow over my mouth so that, G-d forbid, no one would hear my coughing. Walls, in those days, had more ears than ever before.

After a number of months had passed, Mrs. Dinerman suffered a brain hemorrhage and her mental state became confused. She shouted that she wanted to go home, that the war had ended. We were in great danger of being discovered. Unfortunately, after some time she suffered a further attack and became completely paralyzed. For three days she rasped so loudly that Michael's wife and grandmother had to guard the gate at the entry into the farmyard, to prevent anyone from hearing her. These were terrible moments. Finally her suffering ended, and she passed away. The grandfather prepared a coffin and buried her at night in the garden. Later her body was transferred to the cemetery in Kraslava.

Life went on. The warning system used in Plusy helped us a lot. For instance, if police or gendarmes entered Plusy, someone would hang a white sheet on the building near the church on the other side of the lake. Seeing it, we'd enter the safest hiding place.

It's hard to describe all the troubles we faced. The children with us turned pale from the lack of air, poor food and bad living conditions. But despite our suffering, we were toughened by the strong will to stay alive.

Time passed, month after month, year after year, until 1944, when the front began to approach our region. Our fears grew. Rumors spread that the Germans, in their defeat, were expelling residents westward and burning villages. Luckily for us, the Germans became caught in a "pocket," were attacked from all sides, and failed to carry out their plans. But in the area of Dvinsk, residents were forced to move on. For this reason, Michael took in a refugee family that wasn't Jewish. By a miracle, they didn't notice us. We lay in hiding for long days without food, since Michael was afraid to bring us food at that time.

The front moved closer and the Germans prepared a line of defense that passed through the village. But they couldn't hold their position, and they withdrew. The Russians took Plusy. Michael, our savior, let us come out onto the porch, and our presence in the village was no longer a secret. The next day, you can understand our terror when the Germans returned. But there was no longer the fear that someone would hand us over to the Nazis; it was clear to everyone that the Nazi beast was dying.

The battles in the area continued for several days; shells fell all around us, but we were no longer as afraid: Liberation was

[Page 130]

imminent. Soon we met tired Soviet soldiers, dirty but victorious. It's impossible to describe how we felt on emerging from our cramped, narrow holes into the clean open air, filling our lungs with the fragrance of flowers and fields.

It was September 1944 when the Barkan family returned to Kraslava. The grandmother took me to Braslav, where I met with a handful of the beloved Jewish survivors of my town. I found work and stayed in Braslav until 1946. From there, I traveled to Vilna [about 165 kilometers to the southwest].

A few more words about the brave and noble family that saved us. It's very difficult to describe all that they and we experienced over the two years and seven months. Many times all of us were in danger of death and in despair, and it appeared that everything was lost. Sometimes all of us were ready to go to the lake and drown ourselves in it, to stop endangering the lives of the good villagers. But each time they answered: Our fate will be your fate.

During the German occupation --- it seems to me that it was during the second winter of German rule --- the frozen bodies of the Shlosberg family were found on the lake. (They had land near Plusy and also owned a shop. The son was an agronomist, and the daughter ran the shop.) According to Michael, the people who hid them couldn't keep them any longer. So they poisoned the entire family, four souls, and threw the bodies onto the frozen lake. The family of Aharon Zeif was similarly poisoned just before the end of the war.

And another detail: A cousin of Michael's visited from Braslav. This cousin was also from the Kizlo family, but he was one of those who celebrated the destruction of the ghetto. From my hiding place I heard his boasts of how, at the time the ghetto was destroyed, he'd helped the Germans to find Jews who were in hiding. "I pulled out the *Zhids* [Jews] by their hair and grabbed a lot of loot," he said.

After the liberation, I filed a lawsuit against him. The trial took place in Polotsk [115 kilometers east of Braslav], before a panel of three officers of the NKVD.[7] They sentenced the criminal Kizlo and his family to five years of exile in Siberia. That trial, as well as the trial of Yashinski, I brought out of a deep-seated desire for retribution despite the cost, and I'm very satisfied with my actions. I've included a report from the trial [of Yashinski, on pages 134-142 of this memorial book].

About the Trial

For the Poles, the intelligentsia and the lower classes, the arrival of the Germans was like the coming of the Messiah. They felt that the Germans had delivered them from the yoke of Soviet occupation. Many Poles expressed their enthusiasm and willingness to serve the Germans, and organized receptions and banquets for them. Even Dr. Baretzki was swept along with them.

Yashinski, who'd lived through the Soviet occupation [of 1939-41] in constant fear, was among the first to welcome the Nazis. I don't know how he succeeded in catching the eye of the Germans, but he was soon appointed chief of police.

[Page 131]

Who was Yashinski? If I'm not mistaken, he was a sergeant in the border guards of the Polish Army. When the Red Army entered [in September 1939], many soldiers of the Polish Army were arrested. Some of them succeeded in escaping to Lithuania and Latvia. But with the help of a local Jew, Yashinski was registered as a laborer and remained in Braslav. During the first days of the Nazi occupation, the Germans were assisted by volunteers who wore a white band on their sleeves. It should be pointed out that later some of the volunteers resigned; they saw what was likely to happen and didn't want to be among the murderers.

Yashinski played a two-faced game. In the first months [of the German occupation] he murdered no one; on the contrary, he developed good connections with the Judenrat, with its chairman, Yitzchak Mindel, and with Sasha Tempelman. The Judenrat was located in the school opposite our house. Often acquaintances would visit us to talk and drink a cup of tea.

Only a few memories of this time remain with me, except for the incident about which I testified in court: In December 1941, during the time of the Hanukkah holiday, the massacre of the Jews of Yod took place. The killing was carried out by the men of the Braslav police, under Yashinski's orders. Afterward the murderers were seen returning, drunk and full of loot, with Yashinski at their head, drunk and happy.

As I've described, I hid in the house of a farmer from the end of December 1941 until the liberation [around July 1944]. After that, I stayed in Braslav for some time; from there I went to Vilna and later to Poland. Sima Fisher also lived there. She was related to my late husband, and so we often met. One day, in 1962 or 1963, Moshe Fisher and Boris Ulman came to the apartment and told us that they'd testified at the trial of one of the blue policemen,[8] and Yashinski had appeared as a defense witness. At this time, we decided that we must take Yashinski to trial. After some time had passed, Sima and I were called to the court to identify Yashinski, and indeed we identified him among the men who were presented to us. The Warsaw press wrote that Yashinski would receive the death penalty. At the first trial, a writer for the Yiddish newspaper *Folks-Sztyme* --- Tenenbaum [sic] --- was present, and he published an article about the trial.[9]

I'd like to emphasize that immediately after we decided to testify, I sent letters to Masha and Mendel Maron, to Liuba and Eliahu Shmidt, and to Sasha Tempelman in the United States, asking them to send affidavits. I also wrote to Israel, to Reichel and to Yerachmiel Milutin. Their testimonies arrived and were read to the court, but they were rejected and not taken into consideration as evidence.

My situation during the trial was difficult. I hadn't been in the [Braslav] ghetto during the general massacre [on June 3-5, 1942]. I told the court that my brother David [Kantor] had been among the Jews who worked peeling bark from logs near the train station. I'd brought him food every day. One day, I saw how Yashinski and some other policemen shot at Jews who'd been smoking while working. This was my testimony, and throughout the trial I maintained it without change. I see giving this testimony as the most important thing I did in my life.

In the book *Till Eulenspiegel*, the hero of the story avenges the death of his father: "The ashes of Claes always beat in my heart."[10] In my heart beats, and will always beat, the ashes of those who were so cruelly murdered in cold blood.

The trial was delayed a number of times for various reasons. Meanwhile, I wrote a detailed account of the period of occupation in Braslav. This was an affront to all those for whom the period had been like a "celebration at the time of a plague" [that is, those who'd welcomed the Nazi occupation]. In my article, I explained why

[Page 132]

From the bill of indictment [of Stanislav Yashinski]

[Page 133]
I had initiated the trial. The article negatively affected the judges and lawyers.

The court sessions took place in Olshtin [Olsztyn, now in northeastern Poland, about 470 kilometers southwest of Braslav], where most of the Polish refugees who had left Braslav in 1946-47 were then living. Just before the second session of the court, an agronomist named Kovalski [Kowalski] offered silver, gold and jewelry to me and to Sima Fisher, to get us to change our testimony. We reacted sharply. It's interesting: Over several years, they were unable to discredit my testimony, but meanwhile something happened. A committee was sent to Braslav to investigate the location of the incident. In addition a witness was found, a girl I'd never seen before, and she testified behind closed doors. In the hall were present only the judges, her and me. She accused me of collaborating with the Germans in the town of Opsa [18 kilometers southwest of Braslav], of injecting Poles with experimental inoculations, of abusing the Polish population and so on. The worst thing was that the chairman of the court session (the staff had changed completely over time) acted as if he believed all of this, and in front of the witness he expressed his sympathy and sorrow for the torture she'd experienced. Kovalski and the other defense witnesses testified zealously on behalf of Yashinski, although they didn't dare to accuse me, except for that lowlife.

The trial ended with Yashinski's acquittal, and the chairman [of the court session] noted that measures would be taken against certain witnesses.

There was great joy among Yashinski's friends, about 30 to 40 people. Throughout the trial they'd spoken in his favor as witnesses for the defense, but to no avail. Only the final testimony [of the girl] turned the scales in favor of the accused.

After these events, I was broken. I feared that they were planning to charge me with perjury. I traveled to Warsaw, to the chairman of the Jewish Committee, Mr. Domb. He told me that I had nothing to worry about, because any trial of that kind would cause an international uproar and the Polish government couldn't allow that to happen.

No one should get the idea that I wish to present myself as a hero. Everything I wrote was the truth. It was the reality. I don't see my testimony as anything unusual, I simply followed my heart. It was my duty.

Footnotes:

1. Yaisi (Jaisi) was seven kilometers east of Braslav. According to the story of Shneiur Munitz on pages 399-402 of this memorial book, around 14 Jews were killed in Yaisi on July 4 or 5, 1941.
2. According to the *Encyclopedia of Camps and Ghettos, 1933-1945*, Volume II-B (2012), this was the massacre in Latvia on July 28, 1941 of the Jews of Silene, a village that was known until the mid-1930s as Borovka. On July 28, on the pretext of being moved to the Braslav Ghetto, the Jews of Silene were driven on foot to Lake Smilga, three kilometers southeast of their village, and shot by Latvian nationalists. Elderly Jews and children were taken to the killing site in carts. The victims numbered 186 people in 32 families. Following the massacre, local non-Jewish residents dug four large pits and buried the victims. Silene was located about 23 kilometers north of Braslav.
3. The lawsuit is described on pages 134-142 of this memorial book.
4. According to the *Encyclopedia of Camps and Ghettos, 1933-1945*, Volume II-B, the Dvinsk Ghetto was formed on July 31, 1941. In addition to Jews from Dvinsk, it contained Jews from towns such as Rezekne, Subate and Kraslava.

    Thousands of Jews in the Dvinsk Ghetto were killed in a series of Aktions between late July and mid-August 1941, August 15-20, and November 7-9. Following these Aktions, some 1,000 Jews remained in the ghetto, of whom half then died in a typhus epidemic that began in late November or early December 1941. In May 1942 the ghetto suffered another massacre. In October 1943 the ghetto was cleared, and the remaining ghetto inmates were transferred to concentration camps in Kaiserwald and Stutthof.
5. Shemelki was about two kilometers northeast of Plusy, separated from Plusy by a lake. Shemelki was 22 kilometers north of Braslav.
6. The massacre on December 17, 1941 of the Jews of Yod (and of the Jews from other communities who had been brought to Yod), is described in survivor accounts on pages 405-437 of this memorial book.

7. Narodnyi Komissariat Vnutrennikh Del (People's Commissariat for Internal Affairs): The Soviet law enforcement and intelligence agency that existed from 1934 to 1946, after which it evolved into the KGB.

8. Presumably this refers to the uniform of the local police in Braslav (composed of non-Germans), rather than to the Gendarmerie in Braslav (who were the German police). Generally speaking, blue was the color of the uniforms worn by the Polish police during the war in German-occupied Poland. These Polish "blue policemen" were allowed to operate because the German police force in occupied Poland (the Order Police, or Orpo, whose uniforms were green, and which included the Gendarmerie) was too small to operate by itself.

9. This might refer to the newspaper article that appears on pages 134-136 of this memorial book. That article, however, was written by Tenenblatt, not Tenenbaum. The *Folks-Sztyme* (*People's Voice*) was a magazine published in Yiddish/Polish in Communist Poland between 1946 and 1991.

10. Till Eulenspiegel was a figure from German folk literature, dating back to at least the 1500s; there are tales about him in many parts of Europe. In one of them, he had a father named Claes who was betrayed by a neighbor, turned over to the Inquisition and burned at the stake. Eventually Till avenged himself against the authorities for his father's death.

[Page 134]

From the Courtroom: Was It All a Misunderstanding?
By Special Correspondent S. Tenenblatt
[Written for the *Folks-Sztyme* (*People's Voice*) magazine in Poland in 1963]

**Translated from the Hebrew / Donated by Jon Seligman
Revised Based on Laia Ben-Dov's Translation /
Footnotes Added by Jeff Deitch**

We're in the district court of Olshtin [Olsztyn, in what's now northeastern Poland, about 470 kilometers southwest of Braslaw/Braslav].[1] In the corridor outside Hall No. 238, a few tens of people are engaged in a discussion. They're recalling earlier times, some decades before, when they used to meet daily. These people all come from the same town.

"We're starting, please enter the hall," announces the court orderly, cutting short the conversation. People enter and take their places. In the hall, it's quiet. Again the voice of the orderly is heard: "All rise! The court is in session!" Witnesses are sworn in. In the hall only a few people remain, but later the court will fill again with witnesses who have already testified. To the left of the panel of judges, guarded by a policeman, sits a tall man with broad shoulders, 50-something years old --- calm and collected. From time to time, he leans over to his defense attorney and tells him what to ask the witnesses. On his face, it's possible to read his thoughts --- soon everything will become clear, it's only due to a misunderstanding that he's sitting in the dock as the accused.

Is it really so?

The court session continues. The events under discussion took place some 20-odd years ago in the town of Braslav, 180 kilometers from Vilna [as the crow flies, Braslav was about 165 kilometers northeast of Vilna]. Like hundreds of other towns in the Vilna region, the town had been inhabited by a few thousand Jews who were exterminated by the genocidal Nazis.

"Your honors, I saw it with my own eyes," one of the witnesses will later testify. "It was terrible, shocking, they beat, they killed, they laughed, and then they fired . . ."

Of all the Jews of Braslav, who'd numbered several thousand, there survived after the years of terror of Nazi occupation --- only about 30 people [sic].[2] Most of them had fought in the ranks of the partisans.

At the end of 1962, there was a trial in Kashlin [Koszalin, in northwestern Poland]. Present in the courtroom were Sima [Fisher] Zilberman, Niuta Zelikman of Valbzhich [Wałbrzych], and Michael Vinokurovski (formerly Moshe Fisher) of Lodz. They identified one of the witnesses, a person who'd long been sought by the authorities, the former chief of police in Braslav, Stanislav Yashinski [Stanislaw Jasinski]. An investigation began, and an indictment was sent to the district court in Olshtin.

[Q:] Can the witness recognize the accused?

[A:] Of course! Your honor, he was an honest man, he often helped people and we spoke frequently.

[Q:] Please answer the question, does the witness know where the accused worked?

[A:] They say that he worked for the police, but I never saw him in uniform, he was a respectable man.

From the Indictment

Stanislav Yashinski faced the accusation that in 1941, after the Germans occupied Braslav, he had changed sides to serve the Hitlerites as chief of the local *Schutzpolizei* [police force]. He was charged with treason toward the Polish nation, in that he took part in the murder of the civilian population, particularly Jews . . .

If the court found him guilty, wrote the newspaper *Głos Olsztynski* [*Voice of Olsztyn*] before the trial, then based on the 1944 law (according to which he was being judged) he could face the death sentence.

[Page 135]

Q: Did the local police take part in the expulsion of the Jewish population?

A: Yes, but I didn't see Yashinski among them, the hangings and murders were conducted by the Germans.

Q: Did the witness see the accused in uniform? Did he carry a weapon?

A: Yes, but . . .

Q: How did the accused treat the Jewish population?

A: What does this mean? I stated already, the treatment was good. Once he told me, during the war, that he was revolted by the shootings. It was even said that he hid three Jewish women at his place.

Q: Did the witness see them?

A: No.

Q: And what happened to them?

A: I don't know, but . . .

"But he's a respectable man, he had a good name." These words were repeated many times. The face of Yashinski grew more and more animated. He'd been a policeman, chief of the *Schutzpolizei*. During the investigation, he hadn't denied it. According to his statements, he'd avoided atrocities. Was everything just a misunderstanding?

Facts, Facts

The witness Niuta [Anna] Zelikman: It was next to the train station, in the first months of the occupation. My brother was working there among the other people. I brought him food. Suddenly, I saw from a distance . . . yes, I state with full certainty that I saw Yashinski. Shouts were heard, curses and shots. Six Jews were killed.

Q: Who else can confirm this?

The witness was quiet. Was it correct? Did the accused shoot, or not? At this trial, the matter was crucial.

The witness Michael Vinokurovski, age 46 and now living in Lodz, stands up. Formerly he was known as Moshe Fisher.

The witness [Vinokurovski]: Yes, I was born and lived in Braslav. I knew the accused before the war. He was dressed in a uniform with an armband of the *Schutzpolizei*. Like all the policemen, he was armed.

Q: Did he take part in murder?

A: Who among the policemen didn't shoot? They all . . .

Judge: Please be specific . . . facts!

A: I was in the ghetto at the time it was destroyed, in June 1942. I succeeded in escaping. Afterward I hid in the building of the tannery. I hid there with my sister, Sima Zilberman.

She [Sima Fisher Zilberman] is in the hall, listening to the trial. She's an elderly woman and has already testified. During the recess, we walked in the corridor. "I'm already tired of this trial," she says. "To experience the nightmare again. What do you think, who will the court believe?"

The witness [Vinokurovski]: I hid in the attic, there my sister told me that she saw through a crack how they murdered an injured woman. Yashinski fired, she saw him.

Q: What happened next to the witness?

A: I succeeded, your honor, in reaching the partisans. I stayed with them until the end of the war. I was in a special unit. We received an order to catch Yashinski so that he could be tried, but two weeks before the Soviet army entered the area [in July 1944], he escaped.

Q: What did you want to try him for?

A: For what exactly I don't know, but . . .

Again, there was no clarity. After 20-something years, it's impossible to rely on human memory. But is it possible to forget

[Page 136]

those days, full of nightmares?! Who must the court believe? All of the circumstances must be checked.

In Israel lives a man named Yerachmiel Milutin. He's originally from Braslav, a former partisan . . . his written testimony was added to the indictment, as the affidavit of a witness.

The judge reads it. For the first time, the self-confidence drains from the face of the accused, and for a moment he hides his face in his hands. Is it . . .?

[From the affidavit of Yerachmiel Milutin]

I learned of the investigation against Stanislav Yashinski. I lived in Braslav, and I knew him well. I met him when he worked as a policeman. He was especially active in the extermination and dispossession of Jews. Besides his weapon, he always carried with him a white baton, and he liked to use it frequently.

June 3, 1942 is a day especially engraved in my memory: the afternoon of a summer day. The Germans and the police led out the Jews. On that day about 4,000 Jews were murdered in Braslav, and I succeeded in escaping. From my hiding place, I saw Yashinski leading my wife and daughter. At one point he ordered them to stop while the line continued to move. With his hand he signaled them to keep walking, and then he took out his pistol and shot them twice, and it grew quiet. I left my hiding place and approached my dear ones to part from them forever. After that, I joined the partisans and fought in their ranks until the end of the war. I'm prepared to testify in person. [End of Yerachmiel Milutin's affidavit]

We in the courtroom are listening. The judge continues to read affidavits that have arrived from the United States during the investigation. Those of Eliahu and Liuba Shmidt and Sasha Tempelman accuse Yashinski, but because they didn't follow the required procedures their evidence isn't taken into consideration.

A short consultation takes place in the district court of Olshtin. The chairman, D. Yavarski [Jaworski], and the prosecutor --- S. Vatznitzka [Warznitzka?] --- decided that the matter in its present form couldn't be concluded [that is, it was impossible to reach a verdict]. Accordingly, it was decided that the accused would remain in jail and all the documents would be sent to the district attorney in Kashlin, who'd conducted the investigation, to complete the affidavits. It was also recommended that he apply to the office of the chief prosecutor, to receive additional material through him from the judicial department in Belarus.

For a verdict, we must wait.

(*Folks-Sztyme*, Warsaw, November 20, 1963, No. 181)[3]

Footnotes:

1. Following the end of World War II, Braslav was no longer in Poland but in Belarus, as the border had been shifted to the west. On page 133 of this memorial book, Anna (Niuta) Zelikman stated that most of the Polish refugees who left Braslav in 1946-47 resettled in Olshtin, Poland.

2. According to the *Encyclopedia of Camps and Ghettos, 1933-1945*, Volume II-B (2012), approximately 70 Jews from Braslav survived the war.

3. The *Folks-Sztyme (People's Voice)* was a magazine published in Yiddish in Communist Poland between 1946 and 1991. During part of this period, it was also published in Polish. In the 1960s, one of its editors was Samuel Tenenblatt, perhaps the "S. Tenenblatt" mentioned above as the correspondent.

Stanislav Yashinski [Stanislaw Jasinski]: Murderer of the Jews of Braslav

**Translated from the Hebrew / Donated by Jon Seligman
Revised Based on Laia Ben-Dov's Translation /
Footnotes Added by Jeff Deitch**

After World War II, the murderer Yashinski was placed on trial [as described on pages 134-135 of this memorial book, in 1963]. The trial took place in the district court in Olshtin in Poland [Olsztyn, in what's now northeastern Poland, about 470 kilometers southwest of Braslav/Braslaw]. The following are portions of the protocol of the witnesses' testimony. Some of the witnesses testified at the trial in the courtroom, while others gave their testimony in Israel and in the United States [in the form of affidavits]. All were photocopied from the official protocol of the court that was written, obviously, in Polish.

The Witness Sima [Fisher] Zilberman

During the war, I lived in Braslav. On June 3, 1942, in the early hours of the morning, at around 3 a.m., I heard the voices of policemen who were making Jews run through the street. I ran outside

[Page 137]

wearing only my nightgown. After I saw what the police were doing, I became very frightened and ran immediately to the attic of our house. My brother [Moshe] Fisher-Vinokurovski came with me. I hid in a chest that stood there. When the noise in the street subsided, I looked through a crack and saw a woman lying on the sidewalk, screaming, "Oy, my intestines have come out." Many policemen and other people were there. From time to time, shots were heard. With my own eyes, I saw the accused shoot and kill this woman with his pistol. On his lips I saw white foam. I recognized him immediately. When the Jews were taken to forced labor during the German occupation, the accused was also with the Germans. When the ghetto was established in Braslav in [April] 1942 and the Judenrat [Jewish Council] was chosen, the accused would come to them with commands from the Germans to hand over all valuables, as well as fur coats. I met him there and got to know him for the first time. He was dressed in black. Everyone said this was Officer Yashinski. Yashinski came to the Judenrat many times and I knew him very well, because I saw him in daylight. When we hid in the attic, I told my brother that I saw Yashinski shoot and kill the woman from the Biliak family. In the evening, my brother and I went downstairs to change clothes. Outside I heard shouts from the policemen saying, "Come, let's go to the Fisher house, they've got everything." I don't know who looted the house. I knew by her voice the woman who was killed by the accused, and I also saw her husband beside her. I'm sure it was her, there can be no doubt or mistake. I'm convinced that the accused killed the woman. One day before the destruction of the ghetto, I saw him taking furniture from our house. I saw the accused from the front, not only from the side. I saw his entire face and the foam on his lips. On our street where we lived, there weren't many people of other nationalities; most were Jews. Sometimes Yashinski would come to the Judenrat, along with the Germans. In the ghetto, I heard that Chatzkel Vinokur was shot and killed next to the train station. He was killed at a distance from the station. At this time, they were shooting people there almost every day. Ulman was also killed then. Emma Milutin said that Yashinski shot and killed her mother. From the ghetto 100 girls were expelled on foot to Slobodka [the day before the destruction of the ghetto on June 3; Slobodka was about 11 kilometers northeast of Braslav]. I don't know if Yashinski was present at the expulsion. I saw him when he ran us through the snow [presumably this means the winter of late 1941-early 1942].

The Statement of the Witness Anna Zelikman

I was present in Braslav in 1941 in the area of the train station, when the accused Yashinski and other policemen murdered three Jews: Boris Karas, Chatzkel Vinokur and another Jew whose name I don't know, but I recognized him by sight. At the station were many wooden logs, and most of the Jewish men worked at cleaning them. My brother David Kantor worked there too, and I'd bring him food. It was during the early days of autumn 1941, when I brought my brother lunch. He approached me and began to eat. Not far from me, I saw three boys sitting on railroad ties and smoking cigarettes. Suddenly Yashinski and another policeman ran toward them, shouting and moving them to the side. After a moment they shot them, Yashinski with his pistol and the other with his rifle. As far as I can remember, they kicked the bodies and shouted, "That'll teach the others a lesson." Then they turned to the other Jews and ordered them to "remove the carcasses." Upon seeing all this, I fled from the place. Yashinski I'd meet in the street. He ruled the Jews' affairs; he'd rush about in the street with a whip in his hand and drive Jews off the sidewalk. The accused was in constant contact with the Judenrat. All the residents of Braslav knew

[Page 138]

this. Yashinski was the one who communicated with the Jews on behalf of the Germans. Everyone knew him as "Officer Yashinski." Among the Jewish population, he didn't have a good reputation. Maybe things changed after the ghetto was destroyed and maybe that's why several of the witnesses have given evidence in his favor, but they aren't Jews. I was in Braslav until December 24 [1941]. After the liberation [around July 1944], I [returned and] stayed in Braslav for two years. I didn't inform the Soviet authorities about the activities of Yashinski because during that period I was mentally broken. I didn't even concern myself with my mother's inheritance. After that I traveled to Vilna [about 165 kilometers southwest of Braslav], where I stayed until 1958. In that year, I came to Poland and lived in Valbzhich [Wałbrzych, in what's now southwestern Poland].

Yashinski did grave harm to the Jewish population. On the day he killed the Jews, he was dressed in civilian clothes; although I don't remember for certain, he might have worn a military topcoat with a band on his arm. On that day, they shot only three Jews. Before that, right at the beginning of the decrees, a few Jews had already been shot. The entire Jewish population of Braslav numbered 4,000-4,500 souls. From that number, after the liberation only 30 [sic] people remained alive. After the shooting of the Jews by the train station, I stopped taking food to my brother. I was afraid. I'm convinced that the accused committed the murder. Everyone said at the time that Yashinski had done it. In the Christian version of history we, the Jews, are considered responsible for the crucifixion of Jesus. "A Jew isn't a person," people said. Many non-Jewish people from Braslav knew that the liquidation of the ghetto was imminent, but not one person came to warn the Jews.

The Witness Michael Vinokurovski (Moshe Fisher)

During the Nazi occupation, my name was Fisher. From the days of my birth, I'd lived in Braslav. I knew the accused even from before the war. After the outbreak of hostilities, he was appointed chief of police and later acting chief.

A few months [sic] after the arrival of the Germans, they shot and killed some Jews in Dubina [Dubene, 16 kilometers northwest of Braslav].[1] A Jew named Blacher escaped and informed us that the accused, together with a group of policemen, was in Dubina and they had killed Jews. Blacher told me and other Jews who were members of the Judenrat. During the first days of the Nazi occupation, I saw Yashinski speaking beside the church [in Braslav]. After two days, my sister and I fled to a village, where we hid. After that, I joined the partisans. At the time we hid in the attic, my sister told me that she'd seen Yashinski shoot a woman in the stomach. Four years later, at the trial of Kolkovski [Kolkowski] in Kashlin [Koszalin, in northwestern Poland], I met Yashinski again. After the proceedings in court, I was sitting in a restaurant with a group of friends, among them the witness Zapolski. Yashinski appeared and approached me. He called me aside and told me that he'd already been tried for his actions as chief of police in Braslav, and added that he'd hidden and saved one Jewish woman. I don't remember the name of the woman he mentioned. To this, I replied that I knew in fact she'd been shot and killed. When I was with the partisans, we prepared lists of people suspected of collaboration with the Germans. Yashinski appeared on the list as the chief of police in Braslav. In 1941, I worked around the train station loading wood onto freight cars. My cousin Chatzkel Vinokur worked there too. We were sent to work by the Judenrat. I don't know if Germans were also there. The train yard was large. At noon one day, 5-6 people were shot and killed. When the shooting started, I ran from

[Page 139]

the place. I didn't know what was happening, only that [Boris] Karas, [Chatzkel] Vinokur and others had been killed. Ulman wasn't killed on that day. By pleading with the police, he succeeded in saving himself. I took part only a few times in the work near the trains. I used a medical certificate, which I presented to the Judenrat [to forgo further work at the train station]. I didn't see Germans near the station, and I don't know what happened afterward.

The Testimony of Antoliush Zavdazki [Anatoljusz Zawacki]

I met the accused in Braslav. I lived there from 1937 to 1945. I worked in Braslav as a land surveyor. I knew the accused only by sight. I knew that he worked in the police. I don't remember what uniform he wore. It was said that he was chief of the local police. I heard nothing against Yashinski. As far as I recall, the local police didn't take an active part in the destruction of the first [Braslav] ghetto [on June 3-5, 1942]. I worked then in the office of the district governor. One morning, at around 7 o'clock, I saw the arrival of a group of Germans in black uniforms with skull insignias on their caps and maybe also on their arms. I knew that this was a military unit, because a few of its members expressed concern about being sent to the front. The officer of this unit was Bucholtz. Next to the train station, a group of Jewish men were working. The Germans took them to work and also guarded them. The group of Jews numbered several tens of men. I heard that they shot several Jews on the train platform. I didn't see who was shooting. I know that someone told Bucholtz a group of Jews wasn't working properly, and he ordered them brought to the station. I learned this from the Jews who worked there. The men who were brought to the station, numbering 10-11 people, were locked in freight cars. At nightfall they were taken out of the freight cars, moved some distance from the station, and all were shot. Children from our family saw this. The following day, I met a German who was standing and cleaning his weapon. "I'm not doing this for parade," he said, "yesterday we shot Jews." This was the only occasion when Jews were shot near the station. I know that a group of Soviet prisoners fled from the station. Some of them returned and were shot. This happened after the Jews were killed.

The Witness Michael Laffir

I lived in Braslav from the day of my birth until 1946. I know that Yashinski was respected and had a good name in the town. This was noted when he served in the police. He was acting chief of police. I heard that Jews were shot next to the train station. A German army base was there, under the command of Bucholtz. The Germans [also] had an independent police station [in Braslav]. Opposite the station were storerooms and a loading platform. I heard that the Jews didn't want to work loading wood, so they were locked up in freight cars and then they were shot.

The Testimony of Chalbovitz [no first name given]

In 1944, I was drafted into the Polish army. Until then I lived in Braslav, near the train station. At the time of the destruction of the ghetto, I worked in the office of the district governor in Braslav. We received an order to go to the town and to bring shovels. I didn't go. When I passed [through] the town, I saw the Germans leading Jews. Near the

[Page 140]

train station, some Jews were working. There was a German base there, commanded by Bucholtz. When I went to visit my sister, sometimes I went past the train station. There the Germans shot about 13 Jews. This happened in a swamp near the station, shortly after the front moved further away. [Boris] Karas I knew, [Chatzkel] Vinokur I don't remember. The Jews worked loading wood. The area of the station was closed to strangers. People weren't allowed to come near it. I didn't try to approach the Jews.

Testimony of Alexander (Sasha) Tempelman (who died in the United States)

As I was in the Braslav Ghetto during the Nazi occupation, it's my duty to testify in the trial of the accused, Stanislav Yashinski, who was the chief of police in Braslav during the German occupation and whose trial is now being conducted.

Stanislav Yashinski led a reign of terror, imposing fear on the Jews in the ghetto. He didn't allow them to buy food from the farmers, and he imprisoned and beat all those who dared to sell bread and potatoes to the Jews.

Under his command, people were beaten without reason. In December 1941, someone informed the police that Zelig Ulman, who lived with us in the ghetto, had said that the Nazis would be defeated and the Allies would liberate us all. Yashinski imprisoned Zelig and killed him and his family --- five souls. After a few days, I saw Yashinski walking in the ghetto, wearing Ulman's yellow boots. In June, Yashinski caught five wagons in the forest, containing gypsy families. All of them were killed and we, the Jews, were forced to dig pits and bury them. The murdered numbered 23-25 people, among them children.

During the destruction of the ghetto, Yashinski, armed with a pistol, shot indiscriminately at Jews who tried to escape and find shelter. I hid in an attic and with my own eyes I saw how this criminal fired his pistol. I saw him grab Yitzchak Mindel, who had a child in his arms, and shoot them.

A few days after the ghetto was destroyed, the police were able to catch Jews who'd succeeded in hiding, and Yashinski and his policemen killed them.

Victims of Yashinski included my father, my brother-in-law, my sister and her children --- pharmacists in Slobodka, near Braslav. He arrested them, and on the way to the pits he shot them. All this I learned after the war, when I visited Slobodka and Braslav.

Is it at all possible to describe and detail the horrible deeds of Yashinski, a Pole who sold his soul to the Germans and tried to surpass them in brutality and murder? More than once Dr. Kovalski [Kowalski], who was then the town mayor, remarked that Yashinski had gone too far. Later they also murdered Kovalski.

Until my dying day, I won't forget this terrible murderer and his actions to destroy innocent people, among them women and children.

New York, October 26, 1963

[Page 141]
About SS Commander Brodrik (Affidavit)

On August 6, 1947, Alexander Tempelman (born on December 15, 1904) appeared in the office of the honorary court of Vilseck [Wilzak], located at Vilseck camp, at Altnuihauz [Alt-Neuhaus], and he declared the following under oath:

From October 1941 I was in the Braslav Ghetto (Vilna region). The SS commander there was Brodrik. He was especially cruel to the Jews. One of my acquaintances, Zelig Ulman, with his wife and daughter, was shot on the order of Brodrik in December 1942 for no reason. Another acquaintance of mine, Blochin[?], met a similar fate.

On the night of June 2, 1942 [actually on June 3] began the mass murder of the Jews of the Braslav Ghetto. Over five days, 2,000 [sic] Jews were murdered there.[2]

From my hiding place, I saw how Brodrik ordered acts of murder. He personally used his pistol. When I left my hiding place that night to escape the ghetto, I saw many bodies of murdered Jews. From the building of the police, arrested Jews were taken out and arranged in rows of six. Brodrik, together with his men of the SS, brutally beat the men and took them to the pits, to death. In the mass murder of the Braslav Ghetto, my father, my sister and her husband, together with their children, were killed. Of the entire population of the ghetto only 10-12 [sic] people survived. In the ghetto I lived in the house of the Judenrat chairman, Yitzchak Mindel.

Brodrik would talk frequently to Mindel. In these conversations, he'd say that he planned to leave Braslav after all the Jews had been exterminated. This statement was told me by Mindel himself.

The day after Brodrik arrived, the Germans prepared pits in the nearby forest. Within a very short time, they filled the pits with the bodies of gypsies, prisoners of war and Jews. The Jews sent by the Judenrat to dig the pits said that when they walked to work they could hear from the pits the groans of people who'd been buried alive.

In December 1941, Brodrik and his SS men, together with police from Braslav, also destroyed the ghetto in the nearby town of Yod (20 kilometers from Braslav) [sic; actually 25 kilometers southeast of Braslav]. After that Aktion I saw the men returning with packages, joyful and happy.

I name one other witness: Yitzchak Rivosh [Rywosz], Munich, Central Committee.

I swear under oath the truth of the above declaration. I realize the consequences of a false declaration, and I'm prepared to appear as a witness before the court.

Vilseck, August 6, 1947
Signed: Alexander Tempelman
Signature authorized, Vilseck August 6, 1947
Secretary (signed)   Chairman (signed)

[Page 142]

Department of Advocacy in Cases of War Crimes

To the Jewish Community,
Leipzig
Subject: War Criminal Brodrik

According to our information, former Gendarmerie-Meister[3] Brodrik is located in the vicinity of Yena [Jena, 60 kilometers southwest of Leipzig, Germany], even though his exact address is unknown to us.

Brodrik participated in the murder of 2,000 [sic] Jews in the town of Braslav (Vilna region) in the month of June 1942, directing it personally.

We have incriminating evidence against Brodrik, and we are very interested in obtaining his address. We are certain that Brodrik is known in police circles in Yena, since he was active for 25 years in the police or Gendarmerie of Yena and the vicinity.

We ask that you confirm discreetly the place where Brodrik can be found and inform us of his address.

Signature unclear

(Yad Vashem archive M-21/124)

Footnotes:

1. This is incorrect, as the Germans arrived in Braslav in late June 1941 and the Jews in Dubina were attacked in July, probably on July 19.
2. A footnote in the original Hebrew of the memorial book says here: Actually 4,000 people were murdered; Tempelman wasn't from Braslav and underestimated the number.
3. The rank of Gendarmerie-Meister suggests that Brodrik was a member of the *Ordnungspolizei* (Order Police, or Orpo), a police force that operated in Nazi Germany between 1936 and 1945. The Orpo was under the administration of the Interior Ministry but was led by the SS. Their uniforms were green. The Gendarmerie (rural police) was one branch of the Orpo.

    When Germany invaded the USSR, Orpo police battalions were formed into independent units and attached to army security divisions and *Einsatzgruppen*, taking part in mass murder against the civilian population.

    In the *Encyclopedia of Camps and Ghettos, 1933-1945*, Volume II-B (2012), under the entry for Braslav, Brodrik wasn't mentioned. According to the encyclopedia, at the time the Braslav Ghetto was massacred in June 1942, the Gendarmerie post in Braslav was headed by Otto Haymann.

[Page 143]

Boris Ulman
Son of Leah and Zelig

Translated from the Hebrew by Eilat Gordin Levitan

Some individuals from our town have already recounted the story of the murders of Zelig Ulman and the members of his family at the hands of the Nazis. Zelig's son Boris was saved by chance, since he wasn't home at the time of the killings.

This is Boris's story. He succeeded in surviving despite all that he experienced, and today he lives with his family in the United States.

While my family was murdered, the Germans searched for me. They didn't find me, since I was hidden at Leib Sherman's house. Many people were afraid to give us a place to hide, because the police had informed the community that anyone who sheltered a Jew would be killed along with his entire family.

On the day the massacre of the Jews of Braslav began [June 3, 1942], I was at home. At a very early morning hour Hirsh Fridman burst into my house and screamed, "We must escape, they're killing everyone!" Once again I ran to Leib Sherman's house and hid in the basement hideout that Leib had made for his family.

After some time passed, we checked outside; I came out of the hiding place with Nechamka Sherman [Leib's daughter]. We saw wagons filled with bodies of young women who only the day before had been sent to Slobodka [about 11 kilometers northeast of Braslav] to clean the army buildings. We also saw Moshe-Baruch being led by Kizlo the policeman.

We returned to the hiding place. The next day we heard an announcement [in Yiddish] by a Jew from the town of Druya [Druja, about 34 kilometers northeast of Braslav] (his name might have been Ribash). Following the orders of the Germans, he ran between the houses and called for the people in hiding to come out. The day of the massacre was over --- so he said --- and the Germans had promised that they wouldn't kill any more people.

We went outside. I met with Leib Zeif with his two children, the Fridman family and others. Police hurried us along and ordered us to go to the Folkshul [the Yiddish school in Braslav] to register our names.

[Instead] Nechamka and I fled to the cemetery and hid there for a long time. Later, we set out in the direction of Opsa [18 kilometers southwest of Braslav]. On the way, we encountered some local farmers. They were afraid to give us shelter, but they gave us food and told us that in Opsa there were still some Jews. We stayed in Opsa for a while, and from there we moved to Vidz [Widze, about 22 kilometers southwest of Opsa]. [In April 1943] along with many Jews from the Sventzion area [Swieciany, about 45 kilometers southwest of Vidz and in Lithuania], we were all forced into the freight cars of a train. After some time, we learned that the train was headed for Ponar. (We knew by then that it was the killing ground for most Jews from the Vilna area.) When the train arrived in Vilna [on the way to Ponar], a few of us were able to jump off and flee, entering the Vilna Ghetto.

[In the Vilna Ghetto] we began to organize an underground unit and were able to collect some weapons. Here I must write about the heroism and heart of Tevka [Tuvia] Biliak, a beloved young man of our town, who like me had fled from the train

[Page 144]

that would have led us to the killing field of Ponar. Together we arrived at the Vilna Ghetto, and I was near him on the day he attempted to smuggle a weapon into the ghetto and was caught by the [Jewish] ghetto police. He was interrogated and they beat him severely, trying to get information about others in the unit. He refused to say a word! Even [Jacob] Gens, the Jewish head of the ghetto police, couldn't believe how brave he was. They beat him to death. [A description of Tevka Biliak, his bravery and death is given on pages 283-285 of this memorial book.]

Since we had no money to buy weapons, we (together with the Fogel brothers) decided to make a business out of smuggling weapons and the like to the ghetto. [Many Jews wanted weapons and paid good money to those who risked their lives to get them.] One day, we went to meet a Jew at an agreed-upon place to deliver a pistol. At the meeting, the Jewish police fell on us. I succeeded in escaping, but the two brothers were caught and sent to jail.

After some days, our unit was able to escape from the ghetto into the forests. On the way to the area where the partisans had a camp, we had to find food. We had no choice but to show our weapons to farmers in the area and order them to give us food. They went to the Germans and told them about us, and we had to split into two groups and flee. Eventually our unit encountered a Russian partisan unit, but they confiscated our weapons and sent us to a family camp in the woods where other Jews were also located. [By this time, hidden camps had been set up in the forest for Jews who escaped from the Nazis.]

After some time, the partisan commanders arrived at the camp and took Motke [Mottel/Max] Vishkin and me as fighters in their unit. At the beginning our group had only seven people, but within a short time our number expanded to 120 fighters. We were able to take some revenge for the killings of our dear family members and friends. We blew up many German trains, and we took part in many actions against the collaborators. We excelled in these missions, and we were recognized for our bravery and received many medals and awards. We also helped Jewish families who were hiding in the family camps in the forests.

I'd like to say something of Abrashke [Avraham] Ulman, a son of our town. He was able to escape from the Braslav Ghetto at the time of the massacre [on June 3-5, 1942]. On the way to Slobodka, he was caught by three policemen. He wrestled with them with all his might, and despite lacking a weapon he killed two of them. Only the third man succeeded in shooting and murdering him.

My wife Tonia was hidden for three months with a Polish family by the name of Nidzbeidski, despite the fact that one of their family members was a policeman in the Braslav Ghetto.

Immediately after the liberation of our area [in July-August 1944] and our meeting with the Red Army, Motke [Vishkin] and I traveled to Braslav. There we found others who had survived; among them Mendel Maron and Meishke [Moshe] Fisher.

I was appointed to guard German prisoners of war in the town of Postav [Postawy, about 64 kilometers south of Braslav], but after two weeks I volunteered for the Red Army, in which I served until 1949.

Boris Ulman (first on the right) with a group of partisans

[Page 145]

Moshe Vishkin
Son of Sara-Leah and Tuvia

Translated from the Hebrew by Laia Ben-Dov
Footnotes Added / Donated by Jeff Deitch

A few days before the war broke out [on June 22, 1941], rumors and events had already told us it was indeed about to start, but we didn't imagine it would happen so quickly or be as devouring and cruel as it was. At the time my sister Slova, age 20, worked at the meteorology station in the town of Braslav [Braslaw]. My brother Yosef, age 16, studied in a professional school for young people in the town of Opsa [18 kilometers southwest of Braslav]. I was 15 years old and lived with my parents, together with my sister Nechama, age 14, and my little brother, Chaim, age 12.

Life in our house was uneventful until the war broke out between Russia and Germany. The third day after the war started, we saw Russian tanks and tractors bearing artillery moving toward the Russian border [the pre-1939 border, to the east]. We understood that the Russian army was retreating. Fear began to grow. People worried about whether to stay or leave. On the fourth day, when we saw that all of the Russian families were leaving to follow the tanks, there was a great flow of young people and families out of the town. Our family too decided to leave. This was toward evening.

We harnessed our horse, loaded some movable possessions --- not forgetting the cow --- and began to move out. Within a short time it became clear that the movable effects were slowing us down because of their heavy weight, so we stopped in one of the villages and sold most of them. Then we continued on our way until we came to Miory [about 40 kilometers east of Braslav]. There we stopped, and in the morning we continued toward the Russian border. When we arrived at Disna [Dzisna, about 72 kilometers east of Braslav], which was on the border, the German bombing began, and it became clear to us that we couldn't cross to the Russian side. We decided to return, but Slova announced that she wasn't going back. Parting from her was hard. She crossed the border [into Russia] at a checkpoint that permitted single individuals. My mother said she had a feeling we'd never see her again.

Returning home, we found our house broken into and deserted. This was a Friday, the Sabbath, [June 27]. We began to organize ourselves with what remained. By this time, the Germans were already in Braslav. Most of the population remained in the town. Life became difficult; we saw that our situation was getting worse. Our right to live as free people was denied, and we were taken for forced labor with no possibility of appeal. One day [June 27, according to other accounts] they gathered all the residents of the town and took them to the swamp, and the Gentiles were allowed to do as they wished in our homes. Then

[Page 146]

the first two sacrifices took place: Shlomo [Zilber] the *shochet* [ritual slaughterer] and Chaim Milutin, of blessed memory. With my own eyes I saw how Chaim Milutin tried to run away to a field of standing wheat, but he didn't succeed.

The officer of the town was a Pole who was appointed by the Germans; Kovalski [Kowalski] was his name. He was accustomed to riding about on a horse and giving orders. Most of the orders were published on notices hung on a wall. The decrees degrading the Jews began: It was forbidden to walk on the sidewalk, only the middle of the road was permitted. Hats should be removed in the presence of every German. The hours when it was allowed to leave the house were limited. Every radio receiver had to be turned in. It was forbidden to keep animals (cows, horses or goats), and everything we possessed had to be turned in to the Germans.

Immediately with the occupation, a Judenrat [Jewish Council] was organized. At its head stood Yitzchak Mindel, Eliezer Mazeh, Sasha Tempelman and others. A Jewish police force was also organized to keep order. The demands of the Germans were addressed to the Judenrat, which took care to fulfill them. The Germans demanded the immediate resumption of flax processing and rope braiding. They demanded that groups of Jews be sent daily to work as porters and strip bark from wood at the train station. They demanded Jews for the repair and maintenance of roads. Groups of [Jewish] women were kept busy knitting socks for the soldiers and working as servants in the quarters of the German officers. There were demands for silver, gold and copper items, including even candlesticks, doorknobs and dampers; these were sent to Germany for the military industry. After this, occasionally they demanded large sums of money. Along with the claims and demands that had to be fulfilled precisely on time and without appeal, there was always the accompanying threat --- slaughter.

The next 13 martyrs were Jews who worked cleaning logs and loading them on boxcars [at the train station]. Someone slandered them, saying that they were careless in their work, and as a result they were gathered, taken outside the station and killed. The place of their burial is unknown to this day.

When the decrees began, we wore a white ribbon on our arms. But because the local police also had to wear such a ribbon and this made it difficult to distinguish them from Jews, it was decreed that we had to wear a yellow patch on our front and one on our back, with the letter "J" on each patch.

Life in the ghetto was difficult. Even at the beginning, when the ghetto was established [formally on April 1, 1942] and it was open, it was hard to get food. But the will to live was stronger than everything else: In various ways we traded with the farmers of the area, and in exchange for some possessions that we had, or in payment for work we did for them, we got a bit of food to keep ourselves alive. Hunger became like a member of the family, even among the better off. With hunger came sickness. A typhoid epidemic broke out in the ghetto. First, the daughter of [Aharon-Zelig] Singalovski the *shochet* fell ill. The epidemic was kept secret; if it had become known, they would've killed all of us. We notified the Judenrat, and they made sure to send a doctor and medicine. Due to the attentive care, most of the patients recovered.

Because of my young age, I wasn't taken for labor. But one day, a shout woke us: "Jews! Save yourselves!" [Presumably this was June 3, 1942, when the massacre of the Braslav Ghetto began.] We left our house and saw the policeman Grivkov [Krivko, a.k.a. Kriwko] (a notorious murderer of Jews) and other policemen about to surround us. At the last minute, we succeeded in fleeing and hid in the house of Chaim-Aizik [Maron],⁴ where the Maron family also had gone. We hid in the basement of his house for three days.

While we were in the basement, I heard the noise of wagons coming and going. Afterward, I found out that the Germans had left people's possessions unguarded and the local residents had robbed our house and taken everything there in their wagons. We were afraid

[Page 147]

to leave the basement. We feared the anger of those who were collaborating with the Germans. While we were wondering what to do, a local resident discovered the entrance [to the basement] and shouted at us to come out. When we emerged, I managed to flee and hid between the nearby stables. From there I saw how they killed Yoska [Yosef], my big brother, and Masha Maron's father [Chaim Maron]. A few meters away from them, I found my sister [Nechama] lying dead.

The Vishkin family

[Page 148]

With nightfall, it seemed to me that of the three families that had been in the basement [Mendel Maron's family; Masha Maron's family; and the family of Tuvia Vishkin, which included Moshe], only Masha Maron remained alive. I heard the voice of Ribash calling, "Jews! You can come out! The killing is finished." I went out and learned that my mother [Sara-Leah] and my little brother [Chaim] had also survived the massacre. All of us gathered at the police station opposite our house. From there, they took us to the Folkshul [the Yiddish school]. I fled again. I went into the house of Chaim-Reuven [otherwise unidentified], and from there I returned to the previous hiding place in the basement.

After we were caught by the Germans, my mother said words I'll never forget: "My dear children: I gave you the best I could. Save yourselves."

I felt it was now possible to move around without getting hurt. I decided to find out if my father remained alive, but Moshe-Purka [or Moshe-Furka or Masha-Purka, the name is obscure], who I met during my search, told me they'd killed him next to the bathhouse. When night fell, I went up into the attic of Rivel Milutin, where many Jews were gathered. I met a Jew named Schiff, a wealthy man who'd fled from Dvinsk [42 kilometers northwest of Braslav] and sought a way to get out of Braslav. In talking to villagers in the area, he'd made an agreement with one of the Gentiles: If something bad happened, Schiff would go to the villager and the villager would hide him. The problem was that Schiff didn't know the way to the villager's house. The place where he'd met the Gentile was in Balshnitzuvka's cellar, which served as a storeroom for drying seeds. I knew the place. During the night we succeeded in reaching it, but the Gentile wasn't there. We waited an entire day, but he didn't come. Then I said, "There's only one thing to do --- let's go in the direction of Opsa [18 kilometers southwest of Braslav] and Vidz [Widze]." With no other choice, we started out toward evening. On the way I met a policeman with his bride, who I'd studied with at school. She knew me, but we didn't exchange a word. At midnight we arrived in Opsa without any problems. In the first house we saw a couple sitting and smoking a cigarette; we approached and asked them to take us to the ghetto. I knew that the police were located in the middle of Opsa and the ghetto was on the other side, but I didn't know the way there. The man we approached was a policeman, and he asked me for money in exchange for taking us there. We entered the ghetto using a back road. In the Opsa Ghetto, little by little, people from Braslav who'd survived began to gather.[2] That's how Sasha Tempelman arrived with his wife and son.

We decided not to stay in Opsa, but to move on to Vidz [about 22 kilometers southwest of Opsa]. One night we gathered, about 10 people, and started out toward Vidz. It began to rain, and we took the wrong road. All night we looked for the right road; we were soaked to our bones. We decided to wait until morning to see where we were; we'd check the road during the day and go at night. We discovered that we were next to the holding of a landlord who Sasha Tempelman knew. This man gave us food. We waited for night to come. Suddenly, we saw a group of people. We learned that they were Jews who'd come from the Vidz Ghetto to cut trees. In this way, we reached the Vidz Ghetto.[3] Leibka Tvoretzki went with me; he was a resident of Vidz and took me to his house. There was great joy when Leibka returned to the house alive. And so my life in the Vidz Ghetto began. The Judenrat there took care of people who arrived with nothing at all, and so I received food.

Bit by bit, people from Braslav arrived. I stayed in Vidz for a very short time. The decrees of the Germans, who demanded workers for Podbrodz [Pabrade, 72 kilometers southwest of Vidz and in Lithuania], arrived also in this ghetto. It was the end of the summer [1942]. Workers were demanded for labor at a sawmill. From 20 young men, all of them refugees from Braslav, there were six of us who knew each other: Moshe Milutin, Chaim Burat, Borka [Boris] Ulman, Mulka [Shmuel] Maron, Itzka [Yitzchak] Reichel and me.[4] The Judenrat gave us some money, and we went out to work. We decided that all of us would live as a commune. We found a work camp of Jews from Vilna [Podbrodz was about 45 kilometers northeast of Vilna]. The food was scarce, but they allowed us to go out on Sundays to the villages to ask for food. The one responsible for us to the Germans was a Jew named Margolis, and this

[Page 149]

was useful to us. From the Gentiles we received a slice of bread, a bit of meat, and so we didn't feel hunger.

Older Germans guarded us. They'd served during World War I and remembered the local towns. I can't say they were bad men. About them, it could still be said that they treated us decently. They simply fulfilled their tasks.

From Podbrodz we were transferred to Duksht [Dukstas, about 75 kilometers to the northeast and in Lithuania], because the German who was responsible for us bought a sawmill for himself and he needed workers. Most of the labor involved preparing ties for railroad tracks.

We lived in a Jewish house and there we were between 30-40 people, men and women, mostly young. Living here also was the family of a professional, an expert on wood from Sventzion, the Kobruski family.

Winter. At night, it was cold. I felt very bad and didn't go to work until they forced me to. They set a norm for us: the amount of wood that we had to saw by hand. My feet froze. I said to myself, "I won't continue to work, no matter what." I approached the stove. A Jew, whose name I don't remember, said that if I sat next to the stove my condition would get worse. Already I couldn't walk. With difficulty, I took off my boots and saw that my toes were white from the cold.

The next day I went to the doctor and asked for an acknowledgment that I was unable to work. The doctor said to me, "Do you want me to put my own head at risk for your sake?" He had a calendar in which he recorded the condition of health of everyone who was sick, whether he needed to rest or not.

When I stood up to leave, the doctor called me and wrote in his calendar that I was unable to work. I remained in the camp and of course I tried to carry out jobs, as far as I was able. In the house I rubbed coal on my feet, so they'd think my condition was worse than it was. All this I did after receiving information that my uncle, who'd been in the Vidz Ghetto, was now near Nementchin [in Lithuania] in the forest, and it was good there. This intrigued me, and I wanted very much to go to him. My uncle sent me a small amount of money and a letter. I understood that he wanted me to come to him.

I was freed from the camp. I traveled from Duksht to the Sventzion Ghetto [about 50 kilometers to the south and in Lithuania], and from there I began to search for roads in the direction of Nementchin [about 60 kilometers southwest of Sventzion and 20 kilometers northeast of Vilna]. Two girls who worked in Podbrodz came to the place, with a note that allowed them to go out and return. One of them decided to stay there. I received her permission slip, and with it I succeeded in reaching Podbrodz. From there, on a market day, I went out and kept walking until I reached my uncle.

I came to him toward January [1943]. I arrived and found him in a lone house in the forest with a group of about 15 people, who were accustomed to go out every day to cut down trees. There was plenty of food, and life there was pretty normal (insofar as it was possible to call this kind of life normal). We weren't under surveillance, and there was one man who was responsible to the authorities. He told us where to go, but that was all. They took me into their group and thought that in the forest they'd be able to overcome all the problems. They also had freedom to visit the ghetto. [This may refer to the Vilna Ghetto, but it's uncertain.] The situation in the camp was so good that it even had tailors who sewed; they received money, which they shared. Part of it they gave to the supervisor, and part they took for themselves. There were plenty of potatoes in the area, as well as bread.

To my great dismay, this situation didn't continue for long. In March 1943, an order was given to kill all the Jews who remained alive. This ended the delusion. Everyone who was able to flee ran away. The day before the tragedy, two Lithuanians arrived and told us that the Jews had been gathered in wagons and taken to Ponar [Ponary, on April 5, 1943]. I fled with Mendel Vishkin, not knowing where we were going. Surprisingly, I met my cousin Itzka Reichel, who'd fled from Duksht. I'd written a postcard to him in which I pointed out in Polish that the area and the people

[Page 150]

were good. But unfortunately I couldn't take him with me, since I myself was going with a man who was helping me. This was a tailor who knew how to sew furs. A Gentile told his friend that there was a man who knew how to sew, and so both of us sewed furs for the Gentile. In exchange, we received food and a place to sleep. But this too passed very quickly. The tailor left me, and I remained alone.

I'd like to tell of two dreams I had when I was with my cousin during the German occupation: I was sleeping in the attic of a bathhouse. I dreamed that my mother came and said to me, "Get up! The ceiling's about to collapse!" Before I managed to jump from the attic, the ceiling indeed collapsed. The second dream: I was sleeping in a granary. My mother woke me: "Get up, run away! Germans are in the village." Waking, I heard the shouting of Germans. In the darkness of night, I fled into the forest. And indeed, they'd come to search for Jews.

My Gentile became deathly afraid that they'd find me. When I told him what had happened to me, he crossed himself and said, "Your mother's watching over you, and you'll surely stay alive. I was certain they'd find you in the place where you were hiding."

This was the period in which Jews began organizing with weapons, with the aim of self-defense. There was no link between them and the partisans. Among them was Itzka Shur, who was the fear of the Gentiles (he and his entire family remained alive).

Mendel [Vishkin?], who was with me, joined this group. He was killed in one of the attacks on them. Among the men of the group were Zuska, Shepska, Zamka Levin, Mendka Vishkin and Itzka Shur. I wasn't accepted into the group; I had no weapon. So I began to wander from Gentile to Gentile. I knew a farmer who allowed me to work for him, hard labor from dark to dark; I learned to plow, to harvest. The residents were surprised that a Jew knew how to plow and to harvest. I'd learned how to do this when visiting my grandfather [Gershon Vishkin] in Dubina [16 kilometers northwest of Braslav]. The fact that I knew how to plow and harvest made me happy. This might be one of the reasons I remained alive.

Occasionally, the farmer I stayed with would send me away from his house, because he was afraid my presence would become known. The question always arose: Where to go? I knew another farmer, who kept me for one day and night, then sent me away. So I wandered from place to place.

One day a Jewish man came and told me that partisans had arrived and asked him for water. They said they'd come to organize a group of partisans, because they'd heard of a group of Jews who were interested in fighting the Germans. (This was the group that hadn't allowed me to join them.) I took them to the group's hiding place. But here, I made the biggest mistake of my life: I didn't join the partisans, because I felt an obligation toward the farmer who was keeping me. It was harvest time. The man, his name was Bronislav Rymkievitz [Bronislaw Rymkiewicz], helped me so much; he put his life in danger and kept me --- how could I, at a time when I needed him so much, get up and leave? If he'd wanted to, this Gentile could have gotten several good kilograms of salt --- a commodity then in great demand --- in exchange for my head. In any case, the two groups met and together they went to the partisans, to whom I also sent my cousin, Itzka Reichel.

I hoped that within two months I'd join them. But when I arrived at the place where they'd been (I knew the exact place), they told me that if I wanted to join I had to bring a weapon. I had no weapon, nor any chance of getting one. Again I remained alone, with no opportunity of joining the partisans, so I returned to the Gentile. Unfortunately, I was unable to stay

[Page 151]

with him either, because then the Polish partisans[5] began to arrive, and they were worse than the Germans. The Gentile was afraid of them; I lost on both counts.

Several Jews organized themselves; we dug a pit in the forest and stayed there. One day, I fell ill and went to talk to the farmer. I'd begun to suffer from an ulcer; because of this, sometimes there were strong attacks of pain. The farmer's wife felt pity for me and gave me sour milk to drink. There was a doctor in the area; I went to him one night and told him that I was a Jew and I was suffering from ulcer attacks. From him I received some bicarbonate of soda. I went back to the farmer's wife, and again she gave me sour milk and a bed to lie in. The farmer's family behaved decently to me, so did the children and even the neighbors. They knew I was a Jew. In that same village, there was another family of Gentiles who hid a Jew. I became friends with many of the residents and was accustomed to walking around freely during the daylight hours. More than once the Gentiles asked, "Why are you wandering around freely in the afternoon?" I'm convinced the reason they hid me wasn't out of pity but because I was a good worker and my work was done for free, without payment. In exchange, they gave me only food and a place to sleep.

One day, I went to a Gentile woman when I was suffering from some pain. Suddenly, I heard an explosion. I fled back to the forest. I found a ditch, one where I'd used to hide with a woman and her 25-year-old son; the mother had looked like a typical Russian. Later I learned that one day the son had gone to the village to ask for food and met people he thought were partisans. They asked him, "Where are you from?" It became clear that they were Ukrainians who'd been sent by the Germans to search for Jews. [At some point, they must have followed the son back to his hiding place in the ditch.] They threw a grenade into the ditch, where, in addition to the mother and son, four other people were hiding [this was the explosion heard before]. One was killed; two were wounded. One little boy, age 6, remained alive. They took the 25-year-old to Podbrodz; the mother was wounded in her finger. Two other women were taken from the ditch. It was my luck that I'd been at the Gentile's house, and so I remained alive. A good friend of mine, Zalman from Plusa [Plusy, 21 kilometers north of Braslav], was also there.

After that, we organized ourselves, nine people. We dug another pit in the same area and organized a new life. The difficult problem of food arose. The [other] people were wounded, so the burden of finding food was placed on me and Zalman. There was no choice but to enter the [peasants'] pits for storing potatoes and steal some of them. In this place too, we didn't stay long. In the pit we spent the winter of 1943-44, a hard, hungry time. Once a day, we ate a potato and a slice of bread. We got through the winter despite the terrible cold. There were lice and indescribable crowding; we'd press close to each other to get warm. From time to time, I'd go to my Gentile and ask him to let us wash ourselves in his bathhouse. There I caught a skin disease; my entire body became covered with wounds, and I had no medicine. Fortunately for me, I visited a Gentile family on one occasion and they caught the disease from me. After the entire family was examined, they traveled to Vilna and brought back some medicine. With this, I was able to treat my own illness. And so, after some hard suffering, I recovered.

In the spring of 1944, when the snow began to melt and the first flowers appeared, Polish partisans attacked the nine of us and killed eight people; I was the only one who remained alive. They surrounded the pit and drove us out into an open field. I saw a fence and a nursery for plants on the other side. I hid behind a bush, jumped over the fence and passed through a plowed field. My clothing was thin, and my shoes weren't at all useful. I'd made shoes for myself out of wood. For some reason, that morning I hadn't wrapped my feet in rags (I had no socks), and so I ran with my wooden shoes, with a Pole chasing after me. Fortunately,

[Page 152]

it seems that he didn't have enough bullets. The chase continued for two kilometers. I left the field and ran toward the forest, where there was a trench. I don't understand how I was able to jump over it. Then I entered the forest, not knowing where I was going.

Suddenly, I thought I was in the place where the Polish [partisan] headquarters were located. I had no choice but to turn back. Hearing the hoof-beats of a horse, I hid behind a tree. I saw the rider was a Gentile by the name of Shidlovski, one of the officers of the A.K. [Armia Krajowa] (the nationalist anti-Semites), who I'd met in the past through my uncle. I walked up to him, stopped him and said, "Mr. Shidlovski, look what they've done to us!" He asked if I knew which unit had blown up the pit where I'd been hiding, and said that he couldn't give me much help. But he added, "There's a green roof over your head, the trees are blooming, the forest is the best place to hide." He suggested that I leave the area. I had nowhere to go. That night, I slept in the forest.

Toward morning I went back to the pit, to get some bread. I walked in the direction of the place where they'd chased us, and saw the dead: Among them were a boy and two young girls from Podbrodz, who lay there for a few days until the local priest asked that they be brought to burial. Here the cruelty of the Gentiles should be pointed out. Without any embarrassment, they undressed the girls and took their clothes.

I kept walking. I entered a house I hadn't visited before and asked for some water. This house was next to the forest. In it was a Gentile woman with two small daughters who offered me a place to sit and served me water and food. She asked if I'd heard about the Jews who'd just been killed, and I told her that I was one of the survivors. She'd identified me immediately as a Jew, it wasn't hard. At this time I'd begun to grow a beard, and when I saw myself in a mirror I grew alarmed. At this place, I received some shaving articles. The woman didn't ask me to leave, so I decided to stay, which I did until evening. In the evening, guests arrived. She set the table with food and drink and sat me down among the diners. I remained calm. I stayed there until dawn, and the woman offered me a bed to sleep in. The next day, after all the guests had left, I asked if I could work for her. I was sent to the granary to cut hay with a hand-operated machine and to chop wood. The woman told me that her husband had been arrested by the Germans, but she didn't know the reason.

This Gentile woman hid me for close to a month. Her name was Lavusia. In her house there was a pit for storing potatoes; there she placed a board and told me that if I felt danger approaching I should enter it and hide. She told me that she had an elderly mother who'd been staying for a month in succession with her sister and then a month with her. During the month that the mother was at the sister's, I could stay with her. As fate would have it, the elderly mother passed away in the sister's house before the month was over. It seemed to me that the woman kept me out of pity. She also told me that four Jews were hiding at her sister's house. She went and told her sister that she too had a Jew hiding in her house, who was the only survivor of the group that had been killed in the [recent] chase and was known throughout the village.

Eventually the fact that I was in her house reached the ears of unwanted people. The good woman began to worry about her own life and mine, but she didn't know how to tell me we were in danger. She knew that if I left her, my situation would get worse. I understood her anxieties, and one night I left her house.

I knew that there were Jews in the area; earlier they'd asked me to join them. These were Shachna Yavich, Elka Krol, Meir Nisan and Nitka Epshtein, who lived in a pit they'd made and hidden in; they'd also installed a stove for cooking and heating. I joined them and helped them to obtain food, mainly

[Page 153]
potatoes, which I took from the [peasants'] storage pits.

One day, when we were all away, Polish partisans, who we feared as much as the Germans, "visited" us. This was apparently the result of a denunciation by one of the villagers. When we returned, a Gentile friend told us, "It's a miracle you weren't here" and advised us to leave. That same night, he took us to the other side of the river.

We couldn't all stay together, so we separated. Three of us went to acquaintances, while Meir Nisan, who was elderly, and I continued together, directionless. In the course of our wanderings Meir found a Gentile acquaintance, a poor but good man, and he promised to help us. In a certain place he prepared potatoes, half a loaf of bread and a pot of sour milk. We hid in the forest, and once a week we went to take the food that he prepared for us without any compensation.

One day, when we were preparing to go and take our weekly portion, we heard gunshots. The next day, gunshots again. We knew that in the forest there was a road on which heavy wagons passed, but we didn't know what had caused the shooting. For two or three days, we remained without any food. On the fifth day, I said to Meir Nisan, "Come, let's go. I'd rather die from a bullet than die of hunger." At night, when we decided to go out, we heard the sound of an orchestra from the neighboring village. Meir Nisan said to me, "Look how organized the German army is. They go out to battle with music." I recognized the tune, a well-known Russian song.

We continued past the swamp and reached the Gentile's house. Meir Nisan said to me, "You go in, I'm hard of hearing." I said to him, "So be it, I'll enter. If we're to be killed, I'll be first." Quietly I went inside. From the forest, one could hear the mooing of cows and the snoring of pigs; maybe the Gentiles were in the forest. A dog began to bark, and the woman of the house came out. I asked her, "Where are the Polish partisans?" and she replied, "They went to the dogs," a Polish expression. I asked, "What's happening here? Where's the front?" "What are you talking about? It's already five days since liberation!!!" [The region was liberated around July 1944.]

I ran to tell my friend. Meir Nisan saw me running toward him, and he too started running. I couldn't say even a word. I reached him and told him that we were free. It's hard to describe our joy. But then the questions began: Where's my family? Was anyone still alive? And Meir Nisan asked, "Where are my wife and children?"

When the sun came up, we lit a huge bonfire. We undressed and cleaned our clothes. Later, we set out on the road.

I went to the house of the Gentile where I'd hidden for a long time, and asked him to prepare a place where I could wash. I must mention what an emotional encounter this was, as if his family were members of my own. His woman cried and said it was hard for her to believe I was still alive. Several days had passed since liberation and she'd worried: How could it be that I'd survived and not returned to them? I told her all that had happened to me. I'd left a pair of underwear in their house, in case I survived.

After taking a shower, we continued on the road. We arrived in Podbrodz. It looked like the aftermath of destruction: deserted houses; there were no Jews. Meir Nisan entered his house and found a Gentile living there. I searched and met a group that I knew.

[Page 154],

I met Meir Nisan a number of times after that. He married for the second time, and he and this wife had a daughter. When he passed away in Russia, he commanded his daughter and wife to go on *aliyah* to the Land of Israel, and this they did.

I remained with the group that I'd met. I filed a request to be drafted into the police, but was rejected because of my young age. So I decided to join the NKVD,[6] but they said I should wait until they needed me. After that, I learned that my cousin Itzka Reichel was alive and in Sventzion. I traveled there and met groups of acquaintances from the partisans.

And so I joined those working for the NKVD in Sventzion. We worked in the prison, and from there they transferred us to Vilna [80 kilometers southwest of Sventzion], to another prison. There I stayed for nearly two years.

After the war, before moving to Vilna I traveled to Braslav [about 165 kilometers northeast of Vilna], and there I found destruction. There were a number of Jews there who'd survived [and returned]. They began to prepare lists of those who remained alive. In this regard I must mention Zusman Lubovitz, who kept an exact diary of everyone who remained alive.

In Braslav, I learned that my sister Slova had survived and was living in Russia. I received a letter from her. I also found a letter from my cousins Miriam and Asher Reichel.

I went to the graves [in Braslav] to pour out the bitterness of my heart. I returned to Sventzion but at every opportunity I returned to Braslav, to visit the graves of those who'd perished.

In 1946, I moved to Poland. There I met Moshe Bogomolski. I regret that I wasn't able to keep a diary, I would've been able to describe things in more detail.

After liberation the desire of every Jew was to leave the land soaked with Jewish blood and go to the Land of Israel, and so I came to the Land on the ship of illegal immigration *HaMapil HaAlmoni* (*The Unknown Immigrant*).[7] Near its shores, the ship was seized by the British and we were sent to Cyprus [in 1947].

In Cyprus I met my wife [to be], Rayzeleh and, together with her, in 1948 we arrived in the Land of Israel and set up our home there. I raised three children: Sara, Yaacov and Avia, and I even merited grandchildren.

In my mind, I feel the fear to this day. The sights and horrors will stay with me all my life.

Footnotes:

1. This refers to Chaim Maron (the father of Masha Maron), not to Chaim-Aizik Maron (the father of Mendel Maron). The account of Masha Maron and Mendel Maron, on pages 72-79 of this memorial book, touches on some of the events described here by Mr. Vishkin.
2. So far as is known, there was a ghetto in Opsa through at least July 1942, containing some 300 people, according to the *Encyclopedia of Camps and Ghettos, 1933-1945*, Volume, II-B (2012). Subsequently, in August or early September 1942, some 50 of its inmates were transferred to the

ghetto in Braslav, to repopulate that ghetto because its inmates had been slaughtered on June 3-5, 1942, as described in Mr. Vishkin's account.

Because the members of the second, new ghetto in Braslav were from Opsa, the second Braslav Ghetto would also be called the "Opsa" Ghetto. It would be liquidated on March 19, 1943.

3.   According to the *Encyclopedia of Camps and Ghettos, 1933-1945*, Volume, II-B, the Vidz Ghetto had been formed in early 1942. Jews from elsewhere were also brought into Vidz: from Drisviati (Dryswiaty), Druysk (Drujsk), Opsa, Dubina (Dubene), Kozian (Koziany), Ignalina (Ignalino) and Sventzion (Swieciany). Conditions in the ghetto were poor, and a number of the inmates, especially the elderly, died of weakness and disease. (The four women from Dubina whose accounts are on pages 369-388 and pages 390-392 of this memorial book were taken out of the Vidz Ghetto in 1942 to do forced labor elsewhere, and in this way, after suffering terrible privation, they survived the war.)

Sometime around October 1942, most of the Jews in the Vidz Ghetto were transferred to the Sventzion Ghetto, about 45 kilometers southwest of Vidz and in Lithuania. Only about 80 Jews (craftsmen and their families) remained in Vidz at this time, but later they too were sent to Sventzion. As described on page 283 of this memorial book, the majority of the Jews in the Sventzion Ghetto were eventually taken to Ponar outside Vilna and murdered on April 5, 1943.

4.   The account of Moshe Milutin is on pages 227-233 of this memorial book, that of Chaim Burat is on pages 288-292, that of Boris Ulman is on pages 143-144, and that of Yitzchak Reichel is on pages 258-262.

5.   Later in Mr. Vishkin's account, it becomes clear that these were members of the anti-Communist Armia Krajowa (Polish Home Army), which had begun to enter the area from the west by 1943, if not earlier. Sources on wartime partisan activity in the region, such as Allan Levine's *Fugitives of the Forest* (1998) and Yitzhak Arad's memoir *The Partisan* (1979), mention skirmishes and bloodshed between the AK partisan groups and the Soviet and Jewish partisan groups, even as each of them individually battled the Nazis. In part, this was due to deteriorating relations between the Polish government in exile and the Soviets, who had broken off relations in April 1943.

6.   Narodnyi Komissariat Vnutrennikh Del (People's Commissariat for Internal Affairs): The Soviet law enforcement and intelligence agency that existed from 1934 to 1946, after which it evolved into the KGB.

7.   This ship, with approximately 800 passengers, departed from southern France on February 3, 1947, bound for Palestine. On February 17 it was intercepted by British ships, captured after a struggle and towed to Cyprus.

[Page 155]

Eliezer Fisher
Son of Chaya and Feivush

Translated from the Hebrew by Laia Ben-Dov
Footnotes Added / Donated by Jeff Deitch

"They have chased me like a bird,
they are my enemies without cause.
They have cut off my life in the pit
and have cast stones upon me."

--- Lamentations [Eicha] 3:52-53

Braslav [Braslaw] . . .

A small town where I was born to my parents, Feivush and Chaya.[1] The town was surrounded by lakes, with a mountain[2] at its center. Everything was very beautiful and good. Everyone was friendly, and the people were good to each other.

All of a sudden --- the oppressor came to us. He destroyed our home, murdered our relations and friends. They were scattered in every direction; only a few remained alive . . . I too was among the survivors.

I wish to tell how I survived, now that I live in the Land of Israel.

It isn't easy to recall everything that took place many years ago, but I'll never forget all that happened to me. This will be a monument to us and to those who come after us.

When the Germans entered our town, they immediately took Jews out for forced labor. They chose young men and young women and took them under guard to the small train station [in

Braslav], and promised that they would be well paid. These young people didn't return. The Germans did this several times --- they took people away and didn't bring them back . . .

A great fear took hold of everyone. Each day brought with it new troubles. We sent some people to find out what was happening; then the Germans ordered us to choose a Judenrat [Jewish Council] to handle all matters. We chose Yitzchak Mindel, Gershon Klioner, Levi-Yitzchak Veinshtein, Rafael Fisher [a first cousin of Feivush] and others. After that, they announced the decree imposing the yellow patch, which had to measure 10 x 10 centimeters. It was forbidden to walk on the sidewalk, it could only be the middle of the road. We had to take our furniture outside (next to the houses) and give it to the authorities --- whoever didn't do this would be shot. After this, they ordered us to organize a ghetto [established formally on April 1, 1942] and to concentrate all the Jews on the main street --- Pilsudski Street, several families in a single house. The crowding and the fear that came over the Jews can't be described. Each day the situation got worse:

[Page 156]

They ordered us to give them our money, gold and watches --- everything in our possession. And then --- they said --- they'd supply us with work and food, and if we didn't obey --- they'd kill everyone.

We wept bitterly, but it didn't help. We were forced to hand over everything --- who didn't want to remain alive? When we gave everything to the Germans --- nothing remained in our hands --- neither money nor food . . . our men in the Judenrat went to request something for the hungry, small children. The Germans brought a crate of loaves of bread and said that they'd come again to pass it out. We were forbidden to touch the bread.

We waited a long time. The crying of the small children increased, but nobody came. Finally my uncle, Baruch Fisher [a brother of Feivush], said he'd take one loaf of bread and divide it among the children. As soon as he touched the bread, policemen came immediately and threatened to kill him. But this wasn't enough for the Germans. They frequently invented additional ways to break us. One day we learned that the Germans were planning to murder us all. When my father heard this, he became confused and ran to hide in the attic. When he looked out from there to see what was happening in the street --- they shot and killed him. Their plan to destroy us was this: The Gentiles, without our knowledge, dug killing pits that were intended for us. None of us had a chance of being rescued, we were weak like children from the lack of food.

[When the massacre began on June 3, 1942] the German soldiers came at 3-4 o'clock in the morning, ordered everyone out of the houses, and we were taken to the pits in groups. There, they ordered everyone to undress to their underwear and sit on the ground, and not to lift their heads. Whoever lifted his head was shot immediately.

This is how they killed our group within a few minutes. The small children they threw into one pit. They left us lying there and didn't cover us with dirt. There were some who shuddered and collapsed with severe wounds. The pits were located near the forest. Toward evening, when it began to get dark --- I was lying in the pit and heard a buzzing, like bees, flying around me. I tried to raise my hand, my foot, and realized I wasn't dead. I was lying in a puddle of the blood of my dear ones, on a heap of the bodies of children. I gathered a bit of strength, lifted myself up, and entered the nearby forest. There I stayed until night. I wandered the forest for three days, naked and hungry, covered in blood. I wanted to stay alive so that I'd be able to tell of the tortures we'd gone through and all of our sorrows.

I wandered in the forest until I came to a storehouse. With the last of my strength I entered, climbed into a pile of fodder and hid there. I waited to see what would happen. Toward morning, a farmer came with a large wicker basket to get food for his animals. I looked out to see if I knew him. "He senses there's someone's here in the storehouse," I thought. "I've got nothing to lose. Either way, I'll die." So I went out and stood before him. At first, he was terrified. A naked man had suddenly appeared to him, dirty and covered in blood --- but then he recognized me and shouted, "Leizerke, is it you? Lie down, lie down, and I'll bring you some food right away."

This was a farmer who'd frequently come to us to buy meat in our butcher shop. Many times I'd given him meat without charge, because I knew that he was poor.

I thought he'd gone to bring the police, who would kill me, and I lay down in great fear. Finally, I saw him approaching with a military tunic and a pot of cooked potatoes. I felt like I was beginning to return to life once more.

This farmer was very poor and had eight children, but he hadn't forgotten what we'd done for him. Once he'd brought his wife to us; she was very ill and needed an urgent operation, but he didn't have enough money to pay for it. We'd given him the amount he needed, and in this way his wife was saved

[Page 157]

and recovered. They remembered this and repaid good for good. There were times when they brought me into their house to get warm; their house was isolated in the forest, far from the villages. I stayed with them for two years [sic]. The man was Josef Orlovski [Orlowski] from the village of Zwirbli [Zwirble], near the Belmont estate.[3]

In the neighboring forests, the Germans conducted frequent searches, in case they found some Jew wandering free. A neighbor came to my benefactor, said it was rumored that Josef was hiding a Jew, and advised him to drive him out or hand him over to the police. Afterward, Josef said to me: "Listen, Leizerke, I want you to stay alive. Until I find you a new hiding place, I'll dig you a pit in the pigpen. There you'll lie down and I'll bring you food." His devotion gladdened me. And so it happened --- I lay in the pit for eight months.

One day the Germans came, took the entire family outside, stood him, his wife and their eight children in a row as if they were about to shoot them, and ordered them to admit that they were hiding a Jew. The farmer's wife fell to the ground; weeping, she said to them, "You think the life of one Jewish pig is more precious to me than the lives of my eight children?! If we had a Jew here, we'd hand him over to you immediately." The Germans left them alone; they took some tobacco and went away.

After this, Josef came to me, took me out of the hiding place, brought me into his house to warm up, and said to me, "Tell me, what should we do now?" I replied that he should do whatever he decided was the right thing to do . . . I'd obey.

Josef harnessed his horse and traveled to the forest to gather wood. He hoped that in the forest he'd meet some Jew or maybe some partisans (it was rumored that they were in the forest, but it wasn't known where). Reaching the forest, he saw a man armed with a rifle. The man stopped him and wouldn't allow him to travel further. The partisans forbade entry to the forests, so that no one would know their location.

Josef approached the man and said to him, "Listen, an unfortunate Jew is wandering in our village. He has nowhere to hide. Maybe I can bring him to you. Will you accept him?"

The partisan gave him permission to gather wood and said that they didn't usually let people unknown to them into the forest. "But since you've told me about the Jew, you can bring him. Tell no one else, otherwise we'll come and set fire to your house and all that belongs to you. Bring him here to the forest clearing, and I'll wait for him."

Josef thanked him and returned home. He told me the story and asked me if I was willing to go see the partisan. I agreed. The next day Josef again harnessed his horse, filled the wagon with fodder, put the bench on top of it, and laid me down under the bench. In this way he brought me to the forest clearing, the appointed place. I said goodbye to Josef, and he returned to his house while I remained alone in the clearing. I stood there waiting, not knowing what fate G-d had in store for me. While standing there thinking, I heard footsteps approaching and a man appeared, armed with a rifle. Suddenly he moved toward me with a cry of surprise: "Leizerke, is it??!!" This was a son of my town, a relative --- Yerachmiel Biliak. We kissed one another and wept, remembering all that had happened to us. He took me with him, fed me and gave me something to drink. We came to his unit, the partisan unit of Antonov.[4] Conditions in the forest weren't bad in comparison with the earlier places.

The Germans were carrying out periodic sweeps and searches for Jews. At such times we'd flee in all directions, hiding among the trees and bushes, enduring a number of days without food or drink. The Germans were afraid to go deep into the forest; they moved only along the railroad tracks and roads. This kind of search would last for several days, and then we'd re-form and hit back

[Page 158]

in revenge. This is how we lived. We'd attack the routes used by the Germans and their collaborators, hoping to bring a rapid end to Nazi rule.

The partisans gathered food from the farmers of the nearby villages. I was responsible for distributing the food.

Time passed. One day we received an order to leave the forest --- the war was over --- the Russians had liberated us [in July 1944]. We came out and met them with joy and thanks.

[Afterward] I always helped Josef Orlovski and his family as much as I could, with clothing and food. I found his daughter a job in Vilna. I lost touch with him after I made *aliyah* to Israel.[5]

Footnotes:

1. Feivush Fisher was a son of Zelik Fisher and Guta, and a grandson of Morduch Fisher; this Fisher family had lived in Braslav since at least the time of Morduch, born ca. 1800.
2. This location in Braslav, Castle Hill, was also called Castle Mountain, even though it stood only 15 meters or so above the town. It was also called Schloss Berg and the Zamek.
3. Belmont was about seven kilometers southeast of Braslav. Zwirbli was five kilometers south of Belmont.
4. Presumably this refers to the Antonov detachment of the Shirokov brigade, which operated in the region to the south of Braslav.
5. Mr. Fisher lost his first wife and their children in the massacre in Braslav that began on June 3, 1942. Later he remarried, and in Israel he and his second wife raised a family.

[Page 159]

Tzipora (Feiga-Tzipka) Toker
Daughter of Gisia and Chontza [Chona] Biliak

Translated from the Hebrew by Laia Ben-Dov
Footnotes Added / Donated by Jeff Deitch

For me, life out of the ordinary began in the year 1939. The hardest thing for me, an eight-year-old, was the death of my mother, Gisia. There were two other children in the house, younger than me: Tuvia, who was six, and Sara-Gitka, who was three. We had a very strong, close relationship with the family of my father's brother, Yerachmiel [Biliak], his wife Kayla-Malka and their six children: Noachke [Nochka], Gitka [Gita], Chaim-Leib, Leizer-Itza, Sara-Esther and Chana-Feiga.

Events became clearer in memory after the war broke out between Germany and Russia [in June 1941]. There was fear in the town: The Russians began to withdraw back toward their old [pre-1939] border [which was to the east of Braslav/Braslaw], and with them went some of the Jewish population. My uncle had a truck, and there was talk of our two families moving to the Soviet Union, but my aunt refused to part from her house and possessions. We didn't know what would happen, but we were very afraid of the Germans. Relatives and neighbors gathered in our house, with much talk of the war and making of plans.

It seems to me that most of the decrees came to us on Fridays. One Friday, they gathered all of us into a large, fenced-in courtyard next to the Pravoslavic [Eastern Orthodox] church, near the lake. They arranged us in the shape of a U, with women, children, and men separated from each other. It was forbidden to move; we stood there and listened. A German stood in the middle of the yard with a staff in his hand, and shouted that they'd shoot us and drown us all in the water. We didn't understand why we deserved this; we stood there in fear. When he finished speaking, he ordered us to run home, saying, "I don't want to see a Jew in the street."

Another Friday --- a new decree: The Jews must bring to them money and jewelry. We were waiting for the next decree. We began to understand the meaning of the word "Germans." After that, another Friday came; they told us to gather ourselves on the road that left Braslav, next to the mountain [Castle Hill, a.k.a. Castle Mountain].[11] The Germans came armed, riding on motorcycles. They ordered the men to take off their boots and put them in a certain place. My father didn't remove his boots; I began to worry what would happen to him. Again they separated the women from the men. They said that they'd take us to the swamps, pour kerosene over us, and burn us alive.

We stood there in shock. Two men, Shlomo [Zilber] the *shochet* [ritual slaughterer] and Chaim Milutin,

[Page 160]

started to run away. I saw how the Germans shot them. Then they took us to the swamp. Along the way we wanted to hide in a storehouse, but we were afraid that something worse would happen if we did so, and so we continued to walk with everyone, my brother and my sisters next to me. We were hungry. It had been forbidden to take anything with us; we walked with empty hands. The men walked barefoot. My father's boots frightened me, I was afraid I'd be shot. We arrived at the swamp: I very much wanted to stay near my father, but the Germans didn't allow it. Despite this, I picked up a number of branches and put them under father's head --- so that he wouldn't have to lie down in the mud. I lay among everyone. The Germans told us they were waiting for an order to shoot us. They had machine guns. This is how we passed the day and the night. In the morning, they told us to go home. When we got back, we found all of our possessions packed into sacks. The Gentiles had robbed us, they'd stolen their booty but not managed to take it away.

After this, more decrees came, such as the decree about the yellow patch.

I found some suitable material and with my own hands sewed patches for everyone, one for their chest and one for their back. It was forbidden to walk on the sidewalks. Other girls my age were taken to knit hats, gloves and scarves for the Germans. My father didn't let me go to work; he was afraid for me. They took my father to work at the train station and to shovel snow from the streets.

One decree followed another. Now it was necessary to uproot ourselves and go to the ghetto [April 1, 1942]. We moved to the house of the Gebelman family. This was a brick house that had a hiding place. They took toast and water as well as family pictures down there. In part of the house they hadn't yet finished building the floor, and there was a lot of sand. Next to the entrance to the hiding place stood a bookcase with holy books. We felt that something was about to happen; again we gathered and talked. I heard that the Germans were killing Jews in the nearby forests. Then on June 3, 1942, a Wednesday, toward morning, it began. Outside there was a big uproar. They were shouting that everyone must come out of the houses and go to the left of our house. I went outside and walked with the stream of people. My father ran after me, grabbed my hand and took me back into the house. My father, I, my sister Sara-Gitka and Nechama Gebelman went down into the hiding place. My brother hid under the big stove. Nechama's old grandfather, a man with one leg, refused to go down. He hid the entrance to the hiding place with sand and sat himself next to the bookcase and read the Torah. When the Germans entered the house to see if anyone remained inside, they saw him and shot him on the spot. He fell over the entrance to the hiding place. My father made openings in the hiding place, and this allowed us to distinguish between day and night. Hearing shouts and shooting, we stayed inside for a number of days.

On Wednesday, when the destruction began, before entering the hiding place, I'd seen how the Germans were crushing the heads of infants and children on an electric pole. I'd seen how a village wagon was passing and gathering bodies. After the massacre, there were a few days of calm, and then they gathered in the Folkshul [the Yiddish school in Braslav] the few Jews who remained. My brother came out of hiding and went there. He soon returned, and with emotion he shouted to father that if we had any silver and gold, we had to give it to the Germans and in this way it'd be possible to save the Jews. Inside the house, in the ground, was hidden a red box

--- a savings box of PKO, the Polish national bank,[2] and in it was gold. My father took out the gold to give it to the Germans. After delivering it, my brother returned . . .

During these days of calm, my father decided that we'd go to hide with Gentile acquaintances outside the town. We went down to the lake

[Page 161]

and ran along the shore in the direction of the Dubki [Dubkes] forest. We saw that we were being followed. On the shore of the lake, in the natural pasture, horses were grazing; their feet were tied as they ate the green grass. It was hot, and we ran barefoot in light clothing. My father told us to hide behind the horses, and he said that if anyone got hurt we shouldn't make any noise but advance toward the forest. The police didn't see us and returned where they came from. We waited for them to move far away and then we entered the forest, reaching the house of our acquaintance Vincent Kolkovski [Kolkowski]. From him we heard that my uncle Yerachmiel [Biliak, brother of Chontza], with three of his children [Chaim-Leib, Leizer-Itza and Sara-Esther], had passed by earlier. Yerachmiel had told him he thought we'd suffocated in our hiding place, and had asked Kolkovski to travel to Braslav to bury us. When he heard this, father burst into bitter tears. He gave me soap and explained to me that the Gentile had bought himself a great good deed and asked me to give him the soap, so I could "buy" the good deed from him, so to speak.

We continued with wanderings and troubles [apparently they didn't stay long with Kolkovski at this time]. We had no place to hide, no clothes and no food. Each time, we hid in the bathhouse of a different farmer. For a loaf of bread, my father gave a gold pin, a remembrance from my mother. Another time, for a bit of bread, he gave gold teaspoons that we'd used on the Passover holiday. One of the bathhouses where we stayed belonged to Metzatznikov. We stayed there 10 days, lying on the floor and stools. We washed ourselves and passed our clothes through fire to burn off the lice.

The winter of 1942-43 was very difficult; we were on the verge of despair. My uncle Yerachmiel found himself a hiding place with a farmer. My father and my little sister [Sara-Gitka] joined him, without the Gentile knowing it. With no choice, having nowhere to go and with father's agreement, both of us --- me and my brother Tuvia --- on Hanukkah, we entered the second ghetto in Braslav.[3] This ghetto was established in a number of alleyways in a small section of the town, and it was fenced in. Here they put some of the Jews from Opsa who remained after the destruction there, and to them they added the few Jews who survived in Braslav.

I don't remember how my brother entered the ghetto. I snuck in by way of a well; I had to break a board and go inside. Apparently some police saw this and began to look for me, but they failed to catch me. My relative Leizer Biliak hid me in some house in a little room under a bed. The police entered the house, saw in the living room a woman sitting with a boy, and killed them. During this period, I visited a family from Opsa many times. The head of the family was a blacksmith. When I knitted a hat or gloves, they'd give me a bit of food. Once they gave me uncooked rice, which I took to the blacksmith. During the first days in the ghetto, I slept with Nechama Gebelman on a table. I'd meet my brother going around among the houses. People would take pity on us and give us something to eat. After that, I found my father's uncle in the ghetto --- Natan Biliak. He'd sleep on the big stove in the *matzoh* [unleavened bread] factory in the Bogomolski family's house. He'd leave the door open for me, and when everyone was asleep I'd sneak in quietly, go up on a small ladder to the stove and spend the night in the uncle's arms, behind large woven baskets in which the *matzoh* was packed for delivery. Sometimes I slept inside a basket. On this stove with us there was a woman from Opsa whose mind was unbalanced. They called her Sara-Gitka the *meshuggene* [crazy one]. Sometimes she'd break out in screams, which put all of us in danger. The uncle sometimes succeeded in calming her. Early in the morning, I'd get down quietly and flee, because I wasn't registered as a resident of the ghetto and it was forbidden for me to be found in the house. In some houses the people asked me not to come into them. They were afraid that they'd be murdered because of me, so I wandered around outside.

[Page 162]

It was winter; it was cold and a lot of snow fell.

One Sunday, when Vincent Kolkovski traveled to Braslav to go to church, my father gave him a note to pass to us. Kolkovski approached the ghetto fence and threw the note over it. Somebody picked it up and gave it to my brother. In the note, father asked to see us; we should come to Kolkovski's house. My brother refused. After a week, we received another note in which father asked, in fact begged, to see us. Since I missed him very much, I decided to go and see him. My brother didn't want to leave the ghetto this time either, but said to me, "Go to father, I want to die [here]." My eight-year-old brother . . . Somebody gave me boots from among some rags, and I found a light purple scarf that had been my mother's. I put on the shabby boots, wrapped myself in the scarf, put a book under my arm so that it looked like a prayer book, and without anyone seeing me I walked out of the ghetto. I was sick and had a temperature. I passed Pilsudski Street, where our house had stood, the house where I'd been born and grown up. A policeman passed by, who I recognized, but fortunately he didn't see me.

I left the town. Outside, there was snow; the Gentiles were preparing to return to their villages after prayers in church. I approached one of them and asked him to take me. He suggested that I get into his sleigh and wanted to cover me with a blanket, because it was very cold. Then he asked me where I was going. I didn't answer specifically but said, "Today's Sunday and I'm traveling to visit my aunt." I explained to him that I wasn't cold and didn't have far to go. To be safer, I didn't get into the sleigh; I only stood behind it on the step. When I saw the chimney of Kolkovski's house, I asked to get off. I thanked him and began to go in the deep snow toward the house. A dog began to bark. I knocked on the door of the house and immediately was given permission to enter. When I asked to see my father, the lady of the house said he wasn't there. I burst into tears. When she saw this, she moved a small curtain aside and told me that he was on the stove. I found him unwell, a bit unbalanced in his mind. He was suffering from feelings of guilt that he hadn't been able to help us and had allowed two children to enter the ghetto alone. He wanted to save us, but this was beyond his power. I climbed up on the stove; we embraced and wept. I asked him, "Why did you ask for me?" Father replied, "I want us to be together." I refused, explaining that in the ghetto the conditions were a little better, and if it was my fate to die then I preferred to die in the ghetto. Both of us wept. During the night, he woke me and said that we'd go to see Yerachmiel with his children and my little sister. I loved my father and couldn't refuse him. He wept the whole time. The Gentile went out to see if there was a guard on the bridge. We thanked him and parted from him. We found Yerachmiel with only two [of his] children [Leizer-Itza and Sara-Esther], the third [Chaim-Leib] was no longer alive. We stayed with them.

On the day before Purim, 1943, they killed the rest of the Jews in the ghetto [March 19, 1943]. I, my sister and my father were in a hiding place with Yerachmiel [outside the ghetto]. My brother was at that time in the house of the Bogomolski family, which was within the ghetto. In this house, when the enemy came for them, the Jews attacked aggressively. At their head stood my cousin, Leizer Biliak, who'd served in the Polish army. With a pistol he killed a German and a local policeman, and he wounded an additional policeman. Then the gendarmes threw grenades into the house, and it began to burn. Fleeing, Leizer, jumped a fence and took a bullet in his hand that held the pistol. Wounded, tired and barefoot, he reached Yerachmiel's hiding place. The others in the house, and with them my brother, Tuvia, were burned

[Page 163]

alive.

This is how we became tenants of my uncle Yerachmiel, without the agreement of the Gentile. The pit was very crowded: Yerachmiel and his two children, my father, me and my sister Tova, and now also Leizer.

[One day] My father and Leizer left to find a hiding place for us. When the days passed and they didn't come back, Yerachmiel went out to look for them. He learned from a farmer that the two had been grabbed by Gentiles and handed over to the Germans, who'd killed them.

Mourning the loss, Yerachmiel returned to us, discouraged and perplexed, and in a choked voice he told us of the tragedy. We wept quietly at the loss of our dear father.

Our good uncle promised to help us with everything, but his means were limited. All of us were in constant fear, hungry and dirty. When the Gentile heard what had happened to my father and Leizer, he became frightened and told Yerachmiel that he was afraid to keep us any longer. He, his family and his possessions were in danger of annihilation, he said, and he asked us to leave the pit. He advised Yerachmiel to find a way to reach the partisans.

What happened afterward, from this point until the end of the war, is told in Yerachmiel's testimony [on pages 96-107 of this memorial book].

. . . the war ended [the region was liberated around July 1944]. Yerachmiel begged us to stay with him, but we were very young. I felt an obligation to learn and make up for the education I'd lost during the years of the war, and so did my sister. With Yerachmiel's knowledge, but not so much with his agreement, we moved to an orphanage in Vilna [about 165 kilometers southwest of Braslav]. The place suited us, we felt good there. We studied and took care of ourselves. After two years, in 1946, Yerachmiel decided to move from Russia to Poland, and he got us to go with him. In Poland we joined a kibbutz of children of the Dror movement; its general orientation was Zionist-Pioneerist and its purpose was *aliyah* to the Land of Israel. We continued with this kibbutz to Germany, and when our turn came for *aliyah*, they put us on the ship *Exodus*, which was intercepted by British warships and forced to return to the shores of Europe.[4] Again in Germany, we met with Yerachmiel and he asked us to join him and go with him to Canada, but we were already "brainwashed" about the Land of Israel and refused his suggestion.

We returned and came on *aliyah* to Israel in 1948, this time after the state had been established. I joined the youth society in Kibbutz Afek [in northern Israel near Haifa] and my sister Tova the children's society at Givat HaShlosha [a kibbutz in central Israel near Petah Tikva]. We matured, grew up and established families.

Now both of us are grandmothers. We live happily in the present, but we'll never forget the past.

Footnotes:
1. Accounts differ on when the Jews of Braslav were taken to the swamp. Other accounts say it was June 27, and that this happened on the same day the Jews were gathered in the church courtyard.
2. This might refer to Powszechna Kasa Oszczednosci Bank Polski (PKO Bank Polski), a major bank network, established in 1919.
3. In August or early September 1942, some 50 Jews in Opsa (about 18 kilometers southwest of Braslav) were transferred to the former ghetto in Braslav, to repopulate it after the original inmates had been slaughtered on June 3-5, 1942. Because the members of this second, new ghetto in Braslav were from Opsa, the ghetto was also called the "Opsa" Ghetto. It would be liquidated on March 19, 1943.
4. This was a large passenger ship that sailed from France in July 1947, carrying some 4,500 Jewish immigrants as part of Aliyah Bet ("Immigration B" or "second immigration") attempts to enter Palestine in contravention of British restrictions. The ship was intercepted by the British and forced to return with its passengers to Europe, to displaced-persons camps in Germany. The incident deepened international sympathy for the postwar plight of Holocaust survivors and reinforced support for the establishment of Israel.

[Page 164]

Sara Movshenzon
(Widow of Yehuda-Moshe Shmushkovitz)
Daughter of Riva and Mendel Katz

Translated from the Hebrew by Laia Ben-Dov
Footnotes Added / Donated by Jeff Deitch

Our town of Braslav [Braslaw] was a regional town in the Vilna district, which included several towns and villages. Most of the residents of the town were Jews. It was surrounded by pine forests and lakes. At its center stood a hill called Castle Mountain,[1] a name that originated early in its history, so it's said --- when Braslav was a large town and at its center a castle had stood on the hill. The castle was no longer there, but the name remained.

Viewed from the top of the hill, Braslav appeared like a green, blooming island at the heart of forests and water. It was called a "second Venice." The climate there was good and especially comfortable for people who were suffering from diseases of the lung. In the summer months, convalescents came to Braslav from large cities [elsewhere] in Poland such as Warsaw, Lodz and so on. There were two Christian churches in Braslav: Catholic and Pravoslavic [Eastern Orthodox]. On Sundays the town filled with Gentiles from the surrounding area, who came to attend prayers and to buy necessities. The Jews and the Gentiles in the town lived in a neighborly fashion, without major quarrels. No difference was felt between a Jew and a Pole. Life passed in an ordinary way. There were many stores in the town and most of them belonged to Jews, who dealt in trade and various crafts. Among the Jews there were also intellectuals: doctors, lawyers and the like. It's true that among the Jews there were some wealthy people, but the great majority weren't well off economically.

There were four synagogues in our town.[2] Hasidim prayed in three of them, and the Mitnagdim in one. Three rabbis served us: the elderly Rabbi Abba Zahorie [for the Hasidim], whose parents and grandparents had been rabbis in Braslav; Rabbi Zvi-Hirsh Valin [for the Mitnagdim]; and Rabbi Betzalel Orlanski.[3] Each synagogue operated according to its own customs and was managed by *gabbaim* [caretakers] and *shamashim* [sextons] and the congregation. There was a charity fund in the town, which helped the needy Jewish population. The poor of the town were helped with everything: clothing, food and medical assistance. This help was given particularly on the eves of our holidays.

There were three *shochtim* [ritual slaughterers] in the town: Leizer,[4] Shlomo [Zilber] and Aharon-Zelig Singalovski. Reb[5] Shlomo was also a leader of the prayers and a cantor. He was the leader of prayers in one of the Hasidic synagogues; everyone loved him. As in many other cities and towns in Poland, there were sometimes quarrels and disputes in Braslav between the rabbis and the *shochtim*, but in general our town was a town of peace, and events there didn't exceed the bounds of what was acceptable in other Jewish communities. In our town,

[Page 165]

there was also a fire department. All of the firemen were Jews who lived there --- the *pozharnikim* [fire-fighters] --- and they had a large band that played wind instruments.

Braslav had many Jewish young people. Most of them were educated at Jewish schools, which included a Yiddish public school [the Folkshul] that saw many classes complete their studies during the years of its existence; a Tarbut school;[6] a yeshiva and *chederim* [Hebrew primary schools], where many went for study. The town also had a Polish school, operated by the government. The Jewish schools got no support from the Polish government; only the Jewish community was concerned with their existence. Much was done by the Jewish community to ensure their continuance. A number of activities were organized on behalf of the school [referring either to the Folkshul or to all the Jewish schools]: theater presentations, raffles, flower days [when flowers, real or artificial, were given to people in exchange for a donation] and parties.

The Town Government Changes

In 1939, the Red Army entered Braslav and the town's way of life changed immediately. All of the stores and other businesses that belonged to the Jews were shut down, as if they'd never existed. Workers and those looking for work multiplied in the town. The property of many people was nationalized, and their homes were confiscated. Entire families were turned out of the town after they were found to be "unfit" by the new regime. From the outside it appeared that life was continuing as before, but in reality all had changed.

Yeshiva students began coming to town from places where they were now unable to do their Torah studies; they wished to continue their studies at our yeshiva. But we couldn't absorb all of them, and there was also a concern that the authorities would find out. So the people of Braslav would send them, group after group, across the border into Lithuania.

Occasionally refugees would arrive in the town from the region of the German occupation. They spoke of what was happening to the Jews since Hitler had come to power. The Jews of Braslav received them warmly and helped them with everything. Such refugees didn't stay for long in our town. Their fear of the approaching evil drove them onward, and they wandered from place to place.

We in the town had the feeling that a storm was approaching; it was hard to know what was likely to happen. Meanwhile, the relations between Soviet Russia and Germany were good. From Russia various necessities were sent to Germany, and in the town there were theater shows, concerts and cultural life. But this continued for just a short time longer. On the morning of June 22, 1941, Germany attacked Russia.

War Breaks Out

Fright took hold of everyone; the situation changed overnight. It was impossible to recognize the town. The Jews wandered about in sadness; we began to understand more clearly what was coming. This we knew from the stories of the refugees who'd come from the zone of German occupation. But no one knew what to do. The Christians in the town were busy hoarding food. Many of them celebrated openly and waited for the Germans' arrival, so that they'd be able to steal Jewish property. The authorities announced the drafting of several age groups into the

Red Army. German bombings had started immediately, from the first day of the war. German airplanes flew right over the roofs of the houses, bombing indiscriminately. As a result of the bombings, it became impossible to carry out the

[Page 166]

draft. People scattered in every direction. On the evening of the first day, we saw that men of the Red Army and officers of the local soviet were leaving town and heading for the Soviet Union.[7] Braslav was left defenseless. Panic in the town was great; no one knew what to do. Jews began fleeing in every direction, to put distance between themselves and the Germans. Many set out on foot toward Soviet Russia [to the east]; this seemed to be the only sure way of escape. Some people obtained horses and wagons, and there were also a lucky few who succeeded in boarding the train out of town before it stopped operating because of the bombings. But most people remained where they were, among them the wealthier ones. They were happy to be rid of the Bolsheviks. And there were also some who dreamed that the Germans would return to them the keys to their businesses that had been confiscated. For some reason, they saw the Germans not in their present incarnation but as they'd been in the days of World War I. Christians who had cooperated with the Soviets also left town. But there were also those who looked forward to the Germans' arrival, with the aim of collaborating with them.

The Evacuation

Evacuation wasn't easy. German airplanes flew over towns and roads, shooting at every vehicle and person they could find. Movement on the roads became impossible. Many bodies lay scattered on the roads and in the ditches alongside them. Bodies of people lay in the grass and scrub, together with carcasses of horses and broken vehicles, the result of the bombings. After much effort, some lucky people arrived at the old Russian border, but here they encountered a problem they hadn't foreseen: The Red Army soldiers wouldn't allow them to cross to the Russian side. The refugees were told to return to their homes. Disappointed, people began to panic. With no other way out, they turned around to go back to Braslav. Other refugees, at the end of their strength, remained at the border. After three days, these were given permission to cross, and they moved far into the Soviet Union.

Amid the confusion in Braslav, the commissar and several officials had remained [for a time]. Many government workers there had turned to the commissar, asking "What will happen to us?" Acting on his authority, he'd given an order to evacuate as many of them as possible from the town. I'd been working as a teacher, and so they saw me as a propagandist [government supporter]. My adult sister also worked in a government position, and therefore the authorities wanted to join us to the evacuees from the town, together with our children: my son [Luba] and my sister's three children. But we had parents in Braslav and two sisters with their families. How could we leave them to certain death?! So we dropped out of the planned evacuation and on our own we acquired a wagon, onto which we loaded valuable possessions and set out on the road. We encountered many pedestrians who were proceeding with difficulty. We knew them all and had grown up with many of them. We wondered: How much longer can they keep walking like this? So we loaded their suitcases onto our wagon, and all of us continued on foot. The wagon, with its suitcases and children, looked like a wagon loaded to the brim with hay.

After going several kilometers, we found that the horses had grown very weak and there was no hope of their reaching the border. At each farmer's house that we passed, we asked them to rent us a wagon at any price, whether for money or valuables, but none of the farmers agreed to come out on the road with us, out of fear for their lives. After great difficulty, we arrived in our wagon at the town of Podbrodzh.[8] We decided to leave most of the people there and return to Braslav on foot with a small group, in the hope that we could succeed in obtaining another wagon back in town. We set out, I, my sister, my brother-in-law, and Yankel Amdur, son of

[Page 167]

the elderly *shochet* [sic]. His wife and children remained in the town. As we sat down to rest from walking, we saw an engagement between Soviet and German airplanes. A few of the planes burned and then exploded. The air battle was taking place over Dvinsk in Latvia, not far from

Braslav [Dvinsk was actually 42 kilometers northwest of Braslav], but to us it seemed like it was happening above our heads. On the way, we met our neighbor Yoska [Yossel], the son of Yitzchak Peretz. He and his family had traveled from town to town in a wagon, behind which they tied a cow. They told us that we were returning to Braslav for nothing; not a single person from the government was left in the town. In his opinion, we wouldn't be able to get a wagon and the farmers were already robbing the homes of the Jews.

With no other option, we used our last bit of strength to return to Podbrodzh, where we'd left the others. There we found many people who'd returned from the Russian border. Yossel, the son of Yitzchak Peretz, was a militia man for the commissar, and he set out for the border to learn the situation. After some effort, he succeeded in contacting the *ispolkom* [executive committee], where by chance he found his son Meir, who told him that he could do nothing except return home. The Germans, he said, had already surrounded the entire region; the commissar himself and his people didn't know if they'd be able to escape. When we heard this news, we returned to Braslav. After we'd gone some distance, the son of a farmer acquaintance, Vanka Balufka [or Balopka], came out to meet us in his wagon. He'd heard about our situation and came to take us to his house, to his village of Madinki, 14 kilometers from our town. We stayed in his house for a week.

Since I'd been a teacher under the Soviet regime, the Communist Party had asked me to serve as a propagandist. I'd refused, for obvious reasons [not being a Communist], but I did appear on their list of such people, even though I'd never carried out such a task for them. If the Germans saw my name on the list, my fate would be sealed. Since I'd finally decided to return home, those I was with all joined me. We set out on foot [for Braslav] because our "good" Gentile didn't want to take us there. The reason for his refusal became clear to us only later.

Under German Rule

For a week, Braslav was without a government. Then a motorcycle unit appeared, passing through all the streets of the town and then going away. Just a few days later, the German army entered the town in full strength. Immediately it began to issue one decree after another. The first was that the Jews had to choose a committee [Jewish Council, or Judenrat] through which the Germans would manage the Jewish population, and which would carry out the German orders. The members of the committee were people from Braslav: [Yitzchak] Mindel, [Eliezer] Mazeh, [Gershon] Klioner, Leib Valin, and others.

The first [sic] decree was that all the Jews had to wear a yellow patch on which there was a Magen David [Shield of David]. It was forbidden for a Jew to appear outside without the yellow patch. It was forbidden for Jews to come into contact with non-Jews. Bread would be sold to Jews and rationed, at a place set aside for them, to 150 grams per person per day. A night curfew was imposed; it was forbidden to leave one's house after six o'clock in the evening.

Once more, refugees from Latvia and Lithuania arrived in Braslav. The situation grew difficult. Occasionally the Germans would ask for more workers. Each day, the committee had to supply a large number of them, for work without wages. SS men urged the workers to work quickly. Whoever didn't "find favor" in their eyes they killed on the spot, by shooting. The jobs involved construction, work on the railroad, knitting sweaters, manufacturing gloves, ropes and other kinds of services. One day, the workers on the railroad returned but 13 of them

[Page 168]
were missing. These had been taken to another place, and later we learned that all of them had been killed.

The Gestapo Begins to Operate

Every Friday, there was a new decree. Once they took all the Jews of the town from their houses and concentrated them in the square next to the church. They arranged them all in rows, separating the men, women and children. The sight was shocking. The heart cried out to see our elderly rabbi, Rav Abba [Zahorie], with his long beard and holiness radiating from his face, among those who were standing there. They put the refugees who'd come to Braslav in separate rows.

All those who stood there thought this was their last day. Mothers began to hide their children near themselves; they wanted to die together. The men of the SS took their time, enjoying the helplessness of the Jews. From a distance, laughing, they looked at their victims and set their dogs on people to heighten their enjoyment.

After several hours, which to us seemed like forever, they began to count the people in the rows. They counted, and repeated, and counted. They began shouting at the rows of refugees, "Why did you flee your homes? Don't you like the Germans?" After much effort, the men from the committee [the Judenrat] succeeded in explaining to them that the refugees hadn't fled from the Germans. Here too, they said, was a German government. The refugees had come here, they explained, because their homes had been destroyed by the bombings and they had nowhere else to live. This time, the committee succeeded in rescuing everyone. First the women were sent home, and after some hours the children. The men were held for many more hours. In the end they too were freed, and all of us were glad when they returned home.

One day, a large army arrived in Braslav and seized the entire shore of the lake. We were told that they intended to establish an airfield with a length of several kilometers. The Russian air force began to bomb concentrations of Germans, and this continued for hours. After several days, the German army left and moved onward. In the area remained only several heavy vehicles that had been damaged. We didn't know about these losses in the German army. After this event, the Germans accused a hunchbacked Jewish woman, Beilka Deitch, of summoning the Russian airplanes. They tortured her severely, and in the end they murdered her.

Braslav was bombed. Our house stood near the electric power station, which became a target for the bombs. After a difficult night of bombings, we left the house and entered the forest, several kilometers from town. In the forest stood a lone house in which fishermen sold their catch; the house belonged to Shneiur Aron, a wealthy Jew from Braslav. Our family had business ties to him, and the guard stationed at the house knew us well. When we appeared, he gave us a key to the house. We'd fled the town with nothing, not even food; now we had to get something to eat, at least for the children. I set out with my sister to retrieve food from our house, while my other two sisters traveled to other villages.[9] The husband of one of them had been taken prisoner by the Russians, leaving her with three small children; the second sister traveled to other villages looking for food with her husband and their three children. Her oldest son had been taken by the Red Army when Braslav was evacuated. We walked along the shore of the lake, which was full of Germans, but they didn't harm us. We arrived at our home, took all we could carry, and returned to the forest. While we were walking outside, we heard that the Germans were driving everyone outside, out of their homes. We quickly dropped everything and ran to the shore, which had already emptied of soldiers. We continued to run toward the forest. From afar, the shouts

[Page 169]

of the Germans could be heard. We ran to the house where we'd left our families. They were standing outside and didn't know what was happening in town. With them now were more Jews, who'd succeeded in getting away. We told them briefly what we knew. When we looked toward the town, we saw a large line of people moving toward us. We quickly entered the dark room inside the house and sat quietly. The Gentile guard hung a lock on the door of the house from the outside, to show that no one was in the house, and returned to his own house. A short time later, we heard motorcycles approaching. The guard emerged from his house and took his cow out of the cowshed to lead it to pasture, acting as if he didn't know what was happening. The Germans asked him where the road led and if any Jews were there. When I looked outside, I saw my sister and my brother-in-law with their children among the Jews in the procession. After speaking with the guard, the Germans continued on their way.

A number of days later, we learned that the Germans had gathered the Jews [of Braslav] in order to kill them, but they'd been prevented from doing this by the locals, among them Dr. Baretzki [Barecki], who protested vehemently to the town authorities. The Gentiles argued that they knew all of the residents of the town; all of the Jews were locals and there were no Communists among them. In this way, that day they succeeded in rescuing the Jews.

From day to day, the decrees and troubles multiplied. From time to time, the Germans demanded larger sums in ransom. They also took gold, silver and copper. They even took the copper handles off the doors, and clothing. They confiscated everything.

Despite the strict prohibition against Gentiles visiting Jewish homes, they occasionally came anyway. In exchange for the little bit of food they brought with them, they took valuables. After some time, when the houses were empty of all valuables, they began to take furniture. "Why do you need furniture?" they said, "they'll kill you in any case."

The Ghetto

The Jewish committee received an order from the Gestapo to concentrate all the Jews in a ghetto. It was determined that the ghetto would be on the main street, which was two kilometers long: Pilsudski Street, whose name had been changed to Lenin Street under the Soviets. One side of the ghetto, where people lived who were able to go out to work, was called the "live ghetto"; the other side, populated by the elderly, the weak and children, was called the "dead ghetto." Much crying accompanied the ghetto's establishment [formally on April 1, 1942]. Everyone felt that this was just a temporary step before utter destruction. Rumors circulated that in Lithuania and towns near us, all of the Jews had already been killed. Still, everyone lived with a hope in their hearts, which they didn't express openly, that maybe they'd succeed in escaping this hell.

The problem of food in the ghetto was very serious. As mentioned, before the ghetto was established, Gentiles would come with food to the homes of the Jews. They weren't allowed to enter the ghetto freely. And Jews who went to work outside the ghetto were able to get a bit of food and bring it into the ghetto, at great risk. More serious was the situation of the people who weren't taken for work; they simply died of hunger.

Our house stood on the edge of the "live ghetto," so we were allowed to stay where we were. We were near the lake, and there were times when Gentiles brought us a little food by making use of the lake. These were the parents of students I'd taught. My father sat for entire days and ground seeds of grain in a coffee grinder, and from the little bit of flour they baked

[Page 170]

bread. The mutual aid in the ghetto was comprehensive. All the food that arrived was divided equally. The poor of the ghetto weren't charged when ransom was paid to the Germans. On the contrary, they were provided with help.

News reached the ghetto about large excavations that the Germans were making in the nearby forest. This news shocked everyone. The mouth couldn't bring itself to express what was in each heart. In this way, things had continued for nearly an entire year.[10] It wasn't clear to anyone what should be done and what it was possible to do. Many began to divide their possessions among "their" "good" Gentiles for safekeeping, in the hope that they'd succeed in remaining alive with the help of the items they'd entrusted.

But in fact, most of the Gentiles turned into beasts of prey. Even the good ones, who we trusted, saw the Jews of the ghetto as superfluous. Those who'd been given Jewish possessions to safeguard wanted to rid themselves of the Jews as quickly as possible. Among the Jews of Braslav, Zelig Ulman, of blessed memory, gave all of his possessions to his Christian friend, who he'd known for many years. Sometime later he asked the friend for one of the items, and this friend drove him from his house and informed the Gestapo that Ulman was a Communist. The next day the Gestapo arrested Ulman, his wife [Leah] and their daughter [Chasia], took them to the forest and shot them. Their son Borka [Boruch/Boris] wasn't in the house at the time of the arrest, and so he was saved and survived. He married a girl from Braslav, Tania Karasin, and today they live in America. Our "good" Gentile, Vanka Balufka, whose family our father had supported for many years --- they were poor, like all the families of their village --- when we told him that we wanted to return to Braslav, he wasn't prepared to drive us in his wagon, so we went on foot. His behavior surprised us. We didn't see at the time that his dream was to take everything from us; this became clear to us only later. Each day, he'd come to our house in the ghetto with stories: "Why should you live here? In other places, Jews have already been killed. Come to me, I've prepared a hideout for you." We didn't go with him, but he'd always return home with the good things that we gave him. We were four sisters, each of us with her own family, and with parents of good standing. Everything that we had was passed to Vanka to "guard." We believed sincerely that the possessions were only being safeguarded, up until the time when we asked him, "Vanichka, tomorrow bring us a bit of sugar from our sugar, for the children" --- and he didn't bring it.

Intentional Deception

On June 10 [sic],[111] 1942, all the Jews of the region had to concentrate themselves in Braslav. For some time, the residents of the ghetto had been preparing hiding places and bunkers. We heard that the ghetto in Miory, a town 44 kilometers from Braslav, was being destroyed.[112] The Judenrat sent messengers to Miory to investigate, and they returned with the bitter news that it was indeed true. The men of the Judenrat turned to the Gestapo [in Braslav] for clarification but, as always, the Germans denied everything. To Braslav, they said, nothing could happen, because its people were quiet, disciplined and good workers. The day before the destruction of the Jews of Braslav, they gathered a group of young girls and sent them to work in Slobodka, 10 kilometers from Braslav [actually 11 kilometers to the northeast]. That same evening, there arrived in Braslav large vehicles covered with tarpaulins, which the Germans hid in a garage near our house. Nobody knew what these vehicles were. They were vehicles of destruction that people called *dusha-gubki* [soul-destroyers, in Russian].[113]

That night, there was great unrest. The heart guessed that something horrible was about to happen. I suggested that we sleep in the bunker the next night; we'd take with us into hiding only medicine, nothing else. But by the "next night," it was already too late . . .

[Page 171]
Destruction of the Ghetto

On June 3, 1942, the 18th of Sivan, toward morning I heard shouting. I looked out the window and saw that Germans were surrounding the ghetto. And I saw Germans dragging by his feet the little child of Lubka Veis, our neighbor across the street; now and then, his little head was striking the pavement.[114] The Germans began to drive Jews out of their houses and concentrate them in a number of places; among others, next to the building that had once served the militia and been a public school. All around, Germans and [local] volunteers were standing guard. After that, they took the Jews, group by group, to the area of the pits in the forest [north of Braslav]. They ordered them to undress, and they shot them.

Many victims fell in the streets of the town and in the yards; all those who didn't manage to enter the bunkers, or whoever ran into the street. The Germans demanded that Jews gather the dead in wagons. There was great confusion; many became deranged. Our neighbor Maishke, when he heard what was being done, burst out of his house, leaving his wife and children inside. His wife ran after him, searching for him in the streets of the town. The Germans immediately killed Maishke, his wife and his children. This wasn't the only such incident. People who failed to reach their own hiding places entered the bunkers of others. Many hiding places became filled with more people than they could hold. Mothers suffocated their children so that their crying wouldn't reveal the bunker's existence. Before the destruction began, many people tried to give their children, mainly girls, to the Christians, thinking that in this way the children might survive.

This didn't go well. The children were returned to their parents by those same Gentiles. Such an incident happened with Beilka Gans. She dressed her daughter in nice clothes and left her next to the house of a Polish Christian, but the Polish woman recognized the girl and returned her to Beilka. All of them were destroyed.

The Gentiles robbed the homes of the Jews. If they found Jews inside, they handed them over to the Germans. Most of these Gentiles were known to the Jews. The destruction of the Jews of Braslav and the surrounding area continued for a long time.

In those days, there weren't yet any partisans in our area. The local [Jewish] youths had just begun to organize themselves, but it was impossible to get any weapons. It had been thought that organizing such activity required extreme caution, otherwise it would accelerate the destruction.

Right at the start of the ghetto's destruction, the chairman of the committee, the Jew [Yitzchak] Mindel, who was beloved by us all, went to the Gestapo and asked them why they were killing the Jews. They replied, "This is an order." Mindel then asked them to shoot him first, and they killed him on the spot.

I will tell of other acts of bravery.

There was a man from Braslav, Moshe-Baruch was his name. He wasn't a young man, but he was learned in the Talmud and accustomed to crossing the Lithuanian border with the yeshiva students. For a time, he cleaned the stables in our town. He was strong. When local farmers revealed to the Germans the location of their hiding place and they broke into it, Moshe-Baruch fell upon one of them and bit his thumb. Furious, the Germans tied 20 women to each other; among them was my elderly aunt, Riva-Dina. Moshe-Baruch himself they tied up last and, lashing them all with a whip, they made them run to a pasture and there they killed them all.

Another incident, in which a young Jew was involved: When the Germans broke into their house to expel

[Page 172]

them all, he fell upon a German, strangled him, and put on his clothes. He ran outside with the German's weapon in his hands, shooting in every direction. Until the Germans understood what was happening, he managed to kill several of them and their escorts, the farmers. In the end, they surrounded him and shot him and his family.

Moshe Barmapov and several young men from Braslav hid in an attic near the church. From above, they saw the daughter of Yakobson the dentist running toward the church; a bayonet was stuck in her back, and local Polish hooligans were with her. The priest came out to meet her, and the girl --- saying that she could endure no more --- begged him to kill her. That's how she died.

On the morning [of June 3], when we heard the shouts of the Germans, we understood what would happen. I and my two-year-old son immediately went up carefully into our hiding place. My mother also wanted to go up with my father, but they couldn't manage to do so. The Germans were already inside the house and drove them outside. Our mother begged them to let her take a head scarf and the murderers replied, "No need, you won't freeze from the cold." My mother's last words were this request.

I was left alone with my child; my husband had died at the start of the war. We didn't go down into the bunker. I didn't think I'd remain alive, and I didn't want to see, nor my relatives to see, how they'd murder my child. The Germans were killing the children in an extremely cruel way: They'd strike a child's head against a tree or split it in two. Against children, they didn't use ammunition. A "good German" would shoot into the mouths of the children when they cried. I thought that if they found me, they'd kill me first and then I wouldn't have to see the death of my child. So we sat for an entire day in the attic. We were very cold, even though the sun was shining. We'd had no time to dress, and the boy neither ate nor drank. Fear took hold of him as well. We heard everything that was happening around us: the shouts, the running, the shooting. Next to us lived a childless woman, Dinka [Dina] Dagovitz. She was ill with the final stage of tuberculosis and unable to speak even a syllable. When the Germans entered she shouted, "Mama!" and they killed her immediately in her bed.

For an entire day, they robbed and murdered. They failed to find us, even though a German came up to the attic where I and my child were hiding.

In the evening hours, it grew quiet; the Germans were afraid to move around at night. Near our house was located a German guard post. Suddenly I heard people calling my name. I looked outside and recognized my cousin [Benyamin Movshenzon], with two of my sister's children. They came up to us, and we all entered the hiding place. There were six loaves of bread there and a container of drinking water. Nobody touched the food or the water. Fear silenced hunger and thirst.

My Cousin

My cousin [Benyamin Movshenzon] lived in a small town, Rimshan [Rimszan], in the Braslav district [about 45 kilometers southwest of Braslav and now in Lithuania]. This place had also been under Soviet occupation. Formerly, he'd dealt in trade and the rental of lakes. He knew the farmers in the area; he had good relations with them and would buy their products. His wife [Liba] was a seamstress; they had four children [Eli-Yakum, Sara-Ela, Rachel-Leah and Yehuda]. Their family had lived for many years in Rimshan. Since my cousin was accepted by the local men, [before June 1941] they chose him and his Polish friend for the local militia.

Once [during the Soviet occupation], the two of them saw a German parachute into an open field. They took him prisoner and turned him over to the Russian authorities. When the war broke out [in June 1941] and the government authorities began to evacuate, together with the men of the militia, my cousin and his family left their small town in a wagon. On the way they passed Braslav, where

[Page 173]

my cousin's sister [Batia] lived; she was married to Chaim-Yisrael Reichel. This brother-in-law advised my cousin to stop traveling and to remain in Braslav; the security situation on the roads also made it difficult to continue. During those days, more Jews arrived in Braslav from Rimshan. After some time had passed in Braslav, my cousin's wife [Liba] demanded that the family return to Rimshan. "We did no harm to anyone, and everyone respects us," she said, "why shouldn't we return home?" So they set out on the road. When they reached Rimshan, they saw German notices and orders on the walls of the houses. One of the notices stated: "Anyone who succeeds in apprehending Benyamin Movshenzon" --- my cousin's name --- "will receive a prize of 3,000 German marks. He can be brought in alive or dead." Benyamin was a brave man, tall and strong, but this wasn't enough at the time. He was forced to flee the area, while his wife remained in Rimshan. A few days later, the Germans drove all the Jews of Rimshan from their homes. The Jews scattered here and there, to places where they had acquaintances, but this reprieve lasted only a short time. One day, the Germans gathered all the Jews from Rimshan and the surrounding area and took them to one place --- Zarasai, in the heart of a tangled forest in Lithuania --- and murdered them all. In this place were buried 8,500 Jews.[15] The length of the killing pit was half a kilometer. Farmers in the area said that for days after the cruel massacre, groans were heard from the pit.

After Benyamin fled for the second time from Rimshan [leaving his wife behind], he went to his sister in Braslav. It was his intention to stay in Braslav for a while until he was forgotten, but this proved impossible. One day, Germans came to his sister's house to arrest him. They were taken there by a Polish woman from Rimshan whose husband, a Polish policeman, had hidden from the Germans after the Polish-German war [in 1939]. In defaming Benyamin, the policeman's wife sought to gain two things: to clear her husband's name and to get the bounty that had been promised for Benyamin's head. Luckily, when the Germans arrived with the Polish collaborator, Benyamin wasn't in the house.

After this, Benyamin felt that he couldn't hide in Braslav, he'd be captured if he stayed there. So he fled, wandering from place to place, avoiding every acquaintance. Many people from the villages were busy searching for him, attracted by the size of the bounty. At last, after many days of wandering without food, he had to sneak back into Braslav. He was also plagued with worry about his family's safety, and later he decided to go out to the area [around Rimshan] to search for his parents, wife and children. In this way, he arrived at the home of a farmer, one of his father's friends, where he found his father hiding in the bathhouse. On seeing his son, the father --- who was 70 years old --- took off his "four corners" [*tallit katan* or small *tallit*, a four-cornered undergarment with ritual fringes attached to the corners], gave it to his son together with a prayer book, and said to him, "My son, you'll remain alive, but flee from here." Benyamin found his wife and children at the home of another farmer, who was also a friend of his father. His wife begged him to leave the area, because people were searching everywhere for him. She gave him the names of farmers who were their friends, to whom she'd given property to safeguard. She lived in the hope that both of them would be able to make use of this property. Benyamin set out to find a hiding place for himself and his family. It wasn't easy. And then, on a day when he was searching, he learned from a farmer that all of his dear ones had been lost. The Germans had gathered all the Jews of the area, among them his wife and his children, his parents, his sisters, his brother and their children, and killed them all [in the massacre in the Pazemis Forest already described at the beginning of this page]. Anguished and broken, Benyamin returned to Braslav and lived with my sister Raizel Ulman. The roof of her house was attached to the roof of ours. We'd spent many days together before the war. So he also knew the location of our hiding place, and he came to us.

[Page 174]
The Dream
Adults weren't the only ones who were traumatized by this terrible period. [This passage jumps back in time, to the period when Benyamin Movshenzon was living with the narrator's sister, Raizel Ulman, before the massacre of the Braslav Ghetto that began on June 3, 1942.] Children too were wounded in their very souls. Once at midnight, my sister's young son began to feel bad. He began to writhe in convulsions, and white foam appeared on his lips. His condition worsened by the hour, his life was in danger. Where could we find a doctor, especially at this hour? The curfew forbade Jews from going outside before six o'clock in the morning, so who could go? The children were small, their father was a prisoner of the Russians, and only their mother [the narrator's sister, presumably Raizel] was with them. Despite the danger, I ran outside and made my way to the house of the Polish doctor, Dr. Baretzki. Dogs guarded his house, it wasn't easy to reach him. I knocked on his door, and he came out. He listened and understood, but didn't want to go with me to the child. "It's still night-time, and the sick boy is a Jew," he said. But he didn't send me away empty handed; he explained what I should do to ease the boy's suffering. This I did, and the boy improved and passed out of danger.

Another night, Benyamin had a dream. In it, his father, who was no longer among the living, said to him, "My son, this week and perhaps for two weeks more you'll remain here, but after that you must flee from this place. And you'll remain alive." Greatly agitated, Benyamin woke up. He wanted to leave the place immediately, and only my sister's words stopped him. "For the time being," she said to him, "they aren't attacking the Jews; who knows what will happen? A lot can change in one minute." So Benyamin remained.

Two weeks later, it happened [that is, the massacre of the Braslav Ghetto, which began on June 3, 1942]. Suddenly the shouting of Germans was heard. My sister told Benyamin to go quickly to the hiding place in the attic, with two of her children. The third boy, the oldest, ran outside, while she ran outside to tell us and others.[16] Outside, the Germans shot her. Benyamin and the two children were nearby, but in the dark the Germans didn't see them. In the evening, when it grew a bit quieter, they got down from their hiding place and came to me [as already described in the bottom half of page 172]. They'd had no time to take anything, and we too were without clothes, because there had been no time to dress when we fled. The homes of the Jews were robbed and looted. In our house everything was packed up, and Benyamin went there to get clothes and some valuables that had been hidden among the clothing. We dressed ourselves and remained sitting in the bunker for three days and three nights. In the daytime, we heard the voices of local Gentiles who were busy looting; one would go inside and two would come out. When we were in the attic, we held our breath out of worry that they'd sense our presence. In those three days, none of us, neither adult nor child, touched any food or water. On the third night, it grew quiet. Benyamin left the hiding place and entered the house to see whether anything remained and to check if the German guard was still there. He didn't see the guard. When we learned that the German guard had gone, we quickly left the hiding place and ran toward the lake, which was nearby. On the way, we approached my sister's bunker, but there we found no one. So the most terrible thing became clear: In this Aktion [of June 3-5, 1942], I'd lost my parents, three sisters, a brother-in-law and, with them, six children.

[Page 175]
Exit from the Pit
We continued to run toward the lake. We hoped to find a boat on the shore that could take us to the other side, eight kilometers away. We ran along the shore. How happy we were when we saw, in the distance, a boat lying at anchor. Benyamin pulled out two boards from the fence around the power station, to serve as oars. Without anyone noticing, we got into the boat, but to our great disappointment we found it punctured with holes. So we left it and kept running along

the shore. From afar, we saw a bridge that crossed the road leading to Braslav, with men standing nearby. We understood that they were guarding the train tracks and the bridge. We had to get past the road without them seeing us. We continued along the fields, not far from the train tracks. After going a great distance in this way, our strength began to fail and we decided to enter the house of a farmer who was a good acquaintance of ours, Anton Patkovitz. On seeing us, he burst into tears and told us that he'd traveled to Braslav for the market day and seen how the Germans were leading the Jews to destruction. He hadn't continued into the town, but had returned home immediately. Anton took us to his own field and put us in a pit that he used for storing potatoes in the winter; he gave us food and a pail of water, and went away. Meanwhile, the day had dawned.

When he gave us the food, he'd also given me several printed pages and asked me to read them. This surprised us. Long ago, I'd been the teacher of his children. Now he wanted me to give them lessons. I saw this as dangerous and I objected, but asked myself what he intended with the pages. I looked at them and saw that they concerned the trial of Jesus the Christian. Strange, I thought. Later, after it got dark, the farmer took me into his house and said that he couldn't keep us any longer. He was afraid that if the Germans found us, his brother's children would tell them who was keeping us and they'd shoot us all [including the farmer and his family]. A hint of what he said had been in those pages about Jesus, who was likewise judged after being denounced.

We saw that there was nothing for us to do but leave. The farmer's house was a lone house in the area, built in the Polish style: a white house with a red roof. On each side of the house was a main road. One led from Braslav to Opsa, and the other from Braslav to Drisviati [Dryswyaty]. [Opsa was 18 kilometers southwest of Braslav, and Drisviati was 24 kilometers west of Braslav.] Half a kilometer away was a German army base, and Germans, together with the volunteers who served them, were continually loitering on these roads. The Jews and prisoners they captured were shot immediately. That same evening, we left Anton's house and went to the farmer Vanka Balufka, who I've already described. All of our possessions were at Vanka's, and he was continually begging us to come and shelter in his bunker, which he claimed to have prepared for us. To be honest, we doubted the truth of his statements, but at the moment we had no other choice. The path to his house led through a forest, which was near the German base. Several times, in the utter darkness, we lost our way. Toward morning we arrived, tired and exhausted, at Vanka's house and I was overjoyed to find there my sister's son, the oldest of her two children who'd been with us, a 13-year-old boy. In contrast to me, Vanka wasn't at all happy that we'd come. He put me and my son behind his barn, and he took Benyamin and my sister's three children away, to a place unknown to me. His actions displeased me. I asked myself where was the bunker he'd prepared for us, the bunker he was always telling us about. While sitting next to the barn, in the distance I saw Benyamin with the children walking toward me, pale as whitewash and full of fear. They told me that Vanka had taken them far from his house and put them in a deep ditch that dated from the time of World War I. While sitting in the ditch, they'd overheard above them a conversation between passing farmers about searching the ditch to see if any Jews were inside it. The farmers had peered in, and their eyes had met

[Page 176]

those of the children. On seeing the children, the farmers had left immediately. Benyamin and the children got away from that place and came to me as fast as they could. All of us entered the barn and hid under a pile of straw; there was no time to ask Vanka's permission. Once again, we were all together. From what had just happened, we understood that our "friend" Vanka, after acquiring all our possessions, now wanted to rid himself of us. The situation was very dangerous, we had to get away from there and find another place. The destruction of the Braslav Ghetto was still continuing; even now, we could hear the echoes of gunshots. When we left, who knew who else we were likely to encounter?

In the evening, when he couldn't find us outside, Vanka realized that we were in the barn, and he came in to us. We spoke to him and gave him something else that we had with us. We wanted him to understand that all of our possessions in his hands now belonged to him, and we asked him only to give us bread in return. We just wanted bread. The next day, we saw Vanka harness his wagon and leave with his son. This alarmed us; we didn't know where they were going. When they returned in the evening, we saw the wagon piled high with booty. All day long, they'd been robbing the homes of Jews in the town. We worried that one day Vanka was likely to hand us over to the Germans. In exchange for all of our possessions that he was "guarding," he gave us a few slices of dry bread, for which we thanked him a thousand times. We continued to sit in the barn. Every so often, he'd come to us with news: In one place all the Jews had been killed, in another place they'd been destroyed, until one day [shortly thereafter] he told us that his neighbor had come and accused him: Why was he hiding Jews in his house? We knew his story to be an utter lie; none of the village residents had seen us there or knew of us. All of these stories were intended to make us leave his house, and this happened sooner than we expected.

On the third day of our stay at Vanka's, we heard how the wife of his oldest son was having an argument with her husband and Vanka about vulgar things the two had said of us. This caused an enormous quarrel in their family, leading to blows. Afterward, the younger son entered the barn and ordered us to come with him, even though it was still daylight. We followed him into the forest, and there he told us, "You must keep going into the forest, and there you'll find a place with tangled brush." After saying this, he left. Later we learned that when he returned home, he found Germans waiting there.

In the Forest

We continued into the forest. We looked for the tangled growth the son had described, and indeed we found such a place. Benyamin tied the tops of the brush together in such a way that the place became a kind of *sukkah*[17] with a roof. We went inside it in search of calm after all the tension we'd been feeling, especially the children. From what we'd heard, we knew the Germans wouldn't come this deep into the forest, but shepherds from the village were a big danger, and we had to be on the lookout for them. We sat in the undergrowth, saying nothing. The children understood the seriousness of the situation and kept wonderfully silent.

Somehow we organized ourselves in our new surroundings. But where could we obtain a sack of food to stay alive? Around us was only forest, stretching for some distance. Even here, however, shots from the ghetto could be heard, and more than once it seemed to us as if the bullets were flying over our heads. We could also hear shooting from the German base that was near the forest. The birds in the forest were our only true friends, it was a pity they couldn't help us. Benyamin moved about as if he were sleepwalking; the surroundings were strange to him. He knew no one nearby, and he was disheartened. We could see no way out of our situation. I told him that he shouldn't think of us or see himself as responsible for us. I knew that he was the only survivor from his entire family and he was strong; if he were on his own, maybe he could

[Page 177]

save himself. As for me, I was a mother to four children [the narrator's son and the three children of one of the narrator's sisters, presumably Raizel] and I'd never leave them, no matter how small the chance of survival. I thought all of this over, without saying a word to him. I didn't want my words to influence his decision to stay with us. I told myself that if he decided to go we'd divide our small amount of money between us. In the end, he refused to hear of leaving us and we remained together.

In contrast to Benyamin, who was a stranger in this area, I knew all of the local farmers. There'd been a bakery in our house, and my father, of blessed memory, had also traded with the farmers, and they respected him a great deal. Many of them also knew me, because I'd taught their children. So there was less danger of my being caught by the farmers and handed over to the Germans. I went to ask for something to eat, and several of them gave me food out of pity. I could go out only at night; they couldn't see me in the darkness, and so they couldn't see which of them I went to. The trees in the forest were tall and thick, and cast heavy shadows; it was very dark. More than once, while walking on swampy ground, my feet sank into the earth and I got out only with difficulty. Vanka Balufka knew that we had a few more valuables with us, and this brought him to us every few days, to get his bribes and to take the opportunity to frighten us with things he said. Once he told us that the local farmers were very angry with him because of our presence in the forest. Especially, he said, the farmer Fyodor, who blamed Vanka for our being there. One day, while looking for food, it happened that I came face to face with this Fyodor, who'd been orphaned and had grown up in our house, together with his brother. Now, years later, he was married and lived on his own land like all the other farmers. When we met, he was surprised to find me there, and I asked him, "Fyodor, what harm did we ever do to you that you're so angry now at our being here? Would it be easier for you if they killed us?" He crossed himself and began to weep. "How can you say such things? Come to me, and I'll guard you as if you were my sister." I didn't go to him, but said that soon we'd be leaving the place and going away. I didn't mention Vanka's name. I didn't want a quarrel to start between them, lest we become its victims.

One day, Vanka brought to us our former neighbor, a Jew named Maishke [Moshe] Goldin --- the son of Avraham-Yossel. He'd been a trader and had acquaintances among the farmers, among them Vanka. He'd learned from Vanka that I was alive and staying there. Maishke stayed with us. Very dirty and full of lice, he hadn't washed himself in a long time.

At this time, the things that we had included a pot, a tin cup and a small military spade which we'd gotten from Vanka. Benyamin used the cup to wash the children. We didn't have clean water, only moldy water in a pit swarming with insects. We strained this water before using it. Benyamin dug two pits. In one of them we put water for drinking, and in the other we warmed a pot of water for washing and laundry. For the time being, we were clean. I washed Maishke's clothes to prevent the lice from spreading. Maishke would look at the children with pain in his eyes. I understood his thinking and ignored his behavior toward them. He simply couldn't see the point and was angry at us for keeping the children with us. Because of them, he argued, all of us would be lost. Parents were strangling their children, he said, but we paid no attention to what he said. After he'd been with us for some time and gotten familiar with the area and its residents, he'd go out with Benyamin to ask the farmers for food. What he brought they divided in two: Maishke took half, and the other half was for the rest of us: six souls [the narrator, her son, Benyamin, and the three children of one of the narrator's sisters, presumably Raizel]. In the end, Maishke ate from our share and would hide his own among his possessions. This behavior caused me much aggravation.

[Page 178]

The farmers gave me permission to take potatoes from a field. Benyamin and Maishke went out to do this job. The night was long, and they were able to go far while covering their tracks. Benyamin worked quickly and managed to take out more than half a sack of potatoes in a short time. During this potato season, we had plenty to eat.

When Maishke saw that Benyamin knew no fear, he'd turn to him and say, "Why should a man like you risk his life for a woman with many children? It'd be better for both of us if we went somewhere else. We two men would lack for nothing." These things were said to Benyamin when they went out together to look for food. And when Benyamin went out alone, Maishke would turn to me and say, "Why are you acting like a gypsy, running around to get food for him?" His intention was clear: to bring about an argument between me and my cousin and cause a break between us, so that the two of them could go somewhere else together. But his attempt didn't succeed.

Our happiness with the potatoes didn't last long. The farmers harvested the rest of them, taking them from the field. The problem of food grew even more severe, and we became very hungry. We felt that because of the hunger and the cold, we couldn't remain in this place any longer. Maishke would disappear for days before returning. Jews wandered the forest like lost sheep. More than once in the forest, a Jew would encounter another Jew and each would flee, in fear that the other was a Gentile hunting Jews. Once Benyamin and I saw a bonfire in the forest. We went closer and recognized a young man from Braslav, Idel [Yehuda] Rusonik, standing next to the fire, and on the ground next to him lay other people. We couldn't recognize them from a distance, but certainly they were Jews from Braslav. When they heard our approaching footsteps, they quickly fled deep into the forest. It was dangerous to run after them and call them out loud. We never saw them again.

One day, Vanka came to us and said that he was traveling to Opsa, a town where many of our relatives were living; we also knew other people there. We paid him, and he took with him two of my sister's older sons; one was 10 years old and the other was 13. Both of the boys had light-colored hair and didn't look like Jews. We sent them to learn how things were with our relatives. After they left, Benyamin and I went out to get food for us all. In our *sukkah* hiding place, we left my two-year-old son with my sister's son, a boy of eight. We made signs on the trees so that we could find the way back. And when we left the forest, Benyamin made a large sign on one of the trees, so that we'd be able to see it at night on our return. Beyond the forest lay a valley. From a distance we saw a number of houses, and beyond them another forest. It was dangerous to go near the houses, but we had no choice. I asked Benyamin to wait so that I could approach one of the houses alone. And I told him that if anything happened to me, he should return immediately to the children. I went by myself but, as I neared one of the houses, who did I run into but Benyamin. He'd regretted agreeing to my going alone and had run to catch up with me. Both of us entered the house and left it safely with a bit of food in our hands: bread, grain and milk. We were very happy, but our happiness quickly evaporated. We'd just started walking back when a heavy storm broke out, accompanied by pouring rain. A veritable flood spilled over us. The roofs of the houses were lifted upward in the wind, and branches broke off from the trees. All around, there was utter darkness. Only occasional lightning lit up the way. It was impossible to keep walking, but we had to go on, because we'd left the children in the forest *sukkah*. We reached the forest, but not even a trace remained of the signs we'd left. Suddenly we heard the voices of people approaching, riding on bicycles and speaking German among themselves. We

[Page 179]

quickly hid ourselves in the brush at the roadside, and the Germans didn't notice that we were there. After they went away, we got up fearfully from our hiding place. We entered the forest and pushed ahead, not knowing where we were going. After a long walk, somehow we arrived back at the *sukkah*. The children sat inside it, hugging each other and soaking wet to the bone --- a very sad sight. Still, we were happy that we'd found them in spite of the storm and the rain. We celebrated: Benyamin managed to light a fire, and we all sat around it. We dried ourselves out and warmed up a bit, while the fish cooked on the fire. After the meal we lay down to sleep, but I couldn't close my eyes. I was worried about the children who'd gone with Vanka and not yet returned. Given the time that had passed since they'd set out on the road, they should already have gotten back. We waited another night and another day. When at last we asked Vanka about it, he said that the relatives hadn't allowed the boys to return to us, but we doubted what he'd said. Despite the danger, we asked another farmer if he'd heard anything about children being seized by the Germans. Farmers said they'd heard nothing. The matter of the children was a great worry. I turned again to Vanka and paid him to travel to Opsa --- if he found the children there, he should bring them back. But once again he returned empty handed with the same answer as before, and not even a letter. My worry about the children increased.

Maishke now returned to us, bringing with him my brother-in-law Leizer, who he'd met in the forest. They too hadn't heard of any children being seized by the Germans.

After leaving Vanka's house, we stayed in the same place as before [the *sukkah*]. The forest was large and overgrown. It continued for kilometers, and it was hard to pass through on foot. We were alone, with only the visiting birds to keep us company. But by now a path leading to our *sukkah* had become visible, created over time by our going out occasionally to get food and return to the *sukkah*. This path was a great danger. Once, hearing footsteps, we quickly left our shelter and hid in a new place. "Our" birds moved with us.

One evening, Maishke and I went out to search for food. We decided that he'd go to his acquaintances among the farmers and I to mine, and we'd meet up at the home of "my" farmer. When I got there, the farmer's family told me that if I wanted to wash myself I could go to their bathhouse. To this I gladly agreed. The bathhouse was quite far from their house; I entered it and undressed. Suddenly I heard the conversation of people passing by. This frightened me so much that I didn't notice which language they were speaking. I was convinced that they were coming to get me. Their footsteps drew nearer. Now they were next to the bathhouse. I prayed to G-d that they wouldn't torture me a great deal. As I prayed, I heard the footsteps pass by and disappear altogether. I dressed quickly and ran to the farmer's house, thanking him for the bath.

When I left his house I found Maishke, who had arrived breathless. He told me that several Gentiles had chased him and tried to catch him. With a great effort, he'd succeeded in escaping them. We quickly returned to our *sukkah* in the forest. That night, I grew very cold and a hard swelling appeared on my back, which made it difficult for me to move about.

I wanted to go to Opsa to find out what had happened to the children, my sister's sons, but everyone objected. Several days later, after my fever subsided, I got up determined to go to Opsa, no matter what. Maishke said that he too would go, and we both set out on the road. We didn't know that this day was a Christian holiday and there were many people on the roads. We had to hide, but how could we do this in a field where there was only low-lying grain? Somehow we succeeded in hiding from the people who were passing by. This cycle repeated itself several times. After great difficulty,

[Page 180]
we arrived in the Opsa Ghetto toward morning.

The boys (my sister's sons) and the relatives were happy to see that I was still alive. More than once, Gentiles had come to them and said that the teacher (that is, I) had been killed, even adding details about where and when. After resting a bit, I began to ask why the boys hadn't come back with the farmers to join us, as I'd requested. I learned that the relatives hadn't allowed them to go. The older boy was prepared to come to us on his own, but the younger boy was afraid and so the older one kept delaying his departure from day to day. In light of the horrors that took place on the roads, maybe it was a good thing they'd stayed with the relatives. I was very happy to find them alive and to see them again.

I prepared to return to the forest. To this my relatives objected strongly, but on the other hand they knew that my cousin and the other [two] children were back there [meaning the narrator's own two-year-old son (Luba) and her sister's eight-year-old son, referred to on page 178]. I was worried myself; I couldn't easily find a way back to the forest that was relatively safe. But I had to reach a decision. I told myself, "Since the Gentiles know I'm alive, they'll certainly try to catch me again. It's before the holidays at the beginning of our year [in 1942 Rosh Hashanah fell on September 12-13], and the weather has already grown colder. Soon the winter will come and with it rain, snow and severe cold, and we have almost no clothing, nor a roof over our heads. The food is getting used up. It's hard to see how we'll be able to keep ourselves in the forest --- and why should we die alone somewhere out there? Here [in Opsa] our fate and that of other Jews will be shared." So I promised my relatives and friends that I'd return to the forest only to bring Benyamin and the children back to Opsa.

Before I set out on the road, my friend Rachel Shneider, of blessed memory, with whom we'd stayed when we were in Opsa, advised me to take the opportunity to wash myself thoroughly, something I hadn't been able to do for a long time. I washed and enjoyed it. Unfortunately the hot water aggravated the swelling on my back, turning it into one huge sore.

The Germans posted notices in which they ordered all the Jews from around the area to travel to Glubok [Glubokoye] and enter the ghetto there.[18] (Glubok was a town in Belorussia.) In their notices, the Germans said that they'd no longer harm the Jews. Every Jew knew that these words were lies; their purpose was to deceive and delude Jews who'd succeeded in escaping from the ghettos that had been destroyed and who were wandering the roads and forests.

Despite my bad health, I decided to go to the forest. Maishke said that he'd stay in Opsa [for the time being]. The relatives gave me a sack of bread and other necessities. I tied it onto my sore back like a backpack and, early on the morning of the next day, I set out on the road. Benyamin Shneider, of blessed memory, accompanied me the entire length of the town, which I had to pass through to leave on the best road. Between us, we agreed that if we were stopped and asked about where we were heading, we'd say we were going to work. When I left the town, I continued alone. To any question, I intended to reply that I was going to Glubok.

The farmers were already in their fields. When they saw me, certainly more than one of them must have been surprised: What? A Jewess remains? As I approached a large village, I heard someone calling my name from one of the houses. I came closer and went inside. The owner of the house was a Christian who I knew quite well. In the house I found a young man from Braslav: Shlomo Shteinman. He and his family had lived in my sister's apartment in the ghetto. We were happy to find each other. Shlomo didn't want to part from me and decided to go with me to the forest. When we got there, they told me that my little two-year-old son had asked only once, "Where's mother?" He'd been sad all the time and hadn't

[Page 181]
eaten, drunk or slept at night. He hadn't cried, just looked continually in the direction I'd gone when I set out on the road. I told them all about what had happened in Opsa. I told them the opinion of the Jews of the town regarding our stay in the forest, and added my opinion about the coming winter, rain, snow and cold. I finished by saying that I'd decided to follow the wishes of the relatives in Opsa and move there. Whoever wanted to, I said, could come with me, and whoever didn't want to could do as he saw fit.

That same evening, Maishke arrived in the forest. My brother-in-law Leizer suggested that my cousin Benyamin go with him to the front, while Maishke too asked Benyamin to join him. Meanwhile, Shlomo countered these two by suggesting that Benyamin go with him. Each of these men wanted to go with Benyamin, because he was brave and strong, but in the end Benyamin went with none of them. He wouldn't agree to leave me alone with the children.

The farmers of the area were accustomed to travel to Opsa to do their marketing. I succeeded in sending my sister's eight-year-old son with one of them. [This left her two-year-old son, Luba, with her in the forest.] Then, while the bread that I'd brought from Opsa lasted, we sat and argued about what to do. Each of us tried to change the others' minds, but everyone stuck to their own opinion. The bread got used up. My cousin [Benyamin] would go only with me, and I was firmly set on going only to Opsa, where the children remained. At night, Benyamin put my son Luba on his back and I loaded onto my sore back a sack containing all that remained. With the three other men [Maishke, Leizer and Shlomo], we set out for Opsa.

The Road to Opsa

The road was full of dangers and obstacles, especially for me, not just because I was a woman but also because I was ill. The possessions I was carrying on my back worsened the pain until it grew unbearable. The three men walked ahead, light handed, with the idea that if anything happened they'd be able to get away easily. Many farmers' wagons were traveling on the road. Each time they approached, we had to hide from them. Maishke was our guide. He knew the area but in the end he made a mistake, which caused the distance we traveled to nearly double. When we got to the town, the three men went off in another direction and we [the narrator, her son and Benyamin] continued on, not knowing the way. We knew it was dangerous for us to pass through the town, so we went around it and approached the ghetto that way. We were tired and worn out, and it became necessary for us to rest a bit before entering. We sat on the ground; it was completely dark. Suddenly we heard people approaching. We were sure that these were Germans who'd noticed us, and there was nowhere to hide. I was sure that our fate was sealed; our end was at hand. We sat quietly. The footsteps approached, and then we saw the three men who'd parted from us when we'd reached the town. All of us entered the ghetto together, and I went to my relatives to see the children.

In the Opsa Ghetto

The Jews of Opsa had been divided into two groups. Most of them had been transferred to the town of Vidz, 20 kilometers away [actually 22 kilometers to the southwest].[19] The remainder had been concentrated on the side streets of the town [of Opsa], the boundaries of the ghetto.

After the destruction of the Braslav Ghetto [on June 3-5, 1942], the Germans had needed various types of professionals [expert craftsmen]. They demanded that the ghetto [in Opsa]

[Page 182]
supply them with such workers. But the Jews of Opsa, knowing the fate of the Jews of Braslav, refused to travel to work. Once in a while, when the Germans arrived, people would panic and run to their bunkers. For us, survivors from the Braslav Ghetto, it was extremely dangerous to be seen outside, because we'd already been included in the list of the dead. Among the survivors of the Braslav Ghetto were also Chaim-Reuven [Blacher] the baker, his son David, and Zerach

Bogomolski, the watchmaker. They were hiding in an attic of one of the houses. Bogomolski was very sick; his legs were so swollen that he could no longer stand. He was also depressed and had lost his self-confidence. He wept continually and spoke of his wife and daughter, saying that it was certain they were no longer among the living, and he seemed to expect the same fate. He worried about his two sons, Moshe and Yisrael, who'd fled from the Germans. "G-d knows what happened to them," he said, adding, "It wouldn't be hard to die if I knew that they could survive this war and remain alive."

We had a Jewish doctor come and see him in the attic. After examining him, the doctor told us his condition wasn't good, and it was impossible to obtain medicine.

During our time in Opsa, Benyamin and I would visit him, bringing food and drink, and we tried to comfort him.

There were other people from Braslav in Opsa: Yisrael Kort, Shlomo Shteinman, Mashka Biliak, Dveirka Goldin, and others. When Germans appeared all of them would flee, scattering in every direction. With the children, we'd run to the nearby forest and wait. After the Germans left Opsa, we'd be called back. This cycle repeated itself a number of times.

Benyamin and I [eventually] decided that there was no point in staying in the ghetto in Opsa. Destruction was approaching. If they caught us, we had nothing with which to redeem ourselves, and before dying we'd have to endure severe suffering. But every time we began to speak of leaving, our relatives would burst into tears. "Where will you go with the children? Whatever our fate, we should face it together." In this way, we kept putting off our departure. The situation became extremely difficult.

Mashka Biliak wept in front of me. She thought she was pregnant. If she knew her husband was alive, the pregnancy wouldn't have worried her, but there was no news of him. Immediately at the start of the panic in the Braslav Ghetto [presumably the Aktion on June 3-5, 1942], she'd fled with her infant to a large hiding place where there were many Jews. Because the infant was crying, they'd forced her to strangle him. At night, they'd taken him out to a vegetable garden and she'd put him between the rows, and now she was alone and expecting a baby. I gave her some money, and she went to see a doctor.

In Opsa, we suffered three weeks of fear and mental agony. One day, great confusion arose in the ghetto. A woman who'd escaped from the Vidz Ghetto and reached Opsa said that the Germans had concentrated all of the Jews in the ghetto in order to take them all out to be killed. Hours later, Germans came from Braslav and asked for many Jews to go to work. For us, this was a sign to leave Opsa immediately. We took the children and a few possessions, and once again we fled to the forest. This time, we thought, it would be the last time. We fled despite our great doubts as to whether we could succeed in reaching a village and finding there a farmer who'd shelter us in his house. When we heard that the Germans had left Opsa, we returned there to say goodbye to our family and friends.

We decided to head for villages in Lithuania [the Lithuanian border lay about 15 kilometers to the west and north of Opsa]. Benyamin had many acquaintances in these villages, with whom he had longstanding trade connections. But most of the Lithuanians were collaborating with the Germans. And there was also this: Lithuania was the first country that had become "*Judenrein*" ["cleansed of Jews," in German].[20] So we had great doubts about finding

[Page 183]

a farmer who'd shelter a Jew. As always, our relatives and friends were opposed to our going; we decided to go in any case. But what would we do with the children? After much discussion, we decided that Benyamin and I would go out to look for a place for us all, and for the time being the children [meaning her sister's three children, including the eight-year-old son the narrator had been caring for] would remain in Opsa with the relatives. They didn't want to take responsibility for my two-year-old son, so we had to take him with us.

We Leave Opsa

We set out on the road. We were joined by Chaim Ulman, a young watchmaker from Zarasai in Lithuania [about 44 kilometers northwest of Opsa]. I won't describe the moment we parted from the children; I don't have the words to express it. Was this a final goodbye? I didn't dare mention such a worry. We embraced for a long time; crying, I promised to come back soon and take them with us. This was a difficult parting for us. The relatives fainted from sorrow.

After leaving Opsa we headed toward the forest, to get a bundle that we'd left there sometime earlier. But before we could reach it, we heard many shots echoing all over the forest. We thought maybe the Germans had sensed our presence and were shooting at us. We waited for a while to see what would happen, and then continued on the path that left the forest. We had to go onto the main road, despite the ever-present danger. On the road we saw many cars filled with Germans, as well as many people who were on foot. From time to time, we hid near the roadside. In great fear, after much difficulty, we reached a farmhouse where Benyamin hoped to find a hiding place. After we got inside, I discovered that I too knew the farmer well. He and his family received us willingly; they even agreed that we could stay with them. When we came in, we immediately told the farmer that we'd left our three children in Opsa and were prepared to pay him to bring them to us. He agreed to this but unfortunately, before he could harness his wagon to get them, we learned that it was too late. Another farmer reached Minkovitz [Minkowicze, about 12 kilometers northwest of Opsa] and told Anika Beilov (the farmer whose house we were in) that he'd just now returned from Opsa; some of the Jews there had been transferred to Braslav and the rest had been taken to Postav [Postawy], a town further away from Opsa [50 kilometers south of it]. As far as he knew, there were no Jews left in Opsa.

This farmer's story hit us like a hammer blow. We were stunned and didn't know what to do. Where had the children been taken? How could this have happened in just a few hours? We wanted to believe that there was still enough time to get them from Opsa and bring them to us. From the farmer's words, the meaning of the shooting that we'd heard on leaving Opsa became clear. What should we do now to find the children and bring them to us? To learn where they were, we'd have to send two wagons: one to Braslav and one to Postav. I wrote two identical letters. I gave them to two farmers who traveled to these towns and asked them to give the letters to the first Jew they met when they entered each town. In these letters, I begged the recipient to find our children and tell us in a return letter, to be sent with the same farmer.

From Braslav, which was closer to where we were staying [Minkovitz, their presumed location, was 22 kilometers west of Braslav], the farmer returned that same evening with a reply from Shlomo Shteinman, who I'd met in one of the villages when he left Opsa. In his letter, Shlomo wrote that the second ghetto in Braslav was being fenced in with barbed wire.[21] The work hadn't yet been completed. There were many Jews in the ghetto, and he suggested that we come there as well. To my question about the children, he said not a word.

[Page 184]

Sometime later, the farmer returned from Postav with ominous news: "There are no Jews in Postav. All of them have been killed." This burned three deep new wounds into our hearts.[22]

For a week, we lay under a pile of straw in the barn. Anika the farmer would bring us food and water, but we didn't touch this or that. The tragedy of the children [her sister's three children] had depressed us greatly. Now, everything looked different. We felt that we should leave this place immediately. Our barn was near the church; many of the Christians who came to pray would lean their bicycles against the walls of the barn. People walked nearby during the hours of prayer, and they could find us at any moment. A light cough from one of us might give us away. After that, not only would we be tortured to death but the farmer and his family were likely to pay with their lives. Before the farmer could think about all of this, we went out to find a different hiding place.

Connecting with the Partisans

We found another hiding place for all of us a great distance from Minkovitz, in a large village called Pasovitz [Paszewicze, four kilometers west of Minkovitz and just north of the town of Drisviati; on the eastern side of Lake Drisviati, now called Lake Druksiai].[23] The village was divided into *hutorim* (separate, isolated farms). Every house was surrounded by rich vegetation for several kilometers. Here in this village, we found several more Jews who'd escaped from the ghettos, along with some prisoners of war. In a spread-out village like this, it felt more comfortable, because the Germans were afraid to enter such places. Here too, we arranged a hiding place for ourselves in a large pile of straw. During the day, we'd emerge from the hiding place to meet with our companions. Those who sat in bunkers in the houses of the village knew each other. After we'd stayed in the village for some time, the place became oppressive to Chaim Ulman, who was with us. He wanted to explore the surrounding area, which was new to him, and he wanted especially to get some tobacco for smoking, at any cost. We objected to his plan to go out. Why, we argued, should he put himself in greater danger, especially when the local farmer's family had no objection to our remaining with them? We tried to convince him not to go, but he insisted and he left us. After a few days, the farmers told us that Chaim had been seized by the Germans next to the town of Drisviati, not far away [about three kilometers southeast of Pasovitz], and they'd shot him immediately. So Chaim Ulman too was no longer alive. We were sad, very sad.

One evening, when we were sitting in our hiding place, we heard shots from all directions. We didn't know what was happening in the surrounding area, and we didn't dare leave our hiding place to find out. A few hours later, after the shooting stopped, about 20 men arrived --- partisans. They'd come from Belorussia to carry out a mission. The Germans had sensed their presence and opened fire. The partisans had succeeded in getting away without suffering any wounded, and now they entered the house of the farmer near where we were hiding, to rest a bit. While we were all sitting together, the partisans told us that they had to go into Lithuania. There, in one of the forests, lived a forester who'd killed a Soviet general, 18 prisoners and 140 Jews. One of the prisoners had succeeded in escaping, crossing the front lines and reaching Moscow. There, he told of the forester's deceit and evil deeds. The mission of this group of partisans was now to reach the forest and kill the forester. The forest was called Grazuta [Grazutes], and it was 18 kilometers away [the forest's eastern edge was roughly that distance west of Pasovitz, inside Lithuania], in an area that Benyamin was very familiar with; he knew every path. When the partisans heard that Benyamin knew the place, they asked him to serve as their guide. Benyamin agreed, on condition that if the mission succeeded and they came out of it safely, they'd take me and my son back with them to their base. This the partisans promised to do. One

[Page 185]

other Jew who was with us, Moshe Okun from Turmont [Turmontas, 40 kilometers west of Braslav and in Lithuania] (today he lives in Kovno), asked to join Benyamin and the partisans. They agreed. After resting a while, they left to carry out their mission.

The Siege

Every day of our stay with Nikolai Barila [or Varila] we worked at various jobs, as payment for our food and also because we didn't want to sit doing nothing when the farmer's family was helping us. In the morning, after the partisans set out with Benyamin, I went to the field with the farmer's family to gather potatoes. Luba, my child, remained in the house. Outside, it felt like autumn; the trees and undergrowth had already shed many of their leaves. The wind was strong. Soon winter would arrive. [The time was late in 1942.] Outside it was dark, just as the soul was gloomy. Only the work in the field progressed very nicely. While I was caught up in the work and thinking about our situation, one of the prisoners who were hiding in the village ran up in a panic with the shout: "Get away from here quickly! The Germans are in the village and searching every house." With my hands covered in mud, I ran to the farmer's house, grabbed my child and fled deep into the underbrush in the field. There was nowhere else to hide. Among the bushes, in the place we arrived at, I found a little girl of about 12-13 years; her name was Itta, from Drisviati, the daughter of Benyamin the tailor. She asked for my help and protection, and stayed next to me. We sat in the tangled growth, to which I added more scrub to camouflage the place. We sat together, hugging each other, and waited to see what fate had in store for us. I wondered to myself what kind of death awaited us. Gloomy thoughts came to mind. From what had I fled, and where had I got to? Did I know what was in store for my child, after all this? I envied our martyred dead, who were already beyond suffering and torture. My heart cried out, but I didn't want the children to sense my feelings; that would increase their fear.

In this way, we spent an entire day in the tangled brush. When night fell, all of the Germans left. As we'd heard, they indeed searched all the houses of the village, as well as inside burning stoves. Happily, not a single Jew was found. When night fell, they stopped searching. This time, we were saved from death.

The Partisans Return

A number of days passed. From the front, there was news of German victories. The news encouraged our enemies; they turned into beasts of prey, prowling the villages and forests in search of Jews and partisans. For the survivors wandering from place to place, the situation worsened. Every day, we heard of Jews and partisans who'd been caught. Out of fear of the Germans, the farmers who'd given shelter to Jews did all they could to get them to leave. There were cases where farmers had been executed after Jews were found hiding in their homes. In situations like this, the local police did the work of the Germans. They were able to capture Chaim-Yisrael Reichel from Braslav, who'd succeeded in fleeing the massacre when his entire family was destroyed. They tortured him cruelly until he revealed the name of the farmer who'd hidden him. The police killed Chaim-Yisrael as well as the farmer's family. Each moment, we were afraid of what was likely to befall us. Then another fear was added: It was several days

[Page 186]

since my cousin Benyamin and Moshe Okun had gone out on the mission with the partisans, and they hadn't returned. They'd had to go a long way, full of danger. Had they been caught, G-d forbid? After a week Benyamin and Moshe returned, and all of the partisans with them, happy that their mission had succeeded. The partisans protected Benyamin; he'd shown bravery and initiative in the operation and taken them on a relatively short and safe path. When they reached the Grazuta forest behind Salok [Salakas, about 34 kilometers west of Pasovitz and at the forest's southern edge], where the forester lived, Benyamin had been the first to burst into his house. In the house, at the table, sat the forester and another man, a German. They were taken completely by surprise. Benyamin ordered them to raise their hands, and he cut the telephone cables. The partisans killed the forester right there, and they took the German with them as a prisoner. Russian prisoners [who had been rescued by the partisans] exchanged their clothes for ones they found in the house and then left the place. On their way back, the partisans had to cross the train tracks. A villager who was working there told Benyamin that at night a train loaded with weapons was supposed to pass on the way to the front. The partisans hid in the area, and that night they blew up the train, preventing the weapons from reaching their destination. In addition, two local policemen who showed up there were killed. After this, the group continued on its way. They passed a small town named Tilz [Tilze], which was next to Lake Drisviati [on the lake's northern shore, about seven kilometers northwest of Pasovitz]. There, Benyamin suggested that they all rest a bit at the home of a farmer they knew. When they were got to the man's house, the farmer told them that there were police at his neighbor's house. Benyamin and three partisans entered the neighbor's house to "take care" of them. The neighbor's wife hinted to the partisans where the police were located. Benyamin ordered them to come out from behind the stove, and he killed them all. Afterward, the wife said to Benyamin, "You really look to me like Benyamin, but that can't be, because he was killed." To which he replied that he was indeed Benyamin and he was still alive. She asked about his family, wife and children, and he told her that all of them had been lost. She burst into tears and thanked him for rescuing them from the police, who had caused them many problems.

We celebrated their return by resting in the farmer's house. When night fell, we all set out on the road, together with the partisans. Just before we entered a forest, we nearly walked into a German ambush. There were very many of them, and they surrounded the entire forest; it was impossible to pass through the forest in one group. The officer Sarokin, who commanded the partisans, told everyone that there was no option but to separate, and each person would escape the siege on his own.

We Separate from the Partisans

It's hard to describe the barrage of firing that we heard around us. We had to run quickly to escape; Benyamin with the boy on his back, as always, and me behind him, partly running and partly walking. After much difficulty, we arrived out of breath at one of Benyamin's acquaintances who lived in an isolated farmhouse (*hutor*); his name was Chit Beilov. He gave us permission to build a hiding place far from his house, in swampy ground that belonged to him. At its center was an area whose bottom was stone; it appeared like an island in the sea. The stones had to be uprooted and a pit dug, and after that the pit could be covered by a roof. This would be our house. It would be hard work, but we were happy the farmer had agreed to give us the place. Since we were tired and worn out, we decided to rest and start work the next day. We sat down near a small bonfire to warm ourselves. While we were sitting, suddenly some Jews appeared: Nachum Kasimov with his wife and three children. They told us they'd been with several Poles, and after a short time

[Page 187]

the Poles had asked them to leave. They too had been in the village of Pasovitz and had left when the partisans went away. Recently, Nachum told us, the Germans had been blockading Pasovitz from time to time and searching for Jews and partisans. As long as the vegetation was dense and green, this had kept the Germans from entering the area, but now that the leaves had fallen the Germans were appearing from time to time. At the last minute, said Nachum, he and his family had succeeded in escaping. The farmers hadn't wanted to endanger themselves for Jews.

Nachum was happy to see Benyamin. He told us that once, while sitting hidden in the cellar of the house of a farmer, they'd heard a conversation among members of the farmer's family on the need to rid themselves of the Jews by killing them. During one such conversation, he'd heard the farmer's wife tell her husband, "Don't do anything to them, because the news will reach Benyamin and he'll come and kill us all." They were afraid to hurt us, Nachum concluded, and so they'd asked us to leave.

The next day the two men, Nachum and Benyamin, came to build the bunker. My help, and the help of Musia, Nachum's wife, was nothing in comparison to what they did. The work was hard, but when it was finished and we entered the bunker we were the happiest people in the world. We could lay down our heads and relax. From time to time, the farmer's family came to us. They were very good people and took care of us. Seeing how cold I was, the farmer's mother gave me a pair of old felt shoes, and this helped a lot. When we sat in the bunker, we believed that now we could rest for a while. The farmers in the area were acquaintances of Benyamin and Nachum, and both of them were getting food for us. Without saying anything to one another, each of us thought: If only we can stay in this bunker for a long time, G-d will help us and we'll be able to see the Redemption.

But matters didn't develop that way; change came much sooner than expected. One morning, the farmer came to us in a panic and asked us to immediately leave the place and his land. He told us that the Germans were searching the entire area, and if they found us on his property they'd burn down his farm with his family inside it. In tears, we convinced him to let us stay until it got dark.

Where would we go? Nobody knew. In such a situation, we needed to get far away. In the region, certainly all of the farmers knew about the searches by the Germans. One person would tell another, and not one of them would open his door to us. We had no choice but to set out on the main road, despite the danger that we were likely to encounter Germans or others who were hostile.

We Part from Nachum

To avoid arousing too much attention, we had to divide ourselves once more into two groups. Nachum and his family, despite all the pain we felt at separation, turned in one direction, and we in the other. (Today, we know that Nachum and his family remained alive, and they live in America.) Here I write "We went this way, and they went that way," but actually we crawled on all fours at the roadsides, over barbed wire, stones, scrub and other obstacles. Our hands and feet were scratched, wounded and bleeding, and more than once we lost track of each other. More than once, we thought of meeting a "good" German, who'd kill us without torture. But our fates were otherwise. With our last bit of strength, utterly exhausted, we arrived at a village called Malki [presumably Mialka, on the northeastern shore of Lake Drisviati and about 3.5 kilometers north of Pasovitz]. Benyamin approached a small, isolated house, whose owners he knew. This was the farmer Koschuk.

[Page 188]
At Koschuk's

Koschuk immediately took us into his house and agreed to give us shelter. After resting, Benyamin entered the barn and made a pit next to the wall, under a pile of hay. Toward morning, we went down into the pit. It was small, and we arranged ourselves inside it with difficulty. A beam of light came through a narrow crack under the wall of the barn, which was enough for us to distinguish between day and night. We lined the bottom of the pit with straw; we had nothing else. We were happy to have found a hiding place. The farmer took everything from us, worst of all our shoes. His excuse for this was to prevent Benyamin from visiting other farmers in the vicinity. All of the locals knew the farmer and it wasn't desirable for them to know that he, Koschuk, was keeping us in his house. Outside it was already cold; winter had begun and snow had already fallen. Inside the pit, it was very cold. The clothes that we wore were torn and worn out, and they failed to keep us warm. All day we sat hugging each other, to warm up a bit. What saved us in such weather was the forester's large fur coat, which Benyamin had taken with him when he returned from the mission with the partisans. At midnight, Koschuk would bring us into his house to warm up a bit next to the stove. I used this time to wash the boy, but it wasn't possible for Benyamin or me to remove the dirt from our bodies. The farmer's bathhouse was far from the house, and it was dangerous to go there; we had to return when it was still dark outside. One day, I felt that the boy's head was covered entirely with swellings, apparently because of the cold. What to do? The boy still had his golden curls, which he'd had since birth. When we were wandering in the open, it had been possible to keep him clean and I'd wash him occasionally. But now it was impossible. I had no comb. Scissors? Even the farmer had none. The boy suffered from severe pain and couldn't lie down. He'd sit during all hours of the day and night, and I held his head and told him stories that I made up by myself. He loved the stories, and this eased his pain.

Despite the good growing season, the farmer didn't want to give us any of his food, which was plentiful that year. He brought a little, only from what he prepared for his dog. The amount wasn't enough to keep us alive, and we began to feel hunger. Nor did the farmer agree to let Benyamin go out to get food for us. Despite this prohibition, Benyamin went out on the day of a blizzard, in my felt shoes, to ask for food. The falling snow covered his footsteps; in the morning, no trace of them could be seen. Occasionally he'd go searching in this way. When the felt shoes became torn, he'd wrap his feet in sacks and go out to get food. And Benyamin did something else at night without leaving any footprints: Every night, he left the pit and got half a cup of milk for the boy from the farmer's three cows in the barn. Only half a cup, so that the farmer wouldn't know that the cows had been milked. This small amount of milk helped us to keep the boy alive.

The Bread

One night, Benyamin succeeded in bringing bread: food we hadn't eaten in a long time. He sliced a piece for each of us, and I put what was left in a sack under the boy's head, for him to use when he was hungry. Without our knowledge, the boy found the bread and ate it all. The next day, when I wanted to give

[Page 189]
him something to eat, I found that the bread was gone. And then I did something I shouldn't have: As a punishment, I slapped the boy. First of all, why did he take the bread himself without asking? And second, he'd broken some of the bread into crumbs without eating it, and this was a terrible waste. A minute later, I was sorry I'd slapped him. Certainly the conditions were abnormal; everyone did things that weren't always logical, and all of us were affected by our terrible situation. But to harm him? To this day, I can't forgive myself. Since then, I haven't lifted a hand to him. He really was a good boy and he understood the situation very well, despite his young age.

During one of his nightly outings, Benyamin went far from our pit, to one of the farmers who, right at that moment, had taken bread out of the oven. Benyamin described our situation and the farmer, a truly good man, gave him two loaves of bread, which were still warm. Very happily, Benyamin ran back with the bread, reaching us at the pit while it was still dark.

That night, we ate until we were satisfied, after days of utter hunger. The swellings on the boy's head began to heal. Luba was a lucky boy. At nine months old, he'd already known how to walk. He was like a grown man! At the age of one year, he spoke freely and clearly. My mother, may she rest in peace, had 14 grandchildren from five daughters; Luba was the youngest. "He isn't an ordinary child," my mother said. "He'll grow up to become either one of the most important people we've got or, G-d forbid, one of the worst."

I thought the farmers must have owned scissors for shearing sheep, and so I asked a farmer to lend me a pair. With the help of these scissors, I gave my son his first haircut. Outside it was already warm enough, and we were able to go out of the pit. We sat the boy on a pile of straw and I began to cut his golden curls that I loved so much. For the first time in a long time, I saw the boy's head in daylight, and in disbelief I saw that it was crawling with lice. I was so alarmed to see this that I let out a big scream. Benyamin came running to learn what had happened. I showed him the boy's head. What to do? Lacking any of the chemical methods that are used today, we took a clothes brush and with it we brushed the boy's head, and after that I washed it thoroughly. Several hours later, I repeated the action. The boy's mood changed completely, as if he'd woken up, after the great suffering he'd endured without our knowing the reason. His health changed completely for the better.

The Incident with Koschuk

The troubles we'd passed through up to now were dwarfed by the difficulties that awaited us. Koschuk's house was next to a main road, and the Germans passed along it day and night. In addition, next to one of the windows stood a telephone pole, which the Germans visited from time to time to check if it had been sabotaged. During each inspection, they entered the house to warm up a bit and to eat and drink. It happened that one time they glanced outside and saw that their horses, which had been outside, were no longer there. They shouted and ran out, together with Koschuk, to look for the horses. A short time later, they found their horses standing next to the barn where our pit was located. When they ran toward the horses to take them, for some reason the horses grew frightened and began to gallop around the barn. The Germans chased after them with shouts of "Halt!" This continued for some time, until they succeeded in catching them. The whole time, we sat in the pit not knowing what was happening above our heads. We heard

[Page 190]

German voices shouting "Halt!" and were certain that they'd found us. Since we hadn't been warned, we didn't know if we'd left anything that pointed to our presence. We sat with bated breath, waiting. After a long hour all grew quiet, and we understood that this time the danger had passed. We breathed easily.

The incident, as I've described it, was told to us afterward by Koschuk. We sensed that the Koschuks had been shaken by it and wanted to get rid of us. Each day, the farmer's wife came to us and told of a new dream she'd had about Jesus the Christian. These dreams continued for several days, until finally they told us that they were afraid to shelter us any longer and wanted us to leave immediately. I was ill at the time and couldn't stand on my feet. I begged them to let us stay for just a few more days, and in this way we put off our departure.

One night, Benyamin went out as usual to get food. He arrived at the house of a farmer, not far from where we were staying. The farmer gave him some bread and warned him not to come again, to either the village or his house. He didn't explain why. Benyamin took the bread and returned hurriedly to the pit. At night, when we lay down to sleep, suddenly we heard the sound of gunfire. We asked ourselves: Is it possible that the front is approaching? We knew there were no partisans in the area. All night we sat in great fear, not knowing the reason for the shooting. The next day, Koschuk told us that farmers in the neighboring village had killed three Jews. This was the same village where Benyamin had received bread the night before, together with the warning. The three victims had been three brothers from Braslav, and the background to their murder was this: The Germans, knowing that Jews and partisans had been coming to this village, had wanted to punish the villagers by setting the village on fire, together with all its possessions. The farmers had succeeded in getting the decree canceled, but in return the Germans demanded complete cooperation from them, including first and foremost the capture and killing of all the Jews and partisans. The villagers had promised to cooperate, waiting for the moment when they could prove their loyalty to the Germans.

The three brothers didn't know about the agreement the villagers had made with the Germans. Tired and exhausted, they'd arrived in the village the night before, to rest a bit. The villagers surrounded them, beat them, and opened fire on them. As they began to flee, two of them were killed immediately. The third was seriously wounded and asked his attackers to kill him. Hearing all this, we were amazed that the villagers hadn't harmed Benyamin, who'd been in the village that night; he'd only been warned not to return.

Now we knew that to stay in this place was very dangerous. Occasionally, when Koschuk or his family opened the gate to the barn, we thought that now they were coming to kill us. We stopped inventing excuses to delay our departure from there. But --- where to go? There were no Jews anywhere in the surrounding area. In the villages in Belorussia, the Germans were preparing to hunt for partisans. Benyamin decided that we'd head toward the villages that recently belonged to Lithuania, despite the fact that in these villages the Gentiles knew of the bounty the Germans had put on his head. To reach the Lithuanian zone, we had to cross Lake Drisviati, a very large lake. We decided to follow the shore of the lake, on the chance that we'd find a deserted boat.

On May 5 [1943], still in winter weather, barefoot, in torn and worn-out clothes, we left Koschuk's house. When we left, we wanted to give Benyamin's fur coat to Koschuk, because we had no other possessions, but he wouldn't take it from us. His conscience wouldn't allow him to do so. Without

[Page 191]
the fur coat, we would have frozen from the cold. We cried when we parted, and the Koschuks cried too. Would we ever find a place of safety?

On the Way to Lithuania

Benyamin's hunch was correct. On the shore of the lake we found a boat locked with chains, and in it were two oars. We succeeded in breaking the lock, and we immediately rowed away from the shore. The distance to the other side of the lake was great and involved many dangers. How would we find a proper place to anchor in the dark? We put our trust in blind fate, setting a course straight for the other side of the lake. Suddenly, a comet appeared in the sky, falling over us. We were sure that the Germans had sensed our boat and were lighting us up with a rocket, and we sensed that all was lost. Benyamin --- who'd always been the strong one --- had a moment of weakness. He suggested that we throw the boy into the lake, maybe without him we'd be able to get away. I answered that I was prepared to jump into the lake together with the boy. We didn't speak of it again; I knew that Benyamin loved the boy very much. We continued to row toward the other side. Quietly, as quietly as possible, we reached it and arrived happily at the place where Benyamin wanted to go. Having been a fisherman on this lake, Benyamin knew its shores very well.

After hiding the oars, we left the place. Benyamin knew that the forest, which once had been very dense, was now thinned out and unrecognizable. The Germans had thinned out the forest due to fear of the partisans. In front of us, from a distance, we saw the beam of a pocket flashlight; certainly a German was holding it. We couldn't return to the boat; maybe the Germans had already noticed it. So we hid in a nearby Christian cemetery, behind the gravestones. After a while, we continued walking in another direction. When we approached a house, the boy and I remained behind, next to a tree. Benyamin walked up to the house and listened to hear if there was any talking inside, as well as which language it was in. After a few minutes, he knocked on the door. The farmer who came out and saw Benyamin nearly fainted. "How," he asked, "did you succeed in escaping?" He advised Benyamin to quickly leave the area. "This morning," he told him, "a German was killed in the forest. In response, the Germans are preparing to search the entire area." Benyamin returned to us and sadly told us what he'd heard. I said that we should go back to the lake and, if we found the boat, return to the other side. Here we were in the mouth of a wild beast; there was no hope of escaping alive from their clutches. I didn't know a single person in the area. In contrast, Benyamin knew every path, road, tree and bush. He was closely acquainted with many of the farmers; in this area there also lived the farmers to whom his wife, may she rest in peace, had given all of their possessions to guard. Benyamin said he'd try his luck with one of these farmers. We kept walking. Benyamin, with the boy on his back, led me across a swampy path, into which we sank from time to time. After much effort, we arrived at a house. Benyamin knocked on the door. Through a small window, the farmer looked out and when he saw Benyamin he shouted [in Russian], "*Nye osiroti moikh dyetei*" --- "Don't orphan my children" --- and closed the window. We continued onward. I felt sick, and my temperature rose so much that I couldn't take even one more step. Suddenly, I bent over and fell. I told Benyamin to leave me there and keep going, because I'd surely die in any case. I managed to ask him to take the boy with him, maybe they'd succeed in surviving, and then I fainted. I don't know how long I was out. When I opened my eyes, I saw my cousin with the boy next to me; the day had already dawned. Around the place where we sat, there were no

[Page 192]

trees or bushes. It was an open area with no place to hide. In the distance, Benyamin saw a lone tree with some bushes nearby. With his help I got to my feet, and after much effort we succeeded in reaching the tree. We hid among the undergrowth and waited again for the dark. Fortunately, the shepherds in the area, with their sheep and cattle, didn't sense that we were there. The calls of the shepherds and the whistles of the train that passed not far away shook us each time we heard them.

When night fell, after resting a bit, we went out on the road again. The chances were almost zero that a farmer would let us enter his house. Suddenly, not far from the road, we saw large bushes and tall trees, and between the trees was a small stream. We reached it and sat among the bushes. There was nowhere else to go, we said, so we'll make ourselves a hiding place here amid the undergrowth. And we'll scatter among the trees the earth that we dig out.

The Goose

As we began to consider how to prepare the bunker, suddenly we were frightened by the shouts of Germans who were coming out of the forest. One of them blew a whistle and called a dog that ran before them, directly toward the bushes under which we were sitting. We were certain that the dog would smell us and head straight for us. But just as the dog approached the bushes, a wild goose rose up from them in flight, capturing the dog's full attention. The dog began to chase the goose and apparently lost the scent of our footsteps. Once again, chance saved us from certain death.

After this, we decided to start digging a hiding place only after I felt better. Meanwhile, we hadn't eaten any food for two days. The chill and the rain penetrated our bones, and our teeth chattered from the cold. Benyamin decided once more to approach one of the farmers who were holding our possessions and ask for at least a pair of trousers, while I remained behind with Luba. The farmers weren't happy to see him, but they let him come inside and heard out his request. They didn't give him any trousers, however. Their excuse was that if it became known then all of their families would be executed, but they did promise to prepare some bread for the next day. They'd put the bread --- they said --- in their bathhouse, and Benyamin should come and take it.

At this time, it was dangerous to trust what farmers said. More than once, their words had set a trap for people. What should we do? Benyamin risked his life, going at night to the place one of the farmers had showed him. Usually it took Benyamin half an hour to reach the place, but this time, because he crawled and moved carefully, it took more than two hours. After much hesitation and careful listening to what was happening inside the bathhouse, he entered and found a loaf of bread and a bit of milk.

We hadn't yet begun to dig our pit. I was unable to help, and Benyamin couldn't do all the work by himself. We'd been sitting on the ground, and this harmed my health. Again Benyamin went to try his luck with one of the farmers --- maybe he'd find someone who still had some human feelings and would let him hide in his house. The boy and I again stayed to wait. This time, Benyamin had to travel a long distance and it wasn't certain that he'd succeed in getting back to us on the same night. We chose a signal: A whistle from him would let me know that he was coming back, and a whistle from me would tell him that he was going in the right direction. The first night passed, and Benyamin didn't return. All night I listened tensely for the sign. The next day, I thought, he certainly wouldn't return to us in daylight. The second night passed the same way. My fear about Benyamin's fate increased. Every so often, the boy asked me: "Where's my uncle?" Had

[Page 193]

he been caught, G-d forbid, by the Germans or the farmers? The third night, I was alert again to every sound, and then --- I heard a whistle like the signal we'd chosen. I answered as agreed, but heard nothing more. Terrible thoughts passed through my mind: He'd been caught and tortured, and he'd revealed our password. "No," I told myself, "Benyamin wouldn't do that." I was so afraid that I closed my eyes and waited for the end. When I heard a rustle next to me, I opened my eyes and saw two men standing there. I didn't scream, because I was too frightened to speak. The two felt this and turned toward me. I heard Benyamin's voice. He'd returned with another man, Avraham Kasimov, the brother of Nachum Kasimov, who'd been with us earlier. Avraham had been in our group at the start of our wanderings, and had lived with us once as a neighbor. Today Avraham is in Israel, and he lives in Kiryat Ata [near Haifa].

At the Kandzhelevskis

Benyamin explained: When he'd left us the day before yesterday, he'd gone four kilometers to the tiny village of Ilishki [Iliszki, at the western end of Lake Drisviati]. The village was surrounded by forest, underbrush and swampland. Only one road, from Turmont, led into it [Turmont was eight kilometers north of Ilishki, away from the lake]. On the other side of the village was Lake Drisviati, into which flowed a small river; over the river was a narrow bridge of wood. This bridge was the entrance to the village. Strangers didn't go there, and they didn't pass by the village. In this village lived three brothers and their families. The oldest of them, Kazimirzh Kandzhelevski, had been the village head under the Polish regime; Benyamin had business connections with this Kazimirzh. That night, Benyamin approached one of the houses and knocked on the window. This was the house of the youngest brother, Mitzislav. When Mitzislav looked outside and saw Benyamin, he immediately opened the door and brought him inside. All the members of the family got out of their beds and stood around him. They were happy to see him alive. An old grandmother was also in the house. When she saw Benyamin, she crossed herself and kissed his head, with the blessing, "G-d will help you remain alive." They fed him, and after that they laid him to sleep in the barn. All night he didn't close an eye, worrying that they intended to turn him over to the Germans. Toward morning, Mitzislav brought him food. Benyamin was hesitant to touch it. Sensing this, the farmer told him, "Eat, don't be afraid." In the morning, he took Benyamin outside and showed him a path leading to the forest. "Keep going straight," he said to Benyamin, "and there you'll find a 'rabbit' like yourself." Benyamin walked as Mitzislav had directed him, and there he found his good friend, Avraham Kasimov. The two were happy to find each other, as if they'd come from another world. Benyamin told him about me and my child, and about where we were.

Benyamin worried about how to bring me there. The villagers knew his wife and children, and they knew that all of them had been lost. He hadn't told them about me and my child. Who knew, he wondered, if they'd agree to let us join him. Avraham advised Benyamin to not ask for too much, but Benyamin didn't want to lie and he decided to ask for their agreement. In the evening, when all of the Kandzhelevskis gathered to talk in their large dining room, Benyamin told them about me, his "sister," and the boy (for them, a cousin was treated like a sister). The three brothers agreed that he could bring us to them. Benyamin and Avraham were very happy and immediately left to get us.

Now all of us set out on the road. Tired and exhausted, we arrived at the home of Mitzislav Kandzhelevski. We stretched out among the bushes and fell asleep. Toward morning, we decided to build ourselves a hiding place from logs tied

[Page 194]

in bundles. The bundles we placed one on top of the other, like a pile of hay, and in the center of the pile we left an empty space, where all of us could sit. We worked until our strength was gone. Now we had a place to lay our heads.

I don't know exactly why, but at this time my health took a serious turn for the worse. Swellings full of pus appeared on the joints of my hands and feet. The pain was strong, and we had no medicine or other means to lessen it. And of course there was no doctor there or nearby. I had to suffer in silence and pray that the illness would quickly go away.

One day, the old grandmother brought us a live chicken for us to cook for ourselves. I kissed her hands and asked her to take it back. "We don't ask for any luxuries," I said to her, "but only bread and potatoes, which will keep us alive." I begged her to take back the chicken, but she didn't listen. She called Avraham and ordered him to cook the chicken. While we stayed with the Kandzhelevskis, we were well fed and satisfied. We received as much bread, potatoes and fish as we needed.

Yanush Sees Luba for the First Time

My son, Luba, knew many Russian songs, and he sang them in a pleasant voice. One day Yanush, the oldest son of the brother Kazimirzh, came to visit us and met Luba for the first time. "What a nice, quiet boy," he said. Avraham asked the boy to sing a song, and Luba sang about an orphan boy who was among strangers. Yanush was moved by the song and burst into tears. He told everyone in the house about the boy and his sweet voice. The next day, the entire family came to us to see the boy and hear his song. For this, the boy received sweets and a new name: "the nightingale."

At the Kandzhelevskis, we recovered completely. Here we cleaned ourselves in their bathhouse, washing off all the mud and dirt that had accumulated for months. More than once, we stayed to sleep in the warm bathhouse. More than once, we wished for ourselves at least a small house like this one, in which we could live without fear.

We tried to help our benefactors by working as much as we could. The men chopped wood for heating and also helped to make home-made liquor (*samogon*). I helped by plucking feathers to make pillows. Once in a while, we went out to the field. So that their children wouldn't pronounce our Jewish names in the presence of strangers, the Kandzhelevskis called us by Gentile names: Avraham they called "Adamka," Benyamin was "Petkovitch," and I was "Petkovitchova." They called Luba "Spivak."

That year, the winter [of late 1943/early 1944] was very hard. More than once, the temperature was more than 40 degrees below zero. The farmers' sons would come to see that we hadn't frozen from the cold. The forester's fur was what saved us. We'd sit hugging each other under the fur. During this season, the air was already getting warmer during the day; it was very cold only at night.

One day Yanush came to visit us as he did from time to time, but this time I saw that his face didn't look normal. It was obvious that something was bothering him. "What happened, Yanush?" I asked. He hesitated a moment and said, "Mother's very sick. There's nobody to clean the house and prepare for the holiday that starts tonight." I immediately got up and went with him to the house. With his help, by evening the house was

[Page 195]

organized and ready for the holiday. I drew not on physical strength, but on strength of will. I even put paper in the corners of the rooms, as was customary with them. When the entire family gathered, they were very excited and didn't know how to thank me. After that, I went to their house every day to help with something. There was always work for me. The three brothers lived in three houses and an additional large room that they used for cooking and eating.

In Mitzislav's house, moss stuck out between the boards. I asked them to bring thin boards, and with them I covered all the walls. I plastered them with material that they had in the field, and in the end I whitewashed them. Now the house looked like new.

After living in poor conditions for so long, we lacked even a change of clothes. Everything was torn and worn out; it was necessary to try to sew something. I asked the farmers for thread and a needle, and was given a needle for sewing sacks. With it I was able to sew a pair of pants for Luba from a torn dress, and a shirt from another old garment. These two items were so successful that Mitzislav's wife asked me to sew pants for her son from an old garment. I couldn't refuse her, but I was very reluctant --- worried that if I failed it would damage our good relations. But having no choice, I took on the job and succeeded in sewing not just one pair, but two lovely pairs of pants. Mitzislav and his wife didn't know how to thank me.

Sometimes they'd bring us something to eat. We very much appreciated their commitment to us, and we didn't want to upset it. They knew the great danger they faced, sheltering us in their household. Once one of them hinted at this, saying that they were 17 souls and concluding: "G-d said, 'You should love your neighbor as yourself.' All of us are in G-d's hands. What happens to us is His will."

I became a daughter of their house and helped them as much as I could. At night, I'd go to sleep in our hiding place. They appreciated my help very much and said so many times.

I want to tell of an incident that appears funny now, but more than once such a "laugh" could kill a person. One day, when Benyamin and Avraham were chopping wood in the forest, the boy was alone in the stable and I was in the farmers' house, the middle brother --- Michal --- traveled to Turmont to sell the whisky that they'd recently made. Michal was a simple, straightforward man. On the way, some Germans met him and asked what he was bringing to market. Michal made no excuse, but said that he was bringing *samogon* to sell. The Germans asked him to return to the village, and they followed so that they could confiscate the whisky together with the equipment used to make it. When Kazimirzh saw them approaching the house, he understood immediately what had happened. He calmly took the Germans into the large dining room, set the table for them, loaded it with many good things, and said, "Why hurry? Eat and drink, after that you can take everything you want." Kazimirzh put me in the bed, wrapped in a scarf, and next to the bed he stood a cradle in which there was an infant four months old, as if I were his mother and I was very sick. The Germans were afraid to go near a sick person. Yanush succeeded in rescuing the boy from the stable, and Avraham and Benyamin went into the hiding place. Only Stefa [not mentioned before, presumably a woman with the Gentile family] became a bit hysterical as always and said that this time the Germans would shoot everybody. The sisters-in-law got angry with her and drove her from the house.

Kazimirzh fed the Germans and gave them drink until they were drunk and couldn't tell the difference between left and right. Then he gathered all kinds of pots and old wheels and put them in the Germans' car together with some pork, and they went on their way without making a search.

[Page 196]
Another time, Mitzislav asked one of us to help him harvest the hay. He would cut the hay with a scythe, and it would be heaped up in haystacks. Benyamin went out to help him. A short time later, Benyamin came running from the field, pale as whitewash. All of us immediately closed ourselves up in our hiding place, and he told us: They'd been harvesting in the field near the lake. Suddenly they saw a fishing boat approach the shore, and in it was a group of men, among them someone who was a known collaborator with the Germans. All the fishermen of the lake knew Benyamin. He ran immediately from the field toward the bridge, crossed it and ran through the open field to our hiding place. From a distance, he could see the Germans approaching, along with some collaborators. While listening to this we remained sitting, waiting for what would happen. But no one approached us except Mitzislav. He too had seen the men and understood the danger, but he hadn't seen Benyamin leave the field. Mitzislav thought the Germans had caught Benyamin and taken him away, and now he came to tell us this. When he saw Benyamin, he crossed himself and said, "How did you succeed in escaping? You were right next to the Germans."

We stayed with the Kandzhelevski brothers for 10 months. There, we felt as if we were in paradise. We wanted to believe that G-d had had mercy on us and we'd be able to stay there until the days of horror came to an end. Unfortunately, things developed otherwise.

The Turning Point

The Kandzhelevskis secretly kept a radio receiver. Occasionally, they'd listen to news from the front. Recently they'd heard that the Germans were suffering heavy losses and retreating. German officers were patrolling in the vicinity, and they were planning excavations and protective trenches. This meant that in the forest and in the Kandzhelevskis' swampland, strange men were wandering around. In light of all this, the brothers called us to their house and explained the situation. We weighed what could be done under the circumstances. It was clear that our situation there had grown dangerous. The men wandering around would surely discover our presence; we had to start making plans to leave. We supposed that somewhere in Belorussia there were organized partisans; Benyamin and Avraham should try to reach them, as long as there were no great numbers of Germans present. Meanwhile, the boy and I would remain with the Kandzhelevskis and share their fate, whatever happened. But after several days, it became clear to us that our original assessment of the situation was correct and all of us needed to set out immediately.

Like a good father preparing his children to leave their home, that's how the Kandzhelevskis took care of us. They made a small sleigh for the boy, so that we wouldn't have to carry him in our arms on the long journey ahead of us. They told us how to take precautions on the road and gave us bread, meat and sausage, as well as *samogon* vodka for the partisans, who we hoped to meet.

We Leave the Kandzhelevskis

After Christmas night, we left the Kandzhelevskis and set out on the road. Their three families, from the oldest to the youngest, stood outside and cried together with us. They understood very well the risk we faced. We also knew that the chances of reaching a safe place were very small. Death threatened to ambush us at every step. We walked along the length of Lake Drisviati, to arrive as quickly as possible in the territory of Belorussia [the border between Lithuania and Belorussia ran north-south through the lake]. Outside, there was

[Page 197]
deep snow. The little sleigh in which the boy sat was unsuitable for snow that deep, but we held onto it, hoping that things would improve. In the forest Avraham and Benyamin found a rifle and pistol, rusty and covered with leaves and unfit for use. We had no ammunition, but they decided to take the weapons with them, and they came in handy even though they weren't usable. After great difficulty, we arrived in the deep snow at the village of Malki [on the eastern shore of Lake Drisviati and about 10 kilometers east-northeast of Ilishki] and the farmer Koschuk, where we'd stayed for half a year previously. He was happy to see us alive. He brought us into his house and served us some food and a hot drink. All that day, we rested at his place. In the evening, we set out again on the road, in a hurry to meet the partisans.

On the Way to the Partisans

For some time Benyamin had had a long beard, and people could no longer recognize him. He wore the large fur coat and had the rifle on his shoulder, while Avraham belted the pistol on his hip. We hid the boy in the sleigh. In this way, we passed through the village of Malki. Benyamin knew the farmer who had raised the best horse in the village, and he knocked on the door of his house. The farmer opened the door and Benyamin told him that we were partisans and needed a sleigh with a horse. In general, the farmers trembled when they saw the partisans, and Benyamin wanted to take advantage of this. Without any discussion, the farmer harnessed his horse to a sleigh and we quietly got in it and set out on the road, while the farmer led the horse. On the way we spoke not even a syllable, so that he wouldn't know we were Jews.

Unfortunately, the weather took a turn for the worse. A heavy snowstorm began, and it became impossible to see the road. We progressed slowly with much difficulty, until the horse grew weak and unable to continue. By this time, we'd reached a farm settlement. We got out of the sleigh. Benyamin told the farmer to go home, and we approached one of the houses. Benyamin knocked on the door. When the farmer came out, the "partisan officer" [Benyamin] asked for a sleigh with a horse, and this was supplied immediately. We continued on our way, but the journey became harder from hour to hour. We knew that we could travel only at night. We continued to another settlement, and again it became necessary to change horses. The farmer returned home with his horse and his sleigh, and again Benyamin turned to one of the houses to ask for a vehicle, and he received one. This time, the farmer looked like a partisan himself. Because of the deep snow, the horse was advancing now with great difficulty. After traveling for two hours we saw a house in the distance, and we headed for it. As we approached, it became clear that this was the house of the farmer who was leading us; we'd been circling his house by mistake for two hours. We decided to enter the house to warm up and rest. We couldn't stay for long, because dawn was approaching. By this time the distance to the forest wasn't that great, and we decided to finish our journey on foot.

We walked. We passed large villages in which not a single house remained intact. By this time, we were in great fear; not a living soul was to be seen. We reached another village and found a similar situation; everything had been burned. The Germans had burned the villages. At each moment it seemed to us that a German would jump out at us from somewhere, but no one appeared. We kept walking. Outside it was already full daylight; the blizzard was over. We were tired and lacked the strength to go on. We could see nothing in the distance, so we decided to sit down and rest a bit. We ate something and then set out again on the road. Then, in the distance, we saw a sleigh approaching, and in it were many people. We were sure that they were Germans, but there was nowhere to escape to or hide. We were in an open field without a tree or even a bush. We thought that we were lost: Come, let us go to meet death. Then we saw people getting out of

[Page 198]

the sleigh, rifles in their hands, with their faces turned toward us. As they approached, one of them shouted, "*Stoi!*" ("Halt!" in Russian). We understood that they were partisans, and we calmed down. They approached and asked who we were and where we were going. We replied that we were Jews and wanted to reach the partisans. Without speaking, they confiscated the rifle and the pistol. Then they ordered us to get into their sleigh, and they returned with us to the forest. On the way, we talked with them and learned that they were originally from Ikazna [Ikazn], a village 14 kilometers from Braslav [to the east of Braslav]; now they were partisans. They didn't understand how we'd succeeded in arriving from such a distance. The forest, they said, had already been surrounded for days by a large German army. As far as they knew, the army was planning to attack the partisans. As a native of Braslav, from their region, I felt close to them and thought that now we were among friends. Unfortunately, they didn't share this opinion. When we reached the forest, they stopped the sleigh and ordered us to get out and walk toward a gypsy camp inside the forest. They burst into laughter and went on their way.

We remained where we were. The area was very overgrown. What should we do now? We were stunned. We hadn't expected this kind of treatment from partisans. We understood that we couldn't stay there. But --- where to go? Benyamin said that he and the boy would remain there, and Avraham and I should go to look for the partisans' camp and ask the officer to take us into his unit. I disagreed. To me, it wasn't proper for a woman to go looking for the partisans and a man to stay behind and wait. I don't know why it didn't occur to him that we should go together to look for the partisans; exhaustion must have dulled our thinking. In the end, I remained with the boy and Benyamin and Avraham went to look for the partisans.

I sat with the boy under a large tree. We sat and waited. Outside, it was very cold and our nerves were very tense. Hours passed, which seemed to me like many days. Once in a while the boy would ask, "Where's Uncle Benyamin, and where's Avraham?" "Come," he said, "let's go and meet them. I'm cold here, cold." I calmed him, saying, "Don't worry, Luba, they'll return in a little while." But in my heart, I thought: Who knows what's happened to them? What are they doing?

Night is falling, the frost is growing stronger. My child will freeze from the cold. But if we go away from here, what'll happen if they return and can't find us? Who knows whose hands they fell into, and whose hands I'm likely to fall into? Sunk in such thoughts, I suddenly heard the ringing of a little bell: this meant travelers. I woke up. Without thinking, I began to run toward them, ready for anything: life or, G-d forbid, death. The sleigh approached and I saw that in it was sitting a young man wearing a Red Army hat. This must be an officer, I told myself. He stopped next to me and questioned me. Quickly I told him about my situation and the danger to the boy's life because of the great cold. I asked him to rescue us, and if he couldn't do this, then he should shoot and kill us. He calmed me down and told me that he'd send someone to take us away from there. Then he continued on his way.

We Remain in the Forest

I had to stay there and wait; maybe he'd send help as promised, and maybe Benyamin and Avraham would come back. The group of partisans that we'd met earlier passed by again. They looked at me and smiled. Night fell. Around us, it was completely dark. The boy continued to ask about going to look for Benyamin and Avraham, while again and again I said to him, "They'll come in a little while." Then I heard a sleigh approaching. I ran immediately

[Page 199]

to meet it. In it sat an older man with a beard. I told him my situation, as I'd explained it previously to the officer. The man ordered me to get into the sleigh with the boy and our bundle. I was happy to leave. I didn't even ask about our destination; the main thing was to get the boy out of the freezing cold. We set out. The driver didn't turn to me with even a single word, but I knew that he was from the partisans. He kept quiet while I spoke, asking him what was happening outside the forest, were the Germans there? I told him about Benyamin and Avraham, and how they'd gone to find the partisans and left me to await their return. He didn't answer. We traveled onward. On the way, another man got into the sleigh. Occasionally we passed a guard. These would ask for a password and then receive it. We continued in this way until we arrived at a small clay hut built into the ground. They brought us inside, told me to wait there, and then went on their way. I was excited by all that had happened: An hour ago we had been about to freeze, and now the boy and I were in a warm hut that looked like a palace from a children's story. Gradually, I calmed down. People were living in the hut. I began to talk to them, and they told me that there were other huts like this one in the forest, in which lived the families of the partisans: the parents and the children. They received food from the unit's headquarters. The man who'd brought us there was from a different unit. He'd asked them to host me for one night; tomorrow they'd decide what to do with me. I told them of my worries about Benyamin and Avraham, and they calmed me. They said that there were partisans throughout the forest and partisans patrolling outside it. They served us some food. They also promised to help so that I could remain with them, because two daughters of theirs, they said, were about to join the partisans and so some space would be available.

The Partisans' Meeting

While we were talking, the partisans came to call people to a meeting. A representative from Moscow was going to speak on the political situation. I too was invited. At the head of the table sat the representative from Moscow. Next to him I recognized the partisan officer who'd promised me in the forest that they'd come to get me, and indeed they had done so. The only speaker at the meeting was the man from Moscow. He discussed the situation at the front and the tasks facing the partisans. After the meeting, I turned to the Muscovite and said, "As you see, I'm a Jew. With me were two Jewish men. The Germans killed our entire family. After much effort we obtained a rifle and a pistol, and we've traveled a long and dangerous path to join the partisans. All we want is to fight the Germans. When we arrived here in the forest, our weapons were taken and we were directed to a gypsy camp. The men have gone to look for the partisans, and I don't know what's happened to them." "Calm yourself," said the representative. "They'll be found and everything will be all right." The local officer, who was listening to our conversation, told me to go tomorrow morning at nine o'clock to the watchmaker's hut, not far away, and then the two of them went on their way. While I'd been talking with the Muscovite, people had gathered around us but I paid them no attention, thinking that I knew no one there. The next day, however, it became clear to me that I'd made a mistake. People from our region came to find me. They told me how I should present myself to the officer --- as the wife of one of them, not his sister. This was because members of the partisans' families were given some consideration, and they had rights as specified by orders from Moscow. Whereas a mother and her child wouldn't be accepted into the partisans, they said.

[Page 200]

Several hours later, several people from Braslav came to me: Esther Rusonik and Yerachmiel Milutin. Both of them were serving in a unit nearby. They told me that the man who'd ordered me to go the next day to the watchmaker's hut was the officer of the brigade. They also told me that the Muscovite representative had given an order to find Benyamin and Avraham, as well as their weapons. And indeed, after some time they told me that these two had been found in the partisan regiment named after Kutuzov. The weapons taken from them had been found in another unit. The brigade officer asked that the weapons be returned to Benyamin and Avraham, while the officer whose unit held the weapons asked that Benyamin and Avraham be handed over to him. I was happy to hear all of this and calmed down. At last, I knew that Benyamin and Avraham hadn't fallen into German hands.

The Meeting with the Officer

I came early to the meeting. In the watchmaker's hut, many partisans were coming and going. The watchmaker's wife understood that I was new to the place, and she treated me very well. While talking with me, she pointed out the officer of a division in the Kutuzov regiment. I looked at him and saw Leibke Kaplan from the town of Yod [Jod, 25 kilometers southeast of Braslav] (today he lives in Israel). I was very happy and immediately approached him. I told him about Benyamin and Avraham, and asked him to tell Benyamin to register me as his wife, because then I could be accepted into the partisans. Before he could reply, the commissar from the Kutuzov regiment arrived. Before leaving, Leibke hinted to me that this man wasn't among the lovers of Israel. The commissar called to me and told me that Benyamin and Avraham were in his unit, and then he went on his way. I returned to the hut.

My Meeting with Benyamin

The next day, an elderly partisan came to the hut and turned to me: "If you want to see the men you're looking for, come with me. I'm going to that unit, my two sons are serving there." Eagerly, I joined him. When I arrived at the camp, I asked them to call my cousin Benyamin; we were happy to find each other alive. Benyamin told me about the difficulties they'd faced to get accepted into the unit. At the beginning of their interrogation, they'd been shouted at, suspected, and listened to with disbelief. Benyamin and Avraham had asked that the officer keep them in the unit and promised him that within a short time they'd prove their dedication and loyalty. They also told the officer that if he didn't accept them into the partisans, he should order them to be killed on the spot, as the Germans did. Benyamin told the officer how we'd come to the forest and about the place where they'd left me with the boy, and the officer said that he was the one who'd sent for me.

While we were talking to each other, the guard saw that Benyamin was talking with someone "who wasn't theirs" [that is, with the narrator, who didn't belong to their unit]. He approached me and drove me out of the camp. Because of this, I wasn't able to find the old man who'd brought me there along a path that was unknown to me. Despite this, I set out on the way back. While walking, I suddenly encountered Germans on horseback, who gave me a great fright. Only after I got near them did I see that they were partisans disguised in German uniforms, who'd gone out on patrol. Somehow I was able to return to my hut.

[Page 201]

The Germans Attack the Forest

"I'm happy, I'm with my child." These were my thoughts on my way back to the hut. Unfortunately, when I entered the hut my happiness received an immediate blow. My child was sick. His temperature was rising, and he was burning up all over. Speaking in Russian, he told me that he had a headache. Before I could think how to ease his pain, a great tumult arose outside the hut. I stepped outside to learn the reason for this and saw the commissar of the battalion surrounded by many men who were arguing with him: "What can we do?" "Don't be afraid, you won't be left behind; a solution will certainly be found." I asked the officer, "And what about me?" He replied, "You'll be treated like everyone else," and he left. Everyone returned to their huts, and I returned to my sick child. After a short time, five sleighs harnessed to horses were brought and put next to the huts, in case evacuation became necessary. I was worried. Even though all of them had promised to come to my aid if needed, I was afraid that if panic broke out and people ran to the sleighs, no one would remember me.

The next day, we saw that one of the units was preparing to move out. The Germans had attacked its section of the forest. The partisans with children turned to their officer and asked what they should do, and he replied that children who were able to walk should join the partisans; taking the others would only make things harder for the fighters. What was happening in the camp is difficult to describe. Everyone was running about. I sat next to my sick boy; I couldn't help him. He suffered greatly but said not a word, something he'd learned to do in the course of our wanderings. In silence, I awaited the worst. For many hours, we tensely awaited the unknown. Fortunately, this time as well, we were saved. A day passed, and the people congratulated each other and were happy again. We were told that the Germans had penetrated into part of the forest but not encountered any partisans there. In great fear, apparently of falling into a trap, they hadn't dared to go any further and had withdrawn. Again, a spark of hope was ignited in us.

Benyamin and Avraham Are Partisans

After the officer of the Kutuzov unit finished his interrogation of Benyamin and Avraham, he decided to accept them into his unit. At the time of the German attack on the forest, their conduct was tested and trust in them rose a great deal. The officer saw that they could become good partisans. This was told me by Benyamin when he visited our camp for a few hours, with the officer's permission. A few days passed; Luba was still sick, and our hut was very crowded. The commissar ordered me to move to another hut, where an elderly man lived with his wife; their two sons were serving in the unit. Many regarded this old woman as a shrew and warned me against joining them. Nevertheless, I moved there and relations between us were good enough, but it was hard for me to see her going out at night from the forest to gather clothes from dead Germans. She'd undress them completely and take everything. This simply repelled me.

Some weeks passed. The young daughters from the hut where I'd spent my first night in the camp joined battle units, and the residents of that hut invited me to return and live with them. This I did. One day someone from Braslav, Moshe Milutin, came to visit me. He'd served as a partisan in one of the units. After

[Page 202]

being wounded in his hand after a partisan action, he learned in the camp that I was there. When we met, there was no limit to our happiness. For an entire day we sat and talked, and even this wasn't enough for everything we had to tell each other. He had no more time because he had to return to his unit. (Today he's in Israel with his wife Malka [née Shteinman], the doctor; she's also a daughter of Braslav and they already have grandchildren.) They told me that Zusman and Chana Lubovitz and their children were living in the forest not far away. Also with them were Pinchov from Zamosh [Zamosz, 16 kilometers south of Braslav]; two brothers, Yankel-Velvel and Shlomo; a woman and child from Zamosh; and a few more families. They were living separately in the forest, with no connection to the partisan units. After some time, they all visited me. My cousin Yitzchak Reichel from Braslav, who was a partisan in the Lithuanian unit, also came to visit. I told him all that had happened to us and about my conversation with the officer. My cousin revealed to me that this officer was his officer, and he knew him well. Both of us went to him, and he received us very warmly; we became friends. He praised me for the help I'd given to the unit in various jobs and in laundering the partisans' clothes, but to my request to join a fighting unit he answered no: A woman with a child couldn't join the partisans.

This was an elite unit that won many battles. Not many Jews served in it. They took only those with special skills. In this unit served Leib Kaplan from Yod, who was the unit's quartermaster (today he lives in Israel); Pesia, a seamstress (after the war she got married, lived in Riga, Latvia, and passed away there); my cousin Benyamin, who worked at first in administration; and Avraham, who did every kind of job. After that, Shneiur Ritz from Drisviati joined the unit. They accepted him after the recommendations of Benyamin and Avraham, who'd transferred into the ranks of the fighters. Both of them took part in all of the most dangerous operations.

Partisan certificate of Benyamin Movshenzon [of the Klimchenko unit of the Zhukov brigade]

[Page 203]
Receiving Weapons
Weapons for the partisans arrived from Russia; large amounts of them were brought by an airplane that landed from time to time in a temporary airfield next to Disna [Dzisna, 72 kilometers east of Braslav]. The unit for which the weapons were intended would send men to pick them up. Once, it was decided that 100 men from the Kutuzov unit would go and get the weapons. Among those who set out were Benyamin and Avraham, who always stayed together. The men had only 10 rifles among them. Their officer was a good fighter. After several hours of walking, all of them reached a large village and decided to stop there to eat and rest. When they entered the village, they divided into several groups, among the houses of the farmers.

The farmers fed them and served them alcohol until they were drunk. Benyamin, Avraham and the officer didn't touch the *samogon* vodka, and this saved their lives. During the celebration, one of the farmers revealed to Benyamin a secret: A villager had set out to call the Germans.

Benyamin immediately told his officer, who went to the village head and demanded several sleighs harnessed to good horses, or he'd kill him and burn the entire village. With much effort, they succeeded in getting the men who were drunk into the sleighs and escaped the village.

After traveling for hours, the drunk men awoke. The officer ordered them to get out of the sleighs. He sent the farmers with the sleighs back to the village with a warning not to tell anyone who they'd transported or where, otherwise their punishment would be severe. The partisans turned once more toward the temporary landing field. They went all the way to the field without resting, and there they entered only the houses of partisans who were already waiting for them. For a week they waited for the airplane, which was late in arriving. While staying there, they learned that the Germans had indeed entered the village where they'd been earlier, but hadn't found even one partisan.

Returning with the Weapons

When the airplane arrived, the partisans loaded the weapons onto their shoulders and set off immediately to return to base. The job of getting the men back to the base with their equipment was given by the officer of the battalion to a young Georgian officer, a brave man with a lot of initiative. The problem facing him was how to move the men without passing through the same village, where the Germans were now staying. He took them through fields and forests until they reached a river, on which large chunks of ice were floating. They found a place where they could cross, although the water reached up to their necks. The officer ordered them to cross quickly, with full equipment. When they came out of the river on the other side, their clothes froze on them. The men found it difficult to move and asked to be taken to a place where they could warm themselves and dry out, but the officer wanted to keep going no matter what, and he told them that whoever couldn't walk would be shot. Everyone kept going until they reached a large village. There the officer again divided them into groups, putting them into several of the village houses. In front of the houses he set up a guard, and he ordered that no stranger could enter the house and no one could come out. In the evening they continued on their way until they arrived, with all of their equipment, back at the base.

[Page 204]

Partisanchik the Pony

One day, when Benyamin was busy helping Shneiur [Ritz], Leib Kaplan approached and ordered him to go out to help transport partisans to their destination. After Benyamin had traveled for an entire day, the officer of the operation turned to him and told him to take all the sleighs and horses back to the base. Benjamin asked, "How can I do this alone, since I don't know the road?" But the officer insisted: "Get going." Benyamin was bewildered; how would he accomplish this? He stood there, not knowing what to do. An elderly partisan, seeing Benyamin's dilemma, approached him. "Don't worry so much," he told Benyamin. "Take the little pony, the one we call Partisanchik, and harness him at the head of the line of horses. You'll see, he'll take you safely to your destination."

With no alternative, Benyamin decided to do as the old man advised. He tied Partisanchik in front. He drove the first sleigh himself, and they set out on the road. They traveled a long way without knowing if they were on the right path. During the trip back, Benyamin noticed several things that he'd seen on the way there, and this calmed him a bit. He continued in the same direction until they reached the first guard in the forest, who from a distance ordered him to give the password. Benyamin answered with yesterday's password, from the time that they'd set out on the road. In this way, he continued from one guard to the next, until he arrived back at his unit. When he reached his destination, he kissed the pony, who'd brought him back safely to the base.

The Officer Falls

The Kutuzov regiment was an elite unit, to which the most difficult missions were assigned. Their officer was a good, strong-hearted leader. On missions that were difficult to fulfill, he'd go out himself at the head of his men. To his soldiers his word was sacred, they'd follow him through fire and water. In one of the toughest battles, which continued for many hours, he fought a large German force that was accompanied by many volunteers. The partisans succeeded in destroying a large part of this German force, taking 40 prisoners back to the partisan base. The partisans gained a big victory, but their revered officer was killed; a German who'd been taken prisoner shot at him, killing him on the spot. This was too great a price for the partisans to pay; every partisan unit mourned him. After interrogating the German prisoners, they shot them all.

As a sign of appreciation, they called the unit that had taken part in the battle by the name of the beloved officer --- Klimchenko. Before each battle operation, the men of the unit would declare that they were setting out for battle in the name of Klimchenko. He would help them win.

In the Forest

I became a tried-and-true partisan and carried out a number of jobs, among them the task of a nurse. For this, people respected me a great deal. The women would also gather wood for heating, and I was always first among them. I volunteered continually for difficult tasks; people shouldn't say that a Jew was shirking work. As mentioned, when we'd reached the partisans we were barefoot, in torn clothing and worn out. The fighting men had been given clothes and

[Page 205]

boots, while I remained without a change of clothing. Once, a partisan brought a pair of shoes for the boy; this made him the happiest boy in the world. Unfortunately, the shoes were in his possession for just for a few hours. When he went to sleep he took them off, and when he woke up the next day they'd vanished. They simply disappeared . . . Benyamin received a military coat, and I made pants from it with the help of a tailor from another unit.

I don't know who told the unit that I knew how to brew *samogon* vodka. After they heard this, the partisans gathered all that was necessary, including the required tools, and asked me to make vodka for them. In forest conditions this was no easy task, but Benyamin and Avraham also told me to fulfill the request. So I took all the equipment and the boy, and went to find a suitable place in the forest, far from the huts. After finding it, I dug a pit and put all the equipment in it. After several hours, I had *samogon* of sufficiently good quality that was ready for drinking. To thank me for my work, the partisans brought me some fabric and leather for shoes, and with the help of Sonia Pinchov from Zamosh I sewed some clothes for Benyamin and the boy.

One day, confusion arose in the camp. Near us, in a meadow in the forest, a partisan and his wife who were traveling in a wagon had been killed. A German airplane appeared above them, bombed the area and murdered them. It became clear that the Germans were resuming their flights over the forest, something they hadn't dared to do for a long time.

A number of days passed, and the matter was forgotten. Once more, I took the boy and the equipment to prepare *samogon*, and went out to my place in the forest. While I was busy preparing the dough, I heard the sound of an approaching airplane. Since I'd learned to distinguish the sounds of different planes, I knew that it was a German plane. Flying low,

Benyamin Movshenzon (first on the right) with his wife Sara and their son Luba

[Page 206]

he began to circle. I assumed that the smoke from the fire where the *samogon* was cooking would show him our exact location. How could I put out the fire without producing smoke and steam? I began to pour earth on it. Working slowly, I put out the fire and the pilot's target was lost. Frightened, I took the boy back to the hut, and that was the end of *samogon* production.

Cows for the Partisans' Families

The battalion's commissar ordered that a milk cow be given to each partisan family, so that they could enjoy real milk. At this time, the boy and I were living with the elderly Russian woman and her husband, and so we received only one cow. The woman asked that she be allowed to take care of the cow by herself and do all of the necessary work. (To tell the truth, I didn't know how to even approach a cow.) In exchange for taking full care of the cow, it was decided that she'd receive two-thirds of the milk and I'd get just one-third. I accepted this with gratitude. But here too, the evil in the old woman revealed itself. Instead of milk, she gave us water mixed with just a tiny bit of milk. I didn't want to give the boy this water to drink, and so I gave up the entire business and told no one. But on one occasion, after seeing the "milk" the old woman had brought me, our neighbors went and told the commissar. He came the next day, together with the quartermaster. They both became angry and threatened to take the cow away from her. After that, I received real milk from milking that she did in my presence.

Each day, the cows were taken out to pasture. Two people did this, taking turns. When my turn came to go out to pasture, I took Luba with me. The other person that day was an older man. The job of the shepherds was to watch the cows so that they wouldn't wander deep into the center of the forest; there was enough pasture for them in the meadow. When the noon hour arrived, the boy and I remained alone with the cows. Unfortunately, a German plane reappeared.

Before I had time to grab the boy and hide behind a bush, the plane was already over us, flying low. I clearly saw the pilot's face, and it seemed to me that he saw me too. He flew over us several times and then left. I remained with the boy next to the bush for some time, to see if he'd come back, and after that I got up to shepherd the cows. Suddenly, some distance away, I saw something shiny and sparkling. When I approached, I saw a large toy, in the shape of a man riding a horse. How had it gotten there? I didn't touch it until the second shepherd came, and both of us concluded that it was certainly a bomb which could explode at the touch of a hand. We gathered the cows and returned home. The partisans threw the suspicious object into a fire and, indeed, it exploded.

The Klimchenko unit was given a large and difficult mission: It had to pass villages and towns and reach a very important train crossing. From there, trains went out to all sections of the front. The unit's mission was to blow up the station and the train tracks. The day before it set out, the officer sent a unit to patrol the area and check the road leading to the forest. After the patrol returned to base, the entire force went out on the mission.

Benyamin was included in the mission and with him, as always, was Avraham. Both of them were in the advance patrol, which moved some distance away from the main force, an entire squadron. They approached the large village of Pelikan [Pelikany], three kilometers from Opsa [and to the west of it], in the center of which stood a church surrounded by a wall. As they approached, Benyamin turned to the officer and said that they shouldn't enter the village, lest they encounter an ambush. There was

[Page 207]

a good road that bypassed the village. But the officer just laughed at him. "Only yesterday a patrol of ours was here," he said, "the enemy isn't around and we're a large force," and he ordered them to continue. As they approached the wall surrounding the church, heavy fire opened up on them from rifles and artillery. The main force of the partisans returned strong fire and the men of the patrol, who'd gone ahead, were trapped in the crossfire. Many were injured; Benyamin was wounded in both legs. He took eight bullets in one leg and one in the other. Despite this, miraculously he wasn't crippled. The partisans carried him from the area, thinking he was dead. Avraham was wounded in the elbow by shrapnel, but he succeeded in escaping the area.

The partisans took Benyamin and Avraham to a field clinic, and after rapid treatment they came out of danger. But to this day a bullet remains in one of Benyamin's legs, and one of Avraham's hands is a bit weaker than the other.

The Red Army Is Approaching

The front was drawing near [the Braslav region would be liberated around July 1944]. On the roads, we began to see soldiers from the Red Army. The happiness that filled everyone's hearts at this sight cannot be put into words. Everyone burst out of the forest, some on foot, some in vehicles, to see the soldiers. At first, people couldn't believe their eyes: Wasn't it a dream? They surrounded the soldiers, kissing them, covering them with flowers and even more with questions. People cried with joy. Even Benyamin, who still found it difficult to walk, was taken in a wagon to the road so that he could see the soldiers. Later, after some time had passed and Benyamin could walk again, he turned to his officer and asked for some leave, because he wanted to avenge the blood of his wife, his four children and his parents, brothers and sisters. He knew their murderers very well. The officer approved the leave and sent another partisan with him: Shneiur Ritz, who'd expressed a wish to accompany him.

The front line was very close. The Poles began to return from the camps to their homes, and the partisans were sent to fight at the front, near Braslav. In the nearby forest, Germans who'd fled from the front were wandering about, and volunteers who'd served the Germans were hiding in the forest. Many people fell victim to the fleeing murderers.

In the camp of huts, only my son and I remained. The danger was great. I turned to the brigade officer to request a pass certificate to Braslav. This angered him and he shouted, "We've guarded you and your boy all this time with great difficulty. Now you want go and get killed? Stay here and wait until the situation stabilizes, it's safer." After calming down, he asked me where I wanted to move, and I asked to go to a camp where there were people from Braslav. To this he agreed.

When I reached the camp, I found only women; all of the men had gone out to Braslav to look for work and arrange their release from the army. In the camp were four children; Luba was the youngest.

Benyamin knew that his childhood friend, Semyon Labotzki from the village of Kumraz [possibly Kiemerezy, on the southern shore of Lake Drisviati], had helped the Germans to gather all the Jews: men, women and children, among them the members of Benyamin's own family, and take them into the Zigod [Deguciai?] forest, where all of them were shot. In a huge mass grave, half a kilometer in length, 8,500 Jews from Lithuania had been buried. [This appears to be the same massacre that was described on page 173.] People from the surrounding area said that for days after the massacre they could hear moans from the grave. Benyamin captured Labotzki and had him put in jail. Many Gentiles also had complaints against Labotzki, but unlike Benyamin they didn't seek his execution. But the days of leave that Benyamin had received

[Page 208]

weren't enough time for him to see Labotzki executed for his crimes; he had to return and report to his unit. So his trip wasn't able to accomplish anything. And he couldn't take care of Labotzki by himself; he would've been put on trial for taking the law into his own hands and received a heavy punishment. So he handed Labotzki over to the NKVD,[24] but to the dismay of many, the man was freed on the basis of an order that had been issued by the Soviet authorities. In the order, it was stated that every man who had collaborated with the Germans could report to the police and receive a pardon. Labotzki reported and received a pardon. In the eyes of the authorities he was now a decent man, but in fear for his life he left for Poland.

We Return to Braslav

The leave ended, and Benyamin returned to the forest and his unit. He found that in his unit the arrangements had changed. The partisans were transferred to Braslav, and from there to the front line. Only a few of them survived. Among the fallen were Avraham Bik, Bitzon and others.

When he returned from his leave, Benyamin divided among his unit all the items he'd brought back with him. From one of the farmers, in whose hands he'd left many possessions to guard, he got back only a small amount of his property. I asked Benyamin not to divide everything among his unit, but he wouldn't heed my request. He was also reluctant to talk with the officer about his release from the army. And so I turned to the officer and told him our troubles. He listened and said, "Benyamin will take his weapon and travel to the villages on the shores of the lake, and he'll prepare a list of all the fishermen who fish in the lake. In the future, a fishery factory will be built there and Benyamin will be its manager."

We received wagons and set out for Braslav; Chana Lubovitz and her family traveled with us. In Braslav, all of the Jews from there gathered in a house whose owners had all died in the war. There we lived like a commune, sharing everything. I didn't go to see the remains of our house; fear of the horrors that had occurred there was still like a fresh wound in my heart.

With the officer's permission, I brought to Braslav the cow that had been with us in the forest, and it provided plenty of milk for everyone. Benyamin also obtained some meat. All of us cooked and ate together.

After several days, Benyamin took his weapon and set out for the fishermen's villages, while I stayed in Braslav with the group. The roads were dangerous, and when Benyamin was late in returning I began to worry. My anxiety increased when, one day, Shneiur Ritz and Masha Ring from Drisviati came to our apartment and told us that Benyamin had been arrested. Why? They had no explanation. I immediately knew that I had to go and look for him. I left my boy in the house, with the others, and I set out. After going a short distance by train, I'd have to go a long distance on foot. When I stepped off the train at night, I didn't know in which direction to turn. I walked up to one house and knocked on the door, asking the residents to tell me the way to Drisviati. They told me nicely, but advised me not to keep traveling at night. They said that many terrible things had happened recently on the roads. They invited me to sleep that night at their house, and the next day they went with me for part of the way. I thanked them from the bottom of my heart.

I arrived in Drisviati [24 kilometers west of Braslav]. I knew that Avraham's brother Nachum and his family were already there. From what Shneiur had said, I understood that Benyamin had traveled with them. I sought them out, but none of them were in the house. Then I found Benyamin; he was standing and repairing his bicycle. "What happened?" I asked

[Page 209]

with impatience, "Why were you arrested?" He explained: On his way there, he'd met Nachum and his wife Musia, who were traveling around to gather the possessions of Jews that had been given to farmers in the area to guard. Knowing that Benyamin was a brave man, Nachum and Musia had asked him to come with them. After this they encountered some soldiers, who stopped them. The soldiers wanted to confiscate the bicycle, but Benyamin hadn't wanted to hand it over. While Benyamin and the soldiers were arguing, Nachum and his wife had continued on their way without waiting for the conclusion. Shneiur [Ritz] and Mashka [Ring] had also passed by at this time and seen Benyamin standing there with the soldiers, but they too continued on their way. This is how the story got started that Benyamin had been arrested. After this I accompanied Benyamin to several villages, where he registered the fishermen. The fishermen were happy that he'd come, and they registered willingly. Benyamin continued alone to two more villages and I returned to Braslav and my boy, feeling much better. The registration of the fishermen was completed, and all that remained was to present it to the officer.

Benyamin prepared to travel to Braslav. In Duksht [Dukstas, about 25 kilometers southwest of Drisviati and in Lithuania] he met his friend Hershel Aron from Zarasai. Benyamin told him about his work organizing the fishermen and his appointment as their manager. The matter didn't please his friend. "Why should you be the one who has to trouble yourself with farmers?" he asked. Hershel told Benyamin that he was a member of the NKVD and was ready to try to persuade them to let Benyamin join them. Benyamin agreed, seeing this as a chance to bring to justice those who'd collaborated with the Germans. He traveled to Zarasai [about 25 kilometers north of Dukstas and in Lithuania] and was accepted into the NKVD.

Braslav after the War

Our town had been destroyed. Many houses were razed down to the foundation, with nothing else remaining. Many others had been bombed from the air and remained only partly standing. The few houses that survived in their entirety, here and there, looked like orphans, torn away from something that no longer existed.

The house of one of my sisters was utterly destroyed. The house of another sister had survived the war, but the Gentiles had then stripped it to its foundation and looted its contents. The house of my parents stood with its furnishings intact; it had been closed and locked up. With weeping eyes and pounding heart, I saw my parents' house standing undamaged. The house of my third sister was still standing, but not even one person from among its residents remained alive. An unconscious inner will had brought me there. Would I find a photograph or some other item, as a keepsake? I didn't have anything from them. I found nothing but a photograph and torn pieces of photographs lying under the stairs. I thought that my heart would be afflicted, that I'd lose my mind. I fled the place and didn't return.

I went to see the family graves in Braslav. But it became clear that the old Jewish cemetery had been destroyed by the Germans and the Jewish monuments that had stood for generations had been uprooted to pave the sidewalks of the town. The old cemetery was converted into a public park. The [new] Jewish cemetery was now located in the place of the massacre, where there were two mass graves in which were buried the holy [martyrs] of Braslav. Next to them were a few lone graves of Jews who died or were murdered after the war.[25]

[Page 210]

We Leave Braslav

The municipality imposed on me the task of preparing lists for it of the names of the Jews of Braslav: One listed those who'd survived and were in Braslav; the second listed those who'd left the town; and a third was a list of Jews who'd been lost. The preparation of such lists was beyond the ability of one person, and many people came to my assistance.

Once, while walking in the street, I met someone who'd been the manager of the education department in the municipality [before the war]. He was happy to find me alive and asked if I'd [also] compiled a list of teachers. I was stunned: Could I really become a teacher to their children, after the Germans and their Polish collaborators had murdered ours? And he himself, the manager of the education department, was known to be a great hater of Jews. I answered his question positively and immediately turned away.

When I returned to our communal apartment, the *kolkhoz* [collective farm, in Russian] as we called it, I found Benyamin, who'd come to take me with him to Rimshan, where he'd gotten a job in the NKVD. I had few doubts about leaving Braslav. Given my feelings about seeing the manager of the education department again, I was ready to set out immediately. But I also agreed with Benyamin, who said that in the NKVD he'd be able to catch the murderers and criminals who were in hiding and bring them to judgment.

The next morning, we set out on the road. We had almost no possessions. With pain and sadness, we said goodbye to our friends in Braslav. We left them the cow that we'd brought from the forest, and we traveled in a wagon to Rimshan. In a village near Braslav, a farmer came out to meet us. He gave us a pillow filled with feathers and said, "This belongs to you, I received it as a deposit." This farmer even gave us bread, butter and eggs.

I was leaving Braslav. I was parting from the town, from Jews who had lived there and now were no more. I was leaving there the good years of my younger life, and taking with me the bitter memories of the ruin of all that had been dear to us. I was parting from Braslav forever.

Rimshan

We reached Rimshan [about 45 kilometers southwest of Braslav and in Lithuania]. Once this had been a small Jewish town, vibrant and full of life. Now it contained only ruins. Most of the Jewish homes no longer existed. Of all the Jews of Rimshan, only Benyamin remained alive. His house, which had outlasted the war, had been dismantled by a farmer, who transferred it to his own yard and rebuilt it there. In our wagon, we approached a house that had belonged to Jews and was still standing. It had been turned into an office building of the NKVD. A Lithuanian named Birolin came out of this house to meet us; he'd been sent there with his wife to work with Benyamin. They were very happy we'd come, because they knew no one in Rimshan. Until that day, they'd been hungry for bread, not knowing where to get any. Benyamin calmed them, saying, "You won't be hungry anymore."

We found living quarters in an apartment where only the floor and peeling walls remained. There wasn't a single piece of furniture. We were visited by a Jew from Drisviati, Hershel Zilberman, who was a good acquaintance of Benyamin's. He'd survived, together with his wife and their two children, his younger brother and his wife, and their father; all of them had hid in a bunker in the forest. When they learned that Benyamin was in Rimshan, they came to ask for his help, because

[Page 211]

they had no work or means of support. Since Benyamin was the manager of the local NKVD, he suggested that Hershel stay and work with him. Hershel was happy to hear this. Benyamin got food from a farmer, and we sat down to eat together, hoping that better days lay ahead.

The next day we woke up early, because the apartment also served as an office that people could visit about various matters. Likewise, I had to return to Braslav and legally change my address: Braslav belonged to Belorussia, and Rimshan to Lithuania. When I got back to Braslav, I found no changes. There I found [Sasha] Tempelman, a good acquaintance from Vidz [about 40 kilometers southwest of Braslav], who was a teacher. He'd been wandering about and now asked me to take him to Rimshan. He'd look into the situation in Rimshan and then decide where to live. After arranging all of the formal matters in Braslav, we traveled together to Rimshan. There, Tempelman was our house guest. I introduced him to Benyamin, who listened to his problems.

Because we'd decided to stay in Rimshan, we urgently needed a separate apartment; we couldn't live in our office. We went to look for an apartment nearby, but everything had been destroyed and it was dangerous to live further away. The work that Benyamin was doing, catching war criminals, would definitely bring a reaction from them. After searching further, we found a closed-up apartment that belonged to a Polish policeman. Acting on the instructions of the chief manager of the NKVD in Zarasai [28 kilometers northwest of Rimshan and in Lithuania], we entered the apartment to live there. The desire for revenge gave us no rest. Benyamin knew many of the criminals personally, and he received a lot of information about many others. Although he lacked a police force to back him up, he didn't want to delay the start of his work. With the help of several workers and gypsies that he armed, he'd go out to conduct arrests, to bring the criminals to trial. But it was hard to capture them with the tiny number of men he had available. More than once, there weren't even enough men to guard the prisoners. I'd take a rifle and guard the entrance to the jail. Weeks went by until the ranks of the staff filled out and it was possible to operate normally.

The search for the criminals brought results. Many now sat in jail, but many more were still running around freely. It wasn't easy to jail an entire village. Nevertheless, Benyamin was putting his life at risk to arrest the men against whom there was clear evidence. He worked hard and used a number of tactics to find the criminals. More than once, there were large operations in which men from the army came to help him. We knew very well the dangers faced by Benyamin and his men. More than once, we, the women and children, had to go to sleep in the home of a Gentile out of concern about the danger to which we were exposed.

Generally, men of the police guarded our apartment with machine guns. Once in a while, the officer from Zarasai, Smirnov, would sleep at our house. This too required a careful watch. Sometimes, Benyamin would get letters in the mail containing threats of murder. At the NKVD center in Moscow they hadn't known Benyamin, but his signature on the arrest warrants of people who were then transferred to Moscow aroused interest in the name of Movshenzon. He became known there as a brave man.

Several local men and several Jewish survivors helped Benyamin with his dangerous work. We lived together as one family. These were the two Berzon brothers, Chaim and Pesach. When I was in Vidz, I'd met the father of Pesach and Chaim Berzon, and he'd told me about them and added that both of them were tired and worn out. When I told him that both of them could live with us, he was very happy. Both of them indeed came and lived with us. Benyamin told his superior that in men like them, who had served with him in the partisans,

[Page 212]
he had complete trust. They carried out their responsibilities to the full. After that, Benyamin received a free hand in accepting men into the local police (militia). This enabled him to bring in Yankel-Leib Maron from Vidz and Shalom Katz from Duksht. All of them lived with us like one family.

One day, after great difficulty, Benyamin and his men succeeded in arresting a war criminal known throughout the area. After his arrest, this man gave up the name of a Polish citizen, Stramchinski, who he claimed was the leader of a group of criminals. The arrested man didn't say directly where the Pole was, but acting on various hints in his statements they succeeded in finding Stramchinski and arresting him. At his interrogation, the Pole revealed that an entire gang was hiding in a house in the village of Ilisk[?]. Benyamin checked with people in the area, and they confirmed this. Benyamin now understood that the matter was serious. He called for the army's help in carrying out his mission and soldiers came, accompanied by their senior officers. After learning the location and the way to it, they set out under Benyamin's orders. When they reached the house in the village of Ilisk, the house of the farmer Michal Sokshtol, Benyamin was the first to burst into it. To his question, "Where are the men of the gang?" the farmer crossed himself and said that his house didn't contain such people and never had. It was clear that he was lying. A search was made of the house and the farm. In the sheep pen Benyamin sensed that the floor was hollow, and he began to look for an entrance outside the pen. He found it and ran up to it. At that moment, two soldiers approached and told him, "We're younger than you, let us open it." This they succeeded in doing, but just as they prepared to descend shots were fired at them from inside the hiding place, and they were killed on the spot. The shooter then shot and killed himself. An army officer pulled out his pistol, killed the farmer Sokshtol, and ordered Sokshtol's wife to go inside and order the men to come out, otherwise the soldiers would throw hand grenades inside and kill all of them. The men came out of the bunker in a long line, 40 gang members. Nobody had expected so many. A search of the bunker revealed a large room with pictures of leaders on the walls. It was assumed that this was the base of a regional national council with connections to London, from which the gang had received its equipment. Nine wagons of assorted equipment, including weapons and ammunition, were taken from the hiding place. The booty and the prisoners were sent immediately to Rimshan.

The bodies of the farmer and the gang leader who'd shot himself remained under guard for a number of days, next to the local police, as a warning to criminals everywhere.

The farmers who suffered from the Germans and their collaborators would come day and night, despite their great fear, to give news about the criminals: which of them lived alone and who was hiding with an entire gang. These farmers had known Benyamin before the war, and knowing now that he was managing the investigations, they had complete trust in him.

Jan Foiksta

In Rimshan lived a Lithuanian by the name of Jan Foiksta, who'd been a teacher in the Polish school in the days of the Polish government [before September 1939]. In 1939, as the Polish army prepared to evacuate the town, many weapons had been distributed to the residents. Later this Foiksta gathered all the weapons and hid them in a secret place. When the Germans arrived, they saw him as the man for them and appointed him mayor of the town.

[Page 213]

It's hard to describe how much Jewish blood was spilled by this murderer. He tortured and killed Jews as well as Polish and Russian prisoners. He traveled to his friends in the towns of the region, who were mayors of towns like himself, telling them, "Why are you still playing games with the Jews? I got rid of them already."

When the Germans fled, he disappeared. Nobody searched for him. It was as if he'd been forgotten.

The First Passover as Free People

On the eve of the holiday, a number of Jews came to us to celebrate the first Passover in freedom. At the Seder [ritual feast marking the start of Passover] the Jews of Rimshan and friends from Duksht dined with us. We were happy that we were alive and free, and we spoke of memories of our parents' homes that were no more. On the first day of the holiday, several young men from Vilna came to visit: Yisrael Salitan, Shmuel and Chaim. In the numerous conversations, which lasted for many hours, Yisrael Salitan told Benyamin, among other things, that Foiksta, who'd been the mayor in Rimshan during the German occupation and killed many Jews, was now in Vilna [about 125 kilometers southwest of Rimshan]. Benyamin jumped up and began to ply Yisrael with questions: Where had he seen him? In what street? What house? Yisrael remembered the street, but not the house number. After hearing the details, Benyamin got up and announced that he was leaving that day for Vilna. He refused all requests from me and the others to delay his trip until the holiday had passed. Taking two policemen with him, he set out on the road.

The Arrest of Foiksta

When Benyamin reached Vilna, it wasn't easy for him to find Foiksta. There was no point in searching for him at the population registry office, because he'd certainly be under a false name. Benyamin decided to look for him on the same street where Yisrael Salitan had seen him. When they arrived at the place they asked no one, because of the danger, but they set up an ambush for him next to the house he'd been seen coming out of. They sat in ambush until midnight and then the next day, before dawn, they renewed it. On the third day, Benyamin saw him. He immediately jumped him, together with the two policemen. Foiksta didn't even understand what was happening. They took him to the train and transported him to Rimshan. Soldiers who were traveling on the train and had heard about his murderous deeds were ready to kill him on the spot. But Benyamin explained to them that this criminal had also led a gang, and so he had to be interrogated thoroughly and brought to trial.

Benyamin and his men succeeded in bringing Foiksta to Rimshan and putting him in prison. The news of his arrest spread quickly. People from the town and the surrounding area began to come to our house, and each one spoke of how Foiksta had killed his dear ones.

The men of the police brought Foiksta, in handcuffs, to the regional center of the NKVD in Zarasai [about 140 kilometers northeast of Vilna, in the same general region as Rimshan and Dukstas]. The police wouldn't let Benyamin bring him there, out of concern that Benyamin might kill him on the way. We went on with our day-to-day lives. Then one day, some men came and told us that Foiksta had been released from jail. We were alarmed and set out immediately to find the manager of the NKVD in Zarasai, Comrade Smirnov. Benyamin told Smirnov why he'd come: "Where's the criminal Foiksta, the murderer of

[Page 214]

hundreds and thousands of people? Why was he freed? By what law? He was brought to you together with many documents signed by people who testified to the suffering he caused them. If that's not enough, more testimony can be provided. We put our lives at risk to capture him." Smirnov, the head of the NKVD, listened to what Benyamin was saying and his face grew pale. It turned out that he'd known nothing of the matter, it had been done without consulting him. The existence of the prisoner hadn't been reported to him. It was the detective Genichov who'd contended that the material at hand was insufficient to put the prisoner on trial. Smirnov and Benyamin went to the office. A short look at the documents showed Smirnov what a terrible mistake had been made without his knowledge. He shouted at everyone, ordered the arrest of the detective, and turned to Benyamin with the request that he return to Rimshan and try to recapture Foiksta.

We Plan to Leave

Many murderers were still running around, collaborators with the German conqueror, frightened that they'd be captured and tried for their criminal acts. With the publication of the order that everyone who reported to the police and admitted his collaboration with the Germans would be pardoned, there was no more point in our working or endangering our lives. We began to look for ways to be released from the work that we were doing and to leave Rimshan.

Benyamin needed some X-rays, which could be taken in Vilna. Both of us traveled there. In the city, we went to Jewish friends who worked in the local police. The officer Hershel Aron from Zarasai worked there, the one who'd convinced Benyamin to join the NKVD. We were like family with each other, and the meeting was very happy. All night we spent talking in friendship and recalling old memories.

Foiksta Is Caught for the Second Time

In the morning, I stepped out to accompany Benyamin to the hospital for the X-rays. As we left the gate of the yard, Benyamin immediately saw Foiksta across the street, on the opposite sidewalk. Quick as lightning, he ran to him and grabbed him with all the strength he could muster. It was impossible, as well as dangerous, to take Foiksta to the NKVD office by himself. So we returned with him to our friends' yard, and I entered the apartment to get help. Hershel ran with me to the yard, which by now was full of curious onlookers. At their center stood Benyamin, holding Foiksta, who was shouting, "What do you want from me, I have to go to work!" Among the onlookers was an army officer with a lot of medals on his chest. He asked Foiksta for his papers. I suspected that this officer was one of the murderer's men and would likely release him. The officer looked at the papers, looked at Foiksta and again at the papers, and finally told Foiksta, "You must go with them." To Benyamin and Hershel he said, in Yiddish, *"Halt im shtark"* ("Hold him firm") and went on his way. Benyamin and Hershel held onto Foiksta and, with pistols drawn, took him to the local police. I walked behind them. At the police station, they'd already heard of the arrest. When we arrived, they took us into a courtyard between high walls and locked the iron gate. While Benyamin was in the station discussing the matter, Foiksta kept shouting, "What right do you have to hold me, I must go to work in the education ministry!" To this I replied, "Your job is truly a nice one, but how did a scoundrel like you get such a position?" After a

[Page 215]

telephone conversation with Zarasai, they put Foiksta on a truck and, accompanied by 12 policemen, he was taken to Zarasai.

All the material evidence against him had already been prepared, and he was tried immediately. His sentence was also carried out immediately. Foiksta was no more.

Benyamin Is Released

For health reasons, Benyamin was released from the NKVD. All of them were sorry to lose a dedicated man like him, but for us it was difficult to continue. After four years of effort, tension and danger, only now did we feel that we were free. In 1947, after Benyamin received his release papers, we went to Riga [about 235 kilometers northwest of Rimshan and in Latvia] to start a normal life. Luba began to study at school, and he was a good student. Despite difficulties with his health, he matured and succeeded in finishing high school with high grades. Benyamin worked at various jobs. Finally I decided not to teach another nation's children anymore. I did various jobs to assist the family with its livelihood, and in the evenings I took an accounting course, which I completed successfully.

In Riga too, our house was an open one, always full of people. A day with no guests was a sad day for us. Many people who needed assistance of some kind would come to us and receive the necessary help.

We Leave Riga

In 1957, we left Riga. We traveled to Poland with the thought of immigrating immediately to the Land of Israel. Unfortunately, at that time the *aliyah* of those who'd returned from Russia was stopped [presumably this means that former Polish citizens, who'd wound up in Russia during the change in borders at the war's end, were no longer allowed to return to Poland]. None of our efforts to leave the country bore fruit. For 10 months we remained in Poland under difficult conditions, in danger and fear. After that, we were able to immigrate to Israel, having been recognized as war disabled. We arrived in Israel on February 4, 1958 and were sent to Tiberias by the Jewish Agency and the Ministry of Absorption.

In the Land of Israel

During the first part of our life in Israel, we lived in difficult conditions. More than once, we felt we'd gotten off to a bad start. A lot of time passed until we felt that we were standing on solid ground. Benyamin began to work as a fisherman on Lake Kinneret [in northern Israel], and there too we experienced problems. For example, each day a portion of the fish was stolen from us and we didn't know how to prevent it. We lived far from the shore, and it was impossible to guard the fish. Some time passed until we found a solution to the matter.

Immediately after our arrival in Israel, Luba filed a request to be accepted into the Technion in Haifa. He was called to the entrance exams, took them and was accepted as a student there, but because of our unstable financial situation he decided to study instead at the school of military electronics in Haifa. His studies there could be finished more quickly, he said, and then he could help with our finances and join Benyamin at work immediately. We didn't see

[Page 216]

a solution to his future, nor did we see a future for him as a fisherman. Not having a choice, I went out to help Benyamin. After the job of spreading the net and gathering the fish, I'd sit and repair the nets, which sometimes became torn. Everyone thought this was strange; they said they'd never seen a woman working at fishing on the Kinneret. The news reached the ears of reporters, and they came to ask for permission to write an article about it for the newspaper.

We experienced many things in Tiberias. We didn't complain; we asked only that the housing authorities change our dwelling place to an area where both of us could work and find a roof "under which to lay our heads." Unfortunately, they didn't come to our assistance. We faced our troubles like Jews who understood the situation, accepting everything with gratitude. The representatives of the Jewish Agency always described us as exemplary, saying that with people like the Movshenzon family "It's possible to build the Land."

Years passed. Luba married, and he has three children. He has been in the army since we came to Israel. His wife works. We're already at an advanced age; our experiences have left their mark on us. Our health is imperfect, but we're happy with the young and beautiful generation, healthy in body and soul. We can be proud of them.

Footnotes:

1. Also known as Castle Hill, Schloss Berg and the Zamek. It was called a mountain by locals, even though it stood only 15 meters or so above the town.

2. Three of the synagogues were near one another between Castle Hill and Lake Driviata (Drywiaty): the Beit Midrash of the Mitnagdim and the Old Synagogue and New Synagogue of the Hasidim. Some distance from them, around one side of Castle Hill, was the fourth synagogue: the Sandy Synagogue of the Hasidim.

3. The two long-serving rabbis in Braslav were Rabbi Zahorie and Rabbi Valin; sections on them are on pages 66-69 of this memorial book.

4. This might refer to Leizer Fisher (son of Zalman/Zalk), who on a 1941-42 list of Jewish skilled professionals from Braslav, now at Yad Vashem, was called a ritual slaughterer.

5. Reb is an honorific term, something like an exalted "Mr."

6. Tarbut schools (from the Hebrew word for culture) were a network of secular Zionist, Hebrew-language schools, founded in 1922 in Warsaw, that operated mainly in Eastern Europe. Their curriculum included science, humanities and Hebrew studies, including Jewish history.

7. This meant that they were trying to cross from Polish territory that the Soviet Union had occupied in September 1939 (which included Braslav) eastward into Belorussia (that is, the Belorussian Soviet Socialist Republic, part of the Soviet Union). In this account, the border with Belorussia --- the pre-1939 border --- is also called the "old Russian border."

8. Presumably this meant Perebrodia (Przebrodzie), also known as Pirabrod. It was about 25 kilometers east of Braslav, on the way to the pre-1939 border that was further east.

9. Sara Movshenzon's postwar pages of testimony at Yad Vashem named three sisters who were killed: (1) Raizel, the wife of Moshe Ulman, and three children: Avram, Ruvin and David. (2) Tzila, the wife of Leiba Zaks, and four children: Avram-Zalman, Dvora-Pesa, Esther and Leiba. And (3) Yehudit, the wife of Reuven Zilber, and three children: Liuba-Rasa, Moshe and David.

10. By this the narrator meant the period between the time the German occupation started in June 1941 and the liquidation of the Braslav Ghetto in June 1942. The ghetto had been formed officially (enclosed with barbed wire) on April 1, 1942, only three months before it was liquidated, but some Jews from smaller localities were being concentrated in Braslav long before April 1.

11. "June 10" is incorrect, as the massacre of the first Braslav Ghetto began on June 3, 1942. The ghetto had been formally established on April 1, not June 10.

12. Miory was about 40 kilometers east of Braslav. According to the *Encyclopedia of Camps and Ghettos, 1933-1945*, Volume II-B (2012), the Miory Ghetto had been established in either the fall of 1941 or early April 1942, possibly in several stages. In the spring of 1942, a number of Jews were added to it from other places in the region such as Perebrodia (25 kilometers east of Braslav) and Ikazn (14 kilometers east of Braslav).

   At the end of May 1942, an SS officer arrived in Miory, setting in motion the massacre of the Miory Ghetto, which began early on the morning of June 2. On that day, 680-800 Jews were killed; it's thought that a small number of inmates might have succeeded in escaping. The massacre of the Braslav Ghetto began the next day, early on the morning of June 3.

13. This was a Russian term for the mobile gas vans that were used by the Nazi *Einsatzgruppen* (mobile killing squads) on the Eastern Front from the autumn of 1941.

14. The English-language summary of this memorial book says on page 601 that this was the daughter of Lubka Veis, not the son. However, the Hebrew used here in the original ("*v'rosho hakatan*") says that it was the son, not the daughter.

15. This appears to refer to the massacre on August 26, 1941 described briefly in *Encyclopedia of Camps and Ghettos, 1933-1945*, Volume II-B. On that day, a large number of Jews were shot in the Pazemis (a.k.a. Pozejmy) Forest, about three kilometers west of the village of Deguciai (a.k.a. Degucie) in the Zarasai district, and buried in a long ditch. The forest can be found today about 14 kilometers southeast of Dusetos, in Lithuania, along the road from Deguciai to Dusetos.

   According to a source on Jewish communities in the region (*Preserving Our Litvak Heritage*, Volume II, published in 2007), the Jews murdered in the forest on August 26 included those from the surrounding region: the Dusiat (Dusetos) Ghetto, a small ghetto in Salok (Salakas), Ezhereni (Zarasai), Turmont (Turmontas), Antalept (Antaliepte) and Rimshan.

    Sources disagree on the number of those killed in the forest on August 26, ranging from 2,569 (German sources) to 5,000 (*Preserving Our Litvak Heritage*). But the postwar memorial at the massacre site says that the victims numbered 8,000. The site is about 70 kilometers west of Braslav.

16. Raizel Ulman's three children were Avram (born ca. 1930), Ruvin (born ca. 1932) and David (born ca. 1934).

17. A type of temporary hut --- called a tabernacle --- built for use during the week-long Jewish festival of Sukkot.

18. According to the *Encyclopedia of Camps and Ghettos, 1933-1945*, Volume II-B, this happened in August 1942, when the Germans spread news of an amnesty for Jews in hiding, if they surrendered and entered the Glubok Ghetto. (Glubok was about 75 kilometers southeast of Opsa.) As a result, hundreds of Jews came out of hiding in the forests before the onset of winter and went into the Glubok Ghetto. The ghetto would be liquidated in August 1943.

19. The transfer of a large number of the Opsa Ghetto inmates to Vidz was also mentioned by Opsa survivor Mordechai (Motke) Rozenberg on page 341 of this memorial book. Subsequently, according to the *Encyclopedia of Camps and Ghettos, 1933-1945*, Volume II-B, a small ghetto continued to operate in Opsa through at least July 1942, containing some 300 people. In August or early September 1942, some 50 of the Opsa Ghetto inmates were transferred to the ghetto in Braslav, to repopulate that ghetto after its inmates had been slaughtered on June 3-5, 1942. On page 183 of this memorial book, in her account, the narrator mentions that some Jews in Opsa might also have been transferred to Postav (Postawy), 50 kilometers south of Opsa. Subsequently, any Jews who might have remained in Opsa --- women, children, the elderly and others considered unfit for work --- are thought to have died in a final liquidation in Opsa carried out sometime between September 1942 and the year-end.

    According to the *Encyclopedia of Camps and Ghettos*, the Vidz Ghetto had been formed in early 1942. In subsequent months Jews were added to it from Drisviati, Druysk (Drujsk), Opsa, Dubina, Kozian (Koziany), Ignalina (Ignalino) and Sventzion (Swieciany). By August 1942, the official population was 1,505. Sometime around October 1942, most of the Jews in the Vidz Ghetto were transferred to the Sventzion Ghetto, about 45 kilometers southwest of Vidz and in Lithuania. Only about 80 Jews (craftsmen and their families) remained in Vidz at this time, but later they too were sent to Sventzion. The majority of the Jews in the Sventzion Ghetto were taken to Ponar outside Vilna and murdered on April 5, 1943.

20. This refers to the fact that, out of the approximately 208,000-210,000 Jews in prewar Lithuania, an estimated 190,000-195,000 were killed in the Holocaust, most of them between June and December 1941. In carrying out their mass murder in Lithuania, the Germans were greatly assisted by ultranationalist Lithuanian paramilitary groups such as the Shaulists.

21. After the first Braslav Ghetto was massacred on June 3-5, 1942, the Germans repopulated it in August or early September 1942 by bringing in some 50 Jews from Opsa, many of them craftsmen. Because these people were from Opsa, this second Braslav Ghetto was also called the "Opsa" Ghetto. The "Opsa" Ghetto in Braslav would be liquidated on March 19, 1943.

22. According to the *Encyclopedia of Camps and Ghettos, 1933-1945*, Volume II-B, the inmates of the Postav Ghetto were murdered on November 23-25, 1942.

23. Pasovitz and the town of Drisviati were just inside Belorussia at the border with Lithuania, with the border running north-south through Lake Drisviati.

24. Narodnyi Komissariat Vnutrennikh Del (People's Commissariat for Internal Affairs): The Soviet law enforcement and intelligence agency that existed from 1934 to 1946, after which it evolved into the KGB.

25. The old Jewish cemetery in Braslav was in the western part of the town, number 11 in the map on page 21 of this memorial book. This cemetery was destroyed during World War II, and after the war the area was turned into a park. The newer Jewish cemetery in Braslav lies north of the town, where the Jews of the town were killed in June 1942 and March 1943. In the years after the war, it was augmented by burials from the small Jewish community that remained in Braslav.

Chana Lubovitz
Daughter of Sheitel and Rafael-Yaacov Munitz

Zusman Lubovitz
Son of Chaya-Leah and Avraham

Translated from the Hebrew by Laia Ben-Dov
Footnotes Added / Donated by Jeff Deitch

My name is Chana Lubovitz, of the Munitz family, the daughter of Rafael-Yaacov and Sheitel. There were eight children: four sons and four daughters. The family was very close; our home emphasized brotherhood, peace and respect.

During World War I, when the army of the German Kaiser approached our country, we moved deep into Russia, arriving as refugees in the city of Kerch, on the Crimean peninsula. I was then five years old. Economically our situation was good, until the Bolshevik Revolution in 1917, which didn't bring us a blessing. Apart from material shortages [in the Crimea], many hardships and troubles passed over us: pogroms, bombardment and the like.

My father, who was learned and erudite, taught Hebrew and prepared young people for *aliyah* to the Land of Israel. We, the children, studied at a Russian school. Our older brothers and sisters worked and helped to support the family. In 1921 we received permission to return to Poland, but my oldest sister and my big brother remained in Russia, because he was called to serve in the Red Army, together with my sister's husband.

The trip home from the Crimea took more than half a year, due to bureaucratic procedures. At that time, our town was already under Polish rule. First the authorities put us in Minsk [about 195 kilometers south of Braslav/Braslaw], in Belorussia, settling us in a deserted building that had been a synagogue. The conditions were uncomfortable; we suffered from cold and hunger. Father was teaching in the *cheder* [Hebrew primary school], and our situation was difficult.

In the spring of 1922, we received permission to return home [to Braslav]. Fortunately we found relatives of my mother there, who helped us with arrangements. Father opened a small store, and we began a new life. After some time, a Yavneh school[1] was established in the town and father received a position there as a teacher of the Tanach [Hebrew Bible] and Jewish studies.

Our mother passed away in 1929 after a serious illness, and the responsibility of maintaining and managing the household fell on me. My brother Chaim and my sister Matla, the young ones, studied in Vilna in the Yiddish Teachers' Seminary.[2] Later, our youngest brother Boris (Baruch) also traveled there to learn locksmithing.

In 1932, I married Zusman Lubovitz. We opened our own business and lived

[Page 218]

in my father's house. In 1936 our oldest son, Arieh, was born, and in 1939 our second son, Moshe, was born. My brother and sister finished their studies as teachers, returned to Braslav, and began to teach in the popular Yiddish school [the Folkshul]. After a number of years, my brother Chaim traveled to Vilna and was received as an aspirant at the YIVO (Yidisher Visnshaftlekher Institut --- The Yiddish Scientific Institute),[3] where he worked until World War II broke out.

When the war broke out [in September 1939], our brother Baruch was drafted into the army. After that, we don't know what happened to him. In [September] 1939, the Russians entered the town. Our situation grew worse. Our business was confiscated. The Soviet authorities didn't permit ownership of private businesses, and we remained without a source of income. Studies of Judaism and the Hebrew language were forbidden, and father was denied the right to teach at school. This hurt him greatly. He also worried about being exiled to Siberia, because he was known to be an enthusiastic lover of Zion. All of these things affected father's physical and spiritual condition. One day in April 1940, he had a heart attack and died.

For us, this was a heavy blow. Our father was also our teacher, counselor and friend. When he passed away, our world grew dark.

But life went on. We had to overcome the difficulties and contend with the problems. My brother Chaim, who'd returned from Vilna with his wife, and my sister Matla continued to teach in the school [in Braslav]. Zusman, my husband, received a job with the Soviets and our economic situation improved.

On Sunday, June 22, 1941, we heard on the radio that the Nazi oppressor had begun a war against Russia. We wondered what kind of treatment we could expect from the Nazi soldiers.

By the day after the German invasion, the Soviet army had already begun to withdraw. Full of despair and lacking sound advice about what to do, we watched them leave and waited fearfully for what would come. Many Jews also left with the army. We had small children to take care of, so we remained where we were.

After three days, the Germans entered the town. We already knew that they'd passed through Latvia and destroyed [sic] the Jews of Riga and Dvinsk.[4] On Friday [June 27], we received an order to gather in the center of town and leave our homes open. We thought that our end had come. We gathered with the entire Jewish population in the town center, with the children at our side. They arranged us in rows, men alone, women and children alone, and brought us under heavy guard to the Dubki [Dubkes] forest. On the way, the first sacrifices fell: the *shochet* [ritual slaughterer] Shlomo [Zilber], my sister's brother-in-law, and a young lad, Chaim Milutin. The Germans shot them on the excuse that they'd tried to flee. Tired, dejected and hungry, we arrived at a place of deep swamps in the forest. They ordered us to sit and not move. We were surrounded by Germans, their weapons aimed at us. We were sure that they'd kill us.

We sat all night, together with the children. Not a single one cried; it was as if we'd turned to stone. At dawn, they ordered us to get up and go home. We ran home and found total chaos: Everything was broken and turned upside down. The Germans had given permission to the Christian population to rob and steal our possessions. But we weren't especially embittered: The robbery and looting were unimportant in comparison with our remaining alive.

And then the decrees began. First, they ordered us to choose a Judenrat [Jewish Council] of 12 men, who would represent us. We chose this committee from the town's dignitaries. At its head stood Mr. [Yitzchak] Mindel. My brother Chaim was appointed secretary, and the members

[Page 219]
of the Judenrat who were chosen that I remember were [Gershon] Klioner, the teacher [Eliezer] Mazeh, [Hirsh] Fridman and others.

We were asked to pay a bribe of gold. Everyone gave his possessions. Likewise, we had to hand over fur coats and many valuables and expensive items. We were taken to various jobs, women and men alike. At this time we still lived in our house, and we were free to move around. We had connections with the local population, and we could get food in exchange for possessions and clothing.

My husband, Zusman, was registered as a carpenter and worked in carpentry. A large group of men worked at the train station loading logs onto freight cars. One day, 13 men didn't return from the train station. The Germans killed them because a Pole denounced them, saying that they were careless in their work. Among those murdered was my brother-in-law, Yitzchak Blacher. My sister [Batia], now a widow, and her two children moved in to live with us.

At that time, it was decreed that we had to wear the yellow patch, and we were forbidden to walk on the sidewalks. Ten months after entering the town, the Germans established the ghetto [formally on April 1, 1942].

The ghetto was located on the main street, Pilsudski Street, and Jews from nearby towns were also put there. The crowding was terrible. And so in our three-room apartment, which inside the ghetto, four families crowded together. We, my sister Batia with her two children [Bluma and Shaul], my brother Chaim, his wife and their baby, and relatives of the family from Druysk [Drujsk, about 19 kilometers northeast of Braslav], Rachel and Michael Tzipuk and their two daughters, who were sent to our ghetto. My youngest sister, Matla, and her family moved to live in the hotel where our aunts lived, which also was populated by many Jewish families. It was very hard to bear all this, but 70 times worse was the disconnection from the outside world, because it was forbidden for us to go out and obtain food.

We began to think about escaping, self-defense and ways to fight the Germans. Zusman and a few of his friends tried to obtain weapons. When the Judenrat found out, they objected and argued that this would harm everyone. At the time, we already knew that many settlements and towns had been destroyed by the Nazis. Judging that each day was bringing us closer to our end, we decided to prepare hiding places, to hide the families at a time of calamity.

In the yard of my grandfather, Avraham-Hirsh Bik, there was a granary. It was built on foundations of stone. We took out several stones, dug very deep and built a large bunker that could serve us when the time came.

As mentioned, the crowding in the ghetto was terrible. Several families were forced to live in an apartment or even in one room. Despite this, we tried as much as possible to live an ordinary life, to keep clean, bathe frequently and so on. In this way, illnesses and epidemics were prevented. But cultural activities were completely impossible.

In the ghetto, in accordance with German directives, a Jewish police force was organized to keep order, prevent people from leaving the ghetto, and ensure that all the German commands were carried out exactly. In general, the Jewish police behaved tolerably and tried to help as best they could, but there were those who thought it would be better for them if they treated us strictly.

Occasionally Germans would come to our house, to order crates for packages that they would then send to their country. Sometimes we received a bit of food in payment. I don't remember much about our life in the ghetto; it all became foggy over time and was forgotten. But the ghetto's bitter end will never be erased from my memory.

Several days [sic] before the massacre, we learned that the Miory Ghetto had been destroyed [on June 2].[5] We knew our end was near, because no

[Page 220]

ghettos remained [nearby], except for the ghettos of Gleboki [Glubokoye, about 70 kilometers southeast of Braslav] and Druya [Druja, about 34 kilometers northeast of Braslav]. Toward the evening [of June 2], before the destruction of our ghetto, various rumors spread. A feeling of despair, helplessness and fear surrounded us all. We began to prepare to save ourselves.

That day, I baked bread. Every family began to quietly enter the hiding place that had been prepared. Zusman's father came to say goodbye, and even though Zusman asked him to enter the hiding place with us, he refused, saying that he no longer wished to live and couldn't bear to see us suffer. He kissed us all and quietly left the house. His last words were that we should try to stay alive and take revenge on the oppressor. He returned to his house and waited for the Germans to come for him.

By nightfall, all of us were in the hiding place. Many acquaintances and neighbors also joined us. We were about 70 [sic] people. We heard what was being done outside [starting early on June 3]. Every so often, we heard shooting and the shouts of people and the German soldiers. It was very hard to calm the children, but we did everything so that their voices wouldn't be heard.

During the second night, several men went out to get water. The amount of water that I'd prepared wasn't enough, and we hadn't managed to bring the bread that I baked down into the hiding place. In my grandfather's cellar, there was ice; we used that instead of water.

We stayed in the hiding place for five days, until the Germans found us. [By this time] we knew that of all the Jews in the town, only about 500 people remained alive. They and we were found, apparently, because of slander or because people's voices were heard coming from the hiding place. The Germans approached the entrance and told us that if we didn't come out willingly they'd throw grenades inside. There was no choice left for us. We came out exhausted, broken and indifferent to our fate. My brother Chaim emerged with no strength, troubled and in pain, leaving behind his little son Rafulik [Rafael], who had died. My husband, Zusman, tried to encourage us and said that we shouldn't lose hope. They gathered us all in the Judenrat building and kept us under heavy guard. We lay on the floor. Our hearts were torn inside us when we saw our young children suffering. We received almost no food. Some of the men were taken for various kinds of labor.

Our relatives from the Tzipuk family, who'd been moved to the ghetto [from Druysk], divided their possessions among villagers they knew, advising us to try to escape and reach one of the villagers. All of the villagers promised to help in time of need. But they set conditions: that we all not go out together and that we leave the small children. I objected to leaving without my small son. My sister Batia, whose husband [Yitzchak Blacher] had already been killed, said that there was no reason for her to live and she'd stay there with her small daughter [Bluma]. She asked only that we take her son, Shaul, with us.

My younger sister [Matla] was in the ninth month of her pregnancy, and she didn't agree to escape. My brother Chaim also refused, saying that there was no longer a reason for him to live. With a heavy heart and with fear about the fate of those who were staying, Zusman and I decided to leave together, and with us our son Arieh; my sister's son, Shaul; my aunt's daughter; her husband and their daughters. About 10 more people joined us. When this became known to the others who were being held with us in the room, they told us they wouldn't allow us to leave. They were worried that the Germans would kill them if we escaped. Their reasoning didn't convince us, because the Germans didn't know the exact number of people who were there. Besides, we thought that if we stayed there we'd die, even though some Jews believed the Germans would keep them alive because they were needed for work. Our son Arieh, who was six years old, said, "Father, come, let's escape from here, I don't want the Germans to kill us."

The next night we tried once more to go out and this time, with the help of a bribe to the guards, we succeeded [in escaping the Judenrat building and Braslav]. I left with

[Page 221]

a broken heart and without hope; I'd left behind my little son Mosheleh there, and a large part of my family.

My sister Batia told me to leave and save my son and hers and, if we succeeded, we should come back to rescue them. They'd try to do everything to be saved, and if not --- at least we'd remain alive. We thought that we'd be able to rescue them; the villager [outside Braslav] who we reached promised to travel to Braslav and try to bring them back. Toward morning, we heard shooting from the direction of the town. This told us that our dear ones were no more. All day we stayed in the villager's attic and cried. Shaul, who was eight years old, wept bitterly when he learned what had happened.

Of all the eight children [of my parents], only I remained alive. Sometimes the thought gnaws at me: Why did I alone, of all my family, merit life? My sister who remained in Russia after World War I was killed in the Crimea. My oldest brother [who also remained in Russia] managed to flee with his family to Kazakhstan [when the war broke out] and died there a few years later. This we learned after the liberation [in 1944], when we returned to Braslav.[6]

After the flight from Braslav, a period began of wandering from place to place. The first village we reached was very small; its name was Kropishki [probably Kropiszki, about 16 kilometers northeast of Braslav]. It included only a few houses, distant from each other. This helped us, because there were few people and the farmer's neighbors didn't know a thing about us. Ten people arrived at the farmer's house: the four of us; four of our relatives [presumably the Tzipuk family]; Yisrael Kort, the husband of my sister Matla; and his sister's husband from Warsaw, a teacher by profession.

The name of the farmer where we were guests was Benedikt Shakiel. He lived here with his adult son and daughter. The son became a faithful friend to us, and he had a large part in our rescue. Thanks to him, apparently, we remained alive. Benedikt himself was a hard, unpleasant man. He sheltered us only because of the money our relatives paid him. But he was an honest man, and we could rely on him.

After staying with him for several days, my brother-in-law Yisrael Kort left us. He was sure that he'd find a hiding place with other farmers in the vicinity, who he'd traded with before the war. He left us, and we didn't see him again. Later we learned that he'd been caught and killed.

We stayed with Benedikt for two months. Despite the scarce food and difficult living conditions, we were satisfied; we had a place to stay. But after two months Benedikt told us a rumor was circulating in the area that he was hiding Jews, and he said we had to look for another place.

Our relatives had a lot of property, which they divided among farmers in the area. They found another acquaintance who agreed to hide us for a limited time. We lived alternately in the attic, the granary and the pigpen. In this way, we changed places and wandered from village to village. Once we --- 17 people --- stayed with a farmer; it was good for us there, but we couldn't stay for long. If they'd found us, they would've killed him too.

We went out toward evening, not knowing where to turn. Snow began to fall, and with difficulty we arrived at a large forest. We stayed there for an entire day, and in the evening we went out on the road again, looking for a place to stay. We parted from the other people and our relatives again took us to an acquaintance, who hid us without much willingness. He prepared a hiding place for us under the stable, small and narrow, where we lay close to each other. This farmer was very hard. He told us frankly that it wasn't worth it for us to exert ourselves; sooner or later, we'd be killed. After arguing about the payment, he agreed to hide us for just a very short time, in return for merchandise

[Page 222]

that our relatives gave him: skins for boots and various other products.

Some time later, we parted from our relatives. The situation had become difficult; there was now nothing to pay the farmers. We didn't know where to turn to or to whom, and we returned again to Benedikt in the hope that he'd shelter us. He refused. Even the pleas of his son Stanislav didn't help. We had no choice; we went out in the field and lay down under the bushes, covered with rags. Stanislav, who knew where we were, would bring us a bit of food and tell us what was happening at the front. He was a wonderful lad; he wanted very much to help us, but his father didn't allow it.

We searched for other places. Once we found shelter with a farmer we didn't know. He was a good man, a *Starovery* (Old Believer).[7] But we had to leave him after a few days; somebody had noticed us. It was a holiday, Sunday, and all the Gentiles in the vicinity were celebrating.

The farmer told us that in a little while the enemy would come to take us, and Zusman suggested that meanwhile we eat the bread and cereal that the Gentile cooked for us. I looked at him as if he were crazy. In a little while they'll take us away to kill us, and he thinks about food! It began to get dark, but nobody came. The farmer took us out and went with us through fields and bushes; we kept walking, without knowing the destination. We reached a field of tall wheat, with many ditches in it, laid down in the tall wheat. At night, Zusman would go out to search for food. Sometimes the children accompanied him and when they returned, with a bit of vegetables such as peas and radishes, for them it was a celebration. They'd also go to Stanislav, and he sometimes gave them a bit of bread or some potatoes. It was difficult to obtain drinking water. Sometimes we remained without water for days.

The children didn't complain even once. They'd lie there quietly and talk to one another. Sometimes it would rain, and we'd be wet through to our bones. We became dry again only when the sun came out. For nearly half a year, we lay there in the hiding place in the channels between the bushes. We became skin and bones. It was a miracle that we didn't fall ill and were not discovered.

One day, a small boy found us. He was chasing a cow. He saw us and grew very frightened, but recovered and approached us. He knew who we were. We asked him not to tell anyone about us. But he ran home and brought his father. We were afraid; we didn't know who the man was, but we felt he wouldn't harm us.

Zusman promised to pay him, but by this time we had nothing. The farmer replied that he didn't want anything from us, but he suggested that we leave; our situation was very dangerous now that his son had seen us.

That night, Zusman went to consult with Stanislav. He advised us to hide in a nearby destroyed building that was full of hay. There, he said, people came only very infrequently to take hay for their animals. At this time, we learned that the teacher Greenberg was no longer alive. He'd hidden for some time with Stanislav, but someone had denounced him and he'd fled and hidden in the same destroyed building. There, the Germans had found him and murdered him. We entered the building, we had no choice. We dug into the hay and lay down in it.

This was our last shelter before we joined the partisans. Our only connection was

[Page 223]

with Stanislav. He told us that there were partisans not far from the place, and he said he'd try to find out how to contact them.

Winter arrived [in late 1942], but it was warm for us inside the piles of hay. We were dirty and fleas swarmed on our bodies; we hadn't bathed for half a year or more. With a yellow beard and swollen feet wrapped in rags, Zusman looked like a man from another world. No one who met him identified him as a Jew, and he used his appearance to search for food for us.

By this time, we had no strength left. More than once, I wanted to die. I couldn't stand to watch the children suffer. Zusman, in contrast, didn't lose hope, and he encouraged us and strengthened my spirits, saying that eventually we'd be able to immigrate to the Land of Israel.

One day we heard someone enter the building to take some hay, and this scared us. Fortunately the man didn't sense that we were there; he loaded the hay on a wagon and left. But we lived in fear that next time, when he came to get hay, he'd find us. And in fact a week later the man returned and began to load hay. We heard him talking to himself, cursing and wondering why it was so warm inside. This was during the cold, snowy days of December, and here, when he took out the hay, it felt warm.

We decided to come out of our hiding place, and we stood opposite him. He was more surprised and frightened than we were; he thought that maybe he was seeing some ghosts. After he calmed down and understood who we were, Zusman told him that we intended to go to the forest, to the partisans, and that we had contacts with them.

At this time all the farmers in the area knew about the partisans, and everyone was afraid of them. The man promised not to harm us and said that we could stay there until he took out all the hay. He left, but we were afraid to remain. We knew we couldn't stay there any longer, and we decided to go, once and for all, to search for the partisan camps. We told this to Stanislav, and Zusman asked him to watch us while he, Zusman, went to look for the partisans.

I remember how Zusman went out. This was the end of 1942, for the Christians the night of the Christmas holiday. We remained alone, in fear and uncertainty. The second night, Stanislav took us into his house. Before that, he brought us to the bathhouse and left us to wash and clean ourselves of all the dirt that we'd accumulated. Now and then he'd return to see if everything was all right, because he knew that we were exhausted and was worried that we'd faint from the heat in the bathhouse. After we bathed he took us into his house, fed us, and didn't allow us to return to the destroyed building. He put us in the attic and said that we should wait there until Zusman came back. Of course, our happiness knew no bounds.

The next day, our cousin arrived at Stanislav's house to ask for food for his family. They were located somewhere else, and the female cousin [his wife] was no longer alive. She'd died of tuberculosis and was buried somewhere in the forest. The man was broken and completely discouraged. He remained alive, along with his two daughters, and was trying to save them.[8]

That night, Zusman returned. Of course, our happiness and joy can be imagined. He also brought the happy news that he'd succeeded in contacting the partisans, and that in their camp he'd met several people from Braslav, among them Yerachmiel Milutin. After eating at the camp, he had come back to get us. He arranged with the partisans that they'd wait for us somewhere with a horse-drawn wagon, and he hurried to bring us the news. It's impossible to describe the scale of his disappointment and fear when he couldn't find us in the destroyed building. Thinking that the Germans had discovered and killed us, he'd hurried to Stanislav to find out what had happened, and

[Page 224]
to his joy he found us.

We decided to leave that night. It was January 1, 1943. I'll never forget it. A strong and cold wind was blowing, and we were dressed in rags. A snowstorm was raging outside. Stanislav took us in a sled to a clearing in the forest, and gave us a loaf of bread and a bit of salt. We parted from our cousin, who remained there, and Zusman promised him: If we arrived safely and were accepted into the camp, we'd come to get him and his daughters. We parted from Stanislav with kisses and tears; with emotion and excitement, he wished us success.

We began to walk into the heart of the forest. The storm became stronger. Zusman took Arieh on his shoulders, and I carried Shaul in my arms. That's how we walked all night. We weren't afraid of wild animals, but of meeting human ones. Toward morning, we arrived at a small village near Slobodka [about 11 kilometers northeast of Braslav]; we were frozen from the cold. We knocked at the first house. An old woman opened the door. Without asking any questions, she brought us inside and immediately lit the stove, cooked some potatoes, fed us, and gave the children wool socks and gloves. She kissed them and cried when she saw their terrible suffering.

We rested there for several hours, but we couldn't stay. The woman was afraid, even though her house wasn't far from the partisan camp. We thanked her for the compassionate things she'd done for us and continued on our way. Already it was morning, but we weren't afraid to keep going, because the region was under partisan control and the Germans didn't dare to wander about. We walked all day, with short pauses to rest. Toward evening, we arrived at the intended location. There partisans we didn't know were waiting for us, they'd known we were coming. They brought us to a large house full of people. All our strength was gone. They immediately served us a meal. Afterward we washed ourselves and lay down to sleep on the floor. Around us partisans sat and sang songs. I couldn't believe that we were in a place where we no longer needed to be afraid, in warm, human surroundings among good people. One song that the partisans sang reminded me of my brother Chaim. He'd loved to sing it, and I broke into bitter tears at the memory.

The next day, Zusman awoke early and traveled to meet Yerachmiel. The meeting was very emotional. Zusman returned and took us to a village next to the forest. Again, they received us very nicely; they gave us some clothes, and after a day we went back [to the partisan camp].

At the entrance to the forest, a heavy guard had been stationed. We kept going and arrived at the cabins of the forest dwellers. The partisan unit we'd reached was called by the name of the officer Sazykin [part of the Belorussian brigade]. They took us into the cabin of the Pinchov family. They received us with great joy, prepared for us a meal fit for kings, and took us to the bathhouse, where we stayed all night, because there was no room for us in the cabin.

But the Russian partisans weren't so happy. First of all, we'd arrived without any weapons. In addition, they didn't willingly accept families with children. Zusman told them that he was a carpenter and volunteered to make butts for the rifles. In addition, all of the Jews who were in the camp recommended that they accept us, and in the end the partisans consented.

A few days later, they began to build a *zemlyanka* for us --- a cabin, most of which is in the ground --- and they installed a large oven for baking bread. After some time, the family of Shmuel Deitch, Masha and her sister Yenta, joined the camp. They lived together with us, and later my cousin Liuba [Shmidt] and her brother-in-law Eliahu came also. Liuba served the partisans as a nurse, and she was very

[Page 225]

celebrated among them. Since there were no medical teams, she carried out the work of both doctor and nurse. There were many wounded among the partisans from fighting against the Germans. Zusman didn't take part in the fighting, but he'd travel with the partisans to the villages to get food and clothing. We had plenty of food. I'd cook varied foods in large pots, and there always were guests at our meals. That's how we lived, like one big family.

There were almost no complete families in the camp. In general, the camp contained individuals who'd been rescued from the clutches of the Nazis. Our children were the only ones in the camp.

In this way, the first winter in the partisan camp passed over us. Spring arrived, and the forest turned green. In the evenings we'd go out of the cabins, gather together, light bonfires, sit around them and sing.

In the beginning, it was hard for me to understand how people who'd lost their dearest ones could sing and celebrate. The children were very happy. They gained weight because of the good food, and enjoyed the freedom and atmosphere of the forest. There was no room for fear or hiding places. It was possible to go outside to play during the day.

The partisans went out frequently on operations against the Germans. They blew up train tracks and trains and caused the Germans heavy losses. There was also loss of life among the partisans. The Germans were afraid to go deeply into the forest. Fortunately, they didn't know the size of our force. In fact we were very few and not well armed, either in quantity or quality.

One day the news came that a German unit was approaching the forest. An order was given to leave. This was in the winter. Naturally, we didn't wait long; we left the cabin and everything in it, and ran to look for a place of shelter deep in the forest. We walked all day, and toward evening we arrived at another partisan camp. There we found many Jewish acquaintances. We slept there, and the next day --- when they notified us that everything was all right --- we returned to the previous place. Over time, echoes of the battles began to reach us from the front. We'd heard about the defeats of the Germans and their withdrawal, and we believed that soon we'd be liberated; but we worried that before their final collapse they'd want to take revenge on the partisans and kill them. The men prepared shelters for a time of trouble, deep inside the forest. We also prepared a lot of food: smoked meat and toast. But thank G-d, there was no need for it.

The Germans conducted a large hunt for a partisan unit near Disna [Dzisna, about 72 kilometers east of Braslav], in the region where my cousin Luba [sic; possibly the Liuba mentioned on page 224 of this memorial book as a nurse for the partisans] worked as a nurse transferring the wounded to Russia. We were worried about her, but one day she appeared, healthy and whole.

The year 1944 arrived. The Germans were collapsing on all fronts, and as spring approached we were certain that their end had come. The constantly heard thunder of artillery came nearer and nearer. We were witnessing the defeat of the Nazi murderers.

And the longed-for day arrived! On July 9, 1944, the Red Army arrived at our camp and told us that we could go home. After a number of days, Zusman and other men from Braslav took a wagon and traveled to the town to find out if the danger had passed. When he came back, Zusman took us to Braslav. We returned to the town with mixed feelings: We were happy that we could return home, to the place where we'd been born and grown up; but we knew we were coming back to a place that held the graves of our dear ones, a place of blood and tears,

[Page 226]
inhuman suffering and troubles.

When we reached the town, we didn't even enter our house; all of us gathered in one of the empty houses. Slowly, slowly, Jews began to arrive in the town, the remaining refugees from Braslav and its surroundings --- and all of them lived together in several houses.

Letters began to arrive from all over Russia from survivors from our town, and in them were questions about the fate of their dear ones. I answered every letter and passed on all the information known to us. Together with the Red Army, many journalists from abroad arrived and interviewed us. All of them wondered how we'd succeeded in rescuing the children. Through the journalists, we told our relatives in the United States and Israel that we were still alive. In 1945 a daughter was born to us, and we named her Batia, for my sister. We decided not to remain in Braslav and at the first opportunity to make *aliyah* to the Land of Israel. At first the authorities didn't permit this, but later everyone who'd once been a Polish citizen was given permission to leave the Soviet Union.

In January 1946, we left Braslav. We stayed in Germany for three years, and when the state of Israel was established we made *aliyah*, in April 1949.

Exodus from Braslav, 1945

Footnotes:

1. The Yavneh school was part of a network of more than 200 schools established throughout Poland by Mizrahi, the Religious Zionist movement that had been founded in 1902 in Vilna to promote Zionism among observant Jews. Yavneh schools emphasized modern Hebrew (in place of Yiddish), religious education and reconstruction of Jewish life in Palestine. The flagship of the Yavneh school network was the Tachkemoni rabbinical seminary in Warsaw.

2. Vilna was about 165 kilometers southwest of Braslav. The Yiddish Teachers' Seminary had been established in 1921 in Vilna to produce teachers for schools of the Central Yiddish School Organization (Tsentrale Yidishe Shul-Organizatsye), abbreviated as TSYSHO or CYSHO. Although official state recognition was granted to the Yiddish Teachers' Seminary in the 1920s, later governments in Poland proved less supportive and in 1931 the seminary was forced to close.

    TSYSHO itself was established in Warsaw in 1921 and continued to operate until 1939. It was led mainly by the left wing of Poale Zion (the more radically socialist wing of the Labor Zionists) and the Bund (the Jewish socialist party in Poland), which was anti-Zionist but supported the use of Yiddish. Together they sought to create a network of secular Yiddish schools under socialist auspices.

    TSYSHO was administered by a central office in Warsaw and a central education committee in Vilna (which between 1922 and 1939 was part of Poland, as was Braslav). According to *The YIVO Encyclopedia of Jews in Eastern Europe*, the curriculum consisted of Yiddish language and literature, Jewish history and culture, the sciences, math, music, physical education, arts and crafts and, in some cases, Hebrew. In addition, Polish language, literature and history were taught in Polish.

    At its peak in the late 1920s, the TSYSHO network maintained 219 institutions with 24,000 students in 100 locations. These included 46 kindergartens, 114 elementary schools, 6 high schools, 52 evening schools, and the Yiddish Teachers' Seminary in Vilna. The crown jewel of the

TSYSHO network and Yiddish secular education in Poland was the Vilna Realgymnazye, the first modern high school in which Yiddish was the language of instruction.

3. YIVO, founded in 1925 and based in Vilna before the war, sought to preserve, study and teach the history of European Jews and Yiddish. After war broke out in 1939 the headquarters was moved to New York City, where it continues to operate. It's now known in English as the Institute for Jewish Research. A section on Chaim Munitz, including his time at YIVO in Vilna, is on pages 70-71 of this memorial book.

4. Dvinsk (a.k.a. Daugavpils), in Latvia, was 42 kilometers northwest of Braslav. Riga, also in Latvia, was about 245 kilometers northwest of Braslav. According to the *Encyclopedia of Camps and Ghettos, 1933-1945*, Volume II-B (2012), the German army reached Dvinsk on June 26, 1941 and Riga on July 1, after Braslav had been occupied. This was followed by the arrest and murder of some 1,150 Jews in Dvinsk, about one-tenth of that city's prewar Jewish population. A ghetto was established in Dvinsk at end-July 1941 and in Riga between August and October 1941. After suffering periodic Aktions over the following two years, the Dvinsk Ghetto would be shut down in October 1943 and the Riga Ghetto in November 1943.

5. The historian Yitzhak Arad, in *The Holocaust in the Soviet Union* (2009), has noted that most of the Jews of Belorussia were still alive by the end of 1941, unlike the Jews of Lithuania, Latvia and Estonia, many of whom had already been murdered. The winter that began in late 1941 was especially harsh, making it difficult to dig mass graves in the frozen earth, and this halted massacres for a time.

With the winter in Belorussia receding, on March 2, 1942 some 5,000 Jews in the **Minsk Ghetto** (out of 49,000) were shot by German security forces consisting of Belorussians, Ukrainians and Lithuanians. On March 3 some 2,300 Jews from the **Baranovichi Ghetto** (out of 18,000) were shot by German, Belorussian and Lithuanian police. On May 8 some 5,700 Jews in the **Lida Ghetto** (out of some 7,200) were shot. On May 29 the **Dokshits/Dokshitsy Ghetto**, with some 2,653 Jews, was liquidated. On June 1 the **Luzhki Ghetto**, with 528 Jews, was liquidated, as was the **Plissa Ghetto**, with 419 Jews. On June 2 the **Miory Ghetto**, with 779 Jews, was liquidated. The massacre of the Jews in the **Braslav Ghetto** began the next day, on June 3.

Subsequently other ghettos were targeted, including the **Slonim Ghetto** with 10,000-12,000 Jews, the **Glubokoye Ghetto** with 2,200, the **Disna Ghetto** with 2,181, the **Kletsk Ghetto** with 1,500, the **Druya/Druja Ghetto** with 1,318, the **Dunilovichi Ghetto** with 979, the **Postav/Postawy Ghetto** with 848, the **Ghetto in Opsa**, with 300, and the **Sharkovshchitzna/Szarkowszczyzna Ghetto**.

6. The eight children of Rafael-Yaacov Munitz and Sheitel were as follows. (1) The oldest brother, who died in Kazakhstan. (2) The oldest sister, who was killed in the Crimea. (3) Chana, whose account this is and who was married to Zusman Lubovitz; she and he survived the war, together with their son Arieh, but their other son, Moshe, didn't survive. (4) Batia, who was married to Yitzchak Blacher; they didn't survive the war but their son, Shaul, did, cared for by Chana and Zusman. (5) Chaim, who was married to Asya and was the secretary to the Braslav Judenrat; neither they nor their small son, Rafael, survived the war. (6) Matla, who was married to Yisrael Kort; they didn't survive the war. (7) Boris/Baruch, who joined the Soviet army in 1939 and wasn't heard from thereafter. The eighth sibling, not mentioned in this account, was Yekutiel, who was married to Chava/Eva; neither of them is believed to have survived the war.

7. This was a group of Eastern Orthodox Christians that had split from the state-supported Eastern Orthodox Church in the 1600s over differences in liturgy and ritual. Their split provoked government oppression that continued up to the early 20th century.

8. This may refer to Michael and Rachel Tzipuk and their two daughters, who were mentioned on page 219 of this memorial book as relatives who'd come from Druysk.

Moshe Milutin
Son of Sonia and Ber-Leib

Translated from the Hebrew by Laia Ben-Dov
Footnotes Added / Donated by Jeff Deitch

. . . The Germans entered the town on Thursday afternoon [June 26, 1941]. Two patrols riding on motorcycles arrived from the direction of Turmont [Turmantas in Lithuania, about 35 kilometers northwest of Braslav/Braslaw]. They stopped next to our house and looked toward the Catholic church (the tallest building in the town), apparently to make sure that there were no snipers in it. Representatives of the Polish population received them with bread and salt.

Toward evening, they turned around and left the town on the road that passed next to the Christian cemetery [in the western part of town]. At midnight, a large German army began to move in the direction of the village of Plusy [about 21 kilometers to the north]: foot soldiers, artillery, vehicles and more. Few soldiers remained in Braslav. The next day, on Friday [June 27], the Germans announced that the Jews must come out of their houses; they gathered them all next to the "horse market" [a.k.a. the cattle market], separated the men from the women and took all of them into the Dubki [Dubkes] forest, to the peninsula on Lake Driviata [Drywiaty]. From there it was impossible to flee, because all around there was a heavy guard of soldiers with machine guns, and also because the surrounding area was swampy. Only my cousin, Chaim Milutin, and Shlomo [Zilber] the *shochet* [ritual slaughterer] tried to flee on the way, but they were caught. Chaim was hit by a volley of bullets; he turned toward the people around him, called out his final words to everyone, and fell. Shlomo the *shochet* was shot in the head; he kept clearing his throat and then a soldier approached him and shot him again, killing him.

At the place where we were gathered, they ordered us to sit on the ground and not move. We sat that way all night. Only at four o'clock in the morning, after a discussion between the

Germans and the person appointed by them as mayor of the town [of Braslav], a doctor and veterinarian named Kovalski [Kowalski], did they free us and give us permission to return to the town. We found our houses broken into and robbed. After a number of days, they ordered the Jews to hand over their cows to the authorities; they decreed that we had to wear yellow patches on both sides of the body. The ghetto was actually organized only 10 months later, in April 1942.

There was no German police force. Policemen were appointed from among the local Polish and Belorussian population. Exceptionally cruel among them were one Grivkov [Krivko, a.k.a. Kriwko] from Ikazna [Ikazn, about 14 kilometers east of Braslav], Shlachchik [Shliachchik], [Stefan] Zhuk and also Yashinski [Stanislaw Jasinski], who later became the chief of police.[1]

A unit of German gendarmes ruled in the town, and battalion [or regiment or troop] 44 of the SS, which had returned from the front, camped at the train station. There were

[Page 228]
emergency storerooms there. We worked in the garage. Moshe-Chatzkel Milutin worked with me.

Immediately after the Germans entered, the Judenrat [Jewish Council] was appointed by the supervisor Kovalski. He appointed about 10 people. The chairman was [Yitzchak] Mindel and the rest of the members were Sheinkman, Chaim-Yekatriel [Katriel] Deitch, Yankel-Velvel Shapira, [Gershon] Klioner, Falka [Rafael] Fisher, Hirshka Deitch and Leib Valin, who was responsible for sending people out to work.

Chaim Munitz was the secretary. It was said that he kept a diary about life in the ghetto and the events that occurred to the Jews of the town. After the liberation of Braslav [in July 1944] we searched in many places for this diary, but we didn't find it.

The Judenrat had many responsibilities, mainly to carry out the decrees of the German authorities, such as handing over cows and other animals, handing over fur coats, organizing the knitting of hats and wool gloves for the German army, and making ropes out of flax. A group of men worked at the train station stripping the bark from logs that were sent to Germany for paper manufacturing and to the coal mines.

They didn't pay for the work, and they provided no food. Each person worried about himself and his family and the need, of course, was great. We had to sell clothing and possessions to buy food. We sold to the Poles, the Belorussians and the farmers in the area; it was forbidden for us to go to the market. The Gentiles would come into the ghetto, which was concentrated along the length of the main street --- Pilsudski Street.

The Germans also brought Jews from the Jewish village of Yaisi [Jaisi, seven kilometers east of Braslav] into the Braslav Ghetto, and also Jews from the nearby towns --- Druysk [Drujsk] and Dubina [Dubene].[2] The crowding was terrible. Several families lived together in one apartment or house.

There was no medical assistance. In cases of illness, a doctor would be brought secretly. Circumcisions were also done in secret. At night, people shut themselves in their houses. Nobody went out and no one came in, due to the great fear. There also were cases of random murders, without any clear reason.

A large group of 80-90 men would go out to work at the train station. I remember that once 13 men didn't return from the station. Later we learned they'd been put into a boxcar that stood on a side track and shot. Among them were Boris Karas and Yechezkel Vinokur. They were murdered after a warehouse worker denounced them, claiming that they'd been careless in their work.

Several weeks after the Germans had entered, Soviet planes bombed a German army convoy. Local residents, Poles and Belorussians, said that a hunchbacked Jewish woman had been seen signaling to the planes. The Germans seized Zelig Ulman's sister, accused her of spying and murdered her. After that, they arrested Beila Deitch (she too was a hunchback) and accused her, Yaacov Musin from Druya, and Ch.-I. Burat of the same crime. After much running around and many attempts, the head of the Judenrat, [Yitzchak] Mindel, succeeded in freeing Burat. After suffering much torture, Beila Deitch and Yaacov Musin were hanged by the Germans.

They found the member of the Judenrat, Zelig Ulman, his wife and his daughter, who'd hidden themselves in a secret place. They took them to the Karpovitz forest [Karpowicz forest, near the western entrance to Braslav] and killed them there. This happened about a half-year before the destruction of the ghetto.

The women (Esther Rusonik, Lusia Segal, Sonia Aron, Roza Skopitz, Esther Zeif and others) worked mainly in cleaning the offices of the Germans. The attitude of the Polish population was, in general, threatening. No one from [among] the [Gentile] residents helped the Jews with anything. Sometimes their attitude was even worse

[Page 229]

than that of the Germans. The local farmers were more human in their behavior toward the Jews of the town. For instance, the farmers from the villages of Ozravtzi [Ozierawce, about six kilometers southeast of Braslav] and Achremovtzi [Achremowce, about seven kilometers southeast of Braslav] hid several Jewish families until the last day of the occupation. (Natka Fisher, Niuta Kantor, Masha and Mendel Maron and two families from Dvinsk [42 kilometers northwest of Braslav] hid with farmers in the village.)

The son of the Pravoslavic [Eastern Orthodox] priest, Alexi [Aliosha] and his brother Dima Vasilevski [Wasilewski] --- helped more than a little. Especially Alexi, who was the deputy of the *starosta* [town elder/mayor] Kovalski. He helped the prisoners of war of the Red Army, forged documents and certificates, and would send the prisoners to the villages to work. The Germans killed him and the supervisor Kovalski.

Beila Deitch (first on the left) and family

[The other family members shown here are Beila's brother Shaya Deitch, a theater actor; their mother, Fraydel, who was the widow of Pesach-Leib Deitch; and the young Malka Shteinman, a niece of Beila and Shaya. Malka later married Moshe Milutin. Shaya Deitch is also pictured on pages 40-41 of this memorial book.]

The Massacre

The killing began on June 3, 1942 and continued for three days. The day before [the killing began], a group of about 100 women was taken to do cleaning work at the nearby village of Slobodka [11 kilometers northeast of Braslav]; the next day the oppressors returned them and brought them, together with all [the Jews of Braslav], to the site of the massacre [where they were then killed]. A few days before, rumors had spread in the town about the destruction of Jewish populations in the region. The rumors told of massacres in Gleboki and Miory.[3] In the winter of 1941 [on December 17], the Jews of Yod [Jod, 25 kilometers southeast of Braslav] had already been killed.

Knowing all this, we tried to prepare, digging and building secret places. We built them in stables, cowsheds, storerooms and various other places; we'd dig a pit and cover it with boards. There we lived. Matityahu Handler [Gandler?], the blacksmith's son, built a trench like [those] on the front.

[Page 230]

In the night between Tuesday and Wednesday [June 2-3] we heard terrible shouts, accompanied by shooting. I lifted the screen of the hiding place and saw groups of Germans, together with local police, going from house to house and taking people outside. I quietly snuck out of the hiding place and fled in the direction of the house opposite; I entered a hiding place that had been dug under the storeroom. There I found several families who had been hiding there for a few days. All the time, we heard shooting.

I left and crawled between the bushes. I found [people who had been] killed --- Moshe Vishkin's father [Tuvia] and his brother Yosef. I crawled back and entered my Aunt Rivel's kitchen. [This might refer to Rivel Milutin.] There I found some people hiding in a pit under the table. Ch. Pinchov, Esther Rusonik, Moshe-Yechezkel [Moshe-Chatzkel] Milutin, Mendel and Masha Maron and Moshe Vishkin were there. I lay down among them.

From there, we went out at night to see what was happening in the streets. We found many bodies. They'd killed my mother in the yard of our house, while she was trying to flee through the gardens. The policeman Grivkov [Krivko, a.k.a. Kriwko] killed her, and my brother buried her.

The big massacre took place near the train station. Almost all the Jews of the town were brought there [to the pits that had been dug outside the town]. They ordered all of them to undress next to the pits and then they shot them. Mashka Katz ran from the pit; all day she lay hidden among the bushes. In the evening she walked naked to a nearby village and asked for shelter, but the farmers handed her over to the Germans, who killed her. Nioska Yakobson, the daughter of the dentist, ran away when the people were being taken to death. She entered a house that stood on the side of the road and hid there. The police found her and killed her. Many young people were killed in the streets, in their attempts to flee.

The Germans knew that many Jews were still hiding, and so they announced that they'd take no more people out to be killed, because they needed people to work. One of those who passed through the streets and called for the Jews to come out of their hiding places was Epshtein's son, a drunkard and a corrupt Jew. Many Jews believed these announcements and came out of their hiding places. They were immediately imprisoned in the Yiddish school [the Folkshul]. Hundreds of people were there.

Sheinkman, and Ribash from Druya, members of the Judenrat, turned to the Jews who remained alive and asked for money, gold or jewelry from them, to bribe the guards, but this didn't help, and all of them were taken out to be killed. They say that the elderly Rabbi [Avraham-Abba-Yaacov] Zahorie went to be killed wrapped in his *tallit* [prayer shawl], saying, "We must accept death with honor." Several people (such as Hirsh Fridman) drank to excess before they were taken out to be killed and [then they] went with all the Jews on their last journey.

In the ghetto there was an underground organization, consisting mainly of young people and former soldiers. I know that after the destruction of the Miory Ghetto [on June 2], rumors began to spread about the coming destruction of the Braslav Ghetto. People (most of them Jews from the Miory Ghetto who had succeeded in fleeing in time, before the destruction of that ghetto), filtered into the Braslav Ghetto with weapons to defend themselves. I don't know what happened to these weapons. I myself had a pistol that I buried in the ground.

When the men of the Judenrat came to collect money to bribe the guards, we went out into the streets with wagons and gathered the dead, who were lying around outside. We were witnesses to police chasing after some Jews with rods; we saw how they chased after Yitzchak Ulman and grabbed him.

My father was a guard in a leather storeroom. When he learned of the killing, he went up in the attic of the storeroom, took the ladder up with him, and hid there. Earlier we'd taken him to our hiding place, but he didn't want to stay there and told us, "You go, the young ones. I'm already 48 years old." I know

[Page 231]

of several incidents of active opposition. For example, I heard about Eliezer [Leizer] Biliak, who disguised himself as a German they'd killed and who murdered several collaborators among the local residents. And Moshe-Baruch [Bank], who after a struggle was tied to the tail of a horse and dragged through the streets of the town until he died.[4]

The Road to Armed Conflict

At night, we decided to leave the ghetto. Several men, including me, snuck into the garage of the hospital and hid there for a number of days. From there, we set out in the direction of the Karpovitz forest [near the western entrance to Braslav]. In the forest, we came across graves that weren't properly covered; we found bodies with their feet unburied. We covered them and continued onward. We entered the house of a farmer and hid in the attic for an entire day. The Gentile told us that he'd visited the church in town and heard about what was being done there. From his house we went to another farmer, who took us into the granary and gave us food. From him I learned that my father had been killed; the oppressors had also found and killed Ulman's father, who'd hidden in Burat's house. We also learned from the farmer that the Jews of Opsa [18 kilometers southwest of Braslav] had not been destroyed.

We waited for night and set out in the direction of Opsa. We entered the ghetto there by way of the Vidz-Boian road. There I met my uncle Yerachmiel Milutin and Esther Rusonik. Yerachmiel took us to the bathhouse of a farmer, and there we found M.[oshe?] Vishkin and A. Reichel. They gave us a bit of money and a loaf of bread. From there we continued to Vidz [Widze, about 22 kilometers southwest of Opsa]. On the way, we met several Jews from Vidz, and we walked together. In the dark, we couldn't find the bridge over the river. We grew confused. We wandered all night, and found the road again and entered Vidz only toward morning. We stayed there for a week and worked with all of them [the Jews of Vidz]. From there, the police took us to Sventzion.[5] There we worked repairing the train tracks.

The food we received was like in the camp, a bit of soup with a little bit of meat. From there, I'd sometimes travel to the Vilna Ghetto on the train and return to the Podbrodz Ghetto.[6] There was one German there, Shultz. After I repaired his motorcycle, I gained his confidence. The son of the German was always singing the [Nazi Party's] Horst Wessel song: "When Jewish blood spurts from the knife, then it's good and fitting."

After staying a month in the Podbrodz Ghetto, we were sent to Duksht [Dukstas, in Lithuania and about 75 kilometers northeast of Podbrodz]. There too we worked on repairing the train tracks and in the sawmill. In the sawmill many non-Jews, farmers of the area, also worked as hired laborers. The supervisors were two Germans, who'd been disabled in the war.

In the winter, before Christmas of 1942, I made contact with my cousin Moshe-Yechezkel [Moshe-Chatzkel] Milutin, who was in the Sventzion Ghetto; Biliak was with him. At the time, rumors were spreading they wanted to destroy our work camp, and a group was organizing that planned to flee to the partisans.

I asked for permission from my supervisor to visit a family relative, and I received it. I set out on the Dvinsk-Vilna train. When I got off the train at the station in Duksht, gendarmes grabbed me, chained me, took me to the police station and put me in jail. There I learned that some days earlier some of the members of the Sventzion labor camp had fled (Idel Rusonik, Handler, Efraim [sic] and others); they thought that I too was one of the escapees. Rusonik and Handler they sent to Ponar.[7] When Motka from Turmont learned that his friends had been taken to be killed, he knew that if he was caught his fate would be like theirs, and he decided not to fall into their hands alive. He entered a Gentile's house, asked for a knife, and cut his own throat.

[Page 232]

They brought him to the police station as he was dying, and he died there. They killed Arka [Aharon?] Milutin in the place where they buried Motka.

When I was in the jail they abused me, starved me and flogged me at every opportunity. One time the door opened and into my cell burst a violent dog, a German shepherd, which attacked me and bit me on the leg. For a long time after that, I was unable to walk. Scars from the bites and wounds remain with me to this day.

The gendarmes interrogated me; they beat me with murderous blows until the German from whom I'd received the travel permit arrived and asked that I be freed, because he needed me for work. After they released me, the German took me and gave me medicine and food, and in this way I was saved. He also told me that they were going to destroy the camp. By the way, after the war I learned that this German was alive and in Düsseldorf. I wrote to him, but got no reply.

From Duksht, I fled to Sventzion [about 50 kilometers to the south], where I met my cousin Moshe-Chatzkel [Milutin]. We knew that they were sending people to Ponar to be killed. We organized 20 men, we gathered several weapons, grenades and a pistol, and we set out in the direction of Hidotzishok [Hoduchishki a.k.a. Adutiskis in Lithuania and about 27 kilometers east of Sventzion] --- to the forests.

Partisan certificate of Moshe Milutin

[Page 233]

We reached a forester, who told us that there were indeed partisans in the area who carried out sabotage activities, mainly against trains, and that they sometimes came around. With us were Yerachmiel Milutin and Esther, my cousin Moshe-Chatzkel [Milutin], Yochai Barka [sic] and a few other friends. We wandered in the forest for a few weeks, occasionally entering village houses to take food. We slept outside, in the snow, under the trees.

One day we met a Russian, a former commissar of the Red Army, whose name was Vasily Markov. We spoke with him about our wish to join the partisans. He promised us that he'd return to see us after carrying out a sabotage mission. This he did, after a number of days, and he took us to the forests around Postav-Hidotzishok [Postawy-Adutiskis]. On the way we encountered a German ambush, which opened fire on us. Fortunately, only one member [of our group] was injured. We covered him with branches, promised that we'd return for him, and kept walking. Markov and two friends succeeded in crossing the river, and we remained in the forest without a leader. We entered [the house of] one farmer, forced him to harness a horse, and together with him we traveled to the place where we'd left our friend. We took him with us, and at night we crossed the river. We reached a village by the name of Osatzina, on the other side of the river. While we were crossing the river, the partisans opened fire on us, thinking that we were Germans, but in the end the situation became clear. After interrogations, the partisans accepted only those who had weapons of their own. Those with no weapon in hand were sent to procure one, so that they could join up.

From there, we turned in the direction of Braslav. We reached the village of Krasnosletzi [perhaps Krasnosielce, four kilometers west of Braslav], and there we began to carry out actions: we destroyed the houses of collaborators with the Germans, killed local policemen and Germans, derailed trains, and carried out other types of sabotage. I took part in many activities in the areas around Sharkovshchitzna [Szarkowszczyzna, about 40 kilometers southeast of Braslav], Boian [about 28 kilometers southwest of Braslav and now called Bogino], Opsa, Kozian [Koziany, about 40 kilometers southwest of Braslav], Vidz and others. Near Kozian, I was wounded. Our officer was Strikov, a former Soviet pilot. We continued to operate in this way until the summer of 1944. After that, we joined the Red Army. In July 1944, our town of Braslav was liberated. The day after liberation, I asked for and received permission to visit it. There I stayed two days, gathering a lot of information.

Those who'd collaborated with the Germans had fled. I searched for Anton [Burak], who was one of the most despicable informers, but didn't find him. I wanted to execute him. At the time, we had permission to take revenge and execute such people without trial.

When I learned the identity of the man who'd killed Leizer Biliak, we went and told this to the Soviet authorities and asked for permission to capture him. They told us to wait. After a week, they informed us that permission was granted. Avraham Biliak and I then went to the house of the Gentile Promchenko [Primchenko on page 244]. He began to run; we opened fire on him and killed him and his sons.

Footnotes:

1. According to the *Encyclopedia of Camps and Ghettos, 1933-1945*, Volume II-B (2012), on June 30, 1941 --- a few days after entering Braslav --- the local German commandant began to recruit a local police unit from among local ruffians who were sympathetic to the Germans. A Pole named Yashinski [Stanislaw Jasinski] was made the unit's commander. Other policemen in the unit included Kriwko, Stefan Zhuk, Malinowski, Masara, Czeslaw Kolkowski, Zarniewicz and Stanislaw Nowicki. A man named Sucharewicz was one of the most brutal participants in the persecution of the local Jews.

    In autumn 1941, responsibility for the local police was transferred from the German army to the German gendarmes, after a civil administration had been established to replace the military administration. (That is, the German gendarmes supervised the local police unit.) Among the men based at the German gendarmes' outpost in Braslav were Johannes Czapp, Willy Dittmann, Otto Hayman, Paul Kontny, Leo Leidenroth, Ludwig Müller, Ernst Schreiber and Waldemar Schultz.

2. Druysk was about 19 kilometers northeast of Braslav, and Dubina was 16 kilometers northwest of Braslav. The Jews from Dubina stayed in Braslav only a short time and were soon taken to the Vidz

Ghetto. They remained in the Vidz Ghetto until around the autumn of 1942, when that ghetto was closed and the inmates were transferred to the Sventzion Ghetto.

3. Gleboki (Glubokoye) was about 70 kilometers southeast of Braslav, and Miory was about 40 kilometers east of Braslav. According to the *Encyclopedia of Camps and Ghettos, 1933-1945*, Volume II-B, 110 Jews from the Glubokoye Ghetto had been shot by the German Gendarmerie and local police on March 25, 1942, and about 20 more Jews had been killed there in May 1942. On June 2, 1942, one day before the Braslav Ghetto was massacred, the Miory Ghetto was eliminated; estimates of the dead there range from 780 to more than 1,000.

4. An account of Moche-Baruch Bank and the Bank family is given on pages 286-287 of this memorial book.

5. Sventzion (Svencionys), in Lithuania, was 45 kilometers southwest of Vidz. The *Encyclopedia of Camps and Ghettos 1933-1945*, Volume II-B, says that following the massacre of most of the Jewish inhabitants of Sventzion in July and October 1941 a ghetto in Sventzion was formed, comprised initially of the small number of surviving Jews from the town. Around the autumn of 1942, the population increased substantially when most of the Jews from the Vidz Ghetto were transferred to the Sventzion Ghetto. This transfer included the surviving villagers from Dubina, who'd been moved to the Vidz Ghetto from Dubina earlier in 1942.

6. Podbrodz (Pabrade), also in Lithuania, was 32 kilometers southwest of Sventzion. Vilna was 45 kilometers southwest of Podbrodz. According to the *Encyclopedia of Camps and Ghettos 1933-1945*, Volume II-B, the first Podbrodz Ghetto was formed on September 1, 1941, but most of the inmates were killed soon after, in October. In May 1942, 400 Jews were brought to Podbrodz from the Vilna Ghetto and put in a newly built labor camp, and this is presumably the place mentioned by Mr. Milutin in his account. The inmates of the labor camp worked on a railway line for the German Giesler company. In 1943, those among them who were still alive were returned to Vilna.

7. Ponar (Ponary in Polish, Paneriai in Lithuanian) was about eight kilometers southwest of the Vilna train station. It was the major execution site in the Vilna region during World War II and the largest execution site in Lithuania. Between July 1941 and August 1944, an estimated 50,000-70,000 Jews, 2,000-20,000 ethnic Poles and 5,000-8,000 Soviet prisoners were killed there. Typically, small groups of victims were marched to the site on foot from Vilna, while larger groups were taken to Ponar in trains. Upon arrival, they were walked to the killing site inside the adjacent forest and shot. In 1943-44, before the Germans retreated from the area, the corpses of the executed were dug up and burned. In the years since the war, memorials and a small museum have been erected on the site.

On April 5, 1943, an estimated 4,000-5,000 Jews from the Sventzion Ghetto and other small ghettos in the region, on the pretext of being resettled in the larger ghettos in Vilna and Kovno, were instead taken in trains to Ponar and killed. The victims on that day included many villagers from Dubina, who'd been transferred to the Sventzion Ghetto from the Vidz Ghetto around the autumn of 1942.

[Page 234]

Rafael Charat
Son of Isel and Avraham-Baruch

Translated from the Hebrew by Jerrold Landau
Donated by Aron Charad

My father was a small-scale merchant who dealt in the buying and selling of chickens, eggs, fish, fruit and other such products. He would send the merchandise for sale in the regional city of Vilna. During the time of Soviet rule, father worked as a warehouse keeper in the bakery of the Kort family. His job was to receive the flour and deliver the bread. I worked in the tailoring workshop, my brother Yisrael worked as a firefighter, and my brother Moshe worked in a print shop.

After the German invasion of Russia [in June 1941], unrest pervaded the town. The Soviet officials began to withdraw, leaving us to our fate. A portion of the Jewish population, especially the young people, began to escape in the direction of the old Polish-Russian border [to the east, the pre-1939 border], with the hope of entering the Soviet Union and remaining there until the fury had passed.

In our house we thought that all of us must flee, but father was opposed. "What happens to the People of Israel will happen to Reb Yisrael," he said. [In other words, he'd share the fate of whatever befell the Jews of Braslav.] We, the sons, were already of age, and we decided to set out on our own. My sister Sima remained at home with our parents. Along with us, a large group of young people headed toward the town of Druya [Druja, about 34 kilometers northeast of Braslav/Braslaw, next to the Dvina River]. Along the way, we met the wagon driver Pesach Shkolnik and his daughter Libka; they were traveling in the same direction. The next morning, we were shelled from the other side of the Dvina River. We were told that the Russians were prohibiting people from crossing the [pre-1939] border. Discouraged and disappointed, we returned to Braslav. It was difficult for us to walk the 40 [sic] kilometers by foot. We walked only at night, with the flames of burning villages lighting our path.

When we entered Braslav, we learned that the German army had already arrived. In our house we found only our parents, our sister was no longer there. We learned that the Germans had arrested members of the Communist Party as well as the Komsomol youth.[1] My sister was a Komsomol member, and everyone had advised her to quickly leave town, despite rumors that the situation wouldn't last, the Russians would repel the Germans and she'd be able to return. Several months passed, Sima didn't come back, and we became convinced that she'd been killed somewhere.

Several days after the entry of the Germans, Soviet airplanes bombed local concentrations of the German army. The next day, the Germans arrested

[Page 235]

a Jewish girl and two lads [Beilka Deitch, Yaacov Musin and Ch. Burat], accusing them of cooperating with the Soviets by signaling the airplanes and pointing out the bases and shelters. After being tortured, they were taken out and killed.

The next victims were 14 Jews who were murdered based on the slander of a Polish work supervisor, who informed the Germans that the workers had been careless on the job. Our work was stripping bark off logs of wood at the railway station, after which the wood was sent to Germany. We worked without a break. It was forbidden to raise one's head or take a rest.

In Slobodka [about 11 kilometers northeast of Braslav], there were army barracks. The Germans learned that the Russians had hidden weapons there during their retreat. We were sent there. We dug, found the weapons and loaded them onto the railway cars. We loaded barrels of water onto trucks; after we finished the job, a German ordered us to climb onto the barrels. Suddenly we realized that another German was aiming his rifle at us. We were very frightened. One of them photographed the event. We unloaded the barrels at the bakery and received a loaf of bread, a not-insignificant return for the fright.

When the ghetto [in Braslav] was established [officially on April 1, 1942, although Jews in the region were being concentrated in Braslav before that date], we were ordered to leave our homes and enter the ghetto, where we lived together with the family of Leizer Frumin. We gave our cow to our Polish neighbor and asked him to bring us a bit of milk from time to time. We also gave many articles of clothing to sell to a farmer from the village of Diedushki [Dzieduszki, 12 kilometers southeast of Braslav]. In times of need, we exchanged belongings for food.

Nine of us lived in the tiny dwelling. In the ghetto, we already knew that the Germans were liquidating the Jews. News reached us about the liquidation of Jews in neighboring villages. We didn't believe that it was possible to hide and save ourselves. The Germans received a great deal of assistance from the local Christian residents, who knew everything that was happening in the town. Nevertheless, people began to prepare hiding places.

[Meanwhile] the Germans were sending messages of assurance through the Judenrat [Jewish Council], stating that nothing bad would happen to the Jews of Braslav, since they were diligent and obedient workers.

We, the four men in the family, decided to prepare a hiding place to use in case of need. We began to dig together with our neighbors, the Tvoretzki family. Their house seemed suitable to us for this purpose, since it was located some distance from the street and was close to the mountain.[2] The work had to be carried out secretly, in quiet. We had to watch out for not only the police but also the eyes of neighbors. The entrance to the hiding place was below the bathroom.

Early in the morning of Wednesday, June 3, 1942, we heard shouting outside and orders to come out of the houses. Some people managed to hide, but we thought that in all the commotion we'd be able to flee to an outlying village, to our acquaintances. We were mistaken. On leaving the house, we saw that we were surrounded on all sides by armed men, who were leading everyone in one direction. We were forced to advance together with everyone else. Our family walked together, and when we neared the house of Falka Katz we began to run behind the houses to get back to our hiding place. Shots were fired at us from the direction of the mountain, but we succeeded in going down into the shelter. We stayed there for three days, but were captured on Friday, the third day of the slaughter: Someone went out to fetch a bit of rainwater to drink, and a policeman noticed him. They ambushed us like dogs. The police and gendarmes arrived immediately and demanded that we leave our hiding place, or else they'd throw a grenade inside.

[Page 236]

The family of Meir-Yossel Deitch, relatives of the Tvoretzki family, was together with us. Some of them succeeded in getting away. My two brothers also succeeded in escaping from the police. The rest of us were arrested and taken to the gathering place in the building of the tax office. I was taken there along with Matus (Matityahu),[3] with father and mother behind us. In the building, we met other Jews who'd been captured in other hiding places. Everyone's fate was sealed. I recall Chaim-Aizik Maron standing there, weeping bitterly. I remember a large room in which many articles of clothing had been thrown. First names and surnames had been written on the walls, and next to each one was the word *"umgekumen"* ("perished").

While we'd been in the ghetto, mother had given articles of value to each of us, saying that we should keep them until a time of need, so that we might save ourselves and survive. Now, confined in the tax office, I tried my luck, knowing that our end might come the next day. Next to the door sat a policeman, as well as a member of the Judenrat wearing an armband (I won't mention his name). I gathered my courage, approached him and offered him an antique watch made of gold, from the days of Czar Nicholas, if he let us go. He refused and ordered me to move away from the door. Later, I tried again. By this time it was already dark, and next to the door sat just one sleepy policeman. To this day, I can't explain how I slipped past him into the yard. In the yard lay the bodies of people who'd been murdered. I jumped over the corpses and ran through the yards until I reached the house of Leib Gurevitz. There I encountered a Jew, who dragged me to shelter. This time, I was saved. I sat there, frightened and trembling with emotion. There I also found my friend Meir Gurevitz.

But we had to leave this shelter. The police and the Germans were moving from house to house, searching every corner, and it was very difficult to hide from them. Meir's mother, Rachel, told us to flee. My mother, Isel, of blessed memory, was from the village of Diedushki, where several Jewish families had lived previously. Mother had gone to school with the villagers, and many of the girls in the village were her friends. She'd known every farmer there, and in the summer we'd gone there for vacation. Now I decided to flee to that place.

At the entrance to the village was a bridge guarded by the Germans. On the way there, we met the sister of the policeman Kolkovski [Kolkowski] and found ourselves between a hammer and an anvil. But fate was kind to us: The two guards were lying asleep next to the bridge, with their weapons at their sides. We managed to cross the bridge without being noticed, but then they awoke and began shouting at us to halt. Frightened, we ran in different directions; we were separated and never saw each other again. After the war, I heard that Meir had entered the ghetto in Glubok [Glubokoye, about 70 kilometers southeast of Braslav], where he'd been killed.

I lay in the field all night and entered the village early in the morning. I met my older brother, Yisrael, at the home of our good friend Mikita Sevelevitz [Sewelewicz], and later my third brother, Moshe, arrived. Mikita took us to his acquaintance, Vanka, in the village of Buyavshchitzna [Bujewszczyzna, about two kilometers east of Dzieduszki], who belonged to an ancient sect of the Orthodox Christian faith. He hid us in his house for several months. We slept in the attic, dug into piles of fodder and hay, while the lice and the mice ate us alive. When we learned that a second ghetto was being set up in Braslav, we went there.[4] The people in this ghetto numbered several hundred, some of them from Opsa. The Judenrat also consisted of several Jews from Opsa. Mikita and the Polish neighbor with whom we'd left the cow would bring us a bit of food. The ghetto was surrounded by barbed wire and guarded by policemen; one of them was the former conductor of the band in which I'd played. Later Vanka, the farmer with whom we'd hidden, came to us and told us

[Page 237]

of a rumor that our ghetto [the "Opsa" Ghetto in Braslav] would soon be liquidated. He suggested that we return to his house. With his agreement, we dug a hiding place there under the sheep pen.

[In this way] Vanka saved us from certain death. A few days after we left the ghetto, the gendarmes and police arrived, led everyone to the pits, and murdered them. This was on the eve of Purim, 1943.[5]

We stayed with Vanka for a few months. After it became known that he was hiding Jews, he asked that we find another place for ourselves. As always, help came from our friend Mikita. He found for us a farmer in the same village, Kasan was his name; at his place, we dug a shelter in the cowshed. We covered the walls of the pit with the doors of the village bathhouses, which we stole from nearby villages during the night. Once, as we were attempting to take down a door, we saw the shadow of a man and became very frightened. We learned that he was a Russian officer who'd escaped from a prison camp near Dvinsk. He joined us, and we lived together. Later, we found out that the farmer had also hidden Leib Sherman and his children.

[Page 238]

Notice from the War Commissariat informing Sima Charat [sister of Rafael] that two of her brothers, soldiers in the Red Army, had fallen as heroes on the battlefield:
Yisrael Charat, fell on September 9, 1944
Moshe Charat, had been gravely wounded, dying on September 20, 1944

Footnotes:

1. The All-Union Leninist Young Communist League (Komsomol) was the youth organization of the Communist Party.
2. Castle Mountain, also known as Castle Hill and the Zamek. It was called a mountain by locals, even though it stood only 15 meters or so above the town.
3. This might refer to Matityahu Deitch: According to the Yad Vashem database, Meir-Yossel Deitch had a son by that name.
4. Around August-September 1942, some 50 Jews in Opsa were transferred to the former ghetto in Braslav, to repopulate it after the original inmates had been slaughtered on June 3-5, 1942. Because the members of this second, new ghetto in Braslav were from Opsa, the ghetto was also called the "Opsa" Ghetto. It would be liquidated on March 19, 1943.
5. Purim Eve 1943 was March 20. The ghetto was liquidated on March 19.

[Page 239]

Avraham Biliak
Son of Henia-Riva and Natan

Translated from the Hebrew by Laia Ben-Dov
Footnotes Added / Donated by Jeff Deitch

When the Germans and Russians divided Poland between them in September 1939, I was a lad of 15. Suddenly I became an adult. Life's routine was broken; everything changed. We went from being cattle traders in independent Poland to farmers in Soviet Russia. Ten hectares of agricultural land were divided between my father and his two brothers. At home, we were, in addition to our parents, four sisters and three brothers: Masha, Moshe, Shayna, Sara-Gitka, Libka, Tevka [Tuvia] and me. All of us from the Biliak family, a respected family. After the Holocaust, only two of us remained: me and my brother Moshe. Masha --- our big sister --- was married in 1933 to Yankel Glazer. At home, she caused us a lot of problems and anguish, like Hodel in "Tevye the Dairyman."[1] Our Masha was an active member of the Communist Party, which was illegal in Poland. Occasionally they'd arrest her and put her in jail in Braslav [Braslaw] or in Lukishki [Lukiskes Prison] in Vilna. This would happen in the runup toward the workers' holiday, May 1, and also before the anniversary of the Bolshevik Revolution [October-November]. She was [also] arrested when they found Communist propaganda material in the attic. Before the war began, she and her husband had two children, Avraham-Itza and Rivkeleh. The third child --- Velveleh --- was born during the war, and he was half a year old when the Nazis murdered the Jews of Braslav.

We parted from our big brother Moshe with a sad heart. He was drafted into the Polish army, in the war against the Nazi invader, at the beginning of September 1939. Their advance was much faster than expected, and it could be estimated that within a few weeks they'd take all of Poland. We grew worried about our fate; we feared the Germans.

Then came the decision of the Soviet authorities to rule over eastern Poland (as they said, to free the areas of Belorussia and western Ukraine). With flowers and kisses and shows of happiness, we willingly received the Red Army. We began to grow accustomed to a new, strange way of life. We became accustomed to shortages and standing in line for necessities, and we also learned to be afraid. The men of the NKVD[2] would sometimes take unwanted families and send them to distant locations. Jews from Braslav were sent as far away as Siberia.

[Page 240]

We lived under the Soviet regime for about two years [September 1939 to June 1941]. Frightening news reached us about the Nazis' treatment of their Jewish population. Then, before we understood what would happen, it became our turn.

We were astonished when we heard that the Germans had invaded the Soviet Union [on June 22, 1941]. We were shocked by the strength and rapid advance of their army. The Red Army withdrew, sometimes in disorder, deep into Russia. On the fourth day of the war, the last Russian officers and their families left Braslav. The civil government, police and party also left. We remained without a government. There were no Poles, the Russians had fled, and the Germans hadn't yet arrived.

On the fifth day of the war, the Germans entered Braslav. First a number of patrols riding on motorcycles, and then the army. They located themselves opposite our house, in the yard of Skuriat and along the length of Lake Driviata [Drywiaty]. After that, they changed locations and moved the army next to the train [station]. Remaining near us were a number of their workshops and a bakery that was established with three large machines to supply their bread. They grabbed people [Jews] for various types of work. They also took me for work in the bakery, with 20 other men. We worked from morning till night. Each order from them began with "*Du verfluchter Jude*" ["You cursed Jew"]. Many times they dragged me to work at the train [station]. We worked many hours at hard labor. We loaded weapons, hay, wood and other things. Despite our good work, they beat and cursed us. If a Jew had a beard, they'd grab it and shake his head in every direction.

After that came a succession of things: a Judenrat [Jewish Council], Jewish police, yellow patches, a prohibition of walking on the sidewalks and a prohibition of buying in the market; contributions of large sums of money, valuables and good clothing.

The day before Passover 1942 [on March 31, 1942], an order was published requiring Jews to leave their houses and property and move to a ghetto. The ghetto ran along the entire length of Pilsudski Street, and it was divided in two. Across the bridge, in the direction of Slobodka [to the northeast], the elderly and their families had to gather ("*nicht arbeits-fähig*" --- not fit for work), in other words: the "dead ghetto." Our house stood within the elderly ghetto, and we very much wanted to stay in our house. My father went to his friend, Rafael Fisher, a member of the Judenrat, to consult with him. Rafael told him, "You can remain in your house. All of us are sentenced to be destroyed. They might destroy you earlier." We moved to live together with the family of my uncle, Mulka Biliak, my father's brother. Everything was done in a big hurry: the crowding in the house was great, the conditions were terrible, the children were crying. We received a little bit of food from the Gentiles in exchange for some clothes and valuables. We knew that the ghetto was temporary; they were concentrating the Jews before destroying them. We had to find a hiding place and try to remain alive. We dug a pit under the house, pouring the dirt into the river under the bridge. We made an opening in the floor to go down [into the pit], well camouflaged. We prepared water and food in the pit. On June 1, 1942, they ordered the Judenrat to send to Slobodka (10 kilometers from Braslav) 100 young people to clean the army barracks, mostly girls. I and my sister Libka were among those drafted. They gathered us all in the yard of the Judenrat. On June 2, Tuesday morning, we went out on the road. Gendarmes and armed police who rode on bicycles accompanied us. The [Gentile] people of Slobodka pitied us and gave us water and a bit of food. On Wednesday morning, they gathered us again and we were told that we were returning home. Our happiness was boundless. We walked in loose order. Along the entire way, we met patrols.

[Page 241]

As we approached Braslav, a unit of gendarmes met us. Brutally and with curses, they began to crowd us together and speed us up. Shlomke Shapira, walking next to me, said "I have a feeling that something's happening in Braslav. Come, let's run away." At a suitable opportunity, we rushed from the group. Hirshke from Zamosh [Zamosz] joined us. We hid until the group moved far away. Later, I was told by my sister [who stayed with the group]: Only after the group entered Braslav did everything become clear to them. The marches to the extermination pits were at their height. The city was full of Germans, Lithuanian police, Latvians and locals. On every side there were screams and shots, beatings and curses. In the group [coming back from Slobodka] there was fright and confusion. A few tried to escape and succeeded, as did my sister. Others were shot and wounded. The soldiers took most of them to the pits and killed them in cold blood. And my sister further told me: Next to the gate of the cattle market they saw two bodies, of Avramke and Naftal Fisher [Avraham, the son of Baruch Fisher, and Naftali, the son of Zalman-Yaacov Fisher]; they'd fiercely resisted the police who came to take them to the pits, and the police had shot them.

The order to begin the destruction of the Braslav Ghetto on Wednesday, June 3, [1942] came from the *Gebietskommissar* [district commissioner] from Minsk. The night before the massacre, we noticed forces arriving in the town and spreading out around it. These were *Einsatzgruppen* [mobile killing squads], Lithuanians, Latvians and locals. To assist, vehicles arrived loaded with gendarmes from Gleboki [Glubokoye, about 70 kilometers southeast of Braslav]. On this day [June 3] they went wild; they murdered and slaughtered multitudes of the Jews of Braslav.

That night, the street of the ghetto was quiet. Patrols circulated outside. When they went away from our house, I snuck out and entered the family hiding place. My sister Libka had already managed to come. My family was saved from the massacre on the first day, except for my sister Shaynka; we didn't know what had happened to her when we all went down into the hiding place. Apparently, she was grabbed and killed. The next day, the soldiers continued their work: They broke the doors and windows of houses, turned over furniture and looked for hiding places. We were lucky; they found no one in our house and didn't see the entrance to our hiding place. In our hiding place, my sister Masha's baby --- Velveleh --- was crying. We were afraid that his cries would reveal the hiding place and its inhabitants, and my sister put a feather pillow over his mouth, and then the crying stopped. The massacre of the Jews of Braslav continued for three days. In the first massacre, our family lost two of its members [Shaynka and Velveleh].

We knew that our shelter was just temporary; we had to flee. Even before the massacre, my father had gone to speak with farmers from the neighboring villages. They showed a willingness to help us when needed. One of them was our friend Petro --- the priest from the Belmont church [Belmont was about seven kilometers southeast of Braslav]. On Friday night [June 5], we decided to try our luck. We went out: father, my sister Masha and her husband Yankel [Glazer], my sister Libka, my brother Tevka and me. Mother remained in the hiding place with her two grandchildren --- Masha's children. With them also was my sister Gitka [Sara-Gitka], who didn't want to leave mother alone with the children. We decided: We'll find a safe place, then come back and take them with us.

At the entrance to Belmont, there was a large bridge, well guarded by the Germans, so it was necessary to go around it. We asked for help from an acquaintance who lived near the bridge. After midnight he put us all into a boat, made a big detour far from the bridge and brought us into Belmont. The priest was surprised to see us and happy that we'd come. He'd thought for sure that we'd been killed. He received us with food, drink and tears in his eyes, and promised to help us survive. First, he took us into the church and locked it. To his congregation he said, "It's better for the church to be locked and not used as a hiding place by undesirables who are passing through." On Sundays, he'd return us to his house and open the gates of the church to the worshippers.

A number of days after the massacre, the oppressors went around Braslav and announced on loudspeakers that all those who were hiding could come out; nothing

[Page 242]

bad would happen to them. My mother, my sister, the children and many others with them who had survived believed the announcements, and they went outside. All of them were gathered into the yard of the Judenrat, and some days later they were all taken to the pits; their end was like those who'd gone before them.

Yankel [Glazer], Masha's husband, decided to return to Braslav and bring the children, mother and my sister. We didn't yet know that they'd already surrendered themselves and been killed. When he reached Braslav, he was caught; they beat him and killed him.

The priest [in Belmont] began to look for safer places for us. He took Masha to a farmer in the village of Zaravtzi, where they hid her under a large Russian stove; the chickens were also kept there. Father, me, Tevka and Libka he brought to the village of Piatoshki to two brothers who weren't married. They hid us in the cellar under the cowshed, and at night we'd go up in the attic, where we had a lot of air and a larger living space than in the cellar. We paid them generously for all of their kindnesses: the lodgings and the food, their communication with us and the goodness of their hearts. For just one thing was compensation impossible --- the fear. Whoever hid a Jew lived in constant fear. The villagers were warned continuously not to hide Jews, and woe to the person who had a hidden Jew found in his house. His fate, the fate of his family and his possessions, was sealed. The house and its contents would be burned, the animals taken, and the entire family would be killed. Once the brothers hinted to us that a few of us would have to find another place. We heard that in Opsa [18 kilometers southwest of Braslav] a ghetto still existed; we had acquaintances there. We decided to separate: Father and my sister Libka would stay where they were, my sister Masha would move to a neighboring village, and I and Tevka would go to Opsa. We said our goodbyes, and we parted from the brothers who'd put their lives in danger because of us. They told us how to go on the roads and paths, through the forests and villages. On the way, villagers helped us. All the time, we faced dangerous threats; we were afraid but continued onward. Everyone was looking for Jews: the Germans --- naturally --- and the local police --- they were drafted to do this and they did their work faithfully. Every Gentile who caught a Jew and turned him over to the authorities received salt as a reward. (There was a great shortage of this necessity.)

Before the entrance to Opsa, a local Gentile told us how to enter the ghetto without being seen. He pointed to a small wood not far from where we stood, and told us that two bodies were lying there: Mulka and Chemka [Nechemia], the sons of Leib Sherman. They were two young sons of Braslav, like us, who'd been caught, tortured and beheaded. We approached and identified them. We wept. In our minds arose gloomy thoughts. We couldn't stay in the Opsa Ghetto for two reasons. First, it was closed to Jews from outside. And worse: Every day police from Braslav visited, and they might recognize us. If caught, we could expect certain death. We kept going, somehow, for another 20 kilometers. Exhausted, we reached the Vidz Ghetto [in Widze, about 22 kilometers southwest of Opsa]. Here we were allowed to stay for some time. Three weeks passed; we'd only just managed to recover and rest a little. Then an order came for the Judenrat to send a group of young men to the labor camp in Sventzion [about 45 kilometers southwest of Vidz]. They put us in this transport. The camp [in the Sventzion Ghetto] was on Vilna Street, in an area fenced in with barbed wire. They took us inside and separated us into miserable huts. We were about 500 Jews. All of us worked at repairing the train tracks from Sventzion to Podbrodz [Pabrade, about 32 kilometers southwest of Sventzion].[3] They put us to work early in the morning and returned us late. We worked at hard labor for half a year, supervised by the men of "Todt."[4] Then we were told that they were transferring us to the Vilna and Kovno ghettos. From trustworthy sources, we learned immediately

[Page 243]

that the destruction of the labor camp was part of the overall plan for destruction, and that some of us would be sent to Ponar.

Meanwhile, in the autumn of 1942, the Germans established another ghetto in Braslav.[5] When this became known to my father and sisters, who believed the Germans' promises of no more killing --- they went to the ghetto. In March 1943 [March 19], the ghetto was destroyed and all of them were killed. Now from my family, just I and my brother Tevia remained, and unfortunately the two of us became separated. He decided, with his friend Shlomo Yechilchik, to go to the Vilna Ghetto; I, Moshe Milutin, Yerachmiel Milutin and his wife Esther, all of us from Braslav, decided to go to the Kozian forests, where we'd heard partisans were organizing themselves, and join them. We snuck out of the camp [at the Sventzion Ghetto] and went on our way. We arrived at the village of Kamyelnik, near Lintup [Lyntupy, about 13 kilometers southeast of Sventzion]. We asked one of the farmers we met, and who seemed to be a decent man, if there were any partisans in the area. We'd found the right person. Because we were Jews he put his confidence in us, telling us that the partisans had passed by that night and he'd inform us when they came back. The time --- Passover Eve 1943 [April 19]; spring. For a week we hid in the forest and then, when the partisans returned from their mission, the Gentile [arranged for us to meet] with their officer Charitonov. In the course of the conversation we asked him to accept us into the *otriad*,[6] and we showed him our weapons. He was convinced of our desire to fight the Germans, and he agreed to take us.

Now we were partisans. We had to prove our will to fight and revenge ourselves on the Germans and their collaborators. At night, we went out to the base. In the river, near Paltrova, on the way to their mission, the partisans had submerged two boats. Now we had to take them out and use them to cross the river again. But here we met a surprise. A Lithuanian police unit knew of our movements, apparently because of a denunciation, and they were waiting for us. When we approached the place where the boats had been hidden, they directed heavy fire at us. We fled in disorder to the nearby forest and hid. We'd passed a serious baptism of fire. The next day, we met in the partisan base in Paltrova. At first, they joined the Braslav group to the *otriad* in the name of Chapaev, but after a number of weeks they transferred us and a few others to the *otriad* named Spartak [the Spartak brigade]. In the Kozian forests additional Jewish fighters joined us, as well as Russian soldiers who'd fled German imprisonment. Within a short time, they appointed me officer of a section in the second *otriad* and Yerachmiel Milutin the assistant officer of a patrol section. I went out on most missions together with Moshe Milutin.

In Vidz, there were many gendarmes and local policemen. They plotted against the villagers with the excuse that the villagers were helping the partisans; they took their possessions and even burned their homes. It was decided to teach them a lesson. On the orders of Commander Strikov, we went out, hundreds of partisans, to attack the uniformed men in Vidz. In addition, we were ordered to take control of the pharmacy in the town and get medicines from it. In a surprise attack, we killed many. We also lost some [fighters] killed, among them six Jews.

To guard a certain important section of the train track near Voropaivo station [Woropajewo, about 55 kilometers south of Braslav], the Germans built bunkers. From these bunkers, they guarded against attacks by the partisans. We received an order to destroy the bunkers; we had to blow them up with the soldiers inside. According to the report of the patrols that surveyed the target, 500 Germans were there. Under the leadership of Ponomariev [Arkadi Ponomarev] we went out, 250 partisans, to carry out the mission. When we got near the place, we divided into squads. The bunkers were equipped with machine guns. In our hands was a new Russian anti-tank gun (PTR) that was excellent for cracking bunkers. We approached in the dark, without them sensing us, until we were 50 meters away, and on command we opened fire with all of our weapons. Our success was complete; we blew up the bunkers and killed the Germans.

[Page 244]

At the beginning of 1944, I was appointed officer of the punishment section. The group numbered six men, and besides me there was another Jew, Tzalka Malozhki. We received our instructions from the intelligence department next to headquarters. We acted against traitors and collaborators with the Germans, denouncers, murderers of Jews and the like. Sometimes we carried out the death penalty in the place where they lived, and other times we brought them to headquarters.

When they came to destroy the Jews of the second ghetto in Braslav [the "Opsa" Ghetto in Braslav, which was liquidated on March 19, 1943], Leizer Biliak fought against them with all his strength. With his pistol he shot and killed a German, wounded several others and then succeeded in fleeing. The Germans promised a reward to whoever handed him over to their security forces. Leizer knew the village and the place where his relative Yerachmiel Biliak was hiding. When he got there, he found Yerachmiel's brother --- Chontza --- with his children; they also had nowhere to go. Yerachmiel's hiding place was too small to contain them all, so Leizer went out with Chontza to look for another hiding place. In the course of their wandering, they entered the village of Matseshe [Maciesze, 13 kilometers southeast of Braslav], to their acquaintances the Primchenko family [Promchenko on page 233], and asked Alyocha, the head of that family, to allow them to rest and wash. Alyocha agreed, while signaling to his sons that they should notify the Germans that two Jews were in his house, and that one of them was the wanted man --- Leizer Biliak. Within a short time, the gendarmes arrived and arrested Leizer and Chontza. They took them out to a nearby hill and shot them.

Two weeks later, villagers told us the story. We decided to take revenge. Three times we went to the village: I, Yerachmiel Biliak and Moshe Milutin, and with us the partisan Pitka Kasharavski, to kill the father and the sons. Twice we returned, because not all of them were in the house. The third time, we found them all. We were prepared for them to resist or try to escape; three of us took positions around the house. Alone, I entered. They recognized me and immediately understood why I came, and they grew very frightened. They tried to escape. I shot one of the sons and killed him. The second son and Alyocha were killed outside by the friends who'd come with me. Consolation? No, but still it was revenge.

At the end of the war, my brother Moshe and Yehuda Graber retrieved Leizer's and Chontza's bodies and brought them to burial next to the pits [in Braslav]. May their memory be blessed!

In the summer of 1944, the Braslav region was liberated, and much more. The partisan units disbanded. I was drafted into the Red Army, and I continued to fight the Germans in the framework of the first Pre-Baltic front until victory over Hitler and his army. Then I returned to Braslav. I went to see with my own eyes the pits next to the train [station] that were filled with thousands of Jews. I also learned that my brother Tuvia [Tevka] had been killed in the police station of the Vilna Ghetto.[7] With the help of the Red Cross, I located my brother Moshe. I'm not the only orphan. Of our family, we two survived.

Footnotes:

1. Tevye was the fictional narrator of a series of short stories by the eminent Yiddish writer Sholem Aleichem that were first published in 1894 and later published together as a novel. A pious Jewish milkman in czarist Russia, Tevye had a large number of daughters, one of whom --- Hodel --- was politically active and broke away from her traditional upbringing.
2. Narodnyi Komissariat Vnutrennikh Del (People's Commissariat for Internal Affairs), the Soviet law enforcement and intelligence agency that existed from 1934 to 1946, after which it evolved into the KGB.
3. The main rail line linked Pabrade and Svencioneliai (Nowo-Swieciany in Polish, Nei-Sventzion in Yiddish); another rail line linked Svencioneliai to Sventzion (Swieciany in Polish, Sventzion in Yiddish), where the ghetto was located. Svencioneliai was about 11 kilometers northwest of Sventzion.
4. The Organization Todt: A civil and military construction and engineering group founded in 1933 by senior Nazi Party member Fritz Todt. Until 1945, it operated or oversaw many major projects in Nazi-occupied Europe, including the concentration camps, and made extensive use of slave labor.
5. After the first Braslav Ghetto was liquidated on June 3-5, 1942, the Germans repopulated it in August or early September 1942 by bringing in some 50 Jews from Opsa, many of them craftsmen. Because these people were from Opsa, this second Braslav Ghetto was also called the "Opsa" Ghetto. It would be liquidated by the Germans on March 19, 1943.
6. Russian word for a partisan unit.
7. The story of Tevka (Tuvia) Biliak is on pages 283-285 of this memorial book.

[Page 245]

Chaim-Eliahu Deitch
Son of Malka-Rayza [née Deitch] and Yitzchak

Translated from the Hebrew by Jerrold Landau
Footnotes Added / Donated by Jeff Deitch

On September 1, 1939, at the outbreak of the German-Polish war, I was immediately drafted into the army, as were many others from Braslav [Braslaw] and the surrounding area. We were taken on the first train to Sventzion [Swieciany, about 85 kilometers southwest of Braslav and in Lithuania]. Many draftees from different towns and villages arrived there --- a lot of people. In the evening we had a festive gathering, on the initiative of the locals and artists from among the draftees. It was a pleasant and enjoyable event, despite the shock and astonishment of the outbreak of war and the sudden enlistment. But the evening didn't end as planned. In the middle of it, a Polish officer arrived riding on a horse and ordered us all to enter the train cars waiting for us at the station. We were about 2,000 people. All of us were already wearing army uniforms and carrying guns and food. We obeyed the command at top speed, and the train set out. I was able to find a seat, and because I was very tired I fell asleep. We knew that we were being taken to the front to fight the invaders. To tell the truth, I'd no wish to fight for the Poles, but this time I knew I'd be fighting against the enemy of the Jews.

We approached Lomzhe [Lomza, about 380 kilometers southwest of Swieciany], but we couldn't enter the railway station. German airplanes had preceded us and bombed the railways and everything on them --- locomotives, wagons and war equipment. We passed the town. The bombing had also damaged living areas, and houses were burning. We passed wagons carrying the wounded and dead. In some of the places, bearded Jews stood looking out for Jewish soldiers, and they offered us food and drink. We also endured a bombardment as we crossed the bridge

over the Narev [Narew] River outside Lomzhe. The airplanes hunted two targets together ---
a bridge and a large Polish army concentration. We had already crossed the bridge when it
collapsed. Many of our soldiers were killed or wounded, and we hadn't yet hurt even one German.

We were ordered to dig ourselves in and fight. A long time had passed since I'd received any
training, and the others were the same as me --- army reservists. We fought an entire week and
suffered many losses, but we managed to hold the line for a time and inflict losses on the enemy.
Once, we even launched a counterattack; we forced the enemy to withdraw with many dead and
wounded, but this was a passing episode. The next day, they repaid us with such a blow

[Page 246]

that we couldn't recover. Only a few of us were left, and we scattered in every direction.

Three of us ran in one direction; me and two *shkotzim* [a dismissive term for Gentile young
men]. We sought shelter. At night, we walked along a canal. In the morning we were discovered,
and the enemy shot at us. A small grove lay ahead of us. We advanced, bent and crawling, and
one of the Gentiles was hit in the eye by a bullet. We wanted to rest a little in the grove and care
for this wounded man. Suddenly, there was a shout: *"Hände hoch!"* ["Hands up!"]. One of us
succeeded in running away [while I and the wounded Gentile were captured]. We were taken to
a small village and the wounded man was bandaged. After a while, the man who'd escaped was
caught and shot; they suspected him of being a spy. The two of us were transferred to a prisoner
camp in another village.

For several days, I worked in a field bakery and ate well. On the fifth day of our stay in the
village, I noticed increased movement by the Germans around us. The same day, we received a
command --- we organized ourselves like good soldiers. We were taken out of the place, and we
marched . . . We were told that we'd have to march to Hamburg. None of us could estimate the
distance, but it seemed very threatening. We walked. The food was meager, and the drink too
was limited.

All my life, I'll remember that chaotic march and what happened to us on the way. We were
very many prisoners; I can't estimate our number. We arrived in Hamburg two weeks later with
fewer than half our people. A sane man would never be able to understand why they had to kill
so many people on the way. What a satanic idea it was!

We passed through forests, groves and villages, and another forest lay ahead on our route.
We were told to take off our shirts, stand in order and walk in single file, one behind the other.
The path was very narrow, and there were cut trees on the side along the entire path, like markers
along the path. The forest was very dark and dense. As we advanced, some Germans stood on
both sides of the path opposite us, waiting for us, as if greeting a military parade. Our many
guards started to push us forward. As we passed them, they shot anyone who happened to be in
front of their pistol muzzles. We started to run and bend over; we stepped on the bodies of our
fellow soldiers. By the time we came out of the forest, our ranks were much reduced. We
continued the tiring march. We were frightened, tired and wounded. Even the little food we had
I couldn't put in my mouth.

In Hamburg, we were placed in a camp with an electric barbed-wire fence. The guard was
increased, and they were armed with machine guns. We were put into miserable huts, with no
windows or doors. The roofs were sloped to the ground.

Recruits of the Polish army, September 1939. Eliahu Munitz (first from the right) and Hirsh Chepelevitz (third from the right) later fell in battle.

[Page 247]

The Incident with the Coat

On the way to Hamburg, not far from the road we'd passed through, I'd seen a Polish officer lying dead on the ground. It was autumn; it was cold already and raining outside, and our clothes were torn and ragged. I removed his coat from him and put it on. It was ragged, but anyway it was a coat. At night in the open huts we slept huddled together, covering ourselves with it.

There was a well with a hand pump in the camp yard. One morning I went out to wash, and when I came back . . . the coat was gone. "Where's my coat?" I asked. No one in the hut knew anything about it. I went outside, walked around the hut, and there was a Polish prisoner from a nearby hut, holding my coat. I approached him, yelling in anger, "Why'd you take my coat?!" "You damned Jews," he replied. I hit him so hard that he fell against the sloped roof. I took the coat from his hands and returned to the hut.

The camp guards heard shouting, saw prisoners gathering, and called for help and entered the camp. They asked questions, investigated, and took me outside. My friends, Jewish prisoners, grew concerned about my fate. Outside they investigated, asked questions, took photographs, and took me into a nice building. I waited a bit. A door was opened, and I was told to enter; a severe-looking German officer was sitting at a well-ordered desk. I stood there trembling. In one second, many thoughts passed through my mind: "They don't need many reasons to kill a Polish prisoner, let alone a Jew." To the officer's question about how I'd arrived there, I answered that I hadn't wanted to fight, so I'd surrendered. My answer satisfied him. He continued questioning me and wrote down every detail. To his question about where I came from, I replied, "Braslav." He repeated and asked, "From Breslau?" [Breslau, then in Germany, is now Wrocław in Poland.] I responded, "No, from Braslav in Poland, not far from Vilna." He asked me to describe the town. I told him, "It's not a big city. It has several streets, a mountain in the middle [Castle Hill], and is surrounded by large lakes and forests." Then he asked me to describe the region. I mentioned villages and places I knew very well, not understanding why he was so interested. When I mentioned the Belmont estate [about seven kilometers southeast of Braslav], he yelled "*Oh mein Gott!*" and again I understood nothing.

I noticed the man had changed. His tension had disappeared. He grew more relaxed, as did I, a little. He pushed a button, and his adjutant came in. He asked for coffee and bread rolls. It didn't enter my mind that they were for me. He invited me to sit and offered me food. Now it was his turn to confess. He told me that during World War I he'd arrived in Braslav with the German army and been appointed the officer in charge of Belmont --- the yard and the property. I felt that he enjoyed the nostalgic memory. I enjoyed the coffee and the fresh rolls. Now, I thought, he'd do something good for me.

The interrogation and conversation ended. He said, "Now they'll imprison you. You'll also go on trial. You've attacked a *Volksdeutscher* [ethnic German], and you'll have to defend yourself, justify yourself, and prove that the coat is yours. Otherwise you'll be shot." A push on the button, and the adjutant entered. A door was opened, I was taken down to a cellar and placed in a very small, narrow cell. There was no room to lie down, sit or even bend my knees, just to stand up. In the door was a little opening, and on the ceiling a small, flickering lamp. The next day, through the door opening they gave me salted fish and cabbage with water. I knew that I'd be tormented by thirst if I ate the fish, so I tossed it back through the opening. I ate the cabbage and drank the cabbage water. It was hard to stand in the cell; I couldn't find a place for my aching feet. This went on until

[Page 248]
soldiers came and took me to the trial.

German officers were sitting in a row, and I stood in front of them. They began with the question, "Why did you strike a *Volksdeutscher*?" I replied, "Because he stole my coat." "Can you prove that it's your coat?" "Of course," I answered. "Show us," they said. They put the coat on the table, and I pointed out one by one where the tears and patches were. They checked everything. I went on, "Please, look at the belt at the back of the coat. One of the buttons is tied with an iron wire." They checked; it was true. I also said that the right-hand pocket was torn and likewise tied with a wire. They checked --- also true. After consulting among themselves, one of them said, "The proofs are correct. You're released to return to the camp. The coat will be given to the *Volksdeutscher* as compensation for the beating."

My Jewish friends welcomed me back with joy. The next day [September 23, 1939] was Yom Kippur. We fasted and prayed, and at the end of the day food was thrown to us. I couldn't find out who told them we'd fasted or who'd thrown the food . . .

Escape

After several days, an officer came and asked for volunteers for work in the village. I volunteered along with several others. We helped villagers at assorted jobs. They were very satisfied with us, and in return they served us good, varied food. Our guards, every day the same ones, decided that we were all right and there was no need to guard us. They went to enjoy themselves in the farmers' houses. Trains passed nearby, and for some reason they slowed down. We decided to escape. We took advantage of the guards' absence and jumped on a cargo train headed for Poland. After a ride of several hours, we calmed down from the excitement. We were no longer prisoners.

We were six, two of us from my area. In German-occupied Poland, friendly Jews explained to us how to continue on our way. They told us that Bialystok and our entire district were under Russian control. We crossed the area of Poland that was partitioned between Germany and Russia. We crossed relatively easily the new border that divided Russia and Germany and reached Bialystok [some 400 kilometers southwest of Braslav]. I breathed with relief --- the escape had succeeded. But woe to me if I'd been caught.

Many things happened to me during the escape. I'll briefly tell them. We had to hide because of sudden searches. We walked long distances. Sometimes we ate, but we suffered much from hunger. We had to replace the torn clothes with something more sensible. We had to be very wary of Polish policemen --- collaborators with the Germans. My loyal friends were the Jews who helped me a lot on the way.

In Vilna [about 165 kilometers southwest of Braslav], I separated from my friends and took a train that brought me home. I was very happy when I met in the train car one of my townsmen, Yehuda Fisher [probably the merchant son of Avraham-Leib Fisher]. He offered me food and drink, and we talked the entire way. I answered his questions, and he told me what had happened in the town. On the platform in Braslav, I saw women, some of them mothers, who came there daily in the hope of finding their son or husband returning from war. That's how I met my mother, who fainted from the great emotion. Instead of her taking care of me, I ended up taking care of her. Finally, I'd returned home.

[Page 249]
Starting Everything from the Beginning
Mother and I were at home. Father had already died before the war. I couldn't find my brother Zerach, who'd been drafted to serve the new homeland in the Red Army. We only received a few letters from him. Once we got from his commander a letter praising Zerach and saying that we should be proud of him. He was an excellent soldier and an outstanding tankman.

I wanted to return to normal civilian life as soon as possible under the new Soviet authority, which was new to me. Here, you didn't do anything without the authorities' permission. There were permissible things as well as restrictions. You weren't allowed to trade as before and couldn't own a business; everything belonged to the state. It was the employer, the one that provided for you. I was accepted as a fireman, but when they learned that I'd been trading under the former authority, albeit as a small-scale merchant, they fired me. After a while, I was accepted in a government linen company. I returned to normal life.

War Again?! The Germans Again?!
A year and a half passed. I worked, and mother managed the household. In the evenings and on rest days there were meetings with friends, drinking a cup of tea, and conversation. Sometimes, I went to watch a Russian film.

Suddenly, like thunder on a clear day, the war between Russia and Germany broke out [on June 22, 1941]. The Germans were pressing hard and advancing. During the first two days of the war, I was completely beside myself. I ran from place to place and from person to person to hear and see what others were doing. On the third day of the war, I decided to escape to Russia;[1] I was afraid of the Germans. I said goodbye to my mother. She was helpless and didn't know what to say to me. She wept. The escapees all ran in one direction --- to Russia. I went by train for part of the way and continued on foot. There were many Jews along the way.

We arrived in Disna [Dzisna, about 72 kilometers east of Braslav]. A lot of people had arrived there from nearby or further away. All were in a rush, afraid the Germans would precede us and then we'd be lost. We heard airplanes pass above us, on their way to targets in Russia. A train arrived bound for Polotsk, which was our destination [Polotsk was about 35 kilometers southeast of Disna]. The crowd pushed itself onto the platforms and into the compartments. The locomotive whistle blew, and we moved out. We were a day ahead of the Germans, maybe only a few hours, we thought. But the train had only just started to pick up speed when German planes attacked us with guns, dropping bombs on us. A tumult broke out. We tried to hide under anything available, putting something over our heads to avoid getting hurt. Many jumped from the speeding train. I jumped too and was unhurt. The train continued on, and the planes disappeared.

Some of the people from Braslav met in an open field and discussed what to do. Chances of escape were growing slim. Some said that it was better to be back home when the Germans arrived. We decided to go back. The way was long and tiring. Many of us tore our shoes, and it was very hard to walk barefoot. We could get water from anywhere, but we were hungry and it was more difficult to get food.

While we were at the entrance to the town [Braslav], Russian soldiers entered from the direction of Slobodka [the northeast]. We were surprised --- were the Russians still here? At exactly the same time, the German army was entering opposite them, from the direction of Opsa [the southwest]. I went home.

[Page 250]

The Germans Are with Us

On the first Friday after the Germans arrived in Braslav [June 27, 1941], they gathered all the Jews and expelled us to a large swamp behind the city. Gendarmes with guns and machine guns guarded us to prevent our escape. Two Jews were killed during the round-up --- the *shochet* [ritual slaughterer] Shlomo [Zilber] and the youth Chaim Milutin. We were terrified. It was said that they'd kill us all in the marsh. I walked with my mother, and beside me, struggling along, was the elderly rabbi, Rabbi Avraham[-Abba-Yaacov] Zahorie. We lay in the marsh for a day and a night. On Saturday morning, we were told to return home. Most of the houses had been pillaged by the Gentiles. To my good fortune, our home was untouched.

Soon after that, they ordered us to wear the yellow patch on our chest and on our backs. We weren't allowed to walk on the sidewalk. It wasn't permitted to stay outside from evening until morning. It was forbidden to buy from Gentiles. There were many other prohibitions as well. The Judenrat [Jewish Council] was in charge of executing the orders, and they were carried out strictly. It was headed by Yitzchak Mindel, and several Jewish policemen were in his service.

In the spring of 1942, the Jews were ordered to leave their houses and gather along a small street that was announced as the ghetto. We had to leave our houses and belongings, and we moved to a small house with two other families, the Valin brothers. I succeeded in selling a few belongings to the Gentiles. With the money, I bought wheat and hid it behind a woodpile. On Passover Eve [April 1, 1942], several families joined together to bake *matzot* [unleavened bread]; they invited me to join them. We worked for several nights in the cellar of the house of Abba Shmushkovitz, the former bakery owner. I was so happy that I had some wheat and was able to prepare some *matzot* as well. Mother was happy.

The Judenrat received a new demand from the authorities, to send them two men able to do mechanical work and locksmithing, and two more to take care of the horses. At the Judenrat, it was decided that for the mechanical work Moshe-Chatzkel Milutin and another youth from Kovno would be suitable; and for the stable work and taking care of the horses they sent me and Chaim Munitz,[2] the son of Shmuel-Yankel. The stable and the locksmith workshop were near one another. There were many horses in the stable and a fenced yard. Both of us had to care for the horses, clean manure from the stables, feed and water the horses on time, and take care of the equipment. We had to work hard, for many hours, to meet the authorities' demands. But I must admit that the officer in charge treated us nicely. He didn't get angry, yell or hit us. Things continued in this manner for about half a year [actually just two months: early April to early June].

Since it was forbidden to leave the stable unattended, we arranged that one of us would go to visit his family each night. The day before the ghetto was liquidated [on June 3-5, 1942], I left with the German officer to go to one of the villagers in the area to get hay for the horses. He went on horseback, and I went in a wagon hitched to two horses. The German officer went back as soon as we finished loading, and I arrived back at the stable late that night. I told Chaim, "I haven't visited my family for two nights; they [sic] must be worried. I'll wash up a bit and go and see my mother." Chaim said, "While you're washing and getting dressed, I'll go see my family and come back soon. Then you'll go." I agreed. But we didn't know what was about to happen the next day. Chaim couldn't return.

Early in the morning [June 3, 1942], a local policeman came and took me to jail. Before that he told me to take off my clothes, and he took my shoes and trousers, which were in good condition. I didn't understand the reason for my arrest and didn't yet know why Chaim hadn't returned. That morning and throughout the day, I heard a lot of shooting, the sounds of guns and machine guns. I didn't understand why they were shooting, and I didn't know that one kilometer away

[Page 251]

the Jews of the town were being exterminated. In the afternoon, a policeman I knew passed by. Through the bars, I asked him why there was so much shooting, and he told me everything. How can I possibly tell all that I endured during those days and nights?

Several days later, the German officer for whom I worked arrived, released me, and told me to go back and take care of the horses. Could I go back to that life of routine again? Caring for the horses, feeding them? And my mother? I hadn't even said goodbye to her. Perhaps she'd looked for me by the pits, wanting to face the end together. These thoughts raced through my mind. Could it be that I, Chaim-Eli --- son of Malka-Rayza and Yitzchak from the village of Galis and brother of Zerach (maybe he was fighting now against the Germans) --- was the only remaining Jew? [Galis was probably Gajlesze, about 11 kilometers southeast of Braslav.] Why hadn't they taken me with all the others? And why had they thrown me behind bars that morning?! . . .

The next day, my friends returned. Moshe-Chatzkel and the youth from Kovno had run away to the lake and hidden themselves there during the days of the massacre. They said this to the German officer as well. We worked a little, walked around, and talked a lot. The German didn't demand much of us. We saw the Gentiles carrying wagons full of Jewish property from the ghetto.

One week after the massacre, while we were in the stable yard, a Gentile acquaintance passed by the fence and, without stopping, told me that my mother and some other Jews were in the Judenrat yard [alive]. The German allowed us to go. I shouted, "I have a mother!" We were told that policemen had passed along the ghetto street and announced that there'd be no more killings --- this was a German promise. People [presumably including his mother] had come out of their hiding places, which the murderers hadn't managed to find during the days of the massacre. Moshe-Chatzkel found his relative Esther [Rusonik] in one such hiding place. We discussed sending her out to one of the villages.

The German told me to bring him a slaughtered pig from the Ostropolsky sausage factory. He also asked me to get some good bedding, and suggested that I look for them in the houses of the Jews. This was an excellent opportunity to get Esther out of there. I harnessed a horse to a wagon, loaded it with lots of hay, and set out. I put the pig on the wagon and had also found some good bedding for the German. I went to Esther's hiding place and suggested that she come with me. I wrapped her in sheets, took her out from the house, laid her down in the wagon, and covered her with straw. I gave the pig and the bedding to the German, and this time I heard a good word from him --- "*Danke schoen*" ["Thank you"]. Moshe-Chatzkel transferred Esther to a Gentile acquaintance, Slitski, who promised to take care of her and protect her.[3]

On the 10th day after the ghetto massacre, we heard shooting again.[4] This time we guessed what it was. Indeed, on that day they liquidated all those who'd survived the first massacre. Wagons laden with clothes arrived near the stable. When they unloaded the wagons, I recognized my mother's dress. I murmured, "*Baruch Dayan Emet*" ["Blessed Be the Righteous Judge"].[5]

Escaping Again

Now we knew for sure that there were no Jews left in Braslav. Any who survived must have escaped and hidden themselves. It was very dangerous to remain; we decided to run away. But to get out through the gate to the road, even at night, was very risky. There were German forces in their offices and their accommodations. Gendarmes and police also patrolled during the night. Any Jew caught would die. At night, we dug under the foundation of the stable. The place we came out to was an open field. People didn't search there.

[Page 252]
We wanted to go through the fields to some acquaintances in the nearby villages. At the time, we didn't know where the massacre had taken place. There, not far from the train station, we saw the burial places of our beloved ones. There were long, large pits. We saw how the pits were exploding from internal pressure, as if from an earthquake.

We separated. My friends went to a Gentile blacksmith whom Moshe-Chatzkel trusted. I went to the village of Murazha [Murazh, about three kilometers northeast of Braslav] and hid myself under a pile of straw in the barn of an acquaintance, Taduvka [Tadowka]. After two days, he discovered me, gave me food and asked me nicely to go. I wandered from place to place until winter came, eating anything I could get. Winter began, and it started to get too cold to wander around. I went to the village of Pantilayki [Pancielejki, about five kilometers north of Braslav]. It was snowing on the way. I arrived at a house and climbed into the attic of the barn. In the morning, when Anton [the house's occupant] came to feed the cows, he noticed footprints on the snow, climbed up and found me. He was astonished to see me, and willingly agreed to help me.

I remained with him for about a year and a half [roughly the second half of 1942 to early 1944], with a short break --- during a certain period he was afraid that his daughter-in-law would turn me in, and he asked me to leave his place. I went from him to another small village, Zarach [Zaracz, six kilometers west of Braslav], to a farmer named Milevitz [Milewicz]. He had a large family with seven children. They willingly accepted me. They put me in the bath, gave me a change of clothing and food, and hid me in the barn. A short time later, they heard that a Jew from Braslav had been caught by the gendarmes, been unable to withstand the torture, and told them the name of the village and the family that had hidden him. The Germans had killed the family and burned the entire village. The family hiding me became afraid of keeping me any longer. I went back to Pantilayki and met Anton near his house. I asked to stay with him for a while. He agreed that I could stay with him, and he also told me that a new ghetto had been built in Braslav.[6] If I agreed, he was willing to check whether they'd accept me.

Meanwhile, news began to arrive of the Russian victories and German retreats. The evil daughter-in-law now changed her tune; it was convenient now to be nice to me. Once, she came up to the attic and said, "Don't be afraid of Anton. He needs you now and wants to keep you. He's a criminal." She told me that during the great massacre of the Jews of Braslav, two Jewish women had thrown themselves into the pit without being hit by the bullets. They were Aydel and her daughter Chana Munitz [mother and sister of the Chaim-Noach Munitz described on page 250]. At night, after everyone had left, they'd emerged from under the heap of corpses, naked and covered in blood, and come there. He, Anton, had turned them over to the police for salt and a lighter.

After Anton checked in Braslav and told me that I couldn't be admitted into the ghetto, I left him and went to look for the partisans. I went from place to place and from one partisan unit to another, but they didn't want to accept me without weapons. In the *otriad*[7] of Polish partisans I was told clearly, "We don't accept any Jews." Then I went to the village of Babuli near Zamosh [Bobyli a.k.a. Bobyle, about eight kilometers southwest of Zamosh]. I entered the command room of the *otriad* and said to them, "I don't have a gun, but I'm an experienced soldier who wants to fight. I'm not leaving here. Instead of being killed by the Germans, I prefer to be killed by a Russian bullet. Please kill me now." The officer was impressed by my words and asked me to wait, while he went to speak with his superiors. When he returned, he told me that I was admitted to the *otriad*. I was glad. I received an *otrezanka* [sawed-off rifle[8]] and took part in the majority of the *otriad*'s actions. Later I was transferred to a special-mission unit and put in charge of a 12-man force. We were ordered to cross the old border and organize a new *otriad* under Morozov's command.

We proceeded on out-of-the-way roads for many days, avoiding encounters

[Page 253]

with the German army. We crossed the Dvina River near the city of Disna and reached our target. We organized quickly; the new *otriad* under Morozov's command began intensive activity. Now the enemy was between a hammer and an anvil. The Red Army was repelling them, and as they withdrew the Germans encountered our fighting unit. Together, we inflicted on them losses of soldiers and arms.

. . . It was the spring 1944. The Red Army soldiers continued to expel the invaders from their land. In the liberated areas, the partisans had stopped their activity and joined the regular army formations. When Minsk, the capital of Belorussia, was liberated [early July 1944], we applied to join the army. We were concentrated in a camp. In a festive roll call, we were informed that a Polish division was fighting by the side of the Russian army. I joined the Second Army. We began moving. I passed a course in Vilna and received the rank of corporal. We received Polish army uniforms. Around Poznan [about 280 kilometers west of Warsaw], we battled the retreating German army and took part in expelling them from Polish land. We were in Munich [sic] when the Wehrmacht [German army] announced its surrender.[9]

The war ended on May 8, 1945. I remained serving in the Second Army until October of that year. I was released from the army on October 4, 1945.

The next step was *aliyah*, immigration to Israel.

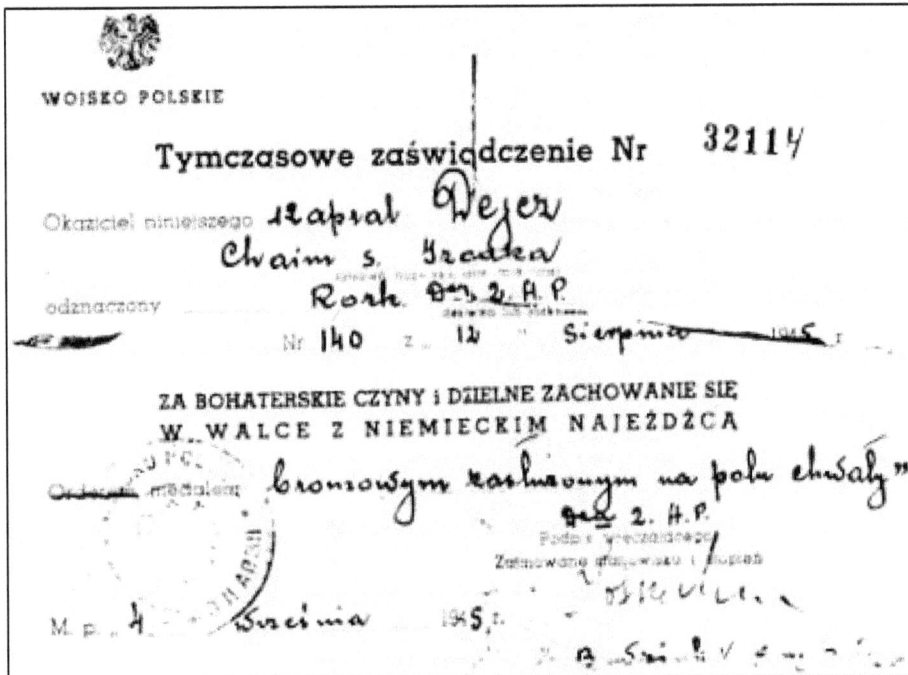

**A bronze medal was awarded by the Polish army to Chaim Deitch
for action and bravery in battle against the German invader.**

Footnotes:

1. Meaning the border of pre-1939 Russia, which was to the east of Braslav.
2. This Chaim Munitz (Chaim-Noach, son of Shmuel-Yankel and Aydel) was different from the Chaim Munitz (son of Rafael-Yaacov and Sheitel) mentioned on pages 70-71 of this memorial book, as well as the Chaim Munitz (son of Levi-Yitzchak and Rachel) who survived and left an account on pages 280-282 of this memorial book.
3. The account of Emma Milutin-Korner (born Esther Rusonik) is on pages 274-279 of this memorial book.
4. Survivors' accounts differ on the number of days that passed between the ghetto liquidation, which began on June 3, 1942, and the time the Germans and their collaborators began killing the remaining Jews who subsequently came out of hiding.
5. The blessing recited upon learning of bereavement.
6. In August or early September 1942, some 50 Jews from the town of Opsa were transferred to a new ghetto in Braslav, to repopulate the Braslav Ghetto after its inmates had been slaughtered on June 3-5, 1942. Because the members of this second, new ghetto in Braslav were from Opsa, the second Braslav Ghetto was also called the "Opsa" Ghetto. It would be liquidated on March 19, 1943.
7. Russian word for a partisan military unit. "Polish partisans" probably refers to the partisans of the nationalist and anti-Communist Armia Krajowa (Polish Home Army).
8. A rifle whose butt had been sawed off and barrel shortened, making it easier to carry; used by the regions' peasants before the war because it could be hidden beneath one's jacket. When the Red Army retreated from the region in June-July 1941, many peasants found soldiers' abandoned rifles and turned them into *otrezankas*.
9. Munich in southern Germany was liberated by the U.S. army on April 30, 1945 and not the Soviet army or Polish troops, neither of which reached southern Germany. Nevertheless, Mr. Deitch said in the Hebrew that he was in "Minchon" (Hebrew for Munich). Munich doesn't seem correct, but an alternative location for the reference hasn't been identified.

[Page 254]

Yerachmiel Milutin
Son of Sima and Avraham-Yitzchak

Translated from the Hebrew by Laia Ben-Dov
Footnotes Added / Donated by Jeff Deitch

"Blessed be the Lord, my Rock,
who traineth my hands for war,
and my fingers for battle."

--- Psalm 144:1

On the second day after entering Braslav [Braslaw] [in late June 1941], the Germans gathered all of the Jews of the town and took them to the area of the [Dubki/Dubkes] swamps opposite the village of Rozeta [just southeast of Braslav], where they kept us all night. When it grew light, they ordered us to go home. Everyone had been driven out [to the swamp], also the elderly and the children. There was a lot of crying. A German accompanied us, and with him was a translator of Polish. We asked the German what they planned to do to us, and the translator passed on his answer: "They'll pour boiling oil on you and burn you." Chaim Milutin and Shlomo [Zilber] the *shochet* [ritual slaughterer] grew frightened and tried to flee. The Germans chased after them, grabbed them, and in the presence of all of us they shot them. Chaim managed to shout, "Jews!

I'm falling in sacrifice, avenge my blood!" Shlomo was killed by the first bullet. Eighteen bullets were fired at Chaim Milutin, until he breathed his last; he was only 20 years old. We took their bodies to the town, to the cemetery, and when we conducted a *taharah*[11] for them, I counted 18 bullet holes in his body. Chaim was my brother's son. We buried them and parted from them forever.

Two days later, again they gathered all the Jews of Braslav, as well as some refugees who'd come from Lithuania and Latvia, and they drove us all out behind the Russian [Eastern Orthodox] church, where they separated the men from the women and children. Again, they held us there all night. The next day, they returned us to our homes.

The German headquarters was located opposite my house. I saw how they arrested Beilka [Beila] Deitch, [Aharon-Zelig] Singalovski the *shochet* from Sventzion [about 90 kilometers southwest of Braslav], and another man. A man by the name of Shliachchik, who lived in Braslav, brought about their arrest; it became clear that he was a German agent. Shliachchik testified that he'd seen Beilka Deitch signaling to Russian aircraft to bomb the German army, which was on the main road at the entrance to Braslav. And indeed, that same day the Russians did bomb the Germans.

I also saw how the police brought Zelig Ulman, his wife and their small daughter to the Karpovitz forest [Karpowicz forest, near the western entrance to Braslav]. Zelig and his family hid with some Gentiles in the village, and these handed them over to the Germans. Jews hid likewise at the *hutor*[2] (farm) of Shavenski [or Svinski] and in the villages of Milashki [Milaszki, about 20 kilometers south of Braslav], Bukashki, Shalia, Rapovshchitzna and others, until they were freed by the Red Army.[3]

[Page 255]

I was in constant contact with Aliosha Vasilevski [Aliosza Wasilewski] (the son of the Russian priest). He worked for the Germans in the regional headquarters and secretly prepared weapons to oppose the Germans. (Vasilevski asked [Gershon] Klioner to send him five men to work, and I was among them.) When I came to work, Vasilevski showed me the weapons he'd hidden in the cellar of the regional headquarters. Gershon Klioner --- a member of the Judenrat --- had a list of 95 healthy young men who were organized to fight.[4] Among them were Yerachmiel Milutin, Leib Valin, Meir Kort, Matus Gandler, Berka Fisher, Volfka Fisher, Hirshka Deitch, Chaim-Berka Deitch, and 22 fighters from Latvia, 18 from Lithuania, 35 fighters from the surrounding towns, and another 15 additional young men, among them Hirsh Levin. The list indeed included 95 [sic] fighters, but in the end none of them took action, because the matter became known to the head of the community, [Braslav Judenrat head Yitzchak] Mindel, and he didn't give permission to take the weapons. The Germans promised him that nothing bad would happen to the Jews of Braslav; but at the time of the destruction [June 3-5, 1942] they killed him and his family first. Vasilevski was also arrested and transferred to the jail in Glubok [Glubokoye], where he was shot by the Germans. It became known that Shliachchik had slandered Vasilevski to the Germans, saying that he was working against them. Aliosha's brother, Dimka [Dima], told me this.

The destruction of the Jews of Braslav began on Wednesday, June 3, 1941 [sic; actually June 3, 1942], at three o'clock in the morning. After the Aktions [of June 3-5, 1942], I joined the partisans. All of the people who survived after that were gathered together with the Jews from Opsa, Dubina [Dubene] and other places in the second ghetto [the "Opsa" Ghetto in Braslav], and they were killed when the German army withdrew.[5] When Braslav was liberated [in July 1944], we found an empty town and a small group of isolated Jews who'd managed to return. Among them were Chaim Kagan, Aronovitz, Elchik Shmidt, the Lubovitz family, Rabinovitz from the pharmacy, the sons of Baruch Fisher, Mendel and Masha Maron, Yentka [Yenta] Fisher and a few others. It was heartbreaking to find my town like that.

When I was with the partisans, we took revenge on many Gentiles who'd helped to destroy the Braslav Ghetto. They were residents of the villages near Zamosh [Zamosz, about 16 kilometers south of Braslav]. We burned them along with their houses, their property and the Jewish property they'd stolen; among them was the policeman [Stefan] Zhuk and his brother-in-law Primchenko and Panish, from the police of Meziazh [perhaps the Maciesze that was 13 kilometers southeast of Braslav] who helped to destroy the Jews of Braslav and, according to information that I saw, also killed the family of Falka [Rafael] Fisher and stole their possessions. I gave testimony about them to the authorized institutions. The policemen were caught near Riga [about 245 kilometers northwest of Braslav, in Latvia]. Others hid under false names in the villages that were in the area of control of our partisan unit. We searched for them and found them. Shliachchik and Antosh had run around the town at the time of the Aktions [in Braslav on June 3-5, 1942] shouting, "Jews, come out of your hiding places. They won't shoot anymore and they won't destroy you." They'd turned over many Jews to the Germans. This Antosh had worked for a long time for Yosef Bik in the beer factory and spoke good Yiddish.

I was invited to the NKVD[6] to testify against them in an investigation managed by Polkovnik Balkashov at two o'clock in the morning. He came out of the room and said to me, "Pass judgment on him the way the partisans would do." I hit him on the head with a stool until he collapsed. After the interrogation, he was hospitalized.

When we were with the partisans, there were people who helped us. One of them was Igor Tominski from Vidz [about 40 kilometers southwest of Braslav], the son of a lawyer. This Igor was a friend of Vasilevski.

[Before the Braslav Ghetto was liquidated] Rabbi [Yisrael-Alter] Fuchs[7] and two women lived with Zerach Bogomolski. He [Bogomolski] was a great help to Jews who'd fled from Dvinsk [about 42 kilometers to the northwest] and come to Braslav. Once I met Bogomolski when he went to see the manager of the forest department in our region, Mindovski [Mindowski]. He was a friend of the Jews and hid in his house

[Page 256]
a few Jews from Dvinsk.

When I was in the [Braslav] ghetto I was sent to work with Mindovski, together with some others: Berka from Opsa [18 kilometers southwest of Braslav], Meir Kort and Matus Gandler and some Russian prisoners. We worked in a factory for drying forest seeds, and we set it on fire. The factory burned down completely.

Artiom, from the village of Lishishki [unidentified, unless it was the village of Leoszki, 14 kilometers northeast of Braslav], who cooperated with the Germans, handed over to them the families of Moshe Goldin, Yerachmiel Bik, and three additional families. All of them were shot.

I pursued and captured him, and after the first interrogation he hung himself in his house.

Of all the fighters, only I and a few partisans remained alive [at the time of liberation in July 1944]. We decided to meet in Braslav and take revenge on those who'd cooperated with the Germans.

We learned that at the time the ghetto was destroyed [the second Braslav Ghetto, that is, the "Opsa" Ghetto in Braslav, in March 1943], Leizer Biliak had killed two Germans and succeeded in fleeing to the village of Kuzmishtzina [perhaps Kuzmovszczyzna, 15 kilometers southeast of Braslav], but the Poles turned him over to the Germans for some money, and they murdered him. We, the partisans, found these Poles, and my nephew Moshe Milutin and his friends executed them. As partisans, we received help from the Soviet army behind the front line. That's how we were given an officer for our unit. His name was Bolovchik. He was a friend of the Jews. With him we carried out many complicated and dangerous activities in the areas near Kovno, Vilna and also in Latvia. We derailed a train that was bringing ammunition to the Germans. We paid in blood for these actions, and our officer Bolovchik fell in one of them. He was an excellent fighter and a good man. He often said to me, "If you meet your brother, that means a Jew, bring them to the headquarters and we'll transfer them to Russia, and if they're the kind who are prepared to fight, we'll accept them." He said with complete confidence that we'd defeat the Germans. All of the orders of operation under his command were carried out successfully, and we received certificates of excellence for this. I fought in the Zhukov brigade, in the Suvorov unit --- a unit that took an active part in the war --- and I took revenge for the people of my nation with all my heart.

[Earlier in the war] Musia-Leah Blacher told me they were driving her family out to Pohost [a.k.a. Novy-Pohost, about 32 kilometers southeast of Braslav] and asked me to save her two sons. Unfortunately I was a wanderer myself at that time and had no chance of finding a safe place for the children. When I finally located one, I searched for the children but couldn't find them. I'm glad that every person who I took out of the Braslav Ghetto is still alive [his meaning becomes clear in the next paragraph]. A few of them live in Israel.

I met Peretz Levin in Minsk on the way to the front.[8] I parted from him then, apparently forever. Michael Rabinovitz came to the headquarters where I worked. At that time, he'd fled from the massacre in Glubok [Glubokoye, about 70 kilometers southeast of Braslav], wounded in his leg.[9] I turned to the officer of the brigade, Siromcha.[10] I asked for and got permission to take in the Jews who'd saved themselves by fleeing the [Braslav] ghetto and to offer them aid. I helped the survivors with food, clothing and other items.

In a unit that comprised 12 men, all of them were educated Christians; among them were paratroopers. I was the only Jew.

In the second *otriad*,[11] the deeds of the Jewish fighter Yerachmiel Milutin from Braslav were mentioned (he served in the position of deputy officer of the patrols). The group of eight men, and Milutin, the only Jew in the group, encountered an ambush (near Sharkovshchitzna [Szarkowszczyzna, about 40 kilometers southeast of Braslav]). Lacking experience against the enemy, the partisans fled, except for Milutin. Firing a machine gun and throwing grenades

[Page 257]

one after the other, he defeated the enemy and saved himself. When Milutin returned alone to the base unharmed, his magazines empty of bullets, the officer of the unit --- Strikov --- gathered the partisans and vehemently denounced them, especially their officer, for cowardice at the crucial moment. In contrast, he praised Yerachmiel Milutin, who he said showed unusual bravery.

--- From *Sefer HaPartizanim HaYehudim*
(*The Book of the Jewish Partisans*), Volume 1
[Published in Israel in 1958]

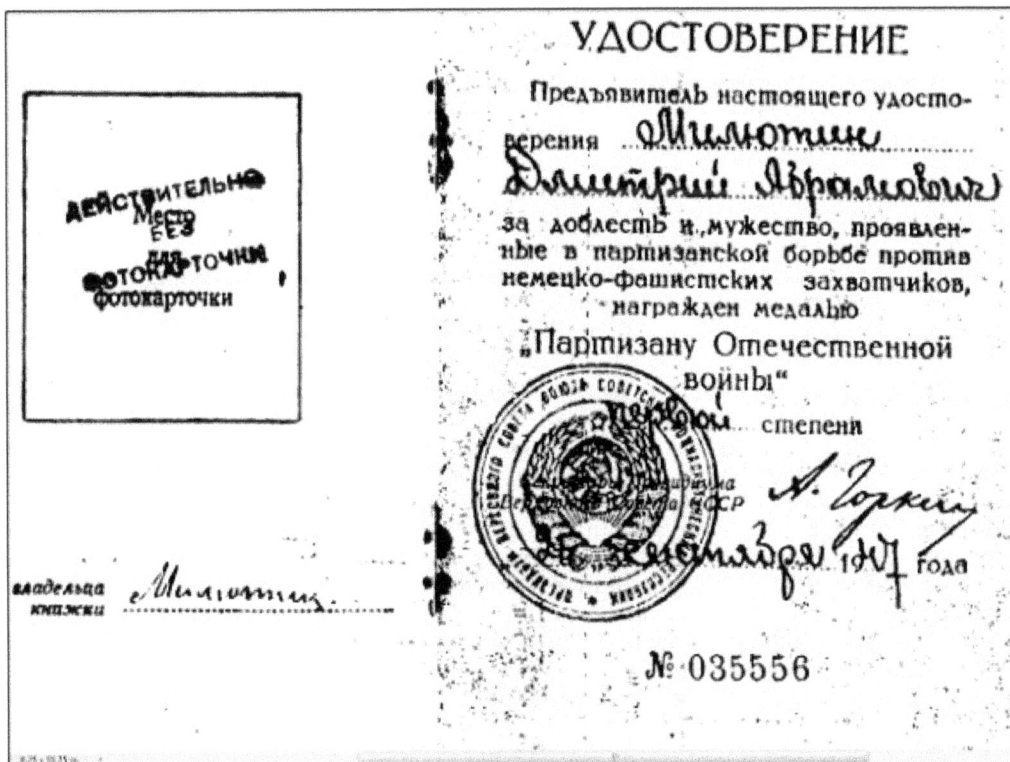

**Partisan certificate of Yerachmiel Milutin, partisan in the Suvorov battalion
of the Zhukov brigade**

Footnotes:

1. Ritual purification of the deceased, including cleansing, ritually washing and dressing of the body, with the recitation of special prayers asking G-d to take the soul into eternal rest.

2. *Hutor* is a Russian word meaning single-homestead settlement/isolated peasant farmhouse.

3. Shalia and Rapovshchitzna might refer to the villages of Sloly and Rzepowszczyzna, which were respectively three kilometers and four kilometers northeast of Milashki.

4. The English-language abridged version in this memorial book (pages 640-569) said that these 95 men were "former Polish soldiers" (page 598). However, this detail didn't appear in the Hebrew version that was translated here (page 255). A comparison of the English abridgement on pages 640-569 with the pages in Hebrew (pages 1-465) sometimes revealed minor differences like these. A second example: The English-language abridgement said that the daughter of Lubka Veis was maltreated by a German soldier (page 601), whereas the Hebrew version said that it was the son of Lubka Veis (page 171). A third example: The English-language abridgement said that the dying Chaim Milutin shouted, "Jews, avenge our blood!" (page 607), whereas the Hebrew version said, "Jews, avenge my blood!" (page 254).

    The reason for such differences between the English-language abridgement and the Hebrew version isn't known for sure. Page 635 suggests that the original material gathered to make this memorial book was mainly in Yiddish. This was then translated into Hebrew (which became pages 1-465), the main part of the book. From this, a Yiddish-language abridged version was then made (which became pages 497-568). From the Yiddish-language abridgement, an English-language abridged version was then made (appearing on pages 640-569). The multiple rounds of translation and abridgement might account for the variants.

5. In August or early September 1942, some 50 Jews from Opsa were transferred to the ghetto in Braslav, to repopulate this ghetto after its inmates had been slaughtered on June 3-5, 1942. Because the members of this second, new ghetto in Braslav were mainly from Opsa, the ghetto was also called the "Opsa" Ghetto. It would be liquidated on March 19, 1943.

    Mr. Milutin said that there were people from Dubina in the "Opsa" Ghetto, but if so they must have been a small number. Because most of the villagers from Dubina had already been transferred to the Vidz Ghetto in late 1941 or early 1942, according to survivors in the Dubina section of this memorial book on pages 367-392.

6. Narodnyi Komissariat Vnutrennikh Del (People's Commissariat for Internal Affairs): The Soviet law enforcement and intelligence agency that existed from 1934 to 1946, after which it evolved into the KGB.

7. Rabbi Fuchs, a rabbi in Dvinsk, had fled to Braslav sometime after the German invasion on June 22, 1941, together with Rachel Citron, a widow and the daughter of his late teacher. Rabbi Fuchs and Mrs. Citron were killed in Braslav in the massacre on June 3-5, 1942. They're mentioned in this memorial book on pages 91 and 93 (in the account of Mottel-Hirsh Fisher), page 110 (in the account of Tuvia Fisher), page 255 (in the account of Yerachmiel Milutin) and pages 258 and 260-261 (in the account of Yitzchak Reichel). The identity of the second woman mentioned above is unknown.

8. An account about Peretz Levin appears on pages 300-301 of this memorial book.

9. It's unclear which massacre in the Glubokoye Ghetto this refers to. According to the *Encyclopedia of Camps and Ghettos, 1933-1945*, Volume II-B (2012), a ghetto had been established in Glubokoye in October-November 1941; Jews from nearby towns were also brought there, raising the ghetto population to 6,000. On June 19, 1942 a massacre of some 2,200-2,500 of them was carried out, but unlike the Braslav Ghetto a large population was also kept alive to work. Later the Germans decided to increase the population of the Glubokoye Ghetto, and they sent the Judenrat chairman outside the ghetto to bring Jews inside. Eventually, the ghetto population rose again, to 7,000. Thus, by 1943 Glubokoye was serving as a temporary refuge for Jews in western Belorussia who weren't in the forests. Eventually, however, as partisan activity in the region increased the Germans decided to liquidate the ghetto, announcing a deportation on August 20, 1943. When the ghetto responded with armed resistance, the Germans set fire to it, killing some 5,000 inmates. It's estimated that about 60-100 ghetto inmates survived the war.

10. On page 440 of this memorial book, Siromcha was called the commander of the partisan Zhukov brigade, and Boloychik its commissar.

11. Russian word for a partisan military unit.

[Page 258]

Yitzchak Reichel
Son of Batia and Yaacov
(From testimony at Yad Vashem)

Translated from the Hebrew by Laia Ben-Dov
Footnotes Added / Donated by Jeff Deitch

When the Russian-German war broke out [in June 1941], I was drafted into the Red Army. The war developed so quickly that they even failed to form us into battle units. The Russians left the town [of Braslav/Braslaw] and withdrew eastward, and we, the draftees, scattered in all directions. I returned to Braslav. As Jews, we knew that we had to leave and escape the approaching Germans. I told my father that our entire family should leave the town, but he disagreed, saying, "The Jews of Braslav won't abandon their homes." With a group of young people, I headed for the Russian border.[1] Unfortunately, the Germans were ahead of us, and so everyone returned to the town.

With the Germans also came decrees, one after another. Shortly after the Germans arrived in Braslav, I and all the [other] Jews were taken to the swamps outside the town [June 27]; the threat of death hovered over us all. There the first martyrs fell from among the sons of Braslav: Shlomo [Zilber] the *shochet* [ritual slaughterer] and Chaim Milutin. After a night of horror, toward morning all of us returned to our homes, which had been broken into and robbed. It felt as if our lives had been returned as a gift, because we hadn't thought that we'd leave the swamp alive.

News arrived in the town about the destruction of the Jews of Yod [Jod, on December 17, 1941] and Dvinsk.[2] Refugees arrived in Braslav from Dvinsk: the famous Rabbi [Yisrael-Alter] Fuchs, the Shlosberg, Kravitz and Solomon families and others. In Braslav itself, things were still quiet. Some men of the town wanted to believe that Braslav was a blessed town and its Jews would live to see the day of redemption.

This situation continued until April 1942. Then came the fateful turning point: The enemy established a ghetto in Braslav [formally on April 1] and shut all the Jews of the town within it. The situation worsened from day to day. Those who were taken for forced labor brought a little bit of food into the ghetto. Each day, Jews were murdered. [For example] a group of men worked on the train tracks. One day, a German from the camp approached us, chose from among us 17 men, and killed them.[3] The bribe that was taken didn't save their lives.

Among the Jews in the ghetto, some called for opposing the Germans, but the majority didn't want to hear about it. We began to prepare hiding places, bunkers that would be ready when needed for children and the elderly. We hoped that the younger people would acquire weapons by then and fight the Germans and their local collaborators. But the hope

[Page 259]

of getting weapons went unfulfilled,[4] and the bitter day of 17 Sivan arrived [June 2, 1942, one day before the massacre began]. On that day, as on previous days, we went out to work next to the train [station]. At a certain moment, a German turned to us and said, "Jews! You're so young; you should live. Hide yourselves, because something bad is about to happen."

When we returned to the town after work, we told this to the members of the Judenrat [Jewish Council] and all the Jews. A great sadness fell over the Jews of Braslav. No one knew what to do to advance the fateful hour and rescue their families. I and some other young people who were in one house decided to remain awake all night. I put a bit of food in my pack and decided to leave the house at the moment of calamity. I asked my father not to stop me, and not to tell my mother about it.

It was three o'clock in the morning. The 18th of Sivan [June 3]. Through a small window, we saw two gendarmes walking. One of the young men said, "Let's go out. Let's attack them and take their weapons and uniforms." Somehow his words reached the ears of the women in the room, and they locked the exit from the house [keeping us inside]. "In Braslav, they won't kill the Jews," they declared. Sometime later, we heard shouts from the street. This was the police, who'd arrived from the direction of the lake and begun to drive everyone out of their homes. The young people from our house went outside; in their hands was anything they could find to defend themselves. They didn't have even one pistol. Among these young people were Naftali Fisher, the son of Zalman-Yaacov, and Avraham Fisher, the son of Baruch.[5] They struggled with a German, trying to take away his rifle. He raised a shout, and other Germans rushed to help him. They opened fire, and a few of our young men fell.

After this, I had no chance of returning to our bunker. I ran toward the lake. I wanted to swim to the other shore, but unfortunately on that side were Germans with machine guns, and they shot anyone who succeeded in approaching. I stayed close to the ground, lacking strength to move. Recovering slightly, I raised my head and saw Jews running toward the priest's yard. I too began to crawl toward his house. A large group of Jews had gathered there, even though the Germans were shooting at us. I entered one of the buildings near the priest's house and went up to the attic. Above I saw an opening, through which it was possible to go down into the granary, which was locked on the outside. I entered and dug myself into a pile of straw.

After a number of hours the Germans arrived, accompanied by local police, and they opened fire on the Jews who were hiding in the priest's buildings. With the first shots, the priest, a good-hearted man, came out and saw the scale of the tragedy that was befalling the Jews of his town. He became distraught, suffered a heart attack and died immediately.

During those hours, the killers didn't enter the granary where I was hiding. I stayed there for three days. On Friday afternoon [June 5], through a small opening I saw two gendarmes, police and firemen coming with the woman who owned the granary, asking her to open the door for them. I didn't know what to do: Go out, attack them and die immediately, or try my fate and keep sitting in my hiding place? I sat there with bated breath. The police entered the granary and then left. Suddenly, I heard them uprooting boards from the floor, yelling "Out!" and shooting. When the shooting stopped, I heard the familiar voice of the policeman Krivko [Kriwko, a.k.a. Grivkov] saying, "Barmapov, come out of there," and Barmapov answered, "I'm seriously wounded and can't move. Fire another bullet so that I won't suffer any more."

After some time, the policemen went away. When night fell, I left my hiding place and saw, next to the granary, the bodies of Moshe Barmapov and Luba Sheiner. I was afraid. I returned to the place where our family's bunker was located. When I got there, to my disappointment I found it empty of people. Only a bit of bread

[Page 260]

and my sister's coat remained. Sadness. I stayed sitting in the bunker until after the Sabbath. I hoped that maybe a relative would come, but no one did.

At night I went to an acquaintance, a [Gentile] farm woman who lived some distance from Braslav. I asked her to go into the town to find out what was happening. She agreed, and after a few hours she returned and told me: "Of your people there's no one. Your father's sister, Sara-Leah Vishkin, and her little son Chaim, are in the Jewish school where all of the refugees from the massacre are gathered." She added, "They're saying that they won't shoot any more Jews." I went to the school [the Yiddish Folkshul]. There were Jews there, among them Chaim Munitz, who'd been a teacher in the Jewish school and become the head of the Judenrat. [The former head, Yitzchak Mindel, had been killed at the start of the massacre.] He [Munitz] recorded the names of everyone who came there. There were adults and young people, elderly and children. The adults adopted the children whose parents were lost, calmed them and promised them, "Your parents will come back soon . . ."

A day passed. Next to the school gate, there was no guard, so I went outside. I met my aunt [Sara-Leah Vishkin, née Reichel], who was in utter shock. [Earlier] when the police had found the bunker and approached, the people [inside] had tried to scatter and flee. The police had opened fire, killing her husband Tuvia [Vishkin], son Yoska [Yosef] and daughter Nechama. My aunt also told me that when they were closed up in the house where they waited for the murderers, others had brought them clothes of Jews from the death pits, and she'd recognized some of these as the clothes of family members. "These were their identification certificates," she said, and gave them to me . . .

I went further into the town. Bodies of Jews were scattered everywhere. Next to my grandfather's house I saw the bodies of my uncle, two children and my cousin. I was stunned. I ran back to the school; maybe my young sister, who was 18 years old, had come. But she wasn't there. She was found by the young people who were busy gathering the bodies, to bring them to burial. A bullet from the murderers had struck her heart, and she'd died without suffering. I didn't weep; I had no more tears. I only asked that they bury her together with the martyrs of the town. Sad. I was sad.

Where should I go? I went up to the attic in Zerach Ginzburg's house, which stood near the lake. There I sat for two days. I wanted to get far away from the town. At night I walked along the lakeshore, and next to the casino[6] I stopped to look around, maybe there were Jews inside. And indeed, upstairs I found several families, among them Rabbi Fuchs with an ailing woman [Rachel Citron] who was the daughter of the Gaon from Rogatchov.[7] The woman told me that a Gentile knew their location, and in exchange for payment he brought them food. I sat with them for an entire day, and at night I returned to my hiding place. While I was with them, I tried to warn them about the Gentile who knew where they were, but they said that there was nowhere to go in any case; what would be, would be.

In the casino they told me of a hiding place where Shachna and Chinka Band were located. After searching, I found their place. In the attic also were Leib Burat with his family and another family. While we were sitting up there, all the time we heard Gentiles coming in and out of the house, looking for things to steal. That same day, I asked Leib Burat to give his older children permission to go with me to the forest, but he wouldn't agree. Only on my second visit to them did he give his son Chaim permission to join me.

When night fell, the two of us went on our way. First we wanted to get to the casino and see the people there. After walking a few minutes, suddenly we encountered a hail of bullets.

We quickly fled in different directions. I lay down for some time until it grew completely quiet and then continued on to the casino. I entered, calling out to the people in a whisper. There was no answer, the place was already deserted. At the time, I didn't know what had happened to these good people. I found out only years later, after the war.

[Page 261]

[After the war] I met a Jew who'd been in the casino attic on that tragic day, and he told me what happened: After their hiding place was discovered, all of them were arrested. They sat in a jail that had been made in Blacher's bakery, guarded by a policeman from Latvia. Rabbi Fuchs spoke continually to the policeman, telling him that he didn't have to carry out the evil deeds of the Germans. The rabbi spoke and spoke, until finally the guard was convinced. He opened the jail door and said, "Go, all of you, to wherever you want." The people went out, and with them Rabbi Fuchs and the daughter of the Rogatchover Gaon. But the woman [Rachel Citron] collapsed and was unable to get to her feet. The policeman told the rabbi, "Leave the woman here and go; you're a young man. I'm giving you your life as a gift." The policeman put the woman back in the jail, and Rabbi Fuchs also went back inside; he said that he wouldn't leave her. Thanks to Rabbi Fuchs, nine Jews were freed at that time, among them Chaim Kagan.

Completely alone, I remained sitting in Riva-Dina's [sic] attic for a week, until all my food was gone. One day, through a crack, I saw Gentiles robbing the neighboring house of Abba Shmushkovitz, and while doing that they found him hiding with his family. Soon the police arrived, drove them outside, and took them, accompanied by blows, to the pits.

Again, I returned to [Leib] Burat's attic, and here too there was no one. The murderers had found them also. Only the son, Chaim Burat, who'd left with me earlier, survived. Today he lives in the Land of Israel.[8]

I decided to go to a village, and at night I set out on the road. Outside, I was greeted by strong rain. In the forest near our town I was unable to find cover. I continued until I reached a small building that served as a bathhouse for a farmer's family that was living nearby. I sat inside it all night, and in the morning I looked out to see if the rain had stopped. Unfortunately, I was seen by a shepherd who was pasturing his cattle close by. He quickly ran to the farmer and told him. The farmer immediately came running, opened the door, and when he saw me he said, "Very good. For you I'll get 50 kilograms of salt." He locked the door and went away. Knowing that he'd gone to call the Germans, I tried to break through the door but failed.

I decided to escape through a small window high up on the wall. I broke the glass and stuck my head outside. The shepherd, who was still nearby, tried to prevent my getting out, but after much effort I succeeded, fleeing to a field of standing wheat and getting away. Crawling slowly, I reached another building, which also was a bathhouse, and I entered. I hoped to rest there before continuing.

After some time, another farmer appeared and saw me. To my great surprise, he turned to me and said, "Don't fear, I won't do anything bad to you like Kazhik [a policeman in the region who was known for his cruelty toward Jews]. Stay here as long as you wish." This man is good-hearted, I felt. The farmer brought me food and something to drink, and told me that the Jews in Opsa and Vidz were living quietly and nobody was harming them. I decided to go there.[9]

Before midnight, I went out on the road, arriving in Opsa toward morning [Opsa was about 18 kilometers southwest of Braslav]. Here I had friends and relatives. There were also survivors from Braslav. I stayed in an apartment with friends, who took me in with love. Unfortunately, after a few days in Opsa I was seen by a policeman from Braslav who'd come to Opsa. His name was Kolkovski [Czeslaw Kolkowski]. He entered the apartment where I was staying and said he was going to arrest me. His argument was that they'd killed all the Jews of Braslav and my fate must be like theirs. The pleas of my hosts didn't help. He told me to come with him. I turned to him and said, "Kill me here. But you've a family in Braslav, and you should know that those of us who survive will take revenge on all the murderers of Jews. Then you'll need our help." My words stopped him from using force. He turned to his companions and said, "What'll

[Page 262]

we gain from killing him?" I quickly exited the house and ran to the cemetery. The police fired in the air and then left. When night fell, my relatives came to the cemetery and took me back to their house. That same night I left Opsa on the way to Vidz, arriving toward morning [Vidz was about 22 kilometers southwest of Opsa].

In Vidz I also had acquaintances. We were a group of 20 people who'd lost their families. We lived together in a deserted house, going outside only at night. The people called us "the rabbits." We stayed there with the hope of obtaining some weapons; we wanted to go to the forest and join the partisans. Unfortunately, after a few days it became clear to us that this was impossible. We couldn't keep sitting in Vidz. We were forced to go out to a labor camp in Podbrodz; the Judenrat in Vidz was obliged to send 20 young men to it [Podbrodz, or Pabrade, was about 70 kilometers southwest of Vidz, in Lithuania]. The way there was difficult, and we suffered many humiliations and tortures. I wasn't content to stay there; it was impossible for me and other young men like me to remain slaves to the Germans. We decided to join the partisans at any cost and found a way to escape from the camp. For half a year we wandered the forests, in indescribable conditions. With time, we acquired weapons and were accepted into the partisan *otriad*[10] Kostas Kalinauskas. The climax of the actions in which I took part was the destruction of two freight trains carrying soldiers and equipment to the [Eastern] Front.

Within the framework of the *otriad*, I was able to see the end of the war.

Footnotes:

1. Meaning the border of pre-1939 Russia, which was to the east of the Braslav region.
2. References to destruction in Dvinsk during this period could refer to any one of a series of major Aktions in July-August 1941 or on November 7-9, 1941.
3. Other accounts, such as that of Chaim Munitz on page 280 of this memorial book, say 13 were killed
4. A major, failed attempt to get weapons is described by Yerachmiel Milutin on page 255 of this memorial book.
5. Naftali Fisher, the son of Zalman-Yaacov, was a grandson of Neftel Fisher and a great-grandson of Morduch Fisher. Avraham Fisher, the son of Baruch, was a grandson of Zelik Fisher and a great-grandson of Morduch Fisher. This Fisher family had been in Braslav since at least the time of Morduch, born ca. 1800.
6. Casino here means a place of entertainment (café or club) or a mess hall, not a gaming house.
7. The Gaon from Rogatchov was Rabbi Yosef Rosen (1858-1936). His daughter was Rachel Citron, a widow who'd come to Dvinsk from Palestine around 1936 to help compile and safeguard her late father's writings. Working in Dvinsk with Rabbi Fuchs, a devoted student of her father and his successor, she was able to publish several volumes of her father's writings and send copies of his notes and correspondence to New York City, before fleeing to Braslav in wartime.
8. The account of Chaim Burat (Chaim Ben-Arieh) is on pages 288-292 of this memorial book.
9. A ghetto in Opsa operated until around August or early September 1942, after which its surviving inmates were transferred to form a new (second) ghetto in Braslav, to repopulate that ghetto after its inmates had been slaughtered on June 3-5, 1942. A ghetto in Vidz had been established in March-April 1942; most of the inmates were transferred to the Sventzion Ghetto in October 1942.
10. Russian word for a partisan unit. The Kalinauskas unit (also called Kalinovskas) was named for a prominent 19th century revolutionary and comprised mainly Lithuanians.

[Page 263]

Liuba Shmidt
(Widow of Leib Gamush and Moshe Kagan)
Daughter of Minda-Faya and Eliezer-Yitzchak Bik

Translated from the Hebrew by Laia Ben-Dov
Footnotes Added / Donated by Jeff Deitch

I was born on 11 Elul 5679 [September 6], 1919 in the town of Disna [Dzisna, about 72 kilometers east of Braslav] on the Disna River, on the Polish-Russian border.[1]

Those years, the years of the final stages of World War I and the Bolshevik Revolution, were years of riots and robbery, carried out by the soldiers of the Russian armies (the Whites and the Reds) and by other rioters and hoodlums. My parents were forced to abandon their property and the flour mill that was the source of their income; together with their three children, they moved to live in Braslav, where my father had been born and where the family of his father and mother lived.

I was then three years old. As if in a dream I recall the main street, Pilsudski Street, which ran the length of the town. On one side of the street, to the west, flowed the waters of the large Lake Driviata [Drywiaty], and on the other side, beyond the mountain[2] that stood in the center of town, was the small and deep Lake Noviata [Nowiata].

At the time of the retreat of the Red Army [in June 1941], I, my husband Leib Gamush, our little daughter Pesia, and my father-in-law, Chaim Gamush, were in the town of Vidz [Widze, about 40 kilometers southwest of Braslav]. A week before the war broke out, my husband had been sent to Minsk to a teachers' conference, since he was the principal of the school in Vidz.

When the news came that war had broken out, the town residents were seized with fear. My father-in-law advised us to return immediately to Braslav to be with the family. We took his advice, and the next day we went there. My father-in-law, his oldest son and his four children, like many other Jews, set out, some by car and some on foot, in the direction of the old Polish-Russian border [east of Braslav]. I remained in Braslav with my brothers and sisters, because we thought it was impossible to leave with small children.

When German planes started to bomb the withdrawing Russian army, the supporters of the Nazis began to raise their heads; they grabbed people, especially Jews who worked as clerks in the government under the Soviet regime, as well as teachers and ordinary citizens who were suspected of being Communists; they were tortured and murdered. In this way, Beila Deitch and Yaacov Musin were caught and killed.

At the initiative of the Germans, a local police force was organized, whose members

[Page 264]
wore the swastika on their sleeves with great pride.[3]

The Germans continued to bomb civilian trains, increasing the number of dead and wounded. Confusion reigned over everything; in addition, the Soviet regime wouldn't allow people trying to save themselves to enter its territory [that is, to cross the pre-1939 border east of Braslav into the USSR], and it even closed the crossing by shooting. Many people returned to Braslav just like they'd left it.

Among the local policemen who volunteered to serve the Nazis were Stankivitz, Kolkovski [Czeslaw Kolkowski], [Stefan] Zhuk and Kozlovski [Kozlowski]. They felt themselves to be our rulers; they would enter the homes of the Jews and rudely demand whatever they wanted. A number of days later, the German army covered the roads and the entire area.

One Sabbath night [presumably June 27], they ordered all the Jews out of their homes. They told them not to take anything with them and to arrange themselves in the main street along the banks of the lake. All the Jews of the town, men, women and children, from young to old, were put in rows of four, surrounded by Germans, armed police and dogs, and ordered to walk toward the Dubki [Dubkes] forest. The Jews walked in the rain, while trying to quiet the cries of the small children. No one knew where they were taking us. Everyone felt certain that this was our last journey. The Germans warned us that it was forbidden to step out of the lines. Anyone who did so would be shot! Two men tried to go out of the line [Shlomo Zilber and Chaim Milutin], and the Germans shot them immediately, killing them.

I walked with my small daughter in my arms. My sister Roza [who was married to Eliahu Shmidt] held the hand of her daughter Sonia, and with her other hand she carried the very young Chayala. The Germans separated us from each other and from our brothers.

My brother-in-law [Eliahu Shmidt], the husband of my sister, wasn't at home at this time. A month before the war broke out, the Soviets had begun building a military airfield next to the town of Skidel (near Grodno), and he was drafted to work together with many other young men

(Chaim-Katriel Deitch, Hirsh Maron, Rafael Deitch and several young men from the towns of Druysk and Slobodka).[4] In the first bombings of the airfield that was under construction, many were killed and those who survived scattered in every direction and tried to return home. But we didn't think that Eliahu, Roza's husband, would be able to return home safely.

They brought us to the swamps [of the Dubki forest] . . . after we stopped, they ordered us to sit on the swampy ground. From among the congregants they took out the elderly *shochet* [ritual slaughterer] [Aharon-Zelig] Singalovski, cut off his beard with a knife, sat him on a motorcycle and drove him through the streets of the town. Due to great fear, the old man died of a heart attack.

We sat in the mud with the children until Sabbath morning [presumably June 28]. Then they told us that we were free to go home. Exhausted in body and spirit, I, my sister and my brother decided to stay with a farmer we knew [outside Braslav]. His name was Franus Kolkovski [Francis Kolkowski].

With our last bit of strength, we reached the farmer's house. He took us inside, gave us lots of food, and my brother went back to town [Braslav] to find out what was happening there.

The next day, many German military officers and men began to arrive in the area where we were staying. General Romuald set up his headquarters not far from Kolkovski's house.

We were seized by fear; the farmer was also very afraid. We sat hidden in his house until my brother came with my husband, Leib Gamush, who'd returned on foot from Polotsk [about 115 kilometers east of Braslav], because the train in which he'd been traveling had been bombed. He told us that on the way he'd seen villages that were burned and destroyed. On the roads and in the forests were many bodies of people who'd been killed. A few days later, Eliahu Shmidt, Roza's husband, also arrived. He was unshaven and wore farmers' clothing, and he told a similar story of the horrors he'd seen on the road.

[Page 265]

Once more, we all were together. We decided to return to our own house [in Braslav], even though we knew that while we were away the Christian neighbors had stolen our possessions.

Toward morning, quiet and fearful, we slipped into the town.

We put the house in some order and tried to live as normally as we could in dangerous times. Our neighbors returned some of the furniture, aiming to atone for what they'd done.

The period of decrees began; the Judenrat [Jewish Council] was established and took orders from the German authorities. Each day men and young girls were taken for various kinds of work. Many men worked at the train station cleaning logs and loading them on freight cars. Those who went out to work were uncertain if they'd be able to return home, and this happened with 13 Jews who went to work at the train station and didn't come back. Every day someone disappeared, and afterward it became known that the Germans or the police had murdered him. Likewise, the Germans frequently forced the Jews to contribute money, jewelry and valuables to their "war effort."

One of the policemen was Shliachchik, a *Volksdeutscher* [ethnic German] who under the Polish regime had worked as an accountant at our windmill; with the help of Eliahu Shmidt, we bribed him to make things a little easier for us.

We suffered from hunger; the farmers were afraid to bring food to town. Even so, we succeeded in obtaining a bit of food. Since we lived at the edge of town, conditions there were more comfortable and enabled us to form ties with the local farmers, who came to grind flour.

Sometime later, it was decreed that we had to wear the yellow patch, on the left side of the chest and also on the back; we were forbidden to walk on the sidewalks; we were allowed to be seen in the street only until sunset. After that, the ghetto was established [officially around April 1, 1942]. All the Jews of the town were concentrated in one street.[5] The rest of the streets were emptied of Jews. The crowding was terrible and caused sickness, hunger and other problems.

The local doctors --- Levsha [Lewsza], Baretzki [Barecki] and Emilianovitz [Emilianowicz] --- lived in hiding [sic] and, putting themselves at risk, helped the Jewish population with medicines and other medical assistance. But it was forbidden for Jews to be hospitalized.

There were no newspapers, and it was impossible to get news from outside about what was happening in the nearby towns or the world in general. Only those who worked outside the ghetto could sometimes bring bits of news and stories of killings and massacres that were being done to the Jews in various places.

We knew that when the Germans were winning we could expect days of relative quiet, but on days of a retreat or loss at the front they'd cruelly revenge themselves on us. Sometimes Jews from other places slipped into the ghetto, from towns where all the Jews had already been murdered and only a few survivors had succeeded in escaping.[6] We hid them and joined their fates to ours.

Men of the Gestapo took Jewish girls for themselves to serve them "with everything." Through these girls, the Judenrat learned what the Germans were planning in the near future, and we also got some news of what was being done at the fronts and in the region. Sometimes we'd find a magazine in the garbage, and in this way we could scrounge another bit of news.

On Tuesday, June 2, 1942, toward morning, 100 young girls were sent to Slobodka nearby, to clean an army barracks. We never saw them again. Toward evening, we heard of the disaster

[Page 266]

that was about to happen [later on the early morning of June 3]. The ghetto was surrounded by Gestapo men, gendarmes and police. It was clear to all what would happen. A few people succeeded in fleeing to the forest or other places.

We stayed in our house and waited nervously for what was coming. After midnight two armed policemen broke in and, with the barrels of their rifles, they pushed us and threw us outside down the stairs. They didn't allow me even to take my little daughter, who was asleep in her bed. They hit us with the barrel of the rifle and took us outside. I wasn't aware of where we were going. Suddenly, I found myself in Rabbi Abba Zahorie's yard. Somebody dragged me there and then took us into an old bathhouse, which already contained several Jews who hoped to find a hiding place there. But after a short time, again were heard voices and shouts, crying and shooting. They discovered us, and with blows they took us outside. One of our group, I think it was Mendel the locksmith, was shot on the spot. We who remained were taken toward the Yiddish school [the Folkshul]. In the confusion, I succeeded in slipping away and fleeing in the direction of my aunt's house. I found my Uncle Yerachmiel [Bik] and went with him. He took me, together with other people from my family, into a hiding place dug under Rozin's crop storerooms. This hiding place had been prepared by my Uncle Yerachmiel. It was dark inside, and I stumbled against the bodies of people who were lying curled up next to the foundation stones of the storeroom. Among them were my uncle [Yerachmiel Bik], my aunt [Mania] and their little daughter [Perela]. Their older daughter [Tzila] was the first sacrifice among the girls who'd been sent to Slobodka. There I also found my cousin Chaim Munitz with his wife and his toddler son; Chana and Zusman; Batia with her two children; and more.[7] The entrance to the hiding place was blocked with a large stone; it was hard to breathe. Occasionally shouts and shooting were heard from outside, as well as footsteps. Each time a child began to cry, they would silence it by suffocation. This is how Chaim Munitz's two-year-old son [Rafulik] was quieted. There was no food and no water. We had to relieve ourselves right there. The stuffy air and the stench were dreadful.

We lay there, like cattle, for three or four days. We lost all sense of time. But despite it all, the gendarmes and the police found us. They stood at the opening and yelled, "Come out, stinking Jews!" They had some Jews standing next to them who advised us to come out, otherwise the police would throw grenades inside, and they promised us that there'd be no more shooting, because we were needed for work.

One by one, we left the hiding place. The clean air almost knocked me out. All of us, filthy, wrapped in infected rags, arrived at the schoolyard. Someone gave me a bit of water; another helped us to wipe off the filth and even found cleaner rags to exchange in a corner of the room.

I saw among them the Jews who remained from the first massacre. In the next room lay Chaim-Aizik Maron and another elderly Jew. Both of them were dying and beset by madness. I understood that we'd reached the last extremity; this was the end of the road. All of us thought of just one thing: how to get out, how to slip out and flee from there. Zusman Lubovitz, his wife Chana and their son Arieh succeeded in escaping and taking with them Shaul [Blacher], the son of Chana's sister Batia. Batia refused to escape and stayed behind with her pretty daughter Bluma [Blacher]. Both of them would be killed.

My uncle [Yerachmiel Bik] also slipped out with his family, through a side door. He said to me, "Take an empty pail and run, as if you're going out to bring water. Tell the guard you're coming right back, but --- don't come back." This is what I did. With the empty pail I entered the cellar of the hotel that had used to belong

[Page 267]

to the Bik family, and I hid in a concealed corner. At night, I quietly approached the entrance of the cellar. There I saw my uncle and the members of his family. He asked me where I was going. I replied that I'd try to reach the farmer's house where we'd stayed after the "march to the swamp" [in late June 1941, when all the Braslav Jews had been marched to a swamp in the Dubkes forest and forced to stay there overnight, as described on page 264]. He joined me, and we went out into the dark night. We tried to see but not be seen.

We knew that the Gentiles were searching for Jews with the help of searchlights and dogs. So we followed the shore and swam in the water of the lake that lapped on the sands. I don't know which path we took, but after some time we reached the forest. I didn't know the area well, but I hoped for the best. The danger and the will to survive sharpened my senses. And so, toward morning we reached the farmer's house. We were afraid to knock on the door because the farmer's nephew was a policeman. We stood close to the walls of the cowshed, so that we'd meet the wife of Franus Kolkovski, who would come to feed the pigs. In the dark I fell into a sewage pit, and my uncle got me out with difficulty.

When the farmer's wife saw us, she burst into tears and couldn't utter a syllable due to her great surprise. She motioned to us not to move from our places and to wait. After a short time, she returned with her husband and brought us food and drink.

Franus opened the gate of the stable for us and told us to go up on the pile of hay. He gathered all of our infected clothing and brought me clean clothes. I felt as if the gate of the Garden of Eden had opened to us.

Washed and full, I warmed myself in the hay and fell asleep. Asleep, I heard the voice of the farmer calling me. He came up to us again, bringing us warm milk and bread, and told us that he'd paid a visit to the town. All of the houses had been sealed up, and they were planning to destroy the rest of the Jews who still remained. He added that my little brother Abrasha [Avraham Bik] was alive and that he, Franus, had taken him in a boat to the other side of the lake, to a farmer by the name of Skuriat in the village of Dukiel [Dukiele, 6.5 kilometers south of Braslav]. He'd also learned that my brother-in-law Eliahu Shmidt was alive.

From our friend the farmer, we learned about the bitter fate of my daughter [Pesia] and my sister [Roza] and her children [Sonia and Chayala], who were murdered by the Nazis. As he told us, tears streamed from his eyes; he cried together with us . . .

We hid with him for five days. After this he told us that one of his neighbors had denounced him and said he was hiding Jews, and he asked that we leave. Toward morning, he brought the four of us [Liuba, her uncle Yerachmiel, and presumably his wife Mania and their daughter Perela] to the other side of the lake and showed us the way to the house of the Skuriat farmers, two brothers and their families. On parting, he told us that if we needed help we should tell him. We parted from him with kisses and tears.

In the morning, when the farmer Skuriat found us in his stable, he told me that my brother Abrasha had already been with him for two weeks. From an excess of emotion, I grew so weak that it was necessary to pour water over me to revive me. The farmer hid all of us in his granary, fed us, and even gave a pillow to my uncle's wife [Mania] and the girl Perela [daughter of Yerachmiel Bik and his wife Mania].

After a number of days, my brother-in-law Eliahu Shmidt arrived and all of us, six souls, stayed with the farmer for a week. Then we were forced to leave. First of all, it was clear that it was hard for him to support six people; second, he worried that our existence at his house would become known in the village, and this could endanger not only our lives but also his and the lives of his family. Eliahu decided that he, my brother and I would leave

[Page 268]

the place and try to reach the forests surrounding the town of Yod [Jod, 25 kilometers southeast of Braslav]. There, according to what he said, his sister Ahuva and her husband Shmuel Mintzer were hiding at the home of one of the farmers (they survived, made *aliyah* to the Land of Israel and became members of Kibbutz Afek).

The name of the village where we hid was Taljie [Taleje, 4.5 kilometers west of Yod], and the farmer was Viktor Beinarovitz [Bejnarowicz]; his brother Paluk, a widower with three children and miserably poor, lived not far away. All of them were good people with a strong will to help others.

My brother-in-law Eliahu helped them with food and other items, and they were so dedicated to him that Viktor was willing to travel to the ghetto to ask my sister to come and hide at his house, because terrible rumors were circulating about the risk of destruction. But my sister refused to escape without her husband Eliahu, who was worried that the Germans would begin looking for him.

When we arrived at the village, we didn't immediately enter the farmer's house, but hid in the bushes and observed what was happening around us. The farmer's small daughter, who tended the cow, saw us and became very frightened. Eliahu signaled to her to approach us, and he explained to her what to do. Despite her youth, she understood what she should do. She ran home and told her father. And we, quietly and in hiding, one by one entered the farmer's house; there we met Ahuva and Shmuel.

As I mentioned, these people were very poor. In the spring they'd pull the straw from the roof to feed their cow. We knew this, and thanks to the connections we had with the farmers in the area, we succeeded in obtaining potatoes, a bit of barley and other commodities. The farmers truly put themselves at risk for us.

Here we found out that my uncle [presumably Yerachmiel Bik] and his family, who'd hidden in the village of Dukiel until the spring, had been turned over by local farmers to the Germans, who murdered them. Eliahu's sister Brayna, her husband and children, were also murdered in this way, and so was his other sister and her family. Misfortune wasn't scarce at this time.

A few other Jews arrived at our farmer's house, searching for a hiding place. Kalman Pinchov, his wife Slava and her brother came also. [The account of Slava Pinchov is on pages 403-426 of this memorial book.] The farmer was a good-hearted, merciful man, but --- he was afraid. Despite his fear, he agreed to let them stay with him. The place was small and narrow, and Shmuel Mintzer began, with the help of us all, to enlarge it. At night, we began to dig a hiding place under the stable. We poured the dirt on the roof of the stable and the cowshed. This is how we built a hiding place for all eight people. Rumors reached us that a farmer would receive a sack of salt for every Jew turned over to the Germans, and by our calculations eight sacks of salt were a sizeable possession. A worry entered our hearts: Maybe the farmer would be tempted and turn us in, but at the same time we knew that if it happened our hiding place would be revealed, and this implicated him. So we calmed ourselves. Only the members of his family were afraid. We decided to split into two groups and ask the farmer's brother-in-law, Strenchevski [Strenczewski], to agree to hide some of us and have the farmer's brother Paluk also hide some Jews from our group. And this is what happened. The members of the farmer's family were partners in our rescue. We saw the farmer calm down, his spirit lightened and he'd travel to our village acquaintances to get food for us. Among these acquaintances were people who cautioned Beinarovitz not to betray us.

I wish to name the villagers who helped us in our distress: Franus Kolkovski,

[Page 269]

Anthony Patzevitz [Pacewicz], Skuriat and his brother from the village of Dukiel and another farmer from a village near Ikazna [Ikazn was about 14 kilometers east of Braslav], Tolstov [Tolstow] was his name. After the liberation we searched for them and found them, and we helped them with all the means at our disposal. To this day, we keep in contact with them and send them money and packages of clothing and food.

In 1943, almost all of the [remaining] ghettos were destroyed. Many Jews in them died of hunger and sickness; and others couldn't find the spiritual and physical strength to keep going and killed themselves, while a few fled to the forests and joined the partisan movement. At the time, there were many rumors about organized groups that stood ready to fight with weapons in hand. They were concentrated mainly in the forests of Kozian [Koziany], Zamosh [Zamosz], Gleboki [Glubokoye] and around Vilna.[8] These groups were attacking German military posts, destroying train tracks and trains that took soldiers and ammunition to the front, and burning bridges and storehouses of food and military equipment. In this way, we learned that the German army was suffering defeats at the front and in many places had begun to retreat. Russian soldiers also joined the partisan groups; they'd succeeded in escaping from imprisonment or had been wandering the forests since the first days of the war. And so a serious fighting force was created, which organized itself in a united framework [under Soviet control].

I decided to join the partisans, but meanwhile something unexpected happened: The Germans, in their fight against the partisans and the Jews, were sending out spies and collaborators to uncover them. These people would wander the forests and the villages and sniff out people like hunting dogs. One day, while we were sitting in the farmer's house, an unknown woman came in and began to chat. Eliahu grasped immediately that she was one of the collaborators sent by the Germans. When she left the house, we immediately fled to the forest. Shortly thereafter the Germans arrived, and they began to burn the village houses with the residents still inside them. It was impossible to run; I, my brother [Abrasha] and Eliahu dug ourselves into the snow under a tree. Eliahu's sister [Ahuva] and her husband [Shmuel Mintzer] remained in the house under the stove, because they hadn't managed to get out. The Germans entered the farmer Strenchevski's house, where the Mintzer family was hiding. They interrogated him about whether any Jews were there, and he told them that if he knew where they were, he'd immediately turn them over, because he needed salt. The farmer's three children stood silent and afraid next to their father, saying nothing. Fortunately, they didn't burn the houses of the Beinarovitz brothers, nor the house of their brother-in-law, Strenchevski.

The Pinchov family escaped to the forest and joined a family camp near the partisan camp. And I, my brother and my brother-in-law went to the forest to meet with Jews. Little by little we were absorbed into the surrounding forests, a not insignificant number of people. We met Jewish partisans who came to visit and help us with food. Our morale improved a great deal, and the food was much better than at the poor farmers' houses.

At this time, the partisans were causing much trouble for the Germans. The Germans were afraid to enter the forests and were forced to send reinforcements to protect their trains.

It wasn't easy to win acceptance into the ranks of the partisans. First of all, they didn't accept people without a weapon, and second it was hard for Jews to gain acceptance into the units because of anti-Semitic feelings among the partisan ranks. But if a Jew brought a weapon, he was accepted. They accepted me as a nurse, because there were wounded who needed care. I and my brother Abrasha, who was then only 15 years old, were accepted into the partisan group Bondarenko. Eliahu, on the other hand, decided not to join the partisans. He wanted to meet with his sister and brother-in-law

[Page 270]

the Mintzer family and stay with them for a while. My brother worked in the kitchen and supervised the horses. He was ready to carry out every type of job.

Several groups of partisans operated in our vicinity. There were brigades named Zhukov, Kosygin, Spartak, Melnikov [or Malenkov], Bilov, Antonov, Lenin, Bazikin [or Bozikin] and others. Most of their officers had been officers in the Red Army, and a few of them were sent to direct the partisans under Soviet command. They had links to the regular Red Army at the front.

I was given a small pistol and took part in operations with the partisans as a nurse caretaker. I organized a small field hospital to collect the wounded. I'd send messages using the local farmers, who would travel to Braslav, contact the local doctors and bring back medicines, bandages and other medical supplies. Later, our officer, Bondarenko (a lieutenant), made contact with other partisan groups from around Polotsk, and on certain days they'd land helicopters [sic; the Hebrew text here said *masokim*] and evacuate the severely wounded to the Soviet Union. I always accompanied the wounded to the meeting place, despite the danger. All around were German forces, which sought to ambush the helicopters, firing at them. Once, when I was accompanying 12 wounded, we encountered a German unit that was withdrawing. Each side began shooting, and the helicopter was unable to land. The pilot flew away and returned; finally he succeeded in landing and taking away the wounded. But we, the group accompanying the convoy, were cut off from our unit and found ourselves caught in a trap. The forest was what saved us. Thanks to the Kozian [Koziany] forests, which extended to the Russian border, we succeeded after much difficult wandering in joining the partisan group of Sazykin and Zhukov, and we returned safely.

In the depths of the forests, there were many marshy swamps. I witnessed the terrible sight of people who, fleeing the Nazis, ran into the swamps and were drowned in them. Every little puddle that looked innocent, green and safe turned into a death trap. There, in these swamps, in a battle with the Germans, the praiseworthy partisan Shlomo Musin from Druya [Druja, about 34 kilometers northeast of Braslav] and his girlfriend died in a battle with the Germans.

Many partisans fell in battle with the Germans while guarding the camps. Once a large enemy force laid siege to the partisan camps with the aim of destroying them. The siege lasted three weeks. After wandering behind the German searches, in the end we approached an area of hard ground. This was near the town of Sharkovshchitzna [Szarkowszczyzna, about 20 kilometers southeast of Yod]. All around, echoes of shelling could be heard. We were very close to the front, which spread out around Polotsk. During this difficult time, I received greetings from my brother Abrasha. The man who brought me the greetings told me that my brother had remained alone in the forest during the siege. Alone, without food, there was no one to help him; he'd been cut off from our group while the Germans were shelling our camp. With the help of several friends, I reached his location and found him broken and exhausted, spiritually and physically. When I saw his poor condition, I didn't know whether to be glad that I'd found him or to cry. Several weeks passed before he recovered. This was close to the time of our liberation from the yoke of the Nazi conqueror. Then I learned that among the saved were also my brother-in-law Eliahu [Shmidt], his sister [Ahuva] and her husband [Shmuel Mintzer], and Zusman Lubovitz and his family. I also met Yerachmiel Milutin, who'd helped many people. Yerachmiel was a valiant hero, one of the excellent partisan fighters.

The front was approaching quickly. Around us, the thunder of shells and bombs was constant. At night, the skies lit up from the fires raging around us. Our unit's scouts

[Page 271]

now told us that we were surrounded in battle and mustn't move without an order, to avoid throwing our lives away. Meanwhile, groups of partisans went out on operations, to destroy the remnants of the retreating German army and to burn bridges, to prevent the enemy from taking anything with him. Liberation was near; it was something to celebrate, but only now did we feel the scale of our tragedy and destruction. I envied those who were no more; I didn't believe in the future. I felt like a man who'd been sentenced to death and then set free, without knowing where he should go or what reason there was to keep living.

And then the big moment arrived. [The region was liberated around July 1944.] At night we were told that we could return to the town, to see the Red Army advance and to catch the local collaborators. We went out to the town of Sharkovshchitzna. They told me to go immediately to the hospital and the drugstore, to safeguard the medicines and organize for emergencies. A group of people was available to help carry out the mission.

There were no Jews in the town. The non-Jewish population tried to justify themselves to us and find favor; the residents expressed a desire to help us. We saw through their hypocrisy, because of the anti-Semitic behavior they'd shown under the Nazis. We had to stay alert, because we knew that many murderers were still walking around, and many of these criminals had fled to the forests. The struggle hadn't yet ended.

The Soviet authorities began to organize life in the liberated areas. When a draft order was issued to young men who'd served in the partisans, my brother decided to join [the regular army] and avenge the blood of our dear ones.

Certificate of decoration of Liuba Gamush [for her service as a partisan nurse]

[Page 272]

He was only 17 years old and lacked experience. He was sent to a unit that was battling German units in the vicinity of Dvinsk and Riga, which hadn't yet surrendered.[9] After fighting for only a few weeks, he fell in battle along with 60 other fighters near Dvinsk. Thus, I lost the last member of my family. My little brother, who'd endured so much suffering for so long, was unable to see the great day of liberation.

At last I was freed from the ranks of the partisans, and I received a decoration from the government of the Soviet Union for my work as a nurse in the partisan movement.

I returned to my town of Braslav, and there I met the Lubovitz family, which had settled in the house of the Blacher family. My brother-in-law Eliahu lived in his house, which was still standing. I met Chaim Kagan, and he told me about his brother Moshe, who was in Russia and planning to return. In Braslav there were a few other Jewish families, from Druysk, Slobodka, Yod and other places. Masha and Mendel Maron were also there, and all of us worked to gather the broken pieces and put them together.

In August 1945 I connected my life with that of Moshe Kagan, who returned from Siberia. He got work in a fisherman's cooperative. This was the work that he loved, since from a young age he had stayed busy, like all the members of his family, fishing and renting lakes from the estate owners.

Almost all of the Jews had been lost. I worked in a clinic. The local farmers, wishing to cleanse themselves morally, would bring us food. They also returned many items that they'd stolen during the Nazi period, saying they'd taken the possessions to "guard" them for us.

The Soviet authorities weren't so enthusiastic about punishing the criminals and collaborators. In the first days after the liberation, several brave Jews took the initiative and with their own hands avenged a number of denouncers and traitors. Shortly after this, those who remained scattered and hid until the anger passed. Now they were living in quiet and contentment.

In Braslav, we felt the oppression of the cold and the aversion to life in the place where the coals still whispered about the graves of our dear ones. We knew of the camps of the Joint [the American Jewish Joint Distribution Committee] and the UNRRA [United Nations Relief and

Rehabilitation Administration], which were in Germany, where the remnant of the surviving Jews of Europe was concentrated. We knew that from there it was possible to travel to the Land of Israel. The borders of Russia were still open; it was possible to leave; there were trains that traveled to Poland and from Poland to Germany. We registered, we left our jobs --- and went out on the road.

We entered anti-Semitic Poland, where a multitude of fallen humanity had collected, the murderers and the hooligans who'd faithfully served the Nazis. The Jews in Poland were aware of this and did everything to unite and protect themselves from the aroused population. It was "as if" the Polish authorities saw nothing, which encouraged the Jew-haters even more.

One morning, my husband Moshe went out to go shopping. Some hoodlums attacked him and beat him murderously; with difficulty he managed to return home. He was beaten and injured all over: on his head, back and other parts of his body. He fainted from the pain. After this incident, we decided to hurry our exit from Poland and together with the Chepelevitz family from Zamosh, the Tzipuk family from Druysk, and another family from Dvinsk, we slipped over the border into Germany. We were caught and with difficulty succeeded, with the help of a bribe, in saving ourselves, but the soldiers of the border guard robbed us and left us with nothing. We returned to Shechichin [Szczecin, now in western Poland, about 840 kilometers southwest of Braslav]. After a week, we tried our luck once more. This time we succeeded and were able to reach Germany. After staying for some time in a displaced persons camp, we arrived in Israel in May 1951, on a ship that brought sick people, among them my husband Moshe, who was suffering from

[Page 273]

an illness of the kidneys. He passed away in 1954, and I and my son Eliezer, who then was four years old, lived in a small government apartment in the Shaaria district in Paja in Petah Tikva. I worked at a health-care organization in my profession as a nurse. My bitter fate didn't forsake me . . .

In 1959 my brother-in-law Eliahu Shmidt, who lived in the United States, came to visit us. Again our paths crossed. He'd rescued me from the Nazi hell, guiding me from one hiding place to another. This time, we decided to continue our path together. With the agreement of my son, we arrived in the United States. Eliahu treated Eliezer as his own son. With the help of the fatherly relation of Eliahu and his support, our son improved his education, finished university, and today he's a professor of art and sculpture. He married; he has two children and the name of one of them is the name of his father --- Moshe.

Footnotes:

1. This refers to the border between Poland and the USSR that existed prior to September 1939, after which Germany and the USSR invaded Poland and divided it between them.
2. Also known as Castle Hill and the Zamek. It was called a mountain by locals, even though it stood only 15 meters or so above the town.
3. According to the *Encyclopedia of Camps and Ghettos, 1933-1945*, Volume II-B (2012), on June 30, 1941 the German commandant in Braslav began recruiting a local police unit from among local ruffians sympathetic to the Germans. Stanislaw Jasinski, a Pole, was the commander. Other policemen included Kriwko, Stefan Zhuk, Malinowski, Masara, Czeslaw Kolkowski, Zarniewicz, and Stanislaw Nowicki. A man named Sucharewicz was described as one of the most brutal participants.

    In autumn 1941, responsibility for the local police was transferred from the Germany army to the German Gendarmerie, after a civil administration had been established. Among the men based at the Gendarmerie outpost in Braslav were Johannes Czapp, Willy Dittmann, Otto Haymann, Paul Kontny, Leo Leidenroth, Ludwig Müller, Ernst Schreiber and Waldemar Schultz.
4. Skidel (Skidziel), then in Poland, was about 310 kilometers southwest of Braslav. Druysk was about 19 kilometers northeast of Braslav, and Slobodka was about 11 kilometers northeast of Braslav.
5. Under the Polish government between the wars, this had been called Pilsudski Street. After the USSR invaded in 1939, it was renamed Leninskaya Street by the Soviets; it was the largest thoroughfare in Braslav. After the Germans arrived in 1941, the street was called Grosse ("big," in German). At various times the street was also called Bolshaya (the equivalent in Russian) and Veliki (the equivalent in Belarusian).

6.   The historian and former partisan Yitzhak Arad, in *The Holocaust in the Soviet Union* (2009), has
     noted that most of the Jews of Belorussia were still alive by the end of 1941, unlike the Jews of
     Lithuania, Latvia and Estonia, large numbers of whom had already been murdered. The winter that
     began in late 1941 was especially harsh, making it difficult to dig mass graves in the frozen earth,
     and this halted massacres for a time.

     With the winter in Belorussia receding, on March 2, 1942 some 5,000 Jews in the **Minsk
     Ghetto** (out of 49,000) were shot by German security forces consisting of Belorussians, Ukrainians
     and Lithuanians. On March 3, some 2,300 Jews from the **Baranovichi Ghetto** (out of 18,000) were
     shot by German, Belorussian and Lithuanian police. On May 8, some 5,700 Jews in the **Lida
     Ghetto** (out of some 7,200) were shot. On May 29, the **Dokshits/Dokshitsy Ghetto**, with 2,653
     Jews, was liquidated. On June 1, the **Luzhki Ghetto**, with 528 Jews, was liquidated, as was
     the **Plissa Ghetto**, with 419 Jews. On June 2, the **Miory Ghetto**, with 779 Jews, was liquidated.
     The massacre of the Jews in the **Braslav Ghetto** began the next day, on June 3.

     Subsequently other ghettos in Belorussia would be targeted, including the **Slonim Ghetto** with
     10,000-12,000 Jews, the **Glubokoye Ghetto** with 2,200, the **Disna Ghetto** with 2,181, the **Kletsk
     Ghetto** with 1,500, the **Druya/Druja Ghetto** with 1,318, the **Dunilovichi Ghetto** with 979, the
     Postav/Postawy Ghetto with 848, the **Ghetto in Opsa**, with 300, and the **Sharkovshchitzna/
     Szarkowszczyzna Ghetto**.

7.   This refers to Chaim Munitz (profiled on pages 70-71 of this memorial book), who was the secretary
     of the Braslav Judenrat, his wife Asya and their young son Rafulik (Rafael); Chana (who was the
     sister of Chaim Munitz and also the wife of Zusman Lubovitz); Batia (who was the sister of Chaim
     Munitz and Chana and also the wife of Yitzchak Blacher); and Batia and Yitzchak Blacher's two
     children, Shaul and Bluma. Although Mrs. Shmidt said later in her account that Rafulik was two
     years old, this should be taken as approximate; sources at Yad Vashem say that Rafulik was born
     ca. 1941 and around one year old.

8.   Kozian was about 32 kilometers southwest of Yod, and Zamosh was about 10 kilometers northwest
     of Yod. Gleboki was about 50 kilometers southeast of Yod, and Vilna was about 155 kilometers
     southwest of Yod.

9.   Dvinsk (now Daugavpils), in Latvia, was about 42 kilometers northwest of Braslav. Riga, also in
     Latvia, was about 245 kilometers northwest of Braslav.

[Page 274]

Emma (Esther) Milutin-Korner
(Widow of Yerachmiel Milutin)
Daughter of Nechama and Yaacov Rusonik

Translated from the Hebrew by Laia Ben-Dov
Footnotes Added / Donated by Jeff Deitch

Under the Soviet regime, our family's situation was normal from an economic standpoint. My brother, Idel [Rusonik], worked as a clerk in the supply chain, the Food and Clothing Authority; my sister Liuba, who was married to Kalman Pinchov from Zamosh [Zamosz, about 16 kilometers south of Braslav/Braslaw], worked at the same company as an accountant; my sister Chasia married Zalman Gamerov and lived in the nearby town of Slobodka [about 11 kilometers northeast of Braslav]; my little sister Ida studied at the Yavneh[1] school [in Braslav]; and I, after completing my studies at school, began to learn the profession of nursing in the hospital in Braslav. I finished my studies some time before the Germans entered the town.

When the German army invaded the Soviet Union [in June 1941], some of the Jews of Braslav left the town and headed east toward the old [pre-1939] Russian border. Some of the youths were drafted into the Red Army. The non-Jewish population still behaved with restraint, out of concern that perhaps the Soviet regime would return. Only some time later, when the Germans entered the town, did the [non-Jewish] residents receive them with bread and salt. They began to collaborate with the Germans and show their hatred for the Jews.

Fearful of what was to come, I, my little sister Ida and my mother fled to the village of Mizerishki [Mizeryszki, 7.5 kilometers southwest of Braslav], where we had a house and a plot of land. After a number of days, I decided to return to Braslav to find out what was happening in the town. As I reached the Jewish cemetery, I met a group of Jews working on the road. Among them was Yerachmiel Milutin, who approached and told me that on the first Friday [June 27] after the Germans' entry into the town, they'd gathered all the Jews, taken them to the swamps in the Dubki [Dubkes] forest and held them there until the next day. He also told me about the killing of Shlomo [Zilber] the *shochet* [ritual slaughterer] and Chaim Milutin when the Jews were taken to the swamps.

Chaim Milutin was my cousin. When I heard this news, I hurried to the house of my Aunt Rivel [Rivka], Chaim's mother. I found her and her children sitting *shiva*.[2]

Rivel Milutin was the widow of Shmuel-Yosef, one of the organizers of the Jewish self-defense against the hooligans who attacked the town during World War I.

Back in the village, I told my mother what was happening in town and asked her

[Page 275]

to return home. She went back to Braslav with my sister. At that time, another disaster befell our family: My sister Liuba, who was in her last months of pregnancy, entered the hospital to give birth. She gave birth to a dead baby, and due to complications and the lack of blood for transfusions, she too died.

A short time after the Germans entered Braslav, they ordered the establishment of the Judenrat [Jewish Council]. This was the institution that communicated between the Germans and the Jewish population. The head of the Judenrat was Yitzchak Mindel. The rest of the members were Gershon Klioner, Hirsh Fridman, Levi-Yitzchak Veinshtein, Leib Valin and a number of others. Hirsh Fridman was in charge of manpower and responsible for carrying out the work the Germans requested. The Judenrat was located in the building of the Yiddish school.

On Passover Eve 1942 [April 1], the ghetto was established in Braslav. All the Jews of the town and a great number of refugees from other places were concentrated on the main street --- Pilsudski Street. The Jews lived there in terrible crowdedness, poverty, hunger and illness.

In June 1942 [June 3-5], they began to destroy the ghetto. They took the Jews to pits that had been dug ahead of time out near the train [station], where they killed them. The day before this, a group of girls had been sent to Slobodka to clean the barracks of the army. The next day, they were returned to Braslav and together with all the Jews they were brought to the pits and murdered.[3] Among them were my sister Ida and my cousin Rachel Milutin [daughter of Rivel].

Some of the Jewish residents [of Braslav], who'd heard about what was happening in the nearby towns and the Nazi massacres of the region's Jews, had prepared hiding places in the hope of saving themselves. We too had prepared a hiding place like this, and during the days of the killing we hid in it: I, my mother, my sister Chasia [Gamerov] and her toddler son, my brother Idel, my Aunt Rivel and her children, and my brother-in-law Kalman Pinchov, his brother [Chalvina Pinchov], his wife [Sonia] and their baby [Esther], Shlomo Shapira and Yerachmiel Milutin. All of us entered the hiding place, which was under the garage.

After the destruction of the ghetto [on June 3-5], the Germans announced that all those in hiding could come out of their hiding places; they wouldn't kill any more and there was no need to worry. Some people believed these deceitful words and left their hiding places. All of them were gathered in one place and murdered.

In the destruction of the remaining Jews of Braslav and Opsa, my mother, my sister Chasia and her son, my Aunt Rivel and her children, and the rest of my relatives were also killed. Of all my family, only I remained.

Sometime after the murders I met Chaim-Eli Deitch, who was traveling outside the ghetto in a wagon harnessed to a horse (at that time, he worked in the Germans' stables). I jumped onto the wagon, and in this way I succeeded in fleeing from the ghetto.[4]

When I left the ghetto, I hurried to an acquaintance by the name of Slitski, a [Gentile] fisherman. His house wasn't far from the old cemetery. He received me nicely, and I stayed in his house to sleep. The next day at dawn he woke me, loaded up the fishing nets, and we went out to Lake Driviata [Drywiaty]. He took me in his boat to the other side of the lake, close to the village of Maishuli [Meiszule, 6.5 kilometers southwest of Braslav and near Mizerishki]. From there I went to the village of Zwirini [Zwirynie, about 1.5 kilometers southwest of Maishuli], where I had an acquaintance named Stepka. I slept at her house and the next day, in the evening, I moved to the house of the farmer Frank Zhuk, who worked our land in the village of Mizerishki. He hid me in the cowshed, in the hay. There I stayed for a week. One day, toward morning, he came and said that I had to flee immediately, because the village was full of Germans. I went out on the road leading to Opsa [11 kilometers southwest of Mizerishki]. The road was long and tiring, and I grew exhausted. Despite the danger and uncertainty, I entered the first house that stood at the edge of a village.

In this house lived a woman. I blessed her with the

[Page 276]

traditional Christian blessing, "Praise the Redeemer Jesus." I told her that I was going to Opsa, where my brother worked in the flour mill; I wanted to find out if he'd finished grinding the wheat, and then I'd return with a wagon to bring home the flour. She believed my story, and I slept in her house that night.

Early in the morning, I left the house and continued toward Opsa. I met a Christian woman, and we went on together. While we were talking, a farm woman came toward us. She warned the woman I was talking to that I was a Jew, and both of them went away from me. This happened at the entrance to Opsa. I entered the town fearful of the threatening atmosphere.

In the first house in the town, I saw a Jew praying, wrapped in a *tallit* [prayer shawl] and *tefillin* [phylacteries]. I approached him and told him that I'd fled from the [Braslav] ghetto. He took me into his house and took care of me. The next morning, in his house, I met my brother Idel, Yerachmiel [Milutin] and Moshe-Chatzkel Milutin, who'd fled before me. [Moshe Milutin, whose account is on pages 227-233 of this memorial book, also appears to have joined them at some point.]

On Sunday morning, all of us went on foot to Vidz [Widze, about 22 kilometers southwest of Opsa]. In the community office we told them that we were from Braslav, survivors of the massacre. They forbade us to tell anyone about it, and to protect us they even changed our names. For example, they called me Etty Skopitz, and Yerachmiel was Yisrael. They sent my brother Idel, Moshe-Chatzkel [Milutin] and Moshe Milutin to Sventzion to work on repairing the train tracks.[5]

As I found out afterward, my brother Idel [later] fled to the Vilna Ghetto, and when they began to destroy the ghetto and send the Jews to Ponar, he, together with a few other young men, tried to flee to the forests and join the partisans. The Germans caught them, murdered them and burned their bodies. Yerachmiel and I were sent to Kiakst [perhaps Kiakszty, about nine kilometers northeast of Vidz], where many Jews from Vidz were working on excavations in chains.

One day, when I was cooking food outside our barracks, I suddenly heard whistles. I looked up and saw three men approaching, with Red Army tags on their hats. They asked what I was doing there. I answered that a group of Jews was there, and they were digging in fetters. The men told me that they were partisans and wanted to speak to one of the workers. I called over Yerachmiel and Sasha Tempelman. The Russians saw them approaching and saw that they were wearing good clothes. They couldn't believe forced laborers would be dressed in such a way, and so they fled into the forest. I went to look for them. When I found them and asked why they'd run away, they replied that they thought I was planning to turn them over to the Germans. I calmed them down, saying they shouldn't be afraid; one of the laborers was my husband and the other was a pharmacist from Vidz; all of us were Jews, and we ourselves had fled from the ghettos. Only then did they agree to meet with our group, and they told us that they were partisans and their mission was to blow up the dairy in Rozovo [perhaps Rozowo, about 2.5 kilometers west of Mizerishki], because it supplied dairy products to the Germans. They also told me that they were in an organized group and their camp was located in the forest near Zagorie village.

We decided to join the partisans and fight the Germans. We went out toward Zagorie. Local residents told to us how to reach the forest where the partisans were located. There were 15 people in our group; I was the only woman.

We met the officer of the partisans and expressed our wish to join them. Unfortunately, they refused to accept people without weapons. They took me because I was a nurse and the camp had no one who knew how to care for the wounded. Yerachmiel and the rest of the men left to search for weapons.

I was joined to a battalion named for Suvorov. In it, there were about 2,000 [sic] fighters.[6] As I looked around, it became clear to me that there were no arrangements for providing medical aid. There was a woman who'd worked

[Page 277]

as a veterinarian, and another girl had been a former clerk in the NKVD.[7] With them, I began to establish and arrange care for the patients. There were very few medical materials, and it was difficult to acquire them. We made contact with Dr. Volotzhink, who worked in the hospital in Braslav. With the help of loyal villagers, we sent him money and lists of the medicines that we needed. Slowly, we established a field hospital.

At this time, the Germans were transferring soldiers, weapons and ammunition to the [eastern] front in trains. The partisans were carrying out sabotage missions on the train tracks and blowing up the trains. Among our men were some wounded and I, as a nurse, had to accompany the groups of fighters to provide medical aid if needed. During an operation, I and a few soldiers would remain a short distance away. The wounded would be brought to us for care and bandaging. Those who were killed were generally left where they fell. First of all, this was because there was no chance of removing them, and also because we had to withdraw quickly from the battlefield.

When winter arrived, snow began to fall. The Germans found our footprints and a bitter battle broke out, in which we suffered many wounded. I was flooded with work, providing aid to the wounded and moving them to safe locations. Many men left the camp and scattered in every direction.

At my request, they transferred me to Kiakst, where I again met Yerachmiel Milutin. He was hiding with a village acquaintance, and I knew where he was. We were together again for two months. In that same village, two brothers and a sister were hiding. When the Germans caught them and took them out to be killed, our acquaintance grew very frightened and asked us to leave.

Winter was at its peak. It was cold and we had nowhere to go besides the forest. We wandered among the bushes and trees during the day, and at night we returned to that same villager's house to warm up and receive some food.

One day when we were in the forest, we suddenly heard shooting and thought that we were being chased. We fled toward a river that flowed in a forest clearing, hoping to cross to the other side. I jumped into the cold water and started swimming, but quickly began to sink. Yerachmiel immediately jumped into the water and saved me. There, that day in the forest, Yerachmiel promised me with a handshake that he wouldn't leave me again and we'd never be separated.

That night we returned to "our" villager. We dried our clothes, warmed ourselves and stayed there all night. Toward morning, he asked us to leave his house. We set out for Sventzion. [It's not certain where they were at this point, but Sventzion was about 54 kilometers southwest of Kiakst.]

In Sventzion we found Moshe-Chatzkel and Moshe Milutin, together with several young men from Vidz and the surrounding area. We were a group of about 50 people. We obtained weapons and went to the forests in the area around Sventzion, where we began to organize ourselves and build bunkers. We were helped by a forester who lived in the place. First, we began a search for ways to supply food.

Spring 1943 arrived; the cold ended. We moved to the Zamosh forests, where we met many partisan groups who'd gathered from various locations. We were also joined by soldiers who'd escaped German imprisonment. Several brigades of partisans were quickly established, among them the Zhukov brigade, in which Yerachmiel and I served. There was also the Spartak brigade, in which Moshe Milutin fought, and a brigade named for Markov, in which Moshe-Chatzkel Milutin fought. Partisan activities increased in number and frequency.

In every brigade, there was a doctor and a nurse. I was the only Jewish nurse on the entire medical staff. The other nurses had been sent from Russia.

[Page 278]

Partisan certificate of Emma Milutin, nurse in the Suvorov battalion of the Zhukov brigade

Generally, we'd provide first aid to the lightly wounded, those who didn't need surgery. The seriously wounded were transferred to Kalazin or Kalinin in the Soviet Union via airplanes that brought us weapons, ammunition, medicines and clothing.[8] The main activities of the partisans focused, as mentioned, on sabotage and bombing of the trains that were bringing German soldiers and weapons to the front, but we also provided help to Jews who hid in the forests. Many of them joined the partisans, becoming daring fighters and taking revenge for the blood of their dear ones.

One day, a group of 80 partisan fighters went out on an operation. I went with them. A difficult battle developed; the Germans surrounded us and we suffered many wounded. Despite this, we succeeded in breaking out and returned to our base. I was very tired and fearful after the battle. I sat in the house of a farmer and dipped my feet into a bowl of water, to relieve some of the weariness from the long, exhausting trek.

Suddenly, one of the camp guards entered and told me that a wounded Jewish boy wanted to come inside. I immediately let him in. He ran to me, hugged me, and crying he asked, "Auntie, are you Jewish? Save me, I'm wounded and I want to live." I examined him and found a bullet wound in his leg. I cleaned and bandaged the leg, fed the boy and gave him something to drink. When Yerachmiel came, I told him what had happened. He approached the brigade officer Siromcha to discuss what to do with the boy. Siromcha advised that Yerachmiel and I adopt him as our son, and this we did. He

[Page 279]

remained with us until the end of the war, and afterward he continued to live with us for a time. His name is Misha Rabinovitz [Rabinowicz], and he lives today in the Land of Israel and works as a train engineer in Haifa.

In the fall of 1943, a typhoid epidemic broke out in the camp. In the unit's clinic lay many sick patients. To our great danger, the Germans began, just at this moment, to bomb us. One day they attacked and we had to withdraw to the area around Vitebsk [roughly 200 kilometers to the east]. There, there were large and strong partisan forces, equipped with heavy weapons and tanks. We remained there until the spring of 1944, and then we returned to the camp.

The mood was gloomy. We began to reorganize the place, but the Germans again began to shell us, and in one of these attacks I was injured in my left hand and left breast. In addition to all this, I fell sick with typhoid while I was pregnant. One night, airplanes arrived and brought us military equipment. With them I, another wounded nurse and several wounded fighters were sent to the rear. From there, we traveled in a train to the hospital in the city of Kalazin. I stayed in the hospital until August 1944, until after the birth of my daughter Liuba. From there I was transferred to Moscow, where I received an apartment and food. A short time later, I returned by train to Minsk [about 195 kilometers south of Braslav].

The partisan headquarters were located in one of the villages [around Minsk]. I reported there, and after the liberation of Braslav and its surroundings I returned to my town [Braslav had already been liberated in July 1944]. I met my husband Yerachmiel, who was busy "taking care" of collaborators with the Nazis.

We began to build a life for our family. Yerachmiel started working at a *leskhoz* (a government company that supplied wood).[9] Life wasn't easy; there were shortages of everything, mainly food. I too began to work, in the Ministry of Health, to ease the burden on the household economy.

Following an agreement between the governments of Poland and the Soviet Union, in 1958 we went to Poland and lived in the city of Valbzhich [Wałbrzych, in what's now southwestern Poland]. In 1960, we made *aliyah* to Israel and were sent to Dimona [in the south]. Both of us worked in the Ministry of Defense. Soon after that, I began working as a nurse at a health care provider, and gradually our lives began to move along the desired path.

To my dismay, Yerachmiel fell ill and after a short time, in June 1968, he passed away. He was buried in the cemetery in Dimona.

Footnotes:

1. The Yavneh school was part of a network of more than 200 schools established throughout Poland by Mizrahi, a Religious Zionist movement that had been founded in 1902 in Vilna to promote Zionism among observant Jews. Yavneh schools emphasized modern Hebrew, religious education and reconstructing Jewish life in Palestine. The flagship of the Yavneh school network was the Tachkemoni rabbinical seminary in Warsaw. From the 1920s, the youth movement of Mizrahi was HaShomer HaDati (The Religious Guard).
2. The week-long period of mourning for first-degree relatives.
3. Accounts differ on when the girls were taken to the pits and killed: on the day the massacre began (June 3, 1942) or the day after the massacre began (June 4).
4. The account of Chaim-Eliahu Deitch is on pages 245-253 of this memorial book; page 251 of his account describes Esther and her escape from Braslav.
5. Sventzion (Swieciany in Polish, Svencionys in Lithuanian), located in Lithuania, was 45 kilometers southwest of Vidz.
6. The battalion was named for Alexander Suvorov, an 18th-century Russian general and hero. Two thousand would be an extraordinarily large number for a battalion, especially a partisan battalion, which tended to have 150-300 people. Two thousand was normally the size of a regiment, not a battalion. So it's possible that 2,000 in the original is a mistake and it should instead read 200.
7. Narodnyi Komissariat Vnutrennikh Del (People's Commissariat for Internal Affairs): The Soviet law enforcement and intelligence agency that existed from 1934-46, after which it evolved into the KGB.
8. Kalazin might refer to the town of Kalyazin in what's now Tver Province. Kalinin might refer to the city of Kalinin (now Tver), also in Tver Province. Both places were to the north of Moscow and respectively about 700 kilometers northeast of Braslav and 560 kilometers northeast of Braslav.
9. *Leskhoz (lesnoye khozyaistvo*, or forest economy) was a Soviet term for a state forestry management enterprise.

[Page 280]

Chaim Munitz
Son of Rachel and Levi-Yitzchak

Translated from the Hebrew by Dr. Ida Schwarcz
Footnotes Added / Donated by Jeff Deitch

A letter written by Chaim Munitz, of blessed memory, at the beginning of 1946 in Izhevsk (the capital of the Autonomous Republic of Udmurt in the Soviet Union) to his sister Munka Shmutzer in Kibbutz Ein Hayam [near Haifa in Israel]:

Dear ones!

I returned to Izhevsk two days ago [Izhevsk was about 1,000 kilometers east of Braslav]. I've been in Braslav [Braslaw], Vilna, Kovno and Riga. I found the postcard from Hannah, a letter from Hannah and David, and the letter written by the three of you together --- Manya, Hannah and Aharon on February 12, 1946.

On the surface, Braslav hasn't changed. The mountain [Castle Hill][1] hasn't split in two, the water in the lakes is peaceful and quiet, as if nothing had occurred. But terrible things did happen there that are hard to talk about, and even harder to write about.

On the first Friday [June 27, 1941], when the Germans entered Braslav, they gathered all the Jews, took them to the deep swamps near the Dubki [Dubkes] forest, and kept them there for an entire day. While the Jews were in the swamps their property was stolen, and when they returned the town looked as if it had undergone a pogrom. Feathers from the ripped-up bedding flew in the air, as in Bialik's poem, "In the City of Slaughter."[2]

While they were being led to the swamps, Shlomo [Zilber] the *shochet* [ritual slaughterer] and Chaim Milutin tried to escape. Both of them were killed. Later another 13 Jews were murdered after they were accused by a Polish overseer of not working hard enough. (They'd been clearing trees at the train station.) The rest of the Jews were killed in the general massacre of June 3, 1942. Until that date, the Jews lived as if in hell.

On one of the Fridays, the Germans made [Aharon-Zelig] Singalovski, the *shochet*, sit on a motorcycle that they drove around the town. After they freed him, he died of a heart attack. Then came the decrees: It was forbidden to walk on the sidewalks, people had to wear the yellow patch on the left side of the chest and right side of the back, and finally all of the Jews were enclosed in a ghetto on Pilsudski Street, surrounded by barbed wire. It was forbidden for Jews to speak to peasants and of course to trade with them.

The Jews were taken out for heavy labor: washing floors for the Germans, loading tree trunks onto train carriages, knitting stockings and gloves from wool. They received 150 grams of bread a day. The Jews used to exchange their possessions with the peasants, starting with clothing and finishing with sofas, chairs, and tables [to get food]. It was forbidden, but they persisted. They also had to give contributions (ransom money) to the Germans; gold, furs, women's coats. The Judenrat [Jewish Council] and the Jewish police collected the goods and obeyed the Germans' orders.

The Judenrat consisted of about 15 members. The chairman was [Yitzchak] Mindel --- the iron merchant. The others were Levi-Itche [Levi-Yitzchak] Veinshtein, [Eliezer] Mazeh the teacher, Sheinkman the defense lawyer

[Page 281]

and others. The policemen were Alter Arlyuk, Leib Valin and others.

The Jews in the ghetto understood that their days were numbered. Some of them prepared hiding places, hoping that they'd be able to survive the dark period. They tried not to anger the enemy, to avoid the killing. Of course, this didn't help.

On June 3 [1942] the Germans, with the assistance of local policemen, began to remove the Jews from their homes. They gathered the Jews into a building next to the [Eastern] Orthodox church. There they undressed them to their underclothes, beat them and then led them to pits that had been prepared in advance in the forest on the way to Dubina (near the Jewish meadow). The mothers carried their children, and they didn't cry. For three days [after the massacre], blood continued to seep from the pit. Peasants brought sand in wagons and poured it on the pit, but the blood kept seeping forth.

[At the time of the massacre] many Jews concealed themselves in hiding places they'd prepared. The policemen searched for them in these hiding places. Anton Burak had worked for a Jew in a beverage factory and spoke Yiddish. He was also a policeman, and he'd go into the houses and courtyards and announce: "Jews you can come out, they're no longer shooting," and so on. Some believed this deceit, came out and were of course caught and shot. Germans and policemen went into houses and shot into the walls, floors, courtyards and the ground. Small children that were in the hiding places would grow frightened and begin to cry. In this way, they found the Jews and caught them. They gave some of them a chance as if they could escape, and shot them when they crossed the wire fence [surrounding the ghetto].

**The Munitz family, including Chaim (on the ground, first on the right)
and Munka (third from the right)**

[Page 282]

The day before the massacre, the Germans sent all of the youths, about 80 in number, to Slobodka [about 11 kilometers northeast of Braslav], as if to work.[3] Afterward they sent them back to Braslav and took them to the pits. [Later that year] they brought the Jews of Opsa to the empty ghetto, and they killed them after some time had passed.[4]

[When the "Opsa" Ghetto in Braslav was liquidated on March 19, 1943] one Jewish youth attacked a German who came to chase the Jews (to bring them to the massacre), subdued him, dressed in his clothes and took his rifle. He went out and tried to kill a policeman but missed, and was caught and killed. Another youth killed a German and two policemen with an iron bar.

Some Jews who had hidden at the time of the massacre escaped to the forests. If a peasant hid a Jew, the Germans would kill him and his family and burn his house. For catching a Jew, they awarded three kilograms of salt. There were cases where peasants caught Jews and handed them over to the police. To allow a Jew to spend the night, the peasants charged five gold rubles.

But there were also cases where peasants hid Jews or gave them bread.

Masha [Maron], the granddaughter of Sliova-Chaya, and Mendel [Maron], the son of Chaim-Aizik, were hidden by two young peasant women until the Red Army came, even though they had no money or clothing to give them in return. Later the same peasant women hid four more Jews who gave them some money. Thus, they saved six souls.

The deacon (assistant to the priest) died of a heart attack [in Braslav] on the day the Jews were murdered. Some priests ordered peasants who came to confess that they were hiding Jews and giving the Jews food and clothing. One priest gave David *habiznai* and his child crosses to wear on their necks --- to save them.[5]

If there'd been a partisan movement in the area at the time, it's possible that more Jews would've been saved. But the partisan movement arose in our area only in 1943, so that only a few people were saved in the woods. Not one of our relatives survived. Those Jews who survived returned to Braslav, took back some of their possessions from the peasants, sold them, earned a bit of money and left for Poland.

The graves of the martyrs (the pits), as is seen here, were surrounded with some wire and branches. Their conscience didn't allow them to put up a good fence.

Nothing was left of our house or our grandmother's house. Only the barn remained. On the two nights that I spent there I slept at the home of Rayzka, daughter of Palka and Benyamin Gans. They lived opposite us, and they received me graciously.

In short, this is all there is of Braslav.

It doesn't help to cry. On the contrary, we must live and grow great to spite the will of our enemies --- *Am Yisrael Hay* [Long live the nation of Israel].

In a few days, I'll write more.

Yours,
Chaim [Munitz]

Footnotes:

1. Castle Mountain in Braslav, also known as Castle Hill and the Zamek. It was called a mountain by locals, even though it stood only 15 meters or so above the town.
2. This work in Hebrew, by the poet Hayyim Nahman Bialik, was written in 1903 about the Kishinev pogrom of that year.
3. This is incorrect; many young people were sent to Slobodka, but not all.
4. This refers to the second Braslav Ghetto, which was formed in August or early September 1942, when the Germans brought some 50 Jews from Opsa to repopulate the ghetto in Braslav, after the original inmates had been slaughtered on June 3-5, 1942. Because the new inmates were from Opsa, this second Braslav Ghetto was also called the "Opsa" Ghetto. It would be liquidated on March 19, 1943.
5. The reference to "David *habiznai*" is unclear; Yad Vashem lists no one by that surname in the Braslav area. If it isn't a surname, it might mean "David the businessman" or perhaps "David from Bicani," referring to Bicani, a very small locality about 60 kilometers north of Braslav, in Latvia.

[Page 283]

About Tevka (Tuvia) Biliak
Son of Henia-Riva and Natan
By Moshe Bogomolski

Translated from the Hebrew by Laia Ben-Dov
Footnotes Added / Donated by Jeff Deitch

"How have the heroes fallen?"

--- Samuel 2:19

When I began to gather material for this book, someone asked me, "Do you know about the actions of Tuvia Biliak, of blessed memory?" I began searching for information on him, among people in Israel and in books. I made a free translation of the resulting material, but only the parts that concerned him.

My first source was Shlomo Yechielchik. His acquaintance with Tevka began in the Vidz [Widze] Ghetto, and they were together from then on, until Tevka was murdered in the basement of the Jewish [police] in the Vilna Ghetto.

Additional sources were the interesting book by Moshe Shutan, a man from Sventzion [Swieciany a.k.a. Svencionys]: Geto un Vald; Sefer HaPartizanim HaYehudim, *published by Sifriyat HaPoalim; and* Churbn Vilna, *by Shmerke Kaczerginski.*[1]

--- M[oshe] B[ogomolski] [one of the editors of this memorial book]

[Shlomo] Yechielchik: I first met Tevka and his brother Avramke when they arrived at the Vidz Ghetto [about 40 kilometers southwest of Braslav/Braslaw], after their flight from Braslav at the time the Jews in the ghetto there were destroyed [on June 3-5, 1942]. Confused and frightened, Tevka and his brother had traveled a long road full of danger until they reached us, searching for a place where Jews weren't being murdered. I got to know them better after they were rounded up by the Germans and sent to a work camp in Nei-Sventzion [Novo-Sventzion a.k.a. Svencioneliai, about 50 kilometers southwest of Vidz and in Lithuania], a camp that was fenced with barbed wire and well guarded by the Germans. They put us in the army barracks and horse stables of the former Polish army and had us work laying railroad tracks on the Vilna-Dvinsk line. We worked many hours from morning till night; the food they gave us was very limited. Because of the terrible conditions, we choose to flee the camp and enter the Sventzion Ghetto, which was 8-10 [sic] kilometers away.[2] In the ghetto we'd meet, talk and make plans.

[Around early March 1943] Jewish police from Vilna arrived in the [Sventzion] ghetto, and at their head was a representative of the Vilna Ghetto and the chief of police there: [Jacob] Gens.[3] He explained that there was a German order to shut down the Sventzion Ghetto and transfer its residents to the Vilna and Kovno ghettos. He promised us that nothing bad would happen to anyone. The people [of the Sventzion Ghetto] accepted the decree, believed his promise and began to organize themselves for the move. Men from the German-Lithuanian government handled the transfer of people to the train station [in Novo-Sventzion] and put them in freight cars. A group of young people decided to evade the transport and go to the forest.[4] There were also a few among the Jewish police who advised the young people to join the partisans.

The freight cars, filled with Jews, stood on the track [at Novo-Sventzion] for a number of days. At this time, Tuvia and I were working in the train station [at Novo-Sventzion] and we knew the area and its surroundings well; we knew of hollows [filled with] orderly stacks of railroad ties, under which it was possible to hide if necessary. The Jewish police were among those accompanying the transport; we'd become somewhat friendly with them, and they said a few things that were useful to us later on. The police said that they were traveling to Vilna and Kovno, but some of them acknowledged, "Who knows? It could also be otherwise."

Since he'd been separated from his brother Avramke, who had fled to the forest, Tuvia was sad; he didn't say much

[Page 284]

and was sunk into himself. Despite his young age, we were friends. He was good-hearted and understanding, tall and athletic --- a strong lad. He awoke to action when events turned dangerous.

From Shlomo Yechielchik's testimony in Moshe Shutan's book: [During the organization of the transport in Novo-Sventzion of the Jews from the Sventzion Ghetto, ostensibly to the Vilna and Kovno ghettos] we located ourselves in the freight car next to the door. One evening [in the runup to the transport's departure on April 4], from the cars ahead of us, the sound reached us of voices, shouts and the slamming of doors. "I think they're locking the cars," I said to Tuvia, "Come, let's get out of here." We only just managed to get out of the car; the police shouted at us to immediately go back inside and not wander around, but we succeeded in getting away from them and hiding. To reach the Vilna Ghetto, we decided, there was no need for freight cars sealed with lead. We carefully approached the [other] cars from the rear and communicated with friends who were inside. "They're deceiving us," we said. "Sealing the cars is suspicious, and you should try to escape." A few of them agreed, but how could they get out when the doors were locked and the little openings above the doors were blocked with barbed wire? Tuvia found a metal pole, and with it we moved the wire away from the opening. The escape began. One by one, people slid through the opening and we helped them to reach the ground. These were Boris Ulman, Motke [Mottel] Vishkin, the Fogel brothers and a few more --- six men in all.[5] The escape nearly succeeded. But suddenly, we were surrounded. Tevka and I again were able to get away and hide under a pile of railroad ties, but the six men were grabbed by the police and put into a freight car, and when they arrived in Vilna [early on April 5] they were put in the ghetto.

When the train began to move [from Novo-Sventzion, on April 4], we got on it and placed ourselves at the front of a freight car that was intended for the escort, but no one was there. The trip [to Vilna], which ordinarily took about two hours, took an entire day. At the freight station in Vilna [presumably on the morning of April 5], we saw trains full of Jews from Grodno and Oshmiany [sic].[6] Opposite us, on the nearby track, stood another train. A maintenance worker was checking the wheels of the cars, tapping them with a small hammer. Suddenly he saw us through a soot-stained window and shouted, "What are you doing here? Run! They're taking all of you to destruction!"

. . . After a fierce argument between Gens and the head of the Gestapo [Martin] Weiss,[7] the latter agreed to free [some of] the Jews intended for the Vilna Ghetto. The others --- thousands --- were taken to Ponar. [This happened on April 5, 1943, whereas from what follows it becomes clear that Tevka succeeded in escaping the massacre at Ponar on April 5 and died later, in August 1943 in Vilna].

. . . [After Tevka was killed in August 1943] The eyes of Shlomke [Shlomo Yechielchik] darkened. Since the time he'd lost his family, he had never been so sad and bitter as now, when he lost Tevka. "Tevka is no more," he muttered.

From Shmerke Kaczerginski: Fleeing the killing in his town of Braslav, Tuvia arrived by way of Sventzion at the Vilna Ghetto [on April 5, 1943], where he organized groups of partisans from among the young survivors from nearby towns who had come to the Vilna Ghetto. As part of this, he sought to buy weapons in the city [i.e., in Vilna outside the ghetto]. He wandered around without a [yellow] patch, like a lion. One day in August 1943, he went with another man, happy and carrying a weapon, by way of the Lidzki Alley to a place where he was supposed to give the weapon to friends, through a gate leading to the ghetto. Unfortunately, just at that time many people and police were walking there, and it was difficult to complete his mission. Suddenly there was a shout in Lithuanian, *"Zydas!"* ("Jew!"), and someone grabbed Biliak by the hand.

Biliak dashed from his place and began to run down the narrow Kommandantska Alley toward Troki Street. The police gave chase and grabbed him, catching him with a pistol in his hand. [Hearing this] Biliak's friends

[Page 285]

became upset; there was great concern as to whether he could withstand the interrogation. At the beginning, he said his name was Kaczerginski. They tortured him so much that the Jews who worked for the Gestapo as black laborers returned from work exhausted and broken from hearing the wild screams and blows that came from the torture cellar where the interrogation was taking place. But the screams hadn't come from Tuvia; he only confessed his real name. The screams were from the torturers, insane with rage at the stubborn lad who uttered not a syllable and didn't even groan.

Weiss, the murderer of Jews, told Gens that he'd never seen such a lad, who died like a hero under torture.

From Moshe Shutan [describing the same incident as above]: The final time Tevka tried to enter the ghetto [in Vilna in August 1943], two agents grabbed him, pulled his hands behind his back and tied them. They searched him, found a pistol and took him to the Gestapo. From the Gestapo, they returned him to the [Jewish] police for investigation of criminal offenses, to Gens.

Weiss himself, the head of the Gestapo of the Vilna Ghetto, stood there and beat him terribly with a whip. Weiss wanted to learn who'd sent him [to the ghetto] and where he'd gotten his weapon. Tevka was lying tied to a table. He was quiet; he didn't speak, he didn't even sigh. Standing to the side, Gens politely took the whip from the hands of the exhausted head of the Gestapo and continued the assault on Tevka. Blue and red stripes appeared on Tevka's tortured body. Gens stubbornly continued the blows until he was covered in sweat. Weiss, who could do no more, ordered Gens: "Throw away the whip." Then Weiss left, slamming the door.

Gens came out of the interrogation room tired and angry. He looked with scorn at the [Jewish] police, who jumped to attention. Suddenly, between his teeth, he muttered: "Idiots!" He stopped for a moment, turned to them and said, "A son, a son like this I should have."

Shmerke Kaczerginski concludes: The Jews of the [Vilna] ghetto admired Biliak, but later events in the ghetto --- where 20,000 Jews were fighting for their lives --- acted to obscure his name. Now his name is known again, and the young hero casts a light in all his brightness.

From *The Book of the Jewish Partisans*: Tevka Biliak tried to shoot at the agents with his pistol, but missed. They succeeded in grabbing him and took him to the ghetto police. He was imprisoned and then cruelly and inhumanly tortured. The police cut up his living body. They tried every method they could to get information from him about his group, its location and direction. He knew every detail, but told them nothing. Summoning great strength of spirit, he withstood all the tortures of the soul, but his body was unable to endure. After terrible suffering, he died; he was 19 years old.

Footnotes:

1. *Geto un Vald* (*Ghetto and Forest*) was published in Israel in Yiddish in 1971 and translated into English in 2005. *Sefer HaPartizanim HaYehudim* (*The Book of the Jewish Partisans*), edited by Chaika Grossman and Abba Kovner, was published in Israel in Hebrew in 1958 by the publisher Sifriyat HaPoalim. *Churbn Vilna* (*The Destruction of Jewish Vilna*) was published in the United States in Yiddish in 1947.

2. As the crow flies, the Sventzion Ghetto was 12 kilometers southeast of Novo-Sventzion. It too was in Lithuania.

3. Vilna was about 80 kilometers southwest of Sventzion. Gens, the former chief of Jewish police in the Vilna Ghetto, had been appointed ghetto representative in Vilna in July 1942, after the Germans disbanded the Vilna Judenrat. By March 1943, Gens had also been given authority over smaller ghettos in the region such as the Sventzion Ghetto. Although subject to Nazi control, within the Vilna Ghetto he held a great deal of power. While carrying out the Nazis' directives, which cost the lives of thousands of fellow Jews, he tried to keep alive as many as he could for as long as possible, in the belief that if the Vilna Ghetto remained productive many inmates could be saved. This led him to alternately repress and conciliate those who wanted to revolt or escape to the partisans, because he feared that if revolt or escape took place too soon the ghetto would be destroyed by the Germans.

Around early March 1943, Gens and a group of his assistants traveled to the Sventzion Ghetto from Vilna. Gens told the Jews in Sventzion that their ghetto would be shut down and they'd be transferred to the Vilna and Kovno ghettos, the two largest ghettos in Lithuania. Gens then returned to Vilna, leaving behind an assistant, Anatol Fried, and a small number of Jewish police from the Vilna Ghetto to supervise the move.

By April 4, 1943, the Jews from the Sventzion Ghetto were moved in wagons by road to a train station at Novo-Sventzion, about 12 kilometers northwest of Sventzion. There they were put into freight cars. The great majority had been assigned to go to the Kovno Ghetto, while a small minority --- comprising the Sventzion Ghetto Judenrat members and their families, as well as skilled craftsmen and their families --- were to go to the Vilna Ghetto. The Vilna Ghetto was considered the safer destination; in return for bribes, some inmates who'd been assigned to Kovno were reassigned to Vilna, displacing poorer inmates and causing much anger.

On the night of April 4, some 40 freight cars departed from Novo-Sventzion station for Vilna (bound thereafter for Kovno, which was further away); 33 or so of these cars were intended for Kovno, two more were to unload in Vilna, and up to five more contained men destined for other labor camps. (Sources don't agree exactly on the precise total of freight cars.) At the request of the Germans, Gens traveled to Novo-Sventzion to oversee the transfer. He and Jewish police from the Vilna Ghetto were in one of the two freight cars bound for the Vilna Ghetto. Once the ghetto inmates had entered all of the trains, all the cars except for the one containing Gens were locked from the outside.

On the morning of April 5, the 40 or so freight cars reached Vilna train station; the two cars containing people for the Vilna Ghetto and the five or so cars carrying people for the labor camps were uncoupled and left there. The train remained at Vilna station for several hours on the morning of April 5, while several thousand Jews from another train transport were being killed at Ponar outside Vilna. (The Jews killed in the morning transport were from the ghettos of Oshmiany, Soly and several other locations.)

After the Jews from Oshmiany, Soly and elsewhere had been killed at Ponar, some 33 of the approximately 40 cars containing the Sventzion Ghetto Jews were taken out of Vilna train station and driven about eight kilometers southwest to Ponar, arriving on the afternoon of April 5. At Ponar these freight-cars were unlocked and, under armed guard, the Jews in them were taken out in small groups and shot for burial in mass graves, by policemen from Lithuania, Latvia and elsewhere, commanded by German policemen under the German SS man Martin Weiss. Some of the Jews from the Sventzion Ghetto resisted the massacre with fists, knives and a few pistols they'd brought with them, killing and injuring some of the policemen. Amid the chaos, a few of the Jews managed to escape; their number was estimated by the Polish Gentile eyewitness Kazimierz Sakowicz at perhaps around 20.

The death toll at Ponar for all of April 5, 1943 was estimated by Avraham Tory, a diarist from the Kovno Ghetto, at 4,000-5,000, including the transports in both the morning and the afternoon and comprising the ghetto inmates of Sventzion, Oshmiany, Soly, Lida, Smorgon, etc. For some of the Jews from the Braslav region, particularly those from Dubina (Dubene) --- many of whom had been transferred to the Sventzion Ghetto from the Vidz Ghetto --- the afternoon transport to Ponar on April 5 was their final journey.

According to *Ghetto in Flames* (1982), by the historian and former partisan Yitzhak Arad, the rerouting of the trains on April 4-5 to destruction at Ponar took place after a last-minute refusal by the Gestapo to accept the Jews into the Kovno Ghetto. According to Arad, the refusal was due to the Gestapo's fear of a link between the thousands of the new ghetto inmates, if they were resettled in Kovno, and the partisans in the forests.

At the time the destruction occurred, Gens was widely believed to have lied to the Sventzion Ghetto inmates about the transfer to the Vilna and Kovno ghettos; the few survivors assumed that he had known they would be sent instead to Ponar and killed. However, documentary materials from the time that came to light in later years --- the diary of Herman Kruk, a highly placed member of the Vilna Ghetto, and the diary of Avraham Tory, secretary of the Jewish Council in the Kovno Ghetto --- showed that Gens and his assistants, though aware of the possibility of deception by the Nazis, were sincere in their belief that the inmates would be transported to Vilna and Kovno, and not to Ponar. Gens was taken by surprise by the Gestapo's last-minute refusal, and it was due to his last-minute efforts at the train station in Vilna that two of the freight cars were unloaded in Vilna and not sent to Ponar.

Gens himself would be shot in Vilna by the Germans on September 14, 1943, after forgoing the opportunity to flee the ghetto. The Vilna Ghetto would be liquidated on September 22-24.

The main sources for the above description of events, besides (1) *Ghetto in Flames* by Arad, published in English in 1982, are (2) Avraham Tory, *Surviving the Holocaust: The Kovno Ghetto*

Diary, published in Hebrew in 1988 and in English in 1990; (3) Herman Kruk, *The Last Days of the Jerusalem of Lithuania,* part of which was published in Yiddish in 1961 and in a more extensive English translation in 2002; and (4) Kazimierz Sakowicz, *Ponary Diary 1941-1943: A Bystander's Account of a Mass Murder,* published in Polish in 1999 and in English in 2005.

4. This group of young people included Yitzhak Rudnitski, who survived the war and immigrated to Israel, taking the name Yitzhak Arad. Information on the group was included by Arad in his memoir *The Partisan,* published in 1979: 21 Jews left the Sventzion Ghetto on March 5, 1943, one month before the deportation. After spending a few weeks in the forest, Arad and another man returned to the Sventzion Ghetto on April 1, and on April 4 Arad actually rode the transport of approximately 40 freight cars into Vilna. He survived because he was in one of the two cars that were unloaded in Vilna.

5. The names of the six men don't appear in the 2005 English translation of Shutan's book, which was consulted at the Holocaust Museum in Washington, D.C. Perhaps they came from another source that Mr. Bogomolski drew on in compiling this account. There are other minor differences between the account by Mr. Bogomolski and the 2005 English translation of Shutan's book.

    From other sources, it's known that Boris Ulman survived the war; he was from Braslav and his account is on pages 143-144 of this memorial book. Motke Vishkin was Mordechai/Mottel Vishkin (later Max Wischkin), born in Dubina and the son of David Vishkin and Dina Kagan. Mr. Wischkin survived the war, married Yetta/Yentka Fisher --- whose account appears on pages 117-119 of this memorial book --- and immigrated to the United States. He didn't give an account in this book.

6. The small ghettos of Oshmiany, Soly, Smorgon and Lida were in the region of Grodno; they were southeast and south of Vilna. Sventzion was in the Vilna region and northeast of Vilna.

7. This refers to Martin Weiss, the SS official in charge of the Vilna Ghetto from October 1941 to July 1944 and a bloodthirsty sadist. During much of the period, he also controlled the prison in Vilna and commanded the killing squads that operated at Ponar. He personally supervised a number of executions at Ponar, including the one on April 5, 1943. Having survived the war, he was put on trial in Germany, convicted of mass murder and imprisoned from approximately 1950 to 1970, before winning release. He died in Germany in 1984.

[Page 286]

About the Bank Family
By Y[aacov]. Levin

Translated from the Hebrew by Dr. Ida Schwarcz
Footnotes Added / Donated by Jeff Deitch

"Our Father, Our King, act on behalf of those
who have gone through fire and water
for the Sanctification of Your Name . . ."[1]

--- From the [Avinu Malkeinu] prayer

If the Baal Shem Tov[2] had lived during the Holocaust, that time of torment when G-d seemed to hide His face, he would have asked of the Holy One, blessed be He, that his place in the Garden of Eden might be among the multitude who were martyred for the Sanctification of the Name, and that he might be seated next to the simple folk who exposed themselves to death and stood up against the Nazi oppressor . . .

Moshe-Baruch Bank was such a simple, G-d-fearing person.

He had a wife and two sons. He toiled from the early days of his youth, was drafted into the Russian czar's army, and in the time

The Bank family

[Page 287]

between the wars he worked at various jobs to feed his family.

At daybreak he hurried to the synagogue to pray, and immediately after prayers he lifted a ladder onto his shoulders or took his tools in hand to start work.

When the time of massacre and destruction was near [on June 3-5, 1942, when the Braslav Ghetto was destroyed], he didn't hesitate. With his bare hands, he stood up to those who sought to murder him and he struggled with them.

As happened in the story by I. L. Peretz about a young Jewish woman from Mainz, the killers tied him to a horse's tail and dragged him through the streets of the town until his soul left his body . . .[3]

His younger son Yosef was drafted into the Red Army in 1941, fought against the Nazis and died in battle near Warsaw. The following notice reached his relatives in Leningrad: "Sergeant Bank, Yosef, son of Moshe, born in 1919, fell in action near Warsaw on September 20, 1944 for the Socialist motherland."

His older son, Yisrael, left his yeshiva studies and immigrated to the Land of Israel in the mid-1930s. He was a member of Kibbutz Sha'ar HaGolan [in northern Israel] and there he raised a family. When the Jewish settlements were in danger, he enlisted and fought in the Palmach.[4]

Footnotes:

1. The Avinu Malkeinu ("Our Father, Our King") prayer, recited on Rosh Hashanah and Yom Kippur, as well as on the 10 Days of Repentance from Rosh Hashanah through Yom Kippur, the 10th of Tevet, the 13th of Adar, the 17th of Tammuz and so on.
2. Israel ben Eliezer (ca. 1700-1760), also called the Master of the Good Name (Baal Shem Tov), was the rabbi and mystic considered to be the founder of Hasidic Judaism.
3. The story referred to is "Dray Matones" ("Three Gifts"), published in 1904 by the eminent Yiddish-language author Isaac Leib Peretz.
4. The elite Jewish strike force that existed between 1941 and the 1948 War of Independence, in the course of which it was absorbed into the Israeli Defense Forces.

[Page 288]

Chaim Ben-Arieh (Burat)
Son of Esther-Musia and Leib

Translated from the Hebrew by Laia Ben-Dov
Footnotes Added / Donated by Jeff Deitch

From the Ghetto to the Ranks of the Partisans and the Palmach

When the Germans came to Braslav [Braslaw; in late June 1941], they immediately organized a police force there. The policemen were young local Poles and Belorussians who collaborated with the Germans. At the head of the police was a great hater of Jews and a known hooligan --- Yashinski [Stanislaw Jasinski]. He was the murderer of the Jews of Yod [Jod, 25 kilometers southeast of Braslav] and Dubina [Dubene, 16 kilometers northwest of Braslav]. He would take bribes from his victims and then kill them. At the time of the destruction of the Braslav Ghetto [June 3-5, 1942], he went from house to house and took the Jews from their hiding places. During the Aktion, when I hid in the attic of our house, I saw with my own eyes through a small window how Yashinski found a Jewish family that lived across the street from us, and he demanded that they give him all the valuables in their possession. The father of the family, a lieutenant in the Polish army who'd fought the Germans at the start of the war, argued with him, "From where would I have money, when I only just now returned home?!" To this, Yashinski replied with a shout, "I killed all the Polish officers some time ago!" He stood the man against the wall and shot him in front of his children. Then he and his assistants killed the children. To this day, this horrible deed of Yashinski's appears before my eyes.[1]

The Aktion in the Braslav Ghetto began in the first days of June 1942. The Germans destroyed the majority of the Jewish settlement in Braslav --- about 4,500 people, men, women, children and the elderly. Only those few who succeeded in hiding remained alive. Two or three days after the terrible murders, the Germans sent a few Jews into the streets of the town and forced them to announce: "They won't kill any more, you can come out from your hiding places." [Some] Jews believed this lie; they left their shelters and reported to the Germans. The Germans held these people for 10 days [sic]. Some of them were kept busy gathering the bodies that had lain in the streets of the town and burying them; after that, all of them were taken to the killing pits and shot.

The second night after the destruction, I came down from the attic where our entire family had been hiding. I went outside the ghetto to search for food to bring back. To my great distress, when I returned the next night to our hiding place

[Page 289]

I found not one living soul of my dearest ones. Shocked and confused, I stood there not knowing what had happened. A Gentile in the street told me that the police had found them toward morning and taken all of them to the police station. They were held there for a short time and then taken to the killing pits. That day I lost my parents, Leib and Esther, my sister Rivka and my brothers Yisraelka, Mulka, Meir, Shimon and Leizer --- the entire family. Only I remained, the sole survivor.

Few of the Jews of Braslav remained alive after the Aktion; I was one of them. I didn't know where to turn or who to ask for shelter. For three days, I wandered from place to place without food and water. On the night of the fourth day, the hunger began to trouble me severely and I saw no way to get a piece of bread other than to turn to a farmer in one of the villages, despite the danger of being betrayed and turned over to the Germans. I knocked on the window of a farmer in the village of Hutory. I heard the voice of a woman saying to her husband, "It must be some poor unfortunate Jew" --- a note of humanity that I hadn't heard in a long time. They opened the door, and I asked for a slice of bread and a place to sleep for one night. They took me to a haystack, and in the morning an old farmer brought me bread and milk. From what he said, I got the impression that he was a wise and religious man, about 70 years old. I told him about myself and the home of my parents, a poor house. I had only an uncle who was a wealthy man, and the farmer knew him well. I told the farmer that I'd seen the place where my uncle had hidden his gold, and I could show it to him when the war ended, if he'd give me shelter in his house. The old man listened to my words and said, "I don't want the property of others," and continued to talk about G-d and his messenger Jesus the Christian. "All the troubles that befall you Jews" --- he said --- "are because you don't believe in Jesus Christus." In my heart I thought, "To save my life, maybe it's acceptable to agree with him." I told him I was prepared, after the war, to convert from my religion. The old man accepted this with great satisfaction and immediately began to teach me the laws of Jesus. From then on, each morning when he entered my hiding place he said, "Praise Jesus Christus," and I had only to answer "Amen." This continued every day for six weeks.

One morning the farmer came to me very frightened and asked me to immediately leave his house. He said that the Germans had found a Jewish family at his neighbor's house and because of this had arrested the farmer's family. I tried to speak to his heart, because he was a good man. I said, "The Germans and their collaborators are mass murderers, with no faith in their hearts, but you're a religious man, you believe in G-d, how can you drive me away to certain death?!" --- "I don't want to drive you from my house, but my daughters are afraid of the Germans." Again I spoke to his heart, and he replied, "Chaimke, go somewhere for a week and after that you can return to me." He gave me a loaf of bread and a bottle of milk. That same night, I left his house. Where should I go? It occurred to me to go to Vidz [Widze], and that's what I did. The distance from Braslav was great, about 40 kilometers [to the southwest]. Before I left his house, the farmer told me which path to take. In the Vidz Ghetto, they received me nicely and made sure that I had everything. The local Judenrat [Jewish Council] joined me to a family with whom I could stay. This was at the end of summer 1942.

One day the Germans gathered 40 young people, myself among them, and took us to a labor camp in Podbrodz,[2] not far from Vilna. In the camp were 100 young men, all of us working at a sawmill. The camp was surrounded by barbed wire and guarded by adult Germans who were above army age. I was there for two months. I became friendly with a young lad, a Gentile, and we'd talk with each other. Once he told me that the forests in the area contained many partisans, and there were also Jews

[Page 290]

among them. If we wanted to join them, he was prepared to take us to them in exchange for a nice payment. There was no better chance to leave the camp; we were five young men who wanted to go to the forest. One Sunday, the day of the week when we didn't work, we left the camp and went out on the road, instructed by the Christian lad. When we entered the forest, he told us to stay where we were and wait for him until he came back. He left but didn't return. We kept walking, without knowing where we were going, until we reached a farmer's house. He told us that in Postavy [Postav a.k.a. Postawy] there were Jews with the local farmers.[3] He said also that he'd seen flyers in which it was written that Jews could come to the Gleboki [Glubokoye] Ghetto without any harm being done to them.[4] We knew that this too was a German trick to mislead the Jews who'd succeeded in escaping the first Aktion and were wandering the area. We continued onward. On the way, we learned that in the Gleboki Ghetto there was a secret organization that helped people who wished to join the partisans, and the help included obtaining personal weapons, without which the partisans didn't accept new members. Having no choice, we went to Gleboki and entered the ghetto. The head of the Judenrat there was a man by the name of [Gershon] Lederman --- a wise and energetic man. He believed, he said, that the young people who went to the partisans in the forest had a chance to remain alive. The others --- the adults, the elderly and the children --- could be saved, he argued, only through dedicated work for the Germans. He had established factories in the ghetto for wool, cotton, felt boots and more, in which Jews would work "until the hard times pass." But even his [own] sons didn't believe in his ideology. In Lederman's house gathered young men who left the ghetto and went out to the forests at night. In his house, there was also a weapons storeroom.

I stayed in the Gleboki Ghetto until May [sic] 1943,[5] when the second Aktion began to destroy the last of the Jews. Together with my good friend, we bought a pistol and decided to escape to the forest. Unfortunately, we delayed our exit from day to day, until the morning when the Germans, equipped with light and heavy weapons, surrounded the ghetto and called to the Jews to come out of their houses [August 20, 1943]. Hearing their shouts, we saw how many Jews ran in the direction of the fence around the camp, broke through it, and continued to run toward the forest, which was about 300 meters from the camp. I and my friend joined the flight. Heavy fire opened up on us; many people fell. The rest continued to flee. At the outset, we'd decided that if one of us was wounded the other wouldn't leave him to suffer. After that, I was wounded in my leg and couldn't continue to run. I thought of putting an end to my life, because the pistol was in my hands. But my friend and another Jew sensed this; they grabbed the weapon from me and dragged me with them into the forest.

A great many, maybe 1,000 Jews, were among those who broke through the fence, but only a small number of them remained alive. Only 20 young people gathered in the forest. Fate took its course, and I and my friend remained alive. The group said that they'd go and look for the partisans. I was a hindrance to them, because I couldn't walk and they had to carry me on their backs. We didn't encounter any Germans on the way; after the heavy fire they had rained down on the escapees, they didn't think anyone remained alive. The Gentiles who we met on the way left us alone, because they knew Jewish partisans were operating in the area and were likely to make them pay a heavy price for any crime. Reaching a village, we decided to wait for the partisans to come. After a short delay a group of them arrived, among them two Jews. One was Abba Kozliner from Luzhki [Luzki, about 65 kilometers southeast of Braslav, near Gleboki] and the second was a lad from Disna [Dzisna, about 72 kilometers east of Braslav] whose name unfortunately I can't recall. The partisans told us to wait until they returned from their mission, which we did. When they came back,

[Page 291]

they hitched up a horse and wagon, sat me inside it, and together we arrived at the Miory forest. This was the camp of the Belorussian brigade, which numbered 500 men, of whom 80 were Jews. Their officer was the war hero Sasylkin. In this brigade there also were gypsies.

I remember that once, when the officer [Sazykin] was a bit tipsy, he gathered two of the children who were with us into his arms. One was a Jew and the other was a gypsy, and he sang a Russian song to them: "Behold, for these I'm fighting." The relations between the partisans were good. They didn't feel any difference between a Jew and a non-Jew. One veteran partisan once said to me, "Look, Yefim --- that's what they called me --- 50 kilometers from here you Jews are thought to be dogs, and here, among us, you're like my brother." The man was a writer and the brigade historian. In the brigade there were Jewish officers, and the Party secretary was a Jew.

After my leg healed, I was joined to the fighters and the unit's patrol and assigned a horse. I was able to take revenge on the murderers of Jews, but my conscience didn't permit me to kill innocent people. One day, there arrived at our partisan headquarters news that in the town of Miory [40 kilometers east of Braslav] they were organizing an A.K. (Armia Krajowa)[6] to fight against the partisans. Among these there also were murderers of Jews. Our unit ambushed them and captured 10 of them; our field court sentenced them to death. I stayed with the partisans until the liberation of the region by the Red Army in August 1944 [sic; other accounts say the region was liberated in July 1944]. The partisans then joined the army's fighting units. I was sent to the partisan headquarters and from there to a military course. All those who received a rank after that were sent to the front.

Here I saw for the first time that Jewish young people were leaving the partisan camp and returning to the forests where they'd lived until the war, with the purpose of searching for their relatives and, if they found any survivors, giving them as much help as possible. The officer of the camp was a Jew. He always found a way to explain the absence of the Jews and thus protect them. My friend Reuven left the camp. After two days, I was called to the exit gate of the camp, where I met a Jew named Fruchtenbaum and his sister, and they told me that my friend Reuven had recommended me to them and they were prepared to help me. That same day, I requested a day's leave from the camp officer and I went with them. We traveled together to a *kolkhoz* [collective farm] in the Chernigov district of Ukraine. There, I found another four Jewish families who, like Fruchtenbaum, had come there from Siberia after the Russian-Polish agreement that allowed Polish refugees to approach the Polish border. They arranged the appropriate certificates for me on behalf of "The Polish Partisan Organization," and in them it was written that I hadn't been drafted into the army.

I stayed at the *kolkhoz* for an entire year. When travel to Poland became possible, I immediately went there. I arrived in Lodz [some 660 kilometers southwest of Braslav] and the preparatory kibbutz of Gordonia.[7] Later I traveled to Shechichin [Szczecin, now in western Poland and some 380 kilometers northwest of Lodz], and from there I continued to Landsberg in Germany, because I'd been told that a kibbutz was there whose members were former partisans [Landsberg was some 660 kilometers southwest of Szczecin, west of Munich and in the U.S. occupied zone]. The manager of the kibbutz was Dr. Blutovitz [sic].[8] I made *aliyah* to the Land of Israel on the immigrant ship *Yagur*, which was intercepted by the British, who exiled all of the immigrants to closed camps in Cyprus.[9] Three months later, I came to the Land. This was at the beginning of 1947.

With the declaration of the State of Israel and the beginning of the War of Independence, I felt that my place had to be among the fighters for the state. I was drafted into the Palmach and the Israel Defense Forces. I was a soldier in the HaPortzim battalion of the Harel-Palmach Brigade, which fought on the Jerusalem front.[10] Among my officers were Poza --- Chaim Poznanski, who fell in the Battle of Nebi-Samuel [April 1948], and Dado --- David Elazar.

[Page 292]
Letter [Written in 1948 by Chaim Ben-Arieh during His Army Service in Israel]

My dear friends Munitz and the Per family,

This is intended mainly for Tova, because I think that you, Tova, can fulfill my request. At this time, I'm near the enemy. Our enemy is strong, and much has to be sacrificed. We cannot know who of us will pass through everything safely to reach the happy day [when the war is over].

So if I fall in battle, don't grieve too much. I'm not more deserving than my brothers the fighters or the six million who were destroyed in Europe. My consolation is that I'll die on the soil of our holy country, in the Land of Israel.

My request to Tova --- that she take charge of my possessions and divide them according to what I write --- is as follows:

Will

Twenty pounds[11] are intended for the planting of trees in the Negev in memory of my father and mother, Arieh ben Yosef Burat and Esther-Musia bat Chona-Zissa Dagovitz.

And 20 pounds for the refugees from Braslav.

The remaining money and my clothing should be transferred to Moshe Goldin from Braslav.

May 18, 1948
Chaim Ben-Arieh (Burat)

May you all be healthy and have much happiness in the State of the Jewish People.

Written in the parking lot of Kibbutz Maale HaHamisha Company 4, HaPortzim [Battalion], Palmach [Brigade]

Footnotes:

1. Yashinski survived the war. Because Braslav became part of Belarus after the war, like many Polish refugees from Braslav he resettled in postwar Poland, to the west. In 1963 he was put on trial in Olshtin [Olsztyn] in what's now northeastern Poland, some 470 kilometers southwest of Braslav, but he was acquitted. For information on his wartime crimes and postwar trial, see pages 130-142 of this memorial book.
2. Podbrodz (in Lithuanian, Pabrade) was in Lithuania, about 70 kilometers southwest of Vidz and 45 kilometers northeast of Vilna.
3. Postav/Postawy was about 65 kilometers northeast of Podbrodz/Pabrade, inside Belorussia.
4. Glubokoye in Belorussia was about 55 kilometers east of Postav/Postawy. According to the *Encyclopedia of Camps and Ghettos, 1933-1945*, Volume II-B (2012), a ghetto had been established in Glubokoye in October-November 1941; Jews from nearby towns were also brought there, raising the ghetto population to 6,000. On June 19, 1942, a massacre of some 2,200-2,500 of them was carried out, but unlike the Braslav Ghetto a large population was also kept alive to work. Later the Germans decided to raise the population of the Glubokoye Ghetto, as a way to attract the Jews who were scattered among the region's forests; Judenrat Chairman Gershon Lederman was sent outside the ghetto to bring Jews inside. Eventually, the ghetto population rose again, to 7,000. Thus, by 1943 Glubokoye was serving as a temporary refuge for Jews in western Belorussia who weren't in the forests. Eventually, however, as partisan activity in the region increased the Germans decided to liquidate the ghetto, announcing a deportation on August 20, 1943. When the ghetto responded with armed resistance, the Germans set fire to it, killing some 5,000 inmates. As Mr. Ben-Arieh's account relates, some Jews managed to break out and join the partisans; it's estimated that about 60-100 ghetto inmates survived the war.
5. The month appears to be mistaken, as the second major Aktion in the Gleboki Ghetto, in which the ghetto was destroyed, took place in August 1943, not May.
6. This was the Polish Home Army, which had begun to enter Belorussia from the west by 1943, if not earlier. It was fervently nationalist and anti-Communist. From late 1943, as partisan activity in Belorussia intensified, AK partisans increasingly opposed Jewish and Soviet partisans as well as the Nazis, and there were skirmishes and bloodshed among the partisan groups. This partly reflected deteriorating relations between the Polish government in exile and the Soviets, who had broken off relations in April 1943. With Nazi power in decline, a further issue of contention was that the anti-Communist Polish government in exile sought to reestablish an independent Poland, which the Soviets opposed.
7. One of several Zionist youth movements in Poland, together with HeChalutz HaTzair and Betar.
8. This might refer instead to Dr. Abrasha Blumowicz, who managed Kibbutz Negev in Landsberg.
9. The *Yagur* sailed from Marseilles, France on July 29, 1946 carrying approximately 750 illegal immigrants. It was sighted by the British on August 11, intercepted and diverted to Cyprus.

10. The Palmach was an elite strike force that operated from 1941 until 1948, after which it was absorbed into the Israel Defense Forces. The Harel Brigade was established within the Palmach in April 1948; HaPortzim was the second of three battalions within the brigade.

11. The Palestine pound was the currency of British Palestine from 1927 to 1948 and the State of Israel from 1948 to 1952, after which it was replaced by the Israeli lira (from 1952 to 1980).

[Page 293]

About Isser Rabinovitz
Son of Gita and Shlomo

Translated from the Hebrew by Jerrold Landau
Footnotes Added / Donated by Jeff Deitch

In an article by Stefan Kharkovsky in *Nasz Glos* [*Our Voice*],[1] published on February 3, 1968 on the participants in the Battle of Stalingrad, there appeared the following excerpt: ". . . in 1945 Lieutenant-General Isser Rabinovitz was among the soldiers in the Fourth Infantry Division near Austrovitz [Ostrowice, now in northwest Poland]. The commander of one of the brigades of the German 163rd Division surrendered himself and his division of 650 soldiers to him, together with their arms and flags."

Isser Rabinovitz, today a lieutenant-general in the reserves, was born in 1914 in Braslav [Braslaw], a small town in the Vilna district. He studied at the Yiddish Real-Gymnasium [Realgymnazye] in Vilna and completed his education at the Vilna technical college of ORT as a qualified electrician.[2]

In 1924 he joined the ranks of the youth wing of the Communist Party and later the Communist Party of western Belorussia.

He was arrested and imprisoned several times for his Party activities. He was a prominent activist from the Jewish sector.

As a Polish soldier, he began his military career at the time of the August operation in the ranks of the Independent Engineering Battalion and fought near Augustov and Grayev [presumably Augustów and Grajewo, both in what's now northeast Poland].

Then, at the beginning of August, after completing the preparation of fortifications for which the battalion was responsible, it was decided to make a foray into east Prussian territory. Among the volunteers for the operation was Private Isser Rabinovitz. He endured his "baptism of fire" during the tragic days of August with a direct attack on the enemy territory of the Nazi invader.

The force succeeded in crossing the border and penetrated deeply into east Prussian territory, destroying several railway stations and immobilizing German troops. When they returned to their base, they couldn't find the soldiers of their unit; in their absence, the unit had received an order to move southwest. As a result, they were unable to take part in the fighting against the Germans. The next military activity of Isser Rabinovitz in the struggle against the Nazi conqueror was with the Red Army, when he was mobilized in the autumn of 1941. A year later, he fought near Stalingrad as a member of special motorized units. In September 1943 he was

[Page 294]

transferred at his own request to the Dombrovski [Dąbrowski] Second Infantry Division that was combined with the Polish Army First Corps in the Russian army. Isser Rabinovitz joined the unit while the division was being organized on the Ouka[?] River near Siltse.[3] In the beginning he was delegated second-in-command of a platoon in an anti-tank unit of the fourth battalion, and later promoted and assigned the role of second-in-command of political affairs of the battalion. He finished the war with the rank of captain.

In his book of his military experiences Rabinovitz relates, among other events, details of the Battle of Pulawy [in eastern Poland] after he and his men crossed the Vistula [Wisla] River.

On the dark night of September 1, 1944, he and his unit floated across the Vistula on a raft. The order was to cross the river in the direction of Adamovki-Dombrovo. When the raft was in the center of the river, the enemy opened up with a heavy artillery barrage. Fearing the complete annihilation of the force, Isser gave the order to abandon the raft and wade across, but the river was deeper than expected and didn't match the information given by the navigator.

Isser Rabinovitz then continued to move with his unit in the direction of Varka [Warka], Warsaw [now in central-eastern Poland] and the province of Pomorze [Pomerania in northwest Poland] as far as the Elbe River [in eastern Germany]. An incident is engraved on his memory from the period of the fighting around the province of Pomorze in the vicinity of Sosnitsa. The area had great strategic importance as a road junction:

"It was during the first days of February 1945. Our battalion was ordered to stand in operational readiness, prepared to attack.

"When I arrived in the area that was held by a unit of our forces, the unit commander told me that there were clear signs of enemy activity. I immediately told my regimental commander and was informed that a unit of the Sixth Division was being hastily organized to come and reinforce the battalion.

"I calmed the troops and informed them that reinforcements were on the way, but unfortunately the information I'd been given was false. Instead of help, we were subjected to a surprise attack by a German armed unit. Confusion spread through our ranks; the results could have been disastrous, but with the help of several officers I managed to control the situation and retreat with our men to a better defensive position in a clearing in the nearby forest.

"We also needed to get to our company headquarters, which was in an area under the heaviest attack. This operation was carried out by one of the company commanders who, despite great peril, succeeded in getting through and warning the staff commanders. Thanks to this operation, our unit was able to move to counterattack.

"At the beginning of March, I had a more pleasant experience. After we crossed the Drava [Drawa] River [now in northwest Poland], our regiment took part in a spearhead pursuit of the enemy. We advanced via a forest in the direction of Lake Sitsina [Lake Siecino, now in northwest Poland]. As we cleared the forest, the enemy opened an attack on us with machine guns and bazookas.

"I was at the head of the unit. I ordered the troops to form an attack formation and open fire. We captured one of the hilltops that commanded the entire area. In front of us was the town of Austrovitza [Ostrowice, the place already mentioned in the first paragraph of page 293], and from there the German unit rained a heavy fire on us.

"The battalion commander, Captain Trobani, who commanded the remaining units, encircled the town from the southwest and began attacking the enemy. A heavy battle began. The enemy began to evacuate part

[Page 295]

of its forces northward. With my remaining men, I encircled a platoon of German soldiers who were defending themselves on the left flank of the town. Our fire forced the Germans to surrender. A white flag appeared in one of the windows of a house. I ordered a ceasefire. A file of enemy soldiers walked out of one of the houses. I approached them together with two privates. Leading the German soldiers was a colonel who identified himself as the commanding officer of the battalion; he was surrendering together with 650 of his men. The Germans laid down their arms. We took also their flag and sent them to our rear. We joined the battalion that was pursuing the remaining enemy forces."

The front-line journal *W.S.W. Sonitza Unit* reported on other military events. Among the articles is one entitled "Forty-eight hours on guard --- 48 hours behind enemy lines," in which we're told about "two days of fighting against the enemy that surrounded our forces on three sides, a fight that was carried out in knee-deep mud, without food or supplies of ammunition. Three times the Germans launched a counterattack and our men repelled them with bullets and bayonets . . . the commander, Captain Trobani, never moved from the front line and personally encouraged his men. Colonel Rabinovitz, the education officer of the unit, was everywhere: He had praise, a good word, a joke and advice for everyone. He fought alongside them the entire time."

Among the many recommendations for valor that the regimental commander put his name to and confirmed was the following:

"Isser Rabinovitz, son of Shlomo, born in 1914 of the Jewish faith, displayed great courage and energy in the battle near Virhof. In the strongest of counterattacks by the Germans that advanced

War commendation received by Isser Rabinovitz

[Page 296]

with a superior force, his battalion became engaged in an especially difficult situation. Thanks to his courage and resourcefulness, Colonel Rabinovitz succeeded in spurring his fighters on and raising their spirits, setting a personal example of heroism. The situation improved and the German counterattack was repelled.

". . . Apart from his activities as education officer that were performed at a high standard, he was also of assistance to his commanding officer in battle. He was always found in the front line of the forces.

"When the deputy commander of the battalion, Lieutenant Nizhnikov, was killed, Rabinovitz assumed command of the force and led it into the attack. In the Battle of Halbe [April 24-May 1, 1945, part of the Battle for Berlin], Rabinovitz was already a captain. After the war he achieved the rank of colonel in the Polish armed forces, one of the many Jews who took active part in the struggle against the Nazi conquerors for a new and just Poland."

--- From *Nasz Glos* [*Our Voice*], an excerpt from *Folks-Sztyme* [*People's Voice*]

Footnotes:

1. This was a Polish-language weekly supplement to the Yiddish daily newspaper *Folks-Sztyme (People's Voice)*. The latter was published in Communist Poland between 1946 and 1991.

2. The Vilna Realgymnazye, the crown jewel of Yiddish secular education in interwar Poland, was the first modern high school in which Yiddish was the language of instruction. Vilna was about 165 kilometers southwest of Braslav. ORT was Obshchestvo Remeslennogo i zemledelcheskogo Truda (Society for Trades and Agricultural Labor), an organization that had been founded in St. Petersburg, Russia in 1880 to provide employable skills for Russia's impoverished Jews.

3. Some of the locations mentioned in this account couldn't be identified with certainty, either because they were obscure or because there was more than one place in Poland by that name.

[Page 297]

Zalman Charmatz
Son of Chaya-Golda and Bentzion

Translated from the Hebrew by Jerrold Landau
Footnotes Added / Donated by Jeff Deitch

I took part in World War II against Nazi Germany. On April 13, 1939, I was drafted into the Polish army with many young men from Braslav [Braslaw]. That same year, in the summer I was sent to the Slovakian border in the Carpathian Mountains.

On September 1, 1939, war broke out between Germany and Poland. I experienced my first "baptism of fire" in the town of Zhibitz [Zabice, in western or southwestern Poland]. The Polish armed forces were unable to withstand the onslaught of the Nazi forces, and our forces retreated to Krakow, while the Germans were already approaching Warsaw; thus, the Polish army was already surrounded. The officers were the first to turn their backs on the enemy and disappear, and the troops simply fled in every direction or were taken prisoner.

In order not to fall prisoner to the Germans, we advanced in small groups at night with a few other Jews and crossed the Bug River (between the German lines). After many nights of walking, we arrived at the railway station of Brest (Brest-Litovsk), which was already in the hands of the Red Army [Brest was about 200 kilometers east of Warsaw, along the Bug River]. There I met my fellow townsman Shimon Shmushkovitz, who later perished. Many Jewish soldiers gathered there at the railway station in Brest. Although the Russians had promised us that we'd be allowed to return home, they took all of us prisoner and shipped us deep into Russia to the city of Vologda [about 410 kilometers north of Moscow]. After spending two months sorting us out, they released us (the soldiers) to go home while keeping the officers in the camp.

When I got home, Braslav was already in the hands of the Soviet regime. My father, who for many years was a *soltys* [village elder or mayor] in our town, was arrested and sent to a labor camp. On April 13, 1940 I was exiled to Siberia, together with my sister Perel, of blessed memory, my aunt Leah, of blessed memory, and some other Jewish families.

In the middle of 1943, I was drafted into the Red Army in the town of Petropavlovsk [in Kazakhstan] and sent on a course for sergeants in the town of Semipalatinsk [now called Semey, in Kazakhstan]. I completed the course with the grade of "excellent" and was sent to the Third Belorussian Front under the command of Marshal [Ivan] Cherniakhovsky.[1] I took part in the battles for the liberation of Vilna, Kovno and Mariampol and also the villages of Vevie [Vievis], Zhezmir [Ziezmariai] and Kausdar [probably Kaisiadorys] in Lithuania, as far as the Prussian border.

[Page 298]

These towns and villages had already been emptied of their Jewish populations. I could sense the destruction that had been visited upon my people, and fought fiercely to take vengeance against the Nazis. I reached the conclusion that the continued existence of the Jewish people would be secured only by the creation of a Jewish state in the Land of Israel.

At the beginning of 1944 our unit was transferred to the southern front, called the First Ukrainian Front, under the command of Marshal [Ivan] Konev [May 1944-May 1945], and integrated into the Red Army's excellent 285th Mortar Regiment (the possessors of the "Red Flag") under the command of Colonel Baylenki --- a Jew from Minsk. With this regiment, a unit with heavy mortars (120 millimeter), we fought to conquer the town of Zheshuv [Rzeszow] in [southeastern] Poland. After hard battles we conquered the town of Tarnovich [Tarnowiec] on the German border and extended our reach to conquer the town of Gleiwitz [Gliwice, now in southern Poland], on German soil. There I was lightly wounded. There was a short pause in the fighting, after which I was again sent to the front and took part in the battles of the Oder River [a river in Czechia and western Poland], the city of Breslau [now Wrocław in Poland] and its surroundings, and the fall of Berlin and the liberation of Prague.

At the end of the war, the regiment was transferred to the vicinity of Lvov (Ukraine) to liquidate the internal enemy --- the Bandera supporters[2] --- who'd played a significant part in the annihilation of the Jews during the Holocaust.

For my part in battle I received four medals: a medal of heroism, a medal of excellence, and two letters of commendation and gratitude from the Superior Command (for the conquest of Berlin and the liberation of Prague).

In December 1945 I was demobilized from the Red Army, and in 1948 I immigrated to Israel.

I praise and thank G-d, who gave me the strength and the right to fight under arms and to take vengeance against the Nazi oppressor, and to see them defeated and humiliated.

And I'm fortunate that I'm a free man in our own country --- Israel.

[Page 299]

**Letter of commendation received by Zalman Charmatz for his participation
in the capture of Berlin**

Footnotes:

1. This front wasn't formed until April 1944; it was commanded by Cherniakhovsky from then until February 1945.
2. The supporters of Stepan Bandera, a Ukrainian ultranationalist who sought an independent Ukraine. During some periods of the war, Bandera and his supporters were allied with Nazi Germany against the Soviet Union and committed atrocities against Jews.

[Page 300]

About Peretz Levin[1]
Son of Chaya-Shayna and Leib-Meir

Translated from the Hebrew by Dr. Ida Schwarcz
Footnotes Added / Donated by Jeff Deitch

Selections from the Letters of Peretz Levin That Were Sent from the Front during World War II:

Peretz Levin was a soldier in the Red Army who was killed on February 8, 1945 in eastern Prussia. He was wounded in his arm [or hand], but refused to leave the battle. Shortly thereafter, he was struck and killed by a shell fragment.

Dear friends!

I'm writing again to you. We passed Kovno and Vilna. So many ruins, so much blood and tears! At the train station in Minsk, I met some young men from my town [Braslav]. I heard a story from a young man of 19, whose voice was that of an old man.

He told me that my family was murdered by the Nazis on June 3, 1942 [in the massacre of the Braslav Ghetto]. My wife's brother carried my only son [Leiba] in his arms. My older brother, Zvi, and his infant daughter hid in the attic. The baby's cries gave them away, and the Germans shot and killed them right there.

The slaughter of the Jews in the town lasted three days [June 3-5]. People were thrown into pits while still alive. They were driven to their deaths with rods, like dogs. Whoever couldn't walk was shot on the way.

No! No! It's impossible to forget.

Many young people died as heroes. Only those who were in the forests as partisans survived, and those who concealed themselves in all manner of hiding places.

I know one thing now: We must kill these barbaric Nazis and their collaborators. The hatred burning in me has strengthened me, given me courage and energy.

They told me that a young man from our town turned to those around him while the bullets were tearing his body into pieces: "Jews, be strong and brave! Avenge our blood!"[2]

. . . I know nothing about my sister, nor about my brother Yehoshua, who was drafted in May 1941.

They killed my mother, my brother [or brothers, it's unclear in the original], my wife and my son.

. . . Why am I writing to you, you who don't know me!? . . . It's difficult for me, I must share all this with someone. I haven't one soul close to me, you must understand.

Does [my brother] Yaacov write to you? I write to him often.

Peace to you.

[Page 301]
Selections from His Last Correspondence (January 24, 1945):

. . . I await a letter from you, write and say how you are and how Yaacov is doing. Why are there no letters? I write to you often.

So little time! We advance night and day. The Red Army is doing great things --- victory over the Germans. We're all resting now between battles, and I, instead of sleeping --- am writing to you. Who knows when I'll be able to write again.

We're striking the enemy.

Peretz

[Another letter]
Dear friends,
Greetings from the front.
I've a bit of free time, so am writing to friends.
We're advancing, pursuing the Germans, the enemy's land is burning, we're taking revenge! We're winning! We march forward proudly.
Lacking sleep, but in high spirits!
I feel good --- I'm taking part in destroying the enemy.

Peretz

Footnotes:
1. The account of Peretz's brother, Yaacov Levin, is on pages 86-89 of this memorial book and includes some information about Peretz.
2. This probably refers to Chaim Milutin, who in late June 1941 was shot, together with Shlomo Zilber, when the Jews of Braslav were taken to a swamp outside the town. See page 254 of this memorial book.

[Page 302]

About the Three Fighting Veinshtein [Weinstein] Brothers

Translated from the Hebrew by Dr. Ida Schwarcz
Footnotes Added / Donated by Jeff Deitch

We wish to write about three brothers, the three Veinshtein brothers: Shmaryahu, of blessed memory, Shmuel, of blessed memory, and Yisrael-Yosef, may he live long, natives of Braslav [Braslaw], sons of Gitel and Uri, of blessed memory, whom the hand of fate separated and scattered far from their birthplace, homes and families, dragging them into the terrible storm of war.

The youngest brother, Yisrael-Yosef, who came to Israel after the war, relates:

"In 1940, I was drafted into the Red Army as a regular soldier. When the war broke out between Russia and Germany [in June 1941], I was sent to the Crimean Peninsula. There were fierce and desperate battles. I took part in the defense of the city of Sevastopol [about 1,310 kilometers southeast of Braslav, on the Crimean peninsula] as an artilleryman.

"One should remember that at the start of the war the Germans were at full strength in men and material. They attacked without pause and advanced quickly.

"In one of the battles, most of the soldiers in my company were killed by the Germans and some were taken prisoner. About 20 of us remained, mainly Jews, who made every effort to avoid falling into the Nazis' clutches. We ran for hundreds of kilometers, together with thousands of Soviet soldiers, retreating to the rear. Eight of us reached Baku [about 1,410 kilometers southeast of Sevastopol], and the local defense office sent us to the city of Molotov [now Perm, about 2,130 kilometers north of Baku] in the Urals, where we were put to work in military factories.

"Within a short time I was made manager of production, with many workers serving under me. I had many successes. After the war I was asked to remain and continue my work, with promises of benefits and a higher rank, but I gave up everything and left Russia.

"I came to Israel in 1948 and met my brother Shmuel, who was still alive. I told him of my war experiences and he told me how he'd brought munitions to the front as a soldier in the Jewish Brigade,[1] for those fighting the Germans. Shmuel also told me of the heroism and death in battle [in 1941] of our brother Shmaryahu, of blessed memory. Both of us already knew that our large family in Braslav had been annihilated by the Germans."

The second brother, Shmuel, came to the Land of Israel in 1939 and was a member of Kibbutz Ramat Rachel [near Jerusalem]. Comrade Moshe Katz writes, "Shmuel was a quiet, gentle man, and faithfully did all that was asked of him. I knew him well, because

[Page 303]

I worked with him for a long time on the railway. He was devoted to his home, Ramat Rachel, and loved the place and his friends.

"With the outbreak of World War II, he volunteered to join the Jewish units within the British army to fight against the Nazis, and he served as a driver in RASC Company 650 from June 22, 1942 until July 1946."[2]

Selections from Letters Sent by Shmuel in the Army to His Home, Ramat Rachel:

Before his army company left for abroad:

We began a new way of life in the company . . . on Sabbath night, we organized the first Sabbath party. Many guests, including women soldiers, came from Givat Brenner [a kibbutz in central Israel] and Rehovot. The Jewish commander spoke about the Nazi hell in which the Jews of Europe find themselves, and it's our duty to avenge the blood that's being spilled like water . . .

To all my comrades [adult members of the kibbutz] and the children, greetings!

I received the packages of newspapers and two packages as a gift for the holiday of freedom [Passover]. I thank you. I also received the gift package from the settlement, and I prepared a nice package for the refugees. I discovered that there'd been an Italian concentration camp here for our brothers, the children of Israel. We talked to them. One of them spoke Hebrew very well; a veteran Zionist. He told us of all the difficulties they'd endured. The Italians' behavior toward them was fair. At the time of the [Allied] invasion [of Italy], they hid in the hills. They showed me the hiding places in the fearful mountains. They sat in niches [in the mountainside] for 13 days without food or water and suffered badly until our army came and saved them. The Italians, the residents of the town, knew where they were hiding, of course, but didn't betray them to the Germans . . . On the Seder night [ritual feast celebrating Passover], many Jewish soldiers from various armies joined us and Gentile guests also came; high-ranking officers as well as refugees sat with us. The children of the refugees asked the four questions [part of the Seder night ritual]. Many people had tears in their eyes . . . After the holiday, Moshe Shertok[3] visited us. A number of Jewish companies gathered, and he gave a talk to us . . .

Write about everything happening in the kibbutz. Peace to all of you, and we shall see you in the Land of Israel after the victory.

Shmuel

December 20, 1943:

. . . I received a diary and a letter from Ben-Zion. I can't describe our joy. All my thoughts are concentrated on what's happening in the Land [of Israel]. This affects me greatly, as it does the other comrades.

On the one hand, we're glad to have the honor of being in the first ranks of the units invading Europe, and on the other hand I'm sorry we aren't with you in the difficult days facing our country.

Shmuel

Shmuel passed away on July 3, 1980 after an illness.

[Selections from Letters Sent by Shmaryahu to His Family]:

Shmaryahu, the oldest, was born in 1913 and immigrated to the Land [of Israel] in 1935 with his wife, Sara. That same year, their son Uri was born. Shmaryahu was one of the first to enlist in the British army for the war against the Nazis. He volunteered for the Land of Israel's "suicide squad" (51st Middle East Commando), fought in Eritrea, and fell in battle on March 5, 1941.[4]

When Shmaryahu was in British army camps in Egypt and elsewhere, he was careful to keep in contact through letters with his wife Sara and his brother Shmuel, who arrived in the Land on the eve of the war's outbreak, as well as with many friends. Here are a few selections from his letters kept by his son, Uri:

[Page 304]
January 22, 1940:

. . . I reached my destination. I was so deep in thought about the family that on the train I lost my pack and its contents. I especially regret the loss of my photographs, addresses and material for a book on my life in the army that I'd started writing . . . Greetings and kisses to Sara and Urileh.

Shmaryahu Veinshtein

January 14 [sic], 1940:

. . . I've returned again to army life. After my leave, I miss the family even more . . . But the main thing is to be healthy and we'll see each other again . . .

Shmaryahu

June 8, 1940:

. . . Please give my greetings to Sara, may she watch over Uri carefully so that he'll be strong. I wanted to send him a gift, but it's not possible at this time. Perhaps another time . . .

Shmaryahu

October 15, 1940:

To Sara and my dear son Uri. I wrote to you only yesterday. Now the situation has changed here. Please don't send me anything except photos . . .

. . . Please don't worry about me, I'm not in dangerous places . . . The boy probably misses me. Tell him that I miss him too, and maybe in three months' time we'll see each other again.

. . . In the next letter I'll write about changes in my life . . . . Happy holidays to you. Urileh, don't cry, and listen to your mother. Be healthy and well. Happy holidays, Happy New Year, and a peaceful year to you.

Shmaryahu Veinshtein

November 22, 1940, somewhere in Egypt:

To my dear wife and my sweet son, Urileh, be well.

. . . I love reading your beautiful letters that you wrote me . . . . I understand that you're in difficulties, I'll try to help as much as I can. On Monday, the 24th of this month, I'll send you lira [Italian currency].

. . . I wrote three letters to my brother Shmuel but didn't receive a reply. If you've received a letter from my mother, please send it to me. And don't forget to take my pants from the laundry . . .

This Is How the Brother Shmaryahu Fought and Fell

From the earliest battles the commando proved itself; even though its numbers were small, it was superior in every way to the enemy, which was 10 times larger. Small scouting parties of 10-15 people appeared everywhere in the rear of the Italians, and their appearance alone aroused fear and anxiety among the enemy. The enemy didn't know rest, either in the daytime or at night, and felt that behind every bush and rock there lurked the soldiers of the commando, whose caps decorated with colorful feathers brought with them fear and death.

--- "Lochem" ["The Fighter"]; from *Sefer HaHitnadvut* [*Jewish Military Volunteers in World War II*, published in Israel in 1949]

[Page 305]

I had the honor of belonging to the third group [presumably of the commando], which was considered the best. We carried out many exemplary missions, such as the unofficial visit to the Italian headquarters in Keren, and it wasn't our fault that all the officers there were sleeping in pajamas and unable to receive us properly. We came saying *"Buona notte"* ("Good evening"), and it was the sentry's fault for not responding to our greeting: he was sleeping and we didn't allow him to wake up. That morning, we lost three good comrades: an English captain and two men in the ranks; one of them was Shmaryahu Veinshtein, and we'll never forget him.

--- Zvi Svet; from *Sefer HaHitnadvut*

Selections from Letters Sent to Shmuel (Brother of Shmaryahu) in Kibbutz Ramat Rachel:

[First selection]

"It is with deep sorrow that we inform you of the death of our comrade Shmaryahu Veinshtein, of blessed memory. He fell as a true hero during one of our attacks on the hills near Keren (Eritrea) on Wednesday, 6 Adar 5701, March 5, 1941. With his courage and bravery, he saved our company. Every one of us, from the chief commander to the regular soldier, value his good heart and his bravery in his last moments. He wasn't the only casualty among us, but we wept only at his death.

"Please receive the sympathies of all his comrades. They are all mourning like you. May his memory be blessed!"

[Second selection]

"On March 4, at six in the evening, the military company in which the departed served --- together with his Jewish friends who are writing this letter --- left to survey three hills in no man's land and see if anyone from the enemy's army was there. They walked for three hours over the hills, until they came to a plain where there were barbed-wire fences.

"A battle started with the Italian army . . . there was a hail of bullets and explosions. The late Shmaryahu Veinshtein distinguished himself in the battle. He was responsible for the company's machine gun, and he fired with speed and energy. The battle lasted for an hour and a half, ending with the retreat of the Italians and the conquest of the hill by the British-Jewish unit . . .

". . . The next day, March 5 in the morning, the Italians began a counterattack to regain the lost position. In this battle, Shmaryahu Veinshtein fell."

The letter ends: "Be proud of your brave brother, who died a hero's death. He gave pride to our company and to all the Jewish people. We're continuing on the path he set, and may G-d enable us to avenge the blood of Shmaryahu, our good comrade, and the blood of our nation spilled in vain in the lands of the world. We're certain that we'll see you soon, after we achieve the victory and freedom for the world, and especially the freedom of the Jewish people.

"We share your deep sorrow."

[Third selection]

May His Soul Be Bound Up in the Bond of Life

"Shmuel! Your brother Shmaryahu wanted you to say Kaddish for him and also that Uri should learn how to say Kaddish. After the *shiva* [seven days of mourning], try to take care of Urileh. We, the friends of Shmaryahu, of blessed memory, have vowed to concern ourselves with Urileh all our lives if we live . . .

". . . Don't despair. This is a time of emergency, and Shmaryahu fell as a hero. Tomorrow it'll be the turn of someone else, perhaps mine. Nevertheless, we don't despair. We'll continue fighting and avenging ourselves on the enemy, despite the danger, until the sinners are wiped from the earth and there are no more tears. *Amen Selah . . .*"

[Page 306]

The first and third selections were written by Levi Perkal, 10690 51st Middle East Commando M.B.T. The second selection was written by his comrades in battle.

The Heroic Actions of the Jewish Fighters

Many Jewish fighters at the front volunteered for units that accepted the most dangerous missions and were called "suicide squads."

The news from the front testifies to the heroism of the Jewish companies and the value of their actions. Shmaryahu Veinshtein, who was killed in the battle opposite Keren (see the *Davar*[5] from Monday), saved an entire company while sacrificing his life.

(From "Palestine and the Middle East")

[Page 307]

Details: Shmaryahu Veinshtein, son of Gita and Uri
Born: In 1913 in Braslav in the Vilna district
Immigrated to the Land of Israel: In 1935
Served: In the British Army (World War II)
Army number: 10696
Date and place where he fell: March 5, 1941 near Keren (Eritrea)
Burial: In the British military cemetery near Keren (Eritrea) [The Keren War Cemetery]

(From "Palestine and the Middle East")

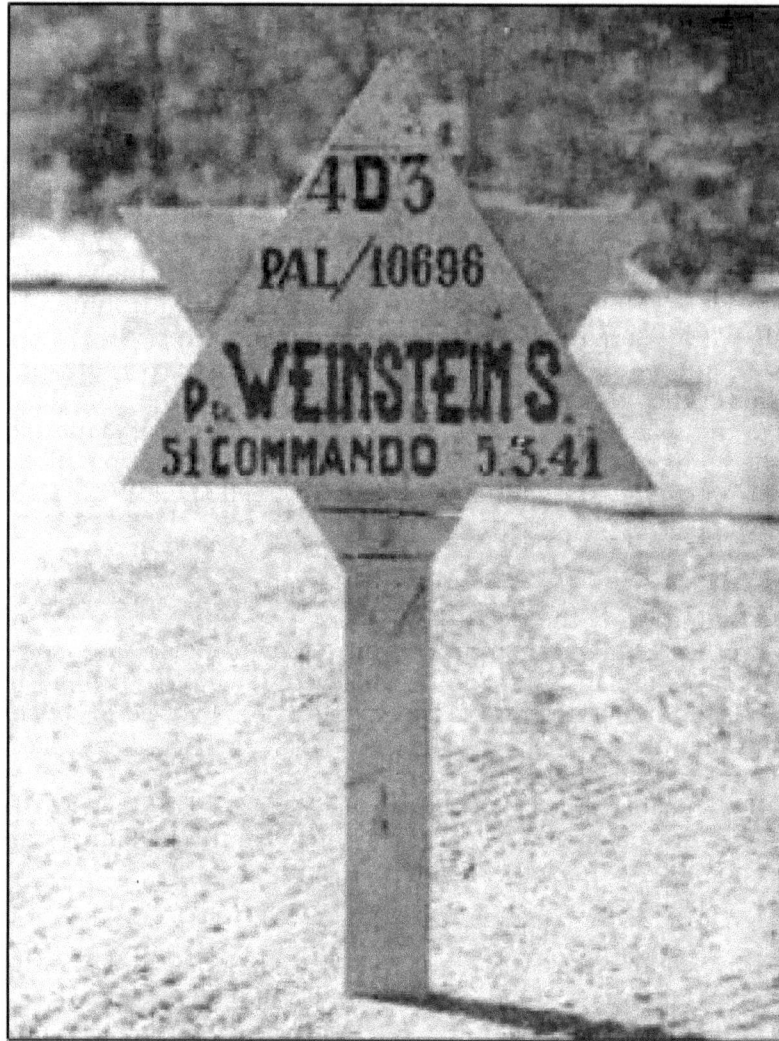

Grave of Shmaryahu Veinshtein

Footnotes:

1. A military unit established within the British army in 1944 and composed mainly of Jews from Palestine. It fought mostly in Italy in 1944 and was disbanded in 1946.
2. Royal Army Service Corps, a part of the British army responsible for transport and supply.
3. Moshe Shertok (later Sharett) (1894-1965), a Zionist leader in British Palestine. Following the establishment of the state of Israel in 1948, he served as foreign minister and later as prime minister.
4. The 51st Commando was formed in 1940 within the British army, from among Jewish and Arab volunteers in Palestine. It was active through 1941, fighting against the Italian forces in Abyssinia (now Ethiopia) and Eritrea. In 1942 the 51st Commando was absorbed into the Middle East Commando, which disbanded later that same year.
5. *Davar (Word)* was a Hebrew-language daily newspaper published in British Palestine from 1925.

[Page 308]

About Gershon Yankelevitz
By Yaacov Levin

Translated from the Hebrew by Dr. Ida Schwarcz
Footnotes Added / Donated by Jeff Deitch

"... And if you find me
Dead on the field
Dead in the snow
Covered with a bit of straw ..."

--- Stanza from a partisan song

In the books *Partizaner Geyen!* by Kaczerginski and *Milhemet HaPartizanim* by Kahanovich, a dramatic battle is described, led by the partisans in the Nacha [Nacza] forest.[1] A son of Braslav [Braslaw], Gershon Yankelevitz, nicknamed Velvel-Gershke, took part in this battle and fell as a hero.

Yankelevitz was born in Braslav in 1910. In the mid-1930s he moved to Lida [about 240 kilometers southwest of Braslav], where he was married and lived until the war. In the summer of 1942 he fled from the [Lida] ghetto to the Nacha forest, where he joined the Kotovsky partisans (Leninsky Komsomol) and was appointed a platoon commander. Thanks to his knowledge of the forest paths, he was often able to break through with his platoon when surrounded by the Germans and White Poles.[2] At the beginning of 1943, he derailed two German trains near Martzikantz [Martsikants].[3] He was instrumental in eliminating a great number of enemies.

Yankelevitz was especially good at sabotaging telephone and telegraph lines. During one such action, on the Martzikantz-Sobakentza [Martsikants-Sobakentsy][4] road, he caught a spy and handed him over to the special division of the platoon.

Kaczerginski's book continues:

... It was September 9, 1943. Grisha [another partisan] tells: "We were on the way to carry out a mission. Suddenly we heard voices: Halt! Halt! We scattered among the bushes with our weapons drawn.

"I looked around: there were 25 soldiers from the [Nazi] garrison that was camped in Martsikants, all armed with automatic rifles. Near me I saw my mother, Gershon Yankelevitz from Braslaw, and Mradin Vintsikovski.[5] Suddenly there was a heavy rain of gunfire. 'No matter what, don't let yourselves be taken alive,' I commanded nervously ..."

Vintsikovski continues telling what happened next: "When Grisha's mother fell, he dashed with his machine gun, upright in the midst of a hail of fire, reached his mother's killer and bashed his face in. To cover Grisha, Yankelevitz and I increased our fire on the enemy, who started to retreat. We began pursuing them, but Yankelevitz was wounded and fell. We also lost sight of Grisha. Where was he?"

Grisha tells: "My dear mother lay there, as if she were smiling at me. She held the rifle close to her body. I took it out of her hands and covered her with twigs and leaves. Afterward I covered Yankelevitz with branches, hid their weapons (lest they fall into enemy hands) and returned to base."

Footnotes:

1.   These refer to *Partizaner Geyen!* (*Partisans on the Move!*), published in Germany in Yiddish in 1947 by Shmerke Kaczerginski, and probably to *Di Milhomeh fun di Yidishe Partizaner in Mizrah-Eyrope* (*The War of the Jewish Partisans in Eastern Europe*) by Moshe Kahanovich, published in Israel in Yiddish in 1954.

2.   The Armia Krajowa (AK), also known as the Polish Home Army: the Polish resistance movement. Sometimes there were skirmishes and bloodshed between the AK partisan groups and the Soviet and Jewish partisan groups, even as each of them separately battled the Nazis.
3.   This might refer to Martsinkantsy, now called Marcinkonys, in Lithuania, about 90 kilometers southwest of Vilna.
4.   This might refer to Sobakentsy, now called Pervomayskaya in Belarus, about 18 kilometers southeast of Martsinkantsy.
5.   The reference is obscure; it could also be read as "and Vintsikovski from Radun."

[Page 309]

About Mikhael (Mendel) Sherman
Son of Rivka and Leib
By Bilha Sherman [His Wife]

Translated from the Hebrew by Dr. Ida Schwarcz
Donated by Jeff Deitch

When the Jews of the Braslav/Braslaw Ghetto were being annihilated, Mikhael escaped from the ghetto and hid in the forests and in the homes of peasants, until after much wandering he was accepted as a partisan in the Zhukov brigade. He took part in operations and inflicted losses of possessions and men on the German enemy.

After the end of the war, toward the end of 1945, he went from Russia to Poland, and came to the Land of Israel with the illegal immigration. He stayed in a kibbutz near Hadera for about a month. Later he volunteered for the Palmach and served in the fifth battalion of the Harel Brigade. Mikhael took part in escorting convoys to Jerusalem, fought the Arabs in the Kastel fortress [1948], and in battles near Ramat Rahel he was seriously wounded and spent about half a year in a hospital in Jerusalem.

As a brave partisan, and after that as a member of the Palmach, he tried with all his strength to combat the malignant disease that [later] befell him, but he wasn't successful.

On May 2, 1979, Mikhael died in Canada. He left his wife, Bilha, and two daughters, Rivka and Leah.

[Page 310]

Sara Shmushkovitz
Daughter of Batia and Leizer Gamush

Translated from the Hebrew by Dr. Ida Schwarcz
Donated by Jeff Deitch

I was born in Braslav [Braslaw], but I don't remember the Braslav of my childhood. My father, Leizer Gamush, left the town when I was three years old. We lived in Novy-Pohost [Novy-Pogost, about 32 kilometers southeast of Braslav], in Miory [about 40 kilometers east of Braslav], and during the years of the war in Ufa in the Urals. I returned to Braslav after World War II in 1946 with my husband Ziske Shmushkovitz and his family. There were very few Jewish families there, mainly survivors of the Holocaust, who by some miracle had escaped the terrible massacre, and a few families that had left Braslav in June 1941 and returned.

I'd heard enthusiastic stories from my husband's family about the beauty of the town, its blue lakes, the pine forests near it and about the thousands of Jews who had lived there. To my sorrow I found huge mass graves in the center of the forest where about 4,500 Jews had been buried, and single graves in the forests and fields where many were murdered when they tried to escape the massacre; and as stated, some tens of families of survivors of the Holocaust [who had returned]. There were additional families from Braslav who'd found safety in cities all over Russia during the war and remained in those places. Sometimes, especially during the summer months, they'd come to Braslav, visit the cemeteries, clean and put the place in order, and return to their homes.

At the beginning of 1976, on the initiative of Chaim Stavski, Shmuel Lubovitz and my family, we decided to organize a reunion. We wrote to all the people from Braslav whose addresses we had and decided to meet in Braslav on July 24. There was a great response. People came from all over Russia: Batia Arklis (Deitch) from Alma Ata; Nisan Konin from Bobruisk; Moshe-Chatzkel Milutin from Kislovodsk; Chaim Stavski from Ufa; Shmuel Lubovitz from Kiev; Chaim Munitz from Vilna; Galya, Chaim and Yehoshua Kanfer from Minsk; my family from Riga; Liuba Maler from Dvinsk [42 kilometers northwest of Braslav; now called Daugavpils]; and more families. Our hosts were of course the few families that still remained in Braslav, among them the families of Shimon Per, Chaim Deitch, Samovar, Shura Milutin, Yisrael Rozenberg and Tisman.

It's hard to describe the joy at this reunion; a meeting of people, friends, neighbors, whose paths had separated more than 35 years before; a meeting of those who'd remained and lived through all the horrors

[Page 311]

of the Holocaust, and those who'd left Braslav in June 1941, before the Germans captured the town.

The first day of the reunion was dedicated to the cemetery. The area was neglected. We collected the dry branches and burned them, we cleaned the paths, we shared memories and united in remembrance of the martyrs. We continued our meeting in the home of Shimon Per. Lunch lasted until late at night. Again and again, each of us related memories and stories of the past.

And then, the parting. Parting from the graves of our dear ones, parting from Braslav, parting from friends with a heavy feeling in our hearts --- would we ever meet again?

"*Di griber*" (the pits): Here the Jews of Braslav and surroundings were murdered

[Page 312]

On the Terrain of Braslav
By Yoel Nimnov

Translated from the Hebrew by Jerrold Landau
Donated by Jeff Deitch

The communal graves are mute
Enveloped in quiet, silent
The living bow their heads
As the past comes before their eyes.

Here are buried thousands
Who were murdered so cruelly
For one and only sin ---
That they were Jews.

Standing silently, in trepidation
Relatives, friends, acquaintances;
Lying here in their eternal rest
Youth, children, and also the elderly.

The ground here is suffused with blood
Tears have been spilled like a river
Is it possible to forget?
How is it that we cannot remember?

May the Nazis be repaid for everything
For the blood, fear, and days of darkness
Your deaths will always be remembered
For all times, from generation to generation.

Never will we forget you
And within our hearts is the hope
That there will be no more war or killing ---
That peace will pervade the world.

This poem was written on June 24-25, 1976, on the day of the gathering in memory of the Jews of Braslav [Braslaw] who were murdered by the Nazis during the years 1941-43. The poem in Hebrew was a free translation from the original in Russian.

[This photo in the memorial book has no caption but shows a memorial gathering at the monument in Braslav. The Hebrew inscription on the monument says, "Here lie more than 4,500 Jews from Braslav and the surrounding region who were cruelly slain by the German murderers / 18 Sivan 1942 / 10 Adar [II] 1943." The dates on the monument correspond to June 3, 1942 and March 17, 1943 (though it should actually be March 19, 1943).]

[Page 313]

In Memory of the Fallen

Translated from Hebrew by Jerrold Landau
Footnote Added / Donated by Jeff Deitch

The war came to an end.
We made families and raised children.
Over grueling paths, we made *aliyah* to the Land of Israel to build a new home.
On the day of need, our children stood to defend the homeland. Not all of them returned
from war.

I Weep over My Son's Passing

To where and for whom
--- Are you, my tears
My weeping
--- For where, and for whom
Do I bring you?

For where and for whom
--- Is my bereavement
Is my loneliness
--- For where, and for whom
Am I bowed down?

For you I bring them
For you I'm bowed down
--- For you, to me
--- I'm bereaved
And my tears
I send forth.

--- A father

[Page 314 = Blank in the original]

[Page 315]

Amitai Kort
Son of Arieh and Esther

He was born on 7 Nisan 5696 [March 30, 1936] in Ramat Gan. His parents, working people, educated their son in the spirit of the workers' movement. From childhood, he was attracted to agriculture and kibbutz life. When he finished his elementary school studies, he wanted to continue at the Kadoorie Agricultural School. But when he considered the feelings of his parents, who were unable to part from their son and send him far away, he agreed to continue his studies at the Shevach School in Tel Aviv. His teachers advised him to dedicate himself to technical studies at a high level, but he didn't agree to this, since he was inspired with the spirit of practical pioneering. At this time he left the HaTzofim movement, to which he'd belonged, and joined the Shomria group of the HaShomer HaTzair movement, which was headquartered in Kibbutz Zikim. He remained with them until he was drafted into the Nahal Brigade of the Israel Defense Forces. In January 1955 he completed Beit Melacha Meshuchlal, as well as his technical studies, so that he could help his kibbutz in the future. In the army he passed a squad commander course, followed by advanced training. When the murderous enemy attacked the archeological convention at Ramat Rahel, he went with his unit to take retaliatory action on 21 Tishrei 5717 (September 26, 1956). He was injured by grenade fragments at the Battle of Husan, but refused to withdraw. He continued to urge his unit to advance, and continued the attack until he was struck by enemy bullets. In one of his letters he'd written, "The true test of our movement is standing in the ranks of defense" --- and he showed his steadfastness when he fell. He was buried in the cemetery at Zikim. On the first anniversary of his death, his parents published a booklet in his memory. Kibbutz Zikim also published a booklet in in memory of him and three other members of the farm who fell. His memory is included in the book *The War of the Paratroopers* by Uri Milstein [published in Hebrew in 1968].

[Page 316]

Chaim Robowitz
Son of Moshe and Shoshana

He was born on 2 Av 5689 [August 8, 1929] in Jerusalem. He studied at the Tachkemoni School. At age 10, he lost his father. He studied labor at the Amal School and began to work in place of his father at the age of 15 at the Egged Company, to relieve the burden on his mother. He then became a driver. He trained in the Gadna military program, enlisting during the War of Independence with a clear understanding of the aims of the war. He participated in actions in Mekor Chaim and others.

He fell with his friends on March 18, 1948 with a convoy taking provisions to Hartuv. They were attacked by 500 ambushers, and fought bravely until the final bullet. He was buried in Sanhedriya in Jerusalem. On 12 Elul 5711 (September 13, 1951), he was transferred to eternal rest on Mount Herzl in Jerusalem.

Zvi (Yehoshua-Heschel) Zeif
Son of Chaim-Abba and Hasia

He was born in Braslav, Vilna District, Poland, in 1912. He studied at yeshiva until the age of 16, but was forced to end his schooling due to his family's difficult circumstances. As the oldest child in the family, he supported his parents. He didn't find satisfaction in work alone, but became active in the HeChalutz chapter in his town, which was in a weakened condition. He put a great deal of effort into the national foundation. He served in the Polish army for two years, and fought in its ranks against the German army in 1939. He was taken prisoner by the Russians and moved from camp to camp in Russia, enduring hunger and cold. When a Polish army was organized in Russia, he left with it, reaching the Land of Israel in 1944. For a year after his arrival in Israel, he worked at Kibbutz Tel Yosef. He was diligent there, but left the farm due to loneliness and became a dairy farmer in Ramat Gan. He joined the Haganah, taking part in the conquest of Tel Litwinsky, Chiria, and other places. He was among the first to go to the front, when the Yarkon was the front line.

He was drafted into the Israel Defense Forces

[Page 317]

as a full recruit, even though he was exempt from the draft due to his vital work as a dairy farmer. He said, "If I, a trained soldier, don't go --- who will go?!" and he proved to be diligent, alert and full of energy. He fulfilled all tasks faithfully and with dedication. He fell during the time of the second truce in Mishlat Midia on 20 Elul 5708 (September 24, 1948) and was buried in Nahalat Yitzhak Cemetery on September 26.

Arieh Levin
Son of Yaacov and Zivia

He was born on 29 Elul 5706 (September 25, 1946) in the Ural Mountains of Russia. He moved with his family to Poland, and set out for Israel at the end of 1958 and early 1959. After a brief time in the Hadassah educational institution of Aliyat HaNoar (Youth Aliya), he went to Kfar-Ruppin, at first through a youth group and later in a boys' class. His father arrived in Israel a few months after his *aliyah*. He was a beloved and good son. The father concerned himself with his son, and his main desire was that he be dedicated and faithful to his nation. Arieh studied in high school, completing his grade 12 studies in Beit-Berl in Tzufit. He was quick to learn, speedily absorbed schoolwork, and became an Israeli youth in all ways. Work wasn't a problem for him, he excelled in diligence, and was happy and open with everyone. He knew how to lose himself in songs, games and dances at the many parties that took place there. He knew not only how to sing and dance but also how to discuss difficult matters without sparing language or compromise, for he had been taught this by the world. He seemed to overcome all difficulties. He joined a good group of people and fit in with his environment. In November 1965 he was drafted into the Israel Defense Forces, serving as an exemplary squad commander at Golani. There were obstacles in his path but he bravely tackled them all, taking part in the Six-Day War [1967] and fighting on the Golan Heights. His unit was prepared to advance at every attack; as the enemy attempted to conquer territory from our land, his unit and others returned fire in kind in a proper fashion. When the day came that his unit broke through the heights, it succeeded in closing accounts with the Syrian enemy and reached Quneitra with the first of the fighters. Throughout the war, the unit had no opportunity to rest during its efforts day and night to achieve all the tasks assigned to it, which it accomplished honorably, and Arieh fulfilled all his roles with excellence throughout the period. When the unit was asked one day to provide choice staff for a special exercise, the best men were selected --- including Arieh. Everything was carried out properly, exceeding expectations. He left the war peacefully, but then came an unexpected incident that felled him. He was severely wounded and lay unconscious for several days. On the morning of 20 Tevet 5728

[Page 318]
(January 21, 1968) he died in the hospital from his wounds. He had carried out his role until the final moments with characteristic dedication and excellence. He was brought to eternal rest at the cemetery in Kfar-Ruppin.

Shmuel Berkman
Son of Halina and Boris

He was born on 15 Adar 5708 (February 26,[1] 1948) in Riga in the Soviet Union. He made *aliyah* to Israel with his parents in 1958. The family settled in Kiryat Yam and later moved to Kiryat Chaim. Shmuel, or as he was called by his parents, Yoneleh, was their firstborn son, their dear, dandled child, to whom they dedicated the best of their time and efforts. His sister was born 11 years after him. After a year of study in Riga, Shmuel completed his elementary education at the Maflusim School in Kiryat Yam. His talents were uncovered there, even though he had no small difficulty in getting used to Hebrew. Shmuel continued to study at the Rodman High School in Kiryat Yam, but it soon became obvious that he tended toward a practical profession. He transferred to the engineering school affiliated with the Technion and was an excellent student. His friend Miki related, "I knew Shmuel from his childhood. When I try to find a constant trait in his personality, what stands out is his drive to advance and succeed. Shmulik came to the engineering school after two years of general high school, without the technical background imparted by a trade school. Because of his aspirations and drive, he quickly excelled in all technical subjects and was named the best student in the class." Shmulik's activities weren't restricted to studies alone. He was a member of the movement for studying and working youth. He took part in regional target shooting contests organized by Gadna and played the accordion. His sister says that he was an ardent patriot. He loved to go on hikes throughout the country, and he was always ready to debate enthusiastically the future of the nation. During the Six-Day War, when his request for an early induction was rejected, he volunteered to work in an ammunition factory.

Shmuel was drafted into the Israel Defense Forces in mid-February 1968 and joined the Ordnance Corps, where he passed a course as a provision technician. He carried out this role throughout his service. Concurrently, Shmulik wrote a book to explain the principles of the Sherman tank cannon and theories of its maintenance, published by the office of the chief ordnance captain. As stated in his certificate of release, "He fulfilled his role in an exemplary fashion and with dedication. He is of a high professional caliber."

Shmuel finished his term of obligatory military service in mid-February 1971. Entering civilian life, he began work at the Soltam enterprise. Along with this, he prepared

[Page 319]

for studies in the faculty of production engineering at the Technion. He was accepted into the Technion, becoming an excellent student. In August 1972 he married his friend Hadassah, who was also a student. They continued their studies, building a family life together. He lived in Neve Shaanan at this time. During the Yom Kippur War [1973], Shmuel joined his unit on the southern front. On 26 Tishrei 5734 (October 22, 1973), during one of the battles that took place between Ismailia and the Great Bitter Lake, his tank was hit by a missile and Shmuel fell. He was brought to eternal rest in the cemetery at Haifa. He left behind a wife, parents and a sister.

Moshe Dayan, then Minister of Defense, wrote in a condolence letter to the family: "Shmuel was a dedicated soldier and faithful friend. He was admired by all who knew him." His beloved sister said of him: "Shmulik was like a father to me. He helped me on my path and was a symbol of modesty. To his friends, he was a leader. Just as I admired him and followed all his orders and requests, so did his friends. But Shmulik was a pleasant leader. He was by nature a warm, family man who honored his parents. He maintained strong relations with our parents and me after getting married, and I was always proud of him. When Shmulik entered the house, the house was full of light." His commander, Lieutenant-Colonel Tuvia, wrote in his memory: "He was thin, with narrow eyes that narrowed even more when he smiled, which he almost always did. He had a well-groomed forelock, and a sly expression --- this is how I first knew Shmulik. His dominant trait was self-assurance. I recall many occasions when we engaged in debate, when Shmulik tried to prove that he understood the issues better. He didn't hesitate to debate with his superiors when he thought that he was right. 'Come, let's wager you're not correct' --- he'd defend himself with theory and argument, seeking to prove that nobody understood the problem better than he did. The debates were always about our work; but if he was proven wrong, he knew how to lose gracefully. At times, I found myself thinking: Where did this young man get the inner strength to debate with such self-assurance officers who were older than him? The pride, self-confidence and talent were so typical of him. With a constant smile on his face, Shmulik drew close the hearts of his friends and brought a cheerful atmosphere to his surroundings, while expressing a healthy sense of humor" (from the memorial book published by the Government of Israel and Ministry of Defense).

Footnote:
1.   February 26 is given in the original, but this doesn't correspond to 15 Adar 5708, which is also given in the original, so one of the dates is presumably off by one day.

[Page 320 = Blank in the original]

[Page 321]

Opsa

Memorial stone for Opsa on Mt. Zion in Jerusalem

[Page 322]

Map of Opsa
(Drawn from memory by Yaacov Aviel)

Translated from the Hebrew by Laia Ben-Dov
Edited / Donated by Jeff Deitch

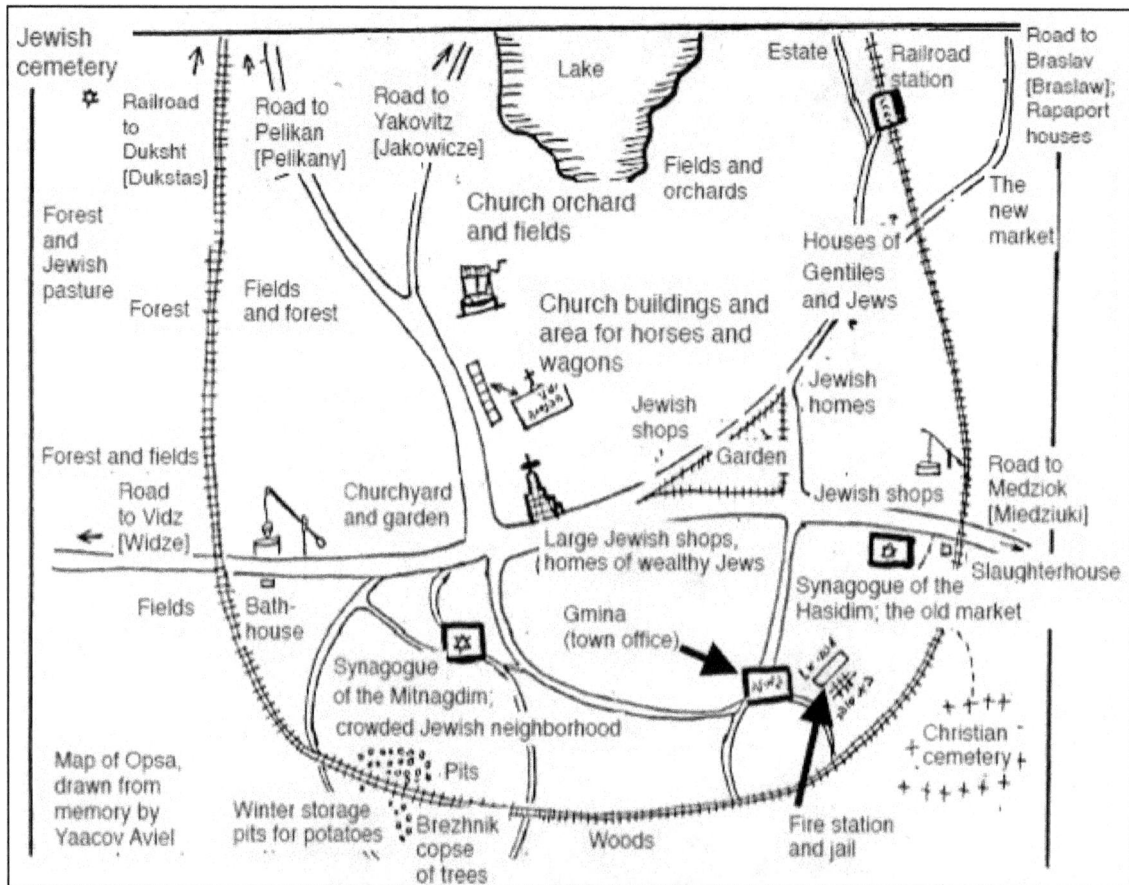

Jewish cemetery

Railroad to Duksht [Dukstas]

Road to Pelikan [Pelikany]

Road to Yakovitz [Jakowicze]

Lake

Estate

Railroad station

Road to Braslav [Braslaw]; Rapaport houses

Forest and Jewish pasture

Forest

Fields and forest

Church orchard and fields

Fields and orchards

The new market

Church buildings and area for horses and wagons

Houses of Gentiles and Jews

Jewish homes

Jewish shops

Garden

Forest and fields

Road to Vidz [Widze]

Churchyard and garden

Jewish shops

Road to Medziok [Miedziuki]

Large Jewish shops, homes of wealthy Jews

Slaughterhouse

Fields

Bath-house

Gmina (town office)

Synagogue of the Hasidim; the old market

Synagogue of the Mitnagdim; crowded Jewish neighborhood

Christian cemetery

Map of Opsa, drawn from memory by Yaacov Aviel

Winter storage pits for potatoes

Pits

Brezhnik copse of trees

Woods

Fire station and jail

[The map contains some inaccuracies, presumably due to a lapse of memory. For
example, the railroad to Duksht actually ran out of Opsa to the west, not the north. The
road to Pelikan went to the west of Opsa, not the north. The road to Vidz went to the
southwest of Opsa, not the west. The road to Medziok went to the southeast
of Opsa, not the east.]

[Page 323]

Yaacov Aviel (Abelevitz)
Son of Esther and Zvi

Translated from the Hebrew by Laia Ben-Dov
(Yiddish Translated by Aaron Krishtalka)
Footnotes Added / Donated by Jeff Deitch

I'll introduce myself.

I wasn't in Europe during the Holocaust, and in my birthplace I wasn't called Aviel.

I'm Yankel Abelevitz from Opsa [18 kilometers southwest of Braslav/Braslaw]. I lived in Opsa until I was 20 years old, and since 1938 I've lived in Israel. Not one member of my large family is alive, except for several cousins on my mother's side [the Rozenberg family]. Of them, the closest to me is Motke [Rozenberg], and it's in his words that I recorded his story of the Holocaust [on pages 339-351 of this memorial book; Motke is also mentioned on page 383].

At the end of the war, in 1945-46, I began to look for my family; I searched among the surviving refugees. I turned to the Jewish Agency's search office and the International Red Cross --- all in vain. They were among the millions who died; may their souls be bound up in the bond of eternal life. Later I thought how good it would be to create a memorial to my family and my town of Opsa, a remembrance of words and feelings for the good Jews I recalled so well --- and I began to write.

Once, in a cemetery [in Israel], alongside the memorials to our loved ones, I met a dear man, a kibbutz member, and he told me that he too was thinking of a written memorial. We joined forces.

All of my sections on Opsa are authentic, but of course from my point of view, sometimes with correct names and sometimes with borrowed names, but all is accurate and exact.

The sections on the Holocaust and the partisans are what I heard from meetings I had with survivors. My cousin Motke told me a lot, and I read and saw a lot on the screen. All were combined into a story [in the second half of this account] and a poem [on page 465 of this memorial book].

As I said, this isn't the testimony of someone who was there; it was written by someone who wasn't there, based on what was told to me by those who were. The bodies of the millions are the real witnesses. Please accept my account as such.

The Time Tunnel

I enter a time tunnel and search for the past. I pace from beginning to end and try to break through the wall of memory, and I begin with my own account of my town. I burrow through my memories, calling up stories of childhood and youth. The dust of years covers it all, the town seems light years away. Does it still even exist!? Despite all my love of the past, I don't want to see you again. I'll describe you in words, in stories unformed by order, continuity or chronology.

[Page 324]

Closing my eyes, I see you in full: streets, people, markets, Gentiles, Jews, loves and arguments, gossip and celebrations, Sabbaths and weekdays mixed together, but everything is clearly seen. Here I see you spread between low hills, orderly and quiet on a Sabbath afternoon, noisy and bustling on weekdays and market days, the image changing with the day, vibrant and alive. I remember people by their names, nicknames both mocking and colorful and I --- one of them --- am standing to one side and recording . . .

Come, we'll take a short stroll through the streets:

We'll begin in the direction of Braslav [to the northeast]. Here you'll see a lot of sky and vegetation, with fields starting to turn green. The road moves ahead between two rows of trees with a thick canopy overhead: the main road to Braslav. Here's the estate of the family of Rapaport, a Jewish landowner with roots in the earth, whose livelihood comes from wagons. It's on his land that the local market, which operates each Monday, is located. The road's paved with cobblestones, and the wagons make a lot of noise on the way to the market. We descend the hill in the direction of the town, cross the railroad tracks and come face to face with the smithies of the Zilber family, Meir and his brother. In their small forge, sparks fly and hammers beat white-hot iron; horseshoes are nailed to the horses' hooves and iron hoops are put on wagon-wheels.

Here the road divides. We turn right and approach the railroad station. On the way, we pass the police station and several Jewish homes. At the railroad station, we see emotional meetings and departures. If you want to continue on, we arrive at a lovely corner --- a very pleasant place, deep in nature. My school was there.

We walk back and make our way to the town center. On the way we pass many houses, large and small, belonging to Gentile families, most of them farmers. This is where Shlomo the wagoner lived with his son Yoske, Yossel Todres and his son Moshe, and a few other Jews. The concentration of Jewish homes really began here, from the home of the *shochet* [ritual slaughterer], [Menachem-Mendel] Liberzon. Opposite lived the two Bikov brothers, Moshe and Gershon. Next door to the house of the *shochet* was the tea-room of Velvel [Levin] and his stout wife, Masha.

This is how the center looked after the [1928] fire:[1]

The Drisviatzki house, a two-story house built of red bricks, and next to it Abrasha Kagan, their son-in-law; both of them owned a *manufaktura*, in the language of the time [meaning shop or workshop, in Polish]. In front of them was the shop of the righteous and respected, thick-bearded Archik; opposite was Feivush the wagon driver and next to him Leizer [Reznik] and his two daughters, Tania and Chasia. In the direction of the town center was the large house of the Levin family, a bakery and a guesthouse. On the corner stood an unfinished structure, just the foundations were laid and it belonged to the Gentile Kondatovitz [Kondatowycz]. He had an artificial leg and was the manager of the railroad station. To the left, in the direction of the village of Medziok [Miedziuki, about 1.5 kilometers southeast of Opsa], was the large shop of the Ulman family, a two-story house with a big courtyard; Ulman was the wealthy man of the town.

Beyond him was the house of the glazier, Chaim-Abba, a short man, "*der kortzer Freitag*" ["the short Friday"], with his sons and daughters. Next to him was the house of his neighbor and eternal opponent in argument, Reb[2] Chaim-Berl Bikov, the father of a dynasty of tailors. Next and on the same side came the bakery of Yisrael, who had a big nose: "Yisrael *der noz*." After him was the home of Zelig the wagon driver, Baruch-Itza [Medziukis] and his crippled daughters, some Gentile houses, a water well, and the synagogue of the Hasidic Jews, the largest in size, with the dignitaries and wealthy of the town. A steep, sandy path led to the Christian cemetery, pine trees whispered in the wind and, on winter nights, so people said, devils went there to dance.

[Page 325]

Some distance from there was the slaughterhouse of Leibel Munitz. A threatening dog, tied with a chain, frightened the children who brought the family chicken for slaughtering for the Sabbath. Behind the slaughterhouse were sandy hills that were crossed by the railroad tracks, forming a deep and formidable ridge. This was the edge of town on this side.

We return to the center. Here we see an unplanted garden in the shape of a triangle, encircled by a low wooden fence. Strong men could pull the planks out of the ground by hand. This was the center of town in the evenings, on the Sabbath and festivals; for gossiping, gambling, spreading rumors and arguing. Around the garden were scattered the shops belonging to the notables of the town; here was the house of Levin, the largest *manufaktura* of them all, owned by Reb Nachum [Levin] and his two homely, single daughters. People said of him that his intelligence was lacking. Next to him were the shops of Zalman Kaiatzki and others. Further along at the rise of the hill was the church, with its crosses glinting in the sun and its bells heard from a distance during festival prayers, funerals and other events. Behind the church was the priest's home, a house with many wings, a large yard and two big dogs. An orchard spread over the ground as far as the lakeshore. Two large, sturdy acacia trees stood upright, with storks nesting in them. Their cry announced the sunset and heralded the coming of spring. A garland of greenery encircled the lake, spotted here and there with estates and villages. If you wish to continue alongside the lake, you can reach the village of Pelikan [Pelikany, about four kilometers west of Opsa]. This is the end of Opsa on this side.

From the center we turn right, toward the road to Vidz [Widze, about 22 kilometers southwest of Opsa]. We sit and rest for a few minutes on the bench outside our house, opposite the church. Now we go down the slope to the left, finding ourselves in the small alleys of the poor: low houses of wood, thatched roofs and impoverished Jews. In local slang, the place was called Srilovka. We pass the house of Leib the tailor, my mother's brother, and continue along the sandy alley and arrive at the synagogue of the Ashkenazim [the Mitnagdim]. We turn right in the direction of the pits, where the potatoes were stored in the ground in winter --- and again we've arrived at the Christian cemetery. We cross the railroad tracks with a jump, and we're passing through a birch grove called the Brezhnik, the lovers' thicket. What didn't people do there! But don't tell who was with whom!

Again we turn left and we reach the local authority building, the Gmina.[3] In the courtyard was the "Sunday" jail, where all the drunks were locked up [after a Saturday night's carousing]. Next to the jail was the fire station, a hall for the orchestra and a netball field.

We return to our house, on the road to Vidz. On the way down the slope stood an ancient acacia tree, completely hollowed out and good for hiding in during games, a water well on the right, the bathhouse and the home of the bath attendant, Reb Mendel. A small stream cut its way across the meadow, and further along the path a bridge was needed. Next to the bridge, a small pool had formed and frogs croaked there at night.

This is Opsa: brick houses in the center, miserable wooden houses in the poor neighborhoods, with smoking chimneys in the winter and the lowing of cattle in the summer. Green hills, a large forest on the horizon, and a blue lake connected to a chain of other lakes. Wagons hitched to tired horses, market days, Sabbath days and the ringing of bells, the Jews hurrying to prayer --- Hasidim and Mitnagdim.[4] Weddings and funerals, grooms and brides, poverty and scarcity, love and disputes --- this is Opsa.

In the winter, the town was clean, fresh and sleepy; bluish smoke rose up from the chimneys of the houses. It was cold outside,

[Page 326]

and cheeks were rosy. Inside the homes, the stove was hot with the cooking of the family meal. The snow lay thick on the ground, and a light wind sent millions of glistening snowflakes whirling. On moonlit nights young scamps would steal a sleigh and fill it with boys and girls. Kisses were exchanged, love blossomed, and people embraced and screamed as the sleigh went down the hill. Then everyone had to push it back up to the hilltop.

In the summer by the lake and on the hills of birch trees, there was talk and yearning for Palestine, as cultural clubs and Zionist groups argued among themselves.

We'll enter the houses again; we'll laugh together and perhaps even cry. Forgive me if I'm not so precise at times. Many years have passed since then --- many years . . .

Fire, Fire

Who doesn't recall the great fire of Opsa [in 1928]?! Everything was reckoned according to this event --- such and such happened before the great fire or, for example, "Do you remember this house before the fire?" and so on. The fire in Opsa was a milestone in the history of the town. That spring Sabbath morning brought calamity. A spark from the dirty chimney of a farmer on the road to Medziok flew into the air and landed on the straw roof of his neighbor, Baruch-Itza. The straw ignited, and the fire destroyed most of the houses in the town.

As is written, there are four causes of damages whose harm is severe --- and fire is one of them.[5]

That same Sabbath morning, the members of the Hasidic synagogue were taking a leisurely stroll; they'd just finished the morning prayers and were on their way home. The synagogues in town had divided Opsa in two: the Hasidim and the Mitnagdim, one against the other. The Hasidim considered themselves the more honorable, the wealthy class. The Mitnagdim were the simple folk, residents of the neighborhood of Srilovka, and they were wagoners, small traders, owners of small shops, shoemakers, tailors, and middlemen of various kinds and the like. There was a barrier between the two groups, even hatred; one side called the other "*Hasidishe kishke*" ["Hasidic tripe"] and was answered in kind with disparaging words. And when there was a potential marriage between the two groups, the issue became very serious. The Hasidim always extended the length of their prayers, and by the time these had finished the Mitnagdim were already halfway through their Sabbath *cholent*.[6]

And so it was on the Sabbath of the catastrophe: The Mitnagdim were already sitting at home eating, while the Hasidim had just begun to leave the synagogue.

I remember this Sabbath as if it were yesterday; I can clearly see pillars of thick, black balls of smoke billowing up through the sloping roof --- and the house was the home of Baruch-Itza.

The people from the Hasidic synagogue stopped walking, they didn't understand what was happening --- was it really a fire?

At that moment, the flames burst out and tongues of fire engulfed the roof and house, spreading wildly from every corner. The spring breeze blew the flames this way and that. The house was soon a mass of flames. In fear and despair, the men from the

[Page 327]

Hasidic synagogue began shouting, "Fire! Fire!"

"There are four causes of damages whose harm is severe --- and fire is one of them." On summer days, a fire could destroy an entire village, down to the foundation. One spark falling on a thatched roof, and the entire village became the fuel --- houses, barns, trees --- nothing would remain.

Communities prepared for catastrophes of this sort. In every town was a fire brigade. In Opsa too there was a fire brigade, located behind the Gmina. There were water-wagons on two wheels, some of them full and some empty, with hoses of fabric and a pump for a crew. To get the water-wagons to the scene of the fire, horses were required. When a fire broke out, our firemen would go into the street and stop any farmers with horses and wagons, take the horses and hitch them to the water-wagon, and gallop quickly to the site of the blaze. The farmers knew that their horses couldn't go very fast, and they objected. This was an opportunity for our firemen to show their speed and determination. In most places, the firemen were young Jewish men.

When a crisis or catastrophe occurred, the church bells would start ringing incessantly. In normal weekday circumstances, as I said, the emergency services would've been ready. But this time it was Jewish homes that were being consumed, and it was the Sabbath and a mealtime --- the men were confused and unprepared.

It was said that one of the men from the synagogue started shouting "Fire!" with his *kapote*[7] fluttering in the wind, and before the church bells started ringing he'd managed to cross the entire town, shouting all the while. The fire spread quickly, igniting every roof, jumping from house to house. Within moments, many houses were ablaze and the town was filled with smoke and the sound of explosions.

The bells rang and rang. Thick smoke covered the sky and people were running around panic-stricken, shouting, pushing wagons filled with belongings and goods, bedding, and other items. No one dared to combat the fire. They only wanted to save as much as they could --- and quickly.

The ringing of the bells was understood by the villagers [outside Opsa]. They came in crowds, some to help and some to loot, but most of them to loot. Bolts of floral-patterned fabric rolled around in the streets, but no one collected them. They rolled loosely among the wheels of the wagons and caught fire. Woe to the eyes, what wealth was rolling around under people's feet! Expensive fabrics that they couldn't afford to buy were rolling in the streets, all they had to do was pick them up and run. And then came the stream of villagers. They came with empty sacks, with wagons waiting outside the town; they filled their sacks and fled through the fields. Even the honorable ones among them were tempted to follow the mob; they looted, emptied their carts and sacks, and returned again and again.

The blaze ran wild; house after house became a fiery torch. My mother held me next to her, and I could see that she was hesitating: to start packing the bedclothes, or wait for a miracle. Our house stood at the edge of town, far from the fire's center.

Suddenly my three brothers arrived --- all firemen --- followed by my father; they all began to pack up everything that they could. First, my mother spread sheets on the floor and piled up all the bedding, pillows and moveable items. She quickly emptied the cupboards, piled up and tied everything, and my brothers loaded the packages onto the wagon and left town at a gallop.

We were flax traders and had a storehouse full of parcels and piles of flax, both processed and raw. Everything was piled onto wagons and moved out of town.

I was appointed to guard over the piled-up belongings, while my father and brothers took away everything that could be moved.

[Page 328]

From the top of the hill, I looked upon the appalling sight of the burning town, at its center the church --- for the church was already engulfed in flames. The entire area, buildings, cowsheds, trees, crosses, everything was wrapped in flames --- and the bells continued to peal out their warning. What wasn't burning? The stained-glass windows with their pictures of saints exploded from the heat; shards of glass flew in all directions, crosses collapsed and torches flamed everywhere.

Suddenly, the bells fell silent. The fire had reached the tall central bell tower. Hundreds of farmers with their sacks of loot froze in place at the sight of the burning crosses; they bent their knees and crossed themselves with shaking hands, crying, "Jesus and Mary, in the name of the Father, the Son and the Holy Ghost, what are we seeing? Oh Mary! What a sight, what a sight!" The Jews also stopped for a moment and wondered, "Will the bell tower fall, or not?!" The tall steeple reared up high into the sky.

People stopped and stared. "Oh Jesus! Mary!" The bells began to fall one by one with loud crashes, making a terrible sound. For a moment all was silent, and the believers held their collective breath and knelt on the ground. The bell tower began to lean to one side. The fire continued to eat away at it. A terrible cry burst from the crowd, they covered their faces in order not to see, and a second later the tower collapsed in flames, in a cloud of fire and smoke. "Woe to the eyes, Jesus, Mary, the end of the world."

All night long, I couldn't sleep. The stars twinkled at me all night, and I was cold. The wind brought clouds of smoke, and tears streamed from my eyes. I sneezed endlessly. The whole town was a mound of flickering embers, and sparks floated here and there and flew up to the heavens.

I awoke at dawn, cold and thirsty, to the sound of birds chirping. My mother was sitting next to me, and she told me that our house was undamaged and my father was there guarding it, to make sure that nothing would be stolen. My brothers were busy driving away the Gentiles and guarding the remaining shops. Later on, wagons began to arrive from Vidz. Our uncles came with bread, milk and candies for me, kissed me on the forehead and disappeared into the remnants of the town.

The Opsa fire brigade

[Page 329]

Mendel the Bath Attendant

Do you remember Mendel? You know --- Mendel *der bader* (bath attendant). If you're from Opsa, you certainly knew him. There were many types of Jews in Opsa, varied and eccentric, wealthy and beggars, those who were satisfied and those whose Sabbath meal was given them in secret by devout ladies who left a basket of food at the entrance of the house before slipping away.

My heart goes out to them, the poor and needy ones, making do with little, lowering their head and mumbling their thanks: "*Gam zu l'tovah*" ["This too is for good"]. Good Jews, making the blessing over a dry slice of bread and refusing all help with a smile. Good Jews, rising early for the morning prayers, sitting quietly in a corner of the synagogue. When they were called to read the Torah, their *aliyah* was "thin" and the blessings they spoke could barely be heard. The weekdays were for toil and labor, Sabbath afternoon was for sleeping, and the time between the afternoon and evening prayers was for reading from the Book of Psalms.

Special, different Jews. In the winter they wore sheepskin hats and faded fur coats, rubbing smelly resin oil on their boots for protection, or wrapping the boots in rags . . . all winter long they kept warm by the stove, and their main food was potatoes, prepared 10 different ways. On market days they sought their livelihood among the Gentiles, and on holidays they looked like wealthy men, going to the synagogue dressed in holiday finery, some to gossip and some to pray. They danced at weddings, drank vodka and burst into song: "When the Messiah comes, what'll we eat --- when the Messiah comes, what'll we drink?" And all the replies were heard only in song.

The women were busy at home, cooking and baking bread; pregnancy followed pregnancy, and then they looked after the children --- many children. A sweater made of coarse wool covered half of a woman's body, including the head, and a sigh accompanied every story or piece of gossip.

There were many people like these in Opsa. One of them was Mendel the bath attendant. There were a few "Mendels" in Opsa, each one with his own occupation and status. This Mendel was the stoker and operated the public bathhouse, which was used mostly for ritual bathing by the members of the Ashkenazi synagogue [the Mitnagdim] and Jews whose homes were nearby.

Mendel served the men and his wife, Yenta, the women. The bathhouse was located on the bank of a stream that crossed the road to Vidz; a creaking wooden bridge passed over the stream. The water next to the bridge formed a large pool covered entirely by plants. Frogs croaked in the pool all summer long, providing an evening melody.

The bathhouse was built of wooden beams, very low and covered with a roof of straw that had turned green with age. The windows were small and the door was low, to prevent the escape of heat. Bathhouses were only built on the shore of a stream or a lake --- who could carry for long distances the huge amounts of water that were needed?

Every Thursday of every week, Mendel would rise before dawn and start to carry buckets of water from the stream: Thursdays for men and Fridays for women. It wasn't easy; he had to fill two gigantic wooden barrels with water, fill the ritual bath, and bring and prepare wood to heat the water. This was Mendel's hardest day.

A massive stove sat in the middle of the bathing room, and low benches lined the walls. The fire heated rounded stones, arranged inside the stove, to an intense heat. Mendel would take the heated stones

[Page 330]

and throw them into the water barrels until the water was almost boiling. Some of the stones he threw in the *mikvah* [ritual bath], so that the water there would be warm. The floor of the bathing room had coarse grooves for the water to drain out, first to the outside and then to the pool next to the bridge. On one side of the bathing room was a raised platform, with stairs up to the ceiling; it was called a *pol* ["floor" in Polish, here meaning a raised platform]. This place, where the lashings in steam were done, showed the quality of the bathhouse.

From the side of the entrance and behind the stove, steps led down to the *mikvah*. A narrow, dark corridor at the entrance, wooden benches for removing boots, nails in the walls for hanging clothes, and a few sparsely scattered sacks underfoot --- this was the entire bathhouse.

Let's go back inside and see what Mendel does on Thursday, his difficult day.

Before dawn, he's already on his feet. In winter, the cold outside penetrates the bones --- you should know that most of his clients come on winter days, because in the summer they can go to the lake outside and bathing there costs nothing. Mendel has a sheepskin coat; it's faded and full of oil stains, but this *peltz* [thick coat of fur or sheepskin] is long and covers about three-quarters of his body, leaving his legs free. When Mendel puts on his coat, his soul is happy; he takes the rope that's always in his pocket, passes it twice around his hips, tightens it firmly and then he's ready. He just has to take the food that Yenta prepared for him --- and he's on his way.

Mendel arrives at the bathhouse, takes the buckets and begins to fill the huge barrels. His fingers are bent like hooks, hardened and callused from the heavy loads he's carried for years. When he's finished filling the barrels about halfway, he lights the stove. The wood has already been arranged carefully so that air can penetrate between the stacks and it'll burn with a nice flame. There are thick branches of birch trees and a few thin branches, so that the fire can catch hold quickly. Mendel sees that the fire's going well, so he takes a break. Sitting opposite the fire, he begins to doze --- but G-d forbid he should fall asleep. He has to get up immediately and continue. There are still many more buckets of water to bring to the barrels, and the *mikvah* too must be prepared. By the time he finishes filling the water, the sun's already high above the treetops; daylight penetrates the bathhouse, the cold abates and it's possible to take off the *peltz*. He says a short prayer without his *tallit* [prayer shawl] or *tefillin* [phylacteries]. He places a low stool opposite the fire; first he makes a blessing and then he takes a bite of the bread and food that Yenta has cooked. He's opposite the fire and it's good for him here, but his eyes are closing and there's still a long time to wait until the bath is ready.

Bathing begins only in the afternoon. Mendel finishes eating and sees that the fire's hot and well arranged. The stones aren't yet hot enough. Mendel lies on the warm floor and dozes off.

There are some days when he wants to go home to snatch a longer sleep --- that would be very good, but it's also dangerous because there's a risk of the bathhouse catching fire, Heaven forbid. A tiny spark is all it takes, when the stove's very hot and the entire structure's built of dry wood . . . Such a catastrophe doesn't bear thinking about. Oy! Oy! He knows of several bathhouses that went up in flames. Heaven forbid!

The sun's now hanging in the center of the sky, and everything seems secure; Mendel goes home for a few hours of good sleep. Mendel lived in a side room attached to the house of my grandfather Mottel and my uncle Leib. My grandfather was known during his life and afterward as very welcoming to guests, and he took Mendel under his roof. The house stood on the lower part of the road to Vidz. It consisted wholly of additions, patches and attachments of walls to walls, under one large roof

[Page 331]

of straw that was green with age. The windows were low and the panes were broken and covered with newspaper; the doors creaked, and a narrow pathway led to the entrance. Mendel's "apartment" consisted of one room that contained a kitchen, a wide bed, a table made of coarse wood and two stools on either side. Mendel also had an "inventory" of livestock --- a big, wild she-goat with large horns and a constant appetite. She was tied with a short rope in the corner of the passageway, with just enough room to allow access to the doors leading to my grandfather Mottel's door and to Mendel's door . . . close by was a ladder leaning against the wall, with a top that reached the attic, where hay for the goat was stored.

There were a couple of reasons for keeping this animal. First of all, she gave milk and that was good for the health, there was nothing better for babies when they had a cough. People would buy milk from Yenta by the cup, paying more than for cows' milk. Second, the goat kept bothersome people from coming to the door and asking, "So, Reb Mendel, can you come to the bathhouse already?" They had to repeat their request a number of times, because Mendel was sleepy and didn't hear well. He'd wake and ask, "Whose are you?" because he didn't know all of the town's young scamps, and the answer was usually "I'm the son of so and so, who's the son of so and so." Mendel's reply was usually based on the fact that he knew who among the people paid generously and who gave only a few small coins. Once someone was seen going to the bathhouse, other people would follow and then it was impossible to refuse them all. Those who came first had the advantage --- why? They had no competition, you could get undressed and there were nails available on which to hang your clothes. You could hum music or sing songs, no one bothered you, and there was plenty of hot water and pails available. And most important, the place was warmed from all the hot steam and there were brooms on the *pol*.

The job of the goat was to scare the children and keep them from coming to Mendel's house: Beware, anyone who dared to approach this wild animal. There were no such adventurers, and if anyone dared to try they were sure to receive a good butt in the behind and a tear in their trousers.

Looking back from a great distance in time and space, I sense how woebegone the place was, how hard it was to make a living, and how impoverished life was. But it was good in our eyes, and we looked to escapades and pleasures, because laughing was healthy and there was nothing better for the body than a steam-bath. And who didn't want to be among the first? The steam rose up like incense with each spray of water on the hot stones, and you could lie on the *pol*, hit all parts of your body with the broom, and encourage yourself by singing prayers. You came early --- no one took your soap, your towel didn't "disappear" or other such pleasantries . . .

Mendel was quick-tempered and disliked those were privileged. For him it was a waste of hot water and steam, and he didn't want first-comers. But how could I refuse my father, who said to me, "*Nu, Yankeleh, gib a shprung tsu Mendlen --- nor freg im! Nu, shoin?*" ["So, Yankeleh, hop over to Mendel's --- just ask him! So, get going."] So Reb Mendel loosened the rope tied to the goat, and our Yankeleh received a good butt on the backside (it shouldn't happen to us!) and returned home crying. On the Sabbath, coming out of the synagogue, my father, of blessed memory, whispered in Mendel's ear, "Did you know your goat attacked my Yankeleh and ruined his trousers?" Mendel replied, "And did I tell him to come to my house? What's this? Am I doing a circumcision or distributing cakes?"

I swore to avenge my disgrace. I took some children with me to help, and away we went. The first thing we had to do was anger the goat so that she'd be ready to attack all comers. Then one of the gang climbed

[Page 332]

into the attic through a hole in the roof, and from there descended the ladder to the rope-end tied to the goat, to release her. Quietly we went out, and then all of us banged on the window in panic shouting, "Mendel, the bathhouse is on fire, it's burning, burning, burning!" We hid behind the fence and yelled, "Great G-d! The bathhouse is burning and he's asleep here in the house and not guarding it! Good Jews, help! Help!" With one hand Mendel grabbed his coat, and with the other he buttoned up his trousers and rushed into the passage --- straight onto the horns of the maddened goat. Oh, what a *zetz* [whack] he got; it should happen to all haters of Israel. And behold --- the bathhouse stood unharmed in its entirety, with just a small wisp of smoke curling up from its chimney; all was in order. Now the children burst into laughter and began to run --- with Mendel after them, chasing and cursing, throwing sticks and whatever came to hand; may his curses fall on the heads of all the Gentiles, *pfui* [ugh], all the unclean scoundrels, and may their names be erased from history!

On Fridays, the ladies' day, Yenta guarded the entrance. She sat on a stool, wrapped in a coarse headdress, with a downcast look so that no one would say an evil eye had harmed a pious woman who'd gone to the *mikvah*. Modesty became those who went to the *mikvah*. Yenta sat there with coins in her lap, not even knowing who went past her.

What did Mendel do on the other four days of the week? People said that he slept, warmed himself next to the stove, prepared wood for heating, and recited Psalms in the synagogue.

On the Sabbath, he rested. He rubbed his boots with resin oil, put on his "four corners" [*tallit katan* or small *tallit*, a four-cornered undergarment with ritual fringes attached to the corners] and his *kapote,* and sat inside the synagogue near the exit. Just once a year, he was called to the Torah --- on the holiday of Simchat Torah.[8] Then the sexton would call out, "Stand up, Reb Menachem-Mendel."

I've No Photograph of My Father

I invited an artist to come, and I said to him: "Take your brushes and paint, and make for me a portrait of my father."

"Where's your father?" asked the artist. I replied, "He went to Heaven in the smoke of the crematoria. I'll describe him to you in words, while you use your brush."

And this is what I said: "Draw me a Jew about 60 years old, a father and grandfather; I haven't decided yet if he'll wear a *yarmulke* [skullcap] or a black, peaked cap. Draw a beard for him, not too long, spreading a little to the sides, brown with a sprinkling of gray hairs. If there's a *yarmulke*, then emphasize the large, bald forehead. Draw him with *payot* [sidelocks] turning gray, his hair at the back cut short.

"Give him a thin nose, a little long with a slight hump. A typical Jewish nose. Draw warm brown eyes with small lashes; they too had some gray hairs. Show him seated and give him a confident gaze, one that inspires belief in the observer and confidence in the listener. Give him a bit of worry in the corners of his eyes, but not fear; give his eyes an expression of comfort and ease with other people, and an understanding of the soul.

"Now draw a mustache that merges with the beard and completes it. Draw him in his holiday attire, in a white shirt without a necktie and with a *surdus* [long coat] open at the back to the hips. The coat is gray, not black, because black was the color of the Hasidim and he belonged to the Mitnagdim. His trousers are black, with the bottoms tucked inside the boots. The boots were originally brown, but they've been oiled with resin to keep out water and dampness in winter, so their color has darkened. Scatter patches of brown and black here and there. I'll wait until you finish, and then we'll continue.

[Page 333]

"Now we'll fill in the background.

"Behind him a sandy pathway leads to the synagogue, and on the sides are low, wooden houses with straw roofs and low entrances, a high threshold and small windows. Artist, please put piles of firewood against the wall. Draw a yard with a stable in it, with the head of a cow or a horse peeking out. Add a little green to the roof, some moss that's grown here and there --- but not too much! No, there are no goats on the roof.

"Drink your coffee, keep listening, and we'll continue.

"I want a few more touches of your brush on the beard. You know, the beard isn't just an emblem of Judaism, it's also a symbol of status."

A survivor told me that my father had [later] cut off his beard so that he could cross from one ghetto to another after becoming separated from my mother.[9] This enabled him to move freely without harassment, you understand, but what mental torture he suffered because of it, what humiliation.

"What did you say? No, Heaven forbid! Don't paint him without the beard or with protruding cheekbones, a humiliated look, ashamed or downcast eyes. No! Not bowed down, not fearful, not weak. Finish up the portrait with balanced colors and a relaxed figure, a forgiving smile and a calm mood --- this is how I see my father."

The Cursed Beet (My Father's Death)

The smell in the freight car was unbearable. People vomited from lack of air, and the vomit added to the stench. It was terribly overcrowded. People were lying next to each other, their bodies touching.

Curled up, they lay in disorder. They couldn't change places or move, lest someone grab the space left empty. They couldn't remember exactly when they'd been loaded onto these freight cars on the way to "work," to toil in factories or on the roads, so they'd been told.

It was already the third day of the journey. At night, it was cold. The packed-together bodies gave off warmth. At first, people complained and quarreled over every centimeter, over parcels of ownerless clothing and muddy shoes, and some were hit in the face unintentionally over a scrap of onion or a cigarette butt.

The women screamed, the men hushed them. At night sleep overtook them, they organized into groups, spoke or remained silent --- Jews imprisoned in freight cars, on the way to an unknown destination.

They stopped briefly at a station on the way. In an unknown country, with a language little understood. Running terrified, some to relieve themselves behind the trees, some to get a hot cup of tea and buy a morsel of food, some to pray, and some to exchange a glance with a relative from another freight car.

At the station, farmers waited for the trains: to buy and sell gold for bread, watches for onions, jewelry for flour, shoes for an egg. They bought and traded quickly, pressed by time and the threats of the accompanying soldiers.

On the third day of the journey, stations along the line had an additional job. The dead had to be taken out of the freight cars and laid at the side of the tracks or under the trees. There was no time for a ritual burial. The dead were covered quickly with earth, and the Kaddish was recited in the freight cars.

My father was in one of the freight cars.

[Page 334]

Something came to him in a strange way: the melodies of Yom Kippur [the Day of Atonement]. Indeed, he was quite used to them when standing before the Holy Ark in the synagogue of the town. The melodies, the musical flourishes, the words came to him --- but why suddenly Yom Kippur?! True, he'd eaten nothing for two days. He wasn't hungry, just weak. He bent over a little, leaning against the side of the freight car and --- as is fitting when serving the Holy One, blessed be He --- he covered his face with his hands and sang in a whisper:

"All vows, personal oaths, pledges and undertakings . . ."[10]

What a sacred melody, and it comes from the heart.

"Vows shall not be considered vows, and pledges not pledges . . ."

What did I promise and not fulfill? What do I owe, and to whom? Only to Thee, O Lord. True, he thought, I lied to the German soldiers. Three times he repeated, "All vows . . ." repeated and recited.

He buried his face in his hands and lowered his head within the collar of his coat. What shame! How will I stand before the Holy Ark with a trimmed beard?[11] What villain had taken hold of his beard with one hand and scissors in the other, cut and pulled, and now he looks like a laughingstock, the pain lasted many days and the embarrassment still hasn't left him. On the third day of the journey, he went out into the station huddled in his coat, bent over, hurrying --- what could he buy, what could he pay with? In his pockets, nothing remained. He stood before the farmer, measuring him with a look, spreading his arms to the side as if to say, "I've got nothing," pointing to the bread in the other's hand --- I've got nothing to give you for it.

The farmer's eyes fell on the ring on my father's hand, and the farmer touched his hand and helped my father to remove it. Then the bargaining began --- a full loaf of bread for the ring --- or half a loaf and a beet. The beet looked good, fresh, with damp earth still clinging to it. Ah --- of course, a beet. When we reach our destination, we can cook some good soup, *borscht*, there's nothing better than hot *borscht*.

For a moment, he thought he'd bargained well. But without the wedding ring on his finger, he felt naked. His maddened thoughts began to turn toward his wife. The children --- where were they all? Oh, Lord of mercy and forgiveness, pardon this foolish deal. Now he'd have to hide his hand. How foolish it had been to take off the ring.

He shoved the beet in among his belongings and began nibbling at the bread. Again the music of Yom Kippur came to him. The tragic story of the 10 Martyrs,[12] of those forced into conversion and martyrdom. He knew most of the Yom Kippur prayers by heart.

With a screeching of brakes and the banging of freight car into freight car, the train came to a halt. Evening was already approaching. Who knew what time it was? All the watches had been sold long ago to pay for bread. In a flash, with an ear-splitting screech, the doors were flung open. Soldiers standing before them began to hurry people out of the freight cars --- "Forward! Forward! *Schnell! Schnell!*" ["Quickly! Quickly!"]

Pushed by a wave of people, pushed and pushing.

What's the hurry? What awaits us at the end of this road? People see buildings, chimneys, surely a factory, and think let's get there already, so that we can rest a bit.

He was pushed, and his parcel of clothes fell from his hand, along with the beet.

"Oy, oy, oy, the hot *borscht*, the soup . . ."

He bent down to pick it up but missed and knelt on his knees, his hand in the mud.

The melodies of the Yom Kippur prayers didn't leave him for a minute . . .

--- "But we bow . . ."[13]

[Page 335]

The cursed beet, after hitting a foot it rolled away . . .

He was kicked and pushed, he fell flat on the ground . . .

". . . in worship . . ."

His face touched the muddy earth.

". . . and thank. . ."

He was stepped on. His face sank into the mud.

". . . the Supreme King of Kings . . ."

They rolled him to the side of the road. His face to the sky --- he saw a great, blinding light. He looked . . .

". . . the Holy One, blessed be He . . ."

He breathed no more.[14]

Partisans

Go there, they told me, in the Kozian forest [stretching south and east of Opsa] you'll find partisans from your area --- but be careful!

I slipped away, and after walking all morning I found myself a hiding-place and waited for night to fall.[15] Before it was dark, I got up and left my hiding-place and began to approach the edges of the forest. The smell of cooking reached me, and my appetite awoke at full strength. I hastened my steps until I was almost running. Ahead of me at the horizon of the forest, I could see a pale blue wisp of smoke rising against the dark sky. I saw a flickering dim light coming from the silhouette of a house --- I made my way there.

With caution, I began to approach the house. I circled around it and moved closer, circled it again and approached the lighted window. With hesitation and great fear, I knocked three times.

There was no response, no sign of life. I knocked again. Suddenly a face appeared in the window pane; the face of a woman --- or was it an evil spirit? Her hair was wild, partly covering her face, partly covering her naked breasts --- she pressed her nose against the glass and took a long look at me; I couldn't take my eyes off her face. Suddenly she screamed, "Pavlo, is it you?" [Then, in Polish] "In the name of the Father, the Son and the Holy Ghost." She touched her hand, her forehead, her chin and shoulders and then disappeared inside.

A few fearful moments passed like a lifetime, it seemed to me I waited there for hours --- until I heard a door creak on its hinges. There in front of me stood Yoske [Shneider] from Opsa. I recognized him immediately. His small black beard framed his pale face, his eyes burned from his black brows, he was slightly stooped and had prominent cheekbones, with eyes piercing like knives and a German rifle on his shoulder. *"Du bist Itzke?"* ["Are you Itzke?"]. He held the door with his free hand. I approached him, and we went inside.

A soft, murky light fell on the walls of the room. The dim light from the kerosene lamp created long shadows. This was the house of poor farmers, made of rough-hewn logs and a floor of pressed earth. A sharp odor of urine rose from the floor, with the smell of sweaty feet. It was one large room with a long table in the center and wooden benches around it. On one side stood two wooden beds, with coats and sheepskins thrown on them. In the far corner stood a huge stove, and from the darkened corner I heard a faint rustling and the murmuring voice of the woman from the window, who

[Page 336]
continued to call, "Pavlo, is that you?"

Yoske sat me at the table and called to two other people, who came out of the shadows. They presented themselves: Chaim from Kozian [Koziany, 28 kilometers south of Opsa] and Moshke from Postav [Postawy, 22 kilometers south of Koziany]. While I told them about the hardships of my journey and the ghetto, Yoske gave me a bowl of potato soup and a quarter-loaf of bread. We sat for more than an hour in conversation that went on into the night. The other two went out to sleep in the stable; Yoske and I remained. The fire in the stove went out, but the coals continued to whisper.

"You must be wondering who the woman is and why she called you Pavlo?" I didn't know Yoske Shneider, the son of Hertzel the shoemaker, all that well. His father had been a courageous man. I heard that the father had been badly tortured by the Gentiles of Opsa at the beginning of the war and they'd killed him. Yoske, his only son, a strong-fisted man, was quick as a knife and bitter in his soul; he'd fled to the partisans. Here in the forest, I'd found him. He spoke quietly in a deep voice, spoke and stopped, playing with the German bayonet in his hand. "We've been in this area since the spring, sometimes in this house, sometimes in the forests and the swamps. Our contact with the rest of the partisans is infrequent and only when Jews are there."

"I'll tell you about the woman," he said. "Pavlo was her husband. They had a son as well, about 15 or 16 years old. One day the boy went to the market and never returned. It happened before we arrived here. Pavlo went looking for him for an entire week, but returned on foot without his son or the horse and wagon. After that, he'd get up every morning and wander around the field or next to the road. Early one morning, we heard a deafening noise in the distance. We understood immediately that German tanks were approaching. We rushed into the forest, and from the dense undergrowth we witnessed a shocking sight. Three tanks approached, one in the middle and one on either side. They were moving slowly, keeping a lookout, stopping for a moment and then advancing. They left deep black furrows in the ground like a plow, throwing clods of fresh earth to either side; trees were bent over and never straightened --- they continued toward the house.

"Pavlo was in the cabbage patch, gathering the heads into a pile. It was the end of summer, and the colorful heads of cabbage stood out against the black earth. The tanks continued toward the cabbage patch, straight toward the place where Pavlo was working. He saw the threat and began running toward the tanks, waving his hands and shouting, 'Please, have pity, turn aside --- they're all I have.'

"The tanks continued straight toward him. At a distance of just a few meters, from the turret of the leading tank appeared a German soldier with a pistol. He fired a shot that was barely heard, and Pavlo fell face down in the muddy earth between the rows of cabbages. Our breathing stopped. The soldier who shot him waved his hand and disappeared inside his tank, and we saw how the tank alongside it drove over Pavlo's body and the rows of cabbage. We've seen so many horrors, Itzke, believe me --- our hearts are made of stone. The others wanted to attack the tanks with bottles of kerosene that they had, but I stopped them. The entire spectacle took just a few minutes. The tank rolled over Pavlo's body and plowed two furrows in the cabbage patch. Body parts and blood were mixed into the muddy earth: here a hand, there a leg, his head. Clods of earth glistened with blood --- the tanks just kept moving.

"Six furrows remained in the field, and parts of Pavlo's body were scattered in two of them. I told you I'd seen horrors. We came running up, and we began to vomit and cry out. When she heard us, the woman came out of the house. She approached the cabbage patch, not knowing what had happened. She got a little nearer and found herself standing next to Pavlo's severed head.

[Page 337]
"After that, she lost her mind. Now she calls everyone Pavlo. The partisans come to the house and they lie with her without shame --- to her deranged mind, everyone's Pavlo."

A Meeting
While the smoke of the crematoria in Europe was abundant with the smell of burning flesh, I was in the blue uniform of His Majesty's Forces.

The renowned German commander [Rommel] got as far as the gates of the land of the Nile. On the edge of the desert, the Allied army blocked him, pitting steel against steel and man against man. The headquarters of my unit --- the Middle East Command --- was moved out of striking distance, deep into the heart of Africa, to central Kenya. Later, witnesses to the horrors that had taken place in Europe began to arrive. Trains of Polish refugees began to pass through to the location of their settlement in Africa [sic].

Searching for my family, I found myself in a refugee camp --- who had seen anything, who had heard? Opsa, Vidz, Braslav --- it was Jews I was searching for, Jews. The refugees were old before their time, some were mentally unbalanced, some were missing limbs. The women cooked sweet potatoes on burners of stones in the blazing sun. Inside, in the cabins, the men were lying down, remnants of men.

Suddenly, I heard [in Polish], "Isn't that young Abelevitz?" I answered, "May the great Name of the Creator of the universe be magnified and sanctified." The man gaped at me: "Don't you recognize me? I was your teacher. Sit here. I know what you're looking for --- but you won't find it." Sunk in thought, he paused and said: "It's a world that's been destroyed --- but I'll tell you."

"The Germans retreated and the Red Army broke through, determined to be the first to reach Berlin. The Oder River, with a bridge across it, was the Germans' last line of fortification. It was necessary to cross the river and prevent the Germans from blowing up the bridge. A suicide mission. The forward Russian command called for volunteers and hundreds of Jewish men volunteered, many of them from our area --- Opsa, yes, Vidz --- maybe your brothers as well." He paused, looked at me and rolled a cigarette. He lit it, drew on it, and continued: "It was war!" [said in Polish]. "What a massacre! The commander, a real hero, tall and straight, gathered them together before dawn. *Nu, Yidn, lomir geyn! Shema Yisroel!* [Come on, Jews, let's go! Hear, O Israel!].

"The night wrapped the river in deep darkness. On the other side were the Germans, dug in and armed. Above our heads the Russian artillery began to rain down a ferocious bombardment. They really gave it to them, the sons of bitches, to break them.

"The commander ordered --- 'To the river!' Some swam, some floated with logs. Hell on earth! Do you hear me, *Pan* [Mr.] Abelevitz, hell on earth, men in hell! Above us shellfire, below us rifle-fire. The Germans shooting nonstop, bullets hitting the water like rain, shellfire creating pillars of flame, and you could see lines of men swallowed up by the river. It drives you mad --- hell, I said, hell. You stand facing the river, and you see bodies of heroes being dragged by the current --- are they alive or dead?

"And here comes a second wave of soldiers diving into the river. They're pushing a few bundles of wood in front of them, on top of which are their rifles and ammunition. Meanwhile, the Germans are raining fire and cracking open the bundles, which explode with a deafening noise and sink to the bottom together with our men.

[Page 338]

"And so it was with a third wave, and the river filled with bodies. Already it's dawn and the red sky illuminates the river and the wild waves, and all the men are dead.

"You know, *Pan* Abelevitz, the Germans allowed the Russian tanks to drive onto the bridge and then blew up the bridge. My G-d! Flames shot up from the bridge and then it collapsed, taking to the bottom all the men and all the tanks. How they flew into the air --- pieces of men and pieces of steel --- and then sank to the depths.

"Silence blanketed the river. The waves grew calm. The sun was already at the edge of the sky, illuminating the river --- and it was red. Tens of bodies floated there. May the Name of the Creator of the world and its destroyer be magnified and sanctified."

A tired morning slowly awoke. From the distance, warning sirens could be heard from Berlin. Once more, the artillery had received permission to speak.

View of Opsa

Footnotes:

1. There was a major fire in Opsa in the spring of 1928. Here Mr. Aviel is describing Opsa after the fire. Later in his account, he describes Opsa during the fire.
2. Reb is an honorific term, something like an exalted "Mr."
3. The Polish term for municipality or township, the smallest unit of regional government in Poland. In other words, a town hall.
4. The Hasidim and Mitnagdim were two important branches within Ashkenazi Judaism. Hasidism (Pietism) emerged in the 1700s in what's now western Ukraine as a movement for spiritual revival, spreading through Eastern Europe. Besides knowledge and observance of the Torah and Talmud, it emphasized immediate religious experience. By the late 1700s, the Mitnagdim (Opponents) came to refer to traditionalist Ashkenazi Jews who opposed Hasidic Judaism, emphasizing intensive study of the Talmud. Opposition to Hasidism was centered in Lithuania, particularly in Vilna.
5. The reference to the four causes of damages is Bava Kamma, Chapter 1, Mishnah 1.
6. Among East European Jews, the traditional stew prepared on Friday and kept hot overnight for Saturday.
7. A *kapote* was a long, thin black topcoat worn by Hasidic men.

8. The holiday marking the conclusion of the annual cycle of readings of the Torah in the synagogue and the start of a new cycle, falling in September or October.

9. Mr. Aviel's parents are also mentioned in Motke Rozenberg's account on page 341 of this memorial book.

10. This line and the line below in quotation marks are from the Kol Nidre prayer, recited in the synagogue at the start of the evening service on Yom Kippur.

11. Leviticus 19:27: "Ye shall not round the corners of your heads, neither shalt thou mar the corners of thy beard."

12. The account of the 10 rabbis who were martyred in the period after the destruction of the Second Temple in 70 A.D., read by Ashkenazi Jews on Yom Kippur.

13. This and the lines below in quotation marks are from the Aleinu Leshabeach prayer, which has a prominent place in the Yom Kippur prayers and in daily prayers.

14. This moving description is the author's poetic conception of his father's fate, since the author noted at the start of his account that he'd left for Palestine in 1938, there were no living witnesses to his father's death, and things the author heard after the war had been combined into a story. Based on Mr. Aviel's page of testimony, given at Yad Vashem in 1999 --- some years after this memorial book was published --- it seems likely that his parents (Abba-Zvi-Hirsh and Esther), whether separately or together, were (1) shot at Ponar outside Vilna on April 5, 1943 or (2) killed in the massacres of the Braslav Ghetto on June 3-5, 1942 or the "Opsa" Ghetto in Braslav on March 19, 1943, if they didn't perish from privation in the interim. Another possibility, based on the *Encyclopedia of Camps and Ghettos 1933-1945*, Volume II-B (2012), is that (3) one or both of the parents died in the liquidation of the remaining Jews in Opsa --- which is thought to have taken place sometime between September 1942 and the year-end. In this liquidation, the women, children, elderly and others left behind in Opsa as unfit for work were killed in Opsa.

15. The narrator in this section on partisans isn't Mr. Aviel, who lived in Palestine from 1938, nor does it seem to be his cousin Motke Rozenberg. Later in this section the narrator is called Itzke, but in the original Hebrew account his relationship to Mr. Aviel and Mr. Rozenberg isn't mentioned.

[Page 339]

Mordechai (Motke) Rozenberg
Son of Leib and Chaya-Pesia

Translated from the Hebrew by Laia Ben-Dov
Footnotes Added / Donated by Jeff Deitch

We sat and talked; Motke spoke, and I wrote. He spoke slowly with pauses, sometimes in a trembling voice, sometimes continuously. He described the smallest details as if they'd happened yesterday, as if the wound was still fresh. He touched parts of his body while speaking, to illustrate his words.

We sat one evening and then more evenings until the late hours. He spoke, and I wrote in the first person. After that, I added descriptions and conditions because his language was poor at describing shades of emphasis and pain. "It was a war on survival, a war on life itself."

He spoke, I wrote.

--- *Yaacov Aviel [one of the editors of this memorial book, whose own account is on pages 323-338 of this memorial book]*

I was a 10-year-old boy when the war broke out. I knew how to play hide and seek and how to play cops and robbers. The game of war was taught to me by life, and the game of hide and seek became a gamble taken on life.

I remember Opsa [18 kilometers southwest of Braslav/Braslaw], the houses, the streets; and how many streets were there? I recall the boys who were my age and those who were older than me. I ran around barefoot on summer days, alone or following the older boys, to the lake or in the forest.

I remember our house at the foot of the hill at the approach to the road to Vidz [Widze, about 22 kilometers southwest of Opsa], not far from the hill of the church. Our house was built of rough boards, with a slanted roof of straw. It had many wings, connected to each other so that tenants could be taken in, both to get rent and out of pity for poor Jews. Where would they live, if not in Grandfather Mottel's house? I'm called Mottel after my grandfather, of blessed memory, a G-d-fearing man who welcomed guests in his lifetime (and after his death it was written on his tombstone). He was a poor tailor, wandering in the surrounding villages, carrying on his back his workshop, in which were contained an iron, scissors and a book of psalms.

My grandmother Hinda, short, wrinkled and bent, was very shy. All her life she worried about their livelihood, food for the Sabbath, and clothing for the children. My father, Leib, followed in grandfather's footsteps. He too was a tailor, but he left the villages, bought a sewing machine and worked at home. I had adult brothers, Gershon and Yisrael, and sisters: Sima and the twins Sorka and Hindka, who were born after me [and apparently another sister, Tzila, mentioned later in this account].

[Page 340]

I was a lad when the war came.

What, in fact, was war? At first, it was thousands of miles away from us and distant as the news; without radio, without a newspaper. Why were they fighting, and how?

So they said: A war broke out --- and I was a boy of 10.

One day, a rumor was passed along: Soldiers were approaching Opsa. And they arrived [in late June 1941]. First it was the Russians, and after that, the Germans. There was a tank battle on the road from Opsa to Vidz. We heard the thunder of artillery from a distance. I didn't see anything.

Before the Germans entered, the Gentiles of Opsa established a kind of police force, a "militia" in the local language. The Gentiles chose the [Jewish] family Drisviatzki's building as militia headquarters. This was a nice two-story building, made of red brick. All the troubles began from this building. Then I began to understand what war was.

One day, I saw something but didn't understand what was happening, or why:

They began to gather all the Jews into the market square. They brought many men and told them to fall on their faces, to lie down and get up, to crawl, to eat grass. They kicked them and beat them. All of this was ordered by the local militia. They grabbed Moshe-Aharon [Donde] the butcher and tied him with a rope to a horse; my G-d, somebody mounted the horse and urged it to run --- and Moshe-Aharon was tied to it by the rope around his neck. They passed through the streets and he was dragged, screaming. At the end they threw him to the side of the road, seriously injured. I don't know if he lived or died.

The Germans spread throughout the town and the surrounding area, and they began to rule with cruelty. At night they entered the houses and took the strong men for hard labor, to repair the road or the railroad. The women they took for cleaning jobs or the preparation of food.

After a number of days, they conducted a parade of the Jews. All of the Jews reported when their name was called. Among them was Leibke Rapaport, a deaf mute. The Germans thought that he was just pretending to be deaf and beat him viciously, as he screamed in terror. The procession was accompanied throughout by beatings and humiliations.

Before the Germans had arrived, during the time of the Soviets, all of the craftsmen had been nationalized: tailors, shoemakers, to help the [Soviet] army. They'd called this a "cartel" and Hertzel Shneider, the shoemaker, had been made the manager.

When the Russians withdrew and the Germans entered, the cartel continued but the managers changed. Hertzel the Jew was removed, and the Gentile Matush [Matusz] was appointed in his place. This Gentile had held a grudge against Hertzel for years, due to professional competition. He was jealous of Hertzel, who was the more successful, and the main thing: Hertzel was a Jew. After his appointment, Matush spread rumors that Hertzel was keeping a stash of hides and this should be punished. Hertzel was a courageous man with strength in his hands, and he didn't want to run away when they came to interrogate him about the stash. I heard that they tortured him terribly, and finally they killed him.

More memories from this time when the armies changed:

Shmuel, the son of Moshe the tailor, was a Komsomolets[1] for the Russians and was accepted by them. When the Germans entered, the men of the militia grabbed him, dragged him through the streets, tortured him, and finally they killed him. In the interval between the Russian retreat and the German entry, the local militia was all-powerful. The Gentile Bludzhin appointed himself commandant of the militia and ruled over everything, deciding life, death or torture. There was no law and no judge --- fear ruled the Jews of Opsa. This Bludzhin began to rape Jewish girls one after another, and as his arrogance increased he also began to rape Christian girls. A local

[Page 341]

teacher denounced him; the Germans arrested him and put him in the prison in Braslav. Shamed by the loss of his power, he hanged himself there. What joy the Jews felt! David Levin, the head of the Judenrat [Jewish Council] in Opsa, didn't hide his happiness and that of all the Jews. On the day of the funeral, they all shut themselves in their houses. Only Shmuel's mother bravely went out into the street, approached Bludzhin's mother and showed her pain and joy as one.

The memories stay with me, year after year. Memories that shocked the soul of an 11-year-old boy. I remember a secret love between Mira, daughter of the tailor Moshe Bikov, and a young Gentile. The Gentile became enraged after he was rejected by Mira's parents, Jews, and he decided to get revenge. He obtained a hand grenade and threw it at their window. The grenade hit the lintel, bounced back and exploded on the road, opposite him, and he lost his leg.

For half a year [roughly September 1941 to March 1942], the Jews of Opsa were left alone. Special prayers were conducted in the synagogues that there wouldn't be killings --- because killings in the vicinity had been heard of. A rumor spread that the Jews of Opsa would be moved to a ghetto in Braslav or Vidz. In Vidz the guards were Lithuanians, murderers, Jew-haters, Shaulists,[2] and this sowed fear among the Jews of Opsa. Whoever was able to pay a bribe in gold was sent to Braslav.[3] The lot fell to my family to travel to Vidz --- we had no bribe to give. They [the militia] told us that they'd already prepared burial pits for us and this would be our end. We saw long lines of Jewish wagons on the way to Vidz, Slobodka, Yaisi [Jaisi] and more [sic].[4] The Gentiles supplied wagons and horses to transport the Jews. We too were put into these wagons. At the exit from Opsa, we crossed the railroad tracks, and passengers began to flee in the direction of the forest. They shot at them, but didn't harm them. A local policeman approached me and asked my father to let me flee. "He's a boy," he said "it's a pity." But I didn't agree to run away, I remained with the family. In this way, we arrived in the convoy at Vidz. This ghetto was crowded and dirty; all the Jews from the [nearby] villages were concentrated there. The Germans immediately began to take out the men for labor. We no longer had any link to Opsa. We heard only that there they'd also concentrated the [remaining] Jews in a ghetto. My uncle, Abba-Zvi [Abelevitz], traveled with us to Vidz, and my aunt Esther remained in Opsa.[5] My uncle wanted very much to return to Opsa to be with his family. He was a religious man; he had a beard and a Jewish appearance. People would know immediately that he was a Jew and turn him in. He absolutely didn't want to remove his beard; his soul pained him and he couldn't decide what to do. I volunteered to take my uncle to Opsa on foot --- I was just a lad.

Toward evening we went out of the ghetto in Vidz, and under cover of night we stole through the fields and villages. Toward morning, we reached Opsa. The ghetto [there] was around my uncle's house.[6] They all were gathered there. After a few days of rest, I returned to Vidz. This time I took courage and walked on the road. Lithuanians stopped me and realized that I was a Jew. But an old Gentile pleaded for my life, and they left me alone.

I returned to the ghetto in Vidz through the same break in the fence that I'd come out of, and along the paths I recognized. I learned that my brother Gershka [Gershon] and my sisters Tzila and Sara had already been taken away.

I began to dare to go out to the villages on the roads I knew, to bring food, exchange valuables for food, buy or beg. I was tall and blond like a Gentile. I grew up too soon.

The Germans began increasingly to search for men for labor. For some reason I, in my innocence, thought I was still a boy and they wouldn't take me. One day, I was sitting with another boy my age on the steps of the synagogue. Lithuanians and Germans came to us, spoke among themselves and decided to take us too for labor. Nothing helped, they wouldn't leave us alone. They loaded all of us on wagons and took us to the town of Dogalishok [Daugeliskis, about 22 kilometers west of Vidz and in Lithuania]. From there,

[Page 342]
they put us on railroad cars and took us to a labor camp.

This was a camp for hard labor. We built a road between Kovno and Vilna (Miligan[7]). I also found my father there. The Jews were forced to work hard from first light until darkness. Food was very scarce. I knew that my mother remained alone with the twins [back in the ghetto], and I was determined to flee to her. I told father of my decision, and he didn't object. Disappearing from the work place, I hid and jumped on a freight train that was on the way to Vilna [about 104 kilometers southwest of Miligan and in Lithuania]. This was my first encounter with a large, unknown city. People had told me that at a labor camp in Vilna there were Jews with work permits and they were centralized in an area called Kalish [Kailis labor camp].[8] I always turned to the elderly for help, and this time too an elderly Gentile assisted me and brought me to the gate of the camp. At the gate I began to speak Yiddish, and they let me enter. They gave me food, but didn't want to leave me because of the danger. They told me how to get to the large ghetto in Vilna. I entered the ghetto. I explained that I wanted to reach my mother in Sventzion [Svencionys, about 80 kilometers northeast of Vilna and in Lithuania].[9] They investigated, asking a lot of questions. In the end, they decided to join me to a transport of children whose parents were dead. In the ghetto there was no food, and I looked for a way to reach my mother. While searching, I found a man from Braslav --- Yerachmiel Milutin.

I and Milutin already knew each other.[10] When I'd been in the Vidz Ghetto, I'd gone to Opsa as a messenger. I got there on the day they were preparing an Aktion. At the last minute, the Germans postponed carrying it out, and we began to plan an escape back to Vidz. At that time, it was thought that Vidz was safer. Milutin [had] succeeded in fleeing the Aktion in Braslav [presumably the one on June 3-5, 1942], and he knew that the group was planning an escape to Vidz and I was the leader. Milutin had joined the group and I, the 12-year-old lad, had led adult men. I knew all the paths and hiding places, the best times to go, and thus I'd succeeded in leading a group of Jewish refugees from Opsa to Vidz. Milutin owed me his life.

Since then, Milutin had arrived in the Vilna Ghetto and been made responsible for a group of laborers with work permits. When I met him [now, in Vilna], he immediately turned to me and promised me safe passage. In his hands were permits for 13 workers. He waited for me near the gate, and there I joined his group. Milutin gave me his permit, putting himself in danger by traveling without a permit. The train was full of Ukrainians. On the way, they searched us [but] I knew that Milutin had succeeded in disappearing. I got off the train in Sventzion. In the ghetto, they didn't believe my story and thought that I'd just fled from an Aktion. I stayed with my mother and began, as I had in Vidz, to wander in the villages, to bring food, to sell. Occasionally I was stopped, but people always had pity on me; "a boy," they said, and they let me go.

Then the Germans wanted to concentrate larger numbers of Jews and decided to eliminate the Sventzion Ghetto. Part of the population would go to the Vilna Ghetto and part to Kovno. Later it became clear that the Jews of the Vilna Ghetto hadn't wanted to receive more refugees, they didn't want a large number. They didn't reveal to us that traveling to Kovno meant Ponar [Ponary] and this was the end of the road.[11]

We had the good fortune that our entire family arrived at the Vilna Ghetto. I was 15 years old.

In the Vilna Ghetto, I was taken for full-time work. My brother Gershon was also in Vilna. From there, he traveled to Panevezh [Panevezys, about 130 kilometers northwest of Vilna and in Lithuania], and after that I didn't see him anymore. My father worked in a bakery so as to bring home a loaf of bread hidden between his clothes. The young ones, myself among them, looked for ways to go out of the ghetto and bring back food. There were four gates, where they did body searches. Despite this I succeeded in smuggling flour, which I hid on my body. I was thin, and they didn't feel it in my clothes.

[Page 343]

My place of work was the railroad. My sisters worked in a place called Prubanek [Porubanek, a suburb of Vilna where there was a labor camp]. Again, the Germans began to gather people and take them out of the ghetto --- in other words, Aktions --- with all kinds of lies. One day, the guards came and took us. They gathered men and women also from other places of work. My sisters were there too. They gathered us together and began to force us into railroad cars. There was a great uproar. People broke out and began to run away. I fled too, jumping into a garden next to the train. The Gentiles yelled at me, "Yid, Yid, Jew, Jew!" I got over the fence and ran. I couldn't stay outside at night, from fear that I'd be caught, so I returned to the ghetto. There they arrested all of the escapees and told us, "Keep calm. Everything will be all right." My parents were there. They suggested that my parents redeem me with a bribe, gold or silver, but my parents had none; all of their requests to free me failed. Again we were loaded on trucks and brought back to the train. We thought the end had come, that they'd send us to Ponar. Instead, they transported us to Estonia.

Estonia, labor camp, Vaivara.[112] A new place, another language, but the same barbed-wire fence, the same guards, the same starving faces, the same lowered eyes and bent back, the same fear of tomorrow, the same conversations about bread, soup and labor.

In preparation for our arrival, they evacuated the Russian prisoners and settled us in their place.

Already the next morning, they divided us into work groups, and . . . forward march! To lay train tracks from morning until evening, hard labor. Our food was a slice of bread and some soup. The crowdedness bothered us; it was impossible to move without stepping on someone. The huts were built without any toilets. Everything was improvised and temporary, built for prisoners. The Latvian and Estonian guards would hit us for every moment of rest, without reason or mercy.

I, Motke, a champion escaper, began here too to plan an escape. I was blond like a Gentile and could easily move among them --- until they caught me once. It was evening, and in the camp they had a roll call. They called names and a number of Jews were missing --- myself among them. The punishment for escape was 25 lashes. One could live with this, I decided, and continued with the escapes. After a few months, they moved us again to another camp, named Narva.[113] There I found my father, of blessed memory. We'd been apart and now we were reunited; I parted from my sisters and met my father. The bonds of affection between father and son can't be expressed; there was no time to talk with him. The conditions in this camp were the very worst. The work was digging, during the winter season, with little clothing and very little food. The guards were murderers and beat us very cruelly. My father fell ill, and they took him to a small hospital. I would come from work and bring him a piece of bread that I'd hidden. I watched him lying there. Once he said a few words and once he just looked at me, lying there with his eyes fixed on the ceiling, as if he was trying to penetrate it and ask for mercy.

One day I came, and they wouldn't let me in. "Your father died," they said. Leaning on the gate, I grabbed the cold iron with both hands, tears wetting my face. I held onto the iron gate, not letting go. There's no G-d, there's not! You're cursed, cursed! I beat the iron with my fists until I finally sensed the pain and blood streamed from my hands. "Cursed, cursed . . . murderers."

I was pursued by the memory of my father, yellow in the face, looking at the ceiling. Again I told myself to live. To live, escape. I wouldn't remain there.

Rumors came that the Russians were advancing, and so now we dug trenches against tanks. There was a scrap

[Page 344]

of hope for survival. We labored in the fields, deep in the earth. I decided: This is the place and time to escape.

There was a strange man among us: a prophet, a rabbi, a genius, crazy --- who knows?

Each day, he gave another sermon. Sometimes according to the weekly Torah portion, sometimes just a sermon. He said that he remembered by heart all of the weekly portions and their order. Sometimes he preached words of reprimand, or prophecy. How did he sermonize on an empty stomach?! How did he stand up to curses and degradations and speak his piece, in Hebrew or in Yiddish?! The guards would point a finger at their heads and leave him alone. Everyone talked about flour, potatoes; he sermonized from hidden books, from the Holy Zohar.[114] Those who knew him said that he was a rabbi, eminent in Torah, but his mind had grown confused. G-d forbid! Thus he went around among the huts or next to the fence, sermonizing and chastising, comforting and proving. Thus he announced that the End of Days had arrived and we should prepare for the coming of the Messiah. Next to the food storeroom, women were standing in line for their daily portion. They spoke there in whispers about "this woman" and "that woman." One of them said she'd seen "such and such a woman" meeting secretly with "the man with the buttons." "Take care when you're around her, she's a foul, disgusting person." Another said, "That piece of filth, screwing an official --- she should die of cholera!" The prophet came and rebuked her. She threw a shoe at him, but he forgave her. Then he approached me. "Moteleh," he said, "today's a lucky day. The war of Gog and Magog is coming to an end. Whoever tries his luck today will succeed."

"Today," I said in my heart, "is my day. I'll run away."

To the clothes of everyone who'd fled and been caught, they'd attached a red patch in front and in back. I already had a patch like this. They guarded me especially. "Let them guard," I thought.

On the way to work, outside the city, we passed through the streets. We'd walk in the shade, in large groups. Ahead of time, I prepared other clothes without the patch, and while walking I put a shirt on my body and waited until we came to those streets. This was the signal. There was a crucified Jesus, "Yoshke Pandera,"[115] hanging there ashamed. I slipped into a side street, ran down another street, made another turn and here, opposite me, was a small house --- maybe here, I thought. I pushed inside. A lone woman sat next to a sewing machine. I spoke Russian and she answered me. "Yes, Jew, I'm ready to help you, but Germans come here to mend clothes --- what'll I do with you?" She took me to the attic. Up there were two Russian orphans; I joined them, becoming like one of them. The Germans who visited the house didn't know me and didn't touch the Russians. I became a helper in the house with household jobs, errands and the like. Since the woman was alone, she was glad to have me as a friend. A number of times she hinted to me that I'd do well to convert to Christianity and come with her to be baptized in church, because I couldn't live as a Jew.

One day, a Gentile came and asked me to go with him. He took me to the local church. There, inside it, there was no war and no fear of the Germans. The organ played notes of prayer and the believers crossed themselves together with the priest and sang the prayers with him. I sat among them and felt safe. After this visit, they began to press me to convert. One Sunday morning, I came down from the attic. In the room I found a bathtub with warm water and the seamstress waiting for me. "Get undressed," she said, "and get in the bathtub." I stood there without moving. I didn't understand the meaning

[Page 345]

of her words. "Wash yourself," she repeated, "and after that, we'll go to church." She approached me and started to nervously unbutton my clothes. I was a grown lad, and all kinds of thoughts began to dance in my brain. She left the room, and I got into the bathtub. After that, I went with them to church. The thoughts pursued me, and on the way I began to plan an escape. While everyone was on their knees and looking at Jesus the savior, I quietly snuck out into the hallway. There, the coats and boots of the congregation were hanging. I took some, put them on and slipped into the street.

I knew that we were near the Russian border, and I knew the direction. Very quickly, I found myself outside the city. I hitched a ride in a sleigh. The Gentile passed along the road where the Jews were digging. They saw me and grew quiet --- here's Moteleh, running away again. I was afraid to say anything. The Gentile took me to his village, which was on the Russian border. I worked in his house at all kinds of jobs, and he gave me food and a place to sleep. I stayed there for a few days. Again, I progressed by hitching rides. Each time, I got closer to the Russian border. I traveled or walked from village to village, passing as a laborer or a Russian orphan. Unfortunately my Russian wasn't that good, and Estonians who spoke Russian realized that

I was a Jew. One evening a woman gave me some food; I sat at the table and ate. Suddenly she pulled out a pistol, aimed it at me and said, "You're a Jew, right? Don't move!" Germans were going around the village, and I was struck with fear. She stood by the window that looked into the street, and it seemed she was waiting for the Germans to pass by, so that she could turn me over to them. The food stuck in my throat; cold sweat covered my body. "Oy, Moteleh," I said to myself, "you got this far, only to fail at the hands of a woman with a pistol?" I'd already seen others like her, and I wasn't afraid. In a flash, I dove outside and got to the street. Walking quickly through the village street, I saw an open door and entered. An old woman sat near the stove, not sensing I was there. I hid under a bed, with my face toward the door. I pulled a bit on the blankets and held my breath. The woman from whom I'd fled was shouting, "A Jew ran away from here. A Jew, a Jew here!" I saw them enter and start looking for me. They asked the old woman. "I've been here the whole time," she said, "and I didn't see anyone come in." They stood up to leave but then felt the blanket that was pulled down to the floor. They got me to my feet and dragged me out. I received many blows and to every question I answered, "I'm not a Jew. I'm a Russian, a Russian." I was without my coat, which I'd left where I was eating; it was cold outside. I trembled from the cold and the beatings, and blood poured down my face. They decided to take me in their wagon to Narva camp, and if they found I wasn't a Jew --- they'd free me. If a Jew --- they'd kill me.

We set out on the road in a horse-drawn wagon. I was dripping with blood and trembling from cold and fear. In the wagon, a young Christian woman sat next to me, and she began to whisper to the German to let me go, to run away. "What'll you do to him, he's only a boy," she said to the guard. She hugged him, took the end of the blanket and wiped the blood off my face. The German put both of his feet on me, so that he knew where I was and I couldn't escape. We traveled like this for half a day, and then night fell. After it got dark, the girl covered me with the blanket, and when she sensed the German guard was asleep, she put her hand under the blanket. I felt a warm hand touching my body. "You're a Jew, right?" she said. A strange warmth passed through me; I hadn't felt the hand of a woman like this. "Quiet!" she said. "I'll give a signal, and you run away." When we passed the area of the trenches that the Jews had dug at the city entrance, she embraced the German. To me, she gave a kick. A dive, and I was out of the wagon. I ran through the streets, to life or death. When somebody ran and there were Germans in the area, they'd start shooting. Learned in escapes, I ran in twists and turns

[Page 346]

and zigzags along the streets and alleys. Where now? Here's the main street, at a crossroad. Here's the cross, and not far from there, the seamstress, the house where they'd hid me. I approached the cross. Next to it knelt a few believers, a man and two women. A thought came to me. I knelt too and began to cross myself.

I lowered my head so that they wouldn't see my face, which was covered with blood. A deep, long breath and a look to the sides. Are they chasing me or not?! There above, the crucified one was looking at me with pity. "Yoshke," I said to him, "do something for me if you care about me; protect me with your cunning smile now, or I'll send you to *kibinimat* [a Russian word for hell]." On the way to the seamstress --- there was a German roadblock. "You there! Halt!" I replied, in Russian: "My mother's sick and I'm running to call a doctor. Quick! Urgent, very urgent!" "*Jawohl* [Yes] --- run, run!" Another few houses, and I was at the door of the seamstress's house. At the sight of my face, she began to cry and took care of my wounds. She fed me and laid me down to sleep. At the side of the house there was an empty structure, and she decided to put me there. She too was afraid of the Germans. Again I returned to routine. Again to errands, helping in the house and the like. One day, I was on an errand to sharpen some scissors, and behind me was the German officer Paniker [Peiniger],[16] riding his bicycle. I was on a bridge. He cut me off and pulled out a pistol. I saw no way to escape. He held me until a German car came that took me to the camp, and he followed.

In the camp, Paniker began interrogations and torture. They said about him that he'd worked in the circus and was alert and daring, with a head for strategy. He looked pleased with himself; finally, he personally had caught the great escaper, Moteleh. Now, he smiled to himself, he'd make a spectacle of me. It was morning, and the prisoners were at work outside the camp. He had time to torment me; we'd see about the champion escaper.

He dragged me to the roof of the building. "Jump!" he shouted. "No!" I answered. "Jump!" he shouted again. I said, "I'm a Jew and my religion forbids me to commit suicide. If you want to kill me, do it, like you killed my father, but to jump, to commit suicide, no. No."

He left me alone and tried a different strategy, more painful, and in his opinion, murderous. He called the Jew appointed in the camp, Diller [the camp elder], to come to his side, and he began to prepare a gallows for me. I was thrown in the corner of the roof and saw how Herr Paniker prepared the hanging for me. First of all he checked the strength of the rope, the knot, the post, the loop, the height of the chair and the entire apparatus. All of this for me, and I was breathing with difficulty.

The circus man leaned over me and told me that everything was ready. He put me up on the chair; he held me because I was trembling all over and my knees had failed. He wound the rope around my neck. I was pushed, I fell and lay flat, but with my hands I stopped the weight of the fall --- I was breathing.

He leaned over me and checked if my elbow was broken. He stopped for a moment: "It isn't broken, amazing, how? What'll we do to this Jew?" He decided on one more try. He called Diller and said, "Look, if he comes out alive this time too, we'll give him his life as a gift. [But] let's find something to kill him; I'm tired of playing with him." Having said this to Diller, he tied my hands behind me. These were the rules and we must follow the rules, like a faithful German. The end of the second hanging I don't remember. I fell with a terrible blow and fainted. When I awoke, Diller stood over me and sprayed me in the face, saying "Du lebst, du lebst" ["You live, you live"].

They left me alone until evening. They brought me into the hut, threw a blanket over me --- and I fell asleep. In the evening, when

[Page 347]

everyone came back from work, Paniker took a roll call. He stood everyone in a semicircle, with me in the middle. He said to me, "And now, you'll shout: 'Hurra, Moteleh ist da!' ['Hurrah, Moteleh's here!'], shout and run around, around the rows." After this, he read the verdict: "Twenty-five lashes, done to he who runs away." I heard the verdict and saw them approaching to whip me. "One, two," each lash cut my flesh. "Three, four, five," and through a fog I heard: "Six, seven." My strength gave out. I yelled, "Shema Yisrael!"[17] and fainted --- and they continued to cut my covered flesh.

From the field they dragged me, tied with ropes, to an empty room, and Paniker ordered them to leave me there for two days without food; if I came out alive --- my life would be a gift. He finished instructing them and gave me over to the Jew who was responsible.

I lay on the floor of the room and cried. It was very cold, and all of my bones ached. Behind the wall were Russian prisoners, who heard my cries. They'd heard the story of the lashes. During the night, they took apart some of the boards [between the rooms] and found me still alive. They untied the ropes, gave me food, and then tied me up again. Then they closed up the boards, and it was impossible to see that anything had happened.

The next day, Herr Paniker came to visit --- was I alive or dead? "The lad's alive? How is it possible?" Again during the night they returned and untied the ropes, gave me food, tied me up again, and closed up the boards.

After two days, Paniker came again and found me alive. For the Germans, a pledge was a pledge. I was freed and left to do work inside the camp, not outside.

All of this happened, it turned out, toward the end of the war. The Russians broke through the German front and were rushing forward. In the camps there was now hope for life and a great awakening. One day they told me that I was being transferred to Vaivara camp, the work camps were being centralized. Paniker's deputy, who was appointed to do the transfer, told me this on the way, in the train. He said that I shouldn't run away, because he feared punishment; he gave me chocolate and food. He brought me to the camp and I was pushed into the officers' room, where they awaited me. When they saw me, they burst into thunderous laughter. They'd thought some strong man would appear, and here before them stood a hungry, beaten lad. They knew I'd survived without food for two days --- how had this lad come out alive? This was the escaper-hero? They laughed and laughed. In the room were their bloodhounds, which were trained to knock down a man and tear out his throat. They stopped the dogs and kept laughing at me. I was known for my many escapes. "You aren't afraid of us?" they asked. "*Ich habe hunger*" ["I'm hungry"], I mumbled. I was thrown outside into the camp. In the huts I met my sisters; they'd heard about me and found me. Again, the family was united.

Here too, rumors were heard about the Russian advance and the German withdrawal. As they retreated, they moved the camps closer to Germany and eliminated as many as they could --- so that there'd be fewer Jews to feed and care for. Because I was guarded especially, I was made Paniker's personal servant; he was responsible for two of the camps. I served him food, cleaned his hut, polished his boots and did all kinds of errands inside the camp. Apparently he liked me, and he began to show a human attitude toward me; the Germans appreciated bravery and initiative. One morning they began to put Jews into trucks, maybe to be moved, maybe to be killed. When the Germans suffered a defeat, they'd liquidate 10% of those in the camp. With frightful German precision, they'd count the prisoners, calculate

[Page 348]

the percentage, choose those to be sacrificed and take them to destruction. During one such Aktion, I hid under the hut. They found me and returned me to the ranks for the roll call. Dr. Bodmann,[18] the German, would walk with a little stick in his hand, counting and pointing, deciding who'd survive for the time being, making a sign with his stick, and the doomed would be taken to the truck.

Here he was, passing before me, his eyes searching --- who's next in line? Enough? They already had 10%. The rows breathed in relief, but wait! Now they're signaling that one's missing from the correct number. And again, they're taking me. All eyes observe the drama, but there's no voice, tear or sigh. I'd already been in a truck like this once, now here I am again. Then here comes Paniker at a run, yelling, "Where's my servant?" He pulled me forcefully from the truck and shouted, "You lazy loafer, quick, go and polish my boots." This time, he gave me my life as a gift. Those put in the truck were murdered.

Over time, the entire Vaivara camp was moved to Sonda camp, a short distance on foot [sic].[19] This camp was like most of the camps of Jews. Our neighbors were Russian prisoners of war; they and we worked in the forest. During this time, I became friendly with a Georgian prisoner; he'd bring me a bit of food, because they were given more. These prisoners knew everything that was happening at the front, and they told me that the Russians were advancing rapidly and the Germans were retreating. He'd heard that they were going to kill all the Jews, he even knew when and where this would happen. There was great cooperation between us; both of us wanted to escape together. We set an appointed time and place for our escape.

But when the day came, many guards arrived at our camp and it was impossible to flee. On that day, they began to load us onto a train that entered the camp. The Georgian friend saw everything on the other side of the fence, and he parted from me in tears.

From the train, they brought us to the port. We were put in the bowels of a ship, and we sailed away. On the ship, I again met my sisters. It was terribly crowded there; people were befouled and vomited, and the dead were thrown into the sea. After several days we arrived in Stutthof, near Gdansk.[20] It was easy to see that the Germans were fleeing and the Russians were advancing and pursuing them.

In Stutthof camp, things were very difficult; it was terribly crowded. Here were concentrated all the survivors of the camps in Europe. There was little food and no regular work. We were a burden on the Germans, and they wanted to be rid of us. In this camp there were cruel, embittered Polish guards. They were the *kapos* there, because whoever didn't want to be a *kapo* was excluded.[21] Severe decrees were issued. It was forbidden for people to be found in the blocks during daylight hours. It was very cold, there was very little clothing, and food --- there was none. For entire days, I went around with an empty stomach. I was always hungry, day and night, and when a man is hungry, thought and logic don't operate. One wants food at any price, even at the cost of life. I was gathering cigarettes in a pail at great risk, and selling them to the cook for bread or a potato. One day, they announced that they'd give half a loaf of bread to whoever came to the gate. Something in my heart told me this was a deception, they wanted to grab us and send us to death. So I didn't approach the gate. Later I learned that those who were caught had been sent to the ovens.

The Russians advanced, and the Germans withdrew more and more toward the border of Germany. We felt the nervousness of the guards, and they said specifically, "We must eliminate the survivors faster, quickly, as fast as possible." Each day, there were roll calls and loading on railway cars, and the cars went away full and came back empty.

[Page 349]

One day, I was pushed along with the elderly and found myself with lads my age in Buchenwald camp [some 700 kilometers southwest of Stutthof and in Germany]. Buchenwald was a big place; it had two camps with a barbed-wire fence dividing them. One camp for us, the Jews, survivors of the camps; thousands of people, mud, dirt, density and hunger. All the time they brought in more people and took some out, shoved and beaten, filling and emptying, and the trains operated at full speed, bringing and taking. On the other side of the fence was a prisoners' camp; it was clean and orderly. There were imprisoned opponents of the regime from Germany and other countries in Europe. Veterans, satiated, in nice dwellings; loudspeakers called them to meals; there were few guards. "What's over there?" we wondered. One day, a well-dressed man came to us. He spoke politely and said that if we wanted to live, we must cross to the other side. But how? He told us, drawing a number of slips of paper from his pocket. "Those who win these will cross to the other side." I was among them. They brought me to a block and showed me a bed. A bed! G-d in Heaven! I hadn't slept in a bed in years. And there was a kitchen, and food, and soup. I ate six portions at once. I ate until I was full for the first time in years. The jobs they gave me were easy. There was no pushing, no beating. Was this a dream, or reality?

The dream didn't last; already as a child, I'd known that a dream didn't last long. One day, Germans passed through the camp between the blocks and announced on the loudspeakers that all those who'd crossed over to the new place must return to the old camp and present themselves at the formation ground. "Anything but this," I said, and I hid between the blocks. Everywhere I hid, they didn't want me; the Czechs and the Russians were afraid to help. All of a sudden, I found myself opposite a German with a bloodthirsty dog. No one could stand up to these dogs, which the Germans trained to attack and tear people to pieces. The Germans trained them to identify Jews by their clothing and smell. Here I was, opposite such a dog. I was pushed to the formation ground. Forward, to a transport!

The Long Journey into Germany

We felt that our end was approaching. They took the survivors of the camps out on a death march. We could sense the end of the war in the eyes of the Germans and those of the guards: these were Ukrainians, Latvians, Estonians, and anyone who'd sold his soul to survive, out of bestial impulses. Everyone in whom burned an appetite for murdering Jews, everyone who'd lost sight of G-d during the blood-soaked years of the war, everyone who saw murder as redemption for himself. Two thousand people, men and women, young and old, we were gathered at the formation ground. I didn't know a single person in the crowd. There were Jews who were survivors from the camps of Europe, a babble of languages, individuals, "eaters of misery," cleaving to life at any price, without G-d, faith or hope to survive, solitary and isolated, each person a lone wolf. They kept us on the ground for two days, closed and locked up. We were guarded with rifles and machine guns, until the order to move was given.

We saw the Germans abandoning us, and it was easy to understand what was happening. With first light, they took us out on our way, through back roads, dirt paths, fields and villages. At night, they let us sleep in granaries and barns. The transporters of food who were with us began, from the start, to slip away one by one. Germans also slipped away, leaving us with the murderous guards.

As we walked, we grabbed whatever we could to eat. We drank from wells in the fields. Whoever had trouble walking was immediately killed. They'd stop with their rifles a group that was lagging, shoot them and throw

[Page 350]

the bodies to the side of the road. The survivors would then break into a run ahead. They were also stopping and killing the first ones. Each day, the procession grew smaller. Every day, fewer and fewer people set out on the road. At night, hunger gnawed at us. In the daytime, walking in the fields, we found some greens or farm plants, stuffed them into our pockets and ate them at night. We went mostly in pairs. My walking partner was a Hungarian Jew, much older than me, who shared the events of this journey. One night, in a barn, we saw that they'd given the cows beets to eat, good beets with healthy tops. My partner grew excited. He prepared a sharp piece of barbed wire and with it, after a number of trials, he succeeded in "fishing" out a nice beet. It was almost morning, and he decided to keep it for the next night; he said that we'd make ourselves a meal fit for a king. But that day, they killed him. The beet remained in my pocket. That night, I didn't have the strength to eat it alone. I whispered the words of the Kaddish, curled up like an animal and chewed on the beet while lying down.

The Journey Continued

In the fields and paths, between villages and forests, beaten and chased, starving and eaten by lice, barefoot and covered with rags or half-naked, without any embarrassment we relieved ourselves in front of everyone. Whoever fell down didn't get back up, and whoever remained alive envied those who had fallen. It was a journey of the sons of death, who wanted to die --- I was among them. I counted my young years; did more time remain for me to live? One must cleave to life at any price, I said, no matter what! To live, to live! One more day, one more day. I want to tell the story of the coat without stripes from the men of the camps, a faded and frayed coat. The value of the coat --- the value of my life:

The guards were busy killing the people who were lagging. One of the dead lay at the side of the road, clad in a civilian coat. I thought of taking the coat, but the guards crossed their rifles and wouldn't let me approach. I slipped under the rifles; I was a young lad, and I quickly grabbed the coat from the dead man. They saw me and began to shout, "This boy, this boy!" I merged into the crowd, and they left me and the coat alone. This coat made me unidentifiable and gave me hope and enough spirit to keep going, no matter what. There's no limit to a young man's wish for life.

The journey continued for a month and a half. From 2,000 people, at the end of the journey there remained only 160. And so we arrived at Lebenoy[?] camp, near Salzburg [in Austria, about 380 kilometers south-southeast of Buchenwald].

Walking skeletons, wounded and eaten by lice, limping and lame with swollen feet, some in rags and some in camp uniforms, we entered the gates of Lebenoy. They told us that the place was a camp for prostitutes of the German army. We heard shots, shouting and large movements; we saw many soldiers running around us. Not recognizing the uniforms of the American soldiers, we thought they were Germans. Among these soldiers were Jews who spoke Yiddish and Polish, and they told us we were free. What is this free? We wanted to express our happiness and fall at their feet, but they stopped us, because . . . how did we look? The American soldiers rained food and clothing on us, and told us that Germany had lost the war, and they were now standing on the land of conquered Germany.

They told us of a Jew, a shoemaker, who'd found the officer of the transport. This German had made himself a canopy on wooden poles and the Jews had carried it. The shoemaker immediately called the Americans and a Jewish chaplain, and they decided to put him on trial. But before they could begin, the Jews attacked him. They

[Page 351]

beat him and tore him to pieces.

Epilogue

Many hardships passed over me until I reached this place in Givatayim [Israel] to tell you, Yaacov, of my Holocaust. My brother Yisrael remained alive; he's in Russia. We write to each other. Attempts were made to bring him to Israel, but he's very ill and unable to leave Russia.

My sister Sima lives in Hadera [in Israel]. She has a family; she came to Israel 20 years ago.

My sister Tzila reached Canada 20 years ago. She's married to a man from Opsa, Meir Zilber, and they have a family.

My sister Sara, one of the twins, made *aliyah* to Israel 20 years ago. She lives in Hadera, and she has a family.

The second twin [Hindka] made *aliyah* from Russia 10 years ago, and she lives in Ashkelon [in Israel]. She has a family.

Footnotes:

1. Member of the All-Union Leninist Young Communist League, the youth division of the Communist Party of the Soviet Union.

2. Literally, "riflemen" (*šauliai* in Lithuanian). These were members of a right-wing, nationalist paramilitary group that had been established in Lithuania in 1919, following Lithuanian independence, and banned after the Soviets took over Lithuania in 1940. The Shaulists violently opposed Communism and all those they saw as enemies of the nation. Those Lithuanians who committed mass murder under Nazi leadership often came from among their ranks.

3. This refers to events around April 1, 1942, when the Braslav Ghetto was officially established. It appears that around this time some Jews of Opsa who could afford to pay bribes were sent to the Braslav Ghetto, while other Jews from Opsa were sent to the Vidz Ghetto. As it turned out, the Braslav Ghetto would be liquidated on June 3-5, 1942; the Vidz Ghetto continued functioning until around October, when most of its inmates were transferred to the Sventzion Ghetto.

4. Slobodka was 27 kilometers northeast of Opsa, and Yaisi was 23 kilometers northeast of Opsa. It's unclear why Jews would be sent to the two small communities of Slobodka and Yaisi; generally, the transfer of Jews was from the smaller villages to the ghettos. It's possible instead that Jews were actually being transferred to Vidz from Slobodka and Yaisi.

5. Zvi and Esther were the parents of Yaacov Aviel (Abelevitz), whose account is on pages 323-338 of this memorial book.

6. So far as is known, there was a ghetto in Opsa through at least July 1942, containing some 300 people (according to the *Encyclopedia of Camps and Ghettos, 1933-1945*, Volume II-B, published in 2012). Presumably it continued operating until August or early September 1942, when some 50 Jews from it were transferred to the ghetto in Braslav, to repopulate that ghetto after its inmates had been slaughtered on June 3-5, 1942. Because the members of this second, new ghetto in Braslav were from Opsa, the ghetto too was called the "Opsa" Ghetto (even though it was in Braslav). It would be liquidated on March 19, 1943. (Meanwhile, according to the *Encyclopedia*, it's thought that the Jews left behind in Opsa as unfit for work --- women and children, the elderly and others --- had been killed in a final liquidation in Opsa carried out sometime between September 1942 and the year-end.)

7. This refers to Mielagenai labor camp, which was about 20 kilometers southwest of Vidz and in Lithuania. This camp was also mentioned by survivors from Dubina (Dubene): Sima Feigin Moretsky on page 371-372, Rivka Maron Rukshin on page 378, and Mira Shneider Lotz on pages 383-384 of this memorial book.

8. Kailis was a small labor camp inside Vilna that operated from October 1941 to July 1944. At its peak capacity, it's estimated to have held about 1,500 Jews.

9. By around October 1942, most of the Jews of the Vidz Ghetto had been transferred to the Sventzion Ghetto. So the narrator is saying that his mother and his twin siblings were now in the Sventzion Ghetto (having been transferred there from the Vidz Ghetto) and he was planning to go to them from the Vilna Ghetto, which he'd just reached by escaping from Miligan labor camp.

10. Yerachmiel Milutin's account appears on pages 254-257 of this memorial book.

11. This refers to events in March-April 1943, when the Jews from the Sventzion Ghetto --- along with the populations of other small ghettos around Vilna --- thought that they were being removed to the Vilna and Kovno ghettos on April 4. Instead, they were taken in trains to the execution site of Ponar outside Vilna and shot on April 5. Only a tiny remnant managed to survive the transport. At the time, it was widely believed that the massacre was due to a refusal by the Vilna Ghetto to take more inmates, but this wasn't the case. For more information, see page 283 of this memorial book.

12. According to the *Encyclopedia of Camps and Ghettos, 1933-1945*, Volume I-B (2009), Vaivara was the largest Nazi concentration/labor camp in Estonia, taking in some 20,000 Jewish prisoners during its time of operation from September 1943 to September 1944. It was about 540 kilometers north of Vilna.

    Vaivara camp had been established to hold the Jews remaining in Lithuania, Latvia and Estonia after the Germans decided to shut down all the ghettos in those countries. For example, the Vilna Ghetto was shut down and the Jews there were dispersed in September 1943. The Kovno Ghetto was taken over by the SS in autumn 1943, reduced drastically in size and converted to a concentration camp. Most of Vaivara's prisoners came from the Vilna and Kovno ghettos.

In mid- to late 1944, as the Soviet army approached, many of the prisoners of Vaivara and its subcamps, including Motke Rozenberg, would be evacuated by ship, executed or sent on death marches.

13. Narva (a.k.a. Narva-Ost), in northeast Estonia, was one of many subcamps of Vaivara concentration/labor camp, operating from September 1943 to February 1944.

14. The foundational work in the literature of Jewish mystical thought known as Kaballah.

15. An irreverent reference to Jesus, called in Jewish texts the son of a Roman soldier named Pandera.

16. This refers to SS-Hauptscharführer (Chief Squad Leader) Kurt Pannicke, who was among the handful of Germans supervising Vaivara concentration/labor camp, assisted by Estonian and Russian guards. He took command of Vaivara in August, shifting to command of Narva camp in September. Camp inmates called him Peiniger (Torturer), rendered in the Hebrew original as "Paniker." He disappeared near the war's end, and postwar efforts to trace him failed. He's mentioned in *Encyclopedia of Camps and Ghettos, 1933-1945*, Volume I-B, in the sections on Narva and Vaivara.

Diller, mentioned later in Mr. Rozenberg's account, was the camp elder, or *Lagerältester*, in other words, the senior prisoner assisting the Nazis with administration of a camp, in return for extra food and other privileges. This enabled the Nazis to operate the camps with fewer of their own personnel.

17. "Shema Yisrael": The affirmation and confession of faith incumbent, when possible, upon Jews *in extremis*, and recited thrice daily in prayers: "Hear, O Israel, the Lord our G-d, the Lord is One!"

18. Franz von Bodmann, SS camp doctor for Vaivara and its subcamps. He would kill himself in May 1945. He's mentioned in *Encyclopedia of Camps and Ghettos, 1933-1945*, Volume I-B, in the sections on Vaivara and other camps.

19. The accuracy of this statement is uncertain; Sonda was a very small camp 55 kilometers west of Vaivara.

20. Stutthof (now Sztutowo, Poland) had been established in September 1939 about 35 kilometers east of the city of Gdansk, in occupied Poland. From the beginning of 1944, with the German army in retreat from the Eastern Front, about 60,000 Jews were transferred there, mainly from labor camps in Latvia, Lithuania and Estonia. In 1945, evacuation of the camp was carried out, by sea and through death marches, during which many prisoners died.

21. A *kapo* was a Nazi concentration camp prisoner who received extra food and other privileges in return for supervising the labor of other prisoners. This enabled the Nazis to operate the camps with fewer of their own personnel.

[Page 352]

Arieh Munitz
Son of Esther-Golda and Yisrael-Yitzchak

Translated from the Hebrew by Joshua Leifer
Donated by Jacob Levkowicz

The Town of Opsa and Its Jews

I haven't found an explanation for the source of the name of Opsa. The buildings and courtyards of the town, those belonging to the Jewish residents and to the Christian peasants, were mixed together. The main street crossed the town, and at its center stood the *platz* --- the marketplace. Houses scattered on the hills, a quiet lake of sweet water, a Christian church with its gardens and fields, pine groves in several directions, and then the forest that stretched into the distance and beyond, to the neighboring towns and peasant villages. On the northern side, the lake washed the steps of the entrance to the mansion that belonged to Polish nobles from the family of Count Plater. It's likely that the noble family's subjects, including its Jewish residents, were concentrated in Opsa.

On one of the sandy hills was the synagogue of the Mitnagdim [traditionalist opponents of the Hasidim], and around it stood the houses of the middle class, who earned a living from the weekly market day. There were tailors, shoemakers, merchant-traders and wagon drivers --- among them, men who walked great distances to the neighboring villages during the week and returned home to greet the Sabbath Queen.

On the eastern side, the street led to the synagogue of the Hasidim; they were the well connected and the wealthy, among them the richest and most influential. There was also a *cheder* [Hebrew primary school], where the learned Reb[1] Yitzchak the *melamed* [teacher] instructed in Torah. Later a second *cheder* was opened, in which the *melamed* was the *shochet* [ritual slaughterer], Reb [Menachem-]Mendel Liberzon. The barn in Reb Mendel's yard was used as the slaughterhouse for small animals (*shechita kalah*). The slaughterhouse for larger animals (*shechita gasa*) was located east of the town.

The weekly market days provided many with their livelihoods. Government clerks and merchants from the large towns would come by train to the market, some from as far away as Vilna [about 140 kilometers southwest of Opsa]. They'd buy milk products, cheeses and butter, eggs and all kinds of agricultural products. On market days, the Jews would open stalls with all kinds of haberdashery, textiles, kerosene, salt and more to sell to the peasants.

Life there went as it did in all the towns. Everyone knew what was cooking in everyone else's pot; a *simcha* [celebration] in the town was a *simcha* for everyone. Families

[Page 353]

intermarried, forming clans of a sort. Of course each social class remained separate, without mixing.

There were also spiritual and cultural endeavors. There was a small Yiddish library. Youth groups tried to organize performances --- in particular, plays by Goldfaden,[2] and people would come to see a "theater" production held in some storeroom or other. In later years, a youth library was set up. At the same time, chapters of Keren HaKayemet [the Jewish National Fund] and Zionist organizations such as HeChalutz and Betar came to be organized.[3] Betar was the largest and most active. A few of those who were in Betar came to Israel, where they're living now (may they live to be 120).

There were also activities and gatherings organized to prepare for *aliyah* to Israel, and of course there were parties just for fun.

The Betar group of Opsa

Footnotes:
1. Reb is an honorific term, something like an exalted "Mr."
2. Abraham Goldfaden (1840-1908), the father of Jewish modern theater.
3. HeChalutz (The Pioneer): A Jewish youth movement founded in Russia and the United States around 1905, advocating the training of Jewish youth for agricultural settlement in Palestine. Betar: A Revisionist Zionist youth movement founded in Latvia in the 1920s, advocating military training for defense and Jewish immigration to Palestine.

[Page 354]

About Melechke [Munitz] the *Geroi* (Hero)
By Arieh Munitz and His Sister, Zehava Bilogoski

Translated from the Hebrew by Joshua Leifer
Donated by Jacob Levkowicz

During the two Aktions or massacres --- the first from June 3-5, 1942, the second in March 1943 --- there were instances of bravery and sacrifice by individuals who fell as martyrs.[1] Those who survived told the stories of these martyrs, so that future generations would remember them.

In the chronicle of heroism and Jewish pride, one chapter of resistance and struggle is the story of Melech Munitz, called Melechke the *geroi* or Melech the brave [*geroi* being the Russian word for hero].

Melech was the youngest child of Yisrael-Yitzchak and Esther-Golda Munitz. He had an older sister, Zehava-Zlotka, who made *aliyah* as a pioneer in 1935, and a brother, the oldest among them, Arieh-Leibke, who made *aliyah* to study at the Hebrew University in Jerusalem in 1936.

Melech was a tailor by trade. When he was starting out, he apprenticed with a member of the Bikov family in Opsa. Later he completed his training and worked for a member of the Rapaport family from Opsa who lived in Vilna [about 140 kilometers southwest of Opsa]. After that he returned and worked in Vidz [Widze, about 22 kilometers southwest of Opsa] for the Sheibel family, to which his family was related by marriage. Although he had opportunities to go to Palestine through one of the channels of Aliyah Bet,[2] he didn't want to leave his mother after she was left a widow by the death of her second husband --- Menachem-Mendel Liberzon, of blessed memory, who had been the *shochet* [ritual slaughterer] and *melamed* [teacher] in Opsa --- or to leave his three young step-siblings: sisters and a brother.

Of the 300 Jews who lived in Opsa when the Germans entered the town [in 1941], within a short time only 50 or 60 remained. Most were transferred and expelled to the ghettos that were set up in Braslav, Vidz and elsewhere, and a few went into the surrounding forests. The only Jews to survive were some who'd left Opsa and immigrated abroad before the Holocaust began and a few who were drafted into the Polish and Russian armies.

Most of those who remained in Opsa [i.e., the 50 to 60] were employed in various types of work and services for the local police and the Germans in the town such as tailoring, shoemaking, chopping wood and cleaning. This remnant of the Jews remained in Opsa, even though in other towns

[Page 355]

of the region all the Jews in the ghettos --- such as Miory, Yod [Jod], Sharkovshchitzna [Szarkowszczyzna], Glubok [Glubokoye], Braslav, Druya, Druysk and so on --- were shot or transferred to death camps.[3] The Jews [in Opsa] were joined secretly by a few Jewish fugitives from the surrounding towns, forests and villages.

These Jews remained in Opsa after the liquidation of the Braslav Ghetto in the first Aktion or massacre (June 3-5, 1942). Then, in August-September 1942, the Germans transferred them to the ghetto of Braslav [making it the second Braslav Ghetto]. Only a few of them escaped, and after great hardship these reached the forests of Kozian [Koziany, to the south] and somehow found refuge among groups of partisans. There they found Jews who'd fled from the Aktions and ghettos before liquidation, and a few of these people remained [in the forests] until they were liberated by the Russians [around July 1944].

[Up to March 1943, after being transferred from Opsa to the second Braslav Ghetto] Melech remained in the ghetto in Braslav, along with a few other craftsmen who the Germans and local police allowed to work for them. In March 1943 there was a sense that something was about to happen, and this time the killers would come for the skilled Jewish workers in their houses. The [Jewish] tailors had uniforms from the Gestapo officers who were at work, as well as lime for disinfecting and whitewashing. Crowds of peasants began to gather nearby in wagons, as they'd done before to claim the spoils [whenever an Aktion took place in the region].

Melech, sensing that a siege was about to begin, given rumors of an impending Aktion and expulsion of the remaining Jews (many of whom were from Opsa), saw at once that there was no hope of survival. He told his comrades to put on the German uniforms, and he did likewise. Next to the entrance [of their house], he prepared buckets of caustic lime. When the first German entered, Melech poured the lime on the man's face and blinded him. Melech then took the man's pistol and killed him on the spot, together with three other Germans. The Jews barricaded themselves in the house and began shooting at the Germans and police who surrounded them. Melech took advantage of the commotion and the fact that he was wearing a German uniform to keep firing at the Germans, who thought that he was shooting at the Jews. As he did so, he told his comrades to flee.

The Jews continued to return fire with the weapons they had in the hiding place. Melech --- dressed like a Gestapo officer, tall, blond and handsome --- went like a lion through the streets of Braslav and shot at the Germans and police, unseen by them. Only at the edge of town did the local Gentiles recognize him, telling the Germans, who caught him and killed him on the spot.

A handful of the Jews who still survived in the surrounded house continued to shoot and kill every German and policeman who tried to reach them; the Germans retreated. Only when the Jews' bullets were exhausted and their firing ceased did the Germans approach and throw grenades into the house. The defense by Melech and his group of comrades came to an end. They fell with their weapons in their hands, dying in sanctification of G-d's name and for the sake of Jewish pride.

Footnotes:

1. This refers to the massacres of the first Braslav (Braslaw) Ghetto on June 3-5, 1942 and the second Braslav Ghetto on March 19, 1943; the second Braslav Ghetto (also called the "Opsa" Ghetto) contained a number of Jews from Opsa who'd been resettled there after the first Braslav Ghetto had been massacred. It was at the liquidation of the second Braslav Ghetto in March 1943 that Melech Munitz, brother of Arieh and Zehava, died heroically.

2. Jewish immigration to Palestine without proper visas, called "Aliyah B." Between 1920 and 1948, much immigration to Palestine occurred in this way, since the British Mandate severely restricted the number of visas.

3. An exception to this was the Vidz Ghetto, which continued until around autumn 1942, when most of its inmates were transferred to the Sventzion (Swieciany) Ghetto. The Sventzion Ghetto functioned until April 4-5, 1943, when most of its inmates were taken in freight cars to Ponar (Ponary) outside Vilna and shot.

[Page 356]

Okmenitz
[Okmienic/Okmianica/Okmyanitsa]

Alexander (Shmaryahu) Dagovitz
Son of Chana[1] and Avraham

Translated from the Hebrew by Laia Ben-Dov
Footnotes Added / Donated by Jeff Deitch

The village of Okmenitz lies on the road between Braslav and Dubina [roughly nine kilometers north of Braslav and seven kilometers southeast of Dubina]. A beautiful place, surrounded by ponds and pine forests; our family lived there for generations. Our father, Avraham Dagovitz, was born there in 1880. In the family, we were six souls. The parents, Avraham and Chana; the daughter, Esther; and three sons: Leibke, Shimonke, and me: Alexander. I was born in 1923. There were no other Jews in the village. Our family's living came from a flour mill, operated by water power, that we rented from the landowners, the Alexandrovitz brothers. We also had a fishpond, in which we grew a unique species of carp.

In Okmenitz, there was a group of pioneers who trained themselves in agriculture; their kibbutz was in Braslav. We'd go there every Sabbath to spend time with them. Our family spent the Jewish holidays in Braslav or Slobodka [about 11 kilometers northeast of Braslav].

Life in Okmenitz was quiet and peaceful, and passed without upheavals. The local young people were good, and we grew up together with very friendly relations. Life continued in this way until World War II broke out [in September 1939]. First, the Soviets came. They took everything, but it was still possible to go on living. The disaster began with the war between Russia and Germany [starting in June 1941]. The Russians evacuated, and many people went with them. Our family didn't manage to leave. We stayed, and our father said, "I survived Kaiser Wilhelm [II], I believe I'll also live to see the last of Hitler."

The German army passed Okmenitz without harming anyone. They began to organize a local police force only days later, into which they drafted young men from the village and its surroundings. Two local men, Kazhik and Malinovski [Malinowski], were appointed at their head. We'd go out each day to Braslav to get news about the Jews there and around the region.

One Sabbath, in July 1941, several Germans, accompanied by local police, came to our house. Father was then standing in prayer, wrapped in his *tallit* [prayer shawl]. The visitors asked us for the horse and wagon and promised to return them in a few hours. They received everything and left. After

[Page 357]

several hours, they did return to Okmenitz; the horse brought them to our house by itself. My brother Leibke went out to untie the horse. As he approached the wagon, the Germans whipped the horse, and it began to gallop. They shouted at Leibke, "Jew! Jew --- forward!" This continued until Leibke entered the pool of water next to our house that served as our reservoir. When Leibke entered the pool, one of the policemen aimed his rifle at him. All of us saw this from the window of our house. Mother raised a great cry, "They're killing Leibke!" We heard a shot, but my brother wasn't hit. Afterward, it became clear why: When the policeman stood up to shoot, the policeman Kazhik jumped toward him and pushed the rifle above Leibke's head, shouting, "What are you doing? He's our Jew (*nash Zhid*) [in Russian]." So Leibke's life was saved. That day, we understood this event as the start of the disasters that would befall us. In the evening, several Jews from Dubina came to us and told us that the Germans, accompanied by the police, had entered their village before noon. They'd robbed the homes of the Jews and killed some of them.[2]

[On August 1, 1941] the day before Tisha B'Av (the ninth of Av), the [Gentile] head of the village --- the *soltys* --- and two Germans came to our house and told father that we all had to move to the ghetto in Braslav, which they were establishing at the time. They further told him to prepare a complete list of all our property and give it to the authorities, and to put on the house a sign with one word: "Jew." All these instructions were to be carried out within a week.

After the Germans left, our father turned to the village head and brought him a nice gift, and he decided to temporarily delay our exit from Okmenitz. Each day, Kazhik and Malinovski came to our house with news about what was happening. These were always the tidings of Job: killing here, robbing there. Our parents began to give away our belongings to our farmer friends, with the thought that later, in time of need, we'd be able to get something back from them. This uncertain situation continued until Hanukkah [December 14-22, 1941], at which time they came and ordered us to move immediately without delay to the Braslav Ghetto, which we did.

In Braslav we stayed in the house of Shimonke, the son of Eli-Chaim, who was a relative of ours. We were registered in the community and went to work with the rest of the Jews of the town. At this time the Jews already understood what was likely to happen, and many began to prepare hiding places for their families. I worked next to the train station, together with young men from Yaisi and Slobodka. While working, we heard news of killings in Miory [about 40 kilometers east of Braslav], Glubok [Glubokoye, about 70 kilometers southeast of Braslav] and other places. In the evenings after work, we passed the news on to others in the [Braslav] ghetto.

On Christmas Eve [1941], many policemen and Germans arrived in Braslav. Worried that they were going to eliminate the ghetto, my brothers and I went at night to one of the villages, where a [Gentile] farmer lived, a good friend of ours. This farmer wanted to shelter all of us on his farm, but to our misfortune another farmer saw us and told others. These put pressure on our friend:

If he didn't drive us out they'd inform on him, and his end would be bitter. Weeping bitterly, our acquaintance asked us to leave his house. We returned to Braslav. Our parents were happy . . . our family was again united. Our parents told us that this time the Germans had been satisfied with a large "contribution" (bribe) in the form of gold, silver and warm clothes for the German army. The Germans carried out a "selection" in the ghetto: they left the professionals on one side of the bridge and put the others on the other side, on the way to the Dubki [Dubkes] forest.[3] We lived with the family of Shneiur Biliak from Slobodka, and worked together with Russian prisoners of war to dig a well.

One day, they sent me with another lad from Yaisi to work serving and cleaning the house and office

[Page 358]

of a German officer. We didn't know who the man was. Once, while both of us were busy cleaning the office, a Gentile appeared, introducing himself as a *soltys* (head) of one of the villages. He told the German officer that at present he couldn't supply the amount of seeds, eggs and the like that they'd ordered him to gather from the farmers of his village, and he asked for more time to comply. The officer heard him out and then ordered his assistant to shoot the *soltys* on the spot. Both of us were horrified. The German assistant very calmly took out a pistol from his holster and shot the farmer. His blood splattered the wall, and the floor filled with blood. They then told us to take the cursed pig out of the office, which I and the lad immediately did. We wanted to take the body even further away, but were told that this would be done by the Russian prisoners. When we returned in great fear to clean the office, the officer asked us to prepare a cup of tea for him, and he continued to play his phonograph as if nothing had happened. The next day, we found out that this officer was none other than [Willy] Dittmann, who was responsible for the entire region.[4]

Food was very scarce, hardly enough to sustain body and soul, and the work we did was very hard. People kept themselves going with difficulty. Whoever wavered at work was shot immediately. At this time, I fell sick and developed a high temperature. We didn't know what my illness was; a medic told us that the symptoms showed it was definitely typhoid. There was no doctor or medicine. Despite this, I succeeded in recovering with the help of some kind of pill, whose contents none of us knew, but I grew very weak.

On June 2, 1942 [Tuesday],[5] two of our acquaintances from the leaders of the local police, Kazhik and Malinovski, surprised us by entering our apartment. "It's just a visit," they said, but we understood that their coming meant something was about to happen. They looked at everyone and then at me, the youngest in the family. Eyeing me, one said to the other, "He certainly will die." To us, these words were a clear hint that they'd come to warn us of a looming disaster. The evening of that same Tuesday, my two brothers, Leibke and Shimonke, left to find us shelter at the house of an acquaintance in a nearby village. A few minutes later, they returned with a yell: "Mother, father, children, save yourselves --- the massacre has begun!" After this, I never saw my brothers again.

Mother got up immediately, and despite my great weakness from the illness, she turned to me and said, "My son, get out of here. Look for somewhere to hide." She gave me clean underwear to take with me, and I left the house. Outside, shots from rifles and machine guns were heard in every direction. Frightened people were being made to run like dogs, some straight to the pits of destruction [that had been dug outside the town near the train station] and many others to the movie house, the study halls, the sports hall and the police station, sites of destruction in the days to come.

A youth ran past me shouting, "Come quick, hide yourself!" I ran with him some distance to a storeroom for wood. We entered and hid like mice between the boards and crates that were there. Also hiding were other Jews who'd gotten there before us. After a few minutes, police and Germans broke in and began to shoot, shouting, "*Juden raus!*" ["Jews out!"]. Many of those inside were killed or injured. A German approached me, and the youth shouted, "Out!" I received a proper blow from the German's rifle butt, but stood up with the help of the youth. The German took both of us to the bridge over the river, the waters of which joined the two lakes, Driviata [Drywiaty] and Noviata [Nowiata], but was stopped by a call from the German patrol. He approached his fellow soldier and began to talk with him. While they were talking distractedly, the youth and I succeeded in getting away. With great effort, I also managed to cross the barbed-wire fence

[Page 359]

and reach the lakeshore. From great exertion, I must have fallen down and fainted. I don't know how long I lay there, unconscious. I do remember that after recovering a bit, I found myself lying in a horrible field of slaughter. Next to me lay a young girl dripping with blood, and I was covered in her blood. I tried to move and found that my limbs responded; apparently I wasn't injured. Around me were killed and wounded, and the cries of people who wanted to die. I heard sighs and moans all around. And then I saw more: how policemen and Gentiles were driving a horse and wagon and putting human bodies in it. A terrible trembling passed through me. If they saw that I was alive and well, they'd shoot me immediately. I tried to crawl, to get away from there, to a nearby house. While fleeing I encountered a boy about 12 years old, Kopke [Gurevitz][6] from Dubina, the grandson of Velvel Blacher. Both of us kept crawling. With our last strength, we succeeded in reaching one of the houses and went inside. I had no strength to go further. There we stayed, because the boy didn't want to leave me. Other Jews were also hiding in the house. Among them was a girl who'd been shot by the police and seriously wounded. From the direction of the pits came the echo of shots --- the destruction was at its height.[7] We decided to remain in the house. We closed the front door and blocked it on the inside, so that it would be difficult to open. Then all of us went up to the attic; we hoped to stay there until dark and then continue our flight. This house had two exits, in two different directions. We thought this might make it easier for us to leave the ghetto.

The young people and those who were stronger left the attic at night and went outside to see what was happening in the ghetto. Because of my weakness, I couldn't go down. Another youth stayed in the attic to guard the wounded girl. Kopke went out with them; after some time, he returned. He told me that he saw how Jews with yellow patches on their clothes were gathering the bodies of those who'd been killed, while the Gentiles were robbing their houses.

These events occurred on Wednesday [June 3]. In our region, the Polish policeman [Stefan] Zhuk excelled in cruelty. The next morning we heard a woman crying; her voice sounded familiar. I looked out through a small crack and saw Germans in the street below leading a group of Jews, adults and children, among them the wife of Shneiur Biliak. In her arms was the baby boy she'd given birth to two weeks earlier, and next to her was her seven-year-old son holding on to her dress. The mother was crying, and now and then a German was hitting her with his rifle butt. After a hard blow, the woman stumbled and fell, and the German shot her on the spot. Then he murdered her baby by stabbing him with his bayonet. I saw more: how the man pulled the bayonet from the infant's body with his boot. Her seven-year-old saw all this and understood. He tried to run away, and the Nazi shot him too. This was the tragic end of Shneiur Biliak's family. The day before this, Shneiur had gone out to one of the villages to get food for the *brit milah* [circumcision] ceremony that was supposed to be held the next day. While he was outside the ghetto, he certainly heard about what was happening there, and didn't know where to go.

After we stayed in hiding for a number of days without food and water, the boy Kopke went down alone to see what was happening. He returned with "news": "They won't harm the Jews any more, that's what people said." I knew that this was just a trick of the Germans. I went out carefully, so that they wouldn't see me in the street, and entered our house: Everything was broken and destroyed, and there were many signs of blood all about. In the basement I recognized, because of the possessions strewn about, that my parents and my sister, Esther, had been there. On the floor I found the pouch of my mother's gold watch, also some dry bread and a bit of fat. I took these items and returned to my hiding place. The boy returned too. It was clear that we couldn't remain in this place; we had to flee

[Page 360]

quickly. But it was only the next night that we succeeded in escaping from the house and the ghetto, because the ghetto was filled with [Gentile] residents of the area who covered the houses of the Jews like birds of prey. I met one survivor who told me, "When the destruction began, a group of us was put into the Sandy Synagogue and guards were set on us. On Thursday afternoon, the guards disappeared. We saw their men through the windows of the synagogue, breaking into the houses of the Jews --- they too wanted spoils. We took advantage of their disappearance and fled."

We went in the direction of Slobodka [about 11 kilometers northeast of Braslav], near the villages Luni [Lunie, about 12 kilometers northeast of Braslav] and Zarach [Zarzecze, about seven kilometers northeast of Braslav and differing from the Jewish village of Zarach, which was six kilometers west of Braslav]. We approached one of the houses [there] and looked through the window. A woman stood in the room, kneading dough. Before we could speak to her, she sensed that we were there and started to shout, "Jews, run away quickly, here you'll get nothing. They'll kill us because of you." We left immediately and kept walking. Next we met a farmer who was about to plow his field. I decided to risk it and asked for something to eat. I told him who I was, and he replied that he knew my father. He promised to bring us some food. We hid in a pile of hay and waited for him, not sure whether he'd keep his promise. But after some time passed, he returned bringing something to eat. In the evening, he asked again what we planned to do. "To cross to the other side of the lake," I answered, "and from there, go to Okmenitz." [Zarzecze was on the eastern side of Lake Strusto --- one of the lakes to the north of Braslav --- and Okmenitz was on the western side.] He agreed to help us, sending his son to take us in his boat to the other side of the lake. We stayed on the shore. After washing ourselves a bit, we sat down to decide where to go next. I'd told the good farmer that we were going to Okmenitz, but how would we get there? Every farmer knew me there, and they were likely to hand us over to the Germans. After thinking about it, I said that we should go to Shvilishki [Szewieliszki, about 1.5 kilometers northwest of Okmenitz], where I'd studied in the past. I knew a farmer there who'd suffered a lot from the Germans. They'd imprisoned his daughter because she belonged to the Komsomol[8] during the time of the Soviets. I hoped he'd give us shelter on his farm.

Okmenitz was on the way to Shvilishki. During a quiet night in the villages, I passed our farm and stopped without emotion. The house and our possessions had been given by the *soltys* to his brother. The dog began to bark, but when I said to him, "Zhuk, be quiet!" he recognized my voice and stopped barking. I wiped away a tear, and we continued on. We passed "our" fish ponds, crossed a little bridge over the river, and arrived at Choltorvitz's house in the village of Shvilishki. When he saw us, he was very frightened. After collecting himself, he told us that the Germans had taken all of the Jews who'd survived the Aktion in Braslav out of their hiding places and killed them. He'd been sure that we too were among them. He took us into the bathhouse and brought us food, together with news from the neighborhood. We arrived there a week after the destruction of the ghetto in Braslav. Every day, Choltorvitz brought us food and gave us news. After we'd stayed a week at his place, he told us that the "Opsa" Ghetto was being organized [in Braslav].[9] When he heard this, the boy Kopke, who longed to see his family members, asked to go to it, because some of his relatives were there. The farmer agreed to take him. One day, he covered Kopke with straw in his wagon and in this way got him to Braslav. I remained alone.

In the Farmer's House

I stayed for some time at farmer Choltorvitz's house. Before Rosh Hashanah [September 1942], I tried to go through the forests to the village of Postoshki, which was closer to Braslav [Pustoszka, about three kilometers south of Okmenitz, was near the road to Braslav]. In this village, I knew, there was a farmer who was a friend of my oldest brother. Once my brother had told me that the farmer promised to give him a rifle,

[Page 361]

one of the rifles the Russian soldiers had left behind when they retreated. I went to the farmer's house at night, and he received me very nicely. He told me that he had a rifle and two hand grenades, and he was willing to give them all to me. I took only the two grenades, because it was difficult to walk undetected with the rifle. I knew how to use the grenades; I put them in my pocket and went out to return to Choltorvitz's house. I told myself I wouldn't give my life to the Germans without them having to pay for it.

One day, rumors reached the farmer's house. One was that the Germans had suffered heavy losses at the front, and the other --- a partisan movement was organizing itself in the forests and already operating in the area. Witness to this were the words of a farmer, who told us that in Okmenitz the dams of the ponds had been blown up, and in response the Germans and police, with Dittmann at their head, had now surrounded the area and were searching the farmers' homes. "This time," I thought, "my end has come for sure." I quickly went down into a storage pit for potatoes. I sat there with an unlocked grenade in my hand. Because of me, the farmer and his family would pay with their lives. I sat there at the ready for some time, until the farmer came and said that the danger had passed, the Germans had left the area. The same day, Vasily, the farmer's son, returned from the forest where he'd taken the cows out to pasture and said that on the way from the forest he'd met two strangers; they'd asked if there were Jews and prisoners in his village. Their words aroused his suspicion that they might be policemen in disguise but, Vasily added, they'd also asked him if his house was near the forest. And indeed, that evening two armed men approached the farmer's house and greeted everyone in Russian. They asked if they could have something to eat and came inside. While eating, they said they were from the same partisan unit that had destroyed the dams in Okmenitz. They also told us they were looking for additional men to recruit for the partisans. They ate and drank and went on their way. Were they telling the truth? I didn't know.

After this news, I decided to join the partisans, to fight and take revenge. But --- where were they? How to reach them? I knew that in that village of Postoshki there was a farmer --- Pentalai was his name --- who had a brother-in-law in the village of Ozravtzi [Ozierawce, about six kilometers southeast of Braslav], a place visited by the partisans. I wanted to reach this farmer, despite the great danger involved. After several days I was able, with the help of my benefactor, to see this Pentalai, and he gave me the details needed to reach the partisans. Outside, there was already a chill of autumn when I left. I walked by way of Kalenkishki [Kalenkiszki, about six kilometers southwest of Braslav, across the lake from it], without passing through Braslav, which as always was full of Germans. I walked only at night; during the day, I hid. One day, I remained sitting in a pile of straw in a field. Suddenly, two members of the farmer's family came to gather the piles and take them home. They took pile after pile, almost reaching the one where I was hiding. Then behold, a real miracle: At this moment, their father called them to come home; I was saved. That night, I went out on the road again.

One night, when outside it was windy and snowing, I came to a bridge whose name I didn't know. The entire surroundings were strange to me. Not far away, I saw a light in a house, and I approached to look inside. Through the window, I saw the hats of three gendarmes. The sight caused me to quickly jump backward, and I hid behind a tree some distance away. From inside the house, I heard a dog barking. The door opened, and in the doorway stood a German and the dog. The German looked around, fired a number of shots into the air, shouted to the dog, and both of them went back inside. After calming down, I continued; I was hungry and tired. I reached the edge of the forest, where I saw a small hut. Despite the danger, I decided again to try my luck. I knocked

[Page 362]

on the window. A young Gentile came outside and asked, "Jew or partisan?" "Partisan," I answered. Before entering, I turned around and shouted, "Comrades, guard well! I'll return immediately." This farmer told me the name of the village and the area. He also warned me not to go around in daylight, because the area was swarming with Germans who were searching for partisans. He gave me food and a bottle of *samogon* (homemade liquor). I thanked him and left. I walked until I reached the village of Siuli, which the Germans had burnt to the ground. There I sat down to rest; I lacked the strength to continue. Suddenly I heard the sound of a wagon. As it approached, I saw a man sitting inside and two women walking beside it. When they came nearer, they shouted "Hands up!" in Russian. They searched me, took away my grenades and asked, "Who are you?" I said that I was a Jew and wanted to reach the partisans. They told me to get into the wagon, and we continued through the forest until we reached some small huts. They locked me inside one of them and went away. After a few hours some men came, took me outside, and gave me some food. Around me I heard people talking among themselves, and to my great surprise I also heard conversations in Yiddish. I looked hard at the men and recognized one of them --- Yerachmiel Milutin. He approached and asked my name; I told him. He came up to me, hugged and kissed me. I told him everything that had happened until I'd come to the forest and about my wish to join the partisans. He said that soon an officer would return from an action; Yerachmiel would talk to him about me and ask what to do. And indeed, soon the officer came, and Yerachmiel told him about me. The officer replied that it wasn't customary to take partisans without weapons but in my case, since he knew my brother Leibke very well, they'd make an exception. And so, he said, he'd talk with the brigade officer. Meanwhile, he suggested that I start training immediately with cold weapons --- a bayonet. I was sent on guard duty together with a Jewish fellow, Zimmerman, and two others, Gentiles.

On Christmas Eve 1943, I went out for the first time with a group of fighters for an actual operation. At this time, German soldiers were traveling on holiday leave. At train stations, they'd leave the railroad cars to eat and drink. Our task was to ambush a few of them, attack and take their weapons. Walking carefully for two days, we reached the objective. Outside it was dark and cold; we lay there and waited. Along came a train, which stopped at the station. The Germans began to get off the train. From my place of ambush, I saw one of the soldiers hang his rifle on a tree and sit down to relieve himself. My only weapon was a bayonet. My officer gave me the signal to act. I quietly approached the Nazi and quickly thrust my bayonet into him; he died before he could utter a sound. I took his rifle, but the officer wasn't satisfied with that. We returned to the German and took all his documents from him. I returned to the base with a coat, boots and weapons like those of everyone else; I'd become a regular partisan.

Our *otriad*,[10] which bore the name of Chkalov, grew. New people joined, and Jews were also taken into it.

During the war, the Germans suffered heavy losses from the partisans' activities. In retaliation, they bombed forests over the entire area from the air, because they didn't dare enter them on the ground. At this time, we were divided into small groups. The brigade to which I was appointed was called Zhukov. We couldn't go out to fight because of the German siege. At this time I didn't meet Yerachmiel Milutin, and I was very worried that, G-d forbid, he'd been wounded in action. After several days of bombing, the Germans lifted their siege of the forest, and partisan activities resumed.

[Page 363]

Our unit received an objective to fire on the Druya-Miory railroad line, to snipe and blow up the tracks. Our base was within a village that had been burnt to the ground; the farmers in the neighborhood would occasionally bring us news of the Germans' movements. One day several cars, loaded with Germans and police, appeared next to our village. We took battle stations and waited. We didn't want to fight an open battle, because there were many of them. Zimmerman and Zaydel and the unit's officer were with me. The police and Germans searched for a while and then began to leave the place. We received an order to attack them with all the weapons we had, as well as grenades. Many of the Germans were wounded, and a few were taken prisoner; we also suffered a number of wounded. During the battle, I saw our unit's deputy officer struggling with a fat German; both of them were rolling on the ground. I grabbed the German by the neck, and my officer overcame him. This German turned out to be none other than Sonderführer[11] Dittmann, the chief murderer of the Jews of Braslav; this was the third time I'd been near him. At the battle's end, as ordered, I was among the soldiers who took the prisoners to headquarters, which was 25 kilometers from the battle location. We sat Dittmann on a horse and tied his legs under the horse's belly. His hands (behind his back) we tied to the saddle. When we arrived at the base, we gave him to the officer of the brigade for questioning. He was interrogated very severely, and handed over important information about local collaborators. At the end of the interrogation, he was sentenced to death; the sentence was carried out immediately.

Not far from Miory was a large camp of gendarmes, policemen and other collaborators who served the Nazis. Their job was to guard the train line and train station. This was a most essential line for the Germans; supplies were sent along it to the front. In the winter of 1943, our unit received the task of ambushing a train loaded with equipment and derailing it. The next day, we arrived at the location at dusk. Here it became clear to us that access to the tracks was difficult and there were guards nearby. The officer of the operation called for some volunteers to eliminate the guards. He decided to send Fisher, who was a good marksman, with three other fighters. They approached in secret, and in a short time they overcame the guards, put explosives under the tracks and blew them up. The entire unit began to withdraw. Our situation was good, only two wounded. We advanced without delays up to a certain point next to a river, not far from the village of Kuzinitz. Suddenly we began taking fire from the other side of the river. We were in an area where there was no cover; nearby was an orchard of fruit trees, but all the trees had been cut down. We entered the orchard, got behind the stumps and returned fire. We were few compared to the enemy.

In my hands was a "seven-battle" machine gun, which had been damaged more than once. I stood it on the stump of a tree and began continuous firing at the Germans. Unfortunately, as had happened more than once, it stopped working after the first shots. I kept trying to operate it; our situation grew very serious. Not far away, I heard the voices of Germans approaching and shouting, "Halt, halt!" Suddenly, like a miracle, the machine gun began firing again; I cut down Germans right and left. Many of them fell, and others began to run away. In these difficult moments, suddenly I sensed Yerachmiel Milutin next to me; he appeared like an angel from Heaven. He moved me aside, grabbed the machine gun and kept shooting. I was covered with blood and mud from the grenades that the Germans had thrown at us.

At the end of the battle, after the Germans fled, I learned that Yerachmiel, with a group of partisans, had arrived to help us, and this decided the battle in our favor. In this difficult battle, we lost a few of our fighters and suffered some wounded, among them Yerachmiel and myself. Among those who fell was a Jewish lad from Zamosh [Zamosz]. We

[Page 364]
took his body and those of the other fallen for burial at the partisan camp in the forest. A few days later, a formation of our unit was held, in which the officer summarized all the actions and accomplishments we'd recently achieved. Unexpectedly, they ordered me to take three steps in front of the row, and in front of everyone the "combrig," brigade commander Siromcha, announced my part in the last battle and said, "Sasha is the one who rescued our unit during the difficult moments we had in the battle." (By the way, my Hebrew name wasn't Alexander, but Shmaryahu; only after my time with the partisans, who called me Sasha, did I adopt the name Alexander [for which Sasha is a nickname in Russian].)

At this same time, the officer praised the Jews fighting the common enemy and also talked about the concern there'd been about receiving Jews into the *otriad* when it was formed. After a series of additional actions, one day I was called to present myself to the officer. He ordered me to prepare a sketch of the area around Okmenitz for a project we'd be carrying out. Our task was to destroy a large supply base that the Germans had established in one of the holdings in Strusta [Strusto], which was next to Okmenitz, an area I knew well from childhood. [Strusto was two kilometers south of Okmenitz.] I fulfilled the order and added extensive information on the area. I was also attached to the group that left to carry out the task. After hiking at night, we arrived in the morning near the destination. We rested in a storehouse during the day, and at night we went out to act. This time, there were no special difficulties. We destroyed the main dam, broke into the fishponds

Alexander Dagovitz, partisan in the Zhukov brigade

[Page 365]

and destroyed the flour mill. Another group of ours destroyed the large pigpen that supplied meat to the front. On the way back, we entered Plushkat, between Dvinsk and Braslav. [Possibly referring to Plauskiety, about 13 kilometers northwest of Braslav.] There, within the forest, we had to find the forester Jan Zinkovitz [Zinkowicz], whose son was the police officer in Opsa. This police officer received information from his father the forester about the movements of the partisans, passing it on to the Germans. Using what they heard from the forester's son, the Germans were bombing the forests, killing farmers and burning their houses. At night, we reached the forester Zinkovitz. A group of partisans, I among them, entered the house. We took the forester outside, his wife went with him willingly, and we moved them both to the road. There, the officer shot the two of them. Inside the house and in the cellar, we found many possessions of Jews; the father and his son had been busy all the time, robbing and stealing from them.

At the end of my story, I'd like to return to Okmenitz, my birthplace and the place of my youth. When we destroyed the flour mill, I'd also wanted to destroy our old house, where the brother of the village head was then living, but the officer didn't allow it. He said, "Maybe after liberation, someone from your family will return here, and this house will then serve him as a place to live." And so it did happen, two years later.

Footnotes:

1. In this memorial book's list of victims (on page 471), the mother's name is given as Nechama-Rayzel. In a page of testimony submitted to Yad Vashem in 1999, Alexander Dagovitz also called his mother Nechama-Rayzel.
2. The attack on Dubina took place on or around July 19, 1941, when 18-25 Jews there were killed. See the Dubina section of this memorial book on pages 367-392.
3. This separation of the Braslav Ghetto into productive and nonproductive sections was also mentioned by Avraham Biliak in his account on page 240.
4. According to the *Encyclopedia of Camps and Ghettos, 1933-1945*, Volume II-B (2012), Dittmann was one of a number of Germans based at the Gendarmerie outpost in Braslav. Others were Johannes Czapp, Otto Haymann, Paul Kontny, Leo Leidenroth, Ludwig Müller, Ernst Schreiber,

and Waldemar Schulz. The German gendarmes were responsible for overseeing the local police after the autumn of 1941, when a civil administration was established in Braslav and responsibility was transferred to the gendarmes by the German army.

5. This Tuesday was the day before the massacre of the Braslav Ghetto began; police and Germans began surrounding it very early on Wednesday morning.

6. Koppel Gurevitz was the son of Tzipa-Chana Gurevitz. Tzipa-Chana was the daughter of Zev (Volf/Velvel) Blacher. Koppel was also mentioned in the account of Mira Shneider Lotz of Dubina on page 383 of this memorial book. According to the testimony at Yad Vashem of David Blacher (a brother of Tzipa-Chana), Koppel didn't survive the war.

7. This refers to the pits just outside Braslav where most of the Jews in Braslav were slaughtered on June 3-5, 1942.

8. The All-Union Leninist Young Communist League, the youth division of the Communist Party of the Soviet Union.

9. After the first Braslav Ghetto was slaughtered on June 3-5, 1942, the Germans repopulated it in August or early September 1942 by bringing in some 50 Jews from Opsa, many of them craftsmen. Because these people were from Opsa, this second Braslav Ghetto was also called the "Opsa" Ghetto. It would be liquidated by the Germans on March 19, 1943.

10. Russian word for a partisan military unit.

11. Specialist officer, a rank in the Wehrmacht as well as the Waffen-SS, Organization Todt and other Nazi organizations, denoting a specialist of some kind.

[Page 366 = Blank in the original]

[Page 367]

Dubina
[Dubene/Dubinovo/Dubinowo]

Caption Translated from the Hebrew by Laia Ben-Dov
Donated by Jeff Deitch

HeChalutz HaMizrahi [The Eastern Pioneer] in Dubina

[The handwritten caption in the top part of the photo is hard to read but might give a date of December 1934. HeChalutz HaMizrahi was a Jewish youth movement affiliated with Mizrahi, the Religious Zionist Party, which had been founded in 1902 in Vilna to promote Zionism among Orthodox Jews.

In the 1990s, most of the people in this photo were identified as follows by Dubina survivor Mira Shneider Lotz, whose account is on pages 381-388 of this memorial book. In a few cases, other information was provided by another survivor from Dubina. Supplementary information in brackets has been added by the donor after the names:

1. **Moshe Toder** {there are two males named Moshe Toder in the list of dead from Dubina on page 485 of this memorial book; it isn't known which of them is in this photo}
2. **Moshe-Nisan Skopitz** {in the list of dead on page 484}
3. **Doba Toder** {in the list of dead on page 485 as the daughter of Sara Toder}
4. **Yudit Toder**
5. **Rachel-Dina Azband** {in the list of dead on page 483 as the wife of Yosef Azband, who is No. 17 in this photo}
6. **Chaya-Rachel Deitch** {in the list of dead on page 483; the mother of Hirsh Deitch, who is No. 28 in this photo. Chaya-Rachel was said to be the sister of Shlomo Zilber, the *shochet* (ritual slaughterer) in Braslav who was killed in June 1941}
7. **Mina Maron** {presumably the Mina, daughter of Volf/Velvel/Zev Deitch and Tova Vishkin, who was married to Betzalel Maron; Mina doesn't appear in the list of dead on

pages 483-485, but a page of testimony identifying her was placed at Yad Vashem in 1956 by a relative, Bunya Vishkin Maron, a sister of Tova}

8. **Avraham Maron** {in the list of dead on page 484; presumably the husband of Bunya Vishkin Maron and the father of Matka, Chasia and Shmuel-Chatra}

9. **Yisrael-Yitzchak Feigin** {in the list of dead on page 484; killed in the attack on Dubina in July 1941}

10. **Shayna-Pesia Skopitz** {in the list of dead on page 484; daughter of Yisrael Skopitz and Zlata}

11. **Chana-Feiga Skopitz** {survived the war; her account is on pages 390-392 of this memorial book; the daughter of Hirsh Skopitz and Esther}

12. **Liuba Toder** {a Liba Toder, daughter of Nachum Toder and Sara, is in the list of dead on page 485}

13. **Feiga Zilber** {presumably the Feiga in the list of dead on page 484 as the wife of Arieh-Leib Vishkin, as his wife's maiden name was known to be Zilber}

14. **Zlata Goron** {in the list of dead on page 483 as the daughter of Pesel Goron}

15. **Not certain; either Nechama Vishkin** {according to Max Wischkin; Nechama is in the list of dead on page 484 and was the daughter of Sara and the late Avraham-Itzik Vishkin} **or Dina Vishkin** {according to Mira Lotz; Dina is in the list of dead on page 483 and was the wife of David Vishkin, who is No. 25 in this photo}

16. **Noach Shtein** {in the list of dead on page 485}

17. **Yosef Azband** {in the list of dead on page 483; the husband of Rachel-Dina, who is No. 5 in this photo}

18. **Yankel Blacher** {in the list of dead on page 483 as the son of Velvel Blacher and Golda}

19. **Hirsh Deitch** {in the list of dead on page 483; presumably the Hirsh who was the son of Avraham and Basia Deitch}

20. **Reuven Vishkin** {in the list of dead on page 484; the husband of Rachel; Reuven was also the son of Gershon Vishkin and Gershon's second wife, Musha-Mera}

21. **Yisrael-Elka Deitch** {in the list of dead on page 483; the husband of Rachel}

22. **Meir Deitch** {in the list of dead on page 483 as the son of Avraham and Basia Deitch}

23. **Betzalel Maron** {in the list of dead on page 484; the father of Shlomo Maron, who is No. 33 in this photo}

24. **Shlomo Levin** {in the list of dead on page 484; the husband of Sara-Ditel or Sara-Disel}

25. **David Vishkin** {in the list of dead on page 483; the father of Efraim Vishkin, who is No. 35 in this photo; David was also the son of Mordechai-Zelig Vishkin}

26. **Son of Noach Shtein** {the list of dead on page 485 notes "two children" of Noach Shtein and Chana but doesn't name them; the boy here might be Ilia, born ca. 1930, who is noted at Yad Vashem as the son of Noach Shtein and Chana}

27. **Not certain; possibly Moshe Vishkin** {Moshe Vishkin survived the war and his account is on pages 145-154 of this memorial book; Moshe was the son of Tuvia Vishkin and Sara-Leah Reichel, and was also the grandson of Gershon Vishkin and his first wife, Slova}

28. **Hirsh Deitch** {in the list of dead on page 483; the son of Chaya-Rachel Deitch, who is No. 6 in this photo}

29. **Sima Feigin** {survived the war; her account is on pages 369-376 of this memorial book; the daughter of Yisrael-Yitzchak Feigin (No. 9 in this photo) and Esther}

30. **Zlata Deitch** {survived the war; the sister of Chava Deitch and also the daughter of Volf/Velvel/Zev Deitch and Tova Vishkin}

31. **Not certain; either Miriam Vishkin** {according to Max Wischkin; Miriam, the daughter of David Vishkin and Dina, survived the war and immigrated to Israel} **or Mira-Zelda Vishkin** {according to Mira Lotz; Mira-Zelda is in the list of dead on page 484 and was the daughter of Sara and the late Avraham-Yitzchak Vishkin}

32. **Not certain; either Rivka Eidelman** {according to Max Wischkin; Rivka was a sister of Zamka Eidelman} **or Chava Deitch** {according to Mira Lotz; Chava, in the list of dead on page 483, was the sister of Zlata Deitch, who is No. 30 in this photo, and also the daughter of Volf/Velvel/Zev Deitch and Tova Vishkin}.

33. **Shlomo Maron** {in the list of dead on page 484 as the son of Betzalel Maron, who is No. 23 in this photo}

34. **Not certain; either Zamka Eidelman** {according to Max Wischkin; Zamka was a brother of Rivka Eidelman} **or Max/Mottel Wischkin** {according to Mira Lotz; Max/Mottel, who survived the war, was the brother of Efraim Vishkin, who is No. 35 in this photo, and was also the son of David Vishkin, who is No. 25 in this photo}

35. **Efraim Vishkin** {in the list of dead on page 483 as the son of David Vishkin, who is No. 25 in this photo, and Dina}]

[Page 368 = Blank in the original]

[Page 369]

Sima Moretsky
Daughter of Yisrael-Yitzchak and Esther Feigin

Translated from the Hebrew by Laia Ben-Dov
Footnotes Added / Donated by Jeff Deitch

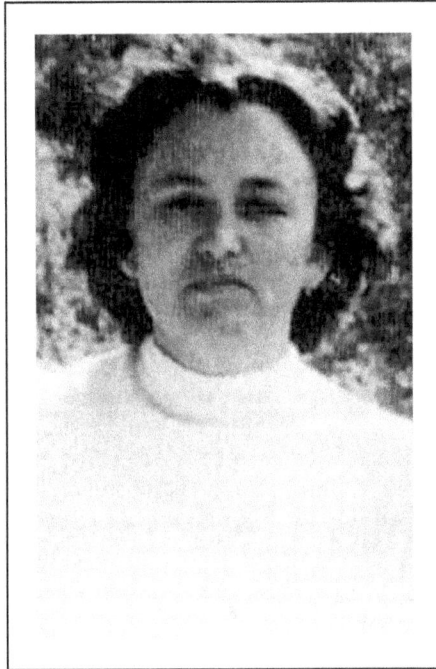

Our family in Dubina [Dubene, 16 kilometers northwest of Braslav/Braslaw] numbered seven souls: my father Yisrael-Yitzchak, born in 1900; my mother Esther, born in 1902; my three brothers: Asher-Ber, age 14; Reuven, age 11; and Feivush, age 7; my sister Shayna-Chaya, age 5; and me --- Sima, age 15.

My father was a farmer. We had a piece of land, a garden of fruit trees, three cows and two horses. In the winter the difficult weather made it impossible to earn anything from agriculture, so my father had to look for another source of income.

Life in the village continued without any major disturbance up until the outbreak of World War II [on June 22, 1941].

A few days after war broke out, German units entered Dubina, and immediately their hand was heavy over the Jews. First, all of the Jews' farm products were confiscated for the German army, which was advancing rapidly toward Moscow in force with tanks and cannons. Airplanes flying very low bombed anything in the area that moved. After a few days, the German units left the area and only a few Germans remained, together with a large number of local collaborators: Poles, Belorussians and others, all of them extreme anti-Semites. They received weapons from the Germans, and they began to oppress the Jews.

This was a very dark period. Each day, news and rumors reached us about murders of Jews here and there in the surrounding area.

The Jews of Dubina formed a system of self-defense to warn the village inhabitants of robbery or plunder by Gentiles, and to protect themselves from the oppressors who had raised their heads. The groups of bandits were joined by Latvians who came from over the border, which was just two kilometers from Dubina. They'd come at night and demand jewelry, money and food, and they threatened to kill us.

We tried to preserve a normal way of life as much as possible. We also kept the Sabbath. Before the Sabbath we baked bread, and those who could afford it also baked *challah* [white bread glazed with egg, a delicacy].

As Sabbath night of July 18, 1941 approached, I prepared

[Page 370]

Sabbath candles for my mother, cleaning the gas lamp and filling it with kerosene so that we could have light during the night. But the candles went out and the kerosene lamp, which was supposed to give light throughout the night, also went out. We couldn't understand why; it was a bad sign.

On Friday my father baked bread, gave me a loaf, and asked me to take it to a family that had succeeded in escaping from the massacre in a neighboring village [probably Plusy, which had been attacked a few weeks earlier was 7.5 kilometers northeast of Dubina]. This was the last time I saw my father [alive].

That Sabbath night, after the prayers, my father went on guard duty. Of course this was done without weapons, in his hand was only a staff. Toward morning on Saturday [July 19], he returned home and lay down to rest. A short time later, we heard loud knocks on the door and the voice of my aunt, who lived next door. She told us that a group of robbers was surrounding the village.

Our house was at the village edge. We saw people coming toward the houses; on their arms were white armbands. Father jumped up immediately and ran toward the village center to warn people of the danger. After an hour, the robbers ordered the women and children to gather in the old synagogue and the men in the new synagogue. We were sure that our end was very near.

In the [old] synagogue it was terribly crowded; there were crying children, thirsty and hungry, and the heart-rending screams of women. The synagogue was surrounded the whole time by the Germans and the local militia. We heard guns shooting nonstop. The policemen took young girls outside and molested them. Later we learned that the Germans' intention had been to burn all of us alive in the synagogue, but because they were afraid the fire would spread to the houses --- which they intended to rob --- they didn't do it. After a few hours, they allowed us to go home.

On the way, we met some men who'd been in the new synagogue, and they told us that the Germans had forced a large number of men outside, assaulted and beaten them, taken them to the Jewish cemetery [just outside Dubina], and murdered them there. My aunt recognized one of the local policemen. She begged him to allow her to go and see what had happened to my father. On the way, I saw Shlomo-Yitzchak Feigin lying dead in a large pool of blood in the yard of the border police building. Later we learned that the first victims had been father, Shlomo-Yitzchak Feigin, Mordechai Levin and Shimon Rukshin. Shimon's mother, Chaya-Hinda, was running about. From her behavior, I could see that she had lost her reason.

Next to her house, we found signs of blood that led to her attic. My mother, I and my aunt Rayna climbed the ladder to the attic, and there we saw a terrible sight. My father was lying on his back in a large pool of blood, with a very deep wound in his stomach. He looked like he was still alive, and my aunt sent me quickly to bring medicine for a compress. With all my strength, I ran to my grandfather and brought the medicine, but it was in vain; my father was dead. Apparently he'd wanted to die peacefully after being shot, and with his last strength had gotten up the ladder to the attic.

They didn't let us take his body; an immediate curfew was declared. Those responsible organized a group of Jews with horses and wagons, and ordered them to collect all the bodies and bury them. My aunt and I managed to sneak into the wagon carrying father, and my aunt put the *tallit* [prayer shawl] over his body.

On Tisha B'Av [the annual day of mourning and fasting to commemorate disaster, falling in 1941 on August 3], we bribed the local policemen and they allowed us to visit the cemetery. We stood there in silence next to the collective grave of 18 of our dear ones who'd been murdered in cold blood.[1]

Some of the village residents had been hiding their valuables and even burying possessions in the ground, so that in time of hunger or other need they could be exchanged for food. Even my uncles from Braslav, Mottel

[Page 371]

Deitch and Beinish Feigin, had brought us some items and asked my father to hide them.

One day, our uncles from Braslav came to take back the valuables that had been hidden. But father was no longer alive, and we didn't know where he'd put them. We dug in different places, but couldn't find them. The uncles were desperate; the money and valuables were needed to pay a bribe. One night my father came to me in a dream and said, "My daughter, in the barn, where the red cow stands, there's a nest with many eggs. Take them." Moved and excited, I explained the dream to my mother and asked her to tell the uncles to try to search in that place. The uncles came, I showed them the location. They dug, and they found everything.

Rumors reached us that Jews were being put into ghettos, but we didn't know what it meant at the time. At the beginning of winter 1942 [late 1941/early 1942], we learned that we'd be sent to the ghettos in Braslav [16 kilometers to the southeast] or Vidz [Widze, 48 kilometers to the southwest]. Because we had relatives in Braslav, we hoped to go there. Before we were expelled [from Dubina], we gave the Poles some valuables for safekeeping. Each family was loaded, together with a few items, into a horse-drawn sleigh; accompanied by militia, we set out on the road. Before my eyes, I saw how the Christian inhabitants fell upon our deserted houses and began taking away anything they could carry. I can still hear the noise and the shouts of those savages.

We were taken to the Vidz Ghetto.[2] On the way, we passed Braslav. There the horses and drivers were changed, and we kept going. That night, we reached Opsa [18 kilometers southwest of Braslav], where we spent the night in the homes of Jewish families. We slept on the floor, a mass of people, in the dirt. In the morning, we continued to the Vidz Ghetto.

In the [Vidz] ghetto typhoid had broken out, and I fell sick with it. The only treatment I could get was a little boiled water from my mother. Through a miracle and because of my young age I recovered, but my hair fell out. After this I had a big appetite, but there was no food and I grew very weak; I couldn't stand on my feet. My mother used to cut a small amount from the food portions of each child, and she fed me so that I could recover. It was very hard for us to get food, and mother, like all of the other women, put herself in danger. She used to sneak out of the ghetto and, in exchange for heavy labor for farmers in the area, she succeeded in bringing us a small bit of food: beetroot leaves, a little flour and potatoes. After some time had passed, we were transferred to a big two-story building. Its windows looked out over the ghetto; we could see Jews being taken to work. Cleaning jobs were arranged for me and some small children.

One day the Germans asked the Judenrat [Jewish Council] for a few people, without saying the purpose. I was among those selected. At night, they put us in the room of the Judenrat. The next morning they took us, accompanied by guards, to the forest. We were very frightened, but we were lucky because among our guards were people of conscience, and they reassured us. "They're taking you to work," they said. We made our way there on foot, without food or drink.

We came to a train station. They put us in freight cars used for transporting cattle and took us to Miligani camp [Mielagenai, about 20 kilometers southwest of Vidz and in Lithuania]. It was surrounded by barbed wire and built of wooden shacks. Most of the camp was already populated. The camp officer was a German; his name was Tseling, and his assistant was named Yoop. Toward evening, a group of Jews returned from work. They told us that general conditions in the camp were terrible; they worked very hard and got little food. Most of the prisoners came from the small town of Oshmiany [about 100 kilometers southwest of Miligani and in Belorussia] and small towns near it.

We worked paving roads and laying railroad tracks. For a bribe, the *Lagerältester*[3] would drive to the ghettos in Sventzion [about 24 kilometers southwest of Miligani and in Lithuania] and Oshmiany, bringing back greetings and news of what was happening there, and he'd also

[Page 372]

pass on news from us. Somehow or other, we learned that all of the Jews in the Vidz Ghetto had been transferred to the Sventzion Ghetto, among them my mother, my brothers and my sister.

Once, my mother sent me some rusks. I wept with emotion; I knew that she'd collected them from the tiny portions of the other family members. I knew that her condition was worse than mine and that every mouth there was starving.

One lady from Dubina, named Feiga, took devoted care of me, as if I were her daughter.

[Presumably around March 1943] We heard rumors that the Sventzion Ghetto would be shut down and all the Jews there would be taken to Ponar and murdered.[4] We bribed the *Lagerältester* (despite his very high position, he was a good man), and he agreed to bring the rest of our families [to Miligani camp] from the Sventzion Ghetto. In this way they were rescued from death for the time being. I was very happy to be reunited with my family. My little brothers, who were 8 and 10 [sic], were sent to hard labor.

At the end of 1943, Miligani camp was shut down. Some of the people were sent to Olia camp in Latvia, 50 [sic] kilometers from Riga.[5] Now we were sure that this would be our last journey. At this camp there were only men from Lodz [in Poland] and the surrounding area. When they saw us they began weeping, because they'd thought that no Jewish women or children remained alive. They treated us as if we were family, and tried to help us and lighten our burdens.

We worked cutting trees and laying railroad tracks. Despite the hard labor and difficult living conditions, we had great satisfaction in seeing, after our work had been finished, trains full of dead and wounded German soldiers moving from the front lines back to Germany.

The *Lagerältester* [in Olia] was a Jew by the name of Dantziger. He treated us with a very hard hand. He had loyal assistants; they would enter the camp with dogs, which they set on anyone they disliked.

One day, a big truck covered with a thick canopy arrived at the camp. There was a selection. All of the children were put in the truck; they also took [two of] my brothers. It's impossible to describe the screaming and crying that accompanied the children. We were forced to stand in formation for hours. Each minute I thought I'd die from desperation and fear. My mother must have felt my agony, and she held me so that I didn't fall. In this selection, two of my younger brothers and my sister, age 4 [sic], were taken. Of the entire family were left only my mother, me, and my brother, age 11.

We were transported to work by train. The guards were German soldiers and policemen from all nations who cooperated with the Nazis. Among the guards was a Polish man by the name of Yanek, who had a good heart. Despite his fear, he used to sneak over to us many times and sing songs to us in Yiddish. Once, when we were traveling to work, the train stopped and we didn't know the reason why. The good Yanek went to find out. He came back and told us that cars full of children were standing on the track, with tiny hands holding onto the bars [at the openings]. We saw them from a distance. We knew that they were being taken to their deaths. We knew, and we were helpless . . .

Sometimes there were guards who still had a spark of humanity left in their hearts; they'd let us go out of the camp to get a little food from farmers in the surrounding area. Once I went with another girl, from Oshmiany, to search for food. The houses were far from the camp and from each other, isolated farmhouses called *hutory* [in Russian]. We knocked on the door of one of them. An old woman gave us a bit of food

[Page 373]

and told us to get away quickly because her son, who was serving in the police, was likely to return any minute. If he found us, he'd certainly kill us. As we fled for our lives we ran into him, and when he saw us he meant to shoot us. But the old mother fell at his feet and begged him to let us go. He ordered us to run, and we fled like deer. We were afraid that at any minute we'd be shot in the back.

In this area [around Olia camp] there were no longer any Jews. The Latvians were crueler than the Germans, they'd killed the Jews immediately after the Germans entered their country.

In July 1944, all of us were transferred to Kaiserwald camp next to Riga [Latvia]. There they gave us numbers; mine was 6757.

Kaiserwald was a huge camp; it looked like a city.[6] Divided into many smaller camps, it was surrounded by several rows of barbed-wire fences, with guard towers along its length. The living quarters were wooden shacks. The women lived separately from the men; there was special housing for the police and the officers.

We reached the camp at night. We were brought to a large shack and ordered to take off our clothes. Naked, we were taken to another shack nearby; there they shaved our hair. From there we were moved to another shack, and each of us got a gray shirt and a dress with blue and white stripes, wooden shoes, and a piece of cloth in the shape of a triangle to cover the head. This was our uniform. We didn't see our old clothes anymore; in our new clothes, we didn't recognize each other.

From there, we passed to a different camp. We were put in a big shack in which there was only one toilet; we had to wait in line for a long time. Many of us got stomachaches and constipation; the situation was unbearable. The next day, we were transferred to a camp with living quarters. In the shacks were wooden bunk-beds with many tiers. Each woman received a blanket. Every few minutes [sic] a formation (*appell,* in German) was ordered, and each time they counted us from the beginning. We were arranged in rows, five women to each row. Very often, Nazis would come to the formations and command us to turn right or left. We knew that this was a selection: to life or to death. Nobody knew when her time would come.

The veterans were sent to labor outside the camp. They were considered happy. I and a few other women worked with anodes [a type of electrical conductor]. We sat at long tables; on them were placed metal parts whose use we didn't understand. With hammers we disassembled the pieces of metal, which were very dusty and dirty, and while we worked the black dust expelled from them would get into our lungs and cover our faces and clothes. We looked like black people. Washing didn't help to keep us clean. Soap wasn't given to us, and water alone didn't wash off the dust.

One day, when I was standing next to the fence, I saw from a distance my brother Bereleh [Asher-Ber?]. He called to me not to worry, because he was among the few children who were still alive, and the adults were taking care of him and other kids like him and giving them a little food. He didn't stay hungry, and he shared his food with me. Once he even threw me a piece of bread, which got stuck on the fence between the barbed wire. A short time later, a large truck came to the camp and took all of the remaining children. After that I didn't see my last brother, Bereleh, any more.

In August 1944, at a time when we were working the night shift, we heard the sound of airplanes over the camp. The airplanes bombed the camp, and the horizon turned red from the huge fires. We understood that they were [also] bombing

[Page 374]

Riga. We knew that the end of the war was coming and we were in great danger. Even in defeat, the Germans wouldn't leave us alive; there was no chance of that.

Now the Germans decided to shut down the entire camp. They put us in lines and took us to the port of Riga; we thought they were going to drown us all. They put us in a big warship, and we sailed off to an unknown destination. They told us they were taking us to a new workplace. Their treatment of us improved slightly: we received some bread, some tinned meat and drinking water. We weren't used to the better food, and so we got diarrhea and stomachaches. Because the toilet was far away and the people who needed it were so many, we used the empty tin cans instead, throwing them into the sea. In this way, we solved a painful problem.

After a few days, they transferred us to a ferryboat. We were very tired and thirsty. In the morning, we were put on the shore and they took us to a big camp, Stutthof.[7] They stood us in formation in a huge, fenced-in lot, where water taps had been installed. We fell upon the taps, and we drank and drank. Next to them, we found small pieces of soap that had apparently been left by the former "residents," and with them we washed ourselves a bit. We were kept in this lot, in terrible heat, until the evening. From a distance, we saw men wearing pajamas.

In the evening, they arranged us again in lines of five people, and we went on foot to the camp. There were many shacks fenced with several rows of barbed wire; the camp looked very similar to Kaiserwald. The guards were Vlasovtsy-Ukrainians,[8] Poles and Latvians, commanded by Germans. Every half-hour, there were formations. We were ordered to report immediately, and because we couldn't all get through the door at once, we jumped out through the windows instead. For this, we were beaten by the *kapo*.[2]

After two days, we were transferred to a camp nearby. Here too there were frequent formations. We slept on bunk-beds and got one meal a day that included a bit of soup and a slice of bread. Our group had a reputation as a group that could work.

Once, when we were standing in the queue for food, we heard terrible screams. We were told that the *kapo* had gotten angry at someone, and he'd thrown her into a vat of boiling water.

Anyone who complained or who the *kapo* disliked was sent to isolation, and from there to the gas chambers. There were days when the smell of the dead from the gas chambers reached us, together with terrible, thick, choking smoke. The fence around the camp was electrified. Many women found their death by touching it.

[Once] we were put in a separate room. Men from the SS told us to take off our clothes, and they examined us. The women whose body condition was bad they put in another room, and we never saw them again. At last, from the entire camp there remained only about 500 women. They ordered us to dress ourselves. The next day, we were moved to another labor camp.

At the new camp, we saw before us a mountain of children's and adults' shoes. Whoever wanted to do so was allowed to choose from it a comfortable pair of shoes. Like many women in the camp, my old [wooden] shoes were very uncomfortable, but it was a terrible feeling to approach this heap and take a pair of shoes, knowing where they'd come from. Despite this, I went to the heap and chose a pair that was very nice. But these shoes weren't suited to work, so I traded them for a loaf of bread. In those days it wasn't at all a bad trade, but I must admit that the bread caused me some problems. If I left it in the shack, I was worried that someone would steal it. I couldn't take it to work, there was no place for me to hide it. And I didn't have the heart to eat it all at once, because I wanted my mother to enjoy it too . . . so I took back

[Page 375]

the wooden shoes and started walking in them again.

One day, we were taken out of the camp, put in small freight cars, and moved to a train station. There we were put in passenger cars and taken to a new labor camp. Here the living quarters were made from plywood, shaped like a doghouse. Over the floor was straw for sleeping on; we also received blankets.

Each morning we heard the shout, "*Kaffee holen!*" ["Get coffee!"], meaning that we were supposed to go and get our morning drink. This camp also had a small shack that was used as a sick room, so to speak. But despite all our aches we were afraid to go there, because we knew that every time a bus came to take the sick on a "rest cure," its path led to the crematoriums. We worked paving roads; the work was difficult and exhausting. Sometimes we had to load heavy stones onto freight cars. The food included a bit of soup and one slice of bread per day.

We worked with prisoners of war --- Polish, French and English. The Poles' behavior toward us was very bad. Sometimes we heard from them poisonous, anti-Semitic remarks such as "It's good the Germans are destroying you" and so on. Compared to them, our treatment by the English and French was good. Sometimes they even threw us a sandwich through the barbed wire or when we were going to work. Another relief was that our German guards allowed us to collect potatoes which had been left in the fields. On Sundays, they'd send us to work for the farmers in the area. The German guards would sometimes take us to a small pool of water, where we washed ourselves among the farmers' cows. The camp was relatively good, because the commander of the camp had a good nature. This gave us hope against a dim future.

One day, a shocking thing happened. Usually, when food was brought to the soldiers, the wagons passed near us, and we'd sneak in and steal a little bit of the food; sometimes a loaf of bread, sometimes a potato or carrot. We'd been warned this was very dangerous, but we were so hungry that we were willing to risk it. This went on for a while, until one day the guards shot and killed a girl. They left her body in the field for some days, and we had to pass her each day on the way to work. After that, the stealing from the wagons stopped.

On Yom Kippur, 1944 [September 27], we decided to fast, despite the hard work. After work and before we returned to the camp, there was a formation as usual, and we were counted. At the entrance of the camp, the camp commander himself welcomed us. He sent away the female guards, and he came to us and whispered that he knew what kind of day it was and what it meant to the Jews. He told us that he wanted both us and himself to see the end of the war. And he promised us that he himself would open the camp gate for us to a new life and freedom. His words warmed our hearts and encouraged us; we were excited to tears. But he wouldn't manage to do it --- when the Red Army liberated us he was among the first to be shot, together with the rest of the guards.

At the beginning of 1945 the camp was shut down, and what we called the "big march" began. For a week, we marched on unknown roads. Heading west, we came to the city of Lauenberg [now Lebork in Poland, about 85 kilometers west of Stutthof]. At night we rested in barns, on the hay. The people of the city looked at us in astonishment. We were forced to walk in the middle of the street, while our German guards went on the sidewalk. Despite our miserable appearance, not one resident offered us a piece of bread. Many

[Page 376]

of us couldn't continue this hard, exhausting journey.

We arrived at a military camp named Gotendorf [Gotetowo, about 8.5 kilometers northeast of Lauenberg], located inside the town. The camp was empty, and that's where they put us.

The situation was unbearable because of the terrible crowding, the cold and the hunger. In the camp there were also some men, and their appearance was miserable and frightening. They wore striped pajamas and looked like the dead. Their *kapo* was a Polish Jew, and he was crueler than the Germans; our *kapo* was a Hungarian woman. These two were the real authority in control of the camp. One of their tortures was a bath in the frozen lake. The Germans and their assistants had permission and freedom to do whatever they wanted with us. They didn't kill us only because they knew that if we perished they'd be sent to the Eastern Front.

On March 9, 1945, they ordered us into lines again, and we set out once more on the road. Many stayed at the camp because they had no strength left to walk; I don't know what became of them.

We reached a main road, full of German soldiers retreating from the Red Army and jammed with equipment and weapons. Airplanes were bombing the withdrawal, there was great disorder. Despite all this, although the end of the Germans was rapidly approaching, they were guarding us and were marching us somewhere. We didn't know if we could get out alive. On the way, we met Polish prisoners of war who called to us to hold on, the end of our troubles was very near. With our last bit of strength, we managed to keep going. Those who couldn't were shot.

The next morning we came to a big village, called Chinhof [Chynowie, about 13 kilometers northeast of Gotetowo]. We were put inside a huge barn filled with machines, cows, chickens and animal feed. Starving, we fell upon some vetch [a type of plant] that was found there. The two *kapos* and our guards prepared resting places for themselves. They had food, even wine. All of a sudden, we heard shooting. We thought that the guards were firing and wanted to kill us. But some of the prisoners, who were sitting inside the entrance, began shouting with joy, "It's the Russians! They've come to liberate us!" Mother and I crawled outside and saw Russian soldiers and tanks. The soldiers waved at us, shouting to not be afraid. They were astonished at our dreadful condition; we looked like the dead.

Every German there was shot by the Russian soldiers. When they liberated us, they warned us not to eat a lot of food at once; this could harm us and even endanger our lives. But we couldn't stand the temptation of so much food that was brought to us, and of course we got diarrhea and vomited.

Among the Russian soldiers there were also Jews, and among them some officers. They helped us, guarded us, and advised us to get away from the front and leave the area.

We took their advice, found a horse and wagon, and we headed east, toward home.

Footnotes:
1. Survivor accounts differ on when the attack on Dubina took place. The account of Sima Feigin Moretsky placed it **after Sabbath night on July 18, 1941 (July 19, a Saturday)**. The account of Rivka Maron Rukshin on pages 377-380 of this memorial book said **June 1941** (which seems too early, since the Germans didn't reach the region until June 26 and several of the accounts say that

the attack on Dubina didn't take place until several weeks afterward). A separate account written by Rivka Maron in 1947 and now at Yad Vashem said that the attack took place **three weeks after June 29, 1941**, a time frame that gives July 19 as the closest Sabbath. The account of Mira Shneider Lotz on pages 381-388 of this memorial book said **July 19, 1941**. The account of Chana-Feiga Berkman on pages 390-392 of this memorial book said that there were rumors of an attack at the beginning of the month of Av (around July 25, 1941) and the attack took place later, which seems too late. Taking these accounts together and discounting what appears to be too early and too late, it seems most likely that the attack on Dubina took place on July 19, 1941.

Accounts also differ on the number of people killed in the attack on Dubina, ranging from 18-25 dead. The variation in numbers might reflect any of the following: Some of the accounts omitted from the total the 3-4 men who were killed individually in the village at the outset of the attack (that is, not killed together near the cemetery), one or more of the victims wasn't from Dubina but from another village (Plusy), one of the victims was a Gentile, and at least one victim was wounded in the attack and died weeks or months later.

Taken together, survivor accounts --- including information at Yad Vashem --- have identified a number of those killed in Dubina in the July attack. Cited as killed were (1) **Mantzik Deitch** (son of Beinish-Antzel), (2) **Shlomo-Yitzchak Feigin**, (3) **Yisrael-Yitzchak Feigin**, (4) **Mordechai Levin**, (5) **Beinish Maron**, (6) **Gershon Maron**, (7) **Natan Maron**, (8) **Shimon Rukshin**, (9) **Gedalia Skopitz**, (10) **Chaim Vishkin** (son of Mordechai-Zelig), (11) **Velvel Vishkin** (son of Shlomo-Leizer Vishkin and Rachel Deitch), (12) **Leibel Vishkin** (son of the murdered Velvel), (13) **Henech Shlosberg from Plusy**, and (14) the Gentile **Grigory Khutzin**, chairman of the local council, who was killed because he was a Communist official. The identities of the remaining victims haven't been established.

Those killed were buried in a mass grave near Dubina's Jewish cemetery; later, the Gentile victim was reburied in a Christian cemetery. The victim who was wounded in the attack and died some time later was **Yitzchak Deitch**, son of Kalman-Yossel.

2. According to the *Encyclopedia of Camps and Ghettos, 1933-1945*, Volume, II-B (2012), before the war Vidz had been a town of about 3,000 people. The majority were Jewish, but there were also Poles, Lithuanians, Belorussians, Tatars, Eastern Orthodox, Old Believers and Roma (gypsies).

    The ghetto in Vidz was formed in early 1942. All of the town's Jews were forced to move to Tatarskaia Street, near the houses of study and the synagogues, and the ghetto was surrounded by a fence, which was guarded by local police. From early 1942, Jews from elsewhere were brought into Vidz: Drisviati (Dryswiaty), Druysk (Drujsk), Opsa, Dubina, Kozian (Koziany), as well as survivors from Ignalina (Ignalino) and Sventzion (Swieciany). Conditions in the ghetto were cramped. There was poor sanitation, people had to sleep on the floor, and the women had to cook in turns, sharing the same stove. Overcrowding in the houses, which held multiple families, led to arguments. A number of ghetto inmates, especially the elderly, died of weakness and disease.

    By August 1942 there were 1,505 Jews living in the Vidz Ghetto, of whom 721 could work and 520 were employed. Sometime around October 1942, most of these Jews were transferred to the Sventzion Ghetto. Horses and carts arrived to move the Jews, each with small bundles, to the railway station in Nei-Sventzion (Nowo-Swieciany a.k.a. Svencioneliai). Only about 80 Jews (craftsmen and their families) remained in Vidz at this time, but later these Jews were also sent to Sventzion.

    From the Sventzion Ghetto, most Jews were later sent on to the Vilna Ghetto or were murdered in Ponar on April 5, 1943. For more information, see page 283 of this memorial book.

3. This term, which meant "camp senior" or "camp elder," referred to the senior prisoner assisting the Nazis with administration of the camp, in return for extra food and other privileges. This enabled the Nazis to operate the camps with fewer of their own personnel.

4. Ponar (Ponary in Polish, Paneriai in Lithuanian), about eight kilometers southwest of Vilna, was the major execution site in the Vilna region during World War II and the largest execution site in Lithuania. Between July 1941 and August 1944 an estimated 50,000-70,000 Jews, 2,000-20,000 ethnic Poles and 5,000-8,000 Soviet prisoners were killed there.

5. Olia (now Olaine, Latvia), was 21 kilometers southwest of Riga.

6. According to the *Encyclopedia of Camps and Ghettos, 1933-1945*, Volume I-B (2009), Kaiserwald had been established in March 1943 at the Mezaparks Forest resort a few kilometers to the north of Riga. At any one time it held 2,000-3,000 prisoners, and an estimated 15,000 Jewish prisoners passed through its 12-14 subcamps. Most of the records in Kaiserwald were destroyed in the war, but it's estimated that at least several hundred Jewish prisoners died there. With the Red Army advancing on Riga, the camp was evacuated between late July and October 1944; most of the inmates were sent to Stutthof.

7. Stutthof (now Sztutowo, Poland) had been established in September 1939 about 35 kilometers east of the city of Gdansk, in occupied Poland. From the beginning of 1944, with the German army in retreat from the Eastern Front, about 60,000 Jews were transferred there, mainly from labor camps in Latvia, Lithuania and Estonia. In 1945, evacuation of the camp was carried out, by sea and through death marches, during which many prisoners died. In addition to this account, information on Stutthof is on pages 378-380, 386-388 and 392 of this memorial book, by three other survivors from Dubina.

8. The Vlasovtsy (in Russian), called the Vlasovics in English, were members of the Russian Liberation Army, formed by the Germans from among Russian prisoners of war and defectors from the Soviet army. Named after Lt. Gen. Andrei Vlasov, a Soviet general who'd gone over to the Nazis, they served the Germans during the war.

9. A *kapo* was a Nazi concentration camp prisoner who received extra food and other privileges in return for supervising the labor of other prisoners. This enabled the Nazis to operate the camps with fewer of their own personnel.

[Page 377]

Rivka Rukshin
Daughter of Chaya and Meir Maron

Translated from the Hebrew by Laia Ben-Dov
Footnotes Added / Donated by Jeff Deitch

The village of Dubina [Dubene] near Braslav [Braslaw] is where I was born. [Dubina was 16 kilometers northwest of Braslav.] In our Maron family, there were five souls: my father, Meir; my mother, Chaya; my brother, Yisrael; my sister, Rayzel; and me, Rivka.

We lived in the village [peacefully] until the beginning of the war between Germany and Russia in June 1941. My parents worked very hard for their living. They managed the household and we, the children, studied. Life in the village was like still water, without disturbance --- the life of a small Jewish community with its worries and daily cares that had mainly to do with livelihood.

At the end of June 1941, the Germans reached even our remote village. With the active assistance of many of our Gentile neighbors, they began to carry out their cruel program, the destruction of the Jews.

From the time the Germans invaded until their defeat in 1945, I endured a long road of hardship and suffering, when death was always near. I was in the Vidz and Sventzion ghettos. I passed through 12 concentration and death camps, among them Miligan, Vievis, Zhezmer, Punivitz, Stutthof and Shteinart. On this long and terrible road I lost my parents, my brother and the majority of my relatives, whose names and memory are bound up in the bond of eternal life with the six million lost in the Holocaust. Only I and my sister Rayzel survived.

I'm not able to describe what happened to me in the death camps. In all those camps, there was one goal: humiliation and extermination. The means were always the same: hard labor, hunger, sickness, beatings, murderous assaults and the crematorium. I want to describe only a few isolated episodes that are branded in my memory.

At the end of June 1941[1] a number of Germans and a mob of Gentiles came to the village, and they put us in the old synagogue. After maltreating us, they took 18 men out to a field and killed them --- in cold blood, without explanation. While we were held in the synagogue, the Gentiles took all of our possessions from our homes; we returned to find the houses empty. The Germans and the mob left the village, and we buried our martyrs in a collective grave near the cemetery.

One day they took my brother Yisrael outside, and on the pretext that he had a pistol they treated him brutally. They laid him down on the road and forced him to eat horse droppings. Only the intervention of my uncle

[Page 378]

Betzalel [Maron], who was the [Dubina] Jews' representative to the Germans, saved him from death.

In October 1941,[2] we were expelled from Dubina and taken to the Vidz Ghetto [Widze Ghetto, about 48 kilometers southwest of Dubina].[3] Here the first selection was made. My mother and my sister, Rayzel, were sent to Miligan camp [Mielagenai, about 20 kilometers southwest of Vidz and in Lithuania]. I, my father and my brother, Yisrael, were sent to the Sventzion Ghetto [Swieciany Ghetto, about 45 kilometers southwest of Vidz and in Lithuania]. After a while, we too were transferred to Miligan camp, and there our family was reunited.

From Miligan camp, we were transferred to Vievis camp [about 120 kilometers to the southwest and in Lithuania, along the road between Vilna and Kovno].[4] There we were forced to build railroad tracks. From there, sometimes we succeeded in going out secretly to the nearby village to trade some clothes and valuables still in our possession for food from the villagers. But on our way back, the policemen stole nearly everything. We remained without clothes or food.

Once, a peasant woman told me that she was hiding a Jew in the attic of her home. I went up there and found a young man, but he looked like he was 60 years old. The only thing he asked of me was to bring him a *tallit* [prayer shawl], *tefillin* [phylacteries] and a *siddur* [prayer book]. Father got what the man wanted, and when I gave them to him he was so moved that he burst into tears.

At this camp, father succeeded in baking *matzot* [unleavened bread] for Passover. We gathered the little bit of flour that we'd been able to hide from the policemen, and father secretly fixed an oven that had been found in the camp. In this way, we succeeded in preparing a bit of "poor bread" for the holiday of freedom.

But we weren't able to eat these *matzot*. About two weeks before the holiday, the Germans came to the camp, ordered us out for a formation, and began to separate us. A part of us was sent to the left, and a part to the right. I was sent to the left but without any forethought, by intuition only, I snuck into the group on the right. The entire group on the left was sent to destruction, to Ponar,[5] while the group on the right remained in the camp. My parents were in the group that was sent to destruction, but during the separation I hadn't seen them. If not for that, without a doubt I would have remained with them and like them would have been sent to Ponar.

It was a terrible day. To this day, I can hear the screams of the mothers whose children were being snatched from them, and the cries of the babies who were separated from their parents. To this day, I see the hands of the children reaching out, the fainting mothers and the sneering policemen, who were dispensing beatings right and left with rubber truncheons. Can it ever be forgotten?

After six weeks, my brother Yisrael was also sent to Ponar. Blind chance sent him to death. The Germans came to the camp with lists in their hands; the lists determined who was sent to be murdered. A man on the list hid in the camp [instead of coming forward], and in his place they took my brother, who I never saw again. From Ponar, nobody came back. It was the end of the road.

Near Vievis camp there was another concentration camp, Zhezmer [Ziezmariai, some 25 kilometers west of Vievis and in Lithuania]. We were sent there for work. In this camp, several men organized themselves; somehow they obtained a pistol and planned an escape to the partisans. But this became known to the Germans, and a young woman who knew the secret couldn't withstand the torture and revealed the man who had the pistol. He was taken outside, and after they tortured him he was killed.

From Zhezmer camp, we were transferred to Punivitz concentration camp [Panevezys, about 104 kilometers north of Zhezmer and in Lithuania], and to another [unnamed] camp 50 kilometers from Kovno [Kaunas, about 98 kilometers southwest of Punivitz and in Lithuania]. From there, we were taken to the terrible death camp, Stutthof [in northern Poland, on the Baltic coast].[6]

It was just by chance that my sister and I came to Stutthof, in a group of several hundred women. In a camp near Kovno (the name of which I can't remember), we were put on an open boat, and after three days of sailing we arrived at a railway station. There we were transferred to freight cars, and after several days' travel we reached Auschwitz [in southern Poland] at night, but the entire camp was lit up. Dozens of policemen were running around,

[Page 379]

guarding us. Before we arrived, another train full of people had come. From them, we could hear shouting and crying. We too began to shout. We were kept on the train, and after a while our train began to move out; I don't know why. Maybe they didn't take us out at Auschwitz because that camp was full, the crematoriums were packed, and there was no room for us. Instead, we were taken to Stutthof [some 480 kilometers north of Auschwitz].

[At Stutthof], a cloud of heavy smoke spread over the camp and the surrounding area. This was smoke from the crematoriums, where thousands were burned, most of them Jews. The smoke came out of giant chimneys 24 hours a day. The death factory worked without stopping.

They put us in a big shack. They took off our clothes, cut our hair, passed us under the showers, and at the exit we received striped clothes. All of our meager possessions, including the clothes we'd arrived in, we never saw again.

By chance, I encountered a policeman of Polish origin called Max (whoever was at Stutthof certainly remembers this cruel man).[7] He "honored" me with a blow to my head. To this day I can feel it, and from that day to this my headaches still recur.

At Stutthof, we didn't work. Instead, three or four times a day we were put in formation, and each time meant long hours of standing in place, in all weather. I remember that once we were put in formation before our food was distributed. In front of us they placed a large container with porridge inside it. A woman standing next to the container looked into it. The female guard, noticing this, pushed her into the porridge, and after the woman succeeded in getting out we had to lick off the porridge that was stuck to her clothes. This was our food portion for the day. The woman got nothing.

One day, they made a list of all those who wanted to travel outside the camp for work. My name was on it. Passing through the camp gate, I managed to take with me my sister, Rayzel, who was 13. I hid her behind me, and that's how we left the camp.

This time, our destination was Shteinart [Steinort] camp. Here we dug trenches and loaded sand onto freight cars. I had to do double quotas each day, for myself and my sister.

In the winter, in December 1944 or January 1945, we were taken out of the camp and, on foot, with snow up to our knees, we were pushed westward for two weeks. The weak ones and the slow ones were killed on the spot. Those days, I prayed for just one thing --- that my sister Rayzel would hold out, that she wouldn't collapse, that Heaven forbid she wouldn't fall. I encouraged her and supported her, although my strength too was running out.

Finally, we reached a giant shack next to the road. They took us inside. We numbered a few thousand. Hundreds died each day from the hunger, cold and sickness; no one even troubled to remove them. So we lay down, the living with the dead, in a big mass together. I remember waking up one morning to find that I was lying on the corpse of Leah, the daughter of Volf [Velvel/Zev Deitch] from Dubina; she'd died in the night. At that time Volf's second daughter, Libka, also died. My aunts Chiena and Zlata were in this shack as well.

We were shut up in the shack for two months. We received 100 grams of bread and two potatoes a day. For drinking we melted snow, and in the spring-time we drank water from the drainage canal near the shack.

One day, they didn't bring us the bread. That afternoon our cook, a girl from Opsa [about 27 kilometers southwest of Dubina], appeared

[Page 380]

with the news that the Germans had fled and we'd been liberated by the American army [sic].[8] We greeted the news with apathy, we lacked the strength to show joy. Several women who were still able to stand, me among them, got up and went to the village of Kolka,[9] about a kilometer away, to look for something to eat. We returned with a little bit of food. From there, we moved to the village.

The food improved, we began to recover, our health started to return. After two weeks, we got on a train and went eastward, toward home. Of the people from Dubina, with us were my sister, Rayzel, and two daughters of Volf [Velvel/Zev Deitch], Minka and Zlata. We arrived at Sventzianka [Nei-Sventzion, also known as Nowo-Swieciany and Svencioneliai, about 90 kilometers southwest of Dubina] in Lithuania, where we met Chana-Feiga Skopitz and Zusia and Zalman Levin, all of them from Dubina. We stayed with them for several weeks, recovered a little more from our wounds, and we went on to Braslav and to Dubina.

In Dubina we found complete destruction. Also in Braslav, we couldn't stay. We went back [sic] to Germany, and after a lot of hardship we immigrated to Israel.

Footnotes:

1. The majority of accounts by Dubina survivors in this memorial book (Sima Feigin Moretsky, Mira Shneider Lotz, Chana-Feiga Skopitz Berkman) say that the attack on Dubina took place in July 1941, not June. In addition, a separate account by Rivka Maron (later Rivka Rukshin), written in 1947 and now at Yad Vashem, said that the Germans first paid a visit to Dubina on June 29, 1941 and then attacked the village three weeks later. Accounts also differ on the number of people killed in the attack on Dubina in July 1941, ranging from 18-25 dead.
2. Survivor accounts differ on when the Jewish villagers were expelled from Dubina, ranging from October 1941 to March 1942, but "early 1942" or "around March 1942" seem most likely. The *Encyclopedia of Camps and Ghettos, 1933-1945*, Volume II-B (2012), says that the Vidz Ghetto was established in early 1942, and that Jews from Dubina and elsewhere were brought there from early 1942. Mira Shneider Lotz said around March 1942. In her account written in 1947 and now at Yad Vashem, Rivka Maron said two weeks before Passover 1942 (that is, in March 1942), but in this memorial book --- compiled four decades later --- she recalled it as October 1941. Sima Feigin Moretsky said the beginning of winter 1942 (that is, late 1941 or early 1942). Chana-Feiga Skupitz Berkman said the end of 1941.
3. According to the *Encyclopedia of Camps and Ghettos, 1933-1945*, Volume II-B, the Vidz Ghetto was formed in early 1942. In subsequent months Jews were added to it from Drisviati (Dryswyaty), Druysk (Drujsk), Opsa, Dubina and Kozian (Koziany), Ignalina (Ignalino) and Sventzion. By August 1942, the official population was 1,505.

   Sometime around October 1942, most of the Jews in the Vidz Ghetto would be transferred to the Sventzion Ghetto, about 45 kilometers southwest of Vidz. Only about 80 Jews (craftsmen and their families) remained in Vidz at this time, but later they too were sent to Sventzion. The majority of the Jews in the Sventzion Ghetto would be taken to Ponar (Ponary) outside Vilna and murdered on April 5, 1943. For more information, see page 283 of this memorial book.
4. Vievis and Zhezmer (mentioned later in this account) were small towns in Lithuania along the road from Vilna to Kovno. During the war, labor camps were set up in them or nearby.
5. Ponar (Ponary in Polish, Paneriai in Lithuanian), about eight kilometers southwest of Vilna, was the major execution site in the Vilna region during World War II and the largest execution site in Lithuania. Between July 1941 and August 1944 an estimated 50,000-70,000 Jews, 2,000-20,000 ethnic Poles and 5,000-8,000 Soviet prisoners were killed there.

   According to Rivka Maron's account written in 1947 and now at Yad Vashem, this large selection in which she lost her parents took place not in Vievis but in Zhezmer --- early in 1944, two weeks before Passover (which began that year on April 8).
6. The concentration camp in Stutthof (now Sztutowo, Poland) was about 310 kilometers west of Kovno and about 35 kilometers east of the city of Gdansk (Danzig). It was the first concentration camp set up outside German borders in World War II and the last camp to be liberated by the Allies. Established in September 1939 as an internment camp, it became a concentration camp in January 1942, operating through end-April/early May 1945, when it was liberated by the Soviet army. Originally a small camp, it was enlarged in 1943 and a gas chamber and crematorium were added.

In early 1945, evacuation of the camp was carried out, by sea and through death marches, during which many prisoners died.

During the war, an estimated 110,000 people were sent to Stutthof or its subcamps, of whom an estimated 63,000-65,000 died, at least 28,000 of whom were Jews. Shteinart (Steinort), mentioned later in this account, was one of approximately 40 subcamps around Stutthof; it was on the Baltic coast about 18 kilometers southeast of Stutthof and is now called Kamienica Elbląska.

In addition to this account, information on Stutthof is on pages 374-376, 386-388 and 392 of this memorial book, by three other survivors from Dubina.

7. This was perhaps Max Musolf/Mosulf, a Polish inmate mentioned in several other books on Stutthof as a *kapo* in charge of the Jewish women's barracks ca. 1944. He was notorious for his cruelty toward the women. See, for example, *We Survived*, published in 1949 by Eric Boehm.

8. According to Rivka Maron's account written in 1947 and now at Yad Vashem, the liberation was carried out by the Soviet army and took place in 1945, about two weeks before Passover (which began that year on March 29). The liberation couldn't have been carried out by the American army, because it didn't reach that area.

9. This probably refers to Kolkau, a subcamp of Stutthof that was about eight kilometers north of Chinhof/Chynow (mentioned on pages 376 and 387 in this memorial book). Kolkau, in Poland, is now called Kolkowo.

[Page 381]

Mira Lotz
Daughter of Rachel-Leah and David Shneider

Translated from the Hebrew by Laia Ben-Dov
Footnotes Added / Donated by Jeff Deitch

I'm a daughter of the village of Dubina [Dubene]. There I was born in 1926. I was 15 when the war between Germany and Russia began, in 1941. I passed through many concentration camps: from the Vidz [Widze] Ghetto to labor and concentration camps --- Miligan [Mielagenai] in Lithuania, Olia and Kaiserwald in Latvia --- and from there to Stutthof death camp and camps Sufenwald [Sophienwalde, a subcamp of Stutthof] and Lauenberg in Germany [sic]. I saw the massacre of thousands and thousands of Jews, among them those dearest and most unforgettable to me --- my family. Each day I met with the bitterness of death and envied the dead; and I was left alive. And so that we do not forget and those who come after us will know, it's my obligation to speak.

Childhood Memories
Amid a thick forest of pines and firs, 18 kilometers from the town of Braslav [Braslaw], and three kilometers from the border between Poland and Latvia, the Jewish village of Dubina was established in 1848.[1] Before the war began, the population in the village was 320 souls,[2] most of them farmers who owned plots of land and livestock --- horses, cows, sheep and chickens. A minority were artisans and small tradesmen.

The village houses were built of wood, with roofs of straw. Due to their age, the houses had settled into the earth, and sometimes in winter the snow would reach up to the chimneys. Almost all the houses were whitewashed. A flower garden, a vegetable garden and fruit trees surrounded each house.

Near the village was a lake, a place for bathing and rest. We children loved this place the most. In the summer, all the residents of the village were busy with agriculture as well as cutting wood in the forest for heating in winter. At every opportunity, the women and children would enter the forest to collect berries and mushrooms.

Most of the Jews in Dubina were religious, and the two synagogues were filled to capacity on Sabbaths and holidays. As in every Jewish community, the rabbi was the head. Everybody also paid respect to the *shochet* [ritual slaughterer], Reb[3] Shmuel-Aba [Deitch]. In one of the synagogues was a *cheder* [Hebrew primary school], and the teacher was Rabbi Shmuel Feigin.

The most important characteristic of the Jews of Dubina was that they were united. The joy of one was the joy of all, and the sorrow of one was the sorrow of the entire community. Decisions

[Page 382]

about all problems in the village were taken at meetings after prayers in the synagogue, and of course after stormy arguments and discussion.

Through community effort, a cooperative dairy was built that produced butter and cheese to sell. There was also mutual aid, and all those in need received support. I remember Malka Gurevitz coming every Friday to all the houses with a big basket in her hand, gathering food for the Sabbath that she distributed among the needy. On Sabbath night, with the lighting of the candles, you could feel the peace and quiet of the Sabbath in the village. And the young people used to gather in groups and enjoy singing and dancing. This is how the Jews of Dubina lived, with their problems and their hopes, working hard as they looked to the future.

And then --- a heavy, black cloud darkened the lives of the Jews. On June 22, 1941, the Germans invaded Russia, and everything collapsed around us. All of us felt the approaching disaster. The roads emptied of people, and we were enveloped by panic and fear. Even during the first nights, farmers from neighboring villages burst into the village and began to plunder, and the nights passed without sleep.

Eight kilometers [northeast] from Dubina, in the village of Plusy, lived eight Jewish families. One morning, the Jews from Plusy came to our village and told us a terrifying story. Two men, Leib Vishkin and Yisrael Milonchik, had been murdered and the rest thrown out of their homes. Naturally they all found shelter with us. From that day, we were in constant fear; we knew that we could meet the same fate.

At night we were afraid to remain inside our homes, and we sat outside without sleeping, ready for anything. Most of the men were armed with bars, sticks, pitchforks and rifles, or whatever came to hand. They guarded us and decided to defend themselves. Heading the group for self-defense was Yisrael-Yitzchak Feigin.

On July 19, early in the morning (it was the Sabbath), a large group of policemen arrived, all of them residents of the neighboring villages, under the command of two German officers. Some of the policemen stayed to guard the exits from our village, to keep anyone who would dare to survive from escaping (Heaven forbid!). Twenty-four policemen, among them the Germans, started banging on doors and breaking windows with their rifle butts. With horrific shouts, they drove us all from our houses and gathered us in the old synagogue.

To cast fear into us, they immediately murdered four men, the first martyrs of Dubina. These were Shlomo-Yitzchak Feigin, who'd come home from guard duty and fell with his weapon, a pitchfork, in hand; Yisrael-Yitzchak Feigin; Gershon Maron; and Mordechai Levin, who was killed while trying to escape to the forest.

After that, the policemen separated the men from the women and transferred the men to the new synagogue. The men were ordered to crawl the distance between the synagogues, which was about 500 meters [sic; the distance was closer to 50 meters]. In the synagogue, all the men were forced to lie on the floor, face down. The policemen trod on their backs, kicked them and beat them viciously. At the end of this torture, they chose 20 men, took them out to the field near the cemetery and killed them all.

After these "heroic" acts, the murderers left the village, and the survivors buried the dead in a collective grave near the cemetery.

Three policemen stayed on in Dubina: the officer Milanovski [Milanowski] and the two Kazhik brothers, who based themselves in

[Page 383]

the house of Meir Gurevitz [near the village entrance]. Later, we were ordered to give the policemen all the horses and cows that we had, and they took them to Braslav.

In March 1942, men from the Gestapo came into the village and announced that they were transferring us to the Vidz Ghetto [48 kilometers to the southwest]. From nearby villages, they recruited horses and sleighs. They put us in the sleighs and drove us toward Braslav. For most of the Jews in Dubina, this would be their last journey. For a few --- me among them, the one who is writing these lines --- this was the start of a long road of wandering that led through the ghettos, labor camps and death camps. Braslav was the first station on the way.

The Jews in Braslav took us into their homes. They fed us, got warm clothes for those who needed them, and cared for us the entire night. "They're taking you to the Vidz Ghetto, where are they planning to send us?" they asked. Early the next morning, we were taken to Opsa (20 kilometers from Braslav [to the southwest]), and from there to the Vidz Ghetto.

While we were in Braslav, the policemen had ordered all of us to report together in the morning. Everyone knew that if we didn't obey, we would die. Despite this, there were people who hid and stayed behind in the town [Braslav]. Among them were Zev-Volf [Velvel] Blacher, his wife, Golda, and their daughter Tzipa-Chana [Gurevitz][4] and her children. All of them were murdered with the Jews of Braslav when the Braslav Ghetto was liquidated [on June 3-5, 1942, when several thousand people were massacred]. Only the son of Tzipa-Chana, Koppel [Gurevitz], escaped and managed to get to the Vidz Ghetto to his grandmother, Mala.

I want to tell you about a family that remained in Dubina, the family of Shlomo Levin. His wife, Sara-Disel, was a dressmaker, and among her pupils was the daughter of the farmer Draygun [Dragun] from a nearby village, Rauhgishki [three kilometers to the north]. The night before the Jews of the village were expelled [from Dubina], Draygun came and promised to hide and save Sara-Disel and her two daughters, Shayna-Rivka and Chayala. He asked only this: that the husband, Shlomo, go with the rest of the Jews to the ghetto. Of course, Draygun's suggestion was accepted. Later the same day, this "compassionate" man took the mother and her daughters to the forest and murdered them, so that he could acquire their meager possessions. All this I was told by farmers from around Dubina who I met in Vidz.

The Vidz Ghetto

Here, part of the town was fenced in with barbed wire. We were ordered to attach a yellow patch to our clothes. In each apartment lived a few families. The crowding and constant hunger helped to spread typhoid fever, and many died each day. Among those from Dubina who died in Vidz were my grandfather Yosef [Shneider]; both my uncles, Yisrael [surname not stated] and Avraham-Yaacov [Shneider]; a woman by the name of Yenta-Leah [Rabinovitz]; and others.

After a number of months, the Germans took 40 people out of the Vidz Ghetto to Miligan labor camp in Lithuania [Miligan, in Lithuania, was about 20 kilometers southwest of Vidz]. I was in this group; I'd just turned 15. Girls my age were Sima Feigin, Dvora Maron, Raizela Maron (who was older than us by maybe a year or two), Dina Deitch, Zlata Deitch, and Feiga Vishkin. Also with us were two girls from Yod [Jod], several people from Druysk [Drujsk], and Motke Rozenberg and his father, Leib, from Opsa.[5] All of the rest were Jews from Vidz. The Germans had told us that they were taking our group to a labor camp, but we couldn't believe it. "It's not possible," some said, "that they'd take to a labor camp girls aged 15." This and the strict way the Germans guarded us --- they didn't let anyone near us --- strengthened our suspicion that they were taking us to be killed. All night, we were locked in the building of the Judenrat [Jewish Council].

In the morning they arranged us and counted us and, on foot and accompanied by policemen, we were taken to Ignalina

[Page 384]

(a distance of 40 kilometers).[6] There they sat us on the ground in the mud, next to the train station, and many hours passed. At last they put us into cattlecars, and in these we came to Miligan camp. The time: August 1942. Before us, they'd brought to the camp hundreds of women from the town of Oshmiany [about 100 kilometers south-southwest of Miligan and in Belorussia], all of them young and brave.

Our representatives there were a wise and brave man by the name of Kretchmer and a woman, Ita Kolar. We lived in temporary shacks with three-tiered bunks. Ita warned us that we should all say we were above the age of 15 and able to work, otherwise they'd mark us for death.

The camp belonged to the military government and was supervised by two Germans. One was named Yoop; the other, Tseling. Germans who were experts at building supervised us and put us to work paving a 25-kilometer road between the small towns of Zhezmer [Ziezmariai] and Vievis.[7] Our work mainly involved making the road level; to do this, we reduced the elevations and filled the depressions with sand. We loaded the sand onto small freight cars, and a small locomotive took it to the required location. There we unloaded the sand and, with the help of stretchers and wheelbarrows, poured it on the outline of the road. Other groups brought stones and paved the road, and in the gaps between the stones we poured sand and gravel. The work was organized in a "wonderful" way, the well-known German system: shouts and beatings from the German experts. They didn't allow us to straighten our backs the entire day, from dawn to dusk.

After the brutal workday, we received "food": 200 grams of bread and a half-liter of water with a few pieces of cabbage floating in it, as if it were soup. In the morning, we drank tea. Our work schedule was the same in the winter, when we had to take the sand and stones from beneath the snow and the frozen ground. In the evening we warmed ourselves next to the stove in the shack, but the heat caused our wounds to open. Our frozen limbs turned blue, and the pain was unbearable. This happened each night: Hungry, freezing and bleeding, we climbed into our beds.

On Sundays, we didn't work. They allowed us to wash ourselves and clean the bunks. There was no need to wash our clothes; they'd been in tatters for a long time, and we couldn't get replacements. Sometimes when we were afflicted by hunger --- when were we not? --- we'd knock on the doors of the Lithuanians to get a piece of bread or a potato. Once, I went with another girl to a house to ask for bread. From the next room, a policeman entered. He drew his pistol and pointed it at us. The woman living there grabbed his hand and begged him not to kill us in her house, and in the meantime we managed to run away.

After I was 10 [sic] months in Miligan camp, the Oshmiany girls learned that the Germans were preparing to liquidate the Jews in the ghettos. So they asked that their families be transferred from the [Sventzion] ghetto to the camp. Apparently the Germans were interested in getting more labor power, so they accepted the request of our representative, Kretchmer. In this way, several of the families from Dubina were transferred [to us] from the Sventzion Ghetto (where they'd been transferred earlier from Vidz). Along with adults, some children also arrived in the camp.[8]

When we finished paving the road, the Germans shut down the camp and transferred the prisoners to other camps. I and members of my family, who'd arrived in the camp from the Sventzion Ghetto, were transferred to Olia camp in Latvia.[9] This was at the end of 1943.

Olia camp belonged to the SS. The entire area was fenced with barbed wire, and in every corner was a watchtower. Here we found Jews from the Lodz Ghetto in Poland, and among them a Jewish policeman (kapo)[10] by the name of Dantziger. In this camp too, we lived in shacks and three-tiered bunks. Each shack was fenced separately

[Page 385]

with barbed wire, and another fence separated the shacks of the women and the men. The policeman Dantziger was very strict about keeping us away from the fence. Anyone who went near the fence, to try to catch a glimpse of family members on the other side, felt the force of his arm and the power of his truncheon. To find favor in the eyes of his German overseers, this Dantziger would beat us viciously whenever we encountered him. We did everything we could to stay out of his way.

One day this cruel man attacked my mother, Rachel-Leah, and he beat her with his truncheon until she fell to the ground. Even then, he didn't leave her alone and continued to beat her. By the morning mother felt deathly ill, and she asked me and my sister not to go to work. But we didn't have the strength to stay with our dying mother. Germans with dogs and the Jewish policeman Dantziger inspected the shacks every day; the dogs would attack anyone who remained in them. Next to my mother stayed only my little sister, Sara-Zelda, and she was with her until the final moments.

That evening, Sara-Zelda told us about the last moments of mother, whose final request was to protect my little sister. Mother and another woman who died that day were buried in a field near the camp. Over there was also buried Aba Vishkin from Dubina.

Once I also saw Dantziger take away the clothes of a young man, tie him to a pole, and call over a German officer to show how dedicated he was to his work. When the German came over, Dantziger let the young man go, ordered him to run and then chased after him, beating him cruelly with his truncheon. This continued until the man fell down, lifeless.

At Olia camp, we built tracks for a railway. This meant the same crushing labor from dawn to evening. For this, we got the same 200 grams of bread and half-liter of soup as at the previous camp.

One evening, when we returned from work, we were all driven out of the shacks into the yard, and the SS men began selecting children under the age of 15. I and others tried to hide my little sister, Sara-Zelda. We put her between us, but the Germans noticed. Under a shower of beatings to the head, she collapsed. I tried to hold this little one in my arms, but she was pulled away from me. I ran after her, to the truck that was standing next to the gate. I was beaten and taken back to the camp.

And so I didn't fulfill the last request of my mother; I couldn't protect my sister. She was taken away from me to the death camp, Auschwitz.

Even now, 40 years later, when I recall that terrible day my world turns black. I don't have the words to describe all that happened. The cries of the children and their parents were heard even in the villages around the camp. We raised our eyes to Heaven, but no miracle took place. The sky was mute, while the savages did their work with calm and skill.

Among the kidnapped were 11 children from Dubina, among them, as I said, my little sister, Sara-Zelda. Our father, David, couldn't bear to part from her, and so he followed her to Auschwitz and from there to the crematoriums.[11] This kind of selection was conducted at many concentration camps. I know that some children of Dubina were [also] murdered in Stutthof camp.

After a number of months, when we returned from work one day, they put us inside closed trucks and transferred us to Kaiserwald camp near Riga.[12] When we arrived, they arranged us next to a big shack. At the entrance to the shack, they took our clothes and cut off our hair. At the exit we received other clothes, with stripes, and the clothes that we'd arrived in we didn't see again. I didn't cry for

[Page 386]

those old rags, but inside them, during all this time of wandering, I'd managed to hide a few family pictures that were dearer to me than anything. These were the only keepsakes I had from the past, the last link with my family. The pictures were taken away from me with the clothes, and the pain of this was unbearable.

Kaiserwald was a camp of transfer and selection. After each selection, most of the people were sent to destruction in Auschwitz, while those of us still able to work were used for heavy labor until the next selection. I learned that the children who'd been taken away from us at Olia camp were held here for a while until they were sent to Auschwitz.

Inside the camp was an isolated shack. In it were kept women who'd lost their minds, most of them mothers of children who'd been taken from them to destruction in Auschwitz. From this shack were heard constantly, day and night, yelling, singing and fighting. Sometimes the inmates would burst outside and we'd see women of all ages, whose appearance frightened us. All of them had no hair, it had been cut off. (We heard that hair on the head was cut before liquidation in the crematorium; it was said that it disturbed the electric current [sic] with which people were killed before being burned.)

We weren't at all surprised by these terrible sights: How could one endure what they'd suffered without losing their minds? But even in those very dark days at Kaiserwald, we also felt a few moments of joy. For example, when we saw German fighter planes getting shot down by Russian pilots.

In summer 1944, every day groups of people were being sent in trains to Auschwitz. But the Russian army and the front were advancing, and each night we heard bombings and saw fires in Riga and the surrounding area. Apparently the Germans decided that they wouldn't be able to remove all of us by train. After two months of living in the camp, we were transferred to the Baltic coast. They put us on a ship, and we sailed. We were taken to Stutthof death camp in Germany [sic].[113]

Like all the camps, this one was surrounded by several electrified, barbed-wire fences. Barbed-wire fences also separated the shacks. Here in Stutthof camp, we weren't forced to work. Instead we had selections nonstop, and after each selection people were sent, group after group, to the crematorium. The air was full of the sickening smell of burnt flesh. From one corner of the camp that we weren't allowed to enter, we saw a continual cloud of thick, black smoke rising into the sky and spreading over the area. We knew that this was the end of the road; this was the crematorium.

Each morning at dawn, we'd wake to the shout of *"Appell!"* ["Line up!"]. With shouts and beatings, we were driven out of the shack. At the exit stood two Russian women with whips in their hands who "honored" us with additional beatings. We'd line up in rows in the square, and two fat German men would sort us. Everyone sent to the left went straight to the crematorium.

In this camp too they gave us 200 grams of bread a day, but not even a drop of drinking water. Each day, we accompanied wagons loaded with the corpses of people who'd died from hunger, thirst and disease. Sometimes I envied these people in my heart, all those whose suffering had ended.

After a month, doctors came to the camp. They had us undress and examined us: They were looking for women who could still work. From a few thousand, they separated about 500 women, me among them. They put us in freight cars, and we started traveling out. We didn't know where to, and we didn't care. We knew only that for the moment we were saved from death, because to kill us they didn't need to take us out of

[Page 387]
Stutthof.

We arrived at a new camp, Sufenwald [Sophienwalde].[114] Within the fenced area, we found several shacks built of plywood. Into each shack, they put 40 women. We were auxiliary labor power for constructing houses, which were being built by prisoners of war from Holland and England. Our job was to prepare and deliver the bricks and other materials. The work was like that at all the previous camps --- from dawn until dark --- and for this, the same 200 grams of bread, half-liter of water ("soup") and vicious beatings all day. Two German policewomen and a Jewish female *kapo* from Hungary beat us.

By February 1945, the inside walls of the shack were covered by a layer of ice several centimeters thick. Because the front was approaching, we were driven out of the camp. On foot, in deep snow and heavy cold, wearing shoes made of wood, we were marched for a week toward Berlin. Many died on the way, and those who fell behind were killed on the spot. Hundreds and hundreds of corpses marked the road we passed through. At the end of the week, they put us in a camp near the city of Lauenberg, near Berlin [sic].[115]

In Lauenberg we stayed about a month. The hunger was terrible. The slice of bread we'd received up to then was withheld from us. We had no water for washing, and lice covered our bodies. Our bed was the frozen earth. Hundreds died each day. As the Russians approached, we were expelled from this camp and marched all night in disorder. At dawn, we were put in a barn and locked inside. We expected death at any moment. It was in the village of Chinhof [Chynowie]. The Russian army, which was rapidly approaching Berlin, passed the village without noticing us.

There were Russian prisoners of war with us in the barn, and they understood from the noise of the tanks that the Russian army had come. They broke through the door, and we got out.

How can I describe that moment? After years of a living nightmare, years when I hadn't known the border between life and death, when I'd lost the ability to feel, become so tough that I cared about nothing at all. And suddenly --- freedom.

At that moment, I plumbed the depth of the terrible disaster. The members of my family, who'd been taken one by one to death, passed before my eyes. I remained alive, with hundreds of others just like me: alone, hardly able to stand. All of us little more than skeletons, barely resembling human beings. Shorn of hair, in striped clothing, over my head a blanket, and wooden shoes on my feet. On my sleeve a Star of David, the symbol of my origin, and my number, 40630.

The Russian soldiers gathered nearby took care not to get too close to us; our appearance was frightening. It was March 10, 1945, two months before the end of the war.

I returned to Braslav. I visited Dubina. I found the place where four years ago my village had stood --- where I'd been born --- burned and destroyed. Only a few houses remained standing.[16] Among them was the house of Meir Gurevitz, the first house at the village entrance. I visited the cemetery. Remnants of memorial stones; everything was covered with grass and weeds.

I went back to Braslav and began to get used to life once more. The man who became my husband, Mendel Lotz, was born in Braslav. He escaped to Russia when the Germans arrived in June 1941. In 1943 he was called into the army, and until the war ended in 1945 he fought at the front against the Germans. All of his family remained in the Braslav Ghetto, and all of them were killed.

[Page 388]

This is the story of my life, a true story. I'm sure that all the Holocaust survivors, all of those who remained alive after that terrible hell, remain broken-hearted like me. Even for one moment, we cannot forget what happened. And we'll never forget our dearest ones, who were taken from us.

Footnotes:

1. As the crow flies, Dubina was about 16 kilometers northwest of Braslav. The Jewish farming colony in Dubina was established in 1847-48, but a place named Dubina already existed by the late 1700s, if not earlier, and Jews were listed in Dubina at least six decades before the 1840s.

   In 1784 a government poll tax listed two Jewish heads of families in Dubina as innkeepers, not farmers. These Jews lacked hereditary surnames; such surnames wouldn't become widespread in the Braslav region until around 1816. (For more information on the Jewish adoption of hereditary surnames in the region, see page 16 of this memorial book.)

   In 1845 a government revision list showed a Jew in Dubina named Vishkin with the occupation of tavern-keeper, not farmer, and another Jew named Milner. It appears that Dubina was located along a road that ran between Braslav to the southeast and Kraslavka to the northeast, and either near or on a road that linked Braslav to the southeast and Dvinsk to the northwest.

   In 1847-48 the Russian government distributed land for Jewish farm settlements in the Braslav region, including in Dubina; some of the local Jews as well as Jews from elsewhere then applied for the land and the status of farmer. Surnames on petitions for land in Dubina in 1847-48 included Vishkin, Deitch, Shneider, Maron, Shtein and Zilber, among others. At the outbreak of World War II, families with these surnames were still living in the village.

2. The population of Dubina in 1941 has been estimated at 320 (according to Mira Shneider Lotz in this account) or 500 (according to Rivka Maron in an account at Yad Vashem, an estimate that seems too high). The list of the dead from Dubina on pages 483-485 of this memorial book shows around 330 Dubina villagers. In addition to these victims were a very small number of Dubina villagers who survived the Holocaust as well as a small number of Gentiles who lived in the village.

   At the outset of the Jewish farming colony's establishment in 1847-48, there were said to have been 18 Jewish families. In 1884 and 1885, it's said that the colony suffered heavy damage by fire. In 1898-99 there were 35 or more families, with the surnames Maron, Deitch, Vishkin, Feigin, Shneider, Vairon, Toder, Abramovitz, Shtein and Zilber. In 1923 the population (Jewish and Gentile) was given as 403. The list of dead from Dubina on pages 483-485 of this memorial book contains the surnames Azband, Eidelman, Blacher, Goldin (a.k.a. Godlin), Gurevitz, Goron, Deitch, Vainer, Vairon, Vishkin, Zak, Zilber, Khatzyanov, Levin, Lotz, Maron, Munitz, Mushkat, Skopitz, Feigin, Zukurya, Rabinovitz, Rukshin, Rapaport, Shtein, Shneider and Toder.

3. Reb is an honorific term, something like an exalted "Mr."

4. Koppel Gurevitz was the son of Tzipa-Chana Gurevitz, who was the daughter of Zev (Volf/Velvel) Blacher. Koppel was mentioned also in the account of Alexander (Shmaryahu) Dagovitz, on

page 359 of this memorial book. According to the testimony at Yad Vashem of David Blacher (a brother of Tzipa-Chana), Koppel didn't survive the war.

5. This Dina Deitch was the daughter of Avraham Deitch of Dubina and/or Plusy. Zlata Deitch was the daughter of Volf/Velvel/Zev Deitch of Dubina and Toba/Teibel Vishkin. The account of Mordechai (Motke) Rozenberg from Opsa is on pages 339-351 of this memorial book.

    In relation to Vidz, Yod was about 38 kilometers east, Druysk was about 56 kilometers northeast, and Opsa was about 22 kilometers northeast.

6. As the crow flies, Ignalina (in Lithuania) was about 32 kilometers west of Vidz.

7. Zhezmer was in Lithuania, 140 kilometers southwest of Miligan. Given the long distance between these two places, it's possible that a mistake has been made somewhere. Vievis, also in Lithuania, was 25 kilometers east of Zhezmer. Zhezmer and Vievis were small towns along the road from Vilna to Kovno. During the war, labor camps were set up in them or nearby.

8. The great majority of those in the Sventzion Ghetto who weren't transferred at this time died on April 5, 1943, when they were taken in freight cars to the killing site of Ponar outside the city of Vilna, unloaded and shot. These dead included many of the former inhabitants of Dubina and the surrounding region, numbering some 4,000-5,000 people. (For more information, see page 283 of this memorial book.) After this massacre, from the village of Dubina it appears that only a small number of people remained alive: the five survivors who left accounts in this memorial book and a few others.

9. Olia (now Olaine, Latvia), was 21 kilometers southwest of Riga.

10. A *kapo* was a Nazi concentration camp prisoner who received extra food and other privileges in return for supervising the labor of other prisoners. This enabled the Nazis to operate the camps with fewer of their own personnel.

11. In testimony submitted to Yad Vashem in 1999, Mira Lotz said that her father died at Auschwitz in April 1944.

12. According to the *Encyclopedia of Camps and Ghettos, 1933-1945*, Volume I-B (2009), Kaiserwald had been established in March 1943 at the Mezaparks Forest resort a few kilometers to the north of Riga. At any one time it held 2,000-3,000 prisoners, and an estimated 15,000 Jewish prisoners passed through its 12-14 subcamps. Most of the records in Kaiserwald were destroyed in the war, but it's estimated that at least several hundred Jewish prisoners died there. With the Red Army advancing on Riga, the camp was evacuated between late July and October 1944; most of the inmates were sent to Stutthof in occupied Poland.

13. Stutthof (now Sztutowo, Poland) was established in September 1939 about 35 kilometers east of the city of Gdansk, not in Germany but in occupied Poland. From the beginning of 1944, with the German army in retreat from the Eastern Front, about 60,000 Jews were transferred there, mainly from labor camps in Latvia, Lithuania and Estonia. In early 1945, evacuation of the camp was carried out, by sea and through death marches, during which many prisoners died. In addition to this account, information on Stutthof is on pages 374-376, 378-380 and 392 of this memorial book, by three other survivors from Dubina.

14. According to the *Encyclopedia of Camps and Ghettos 1933-1945*, Volume I-B, Sophienwalde (now Dziemiany, Poland) was formed in August 1944 as one of the many subcamps of Stutthof; it was about 98 kilometers southwest of Stutthof, away from the Baltic coast. A transport of 500 women was sent to Sophienwalde and worked there under the most primitive conditions. Because of the high number of deaths, new prisoners were brought in to keep the prisoner population continually at about 500.

    On February 10, 1945, the camp was evacuated; it's believed that an order was received to march to the north, to Lauenburg (now Lebork, Poland), which was the destination for a number of groups of prisoners led out of Stutthof and subcamps at the time. On February 17, a group of 347 prisoners from Sophienwalde reached the town of Gotentof (called Gotendorf by Sima Feigin Moretsky elsewhere in this memorial book; now Gotetowo, Poland), after a march of more than 80 kilometers, and they were merged with columns of prisoners evacuated from other subcamps of Stutthof. On March 9, these prisoners were put in columns and marched 15 kilometers overnight to Chynow (called Chinhof by Mira Shneider Lotz; now Chynowie, Poland), to the northeast.

    At Chynow, many other Jewish women who had arrived earlier were already in a huge barn and on the roadside. The next day, on March 10, Russian tanks entered the village and the prisoners were liberated. By this time, no more than 250 of the Jewish women from Sophienwalde were still alive. The Russians shot all of the guards escorting these women, including the commandant with them, SS-Oberscharführer (Senior Squad Leader) Willy Schulz.

15. Lauenberg (now Lebork, Poland) was about 95 kilometers west of Stutthof. It wasn't near Berlin (which was about 250 kilometers to the southwest), and the prisoners on the death march were marched to the north of Sophienwalde, not the west.

16.   At the time of the German invasion, the village was said to contain 74 houses (some of which were "two-sided," holding two households) and 79 families. The village was mostly Jewish, with a few Gentile inhabitants. The village was destroyed in the course of the war, either during German operations against partisans or around the time the Germans retreated from the region. Only a few houses were left standing, the best remembered of which was the one near the village entrance, said to have been the house of a Meir Gurevitz.

After the war the area was resettled by Gentiles, who came from surrounding villages and further away, and houses were put up or rebuilt. When the donor visited in 1991 there were 35 houses, populated by Eastern Orthodox and Catholic families.

[Page 389]

Zalman Levin
Son of Stirel [née Vishkin] and Mottel Levin

Translated from the Hebrew by Laia Ben-Dov
Footnotes Added / Donated by Jeff Deitch

After the war we met, me and my friend Zuska Deitch. Both of us were from Dubina [Dubene, 16 kilometers northwest of Braslav], and both of us were serving in the Novo-Sventzion police.[1] We remember very well what was done to us by the Gentiles in the area who were collaborators of the Nazis. We'll always remember the villager Draygun [Dragun], who killed the seamstress Sara-Disel [Levin] and both of her daughters. We'll always remember the officers among them, and the leaders of the enemy who treated so cruelly the 20 people who were killed that black Saturday, among them our family members.[2] I'd been in the group of those made to dig pits and bury the dead. The bodies had been mistreated so badly that we could hardly recognize them. One of them, Mantzik [Deitch], about 20 years old, Zuska's brother --- we could see how his hair stood on end, probably from the pain and fear.

[After the war] we decided to go to Dubina and take revenge on some of them: on Yanka Vitzikhovitz, Malinovski [Malinowski], and the Kazhik brothers. The first two we couldn't find, and nobody knew where they were. The Kazhik brothers, we were told, had been tried for their crimes against the Jews in Dubina and were in prison. The last one was the killer Draygun. We went at night to his village a few kilometers from Dubina, Raugishki [Raugiszki, three kilometers to the north]. We knocked on his door. To his question, "Who's there?" we answered in Russian, "One of us." He came out, and we asked him to show us the way to a certain place. He didn't recognize us and didn't suspect anything until we left the village. He started to give directions, and we forced him into the woods.

We began questioning him about the murders. He denied everything, from beginning to end. We took him [further] into the woods, tied him tightly to a tree, and when we shot over his head he understood we were serious and confessed that he'd murdered Sara-Disel and both her daughters, Shayna-Rivka and Chayala. He added that he'd been in the wrong.

As we were about to carry out our planned revenge on him, my friend Zuska stopped me and said in Yiddish, "The war's over, Soviet rule has been established. If we kill him, they'll catch us and we'll be judged criminals and murderers." We left Draygun tied to the tree, and we quickly went away.

Footnotes:

1. Novo-Swieciany in Polish, a.k.a. Svencioneliai in Lithuanian, was some 90 kilometers southwest of Dubina, in Lithuania.
2. This refers to the attack on Dubina in July 1941, during which 18-25 people were killed; mentioned also in the accounts by the other survivors from Dubina in this memorial book.

[Page 390]

Chana-Feiga Berkman
Daughter of Hirsh and Esther Skopitz

Translated from the Hebrew by Laia Ben-Dov
Footnotes Added / Donated by Jeff Deitch

I was born in 1915 in the Jewish village of Dubina [Dubene], near Braslav [Braslaw], the only daughter of my parents, Hirsh and Esther Skopitz.[1] I had two brothers, Velvel and Yisrael. Before World War II broke out in 1939, both of my brothers had already established families.

My elder brother, Yisrael, was drafted into the Polish army, but in the chaos of the Polish-German war [in September 1939] he was taken prisoner. Our connection with him was lost, and we never heard more of him. My second brother, Velvel, would be killed with my father in Ponar.

Here I'd like to mention our extended family. Of all the family, which numbered several dozen souls, only I was left alive. May my sad story also serve as their memorial.

Fate was very cruel to us. Zlata, wife of my brother Yisrael, with their three children; her parents, Aba and Mira Zilber; her brother [sic] Lipa; her sisters [sic] Shayna, Chava and their families; her sister Aydel, who was married to my brother Velvel --- all were killed in the extermination camps. [Lipa, Shayna and Chava were actually children of Yisrael Skopitz and Zlata.] Neither were there any survivors from the families of my uncle Leiba and his three aunts who were Aba's sisters [or "my father's sisters," the original is unclear]. My cousin Hirsh Skopitz, his wife Chaya [sic] and their seven children passed along a road full of troubles and wanderings in the Vidz and Sventzion [Widze and Swieciany] ghettos, and they were murdered at Ponar.

Dubina was a small Jewish village of several hundred souls. Almost every family had a little piece of land that had been handed down for generations. In summer they worked their fields, and in winter they looked for other income. These farmers were also shoemakers, tailors and glaziers to the farmers of the neighboring Christian villages. Among these Jewish farmers were business owners and prosperous [sic] merchants. As in every Jewish settlement, here too were a rabbi, a ritual slaughterer, teachers and two synagogues. All of the children studied at a Polish public school and also in the *cheder* [Hebrew primary school] of one of the teachers.

When I grew up, my parents sent me to Vilna to learn an occupation [Vilna was about 165 kilometers to the southwest]. I learned to knit, and when I returned to the village I earned my living honorably. I lived in contentment, with no worries, until the Nazis arrived [in June 1941].

At the beginning of the month of Av [July 25, 1941], there were rumors that the Gentiles of the neighboring villages were planning an attack on Dubina.[2] Our men began to organize a defense. They equipped themselves with weapons such as iron rods,

[Page 391]

pitchforks, axes and anything that came to hand, and at night they went out to stand guard, to call us if danger approached and stop the enemy from carrying out their plot.

That's how it was on Sabbath night. At dawn the guards returned to their homes, but they didn't notice that the village had been surrounded.

Trucks, wagons and people on foot came to Dubina from all around, as well as German gendarmes and armed villagers. As they entered the village, several Jews awoke and tried to warn those who were still asleep, but they were killed immediately. A few others who tried to flee in the direction of the forest were also killed by the murderers.

They drove all of us out of our homes and put us in the synagogues. The women were put in one synagogue, the men in the other. The men were laid on the floor, face down, and the rioters trod on their backs.

The Germans gave freedom of action to the local policemen, collaborators and local villagers. A few Gentiles who had grudges to settle with their Jewish neighbors took them out to the field [near the cemetery] and murdered them. On that bloody Sabbath day, about 20 Jews were killed, as well as one Gentile who served as chairman of the local council under the Soviet regime.[3]

While some of the Gentiles were abusing us in the synagogues, the others were busy robbing, taking away all they could from our homes --- clothes, household equipment, furniture and so on. They took every item of value, leaving nothing. When we returned home, beaten and bleeding, we found only the four walls.

Sometime later, an order arrived from the German regional headquarters in Braslav, saying that we had to hand over our horses and wagons, and they also commanded us to hand over half the number of cows that we had. After a few days, all of the cows were confiscated. Our children were left with no milk to drink.

Fortunately, our land yielded a good harvest that year and we had enough bread and potatoes, so we didn't go hungry. But then the next decree arrived: One day, at the end of 1941, we were expelled from the village.[4] We were driven through Braslaw to Vidz, about 40 kilometers away [as the crow flies, Vidz was 48 kilometers southwest of Dubina].

At Vidz, they put us in a ghetto.[5] This was a street fenced with barbed wire; all the Jews of Vidz were already living there. The Germans took no trouble with our living conditions at all, and we survived on the food that remained from home. Sometimes they sent us to work in the fields of the nearby villages, and that was a holiday for us, because the farmers let us eat.

One day, the Germans came to the Vidz Ghetto and demanded that the Judenrat [Jewish Council] supply them with young people for labor. They took us to Sventzion [about 45 kilometers southwest of Vidz and in Lithuania], and we were put behind a barbed-wire fence. We had to work building railroad tracks, we paved roads, and we worked in the fields of the farmers; in payment we received one serving of food a day, just enough to keep us from dying of hunger. But there were other things I'd like to mention: There were two good men with us in the camp, Ephraim Veinpress [or Veinfers] and Leib Doitch [or Deutsch]. Both of them were born in the place, and they recognized the local population and knew their Lithuanian language. They would wander about the villages, sometimes with permission, usually sneaking in, begging for donations, mainly food. They divided the food among those who needed it, and those in need were all of us.

I spent about half a year in that camp. Around Hanukkah [December] 1942, they transferred a group of people to the Vilna Ghetto [about 80 kilometers southwest of Sventzion], myself among them. We were put in a camp inside the ghetto. It's worth mentioning that inside the Vilna Ghetto

[Page 392]

there were labor camps, and in them were Jews who'd been brought from the rural towns. To carry out every decree and for all hard labor, they used people from these camps.

There the "food" was rotten cabbage and frozen potatoes, which we received in the kitchen managed by the Judenrat. The suffering in the summer was terrible, but in the winter it was really unbearable.

We were taken to work naked and barefoot. As a kind of "winter aid" from the [Jewish] community committee, we received wooden shoes, but the shoes became filled with snow and dropped off our feet.

Finally, the spring of 1943 arrived. The majority of the prisoners were taken from the camps, supposedly to work in Kovno [Kaunas, about 90 kilometers west of Vilna]. In fact they all were taken to Ponar, and there they were killed [on April 5, 1943].[6] A few who were only wounded succeeded in climbing out from under the bodies of the dead, fled from there and returned to the [Vilna] ghetto, and it was they who described what had happened in Ponar. My family was taken on a "transport" to Zhezmer camp [Ziezmariai, about 55 kilometers northwest of Vilna, on the road between Vilna and Kovno]. A short time later my mother was taken from there with the small children in an unknown direction. My father and brother Velvel were employed burning the dead, and they were murdered in Ponar.

I remained for some time in the Vilna Ghetto, then they transferred me to Viwikoni[7] camp in Estonia. Until the beginning of 1944, I passed through several camps. In all of them, there were the same conditions: labor, hunger, cold, illness and degradation; but I didn't break.

At the beginning of 1944, they transferred me to Stutthof extermination camp in Germany [sic].[8] Here too, my portion was hunger and degradation. Each morning, they took out of the block hundreds of people who'd died during the night from hunger and disease. From Stutthof I was transferred to a labor camp near Bidgoshch [Bydgoszcz, about 155 kilometers southwest of Stutthof], and I worked building railroad tracks. Again the same hard labor, from early morning until dark, and the hunger. Only one man in the camp did much to lighten our suffering: a Polish work manager named Josef Radka. Of course he couldn't help a lot, but he tried to make the work easier for us, he insisted that we get food on time, and more.

We were liberated on January 28, 1945.

The Polish population in Bidgoshch received us, and they gave us tea and hot milk.

Footnotes:

1. Dubina was 16 kilometers northwest of Braslav.
2. In 1941 the month of Av began on July 25, but other sources suggest the attack on Dubina took place earlier, on July 19, 1941.
3. This man, Grigory Khutzin, is said to have been killed because he was a Communist official. He was buried near the Jewish cemetery outside Dubina, together with the Dubina Jews who had been murdered that day, and later he was reburied in a Christian cemetery. Those who attacked Dubina included policemen from Plusy (7.5 kilometers northeast of Dubina), who were aided by one or more of the Gentile residents of Dubina.
4. Survivor accounts differ on when the Jewish villagers were expelled from Dubina, ranging from October 1941 to March 1942. The *Encyclopedia of Camps and Ghettos, 1933-1945*, Volume II-B (2012), says that Jews from Dubina and elsewhere were brought into Vidz from early 1942.
5. According to the *Encyclopedia of Camps and Ghettos, 1933-1945*, Volume II-B, before the war Vidz had been a town of about 3,000 people. The majority were Jewish, but there were also Poles, Lithuanians, Belorussians, Tatars, Eastern Orthodox, Old Believers and Roma (gypsies).

   The ghetto in Vidz was formed in early 1942. All of the town's Jews were forced to move to Tatarskaia Street, near the houses of study and the synagogues, and the ghetto was surrounded by a fence, which was guarded by local police. From early 1942, Jews from elsewhere were brought into Vidz: Drisviati (Dryswiaty), Druysk (Drujsk), Opsa, Dubina, Kozian (Koziany), as well as survivors from Ignalina (Ignalino) and Sventzion (Swieciany). Conditions in the ghetto were cramped. There was poor sanitation, people had to sleep on the floor, and the women had to cook in turns, sharing the same stove. Overcrowding in the houses, which held multiple families, led to arguments. A number of ghetto inmates, especially the elderly, died of weakness and disease.

By August 1942 there were 1,505 Jews living in the Vidz Ghetto, of whom 721 could work and 520 were employed. Sometime around October 1942, most of these Jews were transferred to the Sventzion Ghetto. Horses and carts arrived to move the Jews, each with small bundles, to the railway station in Nei-Sventzion (Nowo-Swieciany a.k.a. Svencioneliai). Only about 80 Jews (craftsmen and their families) remained in Vidz at this time, but later these Jews were also sent to Sventzion.

From the Sventzion Ghetto, most Jews would be sent to the Vilna Ghetto or murdered in Ponar on April 5, 1943.

6. Ponar (Ponary in Polish, Paneriai in Lithuanian) was about eight kilometers southwest of the train station in Vilna. It was the major execution site in the Vilna region during World War II and the largest execution site in Lithuania. Most of the inmates of the Sventzion Ghetto and other small ghettos in the region --- on the pretext of transfer to the large ghettos in Vilna and Kovno --- were taken to Ponar and shot on April 5, 1943. For more information, see page 283 of this memorial book.

7. Presumably Viivikonna, one of the many satellite camps around Vaivara concentration camp in northeastern Estonia. (Vaivara, the largest concentration camp in Estonia, took many Jewish inmates from the Vilna and Kovno ghettos.) Viivikonna camp was established by around October 1943. It was about 540 kilometers north of Vilna.

8. The concentration camp in Stutthof (now Sztutowo, Poland) had been established in September 1939. It was in German-occupied Poland, about 760 kilometers southwest of Viivikonna and 35 kilometers east of the city of Gdansk (Danzig). From the beginning of 1944, with the German army in retreat from the Eastern Front, about 60,000 Jews were transferred to Stutthof, mainly from labor camps in Latvia, Lithuania and Estonia. More information on Stutthof and the aftermath is on pages 374-376, 378-380 and 386-388 of this memorial book, by three other survivors from Dubina.

[Page 393]

Zamosh
[Zamosz/Zamoshye/Zamoscie]

Chalvina[1] Pinchov
Son of Tzvia and Menachem-Mendel

Translated from the Hebrew by Jerrold Landau
Footnotes Added / Donated by Jeff Deitch

The village of Zamosh is 12 kilometers from the town of Yod [Jod] and about 18 kilometers from Braslav [Braslaw], nestled among thick forests.[2] The village population was approximately 100 families. About one-tenth (10 families) were Jewish.

The main occupation of the Jews was commerce, but there were also landowners who leased their land to tenants. A small number of Jews were employed as officials.

Like most families in the village, our family earned its living from retailing and the lumber trade. There was no synagogue in the village. Sabbath and festival services took place in the private home of Estrin, a local resident. My father served as the prayer leader and Torah reader during these services.

Jewish children received their primary education from the local Polish primary school in the village, but cultural, social and political activity was conducted in the nearby towns. Most of the older youths joined the institutions, organizations and parties in these towns.

Neighborly relations between Jewish and Christian families, in the village and nearby, were good and proper. During the German conquest, there are witnesses to many instances of help by the local population in hiding Jews, finding hiding places in the neighboring villages, and providing food and clothing.

At the outbreak of war between Poland and Germany [in September 1939], my brother Kalman and I were drafted into the Polish army. In the tumult of war, we were taken captive near the city of Radomsk [Radomsko in central-southern Poland, south of Lodz]. I succeeded in escaping, and after many tribulations and wandering through the area of Pshitik [Przytyk in central-eastern Poland, south of Warsaw] I was able to reach Vilna [about 150 kilometers southwest of Zamosh].

In November 1941, when Jews of Vidz [sic] were brought to the Braslav Ghetto (and from there to the Gleboki Ghetto [Glubokoye Ghetto, about 70 kilometers southeast of Braslav]), we as well --- the Jews of Zamosh --- began to be affected by the German decrees.[3] These demanded that we give them all our valuables and property. The local police commander demanded that we vacate our homes. As they passed through, the Jews of Vidz urged us and even recommended that we move to the Braslav Ghetto with them. Having no choice, we did so. Did we have a choice?!

[Page 394]

My parents, my brother Kalman, and my family lived in Milutin's house [in the Braslav Ghetto]. We were given one room, in which the six of us lived.

The crowding in the ghetto was terrible. Everyone --- the residents of Braslav as well as Jews from nearby towns --- crowded together and were concentrated in one street, the former Pilsudski Street. There was only one Jewish doctor in the ghetto, and his capacity was limited due to the shortage of medication and medical equipment. Obtaining these items from outside the ghetto was fraught with mortal danger for all Jews.

There remained two Christian doctors in the Aryan section of the town: Dr. Baretzki [Barecki] and Dr. Emelianovitz [Emilianowicz]. When my wife, Sonia, went into labor, I succeeded in contacting them. They promised to come when the time arrived and help with the birth. On the day of the birth, I got a permit from the *starosta* [town elder] to leave the ghetto. Late at night, accompanied by a policeman, I went to summon Dr. Baretzki along with a nurse, and they helped my wife give birth to a girl. This took place on the eve of Purim in the month of Adar [March 2, 1942], and we asked the rabbi's advice on what to name her. He advised us to call her Esther, after Queen Esther of the Megillah [Book of Esther]. To our sorrow, the baby didn't survive for long. She died while we were in hiding a few days after the first Aktion [June 3-5, 1942].

The ghetto was fenced off [it appears that this occurred or was completed around April 1, 1942]. Daring individuals went out through the fence at night to fetch food. My brother Kalman reached our village of Zamosh from time to time, and he obtained a bit of food from the villagers with whom we'd been friendly.

We went about tattered and torn, not because we lacked good, proper clothes, but out of suspicion that the policemen and gendarmes would confiscate our clothing as they'd done many times before, taking them for themselves. There was one bathhouse in the ghetto for everyone, and all of the ghetto residents took turns bathing there.

The chairman of the ghetto Judenrat [Jewish Council in Braslav] was Yitzchak Mindel, a former iron merchant. He was a warmhearted, sensitive Jew. It pained him to receive every decree made against the Jews by the Germans and their collaborators, and he tried to soften the decrees as much as possible. The members of the Judenrat --- [Eliezer] Mazeh, [Sasha] Tempelman and others --- also dealt with the ghetto inmates with understanding. Even the Jewish police of the ghetto didn't persecute the Jews, handling the many irregular incidents there with patience.

The slaughter of the Jews of Yod [had taken] place in December 1941. Some of the Jews of Zamosh and Kislovshchitzna [Kislowszczizna, about 17 kilometers southeast of Braslav] were liquidated along with them.

[After that] we went about with the feeling that our turn was approaching. My brother Kalman, who was familiar with construction, built a bunker for 20 people under the garage of the Milutin family. The bunker was well hidden and hard to detect.

The Jews were considered subhuman by the Germans; the murder of a Jewish man, woman or child was nothing to them. A German captain from Gleboki [Glubokoye] shot and killed a Jew for not wearing the yellow patch or for walking on the sidewalk rather than the middle of the road, as was demanded. A local policeman named Krivko [Kriwko, a.k.a. Grivkov] was especially cruel and would often use force.

After the war, Zusman Lubovitz, I, and others in the city of Olshtyn [Olsztyn, in what's now northeastern Poland, about 470 kilometers southwest of Braslav] identified this man. He owned a stall for the sale of meat and sausages. We approached the authorities, and he was arrested. A search of his house found foreign currency, a great deal of jewelry and gold and silver valuables pillaged from ghetto residents. The Jews wanted to bring him to justice on the spot.

[Page 395]

The lot of [Yitzchak] Mindel, the chairman of the [Braslav] Judenrat, was also full of libels and degradation. Once, he was summoned to see the chief of police. Several Jews waited in Mindel's house for his return, to learn why he'd been summoned to appear before the German. When Mindel arrived, he was pale as whitewash: He fell onto the sofa, banged his head against the wall, and cried out in a loud voice. After he calmed down a bit, he told us that the German had been drunk. The German had ordered him to kneel, crawl toward him and lick his boots, as well as perform another contemptible act that he wouldn't describe.

The Germans often demanded large sums (called "contributions") from the Judenrat, and would threaten to kill several people if payment wasn't made. Mindel would say that the money was ready to be collected and would be handed over, but "People --- no!"

He'd go from house to house to collect the requested amount. Once the Jews were forced to swear on a Torah scroll and light candles to prove that they'd give over everything they owned. This was done through the efforts of the Judenrat and in the presence of the local rabbi.

After the first Aktion [June 3-5, 1942], only about 600 people remained. The Germans demanded another 600 gold rubles, or else they'd take out the rest of the Jews for execution. Izia Ribash collected the rest of the money that the Jews had and gave it to the Germans.

On the night before the slaughter [June 3-5, 1942], my brother Kalman woke up and felt that something wasn't right in the ghetto. He summoned all those who were designated to hide in the shelter. We sat there for five days; we were about 20 people. Later, 11 of us succeeded in escaping from Braslav. Sasha Tempelman, and Yerachmiel and Arke [Aron] Milutin were with us. We set out in the direction of Opsa [18 kilometers southwest of Braslav]. Then my brother, my family and I set out for the forests of Zamosh. Our situation was difficult; my wife Sonia was very ill with a high fever. Our young daughter [Esther] died in the hiding place. Moshe-Baruch Bank, a member of the ghetto *chevrah kadisha* [burial society], covered her with a sheet and buried her.

In Zamosh, we hid with farmers with whom we were friends, building a hiding place in one of the barns. One hiding place was even built in a house where Germans lived. I must note the names of several farmers who treated the Jews with friendship and helped us as much as they could: One of them, Yashka [Jaszka] Gasul, was the smith of Zamosh. He and his daughter Tonka, an intelligent, good-hearted girl, fed us and served as our ears for what was happening in the area. They hid us in their house even though they knew that the matter was very dangerous for them and they could have lost their lives. Later, when we were forced to escape again to the forest, I met my brother Kalman and my friend Shlomke [Shlomo] Shapira there. Yashka arranged the meeting, because he knew where they were.

Our friend, the farmer Nikolai Popin, also served as a contact for us. After we escaped from Zamosh in July 1942, he knew where we were hiding, as well as the hiding place that my brother Kalman had prepared in the bogs, among thick vegetation.

At this time, someone reported that Yulian Markievitz [Julian Markiewicz] was hiding Jews, and he was taken out to be killed.

My wife Sonia, myself, and others, wandered from place to place for almost two and a half years. Our friend [Nikolai] Popin, who was very poor, helped us in our difficulties.

Many groups of partisans moved through the forests. Their strength and numbers grew each day. They'd set up ambushes and raids against the Germans, causing a great deal of difficulty for the enemy with their attacks. The Germans were afraid of them and didn't dare to enter the forests. On the other hand,

[Page 396]

they'd burn entire villages as a punishment if they found that an area's farmers were helping the partisans.

There was also a group of gypsies with us. The Germans treated them in the same degrading way as they treated the Jews.

Kalman and I circulated information for the partisans. Since we knew the area, at times we forged contact between friendly farmers and groups of partisans. From time to time, the Germans would move in force to set up blockades over barren areas to subdue the partisans. One day I found Zusman Lubovitz, his wife, and his wife's niece in a very desperate situation in a partisan camp. We helped them as best we could. Together with Yerachmiel Milutin, who was in this partisan camp, we transferred them to our camp, and they remained with us until liberation.

The Red Army arrived on July 9, 1944. Our joy was indescribable. The partisan commander assigned various tasks to us all. We remained in the forest for some time longer and helped them with their work.

In 1941, the Soviet authorities had arrested my father and exiled him to Siberia. A paratrooper who returned from Russia [now] brought us the news that he was living in Gorki [now Nizhny Novgorod, about 400 kilometers east of Moscow] and working as a warehouse operator. Aside from this, we heard nothing more of him. Our mother was with us in the ghetto, and endured all of the tribulations with us. She succeeded in evading the slaughter but she was ill, and we carried her on a stretcher until we arrived in the forest. Her strength didn't hold out, and she died on the journey. My brother Kalman made *aliyah* to Israel, but passed away later due to a malignant illness.

In 1946 I immigrated to Poland, and from there to Germany. I made *aliyah* to Israel at the time of the declaration of independence [in 1948]. I enlisted in the Israel Defense Forces and served for a year and a half, working in military manufacturing.

Footnotes:

1. The Hebrew in this memorial book gives his first name as Chalvina; a more common form of the name is Chlavna.
2. As the crow flies, Zamosh was 10 kilometers northwest of Yod and 16 kilometers south of Braslav.
3. The *Encyclopedia of Camps and Ghettos, 1933-1945*, Volume II-B (2012), mentions a number of transfers of Jewish populations into the Vidz Ghetto from elsewhere, but no transfers of population from Vidz to Braslav or from Vidz to Gleboki. Generally speaking, until the summer of 1942 Jews were concentrated in the Vidz Ghetto, not transferred out of it.

[Page 397]

Zarach
[Zaracz/Zaracze/Zarachye]

Shlomo Reichel
Son of Rayzel and Mendel

Translated from the Hebrew by Laia Ben-Dov
Footnotes Added / Donated by Jeff Deitch

Zarach, a small village about six kilometers [west] from Braslav, is where I was born. At the beginning of the 20th century, there lived in this remote village only two Jewish families: my family --- the Reichel family --- and the Karasin family. I could find no book with any information on where the Jews in our village came from, or when. But what's known to me from my father's stories is that at the end of the 19th century, seeking a way that he could make a living, my grandfather Chaim-Eliahu Reichel settled in the village, bought a parcel of land, opened an inn, and made a living from the Gentiles who came to have their grain ground at the watermill. At about this same time, the Karasin family arrived and settled there. The head of the Karasin family, Michael, leased an estate and a watermill from a count who owned the village and surrounding land.

After World War I the count sold his estate to a Pole named Milevitz [Milewicz], and Michael Karasin and his family left the village and moved to Braslav. Our family remained in Zarach --- my father, Mendel; my mother, Rayzel (who died in 1922); my brothers Gedaliahu, Shneiur, Gershon, Berl and myself.

The entire family supported itself from the watermill; we bought seeds, ground them and sold the flour to bakers in Braslav, Opsa [18 kilometers southwest of Braslav] and Vidz [Widze, about 40 kilometers southwest of Braslav]. One by one, all of the children went to the *cheder* [Hebrew primary school] in Braslav. On Sundays, our father would take all of us to Braslav for the week, and on Fridays he'd take us home to our village for the Sabbath. Apart from our studies at the *cheder*, all of us went to the Polish schools. At the beginning of the 1930s, [two of] my brothers married and left Zarach. Gedaliahu moved to Vilna [about 160 kilometers southwest of Zarach], and Shneiur settled down in Braslav. My father, [my married brother] Gershon and his family, Berl and I remained in the village.

On September 1, 1939, when war broke out between Poland and Germany, I was drafted into the Polish army. I fought against the invaders until the bitter end, until the Germans conquered Poland. Together with the remnants of the Polish army that retreated toward the Romanian border, I arrived in Lvov [in southeastern Poland]. Here we encountered the Soviet army, which took us prisoner. I spent more than a year and a half in a prisoner-of-war camp near Rovno [Rowne, some 500 kilometers south of Braslav]. With the outbreak of war

[Page 398]

between Germany and Russia in June 1941, they transferred us first to Zhitomir [Zhytomyr, in western Ukraine], and from there to Buzuluk near Chkalov [now Orenburg, in a region adjoining Kazakhstan].

In February 1942, I volunteered for Anders' Polish Army.[1] I reached Ashkhabad with them [in Turkmenistan], but before the army left Russia all the Jews were "freed" [released from the army]. This was in September 1942.

We stayed to work at a *kolkhoz* [Soviet collective farm]. At the beginning of 1943 I was mobilized for the third time, this time by the Red Army. After a brief period of training, I was sent to the front to the Kursk-Oriol [Orel] line. I was injured near Oriol [in western Russia]. After a long hospitalization of about four months, I recovered from my wounds and was sent to work in the kerosene industry around Chkalov.

At the beginning of 1945 I moved from Russia to Poland, but after a few months I returned home in the hope of finding someone in my family who'd survived. This hope was in vain; I found only destruction and devastation, and from the information supplied about my family by our Gentile neighbors, I learned the following.

At the beginning of July 1941, the Germans had confiscated our land (about 50 *dunams*[2]) and transferred it to the Gentile neighbors; my brother Gershon, who worked at the watermill, had been expelled. He remained in the village for some time and for sustenance sold his family's clothes and household articles for food. After a few months, the entire family was sent to the Braslav Ghetto. Father, my brothers Shneiur and Gershon, together with their families, were slaughtered in the massacre of the ghetto on 18 Sivan 5702 (June 3, 1942). My brother Berl, together with a large group of young people, was taken to clean the army barracks in Slobodka the day before the slaughter. It's known that this group was returned to Braslav on the day of the massacre, taken straight to the pits and murdered. A few managed to escape, among them my brother Berl. He managed to get to the forests near Zamosh [Zamocz, about 16 kilometers south of Braslav], where he joined the partisans and fought in the Chkalov [Czkalow] brigade against the Nazis and their collaborators, falling in battle. Despite all my efforts, I was unable to learn the day he died or the place where he was buried. My oldest brother, Gedaliahu, was murdered with thousands of Jews from Vilna at Ponar [April 5, 1943; strictly speaking, the Jews killed weren't from Vilna, but from the small ghettos around Vilna, including Oshmiany and

Sventzion]. I remain the sole survivor of my extended family. In 1979, I immigrated with my family to Israel from Russia.

Footnotes:

1. This was a Polish armed force created in the Soviet Union from among Polish prisoners of war, after the USSR established diplomatic relations with the Polish government in exile in July 1941 and began releasing the Polish prisoners that it held. The force was commanded by Wladyslaw Anders. In 1942, many of its members who decided to leave the USSR were evacuated to Iran and later reached Palestine.
2. One Israeli *dunam* = 1,000 square meters or 0.247 acre; 50 *dunams* = 12.4 acres.

[Page 399]

Yaisi
[Jaisi/Jejse/Jajsy]

Shneiur Munitz
Son of Rivka and Avraham-Yaacov

Translated from the Hebrew by Laia Ben-Dov
(Yiddish Translated by Aaron Krishtalka)
Footnotes Added / Donated by Jeff Deitch

*While gathering material for this memoir, I [an editor of the memorial book, not identified here]
met with Munya-Rayza (formerly Vishkin) of Dubina. When she heard about my project, she said:
"Oh --- Shneiur Munitz! He's a relative of my family from the village of Yaisi [Jaisi]. He's here in
Israel and can talk to you about it."*

*He agreed to talk, although not without hesitation and puzzlement. Speaking in Yiddish, he
said, "S'iz shoyn azoy feel yorn fun dan, un der zikorn iz nisht azoy gut, un ikh bin shoyn nisht
azoy yung." ["So many years have passed since then, my memory's weak, and I'm not as young
as I used to be."] Out of curiosity I asked his age and he replied, "Ich bin shoyn ariber di*

zibetziker." ["I'm already past my seventies."] He gave me permission to translate into Hebrew what he said in Yiddish.

The speaker was Shneiur Munitz, from the Jewish agricultural village of Yaisi [seven kilometers east of Braslav/Braslaw]. A few years before the war, he moved to Braslav with his family, where he had a house and a shop. This is what he said:

With the German invasion of Russia on June 22, 1941, there was an immediate general conscription of men into the Red Army. From Braslav and its surroundings 2,000 men were called up, and I was one of them. We boarded a train, from where we were supposed to go to Molodechno [about 150 kilometers to the south] to be enlisted, divided into units and --- of course --- sent to the front to fight the Germans. We got as far as the intermediate station of Krolevshchitzna [Krolewszczyzna, about 60 kilometers southeast of Braslav, between Glubokoye and Dokshitsy]. There I saw more trains with inductees like me waiting around. Alongside one of the freight cars stood groups of men talking and arguing about the war. Naturally they were saying, "They (the Germans) will very quickly break their heads against us (the Russians). We're not Poland or Czechoslovakia." While they were talking, a large squadron of German aircraft suddenly appeared and began bombing the area of the station. The tracks were damaged, along with everything standing on them: locomotives, freight cars loaded with war material, and passenger cars with people inside. The panic was great: Dead and wounded were lying about, people were running this way and that, looking for cover. For the first time in our lives, I and many others saw the damage that could be inflicted by airplanes.

The Germans' applied pressure along the entire front, preventing the Russians from organizing. We, who had to advance, received a notice from our commanding officer: "Since I'm unable to contact our command post and we're likely to be surrounded,

[Page 400]

I hereby release you. You may return to your homes or go further into Russia." I immediately found myself a partner, and together we set out on the road home. Near Gleboki [Glubokoye, about 70 kilometers southeast of Braslav], we endured another bombing from German aircraft. We slept next to the Jewish cemetery that night, and at dawn we went on our way. Fortunately, a Jew who was driving a horse and wagon happened to pass by and gave us a ride, saving us a walk of about 20 kilometers. On the road, we met a large Russian army that was retreating ahead of the German advance. On Thursday --- the fifth day of the war --- I arrived home, tired but glad. There were happiness and kisses, but with sad hearts --- this was war.

On Friday [June 27], the Germans entered Braslav.[1] A large German army continued eastward, leaving behind a small garrison. Russian aircraft tried to obstruct the advance of the Germans with bombing raids over Braslav. It's hard to say how much damage was caused to the enemy, but there were some deaths and injuries among the local population. With the entry of the Germans, fear and worry increased.

As I mentioned, we'd moved to Braslav from Yaisi, where some of our family remained. Yaisi was a Jewish village with about 20 families, most of whom earned their living from agriculture. Braslav was seven kilometers away. Because the situation was unclear, my wife, Sara, suggested that we return temporarily to Yaisi to mother [whether her mother or his isn't clear here, though it could be Sara's mother, since she's mentioned below]. This was a good idea. About two days later, we got to the village together with my cousin Velvel Grinshpan and his family, who joined us. In the village, rumors had reached us that abandoned homes in Braslav were being robbed by the Gentiles. I decided to check; Velvel came with me. We visited Velvel's home [in Braslav] and others as well. There had indeed been incidents of robbery, but my property was undamaged. A few people supported our move to the village, saying that maybe the Germans wouldn't reach us there. This was on Friday [July 4] --- almost two weeks into the war. We returned home early and were at home [in Yaisi] --- preparing for the Sabbath.

The time --- after the Sabbath had begun. Those living at a distance from the synagogue hadn't yet arrived home. I was among them. I was walking along peacefully, my head full of casual thoughts. I heard a shout: "Halt!" I turned my head and received a heavy blow from a German. Around me, I heard shouting and the sound of windows being pounded: "Raus!" [Out!"]

The Germans collected 15 Jews and took us away. At the exit from the village were more Germans waiting for us, together with a Gentile villager with a horse and wagon. In the wagon were some shovels. The Germans began beating us with the butts of their rifles, heavy and painful blows all over our bodies. They hit my face, and some of my teeth were uprooted. Before we could even understand what was happening or why, the order was shouted to take the shovels from the wagon and start digging two pits. We were divided into two groups. The digging proceeded rapidly, hurried along by shouts of "*Schneller! Schneller!*" ["Faster! Faster!"]. I was covered in sweat, from fear and exhaustion. In the next pit, they began to shoot people. I shouted, "Hear, O Israel . . . ."[2] and jumped from the pit: "If there's a G-d in Heaven --- help me!" . . . With my last bit of strength, I began to run through a field of rye. They shot at me, but missed. I was saved.

The shooting at the pits stopped. I dug myself into the rye, tensely expecting that they'd come to search for me. I lay there with my head spinning; I was stunned. In a while it'll be dawn and I, Shneiur Munitz, will return home (so I hoped). How can I tell my family what just happened? How can I explain it --- will anyone believe me? Can there be so many funerals in Yaisi in one day!? Later, acquaintances told me that they attributed the shooting to a platoon of German soldiers who'd passed near the village. People said that these men had been taken for work somewhere. I approached my home slowly, crawling on the ground. Outside, next to the house, I noticed my wife, Sara, searching worriedly for me.

[Page 401]

A lot of people arrived and gathered together. I was talking and crying . . . and everyone was crying with me . . .

This had happened on the Sabbath. The next day, a group of people went out and brought back the corpses. Because of the beatings and shootings, it was impossible to identify the bodies. They were buried in a mass grave. I still remember some of them: There was Nachum Tzipin and his three sons, Paltiel (nicknamed Pailke), Arieh (Leibke) and Chaim-Shmerel; my cousin Velvel Grinshpan, who'd fled from Braslav with me and had a hard life; Yisrael-Yitzchak and Chaim-Reuven, father and son [no surname given]; Shaya-Beinish Tarshish[3]; and my brother Levik. After the incident, I went to Braslav to tell people what had happened and warn them of the situation. The remaining Jews from Yaisi were later sent to the ghetto in Braslav, but not before all their possessions had been confiscated.

The command to enclose in a ghetto the Jews of Braslav, and other Jews who were there, was given on Passover Eve 1942 [April 1, 1942]. Our house was located on a street that was part of the ghetto. Additional residents were quartered in our house. We were ordered to wear a yellow patch, and people were taken for forced labor. There was a serious lack of food; fear and worry over our very existence were our daily lot in the months to come.

One night, I had a dream that my teeth were falling out. Such a dream was a bad sign; someone in the family was going to die. That night, I didn't shut my eyes. I went through the house, checking on everyone: Sara, here's Sara; here's her mother. Here are my beloved children, seven-year-old Avraham-Yankeleh and my little daughter, three-year-old Chaya-Racheleh. Strange thoughts worried me. We'd already heard of the destruction of ghettos in the vicinity, and I could still visualize the slaughter that had taken place in Yaisi. I didn't know it then, but this night was the last time I saw my family. Toward morning [June 3, 1942], the ghetto was encircled by gendarmes, local police and other collaborators. Shooting started, knocking on doors, the breaking of windows and doors, and shouting that everyone had to come outside. I leapt from my bed. There was a large Russian stove in our house that was used to bake bread for the entire week, *challot* [braided loaves of bread] for the Sabbath and *cholent* [traditional Jewish stew]. Beneath the stove was a small opening, narrow at first but gradually widening out. I crawled into the opening. No one knew where I'd gone. Sara quickly dressed the children, and they all went outside. My brother Velvel lived in the house opposite. Sara hurried there to look for me. My brother was surprised to see her and advised her to go down to the hiding place. Sara never saw her children or her mother again. They were driven out, together with everyone else, and murdered near the train station [this refers to the round-up and massacre of Jews in Braslav on June 3-5, 1942]. At that most terrible moment, our little children found themselves without their father and mother. As the day went on, a German leading a large dog came into the house to search for anyone who was hiding, and I could see his shiny boots through the opening. He grabbed a mattress from the bed opposite and blocked up the entrance to my hiding place. For the second time, I was saved. I heard that they caught Sara, together with other Jews who were hiding, and killed her.

The few who remained after the slaughter began looking for more secure hiding places. I thought to myself: I'm a tailor by trade, after all --- I'll go out to the villages and offer my services in exchange for food and a safe place to hide. And so it happened. From the end of summer 1942 through the winter of 1943, I worked for the villagers and wanted for nothing. My situation worsened significantly when a Jew hiding in a nearby village was captured, without even the farmers knowing he'd been hiding there. After relentless torture, he eventually broke and told the Germans the name of the village. They killed him, of course, but they also executed 38 villagers for not checking carefully enough to prevent Jews from hiding in their village. So I was forced to leave the farmers. In a yard in Butzvitz [Buczwicz?] I found a barn full of straw in the courtyard of property owned by Duke Svinski, who'd been exiled to Siberia by the Russians and had his property confiscated. In this straw, I found refuge for eight months.

Partisans had begun operating in the area. After making many requests

[Page 402]

and proving that I was a veteran with experience, I was accepted into one of the partisan units. After the Germans were driven out and Braslav was returned to Soviet control, I was mobilized into the Red Army until the war's end.

It was May 9, 1945. The Germans were defeated, the war was over. The reserve soldiers were demobilized. Everyone was happy, as they returned to their homes and families. I wasn't happy. I had no family and no home, where and to whom should I return? To what destination should I buy a ticket? My entire family had lived in Braslav and its surroundings. I decided to return there, maybe I'd discover someone. A former resident of Dubina, Zlata, returned from the German camps to Braslav. We got to know each other and got married. We decided to leave Braslav and build our home and future in the Land of Israel. One daughter was born to us in Germany, and another daughter in Israel. We had a good life. In 1967, Zlata became ill and died. What's left for me to do at my age? I spend my time visiting my daughters and my five grandchildren.

Footnotes:

1.   Other accounts in this memorial book put the German entry into Braslav a day or two earlier.
2.   "Shema Yisrael": The affirmation and confession of faith made by Jews *in extremis*, and recited thrice daily in prayers: "Hear, O Israel, the Lord our G-d, the Lord is One!"
3.   The memorial book lists a Yeshayahu-Beinish Rukshin, not Tarshish.

[Page 403]

Yod
[Jod/Jody/Iody]

[Page 404 = Blank in the original]

[Page 405]

Slava Pinchov
Daughter of Sara and Chaim-Shalom Bor

Translated from the Hebrew by Laia Ben-Dov
Footnotes Added / Donated by Jeff Deitch

After many years filled to overflowing with pain and suffering, I return to the past to raise from behind a curtain of fog the memory of its Jews, who lived there for generations and then were cut off. Who was the Columbus who discovered Yod [Jod], and who was the first Jew or the first Jewish family to settle there? I've no information and have found no authentic sources on it. I was born in Yod; I grew up and was educated there. I knew Yod well; Jews rooted in the town dwelled there. Jewish families lived there for many generations: parents, children, grandchildren; children of grandchildren and great-grandchildren. Our family was also a large one, with aunts, uncles and cousins on both sides, relatives of our father and our mother.

Yod was a town like all of the towns of exile [from Israel] at that time, before the world war. It can be found on a map in the district of Vilna and the subdistrict of Braslav [Braslaw]. Its neighboring villages were Pohost [a.k.a. Novy-Pohost, about 20 kilometers northeast of Yod],

Sharkovshchitzna [Szarkowszcyzna, about 20 kilometers southeast of Yod] and the commercial center, Gleboki [Glubokoye, about 50 kilometers southeast of Yod]. Many Jews lived in these places as well. The town of Braslav, to which we were connected in all municipal and governmental matters, was 25 kilometers from us [to the northwest]. In the [prewar] Jewish cemetery of Braslav, there was even a separate section where the Jews of Yod were buried.[1] The wagoners of Yod supplemented their livelihoods by driving the Jews of Yod in their wagons through the rain and mud, in summer and winter, to the train [station] in Braslav. On the return trip they'd bring sacks of salt, flour, salted fish and the like for the small shop owners in Yod.

In every town and village there was a market day once a week, which the Jews called a "fair." Our market day was on Tuesdays. The entire town waited for this day; it was the main source of income. The Jews would spread out their wares in stalls in the marketplace; one had cans of paint, another would have barrels of pickles. All the products were brought out to the market, baked goods as well. On this day shopkeepers came to Yod from the entire surrounding area, and the fair also became a meeting place for friends and relatives. The owners of the inns in the town also waited for the fair, among them my Aunt Shayna and her seven children. Each child had a job on this day: one daughter served the table, a second one poured drinks into the glasses; a third refilled cigarettes

[Page 406]

in the stall, and a fourth sold apples. The two sons went around among the farmers at the fair.

Like everywhere else, also among us the Jews were divided into the poor and the prosperous. The latter included the owners of the flour mill and owners of the textile and shoe stores, who were approached more than once to donate to charity and who always responded nicely, whether out of a desire to merit honor or to do a great deed.

There also were craftsmen in the town: shoemakers, tailors and two blacksmiths. They earned their keep by the sweat of their brows from the Gentiles of the area. Their great honesty brought them a good name in the entire region. Yod was the "capital" of several small villages, where there lived only a few isolated Jews. Such villages were Kislovshchitzna [Kislowszczizna, about six kilometers north of Yod], Raflovka [probably Rafalova, about six kilometers northeast of Yod, near Hustat], Hustat [Hustaty, about six kilometers northeast of Yod] and Yuditzin [Judycyn, about eight kilometers south of Yod]. The Jews in these places worked the land. They found solutions in Yod to all of their problems. On Passover Eve, for example, the Jews would come to Yod to buy *matzoh* [unleavened flatbread]; they also came before the High Holy Days, to make sure that they had a seat in the synagogue to pray with the congregation and to wish their families and others a good, blessed year. A good and heartfelt welcome to guests was customary in Yod.

Permit me to remember the goodness of my father, Chaim-Shalom Bor, of blessed memory, who was treated with honor and respect by both the great and small in the town. He knew who lacked a bite of bread in the house for their children and who, in the cold winter, lacked wood for the stove that heated their house. Father always worried that no Jew would be left --- Heaven forbid! --- without *matzoh* on Passover. He was a messenger of the congregation in the full meaning of the word: He led the prayers in the synagogue, read the Torah on the Sabbath, and on Purim he read the Megillah [Book of Esther] for those who were sick in their homes. He worked to improve the only meeting place in town: the synagogue. Engraved in my memory is how, during Hanukkah, he'd pass by with a charity box for Keren Kayemet [the Jewish National Fund] in his hand and call out, "Jews, we must redeem the Land of Israel from the Arabs, for the sake of our children's future." Father deeply studied Herzl's *Altneuland* [*The Old New Land*, a utopian novel published in 1902 by Theodor Herzl]. He was a Zionist in his heart and soul, and in this spirit he educated his children.

Oh! Father, my father, we didn't give you a Jewish burial, and I didn't raise a memorial stone for you. You were holy, and you remained among the holy Jews who are scattered in the fields and forests of Poland; your memory will always shine in my heart. I'll remember you forever.

To our great dismay, at that time the Jews of Yod didn't look sufficiently to the future, and they didn't sense what was happening. Each and every one of them lived only in the present.

"Thank G-d every day," they'd say. They were closely tied to each other. Here we were born, married and brought children into the world, generation after generation. People knew each other by their given names and the nicknames that were attached to them.

There were no Jewish educational institutions in Yod. The children of Israel studied in the morning at the Polish *powszechny* [comprehensive] public school, and in the afternoon at a *cheder* [Hebrew primary school]. My father, Chaim-Shalom, established a loan fund to help the needy of the town. Everyone who was able helped in this matter. Anyone in need could receive an interest-free loan of 100 gold pieces and return it within 10 months. There was a committee that managed the records of the fund. The members of the committee were chairman Avraham Shmushkovitz, secretary Peretz Shkolnik [and] cashier Yaacov Shtein. More than once it happened that some of the borrowers didn't keep up with their payments, and this caused problems and arguments. Father always tried to find a solution. He was also concerned with the spiritual life of the town's Jewish youth. He established a library in our house and made it accessible to the town's young people. With the help of a small participation fee, new books were occasionally bought. Within a short time, the library became known to everyone. There were different kinds of books in the library: textbooks, and simple novels that

[Page 407]

attracted young readers. There also were books in Russian and Polish. Each evening, our house was visited by people who were interested in what was going on in the world. They read the newspapers *Moment* and *Letste Nayes*, which were published in Warsaw.[2] The newspapers arrived once a week, and we received them together with two men from the municipality, Eliahu Rozin and Yitzchak Mushkin. On these evenings, the people who gathered there talked politics; they also enjoyed *makhorka* cigarettes (a cheap type of tobacco) that were always on father's table. When I recall the distant past in Yod, I think that my father was among those who spread culture in our isolated town.

I also want to remember my two uncles, who always took an active part in these same evenings of discussion and argument. They were my uncle Yosef, and my uncle Yaacov [Shtein]. Both of them were eager to know what was happening in the world. My grandmother also took a place of honor at the table.

Our family's livelihood was supplied by a small store, like that of many others in the town. There were shopkeepers who enjoyed great success, and some who merited less. Our store was managed by my father, with the help of my stepmother. My father's ability in Torah was greater than his ability in commerce, and our store wasn't among the successful ones. There was no livelihood from it. Therefore, my father did something he hadn't wanted to do: Having been a yeshiva student for many years in the past, he opened a *cheder* in our house and became a teacher. My father taught not only Torah but also reading and writing, and among his pupils were those who couldn't afford to pay for their lessons. He devoted himself entirely to the *cheder*.

Our family included my father, Chaim-Shalom; the stepmother, Gitel [née Rukshin]; me --- Slava, the eldest daughter --- my sister, Ida; and my brother, Nachum, the only son. Aside from his precious family, my father possessed little: a house, a small garden beside it, and a single cow. Despite this, in our town we were considered to be middle class, because there were people who had even less.

With the progress that was occurring everywhere, even Yod began to change. Many young people left the town and went out into the wide world. Many traveled to the big city of Vilna [about 155 kilometers southwest of Yod], to try their luck there. Many of these expected no help from their parents, even during the early days of getting accustomed to the big, strange city. Among those who left the town was my sister Ida, who was more active than I was. I remained with our parents. Later, among those who left, some became rabbis and scholars, such as [Rabbi] Yosef Fisher and Rabbi Yosef Barnamov. Around this time, development and progress were also felt in the town. The Jewish owners of the flour mill [the Zilberman family] supplied all of the residents of the town, Jews and Gentiles, with electricity. The houses and streets were lit with electric lights. Radio receivers appeared in the homes of the prosperous, evidence of the great progress being made at the time. Neighborly relationships with the Gentiles improved. Jewish young people befriended Christian youths, and life was conducted peacefully. The Jews began to live under the delusion that this situation might continue forever. But suddenly, things reversed: The war broke out; Germany attacked Poland.

When war broke out between Poland and Germany [in September 1939], the feeling grew in the town that the Poles and the Jews belonged to the same nation. Jews and Poles left together to defend the Polish homeland. Jewish parents saw off their sons, women their husbands, and sisters their brothers, when these left for the front. No one knew what would happen or how long the war would last. Immediately, in the first days of the war, those who remained at home felt that something terrible was coming, but they didn't know what. The war

[Page 408]

didn't last long. The Polish army was attacked and defeated, scattering in every direction. Many of those who'd left to fight didn't return. Some fell in the field of slaughter, and some became prisoners of the Germans. And then, in a completely unexpected way, we learned that the Soviet Union, with Stalin at its head, had made an agreement with Nazi Germany with the aim of dividing Poland between them. After this, the political situation was unclear until the division actually took place. Our town of Yod and its surroundings were joined to Soviet Belorussia, whose capital was Minsk [about 180 kilometers south of Yod]. The Jews, who knew the character of the Nazi regime, accepted the Russian government with blessings and love, because they saw it as offering a chance for better conditions. With the change in the political situation, the Russians began immediately to introduce new procedures. Jews who'd been in the Polish government couldn't hope for a government position; they were transferred to other institutions in the town. Many of the Jewish young people turned to their studies, something that previously they'd been unable to do because of limited means. I was accepted at a seminar for teachers in Braslav, where the majority of students were Jews from the surrounding towns. Certainly there were Jews who were dissatisfied with the new government, among them Jews whose businesses were eliminated and those whose possessions were confiscated. Hatred began to sprout between people, between those who were satisfied and those who weren't. This situation aroused from its slumber the great hatred between the Poles and the Jews. "Jews are Communists. Because of them, Poland lost the war," cried the Poles. Many of them didn't hide their longing for the Germans and waited for them to come and take revenge on the traitorous Jews. Relations were tense and boded no good.

Very slowly, the Jews adapted themselves to the new government. Some took part in governmental activity, and some found it possible to deal in small trade. Jews began to make rosy plans for the future, building castles in the air. But this situation lasted only a short time, and then the fog returned. Refugees from German territory arrived in the town with bad tidings, which aroused great concern. As always, there were people who lived under an illusion and argued against the worriers: "Here in Soviet Russia, nothing will happen. The enemy won't come." Unfortunately, they were wrong.

On June 22, 1941, war broke out between Russia and Germany. After several days of fighting the Russians left the area, but the Germans hadn't yet arrived. Fear grew from day to day. Many people left Yod and headed toward the Russian border [the pre-1939 border to the east], to put some distance between themselves and the danger. But there were also those who believed that the war would end and things would return to normal. They didn't want to think that the hard work of generations could be destroyed in a matter of hours. But events developed very quickly. Even before people understood what was happening, the Germans closed all approaches to the town and the surrounding area. There was nowhere to flee, and most of those who'd left Yod returned. The Jews put their lives in the hands of G-d and fate.

While the Jews worried and feared, the Christians exulted and swore to take revenge. The Polish friends from school and the good neighbors of yesterday, who had eaten *gefilte* fish ["stuffed" fish] with Jews on the Sabbath and been served *hamantaschen* [triangular pastries] on Purim or *matzoh* on Passover, all changed their faces. To us it seemed that they couldn't wait until the Germans arrived. A delegation from the Gentiles of Yod went out in a celebratory parade to Zamosh [Zamosz, about 10 kilometers northwest of Yod], to find a quick solution to the problem of the Jews, which they decided to carry out by themselves.

[Page 409]

The first Germans arrived in Yod on July 21, 1941. These were Germans from the special unit (*sonderkommando*), who made decrees against the Jews.[3] On the day that they arrived, some of the Jews locked themselves in their houses, and many left their homes and went into the fields or forests. With the publication of the decrees against the Jews, the Germans transferred the authority in the town to the local Poles, who organized a local police force in a Jewish house that they confiscated. After this action, the Germans left the town.

The next day, these were the orders published on the walls of the Jewish homes:

1. Every Jew must wear a Magen David [Shield of David] on a yellow patch.
2. It was forbidden for a Jew to walk on the sidewalk of a street together with Gentiles, and it was forbidden to walk on the main street of the town.
3. It was forbidden for Jews to mix with a group of non-Jews.

The orders were accompanied by these "pearls":

a. The Jews caused the war, and it was obligatory to crush them like fleas.
b. Jews sucked the blood of Christians, and they must disappear from the world.
c. Jews were a contagious disease; Jews and dogs must be killed.

The decrees took effect immediately. After them came new decrees each day. The local police carefully carried out all the orders and instructions. The Polish population came to their aid, youngsters as well as adults. I remember the names of the first "warriors" of the town: Retzitzki, Yanshik and his sons, Pyotr Matrinank, Olga Mashuk and others. It's very hard to remember all of the decrees; there were a great many. The Jews obeyed them all and gave over everything they had, thinking that in doing so they could perhaps succeed in saving their lives. Jews were also taken for labor. I remember how my father worked on his knees in the market pulling grass from between the stones. And they also did this: One evening the police gathered 20 Jews at the police station, and all of them were beaten until they fainted. Among them was my young husband, Kalman Pinchov. After being tortured, the ones who were beaten had to pay a special bribe; otherwise they'd be beaten again.

Many of the good neighbors of yesterday now showed a different face. They would come to the homes of the Jews for a friendly "visit" and in passing tell hair-raising tales about all that was happening to the Jews in different places. After these "friendly" stories, they'd turn to the Jewish owner of the house and say to him, "Give us your possessions so that we can protect them. When you need them, we'll return them." Having no choice, the Jews gave their possessions to the "friends." Our family also gave the little that we had to people we knew.

In the morning, we didn't know what would happen at noon or in the evening. Fear of the unexpected pulled at our nerve-strings --- and there was no way out. The Jews sat in their closed houses and together discussed what to do; they gathered donations from those who still had some possessions, to give as bribes; they prayed to G-d in Heaven; they announced fast days and recited psalms. They did everything that Jews do in such times, but help was late in coming.

One evening, in August 1941, the shouting of Gentiles and the sound of breaking glass were heard outside. In the streets of the town a large crowd of men, women and children had gathered, with rods and a number of rifles in their hands, shouting, "The end for the Jews." The Jews abandoned their houses and possessions and fled through the alleys to the fields or hiding places. All night, the Gentiles went wild in the Jewish houses. They

[Page 410]

broke, destroyed and stole everything. The next day there appeared leaflets on behalf of the provisional government, in which it was written, "The rule of anarchy has ended. From now on, there will be law and order in the town." This made mockery of the powerless. What could we do? Sad and ashamed, people began to return to their homes, which had been broken into and destroyed.

After the pogrom, the authorities appointed two Jews from the town to be responsible for implementing all of the decrees that the government would apply to the Jews: the first Judenrat [Jewish Council] in Yod. The two men of the Judenrat were Eliahu Rozin and Peretz Shkolnik. At this time, my husband and I lived with my parents and brother. Together we worried about how to survive under the terrible conditions. Each day, we calculated how to get through the day in peace. We grew discouraged about all the possessions that we'd given to the Gentile "friends" to guard, with a promise on their part to help us in times of trouble. Even my long-time good friend, Olga Mashuk, when I asked her to return something to us, replied immediately: "No! I won't return a thing."

One day, an order was sent to the Judenrat: You must bring us all of the gold and jewelry that's in the hands of the Jews. It was already known to everyone that most of the Jews had nothing to give. In the synagogue, after a discussion my father, Chaim-Shalom, stood up and said, "Jews! You should know that charity saves from death" [from Proverbs 10:2]. Immediately, people took off their wedding rings and handed them over to save lives. But this too was for nothing. Each day, groups of [Jewish] men were taken for labor outside the town. Those who went out said goodbye to their families, because they didn't know if they'd return home. This was how things were done at this early stage of liquidation of the town's Jews.

News that reached the town from other places told us the Germans were establishing ghettos and concentrating in them all the Jews of the region. Ghettos like these had already been established in Braslav and Sharkovshchitzna.[4] The ghetto in Sharkovshchitzna was intended for the Jews of Yod. Life in our town had become so difficult and dangerous that the Jews were almost happy to move to the ghetto. They believed that if they stayed together they might succeed in getting through this terrible period and remaining alive. In preparation for entering the ghetto [in Sharkovshchitzna], they took care to obtain warm clothing for the children and a bit of food. They turned to their Gentile friends, to whom they'd given all their possessions to guard, but only a few of these were ready to help and share a little food in exchange for the possessions. Pleading and begging didn't help. Their final answer was "No!" and their consciences were untroubled.

The Jews of Yod were to move to the [Sharkovshchitzna] ghetto in August 1941. But [August arrived and] things went on as usual, and the local administration didn't rush to implement the decree. To the Jews' questions, they replied, "There's still no order from the Germans." This answer aroused deep suspicions. The Jews rushed about to learn what was happening. There was a feeling in the air that something terrible could take place at any moment. As always, the Jews prayed and fasted to cancel the evil decree.

And then [in December 1941] the fateful hour arrived. Instead of an order to move the Jews [of Yod] to the ghetto [in Sharkovshchitzna], the local Poles were given a free hand to riot against them. In cooperation with the local police, when all were drunk and intoxicated, they robbed and stole the little that remained, and when they could find nothing else, they beat people mercilessly. The head of the Judenrat, Eliahu Rozin, was beaten very cruelly. This was a sign that the Judenrat had no more authority or validity.

After a night of rioting, the news arrived that Gentiles from the surrounding area were busy digging huge pits at the approaches to our town. Many among us tried to find an explanation for this, and there were even optimists

[Page 411]

who wished to see the digging as a sign of the Germans' worsening situation. "Maybe they have to withdraw and are using Gentiles to dig to avoid revealing their true condition." We wanted this explanation to be correct, but to the regret of us all, it was a false hope. The next day, immediately in the morning, we saw how the Jews of Kislovshchitzna, Yuditzin and others were brought, under heavy guard, to the Polish school and locked inside. Panic arose among the Jews of our town. What did this mean?

The evening of that same day, my brother-in-law Motke [Pinchov] came to our house, completely frightened, with the news of Job in his mouth: From a reliable source --- he told us --- he'd learned that the pits the Gentiles had dug at the entrance to Yod were intended for the Jews. And he'd found out more: This had come about because of a petition sent to the Germans in which the local residents asked that the lives of the Jews be given over into their hands, together with all of their possessions. The locals had a right to them, and therefore the liquidation should be carried out here, not in some ghetto located elsewhere. My brother-in-law Motke added that the petition had been written by members of the local Polish intelligentsia, among them Adam Kostokovitz, Olga Mashuk, the teacher Kochenska and others.

After we heard what my brother-in-law said, a great fear took hold of us all. What would happen to the Jews of Yod was utterly clear. We discussed what to do and decided to immediately flee our house and the town. Each additional hour might be crucial for us. We decided to leave in two groups and meet at the home of the Mitzkevitz [Mickiewicz] family, who lived 15 kilometers from Yod. We knew the members of the family, and they could be trusted. We'd go straight there --- we determined --- Motke with his family, which also included two children, his sister and their elderly father. They'd try to reach Zalis [presumably Zalesie, about 3.5 kilometers southwest of Yod] and stay there a short time. After several days, we'd meet and decide what to do next.

This was the third day of Hanukkah, December 16, 1941 [most of the Jews of Yod would be killed the next day]. My father lit the candle and prayed for a miracle; only the power of a miracle could help us. Before we went out on the road, we told those close to us what was about to happen. Sad and discouraged, we left the house. In our group were father, with his *tallit* [prayer shawl] and bag for *tefillin* [phylacteries] in his hands, our stepmother Gitel, my brother Nachum and me. Our guide was my husband, Kalman. At this fateful time, my sister Ida was in Vilna; sometime before, she'd given birth to her oldest daughter. We knew nothing of their current situation.

We walked together into the night. It was very cold outside. We walked on side paths, close to each other, not making a sound. We knew it wouldn't be easy to find shelter. We moved ahead quickly; the will to live kept us going. We knew we couldn't cover the distance to our destination in one night; it was too dangerous to walk during the day. So we decided that before dawn we'd go to the house of one of the farmers we knew in the village of Marchinat [Marciniaty, about four kilometers south of Yod]. Some of our possessions were with him, and he'd promised to help us in time of need. We quietly approached his house and knocked on the door. His wife Platnicha opened the door and was very surprised to see us. "Get away from here, quickly," she said. "Run! The farmers of the village got an order to capture all the Jews who escaped from the town, and tomorrow they'll shoot them all." She added, "They'll shoot anyone who gives shelter to Jews!" We left the house. The light of morning burst forth, and with it the danger that an awakening farmer would see us and turn us in. We decided to risk the danger and enter a building along the way. After going some distance, we came across a small building that was used as a bathhouse, and we went inside. Tired and exhausted, we searched in the dark for the wall, so that we could lean against it. Suddenly, we felt there was a body. For a moment we were afraid, but then it became clear that this was a Jew who, like us, had escaped

[Page 412]

from Yod and found shelter here; we shared the same fate. The man was Yisrael Dubinski, who'd fled alone from the town, "Because they said," he told us, "that they'd kill only the men." His wife and children had remained in the town. We stayed together in the bathhouse, and luckily no one entered that day. During the day, each of us tried to squeeze his body into a corner or next to the wall, and prayed to become seeing but unseen.

It was Tuesday [sic; December 17 was a Wednesday]. Farmers returned from the fair in Yod to their villages, as usual. The bathhouse stood near the road on which the farmers' wagons traveled, and we heard some of their conversations quite well. They spoke among themselves about the great killing that had been done to the Jews.[5] How they'd brought men, women and children to the pits at the entrance to Yod, undressed them like the day they were born, and shot them. It was bitter for us to hear. That Tuesday [sic] we saw with our own eyes, through a small crack in the bathhouse, how the farmers were leading two Jews, who they'd taken from their hiding place in the village. These were the seamstress Liba [Pinchov] and her sister Etel. Helpless, we saw this and were unable to help; we knew that a similar fate might await us. The Gentiles rushed around everywhere like wild beasts looking for prey. Many who succeeded in escaping from the town at the time of the great Aktion [on December 17, 1941] were trapped on the roads or in hiding places by the farmers and turned over to the murderers. There were cases where farmers who'd given shelter to Jews were turned in. From the Jews, they took not only their lives but also their possessions.

In these difficult hours, we wondered if there remained any Gentile who was prepared to help the Jews; after what we heard and saw, we understood that we couldn't stay in this place. We had to hurry and get far away. We decided to leave at nightfall and try to reach the farmer who we'd been seeking when we left our town. Yisrael Dubinski didn't come with us. He said that he wanted to share the fate of his wife and children, and so he returned to the town. As we learned later, he didn't find them alive.

Hungry and thirsty, we set out in the night. "We'll do anything," we said, "to keep from falling into the hands of the Nazis. But if even one of us remains alive, he must avenge the Jewish blood that's been spilled." I don't know how, in those dark moments, the thought of revenge arose. How could a Jew take revenge? There was no time to think about it, time was pressing us.

Again we were on the move; on backroads and paths, in the fields and forests, we distanced ourselves from that place with rapid footsteps until we reached a small stream of water. Even though my husband knew the way and the area, we erred. The water in the stream was nearly frozen, but the distance to our destination was still great. We were worn out and tired, and now we were also wet and frozen and --- above all --- night was coming to an end. Again it was essential to enter a village bathhouse and stay there during the hours of daylight. In such a building we might be safe, because usually the villagers came there only at the end of the week. Everything depended on luck. Not one Jew was ever captured in this kind of building.

To our dismay, the dogs in the area sensed us immediately when we entered the bathhouse, and they began to bark loudly. A farmer with a flashlight in his hand immediately appeared outside and saw us. "Don't be afraid," he said, "I won't harm you." This was the farmer Vasil Brezko [Wasil Bresko], whose lone house stood in a field next to the large village of Lonsk [Lonskie, about eight kilometers south of Yod].[6] The farmer was among our acquaintances, and we knew him as a G-d-fearing, merciful man. He took us into his house to dry off and warm up, and he served us potatoes and boiled

[Page 413]

water. Vasil Brezko was a poor farmer, a big drinker with a warm and kind heart. His family consisted of him, his wife and their five children. He suggested that we remain at his house in a hiding place in the attic, among piles of hay. "You can't go on the road now," he told us, "the roads are full of villagers who are busy hunting for Jews." Then he asked us to give him our boots and felt shoes so that he could dry them. In normal times this would've been kind but now, even though our shoes needed drying, his request was cause for worry. Was Vasil plotting something evil? Who knew? With no other option, we put our fate in his hands. Maybe the fact that he was a poor man would help us; he'd see us as a source of help to support his family. We gave him what we had and described the treasures he'd receive in the future, after we took them from the hoard that we'd buried before fleeing from the town. "The war will soon end," we said, and we told him that the merit of saving us would make him a wealthy man. These were stories that we told Vasil, stories. Meanwhile, with worry in our hearts and rags on our feet, we went up into the attic and dug ourselves into a pile of hay. A number of days passed without any shocks, until one morning we asked Vasil for our boots and he replied immediately that he'd sold them all and bought bread for his family and for us. "Stay with me," he added. "As long as it's possible, I won't drive you out." Again --- what could we do? We remained. We wanted to believe that just maybe he was really a good-hearted person and not like all the others during this time.

Despite the fear that never left us, we grew accustomed to the new conditions and our "home" in the attic hay. Things continued this way until January 1, 1942. That day, we heard the sound of an airplane near the house. We heard a call in German, "Halt! Halt!" Without saying a word, all of us thought our last hour had come. The fear of death in such moments was worse than death itself. Every sense grew numb. We sat in the hay and prepared ourselves for the Germans' arrival. We sat there for an entire day, but nothing happened; when it grew dark the farmer Vasil came and told us that not far from his house a German plane had made an emergency landing, and in it were 13 soldiers. They were waiting for technicians to come and repair the plane, and he didn't know how long things would take. Our stay in his house, Vasil added, worried him and his family very much. We were a great danger to them. But to send us on our way now was impossible, because many farmers were in the area to see the plane, and they'd capture us and denounce us. So he asked us not to make any noise in the storehouse. Nevertheless, in the evening he occasionally came up to us as if to take some hay to the cow, bringing a bottle of water. What bread was, we'd already forgotten some time ago. Vasil Brezko was frightened no less than we were.

A few days passed, which seemed to us an eternity. Because of the severe cold, my father got sick and my brother Nachum's foot became frozen. Each one of us considered how to put an end to this miserable life. Vasil, with his bottle of water, hadn't come for several days. Sick, thirsty and hungry, we were fed only by the smell of the foods that the Germans were cooking below in the storehouse. This nightmare continued for eight days, until one evening Vasil took us, half dead, out of the hay. Then we knew that he really was good-hearted. He took us into a well-heated bathhouse. The news that the Germans had left brought us back to life again.

The farmer treated Nachum's frozen foot. With the help of warm water, we were partly freed from

[Page 414]
the lice that had been eating us up. We felt as if reborn. All that night we sat in the cozy bathhouse, warming ourselves and eating potatoes with onions. These were the first good moments we'd known since leaving our home in Yod.

The next day, the troubles and fears returned. Vasil's wife quarreled with him and demanded that he drive out the Jews and not put their family and farm in danger. She lived in the present, she said, not the future. "Who says," she argued, "that the Germans will lose the war?" Once more we told them about the treasure they'd earn after the war ended, but we knew that if Brezko didn't immediately get something helpful from us, all our stories would mean nothing. His wife would gain the upper hand, and they'd drive us from their house. We began to confer. At this time, we knew from news the farmer had brought us that a few Jewish families of craftsmen remained alive in Yod as "necessary Jews." We knew also that among these Jews were my uncle Yaacov [Shtein] the blacksmith and his family. We looked for a way to contact him, hoping to find a solution. Vasil was willing to travel to the town and find Yaacov. We begged his wife to agree that we could stay with them for a few more days.

In the morning, the farmer harnessed his sled, took an axe as if he was intending to have it sharpened by the blacksmith in town, and I wrote a few words to show where we were and hinted at our distress. That same evening, the farmer returned from the town in a good mood, with a warm greeting that had been passed along and a few written words from Uncle Yaacov. Yaacov wrote that he had a connection with a few more Jews who remained alive. He wrote that his brother Motke [or her husband's brother Motke, the original is unclear] was living in hiding. My husband's elderly father, Natan, had been taken to the killing pit. Vasil also told us that Uncle Yaacov had spoken to him and asked him to keep us with him until the times improved a bit and it was possible to move somewhere else. As a sign of appreciation for Vasil's good deed, my uncle had put into the farmer's sled a sack of grain, peas, barley and several loaves of bread, with a bit of butter. This greatly encouraged Vasil and his wife. We also enjoyed this food, but very little. For his part, Vasil offered samogon --- homemade vodka. Crucially for us, Vasil and his wife decided to let us stay with them. Their attitude toward us changed greatly; they saw us as a means of support. From time to time, Vasil would visit Uncle Yaacov, and he never returned with empty hands. Meanwhile, we moved to another hiding place, in the cowshed: the cow on the right, the pig on the left, and us in a corner that remained empty of storage apples. It was a small, narrow space. In the late hours of the evening, Vasil would bring us into his house to warm up a bit.

Winter [early in 1942] arrived in full strength. In days like these, it was impossible to seek another hiding place. It was also certain that there was no shelter in our surroundings, which were overflowing with Jewish blood. Farmers and sons of farmers were swarming on the roads and near the bridges over the rivers, hunting for Jews. For their services, they received from the Germans a kilogram of cooking salt. Many Jews from Sharkovshchitzna fell as a sacrifice on these roads. I was an eyewitness on one of these occasions and it's engraved in my memory to this day: One morning, we heard a terrible scream. I approached a narrow crack in the wall and looked outside. I saw a horse harnessed to a sled, and behind it a woman was being dragged; her heart-rending screams made me tremble. In the evening, Brezko came to our hiding place and told us that his neighbor from the village of Lonsk had grabbed Sara Munitz, who'd come to the village to find the hiding place of an acquaintance of hers. They'd grabbed her and tortured her very cruelly.

It's hard to describe what we felt that day. We saw ourselves, sooner or later, in the place of

[Page 415]

Sara Munitz. We talked with each other and searched for a way to escape the area. We felt that we should meet with Uncle Yaacov, despite the danger. We knew that time was pressing, each day might be crucial. We decided to leave that night. The lot fell to my Aunt[7] Gitel the stepmother and to me, Slava, to carry out this mission.

We parted with much weeping; nesting in our hearts were doubts that we'd see each other again. The situation was urgent, we wanted to reach the town that same night. Father gave us his blessing and said, "G-d is the great father of everyone. He'll protect you. I pray that you return safely."

Outside --- a snowstorm; even a dog wouldn't go out. We walked on backroads, hoping that we could reach our destination on a night like this --- and we succeeded in getting safely to the town without anyone sensing that we were there. The town was quiet, as if after a storm. The homes of the Jews had been broken into, doors and windows were missing and houses were completely empty. It seemed to us that from every house the shadow of a dead Jew accompanied us. We passed our house, which was already peopled with other tenants, Gentiles. With deep emotion, we reached Uncle Yaacov's house and knocked on the window. They hadn't known we were coming and were very frightened. They calmed down only when they saw us, and they were happy to find us still alive. In fear, they told us that according to the order they'd received it was forbidden to bring Jewish refugees into their house, otherwise their lives would be in danger. After they hid us in a secret place, they told us what had happened to the Jews of Yod and themselves. With their own eyes, they'd seen the Jews of Yod, among them our relatives, walking on their last journey to the valley of death. It began on the Tuesday of Hanukkah, December 17, 1941 [sic; December 17 was a Wednesday]. The pits at the entrance to the town were open and waiting for their sacrifice during all eight days of Hanukkah [December 14-22]. Around the pits stood the Gentiles of the area, who celebrated. They searched the clothes of the sacrificed even before these returned their souls to the Creator, taking everything. The massacre had been carried out by two Germans with machine guns. Local police from Yod and Braslav helped them. Gentiles from the area, adults and youths, with rods in their hands, were the ones who brought the sacrificed to the pits from their houses and hiding places. Only a few, a very few, were saved and succeeded in escaping. Among them were Jews who were brought from Kislovshchitzna, who'd been imprisoned in the school. Uncle Yaacov had a connection with a few of them, and he helped them to some extent.

The destruction of the Jews of Yod in such a cruel manner was the first instance of liquidation of Jews in our area. In [other] places they still hadn't harmed the Jews,[8] not in the ghettos and not the people of the town, as "necessary Jews." It was true, Uncle Yaacov told us, that there already were rumors that the "necessary Jews" would also be put in the ghettos, and therefore he'd decided to send his two oldest children, his son Simcha and daughter Sara, to one of his farmer acquaintances to hide; maybe with luck they'd remain alive. Uncle Yaacov and his family knew that a bitter end awaited the Jews in the ghetto. He advised us to remain with Vasil Brezko, if possible, all winter. We took bread with us and boots, mostly of felt, for our feet. At night we parted [from Uncle Yaacov] with much weeping. With a heavy heart and great sadness, we set out [to return to Vasil], hoping that among those who escaped would be some who'd take revenge on the murderers. This hope kept us going. Father, who had a great deal of faith, always encouraged us in difficult moments. All day he'd pray and say: "Jews must remain alive. Our history tells us that after each pogrom Jews remained alive and established later generations of Jews." (After the war, I reached Yod and found there a photographer whose name, to my regret, I've forgotten. He gave me a photograph of the pits

[Page 416]

where 530 Jews from Yod and the surrounding area met their deaths. A huge mass grave. May G-d avenge their blood.)

Days passed. We remained at Vasil Brezko's, living in constant tension and fear. Father bore his suffering in silence. His hair grew whiter day by day. During the last days, he argued that we shouldn't be found together. He said that if, G-d forbid, the oppressor came we should avoid a situation where none of us could be rescued. In the spring, perhaps, we could move to a different hiding place or go into the forest. In the forest, there were Jews whose fate was like ours. From father's words, we understood that he'd lost hope of rescue. He grew apathetic. Depression ruled over us.

Some days passed and we didn't even receive hot water. The distress from hunger was great; we took to sharing the food of the pig and the cow. We took tiny amounts of their food for ourselves, so that Vasil wouldn't find out. The amount wasn't enough for all of us for each day, but once in two days. It was clear to us all that if we didn't die from the sword, we'd die from starvation. We had to leave this place, but . . . where to go? We decided to take a chance, put ourselves in danger and get a bit of food, and maybe also "something" for Vasil Brezko. Our intention was to turn to people who'd received part of our possessions to watch over at the start of the war and who'd promised to come to our aid in time of need. But how could we reach one of them? Despite the danger, my husband and I went out on a stormy, snowy night to a farmer, one of our good and faithful acquaintances, Vincenty. He was a woodsman who lived near the forest. We hoped that he'd help us and not disappoint us.

All the way, we felt as if we were being followed. Full of fear, we arrived at his house and knocked on the door. The people in the house were afraid when they saw before them two pale shadows of human beings. Fortunately, they recognized us immediately. They brought us inside their house, warmed us next to the stove and gave us things to eat that we hadn't enjoyed for a long time. We told Vincenty (who had a great fear of G-d) the entire truth of our situation --- and that not only did we have no food but also the farmer sheltering us wanted us to leave. We asked Vincenty to give us a bit of food and to save us, so that maybe the farmer sheltering us would let us stay. To our surprise, Vincenty agreed to give us real food, seeds, wheat, peas and the like, as well as some items for Brezko's wife. We returned to Vasil's house happy with our treatment. Vasil left in a sled and brought back everything that had been promised us. From this food, we received a loaf of bread a week, for all of us. The important thing was that their attitude toward us improved a lot.

We tried to turn to other acquaintances in the same way, but unfortunately in most cases we returned with empty hands, accompanied by the barking of the dogs they set on us. Vasil traveled to the farmer Vincenty several times and always came back with food. Vincenty was the only man with a kind heart that we met with in those dark days.

Somehow we got through the winter of 1941-42. Spring came, but it didn't bring good news. In the town of Yod, the "necessary Jews" were no more. Uncle Yaacov and his family were moved to the ghetto in Gleboki.[9] From the news that had reached us, we knew that in most of the area's ghettos people were living in constant fear of destruction.

At this moment, we learned for the first time about Jews who had weapons in the area. It was said that with the help of these weapons they'd obtained all the food they needed from the farmers. To find out who they were and where we could meet them, we had to risk our lives once more and go to a farmer, who at the time of the Aktion [in December 1941] was the only one who'd helped and rescued people. His name was Yashke Artsishevski [Jaszka Arciszewski]. He lived in an isolated house far from all the houses

[Page 417]

of the village, and therefore the approach to his house was easy. As in most of our missions, and this time too, I and my husband, Kalman, set out to find Artsishevski, and after several hours of walking we knocked at his door. He immediately took us inside and was happy to find us alive. He told us that he had connections with Jews who'd succeeded in escaping death and finding shelter with him. He also told us that my husband's brother was at the home of his relative and he could meet us here in the house. We waited for night to come, and he traveled to bring my brother-in-law Motke. It wasn't for nothing that people called Artsishevski the "father of the Jews."

About the meeting with my brother-in-law Motke, there isn't much to tell. This was a drama that many experienced, and only someone who lived through that time will understand its importance. Motke told us that after a long stay in a number of hiding places, he and his wife, his two small children and his wife's sister were preparing to enter the ghetto in Miory [about 34 kilometers northeast of Yod]. In their hiding place, it was hard for them to keep up their spirits. From what he said, it seemed that he'd grown apathetic toward life, and he didn't want to continue to look for places to hide. Sooner or later, he said, everyone would die. Until now, they'd endured many troubles and somehow remained alive, but now the farmer who'd given them shelter was asking them to leave immediately. What could they do?

Motke tried to convince us to move to the ghetto. We answered that we thought the situation would improve during the summer, and until then it would be good to stay with some farmer. To this he replied there was hope that in the summer groups of Jews organized in the ghetto would set out for the forests in the area. With sadness, we parted from my brother-in-law. We hoped to meet each other again [later in the year] and set out together for the forest. To our great dismay, this was a false hope. In the summer of 1942 [on June 2], the [Miory] ghetto was liquidated. My brother-in-law and his entire family were killed, along with all [sic] the Jews of Miory.[10]

Under cover of the dark and rainy nights, we tried to reach the "father of the Jews," Artsishevski, not only to obtain a slice of bread but also to hear what was happening in the vicinity. One night, in his house we met Zalman Shkolnik and Shmuel Barnamov. Both of them had weapons. Zalman told us that when all the Jews had been gathered in the square [presumably in Yod in December 1941] before they were taken out to be slaughtered, he'd killed a German. This had caused a great panic that enabled a number of Jews to escape and survive. Others had been shot by the Germans while fleeing. The ones who escaped had reached this area and met here in Artsishevski's house. Among them was Eliahu, Shmuel Barnamov's brother, who'd fled from the Gleboki Ghetto. He told of a brave deed done by Shmuel: He'd entered the stable of one of the policemen, where a lot of weapons were hidden. He took out the weapons and divided them among the young men who'd gone to the forests of Kozian [Koziany].[11] These forests were large and contained swampy areas that couldn't be crossed. In these forests, the Jewish youths who escaped had organized themselves. Together with them were Russian prisoners who'd worked as slaves of the local farmers.

At this time, every Jewish youth had just one goal: to get a rifle or other weapon. Many of them participated in daring missions. In appreciation, I remember the heroes of our town, who are now found in the Land of Israel or abroad, who avenged the spilled blood of the murdered Jews. They killed Germans and local police who murdered hundreds of Jews: Zalman Shkolnik, Mulia [Shmuel] Barnamov, David Shmushkovitz, Pesach Zilberman, Shimon Shragovich and Zvi [Hirsh] Einhorn. They were brave partisans who took part in many missions. One of the first actions they carried out was to set fire to the town of Yod, together with its new residents. These residents were the people who'd murdered the Jews of Yod. The town went up in flames, and the Gentiles scattered in every direction.[12]

Jews made history; Gentile Christians lived in fear of Jewish revenge. Some of them even fled

[Page 418]

their homes. These young Jewish men, with weapons in their hands, took food for themselves and others from the farmers. Life in the forest was safer under the watch of the partisans.

After this awakening, we planned to leave Vasil Brezko's house, to join the Jews in the forest and live there until the Germans were defeated. Vasil agreed that if our plan failed he'd take us in again. We prepared for the appropriate day to set out, but again fate disappointed us. Events developed in a different way.

One morning, Vasil came with a rumor circulating in the village: The Germans were attacking the Jews and partisans in the forests. This action by the Germans had been prompted by the farmers in the area, who told the Germans about the movements of the Jews and partisans in the forest and asked that the Germans do something. The local farmers entered the forest with the Germans and attacked in a large force. Many partisans were killed. Others escaped and wandered from place to place to find shelter with kind farmers.[13]

The hope that we had now disappeared. Hungry and eaten by lice, we begged Vasil to continue to shelter us in his yard until after the winter. The problem was: How would we survive? Recently we'd been going out at night to get food from the farmers, and they, afraid of the Jewish partisans, had given it to us. Now, after the German attacks, everything had changed. It was difficult to go out at night; the danger was great and we didn't know if there were more Jews in the area who were armed. Our hunger was great. We couldn't even get greens from the garden.

The summer came to an end, fall and winter were approaching. Vasil decided, out of great fear, to transfer us to another hiding place, in the stable, between two walls that had a space between them of half a meter. We sat in darkness always, day and night. Only the cry of the rooster told us that day had come. Discouragement penetrated deeply into our hearts. We envied the dog, who lived freely in the yard.

The tragic year --- 1943 --- was about to arrive. The ghettos in the cities and towns were liquidated, the Jews were shot. In the dark, between the walls, we asked ourselves: What are we living for? What are we waiting for? Our nerves grew weak. Our lives had no purpose. Occasionally Vasil came with bitter news. "The Germans," he said one day, "are withdrawing, and while doing so they're burning everything. They aren't leaving a thing in its place." Our father wanted to draw encouragement from the German withdrawal, and he increased his prayers and recital of psalms. As the month of Kislev approached [November 10 to December 8, 1942], he hoped again for a Hanukkah miracle to redeem us.

The miracle didn't occur. One morning the farmer came again, with the news that he and his family were planning to leave the house. Many of the farmers, he said, had left and were fleeing the village. The Germans wanted to destroy the entire area because of the partisans. That night, we came out from between the walls to see what was happening in the vicinity. On every side, we saw fires that appeared to be the result of heavy bombing from the air. The Germans, Vasil told us, were setting the farmers' homes on fire, together with their inhabitants. The villages that had burned: Sabil-Zoravovshchitzna [Sabil-Zorawowszczyzna, about 15 kilometers southwest of Yod], Kushtali [Kusztale, about nine kilometers southwest of Yod] and Lonsk. Horrible cries were carried to us by the wind. What could we do? Wait for death between the walls of the stable? We couldn't flee in the light of day. Where would we run to? We lay down and waited until the smoke rose in our noses and we felt the heat of the fires. I'll remember that night all my life. All around us, we heard the shouts of the Germans.

[Page 419]

Another night came. We reached a point where we could see and hear what was going on outside, and --- silence, the harbinger of approaching tragedy. There was no trace of people, and we heard only the barking of dogs. Near the place where we were, everything was burning. At this moment, father took off his coat, put it on my brother's shoulders, and said, "Children, there's nothing to wait for any more. You're young. Take your fate in your hands, and with the help of G-d some of you will remain alive. Run! Run from here. I can't go with you. Aunt Gitel and I don't have any strength left, we can't go on. And my long beard would give you away. G-d is the great father of everyone. After the war, the ones who remain alive --- search for each other." And he repeated, "Run, run! Every minute is precious." I remember the deep sadness in his eyes and the hushed sobbing of all of us. For a long time, we'd stood together against every difficult situation that faced us. Why should we separate now? Didn't death lie in wait for us at every turn? Father put his hands on our heads, and wordlessly he blessed us as he did on the day before Yom Kippur in our childhood, and we moved away.

The night was lit with flames of fire and the white snow. We ran with all our strength. To life, or to death? To reach the forest edge, we had to travel a great distance and a bridge over a deep valley. On the way, we met people fleeing in every direction. We worried that someone would recognize we were Jews and shoot at us. Next to the bridge, two Germans stopped us. In great fear, we stood frozen in place as if turned to stone; we heard the Germans shouting, "*Mentschen gut, budinki kaput*" ["We're leaving the people alive and burning the houses"], and they directed us to run along a different path. We ran, waiting for the impact of bullets, but they didn't shoot. They must have thought that we were farmers from the area who were fleeing their homes like many others. Running, we crossed the bridge and kept going until we reached the first trees of the forest. There we fell breathless into the snow. After recovering a bit, we lifted our heads for a last look at the way we'd come, and the village that had guarded our lives for so long. The entire village was in flames, as well as the corner where we'd left our parents to await a miracle, wrapped in a huge flame. We knew that with that flame, the holy souls of our father, Chaim-Shalom, and our stepmother, Aunt Gitel, both of blessed memory, had ascended to Heaven.

We felt the severe cold outdoors, which penetrated our bones. We were half naked and nearly barefoot. We rose with sadness and kept walking aimlessly into the forest. We were indifferent to anything that was likely to happen. This was the first instance, since the time of suffering and fear had begun, that we wished death for ourselves. To die somehow, only not to fall into the hands of the Germans or their collaborators. All night we walked in the forest, and toward morning we saw at some distance a house, lit with a weak light, and thick smoke rising from its chimney. Around the house, everything was burned. This surprised us. We came closer. Despite the danger, we told ourselves that we'd test our luck, as our father, of blessed memory, had advised. We knocked on the door, and when it opened, to our surprise we saw a farmer we knew, Beinarovitz [Viktor Bejnarowicz]. He immediately invited us inside. We grew excited. We couldn't believe that there were still people who'd invite Jews, refugees from the sword, into their homes. I kissed his hands. Could we warm our frozen limbs? He sat us on the warm stove,[114] and for a few hours we felt as if we were in the Garden of Eden. After we warmed ourselves, he took us up to the attic, which was filled with hay. In our conversation with him, he revealed that he too was living in danger, not knowing what would happen. We stayed there, hoping that this situation would be temporary. The farmer told us that until recently several Jews had been hiding in his house. They'd left

[Page 420]

when the situation in the area grew worse. Now, he said, the Germans had completed their operations against the partisans in the forest. So he advised us to go to the Zamosh forest [presumably the forest in the vicinity of Zamosh (about 10 kilometers northwest of Yod) that extended to Zoravovshchitzna (about 15 kilometers southwest of Yod) and beyond].

As before, we told the farmer Beinarovitz stories about our wealth that he'd get for saving our lives. Our aim was to find shelter for the [remaining] winter months. In the end, he agreed that we should return to him after the situation improved. We knew that there were few Gentiles willing to endanger themselves by sheltering Jews, and so we were happy that he agreed.

We left his house at night and went to the forest according to his directions. After walking a few hours in the forest, we met some Jews: Shmuel Mintzer and his wife Liba, Eliahu Shmidt and his brother-in-law Liova [or Liuba] Bik. We became a large group sharing a single fate. We sat in the snow next to a large tree, and told each other of the hardships we'd been through. Today, when I think of those days of hunger, lice, snow and frost, I don't know where we got the strength to endure it all and remain alive.

After several days of sitting in the forest, we decided to again divide ourselves into two groups as before. The area was quiet, no fires were seen on the horizon. It was necessary to find shelter for the winter. We set out on the road, with each group not telling the other of its intentions. The destinations were each group's secret, for good or, Heaven forbid, for bad. Thus, we were very surprised when we all met up again at the house of that same farmer, Beinarovitz. We were a large number of people and doubted that he'd take such a grave danger upon himself and let all of us stay with him, but after talking to us he agreed. He said that the danger was equal, whether with one Jew or 10. We remained together, because we knew we had nowhere else to go. The danger was very great, but there was no other choice. And further: For some reason we thought that the winter of [early] 1943 would be a turning point, both for the war and for Jewish survivors. As always, among us there were people who'd already lost their will to live and who argued: What makes you certain the Nazis will lose the war? We hadn't listened to a radio or read a newspaper, but still we believed in and hoped for the downfall of the Germans. So we attached ourselves to the farmer Beinarovitz. We decided to dig a bunker for everyone, and Shmuel Mintzer, who was a laborer and took the initiative, planned it in the cowshed. All of us helped with the digging, and within one night the pit was dug; its shape was that of a large grave. We covered it with boards, and on these we spread the dung of cows and horses. Inside the bunker there was only room to sit. Again we were in continuous darkness, hungry and eaten by lice, not knowing if it was day or night.

We couldn't leave the bunker to get food; the danger was too great. Once a week, we got from the farmer a baked loaf of bread and other products, whose quality we didn't know. We hung the bread above us on a string so that the mice wouldn't reach it; apparently they too were hungry. When it was sliced, the bread would break into crumbs. My brother Nachum would spread his hands under the bread so that not even one crumb was lost. We ate once a day; there wasn't enough food for more than that. We always had to judge when the best time was to eat, during the day or at night. At night, we had to take out of the bunker the waste of the cows and horses that had drained in.

We were in the pit for many days, and each day seemed like a year. We felt like the living dead in the grave. My brother Nachum fell ill with a skin disease and suffered from swellings, and my husband fell ill with a stomach disease. Matters continued this way until March 1943, when something occurred that forced us to flee the bunker, at all costs: One day, gypsies stole our farmer's horse as well as the entire load in his sled (which hinted to us

[Page 421]

that other people were in the forest). In response to the robbery, Beinarovitz called in the Germans and their helpers, the Ukrainians. They entered the forest and made a terrible massacre of the gypsies. After this, the farmer brought all of the gypsies' possessions to his yard, even the clothes of those who'd been killed. He'd become drunk and thirsty for revenge.

The actions of Beinarovitz raised the suspicion that he wasn't one of the righteous people of the world at all, but a German agent. The suspicion was strengthened by the fact that all of the houses in the area had been set on fire and burned down, but his house was untouched. We thought that he might be holding us in the bunker for some purpose, or as a sacrifice for some contingency. The next night, we fled; the bunker now seemed to us to be a death trap. We set out on the road and put our lives in the hands of fate, without saying a parting word to the Gentile.

Our aim was to get to the forest where we'd found Jews and partisans before the Aktion [the German sweep of late 1942, described on page 418], and we hoped to find them there once more. The forest was 10 kilometers away; not a great distance, but it was hard for us to travel. We were weak and sick. My husband, Kalman, had nearly gone blind from sitting in the dark. The glare of the snow in his eyes caused him great pain. When we finally reached the forest, we were exhausted. We rested a bit and continued into the heart of the forest to our destination, a well-known hill named Zhidovka (the Jewess). After an exhausting walk, we arrived at the place. We were happy to find there Jews like ourselves, who'd been forced to leave their hideouts. All of us hoped to stay here, hiding among the trees, for as long as possible. We began to enjoy some comfort. We even put up sukkot[15] to live in. How long we could stay in the forest, we didn't know. Within a few days, more Jews arrived at the camp on the hill; with them were partisans. Most of the Jews were armed with rifles. The problem of food grew worse. The settlements near the forest had gone up in flames, and to obtain food it was necessary to go great distances in operations at night. This was done by the young men who had weapons. We began to grow accustomed to life in the forest.

Summer [1943] passed, and the new winter approached. In the mornings and evenings, we felt the cold becoming stronger. In our hearts, we began to worry: What would we do in the winter months? Some people said that they had no strength left to find a different place of shelter, they wanted to pass the winter in the forest, await some miracle, and mainly get help from the Jewish partisans. My husband, I and my brother didn't think we had the strength to survive in the forest over the difficult winter months, and we decided to try our luck again with the farmers, far from this location, in a village near Braslav [to the north]. The villagers there were living at the time in absolute peace and good relations with the Germans. In one of these villages, there was a farmer who'd promised to help us in times of trouble. We intended to go to him in the hope that the residents there were no longer busy hunting down Jews, since they believed that none were still alive. Thus, in the lion's mouth we sought shelter and protection.

We returned to wandering at night. Finally, we reached an isolated house in a field near the village of Borodzanitz [Borodzienicze a.k.a. Bordzienic, about 20 kilometers southeast of Braslav and 10 kilometers north of Yod], where a farmer lived who'd been a friend of our family. After a knock on the door, the farmer appeared, and he seemed happy to see us alive. But he agreed to let us enter his house only after much hesitation. The experience of years of wandering taught us how to speak to the farmer in such cases. We decided to describe to him the great wealth he'd receive from us in the future. We built castles in the air and wanted him to believe in their existence. We knew there was no way to go back during daylight; the day was only for Christians and dogs. After our efforts, the farmer agreed to let us stay with him during the day, and at night we'd leave

[Page 422]

his house. We thanked him for that. When we were in his house with his agreement, we continued to try to convince him to let us stay there during the winter months, and finally he agreed. It became clear that he was a religious man who wanted to merit the Garden of Eden in the next world. He expressed his willingness to share our troubles. He was a poor farmer who lived with his wife and 10-year-old daughter.

Again we began to spend the days and nights in a stable or in a pit for storing potatoes. Occasionally the farmer would take us into his bathhouse to wash and warm up a bit. He shared with us the little bread that he had, and we promised to help him for the rest of his life. He was a loyal Pole and always claimed that the Germans would be defeated and Poland would rise anew. His faith encouraged us. The village swarmed with Germans; the danger was great that they'd find us there. And then --- not only would our end come, but also the end of the good-hearted farmer and his family. One night, my husband's cousin, Zvi Einhorn (today in the Land of Israel) and Rafael Zilberman came to us. Miraculously, they'd learned that we were living there. They were partisans bearing weapons, and they came to ask if we needed any help. They brought a cow that they'd stolen in a distant village, killed it and gave its meat to the farmer with other food. Both of them, Zvi and Rafael, asked the farmer not to drive us out. They came from time to time, and through them we learned that there were partisans operating in the forest, and Jews among them.

Unfortunately, after a period of quiet, one day the farmer's neighbors discovered us and we had to leave. When we set out on the road the farmer took an old, rusty pistol from its hiding place and gave it to us, saying: "It'll be a great help to you." Its ammunition was a single bullet. We thanked him for everything and went out, accompanied by his blessing.

Another winter was approaching its end [the winter of late 1943/early 1944]. We walked on backroads, not saying a word. Every sound awakened fear in us. The pistol was always in our hands, even though none of us knew how to use it. Everyone wanted to hold it for a while. The pistol was important to us even to commit suicide, so as not to fall into the hands of the Germans or their collaborators. But . . . who had the right to the bullet?

We were unable to reach the forest in one night. In addition to the distance, we had to bypass the town, and this took additional time. With great difficulty, we passed to the other side of Yod [i.e., to the south of Yod], until we reached the road leading to the forest. The little time that remained until dawn, we dedicated to finding shelter. Fate ran its course, and this time too we turned to a good-hearted farmer who was sympathetic toward Jews. In the house there were a husband and wife, Romanonek. They brought us inside, fed us and sat us down next to the stove to warm ourselves. At dawn, they ordered us to go up to the attic in the cowshed, but before we had time to go up, the farmer came running, all frightened. With the words choking his throat, he called out: "Jews! You've brought a tragedy on yourselves and on us. The Germans and their collaborators are spreading through the village and searching the farmers' houses!" With this, he went out. We remained sitting in the pile of hay and put our trust in fate. The farmer and his wife, with baskets on their shoulders, took out the cows as if they were on the way to pasture, and slowly, without hurrying, closed the gate of the yard.

I don't remember how long we sat in the hay. We were afraid even to breathe. I only remember how the farmer entered the cowshed in the evening, and the first words he said were "It's me." Half dead, we came out of the hay. Happily, good fortune hadn't deserted us. The farmer told us that the Germans had been looking for homemade vodka at his neighbors' house and asked if they'd seen any Jews or partisans in the village. When they went past his house, they said,

[Page 423]

"Here there's nothing to look for." He believed, he told us, that the G-d of Israel had saved us all. During the years of troubles and suffering, we had many other heart-stopping incidents like this.

We remained in our hiding place in the attic for several days, until it became clear that the Germans had returned to Sharkovshchitzna [some distance east or southeast of their location]. Again we set out for the forest. We were surprised to find Jews who'd lived there during all the difficult months of the winter. They were full of hope for a better future. At night, they told us, they'd go out to get food and during the day they cooked it in their *sukkot* and ate together. The partisans guarded them. The forest people received us and helped us to build our *sukkah*. We decided not to part from this group of Jews, no matter what. Among the partisans were our relatives: two cousins, Sara and Liuba [or Liova]. Others also had relatives among the partisans, who would come occasionally to the camp and guarded the lives of the Jews, and they told us what was happening in the area and at the front, where the Germans had recently suffered heavy losses and were withdrawing. The partisans told us it was almost certain that the Germans would lose the war. We wanted their statements to be true, it was still difficult for us to believe. Nevertheless, the hope grew in our hearts that Jews would remain alive to see the downfall of the Germans.

We knew the partisan movement was a serious force that carried out important military operations, and this gave us confidence about its protection, but we still felt the need to prepare for a bad situation if one developed. We decided to prepare bunkers for people and supplies if the Germans attacked again. The Jews stopped thinking about the possibility of leaving the forest and seeking shelter with the farmers. All of the addresses of the good people among the Gentiles had been used to the full. The women remained in the *sukkot* and the men went out to the forest, to find suitable places to dig bunkers. For a few days we were busy with digging, and with hard work the mission was accomplished.

One day, we heard the echo of shots near the forest. We didn't know what was happening. The partisans who'd gone out on an operation had yet to return. It looked like we faced an approaching storm. Tense, we waited to learn what had caused the shots. Many men and women went out to the edges of the forest to see and hear what was being done. They returned with the news that a large army was moving in the direction of Svila [Swily, about nine kilometers southwest of Yod]. What was this army? Were they for us or against us? We didn't know. We worried that they were the Germans, and we were afraid of what might happen. Only with the return of the Jewish partisans to the camp did the atmosphere change. They told us that these were Russian soldiers and we shouldn't be afraid. The Russian army was pursuing the German army, which had collapsed along the entire front [around July 1944]. "Jews!" they announced, "Liberation has come!"

I can't describe the feeling in our hearts during these great moments. My strength failed me. Only someone who lived through that terrible period and experienced that moment would understand. I'll remember it all my life.

We were full of fear, but at this moment also gnawed by doubt as to the truth of the news. Was it possible that fate had allowed us to live and see the day of redemption?!

Very carefully we went out again, a group of men and women, leaving the forest to see what was happening. What we saw and heard indeed confirmed what the partisans had told us. The language spoken by the soldiers was Russian, and they sang a Russian army song. An older woman who was with us tied a piece of fabric to a pole and went with it to meet the soldiers. When she reached them, she bowed before a soldier and kissed his dusty boots. We also approached and told them that we were afflicted Jews who were hiding

[Page 424]

in the forest and had been waiting for years for the hour of liberation. At this moment, an officer stepped out from the ranks of soldiers, turned to us and said, "I'm also a Jew. Go and tell everyone in the forest that the hour of liberation has come and everyone is free." After this, the officer ordered that they honor us with some food. He filled a sack with bread and canned pork and gave it to us.

With tears of happiness, we asked each other if everything we were hearing and seeing was real, or was it a dream? With this good news and the food, we hurried back to our people in the forest, who were waiting impatiently.

Only now was the full depth revealed of the tragedy that had struck the Jewish nation and each one of us. The wounds, which until now had been hidden because of each person's struggle to survive, were opened. Only now did we see in our minds' eyes the family members and Jews of our town who'd been lost. The tragedy and hour of redemption hit all of us with a shock that was strong enough to kill. A woman from Sharkovshchitzna, who was with us in the forest, died of a heart attack at the moment that she heard our liberation had come; she was broken by the power of the news. We buried her in the forest. Her grave was added to the many Jewish graves scattered over the paths and forests, before and after liberation. The forest absorbed the tears of those who remained alive, who'd lived until now as if they were the walking dead. Only fate determined who would live. Each moment, death had threatened us all. We'd seen mothers leave their children behind and keep walking. We'd seen husbands fall dead and their wives run ahead with the hope that the German bullets would miss them. We'd seen fathers freeze to death from the cold and their children keep running in the hope that they'd be saved. Their sighs and weeping were borne in the wind, on the paths and in the forests.

The hour of liberation came, unexpectedly, and with it our springs of tears were opened without stopping.

Without our dear ones, without our relatives, faith or a will to live --- where would we go? What next? We'd stopped making plans for the future. We remained in the forest until we were freed from the fear that we'd lived with for many years. Many days passed until the liberation penetrated fully into our minds and we began to grow accustomed to the new reality. Then all of us wanted to return to our places, to the towns where we'd been born. There were those who returned to Gleboki, to Druya [Druja, about 44 kilometers northeast of Yod], to Braslav. We turned toward Sharkovshchitzna. All of us hoped to meet relatives; maybe miraculously they'd remained alive like us. We hoped to live in houses that belonged to relatives or other Jews. The feeling of freedom awoke hatred in us and the will to take revenge on the oppressors.

The date of liberation of the entire area was July 9, 1944. We were freed from the threat of death, but the war continued. Long lines of soldiers of the Red Army advanced westward; their target --- Berlin, the capital of Germany. Many young men from the ranks of the partisans were drafted into the Red Army and continued to fight. The Christian population in the towns was hostile to the remnants of the Jews. The Gentiles acted like beasts of prey who had yet to gain satisfaction. Again we heard of dangers threatening Jews on the roads and even in their homes. We had to be very careful if we were going to live in the towns where we'd been born and grown up.

Our appearance in the town caused great disappointment to the Christians who'd taken the property and blood-soaked houses of the Jews. More than once did they say to people, "What? We didn't kill them all yet?" The many partisans who returned to their homes brought a change for the better. Together with the soldiers, they enforced

[Page 425]

order and established government in the forests. Among these partisans were Jews, and they merited important jobs in the local government. Their first concern was to expel the new residents from the houses that belonged to Jews, and to settle there the survivors who returned to the town. This aroused the anger of the Gentiles against the Jews and the government.

A group of Jews also arrived in Sharkovshchitzna. They were attached to each other and lived together. Every house where Jews lived looked like a small hotel. Happily and with an open heart, they received every Jew who came to the town. We lived together, because we were still worried about the future.

The days passed, and the [Soviet] government became established. The Jews devoted most of their time to recovering Jewish property, that of the survivors who were now settled in the town as well as the property of missing residents of the town who were known to be Jewish. What stolen property was returned, we divided among those who'd saved Jewish lives. These good people visited us occasionally, and the survivors remembered well what they'd done for them and rewarded them for it.

The Jews continued to live without tranquility. They wandered from place to place; they searched, asked and hoped that maybe they'd find relatives alive. They continued these searches for weeks and months. The tension in our lives wasn't yet at an end. We still slept in our clothes at night, and in the daytime we wanted to hear what was happening at the front. We said that if, Heaven forbid, the Red Army had to withdraw again, all of us would accompany it wherever it went. We were happy to hear that the army was going from strength to strength and had already advanced far ahead. In my thoughts I was far away, in Vilna and its surroundings. My sister Ida had lived there before the war. She'd married and borne a child. What had happened to her and the child? I searched for any news or rumor that might tell me, but there was only disappointment: no voice and no answer. I lost all hope of finding them alive.

Time flowed on, running ahead. We grew somewhat accustomed to things. Despite the deep pain in our hearts, we saw no chance of finding survivors from our family. We were discouraged. And then one day, the unbelievable happened: a true miracle. We were sitting in the house. The door opened, and my sister Ida walked in. We jumped up, unable to believe what we were seeing. Was this really my sister Ida? How can I put my feelings into words? She'd returned. We cried, and cried again, and so it was for many hours. She too had endured many troubles and afflictions until liberation. On the day of liberation, she was with the partisans in the Miadel [Miadziol] forests [about 70 kilometers southwest of Yod]. From there, she'd wandered to look for her daughter, who she'd left with a Christian woman at the beginning of the war and who was three months old at the time. After searching, she'd found her; now the girl was three years old. The Christian woman had taken care of the girl with great devotion, like a mother.

After this meeting, we weren't separated again. All our thoughts now were about taking revenge. A *politrok* (political officer) named Nizhimkov, an acquaintance of my husband, Kalman, cooperated with us and helped a great deal. He was an officer in a partisan unit. With his help, we carried out several operations against murderers of Jews, and I brought two Jewish murderers to trial, Retzitzki and Yanashik [sic; on page 409 the name was given as Yanshik], who'd run around like heroes during the war. I was the only witness and ensured that they were found guilty. They were sentenced to exile in Siberia and taken there along with other murderers of Jews. After the trial, I felt some easing of the pain in my heart, which sought revenge.

With the war's end in 1945, the Soviet government decreed that Poles and Jews

[Page 426]
who'd lived in Poland could leave Russia and return to their homeland. Many Poles took advantage of this opportunity to return to Poland [which now lay far to the west of Yod and Braslav].[16] With them went the few who'd helped the Jews during their time of trouble and saved their lives. To us Jews, the Polish "homeland" was no longer an attraction. We wanted to get far away from this cursed land that was soaked with so much Jewish blood.

At the beginning of 1946, the survivors who'd gathered in our area gave notice that they wanted to leave Russia. Again we became refugees wandering in long columns, without a home. For weeks and months we wandered on roads full of danger, from country to country, hoping in our hearts that a guide would appear to take us to safe shores. In columns we passed from Lower Silesia through Czechoslovakia, Austria and Germany, without transit visas. We were the Jewish underground striving for a new life. This continued until 1949, when we arrived in our homeland, the Land of Israel.

Footnotes:
1. According to *From Victims to Victors*, published in 1992 in Canada in English by three survivors from Yod --- Peter Silverman, David Smuschkowitz and Peter Smuszkowicz --- before World War II the Jews of Yod were buried in Sharkovshchitzna as well as in Braslav.
2. The widely read Yiddish newspaper *Der Moment* (*The Moment*) was published in Warsaw between 1910 and 1939. For most of this period it supported Poland's Jewish Folkist Party (Jewish People's

Party), a non-Marxist party that called for Jewish cultural autonomy, Yiddish as the national Jewish language, and a network of Yiddish schools. The newspaper also supported Zionism and settlement in Palestine. It was read particularly by Jewish small merchants and tradesmen. The reference to *Letste Nayes* (*Latest News*) is uncertain, as there was more than one paper with that name.

3. *Sonderkommando* here might refer to sub-units of the *Einsatzgruppen* (mobile killing squads) that operated in eastern territories occupied by the German army. Here it might refer to either (1) *sonderkommando* 1a or 1b of *Einsatzgruppe* A, which carried out mass murder in Latvia, Lithuania and parts of Belarus, or (2) *sonderkommando* 7a and 7b of *Einsatzgruppe* B, which carried out mass murder in Belarus. All of the *Einsatzgruppen* were under the direction of SS chief Heinrich Himmler and his subordinates: Reinhard Heydrich (to May 1942) and Ernst Kaltenbrunner (1943-45).

4. The time period that Slava Pinchov is speaking of here was presumably between August and November 1941. Even though the Braslav Ghetto wasn't formally established (closed off with barbed wire) until April 1, 1942, it appears that some Jews from outside Braslav were being concentrated unofficially in Braslav by August 1941 --- see the account of Alexander (Shmaryahu) Dagovitz on page 357 of this memorial book and the account of Chalvina Pinchov on page 393. According to the *Encyclopedia of Camps and Ghettos, 1933-1945*, Volume II-B (2012), the Sharkovshchitzna Ghetto was established between September and November 1941.

5. According to the book *From Victims to Victors*, published in 1992 in Canada by three survivors from Yod --- Peter Silverman, David Smuschkowitz and Peter Smuszkowicz --- on December 17, 1941 the Jews in Yod were taken to the pits outside town in groups of 20 and shot. The killings were carried out by local police (Belorussians, Russians and some Poles), supervised by German members of the *Einsatzgruppen* (mobile killing squads) who had arrived that morning. The synagogue was also desecrated. Within 10 days of this initial massacre, a large number of Jews who'd succeeded in fleeing the town at the outset --- with the help of local Christians --- but who had later been captured, were also taken to the pit and shot. After about 20 days, the Germans announced that the killings had ended and the surviving Jews could return.

    The total number of victims in Yod in December 1941 was estimated in *From Victims to Victors* at around 400, comprising some 250 Jews from Yod, about 50 Jews from Kislovshchitzna (virtually the entire community of that village), and some 100 who were captured within 10 days and killed. Other accounts, such as Slava Pinchov's account here, give a higher number, of 500-530. In the years since the war, a memorial stone has been placed at the site of the massacre.

6. Page 572 of this memorial book (a list in English of the Gentiles in the Braslav region who helped Jews) says that Wasil Bresko was in the village of Wiazowicz. (a.k.a. Wiazowiec). This village was just to the north of Lonsk and about six kilometers south of Yod.

7. The narrator Slava Pinchov's stepmother Gitel was also Slava's aunt. This Gitel (née Rukshin) was a sister of Ita Rukshin, who was married to Slava's uncle, the blacksmith Yaacov Shtein of Yod.

8. This statement is true in the sense of large-scale killings; the massacre in Yod on December 17, 1941 preceded that of the Braslav Ghetto, whose inmates weren't killed until June 3-5, 1942. On the other hand, several of the smaller local Jewish communities covered in this memorial book had been attacked before Yod: (1) the Jews of Plusy (44 kilometers north of Yod) in late June or early July 1941, when two people were killed; mentioned on page 382 of this memorial book. (2) The Jews of Yaisi (20 kilometers north of Yod) on July 4 or 5, 1941, when approximately 14 people were killed; mentioned on pages 401-402 of this memorial book. And (3) the Jews of Dubina (42 kilometers north-northwest of Yod) on or around July 19, 1941, when 18-25 people were killed; mentioned on pages 370, 377, 382 and 390-391 of this memorial book.

9. According to the *Encyclopedia of Camps and Ghettos, 1933-1945*, Volume II-B, a ghetto had been established in Glubokoye in October-November 1941; Jews from nearby towns were also brought there, raising the ghetto population to 6,000. On June 19, 1942, a massacre of some 2,200-2,500 of them was carried out, but unlike the Braslav Ghetto a large population was also kept alive to work.

    Later the Germans decided to raise the population of the Glubokoye Ghetto, as a way to attract the Jews who were scattered among the region's forests. Eventually, the ghetto population rose again, to 7,000. By 1943, Glubokoye was serving as a temporary refuge for Jews in western Belorussia who weren't in the forests. As partisan activity in the region increased, the Germans finally decided to liquidate the ghetto, announcing a deportation on August 20, 1943. When the ghetto responded with armed resistance, the Germans set fire to it, killing some 5,000 inmates. Some Jews managed to break out and join the partisans; it's estimated that about 60-100 ghetto inmates survived the war.

10. According to the *Encyclopedia of Camps and Ghettos, 1933-1945*, Volume II-B, the Miory Ghetto was established in either the fall of 1941 or early April 1942, possibly in several stages. In the spring of 1942, a number of Jews were added to it from other places in the region such as Perebrodia (Przebrodzie) and Ikazn. The ghetto was liquidated on June 2, 1942 with the deaths of some 680-800 inmates; it's possible that a small number of inmates succeeded in escaping.

11. These were extensive forests around the town of Kozian, which was about 32 kilometers southwest of Yod. According to the book *From Victims to Victors* (1992), these forests became a base of operations for partisan activity from the summer of 1942.

12. A photo of the partisans Pesach Zilberman (later Peter Silverman), his sister Tania and their cousin David Smuschkowitz appears on page 442 of this memorial book. In 1992 in Canada, Peter Silverman, David Smuschkowitz and Peter Smuszkowicz (brother of David) published *From Victims to Victors* in English about their time as partisans during the war and the town of Yod. The book included a street map of the town, with the general locations of a number of Jewish families.

13. According to the book *From Victors to Victims* (1992), the large German sweep through the Kozian forest took place in October 1942. Many partisans in the forest were killed, together with Jews in family camps that had been established near the partisan base. The partisan force melted away, retreating 150 kilometers to the east, returning to the forest only in the spring of 1943. Until then, it was an especially difficult time for Jews in the area who were seeking to hide.

14. In Russia, Belorussia and the Ukraine, ovens were traditionally made of brick masonry that retained heat for long periods of time, and their outer surface was safe to touch. People could sit on top of the oven to keep warm.

15. *Sukkot* (plural), *sukkah* (singular): A type of temporary hut --- called a tabernacle --- built for use during the week-long Jewish festival of Sukkot.

16. In August 1945, the USSR formally annexed much of the eastern Polish territory that it had taken in September 1939, including the Braslav region. This shifted Poland's eastern border roughly 200 kilometers to the west. Many Poles in the territory annexed by the USSR, including those in the Braslav region, subsequently left the territory and moved to the new Poland. Poland was compensated for the loss of its eastern territory with German lands to the west and north.

[Page 427]

Zalman Fisher
Son of Chaya-Sara and Yitzchak

Translated from the Hebrew by Yaacov David Shulman
Footnotes Added / Donated by Jeff Deitch

About 500 Jews lived in my small town of Yod [Jod] --- and I, who was one of them, carry in my heart both the memory of routine, everyday life and the unforgettable and incomprehensible events that befell my family and my town.

It wasn't easy to live there. Earning enough to meet one's basic needs was everyone's concern. Everyone made a living as best he could from various types of work --- in small stores, in small-scale enterprises. My father made a living from trade. He traveled to the surrounding villages and bought produce, horsetail hairs, wool and similar products, which he then sold to larger-scale merchants.

There was a strong bond between Yod and Braslav [Braslaw, about 25 kilometers northwest of Yod]: both in terms of geographical proximity and family ties. In addition, the government regional offices for Yod were located in Braslav. Store owners in Yod would acquire their merchandise there. And once when Sara-Riva lit candles in the *sukkah* [temporary hut constructed for the week-long festival of Sukkot] and set fire to the entire *sukkah* and as a result half of the houses in town went up in flames, the firefighters of Braslav saw it as their duty to [come and] help put it out. We even took our dead to be buried in Braslav.

The children studied at a *cheder* [Hebrew primary school] and at a Polish government school. If someone wanted more than this, he had to travel far from Yod to seek higher education elsewhere.

When I grew up, I left to study in the yeshiva in Braslav. The people who taught were from among the heads of the yeshiva: Rabbi Chaim Tarshish, Rabbi Shalom Rabinovitz and others. Tens of children from Braslav and surrounding places studied in Braslav's synagogues. Like other out-of-town youths at the yeshiva, I ate according to the custom of "days," receiving food from a different householder every day of the week. Each day I was supported by another family, and on Sunday the cycle began anew.

When my study there ended, I was persuaded to continue learning in the yeshiva of Vilna [about 165 kilometers southwest of Braslav].[1] I didn't easily agree to leave Braslav. This was a place buzzing with lively, young students, among whom I had many friends. Many spent the evenings in clubs for youth.

I studied at the Vilna yeshiva for a year and a half. On the eve of the Passover holiday, I received

[Page 428]

a letter from my parents in which they asked that I come home for the holiday. I never returned to Vilna.

On September 1, 1939, the German armies invaded Poland and with lightning swiftness conquered large parts of the country. In the second half of September, the Russians took over the territories of Poland bordering Russia, which they called Belorussia and western Ukraine. We, who lived close to the Russian border, became Soviet citizens.

I was accepted for work in a government store, and on May 1, 1941 I had to appear for active service in the Red Army.

A going-away party in my honor was held in my brother's house. I invited my friends ---who like me had been called to serve in the army --- and relatives. The chairman of the local council was also among those invited. We danced to the notes of a band, and we parted from our comrades and friends. For many, this was a permanent farewell.

We spent the rest of the night waiting for a wagon to come and take us to a collection point in Sharkovshchitzna [Szarkowszczyzna, about 20 kilometers southeast of Yod]. We left our parents and relatives, most of them forever, and we set out on our way. At the collection point, we underwent medical checkups and were told to wait for three days. We waited until the end of the conscription process. After that, freight cars took us to the station at the junction at Krolevshchitzna [about 45 kilometers southeast of Sharkovshchitzna; from Krolevshchitzna, a rail line went in the direction of the Kalinin region]. There I saw many other train cars filled with conscripts.

Our destination was Opotzkeh in the Kalinin region [Opochka was about 220 kilometers northeast of Krolevshchitzna]. We traveled for many days until we arrived. Before we had a chance to organize ourselves, acclimate and enter the routine of training, suddenly . . . war.

That was on June 22, 1941, seven weeks after I'd reported for duty to serve the Soviet state. The German army crossed the borders of the Soviet Union and kept going. The Red Army faced a test; it had to stop the enemy's advance and expel it from its borders. We, the draftees, who hadn't yet learned how to use any kind of weapon, were each equipped with a rifle, grenades, a helmet and other items and then sent to the front.

We came upon the enemy army while it was still at the Latvian border. There we took up defensive positions. The battles were fierce and continued without letup. We fought for days and nights. The two armies used all sorts of weapons. Many soldiers were killed, and many were injured. Finally, we could no longer hold the lines we'd been defending, and we got orders to retreat and take a position behind new lines.

Planes bombed us. A bomb that fell near me buried me alive. Fortunately, my comrades saw me and quickly uncovered me. In shock, I was taken with other wounded to a hospital in the city of Pskov [about 130 kilometers north of Opochka], but enemy aircraft came there as well, bombing the city and damaging the hospital. We were evacuated to another hospital. When

I recovered, I received shortened training and was sent back to the front. The enemy stood at the gates of Leningrad.

By now I was a veteran soldier, tested in battle. I overcame fear and continued to fight. One night, when I was on guard, I heard a rustle from the bushes not far from me. I summoned help. We carefully flanked the location and approached two German saboteurs. We captured them and brought them to headquarters. For this, I received a commendation. At night I'd sneak out under orders to enemy territory and return with captive German soldiers. I don't know where I got the ability and courage to do this. I wasn't afraid of anything. I did all that I could to break the enemy, and for this I received a medal for bravery.

One morning, I was summoned to headquarters. With my weapon, I stood at attention. I was ordered to sit and asked many questions about my past. The officers praised me for being a good soldier and they had no

[Page 429]

complaints against me, but an order had come to remove former citizens of Poland from the front. Who was I to oppose the decision of the Supreme Soviet? We took leave of each other with a handshake and with wishes that soon we'd see the defeat of the enemy.

Many others like me were released. We were all taken to an area where thousands were gathered. We were kept there a long time without knowing what lay before us. In the end we were put on two extremely long trains, and we set off. We didn't know where we were being taken. To my good fortune, I was on the second train. The first train, which preceeded us, was bombed by German airplanes. When we approached it, we saw a shocking sight: Carriages were crushed, and many people had been killed and wounded.

Our trip lasted as many as 16 days. We lay on bunks without padding. The food was meager and of poor quality. Only twice during the entire long trip did we get a warm meal: the first time at the station at Gorki [now Nizhny Novgorod, about 400 kilometers east of Moscow] and the second at the station at Molotov [now Perm, some 830 kilometers east of Gorki]. Our destination was the station at Sverdlovsk [now Yekaterinburg, some 300 kilometers southeast of Perm]. When we arrived, we were housed in barracks and sent to work in military factories that produced goods for the front. Conditions were terrible. In Sverdlovsk, I wore summer military clothing while it was 50 degrees [Centigrade] below zero. Only thanks to my youth was I able to withstand all of these adversities.

We stayed there until the end of the war. Then I was released from the army and received the Medal of Victory for my part in the battle against Germany. I was asked what I intended to do. "Go to Yod," I replied.

My town of Yod had been liberated in the summer of 1944. From then until the end of the war, I'd corresponded with a few of my friends who remained alive. From them, I learned that my entire family had been destroyed.

I wanted to go there and see everything with my own eyes. "To Yod," I said, "That's where I want to go."

I received a travel pass for home, some money and food for a few days. The trip stretched out. On the way, I tried to imagine how my town looked, having read the letters that described the carnage and devastation.

Who could capture the reality? I wandered the streets of the town. Everything was burned and destroyed. I walked and wept. From afar, I saw my brother's house standing ahead of me. I approached and entered. I remembered my brother, his wife and all of my other relatives. In this house, they'd made the going-away party for me on the evening before I was drafted into the army. Now it had been turned into a pharmacy and clinic.

I left the place. Outside, I met a Gentile acquaintance who invited me to stay with him. He told me that Jewish survivors of Yod were in Sharkovshchitzna. In the morning I went to see them, traversing the distance of 18 [sic] kilometers. I was afraid of the meeting, but --- here they were! We kissed, wept and sighed. They told me everything. From them, I learned that Yod was the first town in the area where the Germans had carried out an organized massacre [on December 17, 1941]. First, they prepared pits not far from the town. Afterward, they went from house to house and seized those in hiding. They assembled all of them, from the elderly to infants, in the synagogue, and put a guard over them. From there they were led in groups to the pits, to the slaughter. I was told that was the day they killed my parents and my two brothers. I was also told how two injured youths crawled out of the pits and how they were caught, beaten cruelly and thrown back into the pit.[2]

And I heard the story of how they found Bereleh Mushkat hiding under an oven. The murderers tortured him

[Page 430]

brutally. First, they gouged out his eyes and cut off his ears and fingers. Only after these torments did they kill him. Max [Binkovich] the barber refused to go, and he fought with his murderers until they shot him on the way to the pits. When they led away Liuba Pinchov, the local Gentiles wanted to see how she'd be killed. A contemptible Gentile woman, a friend of Rivka Einhorn for years, searched for Rivka and her mother and found them hiding in the bathhouse. She called a few wretched Gentiles, and they took them to the pits to be murdered.

When the massacre in town began, my brother Aharon-Leizer fled and hid in the forest. One cold winter night, he and a few other Jews from Yod entered a granary in one of the villages and hid in the hay to warm up a little and spend the night under shelter. The Nazis discovered them and burned the hayloft with the Jews inside.

When I was conscripted into the Red Army, I'd left in my parents' house two married brothers and sisters with families and children, my young brother, and many family relatives. What did I find when I returned at the war's end? Woe! I found not a single one of them, all had been murdered.

The local inhabitants, under the leadership of Kublunk, owner of the cheese factory who was under the protection of the Germans, carried out the atrocities against the Jews of Yod.

But the time of retribution arrived: The Jewish partisans from Yod knew what had happened. They

Certificate of the medal awarded to Zalman Fisher for his contribution to the victory over Germany

[Page 431]

waited, and when the right time came they took revenge on the Nazis and their local collaborators. Thus, one day the partisan Zalman Shkolnik entered the town at noon, found the murderer Kublunk and killed him in the street. And one night the partisans came to the house of the Gentile who'd led Liuba Pinchov to the slaughter pits, and they killed him. When the partisans learned that the German officers were staying in one of the houses, they came to the town and killed them. At the time of the occupation, the local Gentiles took possession of the Jews' houses and property. The partisans of Yod organized, and one morning they emerged from the forest and set fire to the houses of the town from every side.

When partisan activity increased, the Germans besieged the forests and sent thousands of soldiers into them to fight. In these battles, other inhabitants of Yod met their death.

The war came to an end. A few Jews gathered and came from various places back to the towns of their birth. They saw the destruction, and they left to build new lives. I too began building my life. On one of my visits to Braslav, I met Chana Gurevitz. We married and established a family. We had a son and daughter. About 20 families assembled in Braslav. We met on various occasions, and prayed together on Sabbaths and holidays. We wanted to leave the land drenched with the blood of the Jews. Only 13 years later were we able to leave Russia, and we came to Israel.

Every year, during Hanukkah, the people in Israel from Yod gather (each year with a different family), tell heart-breaking stories of those days, and recall the holy and pure martyrs who were torn from life and shot down next to the pits near my town of Yod.

Footnotes:

1. This account says "the yeshiva in Vilna," even though there were many yeshivas in Vilna at the time.
2. It's estimated that some 400-500 Jews of Yod were massacred at the pits on December 17, 1941. In the years since the war, a memorial stone has been placed at the site.

[Page 432]

Liuba Yanovski
Daughter of Miriam [Zilberman]
and Moshe Vilkitzki [Wilkicki]

Translated from the Hebrew by Yaacov David Shulman
Footnotes Added / Donated by Jeff Deitch

I was born in 1925 in the town of Yod [Jod] to my parents Moshe and Miriam. I had a brother, Avram [Avraham], older than me by two years, and a younger sister, Hinda, who was born in 1936.

Under Polish rule, we made a living from a textile store, where we sold fabric and woven goods to the local and surrounding populations. Our lives were peaceful and good. In town we were considered well off. I studied at the local school, and my brother continued his education at the Epstein Gymnasium in Vilna.[1] My father, who came from Vilna, would go there occasionally to buy merchandise for the store and to visit his family [Vilna was about 155 kilometers southwest of Yod]. Sometimes I joined him. I'd spend time in the lap of the family and enjoy myself in the big city.

Changes came with the war. When the Russians entered [in September 1939], our family's situation deteriorated. The Russians didn't allow any private business, and it wasn't such a desirable thing to be a merchant under the Soviet regime. If a person was both a merchant and rich, he and his family were sent into exile far from home. We knew that people who weren't [considered] loyal to the regime were sent to Siberia.

Father quickly left home. He went to Novo-Vileyka [now Naujoji Vilnia in Lithuania, seven kilometers east of Vilna], acquired a passport there under another name and got a job as an accountant. Mother, a diligent woman with initiative, assumed the responsibility of taking care of the family. She concerned herself with our day-to-day existence and saw to it that no evil eye should harm us. So that we wouldn't be deported, Mother bribed clerks and police officers and in particular their wives, and they saw to it that nothing bad happened to us. This is how we lived, unhappy and without our father, under the watchful eye of the new regime.

With the outbreak of the German-Russian war [in June 1941], our father returned home and the family was reunited. Only a few days after war began, the German army passed through Yod and advanced toward Russia. I and other children ran to see them. We saw soldiers, tanks and motorcycles that the Gentile population met with joy, bread and salt, calling them liberators. In the market square, the Germans gave speeches to the assembled people. The Germans promised them freedom and announced that the oppressive Soviet regime would not return. As best as I can recall, there were no Jews at the assembly. The

[Page 433]

Gentiles chased away the curious Jewish children, yelling, "The Germans have liberated us from Stalin and the Jews!" On this occasion, the anti-Semitic woman Kastosia Demidovitz, who roused people against the Jews, was especially prominent, but there were others like her. The plundering of the Jews' houses began. It was in essence a pogrom, accompanied by blows and curses. We feared being attacked. We quickly left our houses and sought refuge until the violence passed.

When the winds settled and the plunder ceased, we returned. Weeping and tears were the portion of the Jews of Yod in those days. The Gentiles had taken whatever it was possible to take from the houses and courtyards. They broke the furniture, ripped open the pillows and quilts, shattered the floors, and did everything to find treasures hidden by the Jews.

. . . Afterward, we were ordered to choose a representative committee, and we were told to sew yellow patches on our outer clothes. We had to surrender our sheets, towels and warm clothing for the German soldiers. Women and young girls were required to knit woolen socks in great quantities. We lived in fear and tension until the month of December.

On Hanukkah 1941 [December 14-22, 1941], an acquaintance entered our house and told us that many Germans and police had come to town. Mother's heart told her that something bad was about to happen. She proposed that we leave the house and find shelter among our acquaintances in the village. Already before this, a rumor had come to her ears that the Germans were tormenting and brutalizing the Jewish boys, and she hurried father and Avraham out of the house. She also proposed that we --- mother, me and my sister --- go to acquaintances in another village, to whom we'd sent some of the property and objects from our house. We'd divided our possessions among a few villagers, with the thought that at a time of trouble they'd come to our aid in exchange for the goods we'd deposited with them.

We left the house quickly, but there was no doubt in our hearts that in a short time we'd be able to return and keep living there as before. We locked the door before we left, so that people wouldn't suspect us of fleeing.

The woman peasant to whom we came in the village hurried to hide us in the straw of the granary. As she did so, she told us that the Jews of Yod were being killed [December 17, 1941]. Now the purpose of the Germans' arrival in town became clear to us. The participants in the Aktion searched in the villages for Jews who had fled. A Gentile woman who hated Jews thrust a pitchfork into the straw where we were hiding, but she failed to find us. Toward evening our friend asked us to leave the place, because of threats that any family discovered to be hiding Jews would be killed. Bewildered, not knowing where to go, we left the village. During the night we walked a distance of 25 kilometers. Outside, it was freezing cold and our small sister was with us. We had no food, and instead of drink we sucked icicles. How great was our disappointment in the morning when we found that we were back where we'd started the previous evening. Our [peasant woman] acquaintance told us that the policeman-murderer Retzitzki and others were going through the village looking for Jews. Again we left. When we came to the woods, we found a group of women and children from Yod who'd fled the slaughter. Together, we wept. Then, as though he'd sprung out of the ground, a despicable young Gentile with a scar on his face appeared before us. We recognized him as Jozef, an anti-Semite who helped the Germans hunt for Jews. "Aha!" he roared with glee. "It's a good thing that I found you, the Vilkitzki family." Pointing to the others, he said, "I'll take you to the pits as well. We'll kill you all." Then he whispered to my mother, "If you pay me well, I won't harm you and won't take you. I'll leave you alive." This Gentile with the scar on his face hadn't dreamed that he'd grow rich that day. He took everything my mother had in silver, gold and jewelry.

[Page 434]

We remained with nothing but the assurance that we'd bought our lives. He told us, "If you go in such-and-such a direction, you're likely to meet the officer Retzitzki. If he catches you, neither silver nor gold will save your lives." I remember how I begged the others to redeem their lives with their money. The Gentile left us and went on his way carrying much property, and we scattered in every direction.

At home, we parted from father and Avraham. We agreed that if we didn't return home soon, we'd try to keep in touch through our good friend Mitzkovitz [Mickiewicz], owner of the *hutor*[2] near the town of Kozian [Koziany, about 32 kilometers southwest of Yod]. Now the *hutor* was our destination.

I was astonished at how mother was able to lead us at night on the right path. Our joy had no end when we learned that father and our brother were with the [Mitzkovitz] family. Mitzkovitz and his family, his wife, his two sons and his daughter, took us in with great warmth.

Not far from their house stood a sizable structure that contained a large village stove. This structure with its equipment served as a place for drying flax. We were housed in it. Of course this was no hiding place at all, and anyone who searched for us would have found us at once. The [Mitzkovitz] family was putting itself in great danger, because a directive had been issued, which passed from mouth to ear and also circulated in writing, that any village family found to be sheltering Jews would be executed.

We stayed there for a month. The winter was at its height, and Mitzkovitz was worried. He wanted to help us, but he was afraid of the danger. He apologized to us and told us that he was sorry, but he could no longer keep us. He proposed that we go far from his house into the forest [a large forest covered much of the land between Yod and Kozian]. In this way, he wouldn't endanger his family, and if we remained in the forest he promised to help us.

How would we live in the forest in the cold and snowy winter? Would we die of cold? These and other questions gnawed at our minds. We went deep into the forest.

Mr. Mitzkovitz took his leave of us next to a large haystack and returned home. We warmed ourselves by a fire and fell asleep inside the stack. The next day, we set up a hut. We gathered logs and made them into a floor. We closed in the walls with twigs and branches squeezed together tightly, so that the wind wouldn't penetrate. We bent the ends of the branches and bound them to make a sort of roof, and we paved the floor. This was our new house. We counted the days and weeks that remained until winter would come to an end.

With the coming of spring [in 1942], everything changed for the better. We spent the summer months in relative ease. In addition to the food the Mitzkovitz family brought us, we gathered edible mushrooms, grasses and forest fruits of various kinds.

Toward the end of the summer of 1942, the forest took on a different appearance. We were no longer alone. Survivors of acts of murder, Jews fleeing the ghetto from fear of liquidation or during a liquidation, began to enter the forest. Men came whose protectors refused to endanger themselves and shelter them any longer. Also arriving were Russian soldiers who'd fled German captivity. In the forests of Kozian, groups began to organize and engage in partisan activities. Near us, an *otriad*[3] called Spartak was formed, which my brother Avraham joined. Similarly gathered in the forest were families both together and fragmented, individuals, sick people and old people who'd escaped the Nazi inferno and organized into a family camp, which benefited from the *otriad's* protection. We too joined this camp.

In one partisan action my brother was injured, and due to the lack of good medical assistance he died of blood

[Page 435]

poisoning [in January 1943].[4] He was only 17. The family and his partisan friends buried him in the forest, and my father wrote details identifying him on a wooden board and said Kaddish for his only son. In response to the increased activity of the partisans in the area, the German army organized a campaign of punishment and liquidation. They set a siege around the forest, which lasted from the end of December 1942 to the beginning of January 1943. The partisans fought with great courage, but their resources in manpower and arms weren't enough in a war against a large army with modern weapons. They decided to fall back and sneak out through the encirclement. Many partisans fell in battle, and men from the family camp were killed by the Germans' heavy firing. When we in the camp felt that the siege was closing in on us and the shooting was growing closer, people began to flee in panic. My family too left the *zemlyanka* [dugout], and we ran with everyone else. We didn't know where we were going. The main thing was to get away, to stay alive. We ran, we fell, we hid in the bushes and we started running again. The shooting from behind us hit its targets, and people died. We ran together, holding hands. Then I went a little further ahead, and father cried out that I shouldn't go so far off, I might get lost. And then everyone was hit: father, mother and my sister. I was the only one who remained unhurt. I cried out: "Father! Mother!" I wept, but they didn't reply. I was pulled along with the stream of fleeing people.

It was early evening, and the sun was setting. The shooting stopped until the next morning. I went back to search for my family among those who'd been killed. I found my mother and small Hindeleh lying in the white snow, surrounded by pale splotches of blood. I didn't locate my father. Someone saw him killed not far from where my mother and sister were found. Apparently he'd had the strength to run a few more steps until he staggered and fell.

Night came. People argued that we must leave. During the night, there were many more chances to sneak out.

Where would I go, and what would I do alone? I'd lost my support and anyone I could rely on. To whom would I turn for help, and who'd support me in my grief?

. . . And then a man stood at my side, called my name and embraced me. For a moment I couldn't identify him, but then I knew him. This was my uncle, Rafael Zilberman, my mother's brother, whom I hadn't seen since we'd fled Yod. His wife Lusia, his three-year-old daughter Dvora and grandmother [sic] had been killed by the murderers, together with the other Jews of Yod on the day the Germans came to the town. Only he, the uncle, succeeded in escaping. Now he was my support, and I trusted in him.

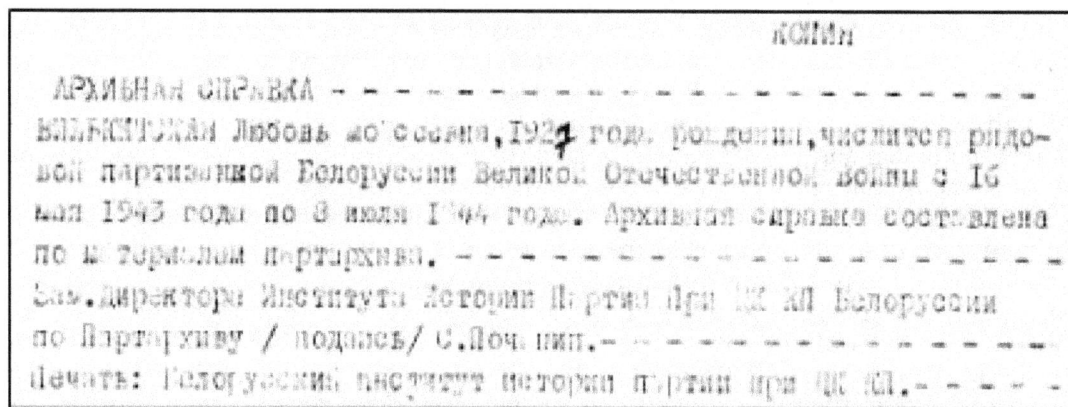

Partisan identification of Liuba Vilkitzki

[Page 436]

As we wandered from place to place, we met our relatives: Yitzchak Shulkin, his wife Brayna, who was in an advanced state of pregnancy, and their children. They too were seeking shelter. We decided to try our luck in one of the villages, where we had many acquaintances. A peasant that we knew took in my uncle and me and gave us refuge, and the Shulkin family took refuge with a peasant named Semyon. After only a few days passed, "our" peasant came to us in a state of agitation and told us that Semyon had denounced our relatives and delivered them to the police. We left to avoid endangering ourselves and this good peasant. I know that partisans from Yod later captured Semyon and hanged him.

During the time of the siege [of the forest], the Germans burned many villages and killed their inhabitants. Those who'd escaped harm were afraid to take us into their houses even for a short time. During this act of vengeance, the Germans set fire to the house of the Mitzkovitz family and burned alive the father, mother and aunt. The sons managed to flee, and they survived. I was in touch with one of them, Vladek, for a long time. In the spring of 1943, my uncle and I presented ourselves to the command of the Spartak brigade and asked to be accepted into their ranks. I was big and developed beyond my 15 years. I was accepted and separated from my uncle, who I only met once more during the remainder of the war.

I had good reasons for joining the partisans. Despite my young age, I felt an obligation to take part in the war against the Nazi oppressor, who had caused me so many tears and so much grief. I saw that I must take vengeance on behalf of my destroyed family and home. In my eyes, it was better to fall in wartime as a partisan fighting the enemy than to be pursued by Gentiles who'd denounce me to the Germans for a handful of salt, or to be captured by a policeman who'd cruelly mistreat me and then kill me. If I fell in battle, I would've lost nothing; I had no one to turn to and no place to live. And if I survived, I'd have no reason to be ashamed of my life. I could be proud that I was a Jewish partisan and had done my part in the war against Nazi Germany.

One day, when I visited the family camp, I met a partisan who'd come looking for people to join his unit called Gastello, which was based in the Narotz [Narach] forest.[5] I wanted to leave Spartak, and this was a good opportunity to do so. I stepped forward as a candidate among young people who volunteered.

In the Gastello unit, we were 34 girls. Besides serving as fighters, we carried out other necessary tasks. Since I was Jewish, I served from time to time as a translator from German to Russian [since Yiddish was close to German]. This happened when we caught a "tongue"[6] (a German soldier) and it was necessary to get information from him that the partisans needed, such as the amount of territory controlled [by the Germans], train movements, how bases were guarded, the number of soldiers and types of weapons. Such interrogations were very interesting.

When I came to the Gastello unit, the brigade commander, [Viktor] Manokhin, summoned me and proposed that I serve as a nurse. He personally taught me how to administer first aid. There were two other nurses with me. When we went out to an action, in addition to my own weapon I carried a knapsack filled with first aid supplies. We returned from many actions with injured fighters, and my hands were filled with work. Our situation improved after a doctor joined us.

In July 1944, our area was liberated. Partisan activity came to an end. Most of the partisans joined fighting units of the Red Army.

For me, the war was over. The hand of fate left me alive to carry in my heart the heavy weight of the calamity to the end of my days. Until the end of my days, I'll remember my dear parents, my brother the partisan, and my sister Hindeleh lying in the snow next to mother. How can I not remember them? . . . I'll never know where they're buried.

[Page 437]
In the summer, only green hyssop covered the field of the massacre.

In 1949 I married, and we established a family. For years we sought a way to leave Russia, but only in 1973, after the Yom Kippur War, did we come to Israel, where we were greeted by my firstborn son, who'd made *aliyah* before we did.

After I left Spartak, my connection with my uncle, Rafael [Zilberman], had ceased, but I met him again in Israel. He related that when partisan combat ended he'd transferred into the Red Army, and he kept fighting in Germany until he made *aliyah* to the Land of Israel. On the way there, in an illegal *aliyah*, his ship was seized by the British and all of the passengers were transferred to internment camps in Cyprus.

In the Land of Israel he reestablished himself, married, and had a son. With time, the son also married and gave his father two granddaughters.

But my uncle suffered from increasing paralysis. I visited him in his home and afterward in an old age home, where he passed away in November 1981.

Footnotes:

1. The prestigious Epstein Gymnasium was established in Vilna in 1915, as a Jewish high school with instruction in Hebrew. The founder and first headmaster was Dr. Yosef Epstein (1873-1916). In the 1920s it was renamed the Tarbut Gymnasium and continued to operate until the summer of 1940, when it was shut down by the Soviets and the building was nationalized. Thereafter it was replaced by a Yiddish high school, which closed at the time of the German invasion in 1941. From 1916, the premises in Vilna were at Pylimo St. 4, which is now occupied by the Lithuanian Jewish Community.

2. Russian word for a single-homestead settlement/isolated peasant farmhouse.

3. Russian word for a partisan unit. According to the book *From Victims to Victors*, published in 1992 in Canada by three former partisans from Yod --- Peter Silverman, David Smuschkowitz, and Peter Smuszkowicz --- the Spartak brigade was the first partisan group established in the Kozian forest, around the summer of 1942.

4. Avraham Vilkitzki is also described on page 443 of this memorial book, in the section titled "Partisans in the Braslav Region." It was in the German attack on the partisans in December 1942-January 1943, described by his sister Liuba in this account, that Avraham was wounded.

5. The Narotz forest was centered around what's now Lake Narotz, which is some 50 kilometers south of the town of Kozian and 50 kilometers southeast of the town of Sventzion [Swieciany]. Like other massive forests in the region --- the Kozian forest west and south of Yod, the Naliboki forest west of Minsk, the Rudnicki forest south of Vilna --- it sheltered partisans as well as family camps.

   According to *Ghetto in Flames*, published in 1982 by the former partisan Yitzhak Arad, partisans under Fyodor Markov were operating in the Narotz forest from 1942. Jewish refugees were also living there by 1942, if not earlier, and by June 1943 such refugees numbered in the hundreds. In September 1943 the Germans carried out a massive sweep of the Narotz forest, killing many refugees in family camps as well as Gentile and Jewish partisans. The partisans retreated north to the Kozian forest, returning to the Narotz forest in October 1943. Thereafter, conditions for Jewish refugees took a turn for the better, as partisan organization improved and weapons were parachuted in from Soviet territories to the east.

6. From the Russian "*iazik*," used to describe a German prisoner who revealed secrets.

[Pages 438-439]
Map: Ghettos and Partisan Camps 1941-44

Translated from the Hebrew by Jerrold Landau
Edited / Donated by Jeff Deitch

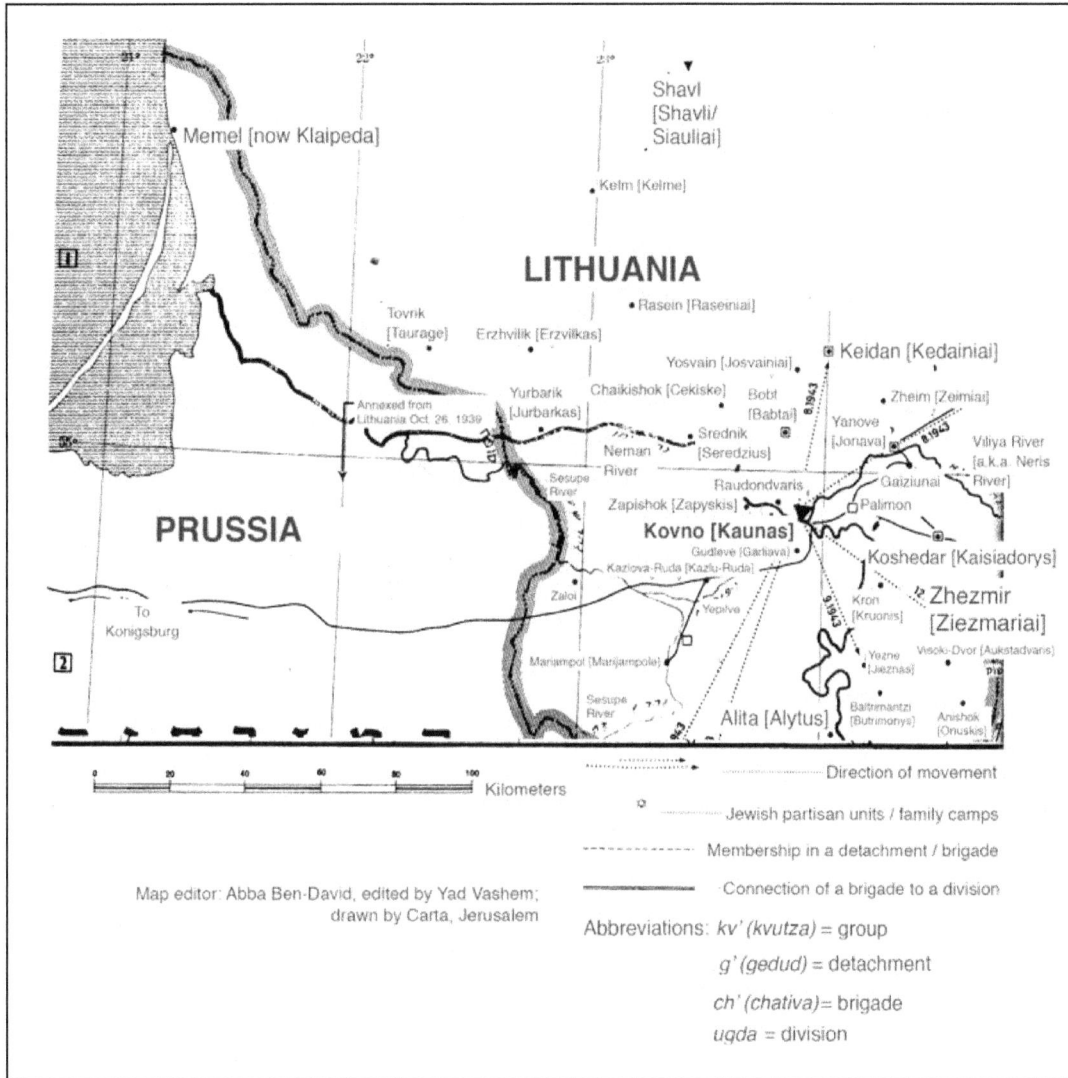

Map editor: Abba Ben-David, edited by Yad Vashem;
drawn by Carta, Jerusalem

Direction of movement

Jewish partisan units / family camps

Membership in a detachment / brigade

Connection of a brigade to a division

Abbreviations: *kv' (kvutza)* = group

g' (gedud) = detachment

ch' (chativa) = brigade

uqda = division

LITHUANIA

25°
Rakishok [Rokiskis]

Dvinsk [now Daugavpils]
27°
Dvina River
28°

[Dubina]
Druya
Belorussian Brigade 4 of Bazikin

Braslav [Braslaw]
Prudnikov-Morozov Brigade
Perebrod
Komar Detachment
Miory
Pohost
Kondrich Detachment

Duksht [Dukstas]
Opsa
Shirokov Brigade
Disna [Dzisna]
Polotsk

Vidz [Widze]
Jod
Bildugi [Bildziugi]
Hermanovitzi [Germanovichi]

Utian [Utena]
Spartak Brigade
Sharkovshchitzna [Sharkowszczyzna]

Dogalishki [Daugeliskis]
Detachment 4
Kozian [Koziany]
Markov Brigade
Malenkov [or Melnikov] Brigade

Vilkomir [Ukmerge]
Novi-Sventzion [Nowo-Swieciany/ Svencioneliai]
[Kostas] Kalinauskas Detachment
Hydutzishek [Adutishkis]
Chapaev Detachment
Varapaeva
Glubok [Glebokoye]
Ushatz [Ushachy]

Shirvint [Sirvintos]
Litayach Brigade
Sventzion [Swieciany/ Svencionys]
Ponomarenko Detachment
Krulevshchina

Transferred from Poland to Lithuania on Oct. 10, 1939
Postav [Postawy]
Danilovitzi [Dunilowicze]
Voroshilov Brigade
50°

Lintup [Lyntupy]
Komai [Komaje]
Porplitzi [Porplasca]
Lepel [Lepiel]

Genis Detachment
Kobilnik [now Narach]
Dokshitz [Dokshytsy]

Svir
Lake Narach
Kalinin Detachment
Parafianova [Parafianow]
Medvedev Brigade

Miadel [Miadziol]
Buid [Budslav]
Kuzin Brigade
BELO-RUSSIA

Vilna [Vilnius]
Michalishok [Michaliszki]
Parkhomenko Detachment
Nechama [Vengeance] Detachment

Trok [Trakai]
Ponar [Ponary]
Lavrishok [Lavoriskes]
Komsomolsky Detachment
Krivitzi [Krzywicze]
Begomi [Biahoml]

Baltoya-Vaka [Biala-Waka]
Transferred to Lithuania
Kutuzov Detachment
Kornitz [Kurzeniec]
Dolhinov [Dauhinava]

Sorok-Tatar
Narach Forest
D[yadya] Kolya's Division

Lithuanian Brigade
Oshmene [Oszmiana]
Vitya River [a.k.a. Neris River]
Hanokeim [Avenger] Detachment

Death to Fascism Group and others
Smorgon [Smarhon]
Vileika
D[yadya] Vasya's Detachment and Group 408

Ilia
Plishnitz

● ○ City or town — Rivers, canals and lakes

○ Village — Railway tracks

○ דורבשצ'ינא Settlement surrounded by forests — Border until Sep. 1939

○ Jewish village — Border with the USSR until June 22, 1941

▼ ▼ Ghetto — District boundaries under the German regime

□ □ Labor camp

[The original map in Hebrew was sourced from *Partizany Vileishchiny (Partisans in the Vileika Region)* by Ivan Frolovich Klimov and Nikita Ermolaevich Grakov, published in 1967 in Minsk in Russian.]

[Page 440]

Partisans in the Braslav Region

Translated from the Hebrew by Jerrold Landau
Footnotes Added / Donated by Jeff Deitch

A brigade called Zhukov operated in the Braslav [Braslaw] region. Its commander was Siromcha, and its commissar was Voloychik.[1] The brigade originated from the Stalin brigade (in the district of Vitebsk-Belorussia) and comprised two detachments that united: Kutuzov and Rokossovsky. The [Zhukov] brigade captured Opsa after liquidating the German garrison there. It united with the regular army on July 9, 1944 and took control of Braslav that day along with the Red Army.

On the importance of the fight conducted by the partisan groups, the material and physical damage inflicted by the partisan movement on the German occupation soldiers, and the psychological impact on the Nazi soldier --- testimony can be read in an excerpt from a diary, found with German captain P. Boshla, who was killed battling a partisan unit:

> With our tanks, we entered the darkness of desolation. There was no living soul in sight, but the shadow of the avengers could be felt everywhere in the forests and bogs. These partisans attack suddenly, as if they've risen from under the ground. They shoot us and hit us, and then disappear like shades from the netherworld. The avengers persecute us at every step, and there's no way to save ourselves.
>
> Hell! I never saw or experienced anything like this at any time or place. I'm not trained to fight spirit-ghosts from the forests. Now I'm writing in my diary, afraid to see the setting sun. It's better not to think. Night falls, and I feel shadows crawling, approaching, stealing their way through the darkness. I'm overtaken by the fear of death.

> --- From the book *Partizany Vileishchiny* (*Partisans in the Vileika Region*)
> by I[van]. F[rolovich]. Klimov and N[ikita]. E[rmolaevich]. Grakov[2]

Footnotes:
1. On page 256 of this memorial book, "Shiromcha" was called the officer of the partisan Zhukov brigade, and "Bolevchik" an officer from the Soviet army who was serving in it. Page 364 of this memorial book also mentions Zhukov brigade commander "Siromcha."
2. Published in Minsk in Russian in 1967; the Hebrew original said the coauthor's name was Kilmov, but in fact it was Klimov.

[Page 441]

Partisans from Yod

All entries below are from *Lexicon of Heroism*[1]

Translated from the Hebrew by Jerrold Landau
Footnotes Added / Donated by Jeff Deitch

Pinchas Iafe [Ioffe/Yaffe], son of Shalom

He was born in the Jewish village of Bildugi [Bildziugi, about 10.5 kilometers northeast of Yod] near the town of Sharkovshchina [Sharkovshchitzna a.k.a. Szarkowszczyzna, about 15 kilometers southeast of Bildugi] in 1895.

He escaped with his 15-year-old son Mordechai (Mottel) at the start of the liquidation of the Jewish population of the town of Yod (Braslav district) to the Zachovshchina [Zachowszcsyna] forest near Kozian [Koziany, about 32 kilometers southwest of Yod] in December 1941. Both were armed.

In the forests, he met with groups of Jews who'd escaped from the ghettos of the area. They organized themselves as a partisan group. They shot a farmer named Obrian in the village of Zalesie [about 3.5 kilometers southwest of Yod] and burned down his farm for the crime of collaborating with the Germans. They killed the family of the farmer Abramei, who'd handed over to the Germans several Jews from Yod who had survived the massacre. They killed the chief of the village of Boyavshchina (near Yod) [Bujewszczyzna, four kilometers southeast of Yod]. In June 1942, this unit was incorporated into the partisan regiment Ponomarenko, led by Meirson, which in turn combined with the Russian division of the same name active in the district of Danilovitzi [Dunilowicze, about 45 kilometers south of Yod].

In July 1942, the Jewish brigade attacked the village of Korsunki [Korszunki] (near Yod) [about four kilometers southeast of Yod], which was the location of the Samachova cell.[2] Together with a Russian detachment that was part of the Spartak unit, they attacked the town of Yod one night and burned down the houses of all collaborators, along with their residents, including two German captains who happened to be housed there. Among the burned buildings was the local council building [this might mean the headquarters of the district command]. Pinchas Iafe carried out this revenge action and distinguished himself in it. His son Mordechai also won praise in the daily records of the command.

When the commander Meirson decided to leave the forests of Kozian and move the base of the Ponomarenko unit in the area of Danilovitzi, Iafe and his son and several other Jews decided to remain and continue their punishment of local collaborators. The group instilled fear in the entire area. In response, the Germans put a price on Iafe's head --- blocks of salt, a rare commodity.

On November 15, 1942, Iafe went with his son to the village of Boyavshchina to take revenge on a farmer who was collaborating. When they didn't find him at home, they decided to spend the night in one of the huts nearby. The farmers found out, broke in during the dark night and captured them. The son was burned alive, and the father was handed over to the Germans. He attempted to escape, but was shot.[3]

--- Hirsh Einhorn (Pachach, portfolio 62) and Kahanovich
(*Milhemet HaPartizanim*, page 368)[4]
[Also appears in *Lexicon of Heroism*, page 183]

Benyamin Dubinski [or Dubinsky], son of Aharon

He was born in 1902 in the town of Vidz (Braslav region) [Vidz, a.k.a. Widze, about 40 kilometers west of Yod]. His father was a leaser of land from landowners. Benyamin became involved in his father's business and was liked by the farmers. Later, he moved to live in the town of Yod.

He escaped to the forest of Milk (between the towns of Yod and Pohost) [perhaps Milki, about nine kilometers northeast of Yod] with several of his friends immediately after the first massacre [in Yod] (December 1941). They joined a group of escaped Russian war prisoners and marched eastward to

[Page 442]

**Partisans of Yod in the Spartak brigade
From left to right: Pesach Zilberman (communications), Tania
Zilberman (nurse), David Smuschkowitz (reconnaissance).**

**[Pesach and Tania, siblings, were related by marriage to David; all
of them survived the war. In 1992, Pesach (Peter Silverman), David,
and David's brother, Peter Smuszkowicz, published in Canada an
English-language account of their experience, *From Victims
to Victors*.]**

[Page 443]

obtain weapons and ammunition.

They returned to the forests of the area in May 1942, well armed, and formed the partisan detachment named Shirokov [Szirokow], after their commander. Dubinski was appointed commander of a sub-detachment.[5] He proved himself in attacks by the brigade on the German regular army in the village of Acremovitzi near Braslav [Achremowce a.k.a. Achremowcy, about seven kilometers southeast of Braslav and 16 kilometers northwest of Yod]. The Germans were defeated, and their weapons and ammunition were taken. Dubinski also proved himself in the ambush against the Germans and their Belorussian collaborators near the village of Perebrodz-Zagorie.

In November 1942, he went to take revenge against a farmer who'd murdered Jews and whose farm was near the former Jewish settlement of Bildugi. To help him, he took several Jews from that settlement who'd been wandering and hiding in the forest. They didn't find the farmer in his home, so they spent the night at a lessee of the farmer's land. Local farmers tipped off the Germans, who surrounded the house, attacked and killed them at night.[6]

--- Hirsh Einhorn (Pachach, portfolio 62)
[Also appears in *Lexicon of Heroism*, page 135]

Avraham Vilkitzki [Wilkicki/Wilkocki], son of Moshe and Miriam

He was born in the town of Yod (Vilna district) in 1925. He studied in Vilna [about 155 kilometers southwest of Yod] until the outbreak of the war. He escaped from the Kozian Ghetto in August 1942 and joined the Spartak brigade in the surrounding forests. He participated in all attacks and battles of the brigade.

He was injured in his hand and leg in a battle, and remained wounded in the field. With his last bit of strength, he crawled to a haystack and hid there. His friends found him a few days later and transferred him to a secure place. Due to the lack of medical services he received inadequate treatment, and he died of blood poisoning on January 13, 1943.[7]

--- Leib Zimmer (Pachach, portfolio 62)
[Also appears in *Lexicon of Heroism*, page 154]

Shimon Zilberman, son of Zalman and Chaya-Sara

He was born in the town of Yod (Braslav region) in 1919. His father was a fisherman. He couldn't continue with his studies at the Polish public school on account of the poverty of his family, and he became an apprentice to a shoemaker.

He escaped to the Kozian forests immediately after the first massacre [in Yod] (December 17, 1941). Throughout the winter and spring months of 1942, he moved about with a group of refugees seeking arms and pursuing murderers of Jews (his entire family who escaped to the forests had been turned in to the Germans by farmers). In the summer of 1942, he was accepted into the Spartak brigade, which had arrived from the region to the east.

He took part in battles against the enemy garrisons in Vidz, Opsa [about 22 kilometers northeast of Vidz] and other places, and in ambushes near the villages of Ustsye [Uscie, about 12 kilometers east of Vidz] and Vasvichi [Wasiewicze, about 16 kilometers southeast of Vidz]. Since the brigade needed a shoemaker, they advised him to return and work at his trade. They settled him in the home of the forester Kobalyunk [Kowalonek] for this purpose.

One morning in January 1943, the house of the forester was surrounded by the Germans. Our partisans who were there succeeded in breaking through the German chain, but Zilberman and Avraham Yair were trapped and burned alive in the house, together with the family of the forester.[8]

--- Hirsh Einhorn (Pachach, portfolio 62)
[Also appears in *Lexicon of Heroism*, page 162]

Shalom Munitz, son of Meir and Sara

He was born in 1900 in Yod (near Braslav). He was a wagon driver.

He escaped with his wife, children and a group of youths to the forests of Kozian in November 1941. At that

[Page 444]

time the ghetto wasn't yet set up in the town [sic], and the partisans hadn't yet organized in the forests.[9] The group began to search for weapons from the farmers of the area; the farmers had hidden weapons that had been cast off by the Soviet soldiers during their retreat. Under the leadership of Munitz, the youths took revenge on those who turned in Jews and who were collaborators. Among others, they killed the farmer Stanislav Kobalyunk [Stanislaw Kowalonek], who turned in the Halpern family and Shayna Rubashin [sic] to the Germans; and the farmer Fyodor Retzinikov [Recznikow], who turned in the Mindov family and Chava Munitz to the Germans.

The group functioned as an independent partisan unit. When escaped Russian prisoners of war began to gather in the forests in the summer of 1942, they joined the by-now experienced Jewish fighters and together launched large-scale procurement actions. They set up the Yatzminov [Jaczminow] brigade (named for the commander), which later became the brigade named for the commander Shirokov.

Munitz was appointed commander of a unit tasked with the provision of weapons. While searching for weapons, they'd wreak vengeance on farmers who collaborated with the Germans. After many complaints were lodged against him for killing farmers, he was made responsible for providing food for the brigade and for the family camp (in which his wife and children lived).

During one of his journeys to collect food in the villages, he encountered a German ambush in the Virov [Wirow] forest. He was killed along with his friend S. Stein in February 1943.[10] His wife and children survived.

--- Hirsh Einhorn (Pachach, portfolio 3)
[Also appears in *Lexicon of Heroism,* page 57]

Feivel Trok [a.k.a. Truk; parents not named]

He was born in 1912 in the town of Yod (Braslav region) to a poor family. From his youth he was forced to help his father, a wagon driver, in earning a livelihood for the family.

He escaped from the Vidz Ghetto on July 5, 1942 and joined the Ponomarenko brigade, which was active in the region of Glubok [Glubokoye, about 50 kilometers southeast of Yod].

He took part in the attack on the standing army in the village of Kamai (near Hoduchishki), in bombing the railway bridge on the Voropayevo-Glubok [Woropajewo-Glubokoye] line, liquidating Polish gangs in the forests of Samische [Szamic], and many other actions.[11]

In March 1944, he went out in a supply action (he was the vice commander of the supply division in the brigade) to the Konstantinova farm near Glubok. Before it left the village, his group was surrounded by the German forces, and he fell in battle.[12]

--- Asher Buchinski (Pachach, portfolio 62)
[Also appears in *Lexicon of Heroism,* page 177]

Footnotes:

1. This refers to *Lexicon Hagevura* by Yehiel Granatstein and Moshe Kahanovich, published in Jerusalem in Hebrew in 1965. An English-language version appears on the JewishGen website as "Biographical Dictionary of Jewish Resistance."
2. Samachova was a voluntary organization under German protection that sought to repel partisans who came to confiscate food from villages.
3. The book *From Victims to Victors,* published in Canada in English in 1992 by members of the Zilberman and Smushkovitz families, survivors from Yod, gave different details. According to them, Pinchas and his son were captured by the peasants and handed over to the Germans to be shot. Pinchas angered the Germans, and they proceeded to burn him and his son alive.
4. Pachach: Information on Jewish partisans compiled by Pachach (Partisans, Soldiers, and Pioneers --- Chalutzim), an organization based in Israel that researches Jewish partisans in World War II. *Milhemet HaPartizanim* (*The War of the Partisans*) probably refers to *Di Milhomeh fun di Yidishe Partizaner in Mizrah-Eyrope* (*The War of the Jewish Partisans in Eastern Europe*) by Moshe Kahanovich, published in Israel in Yiddish in 1954.
5. According to *Lexicon of Heroism,* he was appointed deputy commander.
6. According to the website of the Organization of Partisans Underground and Ghetto Fighters, Benyamin Dubinski died on December 13, 1942 in Bildugi.
7. According to the website of the Organization of Partisans Underground and Ghetto Fighters, Avraham Vilkitzki died on January 15, 1943.
8. According to the website of the Organization of Partisans Underground and Ghetto Fighters, Shimon Zilberman died on January 30, 1943.
9. According to the *Encyclopedia of Camps and Ghettos, 1933-1945,* Volume II-B (2012), the Kozian Ghetto was established in the late summer or fall of 1941.

10. According to the website of the Organization of Partisans Underground and Ghetto Fighters, Shalom Munitz died on February 17, 1943.

11. Hoduchishki (also called Hidotzishok in Yiddish and Adutiskis in Lithuanian) was in Lithuania, about 62 kilometers south-southwest of Braslav and about 52 kilometers southwest of Yod. The village of Kamai was about 10 kilometers to the south of Hoduchishki.

12. According to the website of the Organization of Partisans Underground and Ghetto Fighters, he died on March 17, 1944.

[Page 445]

Slobodka

Boris Berkman
Son of Mira-Leah and Shmuel-Hillel

Translated from the Hebrew / Donated by Guy Elitzur (in honor of his grandmother's family, the Lif family of Slobodka) Revised Based on Laia Ben-Dov's Translation / Footnotes Added by Jeff Deitch

The small town of Slobodka was located on a hill between Braslav [Braslaw] and Druysk [Drujsk].[1] Forests and lakes surrounded it, and at its center stood the large Christian church, whose spires could be seen from a great distance. Its inhabitants weren't many; only about 200 families, of which close to 40 were Jewish. For how many generations had the Jews lived in Slobodka? I don't know. There are no written sources to consult, and unfortunately the Jewish elders of the place are no longer alive. I know only that my mother and her parents were born there.

Jewish community life didn't really exist in the town. All matters involving the Jewish community were centered on Slobodka's single synagogue. My father, Shmuel-Hillel Berkman, was manager (*gabbai*) of the synagogue, and he handled all community matters. As for religious matters, the Jews enjoyed the great assistance of Rabbi Shabtai Rymshinyat, rabbi of the nearby town of Druysk. The Jews found their living in tailoring, the fur trade, shoemaking and petty trading. The Jewish children studied at the Polish school and then went to continue learning in the *cheder* [Hebrew primary school], which held its lessons in the synagogue. The teacher-tutor in the *cheder* was always either a young local man who was a student at one of the yeshivas in the region or a young yeshiva student from elsewhere. The tutor was a "day eater" sustained by the people of the town, the custom for generations in small Jewish communities.[2]

Only a few of the inhabitants of Slobodka left to study elsewhere. My elder sister and I were educated at the Yavneh school in Braslav.[3] Of all the Zionist youth movements, Slobodka had only a small branch of Betar.[4] Neighborly relations between the Jews and Gentiles in Slobodka were very good thanks to the head of the local council, who knew how to build strong ties of friendship with the Jews. Life in the town passed peacefully for many years.

A large base of the Polish army, located in Slobodka, was well known as a camp of the elite brigade of Polish border guards. [At this time, the border with Latvia was roughly 12 kilometers to the north.] When the Polish-German war broke out [in September 1939], the Polish army left the town and there was no one in control. Taking advantage of this time of anarchy, the Gentiles of Slobodka and the surrounding area began to rob Jewish property.

[Page 446]

Our family had six souls. Our parents, Shmuel-Hillel and Mira-Leah; their daughters, Raska and Zisla; and their sons, Boris [me] and Leibke.

Following the Russian-German pact and the division of Poland, the Soviets arrived in Slobodka. Their coming brought the time of anarchy to an end, and life slowly returned to normal. Jews returned without disturbance to their business in crafts and trade. The Russian army occupied the army base and kept order in the town and the surrounding area. Everyone grew accustomed to the new conditions and hoped that they'd continue. But the situation changed when the Russian-German war began on June 22, 1941.

A few days after the war broke out, the entire Soviet army withdrew from Slobodka and the region, heading east. The local authorities left with the army, and Slobodka was once again without a ruling authority. The local Christians, and with them the Poles from the surrounding area, appointed themselves the new rulers. They marched joyfully through the streets of the town, announcing that they were awaiting the arrival of the German liberators, who would free them from the yoke of the Soviets and the Jews. For an entire week, they went wild without restraint.

Among the Poles who were openly proclaiming the end of the Jews, especially prominent was the son of a Polish family in Slobodka by the name of Richter. On the day the Germans arrived, we --- the Jews --- stayed shut up in our homes. No one went outside. Alarmed and fearful, we sat and wondered what would happen. And indeed, we didn't have to wait long. A few days after arriving in Slobodka, the Germans began to impose decrees against the Jews. Every hour, every day, more decrees were announced. "Here, Jews can't go." "There, Jews mustn't stand." From time to time, they demanded a ransom. Sometimes they demanded gold, once they demanded cash, and another time clothes, fur clothing and other items. The Jews were forced to comply with the demands within a few hours. If not, the Germans threatened to kill Jews.

One day the Germans appointed a committee of Jews, headed by Entin, a Jew who formerly had owned a store in the town. In accordance with the Germans' instructions, Entin was linked to the Judenrat [Jewish Council] in Braslav, from whom he received the Germans' orders. We, the residents of the town, worked in groups at various types of forced labor, especially in loading and unloading next to the train. Molka Geskin and Yeshayahu Kanfer worked with me.

One morning a number of trucks entered the town, accompanied by the Germans and their collaborators. They stopped in the town center and announced that they needed Jewish lads to carry out a certain task, whose nature they didn't disclose. The committee decided who among us would go. We got into the trucks and waited for them to move out. There was great fear; a suspicion arose in our hearts that this wasn't about work. We asked ourselves if these hours would be our last. After several hours had passed, the drivers started up the vehicles and we set out on the road, while the sad eyes of our parents followed us to the end of the town.

They drove us to Druya [about 22 kilometers northeast of Slobodka, next to the border with Latvia] and put us in its large synagogue. Inside we found Jews from Druysk, who were sitting there in distress and fear. They'd been brought there a few hours before us. The synagogue looked like the aftermath of a riot; the floor was littered with pieces of parchment from the Torah scrolls and pages from other holy books. Of the young men of Slobodka with me, I remember Molka Geskin, Shneiur Biliak, [Yeshayahu] Kanfer, Falka Zelikman, and a few from the Dagovitz family. We didn't see any Jews from Druya in the synagogue, and we didn't know what had happened to them.

Night fell. We laid ourselves down on the floor and wondered what fate had in store for us. At the crack of dawn they woke us, ordered us into lines, and we started walking. We reached the Dvina River [the border with Latvia]. There they stopped us. There was a raft-bridge over the river. With shouts, the Germans ordered us to immediately dismantle the bridge,

[Page 447]

even though none of us had any idea how to go about it. Nevertheless, we began working. German shouts of "*Jude! Jude!*" ["Jew! Jew!"] accompanied by curses, continued without letup. The task was complicated and difficult. At certain moments Molka Geskin stumbled, and the Germans beat him without mercy. The work continued for two days with no break; finally, the bridge was dismantled. When we were done, the Germans ordered us to return home on foot, some to Druysk and some to Slobodka. Slobodka was 25 kilometers away [as the crow flew it was 22 kilometers, to the southwest]. Very tired, we set out on the road, and after many hours of walking we arrived utterly exhausted in Slobodka.

There everyone had been sitting and waiting tensely for news of what had happened to us. We returned to our parents' houses, and life in the town went on as usual: forced labor, meager bread and "water of oppression."[5] We survived by selling belongings that we'd succeeded in hiding from the eyes of the robbers. Things continued in this way until the middle of winter in [early] 1942.

One winter day, the Germans announced that the Jews of Slobodka would have to leave their homes and the town and, together with the Jews of Druysk, move to the town of Vidz [Widze, about 50 kilometers southwest of Slobodka and 40 kilometers southwest of Braslav]. Winter-wagons were brought to the Jews' houses, driven by their owners --- farmers from the region. Gentiles from the area gathered immediately near the wagons, expressing their joy that at last all of the Jewish property would be theirs. For years, they said shamelessly, they'd waited for this moment.

Weeping and full of sorrow, we loaded a few of our belongings onto the wagons and set out on the road. The road to Vidz passed through Braslav. In Braslav, we knew, the Jews had been shut up in a ghetto, and they too didn't know what to expect.[6] On the way farmers told us, "Behind Braslav, there are pits prepared for the Jews." We listened and kept silent. We continued the journey, none of us uttering a word; only as we approached Braslav did my father, of blessed memory, break the silence. He said, "Children, whoever has the strength to flee should get up and run, find a place to hide, and hopefully you'll be saved. Mother and I no longer have the strength to do it." Our sorrow was deep, we didn't want to part from our parents. We entered Braslav and there, somehow, I took my courage in both hands. I jumped from the wagon and slipped away before the escorts noticed.

Now I was alone. I spent my first days in Braslav at the house of Moshe Milutin's parents. After that, I lived together with the Jews from Yaisi [who were in the Braslav Ghetto after being moved there from Yaisi, which was seven kilometers to the east]. From time to time, I had to move to another apartment. Jews in the Braslav Ghetto were prohibited from letting in Jews from outside the town. I remember once I was staying the night at the home of Moshe Milutin's parents, who took care of me like I was one of their family. At midnight, there was a knock on the door. Moshe's mother called out, "What's wrong with you? Won't you let us sleep at night?" They immediately hid me in the basement and then opened the door. The callers were Jews, messengers from the Judenrat, who'd come looking for Jews from outside Braslav.

I remained in the Braslav Ghetto until that bitter day, 18 Sivan 1942 [June 3, 1942], when the Germans and their collaborators in the local police began to drive the Jews from their houses and run them over to the Pravoslavic [Eastern Orthodox] church. They led us like lambs to the slaughter. From there the Jews were taken away, group by group, to the killing pits [north of town]. In my group of Jews, we whispered among ourselves and agreed to try to escape; we had nothing to lose. We kept walking and when we approached the pits, about 50 meters away, I broke away and ran. I raced toward the railroad tracks, and when I reached them I collapsed. Apparently, I fainted. I don't know how long I lay there unconscious; maybe an entire day, maybe longer.

When I awoke, I was utterly exhausted. I waited for nightfall and began preparing to get away from there. With great difficulty,

[Page 448]

I reached Lake Noviata [also north of town] after dawn. There I sat down in a concealed place to consider my situation: Where should I go? I knew the area around Slobodka well and thought I should go there, but how? To get there it was necessary to cross two bridges, which would certainly be well guarded.

One of them was a railroad bridge. I approached it, laid myself on the ground and looked around. I saw guards on the bridge, maybe they'd leave with the coming of daylight. And indeed, when daybreak came the Germans walked off the bridge. After they left, I took a chance and crossed the bridge to the other side. Then I walked on backroads, taking great care to avoid getting caught. On the road were farmers going to work in the fields. I reached a certain distance from the village of Glinovka [perhaps Glinowka, 4.5 kilometers north of Slobodka]. There the boys of the village noticed me and immediately began shouting, *"Zhid! Zhid!"* ["Jew! Jew!"]. One of the farmers came running toward me with a pitchfork in his hand. As he approached I recognized him, he was called Kishel. He sent the boys away to bring the police from the village. Luckily, before they arrived I succeeded in fleeing from this place and the Gentile, a "friend" who'd visited our home more than once before the war.

At night I continued to walk, and during the day I hid in places I found on the way. After several nights of walking, I arrived at the village of Verkovshchitzna [Wierkowszczyzna, about 4.5 kilometers northeast of Slobodka], at the home of the farmer Milkevitz [Milkewicz], who was a friend of our family. In the first days of the war, my father had given him a large part of our property for safekeeping. I told him what had happened to the Jews and our family, and asked him for a place to hide. To my great joy, he agreed to this immediately. The same day Milkevitz and his sons, who were about my age, prepared a hiding place for me in the barn where I could sit.

I stayed there for a long time. One day, the sons of Milkevitz told me that their father had spoken to the priest in Slobodka and told him he was sheltering me in his house. The priest had replied that it was a very righteous act to save a Jew pursued by the Germans, and it should be done even if it was dangerous. The priest was known for his good relations with Jews. I stayed with the family, quiet and secure, until the day that a neighbor of Milkevitz saw me going out from the barn. After that, unfortunately, I had to leave the place immediately.

With the help of the farmer's son, who had connections with a friend, a pistol was bought for me, which would later add greatly to my security. After the war, I stayed in touch with the Milkevitz family by letter for many years.

Once again, I began wandering. It was now the winter of 1943. Each night, I camped in a different place. The cold was cruel and intense, and I lacked warm clothes. After walking a long distance, I began to feel that my feet were frozen and couldn't move anymore. I was near the village of Gaveiks [Gawejki, about 4.5 kilometers northeast of Slobodka, near Verkovshchitzna]. Having no choice, I decided to knock on the door of one of the homes, hoping to find a farmer who'd let me in. I knocked. An elderly peasant woman opened the door and asked who I was. I explained to her my difficult situation and asked her to go and tell the Germans there was a sick Jew in their home, so that the Germans could come and take me away.

"Heaven forbid!" said the Gentile woman, "I'll tell no one. You can stay with us, and I'll take care of your feet." I was very glad to hear this, and I remained with them. The peasant woman treated my feet, with the help of all sorts of ointments and especially the gall of pigs. Only after a few days had passed did she tell me that local farmers had been asking her: "Why are you constantly asking for the gall of a pig?" She replied that it was for her granddaughter's frozen hands.

She was a very pious woman. She acted as she did out of deep religious feelings and the goodness of her heart. Her family prepared a pit for me in the barn. There I sat until the Germans began searching for Jews in the farmers' houses. Sometime later, I learned that the pit in the barn had been discovered --- at the house of this Savitzki [Sawicki] family. I felt terribly sorry about it. People like them, with human feelings, were very few

[Page 449]
in those days.

Despite the hostile reception that I'd gotten earlier near the village of Glinovka, I decided to return to it and the Murashka [Muraszka] family who lived there. The members of this family were known for their kind hearts. After few nights of walking, I reached them. As I'd hoped, they received me with sympathy and agreed that I could stay with them for as long as I wanted. They were poor farmers who barely earned their living, and feeding me was no doubt a heavy undertaking for them. I decided to help them.

From time to time, I went to the village of Verkovshchitzna to ask the peasant Milkevitz for help, and I always received it. But during one of my "night visits," something happened that nearly scared me to death: Some distance away, a group of young people suddenly appeared, singing and rejoicing, and at a certain moment I heard a shot. It seemed to me that they knew I was a Jew, and I felt trapped. Without hesitating, I pulled out my pistol and began firing. Immediately there were shouts --- "Partisans! Partisans!" --- and they ran off. I quickly got away from there and returned to my hiding place without being seen.

I stayed with the Murashka family until news reached the area that there were heavy German losses at the front and they were starting to retreat. German troops began to appear in the village, and their number increased. The sound of artillery was often heard. It seemed that the Germans' defeat was close at hand. But with their number rising in the village, the risk to my life was growing. I decided to leave the house of Murashka, who'd done so much to help me survive. In peasant clothes, with a rope tied around my waist, I set out on the road to reach the village of Luni [Lunie, about three kilometers southwest of Glinovka and three kilometers northwest of Slobodka], near the lake, and an island near the shore that I knew well.

There too I was lucky --- it was like the hand of fate --- a good man appeared near the lakeshore, a farmer from the village of Luni, and he agreed to take me to the island. He also gave me a little food and water. I regret that I can't remember the name of this farmer; thanks to him and others like him, I survived.

I stayed on the island for several days. Suddenly, a heavy silence fell all around. The front had moved away. [This was probably around July 1944.] One morning, the farmer came in his boat and called out to me: "Young Berkman! Where are you? The war's over!" I was stunned by his words. For years I'd been running like a lone wolf, hunted by those who sought to kill me. Was this good farmer speaking the truth? Had my life been saved? It was hard for me to believe it.

Carefully and in great fear of the evil eye, the farmer took me to his house. I was weak and needed several days of rest, and the farmer's family agreed to let me stay with them for a while. After recovering, I thanked them from the bottom of my heart. I left them and went to Slobodka, hoping to find someone from my own family.

The town was full of Gentiles, who were living in all the houses of the Jews. Of all of Slobodka's Jews, there remained only Shneiur Biliak and the Gans brothers (Shlomo, David and Shalom); the Gans brothers later immigrated to Israel.[7] I didn't stay long in Slobodka; I went to Druya to meet my uncle and my cousin, who had survived. My cousin, Zuska Berkman, immigrated to Israel and lives in Kiryat Motzkin [in northern Israel].

I tried to find out what had happened to my parents, sisters and brother, who I'd left in the wagon in Braslav on the way to Vidz when I ran away. From the few who survived the Vidz Ghetto, I learned only general information that contained no hint at all about my family. Jews from Slobodka and Druysk had indeed gone to Vidz and entered that ghetto. The Germans didn't destroy the Vidz Ghetto, but transferred [some of] the Jews there, group by group, to labor camps scattered around the occupied territory.[8] In the Vidz Ghetto there remained Jews from Vidz,

Druysk, Slobodka and other places in the surrounding area. Only a few succeeded in escaping and reaching the forest where the

[Page 450]

partisans were operating. My family was lost together with other Jews in the camps, without my knowing where or when.[9] I learned only one clear detail: My father, Shmuel Berkman, of blessed memory, had been transferred to a camp in Latvia near Dvinsk [42 kilometers northwest of Braslav], where he met his death together with many other Jews.

Of our immediate family, I was the only survivor. In Druya I was drafted into the Red Army, in which I served until the summer of 1946. I was released from the army in the city of Orsha. I traveled to Riga, Latvia and remained there. There I married Galia Ginzburg from Vitebsk, and there our boy Shmuel was born. In 1957, all of us immigrated to Israel.

Footnotes:

1. Slobodka was about 11 kilometers northeast of Braslav and seven kilometers southwest of Druysk.
2. Under the practice of *essen teg* (eating days, in Yiddish), yeshiva students --- or in this case, the tutor --- were fed by different householders of the community on a rotating basis.
3. The Yavneh school was part of a network of more than 200 schools established throughout Poland by Mizrahi, the Religious Zionist movement that had been founded in 1902 in Vilna to promote Zionism among Orthodox Jews. Yavneh schools emphasized Hebrew (in place of Yiddish), Torah and Talmud study, and reconstruction of Jewish life in Palestine.
4. Betar was the youth section of the right-wing Revisionist Zionist movement, which was led by Vladimir Jabotinsky and had been established in 1925. In the late 1920s and 1930s, the Revisionists were the chief opponent of the World Zionist Organization, which was dominated by the socialist-oriented Labor Zionists. Secular, liberal and nationalist, the Revisionists opposed socialism and sought to establish a Jewish state in Palestine on both sides of the Jordan River. The youth movement of the Revisionist Zionists was Betar, that of the Labor Zionists was HeChalutz.
5. Referring to Isaiah 30:20: "And the Lord shall give you scant bread and water of oppression . . ."
6. The first Braslav Ghetto wouldn't be formed officially until April 1, 1942, when it was enclosed with barbed wire. But Jews were being concentrated there by the German authorities as early as the late summer/early fall of 1941. See, for example, the account of Alexander (Shmaryahu) Dagovitz of Okmenitz (Okmienic) on page 357 of this memorial book and the account of Chalvina Pinchov on page 393.
7. According to Guy Elitzur (a member of the Lif family), other survivors from Slobodka were Yisrael Lif, Yisrael's son Avraham-Yitzchak and Yisrael's daughter Malka. During the war, Mr. Lif and his son Avraham-Yitzchak passed from Slobodka to the Vilna Ghetto and a camp in Estonia, followed by Stutthof and another camp, while Mr. Lif's daughter Malka passed from Slobodka to the Vilna Ghetto and a camp in Estonia, followed by Stutthof and Bergen-Belsen. Avraham-Yitzchak passed away in Europe in 1948, but Mr. Lif and his daughter Malka immigrated to Palestine/Israel in 1947 and 1951, respectively, where Mr. Lif passed away in 1991.
8. Examples of such transfers are described by Sima Feigin Moretsky, Rivka Maron Rukshin, Mira Shneider Lotz and Chana-Feiga Skopitz Berkman, all residents of Dubina who were sent to the Vidz Ghetto, in the Dubina section on pages 367-392 of this memorial book.
9. The Vidz Ghetto had been formed in early 1942, and at some point Jews from other places including Slobodka and Druysk were moved there. Thereafter, some people were removed from the Vidz Ghetto for work in labor camps. Around October 1942, most of the inmates of the Vidz Ghetto were moved to the ghetto in Sventzion (Swieciany, about 45 kilometers southwest of Vidz and in Lithuania). These inmates included many former residents of Dubina, another community covered in this memorial book. The majority of the inmates of the Sventzion Ghetto were murdered on April 5, 1943 at Ponar (Ponary), just outside Vilna. For more information, see the footnotes for page 283 and for page 371 of this memorial book.

[Page 451]

Kislovshchitzna
[Kislowszczizna/Kozlovshchina]

Masha Kapitza
Daughter of Tzvia and Yaacov Rukshin

Translated from the Hebrew by Yaacov David Shulman
Footnotes Added / Donated by Jeff Deitch

I wish to put before you the account of a 12-year-old girl, one of many such stories. It's the story of my life, of what I experienced. I hope it will serve for my children and grandchildren as a memorial to my family that perished in the Holocaust, so that the Nazi atrocities are never forgotten.

I was born into a traditional Jewish home, where love and warmth filled every corner. The house was located in the village of Kislovshchitzna, about seven kilometers from the town of Yod [Jod] and about 20 kilometers from the larger town of Braslav [Braslaw].[1]

In my memory, I can still see the old wooden house where we lived happily and contentedly: my father, my mother, Grandmother Brayna, Uncle Leibke and of course the children: Etka, Masha, Dvora, Bentzion, Shimon and Rachel. I remember well the synagogue that was built close to our house. In particular I remember the chair of my father, who was the synagogue *gabbai* [caretaker]. The chair was made of wood, hand carved, higher than the other synagogue chairs. My father would sit in it with dignity, surrounded by his children, as we prayed together. On cold winter days, when the synagogue couldn't be heated, my father would bring the worshippers into our home to warm up next to the fireplace and pray. In our village of Kislovshchitzna, there were about 32 families --- half of them Jewish and half Polish. The atmosphere of village life was pleasant and calm, with each nationality respecting the other. But little by little, we children began to feel a spirit of anti-Semitism in the air, something in the nature of "Jews, go to Palestine!"

At the end of the summer of 1941 [after Germany had invaded on June 22], when I was 12 years old, news began to arrive in the village that the Germans were killing the Jews. One day, Germans appeared in the village. They loaded the Jews onto the wagons of Gentiles, transported them to the town of Yod, and took them out to be killed.[2] In this incident we were lucky: Because my father was an excellent tailor, the Germans decided to leave our family alone. The days passed as news continued to stream in from the surrounding communities about Jews, who were artisans, taken out to be killed. My father gathered the family together

[Page 452]

and then we split up, fleeing to Gentile friends of the family.

After I fled the village of Kislovshchitzna, I came to the village of Podhaitzi [Podhajce, about three kilometers northeast] to stay with a Polish family. The woman of the house was called Josefa; she hid me in the attic. There wasn't much food, but I didn't complain; I was happy that they'd taken me in. It was potato-planting season, and the woman of the family told me that when everyone went out I should come downstairs and warm myself next to the fireplace.

Fearfully I came down from the attic and gingerly approached the fireplace, careful not to make any noise. Unfortunately, the curtain was open and the daughter of the village policeman was standing outside. She saw me and began to yell, "Jew, Jew!" and ran to the village center to get her father, the policeman. Thoughts raced through my mind; I decided to escape. I ran outside and fled into the field next to the forest. I hid in the field, and through the bushes I saw policemen on bicycles arriving at the house, looking for me. When they found nothing in the house, they decided to continue their search in the field. Many girls my age were in the field, helping their parents to plant potatoes. I rolled up my pants legs and concealed my face and eyes with my headkerchief so that I'd look like one of the other girls, as though I'd moved off a little to the side to "do my business."

The policemen passed very close to me but, naively thinking I was with the other girls, they continued on their way. I remained in the field until darkness fell. When night came, I went to another village named Gardosh [perhaps Girdziusze, about two kilometers northwest of Kislovshchitzna] to look for my father. When we'd fled our house, my father had said that he'd go to this village, where he had friends. When I approached the village at night, I could hear that it was surrounded by Germans looking for Jews, so I didn't enter. Instead, I decided to continue to another village named Badraki, where my parents had a Gentile friend named Igor [Kapusta], a good-hearted and compassionate man who helped every Jew he met.

With great care I approached the village, which was surrounded by trees. Suddenly I heard a voice calling out from the darkness. I stopped immediately and listened. The voice called, "Yaacov, Yaacov . . . ! Yisrael, Yisrael . . . !" and then: "Masha . . . , Masha . . . !" I couldn't believe my ears. I didn't reply, and the words were repeated. Only after the person calling out identified himself as Igor did I go to him, and we fell into each other's arms. Igor, as was his daily custom, had gone out at dusk to graze his horse in the pasture. Recognizing me from a distance, he began to call my name and my father's name, thinking that we were together. Igor had gone out to the edge of the village, because he thought we'd come to him to seek refuge. Since searches were being carried out, going to his house would've been dangerous, and so he preferred to meet us at the village entrance and direct us to the granary, which he owned.

We sat and thought about what I should do. Igor said that if the Germans caught a Gentile helping a Jew, both would be killed. And he added that my uncle Yisrael and my uncle Alter [Rukshin], who'd been staying with him, had been forced to flee to the forest, to another place. As he talked, Igor decided that out of pity for a small girl he'd risk taking me to the granary, which was half empty. He hid me in a corner there and scattered hay around me and on top of me, so that someone coming in wouldn't notice me. While I was staying in the granary, Igor would sneak cooked potatoes from his mother's kitchen and bring them to me, without telling his mother. One day his mother noticed the missing potatoes and decided to help. Without saying anything to her son, she went out to the field, pulled up some nettles, put them in a pot with a little milk, cooked them with a few potatoes and brought them to me in the granary. For a long time, this food was like a royal delicacy to me. This went

[Page 453]

on for four days, until it became known that the Germans were in the next village and about to reach us.

In the morning, she dressed me in clothing that made me look like a Gentile, and Igor took me out of the village. He dug a pit among the trees, put me into it and covered it with branches and twigs, so that I couldn't be seen. I lay in the pit for two days. After that, the Germans left the village, and Igor took me back to his house.

One day, while I was in the granary, I heard the voice of my father, who'd come to look for me. When I met my father, there was no end to my happiness.

The danger in the vicinity of Igor's house increased; father decided that we must escape to the forest. There we met Jewish refugees from Kozian [Koziany, about 32 kilometers southwest of Kislovshchitzna]. Together with them, we experienced all of the attacks that the Germans carried out in the forests.

Let me give you an idea of such a German attack. First, airplanes circled above the forest and dropped bombs. Afterward, they sprayed artillery fire and other heavy ammunition. Then foot soldiers stormed in, killing and destroying everything in their path. During an attack, we'd flee from place to place like people running amok. After one such attack there was a lull in the shelling, and we decided to light a fire to warm ourselves and thaw our freezing bones. As we sat next to the fire, I fell half asleep and moved to a nearby tree. Beneath it, I fell into a deep sleep. Only after a few hours had passed did my father realize I was missing. He searched for me in vain, until someone noticed a pair of feet sticking out of the snow. Apparently while I'd been sleeping, the snow had kept falling and covered me up. If that person hadn't noticed me, I would certainly have frozen to death beneath the snow. When we found a safe place, my father began to remove my frozen clothing from my feet to massage my body --- which was blue from the cold --- with the help of the snow, and to warm me next to a fire. To this day, my feet bear the wounds and scars of that cold.

My situation grew very serious; I couldn't move my feet and the wounds caused great pain. Father decided to look for a place where I could hide and my feet could heal. After some searching, he found a Polish family that agreed to keep me at their house until I healed or recovered. I stayed with them for seven days. They treated me with dedication, placing leaves and various ointments on my feet. To be clear, I didn't stay in their house --- Heaven forbid --- but in the barn together with the cows, where it was warm and my wounds began to form scabs. At the end of the week, the woman of the house came and told me that the Germans were approaching and looking for Jews, and I'd have to leave. In the state I was in, I couldn't go anywhere; I couldn't move my feet. I burst into tears and begged her to let me stay. Her pity was aroused, and she agreed. I dug down in the barn under the cow manure, and lay there for a few days until the Germans left.

After some more time had passed, the Polish woman came again and said that the Germans were coming to the village and I must leave --- otherwise I'd be caught and the family would be taken out and killed. This time the Germans were searching with dogs, and she was afraid. In anguish, with tears in my eyes, I thanked her for her solicitous care and began to drag myself to look for my father. I found him staying with a Pole; together we continued to the forest. After wandering about, we again met the group of Jews from Kozian. We joined them, and in this way the days and months passed.

[Page 454]

One day the Germans staged an attack in the area in the forest where we were staying, and we scattered in every direction. After a month had passed, I met my father again. Like me, he was starving; we shared a few peas that I had in my pocket. One day, when my father went to look for food, he found horses that had been killed in a German attack. He cut a piece of meat from the horse; we lit a fire and put the meat in a tin to cook it. While it was cooking, the smell of the meat apparently reached the Germans, and they began to fire in our direction. We were forced to leave the meat behind and flee. We escaped to another forest, where the survivors of the German attack had gathered, and stayed there for a few months.

While I was in the forest, one day my sister Etka appeared. She told us she'd been in the Kozian Ghetto and from there had come to the forest.[3] While she was talking, a German attack began, with airplanes and heavy ammunition. My sister was hit and died on the spot. In this attack, my Uncle Alter, who was with us, also died.

During the attack, everyone scattered. But since my feet were injured by frostbite, I couldn't run. Alone, I began to weep. A Jewish woman from Bilgioas named Asna passed by. She took me to her, supported me and pulled me after her. We fled until we reached a clearing that had been made to prevent fires from spreading, which separated two forests. Such forest clearings were often surrounded by Germans. As we entered the clearing, we saw a German sentry, and our eyes met his. We froze on the spot. The German, who must have thought we weren't alone and there were partisans were behind us, turned around as though he hadn't seen us [sic]. We took advantage of his hesitation to flee into the forest, as Asna pushed me under a bush until the attack ended. Afterward, we went deep into the forest, where we met families I was related to, and they took care of me.

At this time my father's hand froze, and he was forced to move to the house of Polish acquaintances so that they could help him recover.

Because of the starvation and cold, the [Jewish] family that was taking care of me decided to leave the forest and return to the village they'd come from, where they'd left a great deal of property in the hands of a Gentile friend. This Gentile received the family kindly and told them they had nothing to worry about, he'd provide them with everything they needed. That night, the Gentile went out, got an ax and, when everyone was asleep he killed them all, to the last one.

In the meantime, my father, whose hand had improved somewhat, returned from the Gentile he'd gone to. The Jews in the forest decided to establish a group of partisans, and my father decided to join them. Young people also joined but I wasn't allowed to, since I was too young. We, the children and elders, were called the "families of fighting partisans." From this time, our situation improved a great deal. The partisans would go out at night to Polish villages, carry out raids and bring food and water. The group had a rule that when food was in short supply it shouldn't be distributed to the families; if a member were caught doing so, his blood would be on his head. I remember a youth called Eli Barnamov who risked his life by stealing salt for us from the partisan stores. There were others like him, and with their help we succeeded in overcoming starvation.

One clear day, two partisans went out on horseback to spy on the Germans, to warn against any coming danger. They galloped back to the forest and announced that the Russians were coming --- and with them, freedom. Naturally we were suspicious. After all that we'd experienced, we found it hard to believe that this hell was at an end. But, as they'd said, the Russians indeed came and freed us from the inferno [in the summer of 1944].

With the end of the war, I met my father near the village where I'd been born. Nothing of the village remained --- everything had been burned and destroyed.

[Page 455]

In Germany, I met my husband, Avraham Kapitsa, who was also a Holocaust survivor. We got married, and our first son was born. We --- my father, my husband, and my son ---

made *aliyah* to Israel. After much time, my father, of blessed memory, passed away in his old age. Today I'm a contented mother and grandmother of three children and five grandchildren.

As for the rest of my family, a short story about my six-year-old brother Shimon and my 10-year-old sister Dvora. At the beginning of the disturbances, my parents had placed them in the reliable hands of a Gentile woman in the village of Alchovka [Olchowka, one kilometer east of Kislovshchitzna], where they stayed for two weeks. During that time, the children refused to eat the unkosher food the Gentile woman prepared for them, and so she only cooked them potatoes. In the end, she grew tired of this and decided that they'd have to leave her house. My siblings knew I was with her brother, a man named Kapirosh, whose house stood alone in a place called Alechsandrova [perhaps Aleksandrynowo, about 2.5 kilometers southeast of Kislovshchitzna]. In the middle of the day, while I was at the oven, I heard the Gentile man speaking with my sister and brother, telling them they must go back to where they came from, and that their sister Masha would come to them that night. Despite my desire to go out and embrace my siblings, I held myself back, since the house was filled with guests and I didn't want to get the Gentile arrested. Also, I understood from his behavior toward me that my stay with him was coming to an end.

When darkness fell, I left my hiding place and went to visit my brother and my sister with the Gentile woman in Alchovka. They begged me to take them with me, but I too had nowhere to go. Despite the emotional meeting and their tears, I couldn't take them. I asked them to be patient, promising that in a few days father would come for them.

All of this I told father. When he heard this, he went and hired a Gentile for a great deal of money to get the children and take them into the ghetto in Sharkovshchitzna [Szarkowszczyzna].[4] Mother's sister, Liba, was in that ghetto with her family. She took them in and they stayed in the ghetto until a German attack [on June 18, 1942]. Everyone then fled the ghetto, and when Liba fled, they fled with her. On the way, the Germans killed Liba. She fell, and the children kept running until they reached a place not far from the forest where an empty bathhouse stood. Since they were worn out from running, they told the people with them to tell father and me that they were tired and would stay in the bathhouse, and asked that we come that night to take them. This information reached us but, sadly, after three days had already passed.

People who came to the forest told us what happened: The children were staying in the bathhouse. Toward evening, the forest guard came. He treated them well, gave them food and drink, and said they had nothing to fear. But at the same time, he sent a message to the Germans that two Jewish children were hiding in the bathhouse. Hearing this, the Germans came and killed them.

And another short story about my mother, Tzvia Rukshin, and my two-year-old sister, Rachel.

After a German raid on our village of Kislovshchitzna, the [Jewish] shoemakers and tailors were left alive. The second time, when we learned about another impending raid the Germans were about to carry out, we decided to flee, but my mother Tzvia decided to remain in the house with my [youngest] sister Rachel, because she reasoned that no villager would take her in with an infant in her arms, the crying was liable very quickly to get them arrested and bring disaster on the house and family. Grandmother Brayna, my father's mother, joined her, and they remained in the house. The Germans came and transferred them to the Vidz [Widze] Ghetto.[5] They stayed in this ghetto for a short while until my mother's sister, Grunia, smuggled them out with the help of a Gentile to the Kozian Ghetto, where Grunia lived. Grandmother Brayna remained in the [Vidz] ghetto. She was taken in one of the selections

[Page 456]

carried out by the Germans, and to the best of our knowledge she perished at Ponar.

Mother, who was with her sister in the Kozian Ghetto, felt safe until the Germans carried out an attack against the ghetto. From there, she went to the Glebokie [Glubokoye] Ghetto, staying there until it was liquidated on 19 Av 1943 [August 20, 1943]. There, my mother and my sister Rachel perished.

As for my brother Bentzion, I know only a little. After we fled the house, he joined my Uncle Leibke, who was a tailor by trade. They stayed with a Gentile and worked for him as tailors. When the work came to an end and the Gentile no longer wanted them, he told them to leave.

They had nowhere to go, and they made their way to the Sharkovshchitzna Ghetto, where they perished together with all [sic] of the Jews of that ghetto.

Footnotes:

1.   The distances were probably the distances by road; as the crow flies, Kislovshchitzna was about six kilometers northwest of Yod and 17 kilometers southeast of Braslav.

2.   This might refer to August 1941, when the Jewish residents of Yod were attacked by Gentile villagers from around Yod and their houses were looted. However, most of the Jewish residents of Yod died later, on December 17, 1941, when they were shot and buried in mass graves. See, for example, page 412 of this memorial book.

3.   According to the *Encyclopedia of Camps and Ghettos, 1933-1945*, Volume II-B (2012), the German authorities ordered the establishment of a ghetto in Kozian in the late summer or fall of 1941. This ghetto, which also contained Jewish refugees from other locations in the surrounding area, existed for nearly a year. In August 1942, the Jewish inmates were informed that they'd be resettled in the Postav [Postawy] Ghetto; on hearing this, about 60 Jews fled the Kozian Ghetto, eventually forming a partisan unit in the nearby forests. Those Jews in the Kozian Ghetto who didn't flee, numbering about 300, were transported about 60 kilometers southeast to the Gleboki [Glubokoye] Ghetto, which would be liquidated from August 20, 1943.

4.   The Sharkovshchitzna Ghetto, about 24 kilometers southeast of Kislovshchitzna, had been established between September and November 1941, according to the *Encyclopedia of Camps and Ghettos, 1933-1945*, Volume II-B. At its peak, this ghetto is estimated to have had 1,700 inmates. It was liquidated on June 18, 1942, when the German police and local collaborators surrounded and attacked the ghetto. Some 700 inmates died, but in the confusion nearly 1,000 others managed to break out and flee into the surrounding area. The Germans and collaborators recaptured at least 300 of these and shot them. As many as 500 of the surviving escapees later entered the Gleboki Ghetto.

   Thereafter, in August 1942, the German authorities spread news around the region of an amnesty for Jews in hiding if they gave themselves up and came to the Gleboki Ghetto. This attracted a further number of Jews to this ghetto, but it would be liquidated from August 20, 1943. Fighting broke out during the liquidation and a number of inmates succeeded in escaping into the forests, but more than 3,000 others were shot or burned to death.

5.   According to the *Encyclopedia of Camps and Ghettos, 1933-1945*, Volume II-B, the Vidz Ghetto, about 40 kilometers southwest of Kislovshchitzna, was formed in early 1942. In subsequent months Jews were added to it from Drisviati [Dryswyaty], Druysk [Drujsk], Opsa, Dubina [Dubene] and Kozian. By August 1942, the official population was 1,505. In the fall of 1942, most of the inmates were transferred to the Sventzion [Swieciany] Ghetto, about 45 kilometers southwest of Vidz. From there, most of the inmates were sent to the Vilna Ghetto or taken just outside Vilna to Ponar [Ponary] and killed on April 5, 1943.

[Page 457]

Yizkor [Remembrance]

Translated from the Hebrew / Footnote Added by Jerrold Landau
Donated by Jeff Deitch

[Page 458 = Blank in the original]

[Page 459]

Let the Nation of Israel remember the holy communities
Of Braslav, Opsa, Okmenitz,
Dubina, Zamosh, Zarach, Yaisi, Yod, Slobodka,
Plusy, Kislovshchitzna and Rimshan,
Which were cruelly uprooted, destroyed and annihilated.
May they recall their murdered residents, victims of the evil regime,
Who were tortured physically and spiritually in the death camps.
May they recall all those who were deported to desolate lands, leaving no trace
Who were massacred in marketplaces and roads, hauled to their destruction in death wagons
Who were buried alive, burned, slaughtered, drowned and strangled
Whose honor was violated, and whose blood was spilled, by impure hands, in sanctification of the Divine Name.

May the Nation of Israel remember its dear children, pure ones the children of pure ones
Who were robbed from their parents' bosom by beasts in human disguise and taken like sheep to slaughter
Who were beheaded and murdered, in all manner of unnatural deaths
And piled in heaps in the open ---
Infants and babies who were broken against stone walls, who were tossed down from walls
Whose lives were cut off in their infancy by cruel hands.

May the Nation of Israel remember the pure children, and the splendor of the worlds[1]
And may they not forget the evil and the atrocities
As long as they live upon the earth.

Footnote:
1.   The present world and the world to come.

[Page 460]

Lighting candles on the Memorial Day

Standing (from left to right): Rosa Kastrel, Pesia Eidelman, Sara Movshenzon, Chana Lubovitz, Miriam Rotenberg, Munka Shmutzer

[Page 461]

Statement by Polia (Pesia) Kahat
Daughter of Frida and Sander (Alexander) Veif

Translated from the Hebrew / Footnote Added by Jerrold Landau
Donated by Jeff Deitch

To our community that is no more.

In those days of early summer, in the month of Sivan, when everything was flowering, and the vegetation was renewing its growth, they took our dear ones to annihilation [June 3-5, 1942].

Their souls float and rise higher and higher, and they have a case against the Creator of the world. "Why? For what reason did they destroy us? For what was the great punishment? For which sins? Why did they annihilate us with such terrible death?" And we, who were saved from the great flames, hear the weeping. They accompany us all along the course of our lives. We hear them not only on the days of Yizkor.[1] We see them always, the dear images, known to us, and we see the old houses and paths through which they led the Jewish community to the sacrifice.

The wound is fresh, the agony is great, but one doesn't build life in the cemetery. We, the survivors, left the place that was forever accursed.

Our agonized generation, which knew destruction and annihilation, was also blessed to hear the song of the building and revival of the Land. We merited a state, in which the terrible murderer of the Jews --- Eichmann --- was judged and met his punishment. We mustn't forget the disaster that befell us in the 20th century, in which a third of our nation was murdered. The memory of those who perished will be etched in our hearts and in the hearts of every Jew. We must perpetuate with appropriate honor our parents, brothers and sisters, who were denigrated, starved, beaten and murdered for being Jews.

Blessed be the memory of our martyrs who were tortured in the ghettos, camps, forests and battles --- you who were thrown alive into the pits by the enemy.

Everyone who perished in the terrible storm --- may your memory be honored!

Footnote:
1. The four specific days when the Yizkor service is recited.

[Page 462]

Remove the Shoes from Your Feet . . .[1]

Translated from the Hebrew / Footnotes Added by Jerrold Landau
Donated by Jeff Deitch

A holy silence enveloped us as we, the handful of survivors, paced behind the black stretcher, upon which there was a small earthenware urn with a handful of soil brought [to Israel] from the vale of death of our dear ones, the Jews of our town [Braslav], who were cut down by the German Nazis and their collaborators.

We were a handful, just a few tens of people. We walked with bowed heads. Our footsteps echoed in the silent space of the cemetery, in silence, immersed in searing grief and united in our hearts . . .

He who dwells in the shelter of the Most High . . .[2]

Is this everything? . . .

This is what remains from the bustling Jewish community, its lives, institutions, activities? . . .

An earthenware urn, with soil saturated in blood and torment, lowered into a grave, the dust of the martyrs blended with the Holy Ground . . .

Magnified and sanctified be the Great Name . . .[3]

We stood silently next to the grave, among the graves of the remnants of many Jewish communities of Poland. Memories and forgotten things rose up and flew away. Things forgotten about lives that once were and are no longer, life about which only we, the few survivors, carry memories in our hearts.

Magnified and sanctified be the Great Name . . .

Footnotes:

1. Exodus 3:5, when Moses stood at the burning bush. This section of the memorial book refers to the burial in Holon Cemetery near Tel Aviv, Israel of the urn of soil brought from the killing pits in Braslav. The urn is referred to also on pages 10 and 72 of this memorial book.
2. Psalm 91:1: Yoshev Beseter Elyon.
3. Opening words of the Kaddish prayer.

[Page 463]

Former residents of Braslav and vicinity at the Memorial Day gathering in Israel

[Page 464]

Memorial stone in Holon, Israel

[In Holon Cemetery near Tel Aviv; the Hebrew inscription on the stone says,
"In memory of the martyrs of the community of Braslav and environs[:] Zarach, Yaisi,
Dubina, Rimshan, Zamosh, Opsa, Plusy, Slobodka, Kislovshchitzna, Yod."

[Page 465]

Next to the Monument

A Poem by Yaacov Aviel

I am here, my dear ones, standing silently opposite you
With a silent prayer upon my lips: rest in peace in the soil of the homeland.
--- *Yitgadal veyitkadash* [Magnified and sanctified] . . .

For a moment it seemed to me as if I am talking to you,
Indeed you are known to me by name ---
And the stone monument, roads, roads
A built-up city, a multitude of people!
Towns and villages that I know and remember
--- Did somebody call my name and the name of my father?
Yes, it is I.
I am here, floating around, I was tormented,
Among the towns that I knew.

And see: Everyone had gathered in silence
In the bounds of the eternal city, like a large fair
Of dry bones awaiting resurrection.
Monuments, monuments, with the word "Shoah" engraved upon them,
A large multitude, entire communities,
And what is left of them are ashes and bones.

To me these ashes are family
To me the Holocaust was brothers, parents
And my brethren are many millions such as these,
Millions went, were hauled, and pushed,
And the vale of murder filled up with bones.

And atop all these ashes we set up a monument to guard the place of agony
The story of their deaths cries out, and the searing wound
These and these existed, and thus and thus did they perish
Certainly, they called my name in the final moment
Certainly, they wished that their eternal rest be here.

Here I am, my dear ones, next to your face in stone
With a lowered gaze and a stolen tear
Silently, silently, I recite the prayer,
And I stand silently next to you:
Yitgadal veyitkadash . . .

(The monument [in Holon Cemetery] was erected on 17 Sivan 5741 --- June 19, 1981.)

[Page 466]

I Will Remember These . . .
A List of the Jews of Braslav [Braslaw]
and the Surrounding Area
Who Perished in the Holocaust

Dedicated also to those who are not remembered here
and for whom no redeemer remained . . .

**Translated from the Hebrew by Laia Ben-Dov (page 466)
and Jeff Deitch (pages 467-496) /
Donated by the Latter, with Comments in Brackets**

[The list on pages 467-496 shows the remembered dead for each of 10 out of the 12 communities in this memorial book, omitting mention only of the two very small communities of Okmenitz and Zarach. The period covered was between the time of the Nazi occupation in late June 1941 and the end of the war. For Okmenitz and Zarach, at least some of its dead --- members of the Dagovitz family in Okmenitz and of the Reichel family in Zarach --- were listed instead under Braslav.

The memorial book doesn't say when or how the list was compiled. Presumably it was based mainly on the collective memory of the small number of survivors, gathered sometime between the war's end and the book's publication in Israel in 1986. In some cases, these memories might have been supplemented by the recollections of those who had left the region shortly before the Nazis invaded in June 1941.

The list is fundamentally important but not all-inclusive or error-free. As acknowledged in the book's dedication at the top of this page, some of the dead couldn't be included because there was no one left alive to remember them. For example, the *Encyclopedia of Camps and Ghettos, 1933-1945*, Volume II-B, published in 2012, gave an estimate of 3,000 for the prewar Jewish population of the town of Braslav, of whom only about 70 were said to have survived. For Opsa, which had at least 300 Jewish inhabitants, the number of survivors might have been as few as one: Mordechai Rozenberg. It was impossible for the survivors who compiled the list to recall everyone in their respective communities. Their gathering of names for this memorial book was a heroic attempt.

For those who were recalled and included in the list, mistakes might sometimes have been made; survivors' memories weren't perfect. In a few cases a son or daughter who was married might appear twice, listed under both their parents and separately with their spouse, and so on.

Pages 467-496 list 3,339+ people; the total is approximate because for some families the survivors said that there were children but didn't say how many. If a rough estimate of a Jewish population of 4,000-4,500 in the Braslav region at June 1941 is accurate, then some 660-1,160 of the victims, or 17%-26%, weren't mentioned in the list. But the list gives an approximate idea of the size of each community before June 1941 and the scale of the enormous loss.

The names in the list can be compared with other sources such as the online database of victims at Yad Vashem. That database contains translations of names of many people from this list (not always fully accurate), supplemented by further information and names provided by survivors, as well as by other sources that have come to light. Yad Vashem's database too is fundamentally important but not free of error. So the list in this memorial book can serve as a useful basis for comparison.]

	Number of dead in the list on pages 467-496	Estimate of the Jewish population in each place before June 1941 (in the case of Yod, December 1941)
Braslav	1,734+	Some 3,000 Jews, out of the town's total 5,000 inhabitants, plus some Jewish refugees from elsewhere (according to *Encyclopedia of Camps and Ghettos, 1933-1945*; some survivors' estimates of Braslav's prewar Jewish population are higher)
Yod	435+	450 Jews just before the massacre that began on December 17, 1941, plus some Jewish refugees from Lithuania and Latvia (according to *From Victims to Victors*, a memoir by survivors from Yod)
Dubina	327+	320 Jews (according to page 381 of this memorial book), but was perhaps closer to around 340-350
Opsa	199+	300 Jews (according to page 354 of this memorial book)
Rimshan	192	In the 1921 census, Rimshan had 290 inhabitants, of whom 151 were Jews
Yaisi	144	About 20 Jewish families (according to page 400 of this memorial book)
Slobodka	126+	Close to 40 Jewish families, out of the roughly 200 families there (according to page 445 of this memorial book)
Kislovshchitzna	92	About half of the roughly 32 families there were Jewish (according to page 451 of this memorial book)
Plusy	66	
Zamosh	24	About 10 Jewish families, out of the 100 families there (according to page 393 of this memorial book)
Total	3,339+	The number of Jewish inhabitants killed in the region in 1941-44 has been estimated at approximately 4,000-4,500]

[Page 467]

BRASLAV [Braslaw, Belarus]

[1,734+ dead listed]

[The order of surnames below follows the order in the Hebrew original, not alphabetical order in English. But in most cases the surnames are spelled here in English the way they appear most commonly in Yad Vashem's database.]

Last name	First name	
ABRAMSON,	Berl and Berta Buntza, Katriel-Shmuel	
ABRAMSON,	Chaim-Leib and wife Children [it's assumed this meant at least two]	
ABRAMSON,	Mendel and Yehudit Two children	
ABRAMSON	Shlomo-Zalman and Rachel Three children	[17+]
AUERBACH,	Baruch and Sara	[2]
ULMAN,	Abrasha and Liba A child	
ULMAN,	Eli-Gershon and Matla	
ULMAN,	Eliahu and Matla	
ULMAN,	Dvora-Mirel Musia	
ULMAN,	Zelig and Leah Chasia	
ULMAN,	Zalman and Etel Davidka, Itzka, Taybka	
ULMAN,	Yosef and wife Two children	
ULMAN,	Liuba	
ULMAN,	Leib Liuba	
ULMAN,	Musia	
ULMAN,	Moshe-Anshel	
ULMAN,	Frida	
ULMAN,	Rivka	
ULMAN,	Roza Avraham, Reuven, David	

ULMAN,	Shmerel and wife Nisan-Berl, Leib, and another son	[37]
USTYEV **[or AUSTIEV]**,	Shlomo and Leah David, Mina, and another child	[5]
ASTER,	Tanchum and Sonia A child	[3]
ATLAS,	Nachum and wife Children	[4+]
EIDELSON,	Aharon and Niuta A child	
EIDELSON,	Yitzchak and Sonia Two children	
EIDELSON,	Katriel	
EIDELSON,	Leah	
EIDELSON,	Leib and wife Zaydel, Yehoshua	
EIDELSON,	Leizer and Sonia Leibke and another child	
EIDELSON,	Mendel and Sonia	
EIDELSON,	Ezer and Sara Machla, Shaynka, Chaim	
EIDELSON,	Shaul	
EIDELSON,	Shlomo-Yitzchak Mirka, Esther, Batia	[29]
EINHORN,	Anshel and Dina Yuska and three other children	
EINHORN,	Chloina and Chana	
EINHORN,	Gershon and Chana-Rachel Two children	
EINHORN,	Yerachmiel and Chaya	
EINHORN,	Leib and wife	[16]
ALEKSANDROVICH,	Husband and wife [Yossel and Basya, according to Yad Vashem] Three children	[5]

[Page 468]

Last name	First name	
AMDUR,	Efraim	
AMDUR,	Chasia (daughter of Esther)	
AMDUR,	Yaacov and Chaya Henoch, Asher, Chana, Zelda	[8]
ESTREIKH,	Chaim and Guta Zelda, Peska	[4]
EPSHTEIN,	Wife of Itzka, Merka, and another child	[4]
ARON,	Mina Sonia	
ARON,	Shneiur and Dvora	[4]
ARONOVITZ,	Chaya-Leah Rayvka, Blumka	
ARONOVITZ,	Yisrael and Sonia Leahka, Abrashka, Falka-Eli	
ARONOVITZ,	Slava-Chaya	[9]
ARONCHIK,	Betzalel and Mari	[2]
ARLYUK,	Alter and Chaya Uri, Natan	[4]
ARKLIS,	Nachum and Golda Four children	
ARKLIS,	Rayza	[7]
BASEL,	Liza Chaim-Asher, Shepsel	[3]
BASNER,	Liba-Dina Yitzchak	[2]
BOGOMOLSKI,	Zerach and Chasia-Rachel Sara-Leah	[3]

BUDOVICH,	Chaim and Chaya	[2]
BUDZIN,	Mendel and Gitel Shalom-Moshe, Simcha	[4]
BOR,	Shalom and Alta Simcha and another child	[4]
BURAT,	Leib and Esther-Musia Yisrael, Rivka, Mula, Meir, Shimon, Leizer	[8]
BEILIN,	Benyamin and Doba Leah-Malka, Simcha, Molka, Frumka, Merka, Hoda	[8]
BILIAK,	Avraham and Raytza Velvel, Itka, and another child	
BILIAK,	Itzia-Peretz and Esther	
BILIAK,	David Moshe, Rachel, Leibel	
BILIAK,	David-Shlomo and Sima-Dvora Moshe, Rachel, Tayba	
BILIAK,	Zisla	
BILIAK,	Chone [Chona] and Chava Itzia-Shimshon, Chaya-Shayna, Dvorka, Tevka, Gutka	
BILIAK,	Chontza Tuvia	
BILIAK,	Chaya-Leah Velvel	
BILIAK,	Yossel and Tzipel Beila, Sotzka, Dvora	
BILIAK,	Meir-Yossel and Batia Leizer	
BILIAK,	Natan (Noska) and Henia-Riva Tevka [Tuvia], Libka, Shaynka, Sara-Gitka	
BILIAK,	Sonia Chaim-Meir and two other children	
BILIAK,	Kayla-Malka Nochka, Gitka, Chaim-Leib, Chana-Feiga	
BILIAK,	Simcha	
BILIAK,	Shimon and Leah Velvel, Itka	

[Page 469]

Last name	First name	
BILIAK,	Shneiur and wife Two children	
BILIAK,	Shifra Yankel	[62]
BIMBAT,	Leib and Dvora Two daughters	[4]
BITZON,	Idl and Batia Sender	
BITZON,	Chaim-Yitzchak and Chana-Rachel Chasia-Leah, Michal, Moshe-Henoch	
BITZON,	Katriel-Leib and wife Two children	
BITZON,	Moshe-Henoch and wife Two children	[16]
BIK,	Abrasha (Avraham-Hirsh)	
BIK,	Yosef and Sonia Natan, Leib, and three other sons	
BIK,	Yerachmiel and Mania Tzila, Perela	
BIK,	Musia (Moshe-Hillel)	
BIK,	Feiga	[14]
BLACHER [or BLECHER],	Chaim-Reuven and Musia-Leah Shachna, David	
BLACHER,	Yitzchak and Batia Bluma	
BLACHER,	Moshe-Akiva and Zlata Three children	[12]
BALONOV,	David and Chana A child	
BALONOV,	Yosef and Alta	
BALONOV,	Mantzik and Beila Yosef, Mendel	
BALONOV,	Shalom and Liba-Shayna A child	[12]

BAND,	Avraham-Leib and Chaya-Chana Shachna, Yehoshua	[4]
BANK,	Aba and wife Altka	
BANK,	Alter and wife Chaim-Noach, Chaika, Matla	
BANK,	Zalman-Eli and Golda-Dina	
BANK,	Chaya	
BANK,	Chaim-Ber and Sara A child	
BANK,	Chloina and Tamarl Shepsel	
BANK,	Yankel and Beila A daughter	
BANK,	Katriel and Liuba Rachela, Yisrael, Mila	
BANK,	Moshe and Fraydel Malka and two other children	
BANK,	Moshe-Baruch and Dvora Yuska	[33]
BEK,	Baruch and Mina Zelda, Beila	
BEK,	Father of Baruch	[5]
BER,	Boris and Slava Tzvia and two other children	[5]
BERGAZIN,	Shimon and Tzila Fania, Koba	[4]
BRUN,	Zusia and Rachel Golda, Chana	
BRUN,	Mendel and Matla Yaacov, Aharon-Noach, Michla, Leizer, Brinker[,] Golda	[12]
BERMAN,	Leib	
BERMAN,	Moshe and Batia	[3]

[Page 470]

Last name	First name	
BARMAPOV,	Leib-Meir and Dvora Rivka, Esther, Simcha, Bluma	
BARMAPOV,	Moshe and Sara-Leah Two children	[10]
GANS [or GENS],	Avraham and Esther-Liba Sarala and two other daughters	
GANS,	Bentzion and Chaya Two children	
GANS,	Zlata	
GANS,	Chone and Frumka Two children	
GANS,	Chaim and Rayvka A daughter	
GANS,	Moshe and Tzipa Four children	
GANS,	Shlomo-Zalman and Chana	
GANS,	Sara Four daughters	[30]
GEBELMAN,	Shalom and wife Nechama, Velvel The father of Shalom	[5]
GUTKIN,	Chaim and Rachel-Leah Rayzel, Gitel, Yankel	[5]
GOLDIN,	Avraham-Yossel and Riva-Dina	
GOLDIN,	Bluma	
GOLDIN,	Chone and wife Three children	
GOLDIN,	Leib and Bluma Berele, Michla, Natan, Uri, Zalman-Eli	
GOLDIN,	Leib and Chaya-Ita Dvora	
GOLDIN,	Moshe and Sara Ida, Meir, Leibel, and another child	[24]
GOLDMAN,	Hirsh and wife Avramka and another child	

GOLDMAN,	Mottel and wife Avramka and another child	[8]
GOLDANSKI,	Shimon and Sima Ilia, David	[4]
GUREVITZ,	Idl-Meir	
GUREVITZ,	Chaya	
GUREVITZ,	Yankel and Chaya Meir and two other children	
GUREVITZ,	Nachman-Chaim and Zisla Mendel, Meir, Chana, Liba	[13]
GORDON,	Berl	[1]
GINDLIN,	Gershon and Sara-Pesia Molka, Leah, Lolka	
GINDLIN,	Yitzchak and wife Baruch-Yona, Moshe, Tzipka, Leibke, Bunka	[12]
GINZBURG,	Zerach and wife Rayka	
GINZBURG,	Tuvia and Zelda Three children	[8]
GLAZER,	Yaacov and Masha Avraham-Itzia, Velveleh	[4]
GELISHKOVSKI [or GLUSHKOVSKI],	Aba Avraham, Yeta	[3]
GLAZ,	Leizer and Feiga Yankel, Beinish, Fridka	[5]
GAMUSH,	Leib Pesia	[2]
GAMEROV,	Zalman and Chasia Two children	
GAMEROV,	Fala and Ita Zalman and two other children	[9]

[Page 471]

Last name	First name	
GANDLER,	Shimon and Sara-Rachel Matus	[3]
GRAVITZ,	David and Taybel	[2]
GRABER [or GARBER],	Velvel and wife Children	
GRABER,	Yankel and Feiga Nechama, Matla	
GRABER,	Yitzchak and Sara-Rivka A child	
GRABER,	Rayzka Children	
GRABER,	Shaul and Sara-Riva Two children	[18+]
GRINBOIM,	Hershel and Minka A child	[3]
GRINSHTEIN,	Nachum and wife Elia, Chana	
GRINSHTEIN,	Shalom and wife Two children	[8]
GRINSHPAN,	Velvel and wife Yankel, Tuvia, and two other children	[6]
DAGOVITZ,	Avraham and Nechama-Rayzel Leibke, Shimon, Esther	
DAGOVITZ,	Betzalel-Yankel and Rachel Dobka, Chone-Zisa, and another child	
DAGOVITZ,	Dina	
DAGOVITZ,	Moshe and Ida Monik, David	
DAGOVITZ,	Moshe-Eli and wife Hershel and another son	
DAGOVITZ,	Shmuel and Tzvia Batia	
DAGOVITZ,	Shmerel and wife	[24]

DOBKIN,	Wife of A child	
DOBKIN,	Chaya Chana	[4]
DAVIDOVITZ,	Shneiur and Rachel Vita	[3]
DEITCH,	Aba and Chaya Shepsel	
DEITCH,	Avraham-Itzia and wife Falka	
DEITCH,	Anshel Hirsh	
DEITCH,	Bela Three children	
DEITCH,	Hirsh and wife A child	
DEITCH,	Velvel and Mirel Braynka, Mendel, Milka, Sarala	
DEITCH,	Velvel and wife Two children	
DEITCH,	Ziska and Fraydel Batsheva, Chaya-Brayna	
DEITCH,	Chone	
DEITCH,	Chaim-Katriel and Miriam Fraydel and another child	
DEITCH,	Chloina [sic] and Taybel Children	
DEITCH,	Yosef-Mendel and Hinda Rivka, Matus, Zalman, Golda, Perela	
DEITCH,	Yankel and Guta Two children	
DEITCH,	Yerachmiel	
DEITCH,	Yisrael-Shabtai and Sara-Chaya-Esther Reuven	

[Page 472]

Last name	First name	
DEITCH,	Katriel and wife Chone	
DEITCH,	Levi and Guta Two children	
DEITCH,	Mottel and Sonia Zelda, Zalman, Chana, Yisrael-Berl	
DEITCH,	Malka-Rayza Zerach	
DEITCH,	Mendel and Fania David, Hirsh	
DEITCH,	Slava	
DEITCH,	Fraydel Beilka	
DEITCH,	Shayke and wife	
DEITCH,	Shimon and wife Zelda and another child	[81+]
DIMANTSHTEIN,	Aba and Batia Merka, Mula	[4]
HOLTZ,	Peretz and Gitel Tzvia, Golda, Raika, Leahka	[6]
VORIN,	Etel Hirshel	[2]
VIDEREVITZ,	Shimon and Chana Rishka, Gnesia Israel (brother of Chana)	
VIDEREVITZ,	Brother of Shimon	[6]
VEINSHTEIN,	Ita	
VEINSHTEIN,	Gitel Shmaryahu	
VEINSHTEIN,	Hirsh and Doba	
VEINSHTEIN,	Henoch and Chaya Chaim-Eli	
VEINSHTEIN,	Yosef and Henia Three children	
VEINSHTEIN,	Yaacov and Gnesia Reuven and another child	

VEINSHTEIN,	Levi-Yitzchak and Mirel Shaul	
VEINSHTEIN,	Leib and Gnesia Two sons	
VEINSHTEIN,	Nachum and Chasia Zlatka, Liuba, Chaim	
VEINSHTEIN,	Riva-Dina	
VEINSHTEIN,	Rayza-Matla	
VEINSHTEIN,	Shmerel	[32]
VEIS,	Chaya-Gitel A child	[2]
VEIF,	Berl and wife A son	
VEIF,	Chasia	
VEIF,	Matus and Chaya-Tzesia Zerach, Bentzion, Avka [or Evka], Rivka, Shalom, Matla, Sara-Mirel	
VEIF,	Feiga Moshaka	[15]
VINOKUR,	Chatzkel	
VINOKUR,	Rashel	[2]
VISHKIN,	Tuvia and Sara-Leah Yosef, Nechama, Chaim	[5]
VALIN,	Leib and Dvora Chana-Ita, Rivka, Molka	
VALIN,	Mordechai and wife Children	
VALIN,	Feivush and Elka Pesach, Moshe, Leizer, Shayna-Chaya	

[Page 473]

Last name	First name	
VALIN,	RABBI Zvi-Hirsh and Sara-Hinda Betzalel	[18+]
ZAHORIE [or ZAGORIE],	RABBI Avraham-Aba-Yaacov and Rachel	
ZAHORIE,	Leizer-Itzia	
ZAHORIE,	Mendel	[4]
ZUBOVICH,	Yitzchak and Frida Two children	
ZUBOVICH,	Nachman and Sonia Two children	[8]
ZEIF,	Aharon and Mirel	
ZEIF,	Berl and wife	
ZEIF,	Zalmen-Eli Two daughters	
ZEIF,	Chaim-Aba and Chasia Naftali	
ZEIF,	Chaim-Yisrael and wife Children	
ZEIF,	Yossel and Riva Mendel and two other children	
ZEIF,	Yisrael and Tzirel	
ZEIF,	Leib and Roza Esther, Sonia, Yechiel, and another son	
ZEIF,	Moshe-Anshel and Lifsha Zalman, Feiga, Sonia	[32+]
ZILBER,	Itzia-Yankel and Doba Moshe-Leib, Chaya-Ela, and three other children	
ZILBER,	Baruch and wife	
ZILBER,	Son of Baruch, and the son's wife Children	
ZILBER,	Zalman and Chaya-Dusha	
ZILBER,	Yehoshua and Henia Two children	
ZILBER,	Yosef	
ZILBER,	Yermiyahu and Elka-Mira Mina, Berl, Moshe, Henoch, Shmerka	

ZILBER,	Meir Two children	
ZILBER,	Reuven and Yehudit Liuba, Moshe, David	
ZILBER,	Shlomo the *shochet* [ritual slaughterer] and Sara-Leah Liuba, Bluma, Hirshka	[40+]
ZILBERMAN,	Baruch and Chaya	
ZILBERMAN,	Nisan and Elka Gershka	[5]
ZACHAROV,	Shlomo and Minka Gutka, Meir	[4]
ZLOTOKRYL,	Meir and Fruma Hertzel, Yankel, Sonia	[5]
ZELIKMAN,	Rivka A child	[2]
ZAK,	Velvel and Shayna Efraim, Batka, Paya	[5]
ZAKS,	Tzila Avraham-Zalman, Pesia-Dvora, Leibel, Esther	[5]
ZARZHEVSKI,	Avraham-Meir and Rashka David and two other children	
ZARZHEVSKI,	Efraim and Rachel Three children	
ZARZHEVSKI,	Yosef and Rachel Mosheleh	[13]
KHEDEKEL,	Chaim-Aizik and Olga	[2]
KHARAT [or CHARAT],	Avraham-Baruch and Iska Moshe, Yisrael	
KHARAT,	Itzia-Kopel	

[Page 474]

Last name	First name	
KHARAT,	Yankel and Sonia-Leah Two children	
KHARAT,	Leib and Masha Miriam, Reuven, Sonia, Berka	
KHARAT,	Frayda-Rachel	[16]
TVORETZKI,	Aba-Fishel and wife Liba, Itzka, Lotka	
TVORETZKI,	Leib (Yudl) and Pesia-Rachel Berl, Mula, Danielka, Faytzka, Chana	
TVORETZKI,	Ema	[13]
TODER,	Meir and Sarel Four children	[6]
TODRES,	Chaim and Sara-Rivka Shlomo, Chana	[4]
TOS,	Chone and Esther Yitzchak and three other children	[6]
YAKOBSON [or IAKOBSON],	Gershon and Dora Nioska	[3]
IANKELOVITZ,	Velvel-Gershon and wife Children	[4+]
IAFE [or IOFFE],	Velvel	[1]
KATZ,	Aba and wife Children	
KATZ,	Esther	
KATZ,	Zalman	
KATZ,	Yaacov and wife	
KATZ,	Mendel and Riva	
KATZ,	Sara-Leah	[11+]

LUBARTOV,	Luba and Klara Izia, Veva	[4]
LUBOVITZ,	Avraham and Chaya	
LUBOVITZ,	Mosheleh (son of Chana and Zusman)	[3]
LEVIN,	Bluma	
LEVIN,	Hirsh and Rivka Leibel, Doba-Zlata	
LEVIN,	Velvel and Leah Two children	
LEVIN,	Father of Velvel	
LEVIN,	Velvel and Rayza	
LEVIN,	Chaya-Shayna Tzipka	
LEVIN,	Chaya-Sara	
LEVIN,	Chaim and Batia Tzvia and another child	
LEVIN,	Yehoshua and Iska Malka	
LEVIN,	Yisrael and Chasia Sima	
LEVIN,	Moshe and wife	
LEVIN,	Moshe-Lipa and Sima-Yenta Yehuda, Rachka, Faytzka, Minka, Volfka	
LEVIN,	Peretz and Netzka (Neta) Leibel	
LEVIN,	Rachel-Dita Yerucham	[39]
LOTZ,	Hertz and Zlata [see also under Dubina] Molka, Sima	
LOTZ,	Yitzchak and Slava Rayzla	[7]
LIN,	Moshe-Chone	
LIN,	Reuven and Taybel Sonia	[5]
LIF,	Zalman	

LIF,	Yankel-Hirsh and Hinda Chaim, Mosheka, Mina-Rasha, Bentzka	
LIF,	Shalom-Reuven and Tamarl Paya, Chaim-Feivush, and two other children	[13]

[Page 475]

Last name	First name	
MAGAT,	Yosef and Lena Natan and another child	
MAGAT,	Yitzchak and wife Children	[8+]
MODLIN,	David and Sonia Chana, Mula	[4]
MOVITZ [sic; should be MUNITZ],	Eliahu-Aharon and Tzvia Sonia, Yechiel, Shmuel-Zalman, Isser, Feiga-Tzipa [The Hebrew original says Movitz, but other sources at Yad Vashem show that this family was actually named MUNITZ.]	[7]
MUNITZ,	Efraim and Musia Abrasha, Avka [or Evka], Chaya, Mula	
MUNITZ,	Baruch	
MUNITZ,	Hertz and Gesia Abrasha	
MUNITZ,	Velvel and Beila Katriel-Chone, Tzipka	
MUNITZ,	Velvel and wife A son	
MUNITZ,	Zalman and Hoda Reuven	
MUNITZ,	Chaya Dora	
MUNITZ,	Chaim and Asya Rafael	
MUNITZ,	Chana	
MUNITZ,	Yekutiel and Chava Mira, Avraham	
MUNITZ,	Levi-Yitzchak and Rachel Etzka, Shaynka, Faytzka	
MUNITZ,	Leib	

MUNITZ,	Matus and Leah Two children	
MUNITZ,	Michel-Yankel and Riva-Dina	
MUNITZ,	Sima-Chaya	
MUNITZ,	Shmuel-Yankel and Aydel Chana, Eliahu, Batia, Chaim-Noach	[49]
MUSIN,	Yaacov	[1]
MAZEH [or MAZE],	Eliezer and Liuba A child	[3]
MILUTIN,	Etzka Sarala	
MILUTIN,	Ber-Leib and Sonia Chatzkel, Mina-Rasha	
MILUTIN,	Yisrael	
MILUTIN,	Sarel Sima	
MILUTIN,	Riva Chaim, Arka, Rachka, Abrashka	[14]
MILSHEVITZ,	Etel	[1]
MINDEL,	Yitzchak and wife Three children	[5]
MIRMAN,	Eliahu-Natan and Ditel Chana, Chaya-Mera	
MIRMAN,	Velvel Etzka, Chana	[7]
MALER,	Leib and Zlata-Chava	
MALER,	Frayda Lena, Pesia	
MALER,	Kalman	[6]
MESENGISER,	Velvel	
MESENGISER,	Pesach	[2]
MARGOLIS,	Chaya-Yenta Chana	[2]

MARON [or MERON],	Beila-Esther	
MARON,	Hirsh and Batia Sarala	
MARON,	Zusia and Rachel Golda and another daughter	

[Page 476]

Last name	First name	
MARON,	Chaim and Brayna-Malka Sonia, Lusik, Abrashka, Mosheleh, Rachela, Etzinka	
MARON,	Chaim-Aizik and Sofia Mula	
MARON,	Yosef-Yitzchak and Sonia	
MARON,	Yankel	
MARON,	Yankel and Chana	
MARON,	Yisrael and Sara Three children	
MARON,	Leib and Chana Two children	
MARON,	Shayna	[34]
NIDZVIADOVITZ[?],	RABBI Eliezer-Yehuda and Brayna Children	[4+]
SEGAL,	Reuven and Sara Lusia	[3]
SOLOVEICHIK,	Chaim and Kayla Moshe and two other children	[5]
STAVSKI,	Chaya Esther, Moshe, Relka	[4]
STUL [or STOL],	Simcha-Hertz and Tania Rachel, Hirsh, Sonia, Liuba	
STUL,	Shimon and wife	[8]
SINGALOVSKI,	Aharon-Zelig and Esther Guta, Beni, Shlomo, Yankel	[6]

SLAVIN,	Yosef and Gita Rayzel, Peska	[4]
SAFERN-FUCHS,	RABBI Alter from Dvinsk	[1]
SKUTELSKI,	Reuven and Chana	[2]
SKOPITZ [or SKOPETZ],	Hertz and Ida Rozka, Hirshka, Chayka	
SKOPITZ,	Feiga and husband [this might mean that Skopitz was Feiga's married name, not her maiden name]	[7]
EFRON,	Shimon and Chana Chaim, Hirsh, Zavel	[5]
ETZIN,	Batsheva Ezer	
ETZIN,	Moshe-Aharon and Chana	[4]
PER,	Velvel and wife Children	
PER,	Chone-David and wife Moshe-Leib	
PER,	Chatzkel Dina	
PER,	Yaacov and Rivka Four children	
PER,	Fraydel Two children	[18+]
FEIGIN,	Beinish and Esther Mottel, Mosheleh, Sima-Gitka	[5]
FISHER,	Abrasha and Toiba Three children	
FISHER,	Avraham-Leib and Pesia	
FISHER,	Aharon and Hilda David, Sonia	

FISHER,	Eita and husband [this might mean that Fisher was Eita's married name, not her maiden name] Children	
FISHER,	Ida-Chasinka (daughter of Chana and Tuvia)	
FISHER,	Isser and Sara-Feiga Yisrael, Rivka	
FISHER,	Baruch and Beila-Zelda Zalman-Volf, Avraham, Gutka, Rivka, Zlatka	
FISHER,	Berl and Berta Kulka	

[Page 477]

Last name	First name	
FISHER,	Hillel and Tzirna	
FISHER,	Velvel and Chaya Itzka	
FISHER,	Velvel and Liza-Leah Fruma, Yitzchak	
FISHER,	Zalman-Yankel Neftel [Naftali]	
FISHER,	Chone and Sonia Borka, Avramel	
FISHER,	Chaya-Shayna Feiga-Tzipa, Tevka, Gershon	
FISHER,	Chaim-Ber and Feiga Two children	
FISHER,	Yehuda and Tzila Zelig, Leib-Eli	
FISHER,	Yehoshua and Etel Shayke, Meir[,] Yisrael, and three daughters	
FISHER,	Yehoshua and Henia Chasia, Chatzkel, Neftel, Mirka, Rachka	
FISHER,	Yechezkel and Leah Chika, Guta, Berl, Liuba	
FISHER,	Yankel	
FISHER,	Yisrael and Chaya Dora, Chaim	
FISHER,	Yisrael-Leib	
FISHER,	Leah Gutka, Chaya	
FISHER,	Liuba Sonia, Rachela	
FISHER,	Leizer and Aydel A child	

FISHER,	Lena	
FISHER,	Meir and Dvora Two children	
FISHER,	Moshe and Liuba Kulka	
FISHER,	Nachman and Chaya Two children	
FISHER,	Feivush and Chaya Neftel, Chaim-Hirsh, Gutman, Gutka	
FISHER,	Rafael and Fania Yankel, Neftel [Naftali], Rivka, Esther, Chasinka	
FISHER,	Sara-Gitka	[119+]
FELDMAN,	Daniel and Sara-Leah	
FELDMAN,	Yehoshua and Batia	
FELDMAN,	Yaacov and Fania A child	
FELDMAN,	Moshe	
FELDMAN,	Nachum and Nechama Uri and another child	
FELDMAN,	Shimon Eli-Chaim	[14]
FLEISHMAN,	Shimon and Shayna-Mirel Two children	[4]
FLEISHER,	Shimon and wife Two children	[4]
FRUMIN,	Beila and husband [this might mean that Frumin was Beila's married name, not her maiden name] Children	
FRUMIN,	Gedalia and Lotka Batia and other children	
FRUMIN,	Chaim and wife Three children	
FRUMIN,	Yisrael and wife Two children	
FRUMIN,	Leizer and Bluma Masha and a son	
FRUMIN,	Mendel and Chasia	
FRUMIN,	Nachman and Tzila Velvel	

[Page 478]

Last name	First name	
FRUMIN,	Soska and husband [this might mean that Frumin was Soska's married name, not her maiden name] Children	
FRUMIN,	Slova and husband [this might mean that Frumin was Slova's married name, not her maiden name] Children	[35+]
FRIDMAN,	Hirsh and Hinda	
FRIDMAN,	Niuta	[3]
PERLOV,	Doba Reuven	[2]
PREZMAN [or PRESMAN],	Liuba and husband [this might mean that Prezman was Liuba's married name, not her maiden name] Children	[4+]
CITRON [or TZITRON],	Rachel the *rabbanit* [female Torah scholar/wife of a rabbi], who was also the daughter of Rabbi Yosef Rosen the Rogatchovi [i.e., the late Rogatchover Gaon]	[1]
TZINMAN,	Yisrael and Batia Chava	
TZINMAN,	Rayna A child	[5]
TZIPUK,	Gitel Rachel-Batia, Leah, Golda	
TZIPUK,	Shlomo and Esther	[6]
TZIPIN,	Paltiel	[1]
CHEPELEVITZ,	Liber Hirsh	[2]
KANFER [or KAMFER/ KAMPER],	Yekutiel and Sarel Molka, Abrashka, and another child	[5]

KAGAN,	Yisrael Zalman-Yitzchak	
KAGAN,	Tzila Chasia and another child	[5]
KOBLENTZ,	Yehoshua	
KOBLENTZ,	Leib and Liuba A child	[4]
KOVNAT,	Zalman and Rachel Mosheleh, Chaim-Eli	
KOVNAT,	Mendel and Gita-Rayza Dina, Sima	[8]
KONIN,	Chaya-Gitel	
KONIN,	Pinchas and wife Avramka, Leahka	
KONIN,	Rachmiel-Itza and Mari Fraydel	[8]
KOFKIN,	Eliakim and Malka Three children	
KOFKIN,	Shimon and Liuba A child	[8]
KOCHIN,	Chaim-Yitzchak and Shayna Velvel	[3]
KERBEL [or KORBEL/ KURBEL],	Moshe and Chasia Yankel, Hirshka	[4]
KORT,	Zlata and husband [this might mean that Kort was Zlata's married name, not her maiden name] Shalom-Sender and four other children	
KORT,	Yitzchak and Malka Rafael, Chaim	
KORT,	Yisrael and Matla	
KORT,	Meir and Fania A child	

KORT,	Minka and husband [this might mean that Kort was Minka's married name, not her maiden name] Rotka and another child	
KORT,	Shneiur and Chana Mottel and another child	[24]
KLIONER [or KLYONAR],	Gershon and Sonia	[2]
KANTOR,	David and Sara-Elka Yankel, Perel	
KANTOR,	Rachel	[5]
KANEVSKI [or KUNYAVSKI],	Reuven and Rivka A child	[3]
KASTREL,	Yaacov and Zisla Mashka, Zelig, Leah, and another child	

[Page 479]

Last name	First name	
KASTREL,	Levi-Yitzchak and Sara-Leah	[8]
KAPLAN,	Hirsh and Leah Avramel	
KAPLAN,	Velvel	
KAPLAN,	Velvel and Liba	
KAPLAN,	Yerma and Liba Two children	
KAPLAN,	Ezra and Perel Two children	[14]
KRAUT,	Leib and Shula A child	[3]
KRAVETZ,	Chloina Molka and another child	[3]
KRAVITZ,	Leizer and Brocha [or Bracha] Yehudit and another child	[4]

KARAS,	Boris and Chaya-Sara Tzipka, Esther, Yankel, Kersin-Daniel	[6]
RABINOVITZ,	Zalman and Hota A child	
RABINOVITZ,	Levi-Yitzchak and Roza Sonia, Feiga	
RABINOVITZ,	Shlomo and Gita	
RABINOVITZ,	Shepsel and Dvora Alter, Sonia, Sima, Masha, Tayba	[16]
RUSONIK,	Nechama Idel, Itka [Ida]	[3]
RUKSHIN,	Fishel and Chaya	[2]
RIBASH,	Zalman A son	[2]
REICHEL,	Gitel	
REICHEL,	Gershon and Chiena [or Chayna]	
REICHEL,	Chaim-Yisrael and Batia Sara, Nachman, Velvel, Zalka, Feiga, Bluma, Moshe, Yehoshua	
REICHEL,	Yuska	
REICHEL,	Yaacov and Batia Dvora, Esther, Mina	
REICHEL,	Meir and Feiga Chaim-David	
REICHEL,	Mendel Berl	
REICHEL,	Shneiur and Chasia A child	[27]
RITZ,	Yisrael and Batia Merka, Idel, Matla, and two other children	[7]
RAPAPORT,	Chone-Noach and wife Children	[4+]
SHUTAF[?],	Chana	[1]

SHTEIN,	Aharon and Fania	
SHTEIN,	Melech and Rachel Henoch-Itzka	[5]
SHTERN,	RABBI Moshe and Beila Children	[4+]
SHTEINMAN,	Ema Shayke	
[S]TEINMAN,	Shlomo and Leah Etzka and two other children	
SHTEINMAN,	Shneiur and Rachel-Leah Two children	[11]
SHEIBEL,	Pesia	[1]
SHEINKMAN,	Malka Berta	[2]
SHEINER,	Yosef and Netzka A son	
SHEINER,	Leib and Fraydel Abrasha, Izia	[7]
SHLOSBERG,	Hillel and wife Aba-Zuska and three other children	[6]

[Page 480]

Last name	First name	
SMUSHKOVITZ,	Aba and Esther	
SMUSHKOVITZ,	Yehuda-Moshe	
SMUSHKOVITZ,	Yehoshua and Esther Shaynka	
SMUSHKOVITZ,	Shimon and wife Two children	[10]
SHMIDT,	Roza Chaya-Feiga, Sonia	[3]
SHNEIUR,	Yosef	[1]
SHNEIDER,	Hirsh and Chaya-Merel	

SHNEIDER,	Masha Two sons	
SHNEIDER,	Reuven and Frida Tania, Yosef, Chedva, Mula	[11]
SHAPIRA,	Esther Chava, Matla	
SHAPIRA,	Chone	
SHAPIRA,	Shmuel and Sonia Sima	[7]
SHPERLING,	Michal-Leib and Fruma Moska, Feigel, Dvora, Pinchas, Gitel, Rachel	[8]
SHKOLNIK,	Velvel and Golda A child	
SHKOLNIK,	Matus and Rivka	
SHKOLNIK,	Pesach and Guta Two children	
SHKOLNIK,	Pesach and Matla Lubka, Yuska	[13]
SHERMAN,	Aba and wife Yechiel, Yankel, Liuba	
SHERMAN,	Chaikel	
SHERMAN,	Yerachmiel and wife	
SHERMAN,	Leib and Rivka Mula, Nechemia, Zavel	
SHERMAN,	Leib and Rivka Shlomo, Michal	
SHERMAN,	Rachel	
SHERMAN,	Rayza	
SHERMAN,	Sara	[20]

[Page 481]

OPSA [Belarus]

[199+ dead listed]

[The order of surnames below follows the order in the Hebrew original, not alphabetical order in English. But in most cases the surnames are spelled here in English the way they appear most commonly in Yad Vashem's database.]

Last name	First name	
ABELEVITZ,	Leiba and Tzipora Moshe-Ber, Yehudit, Chaim, Malka	
ABELEVITZ,	Zvi-Hirsh and Esther Leib, Hertzel, Katriel, Batia, Henoch	[13]
ULMAN,	Moshe and Rachel Avraham, Shalom-Meir, Feiga, Gnesia, Rashka	
ULMAN,	Feivush and Fridel Eliahu-Gershon, Rachel, Yehudit	[12]
BAM,	RABBI Eliahu Aharon	[2]
BIKOV,	Aizik and Bela	
BIKOV,	Chaim-Ber and wife Moshe, Chava, Bela-Rasha, Roza, Gershon	
BIKOV,	Leib and Chaya	[11]
BIRMAN,	Ber and wife Moshe, Zisman, Avraham	[5]
BAND,	Nechemia and wife Henoch, Moshe-Yitzchak, Chasia	[5]
BREKERHOV [or BARKAROV],	Chaim-Yisrael and Rachel-Leah Children [it's assumed this meant at least two]	[4+]
BASHKIN,	Avraham and Rachel	[2]
DONDE,	Moshe-Aharon and Chana Yosef	[3]

DRISVIATZKI,	Meir and Mina Eliahu, Gershon, Avraham	[5]
ZILBER,	Aharon and Sara Tzipora	
ZILBER,	Yaacov-Leib and Rivka Chana, Rachel-Leah	[7]
TODRES,	Leib and Chasia	[2]
LEVIN,	Velvel-Zeev and Mariasa Henia, Rivka, Rachel-Leah	
LEVIN,	Chaim-Aba Rayzel, Chaya, Isika	
LEVIN,	Leib and Shayna Chaya, Chana, Bluma	
LEVIN,	Nachum and wife David, Aharon, Liba-Sara, Gita, Dvora	[21]
LIBERZON (Munitz),	Esther-Golda [this might mean that Esther-Golda's maiden name was Munitz] Feiga, Lotka, Henoch	
LIBERZON,	Moshe-Ber and wife Mordechai, Avraham, Rachel, Kayla, Hendel	[11]
LIPINSKI,	Grisha and Rayzel David, Mina	[4]
MEDZIUKIS,	Baruch-Yitzchak and Rachel Tzipa, Chava	[4]
MUNITZ,	Velvel and Rachel-Leah Gnesia, Sara-Rivka	
MUNITZ,	Velvel and Shayna Artzik, Zalman, Sara-Rivka, Ginshka, Rachel-Leah	
MUNITZ,	Zacharia and Feiga Etka, Shmuel-Isser, Leib, Peska	
MUNITZ,	Chone and Etel Leib	
MUNITZ,	Leib and Chana Itel, Sima	
MUNITZ,	Melech	
MUNITZ,	Moshe and Chaya-Riva Kayla, Sara-Leah, Batia, Shneiur, Lipka	

| MUNITZ, | Shlomo and Chaya
Yitzchak, Rachel, Reuven, Chava | |
| MUNITZ, | Shmuel-Hirsh and Chaya | [40] |

[Page 482]

Last name	First name	
FIDLER,	Sima (Shimon) and wife Children	[4+]
FISHMAN,	Leib and wife Matityahu	[3]
PERETZ,	Ber and Lipka	[2]
KAIATZKI,	Zalman and wife Hirsh, Mendel, Rayzel	[5]
ROZENBERG,	Leib and Chaya-Pesia Gershon	[3]
REZNIK,	Leizer and wife Tania, Chasia	[4]
REICHEL,	Aba and Yentl Shmuel, Leib, Yaacov	
REICHEL,	Shmuel and Henia Moshe, Simcha, Feiga, Sara	[11]
RITZ,	Katriel and wife Avraham-Yitzchak, Matityahu, Tanchum	[5]
RAPAPORT,	Shmuel-Hirsh and Yehudit Leibke	
RAPAPORT,	Chaim-Aba and Rachel	[5]
SHNEIDER,	Beila Benyamin, Slava	
SHNEIDER,	Hertzel and Tzirna Yosef	[6]

[Page 483]

DUBINA [Dubene/Dubinovo/Dubinowo, Belarus]

[327+ dead listed]

[The order of surnames below follows the order in the Hebrew original, not alphabetical order in English. But in most cases the surnames are spelled here in English the way they appear most commonly in Yad Vashem's database.]

Last name	First name	
AZBAND,	Yosef and Rachel-Dina	[2]
EIDELMAN,	Malka	[1]
BLACHER [or BLECHER],	Velvel and Golda Yankel	
BLACHER,	Yudel and Chana-Leah	
BLACHER,	Liba Riva-Matla	
BLACHER,	Liuba Sara-Raychka, Gitka, Rachela, Bracha	[12]
GOLDIN [should be GODLIN],	Henoch and Rachel [other sources show that this family's surname was GODLIN, not Goldin] Shayna-Etka, Menucha, Yankel, and another child	[6]
GUREVITZ,	Zacharia and Moshel Rayzla, Mordechai, and another daughter	
GUREVITZ,	Malka	
GUREVITZ,	Tzipa-Chana Serka [Sara?], Kopka [Kopel], Yankel, Rachela	[11]
GORON,	Pesel Zlata	[2]
DEITCH,	Avraham and Basel [Basya?] Mantzik, Hirshka, Meir	
DEITCH,	Avraham and Zelda Leizer-Moshe, Leah, Rayzka, Etzka	
DEITCH,	Avraham and Rasel Shlomo-Itzia, Shimon-Ruvka, Michal	
DEITCH,	Berl and Zelda Serka [Sara?], Yuska	

DEITCH,	Hillel and Sara Chava	
DEITCH,	Velvel and Tayba Leah, Libka, Chuka, Peretz	
DEITCH,	Chaya-Rachel Liba-Hinda, Hirsh, Leizer, Elka	
DEITCH,	Chaim-Aizik and Dina Kayla-Rivka, Itka, Sirka [Sara?], David-Shlomo, Pesia-Feiga, Shayke, Moshka	
DEITCH,	Yuska and Esther Hirsh, Rayzka, Baruch	
DEITCH,	Yitzchak and Liba-Rachel Simka, Kalman-Yossel, Leibel	
DEITCH,	Yisrael-Elka and Rachel Two children	
DEITCH,	Peretz and Chana Michal, Mendel, Velvel, Dusha-Rachka	
DEITCH,	Rivka Mindel	
DEITCH,	Rayna	
DEITCH,	Shmuel-Aba	[67]
VAINER,	Yuska and Liba Three children	[5]
VAIRON,	Avraham and Rivka	[2]
VISHKIN,	Aydel [widow of Meir] Mendel, Gedalia, Batia, Shaynka, Gaska	
VISHKIN,	Gershon and Musha-Mera	
VISHKIN,	David and Dina Efraim, Chaim-Leib, Raynka, Beila-Mashka	
VISHKIN,	Velvel and Leah Serka [Sara?], Chana, Leib	
VISHKIN,	Chaim and Chaya-Batia Four children	

[Page 484]

Last name	First name	
VISHKIN,	Yudel Three children	
VISHKIN,	Leib and Feiga [see also under Plusy] Avraham-Chone	
VISHKIN,	Reuven and Rachel Batia, Molka, and another child	
VISHKIN,	Sara [widow of Avraham-Yitzchak] Mira-Zelda, Nechama, Moshe, Pesia-Rachel, Avraham-Itzka	[43]
ZAK,	Avraham-Itzia and Mina-Elka Three children	[5]
ZILBER,	Aba and Mirel	[2]
KHATZYANOV,	Yisrael and Chana Shaynka, Leibke, Rayzka, Nachka, Davidka	[7]
LEVIN,	Mottel and Stirel Berl, Chaya-Serka, Davidka, Chaim-Elka, Avramka, Shayel [Shaul?]	
LEVIN,	Shlomo and Sara-Ditl [or Sara-Disel] Shayna-Rivka, Chayala	[12]
LOTZ,	Hertz and Zlata [see also under Braslav] Simka, Shmuel, Avramka	[5]
MARON [or MERON],	Avraham Matka, Chasia, Shmuel-Chatra	
MARON,	Beinish and Alta Taybka, Vaytzka, Eli-Ber, Azriel, Braynka, Tzalka	
MARON,	Betzalel Shlomo, Tzirna, Matka, Hirshka, Rachela	
MARON,	Gershon and Sara Three children Gitel (who was the mother of Sara)	
MARON,	Zacharia and Tzvia	
MARON,	Chaim and Sima-Feiga Two children	
MARON,	Yeshika [Yehoshua?] and Tzipka Yisraelka, Feiga-Mera	

MARON,	Meir and Chaya Yisrael	
MARON,	Necha and Sara Two children	
MARON,	Natan and Chana Avraham-Hirsh, David, Shmuel-Feivush, Yaacov	[47]
MUNITZ,	Leah [wife of Afroim/Efroim] Mendel, Chaim-Itzka, Chaya-Rivka, Bentzke	[5]
MUSHKAT,	Tanchum and Sara-China	[2]
SKOPITZ [or SKOPETZ],	Hirsh and Esther	
SKOPITZ,	Hirsh and Fruma-Bracha Mina-Gitka, Gedalia, Liba-Riba, Mantzik	
SKOPITZ,	Velvel and Aydel A child	
SKOPITZ,	Yisrael and Zlata Lipa, Shayna, Chava	
SKOPITZ,	Leib and Doba Isser-Ber and two other children	
SKOPITZ,	Moshe-Nisan and Guta A child	[24]
FEIGIN,	Yisrael-Yitzchak Asher-Ber, Reuvka, Feivka, Shayna-Chaya	
FEIGIN,	Leib and Shayna-Pesia A child	
FEIGIN,	Shlomo-Itzia and Rivka Fraydka, Simka, Gaska, Molka, Shlomo-Itzia, Gitka, Mendel	

[Page 485]

Last name	First name	
FEIGIN,	RABBI Shmuel and Tzirna	[19]
ZUKURYA,	Aizik and Esther-Henia Children [it's assumed this meant at least two]	[4+]
RABINOVITZ,	Yenta-Leah	[1]

RUKSHIN,	Chaya-Hinda Shimon	[2]
RAPAPORT,	Avraham-Yankel and Sonia Anshel	
RAPAPORT,	Chone-Noach and Chana Chaim-David, Gershon-Itzia, Sara-Rivka, Chaynka, Kayla-Dvorka	[10]
SHTEIN,	Hirshel and Chana-Chaya Mantzik, Itzka, Minka	
SHTEIN,	Noach and Chana Two children	[9]
SHNEIDER,	Avraham-Yankel and Stirel Henoch-Isser	
SHNEIDER,	David and Rachel-Leah Sara-Zelda	
SHNEIDER,	Henia	
SHNEIDER,	Yosef	[8]
TODER,	Chana-Musia Moshe	
TODER,	Nachum and Sara Frida, Liba, Tzvia, Moshe	
TODER,	Sara Doba	[10]
[NO SURNAME LISTED],	Beila *die shmiderke* (the wife of the blacksmith) Esther	[2]
[NO SURNAME LISTED],	Natka *der shtumer* (the mute) and his sister Sara [This might have been Nota Vishkin and his sister Sora Vishkin Zalcman, both from Dubina, who were listed together in the Vidz/Widze Ghetto in 1942, with Sora as the head of the household.]	[2]

[Page 486]

<u>ZAMOSH [Zamosz/Zamoshye/Zamoscie, Belarus]</u>

[24 dead listed]

[The order of surnames below follows the order in the Hebrew original, not alphabetical order in English. But in most cases the surnames are spelled here in English the way they appear most commonly in Yad Vashem's database.]

Last name	First name	
GAMEROV,	Chaim and Shayna	[2]
DEITCH,	Hirsh and Esther	[2]
ZACHAROV,	Leib and Lidia Two children	
ZACHAROV,	Menachem-Mendel Batsheva, Yosef	[7]
PINCHOV,	Esther (daughter of Sonia and Chloina [or Chalvina])	
PINCHOV,	Liuba	
PINCHOV,	Tzvia	[3]
RUKSHIN,	Golda Chava	[2]
SHAPIRA,	Batia Feiga, Gershon, Libka, Yenta	
SHAPIRA,	Mari	
SHAPIRA,	Tzipka A child	[8]

[Page 487]

YAISI [Jaisi/Jejse/Jajsy, Belarus]

[144 dead listed]

[The order of surnames below follows the order in the Hebrew original, not alphabetical order in English. But in most cases the surnames are spelled here in English the way they appear most commonly in Yad Vashem's database.
It should be noted that on page 401 of this memorial book the account of Shneiur Munitz clearly stated that his wife, Sara, and their children, Avraham-Yankel and Chaya-Rachel, were killed in the June 1942 massacre of the Braslav Ghetto, but the wife and the two children weren't included in the memorial book's list below.]

Last name	First name	
BERMAN,	Sara-Esther	[1]
KHANIN,	Leib and Feiga Three children	
KHANIN,	Meir-Lipa and Matla Sara, Rachel, and a son	
KHANIN,	Moshe and Sara Two daughters and a son	[15]
KATZ,	Esther A child	
KATZ,	Velvel and Etel Meir and four other children	[9]
MUNITZ,	Yisrael-Getzel and Nechama Chaya, Daniel, Sara	
MUNITZ,	Levik and wife Avraham-Yankel and two daughters	
MUNITZ,	Moshe and Gitel A daughter and two boys	
MUNITZ,	Rivka	[16]
PER,	Yankel and Rivka Three children	[5]
PASTERNAK,	Meir and Rachel	[2]
TZIPIN,	Esther-Rachel	
TZIPIN,	Berl and wife Two daughters	

TZIPIN,	Leib and Rachel-Leah Rayzka, Blumka, Rivka	
TZIPIN,	Falka and Shayna A daughter	
TZIPIN,	Paltiel and Hinda Meir and three other children	
TZIPIN,	Nachum and Rachel Leah, Chana-Tzipa, Chaim-Shmerel, Esther, Shlomo, Rafael, Leib	
TZIPIN,	Nachum-Ber and wife Three children	
TZIPIN,	Shlomo and wife	[35]
RUKSHIN,	RABBI Isser	
RUKSHIN,	Benyamin and wife Mendel, Nechama, and four other children	
RUKSHIN,	Batia and husband [this might mean that Rukshin was Batia's married name, not her maiden name] Mendel, Nechama	
RUKSHIN,	Yeshayahu-Beinish	
RUKSHIN,	Fishel	[15]
SHAPIRA,	Berl and Fraydel	
SHAPIRA,	Yisrael and Malka Meir and four other children	[9]
TARSHISH,	Ida Yitzchak, Chana	
TARSHISH,	RABBI Chaim and Ita-Feiga Mendel	[6]
[NO SURNAME LISTED],	Aizik the *shneiderl* [tailor] and Liba A son and a daughter	[4]
[NO SURNAME LISTED],	Bluma and her husband (the blacksmith) Two children	[4]

[Page 488]

Last name	First name	
[NO SURNAME LISTED],	Berl and Sotzka Two children	[4]
[NO SURNAME LISTED],	Gitel (the widow of Avraham-Yankel, of blessed memory) Esther, Chuka, and two other children	[5]
[NO SURNAME LISTED],	Yankel-Nachum and Feiga Three children	[5]
[NO SURNAME LISTED],	Yisrael-Yitzchak Chaim-Reuven	[2]
[NO SURNAME LISTED],	Shalom the son of Eliahu and wife Two children	[4]
[NO SURNAME LISTED],	Sara the widow Avramel, Musia	[3]

YOD [Jod/Jody/Iody, Belarus]

[435+ dead listed]

[The order of surnames below follows the order in the Hebrew original, not alphabetical order in English. But in most cases the surnames are spelled here in English the way they appear most commonly in Yad Vashem's database.
The memoir *From Victims to Victors*, published in Canada in 1992 by three survivors from Yod, should also be consulted; it contains an appendix listing approximately 370 victims and 116 survivors from Yod.]

Last name	First name	
EIDELMAN,	Shifra Motke, Levik	[3]
EINHORN,	Henia Ita-Riva	
EINHORN,	Mordechai and Henia Zalman-Yitzchak	[5]
ALTHAUZEN,	Shlomo and Riva Two children	[4]
ASTANOV,	Yitzchak-Kopel and Chana Henoch, Tzira, Feivel, Shayke	
ASTANOV,	Leib and Beila Dvora	[9]
BUDIN,	Gavriel and Genia Children [it's assumed this meant at least two]	[4+]
BOR,	Chaim-Shalom and Gitel	[2]
BINKOVICH,	Max and Chana Rivka and a son	[4]
BYCHIN,	Avraham-Yitzchak and Batia	[2]
BIRGER,	Yaacov and Liba-Frida Moshe, Dina, Chana	[5]
BLACHER [or BLECHER],	Chone-Leib and Chana Betzalel, Pesach, Yosef, Golda	[6]

BREZ,	Leib and Rayzel Aba	[3]

BREKHEROV [or BARKHAROV],	David-Shlomo and Rachel-Leah Zalman, Baruch, Velvel	
BREKHEROV,	Chaim and Leah	[7]

BARNAMOV [or BERNAMOV],	Gedalia and Esther Berl, Sara, Shimon	
BARNAMOV,	Henia and Chaim-Zelig [only here is the wife named before the husband] Children	
BARNAMOV,	Hertzel and Riva	
BARNAMOV,	Zelig and Shayna Gitel, Tzirna, Chaim	
BARNAMOV,	Zalman and Shayna-Leah Golda, Chaya-Slova	
BARNAMOV,	RABBI Yosef	
BARNAMOV,	Leib and Liba Velvel	
BARNAMOV,	Shmuel and Pesia Children	[28+]

GUTKOVICH,	Arka and Pesia Zalman, Shulamit	[4]

[Page 489]

Last name	First name	
GUREVITZ,	Gershon and wife Children	
GUREVITZ,	Chaim-Yudel and Sara-Leah	
GUREVITZ,	Yitzchak and Sima Chaim and a daughter	
GUREVITZ,	Michal and Aydel	[12]

GINDLIN,	Alter and Shayna Yehudit, Mula	
GINDLIN,	Shmuel and wife A son	[7]

DAGOVITZ,	Berl and Tzipa Chaya, Esther	

DAGOVITZ,	Yeshayahu and Golda Yosef	[7]
DUBINSKI,	Aba and Chaya-Tzirna	
DUBINSKI,	Benyamin and wife	
DUBINSKI,	Yisrael and Chaya Shprintza, Aharon, Hinda, and another child	[10]
DRUKER,	Moshe and Shayna	[2]
VILKITZSKI,	Moshe and Miriam Avraham, Hinda	[4]
ZILBER,	David-Eli and Esther Berl, Leizer, Batia, Shayna	
ZILBER,	Yosef and Rayzel Mula	[9]
ZILBERMAN,	Chana	
ZILBERMAN,	Zalman and Chaya-Sara Matla, Shimon, Beinish, Etel	
ZILBERMAN,	Yudel and Riva Children	
ZILBERMAN,	Lusia Dvora	
ZILBERMAN,	Palta	[14+]
ZAK,	Eli-Leib and wife Riva, Yaacov	
ZAK,	Baruch and Shayna	[6]
KHIDEKEL,	Avraham and Bela Sara-Miriam	
KHIDEKEL,	Leib and Chana	[5]
TROK,	Feivel and Shayna Meir	[3]
IAFE [or IOFFE],	Pinchas and wife Mordechai, Matus	
IAFE,	Shalom (Silem)	[5]

LEVITANS,	Chaim and wife Two children	
LEVITANS,	Yeshayahu and Slava David, Sara-Miriam	[8]

LEVIN,	Moshe and Necha Mula[,] Leib	[4]

LURIE,	Avraham and Mirka Chaim, Golda	[4]

MEIEROV,	Yaacov and Shayna Esther, Malka, Riva, Yisrael-Yechezkel	
MEIEROV,	Leib and Tzipora	
MEIEROV,	Moshe-Gedalia and Riva Chasia, Chaim, Leibel	[13]

MUNITZ,	Avraham and wife Two children	
MUNITZ,	Hillel and Doba Benyamin, Dina	
MUNITZ,	Hirsh and Matla	

[Page 490]

Last name	First name	
MUNITZ,	Chaim-Yisrael and Sara-Riva Yechezkel	
MUNITZ,	Meir and Ita Sima-Chaya, Shulamit, Bentzion	
MUNITZ,	Reuven and wife Two children	
MUNITZ,	Rachel	
MUNITZ,	Sara Rachel	
MUNITZ,	Sara Shalom, Chava	
MUNITZ,	Sara-Chana	
MUNITZ,	Sara-Leah	[30]

MUSHKAT,	Ema Berl	[2]

MUSHKIN,	Chaya Velvel, Yitzchak, Mula	[4]
SAGLOVA [or SAGALOVA/ SEGAL]	[Only the surname appears here, nothing else]	
STOLAR [or STOLYAR],	Batia Sara	
STOLAR,	Meir and Pesia Mina, Sonia, Moshe	[7]
STAROBIN,	Chaim and Pesia Gitel, Yosef	
STAROBIN,	Chaim and Riva	[6]
SAMOVAR [or SAMOVER],	Chana-Etel Riva	[2]
PEIKIN,	Yisrael and Yocheved	
PEIKIN,	Shmuel and Chaya Shalom	[5]
PINCHOV,	Uri-Yeshayahu and Taybel Aharon, Fishel, Shprintza	
PINCHOV,	Berl-Mordechai and Fruma-Rachel Liba, Esther, Etel	
PINCHOV,	Mordechai and Rayzel Asher, Esther	
PINCHOV,	Natan Liba	
PINCHOV,	RABBI Kalman and wife Children	[20+]
FISHER,	Chaim and Riva	
FISHER,	RABBI Yosef and Feiga Two children	
FISHER,	Yitzchak and Chaya-Sara Aharon-Leizer	[9]
TZEMAKHOVITZ,	Chaya-Gitel	
TZEMAKHOVITZ,	Yehoshua-Avraham and Leah Liba, Hinda, Miriam, Meir	

TZEMAKHOVITZ,	Reuven and Liba Miriam, Rachel-Leah, Meir, Henia	[13]
TZIMERMAN,	Chava Kayla, Yaacov	[3]
TZIPIN,	Chaim-Leizer and Chava Three daughters	
TZIPIN,	Shmuel-Elia and Rachel	[7]
TZEMAKH,	Bentzion	
TZEMAKH,	Leah	[2]
KANFER [or KAMFER/ KAMPER],	Zalman and Riva Mari, Sara, Yehoshua	[5]
KAPLAN,	Idel	
KAPLAN,	Yaacov and Henia Katriel, Azriel	
KAPLAN,	Meir and Chaya-Fruma Rayzel, Berl, Leah-Musia	
KAPLAN,	Feiga Katriel, Shabtai, Tzipora, Melech	

[Page 491]

Last name	First name	
KAPLAN,	Tzadok and Esther Katriel	[18]
RUBINSHTEIN,	Gentel[?] and wife Children	[4+]
ROZIN,	Eliahu and Masha Rivka, Rafael	[4]
RUMIN [or RAMIN],	Avraham and Golda Two children	
RUMIN,	Avraham-Yitzchak and wife Masha, Aharon, Leah	[9]

RUKSHIN,	Isser and Riva Chaya-Sara, Fraydel	
RUKSHIN,	Chana	
RUKSHIN,	Yisrael and Shayna Shmuel, Yitzchak, Tzvia, Etel, Pesia	[12]
RING,	Tzipa Henoch	[2]
RAPAPORT,	Simcha-Bunim and Tzvia	[2]
SHULKIN,	Yitzchak and Brayna Zelda, Nechama, Golda	
SHULKIN,	Meir and Riva-Guta Zalman, David, Peretz	[10]
SHTEIN,	Zusman and Tzira-Feiya[Feiga?] Yitzchak-Kopel	
SHTEIN,	Yaacov-Meir and Ita Chaim-Simcha, Hirsh-Leib, Chaya	[8]
SMUSHKOVITZ,	Benyamin and Bela Pesach	
SMUSHKOVITZ,	David and Chana	
SMUSHKOVITZ,	Leizer	
SMUSHKOVITZ,	Meir and Sonia Pesach, Yenta	[10]
SHMIDT,	Meir-Leib and Malka	[2]
SHAFIR,	Gedalia and Sara Chaim-Nota, Berl	
SHAFIR,	Moshe and Shayna Children	[8+]
SHKOLNIK,	Esther Liba, Rayzel, Yocheved	
SHKOLNIK,	Bluma A daughter	
SHKOLNIK,	David-Shlomo and Sara	
SHKOLNIK,	Yisrael and Riva Yosef	

SHKOLNIK,	Liba Two children	
SHKOLNIK,	Moshe-Aharon and Frida Doba, Yocheved	
SHKOLNIK,	Reuven and Chaya-Feiga Rayzel, Yocheved, Yaacov, Chaim-Yitzchak	[24]
SHRAGOVICH,	Benyamin and Tania Riva	
SHRAGOVICH,	Chaya-Bluma Liba, Ida	
SHRAGOVICH,	Nachman-Leib Masha	[8]

[Page 492]

SLOBODKA [Belarus]

[126+ dead listed]

[The order of surnames below follows the order in the Hebrew original, not alphabetical order in English. But in most cases the surnames are spelled here in English the way they appear most commonly in Yad Vashem's database.]

Last name	First name	
EIDELMAN,	Mottel and Leah A child	[3]
AMDUR,	Leizer and wife A daughter	[3]
ENTIN,	Baruch and Shula Merel	[3]
BILIAK,	Sonia Children [it's assumed this meant at least two]	[3+]
BIMBAT,	Yonah and Chaya-Dina A child	[3]
BIK,	David and Chasia Chaim-Ber and other children	[5+]
BERKMAN,	Shmuel-Hillel and Mira-Leah Raska [Raisa?], Zisla, Leib	[5]
GANS [or GENS],	Bentzion	
GANS,	Sara Children	[4+]
GAMEROV,	Zalman and Chasia Yosef	[3]
GENDELS [or GENDALIS],	David and Chasia Children	[4+]
GESKIN,	Hillel and Sara Molka	[3]

DAGOVITZ,	Chaim-Henoch and wife Sara-Batia, Katriel	
DAGOVITZ,	Mirka and husband [this might mean that Dagovitz was Mirka's married name, not her maiden name]	
DAGOVITZ,	Nachum and wife Shlomka and other children	
DAGOVITZ,	Sender and Chasia A child	
DAGOVITZ,	Shmuel and Shayna-Mirel Leibke, Serka [Sara?], Fromka	
DAGOVITZ,	Shimon-Ber and Chaya-Riva	[21+]
DEITCH,	Ida and husband [this might mean that Deitch was Ida's married name, not her maiden name] DEITCH, Yisrael [a relation of some kind, listed under Ida's household]	[3]
VINOKUR,	Chasia Mindel	[2]
ZELIKMAN,	Chava-Slova Falka [Rafael], Yankel, Rivka	
ZELIKMAN,	Riva A daughter	
ZELIKMAN	[No first name] (was the mother of Riva)	[7]
KHIDEKEL,	Avraham-Yitzchak and Hinda	[2]
KHAZAN,	Taybka and husband [this might mean that Khazan was Taybka's married name, not her maiden name] A child	
KHAZAN,	[No first name] (was the mother of Taybka)	
KHAZAN,	Mottel and Liba Children	[8+]
LIF,	Zerach and wife Children	
LIF,	Frida Avraham-Yitzchak, Zelda, Shalom, Rachela, Mendel	
LIF,	Husband and wife Children	[14+]

[Page 493]

Last name	First name	
SAMOVAR [or SAMOVER],	Avraham-Yossel Luba, Chaya, Bluma, Chone	
SAMOVAR,	[No first name] was the sister of Avraham-Yossel	[6]
SKOP,	Berl and wife	[2]
KANFER [or KAMFER/ KAMPER],	Zelig and wife Children	
KANFER,	Yehuda and Chasia-Leah Chaim-Shayke, Rachel-Rayzel, Aharon-David	
KANFER,	Shlomo and Nechama-Dvora	[11+]
RUSONIK,	Yankel and wife	[2]
SHVARTZ,	Leib and wife Shulamit, Merka	[4]
SHTEINMAN,	Tzvia	[1]
[NO SURNAME LISTED],	Zalka the *katsev* [butcher] and Liba Children [Zalka was presumably Zalka Tamarin, identified by testimony at Yad Vashem as a butcher in Slobodka.]	[4+]

PLUSY [Plussy/Plusa/Plyussy, Belarus]

[66 dead listed]

[The order of surnames below follows the order in the Hebrew original, not alphabetical order in English. But in most cases the surnames are spelled here in English the way they appear most commonly in Yad Vashem's database.]

Last name	First name	
EIDELMAN,	Yitzchak and Leah Golda, Zalman, Rayzka	[5]
BARKAN,	Genia Elik	
BARKAN,	Hillel and Dina Mina	
BARKAN,	Chaya	
BARKAN,	Mariasha	[7]
VISHKIN,	Leib and Feiga [see also under Dubina] Avraham-Chone	[3]
LEVIN,	Leah Chaya-Sara	[2]
MODLIN,	Yosef-Leib and Shifra Avramka, Sara-Rivka	[4]
MILUNCHIK,	Henoch and Chaya-Rivka Rachel-Leah, Shmuel, Shlomo, Rayzka, Ishika [Yehoshua?], Itzka, Berka, Shalom, Nachka	
MILUNCHIK,	Yisrael and Sara-Mala Feivka, Itzka, Kushka, Ishika [Yehoshua?], Feiga, and five other children	
MILUNCHIK,	Feivka and Chanka A child	[26]
MARON [or MERON],	Yudel and Mina Esther	[3]
SHLOSBERG,	Henoch and Fraydel Four children	

SHLOSBERG,	Yisrael and Rachel Manka, Zalman, Noach, Leah, Tayba, and two other children	[15]
[NO SURNAME LISTED],	Esther the daughter of Efraim	[1]

[Page 494]

KISLOVSHCHITZNA
[Kislowszczizna/Kozlovshchina, Belarus]

[92 dead listed]

[The order of surnames below follows the order in the Hebrew original, not alphabetical order in English. But in most cases the surnames are spelled here in English the way they appear most commonly in Yad Vashem's database.]

Last name	First name	
BOR,	Zelda Liba, Nachum	[3]
BAND,	Yaacov and wife Two children	
BAND,	Yerachmiel and Ita	
BAND,	Pesach and Necha Mordechai, Esther	[10]
GOLDMAN,	Alter and Mushka Fraydka, Rivka	[4]
DEITCH,	Moshe-Meir and Sara Sima	[3]
MUNITZ,	Reuven Yisrael, Batsheva, Leib	[4]
MECHANIK,	Baruch	
MECHANIK,	Chaim	
MECHANIK,	Shlomo-Asher and Chana Avraham, Shimon, Shmuel	[7]
SOLOVEI,	Brayna Leib	[2]
KAPLAN,	Avraham and Liba Shlomka, Feiga, Mosheleh, Yenta	
KAPLAN,	Yehuda-Leib and Rayzel Yankel, Yentka, Shlomo	[11]

RUKSHIN,	Avraham and Yenta Liba, Berl-Mordechai	
RUKSHIN,	Avraham-Aba and Sara-Leah Alter	
RUKSHIN,	Berl and Henia Etka, Yitzchak	
RUKSHIN,	Golda Chava	
RUKSHIN,	Heshel and Zelda Zalman, Sara	
RUKSHIN,	Taybka Michla, Elka, Batia, Simka	
RUKSHIN,	Yankel and Sara Fraydka, Moshe-Baruch, Michla	
RUKSHIN,	Slava	
RUKSHIN,	Feiga	
RUKSHIN,	Tzvia Etka, Dvorka, Bentzion, Rachel, Shimon	
RUKSHIN,	Riva-Dina	[36]
SHTEIN,	David-Shlomo and Grunia Sima	[3]
SMUSHKOVITZ,	Yerachmiel and Gita Chaim	
SMUSHKOVITZ,	Shmuel-Grunam and Esther Blumka, Yitzchak, Mordechai	[8]
[NO SURNAME LISTED],	Avraham-Yossel the *melamed* [religious teacher] [This might have been Abram Utkin, a teacher, who appeared on a list of Jews from Kislovshchitzna prepared in 1941-42.]	[1]

[Page 495]

RIMSHAN [Rimszan/Rimšė, Lithuania]

[192 dead listed]

[The order of surnames below follows the order in the Hebrew original, not alphabetical order in English. But in most cases the surnames are spelled here in English the way they appear most commonly in Yad Vashem's database.]

Last name	First name	
EINGORN,	Chana-Henia	
EINGORN,	Leizer and Esther-Shifra A child	
EINGORN,	Leizer and Rachel	
EINGORN,	Moshe and Ita Avraham, Idel, and another daughter	
EINGORN,	Rachel-Leah	[12]
ARON,	Dina	
ARON,	Chaim	
ARON,	Moshe and Leah Gita, Chana	
ARON,	Nechemiah and Mera Nachum	
ARON,	Nachman and Shifra Yaacov, Beila	
ARON,	Pola and Leah Meir, Chana-Ita, Riva	
ARON,	Shmuel-Isser and Berta Avraham, Tova, Mira, Gila	
ARON,	Shmuel-Yosef and Chava Chaim-Reuven, Meir, Chone, and another son	
ARON,	Yosef	[31]
BEIKOVITZ,	Mendel and Tzira Gita	[3]
BRINKER,	Hirshel Leib, Golda, Zalman-David	[4]
GINZBURG,	Avraham-Leib Chaya-Ita, Fishel, Itzia-Ber	[4]

GLOT,	Moshe Chaika, Libka, Peska	
GLOT,	Shimon and Liba Two children	
GLOT,	Shimon and Mera Two children	[12]
DUBINOVSKI,	Shosha	[1]
DEITCH,	Tzirlka and Chaya Three children	[5]
HAMBURG,	Aida A daughter	[2]
VOLFOVITZ,	Meir and Aida A daughter	
VOLFOVITZ,	Shalom and Chana Three children	
VOLFOVITZ,	Shimon-Volf Yenta, Chasia, Riva	[12]
ZAK,	Leizer-Ber and Chaya Yosef, Yitzchak, and two other children	[6]
LEVIN,	Yehoshua-Aba and Beila Yisrael, Sara, Vitka	
LEVIN,	Liba Three children	
LEVIN,	Leib and Shayna Three children	[14]
MOVSHENZON,	Aba and Rachel-Leah Sara-Leah and another daughter	
MOVSHENZON,	Etel Eli-Yakum	

[Page 496]

Last name	First name	
MOVSHENZON,	David and Sara Zusia, Elka	
MOVSHENZON,	Liba Eli-Yakum, Rachel-Leah, Sara-Ela, Yehuda	
MOVSHENZON,	Reuven-Shmerel	[16]
MATZKIN,	David and wife A child	
MATZKIN,	Moshe-Aharon and wife Two children	
MATZKIN,	Shlomo-Yankel and Pesia	[9]
FEIGELMAN,	Chone and Vita Two children	[4]
FISHERMAN,	Yisrael and Mera Mottel	
FISHERMAN,	Moshe-Ber and Dvora A child	[6]
KERBEL [or KORBEL/KURBEL],	Velvel and Elka Baruch, Avraham-Itzia, and another child	[5]
KRITZER,	Aydel Moshe	
KRITZER,	Efraim Avraham-Itzia, Leizer, and another son	
KRITZER,	Yitzchak and Esther Yisrael	
KRITZER,	Yerachmiel and wife Two children	[13]
KARASIN,	Avraham-Shmuel and Riva Sonia, Chana	
KARASIN,	Zerach and Chaya Beila and two other children	
KARASIN,	Yosef and Pesia Two children	[13]
SHADUR,	Hirsh-Berl and Rachel-Leah	[2]

SHALTAISKI,	Chaim-Moshe Feivush, Rachel-Ita, Chana-Sara	
SHALTAISKI,	Lipa-Leizer and Liza Three children	[9]
SHLITEN [or SHALITAN],	Yitzchak and Elka Moshe	[3]
[NO SURNAME LISTED],	Berl the *shochet* [ritual slaughterer] and Feiga Four children	[6]

[Pages 497-568: TRANSLATION OF THE YIDDISH SECTION]

My Perished Town

[The Yiddish section runs from pages 497-568. For the English-language version of the Yiddish section, see the English section, which runs from page 640 backward to page 569.
The Yiddish section contains only one photo, on page 568; it appears below.]

Burial of the urn of earth at Holon Cemetery

[The earth, which had been taken from the massacre site in Braslav, was reburied in Holon Cemetery near Tel Aviv by Braslav region survivors and family members.]

[Pages 640-569: ENGLISH SECTION IN THE ORIGINAL, HEBREW-LANGUAGE MEMORIAL BOOK]

[This section (running from page 640 backward to page 569) contains the English-language equivalent of the Yiddish-language section (which runs from pages 497-568). The English, made by South African translator Rachelle Mann Rachman, appeared in the original, Hebrew-language memorial book that was published in 1986. These Yiddish and English sections essentially are abridged selections from the much-longer Hebrew-language section (which runs from pages 1-465).

The English section on pages 640-569 includes a subsection with a list of names of Gentiles who saved Jews in the area of Braslav/Braslaw. The subsection, which appears only here and not in the Hebrew or Yiddish sections of the book, runs from page 573 backward to page 571.

The English section on pages 640-569 is reproduced here almost exactly as it appeared in the original memorial book, including minor inconsistencies in names, dates, numbers, italics and capitalization. Ms. Rachman's British English spellings, as well as Polish spellings of people's names and place names, have been retained. Corrections to grammar and punctuation are minimal, with factual corrections/other comments added in brackets.

At the time the memorial book was published in 1986, the English section on pages 640-569 was the only part available in English. With the completion in 2020 of translation into English of all 465 Hebrew pages (pages 1-465) --- and book publication of the translations in 2024 in this memorial book --- the full accounts of the contributors have become available in English.]

Darkness and Desolation

In Memory of the Communities of Braslaw, Dubene, Jaisi, Jod, Kislowszczizna, Okmienic, Opsa, Plusy, Rimszan, Slobodka, Zamosz, Zaracz

Association of Braslaw and Surroundings in Israel and America, Ghetto Fighters' House, and Hakibbutz Hameuchad Publishing House

[Page 639]

Editorial Board: Aviel Ya'acov, Levin Ya'acov, Shmutser Aharon
Book Committee: Aviel Ya'acov, Band Chayim, Berkman Boris, Bogomolski Moshe, Cepelewicz Yehuda, Charmatz Zalman, Goldin Moshe, Levin Ya'acov, Munitz Arieh, Rabinowitz Issar, Shmutser Aharon, Wishkin Moshe
American Committee: Chanin Louis, Suran Frederick, Kopacz Michael, Bernamow Sam, Witkin Charles, Fisher Tuvia, Maron Mendel
Editor: Machnes Ariel
Compiled by Bogomolski Moshe
Translation into Hebrew from Yiddish, Polish and Russian, Initial Editing: Aviel Ya'acov, Band Chayim, Bogomolski Moshe, Korner Aharon, Levin Ya'acov, Shmutser Aharon
Yiddish Abridged Version: Levin Ya'acov
Edited by Eisenman Zvi
Translated into English by Mann Rachel
Map of Braslaw (drawn from memory) [on pages 20-21]: Band Chayim
Map of Opsa (drawn from memory) [on page 322]: Aviel Ya'acov
Photographs: From private sources
Typography: Aryeh Velleman

[Page 638]

דאָם וענען די גרינדער

פֿון אינזער סאָסייעטי

ברעסלאָווער אונטערשטיצונגם פֿעראיין

געגרינדעם געוואָרען דעם 2טען מאַרטש, 1913

ברוקלין, נ. י.

שלום הירש העללער, ע'ה

מאיר קענענעק

חיים מענדיל העללער ז

משה אהרן רוקאשין

חיים שמעון רוקאשין

יוסף פֿישער

חיים לייב דיימאָנד

יוסף חיים ווײנפֿילד

גרשון אליעזר אבראמסאָהן, ע'ה

הערי קענענעק

יעקב לעווין

אברהם קאָנטאָראָוויין

זלמן פער

שמחה נינזבורג

ראובן רומאק

אליעזר בעריל דיין

אלמער אולמאן

אורי מרדכי פֿישער

ברעסלאָווער

אונטערשטיצונגם פֿעראיין

נאָך דעם מששאַרטער

ברעסלאָווער

איד סאָסייעטי

געגרינדעם דעם 7טען יאַנואַר, 1913.

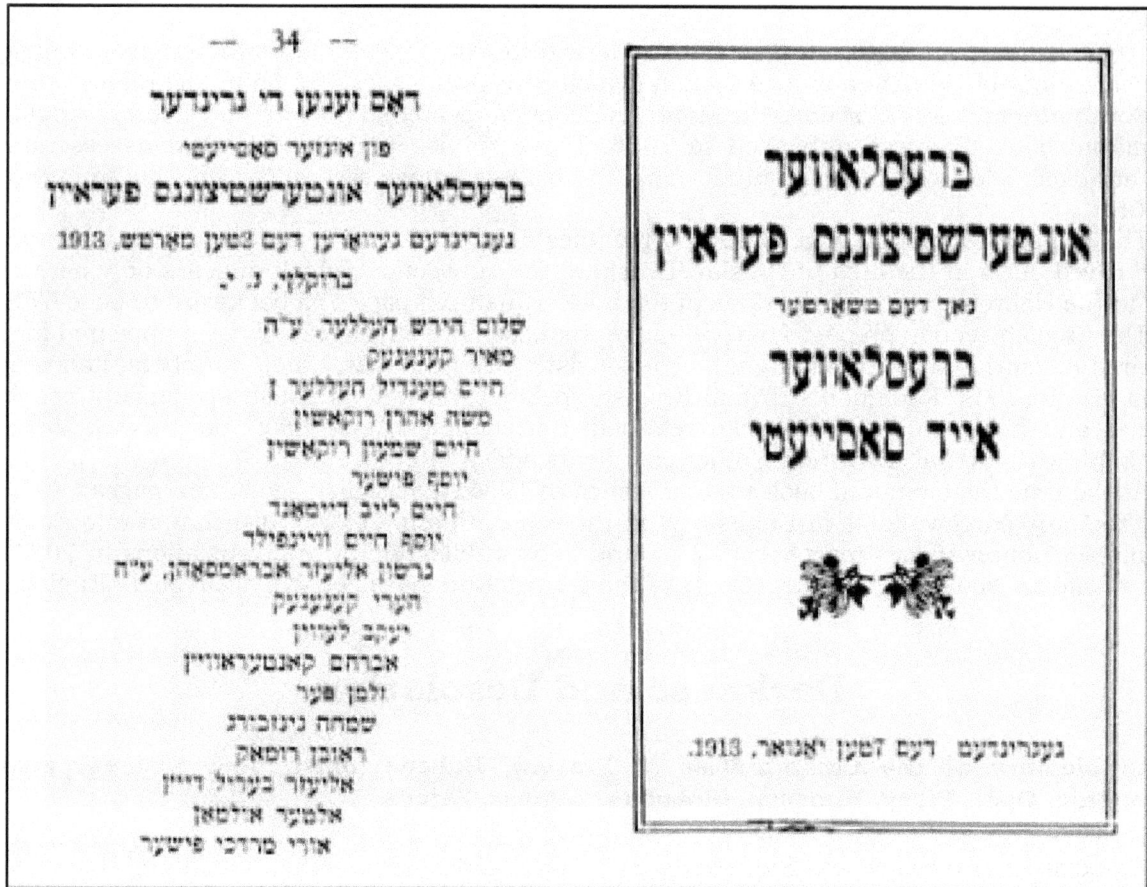

Breslover Assistance Association[1]

From the charter [of the] Breslover Aid Society
Founded on January 7, 1913 [sic][2]

These are the founders of the Breslover Assistance Association, founded on March 2, 1913 [sic] in Brooklyn,[3] New York:

Shalom-Hirsh Heller, o.h.[4]
Meyer Kenenek
Chaim-Mendel Heller[5]
Moshe-Aaron Rukashin
Chaim-Shimon Rukashin
Yosef Fisher
Chaim-Leib Deimond
Yosef-Chaim Veinfild
Gershon-Eliezer Abramson, o.h.
Harry Kenenek
Yacov Levin
Avraham Kantorovitz
Zalman Per
Simcha Ginzburg
Reuven Rumak
Eliezer-Berel Deitz

Alter Ulman
Uri-Mordecai Fisher

Footnotes:

1. This page appeared in the memorial book's English section in Yiddish; the page was translated into English by Aaron Krishtalka and donated by Jeff Deitch.
2. The Breslover Aid Society (for the Braslav in what's now northern Belarus, the subject of this memorial book) was founded in the United States in 1910, not 1913. So the "1913" here would appear to be a printer's error.
3. In the Yiddish original, "Brooklyn" was misprinted as "Brooklny."
4. Olav Hasholem: "May he rest in peace," used after the name of a deceased person is mentioned.
5. In the Yiddish original, "Heller" was given as "Heller n," which appears to be a printer's error.

[Page 637]

[**The sign in the photo says, "A Happy New Year / Thirtieth Anniversary Banquet / Tendered by / Breslover Aid Society / Empire Manor / December 31, 1940."**]

[Page 636]

Preface

This book contains the testimonies, memoirs and experiences of many Jews of Braslaw, Opsa, Okmienic, Dubene, Zamosz, Zaracz, Jajsi, Plusy, Slobodka, Rimszan, Kislowszczyzna and Jod, the survivors of the Holocaust perpetrated by the Nazis during World War Two. Their survival is as varied as it was miraculous: some hid in the ghettoes in all manner of hiding places, some were deported to labour camps, better known as death camps, some escaped, joined the partisans and fought the Nazis and their collaborators, some enlisted in the Allied forces (the Polish, the Red and the British armies).

This book is only being published now [in 1986], forty years --- almost a generation --- after the grim epoch. Yet time has not wiped out the memories as they, the thousands --- nay millions --- of men, women and children, had been wiped out. The book too unveils acts of untold heroism and dedication, man's indomitable will to survive, the relentless struggle and resistance of both individuals and groups --- of the few against the many, the unarmed against the mighty Nazi war machine. It is their courage that helped hasten the victory over the dark forces of evil.

The book is enriched and enlivened by stories of Jewish life in the shtetlach prior to the Holocaust. Jews are shown through the eyes of the storyteller: Jews from every walk of life, rich and poor, Jews in their relations with the Goyim, with one another, their diversified community life with its political parties, groups and circles.

An entire generation has come and gone since the Holocaust. Yet time has not healed the wounds nor silenced the cry. And therefore, let the humble pages of this book be a lasting memorial to them and their suffering. It is a debt that we who survived owe them who perished, and our children --- to remember!

The idea of publishing a book in memory of the Holocaust victims from Braslaw and its surrounding shtetlach originated already in the transit camps to which the survivors flocked after the German surrender. The first memorial service, organised by Zusman Lubowicz, was held in 1947 in the Eshwega camp. The next Yizkor took place in July 1948 in the Hertzog camp and was organised by Zalman Charmatz, Tuvia Fisher and Eliahu Smidt, the late Ben-Zion Charmatz and David Sztrimling.

In 1949, after the survivors had settled in Israel, a Yizkor service was held in David Sztrimling's home in Haifa. A year later a committee of Braslaw survivors was elected and memorial gatherings were held annually. The idea of publishing a book was mentioned on a number of occasions, but the task seemed forbidding, and it was shelved.

However, a nucleus, a committee under the chairmanship of Yehuda Cepelewicz, and consisting of the following members: Moshe Goldin, Moshe Wishkin, Arie Munitz, was formed. The committee kept the memory of the martyrs alive by organising annual gatherings and were subsequently responsible for two vital tasks, namely:

[Page 635]

a. Thanks to the strenuous efforts of Itschak Rajchel, a jar of blood-soaked earth taken from the Braslaw pits --- the mass grave --- was brought by Szlomo Rajchel to the cemetery at Holon, Israel, where an impressive tombstone was erected.

b. It was through their initiative and untiring efforts that the longstanding wish to publish the Memorial Book as a lasting tribute to the memory of the victims came to fruition.

More people were needed, however, both to raise funds and to collect and compile the material for the book. The survivors in America came to the rescue. Mendel Maron, Charles Witkin, and Tuvia Fisher set about to raise funds. Our sincere thanks and appreciation to them for their valiant efforts.

An editorial board was elected consisting of Yaakov Levin, Yaakov Aviel, Moshe Bogomolski, and Aron Shmutser. The latter, though not a Braslavian himself, is married to one --- Monka. He has done a tremendous job collecting and translating the testimonies. The written material was mainly in Yiddish, but also in Polish and Russian. The editorial staff translated and formulated the Hebrew text of this book.

Our sincere thanks and appreciation to the survivors of Braslaw and environs who literally had to draw their breath in pain to tell their story. Each tale is an echo of the cry of the condemned to the pits, of children strangled in shelters.

We also remember the last cry and command of the first victim --- Chayim Milutin --- "Avenge our blood!"

We owe a debt of gratitude to the late Zvi Shner, director of Beit Lochamei Hagetaot (Ghetto Fighters' House) for his encouragement, advice, sharing his knowledge and experience with us, and for offering the patronage of the Ghetto Fighters' House.

Our thanks go to Sarah Shner, Zvika Dror and Itzhak Stemberg [should be Sternberg] of Kibbutz Lochamei Hagetaot for their interest, involvement and encouragement.

Benjamin Anolik, the administrative director, helped us to obtain bibliographic material on the historical background of Braslaw, and a microfilm on the Jasinski trial.

Our appreciation to Ariel Machnes who acted as editor of this book.

Yaakov Levin has done a fine job on abridging the Yiddish version. Zvi Eisenman edited it. Rachelle Mann, a Braslavian presently living in Johannesburg, translated it into English. To all --- our thanks and sincere gratitude.

The "Amos Foundation" of the office of the President of the State of Israel extended financial assistance.

So did the Fund for the Perpetuation of the Memory of Polish Jewry.

Help was also extended by the Breslover Aid Society, Inc. [in the United States].

We have availed ourselves of the following:

1. The Archives of the Ministry of Defence
2. The Congress Library [Library of Congress], Washington
3. The library of Beit Lochamei Hagetaot
4. The National Library of the Jerusalem University
5. The Yad Vashem Archives
6. The Yivo [YIVO] Archives, New York

[Page 634]

To the martyrs who perished in the Holocaust and to the fighters and heroes of Braslaw, its vicinity, and elsewhere --- this book is dedicated.

[Page 633]

Translator's Note:

Though not a survivor in the strict sense of the term, I might --- or might not --- have been one had we not left Braslaw, Poland, two years prior to the outbreak of World War II.

An adolescent, lonely and mute, a stranger in a foreign land, I kept looking back with longing to all I had left behind --- the place of my birth, the friends of my childhood.

Then came the war --- the ominous silence --- and when the clouds lifted, the horrible vision of death and destruction. I felt bereft, desolate, the ground cut from under my feet. Slowly I rallied, tried to live in the present, to strike roots in my new home, and to forget . . .

Years passed. Then, when in Israel, I met up with some of my childhood friends --- survivors. They told me of this book. I felt stirrings of memories long past, the tug of a common bond, and promptly offered to translate it. It was only later that I was to fully grasp what I had but vaguely sensed then.

The manuscript arrived and I began with the poem "Deep, Deep Pits, and Red, Red Loam," its leitmotif. When I came to the words "they who leave no one to speak," I stopped. So this is what the enemy sought. To leave no trace. To sink all into --- silence! So that evil may live and people die! And then I knew that to keep silent is to betray the dead martyrs, the living victims, and to rob those yet unborn of their rightful legacy --- REMEMBRANCE.

Rachelle Mann-Rachman

[Page 632]
Once There Were Shtetlach . . .

[Page 631 = Blank in the original]

[Page 630]
Introduction
Friends,

In these pages, we have endeavoured to give a brief résumé of the personal testimonies of our compatriots, the survivors who bore witness to the bloody events which, like a hurricane, swept over the Jews of Braslaw and environs, its neighbouring shtetlach and yishuvim (small rural Jewish settlements, with yishuv as the singular form; the typical features of the yishuv are described in the *Geographic Dictionary* published in Warsaw in 1886) --- Opsa, Jod, Jajsi, Kislowszczyzna, Dubene, Zamosz, Zaracz, Slobodka, Okmienic, Rymszan and Plusy.

The complete version of these eyewitness accounts appears in the Hebrew section of the book only. Unfortunately, for technical reasons, it was not possible to reproduce them in full in the English section as well. However, in these albeit compressed narratives, we have tried to adhere closely to the facts and to capture both the spirit and essence of their Hebrew counterparts.

It is therefore our sincere hope that the reader will be able to form a picture of that grim epic written in the blood of our dear ones, our never-to-be-forgotten martyrs of blessed memory.

[Page 629]
Poem by Samuel Halkin:

Deep, Deep Pits and Red, Red Loam

Deep, deep pits, and red, red loam ---
Once I too had a home ---
Where the orchards bloomed in spring
And in autumn birds took wing
And in winter soft snow fell.
Now --- the wind his moan howls there.

A disaster struck my home!
Open wide flung doors and gates
The vile murderers, the butchers,
They who slaughter little children,
They who hang the old, the weak
They who leave no one to speak . . .

Deep, deep pits, and red, red loam ---
Once I too had a home.

The years come, the years go,
Brimful are the pits
And redder still the loam.
That loam is now my home.
There my brothers, sisters lie ---
Torn limb from limb
Cut down on the spot
Shot down beside the pit.

Deep, deep pits, and red, red loam ---
Once I too had a home.
Brighter days will dawn again
Fortune will yet smile again
And the pain will slowly wane.
Once again will children sprout
Once again will play and shout
Near the graves of the holy dead
Graves so deep, so full, so red ---
And with the wind will sigh your moan.

[Page 628]

Deep, deep pits, and red, red loam ---
Once I too had a home.

Deep, deep pits, and red, red loam ---
Once I too had a home . . .

Yes, once I too had a home . . .

Translated by the author

My home, Braslaw --- a precious jewel in the heart of thick green forests, deep-blue lakes, which mirror a heaven studded with stars that twinkle and beckon on white moonlit nights, and awaken painful memories and dreams . . .

They well up, bestir, the memories of my old home; ravaged and desolate, it now haunts the minds of a handful --- the *Sh'erit Hapleita* (survivors of the Holocaust) scattered to the four corners of the earth.

Not large was our shelter, a mere 4,000 Jewish souls, but their forebears had struck root there over many centuries. Their cottages, built mostly of wood, huddled as though for comfort and safety around the mountain, "der Schloss Berg" ("Castle Mountain") as it was called.

True, not large was our shtetl, but it hummed and pulsated with burgeoning life --- varied and rich. Synagogues, schools, political parties, cultural and social circles, clubs and societies, lent dignity and meaning to a ceaseless struggle for a meagre existence.

Four decades have passed since Jewish Braslaw and its nearby shtetlach and yishuvim have been wiped off the map, their inhabitants put to death --- four decades since the gruesome destruction.

And so the time has come. It is therefore with awe and trepidation that we, the few, have taken upon us the sacred duty to gather what little testimony is left of the tragic events which befell the Jews of Braslaw and environs, to set it down for all who will come after us --- in eternal memory of our beloved, martyred dead.

[Page 627]
Braslaw --- Brief Historical Background
The history of Braslaw, its ethnic, geographic and communal development, lies hidden in the mists of the distant past.

From the few documents in our possession we learn that Braslaw is already mentioned as far back as the eleventh century --- almost 300 years prior to the founding of Vilna. It belonged to the Potocki duchy which was situated on the Russo-Polish-Lithuanian border and was called Braczislaw, after the reigning duke.

If one examines the geographic-topographic location of the town and its vicinity one cannot but conclude that Braslaw was originally built as a border town. Its checquered topography comprised of mud pans, swamps, forests and hills, lakes and streams, was ideally suited to defence, rendering it a veritable bulwark against attacks from hostile, semi-organised military bands.

The river Dwina, a major waterway which skirts Braslaw, indirectly helped to boost the economic growth of the town.

With the unification of Poland and Lithuania at the beginning of the fifteenth century --- the so-called Jagella [Jagiellonian] period --- Braslaw became part of the Vilna province, and was considered one of its five administrative districts. Incidentally, all official documents of that time refer to Braslaw as Braslaw of Lithuania as opposed to Braclaw near Uman, a city in the Ukraine.

Due to the incessant feuds between the Russian and Polish sovereigns, the town was frequently ravaged by wars, raids and fire. Particularly harsh, though fortunately short-lived, was the Tartar [Tatar] invasion. These rulers who hoisted their flag with its crescent moon on top of the mountain in the very heart of town exacted heavy tributes from the local inhabitants.

In the seventeenth century Braslaw was almost totally destroyed by floods. So vast was the damage that the Warsaw central government by special ordinance exempted the town from taxes for a period of four years.

The town shared the vicissitudes of its rulers, the noble Sapieha family, through whose feuds with rival nobles over several centuries it kept changing hands.

The mountain which, as mentioned earlier, was situated in the centre of town, served not only as a military fortress and prison but also as a Christian religious stronghold, complete with nunnery and church. It was protected by a regular military garrison stationed there.

Legends proliferated about the secrets which it jealously guarded in its

[Page 626]
bowels, about treasures and precious articles buried in it, though in places unknown.

A special order issued by King Stanislaw-August affirms the strategic importance of Braslaw and its contribution to the royal crown. This monarch too designated its emblem: a triangular sundial inset with an eye --- the "watchful eye" --- as a sign of God's vigilance over the town.

There are no documents on the later development of Braslaw as most of them, according to one historian, were burnt or destroyed during the Russo-Napoleonic war.

The Jews of Braslaw and Environs

From historic evidence in our possession we note that Jews are reputed to have lived in Braslaw and environs as far back as the sixteenth century. Thus a report on a population census held in 1559 [should be 1554] cites the names of several Jewish families --- among them Byk, Krawiec and Nemirowicz. [These names are now thought unlikely to have been Jewish; see page 16 of this memorial book.]

The Jews engaged mostly in commerce but were also tradesmen and artisans such as tailors, cobblers, innkeepers and so on. They were organised into communities, some of the larger independent ones like Braslaw, Druja and Vidz, managing the smaller semi-independent ones like Opsa, Slobodka, Drujsk and others.

We shall now briefly trace the history and development of some of the shtetlach and yishuvim of the Braslaw district.

Opsa

A shtetl boasting approximately 300 Jews who were linked with Braslaw by commercial and familial ties.

Opsa is first mentioned in the fifteenth century in a royal decree of the Polish king Alexander in which he ordered a special tax imposed on its pasture lands and on fishing rights in its nearby lakes.

In certain respects its history and development strongly parallel those of Braslaw and other vishuvim. It too kept changing hands as a result of the continual feuding of its rulers. Records show that in 1790 Opsa's population totalled 130 souls, made up of seventeen Christian and two Jewish families.

The year 1794 is a red-letter date in the history of Opsa. It is the year of the famous Kosciuszko revolt against Czarist might when a great battle in which close to 40,000 Polish rebels took part, was fought on its outskirts.

Another fateful date was 28 April 1928, that fine spring Sabbath morning when

[Page 625]

a fire broke out, almost razing the entire shtetl to the ground. Yaakov Aviel describes it as follows:

> I remember it as if it were only yesterday. The fire started in Baruch-Itse's house. The tongues of flame fanned by the spring breeze spread like wildfire, enfolding roof after roof, house after house. The church bells pealed ominously, then suddenly fell silent as the fire began to engulf the sacred building and the burning crosses and massive bells came crashing to the ground.

Opsa was again rebuilt but the fire was not forgotten. Interwoven into the fabric of the lives of its inhabitants it frequently served as a landmark. Thus they would say: "This still happened before the fire." Or: "Do you remember the house before the fire?"

Despite its small Jewish population of barely a few hundred souls the communal and spiritual life of Opsa was multifaceted and replete with cultural activities, clubs, social circles and political parties. It had two synagogues --- a Chassidic and a Mitnaggid synagogue-cum-house of study. The children attended "Cheder," a religious afternoon school, or studied in the Braslaw yeshiva (Torah academy) or in the Hebrew school Yavneh. The Betar was the predominant Zionist movement and attracted a large following among the youth.

As in most Jewish shtetlach in the interwar period the people engaged in business or plied trades. They were tailors, cobblers, tinkers, bakers and so on. The Jews of Opsa, like those of Braslaw and environs, perished at the hands of the Nazis.

Jod

The name of the shtetl, originally Jod-Jody, after Judia or Jehudit, the wife of the then provincial administrator of Brisk (Brzesć), was abbreviated to Jod. An existing report states that the yishuv together with the adjoining land was purchased by this administrator in 1754 and his wife Jehudit (Judita) had a church erected there.

Since then there is utter silence so that even historians can merely hazard a guess at the date of origin of the yishuv or its development and communal life. The only chronicles available are of the interwar period, of the subsequent German occupation, and of the tragic events which overtook Jod and prefigured the liquidation of its Jews.

From the narratives of the survivors Zalke Fiszer, L[i]uba Janowski-Wilkicki and Slawa Pincow of Jod one can reconstruct the economic, cultural and

[Page 624]

communal life of the shtetl, so typical of contemporary Jewish life in general in the interwar period.

The Jews of Jod were mostly shopkeepers, innkeepers, tradesmen and artisans. They too had close familial ties with many Jews in Braslaw. Their children and youth studied in its schools and yeshiva, often graduating to institutions of higher learning in Vilna.

Slobodka

A small yishuv about ten kilometres northeast of Braslaw.

There is little documentary evidence on Slobodka except for a brief mention of the fact that in 1783 its Jewish population consisted of six families and that it belonged to a Polish landowner.

Historians record that the Slobodka inhabitants adopted a negative stance towards the Polish uprising against Russia. With the establishment of the Polish Independent Republic in 1918 a regular military border garrison came to be stationed in Slobodka.

In the interwar period Jewish Slobodka grew and prospered.

General: Social and Economic Position of the Jews

From the report of a certain inspector and envoy-extraordinary of King Stanislaw-August we learn that the Jews of Braslaw and its district enjoyed equal civil rights in Poland, on a par with the Jews of Great Britain and Holland. This report appears to be one-sided, however, as borne out by similar reports and documents which present the situation in a totally different light, if not to the contrary. According to the latter the position of the Jews under Russian and Polish rule was anything if not invidious and they were frequently denounced as spies and enemies of Christianity.

One historian goes so far as to state that he cannot bring himself to put on paper or even attempt to describe the indignities to which the Jews were subjected.

One could possibly try to explain the precariousness of their social position and justify the accusations against them by the fact that in the endless wars and feuds between the kings and the nobles, and the resultant upheavals and changes of power, the Jews found themselves between the hammer and the anvil, each new ruler in turn accusing them of treason or lack of loyalty.

A popular source of income at the time was the inn, so familiar to us from Yiddish folklore and literature. These inns, dotted along the roads and dirt

[Page 623]

tracks, were usually owned by a lord who leased them to a Jew for a fixed sum.

We have no exact numerical or other data about the Jewish inhabitants or their economic position. In existing official papers we read about Jewish colonisation in yishuvim established specifically for this purpose, and about land apportioned to them for cultivation. Some of these yishuvim and villages still exist to this day but, needless to say, they are empty of Jews.

In 1847 the Russian government distributed land for Jewish settlement, thus establishing the villages of Dubene, Jajsi, Drujsk, Plusy, Kislowszczyzna and Ukazne. Some of these later grew into small shtetlach.

To encourage the Jewish colonists the Czarist government, by a law promulgated in 1835, exempted them from military service for a period of fifty or twenty-five years respectively, depending on their numerical strength, and absolved them from head tax for a period of twenty-five to ten years.

However, by the mid-nineteenth century the Czarist regime did an about-face and began to obstruct Jewish settlement on the land until in 1864 it totally prohibited the acquisition of arable land by Jews, or their settlement in villages. In 1866 all existing decrees permitting Jews to work the land were revoked.

While on the subject of Jewish villages we wish to dwell briefly on an item which appeared in the Hebrew periodical *Hamelitz*, No. 91 of January 1885. In it the correspondent Szerman in a specific reference to the agricultural "colony Drujsk" sharply berates the Jews for neglecting agriculture, and for subleasing the land to strangers so that they could engage in trade and commerce. He thus underscores the fact that these Jews are skilled agricultural workers, and it is a great pity that they should abandon this vital means of livelihood.

As regards Braslaw, in the early years of this century, following the pogroms and the Russo-Japanese war, it grew and developed. After World War I many Jewish families who at the onset of war had fled deep into Russia began to return. Not only did they help swell the numbers of the local Jewish population, but [also they] contributed substantially to the social, economic and political ascendancy of Braslaw.

[Page 622]

Braslaw

Scattered on yellowish-brown sand, on the bank of the large lake Drywiata to the west [actually to the south] and the smaller lake Nowiata to the north-east, lie, ranged round the mountain the houses of the shtetl Braslaw.

The main street, once known as "die groisse gass" ("the big street"), after World War I as Pilsudski Street, and with the Soviet entry in 1939 as Lenin Street, spans the entire length of the shtetl.

The street is straight and long. To the east of it, on a hillock, stands dumb, petrified, an old windmill, whose giant wooden wings creak in the autumn nights and cold winds nestle in the crevices of its barred windows. From here the street runs on until it reaches a small wooden bridge beneath which the two lakes meet. It is a fairly wide street, cobblestoned and flanked by wooden sidewalks which shake at every step.

The houses are built mostly of heavy weather-beaten logs. Some, old and decrepit, are half-sunk into the ground, while others stand erect on stone foundations arrogantly flaunting their brightly painted doors and windows.

Squeezed in between the houses is a medley of shops of all shapes and sizes, with an odd assortment of wares: foodstuffs, saddles, whips and other paraphernalia which cater to the needs of the peasants in the outlying villages. On one side where the street intersects "Third of May" street, built on a hill, is a red brick building --- the Roman Catholic Church --- its crosses like pointing fingers pierce the sky.

Opposite, on the edge of the Drywiata, stands demurely the white-blue Greek Orthodox Church with its five onion-shaped domes.

Each day the bells of the two churches ring out, their sounds commingling, as they summon the faithful to prayer.

A short distance away, sloping as though into a valley, is the synagogue courtyard where stand as if abashed, three synagogues known as *Minyanim* or houses of prayer: the Old Minyan, the New Minyan, and the Mithnaggid synagogue-cum-house of study.

In the synagogue courtyard is also situated the fire brigade building. Spacious, built of wood, it housed the fire-fighting equipment: enormous bright red, wooden barrels on wheels, hand pumps, brass pipes, hatchets, firemen's poles, and all sorts of implements. The firemen, all volunteers, are almost all Jews, some middle-aged, broad shouldered, sturdy, most of them sporting beards.

[Page 621]

When a fire breaks out, to the sound of bell and bugle the firemen come pouring forth, and in their wake, from every street and alley, the townsfolk, old and young, armed with buckets, hatchets, picks, or whatever they can lay their hands on, and with much din and excitement help to span the horses hurriedly commissioned for this purpose, to the wagons on which the pumps and barrels full of water are loaded.

Often when the fire is fierce and the pumps cannot pump fast enough, the people form a live chain, filling buckets from the lake and passing them from hand to hand up to the burning house, and so help quench the flames.

The firemen add colour and excitement to the shtetl on a happier note too, for they constitute the practically all-Jewish brass band. On public holidays or on festive occasions the musicians, dressed in their uniforms, bedecked with silver decorations, march along the main street proudly displaying their shiny brass instruments. Here goes Yerachmiel Milutin with his huge booming tuba. Next to him, marching in step to the music, struts the bearded Ezer Eidelson, the teacher with his trombone. Then come Yankel Maron and Ishike Lewin with the horns, followed by a host of others, all led by the bandleader Telmaszewski. Over the entire show presides Beinesz Milutin, serious, dedicated, as though bent on the most grave rather than joyous event.

The theatre hall occupies part of the fire-brigade building. Here the shtetl is entertained by its local dramatic society which stages plays and a variety of performances. The hall also serves as a venue for meetings and gatherings.

The synagogue courtyard, of modest proportions, humped, sandy, comes to life on warm evenings in the month of Ab. The youth of the shtetl flock to it to enjoy the balmy air. Girls stroll past in pairs or clusters, to provoke the boys no doubt, who are quick to take up the challenge. They pelt the girls with burrs and revel in their piercing shrieks of feigned fear.

On Purim the synagogue courtyard is agog. Scores of boys of all ages bang away with keys stuffed with gunpowder against the synagogue walls. The deafening noise from their homemade ammunition aimed at the historical villain Hamman [Haman] --- the Hitler of ancient Persia --- resounds all around.

However, the gaiety and excitement reach fever pitch on the day of a wedding. The Chuppah (wedding canopy) is set up on a flat, clean-swept spot. The shtetl turns out to a man and all gather round the excited families of the young pair. All along the way where the bride and groom are to pass, the windows are lit up with candles which, as though rejoicing in the general festivity, flicker and dance through the misty panes. The street is strewn with fresh yellow sand. The groom, escorted by his close relatives is led to the canopy, accompanied by musicians playing the traditional "dobrydzien"

[Page 620]

(a joyous melody of welcome). Then the bride is brought and she, her mother or female relatives, walk round the groom seven times.

The ceremony over, the groom breaks the glass underfoot --- a reminder of the destruction of Jerusalem --- and joyful cries of Mazel Tov erupt from all mouths. The bride and groom walk hand in hand through the excited crowd, past the poor lined up on either side with buckets of water, into which the groom and guests drop coins. With lit candles in their hands, all escort the newly-weds to the wedding feast.

There is yet another synagogue, the so-called Sandy Minyan, but this is situated further along on the way to the mountain, and like the first two *Minyanim*, belongs to the Chassidic community. The Jewish community, not unlike their former overlords, was not without its disputes and bickerings. D. S. Szerman, the correspondent mentioned earlier, describes in *Hamelitz* of 1884-1885 the sharp differences between the Chassidim and Mitnagdim, the denunciations to the authorities which he regarded as tantamount to blasphemy in the eyes of God. At one time things went so far that the synagogue was closed down, many were arrested, and the town Rabbi and his family suffered want because some of the congregants sided against him.

Mr. Szerman makes an impassioned appeal to the Chassidim to stop persecuting the Mitnagdim and to rebuild their synagogue with had burnt down the year before.

Further along, the street continues until it reaches the mill owned by the Jewish miller Byk. Here too is the power station which supplies the shtetl with electricity.

The street winds like a narrow ribbon between the mountain and the lake, whose waters lap at the sandy banks, often reaching up to the houses.

The lake, Drywiata, is vast and deep and sports a variety of fish which are caught in it all the year round.

With the onset of frost in early December, when the lake is covered with a thin sheet of transparent blue ice, before the snow has had time to blanket it, one can glimpse far down into its dark depths breathtaking sights of magic worlds. On such nights fishermen by the score set out, followed by lovers and idlers whom boredom drives out of doors, to witness a most spectacular, extraordinary mode of fishing.

Armed with long, heavy mallets, iron picks and hooks, the fishermen, with lanterns in their hands, scatter along the tinkling ice and light it up, keeping the lanterns close to the ice.

[Page 619]

The fish, lured by the light, swim up towards it. The fishermen raise their mallets and bring them down with a heavy blow on the ice. A deafening roar reverberates all along its surface. The fish stand still, stunned as though hypnotised, and the fishermen then chop out apertures in the thin ice and with their hooks haul out the fish.

The two lakes which surround and converge on the shtetl have always been a wellspring of fun and pleasure for the youth. On moonlit summer nights the merry laughter and song of young boys and girls who frolicked on its enchanting waters, would ring out until dawn. And in the days, especially weekends, they'd bathe and splash in these magnificent natural swimming pools.

Each year the lakes would claim a victim. Then the entire shtetl would be plunged in deep mourning until the body was recovered and brought to burial . . .

To the west the main street joins the dirt road which leads to Vilna. The road runs along noblemen's estates and villages scattered between pine forests and fields.

To the north of the main street several streets and lanes terminate in the narrow-gauge railway station which adjoins the Christian suburb, the "Gumnes." The train cuts through a sand road on its way to Dubene, a small Jewish yishuv about 18 kms from Braslaw. Its population, numbering less than one hundred families, engaged mainly in agriculture. Each family owned its own plot where it kept horses, cows, sheep, geese and chickens. A vegetable garden, fruit trees and flowers complete the picture. There was the usual sprinkling of shops, the ubiquitous artisans, here especially itinerant tailors who eked out a living from the nearby peasants. In 1927 a cooperative dairy was established in Dubene for the manufacture of butter and Dutch cheese.

Dubene, like most adjacent Jewish yishuvim, was closely linked with Braslaw through commerce, administrative affairs and ties of blood.

Not far from Dubene is Okmienic, a village with only one Jewish family. Villages of this kind were not uncommon in the Braslaw district. Another such village was Zaracz, but there were many more.

The narrow-gauge railway branches off to Druja on the one side, and to Dukszt on the other. There it links up with the wide-gauge railway which runs from Warsaw to Latvia.

Several side streets intersect the shtetl in its length and breadth until they reach the marketplace, the post office, past the printing works owned by the brothers Magat. This press, founded in the thirties, employs local Jewish youth, and publishes a weekly featuring local and regional news.

[Page 618]

One street proceeds beyond the [prewar] Jewish cemetery to the new lush and plush suburb where the Polish intelligentsia --- government officials and others --- live. Here too are situated the government institutions, the civil court and the like. This suburb borders on the Karpowicz forest, a recreational spot renowned for its scenic walks. In view of its proximity to the Polish suburb, however, it was shunned by the Jews. Their favourite haunt was the Dubkes forest at the opposite end of the shtetl. There Jews from all walks of life would flock, stroll and enjoy its beauty and bracing air. This forest, being dense and vast, was an excellent hideout. Little wonder that it served as a central partisan camp during the Nazi occupation.

Another road leads from Braslaw to Jajsi, a Jewish village. Its inhabitants, a few score families in all, engaged in agriculture and particularly in the processing of goat's milk cheese.

The Marketplace

The marketplace, situated on a large empty plain, was surrounded by stalls and houses though, strangely enough and unlike so many other shtetlach, not by shops, most of these, as already mentioned, being interspersed between the houses throughout the shtetl. The marketplace merely served as a centre for the disposal of agricultural produce brought in by the neighbouring peasants who would descend on the shtetl twice weekly, on Wednesdays and Fridays.

They would arrive in their heavily laden wagons, outspan their horses, hitch them to the wagons, and begin to display their produce: potatoes, fruit, vegetables, hay and oats, chicken, hides and hog's hair, and firewood. Jewish small dealers, middlemen or simply loiterers would mill among the wagons, often seen chewing on a straw.

The marketplace was especially lively in autumn when men and women in their hundreds would mingle with the merchants, buying up provisions for the long winter ahead.

The star attraction was the so-called "zadarmenikes" ("givers-away"). Their cries [of] "It's a give-away, give-away . . ." earned them this nickname which stuck. Amid the hubbub, the creaking of wheels, the shouts and curses of drunks, the hoarse cracked voice of the crier, usually an emaciated young man, would rise. Poised high on his wagon he'd proclaim and extol his cheap almost worthless merchandise: combs, scarves, penknives and other knicknacks. Crowds, mostly peasants, would flock, jostle and push --- all eager for bargains. Some peasants who lived on the Latvian border --- redrawn after the rise of Poland --- went in for smuggling, particularly of sugar, since the Polish

[Page 617]

government exported it at a far more competitive price than sold locally. The peasants used to hide a few sacks of sugar in a wagon loaded with hay and sell it to the local shopkeepers.

Trade and Commerce

A number of Braslaw Jews earned their livelihood by transporting goods. The nearest city, Vilna, was situated approximately 180 kms away, and the two-gauge railway system rendered transportation by train prohibitive. Hence it was more economical and convenient to dispatch the goods direct from seller to manufacturer by other means.

Winter was particularly conducive to the transportation of goods. Once the snow had set and the roads frozen hard, loaded sleighs would carry fish and meat, poultry, eggs, flax, hides and other produce to the big city. On their return trip they would bring back manufactured goods such as textiles, footwear, sugar, salt, soap, various kinds of oils and hardware. In summer the horsedrawn sleigh was replaced with trucks, owned by the Milutin and Bielak families.

An important means of livelihood was the fresh fruit trade. Many families would spend all summer and part of autumn watching over the fruit, guarding it, and picking the fruits of their labours --- a rich harvest of apples, pears and many others --- and see to their despatch and sale, both in the shtetl and outside business centres.

Many Jews were also tradesmen, some working as independent artisans and some as journeymen. All occupations were well represented: there were tailors, cobblers, tanners, milliners, watchmakers, carpenters, locksmiths, tinsmiths, ropemakers, bakers and so on.

But the mainstay of the town was the fishing industry, headed by the chief lessee, Szne'er Aron. Braslaw's lakes and rivers were a source of income to many. Entire families engaged in buying and reselling, transporting and packing the fish, which the fishermen caught in their nets. The main fishing season was winter when the lakes were coated with a thick layer of ice. The fishermen would then lower their nets in the apertures, the so-called "windows" which they would chop out in the ice, and a few days later haul out the nets full of sparkling silvery fish.

On the whole the economic position of the Jewish population was precarious. No Jew could hold a government post, the small dealers and shopkeepers, with few exceptions, barely eked out a living. The artisans and unskilled workers were no better off.

[Page 616]

To supplement their income some kept a cow, a goat, a few chickens or geese. Many cultivated small vegetable gardens next to their homes.

Z. Szmuszkowicz vividly depicts the abject poverty and privation of many Jewish families, who often had to seek aid from the community or appeal to the mercy of kindhearted charitable Jews.

Here we wish to mention the inestimable help and support to the poor of the *Gmilut Hesed*, a communal fund which granted interest-free loans to the needy, thereby often virtually saving entire families from starvation and want.

Here too we should mention the honorary communal workers and leaders like Baruch Fiszer, for instance, who did much more for the community as a whole and was among the first to help people in need.

Szne'er Aron, the fishing lessee, was another philanthropist. Every Friday he would freely distribute fish to the poor for the Sabbath, as well as other material aid. One of the founders of the "Yavneh" Hebrew school, he was its pillar. He personally supported the teachers, in addition to caring for the innumerable needs of the community.

Charity and mutual help seemed to be a way of life. Minor philanthropic institutions, often consisting of one or two people, would spring up in a time of crisis and rush to the aid of someone in distress, be it a poor bride who needed a trousseau or refreshments for the wedding feast; or at Passover *Maot Hitim* --- a fund for supplying the poor with Passover needs. And throughout they would do all in their power to observe the traditional and laudable injunction of *Matan BaSether* (secret almsgiving).

Earlier we mentioned fishing as one of the main occupations of the Jewish population. We now wish to add something about the fishermen themselves.

The majority of these fishermen belonged to the old offshoot of the greek-Orthodox church, the "Starowiery" (i.e. members of the old faith) as they were called. They were tall, well-built, powerful men, with bushy beards, who once a year would come from far and wide, even from abroad, and flock to Braslaw to celebrate the festival "Gromnica" (Candlemas, celebrated on February 2, the Feast of the Purification of the Virgin Mary, and the presentation of Christ in the Temple: the day on which the church candles are blessed). This festival, with its pageantry and carnival air, almost invariably coincided with Purim. These men would come sporting magnificent horses, beautifully decorated sleighs, with jingling bells and festooned with coloured ribbons. They would spill out and stroll about the

[Page 615]

streets, the women dressed in all their finery, bedecked with jewels.

While strolling thus, suddenly without warning, a young man would drive up furiously, grab a maiden and drive off with her to an unknown destination. A few days later he'd send matchmakers to her parents. Naturally this was merely a stunt, all agreed upon beforehand, and was not a crime. This folk custom may well derive from the biblical story of the young Benjaminites who too used to snatch maidens in the vineyards after their entire tribe had been practically wiped out.

In the afternoons they would hold horse races on the snow-blanketed lakes, to the delight of the entire shtetl.

On the whole relations between the Braslaw Jews and the peasants were normal, even friendly. More than once the peasants withstood the barrage of antisemitic propaganda of hostile groups which emerged especially after the rise of the "Endek" chauvinist party (N.D. = Narodowa Demokracja --- National Democracy) which raised its head soon after Hitler came to power. When the Germans subsequently entered Braslaw, it became clear that many members of the party were indeed Nazi agents.

During World War I as well there were outbreaks of Jew hatred and dangerous moods presageful of pogroms among the peasantry. The Jews --- proud and firm --- warded off pogroms, looting and pillage with great courage, which is still spoken of to this day.

During the final days of the war [World War I], when Braslaw was without an official government for a while, peasants and marauders from the neighbourhood assembled near the *Gmina* (local administration building), ready to attack the Jews, rob and kill them.

The Jews got wind of this and immediately orgsanised a self-defence. Szmuel Josef Milutin, on horseback, charged among the incited peasants, and brandishing a revolver in one hand and a sword in the other, dispersed and routed the rabble.

Young Yerachmiel-Mendel Meirson fell in this skirmish and Abraham Lubowicz received a leg wound.

Here we might mention that the first victim of the Nazis on their entry into Braslaw during World War II was Chayim Milutin, son of Szmuel Josef.

However, there were also episodes which spoke of the deep friendship and loyalty of many peasants to their local Jews. One such episode concerns the Kagan family from the village Zahorie --- incidentally, the only Jewish family in the village --- who leased the lake Ukla from the local nobleman.

During World War I Polish marauders and virulent Jew-baiters attacked them and sought to burn down their homes and pillage their belongings. The village

[Page 614]

peasants quickly rallied and armed with axes and pitchforks, drove off the attackers.

Religious and Cultural Life

Of the four synagogues in the shtetl [Braslaw], one housed a Yeshiva numbering 60 students, some from the adjacent yishuvim. Since there were no Jewish schools in these yishuvim, the children attended Polish government schools in the morning and Cheder and Talmud Torah in the afternoon. The more affluent sent their children to Braslaw, to its Folkshul, Hebrew school Yavneh, or Yeshiva.

The Yeshiva students were fed from a communal kitchen specially erected for this purpose. Some of them were so-called "day boarders." Each day of the week one family would take one student for a day's board. Naturally this was a makeshift measure, in view of the dire straits in which the teaching institution found themselves, since they received no government subsidy.

Many graduates of the Braslaw Yeshiva continued their studies in the Yeshivot of Volozyn, Myr, Vilna, and Nowogrudek, some even graduating as Rabbis.

Despite constant financial problems, the Yeshiva made a notable contribution to the cultural life of the shtetl.

The shtetl employed two Rabbis who served the people with selfless devotion. The Mitnaggid Rabbi, Reb Hirszl Valin --- tall, broad-shouldered, still in his prime, with a sparse black beard streaked with grey. An outstanding preacher, he also officiated as cantor during the Holy Days. In the thirties he and his family emigrated to Latvia where he took up the position of Rabbi in one of its towns.

The second Rabbi, Reb Abba Zahorie, old, frail, retiring, was the religious leader of the Chassidic community. His mild blue eyes expressed a childlike innocence, as though in wonder at God's world. It is told that when the Jews were led to the pits, he went before them, wrapped in his prayer shawl, and comforted them, saying that man must accept God's will with love, all the while murmuring the verse: *Mima'amakim keraticha* . . . (From the depths I have called thee . . .) [from Psalm 130].

Apart from the Yeshiva, the homeless Yiddish Folkshul too conducted classes in the synagogue --- albeit in the women's section. This naturally often evoked quarrels between the Folkshul and Yeshiva students on account of the permissive dress of the former.

In the thirties a beautiful, commodious Folkshul building, with an adjoining nursery school, was erected in the courtyard of the Jewish Bank. Funds were

[Page 613]

provided by the CYSO (Central Yiddish School Organisation) and the Bank Director, Levi Yitschak Wainsztein. Apart from his financial share in the venture, he also sponsored children from poor homes to enable them to further their studies in Vilna.

The Folkshul was the matrix of the local intelligentsia. Its graduates who took up studies at higher institutions of learning in Vilna, would return as teachers, professionals, technicians, thus enriching the cultural values and quality of life of the youth.

Around the Folkshul cultural circles sprang up, among them a dramatic society, which staged plays and vaudevilles. The moving spirits and gifted artists in this society were Widrewicz, chief bookkeeper of the Jewish Bank, and the tailor Szaie Dejcz. The latter, in addition to being a fine artist, introduced much life and creativity into a number of circles.

In her memoirs, the late Perl Fiszer-Charmac traces the important role played by the Yiddish Folkshul and the cultural circles. She speaks with love tinged with awe and admiration of the Folkshul, its dedicated teachers and of all who spared no effort to maintain this worthy institution. Likewise, Marjasza Rothenberg-Rajchel recalls with love and reverence the multi-faceted activities of the school and its circles.

Thanks to the initiative of a number of townspeople and communal workers, a Hebrew school "Yavneh" was established in the last few years before World War II. Among its renowned teachers was Rafael Jakov Munic, a fine scholar and "Lover of Zion." Already in the twenties he organised the youth to study Hebrew, the Bible, and mobilised young boys to prepare them for Aliyah to Eretz Israel. Young boys went to work on the land, engaged in fishing and other pursuits.

Some of them later emigrated to Eretz Israel, among them Mosze Valin, the Rabbi's son, who joined the Kibbutz Ramat Hakovesh and later founded the Li-La-Lo theatre. He also served as impresario to several famous singers and dancers.

In the shtetl political parties and groupings began to mushroom. There was the Zionist movement made up of the Chalutz group, General Zionists, left- and right-wing Poale Zion. Some of the youth, the Chalutzim, emigrated to Eretz Israel. There was also the Revisionist organisation, the Betar and Brit Hachayal, headed by Advocate Geliszkowski and Zusman Lubowicz.

The adherents of the Yiddish Folkshul were called "Folkisten" and their views were close to those of the "Bund," a strong and influential force among local youth and Jewish worker circles. A staunch supporter of the Folkshul was Lieber Cepelewicz, a colourful personality. His home was a regular venue for

[Page 612]

discussions and a meeting place of the loyal youth.

Braslaw, though lacking in industrial enterprise and a concomitant proletariat, nevertheless featured a Communist party, but its influence on the youth appears to have been negligible.

Despite political differences, there were no signs of any animosity in these youth circles.

All that has been told so far is but a fragment of the history, way of life, and vicissitudes of Braslaw over hundreds of years up to the grim period, the Satanic German-Nazi rule, which ended in the total destruction of many Jewish communities, towns and shtetlach, villages and yishuvim, by Hitler's henchmen.

In 1939 Poland was cut in half. The Red Army advancing from the east and the Nazi hordes from the west split Poland and divided it amongst themselves, thus partitioning it for the fourth time. The two armies stood facing each other across the river Bug. The Jewish population of Poland numbering over three million was likewise split and cut off from one another. However, with the Soviet decision to free the western parts of White Russia and the Ukraine, the dread of falling under the iron heel of the Nazis was dispelled for a time.

The Jews welcomed the Red Army with great joy, with flowers, bread and salt. Chayim Band of Braslaw tells how the draper Aharon Zeif brought out and distributed rolls of red cloth among all who wanted to make flags.

The Jews under Soviet rule knew nothing about the condition of their fellow Jews under German occupation. Only here and there faint echoes would reach them from the other side of the Bug of the deplorable situation of the Jews under Nazi rule. Trickles of refugees would bring sad tidings of the happenings on the western side of the river.

The life of the Jews under Soviet rule was, from a material angle, fairly tolerable, but their cultural, communal and religious life had altered dramatically. One by one the various Yiddish institutions were closed down: schools --- both religious and secular --- and the study of Yiddish was forbidden. Not to speak of the Yeshiva and the Talmud Torah.

Some families were exiled deep into Siberia and the Urals. Ironically, even former avowed communists were not spared, since the Soviets did not trust them.

And so, for close on two years [from 1939 to 1941], Polish Jewry lived in the shadow of suspense and barely contained fear, until the advent of that fateful, bloody era, which plunged the world in blood and tears, suffering and death.

[Page 611 = Blank in the original]

[Page 610]

> Silent perishes the friendless
> Every voice is crushed.
> Bitter days are now upon us ---
> Man dons Satan's mask.

[Page 609]

The fearful tragedy that struck the Jewish people --- and Polish Jewry in particular --- the total obliteration of hundreds of Jewish communities, large and small, the physical extermination of millions --- something unprecedented not only in the annals of Jewish but also of world history --- the systematic genocide perpetrated by the Nazi beast, will never be blotted out nor forgotten.

The holocaust which engulfed the Jewish people must be set down and attested by those who miraculously escaped it, today's living witnesses of all that took place.

Sholem Asch, the great Yiddish writer, introduces as motto to his book *Kiddush Hashem* an extract from an older book:

> We are ashamed to tell what the Cossacks have done with us so as not to dishonour the name [of] man who was created in God's image.

How can we keep silent, fail to speak, to describe what the Nazis did with and to us? The torture, the suffering, the murders, the humiliations, the gas ovens, the valleys of death where our dear ones were butchered --- fathers, mothers, children, brothers and sisters?

In the ghettoes the story went round about the famous Jewish historian Simon Dubnov, who, when led to his death, turned to the Jews next to him and commanded them: "Write down! Record!"

It is therefore with sacred awe that we carry out this last will and testament --- to write down, to record the suffering of our holy martyrs --- as an eternal memorial for the generations to come.

The Jews of Braslaw and environs lived under Russian rule for close on two years.

Then, at dawn on Sunday, 22nd June 1941, the Germans broke the Hitler-Stalin pact, and Nazi hordes began to pour into the Russian zone.

The coming pages describe the early days of the outbreak of this war, the entry of the Germans into Braslaw, the evil decrees and measures introduced by the Nazis, the gruesome events of that period: the ghettoes, the hunger, the torture --- until the dreadful end, the total liquidation of the Jews of Braslaw and its neighbouring shtetlach and yishuvim; and finally the resistance, at first sporadic but later by organised partisans among whom were many of our fellow countrymen.

[Page 608]

In his memoirs Chayim Band of Braslaw describes the first days of the war:

> On the morning of 21nd [22nd] June we heard about the German invasion. The same day a mass meeting was held on the shore of the lake. The Soviet party and government officials gave us their solemn assurance that the enemy would be driven off and the people had therefore nothing to fear.
>
> Next morning Soviet military units, tanks and artillery, were indeed seen passing through Braslaw in the direction of the front, but in the evening the picture had changed and the retreat towards Russia began. Military and government officials and their families made haste to leave the shtetl.
>
> This had a terrible effect on the Jewish population. Plunged into despair and uncertainty, they waited to see what would happen next. Many of the youth left their homes, some on foot or by whatever means they could muster, and headed for the former Polish-Russian border [to the east].
>
> Some Jews consoled themselves and others with the thought that they knew the Germans from World War I days, that they were a civilised and cultured people and one could learn to live with them, as the German axiom goes: "Leben and leben lassen" (Live and let live). Reality however, was to prove otherwise . . .
>
> Meanwhile the German army continued its advance eastwards, destroying in its wake the demoralised and disintegrated Soviet army. Several days after the outbreak of the war, the Germans entered Braslaw and conquered a large portion of the surrounding district.
>
> The non-Jewish inhabitants welcomed them with bread and salt, thereby manifesting their joy at having been liberated from the Russian yoke.
>
> The Poles elected a special council to facilitate collaboration with the Germans. Among its members noted for their antisemitic activity were the Chief of Police, Jasinski, the mayor, Kowalski, the Prison superintendent, Szliachczik, a Volksdeutsch[er] (local German) and notorious sadist, as also the teacher Pawlik and his wife, both local Germans, and others.

Moshe Milutin tells that the Germans entered Braslaw on Thursday, a few days after the outbreak of war between Russia and Germany. First came several intelligence men on motorcycles, [who] looked around, stayed a while and then rode away. During the night massive quantities of military equipment, tanks, artillery and other armaments began to stream into Braslaw. This procession merely passed through, leaving behind a small military contingent which, with the help of the non-Jewish inhabitants, especially the Poles, began to rule the shtetl with an iron hand, introducing draconian laws.

The relations of the Nazi rulers with the Jews were governed by previously determined laws. So, for instance, a document entitled "The brown map"

[Page 607]
contains the following instructions to the German authorities in the occupied eastern zones:

1. All Jews were to be registered and forced to wear the yellow badge.
2. Directions about the movement of Jews.
3. Ghettoes were to be established.
4. Transfer to all Jews from villages and shtetlach to ghettoes.
5. Establishment of Judenraten and a Jewish police force.
6. Confiscation of all Jewish property.
7. Prohibiting Jews from practising their occupations.
8. Introduction of forced labour.

The next day, Friday, the Germans rounded up all the Jews of the shtetl on the horse-market --- men separately and women and children separately --- and drove them at gunpoint to the swamp in the Dubkes forest on the bank of the lake Drywiata.

On the way the first victims fell --- Szlomo Zilber, the ritual slaughterer, and Chayim Milutin --- shot by the Germans on the pretext of trying to escape.

Heartrending is the description of Yerachmiel Milutin, Chayim's uncle:

> On my hands I carried my nephew to the [prewar] cemetery and brought
> him to burial. When I undressed him I counted eighteen bullet holes on his
> body . . . I cleansed him, kissed him twice and took leave of him for ever . .
> .

It is told that when Chayim fell, pierced by bullets, he still managed to cry out, "Jews, avenge our blood! . . ."

The Jews were kept in the swamp all night without food or water. As Yerachmiel Milutin, Feige-Tsippe Toker-Bielak and others relate, they were distraught, being certain that this was the end. However, on the morrow, with daybreak, they were told to go home. The Germans, it seems, merely wanted to intimidate them.

Dejected, afflicted, with sobbing children in their arms, they finally dragged themselves to their homes only to find that these had been looted. Doors and windows stood wide open, and what the robbers could not take with them they threw about or smashed. Their non-Jewish neighbours, with the consent of the Germans, had carried out a pogrom on their deserted homes.

This round-up seemed to be a favourite German pastime, designed not only to frighten the Jews but also to humiliate them. Niuta Kantor describes a day which is indelibly printed on her mind. The Jews of the shtetl had again [sic] been driven to the shore of the lake, and the Poles, especially teachers, government officials and the youth --- the "cream of the youth" --- gathered dressed in their Sunday best and looked on with glee how the Germans humiliated the Jews. [It is clear from Niuta Kantor's account on page 125 of this memorial book that she was describing here the same forced march to the swamp as mentioned earlier, not a different one.]

[Page 606]
They were hoping, it seems, to witness their liquidation.

"One can just imagine," writes Niuta, "what we looked like in their eyes, if our death --- the death of men, women and children --- was to them nothing but a bit of fun."

Slawa Pincow in her testimony tells that the Polish intelligentsia of Jod petitioned the local German authorities for the right to liquidate "their" Jews . . .

And so began the cruel decrees and persecutions.

To facilitate their rule [in Braslaw] the Germans ordered that a Judenrat be elected. It consisted of ten men: Itzchak Mindel acted as chairman, Chayim Munic as secretary, and its members were Gerszon Klioner, [Eliezer] Mazeh, Rafael Fiszer, [Hirsz] Fridman, Szeinkman, Leib Valin and others.

The chairman of the Opsa Judenrat was David Lewin and in Jod there were two members, Peretz Skolnik and Elijahu Razin.

The first decrees introduced were:

--- All Jews had to wear the yellow badge on both front and back.
--- They were forbidden to use the sidewalk but had to walk in the middle of the street.
--- All relations with the non-Jewish population were to be severed.
--- Jews were forbidden to visit a cinema, theatre or similar places of entertainment.
--- In front of every Jewish house a signboard bearing the word "Jude" had to be hung.

At a specially appointed spot, bread was distributed to the Jews --- 175 grammes per head per day.

In terms of a subsequent order, the Jews had to hand over their household animals to the Germans and collect fur coats, felt boots and other warm clothing for the German army. In addition, the Germans from time to time imposed heavy collective fines on them and confiscated all their copper and other metalware.

One day Soviet planes bombed units of the German army. A non-Jew informed the police that he saw Jews signalling to the Soviet pilots directing them to the German positions. The Germans thereupon arrested Beilke Dejcz, Yankel Musin --- a young man from Druja --- as well as Chayim Burt, a young boy. After strenuous efforts by the Judenrat Burt was set free, but Beilke Dejcz and Yankel Musin were tortured and then hanged.

Denunciations were becoming the order of the day. A Polish overseer over some Jewish forced labourers employed at the railway station in stripping bark off logs and loading them onto train coaches, denounced them on the pretext of malingering. Thirteen Jews were shot.

[Page 605]

The Nazis did not lack Polish collaborators and partners-in-crime from every walk of life, from Jasinski, Chief of the Braslaw Police, to the local non-Jewish population. When Jasinski was finally brought to trial [in 1963] at the instigation of Niuta Kantor who accused him of murdering innocent people, the true face of these Polish collaborators came to light.

Anatoljusz Zawacki, a witness at Jasinski's trial, testified:

> The people were brought to the station --- about eleven of them. They were locked in a coach. At nightfall they were let out, driven a short distance away, and shot. This, the children of my family saw. Next day I came across a German cleaning his rifle and he said to me: "I am cleaning the weapon not for a parade. I shot some Jews yesterday."

Zelig Ulman, his wife and little daughter too met their death on the denunciation of a non-Jew. It is rumoured that Zelig had been tortured before he died. His son escaped by a miracle as he was not at home at the time.

The Germans seized Aharon-Zelig Singalowski, the old ritual slaughterer, [and] put him on a military motorcycle driven by a policeman who raced with him through the streets of the shtetl. When he was finally released he was as white as a sheet. A short while afterwards he suffered a heart attack and died the next day. Jewish life was cheap, and the Jews lived in the shadow of constant fear.

Baruch Fiszer, a prominent and respected Braslaw Jew, had been put to work in a German bakery. One day, faint with hunger, he took a piece of bread. The German overseer caught him red-handed, whipped out his revolver to shoot him, but finally relented, yielding to his pleas to spare his life.

In Jod the Germans gathered a group of eminent Jews, forced them to their knees and ordered them to pluck the grass from between the cobblestones. Others were made to dance in the middle of the street.

One night twenty Jews were dragged to the police station and brutally beaten for no rhyme or reason. Each received 25 lashes.

In August of the first year of the Nazi occupation, the peasants from the villages around Jod carried out a pogrom in the shtetl. The Jews fled for their lives and the peasants had a field day looting their homes.

The Jews of Braslaw groaned under the inhuman decrees --- the heavy levies imposed on them by the Nazis. Desperate, they assembled in the synagogue where Chaim Szolem Bor made an impassioned appeal, concluding with the traditional Hebrew words *Tzedaka Tatzil Mimavet* (Charity saves from death). The men and women thereupon took off their ornaments, jewellery, watchers and other valuables and handed them over to the Germans.

In Dubene all agricultural produce and household animals --- cows, goats,

[Page 604]

chickens, etc. --- were confiscated. Seventy-year-old Zechariah Maron, most distressed by all this, dared to resist. A tall strapping German caught him by his sparse grey beard and began to shake him from side to side. The proud old Jew, being short of stature, took a leap and spat full square into the German's face.

On July 19, 1942 [should be 1941] --- in order to intimidate the Jews --- the Germans, aided by local collaborators, surrounded the Jewish village of Dubene and murdered four Jews. They then assembled the rest in the synagogues --- men separately and women and children separately --- ordered the men to crawl on all fours, then drove a number of them to the cemetery, where they tortured and shot them. When the Jews were later brought to burial they were unrecognisable, so brutally had they been beaten. In all, twenty Jews were killed that day [in fact, estimates range from 18-25].

Motke Rosenberg of Opsa tells how as a child of ten he saw the Nazis force Jews to crawl and eat grass on the marketplace, all the while beating and kicking them.

Mosze-Aaron the butcher was tied to a horse and dragged through the shtetl. Herzl Sznaider the shoemaker was tortured to death on the pretext of hiding skins.

The Jews of Jod were the first of the Braslaw district to be murdered. It was winter, December 1941 --- the month of the festival of Chanukah, the festival of lights and miracles. [Before this time some Jews had already been murdered in Braslav, Plusy, Dubene and Jajsi, but Jod was the first place in which the entire population of Jews was targeted for destruction.] The Jews lit the third candle and as they uttered the blessing, the hope that a miracle would descend on the entire House of Israel --- as in days of old --- and on them too, flickered in each breast.

But no miracle came . . .

A few days earlier they had been ordered to get ready for transfer to the Szarkaiszcina ghetto. They packed, prepared food and other necessities, but . . . On December 19 they were taken to the ready-dug pits, ordered to undress and shot.

The same day and at the same time as the Jews of Jod, the Jews of Kislowszczyzna and its neighbouring small yishuvim were killed [in Jod, as they had been brought there] --- all in all over 500 Jews. Some managed to escape prior to the massacre and hid with peasants in nearby villages.

The Jews were "on the move" --- a mass exodus but not to life or freedom. The Jews of Jajsi were brought to the Braslaw ghetto, the Jews of Slobodka to the ghettoes of Vidz and Braslaw. The Opsa Jews were transported to the Vidz ghetto. Some managed to bribe the local police to allow them into the Braslaw ghetto where conditions were said to be more tolerable and because they wanted to be with their relatives. The Jews of Dubene were driven from pillar to post --- from Braslaw to Vidz, from there to Swiencian and to the labour

[Page 603]

camps of Miligan, Wewie, Zezmer, Vilna, Oleina and Kaiserwald --- till Auschwitz and Ponar.

All "actions" (in German, Aktion: round-ups of Jews in the ghettoes, mostly in order to send them to labour camps or death camps), expulsions, murders and denigrations were carried out with typical German punctiliousness and swiftness, after secret planning. Peasants with wagons or sledges, depending on the time of the year, would be mobilised from nearby villages to load the Jews and transport them to far-away places. The police and gendarmes were not mere onlookers but active and zealous participants in the expulsions carried out by the Gestapo. They would urge the Jews with blows and vituperations, forcibly drive them from their homes at a moment's notice so that they would have no time to take along food and clothing for the road. The Lithuanians in particular "excelled" with their bestiality. But the local population too was not found wanting. The non-Jews stood around, watching, waiting to pounce on the Jewish possessions left behind by their owners.

Mire [Mira] Lotz-Szneider in her memoirs of that time, writes:

> Sarah-Disel, wife of Szlomo Lewin, was a dressmaker in Dubene who employed a young apprentice, the daughter of the peasant Dragun from the village Raugiszki. The night before the expulsion of the Jews, Dragun came to the Lewin family and offered to hide Sarah-Disel and her two little girls --- Chayele and Szeina Rivka --- so that only Szlomo would meanwhile enter the ghetto. Naturally this offer was accepted with great joy. Dragun's sleigh was loaded to capacity. With heavy hearts the mother and children bade farewell to the husband and father and rode away in the hope of finding a temporary haven until the evil days would pass.
>
> On the way, as soon as they entered the forest, the peasant killed the mother and her two little girls, and rode off with their belongings.

On Passover eve, early in April 1942, the Gestapo summoned the Braslaw Judenrat and ordered that all Jews living in the side streets vacate their homes and move into the houses on Pilsudski Street (then called Lenin Street). The Germans could not possibly have chosen a more ideal site for a ghetto. On the one side the street bordered on the mountain and on the other, from the west [should be south], was cut off by the lake, the waters reaching up to the houses. All intersecting streets or side streets leading off the main street were cordoned off with barbed wire. And so the Braslaw ghetto came into being. It was divided into two parts: on the one side, up to the bridge, was the so-called "useful ghetto," peopled by the able-bodied fit for work, and on the other, the "dead ghetto,"

[Page 602]

inhabited by the old, the sick and the weak who, unable to work, were earmarked as the first victims.

Abraham Bielak testifies:

> Our house was situated in the "useless ghetto" which meant that we were the first candidates for death, and yet we wanted to stay there and live in our own home. My father went to seek advice from Rafael Fiszer (Folke Lanes), a member of the Judenrat, only to be told, "We are all sentenced to death!"
>
> The ghetto was crowded to overflowing, several families living in each house. Medical services were not to be had and medicine was at a premium. People died of typhus, pneumonia, filth and hunger. This was indeed the beginning of the end --- the physical annihilation.
>
> The non-Jews knew only too well how to exploit the situation. They acquired everything, whatever the Jews still kept --- clothing, furniture, etc. --- for a song, all the while saying: "In any case you'll be killed, so what do you need these things for?"

Death was a frequent visitor in the ghetto. Some lost heart and passively surrendered to cruel fate; others tried to fight despair and sought ways and means of saving their lives; some began to prepare shelters, hiding places, bunkers.

Rumours reached and soon spread through the ghetto about the liquidation of the Jews of Latvia and Lithuania --- two countries bordering on the Braslaw district and where many of their relatives and friends lived --- and of the killings of the Jews from the nearby shtetlach.

The Germans spared no wile to deceive the Jews. They repeatedly lulled the fears of the Judenrat with assurances that the Jews of Braslaw, being law-abiding and hard-working, had nothing to fear.

On Tuesday, the day before the massacre [which began on June 3-5, 1942], the Germans ordered the Judenrat to select one hundred young girls to be sent to Slobodka to clean military barracks. Next day, however, they were returned, led straight to the pits, and murdered with the rest.

Mothers tried to save their little children. They would dress them in their holiday best, steal out of the ghetto, and leave them at the doors of Christian homes. In a day or two the children would be sent back to the ghetto. Such was the fate of Beilke Bank-Gens' little girl.

The night before the massacre, massive police fortifications surrounded the ghetto --- soldiers and police, especially Latvians and Lithuanians. Also, trucks, so-called "gas vans" for suffocating the inmates with exhaust fumes, were brought in.

[Page 601]

On Wednesday, the 18th day of Sivan, the Year 5702, equal to 3 June, 1942, the ghetto awoke to the sounds of heavy shooting and frightful screams, drunken oaths, the wailing of the hunted, beaten and wounded, the smashing of doors and windows, brute orders to get out of the house --- quick --- curses and blows. The killers rummaged and sniffed into every nook and corner to try and ferret out a Jew hiding somewhere.

Liuba Byk testifies:

> It was the eve of the massacre. Police were brought into the shtetl from all around and the entire ghetto was surrounded by guards.
>
> Our house was the first in the ghetto. At about two o'clock past midnight we heard the sound of heavy footsteps, a door wrench open. Two policemen rushed in, started to beat us, and flung us down the stairs. They did not let me take my three-year-old daughter with me, but brutally murdered her in her sleep. I was driven out of the house at the end of a rifle butt. I saw them kill my sister Rosa and her two little girls right next to the barbed wire of the cordoned-off ghetto, near our house.
>
> They drove us to the Folkshul. On the way they shot Mendel the locksmith. I spotted my uncle Rachmiel and followed him. Suddenly he drew me and a few other members of our family into a cellar beneath Rosin's flour store. It was pitch dark inside. I could only feel the huddled bodies crouched against the stone walls. Now and then we heard footsteps above us, followed by shots. Each time a child began to cry it was silenced for ever . . .
>
> We had no food or water. We had to relieve ourselves on the spot. The stench alone was enough to suffocate one. We lay in this living grave for three or four days.
>
> Again we heard footsteps. We'd been discovered. We heard shouts: "Verfluchte, stinkende Juden, Heraus!" [Cursed, stinking Jews, out!] Once in the fresh air, I lost consciousness. Someone gave me a drink of water.

Sarah Katz tells how, looking through the window, she saw a Nazi dragging a little girl --- the infant daughter of Liuba Weiss --- by the legs, her tiny head knocking against the cobblestones.

The ghetto was milling with people. Anyone who sought to flee, whether in the direction of the lake or into a side street, bumped against a policeman or gendarme and was at once shot.

Some went mad. Heartrending scenes took place in the shelters and bunkers. Mothers had to smother their infants so that their crying would not betray those hidden there.

Itzchak Mindel, the chairman of the Judenrat, frantic, ran to the Gestapo to plead for his people, but for his pains he and his family were the first to be

[Page 600]

shot. According to another version, Mindel, on hearing of the impending massacre, took his wife and children and went to the Gestapo. As chairman of the Judenrat, he told them, he ought to be shot first. They thereupon took him at his word and murdered him and his family on the spot.

The Jews of the shtetl were taken to the ready-dug pits, forced to undress, and were shot.

The massacre continued for three days. Then the Germans began mopping-up operations. They searched, hunted, and dragged the Jews out of their hiding places. To help them in their fiendish task they enlisted a non-Jew who was fluent in Yiddish, and also forced some of the victims who had been caught hiding to walk through the ghetto, escorted by police, and exhort the Jews to come out of the bunkers, solemnly promising them --- in the name of the Germans --- that there would be no more shootings. Some, naive enough to believe them, came out and when all had been assembled in the Folkshul building, they were led to the pits and shot.

Peasants from the neighbouring district later told that the earth above the pits was heaving for three days on end, and the blood kept oozing, so that the Germans had to despatch peasants with horsewagons to cart more soil to cover the pits.

Some, no longer able to stand idly by and watch the agony and suffering, bravely resisted the murderers, knowing full well the fate in store for them. Thus, Mosze-Boruch Bank, while wrestling with a gendarme, bit his finger clean off. For this he was meted out the age-old punishment: he was tied to the tail of a horse and driven through the streets until he gave up his soul.

Neftl Zalman-Jankel's (Fiszer) [Neftl Fiszer, who was the son of Zalman-Jankel] and Avremke Fiszer too grappled with the fiends, but what could people armed only with fists do against murderers with rifles and revolvers. Abraszke Ulman took on three policemen singlehanded, killed two, but was fatally shot by the third.

In a letter from the front Peretz Lewin describes his encounter with some young Jewish fugitives from Braslaw at the Minsk railway station:

> I spoke with a young fellow of nineteen but his voice was like that of an old man . . .
>
> ". . . Very few remained alive after the first massacre," he said, "except for those who managed to hide, who escaped to the forest earlier on and joined the partisans, or who were kept hidden by peasants in cow sheds and all manner of hideouts, these peasants virtually risking their own lives and the lives of their families by harbouring Jews."
>
> On the eve of Rosh Hashana 1942 [September 1942] the Germans organised the so-called "second ghetto" in Braslaw, or the "Opsa ghetto" as it was called, because it consisted of Jews brought in from Opsa. This ghetto too was not long-lived. Two days before Purim, 12 days in Adar, 5702 (19 March 1942), the Germans once again surrounded it, drove the Jews to the pits, and murdered them. [In fact, the massacre of the "Opsa" ghetto in Braslav took place on March 19, 1943, not 1942, and on 12 Adar II 5703, not 5702.]

[Page 599]

The liquidation of the second ghetto, however, did not go off quite so smoothly for the Nazis. Many Jews put up a brave fight. Barricading themselves in one of the houses, with what little ammunition they had, they fought fiercely, answering fire with fire. Here the heroic feats of Leiser Bielak of Braslaw and Melech Munic of Opsa are worth mentioning.

In his book *Destruction of Jewish Vilna: Khurbn Vilne* (p. 160), Sh. Kaczerginski recounts the testimony of Sasze Tempelman, former teacher of the Braslaw Folkshul:

> Two months after the first massacre of the Braslaw ghetto (on the 3rd, 4th and 5th June 1942), the Germans brought fifty Jews from Opsa (20 kms from Braslaw) and created what was known as the "second ghetto." This ghetto lasted seven months. In March 1943 the Germans slaughtered the remaining Jews. Some put up a stand.
>
> The resistance took place in a house occupied by ten Jews. They barricaded themselves and held off the German police with rifle fire. When their ammunition gave out the enemy charged the house, but as the first German entered, he was shot dead. One of the Jews donned his uniform, took his rifle, went outside and opened fire on the Germans.
>
> The house was then blown up with hand grenades.

Moshe Kahanovich too in his book *La Lucha de Los Guerrilleros Judios en La Europa Oriental* (*The War of the Jewish Partisans in Eastern Europe*), published in Buenos Aires in 1956, vol. I p. 497, describes the [last] stand of the Jews of the second ghetto in Braslaw.

> A third version is by those who survived the massacre.
>
> Thus it is told that Melech Munic of Opsa, a tailor employed in a workshop along with several other artisans, mobilised some Jews and got ready to put up a stand. They prepared home-made ammunition, consisting of iron implements and buckets of unslaked lime.
>
> When the first German entered the house they threw the lime over him. Melech Munic then shot him, dressed up in his uniform, and went outside and began shooting at the Germans.
>
> In the end he was fatally shot. The Jews inside the house kept up the shooting until the last bullet, and were then pelted with hand grenades.

[Page 598]

Leiser Bielak, it is told, fought back during the liquidation of the second ghetto; he shot a German and two policemen, escaped and managed to hide for a while until, in the end, he was handed over to the Germans by a peasant for a few kilos of salt. After the war and the liberation of the Braslaw district, Mosze Milutin, a young partisan, and Abraham Bielak avenged his death and shot the vile traitor.

Motke (Max) Fiszer, Baruch's son from Braslaw, who relates his experiences under the German occupation, concludes his testimony with the question:

> Why did the Jews not resist?
>
> I have no answer to this question, neither for myself nor for anyone else, but I believe that it could perhaps be explained as follows: in the first place the Germans wore us down through suffering and torture, stripped us of all we had, threatening us daily with death.
>
> And then there is the human will to live, with its eternal hope for a miracle, that things must needs take a turn for the better. Human ties too --- concern for children, parents, the sick, the weak --- more than once quelled the will to fight, as did the belief that this was a punishment from heaven. And how dare man pit himself against God's will . . .?

Max Fiszer's words are but partly true, for despite his aforementioned reasons there were incidents of resistance and heroism, and not all had lost the will to fight. True, mass uprisings were few, but everywhere, whether in the camps or the ghettoes, there were incidents of spontaneous and sporadic resistance, not to speak of the vast partisan movement which spread and grew and played so crucial a role in the victory over the Nazi beast.

It should, however, be mentioned that the most weighty reason of all for the Jews' passivity was the devilish cunning of the enemy designed to weaken their resistance. The oppressors kept telling them, via the Judenraten, that nothing would happen to them, that they were a much-needed work force, and so on. And here it is difficult to entirely absolve the leaders of the Jewish community, the Judenraten, who indiscriminately swallowed the Nazi lies.

This clearly emerges from the testimony of Yerachmiel Milutin. He tells that a resistance group comprising 95 able-bodied young men, most of them former Polish soldiers, was organised in Braslaw. Its initiators were Gerszon Klioner, a member of the Judenrat, and Alexi Wasilewski, son of the Greek-Orthodox priest, employed in the Braslaw town council and trusted by the Germans. Yerachmiel was the go-between and Wasilewski even showed him the cachet of arms and ammunition which lay waiting to be handed over to the fighters. However, immediately the chairman of the Judenrat got wind of this, he fought it tooth and nail and, in order to avoid civil strife, the plan was

[Page 597]
abandoned.

Wasilewski also exerted himself on behalf of Russian war prisoners. He supplied them with forged documents to enable them to obtain work as local residents. Finally he was denounced by a traitor, arrested by the Germans and shot in Glubok.

We wish to end the chapter on life in the ghetto under the Nazi heel, with its privations and hunger, denigrations and death, with the words of Mira Lotz whose fate as a child was the fate of so many children like herself, as also of adults, who shared with her the burden of those dark days. "I witnessed," she writes, "the death of thousands of people, my family among them. I envied the dead, and yet I alone remained alive . . ."

A special chapter in the road of suffering may be found in the innumerable accounts and testimonies of many of our countrymen. For months on end they wandered, driven from pillar to post, here by day and there by night, seeking a haven for themselves and their children, where they would be safe from the claws of the Nazi beast.

Moving in its simplicity is the story of Sarah Katz-Mowszenson.

Hounded and driven, in rain, snow and frost, with an infant in her arms, often without food or water, she wandered --- together with her cousin Benjamin who later became her husband --- from place to place, at times with nowhere to lay down her ailing and aching body.

Days, weeks, months, years, amidst suffering and tribulation, hunger and loneliness, filthy and louse-ridden, uncertain of the morrow, they finally lived to see that happy day --- the defeat and demise of the Nazi beast --- and the day of reckoning when they could avenge themselves on the local hooligans and murderers who helped the Gestapo kill Jews and wipe out entire families and communities.

It was not always easy to track down these collaborators for after the war they assumed the mien of pure, innocent lambs. Such a one was the bloodthirsty butcher and murderer of Jews, Foikste. But, thanks to Sarah and her husband Benjamin, he was caught and received his just des[s]erts.

Such instances of whitewashing were legion, as may be seen from the trial of the war criminal and murderer Jasinski, mentioned earlier, and on which we wish to elaborate somewhat.

From the account of Niuta Kantor we learn of the ways and means whereby these former murderers tried to whitewash themselves. We have in our possession official documents and reports of court proceedings of Jasinski's trial which took place in [Poland in] Olsztin and Kiszalin at Niuta's insistence. Not only do

[Page 596]
these documents reveal Jasinski's brutal attitude towards the Jews of Braslaw and environs, but also the various stratagems, threats and bribery, to which some Poles resorted in an attempt to rehabilitate this murderer.

Another ugly feature of the trial was the patent bias of the Polish law courts which tried to shift the blame onto the innocent victims. The war seemed to have changed nothing --- Polish antisemitism was as alive as ever.

Apart from Jasinski's trial in which Niuta played so vital a part, we wish to dwell briefly on her experiences in Nazi-occupied Braslaw, followed by her life in hiding in a village with a peasant who, at the behest of the local Catholic priest, hid her and an entire Latvian Jewish family.

Niuta relates that after the war when she returned to Braslaw from the village where she lay hidden, the wife of the Polish watchmaker Krzyzanek, their neighbour, told her that she [had] watched through the window the liquidation of the ghetto. Jews in their hundreds were assembled in the courtyard of the Folkshul and in a large hall adjoining the church. They were kept there for three days without food or water. Then, faint and half-dead, they were driven to the pits --- Niuta's mother and sister among them.

She also saw Rabbi Zahorie and his family walking with the rest --- the Rabbi, calm and serene, at the head.

This dark picture was not, however, without its flashes of light. There were non-Jews who helped kill but also non-Jews who helped save the hapless Jews. And this is their story. Many a Jew, faint with hunger, hounded, wandering over fields, forests, dirt tracks and farms, in search of a place where he could find a potato or a piece of bread for himself or his children, was taken in and cared for by a kindhearted Christian. There were many such people whose self-s[a]crifice we now wish to record --- Poles, Russians and even Lithuanians --- who risked their lives and the lives of their families in order to save Jews.

True enough, they did so for various reasons, from humanitarian, to a sense of victory of the Christian faith over the Jewish one, to fear of the morrow which might bring back the Russians who would wreak vengeance on the Nazi collaborators. Often it was simply a matter of gain, of money or possessions. Whatever the case may be, we wish to stress time and again that many Christians, especially village folk, helped Jews in their hour of need. This is borne out by the testimonies of Slawa Pincow, Niuta Kantor, Chayim Dejcz, Hanka Gurewicz and many others.

We recall with deep gratitude all those who, placing their own lives in jeopardy, saved Jews from certain death. There was the Szczerbinski family

[Page 595]

that hid Yetta Fisher and several members of the Grawetz family from Dwinsk for quite a time; the family Kizlo, especially the peasant Michal, who saved Niuta Kantor and the Barkan family from Latvia.

With much warmth and affection we recall the Kandzilewski family which for many months hid Sarah Katz-Mowszenzon, her husband and their small child; Jozefa Siewickaja and the Catholic priest who, despite every danger, hid and cared for the Gurewicz family --- the mother Rachel and her two daughters, Hanka and Riwetka.

How can one ever forget the two sisters Amalia and Jadwiga Czesnowicka and their brother Alfons, who saved Mendel and Masza Maron and also Tewie and Motel Fiszer (Baruch's sons), Chana Fiszer and Motel, son of Zalman Yankel [Fiszer] --- all in all six people.

With reverence we recall Stanislaw Szakiel who hid and cared for seventeen Jews, among them Lubowicz, his wife Chanah and their two children, Leibel and Shaul.

With gratitude we mention Wasil Iwanow and his daughter Irina who kept Chiena Band hidden in their home, without the knowledge of the rest of the family, particularly their own son, a policeman.

With deep regard Slawa Pincow mentions Jaszka Arciszewski, better known as "the father of the Jews."

Slawa, her husband, brother, father and stepmother hid for some time in a village, in the home of the pious, kindhearted Wasil Brezko, until . . .

> Due to the growing activity of the partisans, the Germans began to burn down villages in reprisal. Wasil warned us of the impending danger before he and his family abandoned their home.
>
> Father then turned to us and said: "Children, you are young and must escape. I cannot keep up, my strength has given out. Perhaps a miracle will happen!?" He then placed his hands on our heads and with tears in his eyes gave us his blessing, just as he used to do on the eve of Yom Kippur . . .

The night was bright from the flames and the dazzling snow. We ran for our lives . . . When we reached the edge of the forest, we cast a glance backwards towards the spot where our parents had remained, and saw that all was aflame.

No miracle had happened . . .

In those flames, on that night, the souls of our father, Reb Chayim Szalom, and our stepmother Gitel ascended to heaven.

The kindness of the non-Jewish benefactors did not go unrewarded. After the war, the liberation, many of the Jewish survivors saved by Christians went all

[Page 594]

out to try and compensate and materially assist their rescuers. To name but one instance, Masza and Mendel Maron came specially from America to meet with the sisters Czesnowicki and to hand over their house to them as a token of gratitude.

More than forty years have passed since that tragic epoch, but the memories, the pain and anguish, which the survivors carry in their hearts still well up in all their horror in their consciousness. They clamour for expression nor dare they be allowed to sink into oblivion.

How can one remain unmoved when reading about the Kowno woman who, while in hiding together with the Gurewicz family, was forced to strangle her three-year-old child lest its ceaseless crying give them away, or about the Jod couple, Chayim-Leiser and Chawa Cipin who, no longer able to bear the loss of their three little girls murdered by the Nazis, one day, desperate, took each other by the hand, came out of hiding and gave themselves up to the Germans.

Horrifying in the extreme are the accounts of those who passed through the labour and death camps. Still but children or adolescents, they walked every path of pain and suffering, hunger, loneliness and want.

Particularly shattering is the tale of Rivka Rukszin-Maron. In simple words she describes her experiences during that grim period:

> From the day the Germans entered Dubene until their defeat, I walked an endless road of tribulation and suffering, more than once seeing death before my eyes. I lived in the ghettoes of Vidz and Swiencian, passed through twelve concentration and extermination camps. On that long and tortured road I lost my parents, brothers and all my relatives, and only my sister Reisel and I remained alive.
>
> And in the camps --- humiliations, hunger and sickness, forced labour, blows, until finally --- murder or the gas ovens.
>
> In Camp Miligan we struck a bit of "luck" as it were. We met up with our family. From there we were sent to Camp Wewie, where we worked laying railway lines and then to Zezmer, another camp.
>
> Over many long months we managed to collect a little flour. Father baked matzoth for the Passover, but three weeks before this festival a selection was carried out and my mother, my father, and my brother were sent to Ponar.
>
> That was a terrible day. I can still see the children wrenched from their mothers and their heartrending cries keep ringing in my ears.

[Page 593]
Rivka continues:

> We were put into goods trains and taken to Auschwitz. A trainload of people arrived there before us and they were let out of the coaches. We heard their cries and weeping.
>
> Auschwitz would not accept us. I am certain that the Germans were not frightened off by our cries and laments. It was quite simple; the camp was full, the gas ovens overloaded, and there was no room for us . . .

We moved on to Stutthof. Heavy, thick smoke belched from the chimneys of the gas chambers, which worked day and night. Three or four times a day there would be roll call, and each time we had to stand for hours on end in one spot in all kinds of weather.

One day when the Germans took down the names of people selected for work, mine was among them. I even managed to smuggle my thirteen-year-old sister Reisel through the gate. We were taken to a camp near Danzig where we stayed for ten months, digging trenches.

The fate of Sima Morecki-Fejgin was no better. She writes:

I was one of a group sent from the Vidz ghetto to work in Camp Miligan. Among us were a few Jewish girls from Dubene. We left the ghetto on foot but were later put into cattle trucks and brought to a camp fenced off with barbed wire. It consisted of barracks with three-tier bunks.

Ita Kulak, the woman in charge, noticed that there were many young girls among us. She warned us to say when being registered that we were over fifteen years old or we would be sent to an extermination camp.

In Camp Oleina my two little brothers and four-year-old sister were forcibly taken from us. I cannot describe our sorrow and pain, the cries and screams of the children at parting . . . And so only my mother, eleven-year-old brother, Berele, and I remained.

Every day goods trains would take us to work. Our guards were German soldiers assisted by a multi-national police force, among which was a young Pole, Janek --- a kindhearted fellow.

One day our train stopped midway and remained standing for a long time. Janek told us the reason for the hold-up: a train with many coaches packed with Jewish children.

We looked in the direction in which he pointed and saw hundreds of childish hands stretched out through the window bars. We knew the fate of these children --- the death camps --- but, alas, could do nothing . . .

In 1944 we were transported to Kaiserwald near Riga. Here our heads were shaved, our old rags replaced with striped uniforms and wooden clogs, we were each given a triangular piece of cloth to cover our heads, a louse-ridden blanket and --- of course --- a number. Mine was 6757.

[Page 592]

Every day there were roll calls. From time to time the Germans would come and sort us --- right, left --- to life or death.

From across the barbed wire we would often see little Berele. He told us that the grown-ups took pity on him and gave him a little food. Once he even tried to throw us a piece of bread, but it stuck in the barbed wire. He was upset and Mother cried . . .

Shortly afterwards a truck arrived at the camp and took away the remaining children and so we no longer saw Berele. Only Mother and I remained . . .

When the front began to draw nearer we were transferred to Stutthof, an extermination camp fenced in by several rows of barbed wire. Every half hour there was roll call.

One day, while standing in the queue for our food rations, we heard piercing screams coming from the front of the queue. It turned out that the kapo had plunged a young girl into the pot of boiling soup. Later we were dished out soup from the same pot.

On a certain day, when sent out to work at a different place, I saw a huge pile of shoes --- children's and adults'. I rummaged and found a pair of good, almost brand-new shoes, which I later exchanged for a loaf of bread . . .

The tale of Chana-Fejge Berkman-Skopiec makes painful reading. She describes how her father and brother met their death at Ponar:

We worked in a labour camp near Swiencian, laying a railway line and paving highways. The food barely sufficed to keep body and soul together. On the eve of Chanukah I, along with many others, was transferred to the Vilna ghetto. There were camps into which the Germans put many people who had been brought from the provinces. We were singled out for special hard labour. The conditions were intolerable.

In the spring of 1943 the labour camps were liquidated and all their inmates removed to Ponar. My father and brother were assigned the task of burning the bodies of the murdered, until they too were ultimately killed in Ponar. My mother was murdered in Zezmeri . . .

Tragic is the tale of Mira Lotz-Szneider who paints in vivid though sombre colours all that she herself and so many men, women, adolescents and children had lived through in the labour and extermination camps:

We were working at paving a highway between Zezmeri and Wewie, two shtetlach a distance of 25 kms away from each other. We dared not raise our heads for a second for fear of the shouts and blows of the overseers. We worked long hours.

[Page 591]

In winter, in particular, life was hard. We had to dig under the snow in the frozen earth, stones and sand. Our daily rations --- 200 grammes of bread and a little soup made from rotten cabbage.

We were not guarded, but counted mornings and evenings, with the warning that if anyone were found missing all would answer for it.

Towards the end of 1943 we were transferred to Oleine in Latvia, an SS camp fenced round by the inevitable barbed wire, and surrounded by watchtowers. Germans with bloodthirsty dogs trained to attack Jews only were constantly on the prowl.

And then there were the Jewish kapos, among whom Danziger "distinguished" himself with his brutality. Any Jew who happened to cross his path he beat up mercilessly. One day my mother Rachel-Leah was his luckless victim. He kept beating her until she fell down in a faint. She died the next day . . .

We returned from work one day, dropping from exhaustion, and were immediately driven out of the barracks for roll call. Our children were taken from us and loaded into trucks which stood waiting at the gate. The cries and wails rose to heaven. The peasants in the neighbourhood heard it. Did God hear it too?

The children, eleven of them from Dubene, were taken to Auschwitz. My father David could not bear to part with his little girl Sarah-Zelda, and went along with her . . .

A few months later we were transferred to Kaiserwald, another barbed-wire camp near Riga. At the large barracks, our new home, we were ordered to wash, our heads were shorn, and we were given camp clothes in exchange for our former rags. These rags meant nothing to me in themselves but I was terribly upset and wept bitter tears because of the few family photographs which I had carried with me in all my wanderings and guarded with my very life. They were all I had left of my home, my childhood and my dear unforgettable ones . . .

It was the end of 1944. The Soviet army advanced, frequent bombings were heard. The night sky was lit up with the fires raging in nearby Riga and all around.

The Germans decided to liquidate the camp and we were evacuated to the shore of the Baltic sea and from there to the death camp Stutthof. In one corner of the camp, where entry was strictly forbidden, thick black smoke coiled without a stop. That was the end of the road --- the crematorium.

Roll calls and selections were frequent. Those ordered to the left were sent to the gas chambers. Wagons went round the camp to collect the bodies of those who had died of hunger or disease. We envied the dead for their suffering had ended . . .

[Page 590]

A month after our arrival the Germans came to recruit the able-bodied for work. Of the several thousand inmates a mere few hundred were chosen, I among them. We were put into goods trains and driven to an unknown destination. We knew that once again we had been snatched from death, for why else had we been removed from Stutthof.

We were brought to Sofinwald and set to work helping Dutch and British war prisoners with their building operations. We lived in plywood huts. In winter the thin walls would be covered with thick layers of ice. We slept on the earthen floor . . .

The builders built houses of brick. We carried bricks and cement from the railway coaches to the building site on our shoulders. We also had to dig for loam to make bricks ourselves. The food rations were meagre but then we were not short of blows. In this two SS women, Erika and Walita, excelled, as did a Jewish kapo from Hungary . . .

No less heartrending are the experiences of Motke Rosenberg of Opsa in the ghettoes and camps through which he and his family passed.

We had uncanny "luck." Our entire family was sent to the Vilna ghetto. I was very young and worked near the railway station.

Again the rounding up of people began --- that meant --- actions. People were shoved into coaches, my sisters among them. Pandemonium broke out and many escaped. I too. But we were caught just outside the ghetto gates. My parents were given the option of redeeming me for a bribe but as they did not have the money, I was put back in the coach with my sisters. We were certain that we were being taken to Ponar but were brought to Estonia instead, to the labour camp Wajwary.

Everything was strange and unfamiliar --- the language, the landscape, the surroundings, except for the same barbed-wire fence, the same guards, and in the barracks the all too familiar emaciated faces --- skeletons --- hunched, dejected, half-dead with faded glances . . .

The work --- to put down railway tracks; the working day --- long and hard, punctuated with merciless beatings at the slightest pretext; the food --- a piece of bread and a bit of soup . . .

The punishment for attempted escape was 25 lashes. Not too bad, I thought, one can't die from it. So I decided to run away. Again I was caught, and two months later transferred to Narwe, another camp. There to my great joy I met up with my father. Conditions here were even worse --- we had to dig trenches. Winter, cold, half-naked, starved, the overseers beating mercilessly . . . My father

[Page 589]

became ill and was put into a hospital from which he never returned. I came to visit him one day only to be told that he had died. I leaned against [t]he gate and wept and wept . . .

Once again I ran away . . .

A few days later I was caught. Paniker, the camp commandant, at his wits' end, shouted that he was sick and tired of my attempts at escape and was going to hang me . . .

I lay in the attic and watched Herr Paniker and his Jewish assistant Diler prepare the gallows for me. I saw them test the rope, the beam and the stool on which I was to stand before the hanging . . .

I was led out. I was shaking with fear and Paniker had to support me. I was placed on the stool, the rope round my neck, was given a push and . . . fell to the ground! Once again they tried, and once again I fell to the ground, this time in a faint . . . When I came to I saw Diler standing over me and heard him say: "You're alive, alive!"

At roll call that evening I received 25 lashes and once again fainted . . .

The aforegoing is but a fraction of the suffering endured by so many, told by the few who lived to tell it.

A chapter on its own is the harrowing tale of the so-called "death march" in which thousands of Jews --- young and old --- took part towards the end of the war.

The German extermination machine which worked all out did not slacken to the end, when the Germans knew that they had lost the war, were suffering defeat on every front. Even in the last few weeks before the final capitulation, when the Nazi beast was in its death throes, the demonic murderous plan was not halted. Jews in their thousands were dragged along with the retreating German army --- Jews and war prisoners --- whom they either did not manage to kill or, for some reason or other, could not.

And so they drove worn-out, sick and half-dying human beings, through forests and fields, towns and villages, over highways and byways, in boats and all manner of conveyance --- deep into Germany, and threw them into camps and prisons.

From the memoirs of those who survived the dreadful march unfolds the frenzied race against time by the Germans.

In rain and snow, by day and night, without rest, food or water, ragged and half-naked, dropping by the wayside, desperate, they dragged themselves along. Anyone too weak to go on was ruthlessly killed on the spot. Escorted by

[Page 588]

armed guards, with trained dogs at their sides, the march, the "death march" as it was later called, ended in Germany. Very few of those who set out, completed it.

Mira Lotz, one of the "lucky" survivors, writes:

In February 1945, when the front began to draw near, we were ordered out of the camp and driven on foot, in deep snow and frost, in the direction of Berlin. Many died on the way. Those who lagged behind were shot.

We were kept in a camp near Launberg for a whole month. We slept on the frozen earth, consumed with lice and hungry. Hundreds died every day . . .

When the Red army began to approach we were driven onwards until we came to a village, Chinhof. There we were locked in large barracks together with Russian prisoners-of-war. We were certain that this was the end of the road.

But a miracle happened! The Russian war prisoners recognised the approaching Russian tanks by the sound of their motors. They flung themselves at the gates, pushed with all their might, and forced them open. We were free!

I cannot find words to describe that moment. After so many nightmarish months, years, when the borders between life and death had become blurred in my mind, and suddenly --- free, freedom!!

At that moment I became aware of the abysmal, the horrible disaster. Before my eyes I saw my loved ones --- relatives and friends --- who had been taken from me one by one and only I remained alive.

Lonely and alone, amid hundreds such as I, hardly able to stand on my feet, barely human in my concentration camp clothes with the yellow badge --- the shield of David --- on my sleeve, with a number --- 40630 --- a shaven head, wooden clogs on my feet, and wrapped in a dirty blanket . . .

The Russian shoulders gaped at us in horror . . .

This was 10 March 1945 --- two months before the war ended.

And finally, I visited Dubene, the place where I was born. The village had been burnt down, destroyed, annihilated.

I went to the cemetery but found only smashed tombstones, fragments scattered among the tall wild grass . . .

This is the story of my life. Can I ever forget it?

I will always carry in my heart the memory of my dear ones, the innocent, who were murdered and burnt only because they were Jews . . .

[Page 587]

Similar are the trials and tribulations of Rivka Rukszin, who too took part in the "death march." She relates:

January 1945. For three weeks on end we were driven westwards. Those who could not keep up were murdered on the way. I, though scarcely able to drag myself along, had to support my thirteen-year-old sister Reisel.

Not far from the German village Kulka we were locked in large barracks where we stayed for two months. Of the 3000 people who set out on the march only 500 survived.

At night the Germans used to open the gates, probably to let in the biting cold, which would pierce through us. In the morning we would get up covered with snow. Every day the dead, frozen bodies were removed from the barracks. Our daily rations consisted of 100 grammes of bread and two potatoes.

One day, at midday, the cook, an Opsa woman, came to tell us that we had been liberated by the American army [actually it was the Soviet army]. We greeted the news with apathy as we had no strength even to express our joy . . .

Vivid is the description of Motke Rosenberg of his share in the "death march":

The Germans gathered about 2000 of us for roll call, kept us standing for two days, and then began to drive us. We went along byways, fields and forests. We spent the nights in barns, granaries or any other outbuildings. On the way we scavenged anything that could serve as food. Those who fell behind, the weak, the ill, were shot on the spot and their bodies thrown by the wayside. Our numbers dwindled daily . . .

Hungry, louse-ridden, barefoot, covered in rags and half-naked, half-dead, beaten, we prayed for death.

I recalled my childhood, the days of my youth, the place of my birth, and in my heart the thought kept gnawing: this is the end . . .

The march lasted one month and a half. Of the 2000 men who set out only 160 remained.

On the outskirts of Salzburg we met up with soldiers of uncertain origin --- some spoke Yiddish, some Polish. Then we learned: they were Americans, and we were free!

We wanted to fall at their feet and thank them, but they would not let us --- they were appalled at the sight of us.

Often when reading and listening to the testimonies of those who succeeded in cheating death one cannot but marvel at the part chance played in their destinies. They were tossed like puppets, shunted between death and life, despair and hope . . .

What else could one call the almost incredible, shattering experience of Leiser Fiszer who crawled out of the pit alive after he and so many Jews --- men, women and children --- had been shot and thrown into it [in Braslaw on June 3-5, 1942]. He was lying beneath

[Page 586]

a heap of bodies, covered in their innocent blood. This is his story:

We were driven to the ready-dug pits in batches. It was no use crying, shouting or pleading with God. Many infants were thrown into the pits alive. Some, not yet dead, grappled with death. The murderers did their work and left.

Evening came. Darkness fell. I tried to lift a hand, stretch out a leg, and feel that I am not hurt, but am lying in the blood of my dear friends and on a pile of dead children. With my last strength I crawl out of the pit and make for the nearby woods.

For three days I wandered, naked, bloodstained and famished, until I spotted a barn. I crept in, burrowed into the hay and waited. At dawn the peasant came to fetch some fodder. He was startled to see me but knew at once what I was doing there. He went out and after a while came back with an army coat and a pot of boiled potatoes. I felt alive again.

The peasant, Juzef Orlowski of the village Zwirble near Belmont, hid and kept me for two years until a neighbour told him that the villagers knew that he was harbouring a Jew. He advised him to send me away or hand me over to the police. Juzef told me of this and said, "I want you to live. I will dig you a hole in the pigsty." I lay in that hole for eight months.

One morning the Germans came. They drove everyone out of the house, lined them up ready to be shot, and demanded that they hand over the Jew. Juzef's wife thereupon fell to their feet crying, and said: "Do you think that a swinish Jew is dearer to me than my husband and my eight children?"

The Germans left and I knew that I too must leave.

I set out to look for partisans.

Similar was the fate of the Jajsi Jew, Szneur Munitz who, with a cry of "Shema Israel," leaped out of the pit which he and several Jews had been forced to dig. They were murdered but he remained alive and went home to his family.

The narratives of Fiszer and Munitz evoke pictures of poignant, inhuman suffering, which like furious waves broke over our lives. Hunted like animals, not certain of what tomorrow will bring, Jews from our parts along with all Polish Jews, were prey to affliction and fear, indignities and evil deeds of evil men --- the modern cannibals.

Tragic and bitter are the tales of Yerachmiel Bielak, his brother Chontsze and their little children. Their experiences alone can serve as ample material for a researcher into the happenings of that period --- the frightful Jewish catastrophe under German rule. We shall relate a few incidents.

[Page 585]

Abraham Bielak, a mere eighteen-year-old when the war broke out, soon began to feel the weight of the Nazi iron yoke: life in the ghetto, in underground hideouts (bunkers or shelters as they were called), the hunger and want, watching his sister smother her child to death with a pillow so that its crying should not give away all the inmates of the bunker.

One cannot gloss over or fail to be moved by the tale of Feige-Tsippe Toker-Bielak who, as a child of eight, had known the loneliness and want, the hunger and misery of those trying days.

Her testimony speaks of the anguish of a child who has to console her father in his lonely hideout where he suffers acute mental torture in his longing for his children. She writes:

> When I saw Kalkowski's house from afar I went up and knocked on the door. It was opened to me at once by the housekeeper but when I asked to see my father, she told me that he was not staying with them.
>
> I began to cry. She then took me in, drew away a curtain and told me that I would find him on top of the oven.
>
> I saw him and knew that he was no longer in his right mind. He was tormented by the thought that he could not help us and had to send us, his two children, into the ghetto alone. He wanted to save us but had neither the strength nor the means. I clambered up to him. We embraced and wept silently. After a while I asked him: "Father, why did you call us?" "I want us to be together," he said. I then told him that in the ghetto conditions were better than here, and if one has to die it is much better to die in the ghetto, among Jews. We both cried.
>
> In the night he woke me and told me that he wanted to go and see Yerachmiel and his children, and my little sister. I loved my father and could not oppose his wishes. He cried without a stop. The peasant went outside to see if the coast was clear. We thanked him and took our leave.
>
> We met up with Yerachmiel and two children, the third child had died . . .

She continues:

> On Purim 1943 the last remaining Jews in the ghetto were liquidated. [This refers to the "Opsa" Ghetto in Braslaw, destroyed on March 19, 1943.] My sister, my father and I were with Yerachmiel in his hideout. My brother was in the ghetto in Bogomolski's house, together with some others. They put up a stand when the Nazis came to take them to the pits.
>
> Among the brave Jews was my cousin Leiser Bielak, a Polish ex-solider. He shot a German and a local policeman and wounded another. The German[s] then hurled hand grenades into the house and it caught alight. Leiser, though wounded in the hand, managed to escape.
>
> My brother and all the Jews inside the house were burnt to death . . .

[Page 584]

The Partisan Movement

Not only do we wish to tell of the evil perpetrated against the Jews under the Nazi jackboot, not only record the testimonies about those who, for various reasons, could not put up an armed stand and hence perished by various means --- privation, hunger, burning at the crematoria, brutal torture at the hands of the Gestapo or other Nazis and their local henchmen --- but we are equally duty bound to tell the heroic chapter written by the Jewish partisans and resistance groups in the fight against the common enemy --- the German aggressor.

True, we have told of instances of heroism and courage of Jews in the ghetto and elsewhere, but these were sporadic, spontaneous and isolated cases, which nevertheless manifested the spiritual strength fuelled by hatred and bitterness which swelled in the breasts of proud and undaunted Jews.

However, as an organised, strategic force which was able to make an impact on the war effort on the fronts, and play havoc with the German destruction machine --- such a force was the partisan movement only. Once again, it is difficult, if not impossible, to describe in detail or to give an exhaustive account of numbers, the extent of the damage, and the diversions carried out during that period.

We shall therefore endeavour to extract from the nebulous past what little we have managed to glean from the chronicles and testimonies of those who, with the barest of means, fought in the partisan units in the vicinity of Braslaw, Zamosz, Kazian, Jod and in certain regions of Lithuania and Latvia.

We recall with pride the brave young partisan Tewie Bielak, his self-sacrifice and iron will in wrestling with the enemy forces. Szleimke Ichilczik (in the book *Ghetto and Forest* by Mosze Shutan) tells of him:

> Tewie was a member of a partisan group in Vilna. He used to move about freely, as an Aryan, in the city and supply the partisans with arms. He was tortured to death by the Gestapo without betraying his comrades. We quote:
>
> The last time Tewke had gone outside the ghetto two agents caught him. They caught him at the last moment, near the secret entrance, when his one foot was already inside the ghetto. He did not even manage to turn round, when they pounced on him, twisted his arms backwards, tied him, searched him, found his revolver and took him straight to the Gestapo.

[Page 583]

> He was soon brought back to the ghetto, to the Jewish criminal police, to [Jacob] Gens. This is what the Germans often did --- implicated the Jewish police in the investigation.
>
> [Martin] Weiss, the Gestapo chief of the Vilna ghetto, stands over Tewke and belabours him with a rubber truncheon. He wants to know who sent him and where he found the firearm.
>
> Tewke lies bound on the table. He keeps silent. He does not utter a word. He does not utter a groan.
>
> Gens, who stood aside, intervenes. He delicately takes the truncheon from the Gestapo chief's hand and begins to fleece [flay] Tewke alive. Purple and red stripes swell up on Tewke's writhing body, blood oozes from his every pore --- but he, Gens, beats and beats --- so long and so furiously that he breaks out in a sweat. Even Weiss, the Gestapo chief, can no longer stand it.
>
> "Throw away the truncheon!" he shouts, bangs the door and stomps out.
>
> Gens finally appears from the interrogation chamber --- spent, dishevelled, flustered. His eyes full of hatred, he stares at the Jewish police who jump to attention. With a pained, contemptuous look he meets their quizzical, frightened, cowardly glances.
>
> "Rigged out like a bunch of morons --- idiots!" he hisses through his teeth.
>
> At the door he pauses for a second, turns round and flings at them: "A son, a son like this, I should have!"
>
> And the police, insulted, stare at him in amazement, puzzled at his words, they shake their heads and think that perhaps he, Gens, is not in his right mind at this very moment.

                                                                    (Own translation)

Among the partisans Yerachmiel Milutin, a young man from Braslaw, distinguished himself for his courage and heroism. His exploits are described in *The Book of Jewish Partisans*, page 179.

Yerachmiel was second-in-command of an intelligence group in the partisan unit "Suworow." He and eight others were dispatched on a certain diversion. On the way they hit upon enemy soldiers who opened heavy fire on them. The inexperienced young partisans took fright and fled. Milutin held his ground, and with concerted fire and hand grenades routed the enemy with great loss to them and saved his own men.

Yerachmiel returned to base safe and sound. The commander Strikow then summoned the fighting unit, and sharply reprimanded the intelligence group for their action, while warmly praising Yerachmiel for his courage in taking on such odds.

In his book *Partisans on the March* Sz. Kaczerginski depicts the struggle waged by the partisans in the Natsze forest, in which Gerszon Jankelewicz (known as Welwel-Gerszke) heroically fell. Originally from Braslaw, he married, lived and worked in Lida during the last few years before the war. In summer

[Page 582]
1942 he escaped from the ghetto into the Natsze forest and joined the partisan regiment "Katowski." He was soon appointed company commander. At the beginning of 1943 he derailed two German military trains near Marzinkanz. He took part in liquidating traitors and in diversions. On 9 September he and three partisans set out on an important mission. On the way they chanced upon 25 German soldiers armed with automatic weapons and in the unequal fight two partisans fell. One of them was Gerszon Jankelewicz.

Diverse and fruitful were the operations carried out by Faiwel Trok of Jod in the fight against the Germans. In June 1942 Faiwel escaped from the Vidz ghetto and joined the partisan unit "Ponomarenko" which was active in the Glubok district. He took part in an attack on the garrison stationed in the shtetl Komaj near Haiduciszki (Haidutseszok), in blowing up the railway bridge Woropajewo-Glubok and destroying the Polish-Nazi bands in the Szamic forests, and in countless other partisan ambushes.

In March 1944 he was sent on a so-called "economic mission," was attacked, surrounded by German soldiers, and fell in the skirmish.

Another brave partisan was Abraham Wilkicki, a young man from Jod, who escaped from the Kazian ghetto and finally lost his life fighting the Germans. A member of the unit "Spartak," he participated in all its diversions and battles. In one of the battles he was wounded in the hand and foot and remained lying in the field. With his last strength he crawled into the bushes to hide. There his comrades found him and took him to a place of safety, but as no medical help was to be had, he soon contracted blood poisoning and died on 13 January 1943.

The tale of Pinchas Jaffe and his 15-year-old son from Bildziugi is one of courage and heroism in the fight against the German hooligans and especially their local henchman. Pinchas and his son fled into the Zachowszcsyny forest near Kazian prior to the liquidation of the Jod Jews. Both were armed. In the forest they met up with Jews who had escaped from the ghettoes of the nearby yeshuvim. They formed a partisan unit. In the village Zalesia they shot the peasant and German collaborator Oberjan and burnt down his house and all his property. They also avenged themselves on the family of the peasant Abramei, who handed over to the Germans several Jews from Jod who had survived the massacre. For a similar crime the partisans killed the Soltys (administrator) of the village Bujewszczyzna.

In June 1942 this unit was incorporated into the partisan regiment "Ponomarenko" led by Meirson, which in turn combined with the Russian division of the same name active in the Danilowicz district.

In July 1942 the Jewish regiment attacked the village Korsunki, near Jod, as it

[Page 581]
was a nest of Samachowcy (local youths who organised themselves into units in order to help the Germans fight partisans and Jews).

The Jewish partisans, in a combined operation with the Russian regiment of the "Spartak" division, attacked Jod by night and burnt down the houses together with their inhabitants and German accomplices, including two German officers who happened to be there. One of the buildings set on fire was the headquarters of the district command.

This act of revenge was the brainchild of Pinchas Jaffe and both he and his son Motel distinguished themselves during the attack, winning warm praise from the leaders of their unit.

When Meirson, the partisan leader, decided to leave the Kazian forest and cross over to the base of the "Ponomarenko" division active in the Danilowicz district, Pinchas Jaffe and his son and several other Jews decided to remain and continue their punitive acts against German collaborators. The group sowed fear among the Germans of the district, so much so that the latter fixed a price on the head of this brave partisan.

On December 15, 1942 Pinchas and his son Motel came to the village Bujewszczyzna to carry out an act of revenge against a German accomplice. Not finding him at home they decided to spend the night in one of the hamlets. The peasants got wind of this and in the night forcibly entered the house where Pinchas and his son were sheltering and caught them. Motel was burnt alive and Pinchas handed over to the Germans. He tried to escape but was shot.

Benjamin Dubinski too can serve as a symbol of Jewish courage. With gun in hand he fought against the Nazi military units and their accomplices. Benjamin was born in Vidz in the Braslaw district, and later moved to Jod. He and some friends fled to the forests of Milik between Jod and Pohost. After the massacre of the Jod Jews in December 1941 they joined a group of escaped Russian war prisoners and together began to comb the district for arms.

In May 1942 they returned --- armed --- to the neighbouring forests and formed the partisan unit named "Szirokow," after their commander. It was headed by Dubinski, who excelled himself in the attack on a German garrison stationed in the village Achremowcy near Braslaw. The Germans retreated and the partisans took booty, arms and ammunition. Dubinski also distinguished himself in a battle near the yishuvim Perebrodz-Zagorie against the Germans and their accomplices.

In November 1942 Benjamin set out to avenge himself on a peasant who had

[Page 580]

killed Jews from Bildziugi. He took with him several local Jews who had been hiding and wandering the forest. They did not find the peasant and decided to stay the night at an inn. The local peasants tipped off the Germans, who attacked the inn by night and after a fight all the partisans perished.

One of the first, independent, armed fighters was Szolem Munic. He began to organise fighting units immediately after the Germans entered our district. Szolem, a coachman from Jod, his wife and child, and a group of youths, fled to the Kazian forest in 1941. At that time there were no partisans as yet, nor had the Jod ghetto been erected.

The youths, led by Muic, began to scout for arms among the peasants who were known to have collected and hidden large quantities of arms and ammunition left behind by the retreating Soviet army. This youthful group avenged the Jews handed over to the Germans. They shot the traitors, among them the peasant Stanislaw Kowalonek who denounced the family Halper and Szeine Rubaszin, and the peasant Fiodor Racznikow, who betrayed the Mindow family and Chawah Munic.

The group operated as an independent partisan unit. When escaped Russian prisoners of war began to gather in the forest (summer 1942), they joined the by now experienced Jewish fighters and together launched large-scale plans to obtain food and ammunition, and to form the regiment "Jaczminow" which in time grew into the brigade "Szirakow" mentioned earlier.

Szolem Munic was appointed commander of a division and his task was to provide the unit with arms. While on these missions he used to wreak vengeance on the peasants who had handed over Jews to the enemy. He was later accused of indiscriminately murdering peasants, and as a result was relieved of his post and placed in charge of obtaining provisions for the regiment and the families of the fighters in the partisan camps. His wife and children were among them. On one of his journeys in the villages he came upon a group of Germans. Szolem and his comrade Sztein perished. This took place in the Wirow forest in February 1942.

We cannot help recalling Szimon Zilberman, the young man from Jod who, on 17 December 1941, immediately after the first massacre, fled to the Kazian forest. He spent the entire winter of 1942 there, together with others like him, in search of ammunition as well as tracking down the peasants who had betrayed Jews to the Nazis (his family too perished in this way). In the summer of 1942 he was admitted to the "Spartak" brigade which arrived from the eastern regions. Zilberman partook in battles against the enemy garrison

[Page 579]

from Vidz, Opsa and others, and in attacks against the villages of Usiecza and Wasewicz.

Since the unit was in need of a cobbler (he was a cobbler journeyman in his youth) he was forced to ply his trade, and was se[n]t to repair the partisans' shoes in the house of the forrester (*lesnik*) Kowalionek. One fine morning in January 1943 the Germans attacked the forrester's house. Our partisans succeeded in breaking through the German lines, but Ziberman and Abraham Yair were trapped and burnt alive in the house together with the forrester.

Thrilling is the story of the partisan Alexander Dagowicz who fought valiantly side by side with scores of Jewish fighters. The battle in which the cold-blooded murderer and ringleader, [Willy] Dit[t]man, was caught deserves special mention. He was taken prisoner by Dagowicz and later handed over to the partisan punitive division.

A rich fighting history is that of Chayim Burt of Braslaw who began his "career" as fighter in partisan units in the Braslaw forests, then joined the ranks of the Red Army and finally, on his arrival in Israel, fought in the Palmach for the independence of Israel.

Brave and indefatigable was Benjamin Mowszenzon of Rymszan who joined the Soviet police for the specific purpose of catching the local gangsters and murderers who killed his family and many Rymszan Jews. He carried out his duty with the utmost diligence and together with Soviet punitive units discovered and destroyed the nests of scores of German collaborators who helped to massacre hundreds of Jews.

Abraham Bielak of Braslaw writes about himself, his brother Tewie, his relatives and friends with whom he fought:

> In the Kazian forests we were joined by Jewish fighters as [and] also by Russian soldiers who had escaped from German captivity. Soon afterwards I was appointed leader of a group of partisans of the second division, and Yerachmiel Milutin deputy of an intelligence group. In practically every combat operation I used to go with Mosze Milutin.
>
> Vidz, we were told, was teeming with gendarmes and local police who kept harassing the peasants in the vicinity, accusing them of helping the partisans. They would confiscate their possessions and even burn down their homes.
>
> We decided to teach them a lesson. Hundreds of us, partisans, led by our commander Strikow, set out against the German uniformed men. We also had to occupy the pharmacy and take medicines. In a surprise attack we killed many but there were casualties on our side as well.

[Page 578]

One act of revenge, or rather justice, deserves a place of its own. It is the revenge wreaked on the traitors who handed the heroic Leiser Bielak and Chontsze Bielak to the Germans. Abraham Bielak and Mosze Milutin who carried out the sentence of the partisan court, write:

> Three times we came to the village in order to settle scores with the traitor and his sons. There were three of us --- Yerachmiel Bielak, Mosze Milutin and I --- as well as the partisan Pietka Kaszrowski. Twice we returned empty-handed, as not all were at home. The third time we found them all together. We were prepared for we knew that they would put up a fight or try to make a run for it. Three of us took up strategic positions outside and I entered the house. They recognised me at once, knew the purpose of my coming and

tried to escape. I shot the one son, [and] the second son, Alioch, who denounced and surrendered Jews to the Germans, was shot by my comrades. Poor consolations, but nevertheless, revenge! . . .

After the war my brother Mosze and Yehuda Garber transferred the bodies of Leiser and Chontsze Bielak to the pits and buried them there . . .

Finally, we must mention that apart from the partisans, many Jewish soldiers from our parts too fought the Nazi hordes, whether in the ranks of the regular Red Army, the Polish fighting units, or British formations in Africa and Europe. Many of these soldiers had been mobilised as far back as the beginning of the Polish-German war. Some were captured by the Russians or Germans, some perished in battle or in bombing raids.

After the liberation of the areas where they operated, numerous partisans joined the Red Army, fighting till the Nazi-Fascist beast was totally vanquished. Some of our fellow countrymen attained high officers' ranks and won medals and decorations. One was Isser Rabinowicz of Braslaw who reached the rank of Colonel and was decorated by the Poles.

In the newspaper *Nasz Glos* ("Our Voice"), Stefan Krukowski, the military correspondent, writes that thanks to the courage and determination of Isser Rabinowicz, his unit succeeded in capturing the German Commander of the 163rd division, together with 650 German soldiers.

As mentioned, many of our boys from Braslaw and environs fell on the battlefields of Europe and elsewhere. Obviously, it is not possible for us to give exact details of the time, place or circumstances in which they sacrificed their young lives. Let this chronicle of those dark times, lit up by their brave deeds

[Page 577]

which helped hasten the dawn --- the victory over the Nazis --- be an eternal memorial to their pure and saintly souls.

Some came back and are now scattered throughout the world. Many found a home in our own land --- Israel. Once again we cannot give with any accuracy the names of those who lived to see the great day --- the triumph over the dark forces of evil, horror and death. They too are here remembered with pride.

Epilogue

We have tried to relate, briefly and succinctly, all that has been written down, told and recorded in innumerable documents, testimonies and experiences of the *Sh'erit Hapleita*, the few who survived the almost total destruction of our community and its neighbouring shtetlach and yishuvim.

We feel that the letter by Chayim Munic (Chayim Levi-Itches) written from Russia to his sister in Israel after his visit to Braslaw --- his hometown and ours which is no more --- shortly after the war, can serve as a final note in the dreadful requiem march.

We are reproducing this letter in slightly abridged form which in no way alters its content nor detracts from its worth:

> In Braslaw everything is outwardly as it was: the mountain did not split in half, the waters in the lakes flow calmly, exactly as though nothing had happened. And yet, terrible things happened here which are difficult to speak of and even more difficult to put on paper.
>
> The first Friday after the Germans entered Braslaw they rounded up all the Jews, drove them to a marshy swamp in the Dubkes forest and kept them there for a whole day. While they stood thus in the swamp, whoever wanted looted their homes. When they returned the shtetl looked as if after a pogrom. Feathers were flying from the torn bedding exactly as described in Bialik's "City of Slaughter."
>
> On the way to the swamp Szlomo [Zilber], the ritual slaughterer, and Chayim Milutin tried to escape and were shot dead on the spot. Later another thirteen Jews were shot when their overseer, a Pole, wrote down

that they had been idling when they should have been working. They had been loading logs at the railway station.

The remainder were shot in the wholesale massacre on 3rd June 1942. Till then life for the Jews had also been one hell [an eternal hell]. Once on a Friday night the Germans put the ritual slaughterer Singalowski on a motorcycle and raced with him through the streets of the shtetl. They finally let him go, but the following day he died of apoplexy.

[Page 576]

Next it was decreed that Jews may not walk on the sidewalk, are to wear the yellow badge on the lefthand side of the breast and the right shoulder, and eventually they were shut up in a ghetto. The ghetto was in Pilsudski Street, and was cordoned off with barbed wire. (Our family lived together with Chienke and Gerszon in Stawski's house.)

Jews were forbidden to speak or trade with peasants. The Jews of the ghetto were forced to do unskilled, menial labour, such as washing floors for the Germans, loading logs onto trains, knitting woollen socks and gloves. They received 15 deko (150 grammes) of bread each daily. They lived by bartering with the peasants; everything was bartered from clothing to furniture --- a bench, a wardrobe, a table. It was forbidden but everyone did it. To aggravate matters, the Germans imposed heavy collective fines in the form of gold, fur coats, ladies' coats. The Judenrat and Jewish police collected these on behalf of the Germans and carried out all the Germans' decrees concerning the Jews. The Judenrat consisted of 14-15 people, the most senior member being [Yitzchak] Mindel the hardware merchant. Some of the others were: Levi Itsche Wainsztein, [Eliezer] Mazeh the teacher, Szeinkman the advocate. The policemen were Alter Arliuk, Leib Valin and others.

The Jews in the ghetto sensed that their days were numbered. Some began to prepare hiding places. Since a faint hope glimmered in their breasts that perhaps some will outlive the dark times, like a drowning man clutching at a straw, they did nothing to defy the enemy so as not to precipitate the wholesale slaughter. All this, however, was to no avail. At dawn on 3rd June [1942], the Germans, assisted by the police and Braslaw peasants in the service of the Germans, began to drive the Jews out of their homes. The Jews were assembled in the building opposite the Greek Orthodox Church, stripped of their clothing up to their underwear, brutally beaten, and then led to the ready-dug pits in the forest on the way to Dubene, past the pasture land used by the Jews. Mothers carried their children. No one cried. Three days the blood oozed from the pit. Peasants in wagons carried sand and poured it on top but the blood kept flowing.

Many Jews took refuge in the hideouts they had prepared in advance. For three days the police looked for them. Anton Burak, a tall non-Jew, a policeman, who worked at the brewery and was fluent in Yiddish, would enter the homes, go into the yard and say: "Jews, come out of your hiding places. There will be no more shootings." Some obeyed, came out and were at once led away to the pits to be shot. Germans and police would enter the empty homes and fire at random into the walls and floor, in the yard or even the

[Page 575]

ground. The little children hidden in the bunkers, taking fright, would start crying. In this way they caught the Jews. Some who started to run were shot while trying to scale the barbed wire.

A day before the massacre the Germans sent about 80 young people to Slobodka, ostensibly to work there. Later they were sent back to Braslaw and immediately taken to the pit. The Jews from Opsa were brought into the now empty Jewish ghetto. They too were shot a year later [on March 19, 1943]. During this operation a Jewish fellow killed a German who came to drive them out of the house, donned his uniform, took his automatic rifle and went outside. A policeman was coming towards him, he fired but missed, and was caught. Another fellow killed a German and two policemen with a pick.

The Jews who hid during the first day of the massacre fled to the forests. For hiding a Jew a peasant would be shot and his house set on fire. For catching a Jew the reward was three kilos of salt. There were many instances of peasants catching Jews and handing them over to the police. For spending the night some peasants demanded five rubles in gold.

There were also instances of peasants hiding Jews or giving them a piece of bread. Maszke Slawa Chayes and Mendke Chayim Itziks lay hidden in the home of two young peasant women until the arrival of the Red army. They had no money nor any belongings with them. Later these peasant women took in more Jews from Braslaw. True, these did pay something towards their keep. Thus they saved six people. The Braslaw deacon in the church died of apoplexy the day the Jews were being shot. Some Catholic priests urged the peasants who confessed to harbouring Jews to give them food and clothing. The local Catholic priest supplied David of Bizne and a young boy with crucifixes to wear round their necks. Had the partisan movement existed at the time many more Jews would have been saved, but this movement only emerged in our district in 1943. And so isolated Jews escaped by hiding in the forest, bush[es] or similar hiding places; of our close relatives --- no one.

Those who remained alive returned to Braslaw, claimed some of their possessions from the peasants, sold them, raised a little money and left Poland.

The graves of the martyrs, the "pits" as they are called in Braslaw, were fenced round with a few sticks and barbed wire . . .

This in brief is the story of Braslaw. It's no use crying --- on the contrary --- we must live to spite our enemies.

"Am Israel Chai!" ("Long live the people of Israel!")

Yours, Chayim

[Page 574]
What more can one add to the gruesome tale? What more to the bitter truth? Only the glowing words of our poet [Avraham] Shlonsky [in "A Vow"]:

> In the presence of eyes
> Which witnessed the slaughter . . .
> I have taken an oath: To remember it all.
> To remember, not once to forget!
> Forget not one thing to the last generation . . .

[Page 573]

[List of Gentiles Who Saved Jews in the Braslav/Braslaw Region]

We shall always remember our non-Jewish fellow countrymen from Braslav and country districts --- Poles, Russians and Belorussians --- the kind men and women who risked their lives, those of their families, and their possessions, by taking us in and harbouring us in secret, by sharing their bread with us, serving as eyes and ears for us, for ever on the alert against the Nazi murderers, and by so doing, saved our lives during the long years of terror.

They have earned a place of honour among the annals of our people.

[Page 572]

[The names are presented exactly as they appear in the original, including some not in alphabetical order.]

Aniszka, from the Zalesie village.

Arciszewski, Jaszka.

Awdakim, from Krulewska, near Jacielewszyna.

Barecki, Dr.

Bejnarowicz, Viktor, and his family, from the property Talje, in the vicinity of Jod, and the brother of Viktor, Paluk and brother-in-law Strenczewski.

Borin, war prisoner.

Bresko, Wasil, from the village Wiazowicz, and many others whose names have been forgotten.

Chatkewicz, from the Zalesie village.

Czesnowicki, Emila, Jadzia and Alfons from the village Kochaniszek.

Emilianowicz, Dr.

Gasul, Jaszka and his son Tonka, from Zamosz.

Gibowski, Alfons, from the village of Brodzienice.

Grajczonek, from the village of Pasielie.

Grodz, Anton and Mania, from the village of Mikowszczyzna.

Heskie, from the village Bordzienic.

Ivanow, Wasil and his daughter Irina from the village Zacierewia.

Josefa, from the village Podhajcy.

Kaminitzki, from the village Zorawowszczyzne.

Kajtan, from the village Suchobolcy.

Kapusta, Igor, from the village Badraki.

Kasan, from the village Dziaduszki.

Kizlo, Michal and his family, following the recommendation of the Kreslawa priest. The Kizlo family is from the village Szemelki.

Kole, from the village Wisialowe.

Kolkowski, Francis from the Zaborny-Gumny.

Kolkowski, Vincenty from the Belmont court.

Konachowicz, Zoska, Jurka, Anna, Jadwiga and Jadzia.

Korszak, from the village Puniszcze.

Kosciukewicz, Anton, from the village of Jod.

Kruczkowski, hospital worker.

Kujalowich, Martin, from the village of Jod.

Kurilowicz, from the village Winica.

Labun and Hanusia, from the village of Bisieniec.

Lagun, Albina, Agnieszka and Josef from the village Sizowszczyzna.

Lewsza, Dr.

Lipski, from the village Antonowa.

Markiewicz, Julian.

[Page 571]

Matul, Ignaz.

Mickewicz, from Zurawowszczyzne.

Milkewicz, from the village Berkowszczyzna.

Mindowski, director of the Forest Department.

Muraszka, Jan and his family from the village Glinowka.

Olszewska, Hanka.

Orlowski, Josef, from the village Zwirbli.

Pacewicz, Antony.

Petro, the priest from the Belmont church.

Perchorowicz, from the village Winica.

Pinkewicz, from the village of Jod.

Podoba, Boleslaw.

Podoba, Jan, from the village Jacielewszczyna.

Podoba, Kola, from the village Podoby.

Podoba, Saszka.

Popin, Nikolai.

Priest from the village Prysaroki.

Priest from the village Ikaznia.

Radziewicz, from Zalesie.

Rymkiewicz, Bronislaw, from the village Burzyna.

Sawicki, from the village Gawejkas.

Sewickaja, Josefa, with the help of the local priest from the village Urban.

Siedziukiewicz, Ignacy and Katia.

Siedziukiewicz, Michael, Helena, Maniek, Mietek and Wacia.

Sewelewicz, Mikita, from the village Dziaduszki.

Sklaniewicz, from the village Pupniszcze.

Skuriat, two brothers, from the village Dukiel.

Szakiel, Stanislaw, from the village Kumiesniki.

Szczerbinski, Danat, his wife Josefa and his cousin Wladek from the Kamionka village.

Tolstow, from the village near Ikazna.

Trumpel, from the village of Jod.

Trumpel, from the village of Polinowe.

Vanka, from the village Bujowszczyna.

Wasilewski, Aliosza, son of the Braslaw orthodox priest.

Woronow, of the village Zapolosie.

Zakrzewski, from the village Zalesie.

Zypruk, from Ferma.

[Page 570]

The sun sets in flames
'Tis almost gone from sight
So melts my dream
So comes the night . . .

[Page 569]

Silent, sunk in deep mourning, we, a handful --- the *Sh'erit Hapleita* of the extinct Braslaw community --- followed the wake of the bit of earth brought from the "pit," the mass grave in which our murdered loved ones lay buried.

With bowed heads, choking back the tears and the cry which fought to burst out from the depths of our anguished souls, we drew near the spot on the cemetery at Holon, to bring to burial this handful of earth.

Oh, Heavenly Father . . .

Is this all . . . ?!

Yes! This is all that is left of a living, bustling community, of a town and shtetlach, villages and yishuvim, which flourished and throbbed with teeming life.

Yitgadal veyitkadash sh'mei raba . . . [Magnified and sanctified is the great name of G-d] (from the Kaddish, Hebrew prayer for the dead)

We stood amid the symbolic graves all around, graves of countless Jewish communities that had shared a similar fate, and visions of blood and suffering swam before our eyes . . .

Yitgadal veyitkadash sh'mei raba . . .

Appendix 1: Speech Given by Moshe Bogomolski in 1986 on the Publication of the Memorial Book in Israel[1]

This appendix didn't appear in the original memorial book
that was published in Israel in Hebrew in 1986,
but is included here in the English version
of the book as a supplement.

Translated from the Hebrew by Laia Ben-Dov
Donated /Footnotes Added by Jeff Deitch

Given on 17 Sivan [June 24] 1986, the Memorial Day of the Destruction of the Jews of Braslav and the Surrounding Region

Comrades, friends and acquaintances from Braslav [Braslaw] and the nearby towns,

I stand before you agitated, awed and excited. In my hands is the book of testimony *Emesh Shoah.* As written in the Book of Job [30:3], *"B'chesed ub'kaffan galmud haorkim tziya, emesh shoah um'shoah"* ("In poverty and hunger, alone they flee to the desert, a place of darkness, a desert wasteland").

Today we give ourselves a book that tells something about the distant past of our town and our lives between the two world wars. The book is mainly a collection of testimonies from people who experienced every stage of hell under the Nazi occupation. Some of these people are here with us, and others, who aren't with us, have left us their important writings. May their memory be blessed!

For years we have wanted a book in which the horrific crimes that the Germans and their collaborators inflicted upon us would be told and documented. How they brutally tortured and degraded, how they uprooted people from their homes and livelihoods, their schools and study halls --- from every kind of organized life --- and exiled them to ghettos, labor camps and death camps. We also wanted to tell of acts of bravery and vengeance.

When you turned to me and asked that I take on the work of the book, it was as if you had harnessed me to a wagon that was overloaded and which I felt unable to pull. How could I, with my inadequate ability, contribute to this weighty, important subject? In my heart, I thought that no one could be found to treat it with the necessary care. But at my kibbutz there was a treasured institution --- the Ghetto Fighters' House --- that didn't disappoint, with members whose help could be relied on, with books and many other helpful materials. My friend Zvi Shner, of blessed memory, was the manager of the museum and had extensive knowledge of the Holocaust. At my request, he met with a group of people from our towns who had experienced all the stages of the Holocaust. As he searched and investigated, he was impressed by their stories, concluding that all of them should appear in written form. His opinion was shared by kibbutz members who read the material that had been gathered. In a letter to our organization, Mr. Shner later wrote, "I'm happy to inform you that the managers of the [Ghetto Fighters'] House decided, at their meeting on August 28, 1983, to include the memorial book of your community in our publication plan. We concluded that the testimonies and evidence you gathered make it possible to prepare the book, which will make a serious contribution to Holocaust literature. Together we'll act so that the communities of Braslav and the surrounding towns merit a literary monument that's honorable in form and rich in content."

I received additional support from Ariel Machnes, the book's [co-]editor, who wrote to me as follows: "What can I say to you, Moshe? For someone like me, who didn't experience the trauma of the Holocaust (and neither did my family), these testimonies are the most authentic documents, giving the deepest-possible feelings of pain and shock about what happened to us (individually and as a nation). In my opinion, the material is good from a literary viewpoint, in most cases it's fascinating and powerful, and it definitely deserves to be published in a book. I think that these pages of testimony express the experience of the Holocaust better than many scientific studies."

My friends! We live in a time when a murderer has become president and a doctoral degree is awarded to someone who tried to prove that no Holocaust took place, that no one intended to exterminate the Jews, that there were never any death camps or gas chambers, these were just an invention of the Jews.[2] At such a time, the testimonies in the book --- which record suffering, murder and death, battles, bravery, vengeance and which preserve the memory of the fallen --- show how grotesque are the faces of those who busy themselves with the despicable work of denial. In addition to literature denying the Holocaust, it's possible that someday we'll see the removal of monuments to the destruction of the Jews, leaving us without proof on the ground. Someone who immigrated to Israel from Braslav not too long ago warned of plans there to develop the place where the pits are located, by building factories or even residential neighborhoods, and why not?! Our old cemetery was turned into a public park.[3] If these things come to pass, the place and date of the destruction will remain only in the book.

I wish to highlight two incidents to do with the behavior of the Polish population: The first ones in our region to be destroyed were the Jews of Yod [Jod, about 25 kilometers southeast of Braslav]. This was during Hanukkah 1941 [on December 17, 1941]. In Yod, the cruel attitude of the Gentiles was striking. They volunteered to search for Jews in hiding; they treated the miserable victims brutally and took them happily to the pits. Prior to this, a rumor had spread that the Jews of Yod would be transferred to the ghetto in Sharkovshchina [Szarkowszczyna, about 18 kilometers southeast of Yod]. In response, the local Polish intelligentsia petitioned the Germans, claiming for themselves the right to exterminate the Jews of Yod and take their property.

The destruction of the Braslav Ghetto began on June 3, 1942, but before that the Jews were forced to gather in certain places, to be frightened and threatened with rumors of destruction. Niuta Kantor mentions this, writing, "Especially engraved in my memory is the time when groups of Poles gathered --- among whom were clerks, teachers and those called 'good youths' --- all of them dressed as if for a holiday, happy and joyful. Already at this time, they hoped to see our destruction. It's easy to understand what we were in their eyes on the day of our death. To them, the death of men, women and children was a game."

And something about the Judenrat [the Jewish Council, in Braslav], which served the Germans and met their demands. In its innocence, its members thought that they could succeed in saving the Jews. The head of the Judenrat was Yitzchak Mindel, the affluent former owner of an iron shop. In carrying out his duties, Mindel was assisted by the other members of the Judenrat and by the Jewish police. The Germans treated these Jewish servants like subhumans. As recalled by Chalvina [or Chlavna] Pinchov, ["]Once Mindel was called before the German officer of the town. A few of us awaited his return, to learn why he'd been sent for. When Mindel returned, he was as pale as whitewash. He fell onto the sofa, banged his head on the wall and cried out in a loud voice. After calming down, he told us that the German had been drunk and treated him in the most degrading way. He'd ordered him to kneel, crawl toward him and lick his boots, and perform another contemptible act that Mindel wouldn't describe.["]

More about the attitude of this German is told by Alexander Dagovitz: ["]I was sent with another youth to clean the house and office of the German officer. That day, a village head (soltys) came and requested that a deadline for supplying farm produce be delayed. On the spot, the German ordered his assistant to shoot the man. We took the body outside and returned to clean up the office, but the German merely asked for a cup of tea and kept on playing his phonograph.["]

The situation in the ghetto grew worse: There was hunger and poverty, disease, a lack of medicine and medical assistance. The Jews understood that these were methods of humiliation, to sap their will to live and their ability to fight back when the time of destruction arrived. People sent out to work didn't always return, and their fate was clear. To raise morale, Mindel would go around the ghetto saying that the Germans had promised him not to harm the Braslav Jews, who were good people and good workers for Germany.

Recently I received a letter from a Jew whose name is Leo Korb. He was from Ignalina (in Lithuania). [Ignalina was about 70 kilometers southwest of Braslav.] Attached to his letter was a section from a diary written by his father.[4] From the writing it's possible to understand the problems Mindel faced, his family and his behavior. Here I read from the diary: "I left the doctor and went to the head of the Judenrat, Mr. Mindel. There I met my good friend [Sasha] Tempelman. They invited me to lunch. The table was set nicely and a maid served them. I was amazed and said, 'What's this here? There's a war on. You're keeping a maid, and you still enjoy nice dishes like these?'" Mindel answered him ironically: "What do you think? Here it isn't like in Lithuania. Our *starosta* [mayor] is a very decent man, and even the Germans are different. We aren't afraid of them." The guest found this difficult [to believe] . . . ["]Do you think the destruction of the Jews of Lithuania, which was carried out by the Lithuanians, was started by them and not by an order from Hitler? You have eyes to see. Latvia too is already cleansed of Jews and a harsh wind is still blowing!["] But Mindel, the man wrote, was firm in his opinion and Tempelman also thought that the Jews of Braslav were living in comfort . . .

I return now to the true situation that prevailed in the [Braslav] ghetto: shortages, poverty, disease, murder and more. At this time, we organized groups of opposition. An organizer of one such group was Zusman Lubovitz --- he had led the Betar[5] movement in the town, and he had influence and a talent for persuasion. Yerachmiel Milutin, of blessed memory, described how another group was organized by a man of the Lehi[6] [sic] movement, Gershon Klioner. Klioner found a connection to his acquaintance, Alexi Vasilevski [Wasilewski], who was the son of the Pravoslavic [Eastern Orthodox] priest. The man was loyal to the Germans and worked for them in an important management position. Klioner knew that Vasilevski was [actually] anti-Nazi and was using his position to help the Russian soldiers who were fleeing German imprisonment. Vasilevski promised help to Klioner and even suggested supplying weapons. It was agreed that Yerachmiel Milutin would serve as their go-between. Klioner, a member of the Judenrat, did all of this without Mindel's knowledge.

All or most of the 95 young men [in Klioner's group or in Lubovitz's group] had been in the Polish army. Milutin, in his boldness, knew where the men who were recruited came from, and he also explained the desolation of a few of them [the meaning here is obscure]. When Mindel found out, he objected because he trusted in the promises of the Germans that nothing bad would happen to the Jews of Braslav. He even argued that if, G-d forbid, the Germans learned about the opposition that was being organized, this would be reason enough for them to destroy the ghetto. [Accordingly, nothing further was done.] On June 3, 1942, when the ghetto was attacked by a large, armed force and it was clear to all that the end was at hand, Mindel ran to the Germans and asked them to keep their promise, but they just laughed at him. He understood too late that he had lost the bloody game, and he asked that they kill him first.

During the days of destruction, heartbreaking scenes occurred. One man, who had fallen into the pit without being injured, wrote: "The crying and screams were heard in the surrounding villages; only G-d did not hear us."

People who succeeded in fleeing the destruction wandered about with absolutely nothing. The Germans needed a work force and promised that they wouldn't be harmed, using them to gather bodies from the streets and yards. Later a second ghetto was established for them [in Braslav], and the remaining Jews from Opsa [18 kilometers to the southwest] were moved to them.

This second ghetto existed for about half a year. The day before Purim, 1943 [on March 19, 1943] it was liquidated, and again the inmates were taken to the pits and murdered. There were those who said, "We won't be taken alive." In one house, the tailor Melech Munitz prepared a bucket of whitewash. When the first German broke through the door of the house, Melech poured the whitewash into his eyes and grabbed the rifle[7] from his hands. He shot at the Germans and the police, killing and wounding them, until he was caught and murdered. Gentiles who witnessed the event praised his bravery and called him a hero.

That same day, on the same morning, in a house in the ghetto, a German knocked on the window and ordered the people to come outside. Leizer Biliak shot through the window and killed the German. Police attacked the house and threw grenades inside. The house went up in flames. Leizer managed to kill a policeman, wounded another, jumped over the fence and managed to escape his pursuers. He wandered for a long time, hiding in various places. Signs put up by the

Germans promised a reward to whoever turned him in. When he approached a Gentile acquaintance to ask for shelter, he was turned over to the Germans and killed. Partisans from Braslav searched for the informers, located them and killed them in their house. Leizer and Melech! You bear with honor the words "Jewish fighter." May all of them have strength like you.

There are hair-raising stories of the few who remained alive, of those who wandered from village to village and from Gentile to Gentile, begging for a place to sleep and a slice of bread; of those who joined the partisans and took revenge on the Germans and their collaborators.

We've already spoken of the fact that the majority of the local population was hostile to the Jews, with many of them even helping the Germans in the work of destruction. A few of them were punished. Especially skilled at locating these criminals were Benyamin Movshenzon, Yerachmiel Milutin and Niuta Kantor. But we must remember well that among the Gentiles there were also a few individuals who risked their lives, the lives of their families and all they possessed, and who rescued Jews from certain death. We will never forget them. In the book, we tell of their deeds and their bravery.

The fighters deserve special appreciation. Alone and in groups, they joined the partisans, attacked the enemy and disrupted the Germans' war plans. The diary of a German officer named Boshla[?] describes the partisans like this: "There was no living soul in sight, but the shadow of the avengers could be felt everywhere in the forests and bogs. These were the partisans. Suddenly, as if they came up from under the ground, they fell upon us, tearing and cutting us to pieces, and then vanishing like demons. These avengers persecute us at every step, and there's no rescue from them. Hell! I can't fight against spirit-ghosts from the forests."

After the region was liberated [around July 1944], the partisans joined the battle units of the Red Army and continued to fight the enemy. Many of them fell in battle; those who reached the longed-for day of victory were decorated with medals of excellence and letters of thanks. For example, in a letter to friends Peretz Levin wrote: "Greetings from the front. We're advancing, pursuing the Germans. The enemy's land is burning. We're taking revenge, we're winning, we march forward proudly. I feel good --- I'm taking part in destroying the enemy."

Many pages of the book are dedicated to preserving the memory of our dear ones who were killed cruelly in the place where they lived, in deportations, in the death camps and in battle. The book is dedicated to them and to their memory.

My friends! Six years ago today, we decided on a book. Six years is a long time, but it isn't too much time for a book such as this, more so when all work was done by volunteers. The book has 640 pages and is rich in testimonies and records, photographs, documents and maps. The book contains a list of dozens of Gentiles who deserve an honored place in the list of the Righteous among the Nations.

I have no words to express to you my satisfaction and thanks for putting your confidence in me and appointing me.

I thank the members of the committee and the members of the staff, who were with me from the first day until the book's publication.

A special thanks to Rina Klinov and Ariel Machnes, editors of the book.

Thank you to the publishing house Hakibbutz Hameuchad, which has given us a beautiful book.

My thanks to the members and workers in this house --- the Ghetto Fighters' House --- for the great help of the members. You helped me with everything and answered all of my requests.

Thank you to everyone.

June 24, 1986

Footnotes:
1. Mr. Bogomolski, a member of the Ghetto Fighters' House kibbutz near Acre, Israel, was a former resident of Braslav. The text of his speech, in Hebrew, is in the archive of the Ghetto Fighters' House museum. The speech was handwritten, and some parts of it were hard to read.

    The speech was given in 1986, at the time of publication in Israel of this memorial book. Mr. Bogomolski, a key member of the book's production committee, was involved in gathering, editing and translating the material in the book.

2.   This refers to Kurt Waldheim, who had been elected president of Austria earlier in June 1986, despite having lied about his record in the German army during World War II. And to Henri Roques, a Frenchman who in 1985 had received a doctoral degree from the University of Nantes for a paper that questioned accounts of the gassing of Jews at Belzec and Treblinka. Waldheim was subsequently declared *persona non grata* by the United States and many other countries, and the degree that Roques received was later revoked.

3.   "The pits" refers to the place just to the north of Braslav where several thousand Jews were massacred in June 1942 and March 1943; this site has been preserved and also contains Braslav's postwar Jewish cemetery. (It's number 30 in the map of Braslav on pages 20-21 of this memorial book.) "The old cemetery" refers to Braslav's prewar Jewish cemetery in the western part of town, which has not been preserved. (It's number 11 in the map of Braslav on pages 20-21 of this memorial book.)

4.   The "father" might refer to Yerachmiel Korb of Ignalina, who left extensive accounts of his experiences during the war. He's known to have had a son named Leon (also called Arieh-Leib).

5.   The youth section of the Revisionist Zionist movement, led by Vladimir Jabotinsky, which advocated military training for defense and Jewish immigration to Palestine.

6.   Lehi was a militant Zionist paramilitary organization that had been founded in Palestine in 1940. It sought to expel the British from Palestine, achieve unrestricted immigration of Jews to Palestine, and establish a Jewish state. Its policies were thus opposed to those of Jabotinsky, who believed that working with the British during World War II would better serve the Zionist movement.

7.   The account about Melech Munitz in the memorial book says the weapon was a pistol, not a rifle.

Appendix 2: Map of Yod [Jod/Jody/Iody]

This appendix didn't appear in the original memorial book
that was published in Israel in Hebrew in 1986,
but is included here in the English version
of the book as a supplement.

This map of Yod during the interwar years (ca. 1921-39), as recalled from memory, appeared in *From Victims to Victors*, published in Canada in 1992 by Peter Silverman, David Smuschkowitz and Peter Smuszkowicz. The map is reproduced here courtesy of the publisher, The Canadian Society for Yad Vashem.

Appendix 3: Map and Photos of Dubina [Dubene/Dubinovo/Dubinowo]

This appendix didn't appear in the original memorial book
that was published in Israel in Hebrew in 1986,
but is included here in the English version
of the book as a supplement.

I. Map of Dubina in 1941 (Drawn in 1992 by Mira Lotz)

This map was translated from the Hebrew by Laia Ben-Dov, and donated by Jeff Deitch.

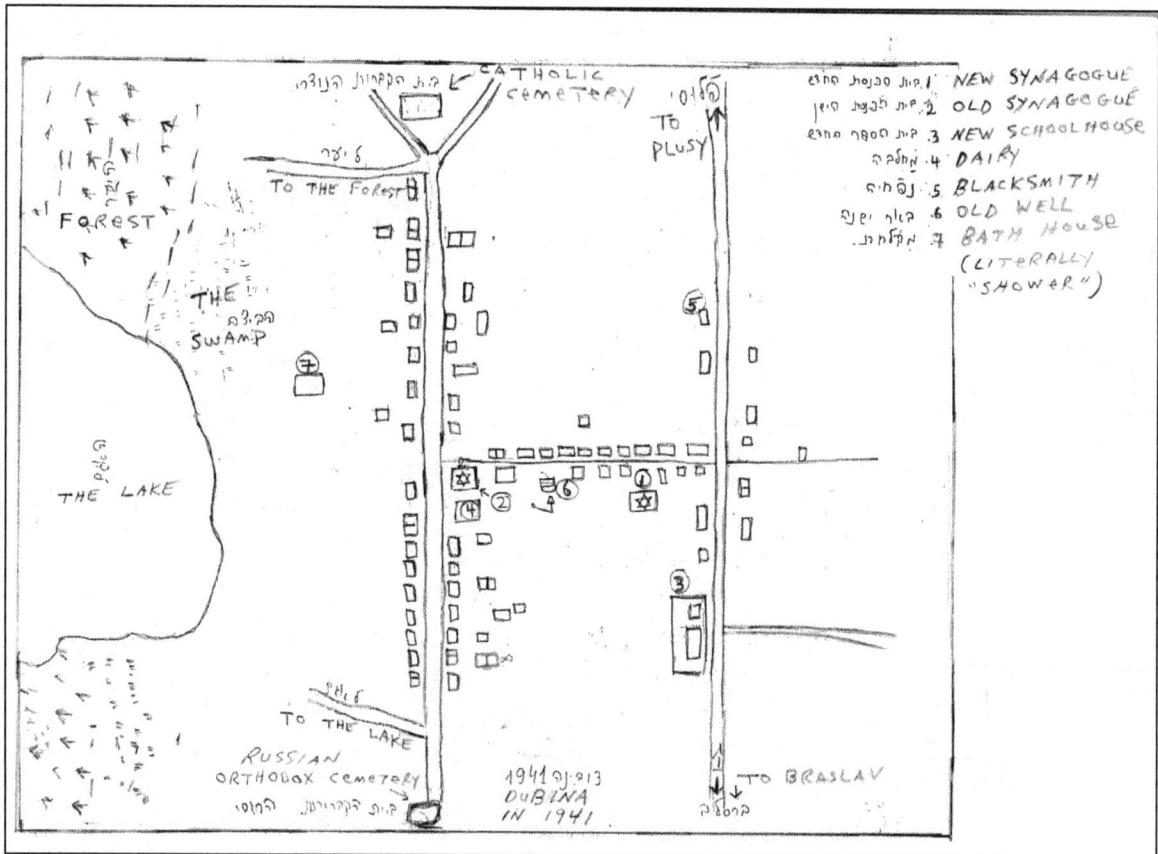

**The map was drawn from memory in 1992 by former resident of Dubina Mira Lotz
and kindly gifted to the donor.**

II. Photos of Dubina

This section contains six photos of the Jewish farming colony at Dubina (a.k.a. Dubinovo, then in Poland) from ORT, an organization that provided financial support to the colony for a time in the late 1920s-early 1930s. The photos, estimated to have been taken ca. 1927-30, are reproduced here courtesy of the World ORT Archive.

ORT (Obshchestvo Remeslennogo i zemledelcheskogo Truda, or the Society for Trades and Agricultural Labor) was founded in St. Petersburg, Russia in 1880 to provide employable skills for Russia's impoverished Jews. After 1917 ORT began expanding its activities to other European countries, opening offices in various cities, and in 1921 a World ORT Union was established in Berlin. The American ORT Society was formed in the United States by 1922, and in 1933 the union's Berlin office relocated to Paris and then Geneva, while ORT's offices in the USSR were shut down in 1938.

Today, although legally based in Switzerland, World ORT operates from offices in London, continuing to carry out education and training driven by Jewish values, and reaching 300,000 people a year in more than 30 countries.

**The agricultural cooperative council in Dubinovo, with the colony's rabbi
seated in the middle (Photo Ref. No. Psa 1964, courtesy of World ORT Archive).
The figures were unidentified by World ORT, but the rabbi is presumed to be Rabbi David Minkin.
Seated at far right might be the council secretary, David Blacher.
Standing at far right might be the visiting ORT specialist, I. Epstein.**

**House of a Jewish farmer in Dubinovo
(Photo Ref. No. Psa 1334, courtesy of World ORT Archive)**

Field workers harvesting hay in Dubinovo
(Photo Ref. No. Psa 1121, courtesy of World ORT Archive)

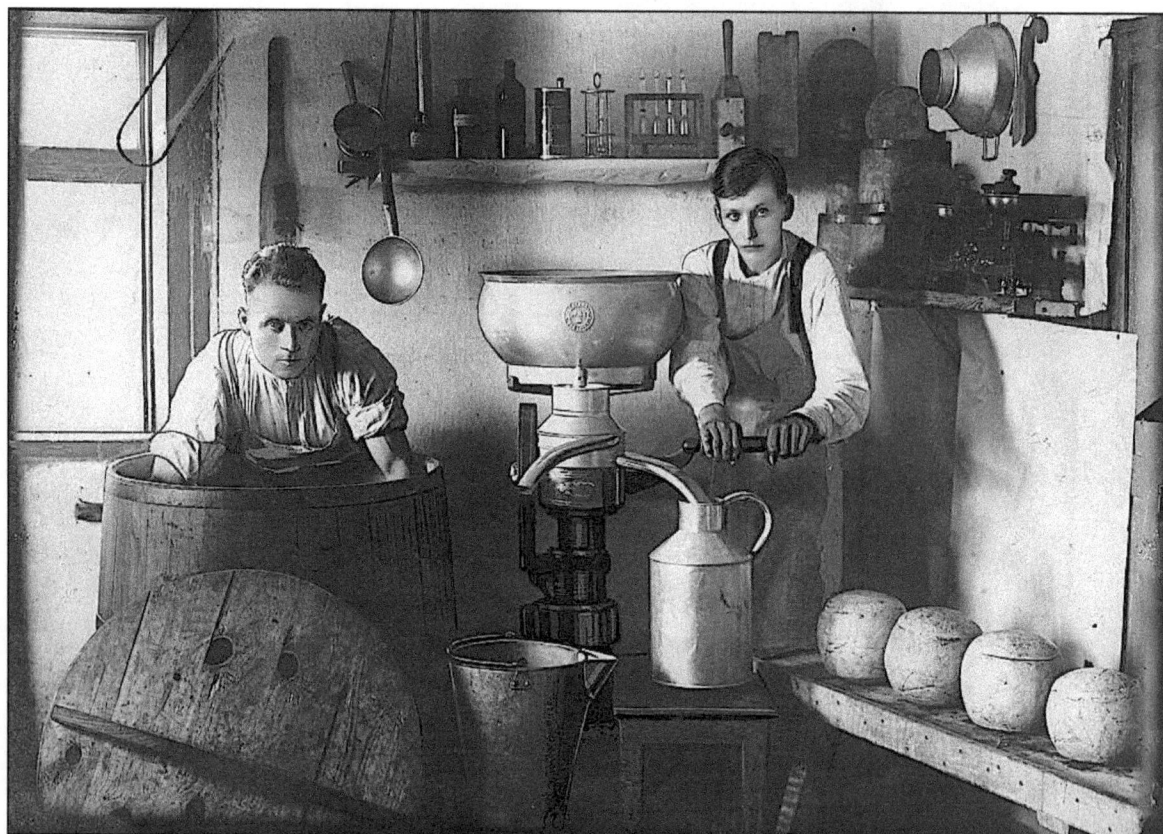

At the dairy in Dubinovo
(Photo Ref. No. Psa 1333, courtesy of World ORT Archive)

ORT agronomist (I. Epstein?) teaching children in Dubinovo
(Photo Ref. No. Psa 1336, courtesy of World ORT Archive)

A herd grazing in Dubinovo
(Photo Ref. No. Psa 1332, courtesy of World ORT Archive)

Appendix 4: Background on Jewish Partisans in Belarus

This appendix didn't appear in the original memorial book
that was published in Israel in Hebrew in 1986,
but is included here in the English version
of the book as a supplement.

By Jeff Deitch

I. Introduction

A number of survivor accounts in the memorial book mentioned joining the partisan struggle against the Nazis and their collaborators. In an attempt to learn more about partisan activity in what's now western Belarus/eastern Lithuania, a range of sources were consulted. The background gathered, although incomplete, is presented here for anyone seeking an overview of Jewish partisans in the region. Some of the groups that appear below were mentioned in parts of the memorial book, and many were listed in the map on page 438.

Making sense of the partisan groups is a challenge. During the war the groups were formed, disappeared, merged with other units and/or changed their names; record-keeping wasn't a priority. Some groups had informal names (often honoring their commanders) that differed from their official names, while their commanders often used both a real name and an alias, either of which could be employed to describe the group they commanded. English-language sources often differed in their descriptions, especially in estimates of partisan strength, geographical distances, and the expanse of forests used by the partisans. Spelling of names often varied, depending on the source language and the document consulted. Terms such as unit, detachment, battalion, regiment, brigade and division were often used interchangeably. Accordingly, information on partisan groups was often conflicting and confusing. The information below may contain some errors of fact/interpretation.

Sources:
Ghetto and Forest (1971 in Yiddish), by Moshe Shutan; English translation published in 2005
The Jewish Resistance (1977), by Lester Eckman and Chaim Lazar
The Partisan (1979), by Yitzhak Arad
Ghetto in Flames (1982), by Yitzhak Arad
Fighting Back: Lithuanian Jewry's Armed Resistance to the Nazis, 1941-1945 (1985), by Dov Levin, translated from the Hebrew
From Victims to Victors (1992), by David Smuschkowitz, Peter Silverman and Peter Smuszkowicz
Fugitives of the Forest (1998), by Allan Levine
There Once Was a World: A 900-Year Chronicle of the Shtetl of Eishyshok (1998), by Yaffa Eliach
Hitler's White Russians (2003), by Antonio Muñoz and Dr. Oleg Romanko
In the Shadow of the Red Banner: Soviet Jews in the War against Nazi Germany (2010), by Yitzhak Arad
Heroism in the Forest: The Jewish Partisans of Belarus (2013), by Zeev Barmatz, translated from the Hebrew
Website of the State Archives of Belarus

For the sake of convenience, the region described below is called Belarus (with boundaries corresponding to the Belarus of today, not the Belorussian SSR of 1939). It should be kept in mind that before 1939 the western part what's now Belarus belonged to eastern Poland. After World War II, the boundaries were shifted: Parts of what had been eastern Poland became part of Belarus, and Poland was compensated with parts of eastern Germany.

II. General Background

Serving as a partisan meant belonging to an irregular military unit formed to resist enemy occupation, fighting behind the front lines. Partisan activity against the Axis Powers wasn't limited to Belarus, taking place also in countries such as Yugoslavia, Italy and France. But Belarus was the largest center of partisan warfare in Europe, for a number of reasons. These included the brutality with which the local populace was treated (in particular, the Jewish population), the region's location in the rear of the German armies that were battling the Soviet armies in a fight to the death, and the fact that Belarus was densely wooded, with forests stretching for hundreds of kilometers.

The number of partisan units established in Belarus in the course of the war has been estimated at a minimum of around 200. The number of partisans in Belarus is said to have grown from some 12,000 in August 1941 to 270,000 by June 1944 (when much of the region was liberated and many partisan units were either disbanded or merged with the Soviet army). Other estimates of the number of partisan units and partisans in Belarus range higher, up to 437 units or more and 370,000, respectively. The number of partisan units and partisan fighters differs according to the source.

It's difficult to determine how many of the partisans in the USSR were Jews; a rough estimate is 10%. For example, sources judged that by summer 1943 there were more than 200,000 men and women in the Soviet partisan movement across the western territories of the USSR, not just in Belarus --- and of these, about 20,000 (10%) were Jews. Some partisan units had a large number of Jews, others had few; it depended on the group. Besides the partisans, it's estimated that half a million Jews served in the Soviet Army; nearly 200,000 of them fell in battle, and 60,772 were decorated.[1]

Partisan activity in Belarus appears to have been relatively small in 1941-42, increasing in scale in 1943-44. It has been claimed that the Soviet authorities in Moscow were at first suspicious of partisan groups formed by the civilian population (as opposed to partisan groups that originated with its own soldiers), and the Soviet authorities didn't begin to encourage partisan activity by civilians on a wide scale until late 1942. With the German defeat at Stalingrad in February 1943, the Germans were thereafter on the defensive. In 1943-44 in particular, as stronger links to the Soviet army were established and Soviet aid to the partisans increased, Soviet control of the groups tightened. Many partisan groups had been Soviet to begin with, but others had formed spontaneously and came under Soviet control only later. Soviet control tended to dilute the Jewishness of a partisan group; promoting Jewish solidarity wasn't a Soviet priority, and the Soviet partisan movement was organized by territory, not nationality. On the other hand, as organization and discipline improved in 1943-44, incidents of anti-Semitism within the Soviet partisan ranks tended to decrease.

By 1943 or 1944, a Soviet partisan brigade could range from 300-2,000 fighters. At full strength, a well-established brigade might have 4-5 detachments of 50-200 fighters each [source: *Fugitives of the Forest*]. But the numbers varied by unit, reflecting the constantly changing conditions.

The partisan camps were generally in the forests. In some cases, if a partisan commander permitted it, attached to these camps were family camps, often consisting of Jews or others who had fled to the forests: the spouses, parents or children of the partisan fighters. Major forest areas, mentioned in a number of sources, were the Kozian/Koziany forest, the Nacha forest, the Naliboki forest, the Narach/Naroch forest, and the Rudnicki forest (see Section VI below). These were described as stretching for hundreds of square kilometers or more, depending on the source. The forests were used as bases for partisan expeditions to targets outside the forests, such as railway lines, supply depots and so on.

From 1943 to mid-1944, there were partisan sabotage actions taking place behind German lines nearly every week. In the Bryansk region of western Russia, from May 1942-April 1943 there were 1,109 railway sabotage actions, an average of more than 90 per month. More than half were judged to have been successful. The raids on train tracks, as well as raids on supply depots and other targets, forced the Germans to cancel night transports by train --- reducing their rail traffic to the front --- and to divert resources and men to defend against the partisans and repair the destruction.

Soviet sources credit the partisans in Belarus for derailing 11,000-12,000 steam engines and train carriages and 34 armored trains, destroying 29 railway stations and 948 headquarters/garrisons, destroying or damaging 819 rail bridges, and destroying more than 7,300 kilometers of phone and telegraph lines as well as thousands of kilometers of railway tracks, besides destroying tanks, armored vehicles and military depots. Many German soldiers and their collaborators were killed. German officials were also assassinated, including in September 1943 Wilhelm Kube, the leader of the occupation government in Belarus.

The Germans depended on the rails in Belarus and Russia, because the road network was in terrible condition. The damage inflicted by the partisans behind German lines was thus a serious problem. Although the partisan activity couldn't be called decisive in terms of winning the war --- since the Soviet/Western armies would have defeated the Germans in any case --- it was important in terms of weakening the enemy and striking back, and helping to bring the war to a faster conclusion.

From time to time, the Germans and their collaborators would launch attacks on the forests. A major one took place in July-August 1943, when the Germans launched Operation Hermann against the Naliboki forest with tens of thousands of soldiers. When attacked, the partisans would generally attempt to escape the encirclement in small groups and flee to another forest, reuniting and returning after the German sweep had ended. As a result, partisan groups tended to move back and forth between the major forests in the region.

Partisan groups sometimes fought each other, even as each of them battled the Germans. This was due to animosity between the Soviet-led groups and the anti-Communist, Polish nationalist-led groups, which complicated the situation for Jews even further. Another problem for Jews was that generally a Jew would be accepted into the ranks of Soviet partisans only if he brought a weapon into the group, whereas a non-Jew (such as a local peasant or an escapee from a prisoner of war camp) was accepted without a weapon.

The attrition rate for Soviet and Jewish partisans was said to be 30%-50%, depending on the group.

A U.S. army study of the Soviet partisan movement has called the partisans in Belarus the "greatest irregular resistance movement in the history of warfare" (*The Soviet Partisan Movement, 1941-1944*, written by Edgar M. Howell and published in 1956). Despite this, the partisan movement in Belarus --- together with Jewish partisan fighters' active resistance against their oppressors --- has received less attention in the English-speaking world than it deserves.

III. Some of the Many Partisan Units in/around Belarus, and a Few Prominent Individuals

ANTONOV: A partisan group mentioned on pages 157 and 270 of the memorial book as operating in the Braslav region. Presumably it was the Antonov detachment of the Shirokov brigade, which operated in the region south of Braslav.

ARIOVITZ, ELIAHU/ELKE (a.k.a. Todras/The Cossack): A Jew from Radun and member of Betar before the war, he established an **independent group of Jewish partisans** in the Nacha forest in summer 1942, after the Radun Ghetto had been massacred. This included a family camp. Many in his group were Jewish refugees from Eishyshok, Radun, Nacha and Dogalishok. After the Soviet-led Leninsky Komsomol brigade under Stankevich established itself in the Nacha forest in early 1943, some of Ariovitz's men joined that brigade. Despite enjoying good relations with Stankevich, in June 1943 Ariovitz was murdered by Communist partisans. Later in June, an assault on the Nacha forest by the Germans and their collaborators is said to have wiped out about three-quarters of his camp, killing about 70 people, mainly civilians [*There Once Was a World*].

ATLAS UNIT: A **Jewish** group came together in July 1942 under Dr. Yeheskel Atlas, initially numbering some 120 Jewish survivors from the Derechin Ghetto, which had just been liquidated. After attacking the Germans/Lithuanians in Derechin in August, killing 44 policemen, Dr. Atlas was allowed to form his own partisan group, officially under the authority of a Soviet partisan commander named Bulat. Dr. Atlas's second in command was Eliyahu Kowienski. Thereafter, the Atlas unit carried out attacks on German trains.

This prompted an attack on the unit by the Germans and their collaborators in the woods near the Schara River.

Dr. Atlas took in families but didn't have the resources to care for them as the Bielski group had done (see Bielski below); thus, many of the families died. In December 1942, the Germans attacked again around the village of Wielka Wola and Dr. Atlas was killed; another Jewish partisan leader, Hirsh Kaplinski, died in the same engagement [*Fugitives of the Forest*].

BAZDERSKI PARTISAN GROUP [*Heroism in the Forest*].

BERIA DETACHMENT (named for Lavrenti Beria, a member of the Soviet government): Partisan group that operated in the Baranovichi region (southwest Belarus) in 1943-44 [State Archives of Belarus].

BIELSKI PARTISAN BATTALION: Included many **Jewish partisans**; formed in late 1941 and commanded by Tuvia Bielski, who was from a village near Novogrudok, after the December 8, 1941 Aktion in Novogrudok that killed 4,000 Jews, after which several Bielski brothers fled to the forest. By March 1942, the group comprised 13 Jews. Around spring/summer 1942, a Gentile named Konstanty Kozlowski turned his farmhouse into a link between Jews escaping from the Novogrudok Ghetto and the Bielskis, enabling the group to grow. In summer 1942, the group was organized into an official Soviet-style *otriad* (detachment), called the Zhukov *otriad*; Tuvia Bielski was the commander, his brother Asael Bielski was deputy, and their brother Zus/Alexander Bielski was head of intelligence. However, the name Zhukov wasn't recognized by the Soviet partisan headquarters [*Fugitives of the Forest*]. A fourth brother, Aron/Arshik, also served with the group.

By October 1942, the Bielski camp had approximately 200 people and Tuvia Bielski had defused a problem with a Lt. Panchenko over the Jews' taking of food from peasants; thereafter, the two leaders (Bielski and Panchenko) worked well together. By autumn 1942, Bielski had decided to accept any Jewish refugee who came to him. Around this time, it appears that his group was in the Zabielowo forest south of Ivia/Iwje. In late 1942, a mission saved about 150 Jews from the Ivia Ghetto north of Novogrudok. In December 1942, the group heard rumors of an upcoming German offensive and moved closer to Ivia; then it returned to the Zabielowo forest. On the way, the Germans attacked a small group of Bielski's family and killed his wife and nine others [*Fugitives of the Forest*].

By early 1943, the group had approximately 300 people around the Zabielowo forest. Shortly afterward, the police followed a trail of animal blood back to the camp and attacked it. Then in the spring, Bielski's third wife's father-in-law and nine others were betrayed by a peasant; the peasant and family were killed. In the early summer 1943, Bielski moved 600 people from the Novogrudok area to the Naliboki forest without being caught. The Soviet partisans there, after some negotiation, allowed them to enter, and they stopped next to Lake Kroman [*Fugitives of the Forest*].

In July-August 1943, the Germans launched Operation Hermann against the Naliboki forest with tens of thousands of soldiers. Instead of leaving the forest, the partisans moved deeper into it, 12 kilometers north, to an island called Kranaya Gorka. They had to walk neck deep through swamps to the island, where they remained without food for 10 days. Then they moved to Jasinowo forest in groups of 40-60 [*Fugitives of the Forest*].

In September 1943, the Soviet headquarters ordered Jewish civilians to return to the Naliboki forest as part of the Kalinin unit, an order that was apparently obeyed. All of the young Jews were to join the Soviet-led Ordzonikidze unit. This left Bielski with about 180 fighters, presumably when they returned to Naliboki forest. By mid-September, the group had 1,000+ Jews; it was especially at this time that many workshops were established within the group [*Fugitives of the Forest*].

After September 1943, the group received support from Belarusian commander Vasily Chernyshev (a.k.a. General Platon) [*Fugitives of the Forest*].

Sometime in late 1943, a man named Israel Kessler was tried and executed for challenging Bielski's authority and lying about him [*Fugitives of the Forest*].

By this time, the Bielski family camp in the Naliboki forest was called Jerusalem; the local peasants called it "Jew town." [*Fugitives of the Forest*]. Including family groups, eventually it totaled some 1,200 people in the forests, a haven for Jews. People came to it mainly from the Lida and Ivia ghettos. It had good relations with the Zorin Jewish partisan group (see Zorin unit), which was also in the Naliboki forest and not far away [*Heroism in the Forest*].

In July 1944, some 1,200 Jews in the Bielski camp began moving back to Novogrudok; the Soviets ordered Bielski to destroy his camp to prevent anti-Communists from using it in the future; at this time, Bielski or someone else killed a Jew named Polonecki because of a disagreement about what could be taken. Later, Tuvia Bielski and his brother Zus fled to Romania with their wives after learning that the Soviet NKVD wished to question them; eventually they reached Palestine and in 1956 they moved to New York City. Their brother Aron also immigrated to Palestine and then the United States. Their brother Asael died fighting the Germans near the war's end.

During its existence, the Bielski camp lost only about 50 of its 1,200 people, an incredible accomplishment. For two or so years, Bielski had had to find food for hundreds of people. In 1998, the 1,150 survivors had more than 13,000 descendants [*Fugitives of the Forest*].

BILOV: Some partisan group mentioned on page 270 of the memorial book as operating in the Braslav region.

BOLAK BATTALION: Partisan unit; in it, a Russian named Kolya Konoplov commanded a **Jewish** company [*Heroism in the Forest*]. This might be the same unit as the one led by Pavel Bulak, a local Belarusian communist near Slonim; in early 1942 it had about 320 fighters [*Fugitives of the Forest*].

BONDARENKO PARTISAN GROUP: Mentioned on page 269 of the memorial book.

BORBA: Partisan unit organized in the forests near Kurenitz by Isaac Einbinder, Ida Galperstein/ Golferstein, Yacob Alperowitz and others. It later joined the Dyadya Kolya (Uncle Kolya) unit [*The Jewish Resistance*]. See the Rudnicki forest.

BUDYONI UNIT OF THE PONOMARENKO BRIGADE: Partisan unit founded sometime after November 1941 by Semyon Ganzenko after he escaped from a POW camp near the Minsk Ghetto [*Heroism in the Forest*].

BULBA: Partisan group that contained **Jews** from Eishyshok [*Heroism in the Forest*].

BYELORUSSIAN BRIGADE NO. 4 OF BOZIKIN (or Bazikin; a.k.a. the Fourth Belorussian Brigade): Mentioned in the memorial book's map on page 438. Contained the Sazykin unit, which operated in the Kazian and Kruki forests. It was also said to operate around Braslav, Druya, Yod/Jody, Miory, Sharkovshchitzna, Disna, Glubokoye and Pogost. Page 270 of the memorial book also mentioned a Bazikin unit operating the Braslav region.

A number of the fighters appear to have been **Jewish**. These included Shimon and Meyer Goldin, Eliahu Korob, Abba and Mayer Kozliner, Leib and Zalman-Ber Chepelevitz, Zusman Shneider, Shaul Nechamchen, Chin, Cymer, the Lifshin brothers, the Berzone brothers, the Estrin brothers, and Moshela Hoffman [*The Jewish Resistance*]. Page 291 of the memorial book also said that 80 of 500 partisans in the brigade were Jewish.

CHAPAEV UNIT (official name, in honor of Vasily Chapaev, a hero of the Russian Civil War): Partisan group that operated in various regions of Belarus. By spring 1942 it had about 60 partisans, commanded by a man named Sidiakin or Sediakin, a.k.a. "Yasnoya Moria" (Clear Sea). Early on, the group was joined by **five Jews** who escaped to the forests in summer 1942. Eventually it numbered about 400 fighters [*Heroism in the Forest*]. A prominent member was Vaska the Black, who'd been a partisan in the forest since the beginning of 1942 [Arad].

The unit was said to have been organized in July 1942 by a man named Semiayin in the Yod/Jody-Koziany forest, initially consisting mostly of Russian former prisoners of war; it was called the Chapaev unit of the Voroshilov brigade [*From Victims to Victors*].

In May 1943, Yitzhak Arad was in this unit in the Koziany forest [*Fugitives of the Forest*].

In autumn 1943, Yitzhak Arad found in the Koziany forest a small family camp that was home to six families from Yod/Jody, 20 people; they had one rifle and one revolver among them. The camp had been established a year earlier for 15 families that had escaped from Yod/Jody, but half of the group had died during the winter from Nazi attacks and sickness. Soviet partisans had taken some of their supplies, and the Spartak Brigade (see below) wasn't helping them [*Fugitives of the Forest*].

Another prominent fighter in the unit was Leibke Volak [*Ghetto and Forest*]. For more on him, see the Spartak brigade.

As part of the Voroshilov battalion, the Chapaev unit was under the overall command of Fyodor Markov (see Markov brigade).

CHERNIGOVSKY'S PARTISAN DIVISION: Partisan group of Fyodorov Chernigovsky [*Heroism in the Forest*].

CHKALOV BRIGADE (named for Valery Chkalov, a celebrated, deceased Soviet test pilot): Partisan brigade that operated in the Baranovichi region (southwest Belarus) in 1942-44 [State Archives of Belarus]. A brigade of 120 men commanded by Gribenov, a Soviet officer who patrolled the forest near Horodok [*Heroism in the Forest*]. Ca. July 1942, merged with a 50-man group commanded by the **Jewish Lidsky brothers** that had escaped from the Horodok Ghetto (which had been liquidated) and was hiding in the Ivenets forest [*Heroism in the Forest*]. At end-1942, the Germans attacked the forest. In December 1942, the Chkalov brigade, including the Jews, attacked German-held Horodok.

DARZINSKI UNIT OF THE PRONZA BRIGADE: Partisan group [*Heroism in the Forest*].

DEATH TO FASCISM (SMERT FASHIZMU): Partisan group that operated in Minsk region (central Belarus) in 1942-44 [State Archives of Belarus]. See the Rudnicki forest.

DESTROYER (ISTREBITEL): partisan: Brigade formed in the Naroch forest around late 1943; included some **Jews** [Arad/*Ghetto in Flames*].

DETACHMENT 4: Partisan group mentioned in the memorial book's map on page 438.

DJALGIRIS: Partisan group of pro-Soviet Lithuanian paratroopers who established a base of operations in the Kozian forest in spring 1943. The Djalgiris group included some **Jews**.

From approximately July 1943, Djalgiris was commanded by Tadeus/Motiejus Shumauskas/Sumauskas (a.k.a. Kasimir/Kazimieras) and his Jewish Lithuanian-Jewish Communist deputy, Henoch/Henrik Ziman (a.k.a. Yurgis). Apparently, this was in the Naroch forest [*Fugitives of the Forest*]. Ziman had been appointed deputy chief of staff of the Lithuanian partisan movement in November 1942. Earlier, in Lithuania during the Soviet occupation in 1940-41, he'd worked to stamp out Zionism [*Fugitives of the Forest*].)

Ziman now allied with the Voroshilov unit and turned to Jewish Zionists and Communists from Vilna [*Fugitives of the Forest*]. Around August 1943, Markov (see below; commander of the Voroshilov battalion) allowed Josef Glazman and 20 of his fighters to leave the Nekama partisan group and join Ziman's Lithuanian group [*Fugitives of the Forest*].

The group became a brigade, and one unit of it was called Vilnius (24 fighters commanded by S. Apivala) sent to the Hoduchishki forest. Yitzhak Arad was part of this unit [Arad]. The brigade was also informally called the Lithuanian brigade [*The Jewish Resistance*].

In late September/early October 1943, a group led by Sumauskas/Kazimieras left the Naroch forest for the Kozian forest ahead of the German sweep [*Fugitives of the Forest*].

Around October 1943, Ziman/Yurgis arrived from the Naroch forest to take charge of the Soviet-Lithuanian units in the Rudnicki forest [*Fugitives of the Forest*; Arad/*Ghetto in Flames* said September 1943].

Ziman led another part of the brigade to the Naroch forest; they blew up train lines near the Cerklishki forest [Arad]. Around November 1943, part of the Vilnius group moved to the Naroch forest, which was safer from the Germans [Arad]. By April

1944, it had some 150 fighters and moved to the Lintup-Hoduchishki-Sventzion region (northwest Belarus/eastern Lithuania). In June 1944, as the Soviet army advanced, it was combined with the Kostas Kalinauskas brigade [Arad].

On October 9, 1943 (around the time of Yom Kippur), Josef Glazman and many of his men were ambushed by the Germans as they tried to destroy the railroad to Polotsk; one girl survived [*The Jewish Resistance*].

DOVATOR (named for General Lev Dovator, a Soviet general who had been killed in action in 1941): Partisan group that operated in the Vileika region (north Belarus) in 1943-44 [State Archives of Belarus].

DUNAEV (also called Boevoi): Partisan group that operated in the Bialystok region (now northeast Poland) in 1942-44 [State Archives of Belarus].

DYADYA (UNCLE) BATTALION: Some kind of partisan group [*Heroism in the Forest*].

DYADYA KOLYA (UNCLE-KOLYA) DIVISION: Partisan group mentioned in the memorial book's map on page 438. Operated in the forests of Pleshnitz [*The Jewish Resistance*].

DYADYA MISHA (UNCLE MISHA): Partisan battalion [*Heroism in the Forest*]. **Jewish partisan unit** operated by civil engineer Misha Gildenman of Korets after many Korets Jews had been killed. In September 1942, Gildenman, his son and about 16 other Jews fled Korets, setting up camp in the forest north of Sarny in the Polesie region. Gildenman's group included a group of Klesov Jews led by Alexander Kutz. In December 1942, they attacked the town of Rozvashev, north of Rovno. Eventually the group linked up with a Soviet partisan brigade led by General Aleksander Saburov (whose group had grown from 15 fighters in September 1941 to 2,800 men by May 1942). In autumn 1943, these joined the Kovpak group of 1,500 partisans under Major General Sidor Kovpak, fighting mainly in north and west Ukraine [*Fugitives of the Forest*]. See Kovpak.

DYADYA PATIA (UNCLE PATIA) PARTISAN UNIT: Some kind of partisan group [*Heroism in the Forest*].

DYADYA VASIA (UNCLE VASIA) DETACHMENT: Partisan group mentioned in the memorial book's map on page 438.

DZERZHINSKY (named for Felix Dzerzhinsky, a deceased Bolshevik leader): Partisan group that operated in various regions of Belarus [State Archives of Belarus].

FIRST BRIGADE OF BARANOVICHI: Partisan group that operated in the Baranovichi region (southwest Belarus) in 1943-44 [State Archives of Belarus].

FRUNZE (named for Mikhail Frunze, a deceased Bolshevik leader): Partisan group that operated in various regions of Belarus in 1942-44 [State Archives of Belarus].

GASTELLO (a.k.a. the Gastello brigade; named for Nikolai Gastello, a Soviet pilot who had been killed in action in 1941): Partisan group that operated in the Vileika region (north Belarus) in 1942-44 [State Archives of Belarus]. At some point, its commander was Victor Manokhin.

GENIS DETACHMENT: Partisan group mentioned in the memorial book's map on page 438.

GLAZER: Gesia Glazer, a **Jewish** Communist (a.k.a. Albina). He helped people in the Kovno Ghetto underground --- the Jewish Fighting Organization (JFO) --- to contact Ziman/Yurgis in the forests. Sometime around 1943, a group from the Kovno Ghetto tried to get to the Augustov forest, but its members were ambushed and killed [*Fugitives of the Forest*].

GOLAYEV PARTISAN UNIT [*Heroism in the Forest*].

GRIZODUBOVA (named for Valentina Grizodubova, a female Soviet pilot and war hero): Partisan group that operated in the Baranovichi region (southwest Belarus) in 1942-44 [State Archives of Belarus].

GROUP 51: Unit of the Shchors detachment based in the forest of Volchi Nory, 32 kilometers south of Slonim [*The Jewish Resistance*]. It was formed mainly by **Jews** from Slonim and was commanded by a Jew named Lt. Yakov Fyodorovitch [*The Jewish Resistance* and *Fugitives of the Forest*] or Jakob Federovitch [*Hitler's White Russians*], who was considered a brilliant tactician. In August 1942, the group successfully raided the town of Kosov northeast of Pinsk, killing 150 Nazis and collaborators and rescuing 300 Jews [*Fugitives of the Forest*]. A few months after August 1942, Fyodorovitch died in battle [*Fugitives of* *the Forest*]. In late 1942, the group was broken up and its members moved to other units [*The Jewish Resistance*].

GROUP 58: Unit formed by **Jews** of Kosov within the Shchors partisan detachment (see Shchors). Around August 1942, Group 58 had some 200 people, most of them women, children and elderly [*The Jewish Resistance*].

GROUP 60: Partisan unit formed by **Jews** from Byten who fled to the Volchi Nory forest. Around August 1942, there were several hundred Jews and non-Jews associated with the group [*The Jewish Resistance*].

GROZNY BATTALION: Partisan unit [*Heroism in the Forest*].

GRYNSZPAN: **All-Jewish partisan unit** led by Yechiel (Chil) Grynszpan from autumn 1942 around the Parczew and Skorodinica forests; protected nearly 1,000 Jews in family camps named Altana and Tabor. Around April 1943, the group was attacked by Germans in the forest, and many in the family camp were killed. In spring 1943, the group was joined by a small group of Jewish fighters led by Moshe Lichtenberg.

From around May 1943, the group was aligned with the Gwardia Ludowa group led by Jana Holod (code name Vanka Kirpiczny) and became known as People's Guard Unit-Chil. Lichtenberg disliked the Gwardia Ludowa; his group separated from them and later he was killed [*Fugitives of the Forest*].

By February 1944, there were 400+ Polish and Jewish partisans in the region. They rebuffed a Nazi offensive and destroyed a town hall in the General Government region of Poland, a first. In mid-May, as the Soviets moved west and they were allowed to remain in the forest, they faced attacks from both the Nazis and the Polish Home Army. There was another Nazi attack in July 1944, before the Soviets arrived. The Jews had 150 fighters and had saved about 200 Jews [*Fugitives of the Forest*].

HANOKEM (AVENGER) DETACHMENT: **Jewish partisan group** mentioned in the memorial book's map on page 438. Led by Abba Kovner of the United Partisan Organization (FPO, in Yiddish), after he led partisans out of the Vilna Ghetto in September 1943 [*Fugitives of the Forest*].

ISKRA (SPARK): Partisan unit. In spring 1942, it operated in the forest between Lida and Novogrudok and had only half a dozen fighters, but eventually it grew into a force of more than 300. Later the Naliboki forest (east of the forest between Lida and Novogrudok) was described as its base. Included many **Jews** [*Fugitives of the Forest*].

IVANOV PARTISAN BATTALION [*Heroism in the Forest*].

KALININ DETACHMENT (named for Mikhail Kalinin, a member of the Soviet government): Partisan group mentioned in the memorial book's map on page 438. Possibly in the forest of Volchi Nory, 32 kilometers south of Slonim [*The Jewish Resistance*] and various other regions [State Archives of Belarus]. The Kalinin detachment (or another detachment with the same name) also operated in the Naroch forest from at least late 1943 [Arad/*Ghetto in Flames*].

KESSLER: Israel Kessler, a **Jew** from Naliboki, formed his own partisan group. In fall 1942, Bielski forced the group to join his own unit after complaints from local peasants. When the Germans attacked the Naliboki forest in August 1943, Bielski allowed Kessler and 50 others to stay in that forest while the rest of Bielski's group moved to the Jasinovo forest. When Bielski returned to Naliboki a month later, Kessler now had 150 Jews. Permitted some autonomy, Kessler started bribing a Soviet commander to be allowed full autonomy and claimed falsely that Bielski had been stealing. Soon after this, Kessler was arrested by Bielski, tried and executed.

KHMELNITSKI (named for Bohdan Khmelnitski, the Ukrainian hetman who had led a bloody revolt in 1648 against the Polish-Lithuanian Commonwealth in which many Jews and Gentiles were killed): Partisan group that operated in the Bialystok region (now northeast Poland) [State Archives of Belarus].

KIROV BRIGADE (named for Sergei Kirov, a member of the Soviet government who had been assassinated in 1934): Partisan unit that included paratroopers, Soviet soldiers and **groups of Jews**; commanded by Mikhail Nedailin from Moscow. Operated in various regions of Belarus [State Archives of Belarus]. At one point it had some 200 fighters, plus 100 others in a family camp. Toward the end of 1943, the brigade included some 700 people [*Heroism in the Forest*].

KOMAR DETACHMENT: Partisan group mentioned in the memorial book's map on page 438.

KOMAROV: Group of partisan commandos [*Heroism in the Forest*].

KOMSOMOLETS: Partisan group that operated in the Baranovichi region (southwest Belarus) in 1942-44 [State Archives of Belarus].

KOMSOMOLSKY DETACHMENT: Partisan group mentioned in the memorial book's map on page 438. Around September 1943, it was in the Naroch forest and commanded by a man named Shaulvitz [Arad] or Vladimir Shaulevitch [*Fugitives of the Forest*]. It might have had some connection to Markov's Voroshilov battalion. The Komsomolsky detachment tended to be unfriendly to Jews, especially family camps [*The Jewish Resistance*]. In late September 1943, when the Germans began a massive sweep of the Naroch forest, the detachment left for the Koziany forest but refused Jewish fighters' pleas to let them join; many Jews, including Josef Glazman, were killed by the Germans [Arad/*Ghetto in Flames*].

KONOVICH DETACHMENT: Partisan unit mentioned in the memorial book's map on page 438.

KOROTKIN (named apparently for S. M. Korotkin): Partisan group that operated in the Vitebsk region (northeast Belarus) [State Archives of Belarus].

KOSTAS KALINAUSKAS (named for a Belarusian nationalist of the 1800s): Partisan unit, apparently comprised of pro-Soviet Lithuanians. In March 1944, many in it were killed in battle with the (anti-Soviet) Polish Home Army. In June 1944, as the Soviet army advanced, the unit was combined with the Vilnius brigade (which comprised pro-Soviet Lithuanians) [Arad]. Called the Kalinovskas detachment in the memorial book's map on page 438.

KOSYGIN: Partisan group mentioned on page 270 of the memorial book as operating in the Braslav region.

KOTOVSKY BATTALION (named for Grigory Kotovsky, a fighter in the Russian Civil War): Partisan unit in or near Kobrin [*Heroism in the Forest*]. Also described as operating in various regions of Belarus [State Archives of Belarus]. This was a unit within the Leninsky Komsomol brigade.

KOTOZOV UNIT OF THE SECOND MINSK BRIGADE: Partisan unit [*Heroism in the Forest*].

KOVNO BRIGADE: Formed under a man named Ziman/Yurgis by late 1943/1944 in the Rudnicki forest. (See the Rudnicki forest.) Eventually it included:

—Death to the Occupiers/Invaders, a group led by Constantine Rodinov, a Lithuanian Communist. **Many Jews** who'd arrived from the Kovno Ghetto served in it. After December 1943, Rodinov and his men were joined by a small group of Jewish prisoners who'd escaped from the Ninth Fort outside Kovno [*Fugitives of the Forest*].

—Vladas Baronas, a group established in January 1944 and led by Karp Ivanov-Seimokov. **Many Jews** who'd arrived from the Kovno Ghetto served in it [*Fugitives of the Forest*].

—Kadima (Forward), a group established in March 1944 and led by a Captain Tziko. **Many Jews** who'd arrived from the Kovno Ghetto served in it [*Fugitives of the Forest*].

KOVPAK: Partisan division numbering some 3,000 fighters at its peak, including **Jewish fighters** [*Heroism in the Forest*]. Originated in mid-September 1941 in the Spadshchansky forest under the command of a Ukrininan Bolshevik, Sidor Kovpak, who'd fled there [*Fugitives of the Forest*]. In October 1941, the group captured two Germans tanks [*Fugitives of the Forest*]. In November 1941, the group was in the Spadshchandky forest in eastern Ukraine with 73 men, then it moved to the Bryansk forest, which offered better protection [*Fugitives of the Forest*]. In September 1942, it moved to the Pinsk region in southwest Belarus. By October 1942, the group had received many airdops of supplies and weapons from the Soviets and numbered 1,500 fighters; it then marched toward Pinsk, crossing the Dnieper River [*Fugitives of the Forest*].

In late 1942/early 1943, the group carried out much sabotage in northern Volhynia and southern Polesie. In spring 1943, it moved to near Rovno and Kovpak was made a major general and supreme partisan commander for the Ukraine west of the Dnieper River [*Fugitives of the Forest*].

In June 1943, the group moved into eastern Galicia to attack oilfields near Drohobycz [*Fugitives of the Forest*]. In autumn 1943, there were 1,500 partisans under Major General Kovpak, fighting mainly in north and west Ukraine; they were joined by a Soviet partisan brigade led by General Aleksander Saburov and Uncle Misha's Jewish group [*Fugitives of the Forest*].

Kovpak welcomed Jewish fighters, but not family camps [*Fugitives of the Forest*]. See Dyadya Misha (Uncle Misha).

KRUK: Partisan unit located around Volkin that contained a family camp of **170 Jews** [*The Jewish Resistance*]. It might also be the nickname of Soviet partisan commander Nikolai Konischchuk, operating in northern Volhynia and who took in Jews from that region, including families. A Ukrainian Communist mayor, Konischchuk had fled to the forest in 1941. Initially he served under Max (see below), but was later given his own detachment. From late 1942, his group became part of Col. Anton Brinsky's brigade [*Fugitives of the Forest*].

KUTUZOV DETACHMENT (named for Mikhail Kutuzov, the Russian general who had fought against Napoleon): Partisan group mentioned in the memorial book's map on page 438. Operated in various regions of Belarus [State Archives of Belarus]. Might be the same as the Kutuzov regiment mentioned on page 200 of the memorial book.

KUZIN BRIGADE: Partisan group mentioned in the memorial book's map on page 438.

LENIN (named for Vladimir Lenin): Partisan group that operated in the Brest region (southwest Belarus) in 1942-44 and the Vitebsk region (northeast Belarus) in 1943-44 [State Archives of Belarus].

LENINSKAIA: Partisan group that operated in the Baranovichi region (southwest Belarus) in 1942-44 [State Archives of Belarus].

LENINSKY KOMSOMOL (LENIN'S KOMSOMOL): Partisan brigade led by Soviet commander and ethnic Pole Anton Stankevich in the Radun forest [State Archives of Belarus]; also described as a group of Belarusian parachutists led by Stankevich [*Fugitives of the Forest*]. The brigade was also said to operate in the Baranovichi region (southwest Belarus) [State Archives of Belarus].

At one point, it contained **90 Jewish fighters** and 30 Soviet fighters [*Heroism in the Forest*]. Within the forests, at some point it had three Jewish family camps: Grodnoites, Lidaites and Hradnaites, numbering around 600 people, all under its protection [*Heroism in the Forest*]. The brigade contained the four Asner brothers (also called the Itzkutzi, after their father, Itzik). The brigade derailed many trains, including rail lines at Oran, Olkeniki, Marchenki and Baston.

By early 1943, the brigade was operating under Stankevich in the Nacha forest south of Vilna [*Fugitives of the Forest*]; the Polish Home Army had also arrived in this forest in late 1942, and there were tensions between the two groups. In mid-June 1943, the Germans launched a sweep of the Nacha forest, and the Leninsky Komsomol partisans moved to the Yureli forest north of Grodno; many Jewish civilians left behind in the Nacha forest were slaughtered [*Fugitives of the Forest*]. In February 1944, Stankevich was severely wounded and then killed by the Armia Krajowa [*There Once Was a World*].

The Kotovsky battalion was part of the Leninsky Komsomol brigade.

LINKOV'S BRIGADE: Commanded by Commander Grigorii Linkov. In late 1942, there were anti-Semitic incidents in which **Jews** were killed by a Lt. Nasyekin. Discipline was improved by a Soviet partisan commander, Col. Anton Brinsky, who ordered Nasyekin's execution [*Fugitives of the Forest*].

LITHUANIAN BRIGADE: Might be the same as the Litayach brigade, a partisan group mentioned in the memorial book's map on page 438. See also Djalgiris.

MAILINKOV BRIGADE: Partisan unit near the town of Lepel [*Heroism in the Forest*].

MARCHENKO (named for A. Y. Marchenko; also called the Third Belorussian group): Partisan group that operated in the Vitebsk region (northeast Belarus) [State Archives of Belarus].

MARKOV BRIGADE: Partisan group commanded by Fyodor Markov; mentioned in the memorial book's map on page 438. Before the war Markov, a Communist, had taught in Swieciany and married a local Jewish woman [*Fugitives of the Forest*]. By August 1941, he was organizing partisan activities in Belarus [Arad]. As early as 1942, he was in the Naroch forest [Arad/*Ghetto in Flames*; *Fugitives of the Forest* said spring 1942]. On May 19, 1942, Markov and a small number of fighters killed three German officers outside Sventzion; they then disappeared until spring 1943 [Arad]. His group grew eventually to become the Voroshilov battalion. (See Voroshilov battalion.)

      The Markov brigade was reported to have taken the guns and valuables of Jews and given the valuables to women with the command [*Fighting Back*].

MAX: Partisan unit mentioned with the Kruk unit [*The Jewish Resistance*]. Possibly the nickname of Soviet partisan commander Josef Sobiesiak, a Polish Communist official operating in northern Volhynia who took in **Jews** from that region. Sobiesiak was one of the more sympathetic partisans toward Jews [*Fugitives of the Forest*].

MAY 1ST BRIGADE (a.k.a. the First of May): Partisan group [*Heroism in the Forest*]. At some point, it was based in the Naliboki forest. It was in the Naliboki forest in July-August 1943, when the Germans launched Operation Hermann with tens of thousands of soldiers; at this time, the partisan group was commanded by a man named Kovalov [*Fugitives of the Forest*].

MEDVEDEV BRIGADE: Partisan group commanded by Dmitri Medvedev; mentioned in the memorial book's map on page 438. This Medvedev might be the same person as the Col. Dmitri Medvedev who accepted Jews from Rovno and Korets into his detachment and kept a family camp of **150 Jews** [*Fugitives of the Forest*].

MELNIKOV (OR MALENKOV) BRIGADE: Partisan group mentioned in the memorial book's map on page 438. Page 270 of the memorial book also mentioned a Melnikov (or Malenkov) unit as operating in the the Braslav region.

MICHKA BATTALION: Partisan group near the town of Mir [*Heroism in the Forest*].

MISYORA UNIT: Partisan group [*Heroism in the Forest*]. It might be the same group as the unit of the Voroshilov battalion commanded by a man named Misyora or Misiyora. He was assisted by a Jew, Eprahim Bakaltzur; nearby was a family camp of **350 Jews** [*The Jewish Resistance*].

MOLOTAVA BRIGADE: Partisan unit led by Misha Gerasimov, with nine detachments of 2,000 fighters. One of five brigades commanded by Major General Vasily Komarov, who'd moved into the Polesie forests in mid-1942. Operated around the town of Pinsk [*Fugitives of the Forest*].

MOLOTOV: Partisan battalion, based around Yanov [*Heroism in the Forest*]. Might be the same as the 19th Brigade, a partisan group that operated in the Baranovichi region (southwest Belarus) in 1942-44 that was described as commanded by a B. M. Molotov [State Archives of Belarus].

MSTITEL (AVENGER): Partisan group that operated in the Gomel region (southeast Belarus) and the Minsk region (central Belarus) in 1943-44 [State Archives of Belarus]. See the Rudnicki forest.

MYANOV UNIT: Partisan unit commanded by Shmuel Gerber Myanov [*Heroism in the Forest*].

NEKAMA (Vengeance/Revenge; called Myest in Russian by the Soviets): Partisan group mentioned in the memorial book's map on page 438. **An independent Jewish unit** formed within Markov's Voroshilov battalion in August 1943 in the Naroch forest on the initiative of Josef Glazman, a Jew who'd come from the Vilna Ghetto with a small group of Jewish fighters in July 1943 [Arad and *Fugitives of the Forest*]. The original idea was to put all the Jewish fighters in it.

      Since Glazman was anti-Communist, the unit was instead commanded by Zerach Rogovsky/Rakovski (alias Butenas), a Soviet Jewish partisan from Kovno who'd been parachuted into the region [*Fugitives of the Forest*]. Glazman served as a staff officer and Chaim Lazar was a unit commander; all of these men were Jews [*The Jewish Resistance*].

Nekama operated in the Naroch forests for about seven weeks, growing from 70 at its creation in August 1943 to 250 fighters in September, all Jews. However, the highest Communist Party authority in the area, Klimov, objected to the existence of a separate Jewish unit, since the Soviet partisan movement was organized on the basis of Soviet territory, not nationality. Anti-Semitism has been cited as another likely factor. In addition, it was feared that separate Jewish partisan activity would raise local opposition and enable German propaganda to paint the partisan movement as largely Jewish [Arad/*Ghetto in Flames*]. Accordingly, the unit was disbanded on September 23, 1943 --- after just a month or two of activity --- and the Nekama fighters were put into the Belorussian Komsomolsky detachment [*Fugitives of the Forest*].

Glazman and a group of about 35 fighters were killed on October 9, 1943 while fleeing a sweep conducted by a massive German force. Chaim Lazar, meanwhile, fled the Naroch forest to the Rudnicki forest [*Fugitives of the Forest*].

NEVSKY (named for the medieval Russian hero Alexander Nevsky, who had defeated German and other invaders): Partisan group that operated in various regions of Belarus in 1943-44 [State Archives of Belarus].

NIKITICHES: Partisan battalion named for its commander. Took in **a very small number of Jews** [*Heroism in the Forest*].

NINETY-NINTH BRIGADE: Partisan group that operated in the Brest region (southwest Belarus) [State Archives of Belarus].

ONE HUNDRED AND FIFTIETH BRIGADE: Partisan group that operated in the Brest region (southwest Belarus) in 1943-44 [State Archives of Belarus].

ORDZHONIKIDZE (named presumably for Sergo Ordzhonikidze, a member of of the Soviet government who had died in 1937): Soviet-led unit mentioned in September 1943, when the Soviet command ordered that **young Jews** from Bielski's group be transferred to it [*Fugitives of the Forest*].

ORLANSKI BATTALION: Partisan group with a Soviet commander, Kolya Vachonin[?] [*Heroism in the Forest*]. This group had **some Jewish fighters**, who might have been former Red Army soldiers [*Fugitives of the Forest*].

PARKHOMENKO UNIT OF THE CHAPAEV BRIGADE: Partisan group [*Heroism in the Forest*]; mentioned in the memorial book's map on page 438. Apparently this was organized by Semyon Ganzenko and Shalom Zorin after they fled to a forest 30 kilometers southwest of Minsk after an Aktion in November 1941. The group eventually grew to 150 fighters, including **Jews**. The growing number of Jews led to tension between Ganzenko and Zorin; Zorin established a family camp for Jews and was at one point sentenced to death. However, in late 1941 or early 1942 Zorin was alllowed to establish the partisan group Unit 106 deep in the Naliboki forest. See also Zorin unit (a.k.a. Unit 106).

In July-August 1943, the Parkhomenko unit was in the Naliboki forest when the Germans launched Operation Hermann with tens of thousands of soldiers [*Fugitives of the Forest*].

PERVOMAISKAYA: Partisan group that operated in the Baranovichi region (southwest Belarus) in 1942-44 [State Archives of Belarus].

POBEDA (VICTORY): Partisan group that operated in the Baranovichi region (southwest Belarus) in 1942-44 [State Archives of Belarus].

PONOMARENKO BRIGADE (named for Panteleimon Ponomarenko, a key leader of the Soviet partisan movement): Partisan group that operated in various regions of Belarus [State Archives of Belarus]. Called a brigade in *Heroism in the Forest*, but elsewhere called a division, regiment or detachment (including in the memorial book's map on page 438). Might be the same partisan group as that created by Nahum Feldman at a base near Koidanov, with **Jews from the Minsk Ghetto**. It was also called an important unit in the vicinity of

Minsk (central Belarus) [*The Jewish Resistance*]. At some point, it was based in the Naliboki forest [*Fugitives of the Forest*], which was west of Minsk.

PRONZA BRIGADE: Partisan group [*Heroism in the Forest*].

PRUDNIKOV-MOROZOV BRIGADE: Partisan group mentioned in the memorial book's map on page 438.

PUGACHOV: Partisan unit commanded by Pugachov, an anti-Semite [*Heroism in the Forest*].

ROKONOVSKI: Partisan unit located in the Voltza-nora forest and commanded by Nikolai Babkov, an anti-Semite. In October 1942, when the Germans were sweeping the forest, he ordered Jewish family camps out of the forest. His group also killed Jews from family camps as well as some Jewish partisans in the area [*The Jewish Resistance*].

ROKOSSOVSKY (named for Konstantin Rokossovsky, a prominent Soviet general): Partisan group that operated in various regions of Belarus [State Archives of Belarus].

SADCHIKOV REGIMENT: Partisan regiment of I. F. Sadchikov that carried out "special assignments" in the Vitebsk region (northeast Belarus) in 1942-44 [State Archives of Belarus].

SECOND MINSK BRIGADE: Partisan group [*Heroism in the Forest*].

SERGEI LAZO UNIT: Partisan group [*Heroism in the Forest*].

SHCHORS (named for Nikolai Shchors, a hero of the Russian Civil War): Partisan battalion [*The Jewish Resistance*]. Operated around various regions of Belarus [State Archives of Belarus]. One of its companies was commanded by Nikolai Bubkov, a vicious anti-Semite. It did, however, have some **Jews** in its 51st company (see Group 51) and other companies (see Group 58 and perhaps Group 60).

SHIROKOV BRIGADE: Partisan brigade, named for its commander; also mentioned in the memorial book's map on page 438. By June 1944, the group was stationed in Yod/Jody [*From Victims to Victors*]. According to the memorial book (page 444), it had evolved from a group of escaped Russian prisoners of war who gathered in the forests in the summer of 1942 and there met **some Jewish fighters**, first taking the name Yatzminow (Jaczminow), after an early commander. See also the Antonov partisan group.

SOKOLOV: Partisan unit based at some point in the Naliboki forest [*Fugitives of the Forest*].

SOVIETSKAYA BELARUS: Partisan group. Operated in the Brest region (southwest Belarus) [State Archives of Belarus]. Possibly in the forest of Volchi Nory, 32 kilometers south of Slonim [*The Jewish Resistance*].

SPARTAK BRIGADE: Partisan group mentioned in the memorial book's map on page 438; also in *Heroism in the Forest*]. **Said to have been the first partisan group established in the Kozian forest**, in summer 1942 [*From Victims to Victors*]. Eventually it included **dozens of Jews**.

It was established by about 30 well-armed Soviet fighters who arrived on foot in summer 1942 from the Kalinin front, having traveled 400-500 kilometers to the Kozian forest to set up there. They formed Spartak, and Avraham Wilkitzki (a cousin of the Zilbermans) was one of first Jews to join it, and the first Jewish partisan in it to die fighting the Germans. He was wounded when the Germans swept through the forest in October 1942, firing to warn his comrades of the German approach, and he died later of his wounds. Hundreds of Jews in family camps in the Kozian forest were also killed around this time [*From Victims to Victors*]. Meanwhile, the Spartak brigade melted away, retreating 150 kilometers to the east [Arad and *Fugitives of the Forest*], to the region of Ushace, where it remained over the winter of 1942/43 [*From Victims to Victors*].

Around the same time, the Germans around Yod/Jody killed many villagers and set towns on fire to cut the partisans' supply lines [*Fugitives of the Forest*]; before leaving for Stalingrad, the Germans called together many of the Gentile villagers to one building and set it on fire, killing them [*From Victims to Victors*]. The Germans were then transferred to the Eastern front, leaving behind a band of Ukrainian collaborators to watch the area [*Fugitives of the Forest*]. The winter of late 1942/early 1943 was long and cold, and the local peasants became more hostile toward Jewish fugitives, as the Soviet partisans had retreated [*Fugitives of the Forest*].

After retreating the region of Usache in late 1942, the Spartak brigade returned to the Kozian forest in April 1943 [*From Victims to Victors*]. By this time, the group had some 300 fighters [*Fugitives of the Forest* and *From Victims to Victors*] or 500 fighters [Arad]. Peter Silverman and his cousin joined Spartak at this time [*Fugitives of the Forest*].

When it returned to the Kozian forest in April 1943, the brigade had two *otriads* (detachments), commanded by Ivanov and Strukov. **A third detachment was created, which the Zilbermans and Shmushkovitzes of Yod/Jody and many others joined, making it mostly Jewish** [*From Victims to Victors*, which estimated that at some point 10%-15% of all of the Spartak brigade consisted of Jews].

Spartak's command structure was a triad: commander, commissar, and chief of staff. (In summer 1943 these were Ponomarev, Ignatieff and Soloviev.) The brigade commander, Arkadi Ponomarev, was superb; he was fair, not an anti-Semite, and he valued the Jewish partisans [*From Victims to Victors*]. A prominent Jewish fighter in the brigade was Leib Wollak/Wollik/Woliach/Volak, commander of the Commandants platoon; he was from Lithuania and the most senior Jew. Before joining Spartak he had been captured by the enemy but had escaped after being wounded. After joining Spartak, he would be killed in the winter of 1943/1944 [Arad and *From Victims to Victors*]. Another Jewish hero was Yankele Natkowicz [*From Victims to Victors*].

By summer 1943, Soviet airdrops had given the Spartak brigade many guns and ammunition [*Fugitives of the Forest* and *From Victims to Victors*]. They blew up trains, railroad tracks and bridges, and destroyed goods and warehouses of food for the Eastern front. They also cut telegraph lines and blocked roads. (There were two rail lines: Leningrad-Warsaw and Polotsk-Vitebsk-Smolensk; the supply lines stretched along 2,000 kilometers and the roads were poor.) In May 1944, they attacked the enemy garrison in Opsa. Around July, as they Red Army approached, the brigade again attacked Opsa again as well as Vidz. In early July, the region was liberated, and the partisans of the brigade came out of the forest.

There was a Spartak brigade cemetery in the forest at Pliaterovo [*From Victims to Victors*].

The memoir *From Victims to Victors*, published in 1992 in Canada by Peter Silverman (Zilberman), David Smuschkowitz and Peter Smuszkowicz, formerly of Yod/Jod, is a valuable description in English of the partisans, with background on the Spartak brigade, the authors' families and the town of Yod.

SPAYEVITZ BATTALION: Partisan group near the town of Mir [*Heroism in the Forest*].

STALIN BRIGADE (named for Josef Stalin): Partisan group that operated in various regions of Belarus. Had some 200 fighters; within it, Marion Spiegel commanded **a small Jewish unit**. At one point, the group fought around Naliboki [*Heroism in the Forest*].

SUSLOV DETACHMENT (named for S. G. Suslov): Partisan group that operated in the Vileika region (north Belarus) in 1942-44 [State Archives of Belarus].

SUVOROV (named for Alexander Suvorov, a Russian general of the 1700s): Partisan group that operated in various regions of Belarus [State Archives of Belarus]. This might refer either to the Suvorov unit within the Zhukov brigade (see Zhukov brigade) or a different unit.

SVERDLOV (named for Yakov Sverdlov, a deceased Bolshevik revolutionary): Partisan group that operated in the Brest region (southwest Belarus) in 1942-44 [State Archives of Belarus].

TWENTY-FIVE YEARS OF THE BSSR (Belorussian Soviet Socialist Republic): Partisan group that operated in the Baranovichi region (southwest Belarus) in 1943-44 [State Archives of Belarus].

UNIT 106: Partisan group [*Heroism in the Forest*]. See Zorin unit.

UNIT 406: Partisan group [*Heroism in the Forest*].

VILNIUS UNIT: See Djalgiris.

VIRNAKOV: Paratroopers (Soviet?) who operated outside Novogrudok [*Heroism in the Forest*].

VO IMIA RODINY (IN THE NAME OF THE MOTHERLAND): Partisan group that operated in the Bialystok region (now northeast Poland) in 1942-44 [State Archives of Belarus].

VOROSHILOV BATTALION (named for Kliment Voroshilov, a general and member of the Soviet government): Partisan group that operated in various regions of Belarus [State Archives of Belarus]. Called the Voroshilov brigade in the memorial book's map on page 438. Was at some time in the Lipchanska forest [*Heroism in the Forest*], but the Naliboki forest was also described as its base [*Fugitives of the Forest*].

       Commanded by Fyodor Markov [Arad and *Fugitives of the Forest*]. At some point (1942?), Markov invited Jews from the Vilna Ghetto to join his group, but most of them refused, because they throught their struggle was in the ghetto [*Fugitives of the Forest*].

       From a "few score" fighters in summer 1942, the group grew to 300 fighters by around May 1943 [Arad]. In 1942-43, the group moved to Lake Naroch [*Fugitives of the Forest*]. By spring 1943, it was called the Voroshilov unit with four detachments of 300+ men [*Fugitives of the Forest*].

       In late September/early October 1943, a huge Nazi force of 70,000 swept through the Naroch Forest; in reponse, the Soviet partisans fled to the Koziany Forest. The Jewish partisans were mostly on their own during this movement. During this sweep, Glazman and his 35-member group were ambushed and killed on the way to Polotsk and the "Rudunick" forest (presumably the Rudnicki forest), except for one nameless girl who survived [*Fugitives in the Forest*].

VPERED (FORWARD): Partisan group that operated in the Baranovichi region (southwest Belarus) in 1942-44 [State Archives of Belarus].

YORAN, SHALOM: Born Selim Szyncer in what's now central Poland, by late 1942/early 1943 he and his brother Musio had fled to the Naroch forest, where they found a group of about 150 Jews in hiding. Eventually they organized an **independent, all-Jewish partisan group**, later joining the Soviet partisans.

ZA RODINU (FOR THE MOTHERLAND/FOR THE HOMELAND): Partisan group that operated in various regions of Belarus [State Archives of Belarus].

       This or another group of the same name was commanded by Major General **Aleksei Fyodorov**, who by 1943 operated in northern Volynia with 1,700 fighters, with a detachment led by Captain Koncha. Eventually **a Jewish platoon** was formed under Isaac Firt. Fyodorov rescued hundreds of Jewish children and protected them in a family camp [*Fugitives of the Forest*].

ZA SOVETSKIU BELARUS (FOR SOVIET BELORUSSIA): Partisan group that operated in the Baranovichi region (southwest Belarus) in 1942-44 [State Archives of Belarus]

ZASLONOV (a.k.a. the Second Brigade; named for Konstantin Zaslonov, a Soviet partisan commander who had been killed in action in 1942): Partisan group that operated in the Vitebsk region (northeast Belarus) in 1943-44 [State Archives of Belarus].

ZHADNOV: Partisan unit [*Heroism in the Forest*].

ZHETLER BATTALION: **Jewish partisan group**, comprised of Jews who'd survived the liquidation of the Zhetel Ghetto and gathered in the Lipchanska forest; commanded by HaShomer HaTzair leader Hirsh Kaplinsky [*Heroism in the Forest*]. Kaplinsky's group (with a small Jewish group led by Dr. Atlas) attacked the Germans/Lithuanians in Derechin in August 1942, killing 44 Lithuanian policemen [*Fugitives of the Forest*].

       In December 1942, the Germans attacked around the village of Wielka Wola and Hirsh Kaplinsky died in the engagement, killed by Soviet partisans for his machine gun; Dr. Atlas was killed in the same engagement [*Fugitives of the Forest*]. After this, the Zhetler battalion was disbanded and merged with the Orlanski battalion [*Heroism in the Forest*].

ZHUKOV BRIGADE (named for Georgy Zhukov, a celebrated Soviet general): See the Bielski partisan battalion. In English-language sources, information on the Zhukov brigade was particularly confusing; one group with this name was mentioned in connection with the Bielski brothers, who were in the Naliboki forest, another one (see next entry) was mentioned as operating in the Braslav region.

Zhukov brigade (perhaps a different unit from the one above): Page 202 of the memorial book mentioned the Klimchenko unit of the Zhukov brigade (Benyamin Movshenzon). Page 257 of the memorial book mentioned the Suvorov unit of the Zhukov brigade (Yerachmiel Milutin), as did page 276 of the memorial book (Esther Milutin-Korner/Esther Rusonik). Page 309 of the memorial book mentioned the Zhukov brigade (Mikhael/Mendel Sherman). Page 364 of the memorial book mentioned the Zhukov brigade (Alexander Dagovitz). Page 440 mentioned that the Zhukov brigade operated in the Braslav region, and that its commander was named Siromcha and its commissar was named Boloychik (page 256 said Siromcha and Bolovchik). Page 270 also mentioned the Zhukov brigade.

Zolotov battalion: Partisan unit [*Heroism in the Forest*].

Zorin unit (a.k.a. Unit 106): Partisan group of **Jewish** fighters commanded by Shalom Zorin, who'd escaped from the Minsk Ghetto after November 1941 and joined the Budyoni partisan group, commanded by Semyon Ganzenko [*Heroism in the Forest*; *The Jewish Resistance* said Guzneko, but this was apparently a corruption of his real name]. Zorin's unit grew to fighters and a family camp of 200 Jews in the Staroye-Selo forest, many of them Jewish escapees from the Minsk Ghetto. The large number caused problems with the Budyoni partisan group (Ganzenko didn't want a family camp), and in late 1941 or early 1942 the partisan command ordered Zorin to separate his unit from the Budyoni group and move to another part of the forest 100 kilometers away [apparently the Naliboki forest].

By spring 1942, there were 60 Jews with 15 guns. Zorin contacted the Minsk Ghetto underground; around May 1942, more Jews from the Minsk Ghetto joined it [*Fugitives of the Forest*].

By June 1943, the group numbered 137 fighters and 300 people in the family camp in the Naliboki forest [*Heroism in the Forest*]. Or 300-350 Jews [*Fugitives of the Forest*]. Zorin's unit had good relations with the Bielski partisan battalion, which wasn't that far away in the same forest [*Fugitives in the Forest*]. Another source said Zorin's unit had 700 Jews, but only 50-60 were armed [*The Jewish Resistance*]. In the Naliboki forest, Zorin rode through camp on a horse, and his partner was a beautiful Russian woman; she demanded most of the fine clothes or goods brought back from missions. Anatoly Wertheim was Zorin's chief of staff for most of the war. A man named Dr. Epstein ran a small hospital. As with Bielski's group, the camp was a small depot, which ensured good relations with the Soviets [*Fugitives of the Forest*].

In July-August 1943, Zorin's people were in the Naliboki forest when the Germans launched Operation Hermann against the Naliboki forest with tens of thousands of soldiers. Afterward, they returned to the camp in the Naliboki forest [*Fugitives of the Forest*].

By September 1943, their group numbered 800 Jews.

By 1944, there were also about 70 orphaned children in the camp; one day, Zorin felt the necessity to shoot one who had disobeyed a curfew to leave the camp [*Fugitives of the Forest*].

In July 1944, the Germans attacked Zorin's unit, killing six fighters and wounding 11, including Zorin. Zorin was taken to a hospital in liberated Minsk, and his leg was amputated [*Fugitives of the Forest*].

IV. From the Partisan Units, Some Individuals Mentioned in This Memorial Book

Antonov partisan group: Pages 105-107 and 157-158 of this memorial book (**Yerachmiel Biliak** from Braslav was a member, **Eliezer Fisher** from Braslav later joined).

Bondarenko partisan group: Page 269 (**Liuba Gamush** from Braslav --- later named Liuba Shmidt --- served as a nurse, and her brother **Avraham/Abrasha Bik** from Braslav was also a member). This partisan group might have been part of Byelorussian Brigade No. 4.

Byelorussian Brigade No. 4: Page 224 (**Zusman Lubovitz** from Braslav). Somewhere within this brigade, **Liuba Gamush** from Braslav --- later named Liuba Shmidt --- served the partisans as a nurse (page 224). Page 291 (**Chaim Burat** from Braslav), which mentioned the officer named Sazykin and said that 80 of 500 partisans in the brigade were Jews.

Chkalov unit: Page 362 (**Alexander Dagovitz** from Okmenitz) and page 398 (**Berl Reichel** from Zarach).

Gastello unit: Page 436 (**Liuba Vilkitzki/Wilkitzki** from Yod).

Kostas Kalinauskas unit: Page 262 (**Yitzhak Reichel** from Braslav), described as a Lithuanian unit (page 202).

Kutuzov detachment: Page 200 mentioned a Kutuzov partisan regiment that was perhaps this detachment. (**Leib Kaplan** from Yod was described as an officer in the regiment and a quartermaster). Pages 201-203 mentioned **Benyamin Movshenzon** from Rimshan and **Avraham Kasimov**.

Leninsky Komsomol brigade: Page 308 (**Gershon Yankelevitz** from Braslav served in the Kotovsky battalion within this brigade).

Markov brigade: Page 277 (**Moshe-Chatzkel Milutin** from Braslav).

Morozov unit: Page 253 (**Chaim-Eliahu Deitch**). This might be part of the Prudnikov-Morozov brigade mentioned above.

Ponomarenko brigade: Page 441 mentioned a group named Ponomarenko, led by Meirson, that combined with another group named Ponomarenko (**Pinchas Iafe** from Bildziugi/Yod was a member). Page 444 also mentioned the Ponomarenko unit (**Feivel Trok** from Yod was a member).

Shirokov unit: Page 443 (**Benyamin Dubinski** from Vidz/Yod) and page 444 (**Shalom Munitz** from Yod).

Spartak brigade: Page 243 (**Avraham Biliak** from Braslav). Page 243 (**Yerachmiel Milutin** from Braslav). Page 277 (**Moshe Milutin** from Braslav, also on pages 201 and 243). Page 436 (**Liuba Vilkitzki/Wilkitzki** from Yod). Page 436 (**Rafael Zilberman** from Yod). Pages 434 and 443 (**Avraham Vilkitzki/Wilkitzki** from Yod, brother of Liuba). Page 442 (**Pesach Zilberman** from Yod, **Tania Zilberman** from Yod and **David Shmushkovitz/ Smuschkowitz** from Yod). Page 443 (**Shimon Zilberman** from Yod).

Pages 417 and 422 mentioned various partisans from Yod (the unit wasn't named, but some of them were identified on other pages as belonging to the Spartak brigade): Besides David Smuschkowitz, Pesach Zilberman and Rafael Zilberman, who were already named above: **Zalman Shkolnik** from Yod, **Mulia/Shmuel Barnamov** from Yod, **Shimon Shragovich** from Yod, and **Zvi/Hirsh Einhorn** from Yod.

Pages 421 and 423 (**Slava Pinchov** from Yod, who spent some time in a family camp attached to the partisans; these were unnamed but were perhaps the Spartak brigade).

Zhukov brigade: Pages 202 and 204 mentioned the Klimchenko unit of the Zhukov brigade (**Benyamin Movshenzon** from Rimshan was a member). Page 257 mentioned the Suvorov unit of the Zhukov brigade (**Yerachmiel Milutin** from Braslav), as did pages 276-277 (**Esther Milutin-Korner/Esther Rusonik** from Braslav served as a nurse and was also mentioned on page 200). Page 309 mentioned the Zhukov brigade (**Mikhael/Mendel Sherman** from Braslav), as did page 362 (**Alexander Dagovitz** from Okmenitz). Page 440 mentioned that the Zhukov brigade operated in the Braslav region, and that its commander was named Siromcha and its commissar was named Boloychik.

Page 270 mentioned brigades named Zhukov, Kosygin, Spartak, Melnikov (or Malenkov), Bilov, Antonov, Lenin, Bazikin [or Bozikin] and Sazykin).

Other individuals were mentioned as having joined partisan units, but their unit wasn't clearly identified: **Peshka Hoffman** (or Pesia Hochman), from Kozian, a nurse or combat medic (page 105). **Froika Boretz** from Glubokoye (page 106). **Mottel/Motke Vishkin** from Dubina (page 144). **Moshe Okun** from Turmont (page 185). **Sara Movshenzon** from Braslav, a nurse (page 204). **Shneiur Ritz** from Drisviati (pages 202 and 207). **Avraham Bik** from Braslav (page 208), **Shlomo Musin** from Druya (page 270). **Shneiur Munitz** from Yaisi (page 402). **Masha Kapitza** from Kislovshchitzna, spent some time in a family camp attached to unidentified partisans (page 454).

V. Other Partisan Forces

The Soviet and Jewish partisans weren't the only forces fighting the Germans in western Belarus. Other forces included those listed below. Two of them, the Armia Krajowa/Polish Home Army and Narodowe Sily Zbrojne/National Armed Forces, were opposed to the Soviets and Communism and were eventually disbanded or suppressed, toward the war's end or soon after. Two other forces, the Gwardia Ludowa/People's Guard and Zwaizek Walki Czynnej/Union for Active Struggle, were groups of Polish Communists who were allied with the Soviets.

ARMIA KRAJOWA (AK, A.K.A. THE POLISH HOME ARMY/THE WHITE POLES): Established in December 1939 as the Union for Armed Struggle and reorganized in February 1942 under Stefan Rowecki. It operated in Poland under the auspices of the Polish government-in-exile in London. It was virulently nationalist and anti-Communist. It carried out many sabotage operations against the Nazis in late 1942 and throughout 1943, but avoided a direct confrontation in battle until 1944, when it began an uprising in Warsaw that was crushed with heavy losses.

    In summer 1943 Tadeusz Bor-Komorowski, a former supporter of the prewar anti-Semitic, anti-Communist National Democratic (Endecja, or N.D.) Party, was apponted the AK's chief commander. From late 1943, as partisan activity in Belarus expanded, AK partisans increasingly opposed Jewish and Soviet partisans as well as the Nazis, and there were skirmishes and bloodshed among the partisan groups [*Fugitives of the Forest*]. In January 1945, after the Soviet army had driven the German forces out of most of Polish territory, the AK was disbanded.

    Although deadly anti-Semitism was frequently found in the ranks of the AK, it wasn't official policy (at least for the government in exile). In some localities, the AK cooperated with Jewish partisans. In some cases, the AK condemned and punished killings of Jews, and hundreds of Jews are said to have served in its ranks. In large cities, AK cells dispensed false papers that enabled Jews to pass as Gentiles. Some AK units executed Poles who were known to have denounced Jews. On the other hand, Jews were often the target of AK attacks.

GWARDIA LUDOWA (GL, OR PEOPLE'S GUARD): A group of Polish Communists established in January 1942. It was the underground movement of the Polish Workers' Party. Unlike its rival, the anti-Communist Polish Home Army (or AK), it was prepared to work with the Soviets to fight the Germans immediately. It was one of the smaller Polish resistance groups; at end-1943 it had only 1,500 partisans, many of whom were Jews and Russians, compared to the National Armed Forces (see below), which had 70,000 allied to the Home Army and which was often anti-Semitic [*Fugitives of the Forest*]. In early 1944, the Gwardia Ludowa was renamed the Armia Ludowa (AL, or People's Army). Eventually it became the army of the postwar Polish Communist state.

NARODOWE SILY ZBROJNE (NSZ, OR NATIONAL ARMED FORCES): A Polish right-wing, anti-Semitic underground group. At its peak in 1943-44, it was estimated to have had 70,000-75,000 members. It didn't accept Jews into its ranks. It suffered a split in 1944, when one wing defected to the Armia Krajowa/Polish Home Army. After World War II ended, the NDZ continued to fight against the Polish Communists and the Soviets, but by 1947 it had been suppressed.

ZWAIZEK WALKI CZYNNEJ (UNION FOR ACTIVE STRUGGLE): A Polish Communist group operating outside the Vilna Ghetto, but it had only 60-80 people [*Fugitives of the Forest*].

VI. Major Forests Sheltering the Partisans

KOZIAN (OR KAZIAN/KOZIANY/KAZIANY) (IN WHAT'S NOW NORTHERN BELARUS): The name of a village as well as a forest (which covered hundreds of square kilometers). Said to be located some 60 to 100 kilometers north of the Naroch forest, depending on the source. The Germans searched the forest intensively in autumn 1942 and in September-October 1943 [Arad]. By the winter of 1943, the Germans burned all the villages and farmhouses close to the forest, to prevent the partisans from getting food supplies [*Fugitives of the Forest*].

Partisan activity in the forest came to an end roughly around July 1944, when the region was liberated by the Soviet army.

NACHA (IN WHAT'S NOW NORTHERN BELARUS): A forest some 130 kilometers south of Vilna [Arad/*Ghetto in Flames*]. In summer 1942, Eliahu Ariovitz, a Jew from Radun, established a Jewish partisan group/family camp in the forest, after the Radun Ghetto had been massacred [*There Once Was a World*]. At various times, a number of other groups were established in the forest, including Jewish partisan groups led by Niomke Rogowski, the Asner brothers and Yoske Lubetski, as well as Russian groups called Sashka and Kolka, comprising soldiers and ex-convicts [*There Once Was a World*]. In early 1943, the Leninsky Komsomol brigade, led by Soviet officer Anton Stankevich, established itself in the forest [*There Once Was a World*]. In June 1943, a German sweep of the forest killed many partisans and civilians and forced many partisans to flee to other forests. In November 1943, a Lithuanian guerilla base was established in the forest, and two Jewish battalions totaling some 100-111 fighters were ordered there, although they had few weapons. These fighters were commanded by Berl Szeresznyevski. The Nacha forest was dangerous at this time, as the Polish Home Army and local peasants were hostile. So the partisans returned to the Rudnicki forest in mid-December 1943 [Arad/*Ghetto in Flames* and *Fugitives of the Forest*]. Partisan activity in the forest came to an end roughly around July 1944, when the region was liberated by the Soviet army.

NALIBOKI (IN WHAT'S NOW CENTRAL BELARUS): A forest southeast of the Naroch forest. Its size differed according to the source; from hundreds of square kilometers to thousands of square kilometers. It held a large number of partisans and Jewish civilians. Jews fled there from the ghettos in Novogrudok, Mir, Ivia/Iwje, Lida, Baranowicze, and others [*Fugitives of the Forest*]. The two major partisan groups in it were the Bielski camp and the Zorin camp. It's estimated that together they saved about 2,000 Jews [*Fugitives of the Forest*]. This breaks down to about 1,200 for the Bielski camp and about 800 for the Zorin camp.

In August 1943, the Germans swept the Naliboki forest with tens of thousands of soldiers [*Fugitives of the Forest*]. Partisan activity in the forest came to an end roughly around July 1944, when the region was liberated by the Soviet army.

NARACH (OR NAROCH/NAROCZ/NAROTZ) (IN WHAT'S NOW NORTHERN BELARUS): A lake and also a forest (the forest was some 50 kilometers southeast of Sventzion and some 150 kilometers east-northeast of Vilna); it also appears in the memorial book's map on page 438. It was northwest of the Naliboki forest. It took about a week to reach from Vilna [*Fugitives of the Forest*]. It covered thousands of square kilometers [Arad/*Ghetto in Flames*]. **Fyodor Markov and his partisans** were there as early as 1942. By 1942 and January-June 1943, there were also hundreds of Jews living in the forest, having fled there after ghettos in the region were liquidated. In July 1943, Josef Glazman and a small group of fighters arrived from Vilna. The Jewish **Nekama/Revenge/Myest** unit operated there in August-September 1943, but was then disbanded. A few days later, the Germans did a massive sweep of the forest, killing many of the Jews who had been disbanded and left to survive on their own, including Josef Glazman [Arad/*Ghetto in Flames*].

In October 1943, the partisans returned to the Naroch forest and the position of the Jews improved slightly, as partisan organization improved and weapons were parachuted in from the Soviet territories east of Belarus [Arad/*Ghetto in Flames*]. Partisan activity in the forest came to an end roughly around July 1944, when the region was liberated by the Soviet army.

RUDNICKI (OR RUDNIKI/RUDNINKAI) (IN WHAT'S NOW SOUTHEAST LITHUANIA): Forest beginning some 20-50 kilometers south of Vilna, depending on the source. Part of the forest was cut by a road called the French Way (60 kilometers), along which Napoleon's army had marched in 1812 [*Fugitives of the Forest*]. Partisan activity began in the forest either in spring 1943, when a small group of Soviet fighters established a base there [*Fugitives of the Forest*], or in summer 1943, when Captain Alko and a group of parachutists set up camp [Arad/*Ghetto in Flames*]. It has also been claimed that partisan activity in the Rudnicki forest began in 1942, when Russian soldiers/Communists arrived there and set up a base around a string of hunting lodges that had once been a hunting camp.

In September 1943, those in the forest were joined by a group of Soviet-Lithuanian partisans who had come from the Naroch forest, as well as some 70 armed **Jews who'd come from the Vilna Ghetto (Yechiel's Struggle Group)**, commanded by Elkhanan Magid, Shlomo Brand and Nathan Ring.

A few weeks after September 1943, these were joined by groups of **FPO/United Partisan Organization Jews from the Vilna Ghetto** led by Abba Kovner and Cheyna Borovska. The Jewish groups had political differences: Kovner and the FPO wanted to ally with the Soviets-Lithuanians, whereas Yechiel's group didn't; nevertheless, the two Jewish groups merged and Kovner became the leader [*Fugitives of the Forest*]. Altogether, these Jews numbered some 140-150 and liaised more closely with Ziman/Yurgis than with Captain Alko [Arad/*Ghetto in Flames*], who was less willing to help them [*Fugitives of the Forest*]. Kovner moved them more deeply into the Rudnicki forest for safety, to an island in the swamp [*Fugitives of the Forest*]. There they were joined by 80 Jews who'd escaped from Kailis labor camp near the Vilna Ghetto, plus some others. By October 1943, the number of Jews had reached about 250 [*Fugitives of the Forest*].

When the number of Jews reached 250, the Jews were divided into three battalions: Mstitel (Hanokem, or Avenger) under Abba Kovner, Za Pobedu (To Victory) under Shmuel Kaplinsky, and Smert Fashizmu (Death to Fascism) under Jacob Brawer [Arad/*Ghetto in Flames*] or Yankel Prenner [*Fugitives of the Forest*]. Later a fourth battalion was formed: Borba (Struggle) under Aharon Aharonowicz [Arad/*Ghetto in Flames*], an FPO member who'd escaped from Kailis labor camp [*Fugitives of the Forest*].

In mid-October 1943, Ziman/Yurgis himself arrived from the Naroch forest and took over command of the Soviet-Lithuanian partisans in all of southern Lithuania. Kovner accepted the authority of Ziman/Yurgis, and the Jewish groups were officially made part of the Lithuanian partisan movement. Ziman/Yurgis commanded the Jewish units to stop bringing more Jewish groups into the forests. Although the Jewish groups weren't disbanded (unlike Glazman's group in the Naroch forest), changes were made to the command structure over the next year that diluted somewhat their Jewish character.

In early November 1943, Ziman/Yurgis sent 111 fighters from the third and fourth Vilna Jewish detachments to the Nacha forest, led by Berl Szeresznyevski, but the Nacha forest wasn't favorable for operations at this time and they returned [*Fugitives of the Forest*].

In November 1943, a Kovno Ghetto group under JFO leader Chaim Yellin was able to escape to the Rudnicki forest; more followed, totaling about 250 people [*Fugitives of the Forest*].

In early 1944, some non-Jews were integrated into the four Jewish battalions and the Jewish commanders were replaced, but the deputy commanders were Jews and the four battalions remained Jewish in character.

By May 1944, those from the Kovno Ghetto (who'd been arriving since November 1943) reached 300 and they were grouped into three battalions of the **Kovno brigade**.

Footnote:

1. Those in the memorial book who served in the Soviet Army --- rather than with the partisans --- included Isser Rabinovitz of Braslav (mentioned on pages 293-296), Zalman Charmatz of Braslav (pages 297-299), Peretz Levin of Braslav (pages 300-301) and Yisrael-Yosef Veinshtein of Braslav (pages 302-307). In addition, Shmuel Veinshtein and Shmaryahu Veinshtein of Braslav served with the British army (pages 302-307).

This three-branched candelabrum, believed to date to the late 1800s if not earlier, was used in Braslav by Esther Kremer (died 1929). Passed down in Esther's family, it was hidden by Gentiles during the Nazi occupation. After the war, it was retrieved by Esther's granddaughter Yetta Vishkin (Wischkin), with the help of Tuvia Fisher, and is now in the United States. Photo courtesy of the family of Yetta Wischkin.